Prayer of the poor

Kabbalistic Daily Prayer Book

KABBALAH
PUBLISHING

www.kabbalah.com™

Edited by YEHUDA BERG

The Kabbalah Centre
155 E. 48th St., New York, NY 10017
1062 S. Robertson Blvd., Los Angeles, CA 90035

First Edition
May 2010

ISBN13: 978-1-57189-673-5

My first Siddur changed my life
and put me back on my path,
may this one also touch at least one soul

I dedicate this to my sons - Andrei and
Vladimir - and my wife Anne Therese

May this Siddur bring Light and Happiness

TABLE OF CONTENTS

TABLE OF CONTENTS

TO THE GREATNESS OF THE VALUE OF THE ASHURIT FONT

And then you should open your mouth with wisdom and say *Keri'at Shema* with intention. This means you should understand the words you are saying and that when you recite the words of *Keri'at Shema* (from the Prayer Book) you should visualize in your mind the shape of each word and its letters. For example when you say the word "*Shema*" you should visualize the letters *Shin, Mem* and *Ayin* the way they are written in Ashurit font in front of your eyes. You should then visualize every word the same way until the end. You should visualize the vowels and the intonations that are above every letter, the same way as they are written in this Prayer Book and by doing so you should merit that each word will excel in its form to the Upper Worlds and every letter shall go to its place and to its root to activate miraculous actions and *tikkunim* (corrections) that are related to you. And by doing so (scanning the Ashurit font) on a daily basis, it will enable you (and it has been proven) to remove all negative thoughts and nonsense that interferes with the purity of our thought and intention in prayers. The more scanning of the Ashurit font a person does with the *Keri'at Shema* and any other part of the prayer will add purity to his thoughts during prayer. This meditation is a simple action and then you are promised to successfully educate yourself with your prayer and all will be desired by God just like the good scent. Amen so be it.

(*Seder HaYom* by Rav Yosef Chaim - The Ben Ish-Chai).

"When you go to sleep you should visualize the Tetragrammaton Name (יְהֹוָה), Blessed Be He, as if it was written capital Ashurit. The eyes should always turn to God and God will protect him falling into a trap".

(*Tziporen Shamir*, par. 68 v. 121 by Rav Chaim Yosef David Azulai - The Chida 1724-1806)

GENERAL GUIDANCE

According to Rav Isaac Luria (the Ari), and Rav Shalom Sharabi (the Rashash), all the words of intention, Holy Names and names of angels that are written in this book, even though they are a part of the text, should not be pronounced verbally. When you get to a word like this, you should scan it with your eyes and not say it.

It is with great honor and appreciation that I write this introduction to the *Kabbalistic Transliterated Siddur*.

It was exactly 20 years ago that the Rav asked me to take on the project of completing the *Kabbalistic Siddur* in Hebrew—my first project for the Centre. It was completed a year later.

It took many years and many attempts to produce an equally comprehensive English *Siddur*, which tells me that the Light it reveals must represent a revolution.

The prayers in this *Siddur* include all the meditations found in the *Zohar* and in the *Gates of Meditation* by Rav Isaac Luria (the Ari), as well as the consciousness given to me by my father, the Rav, who received it from his teacher, Rav Brandwein, who in turn received it from his teacher, Rav Ashlag.

We have called it *Tefila Le'ani* (*The Prayer of the Poor*) because as the *Zohar* in Balak 14:87 teaches us:

> There are three that are considered a prayer: "A prayer of Moses, the man of God" (Psalms 90:1), "A prayer of David" (Psalms 86:1), and "A prayer of the poor" (Psalms 102:1). Which is the most important? One says, "A prayer of the poor:" This prayer takes priority over Moses' prayer, is before David's prayer, and preempts all other prayers of the world.

> The *Zohar* asks: What is the reason? and replies: Because the poor man is broken-hearted and it is written: "The Lord is near to them who are of a broken heart." (Psalms 34:19)

> The *Zohar* continues: As soon as the poor man says his prayer, the Holy One, blessed be He, opens all the windows of the Firmament, and all the rest of the prayers rising above get pushed away by that destitute, broken-hearted man. There exists no other prayer in the world to which the Holy One, blessed be He, will give His immediate attention as [He does] to the poor man's prayer.

> Therefore, the person who puts forth his prayers must make himself poor so that his prayers will be worthy to enter among the prayers of all the poor. All the guardians of the gates do not allow all the prayers in the world to just simply enter as they allow the poor one's prayer, since they enter without permission. If a person makes himself poor and desires constantly to be poor, his prayer ascends and meets up with the poor's prayers. It joins up with them and rises together with them, and enters in combination with theirs. And it is received with willingness before the Holy King. (Balak 187-200)

This *Siddur* represents both the culmination of three generations of study as well as the revelations made by a lineage of teachers who came before us and who suffered great personal harm to make this technology for a fulfilled life available to us so that with the power of this knowledge, we could be the generation that brings about the transformation of this world and the removal of chaos forever.

Words are inappropriate to describe my gratitude for allowing me to be part of this gift to humanity.

Yehuda Berg

When the first *Kabbalistic Siddur* appeared some 12 years ago, we were aware that most people around the world are looking for a meaningful tool to connect with God. While *Siddurim* were always available, history nevertheless bears witness to the fact that for the most part, the prayers of humanity have remained unanswered. This can be attributed to the fact that never before in history has there been a prayer book that included the necessary meditations. Our purpose in presenting this *Siddur* is so that each person can now begin to remove chaos from his or her life.

The *Siddur* was established by the Sages of the Greater Assembly following the destruction of the Second Temple to replace the sacrifices that were no longer performed because the Temple had been destroyed. The purpose of the *Siddur* was to fill the void that was created by the absence of the sacrifices. However, what seems to have been misinterpreted is the purpose of the sacrifices in the first place.

Some say that sacrifices were brought to the Temple for the express purpose of thanking God for His beneficence toward us. Others teach that the sacrifices were used to appease or quiet the wrath of God. And for some, the sacrifices took the form of atonement by which the perpetrator of some violation could have his sin removed.

Kabbalistically speaking, all of the aforementioned do not begin to touch the heart of the objective of either the sacrifices or the *Siddur*. Nor would the *Siddur* play the same role in man's attempt at achieving a life devoid of chaos.

The Hebrew word for sacrifice, *korban* קָרְבָּן is derived from the word *krav* קְרָב, meaning "warfare." Appeasing or thanking God, however, does not appear to have any relationship with the word "warfare." With whom would the worshipper be conducting war? Furthermore, the idea that the purpose of the *Siddur* is for prayer does not correspond to the definition of the word *Siddur*. *Siddur* סִידוּר means "order" סֵדֶר. How does atonement or gratitude relate to order? In fact, even the idea of prayer is confusing. The Torah is very clear about how God relates to our devotion to Him.

At the Splitting of the Red Sea, the Israelites found themselves facing death: Either they would fall victim to the Egyptians who were bent on their annihilation, or they would continue to move into the sea and drown. Naturally, they appealed to the Creator for help, a plea to which the Lord answered, "Why are you praying to Me?" (Exodus 14:15), which is a strange reply from a compassionate, sensitive, and loving Creator.

The *Zohar* raises the obvious question regarding God's response to the Israelites: To whom would the Israelites pray in their time of need, if not to God.

Religionists have always answered such questions with comments such as, "God, in His mysterious ways, knows what He is doing." Just what did religionists have in mind over the past three millennia: that the reason for the chaos of this world is a mystery that only God is privy to? The *Zohar* rejects this kind of inference by the religionists, stating that God would never create chaos in our universe because God is good. If this is true—and it is—where did chaos originate?

The answer, states the *Zohar*, can be found in the kabbalistic principle known as Bread of Shame. In brief, this means that humankind demanded that the Creator cease His uninterrupted flow of beneficence towards us, that we could not accept the Light shared by God without having first earned the right to receive His abundance. This was the reason that humankind was placed in this universe: to choose between right and wrong, to restrict from any activity that would result in treating others with anything less than dignity.

So it has never been God working in mysterious ways, gloating over the chaos that afflicts humanity. Rather, He has always looked on with compassion, knowing that it was we who have tied His hands.

Approximately 2200 years after the sin of Adam, God saw that humanity was not capable of removing the Bread of Shame, so He assisted us with the Revelation that took place on Mount Sinai. Through this Revelation, God revealed the tools and methodology by which humanity would have a chance to achieve its ultimate objective. This was the first opportunity after Adam failed, for humankind to remove chaos from the landscape of human endeavor.

The way the *Zohar* interpreted the event at Mount Sinai was forgotten, replaced with a misinterpretation that introduced the idea that without the intervention of ecclesiastic authority, chaos could not be removed from the environment. Consequently, when chaos could not be removed, blame would be placed at the doorstep of God, with the assumption that God knows best. And because we do not understand God, He afflicts this universe with chaos, pain, and suffering.

In Exodus 14:15, God said, "Why are you praying to Me?" when the Israelites prayed to Him at the shore of the Red Sea. What the Creator then said to Moses is even more incredible. God said, "*Va isa'u,*" meaning literally, "Jump into the sea." One does not have to be a scholar to take notice of how damaging this response is to the whole concept of religion.

The *Zohar* explains that just before the Israelites reached the Red Sea, they were provided with complete instructions for removing chaos. This technology provided the Israelites—and the entire world—with the power of mind-over-matter. This technology can be found in Exodus 14:19-21. The key is that each of these three verses contains exactly 72 letters. I had read these verses hundreds of times and yet had not noticed this peculiarity until I encountered the *Zohar*. The *Zohar* deciphers that incomprehensible instrument and compendium known as the Bible and gleans from it the truths about the Revelation on Mount Sinai. The purpose of the Revelation of the Bible on Mount Sinai was to provide humanity with the methodology, instructions, and tools by which to eliminate the source of chaos—the Satan and his army of destroyers—and by doing so, to subsequently remove pain and suffering from the entire universe.

BY RAV BERG

This was the reason for God's question: "Why are you praying to Me?" God was saying to Moses: "I hear the prayers of the Israelites, and it pains Me that I must restrict sharing My abundance and removing the chaos that confronts the Israelites more than the pain that the Israelites themselves feel about their impending disaster. Why don't the Israelites remember and apply the technology that already has been furnished for them?"

When the Israelites stood at the Red Sea, they were provided with the technology of mind-over-matter—the ability to influence the cosmos—although complete dominion over the physical universe would have to wait until the Revelation on Mount Sinai. With mind-over-matter, the Israelites could split the Red Sea and walk through it. There was, however, a prerequisite for the use of this technology: The Israelites had to exercise certainty. If the consciousness of the Israelites contained any trace of doubt about whether they could indeed split the Red Sea, they would not have succeeded. We are told that a man, Nachshon ben Aminadav, upon hearing the words "Jump into the sea," did just that. To the astonishment of the other Israelites, the waters did not split, and they began to cry out, "You see! It does not work! The sea is not splitting!"

This uncertainty on the part of the other Israelites did not deter Nachshon from his certainty. He continued to walk into the sea until the water reached his nostrils. Only then did the waters part. This miracle clearly drove home the message to the Israelites that certainty plays a major role in achieving the ultimate consciousness of mind-over-matter, thereby relieving the universe of its pain and suffering. Without certainty, humankind, already privileged with the technology to control matter, cannot make this technology become manifest within the physical reality realm.

The *Zohar* contains the wisdom of mind-over-matter consciousness. But for reasons known only to the authors of the *Zohar*, the time for this revelation could come about only in this Age of Aquarius.

The Revelation on Mount Sinai empowered the people to recapture control over their destiny, thereby removing chaos from their lives. The sin of Adam had removed the information and technology that had empowered humankind with the ability to control its own destiny, the years leading up to the Exodus from Egypt and the Revelation on Mount Sinai would be filled with the familiar landscape of pain and suffering.

The Golden Calf incident, which was the result of the Israelites falling from certainty-consciousness to uncertainty, pushed humankind into the abyss of chaos. When Moses did not return from his encounter with God, the Israelites assumed he was dead. At that moment, they forgot that what had taken place earlier on Mount Sinai was their own empowerment and that Moses would no longer be their intermediary with God.

Moses was to return after 40 days. The Israelites miscalculated the time that he was away, thinking that the 40 days had passed while it was only 39 days and 18 hours. Feeling abandoned, they decided that they needed another intermediary. These six hours of miscalculation were just what the Satan needed to create doubt. In their uncertainty-consciousness, the Israelites forgot for a moment the message of Mount Sinai, and they chose the golden calf (our modern-day computer) as their intermediary—and were no longer the empowered people.

What emerges from the *Zohar* is that to restore order and remove chaos is exactly what the term *Siddur* means. This restoration of order was the purpose of the sacrifices presented during the time of the Temples. The word "sacrifice" describes the actual intent of a worshipper bringing sacrifices to the Temple. The objective of the sacrifice was not to thank, appease, praise, or pacify the Creator. The person presenting an animal in the Temple was making use of a tool provided by the Torah to wage war against the negativity that he or she had created. The purpose of the sacrifice was to restore order and balance in the life of the violator by removing the violation. This need to restore order is the reason why this compendium, known traditionally as the *Siddur* (prayer book), was established in the place of sacrifices.

When the Israelites came to the Red Sea, Moses shared with them the knowledge that is contained in our *Siddur*, which prevented the chaos that was about to befall them and permitted the manifestation of mind-over-matter, of consciousness over physicality.

The *Zohar* makes it very clear that the *Siddur* that was intended by the Sages of the Great Assembly must contain the meditations outlined in the *Zohar* and in *Gates of Meditation* by medieval Kabbalist Rabbi Isaac Luria (the Ari). Furthermore, continues the *Zohar*, a compilation of prayers that fails to include the meditations to remove chaos from our lives renders the prayers useless and worthless. This is an extreme and revolutionary statement.

What are we to think about the *Siddur* of the past two millennia? According to the *Zohar*, it was worthless for the well-intentioned worshipper's attempt to remove chaos, pain, and suffering from his or her life. I have to admit that when I read these words in the *Zohar*, they appeared to me to be too harsh to accept.

However, once we understand the intention of the Sages of the Great Assembly in compiling a prayer book, we can sigh with relief and thank the Creator that permission was granted to The Kabbalah Centre to produce and share with people this connection book, this *Siddur*. The fact that for the very first time the layman can now access the power of the Creator Himself, avoiding the pitfalls, pain, and suffering that has created the rubble strewn along the highway of human history, should be considered a blessing and not taken lightly. That we, in the 21st century, are privileged to have an opportunity to remove the usual chaos that has become a trademark of humanity should awaken within us the need to share this remarkable work with as many people as we possibly can. Indeed, one of the prerequisites that come with this blessing is the idea that we must not consider ourselves a privileged class and that it behooves us to assist as many unfortunate people around us as possible with this unprecedented opportunity to remove chaos from our environment.

The notion that we were to accept the misery inflicted upon us because God in His mysterious ways knows precisely what He is doing is contrary and opposite to the very essence and character of God. Today we no longer need accept this and other contradictory ideas concerning our Lord. God is good. His essence and character is one of sharing. The aspect of negativity simply does not apply, nor can be it be associated with the consciousness of a Desire to Share.

At this point, I would like to address the question that I am certain many readers of this introduction have asked: How can I benefit from the *Siddur* if I don't read Hebrew.

The Hebrew letters are not merely a vehicle by which ideas are expressed and a language established. The biblical narrative of the Tower of Babel claims that "the whole earth was of one language and of unity." (Genesis 11:1) Language was formed some 2000 years before the creation of Adam, says the *Zohar*. The basic building blocks of this language were the 22 letters of the Hebrew *Alef Bet* provided by the biblical text. The purpose of this language was to provide a means of communication with the subconscious of every life-form. The *Alef Bet* and the words structured by it provide an unlimited vocabulary. These letters and words transcend the limited realm of our consciousness and can clarify and express more precisely our thoughts and the observable world around us.

The idea that the Hebrew language is exclusively for Israeli people is, from a *Zoharic* viewpoint, a misconception of the language's inherent purpose. The objective of Hebrew is to provide our thought-consciousness with an opportunity to reveal itself. The *Zohar* describes how our thoughts ultimately become manifested in the spoken word, instantaneously converted into vocal manifestations. This process seems to be completely robotic. It is beyond question that speakers apply no conscious thought to each word that leaves their mouth. They never truly think about which word to use or what word will be coming next. Where do these words come from then? They appear to be from a prepared text or cassette, which has been established in our mental computer.

To consider Hebrew the language of Israel exclusively is a complete corruption and should be considered a ploy by the Satan to prevent the flow of the awesome power of the Lightforce of God. It is only when we employ the Hebrew language that we can be assured of a proper connection with the Lightforce of the Tree of Life Reality.

We are all familiar with bar codes. When scanned, bar codes provide a vast amount of information, which the scanner processes in seconds. The scanner eliminates pricing errors and saves time, effort, and money. Similarly, the *Zohar* is replete with examples where scanning by the human eye has improved the ability of our minds to see things around us as they actually are. If an inanimate object such as a bar code scanner can produce such activity, imagine what the human mind can do. The scanner in a department store certainly does not have the potential or the ability to comprehend and understand the many aspects that a human mind can process through scanning the *Siddur*.

INTRODUCTION
BY RAV BERG

The eye is the most powerful vehicle by which we can acquire an understanding of everything around us. As we scan, our eyes, more than our rational consciousness, make the absolute connection, thereby permitting us to tap into the awesome, Flawless Universe of the Tree of Life.

Ever since we opened the door to the study of Kabbalah to the layman without any prior background in the Hebrew language, we knew that the most difficult bridge we would be crossing was the one built of complacency. Because humankind has lived for many millennia within a certain structure, to make any changes would require a monumental effort on our part to enlighten peoples of the world to a new idea. Given that human nature opposes change even on the physical reality level, imagine how much greater the difficulty would be in fostering change on a level that the five senses could not cope with, not because of lack of intelligence or education, but simply because delving into and penetrating the immaterial realm is an exercise that, unfortunately, we are all too unfamiliar with.

The difficulty that readers and scanners of the *Siddur* may have is how to adjust to the idea that although we cannot understand the content of what is written or we lack the educational tools to begin to comprehend the content, we can step in and accept—purely on faith alone— that the *Siddur* is the ultimate answer to the removal of chaos in our life?

The cosmos contains a great deal of positivity and negativity that constantly bombards our brain and confuses us. Hebrew is the language that will best serve us in bypassing this interference. When a reader/scanner of the *Siddur* meditates with a desire to become connected with the Tree of Life Reality, there is much going on between the confusion-filled terrestrial realm and the chaos-free Tree of Life Reality. What is thus required is a cable or channel that will be impervious to outside influences when our thought-consciousness wishes to connect with the Flawless Universe of the Tree of Life. This cable or channel is the Hebrew *Alef Bet*.

Hebrew is foreign to the large majority of Earth's inhabitants, and so its use for the *Siddur* will create an awkward experience for the reader/scanner. Nonetheless, once we have come to the realization that we have no other choice in our efforts to rid the universe of chaos, we will accept the premise that reading/scanning establishes a connection with the Tree of Life Reality. When an individual begins to tap this awesome Lightforce of God, he or she instantaneously experiences the sensation of being surrounded by the warmth of the Lightforce.

We do not refuse to use the telephone simply because we have no idea how the instrument works. We do not hesitate to take medications if the physician assures us that they will be helpful. If the practitioner of Kabbalah will permit the Lightforce to enter his or her very essence of being, the rewards that we have spoken about previously will become a part of humanity.

The purpose of this particular connection book, this *Siddur*, is simply to remove chaos, pain, and suffering; to recharge our batteries when we feel drained or to reinvigorate our tired bodies. For those of us who truly believe in the process of immortality, this *Siddur* will support us in our attempt to regenerate our body. The *Kabbalistic Siddur* strongly opposes any idea that when we reach the age of 20, our body enters the portal of degeneration, the aging process takes over, and we face the inevitable downhill of physical breakdown.

We must have a consciousness and awareness that this familiar landscape of human degeneration is not one of the facts of life. Science has confirmed that degeneration and process of aging is a reality. However, let us clearly understand that science has never proven the reliability or cause of any aging factor other than the observance by the naked eye of a process that seems to resemble aging in the human body.

From a kabbalistic perspective, this is precisely why, up until the present, we have not been capable of reversing the aging process. As a result of our observation, we have determined that every human being and every creature within the animal, vegetable, or inanimate kingdoms must inevitably undergo aging. The idea of "show me and I will believe it" contributes to the idea that all we can observe outside of ourselves is the decay of any living organism. However, were we to change our consciousness and consider the aging process as something temporary and illusionary and that aging or degeneration is not an absolute truth, then we will have entered a new dimension in human history. This is the new path of kabbalistic thinking and will become the consciousness of the 21st century—that "matter" and any other physical material is governed and determined by our consciousness, that as we "will it, so will it be." Rather than "show me and I will believe it," the kabbalistic awareness of consciousness and its significance will reverse this process and declare "that which I believe, I shall see."

I am well aware of the difficulties that humankind will encounter with this revolutionary idea of mind-over-matter in general, or degeneration and aging in particular. Our rational minds, having been programmed over the past five millennia with a "show me and I will believe it" approach to reality, will obviously find it extremely difficult to cope with so radical an idea as reversing many of the "irrevocable and irreversible" laws and principles that we are so familiar with. Everything around us will now have to undergo a complete overhaul in terms of how we perceive it.

This agonizing step of crossing over the threshold of a new dimension will affect the practitioner no less than when people were forced to change from the concept of gathering and processing information manually to doing the same thing with the computer. However, there is quite a difference between these two situations. There are individuals who simply will not become attached to a computer, despite all of its benefits, and who thus depend upon others to do the required information-related tasks. However, when we are involved with a dramatic step towards a complete overhaul of our predestined path in life—a step that involves the removal of chaos from our lives—we have no other choice to make. We cannot remove pain and suffering from our landscape without a personal and individual involvement.

To achieve the goal of reversing the aging process, humankind will be compelled to reverse and completely change the way it thinks. Kabbalistically speaking, and with science slowly but surely creeping up to and closing the gap with Kabbalah, we are composed of nothing more than our consciousness. Our rational consciousness, which is connected to and completely dependent upon the body, serves a very minor role in the way we think or behave. This may sound very strange to the newcomer.

Scanning of the *Siddur* has proven over and over again its reliability in achieving a heightened awareness of our consciousness. Science, too, has recognized the limitations of our rational consciousness and has stated that we do not realize our full potential consciousness. It is to the major but unused segment of our consciousness that scanning/reading of the *Siddur* will be extremely beneficial.

To both the kabbalist and the modern-day scientist, the rational consciousness connected with the five senses is totally limited in function. To achieve a chaos-free society, we must transcend this limited perfunctory means of thought and begin the process of elevating our consciousness to a heightened awareness of things around us.

What Kabbalah is demanding is that to remove chaos from our lives and environment, we have no other choice than to add to our rational consciousness. What this in effect means is that we must make a determined effort to reveal and make manifest the heretofore unused segment of our consciousness—the 99 percent of our potential consciousness—so that this segment becomes as fully operational as our familiar 1 percent rational consciousness.

It has become quite obvious that society cannot rid itself of all the liabilities surrounding chaos unless a greater and broader picture of events around us is reached. How can we possibly determine what represents chaos when the major portion of our observation is limited to this 1 percent of rational consciousness.

Consequently, this introduction serves to emphasize the limited ability of our mind. Without expanding conscious awareness, Earth's inhabitants have little hope that the historical pattern of chaos can be interrupted. The significance of our consciousness has been so downplayed in relation to our daily activities that I consider this hurdle to be the major factor, if not the only factor, that prevents humankind from overcoming and removing chaos from our world.

Unfortunately, our consciousness is stimulated more by our reactive behavior, which comes into play when our egos are touched or damaged by others. We immediately respond to this outside influence or stimulation, usually in a negative way, by becoming defensive. Aside from this situation, we rarely become familiar with the notion that we are not functioning at full potential capacity, beyond our rational limited consciousness.

This limited ability, although known to science for a very long time, simply has not filtered down to most people. The reason, I believe, that science has failed to actively address this lack of consciousness is because of the lack of available tools to expand our rational consciousness to occupy a higher percentage of our total mind. While there are many "new" disciplines that attempt to improve or increase the ability of our consciousness, there is very little credibility that can be attributed to these new methods because they have not weathered the storm of millennia of obstruction. The contents of the *Siddur* and its varied meditations have been with us for close to four millennia. The mere fact that this book has endured indicates that it has a life of its own—a life that has withstood the chaos and destruction that has engulfed all other written disciplines of the past.

According to the discipline of Kabbalah, to raise the level of our active consciousness from the rational consciousness level of 1 percent to the 99 percent of our available consciousness can be achieved only when we have made a connection with the Tree of Life Reality—the Flawless Universe mentioned in Genesis.

This *Siddur* provides that very connection with the Tree of Life Reality. Yes, each one of us will have to devote time and effort to making use of this tool, and I can just hear the comments that will be made by the practitioner when he or she is suddenly faced with being late for an appointment or is pressed for time. What can possibly happen if I skipped making a connection this one time? Will my failure to connect with the Tree of Life Reality truly make a difference in just one day? The Satan constantly bombards us with these thoughts, just as we are subject, as we have stated previously, to a 24-hour-a-day bombardment of many other negative thoughts that we have no control over and cannot prevent from entering our minds.

How important is it for us to regain control over our minds? This is the question that should confront us each and every day. If we were to consider the amount of time that we of necessity waste each day because of our connection to our rational 1 percent consciousness, we would find that the total far exceeds the miniscule amount of time that we must devote to achieve the barest modicum of control over our minds.

The results of our efforts in connecting with the Tree of Life Reality are unquestionably absolute. Of this, I have no doubt. The greatest difficulty that we all share in terms of control over both our destiny and our daily affairs is the Satan's interference with our ability to come to grips with the idea that we are constantly under siege from him. The Satan is present in our consciousness for the full 24 hours of our day—yes, even when we are asleep. Our inability to be constantly aware of this threat and danger is the Satan's strongest weapon. The Satan can supply us with more reasons than we can ever dream of as to why he is *not* involved. His arsenal of distractions and methods of turning our attention away from the Tree of Life Reality is far beyond anything we can think of.

Actual chaos, pain, or suffering does not require nor does it involve the Satan's personal attention. To administer and execute chaos in whatever form it may present itself is left to his armada filled with an infinite number of warriors. The Satan knows full well that the crucial and decisive factor—the factor that inflicts chaos upon every aspect of this universe—lies within the consciousness of all human beings. If the Satan can only instill within our consciousness the idea of uncertainty, lucky or unlucky, or that every good thing must ultimately come to an end, or at the very least, some form of correction or interruption, then the success of his effort to leave the landscape of this universe filled with rubble is already certain.

Let us consider the role of our consciousness in determining whether we will raise or lower our hand. The physical hand, a vital part of our body, has absolutely no involvement in this decision. In the same way, every physical manifestation that comes about depends upon the state of our consciousness. We must become fully and totally aware of the significance that our consciousness has in determining the outcome of any decision we make concerning some physical activity or manifestation. It is precisely in this area where the Satan has, since Creation, been in total control. His influence over both our inability to be constantly aware of the significance of our consciousness and our failure to make use of our total mind is where chaos, pain, and suffering have their origin.

We forget the importance that consciousness plays in the ultimate outcome of any of our actions and activities. For the most part, we have adapted our rational consciousness to accept that once physical or emotional contact ceases on this material level, then we no longer exercise any form of control over the ensuing stages of the action until its conclusion.

This is precisely what the Satan would have us believe. He makes every attempt to disengage the physical, material realm from the metaphysical, immaterial realm. This is what the "show me and I will believe it" principle is all about. This in effect means that consciousness plays no role in our reality. Our reality either presents itself as something very physical or it simply does not exist. Consciousness, that immaterial force, is totally disregarded, and rarely does it assume its rightful place in the manifestation of all physical existence.

Therefore, when we consciously decide to create something, the moment this consciousness crosses over into the physical realm, we believe that for all intents and purposes, our original consciousness no longer plays a role in any further development and result. This is exactly what the Satan wants us to believe, even though kabbalistically, there is nothing further from the truth.

So consequently, we maintain a society that is governed by the Uncertainty Principle established by science. It then follows logically that whatever is determined by our consciousness, anything we do, any decision that we arrive at, will retain this uncertainty-energy. As to our further involvement in any matter, this uncertainty-consciousness plays the greater role in the process of development. Therefore, chaos must ultimately settle into any given situation, inasmuch as the energy of our uncertainty does not cease when we have stopped thinking about or have discontinued being involved in the process. While we do not appear to continue our physical involvement, the original energy of uncertainty of our consciousness nevertheless continues far beyond the apparent "show me the physical relationship." Our uncertainty state of consciousness dictates that what we do not see does not exist. And this is precisely what the Satan would have us believe.

To provide several examples of what the kabbalists mean concerning consciousness, let us examine the biblical references pertaining to this matter.

Having spent more than three millennia exploring the interrelatedness of man and his cosmos, kabbalists are unique among celestial investigators in providing a unified description of Creation. Since the Golden Age of Safed some four centuries ago, kabbalists have had a fully detailed metaphysical model of the universe. How did they develop so radical, yet so amazingly clear a picture of the universe?

The real 99 Percent World is hidden from view by veils of negativity, symptoms and appearances. However, like kabbalists before and after him, the Ari found the answer, at least in part, in the blueprint provided for us by the cosmic code known as the Bible.

"When you come to the land of Canaan… and I put a plague of leprosy in a house of the land of your possession…" (Leviticus 14:34).

The Canaanites were of a negative, evil consciousness. Whenever they erected a building, they made use of and connected with evil forces that roam at random throughout the universe, thus causing these evil forces to become expressed within the building. The negative energy of these forces manifested as the leprosy described in the above quote.

The kabbalists say when a person begins to erect a building that he or she should declare that he is building it for the service of the Lightforce. The *Zohar* states that when the women brought articles for the Tabernacle they used to "specify what part each was for… and all the women whose heart stirred them up in wisdom…" (Exodus 35:26). The women with wisdom understood the power of the mind and human activity. They were stirred up in wisdom, and each thing became connected with the Lightforce.

What seems to emerge from the biblical narrative is the direct relationship that exists between the inanimate reality and its constant interaction on the subtlest levels. The kabbalist knows that all events on the physical level are directed by an internal energy-force of intelligence, which evolves into that which we observe in manifest form.

Herein lies the essential difference between the worldview of the kabbalist and that of the scientist. For the kabbalist, everyone and everything, including a rock or a table, has a level of intelligence and consciousness. A table talks, and so does food. A person seated in a restaurant where the previous occupant of the table threw off enormous negative vibrations may become very uncomfortable during the meal and never knows why. A house with negative vibrations talks and may make a new purchaser or tenant agitated (Rav Berg, *Kabbalah for the Layman*, Vol. III, 140-142). The table and the house have intelligence.

Whether or not we understand the language of the inanimate inhabitants of our universe, or are conscious of their intrinsic language, they reveal much of what is going on around us. The kabbalist or student of Kabbalah knows perfectly well that a home, apartment, or business that has become corrupted by the negative, evil consciousness of human beings is a place to stay away from. The kabbalist will pick up the intelligence of these inanimate entities and act appropriately.

Every vessel of an inanimate structure has a certain note that causes it to reverberate louder than at any other frequency. Gently encircle the rim of a wine glass with a moistened finger to find that vessel's resonant harmonic. The trick of a singer breaking wineglasses is accomplished by singing a particular pitch at a volume sufficient to cause the glass to explode from the force of its own vibrations.

Another example to those of us familiar with the game of tennis is the idea of follow-through when hitting the ball. Tennis professionals all agree that when the racket has struck the ball and there is no longer any physical contact between the ball and the racket, the player should still continue to swing the racket beyond the initial contact. One might ask why it is necessary to continue swinging the racket to the end of its arc, when the movement of the racket merely brings it in contact with the air. I am certain that from the point of view of both the professional tennis player and the scientist, this follow-through affects the speed, spin, and direction of the ball. And the movement of the racket following the point of impact will enhance and influence the behavior of the ball beyond that impact. However, the question as to why the consciousness of the player extends beyond impact is not addressed.

Therefore, if our consciousness is one of uncertainty at the beginning of any endeavor, we should understand that this will have a material effect upon the outcome of the undertaking. Similarly, if we maintain a positive attitude of certainty, then this consciousness will also continue beyond the point of our physical involvement. Consequently, if we could connect our uncontrolled and uncertain mind to the realm of the Tree of Life Reality and infuse our mind with the energy of this flawless reality, then this positive consciousness is what would permeate and extend throughout our physical activities and beyond.

THE PURPOSE OF THE *SIDDUR*

We have the choice of either being influenced by the prevailing atmosphere of uncertainty and the resulting chaos or connecting through the *Kabbalistic Siddur* with the Tree of Life Reality, which will assuredly clear the air of all negative interferences and uncertainty. And just as the planting of a seed governs what will subsequently emerge from that seed, so, too, is our consciousness the seed of all future activities. How and what this consciousness consists of and how this consciousness will behave will depend entirely upon our efforts and our input into our existing consciousness.

To commence activities without a connection with the Tree of Life Reality is literally seeking impending chaos. History, with its evidence of uninterrupted chaos, is a testimonial to the inability of humankind to bring to an end the rampant chaos that affects all of humanity. Humankind in the past has always sought solutions outside of himself. With the advent of the Age of Aquarius, this all will come to an end. The kabbalistic perspective of how chaos will come to an end includes first and foremost the participation of man him- or herself. The tools and methodology to eliminate a chaotic society once and for all are now available to all humanity. No doubt, the past five millennium-programmed consciousnesses will still play a major part in the acceptance of this new role that places humankind at the center of all activity.

With the introduction of the comprehensive first-ever *Kabbalistic Transliterated Siddur*, humankind, for the first time in history, finds itself in a position to become master of its destiny and captain of its ship. However, the removal of environmental and personal chaos now becomes one of personal responsibility. To shirk this awesome burden can only invite the continuity of chaos within our life. The idea that we no longer can, nor do we have to, search elsewhere will indeed seem very revolutionary and strange to most. But this is the Age of Aquarius, and with it comes the enormous support of the Lightforce to assist us in this novel and radical change regarding the problem of chaos. The Satan will provide us with infinite and sufficient cause at every step along this new spiritual journey as to why we may not be able or capable of undertaking so monumental a task. The idea that each and every day requires our time, effort, and participation towards the elimination of chaos within our life is certainly one that can create a little havoc in our schedules and habits.

For those of us who take the time and effort to restore our consciousness to one of certainty and positivity, the observation of the changes that will inevitably occur in our life will be mind-boggling.

The *Kabbalistic Siddur* takes into consideration the cosmic influences for each day of the week. These differences are taken into account, and methodologies are provided that will tap the positive energy of each unique day. The Ari in his book *Gates of Meditation* also states that the support and assistance of angels plays an intrinsic part in ensuring man's well-being. Furthermore, angels are designated for the purpose of further protection from chaos and uncertainty, and one or more angels will not minister from one particular day to the next. Consequently, there is included within this *Siddur* the proper meditation that will ensure the presence of angels on any given day.

Newfound miracles, where we least expect them to occur, will serve to reinforce our conviction and understanding as to why chaos has been a "friend" that has accompanied us and been bound to us for the past five millennia. The *Kabbalistic Siddur* will become the tool that allows us to successfully disengage the Satan from our presence and to enjoy that God-given right to a Flawless Universe free of the chaotic lives that we were forced to live in the past.

THE LETTER OF THE RAMBAN (RAV MOSES NACHMANIDES 1194-1270)

The following letter was written by the Ramban to his son, teaching him humility and modesty. The Ramban instructed his son to read this letter at least once a week and promised him that every day he reads this letter all his prayers will be answered. He also said that all who say it will be protected from harm or suffering and they are promised their share in the World to Come.

שְׁמַע shema בְּנִי beni מוּסַר musar אָבִיךָ avicha, וְאַל ve'al תִּטֹּשׁ titosh

תּוֹרַת torat אִמֶּךָ imecha. תִּתְנַהֵג titnaheg תָּמִיד tamid לְדַבֵּר ledaber כָּל kol

דְּבָרֶיךָ devarecha בְּנַחַת benachat לְכָל lechol אָדָם adam וּבְכָל uvchol עֵת et,

וּבָזֶה uvaze מִדָּה mida שֶׁהִיא shehi, הַכַּעַס haka'as מִן min תִּנָּצֵל tinatzel

רָעָה ra'a לְהַחֲטִיא lehachati בְּנֵי benei אָדָם adam. וְכֵן vechen אָמְרוּ amru

רַבּוֹתֵינוּ rabotenu ז"ל zal: כָּל kol הַכּוֹעֵס hako'es כָּל kol מִינֵי minei

גֵּיהִנֹּם Gehinom שׁוֹלְטִין sholtin בּוֹ bo שֶׁנֶּאֱמַר shene'emar: וְהָסֵר vehaser

כַּעַס ka'as מִלִּבֶּךָ milibecha, וְהַעֲבֵר veha'aver רָעָה ra'a מִבְּשָׂרֶךָ mibesarecha,

וְאֵין ve'en רָעָה ra'a אֶלָּא ela גֵּיהִנֹּם Gehinom, שֶׁנֶּאֱמַר shene'emar: וְגַם vegam

רָשָׁע rasha לְיוֹם leyom רָעָה ra'a. וְכַאֲשֶׁר vecha'asher תִּנָּצֵל tinatzel מִן min

הַכַּעַס haka'as תַּעֲלֶה ta'ale עַל al לִבְּךָ libecha מִדַּת midat הָעֲנָוָה ha'anava

שֶׁהִיא shehi מִדָּה mida טוֹבָה tova מִכָּל mikol הַמִּדּוֹת hamidot טוֹבוֹת tovot,

שֶׁנֶּאֱמַר shene'emar: עֵקֶב ekev עֲנָוָה anava יִרְאַת yir'at יְהֹוָה Adonai

וּבַעֲבוּר uva'avur הָעֲנָוָה ha'anava תַּעֲלֶה ta'ale עַל al לִבְּךָ libecha מִדַּת midat

הַיִּרְאָה hayir'a, כִּי ki תִתֵּן titen אֶל el לִבְּךָ libecha תָּמִיד tamid,

מֵאַיִן me'ayin בָּאתָ bata, וּלְאָן ul'an אַתָּה ata הוֹלֵךְ holech, וְשֶׁאַתָּה veshe'ata

רִמָּה rima וְתוֹלֵעָה vetole'a בְּחַיֶּיךָ bechayecha, וְאַף ve'af כִּי ki

בְּמוֹתָךְ vemotach, וְלִפְנֵי velifnei מִי mi אַתָּה ata עָתִיד atid לִיתֵּן liten

דִּין din וְחֶשְׁבּוֹן vecheshbon, לִפְנֵי lifnei מֶלֶךְ Melech הַכָּבוֹד haKavod,

---

THE LETTER OF THE RAMBAN

"Hear, my son, the instruction of your father and don't forsake the teaching of your mother." (Proverbs 1:8). Get into the habit of always speaking calmly to everyone. This will prevent you from anger, a serious attribute flaw which causes people to sin. As our Teachers said: "Whoever flares up in anger is subject to the discipline of Gehinom" (Nedarim 22a) as it is said: "Cast out anger from your heart, and remove evil from your flesh." (Ecclesiastes 12:10) here Evil means Gehinom, as we read: "and the wicked are destined for the day of evil." (Proverbs 16:4) Once you have saved yourself from anger, the quality of humility will enter your heart. This radiant attribute is the finest of all admirable attributes (see Avoda Zara 20b), "Following humility comes the fear (awe) of the Lord." (Proverbs 22:4), and through humility, the attribute of awe will enter your heart. It will cause you to always think about where you came from and where you are going, and that while alive you are only like a maggot and a worm, and the same after death. It will also remind you before Whom you will be judged, the King of Glory (see Avot 3:1),

שֶׁנֶּאֱמַר shene'emar הִנֵּה hine הַשָּׁמַיִם hashamayim וּשְׁמֵי ushmei

הַשָּׁמַיִם hashamayim לֹא lo יְכַלְכְּלוּךָ yechalkelucha אַף af כִּי ki לִבּוֹת libot

בְּנֵי benei אָדָם adam וְנֶאֱמַר vene'emar הֲלֹא halo אֶת־ et

הַשָּׁמַיִם hashamayim וְאֶת־ ve'et הָאָרֶץ ha'aretz אֲנִי Ani מָלֵא male נְאֻם־ ne'um

יְהוָה Adonai וְכַאֲשֶׁר vecha'asher תַּחְשׁוֹב tachshov אֶת et כָּל kol

אֵלֶּה ele תִּירָא tira מִבּוֹרַאֲךָ mibor'echa וְתִשָּׁמֵר vetishamer מִן min

הַחֵטְא hachet וּבְמִדּוֹת uvmidot הָאֵלֶּה ha'ele תִּהְיֶה tih'ye שָׂמֵחַ same'ach

בְּחֶלְקֶךָ bechelkecha וְכַאֲשֶׁר vecha'asher תִּתְנַהֵג titnaheg בְּמִדַּת bemidat

הָעֲנָוָה ha'anava לְהִתְבּוֹשֵׁשׁ lehitboshesh מִכֹּל mikol אָדָם adam

וּלְהִתְפַּחֵד ulhitpached מִמֶּנּוּ mimenu וּמִן umin הַחֵטְא hachet אָז az

תִּשְׁרֶה tishre עָלֶיךָ alecha רוּחַ ru'ach הַשְּׁכִינָה haShechina וְזִיו veziv

כְּבוֹדָהּ kevoda וְחַיֵּי vechayei עוֹלָם olam הַבָּא haba וְעַתָּה ve'ata בְּנִי beni

דַּע da וּרְאֵה ur'e כִּי ki הַמִּתְגָּאֶה hamitga'e בְּלִבּוֹ belibo עַל al

הַבְּרִיּוֹת haberiyot מוֹרֵד mored הוּא hu בְּמַלְכוּת bemalchut שָׁמַיִם shamayim

כִּי ki מִתְפָּאֵר mitpa'er הוּא hu בִּלְבוּשׁ bilvush מַלְכוּת malchut

שָׁמַיִם shamayim שֶׁנֶּאֱמַר shene'emar יְהוָה Adonai מָלָךְ malach

גֵּאוּת ge'ut לָבֵשׁ lavesh וְגוֹ' vegomer וּבַמֶּה uvame יִתְגָּאֶה yitga'e

לֵב lev הָאָדָם ha'adam אִם im בְּעוֹשֶׁר be'osher יְהוָה Adonai

מוֹרִישׁ morish וּמַעֲשִׁיר uma'ashir וְאִם ve'im בְּכָבוֹד bechavod,

הֲלֹא halo לֵאלֹקִים lelokim הוּא hu שֶׁנֶּאֱמַר shene'emar וְהָעֹשֶׁר veha'osher,

וְהַכָּבוֹד vehakavod מִלְּפָנֶיךָ milfanecha וְאֵיךְ ve'ech מִתְפָּאֵר mitpa'er

בִּכְבוֹד bichvod קוֹנוֹ kono וְאִם ve'im מִתְפָּאֵר mitpa'er בְּחָכְמָה bechochma,

---

as it is written, "Even the heaven and the heavens of heaven can't contain You, How much less the hearts of people!" (I Kings 8:27; Proverbs 15:11) It is also written: "Do I not fill heaven and earth? says the Lord." (Jeremiah 23:24) When you think about all these things, you will come to fear Your creator, and you will protect yourself from sinning and therefore with these attributes you will be happy with your share. Also, when you act humbly and modestly before everyone, and are afraid of God and of sin, then the spirit of the Shechinah and its glorious radiance will rest upon you, and you will live the life of the World-to-Come! And now, my son, understand and see that whoever his heart proud and feels that he is greater than others is rebelling against the Kingdom of heaven, because he is adorning himself with the garments of the kingdom of heaven, as it is written: "The Lord reigns, He wears clothes of pride." (Psalm 93:1) Why should one's heart feel proud? Is it because of wealth? "The Lord makes one poor or rich." (I Samuel 2:7) Is it because of honor? It belongs to God, as we read: "Wealth and honor come from You." (I Chronicles 29:12) So how could one adorn himself with his master's honor? And one who is proud of his wisdom

mesir מֵסִיר safa שָׂפָה lene'emanim לְנֶאֱמָנִים, veta'am וְטַעַם zekenim זְקֵנִים

yikach יִקָּח. nimtza נִמְצָא hakol הַכֹּל shave שָׁוֶה lifnei לִפְנֵי haMakom הַמָּקוֹם,

ki כִּי ve'apo בְּאַפּוֹ mashpil מַשְׁפִּיל ge'im גֵּאִים, uvirtzono וּבִרְצוֹנוֹ

magbiha מַגְבִּיהַ shefalim שְׁפָלִים, lachen לָכֵן hashpil הַשְׁפִּיל atzmecha עַצְמְךָ

vinas'acha וִינַשַּׂאֲךָ haMakom הַמָּקוֹם. al עַל ken כֵּן afaresh אֲפָרֵשׁ lecha לְךָ

ech אֵיךְ titnaheg תִּתְנַהֵג bemidat בְּמִדַּת ha'anava הָעֲנָוָה lalechet לָלֶכֶת ba בָּהּ

tamid תָּמִיד, kol כָּל devarecha דְּבָרֶיךָ yih'yu יִהְיוּ benachat בְּנַחַת,

veroshcha וְרֹאשְׁךָ kafuf כָּפוּף, ve'enecha וְעֵינֶיךָ yabitu יַבִּיטוּ lemata לְמַטָּה

la'aretz לָאָרֶץ, velibecha וְלִבְּךָ lem'ala לְמַעְלָה, ve'al וְאַל tabit תַּבִּיט bifnei בִּפְנֵי

adam אָדָם bedabercha בְּדַבֶּרְךָ imo עִמּוֹ, vechol וְכָל adam אָדָם yih'ye יִהְיֶה

gadol גָּדוֹל mimecha מִמְּךָ be'enecha בְּעֵינֶיךָ, ve'im וְאִם chacham חָכָם oh אוֹ

ashir עָשִׁיר hu הוּא, alecha עָלֶיךָ lechabedo לְכַבְּדוֹ. ve'im וְאִם rash רָשׁ

hu הוּא ve'ata וְאַתָּה ashir עָשִׁיר oh אוֹ chacham חָכָם mimenu מִמֶּנּוּ,

chashov חֲשֹׁב belibecha בְּלִבְּךָ ki כִּי ata אַתָּה chayav חַיָּב mimenu מִמֶּנּוּ,

vehu וְהוּא zakai זַכַּאי mimach מִמָּךְ, she'im שֶׁאִם hu הוּא chote חוֹטֵא hu הוּא

shogeg שׁוֹגֵג ve'ata וְאַתָּה mezid מֵזִיד. bechol בְּכָל devarecha דְּבָרֶיךָ

uma'asecha וּמַעֲשֶׂיךָ umach'shevotecha וּמַחְשְׁבוֹתֶיךָ, uvchol וּבְכָל et עֵת,

chashov חֲשֹׁב belibach בְּלִבָּךְ ke'ilu כְּאִלּוּ ata אַתָּה omed עוֹמֵד lifnei לִפְנֵי

Kadosh קָדוֹשׁ Baruch בָּרוּךְ Hu הוּא, uSh'chinato וּשְׁכִינָתוֹ alecha עָלֶיךָ,

ki כִּי kevodo כְּבוֹדוֹ male מָלֵא ha'olam הָעוֹלָם, udvarecha וּדְבָרֶיךָ yih'yu יִהְיוּ

be'ema בְּאֵימָה uvyir'a וּבְיִרְאָה ke'eved כְּעֶבֶד lifnei לִפְנֵי rabo רַבּוֹ,

vetitbayesh וְתִתְבַּיֵּשׁ mikol מִכָּל adam אָדָם, ve'im וְאִם yikra'acha יִקְרָאֲךָ

ish אִישׁ al אַל ta'anehu תַּעֲנֵהוּ bekol בְּקוֹל ram רָם,

rak רַק benachat בְּנַחַת ke'omed כְּעוֹמֵד lifnei לִפְנֵי rabo רַבּוֹ.

---

surely knows that God "takes away the speech of assured men and reasoning from the sages." (Job 12:20) So we see that everyone is the same before God, since with His anger He lowers the proud and when he wishes He raises the low. So lower you and God will lift you up! Therefore, I will now explain to you how to behave humbly and always follow this attribute. Speak gently at all times, with your head bowed, your eyes looking down to the ground and your heart up (towards God). Don't look at a person's face while you speak to them. Consider everyone as greater than yourself. If he is wise or rich, you should give him respect. If he is poor and you are richer or wiser than he, consider yourself (in your heart) to be more guilty than he, and that he is more innocent than you, since when he sins it is err, while your sin is deliberate! In all your words, all your actions, all your thoughts and in any time regard yourself as standing before The Holy One Blessed Be He, and His Shechinah is above you, for His glory fills the whole world. Speak with fear and awe, as a slave standing before his master. Act with restraint in front of everyone. When someone calls you, don't answer loudly, but gently, as one who stands before his master. Torah should always be learned diligently, so you will be able to vehevei וֶהֱוֵי zahir זָהִיר likrot לִקְרוֹת batorah בַּתּוֹרָה tamid תָּמִיד asher אֲשֶׁר

tuchal תּוּכַל lekayema לְקַיְּמָה, vecha'asher וְכַאֲשֶׁר takum תָּקוּם min מִן

hasefer הַסֵּפֶר, techapes תְּחַפֵּשׂ ba'asher בַּאֲשֶׁר lamadeta לָמַדְתָּ im אִם yesh יֵשׁ

bo בּוֹ davar דָּבָר asher אֲשֶׁר tuchal תּוּכַל lekayemo לְקַיְּמוֹ,

uva'erev וּבָעֶרֶב, baboker בַּבֹּקֶר bema'asecha בְּמַעֲשֶׂיךָ utfashpesh וּתְפַשְׁפֵּשׁ,

vehaser וְהָסֵר bit'shuva בִּתְשׁוּבָה yamecha יָמֶיךָ kol כָּל yih'yu יִהְיוּ uvaze וּבָזֶה

be'et בְּעֵת milibecha מִלִּבְּךָ ha'olam הָעוֹלָם divrei דִּבְרֵי kol כָּל

haMakom הַמָּקוֹם lifnei לִפְנֵי libecha לִבְּךָ vehachen וְהָכֵן, hatefila הַתְּפִלָּה

vachashov וַחֲשׁוֹב, ra'yonecha רַעְיוֹנֶיךָ vetaher וְטַהֵר, Hu הוּא Baruch בָּרוּךְ

bechol בְּכָל hevlecha הֶבְלֶךָ chayei וְחַיֵּי yemei יְמֵי kol כָּל ta'ase תַּעֲשֶׂה

yih'yu יִהְיוּ uvaze וּבָזֶה. techeta תֶחֱטָא velo וְלֹא vedavar וְדָבָר davar דָּבָר

umachshevotecha וּמַחְשְׁבוֹתֶיךָ uma'asecha וּמַעֲשֶׂיךָ devarecha דְּבָרֶיךָ

uvara וּבָרָה zaka זַכָּה tih'ye תִּהְיֶה utfilatcha וּתְפִלָּתְךָ, yesharim יְשָׁרִים

lifnei לִפְנֵי umekubelet וּמְקֻבֶּלֶת umechuvenet וּמְכֻוֶּנֶת unkiya וּנְקִיָּה

tachin תָּכִין :shene'emar שֶׁנֶּאֱמַר, Hu הוּא Baruch בָּרוּךְ haMakom הַמָּקוֹם

ha'igeret הָאִגֶּרֶת tikra תִּקְרָא oznecha אָזְנֶךָ. takshiv תַּקְשִׁיב libam לִבָּם

tifchot תִּפְחוֹת, velo וְלֹא bashavu'a בַּשָּׁבוּעַ achat אַחַת pa'am פַּעַם hazot הַזֹּאת

achar אַחַר tamid תָּמִיד ba בָּה velalechet וְלָלֶכֶת lekayema לְקַיְּמָה

bechol בְּכָל tatzli'ach תַּצְלִיחַ lema'an לְמַעַן, yitbarech יִתְבָּרֵךְ hashem הַשֵּׁם

hatzafun הַצָּפוּן haba הַבָּא la'olam לָעוֹלָם vetizke וְתִזְכֶּה derachecha דְּרָכֶיךָ

shetikra'ena שֶׁתִּקְרָאֶנָּה yom יוֹם uvchol וּבְכָל. latzadikim לַצַּדִּיקִים

ya'ale יַעֲלֶה ka'asher כַּאֲשֶׁר hashamayim הַשָּׁמַיִם min מִן ya'anucha יַעֲנוּךָ

sela: סֶלָה amen אָמֵן olam עוֹלָם ad עַד lish'ol לִשְׁאוֹל libecha לִבְּךָ al עַל

---

fulfill its commands. When you arise from your learning reflect carefully on what you have studied, in order to see what in it you can put into practice. Examine your actions every morning and evening, and in this way every one of your days will be spent in Teshuvah (repentance). During your prayers, remove all worldly concerns from your heart. Prepare your heart before the Lord, purify your thoughts and think about what you are going to say before saying it. If you follow this in all your daily actions, you will not come to sin. This way everything you say, do or think will be proper, and your prayer will be pure, clear, clean, devout and acceptable before the Lord blessed Be He, as it is written: "When their heart is directed to You, listen to them." (Psalms 10:17) Read this letter at least once a week and neglect none of it. Fulfill it, and in so doing, walk with it forever in the ways of the Lord, may He Be Blessed, so that you will succeed in all your ways, and merit the World to Come which lies hidden away for the righteous. Every day that you shall read this letter, heaven shall answer your heart's desires eternally. Amen, Sela.

SPECIAL MEDITATION FOR SPIRITUAL MEMORY

Rav Chaim Vital writes (Gate of Divine Inspiration, pg. 87), "One *Yichud* (unification) that augments the memory of every person is the secret of the two Names of *Yud* and *Hei* spelled out with *Yud* and with *Hei*. Their letters are combined together, one letter from each at a time, as follows:

יּוּדּדּהּהּיּ יּוּדּהּהּהּיּ יּוּוּדּהּהּיּ

The time for this meditation is every morning at dawn.

MORNING BLESSINGS

You should say the Morning Blessings from midnight onward. And you should be aware to say all of the blessings as soon as you rise after midnight, and if you don't say them completely upon rising after midnight, you are preventing the abundance of the Upper World and the *Mochin* from infusing the Upper *Partzufim*. And you also cause the *klipot* to remain attached in the upper places. Also, the *klipot's* power spreads into your *Nefesh, Ruach, Neshamah, Chaya, Yechida*, and your senses. Using your senses now, together with the *klipot*, attached, you become drained of energy instead of grasping the opportunity to use the power to remove and cancel the *klipot*. And this is one of the reasons that other kinds of misfortune and chaos occur in our lives, Heaven Forbid, and for this reason it is important to say all the Morning Blessings when you rise at midnight, even if you plan to go to sleep afterwards, this does not apply to sleeping during the day – as there is no negative energy attached to daytime sleep. When you rise after midnight, or do not sleep at all and begin studying after midnight, you should also say the Morning Blessings (excluding the Torah Blessings, which will be said at dawn). As it is mentioned in the *Zohar, Vayakhel* 14-25: "Rav Elazar and Rav Yossi were studying from the beginning of the night, when midnight came they heard the cry of the rooster and they did say the Morning Blessings." (*Nahar Shalom*, pg. 88)

MODEH ANI

Every night, when our souls ascend to the Upper Worlds, a powerful force attempts to stop us from awakening and seeing the light of a new day. This force resides within each one of us. It is our negative side, or, what the kabbalists call our "Evil Inclination," fueled by our negative behavior from the previous day. However, the Creator gives us another chance each day to change and reveal the Light that we failed to reveal the day before. The connection of *Modeh Ani* allows us to take advantage of this opportunity. This sequence of Aramaic letters arouses our appreciation for the return of our soul to our body. This act of appreciation helps to strengthen and protect all the blessings we receive.

When you wake up, even though your hands are not clean, you can still say the verse "*modeh ani*" since it does not contain one of the Holy Names.

ס"ג מ"ה ב"ן lefanecha לְפָנֶיךָ ani אֲנִי (moda מוֹדָה :Women say) modeh מוֹדֶה

bi בִּי shehechezarta שֶׁהֶחֱזַרְתָּ vekayam וְקַיָּם chai וְחַי melech מֶלֶךְ

emunatecha אֱמוּנָתֶךָ؛ raba רַבָּה ◆bechemla בְּחֶמְלָה nishmati נִשְׁמָתִי

MORNING BLESSINGS
MODE ANI

I give thanks before You, living and existing King,
for restoring my soul to me, compassionately. Great is Your trustworthiness. (Beresheet Rabba, Ch 68)

WASHING OF THE HANDS

When we sleep at night, many negative forces latch onto our body. When our soul returns and reconnects with our body, it removes most of that negativity, but not from our hands. By washing our hands each morning upon waking, we accomplish three important objectives:
1) To cleanse and wash away all negative forces that cling to our hands during the night;
2) To connect ourselves to the cause and seed level of reality (proactive) and not just the effect (reactive);
3) To detach ourselves from the energy of *ani* (poor) and connect ourselves to the energy of *ashir* (rich).

Wash your hands in the water of *Chesed* (mercy) to remove the filth of the *klipa* that is attached to the 5 *Gevurot* (judgments) מנצפך that are revealed by the ten fingers of the hands of *Zeir Anpin* of *Asiyah*. **First**, hold the washing vessel in your right hand and fill it with water, and then hand it over to the left hand. **Then**, pour the water from the left onto the right and then pour water from the right onto the left. This process should be repeated a second and a third time. In a way that every hand would be washed three times. You should not wash one hand three times in a row, but alternate between right and left and in doing so the impure spirit that is called "*Shiv'ta* (**do not pronounce this name**) the daughter of a king" jumps from one hand to the other until it is completely removed from the hands. And if you don't follow this order, this impure spirit is not removed. Before the blessing, you should open the palms of your hands like someone who wants to receive something, and meditate to raise *Asiyah* by the 42-Letter Name of *Yetzirah*, which is the numerical value of three hands:

Right hand (*HaGedola*) יהוה אלהינו יהוה, the secret of the first half of the Name יוד ואו דלת הא אלף
Left hand (*HaChazaka*) כוזו במוכסז כוזו, the secret of the last half of the Name ואו אלף ואו הא אלף
Middle Hand (*Rama*) יהוה יוד הא ואו הא Is the root of the Name itself and from it spreads those three hands and therefore it is in the middle. And by these three hands of *Yetzirah* we raise *Asiyah*.

The washing of the hands is the *tikkun* of the Inner Light, its interior and exterior (*Netzach, Hod, Yesod*) of *Asiyah*. **The blessing** is the *tikkun* of the Surrounding Light of the exterior (*Netzach, Hod, Yesod*) of *Asiyah*. 13 words correspond to the Thirteen Attributes of *Asiyah*.

Wash your hands, go to the bathroom as necessary, and then wash your hands again. The way to wash our hands: Hold the washing vessel in your right hand and fill it with water, and then hand it over to your left hand. Then, pour the water from the left over the right and then pour water from the right onto the left. That process should be repeated a second and a third time. You should not wash them three times in a row, but alternate between right and left. Rub your hands together 3 times and raise them to the level of the eyes and say the blessing before drying the hands.

בְּרוּךְ baruch (אל)   אַתָּה Ata (רוזם)   יְהֹוָה Adonai (וזנון)

אֱלֹהֵינוּ Elohenu (ילה)   מֶלֶךְ melech (ארך)   הָעוֹלָם ha'olam (ורב וזסד)

אֲשֶׁר asher (ואמת)   קִדְּשָׁנוּ kideshanu (נצר וזסד)   בְּמִצְוֹתָיו bemitzvotav (לאלפים)

רְצֹוָנוּ vetzivanu (נשא עון)   עַל al (ופשע)   נְטִילַת netilat (וזטאה)   יָדָיִם yadayim (ונקה)

The last three words of this blessing are *Al Netilat Yadayim*: The first letter from each of these three words spells *ani* עני, Aramaic for "a poor person," and has the numerical value as the Holy Name *Mem Hei* (יוד הא ואו הא). The last 2 letters of each of these 3 words, *Ayin Lamed* עַל, *Lamed Tav* לֹת, and *Yud Mem* ימ, have the same numerical value as the word *ashir* עָשׁיר, meaning "a rich person."

WASHING OF THE HANDS
Blessed are You, Lord, our God, the King of the world,
Who has sanctified us with His commandments and obliges us with the washing of the hands.

ASHER YATZAR

Reciting *Asher Yatzar* after each time we have been to the bathroom connects us to the original spiritual DNA and blueprint of a human being. We may wake up in the morning feeling depleted of spiritual energy, depressed, fearful, moody, or even full of dread for the day to come. Through the power of *Asher Yatzar*, we inject the Light of Creation into our immune system; strengthening and boosting it so that we become filled with Light and spiritually recharged for the entire day.

In this section, there are 45 words, which are equal to the numerical value of the word *Adam* (human being) and the same numerical value of the name *Mem-Hei*, which was created by *Chochmah*. The word *Chochmah* is divided to two other words which mean strength (*Ko'ach*) to the *Mem-Hei*. You should meditate on the Holy Name *Mem-Hei*:

יוד הא ואו הא

The blessing is the *tikkun* of Surrounding Light of the interior (*Netzach, Hod, Yesod*) of *Asiyah*.

Adonai יְהֹוָהאדנייאהדונהי Ata אַתָּה baruch בָּרוּךְ *(Abba of Asiyah)*

yatzar יָצַר asher אֲשֶׁר ha'olam הָעוֹלָם melech מֶלֶךְ Elohenu אֱלֹהֵינוּ

bechochma בְּחוֹכְמָה ha'adam הָאָדָם et אֶת

uvara וּבָרָא

chalulim וַחֲלוּלִים nekavim נְקָבִים nekavim נְקָבִים vo בּוֹ

chalulim וַחֲלוּלִים

chevodecha כְּבוֹדֶךָ chise כִּסֵּא lifnei לִפְנֵי veyadu'a וְיָדוּעַ galuy גָּלוּי

she'im שֶׁאִם

im אִם oh אוֹ mehem מֵהֶם echad אֶחָד yisatem יִסָּתֵם

echad אֶחָד yipate'ach יִפָּתֵחַ

afilu אֲפִלּוּ lehitkayem לְהִתְקַיֵּם efshar אֶפְשָׁר ei אִי mehem מֵהֶם

Adonai יְהֹוָהאדנייאהדונהי Ata אַתָּה baruch בָּרוּךְ echat אֶחָת sha'a שָׁעָה

la'asot לַעֲשׂוֹת umafli וּמַפְלִיא basar בָּשָׂר chol כָּל rofe רוֹפֵא

ASHER YATZAR

Blessed are You, Lord, our God, the King of the world, Who made man with wisdom and created in him many openings and many cavities. It is obvious and known before Your Throne of Glory that should any one of them become blocked or should any one of them break open, then it would be impossible to remain alive for even one hour. Blessed are You, Lord, the Healer of all flesh and Who amazes by what He does.

ELOHAI NESHAMAH: CONNECTING WITH OUR SOUL

Kabbalah teaches us that there are five main levels of our soul: *Nefesh, Ruach, Neshamah, Chaya* and *Yechida*. In our day-to-day lives, most of us are not fully connected to all five levels. An umbilical-like cord constantly runs through the five levels of the soul, feeding us the minimum amount of Light we need to keep the "pilot light" glimmering in our soul. We recite *Elohai Neshamah* every morning to connect our conscious mind to the five levels of our soul so that we can awaken our true purpose and meaning in life.

The name of a person is not merely a word; it is also the spiritual connection to the soul. Each letter of a name is part of the spiritual genetic alphabet that infuses the soul with the particular form of energy that the name creates. The power of this blessing is that it tunnels through the Upper Worlds and creates a connection to all five parts of our soul. We deepen our connection to this prayer by combining our Hebrew name with the word *Neshamah* (soul). To merge your name with *Neshamah*, from right to left, insert the first letter of your name followed by the first letter of *Neshamah*. Then insert the second letter of your name followed by the second letter of *Neshamah,* and so on. Meditate on the entire sequence of letters before connecting to the prayer. For example, with the name *Yehuda*, the combination will look as follows:

Not every person merits the part of the soul called *Neshamah*, however, we all still have a part of the soul of Adam (the first man) that encompasses all of Creation. In this blessing, there are 47 words, which are equal to the numerical value of:

יאהדונהי

(Pause here)   יל״ה   ;   דמב   ע״ב,   מילוי   Elohai **אֱלֹהַי**   *(Ima of Asiyah)*

(five aspects of the collective Atzilut, Beriah, Yetzirah and Asiyah) neshama **נְשָׁמָה**

◆*(Chayah from Atzilut)* tehora **טְהוֹרָה** (in the soul of *Adam*) bi **בִּי** shenatata **שֶׁנָּתַתָּ**

Ata **אַתָּה** ◆*(Neshamah from Beriah)* verata **בְרָאתָהּ** Ata **אַתָּה**

nefachta **נְפַוְֹתָהּ** Ata **אַתָּה** ◆*(Ruach from Yetzirah)* yetzarta **יְצַרְתָּהּ**

meshamera **מְשַׁמְּרָהּ** veAta **וְאַתָּה** ◆*(Nefesh from Asiyah)* bi **בִּי**

litela **לִטְּלָהּ** atid **עָתִיד** veAta **וְאַתָּה** עתידי◆ bekirbi **בְּקִרְבִּי**

◆lavo **לָבֹא** le'atid **לֶעָתִיד** bi **בִּי** ulhachazira **וּלְהַחֲזִירָהּ** mimeni **מִמֶּנִּי**

ELOHAI NESHAMAH
My God,
the soul that You have given in me is pure. You have formed it. You have created it. You have breathed it into me and You preserve it within me. You shall eventually take it away from me yet return it to me in the coming future.

עֹדִי **בְּקִרְבִּי** vekirbi שֶׁהַנְּשָׁמָה shehaneshamah זְמַן zeman יל״י **כָּל** kol

ב״ן מ״ה ס״ג אֲנִי ani **אֲנִי** lefanecha **לְפָנֶיךָ** **מוֹדֶה** modeh

velohei **וֵאלֹהֵי** ; יל״ה דמב, ע״ב, מילוי Elohai **אֱלֹהַי** אדנ״יאהדונה״י Adonai **יְהוָ֨ה**

ע״ב מ״ה ס״ג ב״ן יהוה ribon **רִבּוֹן** avotai **אֲבוֹתַי** ; יל״ה דמב, ע״ב, מילוי ; לכב

יל״י kol **כָּל** אני adon **אֲדוֹן** ◆hama'asim **הַמַּעֲשִׂים** יל״י kol **כָּל**

Adonai אדנ״יאהדונה״י Ata **אַתָּה** baruch **בָּרוּךְ** ◆haneshamot **הַנְּשָׁמוֹת**

◆metim **מֵתִים** lifgarim **לִפְגָרִים** neshamot **נְשָׁמוֹת** hamachazir **הַמַּחֲזִיר**

THE EIGHTEEN BLESSINGS

The purpose of the Eighteen Blessings is to reconnect our soul to our physical body after it has been almost totally disconnected during the previous night's sleep. All of us are blessed with various gifts that, most of the time we do not appreciate, such as the connection of our soul to our body. Unfortunately, most of us only start to appreciate our gifts once we have lost them. Through the power of these Eighteen Blessings, we can inject a proactive energy force of appreciation, which, in turn, protects and preserves all that we hold dear.

The Eighteen Blessings correspond to *Yesod* of *Asiyah*. With these blessings, we draw great abundance and great illumination to the three upper *Sefirot* of *Asiyah*, and by that, their external part is blessed and receives this great Light and the external becomes equal to the internal.

THE FIRST BLESSING - DISTINGUISHES BETWEEN DAY AND NIGHT

The greatest gift we have as human beings is the power of free will. The phrase "distinguishing between day and night" refers to the ability we have to choose the Light of the Creator over darkness or good over evil. By saying this blessing, we are given clarity to see these two opposing forces that are usually concealed from us.

The First Blessing is in the three *Partzufim* of *Keter*: external, middle and internal of Direct Light of the middle *Partzuf* of *Zeir Anpin* of *Asiyah* of *Atzilut*, and of Lower *Asiyah*.

יל״ה Elohenu **אֱלֹהֵינוּ** Adonai אדנ״יאהדונה״י Ata **אַתָּה** baruch **בָּרוּךְ**

ושׁ״ר אבגית״ץ, hanoten **הַנּוֹתֵן** ha'olam **הָעוֹלָם** melech **מֶלֶךְ**

; אהיה אהיה יהוה vina **בִּינָה** גבריאל מלאך = ע״ה שכוי lasechvi **לַשֶּׂכְוִי**

lehavchin **לְהַבְחִין** אדנ״י כלה, = וס״ת (sweetening the night's judgment) ס״ג מילוי ר״ת

◆יהוה פ״ג = ר״ת ; מלה layla **לַיְלָה** uven **וּבֵין** אל יהוה זן, מזבח, נגד, ע״ה yom **יוֹם** ben **בֵּין**

As long as the soul is within me, I am grateful to You, Lord, my God and the God of my fathers, the Governor of all actions. The Master of all souls. Blessed are You, Lord, Who restores souls to dead corpses.

THE EIGHTEEN BLESSINGS - THE FIRST BLESSING

Blessed are You, Lord, our God,
the King of the world, Who gives the rooster the understanding to distinguish between day and night.

THE SECOND BLESSING - GIVES SIGHT TO THE BLIND

King David said: "*We have eyes, but see not. We have ears, but hear not.*" Too often, we are blinded by a lucrative opportunity or we fail to anticipate the chaos of an impending situation. The real power of this blessing is that it helps heighten our senses of perception and intuition so that we can see the truths that are normally concealed from us.

The Second Blessing is in the three *Partzufim* of *Keter*: external, middle and internal of Returning Light of the middle *Partzuf* of *Zeir Anpin* of *Asiyah* of *Atzilut*, and of Lower *Asiyah*.

ילה Elohenu אֱלֹהֵינוּ	Adonai יְהֹוָאהדיאהדונהי	Ata אַתָּה	baruch בָּרוּךְ
ivrim עוְרים	poke'ach פּוֹקֵחַ	ha'olam הָעוֹלָם	melech מֶלֶךְ

THE THIRD BLESSING - RELEASES THOSE WHO ARE BOUND

Often we become prisoners of our jobs, our mortgage payments, our relationships, our careers, or even other people's perceptions of us. In essence, to one degree or another, everyone is a prisoner, held captive by his *Desire to Receive for the Self Alone*. The energy that emanates from this blessing has the power to release us from the clutches of this powerful and self-destructive desire.

The Third Blessing is in the three of *Partzufim* of *Chochmah*: external, middle and internal of Direct Light of the middle *Partzuf* of *Zeir Anpin* of *Asiyah* of *Atzilut*, and of Lower *Asiyah*.

ילה Elohenu אֱלֹהֵינוּ	Adonai יְהֹוָאהדיאהדונהי	Ata אַתָּה	baruch בָּרוּךְ
asurim אֲסוּרים	matir מַתִּיר	ha'olam הָעוֹלָם	melech מֶלֶךְ

THE FOURTH BLESSING – STRAIGHTENS THOSE WHO ARE BENT OVER

The inner meaning of this blessing pertains to the often skewed view we have of the world and the people around us. Our self-centered ego distorts our perception of reality to the point where everyone else appears crooked, imperfect, and wrong. This particular sequence of Aramaic letters has the power to imbue us with acceptance and understanding so that we can transform the negative part of our character which perceives others as bent.

The Fourth Blessing is in the three *Partzufim* of *Chochmah*: external, middle and internal of Returning Light of the middle *Partzuf* of *Zeir Anpin* of *Asiyah* of *Atzilut*, and of Lower *Asiyah*.

ילה Elohenu אֱלֹהֵינוּ	Adonai יְהֹוָאהדיאהדונהי	Ata אַתָּה	baruch בָּרוּךְ
kefufim כְּפוּפים	zokef זוֹקֵף	ha'olam הָעוֹלָם	melech מֶלֶךְ

THE SECOND BLESSING
Blessed are You, Lord, our God, King of the world, Who gives sight to the blind.

THE THIRD BLESSING
Blessed are You, Lord, our God, King of the world, Who releases those who are bound.

THE FOURTH BLESSING
Blessed are You, Lord, our God, King of the world, Who straightens those who are bent over.

THE FIFTH BLESSING - CLOTHES THE NAKED

Kabbalah explains that the body is the clothing of the soul. Just as a negative person cannot change his character by donning an expensive suit, we cannot bring about personal change or lasting fulfillment without connecting to a world beyond our body consciousness. The sequence of letters in this blessing gives us the power to rise above our body consciousness and connect with our soul consciousness.

The Fifth Blessing is in the three *Partzufim* of *Binah*: external, middle and internal of Direct Light of the middle *Partzuf* of *Zeir Anpin* of *Asiyah* of *Atzilut*, and of Lower *Asiyah*. At the end of the blessing meditate to draw 378 illuminations from the Face of *Arich Anpin* to the Face of *Chashmal* of *Zeir* and *Nukva* of *Atzilut* which is the secret of *malbush* (*Malbush* means clothing which has the same numerical value of *Chashmal* – electricity).

ילה Elohenu אֱלֹהֵינוּ Adonai יְהֹוָאדֹנֵיאהדונהי Ata אַתָּה baruch בָּרוּךְ

arumim עֲרוּמִים malbish מַלְבִּישׁ ha'olam הָעוֹלָם melech מֶלֶךְ

THE SIXTH BLESSING - GIVES STRENGTH TO THE WEARY

We often try to affect positive change within ourselves. We attempt to face down our fears, rid ourselves of anger, and overcome our jealousies. But Satan, a negative intelligence, battles us from the inside, and can prevent these changes from happening. The sequence of letters in this blessing gives us that extra help and energy we need to defeat Satan.

The Sixth Blessing is in the three *Partzufim* of *Binah*: external, middle and internal of Returning Light of the middle *Partzuf* of *Zeir Anpin* of *Asiyah* of *Atzilut*, and of Lower *Asiyah*. At the end of the blessing meditate to draw 378 illuminations from the Face of *Arich Anpin* to the Face of *Chashmal* of *Zeir* and *Nukva* of *Atzilut* which is the secret of *malbush* (*Malbush* means clothing which has the same numerical value of *Chashmal* – electricity).

melech מֶלֶךְ ילה Elohenu אֱלֹהֵינוּ Adonai יְהֹוָאדֹנֵיאהדונהי Ata אַתָּה baruch בָּרוּךְ

ko'ach כּוֹחַ laya'ef לַיָּעֵף ושיר אבויתך, hanoten הַנּוֹתֵן ha'olam הָעוֹלָם

THE SEVENTH BLESSING - KEEPS THE LAND OVER THE WATER

The kabbalists teach that before the creation of the world, water filled all of reality and existence. Water is a physical expression of the energy force of mercy and the Lightforce of the Creator, also known as the *Desire to Share*. Physical matter has the inherent essence of the *Desire to Receive*, represented by the creation of the land on our planet. God created a delicate balance between the *Desire to Share* and the *Desire to Receive*, manifested in the balance between the water and the land. This blessing helps us achieve and maintain this balance.

THE FIFTH BLESSING

Blessed are You, Lord, our God, King of the world, Who clothes the naked.

THE SIXTH BLESSING

Blessed are You, Lord, our God, King of the world, Who gives strength to the weary.

The Seventh Blessing is in the three *Partzufim* of *Chesed*: external, middle and internal of Direct Light of the middle *Partzuf* of *Zeir Anpin* of *Asiyah* of *Atzilut*, and of Lower *Asiyah*.

ילה Elohenu אֱלֹהֵינוּ Adonai יְהֹוָוֹאדֹנָיאהדונהי Ata אַתָּה baruch בָּרוּךְ

ע"ה דההין אלהים ha'aretz הָאָרֶץ roka רוֹקַע ha'olam הָעוֹלָם melech מֶלֶךְ

hamayim הַמָּיִם al עַל

THE EIGHTH BLESSING - PROVIDES FOR THE FOOTSTEPS OF MAN

When a person embarks on a spiritual path, he or she will inevitably face obstacles and challenges along the way. This particular sequence of Aramaic letters gives us the power of certainty, to know that the spiritual path we are on is the correct one, even when the road before us is temporarily dim.

The Eighth Blessing is in the three *Partzufim* of *Chesed*: external, middle and internal of Returning Light of the middle *Partzuf* of *Zeir Anpin* of *Asiyah* of *Atzilut*, and of Lower *Asiyah*.

ילה Elohenu אֱלֹהֵינוּ Adonai יְהֹוָוֹאדֹנָיאהדונהי Ata אַתָּה baruch בָּרוּךְ

gaver גָּבֶר mitz'adei מִצְעֲדֵי hamechin הַמֵּכִין ha'olam הָעוֹלָם melech מֶלֶךְ

THE NINTH BLESSING - PROVIDES FOR ALL MY NEEDS

We do not recite this blessing on *Tisha B'Av* (9th of Av) or on *Yom Kippur*.

This ancient sequence of letters ensures that we receive what our soul truly desires and not what our short-term reactive impulses cause us to crave.

The Ninth Blessing is in the Three *Partzufim* of *Gevurah*: external, middle and internal of Direct Light of the middle *Partzuf* of *Zeir Anpin* of *Asiyah* of *Atzilut*, and of Lower *Asiyah*.

ילה Elohenu אֱלֹהֵינוּ Adonai יְהֹוָוֹאדֹנָיאהדונהי Ata אַתָּה baruch בָּרוּךְ

עליונים דפנים נהורין (ע"ע she'asa שֶׁעָשָׂה ha'olam הָעוֹלָם melech מֶלֶךְ שָׂע (ע"ע

להמתיק דיני ע"ה דלהן) = אלף למד אלף למד [אל א' = יהוה ד' אותיות והכולל ואל ב' = יא"י דס"ג](

tzorki צָרְכִּי ילי kol כָּל li לִי אלהים אותיות וה' = אלהים דיורין וה' אותיות עה

THE SEVENTH BLESSING
Blessed are You, Lord, our God, King of the world, Who keeps land over the water.
THE EIGHTH BLESSING
Blessed are You, Lord, our God, King of the world, Who provides for the footsteps of man.
THE NINTH BLESSING
Blessed are You, Lord, our God, King of the world, Who provides for all my needs.

THE TENTH BLESSING - STRENGTHENS ISRAEL WITH MIGHT

In Aramaic, the word for "strength" is *Gevurah*. *Gevurah* has the same numerical value (216) as the three-letter sequences of the 72 Names of God (72 x 3 = 216), which helps us achieve mind over matter and overcome our reactive nature. Another secret can be found in the last three words of the blessing. The first three letters of the last three words (*Alef* א, *Yud* י, and *Bet* ב) have the same numerical value (13) as the Aramaic word for *Ahavah* (אהבה) which means "love." If we have love in our lives, we will always have the ability to tap into the power of the 72 Names of God.

The Tenth Blessing is in the three *Partzufim* of *Gevurah*: external, middle and internal of Returning Light of the middle *Partzuf* of *Zeir Anpin* of *Asiyah* of *Atzilut*, and of Lower *Asiyah*.

ילה Elohenu אֱלֹהֵינוּ Adonai יְהֹוָאדֹנִיאַהדונהי Ata אַתָּה baruch בָּרוּךְ

Yisrael יִשְׂרָאֵל ozer אוֹזֵר ha'olam הָעוֹלָם melech מֶלֶךְ

bigvura בִּגְבוּרָה רי"ו ; ר"ת = אהבה, אוזר, דאגה

THE ELEVENTH BLESSING - CROWNS ISRAEL WITH SPLENDOR

The word for "splendor" in Aramaic is *Tifara*, from the root *Tiferet*. *Tiferet* is the *Sefirah* or the specific dimension that connects the Upper Worlds to our physical world. The sequence of letters that make up this blessing gives us the ability to capture and store the Light—like a portable battery that can fuel us—even after we close the Siddur.

The Eleventh Blessing is in the three *Partzufim* of *Tiferet*: external, middle and internal of Direct Light of the middle *Partzuf* of *Zeir Anpin* of *Asiyah* of *Atzilut*, and of Lower *Asiyah*.

ילה Elohenu אֱלֹהֵינוּ Adonai יְהֹוָאדֹנִיאַהדונהי Ata אַתָּה baruch בָּרוּךְ

betifara בְּתִפְאָרָה Yisrael יִשְׂרָאֵל oter עוֹטֵר ha'olam הָעוֹלָם melech מֶלֶךְ

THE TWELFTH BLESSING - DID NOT MAKE ME A GENTILE/GENTILE WOMAN

On the surface level, this blessing appears to be discriminatory. Kabbalistically, the word gentile has nothing to do with a person's religious affiliation. Rather, it is a code word which represents someone who does not have a powerful and intense *Desire to Receive*. This blessing ignites our desire for spiritual growth, inner change, and positive transformation.

THE TENTH BLESSING
Blessed are You, Lord, our God, King of the world, Who strengthens Israel with might.
THE ELEVENTH BLESSING
Blessed are You, Lord, our God, King of the world, Who crowns Israel with splendor.

The Twelfth Blessing is in the three *Partzufim* of *Tiferet*: external, middle and internal of Returning Light of the middle *Partzuf* of *Zeir Anpin* of *Asiyah* of *Atzilut*, and of Lower *Asiyah*.

יכה baruch בָּרוּךְ Ata אַתָּה Adonai יְהֹוָואדנֹיאהדונֹהי Elohenu אֱלֹהֵינוּ

melech מֶלֶךְ ha'olam הָעוֹלָם shelo שֶׁלֹא asani עָשַׂנִי goi גּוֹי:

Women say: בָּרוּךְ baruch Ata אַתָּה Adonai יְהֹוָואדנֹיאהדונֹהי Elohenu אֱלֹהֵינוּ יכה

melech מֶלֶךְ ha'olam הָעוֹלָם shelo שֶׁלֹא asani עָשַׂנִי goya גּוֹיָה:

THE THIRTEENTH BLESSING – DID NOT MAKE ME A SLAVE/MAIDSERVANT

This blessing gives us the support we need so that we are not governed and held captive by our reactive nature and the material world.

The Thirteenth Blessing is in the three *Partzufim* of *Netzach*: external, middle and internal of Direct Light of the middle *Partzuf* of *Zeir Anpin* of *Asiyah* of *Atzilut*, and of Lower *Asiyah*.

יכה baruch בָּרוּךְ Ata אַתָּה Adonai יְהֹוָואדנֹיאהדונֹהי Elohenu אֱלֹהֵינוּ

melech מֶלֶךְ ha'olam הָעוֹלָם shelo שֶׁלֹא asani עָשַׂנִי aved עֶבֶד:

Women say: בָּרוּךְ baruch Ata אַתָּה Adonai יְהֹוָואדנֹיאהדונֹהי Elohenu אֱלֹהֵינוּ יכה

melech מֶלֶךְ ha'olam הָעוֹלָם shelo שֶׁלֹא asani עָשַׂנִי shifcha שִׁפְחָה:

THE FOURTEENTH BLESSING –
DID NOT MAKE ME A WOMAN/ MADE ME ACCORDING TO HIS WILL

Although this blessing appears to be chauvinistic, it is not. Kabbalistically, the inherent energy of the dimension of *Zeir Anpin* (comprising the Sefirot of *Chesed* to *Yesod*)--the pipeline through which the Light flows from the Upper Worlds into our world--is masculine. *Malchut*, our world has an inherent feminine energy. This prayer ignites appreciation for our ability to generate spiritual Light through the two energy forces of male and female, and helps the two halves of the soul--male and female--to unite.

The Fourteenth Blessing is in the three *Partzufim* of *Netzach*: external, middle and internal of Returning Light of the middle *Partzuf* of *Zeir Anpin* of *Asiyah* of *Atzilut*, and of Lower *Asiyah*.

יכה baruch בָּרוּךְ Ata אַתָּה Adonai יְהֹוָואדנֹיאהדונֹהי Elohenu אֱלֹהֵינוּ

melech מֶלֶךְ ha'olam הָעוֹלָם shelo שֶׁלֹא asani עָשַׂנִי isha אִשָּׁה:

Women say: בָּרוּךְ baruch she'asani שֶׁעָשַׂנִי kirtzono כִּרְצוֹנוֹ:

THE TWELFTH BLESSING
Blessed are You, Lord, our God, King of the world, Who did not make me a gentile / gentile woman.
THE THIRTEENTH BLESSING
Blessed are You, Lord, our God, King of the world, Who did not make me a slave / maidservant.
THE FOURTEENTH BLESSING
Blessed are You, Lord, our God, King of the world, Who did not make me a woman. /
Blessed is He Who made me according to His Will.

THE FIFTEENTH BLESSING - REMOVES THE BOND OF SLEEP FROM MY EYES

Kabbalists have said that humanity has been asleep for 2000 years. Unfortunately, some people live their entire lives asleep. They never raise their level of consciousness, and fail to affect true inner change. The Aramaic letters in this blessing help to awaken us from that coma.

The Fifteenth Blessing is in the three *Partzufim* of *Hod*: external, middle and internal of Direct Light of the middle *Partzuf* of *Zeir Anpin* of *Asiyah* of *Atzilut*, and of Lower *Asiyah*.

ילה Elohenu אֱלֹהֵינוּ Adonai יְהֹוָאדְנִיאהדונהי Ata אַתָּה baruch בָּרוּךְ

chevlei וְחֶבְלֵי hama'avir הַמַּעֲבִיר ha'olam הָעוֹלָם melech מֶלֶךְ

me'afapai מֵעַפְעַפָּי utnuma וּתְנוּמָה מ"ה ריבוע me'enai מֵעֵינָי shena שֵׁנָה

This blessing does not end here but in the end of the next section ("gomel chasadim tovim le'amo Yisrael"), so that is why we don't answer AMEN here.

VIHI RATZON
This prayer helps us to remove the forces of negativity that lie within us.

Vihi Ratzon removes the control of the *chitzoniyim* (negative external forces) from the internal aspect.

milfanecha מִלְּפָנֶיךָ מהע ע"ה, ע"ב בריבוע קס"א ע"ה, אל שדי ע"ה ratzon רָצוֹן vihi וִיהִי

ס"ג מ"ה ב"ן Adonai יְהֹוָאדְנִיאהדונהי Elohai אֱלֹהַי מילוי ע"ב, דמב ; ילה

shetargileni שֶׁתַּרְגִּילֵנִי avotai אֲבוֹתַי ; ילה ; מילוי ע"ב, דמב ; לכב velohei וֵאלֹהֵי

bemitzvoteicha בְּמִצְוֹתֶיךָ vetadbikeni וְתַדְבִּיקֵנִי betoratecha בְּתוֹרָתְךָ

lidei לִידֵי velo וְלֹא chet וְחֵטְא lidei לִידֵי tevi'eni תְּבִיאֵנִי ve'al וְאַל

lidei לִידֵי velo וְלֹא nisayon נִסָּיוֹן lidei לִידֵי velo וְלֹא avon עָוֹן

hara הָרָע miyetzer מִיֵּצֶר vetarchikeni וְתַרְחִיקֵנִי vizayon בִּזָּיוֹן

et אֶת vechof וְכוֹף hatov הַטּוֹב beyetzer בְּיֵצֶר vetadbikeni וְתַדְבִּיקֵנִי

hayom הַיּוֹם utneni וּתְנֵנִי lach לָךְ lehisht'abed לְהִשְׁתַּעְבֶּד yitzri יִצְרִי

ע"ה נגד, מזבוח, זן, אל יהוה yom יוֹם לכב ב"ן, uvchol וּבְכָל ע"ה נגד, מזבוח, זן, אל יהוה

THE FIFTEENTH BLESSING
Blessed are You, Lord,
our God, King of the world, Who removes the bonds of sleep from my eyes and slumber from my eyelids.

VIHI RATZON
And may it be Your will, Lord, our God and God of our fathers, that You accustom me to Your Torah and cause me to cleave to Your precepts, and do not bring me to the hands of sin, iniquity, temptation, nor shame. And cause me to distance myself from the Evil Inclination, and cling me to the Good Inclination, and compel my will to be subservient to You. Grant me this day and every day,

יהוה   ריבוע   ע"ב,   ulchesed וּלְחֶסֶד   בריבוע   מ"ה   מילוי,   מוזי,   lechen לְכֵן

מ"ה   ריבוע   ;   קס"א   ע"ה   be'enecha בְּעֵינֶיךָ   ulrachamim וּלְרַחֲמִים

vegomleni וְגָמְלֵנִי   רוֹאִי ro'ai   ילי   chol כָּל   מ"ה   ריבוע   uv'enei וּבְעֵינֵי

Adonai יְהֹוָאדֹנָיאהדונהי   Ata אַתָּה   baruch בָּרוּךְ   tovim טוֹבִים   chasadim חֲסָדִים   וְחֶסֶד

:Yisrael יִשְׂרָאֵל   le'amo לְעַמּוֹ   tovim טוֹבִים   chasadim חֲסָדִים   וְחֶסֶד   gomel גּוֹמֵל

YEHI RATZON

Too often we attract negative people and unfavorable situations into our lives. We find ourselves in the wrong place at the wrong time. We do business with the wrong people. Here, we gain the ability to remove all external negative events from intruding into our lives. We also remove eleven distinct areas of negativity that can invade our environment.

Yehi Ratzon removes the control of the *chitzoniyim* (negative external forces) from the external aspect. In this section we mention 11 aspects corresponding to the 11 incenses of the *Ketoret*.

milfanecha מִלְפָנֶיךָ   מהש ע"ה, ע"ב בריבוע קס"א ע"ה, אל שדי ע"ה,   ratzon רָצוֹן   yehi יְהִי

velohei וֵאלֹהֵי   אֱלֹהַי Elohai מילוי ע"ב, דמב ; ילה   Adonai יְהֹוָאדֹנָיאהדונהי   ס"ג מ"ה ב"ן

hayom הַיּוֹם   shetatzileni שֶׁתַּצִּילֵנִי   avotai אֲבוֹתַי   ילה ; דמב ; ע"ב מילוי ; לכב

יום אל יהוה   זן, מזבוח, נגד ע"ה   yom יוֹם   לכב   ב"ן,   uvchol וּבְכָל   נגד, מזבוח, זן, אל יהוה ע"ה

אדני אהיה ע"ה, אלהים אל יהוה, זן, מזבוח, נגד ע"ה   me'azei מֵעַזֵּי   vayom וְיוֹם

ra רָע me'adam מֵאָדָם   panim פָּנִים   ume'azut וּמֵעַזּוּת   fanim פָּנִים

ra רָע mishachen מִשָׁכֵן   ra רָע mechaver מֵחָבֵר   ra רָע miyetzer מִיֵּצֶר

hara הָרָע   מ"ה ריבוע   me'ayin מֵעַיִן   ra רָע mipega מִפֶּגַע

kashe קָשֶׁה   midin מִדִּין   hara הָרָע   umilashon וּמִלָּשׁוֹן

shehu שֶׁהוּא   ben בֵּן   kashe קָשֶׁה   din דִּין   umiba'al וּמִבַּעַל

:berit בְּרִית   ven בֶן   she'eno שֶׁאֵינוֹ   uven וּבֵין   berit בְּרִית   ven בֶן

---

grace, loving kindness, and mercy in Your sight and in the sight of all that behold me, and bestow upon me loving kindness. Blessed are You, Lord, Who bestows loving kindness on His people Israel.

YEHI RATZON

May it be Your will, Lord our God and God of our forefathers, to save me this day and every day from an arrogant man and from arrogance, from an evil man, from the Evil Inclination, from an evil companion, from an evil neighbor, from an evil happening, from evil eye, and from evil speech, from harsh judgment, and a harsh opponent, whether he be a son of the covenant or not a son of the covenant.

BLESSINGS OF THE *TORAH*
The next three blessings are known as *Birkot haTorah* (Blessings of the Torah).

THE SIXTEENTH BLESSING -TEACHINGS OF THE TORAH
The kabbalists teach that without a connection to the *Torah*, we do not stand a chance affecting genuine positive change in our lives or in the world around us. According to Kabbalah, reference to the *Torah* refers to spiritual work and spiritual study, and to using spiritual tools. This blessing connects us to the inner essence of the *Torah* giving us the energy and fuel we need to ignite all the other blessings we have recited, and to imbue our lives with passion and spiritual energy.

The Sixteenth Blessing has two aspects:
1) The aspect of the *Mitzva* of *Esek* ("involved") of the *Torah* which is in *Zeir Anpin* of *Atzilut*.
2) The aspect that is in the three *Partzufim* of *Hod*: the external, middle and internal of Returning Light of the middle *Partzuf* of *Zeir Anpin* of *Asiyah* of *Atzilut*, and of Lower *Asiyah* (as in the other blessings). While saying this blessing, you should meditate on both aspects, and while saying the words *"asher kideshanu..."* you should also meditate to draw the *Tzelems* into *Chochmah, Binah, Da'at* of *Zeir Anpin* of *Atzilut*, as we meditate on the other precepts of the *Torah*.

ילה Elohenu אֱלֹהֵינוּ   Adonai יְהֹוָהֿאדניֿיאהדונהי   Ata אַתָּה   baruch בָּרוּךְ

kideshanu קִדְּשָׁנוּ   asher אֲשֶׁר   ha'olam הָעוֹלָם   melech מֶלֶךְ

‡torah תּוֹרָה ראה   divrei דִּבְרֵי   al עַל   vetzivanu וְצִוָּנוּ   bemitzvotav בְּמִצְוֹתָיו

According to the Ari:
We answer AMEN after this blessing, as this is a separate blessing from the next one.

THE SEVENTEENTH BLESSING - TEACHES *TORAH* TO THE NATION
We say this blessing with the consciousness to help everyone make a connection to the energy of the *Torah*. This is our opportunity to genuinely care about others and to share the Light of the Creator - one of the most powerful ways to transform our reactive nature into a proactive one.

The Seventeenth Blessing is in the three *Partzufim* of *Yesod*: external, middle and internal of Direct Light of the middle *Partzuf* of *Zeir Anpin* of *Asiyah* of *Atzilut*, and of Lower *Asiyah*.

ילה Elohenu אֱלֹהֵינוּ   Adonai יְהֹוָהֿאדניֿיאהדונהי   na נָא   veha'arev וְהַעֲרֶב

befinu בְּפִינוּ   toratcha תּוֹרָתְךָ   ראה   divrei דִּבְרֵי   et אֶת

♦Yisrael יִשְׂרָאֵל   ראה בׄ"פ   bet בֵּית   amecha עַמְּךָ   uv'fifiyot וּבְפִיפִיּוֹת

BLESSINGS OF THE *TORAH*
THE SIXTEENTH BLESSING
Blessed are You, Lord, our God, King of the world,
Who has sanctified us with His commandments and obliged us regarding the teachings of the Torah.
THE SEVENTEENTH BLESSING
And sweeten for us, Lord,
our God, the words of Your Torah in our mouths and the mouths of Your Nation, the House of Israel.

venih'ye וְנִהְיֶה   anachnu אֲנַחְנוּ   vetze'etza'enu וְצֶאֱצָאֵינוּ

(You should meditate for your children to be righteous, connected to the *Torah* and to the Light)

vetze'etza'ei וְצֶאֱצָאֵי   tze'etza'enu צֶאֱצָאֵינוּ   vetze'etza'ei וְצֶאֱצָאֵי

amecha עַמְּךָ   bet בֵּית   ב"פ   ראה   Yisrael יִשְׂרָאֵל   kulanu כֻּלָּנוּ

yod'ei יוֹדְעֵי   shemecha שְׁמֶךָ   velomdei וְלוֹמְדֵי   toratcha תּוֹרָתֶךָ

lishma לִשְׁמָה♦   baruch בָּרוּךְ   Ata אַתָּה   Adonai יְהוָֹואדניאהדונהי

hamelamed הַמְלַמֵּד   torah תּוֹרָה   le'amo לְעַמּוֹ   Yisrael יִשְׂרָאֵל‡

THE EIGHTEENTH BLESSING - GIVES THE TORAH

The Aramaic word *chai* וי ("life") has the numerical value of 18. This blessing connects us to the Tree of Life, (*Etz HaChayim* – עֵץ הַחַיִּים) the dimension where only fulfillment, order, and endless bliss exist.

The Eighteenth Blessing is in the three *Partzufim* of *Yesod*: external, middle and internal of Returning Light of the middle *Partzuf* of *Zeir Anpin* of *Asiyah* of *Atzilut*, and of Lower *Asiyah*.

baruch בָּרוּךְ   Ata אַתָּה   Adonai יְהוָֹואדנייאהדונהי   Elohenu אֱלֹהֵינוּ   ילה

melech מֶלֶךְ   ha'olam הָעוֹלָם   asher אֲשֶׁר   bachar בָּחַר

banu בָּנוּ   mikol מִכָּל   ילי   ha'amim הָעַמִּים   venatan וְנָתַן

lanu לָנוּ   אלהים,   אהיה   אדני   et אֶת   torato תּוֹרָתוֹ♦   baruch בָּרוּךְ

Ata אַתָּה   Adonai יְהוָֹואדנייאהדונהי   noten נוֹתֵן   אבגיתץ, וסר   hatorah הַתּוֹרָה‡

THE BLESSING OF THE *KOHANIM*

Finishing the Eighteen Blessings, we make an immediate connection to the *Torah*. The verses that we recite are the blessings of the priests (*Kohanim*). In ancient times, when the *Kohen* blessed the congregation in the Temple, he used the formula *Yud, Yud, Yud* יוי one of the 72 Names of God. Each of the following three sentences begins with a *Yud*. When we recite this prayer, we activate and reveal tremendous powers of healing in our lives.

And may we and our offspring, and the offspring of our offspring, and the offspring of all Your Nation, the House of Israel, all of us know Your Names and be learners of Your Torah for its own sake. Blessed are You, Lord, Who teaches the Torah to His Nation, Israel.

THE EIGHTEENTH BLESSING

Blessed are You, Lord, our God, King of the world, Who has chosen us from among all the nations and has given us His Torah. Blessed are You, Lord, Who gives the Torah.

וַיְדַבֵּר vaydaber   ראה   יְהֹוָה Adonai   אֶל־ el   מֹשֶׁה Moshe

מהע, ע"ב בריבוע קס"א, אל שדי, ד"פ אלהים ע"ה   לֵּאמֹר :lemor   דַּבֵּר daber   ראה

אֶל־ el   אַהֲרֹן Aharon   וְאֶל־ ve'el   בָּנָיו banav   לֵאמֹר lemor

כֹּה ko   היי   תְבָרְכוּ tevarchu   יהוה ריבוע יהוה ריבוע יהוה מ"ה

אֶת־ et   בְּנֵי benei   יִשְׂרָאֵל Yisrael   אָמוֹר amor   לָהֶם lahem:

The initials of the three verses give us the Holy Name: '''.
In this section, there are 15 words, which are equal to the numerical value of the Holy Name: יההו.

(Right – *Chesed*)

יְבָרֶכְךָ yevarechecha   יְהֹוָה Adonai   וְיִשְׁמְרֶךָ veyishmerecha

ר"ת = יהוה ; וס"ת = מ"ה:

(Left - *Gevurah*)

יָאֵר ya'er   כף   ויי   זין   ויי   יְהֹוָה Adonai | פָּנָיו panav

אֵלֶיךָ elecha   וִיחֻנֶּךָּ vichuneka   מנד   ;   יהה   אותיות   בפסוק:

(Central – *Tiferet*)

יִשָּׂא yisa   יְהֹוָה Adonai | פָּנָיו panav   אֵלֶיךָ elecha

וְיָשֵׂם veyasem   לְךָ lecha   שָׁלוֹם shalom   האא   תיבות   בפסוק:

(*Malchut*)

וְשָׂמוּ vesamu   אֶת־ et   שְׁמִי shemi   עַל־ al   בְּנֵי benei   יִשְׂרָאֵל Yisrael

וַאֲנִי va'ani אני   אֲבָרְכֵם avarchem:

Shacharit Prayer can be found on pg. 57 and on. *Talit* and *Tefilin* order can be found on pg. 63.

THE BLESSING OF THE *KOHANIM*

"And the Lord spoke to Moses and said:
Speak to Aaron and his sons saying: So shall you bless the Children of Israel,
Say to them: May the Lord bless you and protect you.
May the Lord enlighten His countenance for you and give you grace.
May the Lord lift His countenance towards you and give you peace.
And they shall place My Name upon the Children of Israel and I shall bless them." (Numbers 6:22-27)

IMMERSION IN THE *MIKVEH*

Purity leads a person to holiness. Since purity of the body causes the soul's purity, a person should make an effort to purify the body so that with this action he might strengthen himself with *Torah* and with awe, love, happiness and true unconditional spiritual work. It is worthwhile for him to make as much effort as possible and spend as much money as is necessary to achieve purity of body, because through purifying the body he will gain some additional assistance in his spiritual work. Therefore, you should make the necessary effort to immerse in a *Mikveh* as often as you can, to repent and purify yourself from the impurity of your general negative actions, especially if you were made impure by something specific. You should be cautious to pray only if you are purified, because the reward is doubled when you do the spiritual work with purity. It is known that the impurity that comes from the body is very severe and therefore, you should immerse in the *Mikveh* for *keri* (male ejaculation) after having sexual relations at night, and all the more so, if the *keri* was unintentional. It is important to be cautious, therefore, you should not delay going to immerse in the *Mikveh* so that you might have long term peace.

The students of the Ari wrote that mercy would descend upon a person and erase the *mazik* (negative entity) that was created from that *keri*, from anyone who experienced an accidental *keri* (Heaven forbid), if he immersed himself in the *Mikveh* that day and repented. Also, whoever has pity on his soul should run and immerse in the *Mikveh*. Anyone who had awe and admiration for the Creator will be careful not to mention the Holy Names of God while being impure, as it is written: "for those who honor Me, I will honor." (I Samuel 2:30).

The sages used to immerse in the *Mikveh* every day before their prayers, not as an obligation but as an important spiritual tool, so that they would be pure from any impurity. The Ari wrote that there are some cases where a person can become impure without being aware (based on Tractate *Niddah* pg. 13b). Regarding the essence of the purity of the *Mikveh*, one of the Ari's students also mentioned: "the one who is cautious with immersing (*Tevilah* - טבילה) connects with God to become one (immerse טבל in the Name of God יה) and praiseworthy is he."

TIKKUN CHATZOT

Kabbalah teaches us that our negative actions create space (represented by the destruction of the Holy Temple) between the physical reality and the spiritual reality, and that chaos has domain in this space. This gap causes the *Shechinah* (our spiritual protection shield and sustainer) some pain as She cannot nourish us. Reciting *Tikkun Chatzot* helps to restore this gap and remove the separation between us, the *Shechinah* and the Creator.

1. *Tikkun Chatzot* is recited only after the cosmic midnight until dawn.
2. *Tikkun Chatzot* is **not** recited on the following days:
   Friday night, *Pesach* (all seven days), *Shavuot*, *Rosh Hashanah*, *Yom Kippur*, first day of *Sukkot* and *Simchat Torah*.
3. **Only** *Tikkun Leah* is recited on the following days: Eve of *Rosh Chodesh*, the days between *Rosh Hashanah* and *Yom Kippur*, *Sukkot Chol Hamo'ed*, days of the *Omer*, the Sabbatical year (*Shemita*), and in any other day that *Tachanun* is not recited.
4. **Only** *Tikkun Rachel* is recited on the following days: *Tisha B'Av* (the 9th of *Av*).

לְשֵׁם leshem יִווּד yichud קוּדְשָׁא kudsha בְּרִיך berich הוּא hu

(יאהדונהי) ush'chintei וּשְׁכִינְתֵּיה bid'chilu בִּדְחִילוּ ur'chimu וּרְחִימוּ

(יאהוויהה), ur'chimu וּרְחִימוּ ud'chilu וּדְחִילוּ (איההיוהה),

לְיַחֲדָא leyachada שֵׁם shem יוּ"ד yud קֵי kei בּוּא"ו bevav קֵי kei

בְּיִחוּדָא beyichuda שָׁלִים shelim (יהוה) beshem בְּשֵׁם כָל kol ילי

יִשְׂרָאֵל Yisrael הֲרֵינִי hareni מוּכָן muchan לוֹמַר lomar:

:(when you say only *Tikkun Leah*) תִּקּוּן tikkun לֵאָה Leah

:(when you say only *Tikkun Rachel*) תִּקּוּן tikkun רָחֵל Rachel

:(when you say both) תִּקּוּן tikkun רָחֵל Rachel וְתִקּוּן vetikkun לֵאָה Leah

כְּמוֹ kemo שֶׁסִּדְרוּ shesidru לָנוּ lanu אלהים, אהיה אדני רַבּוֹתֵינוּ rabotenu

זִכְרוֹנָם zichronam לִבְרָכָה livracha לְתַקֵּן letaken אֶת et שָׁרְשָׁם shorsham

בִּמְקוֹם bemakom עֶלְיוֹן elyon לַעֲשׂוֹת la'asot נַחַת nachat רוּחַ ru'ach

לְיוֹצְרֵנוּ leyotzrenu וְלַעֲשׂוֹת vela'asot רָצוֹן retzon מהשע ע"ה, ע"ב בריבוע וקס"א ע"ה,

בּוֹרְאֵינוּ bor'enu• וִיהִי vihi נֹעַם no'am אֲדֹנָי Adonai ללה אל שדי ע"ה

אֱלֹהֵינוּ Elohenu ילה עָלֵינוּ alenu וּמַעֲשֵׂה uma'ase יָדֵינוּ yadenu

כּוֹנְנָה konena עָלֵינוּ alenu וּמַעֲשֵׂה uma'ase יָדֵינוּ yadenu כּוֹנְנֵהוּ konenehu:

TIKKUN CHATZOT

For the sake of unification between the Holy Blessed One and His Shechinah, with fear and love and with love and fear, in order to unify the Name Yud, Kei and Vav, Kei in perfect unity, and in the name of all Israel, I'm hereby to pray Tikkun Leah / Tikkun Rachel / Tikkun Rachel and Tikkun Leah, that was established by our sages of blessed memory, to correct its root in the supernal place to bring satisfaction to our Maker, and to fulfill the wish of our creator "May the pleasantness of the Lord our God be upon us and may He establish the work of our hands for us and may the work of our hands establish Him." (Psalms 90:17)

For *Tikkun Leah* go to page 34.

ASHAMNU (VIDUI)

Our consciousness during the *Ashamnu* should be one of recognizing our shortcomings and wrong choices in order to get closer to the Light. Self-denial, whether intentional or not, creates many layers of separation between us and the Creator. The *Ashamnu* has been designed by the sages in the order of the Aramaic alphabet. We recite or scan each of the words and strike our chest gently with our right hand in order to ignite the Light of the Creator inside us, and to remove the residue and cleanse the negativity created by our selfish and intolerant past actions. Every time we make a wrong choice or do something negative, we place the Light inside of us into dormancy. Our consciousness and desire to change is what awakens the Light. We must make an attempt to feel and experience the pain that we've caused others through our emotions, and not by the physical pain we could feel if we struck our chest too hard.

> While reciting the *Vidui*, you should strike your chest with the right hand to shake the *Chasadim* (mercy) and the *Gevurot* (judgment) so they can grow up for the sake of the *Zivug* (unification). Even if you know that you didn't commit one of the below-mentioned negative actions, you should still say the *Vidui*. Because we all act as guarantors to each other - The *Vidui* is said in plural because the *Vidui* is about other lifetimes and other people who are connected to your soul's root.
>
> The 22 letters are the numerical value of the Holy Name אכא.

velohei וֵאלֹהֵי ילה Elohenu אֱלֹהֵינוּ Adonai יְהוָֹה(אדני־יאהדונהי) ב״ן ana אָנָּא

lefanecha לְפָנֶיךָ tavo תָּבֹא avotenu אֲבוֹתֵינוּ ילה ; דמב , ע״ב, מילוי ; לכב

malkenu מַלְכֵּנוּ tit'alam תִּתְעַלַּם ve'al וְאַל tefilatenu תְּפִלָּתֵנוּ ב״ן מ״ה ס״ג

azei עָזֵי anachnu אֲנַחְנוּ she'ein שֶׁאֵין mit'chinatenu מִתְּחִנָּתֵנוּ

lomar לוֹמַר oref עוֹרֶף ukshei וּקְשֵׁי fanim פָּנִים אדני ע״ה, אהיה אדני ע״ה, אלהים ע״ה,

ילה Elohenu אֱלֹהֵינוּ Adonai יְהוָֹה(אדני־יאהדונהי) ב״ן מ״ה ס״ג lefanecha לְפָנֶיךָ

avotenu אֲבוֹתֵינוּ ; דמב , ע״ב, מילוי ; לכב ilה velohei וֵאלֹהֵי

chatanu וְחָטָאנוּ velo וְלֹא anachnu אֲנַחְנוּ tzadikim צַדִּיקִים

anachnu אֲנַחְנוּ pashanu פָּשַׁעְנוּ avinu עָוִינוּ chatanu וְחָטָאנוּ aval אֲבָל

ראה: ב״פ vetenu בֵּיתֵנוּ ve'anshei וְאַנְשֵׁי va'avotenu וַאֲבוֹתֵינוּ

dofi דוֹפִי dibarnu דִּבַּרְנוּ gazalnu גָּזַלְנוּ bagadnu בָּגַדְנוּ ashamnu אָשַׁמְנוּ

vehirshanu וְהִרְשַׁעְנוּ he'evinu הֶעֱוִינוּ hara הָרַע velashon וְלָשׁוֹן

ASHAMNU (VIDUI)

We beseech You, Lord, our God and the God of our fathers. May our prayer come before You and may Our King not ignore our plea. For we are not arrogant and stiff necked to say before You Lord, our God and the God of our fathers that we are righteous and we did not sin. For we have sinned, we have committed iniquity, we have transgressed, we and our fathers and the people of our household. א We are guilty, ב we betrayed, ג we stole, ד we spoke gossip and evil speech, ה we caused iniquity, ו we convicted, zadnu זַדְנוּ • chamasnu וְחָמַסְנוּ • tafalnu טָפַלְנוּ • sheker שֶׁקֶר • umirma וּמִרְמָה•

ya'atznu יָעַצְנוּ • etzot עֵצוֹת • ra'ot רָעוֹת • kizavnu כִּזַּבְנוּ • ka'asnu כָּעַסְנוּ•

latznu לַצְנוּ • maradnu מָרַדְנוּ • marinu מָרִינוּ • devarecha דְּבָרֶיךָ•

ni'atznu נִאַצְנוּ • ni'afnu נָאַפְנוּ • sararnu סָרַרְנוּ • avinu עָוִינוּ • pashanu פָּשַׁעְנוּ•

pagamnu פָּגַמְנוּ • tzararnu צָרַרְנוּ • tzi'arnu צִעַרְנוּ • av אָב • va'em וָאֵם•

kishinu קִשִּׁינוּ • oref עֹרֶף • rashanu רָשַׁעְנוּ • shichatnu שִׁחַתְנוּ•

ti'avnu תִּעַבְנוּ • ta'inu תָּעִינוּ • veti'atanu וְתִעְתַּעְנוּ • vesarnu וְסַרְנוּ

mimitzvotecha מִמִּצְוֺתֶיךָ • umimishpatecha וּמִמִּשְׁפָּטֶיךָ • hatovim הַטּוֹבִים

velo וְלֹא • shava שָׁוָה lanu לָנוּ • veAta וְאַתָּה • tzadik צַדִּיק

al עַל • kol כָּל • haba הַבָּא • alenu עָלֵינוּ • ki כִּי • emet אֱמֶת

asita עָשִׂיתָ • va'anachnu וַאֲנָחְנוּ • hirsha'nu הִרְשָׁעְנוּ

> Meditate to ensure that your negative actions are part of the past and are not part of your present anymore

ma מַה nomar נֹאמַר • lefanecha לְפָנֶיךָ yoshev יוֹשֵׁב

marom מָרוֹם • uma וּמַה nesaper נְסַפֵּר lefanecha לְפָנֶיךָ

shochen שׁוֹכֵן shechakim שְׁחָקִים halo הֲלֹא chol כָּל

hanistarot הַנִּסְתָּרוֹת vehaniglot וְהַנִּגְלוֹת Ata אַתָּה yode'a יוֹדֵעַ•

Ata אַתָּה yode'a יוֹדֵעַ razei רָזֵי olam עוֹלָם • veta'alumot וְתַעֲלוּמוֹת

sitrei סִתְרֵי kol כָּל chai חַי•

Ata אַתָּה chofes וְזֵפֶשׁ kol כָּל chadrei וְחַדְרֵי vaten בֶּטֶן•

ז *we were wanton,* ח *we robbed,* ט *we accused falsely and deceitfully,* י *we gave bad advice,* כ *we lied,* ך *we have anger,* ל *we mocked,* מ *we revolted,* ם *we rebelled Your commandments,* נ *we were contemptuous,* ן *we committed adultery,* ס *we have been perverted,* ע *we caused wickedness,* פ *we transgressed,* ף *we damaged,* צ *we have oppressed,* ץ *we gave sorrow to our mother and father,* ק *we were stubborn,* ר *we have been wicked,* ש *we have corrupted,* ת *we committed abominations, we have gone astray from Your commandments and good laws, and it has not benefited us. For You are righteous regarding whatever has befallen us, for You have acted truthfully and we have caused wickedness. What shall we say before You, Who dwells on high? and what shall we recount before You, Whose abode is in the lofty heights? for do you not know all the hidden and revealed things. You know the mysteries of the world and the inner secrets of all living. You search the innermost parts of man,*

רֹאֶה r'oe   כְּלָיוֹת chelayot   וָלֵב valev   אֵין en   דְּבָר davar   ראה

נֶעְלָם ne'elam   מִמָּךְ mimach   וְאֵין ve'en   נִסְתָּר nistar   מ"צ ב"פ

מִנֶּגֶד mineged   מזבח, זו, אל יהוה   עֵינֶיךָ enecha   ע"ה קס"א ; ריבוע מ"ה:

יְהִי yehi   רָצוֹן ratzon   מהש ע"ה, ע"ב בריבוע וקס"א ע"ה, אל שדי ע"ה   מִלְּפָנֶיךָ milefanecha

יְהֹוָה Adonai   אֱלֹהֵינוּ Elohenu   וֵאלֹהֵי velohei   ס"ג מ"ה ב"ן ; מילוי כבה

אֲבוֹתֵינוּ avotenu   שֶׁתִּמְחוֹל shetimchol   לָנוּ lanu   ע"ב, דמב ; אלהים, אהיה אדני

אֶת et   כָּל kol   וְחַטֹּאתֵינוּ chatotenu   וּתְכַפֵּר utchaper   לָנוּ lanu

אֶת et   כָּל kol   עֲוֹנוֹתֵינוּ avonotenu   וְתִמְחוֹל vetimchol   אלהים, אהיה אדני

וְתִסְלַח vetislach   יהוה ע"ב   לְכָל lechol   יה אדני   פְּשָׁעֵינוּ peshaenu:

AL NAHAROT BAVEL

Here (until *"Nidchei Yisrael Yechanes"* – on bottom of pg. 30), you should sit on the ground and cry over the destruction of the Temple, the death of the righteous and feel the pain of the *Shechinah*.

עַל al   נַהֲרוֹת naharot   בָּבֶל Bavel   שָׁם sham   יָשַׁבְנוּ yashavnu   גַּם gam

בָּכִינוּ bachinu   בְּזָכְרֵנוּ bezochrenu   אֶת et   צִיּוֹן Tziyon   יוסף, ו הויות, קנאה:

עַל al   עֲרָבִים aravim   בְּתוֹכָהּ betocha   תָּלִינוּ talinu   כִּנֹּרוֹתֵינוּ kinorotenu:

כִּי ki   שָׁם sham   שְׁאֵלוּנוּ she'elunu   שׁוֹבֵינוּ shovenu   דִּבְרֵי divrei   ראה

שִׁיר shir   וְתוֹלָלֵינוּ vetolalenu   שִׂמְחָה simcha   שִׁירוּ shiru   לָנוּ lanu

אֵיךְ ech   מִשִּׁיר mishir   צִיּוֹן Tziyon   אֲדֹנָי   אלהים, אהיה אדני   יוסף, ו הויות, קנאה:

נָשִׁיר nashir   אֶת et   שִׁיר shir   יְהֹוָה Adonai   עַל al   אַדְמַת admat

נֵכָר nechar: אִם im   יוהך, מ"א אותיות דפשוט, דמילוי ודמילוי דמילוי דאהיה ע"ה

אֶשְׁכָּחֵךְ esh'kachech   יְרוּשָׁלַיִם Yerushalayim   תִּשְׁכַּח tishkach   יְמִינִי yemini:

---

and see the reins and the heart. Nothing is hidden from You, and nothing from before Your eyes. May it be Your will, Lord, our God and the God of our fathers, to be merciful to us, to pardon us for all our sins, to grant us atonement for all our iniquities and to pardon and forgive us for all our transgressions.

AL NAHAROT BAVEL

"By the rivers of Babylon, there we sat down, yea, we wept, when we remembered Zion. Upon the willows in the midst we hanged up our harps. For it was there they that led us captive asked of us words of song, and our tormentors asked of us mirth: 'Sing us one of the songs of Zion.' How shall we sing Lord's song in a foreign land? If I forget you, Jerusalem, let my right hand forget her cunning.

תִּדְבַּק tidbak לְשׁוֹנִי leshoni לְחִכִּי lechiki אִם־ im   יוהר, מ"א אותיות דפשוטו, דמילוי

אֹזְכְּרֵכִי ezkerechi לֹא lo אִם־ im   יוהר, מ"א אותיות דפשוטו, ורדמילוי דמילוי דמילוי דאהיה ע"ה

אַעֲלֶה a'ale לֹא lo אֶת־ et יְרוּשָׁלַיִם Yerushalayim   דמילוי ורדמילוי דמילוי דאהיה ע"ה

עַל al רֹאשׁ rosh רבוע אלהים ואלהים דיודין ע"ה שִׂמְחָתִי simchati: zechor זְכֹר

יְהֹוָה אהדונהי Adonai (סוד המשכת העשפע מן ד' שמות ליסוד הנקרא זכור) ע"ה יהי אור ע"ה, ע"ב קס"א,

לִבְנֵי livnei אֱדוֹם Edom אֵת et יוֹם yom ע"ה   נגד, מזבוח, זן, אל יהוה

יְרוּשָׁלַיִם Yerushalayim הָאֹמְרִים ha'omrim עָרוּ aru עָרוּ aru עַד ad

הַיְסוֹד hayesod ההע בָּהּ ba: בַּת־ bat בָּבֶל Bavel הַשְּׁדוּדָה hasheduda

אַשְׁרֵי ashrei שֶׁיְשַׁלֶּם־ sheyeshalem לָךְ lach אֶת־ et גְּמוּלֵךְ gemulech

וְנִפֵּץ venipetz אֶת־ et עֹלָלַיִךְ olalayich אֶל־ el הַסָּלַע hasala: אַשְׁרֵי ashrei שֶׁיֹּאחֵז sheyochez שֶׁגָּמַלְתְּ shegamalt לָנוּ lanu אלהים, אהיה אדני: שֶׁגָּבְלַתְּ

מִזְמוֹר mizmor לְאָסָף leAsaf אֱלֹהִים Elohim אהיה אדני ; ילה בָּאוּ ba'u

גּוֹיִם goyim בְּנַחֲלָתֶךָ benachalatecha טִמְּאוּ time'u אֶת־ et הֵיכַל hechal

קׇדְשֶׁךָ kodshecha אדני, ללה שָׂמוּ samu אֶת־ et יְרוּשָׁלַיִם Yerushalayim

לְעִיִּים le'iyim: נָתְנוּ natnu אֶת־ et נִבְלַת nivlat עֲבָדֶיךָ avadecha

בָּשָׂר besar מַאֲכָל ma'achal לְעוֹף le'of הַשָּׁמָיִם hashamayim י"פ טל, י"פ כוזו

שָׁפְכוּ shafchu דָּמָם damam כַּמַּיִם kamayim סְבִיבוֹת sevivot וַחֲסִידֶיךָ chasidecha לְחַיְתוֹ lechayto אָרֶץ aretz:

לְשִׁכְנֵנוּ lishchenenu לַעַג la'ag וָקֶלֶס vakeles לִסְבִיבוֹתֵינוּ lisvivotenu: יְרוּשָׁלַיִם Yerushalayim וְאֵין ve'en קוֹבֵר kover: הָיִינוּ hayinu וְחֶרְפָּה cherpa

---

Let my tongue cleave to the roof of my mouth, if I remember you not; if I set not Jerusalem above my greatest joy. Remember, Lord, against the children of Edom the day of Jerusalem; who said: 'Raise it, raise it, even to the foundation.' daughter of Babylon, that art to be destroyed; happy shall he be, that repays you as you have served us. Happy shall he be, that takes and dashes your little ones against the rock." (Psalms 137).

"A Psalm of Asaf: God, the heathen are come into Your inheritance; they have defiled Your holy temple; they have made Jerusalem into heaps. They have given the dead bodies of Your servants to be food to the fowls of the heaven, the flesh of Your saints to the beasts of the earth. They have shed their blood like water round about Jerusalem, with none to bury them. We are become a taunt to our neighbors, a scorn and derision to them that are round about us.

עַד־ ad   מָה ma   מ"ה   יְהֹוָה Adonai אהדונהי   תֶאֱנַף te'enaf   לָנֶצַח lanetzach

תִּבְעַר tiv'ar   כְּמוֹ kemo   אֵשׁ esh   קִנְאָתֶךָ kin'atecha׃   שְׁפֹךְ shefoch

וַחֲמָתְךָ chamatcha   אֶל־ el   הַגּוֹיִם hagoyim   אֲשֶׁר asher   לֹא lo

יְדָעוּךָ yeda'ucha   וְעַל ve'al   מַמְלָכוֹת mamlachot   אֲשֶׁר asher

בְּשִׁמְךָ beshimcha   לֹא lo   קָרָאוּ kara'u׃   כִּי ki   אָכַל achal

אֶת et   יַעֲקֹב Yaakov   ו' הויות, יאהדונהי אידהנויה   וְאֶת־ ve'et   נָוֵהוּ navehu

הֵשַׁמּוּ heshamu׃   אַל־ al   תִּזְכָּר־ tizkor   לָנוּ lanu   אלהים, אהיה אדני

עֲוֹנֹת avonot   רִאשֹׁנִים rishonim   מַהֵר maher   יְקַדְּמוּנוּ yekademunu

רַחֲמֶיךָ rachamecha   כִּי ki   דַלּוֹנוּ dalonu   מְאֹד me'od׃   עָזְרֵנוּ ozrenu

אֱלֹהֵי Elohei   מילוי ע"ב, דמב ; ילה   יִשְׁעֵנוּ yish'enu   עַל־ al   דְּבַר devar   ראה

כְּבוֹד־ kevod   שְׁמֶךָ shemecha   וְהַצִּילֵנוּ vehatzilenu   וְכַפֵּר vechaper   עַל־ al

וְחַטֹאתֵינוּ chatotenu   לְמַעַן lema'an   שְׁמֶךָ shemecha׃   לָמָה lama

יֹאמְרוּ yomru   הַגּוֹיִם hagoyim   אַיֵּה aye   אֱלֹהֵיהֶם Elohehem   ילה

יִוָּדַע yivada   בַּגּוֹיִם bagoyim   (כתיב: בגיים)   לְעֵינֵינוּ le'enenu   ריבוע מ"ה

נִקְמַת nikmat   דַּם־ dam   עֲבָדֶיךָ avadecha   הַשָּׁפוּךְ hashafuch׃   תָּבוֹא tavo

לְפָנֶיךָ lefanecha   ס"ג מ"ה ב"ן   אֶנְקַת enkat   אָסִיר asir   ע"ה ריבוע יהוה וריבוע אלהים ;

בְּנֵי benei   הוֹתֵר hoter   זְרוֹעֲךָ zero'acha   כְּגֹדֶל kegodel   ר"ת = ב"פ רי"ו

תְמוּתָה temuta׃   וְהָשֵׁב vehashev   לִשְׁכֵנֵינוּ lishchenenu   שִׁבְעָתַיִם shiv'atayim

אֶל־ el   חֵיקָם cheikam   וְחֶרְפָּתָם cherpatam   אֲשֶׁר asher   וְחֵרְפוּךָ cherfucha

אֲדֹנָי Adonai   ללה׃   וַאֲנַחְנוּ va'anachnu   עַמְּךָ amecha   וְצֹאן vetzon

מַרְעִיתֶךָ mar'itecha   נוֹדֶה node   לְךָ lecha   לְעוֹלָם le'olam   ריבוע דס"ג ו' אותיות דס"ג

לְדֹר ledor   וָדֹר vador   רי"ו   נְסַפֵּר nesaper   תְּהִלָּתֶךָ tehilatecha׃

How long, Lord, Will You be angry forever; How long will Your jealousy burn like fire? Pour out Your wrath upon the nations that know You not, and upon the kingdoms that do not call upon Your Name. For they have devoured Jacob, and laid waste his habitation. Remember not against us the iniquities of our forefathers; let Your compassions speedily come to meet us; for we are brought very low. Help us, God of our salvation, for the sake of the glory of Your name; and deliver us and forgive our sins, for Your Name's sake. Wherefore should the nations say: 'Where is their God?' Let the avenging of Your servants' blood that is shed be made known among the nations in our sight. Let the groaning of the prisoner come before You; according to the greatness of Your power set free those that are appointed to death. And render unto our neighbors sevenfold into their bosom their reproach, where they have reproached You, Lord. So we that are Your people and the flock of Your pasture will give You thanks forever. We will tell of Your praise to all generations." (Psalms 79)

זְכֹר zechor ע"ב קס"א, יהי אור ע"ה (סוד המשכת השפע מן ד' שמות הנקרא זכור)

Adonai אֲדֹנָי me מַה־ haya הָיָה lanu לָנוּ אלהים, אהיה אדני

habita הַבִּיטָה (כתיב: הביט) ur'eh וּרְאֵה ראה et אֶת־ cherpatenu וְחֶרְפָּתֵנוּ:

nachalatenu נַחֲלָתֵנוּ nehefcha נֶהֶפְכָה lezarim לְזָרִים batenu בָּתֵּינוּ

lenochrim לְנָכְרִים: yetomim יְתוֹמִים hayinu הָיִינוּ ve'en וְאֵין (כתיב: אין)

av אָב imotenu אִמֹּתֵינוּ ke'almanot כְּאַלְמָנוֹת: memenu מִמֶּנוּ

bechesef בְּכֶסֶף shatinu שָׁתִינוּ etzenu עֵצֵינוּ bimchir בִּמְחִיר yavo'u יָבֹאוּ:

al עַל tzavarenu צַוָּארֵנוּ nirdafnu נִרְדָּפְנוּ yaganu יָגָעְנוּ velo וְלֹא (כתיב: לא)

hunach הוּנַח lanu לָנוּ אלהים, אהיה אדני Mitzrayim מִצְרַיִם natanu נָתַנּוּ מצר

yad יָד Ashur אַשּׁוּר lisbo'a לִשְׂבֹּעַ lachem לָחֶם ג' הויות: avotenu אֲבֹתֵינוּ

chat'u חָטְאוּ ve'enam וְאֵינָם (כתיב: אינם) va'anachnu וַאֲנַחְנוּ (כתיב: אנחנו)

avonotehem עֲוֹנֹתֵיהֶם savalnu סָבָלְנוּ: avadim עֲבָדִים mashlu מָשְׁלוּ

vanu בָנוּ porek פֹּרֵק en אֵין miyadam מִיָּדָם: benafshenu בְּנַפְשֵׁנוּ

navi נָבִיא lachmenu לַחְמֵנוּ mipnei מִפְּנֵי cherev וְחֶרֶב hamidbar הַמִּדְבָּר:

orenu עוֹרֵנוּ ketanur כְּתַנּוּר nichmaru נִכְמָרוּ mipnei מִפְּנֵי zal'afot זַלְעֲפוֹת

ra'av רָעָב: nashim נָשִׁים beTziyon בְּצִיּוֹן יוסף, ר' הויות, קנאה inu עִנּוּ

betulot בְּתוּלֹת be'arei בְּעָרֵי Yehuda יְהוּדָה: sarim שָׂרִים beyadam בְּיָדָם

nitlu נִתְלוּ penei פְּנֵי חכמה בינה zekenim זְקֵנִים lo לֹא nehdaru נֶהְדָּרוּ:

bachurim בַּחוּרִים techon טְחוֹן nasa'u נָשָׂאוּ une'arim וּנְעָרִים

ba'etz בָּעֵץ kashalu כָּשָׁלוּ: zekenim זְקֵנִים misha'ar מִשַּׁעַר

shavatu שָׁבָתוּ bachurim בַּחוּרִים mineginatam מִנְּגִינָתָם: shavat שָׁבַת

mesos מְשׂוֹשׂ libenu לִבֵּנוּ nehpach נֶהְפַּךְ le'evel לְאֵבֶל mecholenu מְחֹלֵנוּ:

"Remember, Lord, what is come upon us; behold, and see our reproach. Our inheritance is turned unto strangers, our houses unto aliens. We are become orphans and fatherless, our mothers are as widows. We have drunk our water for money; our wood comes to us for price. To our very necks we are pursued; we labor and have no rest. We have given the hand to Egypt, and to Assyria, to have bread enough. Our fathers have sinned, and are not; and we have borne their iniquities. Servants rule over us; there is none to deliver us out of their hand. We get our bread with the peril of our lives because of the sword of the wilderness. Our skin is hot like an oven because of the burning heat of famine. They have ravished the women in Zion, the maidens in the cities of Judah. Princes are hanged up by their hand; the faces of elders are not honored. The young men have borne the mill, and the children have stumbled under the wood. The elders have ceased from the gate, the young men from their music. The joy of our heart is ceased; our dance is turned into mourning.

נָפְלָה nafla עֲטֶרֶת ateret רֹאשֵׁנוּ roshenu ר"ת = ש"ך דינים אוֹי oy נָא na

לָנוּ lanu אלהים, אהיה אדני ze זֶה הָיָה haya יהה כִּי ki וְחָטָאנוּ chatanu עַל־ al

דָוֶה dave ההוד הפך דוה libenu לִבֵּנוּ al עַל־ ele אֵלֶּה vesh'chu וְשָׁכוּ chash'chu

עֵינֵינוּ enenu ריבוע מ"ה: al עַל־ הַר־ har Tziyon צִיּוֹן יוסף, ו הויות, קנאה

שֶׁשָּׁמֵם sheshamem שׁוּעָלִים shu'alim הִלְּכוּ hilechu בוֹ vo: אַתָּה Ata

יְהֹוָאדנֹי teshev תֵּשֵׁב le'olam לְעוֹלָם ריבוע ס"ג ו' אותיות דס"ג Adonai

כִּסְאֲךָ kis'acha לְדֹר ledor וָדוֹר vador רי"ו: לָמָּה lama לָנֶצַח lanetzach

הַשִׁיבֵנוּ hashivenu יְהֹוָאדנֹי Adonai | אֵלֶיךָ elecha וְנָשׁוּבָה venashuva

(כתיב: וְנָשׁוּב) chadesh וְחַדֵּשׁ י"ב הויות, קס"א קנ"א יָמֵינוּ yamenu כְּקֶדֶם kekedem:

כִּי ki אִם־ im מָאֹס ma'os יוהך, מ"א אותיות דפשוט, דמילוי ודמילוי דמילוי דאהיה ע"ה

מְאַסְתָּנוּ me'astanu קָצַפְתָּ katzafta עָלֵינוּ alenu עַד־ ad מְאֹד me'od:

הַשִׁיבֵנוּ hashivenu יְהֹוָאדנֹי Adonai | אֵלֶיךָ elecha וְנָשׁוּבָה venashuva

(כתיב: וְנָשׁוּב) chadesh וְחַדֵּשׁ י"ב הויות, קס"א קנ"א יָמֵינוּ yamenu כְּקֶדֶם kekedem:

הַבֵּט habet מִשָּׁמַיִם mishamayim י"פ טל, י"פ כוזו ur'eh וּרְאֵה ראה מִזְּבֻל mizevul

קָדְשְׁךָ kodshecha וְתִפְאַרְתֶּךָ vetifartecha אַיֵּה aye קִנְאָתְךָ kin'atcha

וּגְבוּרֹתֶךָ ugvurotecha הֲמוֹן hamon מֵעֶיךָ me'echa וְרַחֲמֶיךָ verachamecha

אֵלַי elai הִתְאַפָּקוּ hit'apaku: כִּי ki אַתָּה Ata כִּי ki אָבִינוּ avinu

אַבְרָהָם Avraham וז"פ אל, רי"ו ול"ב נתיבות החכמה, רמ"ח (אברים), עסמ"ב וט"ז אותיות פשוטות

לֹא lo יְדָעָנוּ yeda'anu וְיִשְׂרָאֵל veYisrael לֹא lo יַכִּירָנוּ yakiranu אַתָּה Ata

יְהֹוָאדנֹי Adonai אָבִינוּ avinu גֹּאֲלֵנוּ go'alenu מֵעוֹלָם me'olam

---

The crown is fallen from our head; woe unto us! For we have sinned. For this our heart is faint, for these things our eyes are dim; for the mountain of Zion, which is desolate as the foxes walk upon it. You, Lord, are enthroned for ever, Your throne is from generation to generation. Wherefore do You forget us forever, and forsake us so long time? You turn us unto You, Lord, and we shall be turned; renew our days as of old. You can not have utterly rejected us, and be exceeding angry against us!" (Lamentations 5)

"Look down from heaven, and see, even from Your holy and glorious habitation; Where are Your zeal and Your mighty acts, the yearning of Your heart and Your compassions, now restrained toward me? For You are our Father; for Abraham knows us not, and Israel does not acknowledge us; You, Lord, our Father, our Redeemer, everlasting

שְׁמֶךָ: shemecha לָמָּה lama תַּתְעֵנוּ tat'enu יְהֹוָה Adonai

מִדְּרָכֶיךָ midrachecha תַּקְשִׁיחַ takshi'ach לִבֵּנוּ libenu מִיִּרְאָתֶךָ miyir'atecha

שׁוּב shuv לְמַעַן lema'an עֲבָדֶיךָ avadecha שִׁבְטֵי shivtei

עַם־ am יָרְשׁוּ yarshu לַמִּצְעָר lamitz'ar נַחֲלָתֶךָ: nachalatecha

קָדְשֶׁךָ kodshecha צָרֵינוּ tzarenu בּוֹסְסוּ bosesu מִקְדָּשֶׁךָ: mikdashecha

וְעַתָּה ve'ata יְהֹוָה Adonai אָבִינוּ avinu אַתָּה Ata אֲנַחְנוּ anachnu

הַחֹמֶר hachomer וְאַתָּה veAta יֹצְרֵנוּ yotzrenu וּמַעֲשֵׂה uma'ase יָדְךָ yadcha

כֻּלָּנוּ: kulanu אַל־ al תִּקְצֹף tiktzof יְהֹוָה Adonai עַד־ ad

מְאֹד me'od וְאַל־ ve'al לָעַד la'ad תִּזְכֹּר tizkor עָוֹן avon הֵן hen

הַבֶּט habet נָא na עַמְּךָ amecha כֻלָּנוּ: chulanu עָרֵי arei קָדְשֶׁךָ kodshecha

הָיוּ hayu מִדְבָּר midbar צִיּוֹן Tziyon מִדְבָּר midbar

הָיְתָה hayata יְרוּשָׁלַ͏ִם Yerushalaim שְׁמָמָה shemama: בֵּית bet

קָדְשֵׁנוּ kodshenu וְתִפְאַרְתֵּנוּ vetifartenu אֲשֶׁר asher הִלְלוּךָ hilelucha

אֲבֹתֵינוּ avotenu הָיָה haya לִשְׂרֵפַת lisrefat אֵשׁ esh

וְכָל vechol מַחֲמַדֵּינוּ machamadenu הָיָה haya לְחָרְבָּה: lechorba

הַעַל ha'al אֵלֶּה ele תִּתְאַפַּק tit'apak יְהֹוָה Adonai

תֶּחֱשֶׁה techeshe וּתְעַנֵּנוּ ut'anenu עַד ad מְאֹד: me'od

עַל al וְחוֹמֹתַיִךְ chomotayich יְרוּשָׁלַ͏ִם Yerushalaim הִפְקַדְתִּי hifkadeti

שֹׁמְרִים shomrim כָּל kol הַיּוֹם hayom וְכָל vechol

הַלַּיְלָה halayla תָּמִיד tamid לֹא lo יֶחֱשׁוּ yecheshu

---

is Your Name. Lord, why do You make us err from Your ways, and harden our heart from Your fear? Return for Your servants' sake, the tribes of Your inheritance. Your holy people they have nearly well driven out, our adversaries have trodden down Your sanctuary." (Isaiah 63:15-18)

"But now, Lord, You are our Father; we are the clay, and You our potter, and we all are the work of Your hand. Be not so very angry, God, neither remember iniquity for ever; behold, look, we beseech You, we are all Your people. Your holy cities are become a wilderness, Zion is become a wilderness, Jerusalem a desolation. Our holy and our beautiful house, where our fathers praised You, is burned with fire; and all our pleasant things are laid waste. Will You refrain Yourself for these things, Lord? Will You hold Your peace, and afflict us very sore?" (Isaiah 64:7-11)

"I have set watchmen upon your walls, Jerusalem, they shall never hold their peace day nor night:

הַמַּזְכִּרִים hamazkirim אֶת־ et יְהֹוָה Adonai אַל־ al דֳּמִי domi

לָכֶם lachem ר"ת אדל, אגל"א (בעת רצון הוא בצירוף אל"ד, ובעת הזעם נהפך לאד"ל רומז לדלות:)

וְאַל־ ve'al תִּתְּנוּ titenu דֳמִי domi לוֹ lo עַד־ ad יְכוֹנֵן yechonen

וְעַד־ ve'ad יָשִׂים yasim אֶת־ et יְרוּשָׁלַ͏ִם Yerushalaim תְּהִלָּה tehila

בָּאָרֶץ ba'aretz ס"ג, ז"פ אהיה, אהיה פעמים אמת, ע"ה נִשְׁבַּע nishba

יְהֹוָה Adonai בִּימִינוֹ bimino וּבִזְרוֹעַ uvizro'a עֻזּוֹ uzo אִם־ im יוהך,

אֶתֵּן eten אֶת־ et דְּגָנֵךְ deganech מ"א אותיות דפשוט, דמילוי ודמילוי דמילוי דאהיה ע"ה

עוֹד od מַאֲכָל ma'achal לְאֹיְבַיִךְ le'oyvayich וְאִם־ ve'im יוהך, מ"א אותיות דפשוט,

בְּנֵי venei נֵכָר nechar דמילוי ודמילוי דמילוי דאהיה ע"ה יִשְׁתּוּ yishtu

תִּירוֹשֵׁךְ tiroshech אֲשֶׁר asher יָגַעַתְּ yaga'at בּוֹ bo כִּי ki מְאַסְפָיו me'asfav

יֹאכְלֻהוּ yochluhu וְהִלְלוּ vehilelu אֶת־ et יְהֹוָה Adonai

וּמְקַבְּצָיו umkabtzav יִשְׁתֻּהוּ yishtuhu בְּחַצְרוֹת bechatzrot קָדְשִׁי kodshi

אַתָּה Ata תָקוּם takum ג"פ רי"ו; אברהם, וו"פ אל, תְּרַחֵם terachem כ"א ההויות שבתפילין

צִיּוֹן Tziyon רי"ו ול"ב נתיבות החוכמה, רמ"ח (אברים), עסמ"ב וט"ז אותיות פשוטות יוסף, ו' הויות, קנאה

כִּי ki עֵת et לְחֶנְנָהּ lechenena כִּי־ ki בָא va מוֹעֵד mo'ed

כִּי ki רָצוּ ratzu עֲבָדֶיךָ avadecha אֶת־ et ר"ת = אלהים דאלפין

אֲבָנֶיהָ avaneha ס"ת = אמת, ע"ה = אהיה פעמים אהיה, ז"פ ס"ג וְאֶת־ ve'et עֲפָרָהּ afara

יְחֹנֵנוּ yechonenu ר"ת = אלהים (על ידי האמת שומרומו בתוזלת הפסוק, מתקיים אפילו עולם התהו

בּוֹנֶה bone ס"ג יְרוּשָׁלַ͏ִם Yerushalayim יְהֹוָה Adonai המרומם בס"ת:)

נִדְחֵי nidchei ע"ב, רביעי יהוה יִשְׂרָאֵל Yisrael יְכַנֵּס yechanes

---

'Ye that are Lord's remembrances, take ye no rest. And give Him no rest, till He establish, and till He make Jerusalem a praise in the earth.' God has sworn by His right hand, and by the arm of His strength: Surely I will no more give you corn to be food for your enemies; and strangers shall not drink your wine, for which you have labored. But they that have garnered it shall eat it, and praise the Lord, and they that have gathered it shall drink it in the courts of My sanctuary." (Isaiah 62:6-9)

"You will arise, and have compassion upon Zion; for it is time to be gracious unto her, for the appointed time is come. For Your servants take pleasure in her stones, and love her dust." (Psalms 102:14-15)

"The Lord does build up Jerusalem; He gathers together the dispersed of Israel." (Psalms 147:2)

AMAR RABBI SHIMON

The essence of this passage from the *Zohar, Noah*, 122-127 concerns the hands. Since the hands are the tools with which we carry out life's actions, the forces of darkness latch onto them in order to influence our deeds. We can infuse our hands with the positive energy that dwells in the Upper Worlds so that they bring blessing and good fortune to all our endeavors.

amar אָמַר · Rabbi רַבִּי · Shimon שִׁמְעוֹן · aremat אֲרֵימַת · yedai יְדַאי

bitzlotin בִּצְלוֹתִין · le'ela לְעֵילָא · dechad דְּכַד · re'uta רְעוּתָא · ila'a עִלָּאָה,

le'ela לְעֵילָא · le'ela לְעֵילָא, · kayma קָיְימָא · al עַל · hahu הַהוּא

re'uta רְעוּתָא, · dela דְּלָא · ityeda אִתְיְדַע, · velo וְלָא · itpas אִתְפַּס · kelal כְּלָל

le'almin לְעָלְמִין, · reisha רֵישָׁא · desatim דְּסָתִים · yatir יַתִּיר · le'eila לְעֵילָא,

vehahu וְהַהוּא · resha רֵישָׁא · apek אַפֵּיק · mai מַאי · de'apek דְּאַפֵּיק, · vela וְלָא

yedi'a יְדִיעַ, · venaher וְנָהִיר · mai מַאי · denaher דְּנָהִיר, · kola כֹּלָא

bistimu בִּסְתִימוּ. · re'o רְעוּ · demachashava דְּמַחֲשָׁבָה · ila'a עִלָּאָה

lemirdaf לְמִרְדַּף · avatrei אֲבַתְרֵיהּ, · ule'itnehara וּלְאִתְנַהֲרָא · minei מִנֵּיהּ.

chad וְחַד · perisu פְּרִיסוּ · itpereis אִתְפְּרֵיס, · umigo וּמִגּוֹ · hahu הַהוּא

perisa פְּרִיסָא, · birdifu בִּרְדִיפוּ · dehahi דְּהַהִיא · machashava מַחֲשָׁבָה

ila'a עִלָּאָה, · matei מָטֵי · vela וְלָא · matei מָטֵי · ad עַד

hahu הַהוּא · perisa פְּרִיסָא · naher נָהִיר · ma מַה · denaher דְּנָהִיר.

uchden וּכְדֵין · ihu אִיהוּ · machashava מַחֲשָׁבָה · ila'a עִלָּאָה,

naher נָהִיר · binhiru בִּנְהִירוּ · satim סָתִים · dela דְּלָא · yedi'a יְדִיעַ,

vehahu וְהַהוּא · machashava מַחֲשָׁבָה · la לָא · yada יְדַע.

AMAR RABBI SHIMON

Rav Shimon said: "I raise my hands on high to pray. When the Supernal desire at the highest point Above, is established upon the forever unknown and ungraspable desire, it becomes the most concealed Head Above. And that Head emanates all that He emanates and all that is unknown. And He illuminates all that he illuminates in a concealed manner. The desire of the Supernal Thought runs after it to be illuminated from it. But a veil spreads and from its spreading and the running after it, it is allowed to reach - and to not reach - the Light. The Light shines upward toward the veil. Therefore the Supernal Thought shines with Unrevealed Illumination, and with Light unknown to the 'Mind (Moach) of air.' And the Thought itself is considered unknown.

כְּדֵין keden בָּטַשׁ batash הַאי hai נְהִירוּ nehiru דִּמַחֲשָׁבָה demachashava

דְּלָא dela אִתְיְידַע ityeda, בִּנְהִירוּ binhiru דְּפַרְסָא defarsa

דְּקָיְימָא dekayma, דְּנָהִיר denaheir מִמַּה mima דְּלָא dela יְדִיעַ yedi'a

דָּא da uchden וּכְדֵין itgalya אִתְגַּלְייָא vela וְלָא ityeda, אִתְיְידַע vela וְלָא

אִתְיְידַע ityeda דְּלָא dela דְּמַחֲשָׁבָה demachashava נְהִירוּ nehiru

וְנָהֲרִין venaharin דִּפְרִיסָא difrisa, binhiru בִּנְהִירוּ batash בָּטַשׁ

הֵיכָלִין hechalin תֵּשַׁע tesha וְאִתְעֲבִידוּ ve'it'avidu, kachada כַּחֲדָא

וְלָאו velav, נְהוֹרִין nehorin inun אִינּוּן lav לָאו vehechalin, וְהֵיכָלִין

אִינּוּן inun nishmatin נִשְׁמָתִין inun אִינּוּן velav וְלָאו ruchin רוּחִין inun אִינּוּן

dechol דְּכָל re'uta, רְעוּתָא beho בְּהוּ dekayma דְּקָיְימָא man מָאן it אִית

kolho כֻּלְּהוּ dekaymei דְּקָיְימֵי nehorin, נְהוֹרִין tesha תֵּשַׁע

מִנַּיְיהוּ minayhu chad וְחַד de'ihu דְּאִיהוּ bemachashava, בְּמַחֲשָׁבָה

batrayhu, בַּתְרַיְיהוּ lemirdaf לְמִרְדַּף kolho כֻּלְּהוּ bechushbena בְּחוּשְׁבְּנָא

vela וְלָא bemach'shava בְּמַחֲשָׁבָה dekaymei דְּקָיְימֵי besha'ata בְּשַׁעֲתָא

la לָא ve'ilen וְאִלֵּין ityeda'u, אִתְיְידָעוּ vela וְלָא mitdabkan מִתְדַּבְּקָן

bemachashava בְּמַחֲשָׁבָה vela וְלָא bir'uta, בִּרְעוּתָא la לָא kaymei קָיְימֵי

tafsin תָּפְסִין vela וְלָא ba בָּהּ tafsin תָּפְסִין ila'a עִלָּאָה

Then, the illumination of the Unknown Thought hits upon the illumination of the veil that stands and shines of what is unknown, what is not known, and what is unrevealed. Thus, the illumination of the Thought that is not known hits upon the veil's illumination, and they shine together. And from them, nine Chambers are made. These Chambers are not Light. And they are neither Ruchot nor Neshamot, and nobody can understand what they are. The desire of all nine Lights is standing in the Thought and is also considered one of Them. And all desire to pursue them while the nine Lights are located in the Thought. Nevertheless, the Chambers are not attained and not known because they are not established as either an aspect of desire or as an aspect of Supernal Thought. They grasp and do not grasp.

בְּאִלֵּין be'ilen קַיְּימֵי kaymei כָּל kol רָזֵי razei דִּמְהֵימְנוּתָא dim'hemenuta,

וְכָל vechol אִינּוּן inun נְהוֹרִין nehorin מֵרָזָא meraza

דְּמַחֲשָׁבָה demachashava עִלָּאָה ila'a כֻּלְּהוּ kolho אִקְרוּן ikrun אֵין en

סוֹף sof. עַד ad הָכָא hacha מָטוֹ mato נְהוֹרִין nehorin וְלָא vela

מָטוֹן maton, וְלָא vela אִתְיְידָעוּ ityeda'u, לָאו lav הָכָא hacha

רְעוּתָא re'uta, וְלָא vela מַחֲשָׁבָה machashava. כַּד kad נָהִיר naher

מַחֲשָׁבָה machashava, וְלָא vela אִתְיְידַע ityeda מִמָּאן miman גּוֹ go

דְּנָהִיר denaher, כְּדֵין keden אִתְלַבַּשׁ itlabesh וְאַסְתִּים ve'astim גּוֹ go

בִּינָה bina, וְנָהִיר venaher לְמָאן leman דְּנָהִיר denaher וְאָעִיל ve'ael דָּא da

בְּדָא beda, עַד ad דְּאִתְכְּלִילוּ de'itkelilu כֻּלְּהוּ kolho כַּחֲדָא kachada.

וּבְרָזָא uv'raza דְּהַקְרְבָּנָא dekorbana כַּד kad סָלֵיק salek, כֹּלָּא kola

אִתְקַשַּׁר itkashar דָּא da בְּדָא beda, וְנָהִיר venaher דָּא da בְּדָא beda,

כְּדֵין keden קַיְּימֵי kaymei כֻּלְּהוּ kolho בִּסְלִיקוּ bisliku,

וּמַחֲשָׁבָה umachashava אִתְעַטַּר it'atar בְּאֵין be'en סוֹף sof.

הַהוּא hahu נְהִירוּ nehiru דְּאִתְנְהִיר de'itneher מִנֵּיהּ minei

מַחֲשָׁבָה machashava עִלָּאָה ila'a, אִקְרֵי ikrei אֵין en סוֹף sof.

וּמִנֵּיהּ uminei אִשְׁתְּכַח ishtechach וְקָיְימָא vekayma וְנָהִיר venaher

לְמָאן leman דְּנָהִיר denaher, וְעַל ve'al דָּא da כֹּלָּא kola

קָאִים ka'em. זַכָּאָה zaka'a וְזוּלְקֵיהוֹן chulakehon דְּצַדִּיקַיָּיא detzadikaya

בְּעָלְמָא be'alma דֵּין den וּבְעַלְמָא uve'alma דְּאָתֵי de'atei.

With these all the secrets of Faith are based upon. And all of these Lights come from the secret of the supernal Thought and all are called the Ein Sof. Because the Lights reach and do not reach, and are not known, there is neither desire nor thought at this point. When Unknown Thought shines from its source, it shines upon whom She shines, and they enter each other until they are as one. Returning to the secret of the sacrifice: when it is raised, all are enmeshed within one another and shine one upon the other. Now all the stages are in the secret of the 'Ascending' and, when it ascends to the Unknown Head, Thought is crowned by the Ein Sof. This illumination that the supernal thought illuminates from is called Ein Sof. And from there it comes. It is established and shines upon whom It shines. And all is based upon this. Happy are the righteous in this world and the World to Come.

TIKKUN LEAH

Meditate here to connect to the moment (cosmic midnight) when the Creator enters the Garden of Eden to joyously connect with all the righteous souls (as is mentioned in the *Zohar*).

שְׂאוּ se'u שְׁעָרִים she'arim כתר רָאשֵׁיכֶם rashechem וְהִנָּשְׂאוּ vehinase'u

ר׳ (ז״א) וה׳ (מלכות) נטאו פִּתְחֵי pitchei עוֹלָם olam וְיָבוֹא veyavo מֶלֶךְ melech

פ״ז בסוד כתם טהור = פ״ז = ר״ת melech מֶלֶךְ ze זֶה ילי mi מִי: לאו hakavod הַכָּבוֹד

יוד הי ואו הה = יהוה כבוד ; Adonai יְהֹוָאדְנִיאהדונהי lau hakavod הַכָּבוֹד עִזּוּז izuz

וְגִבּוֹר vegibor יְהֹוָאדְנִיאהדונהי Adonai גִּבּוֹר gibor מִלְחָמָה milchama:

שְׂאוּ se'u שְׁעָרִים she'arim כתר רָאשֵׁיכֶם rashechem וּשְׂאוּ use'u

ר׳ עילאה שהוא ת״ת נטא פִּתְחֵי pitchei עוֹלָם olam וְיָבֹא veyavo מֶלֶךְ melech

hakavod הַכָּבוֹד melech מֶלֶךְ ze זֶה hu הוּא ילי mi מִי: לאו hakavod

לאו Adonai יְהֹוָאדְנִיאהדונהי ; כבוד יהוה = יוד הי ואו הה tzeva'ot צְבָאוֹת

פני שכינה hu הוּא מֶלֶךְ melech הַכָּבוֹד hakavod לאו סֶלָה sela:

This Psalm and the following are based on the yearning of *Malchut* to be elevated with her mate, *Zeir Anpin*.

לַמְנַצֵּחַ lam'natze'ach מַשְׂכִּיל maskil לִבְנֵי livnei קֹרַח Korach:

כְּאַיָּל ke'ayal תַּעֲרֹג ta'arog עַל al אֲפִיקֵי afikei מַיִם mayim כֵּן ken

נַפְשִׁי nafshi תַּעֲרֹג ta'arog אֵלֶיךָ elecha אֱלֹהִים Elohim אהיה אדני ; ילה:

צָמְאָה tzam'a נַפְשִׁי nafshi לֵאלֹהִים lelohim אהיה אדני ; ילה לְאֵל leEl

יא״י (מילוי דס״ג) חי chai וְ- מָתַי matai אָבוֹא avo וְאֵרָאֶה ve'era'e ראה פְּנֵי penei

וחכמה בינה אֱלֹהִים Elohim אהיה אדני ; ילה: הָיְתָה hayta לִּי li דִמְעָתִי dim'ati

לֶחֶם lechem ג׳ הויות יוֹמָם yomam וָלַיְלָה valayla מלה בֶּאֱמֹר be'emor אֵלַי elai

כָּל kol ילי הַיּוֹם hayom ע״ה נגד, מזבח, זך, אל יהוה אַיֵּה aye אֱלֹהֶיךָ elohecha ילה:

TIKKUN LEAH

"Lift up your heads gates, and be lifted up, everlasting doors; that the King of glory may come in. 'Who is the King of glory?' 'The Lord strong and mighty, 'The Lord mighty in battle. Lift up your heads gates, lift them up, everlasting doors; that the King of Glory may come in. 'Who then is the King of Glory?' 'Lord of Hosts; He is the King of Glory.' Selah." (Psalms 24:7-10).

"For the Leader; Maschil of the sons of Korach: As the hart pants after the water brooks, so pants my soul after You, God. My soul thirsts for God, for the living God: 'When shall I come and appear before God?' My tears have been my food day and night, while they say unto me all the day: 'Where is your God?'

אֵלֶּה ele | אֶזְכְּרָה ezkera | וְאֶשְׁפְּכָה ve'eshpecha | עָלַי alai

נַפְשִׁי nafshi | כִּי ki | אֶעֱבֹר e'evor | בַּסָּךְ basach | אֶדַּדֵּם edadem

In the time of the Omer you should meditate:
"אֶעֱבֹר בְּסָךְ אֲדַדֵּם" אֶל מִסְפַּר יְמֵי הַסְּפִירָה עוֹלֶה מ"ט כְּמִנְיָן "אֲדַדֵּם")

עַד ad | בֵּית bet | אֱלֹהִים Elohim | בְּקוֹל bekol | רִנָּה rina

וְתוֹדָה vetoda | הָמוֹן hamon | חוֹגֵג chogeg | מַה־ ma

תִּשְׁתּוֹחֲחִי tishtochachi | נַפְשִׁי nafshi | וַתֶּהֱמִי vatehemi | עָלַי alai

הוֹחִילִי hochili | לֵאלֹהִים lelohim | כִּי ki | עוֹד od | אוֹדֶנּוּ odenu

יְשׁוּעוֹת yeshu'ot | פָּנָיו panav | אֱלֹהַי Elohai | עָלַי alai

נַפְשִׁי nafshi | תִּשְׁתּוֹחָח tishtochach | עַל־ al | כֵּן ken | אֶזְכָּרְךָ ezkorcha

מֵאֶרֶץ me'eretz | יַרְדֵּן Yarden | וְחֶרְמוֹנִים veChermonim

מֵהַר mehar | מִצְעָר Mitz'ar | תְּהוֹם־ tehom | אֶל־ el | תְּהוֹם tehom

קוֹרֵא kore | לְקוֹל lekol | צִנּוֹרֶיךָ tzinorecha | כָּל־ kol

מִשְׁבָּרֶיךָ mishbarecha | וְגַלֶּיךָ vegalecha | עָלַי alai | עָבָרוּ avaru

יוֹמָם yomam | יְצַוֶּה yetzave | יְהֹוָה Adonai | וְחַסְדּוֹ chasdo

וּבַלַּיְלָה uvalayla | שִׁירֹה shiro

עִמִּי imi | תְּפִלָּה tefila

לְאֵל leEl | וְחַיָּי chayai | אוֹמְרָה omra

לְאֵל leEl | סַלְעִי sal'i | לָמָה lama | שְׁכַחְתָּנִי shechachtani

לָמָה־ lama | קֹדֵר koder | אֵלֵךְ elech | בְּלַחַץ belachatz | אוֹיֵב oyev

---

These things I remember, and pour out my soul within me, how I passed on with the throng, and led them to the house of God, with the voice of joy and praise, a multitude keeping holyday. Why are you cast down, my soul? And why moan you within me? Hope you in God; for I shall yet praise Him for the salvation of His countenance. My God, my soul is cast down within me; therefore do I remember You from the land of Jordan, and the Hermons, from the hill Mizar. Deep calls unto deep at the voice of Your cataracts; all Your waves and Your billows are gone over me. By day the Lord will command His loving kindness, and in the night His song shall be with me, even a prayer unto the God of my life. I will say to God my Rock: 'Why have You forgotten me? Why go I mourning under the oppression of the enemy?'

בְּרָצוֹ beretzach — בְּעַצְמוֹתַי be'atzmotai — וְחֶרְפוּנִי cherfuni — צוֹרְרָי tzorerai

בְּאָמְרָם be'omram — אֵלַי elai — כָּל kol — הַיּוֹם hayom — (ע"ה נגד, מזבח, זן, אל יהוה)

אַיֵּה aye — אֱלֹהֶיךָ elohecha — מַה ma — תִּשְׁתּוֹחֲחִי tishtochachi

נַפְשִׁי nafshi — וּמַה uma — תֶּהֱמִי tehemi — עָלָי alai — הוֹחִילִי hochili

לֵאלֹהִים lelohim — כִּי ki — עוֹד od — אוֹדֶנּוּ odenu

יְשׁוּעֹת yeshu'ot — פָּנַי panai — וֵאלֹהַי velohai

שָׁפְטֵנִי shofteni — אֱלֹהִים Elohim — וְרִיבָה veriva

רִיבִי rivi — מִגּוֹי migoy — לֹא lo — וְחָסִיד chasid — מֵאִישׁ me'ish

מִרְמָה mirma — וְעַוְלָה ve'avla — תְפַלְּטֵנִי tefalteni — כִּי ki — אַתָּה Ata

אֱלֹהֵי Elohei — מָעוּזִּי ma'uzi — לָמָה lama — זְנַחְתָּנִי zenachtani

לָמָה lama — קֹדֵר koder — אֶתְהַלֵּךְ et'halech — בְּלַחַץ belachatz — אוֹיֵב oyev

שְׁלַח shelach — אוֹרְךָ orcha — וַאֲמִתְּךָ va'amitecha — הֵמָּה hema — יַנְחוּנִי yanchuni

יְבִיאוּנִי yevi'uni — אֶל el — הַר har — קָדְשְׁךָ kodshecha — וְאֶל ve'el

מִשְׁכְּנוֹתֶיךָ mishkenotecha — וְאָבוֹאָה ve'avoa — אֶל el — מִזְבַּח mizbach

אֱלֹהִים Elohim — אֶל el — אֵל El (נגד, זן, אל יהוה, ייא"י מילוי דס"ג)

שִׂמְחַת simchat — גִּילִי gili — וְאוֹדְךָ ve'odcha — בְכִנּוֹר vechinor — אֱלֹהִים Elohim

אֱלֹהַי Elohai — מַה ma

נַפְשִׁי nafshi — וּמַה uma — תֶּהֱמִי tehemi — עָלָי alai — תִּשְׁתּוֹחֲחִי tishtochachi

הוֹחִילִי hochili — לֵאלֹהִים lelohim — כִּי ki — עוֹד od — אוֹדֶנּוּ odenu

יְשׁוּעֹת yeshu'ot — פָּנַי panai — וֵאלֹהָי velohai

As with a crushing in my bones, my adversaries taunt me; while they say to me all the day: 'Where is your God?' Why are you cast down, my soul? And why moan you within me? Hope you in God; for I shall yet praise Him, the salvation of my countenance, and my God." (Psalms 42).

"Be You my judge, God, and plead my cause against an ungodly nation; deliver me from the deceitful and unjust man. For You are the God of my strength; why have You cast me off? Why go I mourning under the oppression of the enemy? Send out Your light and Your truth; let them lead me; let them bring me to Your holy mountain, and to Your dwelling-places. Then will I go to the altar of God, to God, my exceeding joy; and praise You upon the harp, God, my God. Why are you cast down, my soul? And why moan you within me? Hope in God; for I shall yet praise Him, the salvation of my countenance, and my God." (Psalms 43)

YA'ANCHA

During the days when we don't recite the *Tachanun*, we skip this Psalm.

In this Psalm, there are 70 words, which correspond to the 70 voices of the *Ayala* (doe).

לַמְנַצֵּחַ lam'natze'ach   מִזְמוֹר mizmor   לְדָוִד leDavid: יַעַנְךָ ya'ancha

יְהוָֹהאהדונהי Adonai   בְּיוֹם beyom   ע"ה נגד, מזבח, זן, אל יהוה   צָרָה tzara

שֵׁם shem   יְשַׂגֶּבְךָ yesagevcha   אלהים דההין ; ר"ת = יב"ק, אלהים יהוה, אהיה אדני יהוה

אֱלֹהֵי Elohei   יַעֲקֹב Yaakov   ו' הויות, יאהדונהי אידהנויה ; ס"ת = ב"ן:

יִשְׁלַח yishlach   עֶזְרְךָ ezrecha   מִקֹּדֶשׁ mikodesh   וּמִצִּיּוֹן umiTziyon

יִסְעָדֶךָּ yis'adeka: יִזְכֹּר yizkor   כָּל kol   יוסף, ו' הויות, קנאה י"ת וס"ת = י' הויות

מִנְחֹתֶךָ minchotecha   וְעוֹלָתְךָ ve'olatcha   יְדַשְּׁנֶה yedashne   סֶלָה sela

יִתֶּן yiten: לְךָ lecha   כִלְבָבֶךָ chilvavecha

וְכָל vechol   עֲצָתְךָ atzatcha   יְמַלֵּא yemale: נְרַנְּנָה neranena

בִּישׁוּעָתֶךָ bishu'atecha   וּבְשֵׁם uvshem   אֱלֹהֵינוּ Elohenu

נִדְגֹּל nidgol   יְמַלֵּא yemale   יְהוָֹהאהדונהי Adonai

כָּל kol   מִשְׁאֲלוֹתֶיךָ mish'alotecha: עַתָּה ata   יָדַעְתִּי yadati   כִּי ki

הוֹשִׁיעַ hoshi'a   יְהוָֹהאהדונהי Adonai   מְשִׁיחוֹ meshicho

יַעֲנֵהוּ ya'anehu   מִשְּׁמֵי mishmei   קָדְשׁוֹ kodsho   בִּגְבֻרוֹת bigvurot

יֵשַׁע yesha   יְמִינוֹ yemino:

YA'ANCHA

"For the Leader; A Psalm of David.

The Lord answer you in the day of trouble; the name of the God of Jacob set you up on high; Send forth your help from the sanctuary, and support you out of Zion. Receive the memorial of all your meal-offerings and accept the fat of your burnt-sacrifice; Selah. Grant you according to your own heart and fulfill all your counsel. We will shout for joy in your victory, and in the name of our God we will set up our standards; Lord fulfills all your petitions. Now know I that the Lord saves His anointed; He will answer him from His Holy Heaven with the mighty acts of His saving right hand.

You should meditate here to be protected from the *Gog uMagog* (Armegadon) war.

אֵלֶּה ele בְּרֶכֶב varechev וְאֵלֶּה ve'ele ר"ת וס"ת = אהיה ; ועם ר"ת וס"ת בסוסים = ס"ג

בַסּוּסִים vasusim וַאֲנַחְנוּ va'anachnu בְּשֵׁם beshem יְהֹוָה Adonai

אֱלֹהֵינוּ Elohenu ילה נַזְכִּיר nazkir הֵמָּה hema כָּרְעוּ kar'u

וְנָפָלוּ venafalu וַאֲנַחְנוּ va'anachnu קַמְנוּ kamnu וַנִּתְעוֹדָד vanit'odad

יְהֹוָה Adonai הוֹשִׁיעָה hoshi'a ר"ת = יב"ק, אלהים יהוה, אהיה אדני יהוה.

הַמֶּלֶךְ hamelech ר"ת יהה ; עם ו' נהורין ו' הונתעודד = יהוה

יַעֲנֵנוּ ya'anenu בְיוֹם־ veyom ע"ה נגד, מזבוז, זז, אל יהוה קָרְאֵנוּ kore'nu

ר"ת יב"ק, אלהים יהוה, אהיה אדני יהוה ; ס"ת = ב"ן ; ועם אות כף דהמלך = ע"ב:

לְדָוִד leDavid מִזְמוֹר mizmor לַיהֹוָה ladonai הָאָרֶץ ha'aretz

וּמְלוֹאָה umlo'a ע"ה תֵּבֵל tevel ב"פ רי"ו וְיֹשְׁבֵי veyoshvei אלהים דההין ע"ה בָהּ va

כִּי ki הוּא hu עַל־ al יַמִּים yamim יְסָדָהּ yesada וְעַל־ ve'al

נְהָרוֹת neharot יְכוֹנְנֶהָ yechoneneha עם התיבה וע"ה קמ"ג: מִי mi יַעֲלֶה ya'ale

בְהַר־ vehar ר"ת יבמ, ב"ן יְהֹוָה Adonai וּמִי־ umi יָקוּם yakum

בִּמְקוֹם bimkom קָדְשׁוֹ kodsho ר"ת יבק, אלהים יהוה, אהיה אדני יהוה ;

נְקִי neki ע"ה קנ"א, אדני אלהים חפים ע"ה קס"א chapayim ס"ת מום, אלהים, אהיה אדני יהוה:

(מזרע לבטלה) וּבַר־ uvar יצחק, ד"פ ב"ן levav לֵבָב בוכו ; בר לבב = ע"ב ס"ג מ"ה ב"ן,

אֲשֶׁר asher (למתק את ז' המלכים עמתו) הברכה נָשָׂא nasa לֹא־ lo לַשָּׁוְא lashav

נַפְשִׁי nafshi (כתיב: נפשו) וְלֹא velo נִשְׁבַּע nishba לְמִרְמָה lemirma:

Some trust in chariots, and some in horses; but we will make mention of the Name of the Lord our God. They are bowed down and fallen; but we are raised, and stand upright. Save, Lord; let the King answer us in the day that we call." (Psalms 20)
"A Psalm of David: The earth is Lord's, and the fullness thereof; the world, and they that dwell therein. For He has founded it upon the seas, and established it upon the floods. Who shall ascend into the mountain of the Lord? And who shall stand in His holy place? He that has clean hands, and a pure heart; who has not taken My Name in vain, and has not sworn deceitfully.

יִשָּׂא yisa בְּרָכָה veracha מֵאֵת me'et ר"ת יבמ, ב"ן יְהֹוָ‎ה‎אדני‎אהדונהי Adonai

וּצְדָקָה utz'daka מֵאֱלֹהֵי meElohei ע"ה ריבוע אלהים ; יהה ; ילה , דמב , ילה

יִשְׁעוֹ yish'o שכינה ע"ה ; ס"ת יהוה זֶה ze דּוֹר dor דֹּרְשָׁיו dorshav

(כתיב : דרשו) מְבַקְשֵׁי mevakshei פָּנֶיךָ fanecha ס"ג מ"ה ב"ן

יַעֲקֹב Ya'akov ז' הויות, יאהדונהי אידהנויה יאהדונהי סֶלָה sela שְׂאוּ se'u שְׁעָרִים she'arim כתר

רָאשֵׁיכֶם rashechem וְהִנָּשְׂאוּ vehinase'u ו' שהוא זעיר אנפין וה' שהיא מלכות - נעשאו

פִּתְחֵי pitchei עוֹלָם olam וְיָבוֹא veyavo מֶלֶךְ melech הַכָּבוֹד hakavod לאו:

מִי mi ילי זֶה ze מֶלֶךְ melech ר"ת = פ"ז בסוד כתם טהור פז

הַכָּבוֹד hakavod לאו יְהֹוָ‎ה‎אדני‎אהדונהי Adonai ; כבוד יהוה = יוד הי ואו הה עֻזּוּז izuz

וְגִבּוֹר vegibor יְהֹוָ‎ה‎אדני‎אהדונהי Adonai גִּבּוֹר gibor מִלְחָמָה milchama:

שְׂאוּ se'u שְׁעָרִים she'arim כתר רָאשֵׁיכֶם rashechem

וּשְׂאוּ use'u ר' עילאה שהוא ת"ת נעשא פִּתְחֵי pitchei עוֹלָם olam

וְיָבוֹא veyavo מֶלֶךְ melech הַכָּבוֹד hakavod לאו:

מִי mi ילי הוּא hu זֶה ze מֶלֶךְ melech הַכָּבוֹד hakavod לאו

יְהֹוָ‎ה‎אדני‎אהדונהי Adonai כבוד יהוה = יוד הי ואו הה צְבָאוֹת tzeva'ot פני שכינה

הוּא hu מֶלֶךְ melech הַכָּבוֹד hakavod לאו סֶלָה sela:

LAMNATZE'ACH

By meditating upon the *Magen David* (Shield of David), we harness the power, strength, and valor of King David so that we can defeat our personal enemies. Our real enemies are not found in the outside world, regardless of what our ego tells us. Our real enemy is our *Desire to Receive for the Self Alone*. When we defeat the enemy within, external enemies suddenly disappear from our lives.

He shall receive a blessing from the Lord and righteousness from the God of his salvation. Such is the generation of them that seek after Him that seek Your Face, even Jacob. Selah. Lift up your heads gates, and be lifted up, everlasting doors; that the King of Glory may come in. 'Who is the King of Glory?' The Lord strong and mighty, the Lord mighty in battle. Lift up your heads, gates, lift them up, everlasting doors; that the King of Glory may come in. 'Who then is the King of Glory?' Lord of Hosts; He is the King of Glory.' Selah." (Psalms 24)

God revealed this Psalm to King David by Divine Inspiration. It was written on a golden plate made in the shape of the *Menorah* (shown on pg. 41). God also showed it to Moses. King David carried this Psalm written and engraved on the gold plate on his shield, the Shield of David. When King David went to war, he would meditate on the secrets of the *Menorah* and the seven sentences of this Psalm engraved in it, and his enemies would literally fall in defeat before him. By meditating upon it (reading the letters without turning the image upside down), we harness that power (*Midbar Kdemot*, by the Chida and also in *Menorat Zahav*, by Rav Zusha.)

לַמְנַצֵּחַ lam'natze'ach   בִּנְגִינֹת binginot   מִזְמוֹר mizmor   שִׁיר shir:

אֱלֹהִים Elohim   אהיה אדני ; ילה   יְחָנֵּנוּ yechonenu   וִיבָרְכֵנוּ vivarchenu

יָאֵר ya'er   כף ויו זין ויו   פָּנָיו panav   ר"ת פאי, אמן (יאהדונהי)   אִתָּנוּ itanu   סֶלָה sela:

לָדַעַת lada'at   ר"ת סאל, אמן (יאהדונהי)   בָּאָרֶץ ba'aretz   דַּרְכֶּךָ darkecha

בְּכָל bechol   ב"ן, לכב   גּוֹיִם goyim   יְשׁוּעָתֶךָ yeshu'atecha:

יוֹדוּךָ yoducha   עַמִּים amim   אֱלֹהִים Elohim   אהיה אדני ; ילה

יוֹדוּךָ yoducha   עַמִּים amim   כֻּלָּם kulam: יִשְׂמְחוּ yismechu   וִירַנְּנוּ viranenu

לְאֻמִּים le'umim   ר"ת ע"ה = איהויהה   כִּי ki   תִשְׁפֹּט tishpot   עַמִּים amim

מִישׁוֹר mishor   וּלְאֻמִּים ul'umim   בָּאָרֶץ ba'aretz   תַּנְחֵם tanchem   סֶלָה sela:

יוֹדוּךָ yoducha   עַמִּים amim   אֱלֹהִים Elohim   אהיה אדני ; ילה   יוֹדוּךָ yoducha

עַמִּים amim   כֻּלָּם kulam: ר"ת ישמוו יודוך ארץ = יא"י (מילוי דס"ג)

אֶרֶץ eretz   נָתְנָה natna   נתה, קס"א קנ"א קמ"ג   ועם ר"ת אלהים לדעת יברכנו = ע"ב, ריבוע יהוה

יְבוּלָהּ yevula   ר"ת אני   יְבָרְכֵנוּ yevarchenu   אֱלֹהִים Elohim   אהיה אדני ; ילה

אֱלֹהֵינוּ Elohenu   ילה: יְבָרְכֵנוּ yevarchenu   אֱלֹהִים Elohim   אהיה אדני ; ילה

וְיִירְאוּ veyir'u   אוֹתוֹ oto   כָּל kol   ילי   אַפְסֵי afsei   אָרֶץ aretz:

LAMNATZE'ACH

"For the Leader; with string-music: A Psalm, a Song. God be gracious unto us, and bless us; may He cause His face to shine toward us; Selah. That Your way may be known upon earth, Your salvation among all nations. Let the people give thanks to You, God; let the people give thanks to You, all of them. Let the nations be glad and sing for joy; for You will judge the people with equity, and lead the nations upon earth. Selah Let the people give thanks to You, God; let the people give thanks to You, all of them. The earth has yielded her increase; may God, our own God, bless us. May God bless us; and let all the ends of the earth fear Him." (Psalms 67)

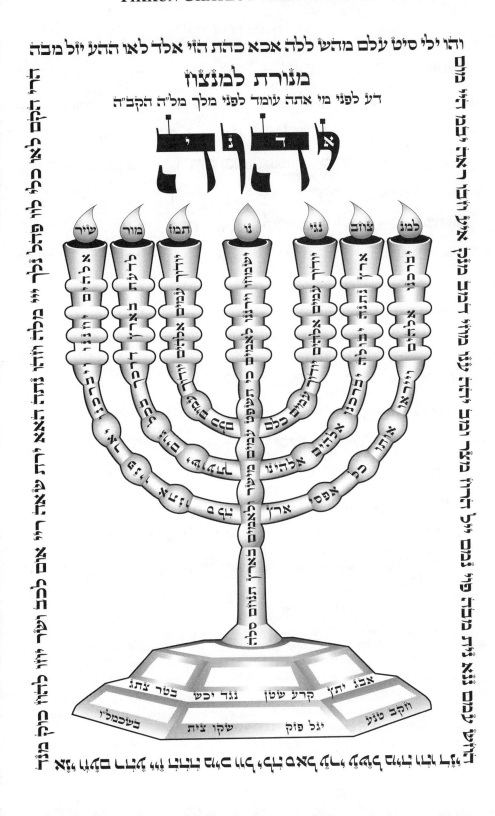

HALELUYAH

Reciting this Psalm is for the *Zivug* (unification) of *Leah* and her connection.

Adonai יְהֹוָׁהאלהיםואדני ode אוֹדֶה לכלה ; ילה ; אהיה אדני, אהיה אלהים, haleluya הַלְלוּיָה

besod בְּסוֹד מוכ, י"פ האא בוכו levav לֵבָב לכב, ב"ן, בֶּחַל bechal בְּכָל

ma'asei מַעֲשֵׂי gedolim גְּדֹלִים סיט: ve'eda וְעֵדָה yesharim יְשָׁרִים

lechol לְכָל־ אדני יה derushim דְּרוּשִׁים Adonai יְהֹוָׁהאלהיםואדני

pa'olo פָּעֳלוֹ vehadar וְהָדָר ההה hod הוֹד־ cheftzehem וְחֶפְצֵיהֶם:

zecher זֵכֶר ב"פ la'ad לָעַד omedet עֹמֶדֶת vetzidkato וְצִדְקָתוֹ

verachum וְרַחוּם chanun חַנּוּן lenifle'otav לְנִפְלְאֹתָיו asa עָשָׂה

lire'av לִירֵאָיו natan נָתַן teref טֶרֶף :עשׂה = יהוה וחנן ורחום Adonai יְהֹוָׁהאלהיםואדני

berito בְּרִיתוֹ: אותיות ו' דס"ג ריבוע le'olam לְעוֹלָם yizkor יִזְכֹּר

lahem לָהֶם latet לָתֵת le'amo לְעַמּוֹ higid הִגִּיד ma'asav מַעֲשָׂיו ko'ach כֹּחַ

emet אֱמֶת yadav יָדָיו ma'asei מַעֲשֵׂי goyim גּוֹיִם nachalat נַחֲלַת

ne'emanim נֶאֱמָנִים אלהים ה"פ ז"פ ס"ג ע"ה umishpat וּמִשְׁפָּט ז"פ ס"ג, אהיה פעמים

kol כָּל־ ילי pikudav פִּקּוּדָיו מנק: semuchim סְמוּכִים la'ad לָעַד ב"פ ב"ן

be'emet בֶּאֱמֶת asuyim עֲשׂוּיִם אותיות ו' דס"ג ריבוע le'olam לְעוֹלָם

le'amo לְעַמּוֹ shalach שָׁלַח pedut פְּדוּת veyashar וְיָשָׁר: ז"פ ס"ג, אהיה פעמים

berito בְּרִיתוֹ אותיות ו' דס"ג ריבוע le'olam לְעוֹלָם tziva צִוָּה־

kadosh קָדוֹשׁ venora וְנוֹרָא shemo שְׁמוֹ: ע"ב בריבוע קס"א ע"ה, אל שדי ע"ה, מהש ע"ה

HALELUYAH

"Praise the Lord!"

א I will give thanks to the Lord with my whole heart, ב in the council of the upright, and in the congregation. ג The works of the Lord are great, ד sought out of all them that have delight therein. ה His work is glory and majesty; ו and His righteousness endures forever. ז He has made a memorial for His wonderful works; ח the Lord is gracious and full of compassion. ט He has given food to those that fear Him; י He will ever be mindful of His covenant. כ He has declared to His people the power of His works, ל in giving them the heritage of the nations. מ The works of His hands are truth and justice; נ all His precepts are sure. ס They are established for ever and ever, ע they are done in truth and uprightness. פ He has sent redemption unto His people; צ He has commanded His covenant for ever; ק Holy and awesome is His Name.

רֵאשִׁית reshit וְחָכְמָה chochmah = בְּמִלּוּי תרי"ג (מצוות) יִרְאַת yir'at

יְהֹוָה Adonai שֵׂכֶל sechel טוֹב tov והו לְכָל lechol יה אדני

עֹשֵׂיהֶם osehem תְּהִלָּתוֹ tehilato עֹמֶדֶת omedet לָעַד la'ad ב"פ ב"ן:

You should meditate on the five final letters —מנצפ"ך— in order to complete the 27 letters which are the illustration of the newborn. You should also meditate: כל"ך סעפ"ה יאעצ"ה. Then, meditate: אלד (this Name is the secret of the birth of Leah and has the same numeral value of Leah).

During the days when we say only *Tikkun Leah*, we recite the following verses:

נוֹעַ no'a תָּנוּעַ tanu'a אֶרֶץ eretz כַּשִּׁכּוֹר kashikor וְהִתְנוֹדְדָה vehitnodeda

כִּמְלוּנָה kameluna וְכָבַד vechavad עָלֶיהָ aleha פֶּשַׁע pish'a פהל

וְנָפְלָה venafla וְלֹא velo תֹסִיף tosif קוּם kum וְהָיָה vehaya יהוה ; יהוה

בַּיּוֹם bayom ע"ה נגד, מזבוח, זן, אל יהוה הַהוּא hahu יִפְקֹד yifkod

יְהֹוָה Adonai עַל al צְבָא tzeva הַמָּרוֹם hamarom בַּמָּרוֹם bamarom

וְעַל ve'al מַלְכֵי malchei הָאֲדָמָה ha'adama עַל al הָאֲדָמָה ha'adama:

Before reciting the following Psalm,
You should cry for your negative actions and ask for forgiveness:

לַמְנַצֵּחַ lam'natze'ach מִזְמוֹר mizmor לְדָוִד leDavid: בְּבוֹא bevo אֵלָיו elav

נָתָן Natan הַנָּבִיא hanavi כַּאֲשֶׁר ka'asher בָּא ba אֶל el בַּת-שֶׁבַע Batshava:

חָנֵּנִי choneni אֱלֹהִים Elohim אהיה אדני ; ילה כְּחַסְדֶּךָ kechasdecha כְּרֹב kerov

רַחֲמֶיךָ rachamecha מְחֵה meche פְּשָׁעָי fesha'ai: הֶרֶב herev (כתיב: הרבה)

כַּבְּסֵנִי kabeseni מֵעֲוֹנִי me'avoni וּמֵחַטָּאתִי umechatati טַהֲרֵנִי tahareni:

ר *The fear of the Lord is the beginning of wisdom;*
ש *a good understanding have all they that do thereafter;* ת *His praise endures for ever." (Psalms 111)*

"The earth reels to and fro like a drunken man, and sways to and from as a lodge; and the transgression thereof is heavy upon it, and it shall fall, and not rise again. And it shall come to pass in that day, that Lord will punish the host of the high heaven on high, and the kings of the earth upon the earth." (Isaiah 24:20-21)

For the Leader: A Psalm of David; When Nathan the prophet came to him, after he had gone in to Bathsheba. Be gracious unto me, God, according to Your mercy; according to the multitude of Your compassions blot out my transgressions. Wash me thoroughly from mine iniquity, and cleanse me from my sin.

וְחַטָּאתִי vechatati — אֵדָע eda — אֲנִי — ani אֲנִי — fesha'ai פְּשָׁעַי — ki כִּי

קס"א קנ"א קמ"ג — tamid תָמִיד — ע"ה יהוה אֶל — זֶ, מִזְבּוֹ, — negdi נֶגְדִּי

be'enecha בְּעֵינֶיךָ — vehara וְהָרַע — chatati וְחָטָאתִי — levadecha לְבַדְּךָ — lecha לְךָ

titzdak תִּצְדַּק — lema'an לְמַעַן — asiti עָשִׂיתִי — מ"ה רִיבּוּעַ ; — קס"א ע"ה

hen הֵן — veshoftecha בְּשָׁפְטֶךָ — tizke תִּזְכֶּה — bedovrecha בְּדָבְרֶךָ

imi אִמִּי — yechematni יֶחֱמַתְנִי — uv'chet וּבְחֵטְא — cholalti וְחוֹלָלְתִּי — be'avon בְּעָווֹן

vatuchot בַּטֻּחוֹת — chafatzta וְחָפַצְתָּ — אֶהְיֶה פְּעָמִים אֶהְיֶה, ז"פ ס"ג — emet אֱמֶת — hen הֵן

todi'eni תּוֹדִיעֵנִי — (מִצְוֹת) תרי"ג = בְּמִלּוּי — chochmah וְחָכְמָה — uvsatum וּבְסָתֻם

techabseni תְּכַבְּסֵנִי — ve'et'har וְאֶטְהָר — ve'ezov בְאֵזוֹב — techat'eni תְּחַטְּאֵנִי

tashmi'eni תַּשְׁמִיעֵנִי — albin אַלְבִּין — (ר"ג אהי"ה) אֶלֶף אֶלֶף אֶלֶף — umisheleg וּמִשֶּׁלֶג — tashmi'eni תַּשְׁמִיעֵנִי

dikita דִּכִּיתָ — atzamot עֲצָמוֹת — tagelna תָּגֵלְנָה — vesimcha וְשִׂמְחָה — sason שָׂשׂוֹן

mechata'ai מֵחֲטָאָי — panecha פָּנֶיךָ — ב"פ מ"ה ס"ג מצר — haster הַסְתֵּר

אכא י"פ — tahor טָהוֹר — lev לֵב — meche מְחֵה — avonotai עֲוֹנֹתַי ילי — vechol וְכָל

בְּרָא קנ"א ב"ן, יהוה אֱלֹהִים אֲדֹנָי, מִלּוּי קס"א וס"ג, מ"ה בְּרָבוּעַ וע"ב ע"ה ; — bera בְּרָא

לֵב טָהוֹר בְּרָא = קס"א קנ"א קמ"ג ; יְלָה ; לִי אֱלֹהִים = רִיבּוּעַ אֲדֹנָי — Elohim אֱלֹהִים אהי"ה אֲדֹנָי — li לִי

שׂהי bekirbi בְּקִרְבִּי — קס"א קנ"א י"ב הֲוִיוֹת, — chadesh וְחַדֵּשׁ י"ב הֲוִיוֹת — nachon נָכוֹן — veru'ach וְרוּחַ

veru'ach וְרוּחַ — milfanecha מִלְּפָנֶיךָ ס"ג מ"ה ב"ן — tashlicheni תַּשְׁלִיכֵנִי — al אַל

li לִי — hashiva הָשִׁיבָה — mimeni מִמֶּנִּי — tikach תִּקַּח — al אַל — kodshecha קָדְשְׁךָ

tismecheni תִּסְמְכֵנִי — nediva נְדִיבָה — veru'ach וְרוּחַ — yish'echa יִשְׁעֶךָ — seson שְׂשׂוֹן

For I know my transgressions; and my sin is ever before me. Against You, You only, have I sinned, and done that which is evil in Your sight; that You may be justified when You speak, and be in the right when You judge. Behold, I was brought forth in iniquity, and in sin did my mother conceive me. Behold, You desire truth in the inward parts; make me, therefore, to know wisdom in my inmost heart. Purge me with hyssop, and I shall be clean; wash me, and I shall be whiter than snow. Make me to hear joy and gladness; that the bones which You have crushed may rejoice. Hide Your face from my sins, and blot out all my iniquities. Create me a clean heart, God; and renew a steadfast spirit within me. Cast me not away from Your presence; and take not Your Holy Spirit from me. Restore unto me the joy of You salvation; and let a willing spirit uphold me.

אֲלַמְּדָה alamda — פֹשְׁעִים fosh'im — דְּרָכֶיךָ derachecha — וְחַטָּאִים vechata'im

אֵלֶיךָ elecha — יָשׁוּבוּ yashuvu — הַצִּילֵנִי hatzileni — מִדָּמִים midamim

אֱלֹהִים Elohim ; אהיה אדני ילה — אֱלֹהֵי Elohei מילוי ע"ב, דמב ; ילה

תְּשׁוּעָתִי teshu'ati — תְּרַנֵּן teranen — לְשׁוֹנִי leshoni — צִדְקָתֶךָ tzidkatecha

אֲדֹנָי Adonai ללה — שְׂפָתַי sefatai — תִּפְתָּח tiftach — וּפִי ufi

יַגִּיד yagid ייי (כ"ב אותיות [=אכא] · ה' אותיות סזכזכזר) ס"ת = בוכו — תְּהִלָּתֶךָ tehilatecha

כִּי ki — לֹא lo — תַחְפֹּץ tachpotz — זֶבַח zevach — וְאֶתֵּנָה ve'etena נתה, קס"א קנ"א קמ"ג

עוֹלָה ola — לֹא lo — תִרְצֶה tirtze — זִבְחֵי zivchei — אֱלֹהִים Elohim אהיה אדני ; ילה

רוּחַ ru'ach — נִשְׁבָּרָה nishbara ר"ת = ג"פ אלהים (יומתיקם בשם ס"ג עובס"ת)

לֵב lev — נִשְׁבָּר nishbar — וְנִדְכֶּה venidke ר"ת = אלהים, אהיה אדני Elohim

לֹא lo — תִבְזֶה tivze ר"ת = ה"פ אלהים ע"ה ; וס"ת מילוי ע"ב

הֵיטִיבָה hetiva — בִרְצוֹנְךָ virtzoncha — אֶת et — צִיּוֹן Tziyon יוסף, ו' הויות, קנאה

תִּבְנֶה tivne — חוֹמוֹת chomot ע"ה קס"א קנ"א קמ"ג — יְרוּשָׁלָיִם Yerushalayim

אָז az — תַחְפֹּץ tachpotz — זִבְחֵי zivchei — צֶדֶק tzedek — עוֹלָה ola

וְכָלִיל vechalil — אָז az — יַעֲלוּ ya'alu — עַל al — מִזְבַּחֲךָ mizbachacha — פָרִים farim

While reciting these verses, one should meditate that the word *Tzion* corresponds to *Rachel* and the word *Yerushalayim* corresponds to *Leah*, and ask the Creator to raise them up from their fall.

When we don't say *Tikkun Rachel* we skip this verse:

עַד ad — אָנָה ana ריבוע מ"ה — בְּכִיָּה bichya מילוי דס"ג — בְצִיּוֹן veTziyon (Rachel)

וּמִסְפֵּד umisped ריבוע ע"ב — בִּירוּשָׁלָיִם birushalayim יוסף, ו' הויות, קנאה (Leah)

Then will I teach transgressors Your ways; and sinners shall return unto You. Deliver me from blood guiltiness, God, You are God of my salvation; so shall my tongue sing aloud of Your righteousness. God, open You my lips; and my mouth shall declare Your praise. For You delight not in sacrifice, else would I give it; You have no pleasure in burnt-offering. The sacrifices of God are a broken spirit; a broken and a contrite heart, God, You will not despise. Do good in Your favour unto Zion; build You the walls of Jerusalem. Then will You delight in the sacrifices of righteousness, in burnt-offering and whole offering; then will they offer bullocks upon Your altar." (Pslams 51)

How long it will be crying in Zion and mourning in Jerusalem?

כ"א היות שבתפילין תְּרַחֵם terachem ג"פ רי"ו ; אברהם, וח"פ אל, רי"ו ול"ב נתיבות תָּקוּם takum

הוזכמה, רמ"וז (אברים), עסמ"ב וט"ז אותיות פשוטות צִיּוֹן Tziyon (Rachel) יוסף, ו היות, קנאה

תִּבְנֶה tivne וְחוֹמוֹת chomot ע"ה קס"א קנ"א קמ"ג יְרוּשָׁלַיִם Yerushalayim (Le'ah):

אֱלֹהֵינוּ Elohenu ילה ; מילוי ע"ב, דמב ; ילה וֵאלֹהֵי velohei לכב אֲבוֹתֵינוּ avotenu•

מֶלֶךְ melech רַחֲמָן rachaman רַחֵם rachem אברהם, וח"פ אל, רי"ו ול"ב נתיבות הוזכמה,

umetiv וּמֵטִיב וחו tov טוֹב alenu• עָלֵינוּ אותיות פשוטות ט"ז וט עסמ"ב (אברים), רמ"וז

alenu עָלֵינוּ הוזע shuva שׁוּבָה אדני• ארה אלהים, לָנוּ lanu hidaresh הִדָּרֵשׁ

she'asu שֶׁעָשׂוּ avot אָבוֹת biglal בִּגְלַל rachamecha רַחֲמֶיךָ bahamon בַּהֲמוֹן

kevatechila• כְּבַתְּחִלָּה ב"פ ראה vetcha בֵּיתְךָ bene בְּנֵה retzonecha• רְצוֹנֶךָ

mechono• מְכוֹנוֹ al עַל mikdashcha מִקְדָּשְׁךָ בית bet כוכ ב"פ ראה konen כּוֹנֵן

betikuno• בְּתִקּוּנוֹ samchenu שַׂמְּחֵנוּ bevinyano• בְּבִנְיָנוֹ har'enu הַרְאֵנוּ

letocho• לְתוֹכוֹ shechinatcha שְׁכִינָתְךָ vehashev וְהָשֵׁב

uleviyim וּלְוִיִּם la'avodatam לַעֲבוֹדָתָם kohanim כֹּהֲנִים vehashev וְהָשֵׁב

vehashev וְהָשֵׁב ulzimram• וּלְזִמְרָם leshiram לְשִׁירָם leduchanam לְדוּכָנָם

na'ale נַעֲלֶה vesham וְשָׁם linvehem• לִנְוֵיהֶם Yisrael יִשְׂרָאֵל

lefanecha לְפָנֶיךָ ס"ג מ"ה ב"ן: venishtachave וְנִשְׁתַּחֲוֶה ראה venerae וְנֵרָאֶה

You shal redeem us, and be mercifull to Zion, and You shal build Jerusalem's walls.

Our God and God of our fathers, Compassionate King,
have mercy upon us. Good and Kind, seek us. Return to us with Your mass compassion.
Because of Your fathers who obeyed Your will. Build Your house as before. And bring back
the Temple to its place. Show us its rebuilding. Let us be happy with its restoration. Bring Your Shechinah
and bring back the Kohanim to their works, the Levites to their stand, their singing and chanting. Bring
Israel back to their dwelling place. And there we will ascend and appear prostrate ourselves before you.

yehi **יְהִי** ratzon **רָצוֹן** מהע ע"ה, ע"ב ע"ה, בריבוע וקס"א ע"ה, אל שדי ע"ה

milfanecha **מִלְפָנֶיךָ** Adonai **יְהֹוָהאדניאהדונהי** ס"ג מ"ה ב"ן Elohenu **אֱלֹהֵינוּ** ילה

sheta'alenu **שֶׁתַּעֲלֵנוּ** avotenu **אֲבוֹתֵינוּ** ילה ; מילוי ע"ב, רמב velohei **וֵאלֹהֵי** לכב ;

bigvulenu **בִּגְבוּלֵנוּ** vetita'enu **וְתִטָּעֵנוּ** le'artzenu **לְאַרְצֵנוּ** besimcha **בְּשִׂמְחָה**

vesham **וְשָׁם** na'ase **נַעֲשֶׂה** lefanecha **לְפָנֶיךָ** ס"ג מ"ה ב"ן

et **אֶת** korbenot **קָרְבְּנוֹת** chovotenu **וֹזוֹבוֹתֵינוּ** temidim **תְּמִידִים**

kesidram **כְּסִדְרָם** umusafim **וּמוּסָפִים** kehilchatam **כְּהִלְכָתָם**׃

shir **שִׁיר** hama'alot **הַמַּעֲלוֹת** beshuv **בְּשׁוּב** Adonai **יְהֹוָהאדניאהדונהי** et **אֶת**

shivat **שִׁיבַת** Tziyon **צִיוֹן** יוסף, ו' הויות, קנאה hayinu **הָיִינוּ** kecholmim **כְּחֹלְמִים**׃

az **אָז** yimale **יִמָּלֵא** sechok **שְׂחוֹק** pinu **פִּינוּ** ulshonenu **וּלְשׁוֹנֵנוּ** rina **רִנָּה**

az **אָז** yomru **יֹאמְרוּ** vagoyim **בַגּוֹיִם** higdil **הִגְדִיל** Adonai **יְהֹוָהאדניאהדונהי**

la'asot **לַעֲשׂוֹת** im **עִם** ele **אֵלֶּה**׃ higdil **הִגְדִיל** Adonai **יְהֹוָהאדניאהדונהי**

la'asot **לַעֲשׂוֹת** imanu **עִמָּנוּ** ריבוע דס"ג, קס"א ע"ה ור' אותיות hayinu **הָיִינוּ**

semechim **שְׂמֵחִים**׃ shuva **שׁוּבָה** הושע Adonai **יְהֹוָהאדניאהדונהי** et **אֶת**

shevitenu **שְׁבִיתֵנוּ** (כתיב: שבותנו) ka'afikim **כָּאֲפִיקִים** banegev **בַּנֶּגֶב**׃

hazor'im **הַזֹּרְעִים** bedim'a **בְּדִמְעָה** berina **בְּרִנָּה** yiktzoru **יִקְצֹרוּ**׃

haloch **הָלוֹךְ** yelech **יֵלֵךְ** uvacho **וּבָכֹה** nose **נֹשֵׂא** meshech **מֶשֶׁךְ**

hazara **הַזָּרַע** bo **בֹא** yavo **יָבֹא** verina **בְרִנָּה** nose **נֹשֵׂא** alumotav **אֲלֻמֹתָיו**׃

May it be pleasing before You, Lord, our God and God of our forefathers, that You will take us up joyfully to our land and plant us within our boundaries, and there we will perform before You the rites of our compulsory offerings, the Tamid-offerings, in their order, and the Musaf-offerings, according to their laws.

"A Song of Ascents. When Lord brought back those that returned to Zion, we were like unto them that dream. Then was our mouth filled with laughter; and our tongue with singing; then said they among the nations: 'The Lord has done great things with these.' The Lord has done great things with us; we are rejoiced. Turn our captivity, Lord, as the streams in the dry land. They that sow in tears shall reap in joy. Though he goes on his way weeping that bears the measure of seed, he shall come home with joy, bearing his sheaves." (Psalms 126)

PETICHAT ELIYAHU HANAVI – THE OPENING OF ELIJAH THE PROPHET

Reciting these paragraphs can help you open your heart to spiritual wisdom.

vihi וִיהִי no'am נֹעַם Adonai אֲדֹנָי ללה Elohenu אֱלֹהֵינוּ ילה alenu עָלֵינוּ

uma'ase וּמַעֲשֵׂה yadenu יָדֵינוּ konena כּוֹנְנָה alenu עָלֵינוּ

uma'ase וּמַעֲשֵׂה yadenu יָדֵינוּ konenehu כּוֹנְנֵהוּ:

patach פָּתַח Eliyahu אֵלִיָּהוּ לכב hanavi, הַנָּבִיא zachur זָכוּר, ע"ב קס"א,

letov לְטוֹב (סוד המשכת השפע מן ד' שמות ליסוד הנקרא זכור) יהי אור ע"ה ; והו

ve'amar וְאָמַר: זכור לטוב = בוזו, ערי ; אליהו הנביא זכור לטוב = ת' כנגד ת' כוונות הס"א

ribon רִבּוֹן יהוה ע"ב ס"ג מ"ה ב"ן almin עָלְמִין de'ant דְּאַנְתְּ hu הוּא וְזֹד chad

vela וְלֹא כָּל kol al עַל ila'a עִלָּאָה hu הוּא ant אַנְתְּ bechushban בְּחֻשְׁבָּן,

setimin סְתִימִין, ila'in עִלָּאִין ; עמם kol כָּל al עַל setima סְתִימָא, setimin סְתִימִין ; עמם

ant אַנְתְּ let לֵית machashava מַחֲשָׁבָה tefisa תְּפִיסָא bach בָּךְ kelal כְּלָל. אַנְתְּ

hu הוּא de'apakt דְּאַפְּקָת eser עֲשֶׂר tikunin תִּקּוּנִין, vekarenan וְקָרֵינָן

lon לוֹן eser עֲשֶׂר sefiran סְפִירָן, le'anhaga לְאַנְהָגָא behon בְּהוֹן

almin עָלְמִין setimin סְתִימִין dela דְּלָא itgalyan אִתְגַּלְיָין vealmin וְעָלְמִין,

de'itgalyan דְּאִתְגַּלְיָין. uv'hon וּבְהוֹן itkasi'at אִתְכַּסִּיאַת mibenei מִבְּנֵי

nasha נָשָׁא. ve'ant וְאַנְתְּ hu הוּא dekashir דְּקָשִׁיר lon לוֹן umyached וּמְיַחֵד

lon לוֹן. uvgin וּבְגִין de'ant דְּאַנְתְּ milgav מִלְגָּאו kol כָּל ילי man מָאן

de'afrish דְּאַפְרִישׁ chad וְזֹד min מִן chavrei וְחַבְרֵיהּ chavrei מֵאִלֵּין

eser עֲשֶׂר, itchashiv אִתְחֲשִׁיב lei לֵיהּ ke'ilu כְּאִלּוּ afrish אַפְרִישׁ bach בָּךְ.

PETICHAT ELIYAHU HANAVI

"And may the pleasantness of the Lord, our God, be upon us and may He establish the work of our hands for us and may the work of our hands establish Him" (Psalms 90:17). Elijah opened, saying: Master of the worlds, You are One without enumeration. You are above all high ones, the most concealed of all. No thought can grasp You at all. You are the one that produced the ten emanations. And we named them ten Sefirot, to conduct with them obscure worlds that are not revealed, and revealed worlds. And through them, You are screened from human beings. And You are the One who connects them and unites them. And because you are from within, thus, anyone who separates these ten one from the other, to give dominance to that one alone, it is considered for him, as if he separates in You.

וְאִלֵּין ve'ilen · עֶשֶׂר eser · סְפִירָן sefiran · אִינוּן inun · אַזְלִין azlin

כְּסִדְרָן kesidran, · וְוַד chad · אָרִיךְ arich, · וְוַד vechad, · קָצֵר katzer,

וְוַד vechad · בֵּינוֹנִי benoni · וְאַנְתְּ ve'ant · הוּא hu · דְּאַנְהִיג de'anhig · לוֹן lon,

וְלֵית velet · מָאן man · דְּאַנְהִיג de'anhig · לָךְ lach · לָא la · לְעֵילָא le'ela,

וְלָא vela · לְתַתָּא letata, · וְלָא vela · מִכָּל mikol · יל"י · סִטְרָא sitra

לְבוּשִׁין levushin · תַּקָּנַת takant · לוֹן lon, · דְּמִנַּיְהוּ deminayhu · פַּרְחִין farchin

נִשְׁמָתִין nishmatin · לִבְנֵי livnei · נָשָׁא nasha · וְכַמָּה vechama · גוּפִין gufin

תַּקָּנַת takant · לוֹן lon, · דְּאִתְקְרִיאוּ de'itkeri'u · גוּפָא gufa · לְגַבֵּי legabei

לְבוּשִׁין levushin · דִּמְכַסְיָן dim'chasyan · עֲלֵיהוֹן alehon · וְאִתְקְרִיאוּ ve'itkeri'u

בְּתִקּוּנָא betikuna · דָּא da, · וְחֶסֶד Chesed · ע"ב, רִיבוּע יהוה · דְּרוֹעָא dero'a

יְמִינָא yemina, · גְּבוּרָה Gevurah · רי"ו · דְּרוֹעָא dero'a · שְׂמָאלָא semala,

תִּפְאֶרֶת Tiferet · גוּפָא gufa, · נֵצַח Netzach · וְהוֹד veHod · ההה · תְּרֵין teren

שׁוֹקִין shokin, · יְסוֹד Yesod · ההע · סִיּוּמָא siyuma · דְּגוּפָא degufa · אוֹת ot

בְּרִית berit · קֹדֶשׁ kodesh · מַלְכוּת Malchut · פֶּה pe מילה; וע"ה אלהים, אהיה אדני·

תּוֹרָה torah · שֶׁבְּעַל shebe'al · פֶּה pe מילה; וע"ה אלהים, אהיה אדני · קָרֵינָן karenan

כָּה la · וְחָכְמָה Chochmah בְּמִלּוּי = תרי"ג (מצוות) · מוֹחָא mocha, · אִיהוּ ihu

מַחֲשָׁבָה mach'shava · מִלְּגָאו milgav, · בִּינָה Binah ע"ה וזיים, אהיה יהוה · אהיה יהוה

לִבָּא liba · וּבָה uva · הַלֵּב halev · מֵבִין mevin · וְעַל ve'al · אִלֵּין ilen · תְּרֵין teren

כְּתִיב ketiv: הַנִּסְתָּרֹת hanistarot · לַיהוָה ladonai · אֱלֹהֵינוּ Elohenu ילה

And these ten Sefirot follow their order, the one is long, and one, is short. And the one is average. And You conduct them, and there is no other who will lead You, neither Above, nor Below, nor in any other side. You prepared garments, from which the Neshamot fly to the human beings and you prepared several bodies. And they are named bodies in relation to the clothing, in which they are attired. The Sefirot are named by this emendation, Chesed being the right arm, Gevurah being the left arm. Tiferet means the body. Netzach and Hod, the two thighs, Yesod the final part of the body, the sign of the Holy Covenant, Malchut, the mouth, we call it the Oral Torah. Chochmah is the brain, the thought within. Binah is the heart, and through it, the heart understands. And about these two, it is written, "The secret things belong to the Lord our God" (Deuteronomy 29:28).

ihu **אִיהוּ**, elyon **עֶלְיוֹן** (באתב"ע גאל) יהוה מלך יהוה מלך יהוה ימלוך לעולם ועד Keter **כֶּתֶר**

malchut **מַלְכוּת** (באתב"ע גאל) יהוה מלך יהוה מלך יהוה ימלוך לעולם ועד keter **כֶּתֶר**

mereshit **מֵרֵאשִׁית** magid **מַגִּיד**: itmar **אִתְּמַר** פהל ve'alei **וַעֲלֵיהּ**

ditfilei **דִתְפִלֵּי** karkafta **קַרְקַפְתָּא** ve'ihu **וְאִיהוּ** acharit **אַחֲרִית**

ve'ot **וְאוֹת** He **ה"א** ve'ot **וְאוֹת** Yud **יו"ד** ot **אוֹת** ihu **אִיהוּ** milgav **מִלְגָּאו**

atzilut **אֲצִילוּת**, orach **אֹרַח** de'ihu **דְאִיהוּ**, He **ה"א** ve'ot **וְאוֹת** Vav **וָא"ו**

ve'anpoy **וְעַנְפוֹי** bidro'oy **בִּדְרוֹעוֹי** de'ilana **דְאִילָנָא** shakyu **שַׁקְיוּ** ihu **אִיהוּ**

ve'itrabei **וְאִתְרַבֵּי** le'ilana **לְאִילָנָא** de'ashkei **דְאַשְׁקֵי** kemaya **כְּמַיָא**

behahu **בְּהַהוּא** shakyu **שַׁקְיוּ** ribon **רִבּוֹן** יהוה ע"ב ס"ג מ"ה ב"ן, almin **עָלְמִין**

hasibot **הַסִבּוֹת**, vesibat **וְסִבַּת** ha'ilot **הָעִלּוֹת**, ilat **עִלַּת** hu **הוּא** ant **אַנְתְּ**

nevi'u **נְבִיעוּ** behahu **בְּהַהוּא** le'ilana **לְאִילָנָא** de'ashkei **דְאַשְׁקֵי**

legufa **לְגוּפָא**, kenishmeta **כְּנִשְׁמְתָא** ihu **אִיהוּ** nevi'u **נְבִיעוּ** vehahu **וְהַהוּא**

uvach **וּבָךְ** legufa **לְגוּפָא**, chayim **וְחַיִּים** אהיה אהיה יהוה, בינה ע"ה de'ihi **דְאִיהִי**

mikol **מִכָּל** ילי, diyukna **דְיּוּקְנָא** velet **וְלֵית**, dimyon **דִּמְיוֹן** let **לֵית**

shemaya **שְׁמַיָא** uvarata **וּבָרָאת** ulvar **וּלְבַר** dilgav **דִּלְגָּאו** ma **מַה** מ"ה

shimsha **שִׁמְשָׁא** minehon **מִנְּהוֹן** ve'apakt **וְאַפֵּקְת**, ve'ar'a **וְאַרְעָא**

uve'ar'a **וּבְאַרְעָא**, umazalei **וּמַזָּלֵי** vechochvaya **וְכֹכְבַיָּא** vesihara **וְסִיהֲרָא**

ve'isbin **וְעֶשְׂבִּין** de'eden **דְעֵדֶן** veginta **וְגִנְתָּא** udsha'in **וּדְשָׁאִין** ilanin **אִילָנִין**

uvnei **וּבְנֵי** uv'irin **וּבְעִירִין** venunin **וְנוּנִין** ve'ofin **וְעוֹפִין** vechevan **וְזֵינִין**

ila'in **עִלָּאִין**, behon **בְּהוֹן** le'ishtemode'a **לְאִשְׁתְּמוֹדְעָא** nasha **נָשָׁא**

vetata'in **וְתַתָּאִין** ila'in **עִלָּאִין** behon **בְּהוֹן** yitnahagun **יִתְנַהֲגוּן** ve'ech **וְאֵיךְ**

The Supernal Keter is the crown of Malchut. And about this is said, "Declaring the end from the beginning" (Isaiah 46:10). And that is the skull of the Tefilin. Within is Yud-Vav-Dalet, Hei-Alef, Vav-Alef-Vav, Hei-Alef, which is in the path of Atzilut. It is the watering of the tree in its arms and branches, as waters that water that tree and it multiplies by this watering. Master of the Worlds, You are the Cause of all Causes, and the Reason for all Reasons, that waters the tree by that stream, and that spring is like a soul to the body, that is the life of the body. And to Yourself there is no likeness nor form inside or outside. And You created heavens and earth and produced from them sun and moon and stars and constellations. And in the earth, trees and grasses, and the Garden of Eden, and plants, and animals and fowl and fish and human beings, through them to acknowledge the high ones, and how the higher and lower ones behave.

וְאֵיךְ ve'ech אִשְׁתְּמוֹדְעָן ishtemode'an מֵעִלָּאֵי me'ila'ei וְתַתָּאֵי vetata'ei

וְלֵית velet דְּיָדַע deyada בָּךְ bach כְּלָל kelal, וּבַר uvar (יִצְחָק, ד"פ ב"ן)

מִנָּךְ minach לֵית let יְוֹזוּדָא yichuda בְּעִלָּאֵי be'ila'ei וְתַתָּאֵי vetata'ei

וְאַנְתְּ ve'ant אִשְׁתְּמוֹדְעָ ishtemoda אֲדוֹן adon (אני) עַל al כֹּלָּא kola

וְכָל vechol סְפִירָן sefiran, כָּל kol חַד chad אִית it לֵיהּ lei שֵׁם shem

יְדִיעַ yedi'a, וּבְהוֹן uvhon אִתְקְרִיאוּ itkeri'u מַלְאָכַיָּא mal'achaya

וְאַנְתְּ ve'ant לֵית let לָךְ lach שֵׁם shem יְדִיעַ yedi'a, דְּאַנְתְּ de'ant הוּא hu

מְמַלֵּא memale כָּל kol שְׁמָהָן shemahan, וְאַנְתְּ ve'ant הוּא hu

שְׁלִימוּ shelimu דְּכֻלְּהוּ dechulhu, וְכַד vechad אַנְתְּ ant תִּסְתַּלָּק tistalak

מִנְּהוֹן minehon אִשְׁתְּאָרוּ ishte'aru כֻּלְּהוּ kulehu שְׁמָהָן shemahan

כְּגוּפָא kegufa בְּלָא bela נִשְׁמָתָא nishmata. אַנְתְּ ant וְזַכִּים chakim

וְלָאו velav בְּחָכְמָה beChochmah (במילוי = תרי"ג (מצוות)) יְדִיעָא yedi'a, אַנְתְּ ant

הוּא hu מֵבִין mevin וְלָאו velav מִבִּינָה miBinah (ע"ה וזיים, אהיה אהיה יהוה) יְדִיעָא yedi'a

יְדִיעָא yedi'a. לֵית let לָךְ lach אֲתַר atar יְדִיעָא yedi'a

אֶלָּא ela לְאִשְׁתְּמוֹדְעָא le'ishtemode'a תֻּקְפָּךְ tukfach וְזֵילָךְ vechelach

לִבְנֵי livnei נָשָׁא nasha, וּלְאַחֲזָאָה ule'achza'a לוֹן lon, אֵיךְ ech

אִתְנְהִיג itnehig עָלְמָא alma בְּדִינָא vedina וּבְרַחֲמֵי uvrachamei,

דְּאִינוּן de'inun צֶדֶק tzedek וּמִשְׁפָּט umishpat (ע"ה ה"פ אלהים)

כְּפוּם kefum עוֹבְדֵיהוֹן ovadehon דִּבְנֵי divnei נָשָׁא nasha.

And how the lower ones recognize to attain from the higher ones; and in you, there is absolutely nobody who is knowledgeable. And besides your unification, there is no such unique unity in the upper and lower ones, and You are recognized as the Master over all. Each of the Sefirot has a recognizable name, of its own. And by them the angels are named. Yet you have no known name, You are He, who fills all the names. And it is You who completes them all. And when You are gone from them, all the names remain as body without a soul. You are wise, but not with known wisdom. You understand, but not with any known understanding. And You do not occupy any known place so that human beings should perceive His strength and might and to show them how the world conducted with justice and mercy that are righteousness and just trial, according to the deeds of the lower ones.

דִּין, din — אִיהוּ ihu — גְּבוּרָה gevurah — ר"י. — מִשְׁפָּט mishpat — ע"ה ה"פ אלהים

עַמּוּדָא amuda — דְּאֶמְצָעִיתָא de'emtza'ita — צֶדֶק tzedek, — מַלְכוּתָא malchuta

קַדִּישָׁא kadisha. — מאזֽנֵי moznei — צֶדֶק tzedek, — תְּרֵין teren — סַמְכֵי samchei

קָשׁוֹט keshot. — הִין hin — צֶדֶק tzedek, — אוֹת ot — בְּרִית berit. — כְּלָא kula

לְאַחֲזָאָה le'achza'a — אֵיך ech — אִתְנְהִיג itnehig — עָלְמָא alma. — אֲבָל aval

לָאו lav — דְּאִית de'it — לָך lach — צֶדֶק tzedek — יְדִיעָא yedi'a — דְּאִיהוּ de'ihu

דִּין din, — וְלָאו velav — מִשְׁפָּט mishpat ע"ה ה"פ אלהים — יְדִיעָא yedi'a — דְּאִיהוּ de'ihu

רַחֲמֵי rachamei, — וְלָאו velav — מִכָּל mikol ילי — אִלֵּין ilen — מִדּוֹת midot

כְּלָל kelal. — קוּם kum — רִבִּי Ribi — שִׁמְעוֹן Shimon — וְיִתְחַדְּשׁוּן veyitchadeshun

מִלִּין milin — עַל al — יְדָך yedach, — דְּהָא deha — רְשׁוּתָא reshuta — אִית it — לָך lach

לְגַלָּאָה legala'a — רָזִין razin — טְמִירִין temirin — עַל al — יְדָך yedach — בַּמַ ma מ"ה

דְּלָא dela — אִתְיְהִיב ityehiv — רְשׁוּ reshu — לְגַלָּאָה legala'a — לְשׁוּם leshum

בַּר bar — נָשׁ nash — עַד ad — כְּעָן ke'an. — קָם kam — רִבִּי Ribi — שִׁמְעוֹן Shim'on,

פָּתַח patach — וְאָמַר ve'amar: — לָך lecha — יְהֹוָה Adonai — הַגְּדֻלָּה haGedula

וְהַגְּבוּרָה vehaGevurah ר"י — וְהַתִּפְאֶרֶת vehaTiferet — וְהַנֵּצַח vehaNetzach

וְהַהוֹד vehaHod ההה — כִּי ki — כָּל chol ילי — בַּשָּׁמַיִם bashamayim י"פ טל, י"פ כוזו

וּבָאָרֶץ uva'aretz — לָך lecha — יְהֹוָה Adonai — הַמַּמְלָכָה hamamlacha

וְגֹו' vegomer, (Here, you should give three coins to charity) — עֶלָאִין ila'in

שִׁמְעוּ shema'u, — אִינּוּן inun — דְּמִיכִין demichin — דְּחֶבְרוֹן deChevron

וְרַעְיָא veRaya — מְהֵימְנָא Mehemna, — אִתְעָרוּ it'aru — מִשְּׁנַתְכוֹן mishenatchon.

Judgement is Gevurah, judicial trial is the Central Column, Righteousness - the holy Malchut; just scales are two supports of truth. A truly measured hin is this sign of the covenant of Yesod. All to show the leadership of the world, but it is not as if there is certain justice that is strictly judgmental, and not a certain just trial that is strictly of mercy, and or of any of these attributes, at all. Rise, Rabbi Shimon and let new ideas come through you, as you have permission, that through you obscure mysteries will be revealed, because permission was not granted to any person until now to reveal them. Rabbi Shimon rose, opened and said, "Yours, Lord, is the greatness, and the power..." (1 Chronicles 29:11). Listen, Supreme Ones, they who rest in Chevron, and the Faithful Shepherd, be shaken off from your sleep.

הָקִיצוּ hakitzu וְרַנְּנוּ veranenu שֹׁכְנֵי shochnei עָפָר afar, אֵלִין ilen אִנּוּן inun

צַדִּיקַיָּא tzadikaya, דְּאִנּוּן de'inun מִסִּטְרָא misitra דְּהַהוּא dehahu

דְּאִתְמַר de'itmar בָּה: ba אֲנִי ani יְשֵׁנָה yeshena וְלִבִּי velibi עֵר er,

וְלָאו velav אִנּוּן inun מֵתִים metim, וּבְגִין uvgin דָּא da

אִתְּמַר itmar בְּהוֹן vehon הָקִיצוּ hakitzu וְרַנְּנוּ veranenu וְגוֹ' vegomer.

רַעְיָא Raya מְהֵימְנָא Mehemna, אַנְתְּ ant וַאֲבָהָן va'avahan, הָקִיצוּ hakitzu

וְרַנְּנוּ veranenu לְאִתְעָרוּתָא le'it'aruta דִּשְׁכִינְתָּא dish'chinta דְּאִיהִי de'ihi

יְשֵׁנָה yeshena בְּגָלוּתָא vegaluta. דְּעַד de'ad כְּעַן ke'an צַדִּיקַיָּא tzadikaya

כֻּלְּהוּ kulhu דְּמִיכִין demichin וְשֵׁנְתָּא veshinta בְּחוֹרֵיהוֹן vechorehon.

מִיָּד miyad יְהִיבַת yahivat שְׁכִינְתָּא shechinta תְּלַת telat קָלִין kalin

לְגַבֵּי legabei רַעְיָא Raya מְהֵימְנָא Meheimna וְיֵימָא veyima לֵיהּ lei

קוּם kum רַעְיָא Raya מְהֵימְנָא Mehemna, דְּהָא deha עֲלָךְ alach

אִתְּמַר itmar קוֹל | kol דּוֹדִי dodi דּוֹפֵק dofek מנק לְגַבַּאי legabai,

בְּאַרְבַּע be'arba אַתְוָן atvan דִּילֵיהּ dilei. וְיֵימָא veyima בְּהוֹן vehon

פִּתְחִי pitchi לִי" li אֲחוֹתִי achoti רַעְיָתִי rayati יוֹנָתִי yonati תַמָּתִי tamati.

דְּהָא deha תַּם tam עֲוֹנֵךְ avonech בַּת bat צִיּוֹן Tziyon יוסף, ו' הויות, קנאה

לֹא lo יוֹסִיף yosif לְהַגְלוֹתֵךְ lehaglotech. שֵׁרֹאשִׁי sheroshi נִמְלָא nimla

טַל tal נִמְלָא nimla מַאי mai טַל, כוזו יוד הא ואו, נִמְלָא nimla טָל tal. יוד הא ואו, כוזו.

"Awake and sing, you that dwell in dust" (Isaiah 26:19). It is those righteous that are from this aspect about which is said, "I sleep, but my heart wakes" (Song of Songs 5:2). And they are not dead, therefore it says about them, "Awake and sing..." Faithful Shepherd, you and the Patriarchs, awake and sing to the waking of the Shechinah that sleeps in exile, as up to now all the righteous are sleeping, and the sleep is in the caverns. Instantly, the Shechinah emits three sounds towards the Faithful Shepherd, and says to him 'Rise, faithful Shepherd. As about you it was said, "hark, my beloved is knocking" (Ibid.) by me, with His four letters. And he will say with them, "Open to me, my sister, my love, my dove, my undefiled" (Ibid.). Since, "The punishment of your iniquity is accomplished, daughter of Zion; he will no more carry you away into exile" (Lamentations 4:22). "For my head is filled with dew" (Song of Songs 5:2). He asks, 'What is that which means 'Filled with dew'?

אֶלָּא ela, אָמַר amar, קֻדְשָׁא kudsha, בְּרִיךְ berich, הוּא hu,

אַנְתְּ ant, וְחָשַׁבְתְּ chashavt, דְּמִיּוֹמָא demiyoma, דְּאִתְחֲרַב de'itcharav

בֵּי bei, מַקְדְּשָׁא makdesha, דְּעָאלְנָא de'alna, בְּבֵיתָא beveta, דִּילִי dili

וְעָאלְנָא ve'alna, בְּיִשׁוּבָא veyishuva, לָאו lav, הָכִי hachi, דְּלָא dela

אָלְנָא alna, כָּל kol, זִמְנָא zimna, דְּאַנְתְּ de'ant, בְּגָלוּתָא begaluta,

הֲרֵי harei, לָךְ lach, סִימָנָא simana, שֵׁרֹאשִׁי sheroshi, נִמְלָא nimla

טַל tal, הֵ"א He, שְׁכִינְתָּא shechinta, בְּגָלוּתָא begaluta,

שְׁלִימוּ shelimu, דִּילָהּ dila, וְחַיִּים vechayim, דִּילָהּ dila,

אִיהוּ ihu, טַל tal, וְדָא veda, אִיהוּ ihu, אוֹת ot, יוֹ"ד Yod

וְאוֹת ve'ot, הֵ"א He, וְאוֹת ve'ot, וָא"ו Vav, וְאוֹת ve'ot, הֵ"א He, אִיהִי ihi

שְׁכִינְתָּא shechinta, דְּלָא dela, מְחֻשְׁבָּן mechushban, טַ"ל tal

אֶלָּא ela, יוֹ"ד Yod, הֵ"א He, וָא"ו Vav, דִּסְלִיקוּ disliku, אַתְוָן atvan

לְחֻשְׁבָּן lechushban, טַ"ל tal, דְּאִיהוּ de'ihu, מַלְיָא malya

לִשְׁכִינְתָּא lishchinta, מִנְּבִיעוּ minevi'u, דְּכָל dechol, מְקוֹרִין mekorin

עִלָּאִין ilai'n, מִיָּד miyad, קָם kam, רַעְיָא Raya, מְהֵימְנָא Mehemna,

וַאֲבָהָן va'avahan, קַדִּישִׁין kadishin, עִמֵּיהּ imei, עַד ad, כָּאן kan, רָזָא raza

דְּיִחוּדָא deyichuda, בָּרוּךְ baruch, יְהֹוָה Adonai, לְעוֹלָם le'olam

אָמֵן amen, וְאָמֵן ve'amen

But the Holy One, blessed be He, said, You think that from the day of the Temple's destruction, I entered My own abode, and I entered the settlement? Not so, as I have not entered as you are in exile. And here is your proof, "For my head is filled with dew". Hei-Alef is the Shechinah, and she is in exile. Her perfection, and her life is dew (Heb. tal = 39), and that is Yud-Vav-Dalet, Hei-Alef, Vav-Alef-Vav numerically tal (= 39). And the Hei-Alef, the Shechinah, was not in the reckoning of tal, only the Yud-Vav-Dalet, Hei-Alef, Vav-Alef-Vav, which amount to tal. And it is He, who fills the Shechinah from the fountain of all the Supernal sources. The Faithful Shepherd immediately rose up, and the holy Patriarchs with him. Up to here the mysteries of unification. "Blessed be the Lord forever, Amen and Amen!" (Psalms 89:53)

veyehe וִיהֵא ra'ava רַעֲוָא min מִן kodam קָדָם atika עַתִּיקָא

kadisha קַדִּישָׁא dechol דְּכָל ילי kadishin קַדִּישִׁין temira טְמִירָא

dechol דְּכָל ילי temirin טְמִירִין setima סְתִימָא dechola דְּכֹלָּא,

deyitmeshach דְּיִתְמְשַׁךְ tala טַלָּא ila'a עִילָּאָה minei מִנֵּיה lemalya לְמַלְיָא

reshei רֵישֵׁיה dize'ir דִּזְעֵיר anpin אַנְפִּין ulehatil וּלְהַטִּיל lachakal לַחֲקַל

kadishin קַדִּישִׁין tapuchin תַּפּוּחִין (עלמו על מישויזו) מנוזם, אדני, יהוה יהוה אהיה

ubchedvata וּבְחֶדְוָתָא bera'ava בְּרַעֲוָא de'anpin דְּאַנְפִּין binhiru בִּנְהִירוּ

atika עַתִּיקָא kodam קָדָם min מִן veyitmeshach וְיִתְמְשַׁךְ dechola דְּכֹלָּא.

temira טְמִירָא kadishin קַדִּישִׁין dechol דְּכָל ילי kadisha קַדִּישָׁא

dechola דְּכֹלָּא. setima סְתִימָא temirin טְמִירִין dechol דְּכָל ילי

vechisda וְחִסְדָּא china חִנָּא verachamei וְרַחֲמֵי re'uta רְעוּתָא

vechedva וְחֶדְוָה bire'uta בִּרְעוּתָא ila'a עִילָּאָה binhiru בִּנְהִירוּ

ve'al וְעַל veti בֵּיתִי ב"פ ראה benei בְּנֵי kol כָּל עמם ; ילי ve'al וְעַל alai עֲלַי

veyifrekinan וְיִפְרְקִינָן amei עַמֵּיה. Yisrael יִשְׂרָאֵל benei בְּנֵי עמם ; ילי kol כָּל ילי

le'alma לְעָלְמָא. deyetun דְּיֵיתוּן bishin בִּישִׁין aktin עֲקָתִין ילי mikol מִכָּל

ulchol וּלְכָל ה ארני lana לַנָא veyityehiv וְיִתְיְהִיב veyazmin וְיַזְמִין

vechayei וְחַיֵּי vechisda וְחִסְדָּא china חִנָּא nafshatana נַפְשָׁתָנָא

min מִן verachamei וְרַחֲמֵי revichei רְוִיחֵי umzonei וּמְזוֹנֵי arichei אֲרִיכֵי

ratzon רָצוֹן yehi יְהִי ken כֵּן amen אָמֵן יאהדונהי kodamei קָדָמֵיה.

ve'amen וְאָמֵן יאהדונהי: amen אָמֵן יאהדונהי מהטע ע"ה, ע"ב בריבוע וקס"א ע"ה, אל שדי ע"ה

And may it be pleasing before the holy of holiest Atika, the hidden of all and the most concealed, that a supernal dew will be drawn from him to fulfill the head of Zeir Anpin, and to drop to Chakal Tapuchin Kadishin from this shining face with desire and happiness for all. And also will be drawn from the holy of holiest Atika, the hidden of all and the most concealed willingly, mercy, grace, kindness, with supernal illumination with desire and happiness, for me and for my household, and for all of Your people, Yisrael. And he will save us from all negative incidents that exist in our world. And he will bring and give us and all the rest of the people, grace and kindness, long life and sustenance, welfare and mercy from before him. Amen shall it be. Amen and Amen.

יְדִיד yedid   נֶפֶשׁ nefesh   אָב av   הָרַחֲמָן harachaman   מְשׁוֹךְ meshoch

עַבְדְּךְ avdach   (פוי, אל אדני)   אֶל el   רְצוֹנָךְ retzonach   יָרוּץ yarutz

עַבְדְּךְ avdach   (פוי, אל אדני)   כְּמוֹ kemo   אַיָּל ayal   יִשְׁתַּחֲוֶה yishtachave   אֶל el

מוּל mul   הֲדָרָךְ hadarach   (ב"פ יבק, ס"ג קס"א+)   יֶעֱרַב ye'erav   לוֹ lo

יְדִידוּתָךְ yedidutach   (ר"ת ילי+)   מִנֹּפֶת minofet   צוּף tzuf   וְכָל vechol   טָעַם ta'am

הָדוּר hadur   נָאֶה na'e   זִיו ziv   הָעוֹלָם ha'olam   נַפְשִׁי nafshi

חוֹלַת cholat   אַהֲבָתָךְ ahavatach   אָנָּא ana   ב"ן   אָל El   יָ"א"י (מילוי דס"ג)

נָא na   רְפָא refa   נָא na   לָהּ la   ♦(11-Letter Name for healing)

בְּהַרְאוֹת behar'ot   לָהּ la   נֹעַם no'am   זִיוָךְ zivach   אָז az   תִּתְחַזֵּק titchazek

וְתִתְרַפֵּא vetitrape   וְהָיְתָה vehayta   לָהּ la   שִׂמְחַת simchat   עוֹלָם olam

וָתִיק vatik   יֶהֱמוּ yehemu   רַחֲמֶיךְ rachamecha   וְווּסָה vechusa

נָא na   עַל al   בֵּן ben   אֲהוּבָךְ ahuvach   כִּי ki   זֶה ze

כַּמָּה chame   נִכְסוֹף nichsof   נִכְסַף nichsaf   לִרְאוֹת lir'ot

בְּתִפְאֶרֶת betiferet   עֻזָּךְ uzach   אָנָּא ana   ב"ן   אֵלִי Eli   וְחֶמְדַּת chemdat

לִבִּי libi   וְחוּשָׁה chusha   נָא na   וְאַל ve'al   תִּתְעַלָּם tit'alam

הִגָּלֶה higale   נָא na   וּפְרוֹשׂ ufros   חָבִיב chaviv   הֵ★   עָלַי alai   אֶת et   סֻכַּת sukat

שְׁלוֹמָךְ shelomach   תָּאִיר ta'ir   אֶרֶץ eretz   מִכְּבוֹדָךְ mikevodach   (ב"ן, לכב+)

נָגִילָה nagila   וְנִשְׂמְחָה venismecha   בָּךְ vach   מַהֵר maher   אָהוּב ahuv

כִּי ki   בָא va   מוֹעֵד mo'ed   וְחָנֵּנוּ vechonenu   כִּימֵי kimei   עוֹלָם olam

---

י *Beloved of the soul, Compassionate Father, draw Your servant to Your desire. Your servant will run like a hart, he will bow before Your majesty. Your friendship will be sweeter than the dripping of the honeycomb and any taste.* ה *Majestic, Beautiful, Radiance of the world, my soul pines for Your love. Please, God, heal her, by showing her the pleasantness of Your radiance. Then she will be strengthened and healed, and she will have the gladness of the world.* ו *All Worthy One, may Your mercy be aroused and please take pity on the sons of Your beloved, because it is so very long that I have yearned intensely, speedily to see the splendor of Your strength. Only these my heart desired, so please take pity and do not conceal Yourself.* ה *Reveal and spread upon me, my Beloved, the shelter of Your peace. Illuminate the world with Your glory that we may rejoice and be glad with You. Hasten, show love, for time has come, and show us grace as in day of old.*

LeShem Yichud

הוּא hu — בְּרִיךְ berich — קוּדְשָׁא kudsha — יִחוּד yichud — לְשֵׁם leshem

וּרְחִימוּ ur'chimu — בִּדְחִילוּ bid'chilu — (יאהדונהי) — וּשְׁכִינְתֵּיה ush'chintei

לְיַחֲדָא leyachada, (אההיויהה) — וּדְחִילוּ ud'chilu — וּרְחִימוּ ur'chimu — (אההיויהה)

בְּיִחוּדָא beyichuda — בְּוָא״ו bevav — קֵי kei — יוֹ״ד yud — שֵׁם shem — קֵי kei

יִשְׂרָאֵל Yisrael — כָּל kol — בְּשֵׁם beshem — (יהוה) shelim — שְׁלִים

יִתְבָּרֵךְ yitbarach — אֱלֹהוּתוֹ Elohuto — עָלַי alai — מְקַבֵּל mekabel — הֲרֵינִי hareni

עֶבֶד eved — וְהִנֵנִי vehineni — וְאַהֲבָתוֹ ve'ahavato — וְיִרְאָתוֹ veyir'ato

מְקַיֵּם mekayem — וַהֲרֵינִי vehareni — יִתְבָּרֵךְ yitbarach — לְהַשֵׁם leHashem

לְרֵעֲךָ lere'acha — ב״פ אור, ב״פ רז, ב״פ א״ס — וְאָהַבְתָּ ve'ahavta — מִצְוַת mitzvat

אָדָם adam — כָּל kol — אֶת et — אוֹהֵב ohev — וַהֲרֵינִי vehareni — כָּמוֹךָ kamocha

מְכַוֵּן mechaven — וַהֲרֵינִי vehareni — כְּנַפְשִׁי kenafshi — מִיִשְׂרָאֵל miYisrael

תְּפִלִין tefilin — וּמִצְוַת umitzvat — צִיצִית tzitzit — מִצְוַת mitzvat — לְקַיֵּם lekayem

מְכַוֵּן mechaven — וַהֲרֵינִי vehareni — רֹאשׁ rosh — וְשֶׁל veshel — יָד yad — שֶׁל shel

וּתְפִלַת utfilat — שְׁמַע shema — קְרִיאַת keri'at — מִצְוַת mitzvat — לְקַיֵּם lekayem

הַנִלְוֹת hanilvot — וְהַמִצְוֹת vehamitzvot — הֵם hem — שַׁחֲרִית shacharit

מְכַוֵּן mechaven — וַאֲנִי va'ani — בָּהֶם bahem — וְהַכְּלוּלוֹת vehakelulot

לְיוֹצְרֵנוּ leyotzrenu — רוּחַ ru'ach — נַחַת nachat — לַעֲשׂוֹת la'asot — ב״ף, לכב — בְּכָל bakol

בְּשׁוּם beshum — פְּרָס peras — לְקַבֵּל lekabel — מְנַת menat — עַל al — שֶׁלֹא shelo

לָדַעַת leda'at — ב״ף, לכב — בְּכָל bakol — מְכַוֵּן mechaven — וַאֲנִי va'ani — צַד tzad

הַקָּדוֹשׁ hakadosh — יוֹחַאי Yochai — בֶּן ben — שִׁמְעוֹן Shimon — רַבִּי Rabbi

---

LeShem Yichud

For the sake of unification between the Holy Blessed One and His Shechinah, with fear and love and with love and fear, in order to unify the Name Yud-Kei and Vav-Kei in perfect unity, and in the name of all Israel, I hereby accept upon myself His divinity, blessed be He, and the love of Him and the fear of Him, and I hereby declare myself a servant to God blessed be He. And I hereby accept upon myself the obligatory commandment of "Love your fellow as you do yourself." And I hereby declare that I love each one of Israel with my soul. And I am hereby prepared to fulfill the obligatory precept of wearing the Tzitzit, the hand Tefilin and the head Tefilin. And I am hereby prepared to fulfill the obligatory precept of The Shema and the prayer of Shacharit and all the precepts that are concerned with it. And I meditate to bring satisfaction to our maker, not for the sake of receiving any prize. And all my intention is according to the holy Rabbi Shimon Bar Yochai.

וַהֲרֵינִי vehareni מְקַבֵּל mekabel עָלַי alai כֹּל kol יל׳ תרי"ג taryag

מִצְוֹת mitzvot דְּאוֹרַיְיתָא de'orayta וּמִצְוֹת umitzvot דְּרַבָּנָן derabanan

הֵם hem וְעִנְפֵיהֶם ve'anfehem ◆ וְאַתָּה veAta הָאֵל haEl (יא"י ; מילוי דס"ג) לאה

הַטּוֹב hatov והו בְּרוֹב berov י"פ אהיה רַחֲמֶיךָ rachamecha

תַּצִּילֵנוּ tatzilenu מִיֵּצֶר miyetzer הָרַע hara וּתְזַכֵּנוּ ut'zakenu

לְעׇבְדְּךָ le'ovdecha בֶּאֱמֶת be'emet ס"ג אהיה פעמים אהיה, ז"פ ס"ג פוי, אל אדני

אָמֵן amen יאהדונהי יְהִי yehi כֵּן ken רָצוֹן ratzon מהש ע"ה, ע"ב בריבוע וקס"א ע"ה, אל שדי ע"ה,

וִיהִי vihi נֹעַם no'am אֲדֹנָי Adonai ללה אֱלֹהֵינוּ Elohenu ילה

עָלֵינוּ alenu וּמַעֲשֵׂה uma'ase יָדֵינוּ yadenu כּוֹנְנָה konena

עָלֵינוּ alenu וּמַעֲשֵׂה uma'ase יָדֵינוּ yadenu כּוֹנְנֵהוּ konenehu:

יְהִי yehi רָצוֹן ratzon מהש ע"ה, ע"ב בריבוע וקס"א ע"ה, אל שדי ע"ה

מִלְפָנֶיךָ milfanecha ס"ג מ"ה ב"ן יְהֹוָה אדני יאהדונהי Adonai

אֱלֹהֵינוּ Elohenu ילה וֵאלֹהֵי velohei ילה לכב ; מילוי ע"ב, דמב ; ילה

אֲבוֹתֵינוּ avotenu שֶׁתַּכְנִיעַ shetachni'a כֹּל kol יל׳

הַמְקַטְרְגִים hamekatregim וְכֹל vechol יל׳ הַקְּלִיפוֹת hakelipot

הַחִיצוֹנִים hachitzonim הַמְשׁוֹטְטִים hameshotetim בָּעוֹלָם ba'olam

וּמְעַכְּבִים ume'akvim תְּפִלָּתִי tefilati לַעֲלוֹת la'alot לְפָנֶיךָ lefanecha ס"ג מ"ה ב"ן

כִּי ki אַתָּה Ata יוֹדֵעַ yode'a שֶׁרְצוֹנִי shertzoni לַעֲשׂוֹת la'asot

רְצוֹנְךָ retzoncha, אַךְ ach אהיה שְׂאוֹר se'or שֶׁבְּעִיסָה shebe'isa

מְעַכֵּב me'akev אוֹתִי oti, לָכֵן lachen גְּעוֹר ge'or בָּהֶם bahem שְׁאַל she'al

יְזִיקוּנִי yezikuni וְאַל ve'al יְעַכְּבוּ ye'akvu אֶת et תְּפִלָּתִי tefilati

---

And I hereby accept upon myself all the 613 precepts of the Torah and the sages and its outcomes. And You, the good God, with your mighty mercy will save us from the evil inclination and allow us the privilege of serving you with truth Amen, so may His will be. "May the pleasantness of the Lord, our God, be upon us and may He establish the work of our hands for us and may the work of our hands establish Him." (Psalms 90:17)

May it be pleasing before You, Lord, my God and God of my forefathers, that You would subjugate all the denouncers and the external klipot that exist in the world, and they deferred my prayer to come before You. And You know that my only desire is to follow your desire, but the leaven in the dough deferred me. So castigate them so they would not harm me and they would not defer my prayer,

וְלֹא velo בְּגוּפִי begufi לֹא lo בִּי bi יִשְׁלְטוּ yishletu וְאַל ve'al

רְצוּיָה retzuya תְּפִלָּתִי tefilati וְשֶׁתְהֵא veshetehe ,בְּנִשְׁמָתִי benishmati

כֵּן ken אָמֵן amen לְפָנֶיךָ lefanecha וּמְקֻבֶּלֶת umkubelet

יְהִי yehi רָצוֹן ratzon

כְּאִלּוּ ke'ilu בְּתְפִלָּתִי bitfilati מְכַוֵּן mechaven הֲרֵינִי hareni

אֲנִי ani עוֹמֵד omed בִּירוּשָׁלַיִם birushalayim בְּבֵית bevet

בֵּית bet כְּנֶגֶד keneged וּמְכַוֵּן umchaven הַמִּקְדָּשׁ hamikdash

שֶׁנֶּאֱמַר shene'emar כְּמוֹ kemo הַקֳּדָשִׁים hakodashim קֹדֶשׁ kodesh

וְהִתְפַּלְלוּ vehitpalelu אֶל el הַמָּקוֹם hamakom הַזֶּה haze

יְהִי yehi רָצוֹן ratzon

מִלְפָנֶיךָ milfanecha יְהֹוָה Adonai אֱלֹהֵינוּ Elohenu

לִבִּי libi שֶׁיְּהֵא sheyehe אֲבוֹתֵינוּ avotenu וֵאלֹהֵי velohei

נָכוֹן nachon וּמָסוּר umasur בְּיָדִי beyadi שֶׁלֹּא shelo אֶשְׁכָּחֶךָ eshkachecha

RIBON ALMA

Rabbi Shimon says in the Zohar, Idra Rabba 303: "The soul of man is taken from the higher levels downward to Malchut. By that, it causes everything to be in single union. Whoever interrupts this union from the world is as if he severs the above mentioned soul, and indicates that another soul exists besides this one. As a result he and his memory will disappear from this world for generations upon generations." Saying "Ribon Alma" before the prayer protects us from doing intellectual mistakes throughout our spiritual work.

רִבּוֹן ribon עָלְמָא alma יְהֵא yehe רַעֲוָא ra'ava קָמָךְ kamach לְמֶיהַב lemehav

כֵּן lan וְזֵילָא chela חֵילָא le'it'ara לְאִתְעָרָא vikarach בִּיקָרָךְ ulme'ebad וּלְמֶעְבַּד

רְעוּתָךְ re'utach וּלְסַדְּרָא ulesadara כֹּלָא chola כְּדְקָא kedeka יָאוּת ya'ut

---

and they would not control me, not my body and not my soul.
And my prayer would be accepted by You, Amen, so may His will be.

I hereby meditate in my prayer
as if I am standing in the temple in Jerusalem, and tuned against the Holy of Holies. As it says:
"and they shall pray toward this place" (1 kings 8:35). May it be pleasing before You, Lord, my God
and God of my forefathers, that my heart will be founded and devoted by me so I will not forget You.

RIBON ALMA
Master of the World, may it be pleasing before You
to give us strength, to stir ourself to honor You, to do Your will and to put everything in the right direction.

וְאַף (ve'af) עַל (al) גַּב (gav) דְּלֵית (delet) אֲנַן (anan) יָדְעִין (yad'in) לְשַׁוָּאָה (leshava'a)

רְעוּתָא (re'uta) וְלִבָּא (veliba) לְתַקָּנָא (letakana) כְּלָא (chola), יְהֵא (yehe) רַעֲוָא (ra'ava)

קַמָּךְ (kamach) דְּתִתְרְעֵי (detitre'ei) בְּמִלִין (vemilin) וּצְלוֹתָא (utzelota) דִּיכַן (dilan)

לְתַקָּנָא (letakana) תִּקּוּנָא (tikuna) דִּלְעֵלָּא (dil'ela) כְּדְקָא (kideka) יָאוּת (ya'ut)

וּלְהֵבוֹ (ulehevo) הֵיכָלִין (hechalin) עִלָּאִין (ila'in) וְרוּחִין (veruchin) עִלָּאִין (ila'in)

עַיְלֵי (ayle) הֵיכָלָא (hechala) בְּהֵיכָלָא (behechala) וְרוּחָא (verucha) בְּרוּחָא (verucha)

עַד (ad) דְּמִתְחַבְּרָן (demitchaberan) בְּדוּכְתַּיְהוּ (beduchtayho) כְּדְקָא (kideka)

וְזִי (chazei), שִׁיפָא (sheyafa) בְּשִׁיפָא (besheyafa), וְאִשְׁתְּלִימוּ (ve'ishtelimu) דָּא (da)

בְּדָא (veda) וְאִתְיַחֲדוּ (ve'ityachadu) דָּא (da) בְּדָא (veda) עַד (ad) אִנּוּן (inun) וְזַד (chad),

וְנָהֲרִין (venaharin) דָּא (da) בְּדָא (veda). וּכְדֵין (ucheden) נִשְׁמָתָא (nishmeta)

עִלָּאָה (ila'a) דְּכֹלָּא (dechola) אַתְיָא (atya) מִלְּעֵלָּא (mile'ela) וְנָהֵר (venaher) כּוֹן (lon)

וְלְהֵבוֹ (velehevu) נְהִירִין (nehirin) כֻּלְּהוּ (kolehu) בּוֹצִינִין (vutzinin) בְּשְׁלֵימוּ (bishlemu)

כְּדְקָא (kideka) וְזִי (chazei), עַד (ad) דְּהַהוּא (dehahu) נְהוֹרָא (nehora) עִלָּאָה (ila'a)

אִתְעַר (ite'ar), וְכֹלָּא (vechola) אַעֵיל (a'el) לְגַבֵּי (legabei) קֹדֶשׁ (kodesh)

קָדְשִׁים (kodashim) וְאִתְבָּרְכָא (ve'itbarcha) וְאִתְמַלְיָא (ve'itmalya) כְּבֵירָא (kevera)

דְּמַיִן (demayin) נָבְעִין (nav'in) וְלָא (vela) פָּסְקִין (faskin) וְכֻלְּהוּ (vecholho)

מִתְבָּרְכָן (mitbarchan) לְעֵלָּא (le'ela) וְתַתָּא (vetata). וְהַהוּא (vehahu) דְּלָא (dela)

אִתְיְדַע (ityeda) וְלָא (vela) אַעֵיל (a'el) בּוֹשְׁבְּנָא (bechushbena), רְעוּתָא (re'uta)

דְּלָא (dela) אִתְפַּס (itpas) לְעָלְמִין (le'almin), בָּסִים (basim) לְגוֹ (lego) לְגוֹ (lego)

בְּגַוַּיְהוּ (begavayho), וְלָא (vela) אִתְיְדַע (ityeda) הַהוּא (hahu) רְעוּתָא (re'uta)

And although we do not know how to be mindful and to direct our heart, to correct everything, may it be pleasing before You, that our words and prayer will be accepted to correct the Supernal tikkun in the right direction, so the Supernal chambers and the Supernal souls are elevated, one chamber penetrates the other, and one soul the other, until they all rest in their proper places as is suitable. One organ is within the other and one complements the other. The elements merge until they become one and shine within each other. Consequently, this most Supernal soul descends and shines on them, and all the candles (Sefirot) are becomingly lit in all their perfection, until this Supernal Light is aroused and all the chambers enter the Holy of Holies, and it is blessed and filled like a well of spring water that never ceases to flow, and all the Upper and Lower are blessed. The innermost of secrets that cannot be conceived and is taken account, it is a desire that can never be grasped, is sweetened deep within the Sefirot, and its desire cannot be conceived

vela וְלָא itpas אִיתְפַּס leminda לְמִנְדַּע ucheden וּכְדֵין, kola כְּלָא re'uta רְעוּתָא

chada וְזָדָא ad עַד en אֵין sof סוֹף vechola וְכֹלָא ihu אִיהוּ vishlemu בְּשְׁלִימוּ

miletata מִלְּתָתָא umigo וּמִגּוֹ lego לְגוֹ ad עַד de'it'aved דְּאִתְעֲבֵד kola כְּלָא

chad וְזָד, ve'itmali'a וְאִתְמַלְיָאה kola כְּלָא ve'ashlem וְאִשְׁלֵם kola כְּלָא

ve'itnahir וְאִתְנְהִיר ve'itbasem וְאִתְבַּסַּם kola כְּלָא kideka כְּדְקָא ya'ut יָאוּת.

ribon רִבּוֹן alma עָלְמָא yehe יְהֵא re'utach רְעוּתָךְ im עִם amach עַמָּךְ

Yisrael יִשְׂרָאֵל le'alam לְעָלַם. ufurkan וּפֻרְקַן yeminach יְמִינָךְ achazei אַחֲזֵי

le'amach לְעַמָּךְ bevet בְּבֵית makdeshach מַקְדְּשָׁךְ ule'amtuyei וּלְאַמְטוּיֵי

lana לָנָא mituv מִטּוּב nehorach נְהוֹרָךְ ulekabela וּלְקַבְּלָא tzelotana צְלוֹתָנָא

berachmei. יְהֵא yehe רַעֲוָא ra'ava קֳמָךְ kamach דְּתֶהֱוֵי detehevei

sa'ed סָעֵד vesmech וּסְמַךְ lan לַן denema דְּנֵימָא milin מִלִּין be'orach בְּאֹרַח

mishor. מֵישׁוֹר betikuna בְּתִקּוּנָא dil'ela דִּלְעֵלָּא betikunin בְּתִקּוּנִין

demalka דְּמַלְכָּא kadisha קַדִּישָׁא umatronita וּמַטְרוֹנִיתָא kadisha קַדִּישָׁא

uleme'ebad וּלְמֶעֱבַד yichuda יִחוּדָא shelim שְׁלִים le'ashalfa לְאַשְׁלָפָא

lehahi לְהַהִיא nishmeta נִשְׁמְתָא dechol דְּכָל chayei וְחַיֵי midarga מִדַּרְגָּא

ledarga לְדַרְגָּא ad עַד sofa סוֹפָא dechol דְּכָל dargin דַּרְגִּין.

begin בְּגִין dihevei דִּיהֵוֵי hahi הַהִיא nishmeta נִשְׁמְתָא

mishtechacha מִשְׁתְּכַחָא bechola בְּכֹלָא umitpasheta וּמִתְפַּשְׁטָא

bechola בְּכֹלָא deha דְּהָא ela עֵלָּא vetata וְתַתָּא telayin תַּלְיָין

behai בְּהַאי nishmeta נִשְׁמְתָא umitkayemei וּמִתְקַיְּמֵי va בַּה:

---

or directed at knowing him. Thus, all the levels up to Ein Sof (The Endless World) unite into one, and everything is perfected from Above, Below, and within. All the levels are filled with his Light, all reach completion and all shine because of him and are suitably sweetened as it should be.

Master of the World, May Your desire be with Your nation Israel forever. The redemption of Your Right may You show to Your nation in Your Temple. May You fill us with the best of Your enlightenment and may You receive our prayers with mercy. May it be pleasing before You to assist and support us to say the words in the right way, for the Supernal tikkun and the tkkun of the holy King and the holy Matron. So it will create a complete unification which will draw out this soul which gives life to all from one height to another, all the way to the end of all levels. Because of the existence of this soul in everything and its extention in everything, Above and Below idepend on this soul and exist because of it.

SHACHARIT – MORNING PRAYER
PREPARATION OF THE VESSEL

ADON OLAM

The two words *Adon Olam* (אדון עולם) are equal to the numerical value of the Aramaic words *Ein Sof* (207), meaning the "Endless World"—our true origin. *Adon Olam* is also the numeric value of the Aramaic word *Or*, which means "Light." The actual words *Adon Olam* translate into English as "Master of the Universe." Through this prayer, we want to arouse a sense of awe and wonderment toward the knowledge and understanding of the spiritual system and the order and perfection of the world and of the Light of the Creator.

adon אֲדוֹן olam עוֹלָם אני אור, רו, א"ס asher אֲשֶׁר malach מֶלֶךְ♦

beterem בְּטֶרֶם kol כָּל ילי yetzir יְצִיר nivra נִבְרָא: le'et לְעֵת na'asa נַעֲשָׂה

vecheftzo בְּחֶפְצוֹ kol כָּל ילי azai אֲזַי♦ melech מֶלֶךְ shemo שְׁמוֹ מהש" ע"ה,

kichlot כְּכְלוֹת ve'acharei וְאַחֲרֵי nikra נִקְרָא: ע"ה אל סדי ע"ה, ע"ב בריבוע וקס"א

hakol הַכֹּל ילי♦ levado לְבַדּוֹ מ"ב yimloch יִמְלוֹךְ nora נוֹרָא:

vehu וְהוּא yhvh היה haya הָיָה vehu וְהוּא♦ hove הֹוֶה vehu וְהוּא yihye יִהְיֶה יי

betifara בְּתִפְאָרָה: vehu וְהוּא echad אֶחָד אהבה, דאגה ve'en וְאֵין sheni שֵׁנִי♦

lehamshilo לְהַמְשִׁילוֹ beli בְּלִי resheet רֵאשִׁית ulhachbira וּלְהַחְבִּירָה: beli בְּלִי

beli בְּלִי tachlit תַּכְלִית♦ velo וְלֹא ha'oz הָעֹז vehamisra וְהַמִּשְׂרָה: beli בְּלִי

erech עֶרֶךְ beli בְּלִי dimyon דִּמְיוֹן♦ beli בְּלִי shinuy שִׁנּוּי utmura וּתְמוּרָה:

beli בְּלִי chibur וְחִבּוּר beli בְּלִי perud פֵּרוּד♦ gedol גָּדוֹל להו ; עם ד' אותיות =

ko'ach כֹּחַ ugvurah וּגְבוּרָה ריו: vehu וְהוּא♦ Eli אֵלִי vechai וְחַי מבה, יזל, אום

go'ali גֹּאֲלִי♦ vetzur וְצוּר אלהים דההין ע"ה chevli וְחֶבְלִי beyom בְּיוֹם ע"ה נגד,

tzara צָרָה אלהים דההין vehu וְהוּא: nisi נִסִּי umanusi וּמָנוּסִי♦ מזבוח, זן, אל יהוה אל

menat מְנָת kosi כּוֹסִי beyom בְּיוֹם ע"ה נגד, מזבוח, זן, אל יהוה אל ekra אֶקְרָא:

ADON OLAM

Master of the Universe, Who reigned before any form was created and, when everything was made according to His will, His Name was proclaimed as King. And after everything has expired, He, the Awesome One, shall reign alone. He was, He is, and He shall remain in splendor. He is One and there is no other to compare to Him or to declare as His equal. Without beginning, without conclusion, His is the power and dominion, unfathomable and unimaginable, unchanging and irreplaceable. He is without connections or separation. His strength and valor are great. He is my God and my living Redeemer; the forbearance of pain in time of distress. He is my banner, my refuge, and the portion of my cup on the day that I call out.

וְהוּא vehu רוֹפֵא rofe וְהוּא vehu ◆marpe מַרְפֵּא vehu וְהוּא tzofe צוֹפֶה

וְהוּא vehu עֶזְרָה ezra: בְּיָדוֹ beyado אַפְקִיד afkid רוּחִי ruchi

◆be'et בְּעֵת ר"ת = קנ"א ב"ן, יהוה אלהים יהוה אדני, מילוי קס"א וס"ג, מ"ה ברבוע וע"ב ע"ה.

אִישָׁן ishan ◆ve'a'ira וְאָעִירָה ve'im וְעִם ruchi רוּחִי geviyati גְּוִיָּתִי◆

אֲדֹנִי Adonai ללה li לִי velo וְלֹא ira: אִירָא bemikdasho בְּמִקְדָּשׁוֹ

תָּגֵל tagel nafshi נַפְשִׁי◆ meshichenu מְשִׁיחֵנוּ yishlach יִשְׁלַח mehera: מְהֵרָה

וְאָז ve'az נָשִׁיר nashir בְּבֵית bevet ב"פ ראה kodshi קָדְשִׁי◆

אָמֵן amen יאהדונהי shem שֵׁם יאהדונהי amen אָמֵן hanora: הַנּוֹרָא

THE SMALL TALIT

The connection of the small *Talit* (*Talit katan* or *Tzitzit*) refers to a garment worn underneath the shirt. The small *Talit* creates a protective security shield around the wearer's skin and body so that evil forces cannot infiltrate or penetrate them. Our skin has the energy of *Malchut,* which is connected to the one percent realm. The small *Talit* controls the energy field around the skin and protects it.

It says in the *Zohar* that the *Tzitzit* is a talisman which covers and protects the wearer from all evil spirits and negative angels. Rabbenu Bachye says that the precept of the *Tzitzit* is linked to the Resurrection of the Dead. The *Tzitzit* represents the Surrounding Light, and for that reason, the *Talit* needs to be large in order to cover the head and the body, back and front, all the way down to the chest. The small *Talit* represents the Surrounding Light of *Katnut.*

If you do not use a *Talit* for the prayers you should only recite this blessing.
If you slept with a small *Talit* you should touch the *Tzitzit* first.

ילה Elohenu אֱלֹהֵינוּ Adonai יְהֹוָאדֹנָיאהֹדוֹנָהי Ata אַתָּה baruch בָּרוּךְ

kideshanu קִדְּשָׁנוּ asher אֲשֶׁר ha'olam הָעוֹלָם melech מֶלֶךְ

tzitzit: צִיצִת mitzvat מִצְוַת al עַל vetzivanu וְצִוָּנוּ bemitzvotav בְּמִצְוֹתָיו

He is a healer and a remedy. He watches and He helps. In His Hands, I surrender my spirit when I sleep and when I awaken. With my spirit shall my body remain. The Lord is with me, I shall not fear. In His Temple shall my spirit rejoice. He shall send our Mashiach speedily. Then we shall sing in His Temple: Amen, Amen, the Awesome Name.

THE SMALL TALIT

Blessed are You, Lord, our God, the King of the Earth,
Who has sanctified us with His commandments and obliged us with the commandment of Tzitzit.

THE TALIT

The *Talit* is a shawl that is draped over the shoulders of the wearer, over his clothes. It surrounds him with a spiritual protective layer of illumination. The four corners of the *Talit*, with their tassels, connect us to the four corners of the universe and to the quantum level of our world, helping us gain control over our lives. The *Talit* connects us to the Surrounding Light—our soul's potential. Generally, only married men wear it, because the energy awakened by the *Talit* is manifested through the man's connection with his wife.

LESHEM YICHUD

LeShem Yichud is a spark plug that activates the next series of prayers and actions, joining the Upper Worlds with our physical world.

לְשֵׁם leshem יְוזוּד yichud קוּדְשָׁא kudsha בְּרִיךְ berich הוּא hu

(יאהדונהי) ush'chintei וּשְׁכִינְתֵּיהּ bid'chilu בִּדְוזִילוּ ur'chimu וּרְוזִימוּ

leyachada לְיַוזְדָא (איההויהה) ud'chilu וּדְוזִילוּ ur'chimu וּרְוזִימוּ (יאההויהה),

shem שֵׁם yud יו"ד kei קֵי bevav בְּוא"ו kei קֵי beyichuda בְּיִוזוּדָא

shelim שְׁלִים (יהוה) beshem בְּשֵׁם kol כָּל יכ Yisrael יִשְׂרָאֵל, hareni הֲרֵינִי

muchan מוּכָן lilvosh לִלְבּוֹשׁ talit טַלִּית metzuyetzet מְצֻיֶּצֶת

kehilchata כְּהִלְכָתָה kemo כְּמוֹ shetzivanu שֶׁצִּוָּנוּ Adonai יְהֹוָהאדנייאהדונהי

Elohenu אֱלֹהֵינוּ יכה vetorato בְּתוֹרָתוֹ hakedosha הַקְּדוֹשָׁה: ve'asu וְעָשׂוּ

lahem לָהֶם tzitzit צִיצִת al עַל־ kanfei כַּנְפֵי vigdehem בִגְדֵיהֶם, kedei כְּדֵי

la'asot לַעֲשׂוֹת nachat נַוזַת ru'ach רוּוזַ leyotzri לְיוֹצְרִי vela'asot וְלַעֲשׂוֹת

retzon רָצוֹן מהע ע"ה, ע"ב בריבוע וקס"א ע"ה, אל שדי ע"ה, bor'i בּוֹרְאִי, vehareni וְהֲרֵינִי

muchan מוּכָן levarech לְבָרֵךְ al עַל atifat עֲטִיפַת hatalit הַטַלִּית

ketikkun כְּתִקּוּן razal רֹז"ל, vehareni וְהֲרֵינִי mechaven מְכַוֵּין liftor לִפְטוֹר

bivracha בְּבְרָכָה zo זוֹ gam גַּם talit טַלִּית hakatan הַקָּטָן she'alai שֶׁעָלַי◆

THE TALIT
LESHEM YICHUD

For the sake of unification between The Holy Blessed One and His Shechinah, with fear and love and with love and fear, in order to unify the Name Yud-Kei and Vav-Kei in perfect unity, and in the name of all Israel, I am hereby prepared to wear a Talit with Tzitzit, according to the law and as we were commanded by the Lord, our God, in His holy Torah: "And they made for themselves Tzitzit on the corners of their clothes." (Numbers 15:38) In order to give pleasure to my Maker and to fulfill the wish of my Creator, I am hereby prepared to bless upon the enwrapping with the Talit, as was established by our Sages of blessed memory. I hereby intend to exempt the small Talit that I am wearing, with this blessing.

vihi וִיהִי ילה   no'am נֹעַם   Adonai אֲדֹנָי ללה   Elohenu אֱלֹהֵינוּ ילה

alenu עָלֵינוּ   uma'ase וּמַעֲשֵׂה   yadenu יָדֵינוּ   konena כּוֹנְנָה

alenu עָלֵינוּ   uma'ase וּמַעֲשֵׂה   yadenu יָדֵינוּ   ❖konenehu כּוֹנְנֵהוּ

WRAPPING THE TALIT: After the blessing, you wrap the *Talit* over your head, leaving your face uncovered and the four corners falling on your chest. Then you grab the two right side *Tzitzits* and throws them over your left shoulder so they drape at the back – then you wait a bit, then take hold of the two left side *Tzitzits* and throw them over your left shoulder, draping them to the back in a way that the four *Tzitzits* will be hanging over your left shoulder towards and down the back. You should wait like that for about four seconds, before allowing the *Talit* to drop down, so it can hang comfortably and loosely over both shoulders with two *Tzitzits* in the front and two in the back.

> The *Talit* is the aspect of the Surrounding Light of *Gadlut*.
> The *Talit* is the *tikkun* of the external part (*Netzach, Hod, Yesod*) of *Yetzirah*.
> **The blessing** is the *tikkun* of the Surrounding Light, and
> **The wearing** of the *Talit* is the *tikkun* of the Inner Light.

melech מֶלֶךְ ילה   Eelohenu אֱלֹהֵינוּ   Adonai יְהֹוָאדְהֹאַהדוֹנָהי   Ata אַתָּה   baruch בָּרוּךְ

bemitzvotav בְּמִצְוֹתָיו   kideshanu קִדְּשָׁנוּ   asher אֲשֶׁר   ha'olam הָעוֹלָם

vetzivanu וְצִוָּנוּ   lehit'atef לְהִתְעַטֵּף   betzitzit בַּצִּיצִית ר"ת ל"ב נתיבות החוכמה❖

Yichud of the *Talit*: At first, you should meditate on the *Yichud* (unification) of *Zeir Anpin*, which is: יהוה, which has the numerical value of 32 paths of wisdom (ל"ב נתיבות החוכמה). In particular, you should meditate to connect the letters יה, which are *Abba* and *Ima*, with the letter ו, which is *Zeir Anpin*, so that it becomes the Surrounding Light which is the *Talit*. Then, you should meditate to connect the letter ו (*Zeir Anpin*) with the last letter ה, to draw the Surrounding Light to the letter ה, which is the *Tzitzit*.

THE TEFILIN (PHYLACTERIES)

The *Tefilin* acts like an antenna, drawing spiritual energy which allows the wearer to bind, harness, and control his selfish desires and to transform them into the *Desire to Receive for the Sake of Sharing*. The letters and words of *LeShem Yichud* help run a current of energy into the *Tefilin* activating it by joining the Upper Worlds to our lower world.

"May the pleasantness of the Lord our God be upon us and may He establish the work of our hands for us and may the work of our hands establish Him." (Psalms 90:17)

Blessed are You, Lord, our God, the King of the World,
Who has sanctified us with His commandments and obliged us with enwrapping ourselves with Talit.

LESHEM YICHUD

LeShem Yichud is like a spark plug that activates the next series of prayers and actions, joining the Upper Worlds with our physical world.

לְשֵׁם leshem · יִחוּד yichud · קוּדְשָׁא kudsha · בְּרִיךְ berich · הוּא hu

וּשְׁכִינְתֵּיהּ ush'chintei · (יאהדונהי) · בִּדְחִילוּ bid'chilu · וּרְחִימוּ ur'chimu

(יאההויהה), · וּרְחִימוּ ur'chimu · וּדְחִילוּ ud'chilu · (איההיוהה) · לְיַחֲדָא leyachda

שֵׁם shem · יוּ"ד yud · קֵי kei · בְּוָא"ו bevav · קֵי kei · בְּיִחוּדָא beyichuda

שְׁלִים shelim · (יהוה) · בְּשֵׁם beshem · כָּל kol · יִשְׂרָאֵל Yisrael · הֲרֵינִי hareni

מוּכָן muchan · לְקַיֵּם lekayem · מִצְוַת mitzvat · עֲשֵׂה ase · לְהָנִיחַ lehani'ach

תְּפִילִין tefilin · בְּיָדִי beyadi · וּבְרֹאשִׁי uvroshi, · כְּמוֹ kemo · שֶׁצִּוָּנוּ shetzivanu

יְהֹוָה Adonai · אֱלֹהֵינוּ Elohenu · וּקְשַׁרְתָּם ukshartem · אֹתָם otam

לְאוֹת le'ot · עַל al · יָדְכֶם yedchem · וְהָיוּ vehayu · לְטֹטָפֹת letotafot

בֵּין ben · עֵינֵיכֶם enechem · וְהֲרֵינִי vehareni · מוּכָן muchan

לְבָרֵךְ levarech · הַבְּרָכָה haberacha

שֶׁתִּקְּנוּ shetiknu · רֹז"ל razal · עַל al · מִצְוַת mitzvat · הַתְּפִילִין hatefilin,

וְיַעֲלֶה veya'ale · לְפָנֶיךָ lefanecha · יְהֹוָה Adonai

אֱלֹהֵינוּ Elohenu · וֵאלֹהֵי velohei · אֲבוֹתֵינוּ avotenu

כְּאִלּוּ ke'ilu · כִּוַּנְתִּי kivanti · בְּכָל bechol · הַכַּוָּנוֹת hakavanot

הָרְאוּיוֹת hare'uyot · לְכַוֵּן lechaven · בַּהֲנָחַת behanachat · הַתְּפִילִין hatefilin

וּבַבְּרָכָה uvaberacha · וִיהִי vihi · נֹעַם no'am · אֲדֹנָי Adonai

אֱלֹהֵינוּ Elohenu · עָלֵינוּ alenu · וּמַעֲשֵׂה uma'ase · יָדֵינוּ yadenu

כּוֹנְנָה konena · עָלֵינוּ alenu · וּמַעֲשֵׂה uma'ase · יָדֵינוּ yadenu · כּוֹנְנֵהוּ konenehu

---

THE TEFILIN (PHYLACTERIES) - LESHEM YICHUD

For the sake of unification between the Holy Blessed One and His Shechinah, with fear and love and with love and fear, in order to unify the Name Yud-Kei and Vav-Kei in perfect unity, and in the name of Israel, I am hereby prepared to fulfill the obligatory precept of wearing the Tefilin on my arm and on my head as we have been commanded by the Lord, our God: "And you shall bind them as a sign on your hands and they shall be as frontlets between your eyes." (Deuteronomy 11:18) I am hereby prepared to say the blessing that was established by our Sages, of blessed memory, concerning the precept of Tefilin. May it appear before You, Lord, our God and the God of our fathers, as if I have intended all the correct and fitting meditations while wearing the Tefilin and while saying the blessing. "May the pleasantness of the Lord our God be upon us and may He establish the work of our hands for us and may the work of our hands establish Him." (Psalms 90:17)

THE LEFT ARM TEFILIN (*MALCHUT*)

The purpose of binding the *Tefilin* on our left hand and arm is to overcome the *Desire to Receive for the Self Alone* that exists in our heart. *Tefilin* helps bind the gravitational pull of the left side, transforming our *Desire to Receive for the Self Alone* into the *Desire to Receive for the Sake of Sharing*.

LAYING THE HAND TEFILIN: First, place the *Tefilin* on your left bicep, facing your heart, and recite the first blessing. Then wrap the strap around your left bicep three times, to create the Aramaic letter *Shin* שׁ on your bicep. This action also connects you to the three highest dimensions, or *Sefirot*, of our universe: *Chochmah*, *Binah* and *Da'at*. After the *Shin* is complete, wrap the strap seven times around your left forearm to connect you to the seven major *Sefirot* that influence our world—*Chesed, Gevurah, Tiferet, Netzach, Hod, Yesod,* and *Malchut*. This action also connects us to the seven sages: Abraham, Isaac, Jacob, Moses, Aaron, Joseph, and David, who are the codes and channels for these *Sefirot*. When these seven wrappings are complete, wind the remaining leather around your hand, leaving it as such. You will come back to complete it after the laying of the forehead strap with your *Head Tefilin*.

The Hand *Tefilin* atones for bloodshed.
It is the *tikkun* of the external aspect (*Netzach, Hod, Yesod*) of *Beriah*. **The blessing** is the *tikkun* of the Surrounding Light and **the laying** of the *Tefilin* is the *tikkun* of the Inner Light.

יכה Elohenu אֱלֹהֵינוּ Adonai יְהֹוָאדְנִילִיאהדונהי Ata אַתָּה baruch בָּרוּךְ

kideshanu קִדְּשָׁנוּ asher אֲשֶׁר ha'olam הָעוֹלָם melech מֶלֶךְ

tefilin תְּפִילִין lehani'ach לְהָנִיחַ vetzivanu וְצִוָּנוּ bemitzvotav בְּמִצְוֹתָיו

THE HEAD TEFILIN (*ZEIR ANPIN*)

LAYING THE HEAD TEFILIN: Place the *Head Tefilin* directly on the center point of your forehead where the hairline starts. Then loop the circle over your skull, placing the knot of the straps behind your skull just above your neck. The Evil Inclination usually targets our mind first, bombarding us with negative thoughts, which, in turn, lead to negative actions. By placing the *Head Tefilin* on your forehead, you are overriding Satan's signal. As you tighten the *Head Tefilin* on your head, recite the blessing, while allowing the two straps to hang loosely over your shoulders to rest on your chest.

The Head *Tefilin* atones for pride.
It is the *tikkun* of the External aspect (*Netzach, Hod, Yesod*) of *Atzilut*. **The blessing** is the *tikkun* of the Surrounding Light, and **the laying** of the *Tefilin* is the *tikkun* of the Inner Light.

יכה Elohenu אֱלֹהֵינוּ Adonai יְהֹוָאדְנִילִיאהדונהי Ata אַתָּה baruch בָּרוּךְ

kideshanu קִדְּשָׁנוּ asher אֲשֶׁר ha'olam הָעוֹלָם melech מֶלֶךְ

tefilin תְּפִילִין mitzvat מִצְוַת al עַל vetzivanu וְצִוָּנוּ bemitzvotav בְּמִצְוֹתָיו

(Whisper:) יוזו אותיות malchuto מַלְכוּתוֹ, kevod כְּבוֹד shem שֵׁם baruch בָּרוּךְ

רִיבּוּעַ ס"ג ו"י אותיות דס"ג va'ed וָעֶד le'olam לְעוֹלָם

THE LEFT ARM TEFILIN
Blessed are You, Lord, our God, the King of the World,
Who has sanctified us with His commandments and has required us to put on the Tefilin.

THE HEAD TEFILIN
Blessed are You, Lord, our God, the King of the World,
Who has sanctified us with His commandments and obliged us with the commandment of Tefilin.
"Blessed is the Holy Name, His reign is forever and for all eternity." (Pesachim 56:1)

According to the *Zohar*, the Creator is laying *Tefilin* and is adorned with four illuminations which are: *Chochmah, Binah, Chesed* and *Gevurah*.

ta'atzil תַּאֲצִיל elyon עֶלְיוֹן (מילוי דס"ג) יא"י El אֵל umechochmatcha וּמֵחָכְמָתְךָ

vechasdecha וְחַסְדְּךָ tevineni תְּבִינֵנִי umibinatcha וּמִבִּינָתְךָ alai עָלַי

oyvai אוֹיְבַי tatzmit תַּצְמִית uvigvuratcha וּבִגְבוּרָתְךָ alai עָלַי tagdil תַּגְדִּיל

al עַל tarik תָּרִיק והו hatov הַטּוֹב veshemen וְשֶׁמֶן ◆vekamai וְקָמַי

tuvcha לאו טוּבְךָ lehashpi'a לְהַשְׁפִּיעַ menora מְנוֹרָה kenei קְנֵי shiv'a שִׁבְעָה

yadecha יָדְךָ et אֶת pote'ach פּוֹתֵחַ ◆livriyotecha לִבְרִיּוֹתֶיךָ

ר"ת פאי וס"ת וחתך = דִּיקְרְנוֹסָא ובא"ת ב"ש סאל, פאי, אמן, יאהדונהי;

ועוד יכוין עם וחתך umasbi'a וּמַשְׂבִּיעַ וחתך - יְוֹהְתֻכֶה (עם ג' אותיות =

דִּיקְרְנוֹסָא ובא"ת ב"ש סאל, פאי, אמן, יאהדונהי ; ועוד יכוין עם וחתך בעילוב יהוה - יְוֹהְתֻכֶה)

לְכָל lechol ה יה ארני = אהיה אהיה יהוה, בינה ע"ה, וזיים כל וזי = chai וְזִי

רָצוֹן ratzon מהש ע"ה, ע"ב בריבוע וקס"א ע"ה, אל שדי ע"ה ; ר"ת רוזל שהיא המלכות הצריכה לשפיעֵ:

COMPLETING THE LEFT HAND

The Ari explains that by placing the strap on our fingers, we also create a ring. This ring connects us to the Light just as a wedding ring connects a bride and groom. It is important to remember that these connections are not just symbolic or metaphorical; they are a technology by which we connect to the Light.

LAYING THE HAND TEFILIN: Now you return to the strap on your left hand. You unwrap it back to the wrist, then wrap the strap twice around the middle of the middle finger, then once around the middle and the ring fingers, close to the palm. This action creates the Aramaic letters *Yud* י and *Dalet* ד with the straps. You have now created an important sequence of Aramaic letters known as the *Shin, Dalet, Yud* שׁדּי, the Holy Name that has the power to combat negative forces.

Here we sanctify *Malchut* by *Zeir Anpin*.

When you bind the *Tefilin* three times around your middle finger, you should say:

אותיות דס"ג וי' ריבוע דס"ג le'olam לְעוֹלָם li לִי ve'erastich וְאֵרַשְׂתִּיךְ

ע"ה ה"פ אלהים uvmishpat וּבְמִשְׁפָּט betzedek בְּצֶדֶק li לִי ve'erastich וְאֵרַשְׂתִּיךְ

מצפצ, ריבוע יהוה י"פ יי, אלהים דיודין: uvrachamim וּבְרַחֲמִים uvchesed וּבְחֶסֶד ע"ב,

veyada'at וְיָדַעַתְּ be'emuna בֶּאֱמוּנָה li לִי ve'erastich וְאֵרַשְׂתִּיךְ

◆Adonai יאהדונהי יְהוֹוָאהדונהי et אֶת־

Emanate upon me Your wisdom, Supernal God; from Your understanding, give me understanding. Increase Your kindness with me. With Your might, may You smite all my enemies and adversaries. Pour good oil upon the seven stems of the Candelabra, so that Your goodness shall flow to Your creatures. "Open Your Hands and give fulfillment to every living creature's desire." (Psalms 145:16.)

COMPLETING THE LEFT HAND

"I shall betroth you to Me forever; I shall betroth you to Me with righteousness, justice, kindness, and mercy; I shall betroth you to Me with faith. And you shall know the Lord." (Hosea 2:21-22)

KADESH LI

The next two connections, *Kadesh Li* and *VeHayah Ki Yevi'acha* are powerful sequences that are contained on the parchment inside the *Tefilin* boxes. When we recite these sequences, we are powering up the *Tefilin*.

After putting on the *Tefilin*, you should say the two following paragraphs. If you cannot say them now, because you are in a rush, you should say them after the Morning Prayer, before removing the *Tefilin*.

Moshe מֹשֶׁה el אֶל Adonai יְהוָֹה vaydaber וַיְדַבֵּר

li לִי kadesh קַדֶּשׁ lemor לֵאמֹר מהע, ע"ב בריבוע קס"א, אל שדי, ד"פ אלהים ע"ה

peter פֶּטֶר רפ"ח ע"ה bechor בְּכוֹר ר"ת לכב chol כָּל ילי

rechem רֶחֶם ילי kol כָּל (להעלות רפ"ח ניצוצות שנפלו לקליפה דמעם באים התוכלאים) אברהם,

bivnei בִּבְנֵי וז"פ אל, רי"ו ול"ב נתיבות החוכמה, רמ"ח (אברים), עסמ"ב וט"ז אותיות פשוטות

Yisrael יִשְׂרָאֵל ba'adam בָּאָדָם מ"ה uvabehema וּבַבְּהֵמָה ב"ן li לִי hu הוּא׃

el אֶל Moshe מֹשֶׁה מהע, ע"ב בריבוע קס"א, אל שדי, ד"פ אלהים ע"ה vayomer וַיֹּאמֶר

ha'am הָעָם ע"ב קס"א, יהי אור ע"ה (סוד המושכת העופע מן ד' שמות הנקרא זכר) zachor זָכוֹר

et אֶת hayom הַיּוֹם ע"ה נגד, מזבוח, זן, אל יהוה haze הַזֶּה והו asher אֲשֶׁר

yetzatem יְצָאתֶם miMitzrayim מִמִּצְרַיִם מצר mibet מִבֵּית ב"פ ראה

avadim עֲבָדִים ki כִּי bechozek בְּחֹזֶק פהל yad יָד hotzi הוֹצִיא

Adonai יְהוָֹה etchem אֶתְכֶם mize מִזֶּה velo וְלֹא ye'achel יֵאָכֵל

chametz וְחָמֵץ hayom הַיּוֹם ע"ה נגד, מזבוח, זן, אל יהוה atem אַתֶּם yotz'im יֹצְאִים

bechodesh בְּחֹדֶשׁ י"ב הוויות, קס"א קנ"א ha'aviv הָאָבִיב׃ vehaya וְהָיָה יהוה ; יהוה

chi כִּי yevi'acha יְבִיאֲךָ Adonai יְהוָֹה el אֶל eretz אֶרֶץ

haKena'ani הַכְּנַעֲנִי vehaChiti וְהַחִתִּי vehaEmori וְהָאֱמֹרִי vehaChivi וְהַחִוִּי

vehaYevusi וְהַיְבוּסִי asher אֲשֶׁר nishba נִשְׁבַּע la'avotecha לַאֲבֹתֶיךָ

KADESH LI

"And the Lord spoke to Moses and said: Sanctify unto Me every firstborn; The first bud of every womb in the Children of Israel, among men or among beasts, it is Mine. And Moses said to the people: Remember this day on which you had come out from Egypt, from the house of slavery. Because, with the strength of His Hand did Lord take you out of this, thus leaven may not be eaten. Today, you are leaving in the month of the spring. And if it shall pass that Lord shall bring you to the land of the Canaanites, Hittites, Amorites, Hivites and Yevusites, which He had pledged to your forefathers

udvash וּדְבָשׁ chalav וְחָלָב zavat זָבַת eretz אֶרֶץ lach לָךְ latet לָתֵת

et אֶת־ ve'avadeta וְעָבַדְתָּ דִּינִין דִּגְדֹלוֹת עי"ך = (הַאַוויר) וי"ד (דְּעֹופֶר) עֹור

bachodesh בַּחֹדֶשׁ hazot הַזֹּאת ha'avoda הָעֲבֹדָה קֹ"א קָנְ"א י"ב הֲוָיֹות,

matzot מַצֹּת tochal תֹּאכַל נלך yamim יָמִים shiv'at שִׁבְעַת והל: haze הֶזֶה

chag וְחַג hashevi'i הַשְּׁבִיעִי אֶל יהוה ז, מִזְבֵּחַ, נֶגֶד, ע"ה uvayom וּבַיֹּום

shiv'at שִׁבְעַת et אֵת ye'achel יֵאָכֵל matzot מַצֹּות ladonai לַיהוָאדֹנָי לַיהוֹ

chametz וְחָמֵץ lecha לְךָ yera'e יֵרָאֶה velo וְלֹא־ hayamim הַיָּמִים ריי נלך

se'or שְׂאֹר lecha לְךָ yera'e יֵרָאֶה velo וְלֹא־ מֵחוֹזֶן דְּאֱלֹהִים דְּקְטֹנוֹת

bechol בְּכָל (אֱלֹהִים) רִיבֹּוּעַ = ר' ; אֱלֹהִים עִם כְּלָלֹות א' ; דְּיֹודִין אֱלֹהִים = (ע' בְּ"ן, לכב

bayom בַּיֹּום levincha לְבִנְךָ vehigadeta וְהִגַּדְתָּ gevulecha גְּבֻלֶךָ:

ba'avur בַּעֲבוּר lemor לֵאמֹר hahu הַהוּא אֶל יהוה ז, מִזְבֵּחַ, נֶגֶד, ע"ה

betzeti בְּצֵאתִי li לִי Adonai יהוָאדֹנָי asa עָשָׂה ze זֶה

le'ot לְאֹות lecha לְךָ יהוה ; יהוה vehaya וְהָיָה miMitzrayim מִמִּצְרָיִם: מצר

ulzikaron וּלְזִכָּרֹון (You should touch the Hand *Tefilin*) yadcha יָדְךָ al עַל־ ע"ב קֹסְ"א וֹנֶ"ב

enecha עֵינֶיךָ (You should touch the Head *Tefilin*) ben בֵּין ע"ה רִיבֹּוּעַ ; קֹסְ"א מֹ"ה

Adonai יהוָאדֹנָי torat תֹּורַת tih'ye תִּהְיֶה lema'an לְמַעַן

hotzi'acha הֹוצִאֲךָ פהל chazaka וְחֹזְקָה beyad בְּיָד ki כִּי beficha בְּפִיךָ

miMitzrayim מִמִּצְרָיִם Adonai יהוָאדֹנָי מצר ; ר"ת ; מֹיה:

hazot הַזֹּאת hachuka הַחֻקָּה et אֶת־ veshamarta וְשָׁמַרְתָּ

yamima יָמִימָה: miyamim מִיָּמִים נלך lemo'ada לְמֹועֲדָה

---

that He shall give to you, a land flowing with milk and honey, then you shall perform this service in this month: For seven days, you shall eat Matzot and the seventh day shall be a festival to the Lord. Matzot shall be eaten during those seven days, Chametz may not be seen by you nor may leaven be seen by you within all your boundaries. You shall relate this to your son and say: It is because of this that Lord did so for me upon my leaving Egypt. And it shall be a sign for you on your arm and a reminder between your eyes, so that Lord's Torah shall be in your mouth, because by a mighty Arm did Lord take you out of Egypt. And You shall observe this law at its destined time, from one year to another." (Exodus 13:1-10)

VeHayah Ki Yevi'acha

וְהָיָה֩ vehaya ; יהוה כִּי־ ki יְבִיאֲךָ֨ yevi'acha יְהֹוָ֜ה Adonai אֶל־ el

אֶ֣רֶץ eretz הַֽכְּנַעֲנִ֗י haKena'ani כַּאֲשֶׁ֨ר ka'asher נִשְׁבַּ֧ע nishba לְךָ֛ lecha

וְלַֽאֲבֹתֶ֖יךָ vela'avotecha וּנְתָנָ֥הּ untana נתה, קס"א קנ"א קמ"ג lach לָֽךְ׃

וְהַֽעֲבַרְתָּ֥ veha'avarta כָל־ chol ילי פֶּֽטֶר peter רפ"זו ע"ה (להעלות רפ"זו ניצוצות

אברהם, וז"פ אל, רי"ו ול"ב נתיבות החוכמה, רֶ֖חֶם rechem עונפלו לקליפה דמעם באים התחלואים)

לַֽיהֹוָ֑ה ladonai וְכָל־ vechol ילי עסמ"ב וט"ז אותיות פשוטות, רמ"זו (אברים),

פֶּ֣טֶר peter שֶׁ֤גֶר sheger רפ"זו ע"ה (להעלות רפ"זו ניצוצות שנפלו לקליפה דמעם באים התחלואים)

בְּהֵמָ֣ה behema אֲשֶׁ֣ר asher בן יִֽהְיֶ֥ה yih'ye לְךָ֛ lecha הַזְּכָרִ֖ים hazecharim

לַֽיהֹוָֽה׃ ladonai וְכָל־ vechol פֶּ֥טֶר peter רפ"זו ע"ה (להעלות רפ"זו ניצוצות

וַֽחֲמֹר֙ chamor (דמעם באים התחלואים) תִּפְדֶּ֣ה tifde בְשֶׂ֔ה vese

וְאִם־ ve'im יוהך, מ"א אותיות דפשוטי, דמילוי ודמילוי דמילוי דאהיה ע"ה לֹ֥א lo תִפְדֶּ֖ה tifde

וַֽעֲרַפְתּ֑וֹ va'arafto וְכֹ֨ל vechol ילי בְּכ֥וֹר bechor אָדָ֛ם adam מ"ה

בְּבָנֶ֖יךָ bevanecha תִּפְדֶּֽה׃ tifde וְהָיָ֞ה vehaya יהוה ; יהוה ki כִּֽי־ מ"ה

יִשְׁאָלְךָ֥ yish'alcha בִנְךָ֛ vincha מָחָ֖ר machar לֵאמֹ֣ר lemor מַה־ ma מ"ה

זֹ֑את zot וְאָֽמַרְתָּ֣ ve'amarta אֵלָ֔יו elav בְּחֹ֣זֶק bechozek פהל יָ֗ד yad

הוֹצִיאָ֧נוּ hotzi'anu יְהֹוָ֛ה Adonai מִמִּצְרַ֖יִם miMitzrayim מצר

מִבֵּ֥ית mibet ב"פ ראה עֲבָדִֽים׃ avadim וַיְהִ֗י vayehi כִּֽי־ ki הִקְשָׁ֣ה hiksha

פַּרְעֹה֮ Far'o לְשַׁלְּחֵנוּ֒ leshalchenu וַיַּֽהֲרֹ֨ג vayaharog יְהֹוָ֜ה Adonai

כָּל־ kol ילי בְּכוֹר֙ bechor בְּאֶ֣רֶץ be'eretz מִצְרַ֔יִם Mitzrayim מצר

VeHayah Ki Yevi'acha

"And it shall be that when the Lord has brought you to the land of the Canaanites, as He had pledged to your forefathers and has given to you, you shall deliver every first bud of a womb to the Lord and every first offspring of every beast that you own, the males to the Lord. And every firstborn donkey, you shall redeem with a sheep; if you do not redeem it, then you must decapitate it. And every firstborn human of your sons, you must redeem. And if it happens that your son may ask you later and say: What is this? You shall say to him: With the might of His Hand did Lord bring us out of Egypt, from the house of slaves. And it was that when Pharaoh was stubborn in his refusal to send us out, the Lord killed every firstborn in the land of Egypt,

בֵּין behema בְּהֵמָה bechor בְּכוֹר ve'ad וְעַד מ"ה adam אָדָם mibechor מִבְּכֹר

ladonai לַיהֹוָאדֹנָי‌אֱלֹהִים zove'ach זֹבֵחַ אֲנִי ani אֲנִי ken כֵּן al עַל

כֹּל kol יל"י פֶּטֶר peter רפ"ח ע"ה (לְהַעֲלוֹת רפ"ח נִיצוֹצוֹת שֶׁנָפְלוּ לִקְלִיפָּה דְמֵהֶם בָּאִים הַתוֹלָלוּאִים)

רֶחֶם rechem אברהם, וֹ"פ אל, רי"ו ול"ב נְתִיבוֹת הַחוֹכְמָה, רמ"ח (אברים), עסמ"ב וט"ו אוֹתִיוֹת פְשׁוּטוֹת

הַזְכָרִים hazecharim וְכָל vechol יל"י בְּכוֹר bechor בָּנַי banai אֶפְדֶּה efde:

וְהָיָה vehaya יהה ; יהה le'ot לְאוֹת עַל al יָדְכָה yadcha

וּלְטוֹטָפֹת ultotafot בֵּין ben עֵינֶיךָ enecha (You should touch the Hand *Tefilin*)

כִּי ki ; ע"ה קס"א בְּחֹזֶק bechozek פהל ki ; רִיבוֹע מ"ה ; יָד yad (You should touch the Head *Tefilin*)

הוֹצִיאָנוּ hotzi'anu לַיהֹוָאדֹנָי‌אֱלֹהִים Adonai מִמִּצְרַיִם miMitzrayim מצר ; ר"ת מ'ה':

יְהֹוָאדֹנָי‌אֱלֹהִים Adonai שׁוֹמְרִי shomri יְהֹוָאדֹנָי‌אֱלֹהִים Adonai צִלִּי tzili

עַל al יָד yad yemini יְמִינִי יְהֹוָאדֹנָי‌אֱלֹהִים Adonai יִשְׁמֹר yishmor

צֵאתִי tzeti לְחַיִּים lechayim וּבוֹאִי uvo'i לוֹזִיִים אֶהֱיֶה ; אהיה יהוה ; בִּינָה ע"ה

טוֹבִים tovim וּלְשָׁלוֹם ulshalom מֵעַתָּה me'ata וְעַד ve'ad עוֹלָם olam

אֵל El עֹדִּי Shadai (מִילוּי דס"ג) יא"י אל עֹדִי = מוּשָׁה, מוּהֵל, ע"ב בְּרִיבוֹע וּקס"א, ד"פ אלהים ע"ה

יְבָרֵךְ yevarech עסמ"ב, הַבְּרָכָה (יְכוּין לְמְתַק אֶת ז' הַמְלָכִים שְׁמְתוּ) אוֹתִי oti

וְיִתֶּן veyiten לִי li רַחֲמִים rachamim:

VA'ANI
COMMUNICATING WITH THE THREE PILLARS OF PRAYER (ABRAHAM, ISAAC AND JACOB)

There are three forces present in the universe that are required to generate power, be it physical or spiritual. These forces are the Right Column positive, sharing energy, of which Abraham is the channel; the Left Column receiving, negative energy, of which Isaac is the channel, and the Central Column of balance, resistance, of which Jacob is the channel. The ancient kabbalists explain that Abraham, Isaac and Jacob are the foundation of every prayer. Their names are transmitters that activate and give power to all blessings and prayers that we perform throughout this Siddur.

---

from the firstborn of man to the firstborn of beast. Hence, I offer for the Lord the firstborn male buds of a womb and all my firstborn sons I redeem. And it shall be a sign upon your arm and as frontlets between your eyes, because with a strong Arm did the Lord take us out of Egypt." (Exodus 13:11-16)

"The Lord is my guardian,
the Lord is my shade at my right hand." (Psalms 121:5) "the Lord will guard my departure and my arrival, for life and for peace, from this time and forever." (Psalms 121:2) God will bless me and give me mercy.

You should say the verse below while entering the temple, standing at the doorpost wearing the *Talit* and the *Tefilin*:

Abraham (Right)

אבגיתץ   chasdecha וַחַסְדְּךָ   אהיה י"פ   berov בְּרֹב   אני   va'ani וַאֲנִי

ב"פ ראה vetecha בֵּיתֶךָ   avo אָבוֹא

Isaac (Left)

ר"ת = יהוה ; אדני, ללה, hechal הֵיכַל   el אֶל־ ע"ב י"פ   eshtachave אֶשְׁתַּחֲוֶה

kodshecha קָדְשְׁךָ

Jacob (Central)

:beyir'atecha בְּיִרְאָתֶךָ

Then bow down and enter.

Right

imanu עִמָּנוּ   פני שכינה   Tzeva'ot צְבָאוֹת   Adonai יְהֹוָֹ אדני יאהדונהי

ריבוע ס"ג, קס"א ע"ה וד' אותיות, מהזע, ריבוע ע"ב וקס"א, אל שדי,   misgav מִשְׂגָּב־ משה,

ד"פ אלהים ע"ה ; ילה Elohei אֱלֹהֵי   אדני אהיה אלהים, מילוי ע"ב, דמב   lanu לָנוּ

:sela סֶלָה   אידהנויה   יאהדונהי   הויות,   י   Ya'akov יַעֲקֹב

Left

ashrei אַשְׁרֵי   שכינה   פני   Tzeva'ot צְבָאוֹת   Adonai יְהֹוָֹ אדני יאהדונהי

bote'ach בֹּטֵחַ   תפארת = אדם אשרי צבאות ה' ; מ"ה adam אָדָם

bach בָּךְ   מילוי ע"ב ע"ה: בך = בוטח (יאהדונהי) ע"ה ; אמן = בך בוטח אדם bach

Central

hamelech הַמֶּלֶךְ ר"ת יהה   יהוה וס"ע נהורין ויט"ע hoshi'a הוֹשִׁיעָה   Adonai יְהֹוָֹ אדני יאהדונהי

kor'enu קָרְאֵנוּ   אל יהוה זך, מזבזו, נגזר, ע"ה veyom בְּיוֹם   ya'anenu יַעֲנֵנוּ

ר"ת יב"ק, אלהים יהוה, אהיה אדני יהוה ; ס"ת = ב"ן ועם אות כי דהמלך = ע"ב:

VA'ANI
"And I, with the profusion of Your kindness,
come to Your House and bow towards Your Holy Ark, in awe of You." (Psalms 5:8)

"The Lord of Hosts, joyful is one who trusts in You." (Psalms 84:13)
"The Lord of Hosts is with us. The God of Jacob is a refuge for us, Selah.
Lord redeem us. The King shall answer us on the day we call Him." (Psalms 46:12)

SHACHARIT – MORNING PRAYER
PREPARATION OF THE VESSEL

ESH TAMID - MEDITATION TO CONTROL OUR THOUGHTS

Our brain is a receiver and there are two transmitting stations that send signals/thoughts to our brain. One source is the Light and the other is Satan. These verses disrupt and override any negative thoughts that might enter our minds.

Each verse is recited seven times:

אֵשׁ esh עה׳׳ קס׳׳א קנ׳׳א קמ׳׳ג tamid תָּמִיד tukad תּוּקַד al עַל־

הַמִּזְבֵּחַ hamizbe'ach נגד, זן, אל יהוה lo לֹא tichbe תִכְבֶּה:

Recite seven times

סְעַפִים se'afim שָׂנֵאתִי saneti וְתוֹרָתְךָ vetoratcha אָהָבְתִּי ahavti:

Recite seven times

לֵב lev טָהוֹר tahor י׳׳פ אכא בְּרָא־ bera

קנ׳׳א ב׳׳ן, יהוה אלהים יהוה אדני, מילוי קס׳׳א וס׳׳ג, מ׳׳ה ברבוע וע׳׳ב עה׳׳

לב טהור ברא = קס׳׳א קנ׳׳א קמ׳׳ג

לִי li אֱלֹהִים Elohim אהיה אדני ; ילה ; לי אלהים = ריבוע אדני

וְרוּחַ veru'ach נָכוֹן nachon חַדֵּשׁ chadesh י׳׳ב הויות, קס׳׳א קנ׳׳א בְּקִרְבִּי bekirbi עדיי:

Recite seven times

AYIN LAMED MEM

This three-letter combination of the 72 Names of God gives us control over unwanted thoughts such as worry, pessimism, and obsessive or compulsive ideas. Besides using this meditation in the morning prayers, we can use it throughout the day as needed.

You should meditate on the Holy Name:

עלם

This helps to control your thoughts.

ESH TAMID

"And the Eternal Fire shall burn upon the Altar and shall never extinguish." (Leviticus 6:6)
"I hate scattered thoughts but Your Torah, I love." (Psalms 119:113)
"Create for me a pure heart, God, and renew a correct spirit within me." (Psalms 51:12)

OLAM ASIYAH - יוד הה וו הה – אל אדני

THE MORNING PRAYER

You should be very careful not to speak, even a single word, during the prayers and meditations.

According to Kabbalah, there are three distinct energy forces that govern three specific times of the day: Right Column (Abraham): morning, Left Column (Isaac): afternoon, and Central Column (Jacob): evening. The prayers of *Shacharit* correspond to the Right Column (Abraham)—sharing, merciful, positive energy. Too often we awake in a bad mood, and this negative state of mind remains with us throughout the day. To counteract this negativity, we have the connection of *Shacharit*, which imbues us with the energy of happiness and vitality, motivating us to reveal Light throughout the day.

THE WORLD OF *ASIYAH* (ACTION)

From here ("Leshem Yichud") until "Baruch She'amar" (pg. 134) you are in the World of Asiyah.

THE FOUR WORLDS

Phase – בחינה	World – עולם	Sefira – ספירה	Element – יסוד	Organ	Body structure
One – א	Atzilut – אצילות	Chochmah – וזכמה	Fire – אש	Eyes	Bones
Two – ב	Beriah – בריאה	Binah – בינה	Water – מים	Ears	Tendons
Three – ג	Yetzirah – יצירה	Zeir Anpin – זעיר אנפין	Air – אויר	Nose	Flesh
Four – ד	Asiyah – עשיה	Malchut – מלכות	Earth – אדמה	Mouth	Skin

LESHEM YICHUD

לְשֵׁם leshem יְוזוד yichud קוּדְשָׁא kudsha בְּרִיךְ berich הוּא hu

וּשְׁכִינְתֵיהּ ush'chintei (יאהדונהי) בִּדְוזִילוּ bid'chilu וּרְוזִימוּ ur'chimu

(יאההויהה) ur'chimu וּרְוזִימוּ ud'chilu וּדְוזִילוּ (איההיוהה) לְיַוזְדָא leyachda

שֵׁם shem יוֹ"ד yud קֵי kei בְּוֹא"ו bevav קֵי kei בְּיִוזוּדָא beyichuda

שְׁלִים shelim (יהוה) בְּשֵׁם beshem כֹּל kol ילי יִשְׂרָאֵל Yisrael,

הִנֵּה hine אֲנַוְזנוּ anachnu בָּאִים ba'im לְהִתְפַּלֵל lehitpalel

תְּפִלַת tefilat שַׁוְזַרִית shacharit שֶׁתִּקֵן shetiken אַבְרָהָם Avraham וז"פ אל,

אָבִינוּ avinu עָלָיו alav

הַשָּׁלום hashalom עִם im כֹּל kol ילי הַמִּצְוֹת hamitzvot הַכְּלוּלות hakelulot

רי"ו ול"ב נתיבות הוזכמה, רמו"וז (אברים), עסמ"ב וט"ו אותיות פשוטות

THE MORNING PRAYER
THE WORLD OF *ASIYAH* (ACTION) - LESHEM YICHUD

For the sake of unification of The Holy Blessed One and His Shechinah, with fear and love and with love and fear, in order to unify the Name Yud-Kei and Vav-Kei in perfect unity, and in the name of Israel, we have hereby come to pray the Morning Prayer, established by Abraham, our forefather, may peace be upon him, with all its commandments,

בְּךָ ba   לְתַקֵּן letaken   אֶת et   שׁוֹרְשָׁהּ shorsha   בְּמָקוֹם bemakom

עֶלְיוֹן elyon   לַעֲשׂוֹת la'asot   נַחַת nachat   רוּחַ ru'ach   לְיוֹצְרֵנוּ leyotzrenu

וְלַעֲשׂוֹת vela'asot   רָצוֹן retzon מהש ע"ה, ע"ב ברבוע וקס"א ע"ה

בּוֹרְאֵינוּ bor'enu   וִיהִי vihi   נֹעַם no'am   אֲדֹנָי Adonai לכה

אֱלֹהֵינוּ elohenu ילה   עָלֵינוּ alenu   וּמַעֲשֵׂה uma'ase   יָדֵינוּ yadenu   כּוֹנְנָה konena

עָלֵינוּ alenu   וּמַעֲשֵׂה uma'ase   יָדֵינוּ yadenu   כּוֹנְנֵהוּ konenehu

A COMMITMENT FOR LOVE AND UNITY - ELEVATING OUR CONSCIOUSNESS

A thin, weak string cannot lift a treasure chest. However, when we weave together many thin strings, we form a rope. By uniting ourselves with the rest of the world through making a Commitment for Love, we can pull down the greatest spiritual treasures, even though we might not be worthy or strong enough to accomplish this individually.

Regarding the danger of deviation, the Kaf-Hachayim says: "In a place of deviation, the blessing removes itself, and people who had disagreements end up with damage and accidents to their bodies as well as their wealth. Those who care for themselves should stay away from any deviation."

The *Ari* writes in the Gate of Meditations: before you start your connections and prayers, you should accept within yourself the precept of "love your fellow as you do yourself." Meaning, you must meditate to love all people who are doing spiritual work as if they are part of your soul, so that your prayers will be included and elevated with the universal prayer and bring results. It is especially important to have love for the *Chaverim* (people who dedicate their lives to spiritual work) and to recognize that praying for others enables and allows our prayers to be accepted.

שֶׁל shel   עֲשֵׂה ase   מִצְוַת mitzvat   עָלַי alai   מְקַבֵּל mekabel   הֲרֵינִי hareni

וְאָהַבְתָּ ve'ahavta ב"פ אור, ב"פ רו, ב"פ א"ס   לְרֵעֲךָ lere'acha   כָּמוֹךָ kamocha

וְהֲרֵינִי vehareni   אוֹהֵב ohev   אֶת et   כָּל kol ילי   אֶחָד echad אהבה, דאגה

מִבְּנֵי mibenei   יִשְׂרָאֵל Yisrael   כְּנַפְשִׁי kenafshi   וּמְאוֹדִי ume'odi

וְהֲרֵינִי vehareni   מְזַמֵּן mezamen   פֶּה pe מילה; ע"ה, אלהים, אהיה אדני

שֶׁלִּי sheli   לְהִתְפַּלֵּל lehitpalel   לִפְנֵי lifnei   מֶלֶךְ melech   מַלְכֵי malchei

הַמְּלָכִים hamelachim   הַקָּדוֹשׁ hakadosh   בָּרוּךְ baruch   הוּא hu

---

to correct its root in the supernal place, to bring satisfaction to our Maker, and to fulfill the wish of our Creator. "And the pleasantness of the Lord, our God, be upon us and may He establish the work of our hands for us and may the work of our hands establish Him." (Psalms 90:17)

A COMMITMENT FOR LOVE - ELEVATING OUR CONSCIOUSNESS

I hereby accept upon myself the obligatory commandment of "Love your fellow as you do yourself." I hereby declare that I love each one of Israel with my soul and my strength. And I hereby prepare my mouth to pray before the King of all Kings, The Holy Blessed One.

THE BINDING OF ISAAC

By reciting this verse which describes Abraham binding Isaac, we connect to the power of mercy. Simultaneously, we bind our judgment as part of our internal cleansing, and we receive help to bind the negative thoughts of people who come against us in judgment.

Elohenu ילה אֱלֹהֵינוּ velohei ילה ; דמב , מילוי ע"ב ; לכב וֵאלֹהֵי avotenu אֲבוֹתֵינוּ

zochrenu זָכְרֵנוּ bezichron בְּזִכְרוֹן ע"ב קס"א וֹגֵּעָ"ב tov טוֹב והו

milfanecha מִלְפָנֶיךָ ס"ג מ"ה בֵ"ן ufokdenu וּפָקְדֵנוּ bifkudat בִּפְקֻדַּת

yeshu'a יְשׁוּעָה verachamim וְרַחֲמִים mishmei מִשְׁמֵי shemei שְׁמֵי

kedem ♦ קֶדֶם uzchor וּזְכָר lanu לָנוּ אלהִים, אֶהֱיֶה אֲדֹנָי (אֲדֹנָיאהֹדֹנִי) יְהֹוָה Adonai

Elohenu אֱלֹהֵינוּ ילה ahavat אַהֲבַת hakadmonim הַקַּדְמוֹנִים

Avraham אַבְרָהָם ו"פ אל, רי"ו ול"ב נתיבות החוכמה, רמ"ח (אברים), עסמ"ב וט"ז אותיות פשוטות

Yitzchak יִצְחָק ד"פ בֵּ"ן veYisrael וְיִשְׂרָאֵל avadecha ♦ עֲבָדֶיךָ

et אֵת haberit הַבְּרִית ve'et וְאֵת hachesed הַחֶסֶד ע"ב, ריבוע יהוה

ve'et וְאֵת hashevu'a הַשְׁבוּעָה shenishbata שֶׁנִשְׁבַּעְתָּ le'Avraham לְאַבְרָהָם

avinu אָבִינוּ ו"פ אל, רי"ו ול"ב נתיבות החוכמה, רמ"ח (אברים), עסמ"ב וט"ז אותיות פשוטות

behar בְּהַר haMoriya ♦ הַמוֹרִיָּה ve'et וְאֵת ha'akeda הָעֲקֵדָה

she'akad שֶׁעָקַד et אֵת Yitzchak יִצְחָק ד"פ בֵּ"ן beno בְּנוֹ al עַל gabei גַּבֵּי

hamizbe'ach הַמִּזְבֵּחַ נגד, ז, אל יהוה kakatuv כַּכָּתוּב betoratach בְּתוֹרָתֶךָ ‡

THE BINDING OF ISAAC

Our God and the God of our forefathers, remember us favorably before You, and evoke for us the remembrance of salvation and mercy, from the earliest and the highest Heavens. And remember, for our sake, Lord, our God, the love of the ancients: Your servants, Abraham, Isaac, and Israel. And remember, also the Covenant, the compassion, and the oath that You pledged to Abraham, our forefather, on Mount Moriah, when he bound his son, Isaac, upon the altar, as it is related in Your Torah:

OLAM ASIYAH - אל אדני – יוד הה וו הה

THE PORTION CONCERNING THE BINDING

Reciting the portion concerning the Binding of Isaac every day allows us to atone for all our sins and create a shield of protection against all sickness, which cancels death from humanity.

vay'hi וַיְהִי achar אַחַר hadevarim הַדְּבָרִים ha'ele הָאֵלֶּה

vehaElohim וְהָאֱלֹהִים nisa נִסָּה et אֶת־ Avraham אַבְרָהָם

vayomer וַיֹּאמֶר

elav אֵלָיו Avraham אַבְרָהָם

vayomer וַיֹּאמֶר hineni הִנֵּנִי vayomer וַיֹּאמֶר kach קַח־

na נָא et אֶת־ bincha בִּנְךָ et אֶת־ yechidcha יְחִידְךָ asher אֲשֶׁר־

ahavta אָהַבְתָּ et אֶת־ Yitzchak יִצְחָק velech וְלֶךְ־ lecha לְךָ

el אֶל־ eretz אֶרֶץ haMoriya הַמֹּרִיָּה veha'alehu וְהַעֲלֵהוּ sham שָׁם

le'ola לְעֹלָה al עַל achad אַחַד heharim הֶהָרִים asher אֲשֶׁר

omar אֹמַר elecha אֵלֶיךָ vayashkem וַיַּשְׁכֵּם Avraham אַבְרָהָם

baboker בַּבֹּקֶר

vayachavosh וַיַּחֲבֹשׁ et אֶת־ chamoro חֲמֹרוֹ vayikach וַיִּקַּח et אֶת־

shenei שְׁנֵי ne'arav נְעָרָיו ito אִתּוֹ ve'et וְאֵת Yitzchak יִצְחָק beno בְּנוֹ

vayevaka וַיְבַקַּע atzei עֲצֵי ola עֹלָה vayakom וַיָּקָם vayelech וַיֵּלֶךְ

el אֶל־ hamakom הַמָּקוֹם asher אֲשֶׁר־ amar אָמַר lo לוֹ

haElohim הָאֱלֹהִים bayom בַּיּוֹם

hashelishi הַשְּׁלִישִׁי vayisa וַיִּשָּׂא Avraham אַבְרָהָם

enav עֵינָיו et אֶת־

vayar וַיַּרְא et אֶת־ hamakom הַמָּקוֹם merachok מֵרָחֹק

THE PORTION CONCERNING THE BINDING

"And it came to be that after those events, God tested Abraham and said to him: 'Abraham' and he replied: 'Here I am'. And He said: 'Please take your son, your only one, whom you love; Isaac, and go to the land of Moriah. Place him as a burnt-offering upon one of the mountains that I shall tell you.' And Abraham rose early in the morning, saddled his donkey, and took two lads with him, together with his son, Isaac. Abraham split wood for the offering then got up and went towards the place of which God told him. On the third day, Abraham lifted his eyes and saw the place from afar.

וַיֹּאמֶר vayomer אַבְרָהָם avraham וו"פ אל, רי"ו ול"ב נתיבות החכמה, רמ"ח (אברים),

אֶל el נְעָרָיו ne'arav שְׁבוּ shevu לָכֶם lachem פֹּה po עסמ"ב וט"ז אותיות פשוטות

עִם im הַחֲמוֹר hachamor מילה (להכניע הקליפות בסוד החמור) ; ע"ה אלהים, אהיה אדני

וַאֲנִי va'ani אני וְהַנַּעַר vehana'ar נֵלְכָה nelcha עַד ad כֹּה ko

וְנִשְׁתַּחֲוֶה venishtachave וְנָשׁוּבָה venashuva אֲלֵיכֶם aleichem וַיִּקַּח vayikach

וַיִּקַּח Avraham אַבְרָהָם וו"פ אל, רי"ו ול"ב נתיבות החכמה, רמ"ח (אברים), עסמ"ב וט"ז אותיות פשוטות

אֶת et עֲצֵי atzei הָעֹלָה ha'ola וַיָּשֶׂם vayasem עַל al יִצְחָק Yitzchak ד"פ ב"ן

בְּנוֹ beno וַיִּקַּח vayikach וועם בְּיָדוֹ beyado אֶת et הָאֵשׁ ha'esh שאה בְּנוֹ beno

וְאֶת ve'et הַמַּאֲכֶלֶת hama'achelet וַיֵּלְכוּ vayelchu שְׁנֵיהֶם sheneihem

יַחְדָּו yachdav וַיֹּאמֶר vayomer יִצְחָק Yitzchak ד"פ ב"ן אֶל el

אַבְרָהָם Avraham וו"פ אל, רי"ו ול"ב נתיבות החכמה, רמ"ח (אברים), עסמ"ב וט"ז אותיות פשוטות

אָבִיו aviv וַיֹּאמֶר vayomer אָבִי avi וַיֹּאמֶר vayomer הִנֶּנִּי hineni בְּנִי veni

וַיֹּאמֶר vayomer הִנֵּה hine הָאֵשׁ ha'esh שאה וְהָעֵצִים veha'etzim וְאַיֵּה ve'aye

הַשֶּׂה hase לְעֹלָה le'ola וַיֹּאמֶר vayomer אַבְרָהָם Avraham וו"פ אל, רי"ו ול"ב

אֱלֹהִים Elohim אהיה אדני ; ילה נתיבות החכמה, רמ"ח (אברים), עסמ"ב וט"ז אותיות פשוטות

יִרְאֶה yir'eh רי"ו לּוֹ lo הַשֶּׂה hase לְעֹלָה le'ola בְּנִי beni ר"ת הבל (למתק או"וז

וַיֵּלְכוּ vayelchu שְׁנֵיהֶם sheneihem יַחְדָּו yachdav ע"מ לתקן עון הבל שהוטא בראיה)

וַיָּבֹאוּ vayavo'u אֶל el הַמָּקוֹם hamakom אֲשֶׁר asher אָמַר amar לּוֹ lo

הָאֱלֹהִים haElohim אהיה אדני ; ילה וַיִּבֶן vayiven שָׁם sham אַבְרָהָם Avraham

אֶת et וו"פ אל, רי"ו ול"ב נתיבות החכמה, רמ"ח (אברים), עסמ"ב וט"ז אותיות פשוטות

הַמִּזְבֵּחַ hamizbe'ach נגד, זן, אל יהוה וְאֶת et הָעֵצִים ha'etzim וַיַּעֲרֹךְ vaya'aroch

וַיַּעֲקֹד vaya'akod אֶת et יִצְחָק Yitzchak ד"פ ב"ן בְּנוֹ beno וַיָּשֶׂם vayasem

---

And Abraham said to his lads: Stay here with the donkey, while I and my son go until there, where we shall prostrate ourselves then return to you. And Abraham took the wood for the burnt-offering and placed it upon Isaac, his son. He took in his hand the fire and the knife as they went together. And Isaac said to his father: 'My father.' and he said: 'Here I am, my son.' And Isaac said: 'Behold the fire and the wood, but where is the lamb for the burnt-offering?' And Abraham said: 'God shall show the lamb for the burnt-offering, my son.' And they went together. And they came to the place God showed him, There, Abraham built an Altar and arranged the wood. He bound his son, Isaac, and placed

עלם mima'al מִבְּעַל אל יהוה, זן, נגד, al הַמִּזְבֵּחַ hamizbe'ach עַל־ oto אֹתוֹ

נתיבות ר"ב ול רי"ו אל, וז"פ Avraham אַבְרָהָם vayishlach וַיִּשְׁלַח la'etzim לַעֵצִים

וחעם vayikach וַיִּקַּח yado יָדוֹ et אֶת־ אותיות פשוטות ט"ו עסמ"ב (אברים), רמ"ח החכמה,

beno בְּנוֹ et אֶת־ lishchot לִשְׁחֹט hama'achelet הַמַּאֲכֶלֶת et אֶת־

mal'ach מַלְאָךְ elav אֵלָיו ב"פ קס"א = אותיות ה' עם vayikra וַיִּקְרָא

ר"ת מ"ה ; כוזו י"פ טל, י"פ hashamayim הַשָּׁמַיִם min מִן־ Adonai ואדונהיאהדונהי יְהֹוָה

(אברים), רמ"ח החכמה נתיבות ול"ב רי"ו אל, וז"פ | Avraham אַבְרָהָם vayomer וַיֹּאמֶר

(אברים), רמ"ח החכמה, נתיבות ול"ב רי"ו אל, וז"פ Avraham אַבְרָהָם פשוטות אותיות ט"ז עסמ"ב

al אַל־ vayomer וַיֹּאמֶר hineni הִנֵּנִי vayomer וַיֹּאמֶר פשוטות אותיות ט"ז עסמ"ב

ta'as תַּעַשׂ ve'al וְאַל־ hana'ar הַנַּעַר el אֶל־ yadcha יָדְךָ tishlach תִּשְׁלַח

yere יָרֵא ki כִּי־ yadati יָדַעְתִּי ata עַתָּה | ki כִּי me'uma מְאוּמָה lo לוֹ

et אֶת־ chasachta חָשַׂכְתָּ velo וְלֹא Ata אַתָּה אהיה אדני ; ילה Elohim אֱלֹהִים

vayisa וַיִּשָּׂא mimeni מִמֶּנִּי yechidcha יְחִידְךָ et אֶת־ bincha בִּנְךָ

פשוטות אותיות ט"ו עסמ"ב (אברים), רמ"ח החכמה, נתיבות ול"ב רי"ו אל, וז"פ Avraham אַבְרָהָם

achar אַחַר ayil אַיִל vehine וְהִנֵּה vayar וַיַּרְא רביע מ"ה enav עֵינָיו et אֶת־

בקרניו בסבך נאחז כשאומר bekarnav בְּקַרְנָיו basevach בַּסְּבַךְ ne'echaz נֶאֱחַז

יצחק. שישחוט כדי האיל, מרוזיו היה העגל קיטרוג בעבור והשטן, עגל הם סבך שאומר לתיבות יכוין
העטן את הכניע הקטורת) סממני (= עס"ח = בקרניו נאחז אוזר (= נגנא איל, הנה (= ומיכאל

החכמה, נתיבות ול"ב רי"ו אל, וז"פ Avraham אַבְרָהָם כלי vayelech וַיֵּלֶךְ

et אֶת־ וחעם vayikach וַיִּקַּח פשוטות אותיות ט"ז עסמ"ב (אברים), רמ"ח

beno בְּנוֹ tachat תַּחַת le'ola לְעֹלָה vaya'alehu וַיַּעֲלֵהוּ ha'ayil הָאַיִל

נתיבות ול"ב רי"ו אל, וז"פ Avraham אַבְרָהָם ב"פ קס"א = אותיות ה' עם vayikra וַיִּקְרָא

hamakom הַמָּקוֹם shem שֵׁם־ פשוטות אותיות ט"ז עסמ"ב (אברים), רמ"ח החכמה, הוזכמה

---

him upon the altar, on top of the wood. And Abraham reached out with his hand and took the knife to slaughter his son. The Angel of the Lord called to him from the Heavens and said: 'Abraham, Abraham.' And he said: 'Here I am.' And He said: 'Do not send your hand forth against the lad and do not do anything to him, for I now know that you fear God and you did not withhold your son from Me.' And Abraham lifted his eyes and saw and beheld a ram, entangled in a bush by his horns. Abraham went forth and took the ram; he burnt it as an offering, instead of his son. And Abraham called the name of this place

הַהוּא hahu יְהֹוָה Adonai | יִרְאֶה yir'e רי"ו אֲשֶׁר asher

יֹאמֵר ye'amer הַיּוֹם hayom ע"ה נגד, מזבח, זז, אל יהוה בְּהַר behar

יְהֹוָה Adonai יֵרָאֶה yera'e רי"ז וַיִּקְרָא vayikra עם ה' אותיות = ב"פ קס"א min מִן

מַלְאַךְ mal'ach יְהֹוָה Adonai אֶל el אַבְרָהָם Avraham וז"פ אל,

שֵׁנִית shenit רי"ו ול"ב נתיבות הוחכמה, רמ"ח (אברים), עסמ"ב וט"ז אותיות פשוטות

הַשָּׁמַיִם hashamayim י"פ טל, י"פ כוזו ; ר"ת מ"ה: וַיֹּאמֶר vayomer בִּי bi

נִשְׁבַּעְתִּי nishbati נְאֻם־ ne'um יְהֹוָה Adonai כִּי ki יַעַן ya'an

אֲשֶׁר asher עָשִׂיתָ asita אֶת־ et הַדָּבָר hadavar ראה הֲזֶּה haze והו וְלֹא velo

כִּי ki חָשַׂכְתָּ chasachta אֶת־ et בִּנְךָ bincha אֶת־ et יְחִידֶךָ: yechidecha

בָּרֵךְ varech אֲבָרֶכְךָ avarechecha וְהַרְבָּה veharba אַרְבֶּה arbe יצחק, ד"פ ב"ן

אֶת־ et זַרְעֲךָ zar'acha כְּכוֹכְבֵי kechochvei הַשָּׁמַיִם hashamayim י"פ טל, י"פ כוזו

וְכַחוֹל vechachol אֲשֶׁר asher עַל־ al שְׂפַת sefat הַיָּם hayam ילי

וְיִרַשׁ veyirash זַרְעֲךָ zar'acha אֵת et שַׁעַר sha'ar אֹיְבָיו: oyvav

וְהִתְבָּרְכוּ vehitbarchu יהוה ריבוע יהוה ריבוע מ"ה בְּזַרְעֲךָ vezaracha

כֹּל kol ילי גּוֹיֵי goyei הָאָרֶץ ha'aretz ע"ה דההין אלהים עֵקֶב ekev ב"פ מום

אֲשֶׁר asher שָׁמַעְתָּ shamata בְּקוֹלִי: bekoli וַיָּשָׁב vayashov

אַבְרָהָם Avraham וז"פ אל, רי"ו ול"ב נתיבות הוחכמה, רמ"ח (אברים), עסמ"ב וט"ז אותיות פשוטות

אֶל־ el נְעָרָיו ne'arav וַיָּקֻמוּ vayakumu וַיֵּלְכוּ vayelchu יַחְדָּו yachdav

אֶל־ el בְּאֵר Be'er קנ"א ב"ן, יהוה אלהים יהוה אדני, מילוי קס"א וס"ג, מ"ה ברבוע וע"ב ע"ה

שֶׁבַע Shava וַיֵּשֶׁב vayeshev אַבְרָהָם Avraham וז"פ אל,

בִּבְאֵר biVe'er רי"ו ול"ב נתיבות הוחכמה, רמ"ח (אברים), עסמ"ב וט"ז אותיות פשוטות

שֶׁבַע: Shava קנ"א ב"ן, יהוה אלהים יהוה אדני, מילוי קס"א וס"ג מ"ה ברבוע וע"ב ע"ה

---

as: Lord shall see, when what is said on the Mount of the Lord shall be seen. Then the Angel of the Lord called to Abraham a second time from the Heavens, and said: 'I have sworn upon My Being, proclaimed the Lord, that since you have done this thing and you did not withhold your son, your only one, I shall surely bless you and I shall greatly multiply your seed, like the stars of the sky and the sand upon the seashore. Your seed shall inherit the gate of his enemies. All nations of the world shall be blessed by your seed, because you have listened to My Voice.' And Abraham returned to his lads. They got up and went to Be'er Sheva. And Abraham resided in Be'er Sheva." (Genesis 22:1-19)

SHACHARIT – MORNING PRAYER
OLAM ASIYAH - אל אדני – יוד הה וו הה

RIBONO SHEL OLAM

Light can never be revealed without a Vessel. *Ribono Shel Olam* helps us build our personal Vessel to draw all the Light that Abraham generated by virtue of his actions.

רִבּוֹנוֹ ribono שֶׁל shel עוֹלָם olam• כְּמוֹ kemo שֶׁכָּבַשׁ shekavash

אַבְרָהָם Avraham וֹ"פ אל, רי"ו ול"ב נתיבות הוחכמה, רמ"זז (אברים), עסמ"ב וט"ז אותיות פשוטות

אָבִינוּ avinu אֶת et רַחֲמָיו rachamav לַעֲשׂוֹת la'asot רְצוֹנְךָ retzoncha

בְּלֵבָב belevav בוכו שָׁלֵם shalem• כֵּן ken יִכְבְּשׁוּ yichbeshu

רַחֲמֶיךָ rachamecha אֶת et כַּעַסְךָ ka'asecha• וְיִגוֹלוּ veyigolu

רַחֲמֶיךָ rachamecha עַל al מִדּוֹתֶיךָ midotecha• וְתִתְנַהֵג vetitnaheg

עִמָּנוּ imanu אֲדֹנִיאהדונהי Adonai ריבוע דס"ג, קס"א ע"ה וד' אותיות יְהֹוָאדנייאהדונהי אֱלֹהֵינוּ Elohenu

יֵלה בְּמִדַּת uvmidat ריבוע יהוה ע"ב, הַחֶסֶד hachesed בְּמִדַּת bemidat

הָרַחֲמִים harachamim• וְתִכָּנֵס vetikanes לָנוּ lanu אלהים, אהיה אדני

לִפְנִים lifnim לאו מִשּׁוּרַת mishurat הַדִּין hadin• וּבְטוּבְךָ uvtuvcha

הַגָּדוֹל hagadol להוו ; עם ד' אותיות = מבה, יזל, אום יָשׁוּב yashuv וְזָרוֹן charon

אַפְּךָ apach מֵעַמָּךְ me'amach וּמֵעִירָךְ ume'irach וּמֵאַרְצָךְ ume'artzach

וּמִנַּחֲלָתָךְ uminachalatach• וְקַיֵּם vekayem לָנוּ lanu אלהים, אהיה אדני

יְהֹוָאדנייאהדונהי Adonai יֵלה אֱלֹהֵינוּ Elohenu אֶת et הַדָּבָר hadavar ראה

שֶׁהִבְטַחְתָּנוּ shehivtachtanu בְּתוֹרָתָךְ betoratach עַל al יְדֵי yedei

מֹשֶׁה Moshe מהוע, ע"ב בריבוע וקס"א, אל שדי, ד"פ אלהים ע"ה עַבְדָּךְ avdach פוי, אל אדני

כָּאמוּר ka'amur: וְזָכַרְתִּי vezacharti אֶת־ et בְּרִיתִי beriti

יַעֲקוֹב Yaakov יי הויות, יאהדונהי אידהנויה Adonai וְאַף ve'af אֶת־ et בְּרִיתִי beriti

---

RIBONO SHEL OLAM

Master of the Universe, just as Abraham, our father, suppressed his compassion to wholeheartedly fulfill Your will, so may Your compassion suppress Your wrath and may Your compassion reveal itself above Your other attributes. Behave with us, Lord, our God, according to the attributes of kindness and of compassion; for our sake, act towards us from beyond the framework of strict judgment. By Your great benevolence, Your anger shall be retracted from Your Nation, Your City, Your Land, and Your Heritage. Fulfill for us, Lord, our God, what You have promised to us in Your Torah, through Moses, Your servant, as it states: "I shall remember My Covenant with Jacob and My Covenant

בְּרִיתִי beriti אֶת־ et וְאַף ve'af בּ"ן ד"פ יִצְחָק Yitzchak

אַבְרָהָם Avraham וו"פ אל, רי"ו ול"ב נתיבות הוחכמה, רמ"ח (אברים), עסמ"ב וט"ז אותיות פשוטות

אֶזְכֹּר ezkor וְהָאָרֶץ veha'aretz אלהים דההין ע"ה אֶזְכֹּר ezkor וְנֶאֱמַר: vene'emar

וְאַף־ ve'af גַּם־ gam זֹאת zot בִּהְיוֹתָם bihyotam בְּאֶרֶץ be'eretz

אֹיְבֵיהֶם oyvehem לֹא־ lo מְאַסְתִּים me'astim וְלֹא־ velo גְעַלְתִּים ge'altim

לְכַלֹּתָם lechalotam לְהָפֵר lehafer בְּרִיתִי beriti אִתָּם itam כִּי kiי אֲנִי ani אני

וְזָכַרְתִּי vezacharti יל"ה אֱלֹהֵיהֶם Elohehem יְהֹוָה Adonai

לָהֶם lahem בְּרִית berit רִאשֹׁנִים rishonim אֲשֶׁר asher הוֹצֵאתִי hotzeti

אֹתָם otam מֵאֶרֶץ me'eretz מִצְרַיִם Mitzrayim מצר לְעֵינֵי le'enei ריבוע מ"ה

הַגּוֹיִם hagoyim לִהְיוֹת lih'yot לָהֶם lahem לֵאלֹהִים lelohim אהיה אדני ; יל"ה

אֲנִי ani אני יְהֹוָה Adonai וְנֶאֱמַר: vene'emar וְשָׁב veshav

יְהֹוָה Adonai אֱלֹהֶיךָ Elohecha יל"ה אֶת־ et שְׁבוּתְךָ shevutcha

וְרִחֲמֶךָ verichamecha וְשָׁב veshav וְקִבֶּצְךָ vekibetzcha מִכָּל־ mikol ילי

הָעַמִּים ha'amim אֲשֶׁר asher הֱפִיצְךָ hefitz'cha יְהֹוָה Adonai

אֱלֹהֶיךָ Elohecha יל"ה שָׁמָּה shama: אִם־ im מ"א אותיות דפשוטות, יוהך,

הַשָּׁמַיִם hashamayim יל"פ טל, י"פ כוזו יִהְיֶה yihye דאהיה ע"ה נִדַּחֲךָ nidachacha יײ בִּקְצֵה biktze דמילוי ודמילוי דמילוי

אֱלֹהֶיךָ Elohecha יל"ה מִשָּׁם misham יְקַבֶּצְךָ yekabetzcha

יְהֹוָה Adonai אֱלֹהֶיךָ Elohecha יל"ה וּמִשָּׁם umisham

יִקָּחֶךָ: yikachecha וֶהֱבִיאֲךָ vehevi'acha יְהֹוָה Adonai

אֱלֹהֶיךָ Elohecha יל"ה אֶל־ el הָאָרֶץ ha'aretz אלהים דההין ע"ה אֲשֶׁר־ asher

---

*with Isaac and even My Covenant with Abraham, I shall remember, and also the Land, I shall remember."
(Leviticus 26:42) And as it also states: "And despite Israel's inequities, when they were to be in
the land of their enemies, I did not despise them nor loathe them such as to destroy them and nullify
My Covenant with them, because I am the Lord, their God. And for their sake, I shall remember
the covenant of the first generation that I had brought out of the land of Egypt for the nations to behold,
in order to be God unto them. I am the Lord." (Leviticus 26:44-45) And as it also states:
"And the Lord shall bring you back from captivity and shall have mercy upon you. And He shall
again gather you from among all nations where the Lord, your God, had dispersed you.
If you have been forsaken at the end of the Heavens, then from there the Lord, your God, shall gather
you and, from there, He shall fetch you. And the Lord, your God, shall lead you to the Land which*

yarshu יִרְשׁוּ   avotecha אֲבֹתֶיךָ   virishta וִירִשְׁתָּהּ   vehetivcha וְהֵיטִבְךָ

vehirbecha וְהִרְבְּךָ   me'avotecha מֵאֲבֹתֶיךָ:   vene'emar וְנֶאֱמַר   al עַל

yedei יְדֵי   nevi'echa נְבִיאֶךָ:   Adonai יְהֹוָהאדנייאהדונהי   chonenu וְחָנֵּנוּ

lecha לְךָ   kivinu קִוִּינוּ   heye הֱיֵה יהה   zero'am זְרֹעָם   labekarim לַבְּקָרִים

af אַף־ (reference to the "Ten martyrs of the kingdom")   yeshu'atenu יְשׁוּעָתֵנוּ

be'et בְּעֵת   tzara צָרָה   אלהים דההין.   vene'emar וְנֶאֱמַר: ve'et וְעֵת־

tzara צָרָה   אלהים דההין   hee הִיא   leYaakov לְיַעֲקֹב   הויות, יאהדונהי אידהנויה

umimena וּמִמֶּנָּה   yivashe'a יִוָּשֵׁעַ.   vene'emar וְנֶאֱמַר: bechol בְּכָל־ ב"ן, לבב

tzaratam צָרָתָם | lo לֹו (לא :כתיב)   tzar צָר   umal'ach וּמַלְאַךְ

panav פָּנָיו   hoshi'am הוֹשִׁיעָם   be'ahavato בְּאַהֲבָתוֹ   uvchemlato וּבְחֶמְלָתוֹ

hu הוּא   ge'alam גְּאָלָם   vaynatlem וַיְנַטְּלֵם   vaynas'em וַיְנַשְּׂאֵם

kol כָּל־   יְלי   yemei יְמֵי   olam עוֹלָם.   vene'emar וְנֶאֱמַר:

THE THIRTEEN ATTRIBUTES

The *Thirteen Attributes* are 13 virtues or properties that reflect the 13 different aspects of our daily relationship with the Creator. They work like a mirror. If we perform a negative action in our world, the mirror reflects this negative energy back onto us. As we attempt to transform our reactive nature into a proactive one, this direct feedback from the world of *Yetzirah* helps to guide and correct us. The number 13 also represents "one above the 12 signs of the zodiac." The 12 astrological signs dictate our instinctive, reactive behaviors. The number 13 gives us control over the 12 signs, thus giving us control over our reactive nature.

An astrological chart is best understood as a DNA blueprint of a person's soul, revealing what the person came into this world to do, and what he or she needs to correct and transform in this lifetime. We are supposed to use the positive aspects of our astrological sign to overcome and transform all the negative aspects imbued in our inner character. It is important to understand that our personal astrological profile is not the *cause* of our nature; it is the *effect*. We are handed a particular DNA blueprint based on our past-life track record. This past-life behavior—and the subsequent spiritual credits and debits that it produced—dictated the time and sign under which we were born. Astrology is merely the mechanism by which we acquire the required traits necessary for our inner growth and change.

---

your forefathers have inherited, and you shall inherit it. He shall benefit you and multiply your numbers over that of your forefathers." (Deuteronomy 30:3-5) And it is also said, through Your prophets: "Lord, be gracious to us, for we have hoped for You. Be their strong Arm in the mornings and also our salvation in times of trouble." (Isaiah 33:2) And as it is said: "It is a time of trouble for Jacob, but he shall be saved from it." (Jeremiah 30:7) Also: "God was distressed by their distress, so the angels that are before Him, redeemed them. With His love and His compassion, He had saved them. He took them and carried them throughout eternity." (Isaiah 33:9) And it is said:

(1) אל   מִי mi   אֵל El יל־י   (מילוי) דס״ג   כָּמוֹךָ kamocha

(2) רחום   נֹשֵׂא nose עָוֹן avon

(3) וחנון   וְעֹבֵר ve'over עַל־ al פֶּשַׁע pesha

(4) ארך   לִשְׁאֵרִית lish'erit נַחֲלָתוֹ nachalato

(5) אפים   לֹא־ lo הֶחֱזִיק hechezik לָעַד la'ad בּ״ן פ״פ אַפּוֹ apo

(6) ורב וחסד   כִּי־ ki חָפֵץ chafetz חֶסֶד chesed ע״ב, ריבוע יהוה הוּא hu

(7) ואמת   יָשׁוּב yashuv יְרַחֲמֵנוּ yerachamenu

(8) נצר וחסד   יִכְבֹּשׁ yichbosh עֲוֹנֹתֵינוּ avonotenu

(9) לאלפים   וְתַשְׁלִיךְ vetashlich בִּמְצֻלוֹת bimtzulot

   יָם yam יל־י כָּל־ kol יל־י חַטֹּאותָם chatotam

(10) נשׂא עון   תִּתֵּן titen אֱמֶת emet ב״פ כהת אהיה פעמים אהיה, ז״פ ס״ג לְיַעֲקֹב leYaakov ז הויות, יאהדונהי אידהנויה (וחיבור ז׳׳א ומלכות)

(11) ופשע   חֶסֶד chesed ע״ב, ריבוע יהוה לְאַבְרָהָם leAvraham ח״פ אל, רי״ו ול״ב נתיבות החכמה, רמ״ח (אברים), עסמ״ב וט״ז אותיות פשוטות

(12) וחטאה   אֲשֶׁר asher נִשְׁבַּעְתָּ nishbata לַאֲבֹתֵינוּ la'avotenu

(13) ונקה   מִימֵי mimei קֶדֶם kedem

THE THIRTEEN ATTRIBUTES

"1) Who is a God like You? 2) Who bears iniquity. 3) And overlooks sin. 4) For the remnant of His heritage. 5) He did not retain His anger forever. 6) For He desires kindness. 7) He shall again have mercy over us. 8) And suppress our iniquities. 9) You shall cast into the depths of the sea all their sins. 10) You grant truth to Jacob. 11) and kindness to Abraham. 12) As You have vowed to our forefathers. 13) From the earliest days." (Micah 7:18-20)

OLAM ASIYAH - יוד הה וו הה – אל אדני

har הַר el אֵל vahavi'otim וַהֲבִיאוֹתִים vene'emar וְנֶאֱמַר

בְּ"פ ראה kodshi קָדְשִׁי vesimachtim וְשִׂמַּחְתִּים bevet בְּבֵית

leratzon לְרָצוֹן vezivchehem וְזִבְחֵיהֶם olotehem עוֹלֹתֵיהֶם tefilati תְּפִלָּתִי

ki כִּי mizbechi מִזְבְּחִי al עַל

veti בֵיתִי tefila תְּפִלָּה bet בֵּית

ha'amim הָעַמִּים lechol לְכָל yikare יִקָּרֵא

ELU DEVARIM

shi'ur שִׁעוּר lahem לָהֶם she'en שְׁאֵין devarim דְּבָרִים elu אֵלּוּ

ugmilut וּגְמִילוּת vehare'ayon וְהָרֵאָיוֹן vehabikurim וְהַבִּכּוּרִים hape'a הַפֵּאָה

elu אֵלּוּ torah תּוֹרָה vetalmud וְתַלְמוּד chasadim חֲסָדִים vezasim וְזֶהָ

otam אוֹתָם ose עוֹשֶׂה she'adam שֶׁאָדָם devarim דְּבָרִים

haze הַזֶּה ba'olam בָּעוֹלָם miperotehem מִפֵּירוֹתֵיהֶם ochel אוֹכֵל

le'olam לְעוֹלָם lo לוֹ kayemet קַיֶּמֶת vehakeren וְהַקֶּרֶן

va'em וָאֵם av אָב kibud כִּבּוּד hen הֵן ve'elu וְאֵלּוּ haba הַבָּא

cholim חוֹלִים uvikur וּבִקּוּר chasadim חֲסָדִים ugmilut וּגְמִילוּת

vehashkamat וְהַשְׁכָּמַת orchim אוֹרְחִים vehachnasat וְהַכְנָסַת

ben בֵּין shalom שָׁלוֹם vahava'at וַהֲבָאַת hakeneset הַכְנֶסֶת bet בֵּית

le'ishto לְאִשְׁתּוֹ ish אִישׁ uven וּבֵין lachavero לַחֲבֵירוֹ adam אָדָם

kulam כֻּלָּם keneged כְּנֶגֶד torah תּוֹרָה vetalmud וְתַלְמוּד

And it is also said: "I have brought them to My holy Mountain and have rejoiced them in My House of Prayer. Their burnt-offerings and their sacrifices shall be accepted upon My Altar, for My House shall be called: 'My House of Prayer' for all nations." (Isaiah 56:7)

ELU DEVARIM

"The following items have no set measure: the corner of the field, the first fruit, the viewing-offering, giving kindness, and the study of Torah. The following things one person can do and benefit from their fruit, both in this world and, as the capital remains intact for him, in the World to Come. And these are: Honoring the father and mother, Bestowing kindness, Visiting the sick, Showing hospitality to guests, Arriving early at the synagogue, Bringing peace between man and his fellow and between man and his wife, and the study of Torah is equivalent to them all." (Pe'ah Ch.1:1, Shabbat 127a)

OLAM ASIYAH - יוד ה"ה וו ה"ה – אל אדנ"י

LE'OLAM YEHE ADAM

It is important to maintain a sense of awe of the Creator and to have a healthy fear of disconnecting from the Light by behaving dishonestly, whether we are alone or among others. Awe helps us realize that it is our opponent—*Satan*—who is attempting to control our behavior, and not our true nature.

le'olam לְעוֹלָם ריבוע דס"ג ו"י אותיות דס"ג yehe יְהֵא adam אָדָם yere יְרֵא

shamayim שָׁמַיִם י"פ טל, י"פ כוזו ב"ף מצר baseter בַּסֵּתֶר kevagalui כְּבַגָּלוּי◆

umode וּמוֹדֶה עַל al הָאֱמֶת ha'emet אהיה פעמים אהיה, ז"פ ס"ג◆

vedover וְדוֹבֵר emet אֱמֶת אהיה פעמים אהיה, ז"פ ס"ג bilvavo בִּלְבָבוֹ◆

veyashkim וְיַשְׁכִּים veyomar וְיֹאמַר: ribon רִבּוֹן יהוה ע"ב ס"ג מ"ה ב"ן

ha'olamim הָעוֹלָמִים va'adonei וַאֲדוֹנֵי ha'adonim הָאֲדוֹנִים◆ lo לֹא al עַל

tzidkotenu צִדְקוֹתֵינוּ anachnu אֲנַחְנוּ mapilim מַפִּילִים tachanunenu תַחֲנוּנֵינוּ

lefanecha לְפָנֶיךָ ס"ג מ"ה ב"ן ki כִּי al עַל rachamecha רַחֲמֶיךָ harabim הָרַבִּים:

Adonai | אֲדֹנָי ללה shema'a שְׁמָעָה ללה Adonai | אֲדֹנָי selacha סְלָחָה

Adonai אֲדֹנָי ללה hakshiva הַקְשִׁיבָה va'ase וַעֲשֵׂה al אַל te'achar תְּאַחַר

lema'ancha לְמַעַנְךָ Elohai אֱלֹהַי מילוי ע"ב, דמב ; ילה ki כִּי shimcha שִׁמְךָ

nikra נִקְרָא al עַל ircha עִירְךָ ve'al וְעַל amecha עַמֶּךָ: ma מַה מ"ה

anachnu אֲנַחְנוּ ma מַה מ"ה chayenu וְחַיֵּינוּ◆ ma מַה מ"ה chasdenu וְחַסְדֵּנוּ

ma מַה מ"ה tzidkotenu צִדְקוֹתֵינוּ◆ ma מַה מ"ה kochenu כּוֹחֵנוּ ma מַה מ"ה

gevuratenu גְּבוּרָתֵנוּ◆ ma מַה מ"ה nomar נֹאמַר lefanecha לְפָנֶיךָ ס"ג מ"ה ב"ן

Adonai יְהוָֹהאהדונהי velohei וֵאלֹהֵי ילה ; מילוי ע"ב, דמב ; ילה Elohenu אֱלֹהֵינוּ ילה לכב

avotenu אֲבוֹתֵינוּ halo הֲלֹא kol כָּל ילי hagiborim הַגִּבּוֹרִים ke'ayin כְּאַיִן

lefanecha לְפָנֶיךָ ס"ג מ"ה ב"ן ve'anshei וְאַנְשֵׁי◆ hashem הַשֵּׁם kelo כְּלֹא hayu הָיוּ◆

LE'OLAM YEHE ADAM

You should always have fear of the Heavens in private and in public and should admit to truth and speak truth in your heart. You should rise early and say: Ruler of the worlds, Master of all Masters, "do not present our pleas before You because of our righteousness but because of Your abundant compassion. Lord, hear us. Lord, forgive us. Lord, listen and act and do not delay. My God, do so for Your sake, for Your Name is invoked upon Your City and upon Your Nation." (Daniel 9:18-19) What is our worth and to what avail are our lives, our righteousness, our strength, and our valor? What can we say before You, Lord, our God and the God of our forefathers? All the powerful ones are as nothing before You. Those men of fame are now as if they had never existed.

וְהַחֲכָמִים vachachamim   מַדָּע mada   כִּבְלִי kivli   וּנְבוֹנִים unvonim

כִּבְלִי kivli   הַשְׂכֵּל haskel   כִּי ki   כָּל chol   מַעֲשֵׂינוּ ma'asenu

תֹהוּ tohu   וִימֵי vimei   וְחַיֵּינוּ chayenu   הֶבֶל hevel

לְפָנֶיךָ lefanecha   וּמוֹתַר umotar   הָאָדָם ha'adam   מִן min

הַבְּהֵמָה habehema   אַיִן ayin   כִּי ki   הַכֹּל hakol   הֶבֶל havel

LEVAD HANESHAMAH (EXEPT FOR THAT PURE SOUL)

The only thing of genuine value and importance is our soul, for the soul is an actual part of God. If we make the mistake of forgetting that everyone around us is also part of the Creator, we immediately disconnect ourselves from the Light. *Levad HeNeshamah* helps us value and appreciate the godliness in all creatures and respect the spiritual essence of our world.

לְבַד levad   הַנְּשָׁמָה haneshamah   הַטְּהוֹרָה hatehora   שֶׁהִיא shehi

עֲתִידָה atida   לִתֵּן liten   דִּין din   וְחֶשְׁבּוֹן vecheshbon   לִפְנֵי lifnei   כִּסֵּא chise

כְּבוֹדֶךָ chevodecha   וְכָל vechol   הַגּוֹיִם hagoyim   כְּאַיִן ke'ayin

נֶגְדֶּךָ negdecha   שֶׁנֶּאֱמַר shene'emar   הֵן hen   גּוֹיִם goyim

כְּמַר kemar   מִדְּלִי midli   וּכְשַׁחַק uch'shachak   מֹאזְנַיִם moznayim

נֶחְשָׁבוּ nechshavu   הֵן hen   אִיִּים iyim   כַּדַּק kadak   יִטּוֹל yitol

AVAL

We are all descendants of Abraham, Isaac, and Jacob. These great biblical patriarchs came into this world and created a spiritual architecture with them as conduits, connecting with specific aspects of the Light, so that you and I and all the people of the world can tap into the same energy that they themselves embodied. It is because of the merit of these spiritual giants that we may now make the highest possible spiritual connections.

All the wise men are as if without any knowledge and all the sensible ones, as if without intelligence. All of our deeds are chaotic and the days of our lives arevain before You. (Tana Devei Rabbi Eliezar Ch. 21) And man is not superior to beasts, for all is vanity. (Ecclesiastes 3:19)

LEVAD HANESHAMAH
Except For that pure soul

that is destined to stand in judgment and be accountable before Your Throne of Glory. The nations are as nothing before You, as it is said: "Truly all nations are as a drop in a bucket and are considered as the dust upon the scales. He removes the lands as easily as dust." (Isaiah 40:15) benei בְּנֵי veritecha בְּרִיתֶךָ benei בְּנֵי amecha עַמְּךָ anachnu אֲנַחְנוּ aval אֲבָל

וֹ״פ אל, רי״ו ול״ב נְתיבות הַחכמה, רמ״ח (אברים), עסמ״ב וט״ז אותיות פשוטות Avraham אַבְרָהָם

behar בְּהַר lo לוֹ shenishbata שֶׁנִּשְׁבַּעְתָּ ohavecha אֹהַבְךָ

akedecha עֲקֵדֶךָ ד״פ ב״ן Yitzchak יִצְחָק zera זֶרַע ◆haMoriya הַמּוֹרִיָּה

אל יהוה זׁ, נגד hamizbe'ach הַמִּזְבֵּחַ gabei גַּבֵּי al עַל־ shene'ekad שֶׁנֶּעֱקַד

bincha בִּנְךָ אידהנויה יאהדונהי הויות, י Yaakov יַעֲקֹב adat עֲדַת

she'ahavta שֶׁאָהַבְתָּ sheme'ahavatcha שֶׁמֵּאַהֲבָתְךָ ◆vechorecha בְכוֹרֶךָ

bo בּוֹ shesamachta שֶׁשָּׂמַחְתָּ umisimchatcha וּמִשִּׂמְחָתְךָ oto אוֹתוֹ

✝vishurun וִישֻׁרוּן Yisrael יִשְׂרָאֵל oto אוֹתוֹ karata קָרָאתָ

LEFICHACH

Lefichach awakens a sense of appreciation, ensures our good fortune, and protects all that we hold dear. There is nothing spiritually wrong with striving for bigger and better things in life, but it is our soul consciousness, not our body consciousness, that will determine whether we receive inner happiness and contentment or dissatisfaction and frustration. The deeper message is that we must be happy with our lot in life whatever it may look like, because that experience of happiness and appreciation is exactly what we need to achieve our spiritual growth.

lach לָךְ lehodot לְהוֹדוֹת chayavim וְחַיָּבִים anachnu אֲנַחְנוּ lefichach לְפִיכָךְ

ulromemach וּלְרוֹמְמָךְ ulfa'arach וּלְפָאֶרְךָ ulshabechach וּלְשַׁבֵּחַךְ

leshimcha לְשִׁמְךָ vehoda'a וְהוֹדָאָה shevach שֶׁבַח shir שִׁיר veliten וְלִתֵּן

vechayavim וְחַיָּבִים עם ד׳ אותיות = מבה, יזל, אום ; להו hagadol הַגָּדוֹל

shira שִׁירָה ס״ג מ״ה ב״ן lefanecha לְפָנֶיךָ lomar לוֹמַר anachnu אֲנַחְנוּ

◆tamid תָּמִיד אל יהוה זׁ, מזבוח, נגד ע״ה yom יוֹם ב״ק, לכב bechol בְּכָל־ ע״ה קס״א קנ״א קמ״ג׳ ע״ה קס״א

AVAL

But we are Your Nation, the members of Your Covenant: the Children of Abraham, who had loved You and to whom You had sworn upon Mount Moriah; the Offspring of Isaac, Your bound one, who was bound upon the altar; and the Congregation of Jacob, Your son, Your firstborn, that out of the love and joy You had for him, You had rejoiced in him and called him Israel and also Yeshurun.

LEFICHACH

Consequently, we have an obligation to give thanks to You, to praise, glorify, and exalt You, and give a song of praise and gratitude to Your great Name. We are obligated to say before You, daily and forever,

chelkenu וְחֶלְקֵנוּ · וֹהוּ · tov טוֹב · מ"ה · ma מַה · ashrenu אַשְׁרֵנוּ

מ"ה · uma וּמַה · ♦goralenu גּוֹרָלֵנוּ · na'im נָעִים · מ"ה · uma וּמַה־

ashrenu אַשְׁרֵנוּ · ♦yerushatenu יְרֻשָׁתֵנוּ · me'od מְאֹד · yafa יָפָה

uma'arivim וּמַעֲרִיבִים · mashkimim מַשְׁכִּימִים · she'anachnu שֶׁאֲנַחְנוּ

♦midrashot מִדְרָשׁוֹת · uvevatei וּבְבָתֵּי · chenesiyot כְּנֵסִיּוֹת · bevatei בְּבָתֵּי

לכב · ב"ג · bechol בְּכָל · shimcha שִׁמְךָ · umyachadim וּמְיַחֲדִים

קמ"ג קנ"א קס"א · נתה, · ע"ה · tamid תָּמִיד · אל יהוה זן, מזבוז, נגד, ע"ה · yom יוֹם

דאגה: · אוזד, · be'ahava בְּאַהֲבָה · pa'amayim פַּעֲמַיִם · omrim אוֹמְרִים

SMALL SHEMA

This version of the *Shema* acts as a rocket booster, helping to launch us into *Shacharit*, the morning connection. First we scan the meditations that precede the *Shema* to prepare our internal Vessel. When we recite the *Shema*, we unite the Upper Worlds with the physical world. We acknowledge that there is only one Creator, one Source, and that the past, the present and the future are one. We overlay our physical reality with the Tree of Life Reality, creating a bridge with your consciousness, meditating that all is one.

Inside the *Shema* are two large Aramaic letters: *Ayin* ע and *Dalet* ד. Together, they spell the Aramaic word for "witness," עד. The Light is a witness to all we do, and we are always accountable for our actions, even if we think nobody saw us perform them. This is the law of Cause and Effect.

First, meditate in general, on the first *Yichud* of the four *Yichuds* of the Name: יהוה, and in particular, to awaken the letter ה, and then to connect it with the letter ו. Then connect the letter י and the letter ה together in the following order: Hei (ה), Hei-Vav (ה"ו), then Yud-Hei (י"ה), which adds up to 31, the secret of י"א of the Name ס"ג. It is good to meditate on this *Yichud* before reciting any *Shema* because it acts as a replacement for the times that you may have missed reading the *Shema*. This *Yichud* has the same ability to create a Supernal connection like the reading of the *Shema* - to raise *Zeir* and *Nukva* together for the *Zivug* of *Abba* and *Ima*.

how fortunate we are; how good is our lot; how pleasant is our destiny; and how beautiful is our inheritance. We are joyful for being able to rise early and return late, in and from the synagogues and houses of study, and to proclaim the unity of Your Name, daily and forever, and we say twice, lovingly:

Shema - שְׁמַע

General Meditation: שֹם ע — to draw the energy from the seven lower *Sefirot* of *Ima* to the *Nukva*, which enables the *Nukva* to elevate the *Mayin Nukvin* (awakening from Below).

Particular Meditation: שֹם = יהוה ♦ שׁדִּי and five times the letters י and ה of ב"ן = ע [The letter *Hei* (ה) is formed by the letters *Dalet* (ד) and *Yud* (י), so in ב"ן we have four times the letter ה plus another time the letters י and ד from יוד of ב"ן.]. Also the three letters ו (18) that are left from ב"ן, plus ב"ן itself (52) equals ע (70).

Yisrael – יִשְׂרָאֵל

General Meditation: שׁיר אל — to draw energy from *Chesed* and *Gevurah* of *Abba* to *Zeir Anpin*, to do his action in the secret of *Mayin Duchrin* (awakening from Above).

Particular Meditation: (the rearranged letters of the word *Yisrael*) – שׁר אלי

ע"ר = מילוי דעד"רי (ין לת ור),

אלי = מ"א אותיות שבאהיה דאלפין פשוט ומלא ומלא דמלא

(אהיה אלף הא יוד הא אלף למד פא הא אלף יוד הא ואו דלת הא אלף).

Meditate to draw the Surrounding Light of *Ima* and the Inner Light of *Abba* of *Katnut* into *Zeir Anpin*.

Adonai Elohenu Adonai - יהוה אלהינו יהוה

General Meditation: to draw energy to *Abba*, *Ima* and *Da'at* from *Arich Anpin*,

Particular Meditation: ע"ב (יוד הי ויו הי) ע"ב (אלף הי יוד הי) קס"א (יוד הי ויו הי)

Echad – אֶחָד

(The secret of the complete *Yichud-Unification*)

The letters *Alef* א and *Chet* ח from *Echad* אחד are *Zeir Anpin* and the letter *Dalet* ד is *Nukva*.

You should meditate to devote your soul for the sanctification of the Holy Name, thereby elevating your *Nefesh*, *Ruach*, *Neshamah* and *Neshamah* of *Neshamah* with *Zeir Anpin* and *Nukva* (using the Names: ע"ב and ס"ג) to *Abba* and *Ima* as the secret of *Mayin Nukvin*, and by that energy, *Abba* and *Ima* will be unified in the secret of the Name: יאההויה.

Also meditate to draw out the Surrounding Light of *Katnut* of *Abba* and the Inner Six Edges of *Gadlut* of *Ima* into *Zeir Anpin*. The Drop, which is ע"ב, is drawn out from the Internal of *Arich Anpin*, and descends to *Yesod* of *Ima*, where it becomes: ע"ב ס"ג מ"ה ב"ן, and the four spelled out אהיה (אלף הי יוד הי, אלף הא יוד הא, אלף הה יוד הה) become Her clothing.

As a result, *Zeir Anpin* now has four spelled out יה"ו (יוד הי ויו, יוד הא ואו, יוד הי ואו, יוד הה וו), four spelled out אה"י (אלף הי יוד, אלף הי יוד, אלף הא יוד, אלף הה הא יוד) and the Inner Six Edges of *Gadlut* of *Ima*. **Also meditate** on the Name: אל"ף ה"י וי"ו ה"י, which is the entire *Mochin* in the secret of *Da'at*. **And also meditate** (according to the Ramchal) on the four spelled out *Alef* (אלף=111) of the Name: אהי"ה that is equal to the word *Midat* (444), making the *Keter* for *Leah*.

Baruch Shem Kevod Malchuto Le'olam Va'ed
בָּרוּךְ שֵׁם כְּבוֹד מַלְכוּתוֹ לְעוֹלָם וָעֶד

Baruch Shem Kevod – *Chochmah*, *Binah*, *Da'at* of *Leah*;
Malchuto – Her *Keter*; ***Le'olam*** – the rest of Her *Partzuf*;
Va'ed – the four הי"ה (4 times 20 equal to *Va'ed*=80) will make the *Keter* for *Rachel*.

And the four spelled out הי"ה (הי יוד הי, הי יוד הי, הא יוד הא, הה יוד הה) will make the rest of Her body.

Adonai יְהֹוָה‎אהדינ"יאהדונהי Yisrael יִשְׂרָאֵל ע"ו רבתי shema שְׁמַע

אֱלֹהֵינוּ Elohenu ילה | Adonai יְהֹוָה‎אהדינ"יאהדונהי ד' רבתי echad אֶחָד‎ | אהבה, דאגה:

malchuto מַלְכוּתוֹ, kevod כְּבוֹד shem שֵׁם baruch בָּרוּךְ יזזו אותיות (: Whisper)

va'ed וָעֶד‎ le'olam לְעוֹלָם ריבוע דס"ג ו"י אותיות דס"ג:

ATA HU

The following *Ata Hu* occupies the metaphysical realm—*Ein Sof* (the Endless World)—that existed before our world was created. The second *Ata Hu* dwells in our physical world, which, was created after the universe came into being. This knowledge helps to reinforce that there is only one Light which encompasses both the spiritual and physical domains.

kodem קוֹדֶם עמם echad אֶחָד‎ דאגה, אהבה hu הוּא Ata אַתָּה

echad אֶחָד‎ hu הוּא veAta וְאַתָּה ha'olam הָעוֹלָם shebarata שֶׁבָּרָאתָ

Ata אַתָּה ha'olam הָעוֹלָם shebarata שֶׁבָּרָאתָ le'achar לְאַחַר אהבה, דאגה

veAta וְאַתָּה והו haze הַזֶּה ba'olam בָּעוֹלָם (דס"ג מילוי) יא"י El אֵל hu הוּא

veAta וְאַתָּה haba הַבָּא ba'olam בָּעוֹלָם (דס"ג מילוי) יא"י El אֵל hu הוּא

kadesh קַדֵּשׁ yitamu יִתַּמּוּ lo לֹא ushnotecha וּשְׁנוֹתֶיךָ hu הוּא

mekadshei מְקַדְּשֵׁי am עַם al עַל be'olamach בְּעוֹלָמְךָ shemach שְׁמָךְ

tarum תָּרוּם malkenu מַלְכֵּנוּ uvishu'atcha וּבִישׁוּעָתְךָ shemecha שְׁמֶךָ

vekarov בְּקָרוֹב vetoshi'enu וְתוֹשִׁיעֵנוּ karnenu קַרְנֵנוּ vetagbiha וְתַגְבִּיהַ

hamekadesh הַמְקַדֵּשׁ baruch בָּרוּךְ shemecha שְׁמֶךָ lema'an לְמַעַן

varabim בְּרַבִּים אל עדי וקס"א ע"ב ברריבוע ע"ב מהש ע"ה shemo שְׁמוֹ:

SMALL SHEMA
"Hear Israel, the Lord our God, The Lord is One." (Deuteronomy 6:4)
"Blessed is the Name of Glory, whose Kingdom is forever and for eternity." (Pesachim 56a)

ATA HU
You are One before You had created the world and You are One after You had created the world. You are Divine in this world and You are Divine in the World to Come. It is You, and Your years are Endless. (Psalms 102:28) Sanctify Your Name, in Your world, upon the nation which sanctifies Your Name. With Your salvation, our King, You shall raise and exalt our worth. Redeem us soon for the sake of Your Name. Blessed is He, Who sanctifies His Name upon the masses.

haElohim הָאֱלֹהִים   Adonai יֱהֹוִה   hu הוּא   Ata אַתָּה

אהיה אדני ; ילה ; ר"ת אהיה עלם mima'al מִבּוּעַל bashamayim בַּשָּׁמַיִם י"פ טל, י"פ כוזו

bishmei בִּשְׁמֵי mitachat מִתַּחַת אלהים דההין ע"ה ha'aretz הָאָרֶץ ve'al וְעַל

ha'elyonim הָעֶלְיוֹנִים י"פ טל, כוזו hashamayim הַשָּׁמַיִם

veAta וְאַתָּה rishon רִאשׁוֹן hu הוּא Ata אַתָּה ◆ vehatachtonim וְהַתַּחְתּוֹנִים

Elohim אֱלֹהִים en אֵין umibal'adecha וּמִבַּלְעָדֶיךָ acharon אַחֲרוֹן hu הוּא

me'arba מֵאַרְבַּע kovecha קוֹוֶךָ nefutzot נְפוּצוֹת kabetz קַבֵּץ ◆ ילה ; אהיה אדני

yakiru יַכִּירוּ ◆ אדני = ר"ת ; ע"ה אלהים דההין ha'aretz הָאָרֶץ kanfot כַּנְפוֹת

hu הוּא Ata אַתָּה ki כִּי olam עוֹלָם ba'ei בָּאֵי ילי chol כָּל veyedu וְיֵדְעוּ

haElohim הָאֱלֹהִים ; ילה ; אהיה אדני יה אדני levadecha לְבַדֶּךָ lechol לְכֹל

asita עָשִׂיתָ Ata אַתָּה אלהים דההין ע"ה ha'aretz הָאָרֶץ mamlechot מַמְלְכוֹת

ha'aretz הָאָרֶץ ve'et וְאֶת כוזו י"פ טל, י"פ hashamayim הַשָּׁמַיִם et אֶת

asher אֲשֶׁר kol כָּל ילי ve'et וְאֶת hayam הַיָּם ילי et אֶת אלהים דההין ע"ה

yadecha יָדֶיךָ ma'ase מַעֲשֵׂה ב"ן, לכב vechol בְּכֹל ילי umi וּמִי bam בָּם מ"ב

lach לָךְ sheyomar שֶׁיֹּאמַר uvatachtonim וּבַתַּחְתּוֹנִים ba'elyonim בָּעֶלְיוֹנִים

avinu אָבִינוּ ◆ tif'al תִּפְעַל מ"ה uma וּמַה ta'ase תַּעֲשֶׂה מ"ה ma מַה

ase עֲשֵׂה vekayam וְקַיָּם chay וְזֹי כוזו י"פ טל, י"פ shebashamayim שֶׁבַּשָּׁמַיִם

imanu עִמָּנוּ ריבוע ע"ב, ריבוע יהוה chesed וְחֶסֶד ע"ב, אותיות ע"ה קס"א ס"ג ריבוע

ba'avur בַּעֲבוּר kevod כְּבוֹד shimcha שִׁמְךָ hagadol הַגָּדוֹל להו' ; עם ד' אותיות =

alenu עָלֵינוּ shenikra שֶׁנִּקְרָא vehanora וְהַנּוֹרָא hagibor הַגִּבּוֹר מבה, יזל, אום

You are the Lord, the God in the Heavens Above and upon the earth Below. In the lights of the Heavens Above and the Earth Below, You are first and You are last and apart from You there is no other God. Gather the dispersed of those who have hope in You from the four corners of the earth. Let all humanity come to recognize and to know that it is You alone Who is God of all the kingdoms of the Earth. You have made the Heavens, the Earth, the sea, and all that they contain. And who among all those who Your hands have made Above and Below can tell You what to do and how to perform? Our Father in the Heavens, Who lives and Who exists, bestow kindness to us for the sake of the glory of Your great, powerful, and awesome Name, that has been invoked upon us.

vekayem וְקַיֵּם lanu לָנוּ אלהים, אהיה אהיה אדני יְהֹוָ(אדני־אהדונהי) Adonai

Elohenu אֱלֹהֵינוּ et אֶת־ ילה hadavar הַדָּבָר ראה shehivtachtanu שֶׁהִבְטַחְתָּנוּ

al עַל yedei יְדֵי Tzefanya צְפַנְיָה chozach וֹזָךְ ka'amur כָּאָמוּר: ba'et בָּעֵת

hahi הַהִיא avi אָבִיא etchem אֶתְכֶם uva'et וּבָעֵת kabetzi קָבְּצִי

etchem אֶתְכֶם ki כִּי eten אֶתֵּן etchem אֶתְכֶם leshem לְשֵׁם

velitehila וְלִתְהִלָּה bechol בְּכֹל amei עַמֵּי

ha'aretz הָאָרֶץ beshuvi בְּשׁוּבִי et אֶת־ shevutechem שְׁבוּתֵיכֶם

le'enechem לְעֵינֵיכֶם amar אָמַר Adonai יְהֹוָ(אדני־אהדונהי):

THE SACRIFICES – KORBANOT

The word *Korbanot* means "sacrifices." *Korbanot* comes from the Aramaic word *krav*, meaning "war," and also from the Aramaic word *kiruv*, meaning "to bring close." Obviously, we no longer bring physical sacrifices to a Temple, but through this connection, we can still go to war against Satan and bring ourselves closer to the Upper Worlds. By reciting the *Korbanot* prayers with an open mind and trusting heart, we are generating the same amount of power as if we were carrying out all the proper actions in the Temple.

THE OLAH (GRAIN) SACRIFICE

According to the *Zohar* (Zohar Chadash 41d), we say this section to cleanse the night of negative thoughts.

vaydaber וַיְדַבֵּר ראה Adonai יְהֹוָ(אדני־אהדונהי) el אֶל Moshe מֹשֶׁה

lemor לֵאמֹר: tzav צַו et אֶת־

Aharon אַהֲרֹן ve'et וְאֶת־ banav בָּנָיו lemor לֵאמֹר zot זֹאת torat תּוֹרַת

ha'ola הָעֹלָה hee הִוא ha'ola הָעֹלָה al עַל mokda מוֹקְדָה al עַל־

hamizbe'ach הַמִּזְבֵּחַ kol כָּל־ halayla הַלַּיְלָה ad עַד־

May You fulfill for us, Lord, our God, what You have promised us through Tzefaniah, Your seer, as it was said: "At that time, I shall bring you and, at that time, I shall gather you. Because I shall give you fame and praise from among all the nations of the world. I shall return you from captivity before your own eyes. says the Lord." (Tzefaniah 3:20)

THE SACRIFICES – KORBANOT - THE OLAH (GRAIN) SACRIFICE

"And the Lord spoke to Moses and said: Command Aaron and his sons, saying, this is the law of the burnt-offering. It is the burnt-offering that is burnt upon the Altar, throughout the night until

הַבֹּקֶר haboker   וְאֵשׁ ve'esh   הַמִּזְבֵּחַ hamizbe'ach   נגד, ז, אל יהוה   תּוּקַד tukad

בּוֹ bo: וְלָבַשׁ velavash   הַכֹּהֵן hakohen   מלה   מִדּוֹ mido   בַד vad

וּמִכְנְסֵי umichnesei   בַד vad   יִלְבַּשׁ yilbash   עַל al   בְּשָׂרוֹ besaro

וְהֵרִים veherim   אֶת et   הַדֶּשֶׁן hadeshen   אֲשֶׁר asher   תֹּאכַל tochal

הָאֵשׁ ha'esh   שׂאה   אֶת et   הָעֹלָה ha'ola   עַל al   הַמִּזְבֵּחַ hamizbe'ach

וְשָׂמוֹ vesamo   אֵצֶל etzel   הַמִּזְבֵּחַ hamizbe'ach   נגד, ז, אל יהוה:

וּפָשַׁט ufashat   אֶת et   בְּגָדָיו begadav   וְלָבַשׁ velavash   בְּגָדִים begadim

אֲחֵרִים acherim   וְהוֹצִיא vehotzi   אֶת et   הַדֶּשֶׁן hadeshen   אֶל el

מִחוּץ michutz   לַמַּחֲנֶה lamachane   אֶל el   מָקוֹם makom   טָהוֹר tahor   י"פ אכא:

וְהָאֵשׁ veha'esh   שׂאה   עַל al   הַמִּזְבֵּחַ hamizbe'ach   נגד, ז, אל יהוה   תּוּקַד tukad

בּוֹ bo   לֹא lo   תִכְבֶּה tichbe   וּבִעֵר uvi'er   עָלֶיהָ aleha   פהל   הַכֹּהֵן hakohen   מלה

עֵצִים etzim   בַּבֹּקֶר baboker   בַּבֹּקֶר baboker   וְעָרַךְ ve'arach   עָלֶיהָ aleha   פהל

הָעֹלָה ha'ola   וְהִקְטִיר vehiktir   עָלֶיהָ aleha   פהל   וְחֶלְבֵי chelvei

הַשְּׁלָמִים hashelamim: אֵשׁ esh   תָּמִיד tamid   ע"ה קס"א קנ"א קמ"ג (מילוי אהיה)

עַל al   הַמִּזְבֵּחַ hamizbe'ach   נגד, ז, אל יהוה   לֹא lo   תִכְבֶּה tichbe: תּוּקַד tukad

THE TAMID – (DAILY) OFFERING

The second sacrifice is the daily offering. The Aramaic word *olat* עילת, meaning "elevated," can be rearranged to spell *tola* תולע, a negative force that is awakened each morning. By adding the word *olat*, as in *Olat Tamid*, we uproot and nullify the negative forces of the morning. *Olat* has the same numeric value (506) as the first sentence in the *Ana Beko'ach*, which corresponds to the *Sefirah* of *Chesed*, which is mercy. It also represents the seed level of our soul - a realm where separation and negativity do not exist. By changing the letters in *tola* to *olat* and meditating on the first sentence of the *Ana Beko'ach*, we remove the negative force and return to the seed of unconditional love and oneness.

---

the morning, and the fire of the Altar shall be kept burning thereon. The Kohen shall put on his linen garment; his linen trousers he shall wear on his flesh. He shall remove the ashes when the fire has consumed the offering on the Altar; he shall place them beside it. He shall then take off his clothes, put on other garments, and carry the ashes outside the camp to a clean place. And the fire on the Altar shall remain burning and shall not be extinguished. The Kohen shall place wood upon it early in the morning. He shall lay the offering upon it and shall burn the fat as incense of the peace-offerings. The eternal fire shall burn upon the Altar and not be extinguished." (Leviticus 6:1-6)

By saying this section, we raise the inner part of the three Upper Sefirot of *Asiyah* to the Upper Level. This is the secret of the *Tamid* Offering, to bring closer the Upper and the Lower, and to elevate the Lower all the way up (Writings of the Ari: Gates of Meditation Vol. 1 Ch. 3).

יְהִי yehi רָצוֹן ratzon מהשע ע"ה, ע"ב, ע"ב בריבוע וקס"א ע"ה, אל שדי ע"ה

מִלְפָנֶיךָ milfanecha ס"ג מ"ה ב"ן יהוַאדניאהדונהי Adonai אֱלֹהֵינוּ Elohenu ילה

וֵאלֹהֵי velohei לכב ; מילוי ע"ב, דמב ; ילה אֲבוֹתֵינוּ avotenu שֶׁתְּרַחֵם sheterachem

עָלֵינוּ alenu אברהם, וז"פ אל, רי"ו ול"ב נתיבות החוכמה, רמ"ח (אברים), עסמ"ב וט"ז אותיות פשוטות

וְתִמְחוֹל vetimchol לָנוּ lanu אלהים, אהיה אדני אֶת־ et כָּל־ kol ילי

וְחַטֹּאתֵינוּ chatotenu. וּתְכַפֵּר utchaper לָנוּ lanu אלהים, אהיה אדני אֶת־ et

כָּל־ kol עֲוֹנוֹתֵינוּ avonotenu. וְתִמְחוֹל vetimchol וְתִסְלַח vetislach יהוה ע"ב

לְכָל lechol פְּשָׁעֵינוּ pesha'enu. וְשֶׁתִּבְנֶה veshetivne בֵּית bet ב"פ ראה

הַמִקְדָּשׁ hamikdash בִּמְהֵרָה bimhera בְיָמֵינוּ veyamenu וְנַקְרִיב venakriv

לְפָנֶיךָ lefanecha ס"ג מ"ה ב"ן ע"ה קס"א קנ"א קמ"ג קָרְבַּן korban הַתָּמִיד hatamid

עָלֵינוּ alenu בְתוֹרָתֶךָ vetoratach עַל־ al עַל־ al יְדֵי yedei מֹשֶׁה Moshe

עַבְדָּךְ avdach פו"י, אל אדני כָּאָמוּר ka'amur: מהשע, ע"ב בריבוע וקס"א, אל שדי

There is a *tola'at* (worm) in the Holy Side which is the secret of *Chesed* that increases and reveals and shines every morning. And similar to that, there is another *Tola* in the *klipa* (The Impure Side). This negative worm awakens every morning to destroy the world, and God, with mercy, reveals the worm of the Pure Side which is the Light of *Chesed* (that is mentioned above). And this is the secret of the *Tamid* (Daily Offering) that is called "*Olat HaTamid*," as the word *olat* has the same letters as *tola*, just in a different order. Through the *Olat HaTamid* that is recited every morning, the *tola* of the Impure Side will surrender. In this section you should meditate to purify the Worlds and to prepare them to receive the abundance from the aspect of *Shabbat*, even though they are purified from the aspect of the weekdays.

THE TAMID – (DAILY) OFFERING

May it be Your will, Lord, our God and the God of our forefathers, that You shall have mercy upon us, forgive our sins, atone all our iniquities, and forgive and pardon all our transgressions. May You build the Temple, speedily and in our times, so that we may sacrifice before You our daily offerings that shall atone for us, as You wrote in Your Torah, through Moses, Your servant, as it says:

OLAM ASIYAH - יוד הה וו הה – אל אדני

Moshe מֹשֶׁה el אֶל Adonai יְהֹוָה ראה vaydaber וַיְדַבֵּר

מהעש, ע״ב ברריבוע וקס״א, אל עדי tzav צַו פוי, אל אדני lemor לֵאמֹר benei בְּנֵי et אֶת

korbani קָרְבָּנִי et אֶת alehem אֲלֵהֶם ve'amarta וְאָמַרְתָּ Yisrael יִשְׂרָאֵל

tishmeru תִּשְׁמְרוּ nichochi נִיחֹחִי re'ach רֵיחַ le'ishai לְאִשַּׁי lachmi לַחְמִי

lahem לָהֶם ve'amarta וְאָמַרְתָּ bemo'ado בְּמוֹעֲדוֹ li לִי lehakriv לְהַקְרִיב

ladonai לַיהֹוָה takrivu תַּקְרִיבוּ asher אֲשֶׁר ha'ishe הָאִשֶּׁה ze זֶה

shenayim שְׁנַיִם temimim תְּמִימִם shana שָׁנָה benei בְּנֵי kevasim כְּבָשִׂים

לַיּוֹם layom ע״ה נגד, מזבוח, זן, אל יהוה ola עֹלָה ר״ת עשל tamid תָּמִיד ע״ה קס״א קנ״א קמ״ג:

vaboker בַּבֹּקֶר ta'ase תַּעֲשֶׂה אהבה, דאגה echad אֶחָד hakeves הַכֶּבֶשׂ et אֶת

ben בֵּין ta'ase תַּעֲשֶׂה hasheni הַשֵּׁנִי hakeves הַכֶּבֶשׂ ve'et וְאֵת

solet סֹלֶת ha'efa הָאֵיפָה va'asirit וַעֲשִׂירִת ha'arbayim הָעַרְבָּיִם:

beshemen בְּשֶׁמֶן belula בְּלוּלָה ב״ן ב״פ ב״ן ע״ה leamincha לְמִנְחָה

katit כָּתִית revi'it רְבִיעִת hahin הַהִין: olat עֹלַת ועֵר, אבגיתץ

(Meditate here to surrender the *klipa* named *Tola* using the Name: אבגיתץ)

tamid תָּמִיד ע״ה קס״א קנ״א קמ״ג ha'asuya הָעֲשֻׂיָה

behar בְּהַר Sinai סִינַי נמם, ה׳ הוויות (ה׳ גבורות) lere'ach לְרֵיחַ nicho'ach נִיחֹחַ

ishe אִשֶּׁה ladonai לַיהֹוָה: venisko וְנִסְכּוֹ revi'it רְבִיעִת

hahin הַהִין lakeves לַכֶּבֶשׂ ha'echad הָאֶחָד בַּקֹּדֶשׁ bakodesh

hasech הַסֵךְ nesech נֶסֶךְ shechar שֵׁכָר י״פ ב״ן ladonai לַיהֹוָה:

"And the Lord spoke to Moses and said, Command the Children of Israel and say to them, My offering, the bread of My fire-offering, My pleasing fragrance, you shall take care to sacrifice to Me at its specified time. And you shall say to them: This is the fire-offering that you shall sacrifice to God, perfect one-year-old sheep, two per day, as a regular daily offering; one sheep you shall do in the morning and the second sheep you shall do in the late afternoon. And one tenth of ephahof fine flour, for a meal-offering, mixed with one quarter of a hin of pressed oil. This is a regular burnt-offering that is made at Mount Sinai as a pleasing fragrance and as a fire-offering before the Lord. Its libation is one quarter of a hin for the one sheep in the Sanctuary, pour a libation of old wine before the Lord.

ben בֵּין   ta'ase תַּעֲשֶׂה   hasheni הַשֵּׁנִי   hakeves הַכֶּבֶשׂ   ve'et וְאֵת

uchnisko וּכְנִסְכּוּ   haboker הַבֹּקֶר   keminchat כְּמִנְחַת   ha'arbayim הָעַרְבַּיִם

(elevation to *Beriah*) re'ach רֵיחַ   (elevation to *Yetzirah*) ishe אִשֶּׁה   ta'ase תַּעֲשֶׂה

✦(elevation to the Endless World) ladonai לַיהוה   (elevation to *Atzilut*) nicho'ach נִיחֹחַ

THE INCENSE

These verses from the *Torah* and the *Talmud* speak about the 11 herbs and spices that were used in the Temple. These herbs and spices were used for one purpose: to help us remove the force of death from every area of our lives. This is one of the few prayers whose sole goal is the eradication of death. The *Zohar* teaches us that whoever has judgment pursuing him needs to connect to this incense. The 11 herbs and spices connect to 11 Lights that sustain the *klipot* (shells of negativity). When we uproot the 11 Lights from the *klipot* through the power of the incense, the *klipot* lose their life-force and die. In addition to bringing the 11 spices to the Temple, the people brought resin, wine, and other items with metaphysical properties to help battle the Angel of Death.

It says in the *Zohar*: "Come and see, whoever is pursued by judgment is in need of incense and must repent before his master, for incense helps judgment to disappear from him." The 11 herbs and spices correspond to the 11 holy illuminations that revive the *klipa*. By elevating them, the *klipa* will die. Through these 11 herbs, the *klipot* are pushed away and the energy-point that was giving them life is removed. And since the Pure Side and its livelihood disappear, the *klipot* is left with no life. Thus the secret of the incense is that it cleanses the force of plague and cancels it. The incense kills the Angel of Death and takes away his power to kill.

Elohenu אֱלֹהֵינוּ   Adonai יְהוָה   hu הוּא   Ata אַתָּה

shehiktiru שֶׁהִקְטִירוּ   avotenu אֲבוֹתֵינוּ   lefanecha לְפָנֶיךָ

et אֶת   ketoret קְטֹרֶת   hasamim הַסַּמִּים

bizman בִּזְמַן   shebet שֶׁבֵּית   hamikdash הַמִּקְדָּשׁ   kayam קַיָּם

ka'asher כַּאֲשֶׁר   tzivita צִוִּיתָ   otam אוֹתָם   al עַל   yad יַד   Moshe מֹשֶׁה

nevia'ch נְבִיאָךְ   kakatuv כַּכָּתוּב   ✦betoratach בְּתוֹרָתֶךָ

The second sheep you shall do in the afternoon like the meal-offering of the morning; its libation you shall do as a fire-offering of a fragrance which is pleasing to the Lord." (Numbers 28:1-8)

THE INCENSE

It is You, Lord, our God, before whom our forefathers burned the incense spices, during the time when the Temple existed, as You had commanded them through Moses, Your Prophet, and as it is written in Your Torah:

THE PORTION OF THE INCENSE

To raise the *Sefirot* from all of *Nogah* of *Atzilut*, *Beriah*, *Yetzirah* and *Asiyah*.

וַיֹּאמֶר vayomer יְהֹוָה Adonai אֶל el מֹשֶׁה Moshe

קַח kach לְךָ lecha סַמִּים samim (*Tiferet, Netzach*)

נָטָף nataf (*Hod*) | וּשְׁחֵלֶת ushchelet (*Yesod*) וְחֶלְבְּנָה vechelbena

(*Malchut*) סַמִּים samim (*Keter, Chochmah, Binah, Chesed, Gevurah*)

וּלְבֹנָה ulvona זַכָּה zaka (*Surrounding Light*) בַּד bad בְּבַד bevad

יִהְיֶה yih'ye וְעָשִׂיתָ ve'asita אֹתָהּ ota קְטֹרֶת ketoret

רֹקַח rokach מַעֲשֵׂה ma'ase

רוֹקֵחַ roke'ach מְמֻלָּח memulach טָהוֹר tahor קֹדֶשׁ kodesh

וְשָׁחַקְתָּ veshachakta מִמֶּנָּה mimena

הָדֵק hadek וְנָתַתָּה venatata מִמֶּנָּה mimena לִפְנֵי lifnei הָעֵדֻת ha'edut

בְּאֹהֶל be'ohel מוֹעֵד mo'ed אֲשֶׁר asher אוּעֵד iva'ed לְךָ lecha שָׁמָּה shama

קֹדֶשׁ kodesh קָדָשִׁים kadashim תִּהְיֶה tihye לָכֶם lachem וְנֶאֱמַר vene'emar:

וְהִקְטִיר vehiktir עָלָיו alav אַהֲרֹן Aharon קְטֹרֶת ketoret

סַמִּים samim בַּבֹּקֶר baboker בַּבֹּקֶר baboker בְּהֵיטִיבוֹ behetivo

אֶת et הַנֵּרֹת hanerot יַקְטִירֶנָּה yaktirena: וּבְהַעֲלֹת uveha'alot

אַהֲרֹן Aharon אֶת et הַנֵּרֹת hanerot בֵּין ben הָעַרְבַּיִם ha'arbayim

יַקְטִירֶנָּה yaktirena קְטֹרֶת ketoret

תָּמִיד tamid

לִפְנֵי lifnei יְהֹוָה Adonai לְדֹרֹתֵיכֶם ledorotechem:

THE PORTION OF THE INCENSE

"And the Lord said to Moses: Take for yourself spices, balsam sap, onycha, galbanum, and pure frankincense, each of equal weight. You shall prepare it as an incense compound: the work of a spice-mixer, well-blended, pure, and holy. You shall grind some of it fine and place it before the Testimony in the Tabernacle of Meeting, in which I shall meet with you. It shall be the Holy of Holies unto you." (Exodus 30:34-36) And God also said: "Aaron shall burn upon the Altar incense spices early each morning when he prepares the candles. And when Aaron raises the candles at sundown, he shall burn the incense spices as a continual incense-offering before the Lord throughout all your generations." (Exodus 30:7-8)

THE WORKINGS OF THE INCENSE

The filling of the incense has two purposes: First, to remove the *klipot* in order to stop them from going up along with the elevation of the Worlds, and second, to draw Light to *Asiyah*. So meditate to raise the sparks of Light from all of the *Nogah* of *Azilut*, *Beriah*, *Yetzirah* and *Asiyah*.

Count the incense using your right hand, one by one, and don't skip even one, as it is said: "If one omits one of all the ingredients, he is liable to receive the penalty of death." And therefore, you should be careful not to skip any of them, because reciting this paragraph is a substitute for the actual burning of the incense.

תָּנוּ tanu רַבָּנָן rabanan פִּטוּם pitum הַקְּטֹרֶת haketoret י"א פעמים אדני

(הֲנֶּבְרָרִים מֵהַקְּלִיפוֹת ע"י י"א הַסַּמָּנִים) קְטֹרֶת – הַק' בֹּאתב"ש ד' = תרי"ג (מצוות);

פִּטוּם הַקְּטֹרֶת = יְהֹוָה יְהֹוָה יה אדני אל אלהים מצפצ מצפצ (ו' מרגלאין דשבת);

כֵּיצַד ketzad שְׁלֹשׁ shelosh מֵאוֹת me'ot המספר = ע, אלהים דיודין

וְשִׁשִּׁים veshishim המספר = מילוי הע' (ין) וּשְׁמוֹנָה ushmona מָנִים manim הָיוּ hayu

בָּה va שְׁלֹשׁ shelosh מֵאוֹת me'ot המספר = ע, אלהים דיודין וְשִׁשִּׁים veshishim

הַחַמָּה hachama מָנֶה mane ע"ה פוי, אל אדני בְּכָל bechol ב"ן, לכב

יוֹם yom ע"ה נגד, מזבח, זן, אל יהוה מֽחֲצִיתוֹ machatzito בַּבֹּקֶר baboker

וּמֽחֲצִיתוֹ umachatzito בָּעֶרֶב ba'erev וּשְׁלֹשָׁה ushlosha מָנִים manim

יְתֵרִים yeterim קס"א, קנ"א וקמ"ג שֶׁמֵהֶם shemehem מַכְנִיס machnis כֹּהֵן kohen מלה

גָּדוֹל gadol לתוֹו ; עם ד' אותיות = מבה, יזל, אום וְנוֹטֵל venotel מֵהֶם mehem

מְלֹא melo וְזֽפְנָיו chofnav בְּיוֹם beyom ע"ה נגד, מזבח, זן, אל יהוה הַכִּפּוּרִים hakipurim

מֽחֲזִירָן machaziran לַמַּכְתֶּשֶׁת lamachteshet בְּעֶרֶב be'erev

יוֹם yom ע"ה נגד, מזבח, זן, אל יהוה הַכִּפּוּרִים hakipurim כְּדֵי kedei לְקַיֵּם lekayem

מִצְוַת mitzvat דַּקָּה daka מִן min הַדַּקָּה hadaka וְאֶחָד ve'achad אהבה, דאגה

עָשָׂר asar סַמָּנִים samanim הָיוּ hayu בָּה va וְאֵלּוּ ve'elu הֵן hen

---

THE WORKINGS OF THE INCENSE

Our Sages have taught: How was the compounding of the incense done? Three hundred and sixty-eight portions were contained therein. These corresponded to the number of days in the solar year, one portion for each day: Half of it in the morning and half at sundown. As for the remaining three portions, the High Priest, on Yom Kippur, filled both his hands with them. On the Eve of Yom Kippur, he would take them back to the mortar to fulfill the requirement that they should be very finely ground. Each portion contained eleven spices:

1) הַצֳּרִי haTzori (Keter) מצפצ, אלהים דיודין, י״פ יי׳׳. 2) וְהַצִּפּוֹרֶן vehaTziporen (Yesod)

3) וְהַחֶלְבְּנָה vehaChelbena (Malchut) ע״ה פוי, אל אדני׳. יהוה אדני אהיה עדי׳.

4) וְהַלְּבוֹנָה vehaLevona (Surounding Light) – שהוא אור לבן והוא יוזידי הנקרא אדון יוזיד׳

מִשְׁקָל mishkal שִׁבְעִים shiv'im שִׁבְעִים shiv'im מָנֶה mane ע״ה פוי, אל אדני׳.

5) מוֹר Mor (Chesed). וּקְצִיעָה uKtzi'ah רהע (Gevurah) – "כי מצפון תפתח הרעה",

6) 7) וְשִׁבֹּלֶת veShibolet נֵרְדְּ Nerd (Tiferet). צפון. סוד רווח והגבורה.

8) וְכַרְכֹּם veCharkom (Netzach) בזֳ׳ךוֹר, סגדלפוֹן, ערי׳. מִשְׁקָל mishkal עָשָׂה shisha

9) קוֹשְׁטְ Kosht עָשָׂה shisha עָשָׂר asar מָנֶה mane ע״ה פוי, אל אדני׳.

10) שְׁלֹשָׁה shelosha (Binah) קִלוּפָה Kilufa עָשָׂר asar. שְׁנַיִם sheneim (Chochmah) עָשָׂר sheneim asar.

11) קִנָּמוֹן Kinamon (Hod) ר״ת ג״פ ק׳ (בסוד קדוש קדוש קדוש). תִּשְׁעָה tish'ah.

בּוֹרִית borit כַּרְשִׁינָא karshina תִּשְׁעָה tish'ah קָבִין kabin. יֵין yen מיכ, י״פ האא.

קַפְרִיסִין Kafrisin סְאִין se'in תְּלַת telat וְקָבִין vekabin תְּלָתָא telata אהיה קבן

וְאִם ve'im יוהך, מ״א אותיות דפשוטו, דמילוי ודמילוי דמילוי דאהיה ע״ה לֹא lo מָצָא matza

יֵין yen מיכ, י״פ האא קַפְרִיסִין Kafrisin מֵבִיא mevi וְחַמֵר chamar וְזִיּוֹר chivar

עָתִּיק atik. מֶלַח melach סְדוֹמִית Sedomit רוֹבַע rova. מַעֲלֶה ma'ale

עָשָׁן ashan כֹּל kol יל שֶׁהוֹא shehu. רִבִּי Ribi נָתָן Natan הַבַּבְלִי haBavli

אוֹמֵר omer: אַף af כִּפַּת kipat הַיַּרְדֵּן haYarden ׳ הויות וד׳ אותיות כֹּל kol יל׳

שֶׁהִיא shehi im אִם יוהך, מ״א אותיות דפשוטו, דמילוי ודמילוי דמילוי דאהיה ע״ה נָתַן natan

בַּה ba דְּבֵשׁ devash עֹר (דשׁופר) וי״ד (האוויז) = ש״ר דינין הגדלות פְּסָלָהּ pesala.

וְאִם ve'im יוהך, מ״א אותיות דפשוטו, דמילוי ודמילוי דמילוי דאהיה ע״ה וְחִסֵּר chiser

אַחַת achat מִכָּל mikol יל׳ סַמְּמָנֶיהָ samemaneha וְזִיּ״ב chayav מִיתָה mita:

---

1) Balsam. 2) Onycha. 3) Galbanum. 4) Frankincense; the weight of seventy portions each. 5) Myrrh.
6) Cassia. 7) Spikenard. 8) And Saffron; the weight of sixteen portions each. 9) Twelve portions of Costus.
10) Three of aromatic Bark 11) Nine of Cinnamon. Further, nine kavs of Lye of Carsina. And
three kavs and three se'ehs of Cyprus wine. And if one should not find any Cyprus wine, he should bring an
old white wine. And a quarter of the salt of Sodom. And a small measure of a smoke raising herb.
Rabbi Natan, the Babylonian, advised also, a small amount of Jordan resin. If he added to it
honey, he would make it defective. If he omits even one of all its herbs, he would be liable to death.

רַבָּן Raban   שִׁמְעוֹן Shimon   בֶּן ben   גַּמְלִיאֵל Gamli'el   אוֹמֵר omer:

הַצֳּרִי haTzori   (מצפצ, אלהים בַּיּוֹדִין, י"פ יְיָ)   אֵינוֹ eno   אֶלָּא ela   שְׂרָף seraf

הַנּוֹטֵף hanotef   מֵעֲצֵי me'atzei   הַקְּטָף haketaf   בּוֹרִית borit

כַּרְשִׁינָא karshina   לָמָה lema   הִיא hee   בָּאָה va'a   כְּדֵי kedei

לְשַׁפּוֹת leshapot   בָּהּ ba   אֶת et   הַצִּפּוֹרֶן haTziporen   (יְהֹוָה אֲדֹנָי אֶהְיֶה עֵדִי)

כְּדֵי kedei   שֶׁתְּהֵא shetehe   נָאָה na'a   יַיִן yen   (ע' כנגד ע' אומות העולם התלויים בסמאל)

לְשָׁרוֹת lishrot   בּוֹ bo   אֶת et   הַצִּפּוֹרֶן haTziporen   (יְהֹוָה אֲדֹנָי אֶהְיֶה עֵדִי)

כַּפְרִיסִין Kafrisin   לָמָה lema   הוּא hu   בָּא va   כְּדֵי kedei

כְּדֵי kedei   שֶׁתְּהֵא shetehe   עָזָה aza   וַהֲלֹא vahalo   מֵי mei   רַגְלַיִם raglayim (ילי)

יָפִין yafin (ילי)   לָהּ la   אֶלָּא ela   שֶׁאֵין she'en   מַכְנִיסִין machnisin   מֵי mei

רַגְלַיִם raglayim   בַּמִּקְדָּשׁ bamikdash   מִפְּנֵי mipenei   הַכָּבוֹד hakavod (לאו):

תַּנְיָא tanya   רִבִּי Ribi   נָתָן Natan   אוֹמֵר omer: כְּשֶׁהוּא keshehu

שׁוֹחֵק shochek   אוֹמֵר omer   הָדֵק hadek   הֵיטֵב hetev   הֵיטֵב hetev

הָדֵק hadek   מִפְּנֵי mipenei   שֶׁהַקּוֹל shehakol   יָפֶה yafe   לַבְּשָׂמִים labesamim

פִּטְּמָהּ pitema   לַחֲצָאִין lachatza'in   כְּשֵׁרָה keshera   לְשָׁלִישׁ leshalish

וְלִרְבִיעַ ulravi'a   לֹא lo   שָׁמַעְנוּ shamanu   אָמַר amar   רִבִּי Ribi

יְהוּדָה Yehuda: זֶה ze   הַכְּלָל hakelal   אִם im (יוֹהך, מ"א אותיות דפשוט, דמילוי)

כְּמִדָּתָהּ kemidata (ע"ה דאהיה דמילוי ודמילוי)   כְּשֵׁרָה keshera   לַחֲצָאִין lachatza'in

וְאִם ve'im (יוֹהך, מ"א אותיות דפשוט, דמילוי ודמילוי דמילוי דאהיה ע"ה)   חִסֵּר chiser

אַחַת achat   מִכָּל mikol (ילי)   סַמְּמָנֶיהָ samemaneha   וְחַיָּב chayav   מִיתָה mita:

Rabban Shimon ben Gamliel says: The balsam was a sap that only seeped from the balsam trees. For what purpose was the lye of Carsina added? In order to rub the Onycha with it to make it pleasant looking. For what purpose was the Cyprus wine added? In order to steep in it the Onycha. Urine is more appropriate for this, but urine is not brought into the Temple out of respect. It was taught that Rabbi Natan said: When he ground, he said: 'Grind it fine, grind it fine.' This is because voice is beneficial to the spices. If he compounds half the amount it is still valid, yet regarding a third or a quarter, we have no information. Rabbi Yehuda said: This is the general rule: If it is in its correct proportions, then half is valid. Yet if he omits one of all its spices, he is liable to death.

o **אוֹ** leshishim **לְשִׁשִׁים** achat **אַחַת** Kapara **קַפָּרָא:** Var **בַּר** tanei **תְּנֵי**

shel **שֶׁל** va'a **בָּאָה** hayta **הָיְתָה** shana **שָׁנָה** leshiv'im **לְשִׁבְעִים**

Var **בַּר** tanei **תְּנֵי** ve'od **וְעוֹד** ◆lachatza'in **לַחֲצָאִין** shirayim **שִׁירַיִם** עִירִים

ba **בָּה** ושר, אבגיתץ noten **נוֹתֵן** יהה haya **הָיָה** ilu **אִלוּ** Kapara **קַפָּרָא:**

kortov **קוֹרְטוֹב** shel **שֶׁל** devash **דְּבַשׁ** שוי (דְּשׁוֹפֵר) ווּ"ד (הָאווּזז) = ש"ך דִינִין דִּגְדוֹלוֹת

en **אֵין** adam **אָדָם** מ"ה yachol **יָכוֹל** la'amod **לַעֲמוֹד** mipenei **מִפְּנֵי**

recha◆ **רֵיחָה** velama **וְלָמָה** en **אֵין** me'arvin **מְעָרְבִין** ba **בָּה** devash **דְּבַשׁ**

mipenei **מִפְּנֵי** ש"ך דִינִין דִּגְדוֹלוֹת = שוי (דְּשׁוֹפֵר) ווּ"ד (הָאווּזז) shehatorah **שֶׁהַתּוֹרָה**

amra **אָמְרָה:** ki **כִּי** chol- **כָּל-** ילי se'or **שְׁאֹר** ג' מווּזזין דְּאָלֹהִים דִּקְטָנוֹת

(ע' = אָלֹהִים דְּיוּדִין ; א' = כְּלָלוּת עִם אָלֹהִים ; ר' = רִיבּוּעַ אָלֹהִים) vechol **וְכָל-** ילי devash **דְּבַשׁ**

taktiru **תַּקְטִירוּ** lo **לֹא-** שוי (דְּשׁוֹפֵר) ווּ"ד (הָאווּזז) = ש"ך דִינִין דִּגְדוֹלוֹת mimenu **מִמֶּנּוּ**

ishe **אִשֶּׁה** לַיהו**ה(ואהדונהי/אדני)** ladonai: שוכן הם בּחִינַת דִינִין דִּקְטָנוֹת ורִגְדוֹלוֹת לכן נָאסְרָה הַקְרָבָתָן

Right

Adonai **יהו**ה(ואהדונהי/אדני) Tzeva'ot **צְבָאוֹת** פני שׁכִינָה imanu **עִמָּנוּ**

misgav **מִשְׂגָּב-** משה, מהטי, ע"ב בּרִיבּוּעַ וקס"א, אל שׁדִי, קס"א ורד' אותיות ע"ה רִיבּוּעַ דס"ג

lanu **לָנוּ** אָלֹהִים, אהיה אדני אלהי ד"פ אלהים ע"ה Elohei **אֱלֹהֵי** מִילוּי ע"ב, דמב ; יֵלֵה

Yaakov **יַעֲקֹב** י' הֲוָיוֹת, יאהדונהי איהדנויה sela **סֶלָה:**

Left

Adonai **יהו**ה(ואהדונהי/אדני) Tzeva'ot **צְבָאוֹת** פני שׁכִינָה ashrei **אַשְׁרֵי**

adam **אָדָם** מ"ה ; יהוה צְבָאוֹת אַשְׁרֵי אָדָם = תִּפְאֶרֶת bote'ach **בֹּטֵחַ**

bach **בָּךְ:** אָדָם בּוֹטוֹ בָּךְ = אָמֵן (יאהדונהי) ע"ה ; בּוֹטוֹ בָּךְ = מִילוּי ע"ב ע"ה:

Bar Kappara taught that once every sixty or seventy years the leftovers would accumulate to half the measure. Bar Kappara also taught that if one would add to it a Kortov of honey, no man would withstand its smell. Why is honey not mixed with it? Because the Torah had stipulated: Because any leaven or honey, you must not burn any of it as burnt-offering to the Lord. (Kritut 6; Yerushalmi, Yoma: ch.4)
(Right) *"The Lord of Hosts is with us, our strength is the God of Jacob, Selah."* (Psalms 46:12)
(Left) *"The Lord of Hosts, joyful is one who trusts in You."* (Psalms 84:13)

SHACHARIT – MORNING PRAYER
יוד הה וו הה – אל אדני - OLAM ASIYAH

Central

יְהֹוָאֲדֹנִיאַהדֹנֹהִי ר"ת יהה hamelech הַמֶּלֶךְ נְהוֹרִין ועש"ע יהוה hoshi'a הוֹשִׁיעָה Adonai יהוה

יְעֲנֵנּוּ אל יהוה ע"ה, ז"ן, מזבח, נגד, veyom בְּיוֹם ya'anenu

קָרְאֵנוּ ר"ת יב"ק, אלהים יהוה, אהיה אדני יהוה ; ס"ת = ב"ן ועם כף דהמלך = ע"ב: kor'enu

ve'arva וְעָרְבָה לַיהֹוָאֲדֹנִיאַהדֹנֹהִי ladonai

virushalaim וִירוּשָׁלַםִ Yehuda יְהוּדָה minchat מִנְחַת

kimei כִּימֵי olam עוֹלָם uch'shanim וּכְשָׁנִים kadmoniyot קַדְמֹנִיּוֹת:

THE ORDER OF THE ALTAR SERVICE RITUAL

We recite all the activities and actions that were performed in the Temple. Utilizing the energy transference of the Aramaic letters, it is as though we are actually performing these rites and rituals ourselves. The organs of the animals that were used as sacrifices in the Temple represent our internal organs and when we recite the words of these specific sacrifices, we bring healing and order to our lives.

◆Abayei אַבַּיֵי (pause here) hava הֲוָה mesader מְסַדֵּר seder סֵדֶר

hama'aracha הַמַּעֲרָכָה mishema מִשְּׁמָא digmara דִּגְמָרָא ve'aliba וְאַלִּבָּא

deAba דְּאַבָּא ◆Sha'ul שָׁאוּל ma'aracha מַעֲרָכָה gedola גְּדוֹלָה

kodemet קוֹדֶמֶת lema'aracha לְמַעֲרָכָה sheniya שְׁנִיָּה shel שֶׁל

ketoret קְטֹרֶת י"א פעמים אדני (הנבררים מהקליפות ע"י י"א הסממנים) ; קטרת – הק' באתב"ש ד' =

uma'aracha וּמַעֲרָכָה◆ sheniya שְׁנִיָּה shel שֶׁל ketoret קְטֹרֶת (מצוות) תרי"ג

י"א פעמים אדני (הנבררים מהקליפות ע"י י"א הסממנים) ; קטרת – הק' באתב"ש ד' = תרי"ג (מצוות)

kodemet קוֹדֶמֶת lesidur לְסִדּוּר shenei שְׁנֵי gezirei גְּזִירֵי etzim◆ עֵצִים

(Central) *"Lord save us. The King shall answer us the day we call."* (Psalms 20:10) *"May the Lord find the offering of Yehuda and Jerusalem pleasing as He had always done and as in the years of old."* (Malachi 3:4)

THE ORDER OF THE ALTAR SERVICE RITUAL

Abayei, he listed the order of the ritual
according to the Gemara and Abba Shaul. The large pyre order preceded the second pyre order of incense. The second pyre of incense preceded the arrangement of the two wooden logs.

וְסִדּוּר vesidur — שְׁנֵי shenei — גְּזִירֵי gezirei — עֵצִים etzim — קוֹדֵם kodem — עמם

לְדִשּׁוּן ledishun — מִזְבֵּחַ mizbe'ach — נגד, זז, אל יהוה — הַפְּנִימִי hapenimi◆

וְדִשּׁוּן vedishun — מִזְבֵּחַ mizbe'ach — נגד, זז, אל יהוה — הַפְּנִימִי hapenimi

קוֹדֵם kodem — עמם — לַהֲטָבַת lahatavat — וְחָמֵשׁ chamesh — נֵרוֹת nerot◆

וַהֲטָבַת vahatavat — וְחָמֵשׁ chamesh — נֵרוֹת nerot — קוֹדֶמֶת kodemet

לְדַם ledam — הַתָּמִיד hatamid — ע"ה, קס"א, קנ"א, קמ"ג◆ — וְדַם vedam

הַתָּמִיד hatamid — ע"ה, קס"א, קנ"א, קמ"ג — קוֹדֵם kodem — עמם

לַהֲטָבַת lahatavat — שְׁתֵּי shetei — נֵרוֹת nerot◆ — וַהֲטָבַת vahatavat

שְׁתֵּי shetei — נֵרוֹת nerot — קוֹדֶמֶת kodemet — לִקְטֹרֶת liktoret — י"א פעמים אדני

(הנזברים מהקליפות ע"י י"א הסממנים) ; קטרת – הק' באתב"ש ד' = תרי"ג (מצוות)◆ וּקְטֹרֶת uktoret

י"א פעמים אדני (הנזברים מהקליפות ע"י י"א הסממנים) ; קטרת – הק' באתב"ש ד' = תרי"ג (מצוות)

לְאֵבָרִים le'evarim◆ — וְאֵבָרִים ve'evarim — לְמִנְחָה lemincha — ע"ה, ב"פ, בן

וּמִנְחָה umincha — ע"ה, ב"פ, בן — לַחֲבִיתִין lachavitin◆ — וַחֲבִיתִין vachavitin

לִנְסָכִין linsachin◆ — וּנְסָכִין unsachin — לְמוּסָפִין lemusafin◆ — וּמוּסָפִין umusafin

לְבָזִיכִין levazichin◆ — וּבָזִיכִין uvazichin — קוֹדְמִין kodmin — כְּתָמִיד letamid

שֶׁל shel — קס"א, קנ"א, קמ"ג ע"ה — בֵּין ben — הָעַרְבַּיִם ha'arbayim◆ — שֶׁנֶּאֱמַר shene'emar:

וְעָרַךְ ve'arach — עָלֶיהָ aleha — פהל — הָעֹלָה ha'ola — וְהִקְטִיר vehiktir

עָלֶיהָ aleha — פהל — וְחֶלְבֵי chelvei — הַשְּׁלָמִים hashelamim◆ — עָלֶיהָ aleha — פהל

הַשְׁלֵם hashlem — כָּל kol — ילי — הַקָּרְבָּנוֹת hakorbanot — כֻּלָּם kulam:

The arrangement of two wooden logs preceded the removal of ashes from the inner Altar. The removal of ashes from the inner Altar preceded the preparation of the five candles. The preparation of the five candles preceded the blood of the daily offering. The blood of the daily offering preceded the preparation of the two candles. The preparation of the two candles preceded the incense. The incense preceded the limbs and the limbs preceded the meal-offerings. The meal-offerings preceded the baked-offerings. The baked-offerings preceded the wine libations. The wine libations preceded the Musaf sacrifices. The Musaf sacrifices preceded the daily offering at sundown. As was said, He set the burnt-offerings on it as incense. And upon it, you shall complete all of the sacrifices. (Yoma 33a)

SHACHARIT – MORNING PRAYER

OLAM ASIYAH - אל אדני – הוה וו הה יוד

ANA BEKO'ACH

The *Ana Beko'ach* is perhaps the most powerful prayer in the entire universe. Second-century Kabbalist Rav Nachunya ben HaKana was the first sage to reveal this combination of 42 letters, which encompass the power of creation.

The *Ana Beko'ach* is a unique formula, built of 42 letters written in seven sentences, that gives us the ability to transcend this physical world with all its limitations. It is known as the 42-letter Name of God. The *Ana Beko'ach* can literally remove all friction, barriers, and obstacles associated with our physical existence. It injects order into chaos, removes Satan's influence from our nature, generates financial sustenance, arouses unity with and love for others, and provides healing energy to the body and soul. We recite or scan the *Ana Beko'ach* every day, as many times as we want.

There are four elements that we connect to, using the *Ana Beko'ach*. They are:

1) **SEVEN SENTENCES** - The seven sentences correspond to the seven *Sefirot*, from *Chesed* to *Malchut*. Although there are ten *Sefirot* in total, only the lower seven exert influence in our physical world. By connecting to these seven, we seize control over this physical world.

2) **LETTERS OF THE MONTH** - Abraham the Patriarch revealed the astrological secrets of the Aramaic letters and of the signs of the zodiac in his kabbalistic treatise, *The Book of Formation* (*Sefer Yetzirah*). Each month of the year is governed by a planet, and each planet has a corresponding verse in the *Ana Beko'ach*; therefore, we also meditate upon the planet and the Aramaic letter that created both the planet and the zodiac sign of that month. (See chart on pg. 108) In doing so, we connect to the positive energy of each planet and not to its negative influence. For example, the Aramaic letter *Ayin* created the sign of Capricorn, *Tevet*. Capricorn is governed by the planet Saturn. The Aramaic letter that gave birth to Saturn is *Bet*; therefore, each day during the month of *Tevet*, we meditate upon the the letters *Ayin* and *Bet* following the recital and meditation of the first verse of the *Ana Beko'ach*.

3) **CORRECTION OF THE SOUL - TIKKUN HANEFESH** - Throughout history, kabbalists have used this healing meditation twice a day, seven days a week, to regenerate and revitalize all the organs of the body. When we reach the sentence in the *Ana Beko'ach* that governs the particular month we are in, we stop and meditate on the letters of the month, and then do the *Tikkun HaNefesh*. (See pg. 561) Using the chart as a guide, hold your right hand over the particular part of the body to which you are channeling energy. Look at the Aramaic letter combination for the specific area of the body that you are focusing on, and allow the Light to penetrate through your right hand, into that part of the body.

4) **ANGELS OF THE DAY** - Angels are distinct packets of spiritual energy that act as a transportation system for our prayers. They carry our words and thoughts to the Upper Worlds. There is a line of *Ana Beko'ach* for each day of the week, and there are unique angels that govern each day. (See pg. 563-564)

OLAM ASIYAH - יוד הה וו הה – אל אדני

Chesed, Sunday *(Alef Bet Gimel Yud Tav Tzadik)* אבג יתץ

אָנָּא ana   בְּכֹחַ beko'ach •   גְּדוּלַת gedulat   יְמִינֶךָ yeminecha•

תַּתִּיר tatir   צְרוּרָה tzerura‡

Gevurah, Monday *(Kuf Resh Ayin Sin Tet Nun)* קרע שטן

קַבֵּל kabel   רִנַּת rinat•   עַמְּךָ amecha   שַׂגְּבֵנוּ sagevenu•

טַהֲרֵנוּ taharenu   נוֹרָא nora‡

Tiferet, Tuesday *(Nun Gimel Dalet Yud Kaf Shin)* נגד יכש

נָא na   גִּבּוֹר gibor•   דּוֹרְשֵׁי dorshei   יִחוּדְךָ yichudecha•

כְּבָבַת kevavat   שָׁמְרֵם shomrem‡

Netzach, Wednesday *(Bet Tet Resh Tzadik Tav Gimel)* בטר צתג

בָּרְכֵם barchem   טַהֲרֵם taharem•   רַחֲמֵי rachamei   צִדְקָתְךָ tzidkatecha•

תָּמִיד tamid   גָּמְלֵם gomlem‡

Hod, Thursday *(Chet Kuf Bet Tet Nun Ayin)* חקב טנע

חֲסִין chasin   קָדוֹשׁ kadosh•   בְּרוֹב berov   טוּבְךָ tuvcha•

נַהֵל nahel   עֲדָתֶךָ adatecha‡

Yesod, Friday *(Yud Gimel Lamed Pei Zayin Kuf)* יגל פזק

יָחִיד yachid   גֵּאֶה ge'e•   לְעַמְּךָ le'amecha   פְּנֵה pene•

זוֹכְרֵי zochrei   קְדֻשָּׁתֶךָ kedushatecha‡

Malchut, Saturday *(Shin Kuf Vav Tzadik Yud Tav)* שקו צית

שַׁוְעָתֵנוּ shav'atenu   קַבֵּל kabel•   וּשְׁמַע ushma   צַעֲקָתֵנוּ tza'akatenu•

יוֹדֵעַ yode'a   תַּעֲלוּמוֹת ta'alumot‡

BARUCH SHEM KEVOD

Whispering this final verse brings all the Light from the Upper Worlds into our physical existence.

(Whisper): יֵלֵּו אותיות   בָּרוּךְ baruch   שֵׁם shem   כְּבוֹד kevod   מַלְכוּתוֹ malchuto

לְעוֹלָם le'olam   ריבוע ס"ג וי' אותיות דס"ג   וָעֶד‡ va'ed

OLAM ASIYAH - יוד הה וו הה – אל אדני

The Month and the Letters		The Astrological Sign And the Letter		The Planet And the Letter		Ana Beko'ach meditation
Tevet	עׄבׄ	Capricorn	עׄ	Saturn	בׄ	אבׄג יתׄץ
Shevat	צׄבׄ	Aquarius	צׄ	Saturn	בׄ	אבׄג יתׄץ
Kislev	סׄגׄ	Sagitarius	סׄ	Jupiter	גׄ	קרׄע שׄטן
Adar	קׄגׄ	Pisces	קׄ	Jupiter	גׄ	קרׄע שׄטן
Nissan	דׄה	Aries	ה	Mars	דׄ	נגׄד יכׄש
Cheshvan	דׄנ	Scorpio	נׄ	Mars	דׄ	נגׄד יכׄש
Av	כׄט	Leo	טׄ	Sun	כ	בׄטר צׄתג
Iyar	פׄו	Taurus	ו	Venus	פׄ	וׄחקׄב טנׄע
Tishrei	פׄל	Libra	ל	Venus	פׄ	וׄחקׄב טנׄע
Sivan	רׄו	Gemini	וׄ	Mercury	ר	יגׄל פׄזק
Elul	רׄי	Virgo	י	Mercury	ר	יגׄל פׄזק
Tammuz	וׄות	Cancer	וׄו	Moon	ת	שׄקׄו צׄית

ANA BEKO'ACH

Chesed, Sunday אבׄג יתׄץ

We beseech You, with the power of Your great right, undo this entanglement.

Gevurah, Monday קרׄע שׄטן

Accept the singing of Your Nation. Strengthen and purify us, Awesome One.

Tiferet, Tuesday נגׄד יכׄש

Please, Mighty One, those who seek Your unity, guard them like the pupil of the eye.

Netzach, Wednesday בׄטר צׄתג

Bless them. Purify them. Your compassionate righteousness always grant them.

Hod, Thursday וׄחקׄב טנׄע

Invincible and Mighty One, with the abundance of Your goodness, govern Your congregation.

Yesod, Friday יגׄל פׄזק

Sole and proud One, turn to Your people, those who remember Your sanctity.

Malchut, Saturday שׄקׄו צׄית

Accept our cry and hear our wail, You that knows all that is hidden.

BARUCH SHEM KEVOD

"Blessed is the Name of Glory. His Kingdom is forever and for eternity." (Pesachim 56a)

RIBON HAOLAMIM

God has given us specific instructions regarding the sacrifices that were to be carried out in the *Beit HaMikdash* (Holy Temple of Jerusalem). Because of the destruction of the Temple, we are not able to carry out those instructions. Here, we ask God to allow us to use the power of these Aramaic letters as a replacement for those sacrifices.

רִבּוֹן ribon יהוה ע"ב ס"ג מ"ה ב"ן הָעוֹלָמִים ha'olamim אַתָּה Ata צִוִּיתָנוּ tzivitanu

לְהַקְרִיב lehakriv קָרְבָּן korban הַתָּמִיד hatamid ע"ה קס"א קנ"א קמ"ג

בְּמוֹעֲדוֹ bemo'ado ♦ וְלִהְיוֹת velihiyot כֹּהֲנִים Kohanim בַּעֲבוֹדָתָם ba'avodatam

וּלְוִים uLeviyim בְּדוּכָנָם beduchanam וְיִשְׂרָאֵל veYisrael

בְּמַעֲמָדָם bema'amadam ♦ וְעַתָּה ve'ata בַּעֲוֹנוֹתֵינוּ ba'avonoteinu וְחָרַב charev

בֵּית bet ב"פ ראה הַמִּקְדָּשׁ hamikdash וּבָטַל uvutal הַתָּמִיד hatamid

וְאֵין ve'en לָנוּ lanu אלהים, אהיה אדני ע"ה קס"א קנ"א קמ"ג Chohen כֹּהֵן lo לֹא Chohen מלה

בַּעֲבוֹדָתוֹ ba'avodato ♦ וְלֹא velo לֵוִי Levi בְּדוּכָנוֹ beduchano ♦

וְלֹא velo ♦ יִשְׂרָאֵל Yisrael בְּמַעֲמָדוֹ bema'amado ♦ וְאַתָּה veAta

אָמַרְתָּ amarta ♣ וּנְשַׁלְמָה un'shalma פָרִים farim שְׂפָתֵינוּ sefatenu ♣

לָכֵן lachen יְהִי yehi רָצוֹן ratzon מהש ע"ה, ע"ב בריבוע וקס"א קס"א ע"ה, אל שדי ע"ה

מִלְּפָנֶיךָ milfanecha ס"ג מ"ה ב"ן יְהֹוָ‎וַ‎אֹהִ‎יָאֲהֹ‎וָדֹנָ‎הִי Adonai אֱלֹהֵינוּ Elohenu ילה

וֵאלֹהֵי velohei לכב ; מילוי ע"ב, דמב ; ילה אֲבוֹתֵינוּ avotenu שֶׁיְהֵא sheyehe

זֶה ze שִׂיחַ si'ach שִׂפְתוֹתֵינוּ siftotenu וְחָשׁוּב chashuv וּמְקֻבָּל um'kubal

וּמְרֻצֶּה um'rutze לְפָנֶיךָ lefanecha ס"ג מ"ה ב"ן כְּאִלּוּ ke'ilu הִקְרַבְנוּ hikravnu

קָרְבָּן korban הַתָּמִיד hatamid ע"ה קס"א קנ"א קמ"ג בְּמוֹעֲדוֹ bemo'ado

וְעָמַדְנוּ ve'amadnu עַל al בְּמַעֲמָדוֹ ma'amado כְּמוֹ kemo שֶׁנֶּאֱמַר shene'emar ♣

RIBON HAOLAMIM

Master of all Worlds, You have commanded us to sacrifice the daily offering at its appointed time, that the Kohens shall do their service, the Levites shall be on their platforms, and the Israelites shall be in their situations. Yet now, due to our sins, the Temple has been destroyed and the daily offering has ceased. We now have no Kohen to do his service; No Levite to stand his platform; and no Israelite in his situation. But we asked: "May we compensate for the bull-offerings with our lips?" (Hosea 14:3) Therefore, may it be Your will, Lord, our God and the God of our fathers, that those words that come out of our lips shall be worthy, acceptable and favorable before You, as if we had sacrificed our daily offering at its appointed time and as if we had stood at that occasion, as it was said:

un'shalma וּנְשַׁלְּמָה   farim פָרִים   sefatenu שְׂפָתֵינוּ •   vene'emar וְנֶאֱמַר :

veshachat וְשׁוֹחֵט   oto אוֹתוֹ   al עַל   yerech יֶרֶךְ   hamizbe'ach הַמִּזְבֵּחַ נגד,   אל יהוה

tzafona צָפֹנָה יה פעמים יה וע"ה ע"ב ס"ג מ"ה ב"ן, הברכה (מכוון למאמרם ז"ל הרוצה להעשיר יצפין)

lifnei לִפְנֵי   Adonai יְהֹוֹוּאֲדֹנָיאאהדונהי   vezarku וְזָרְקוּ   ס"ת   יהוה

benei בְּנֵי   Aharon אַהֲרֹן   hakohanim הַכֹּהֲנִים   et אֶת־   damo דָּמוֹ

al עַל־   hamizbe'ach הַמִּזְבֵּחַ נגד, זך, אל יהוה   saviv סָבִיב :

vene'emar וְנֶאֱמַר :   zot זֹאת   hatorah הַתּוֹרָה   la'ola לָעֹלָה

lamincha לַמִּנְחָה ע"ה ב"פ ב"ן   velachatat וְלַחַטָּאת   vela'asham וְלָאָשָׁם

velamilu'im וְלַמִּלּוּאִים   ulzevach וּלְזֶבַח   hashelamim הַשְּׁלָמִים :

THE POWER OF PEACE

It is important to connect to all levels of the Torah during the day; therefore, we read these verses from the *Mishnah*, followed by verses from the *Gemara* (both are aspects of the *Talmud*). This specific section from the *Talmud* helps to imbue us with the power of truth, unity and peace because it is the only chapter containing no debate or opposing views about the interpretations of the Torah.

TALMUD

There are four levels to understanding the Torah: *Peshat, Remez, Drash* and *Sod. Peshat* corresponds to the literal meaning, *Remez* corresponds to the hints and metaphors within, *Drash* relates to the interpretation of each story, and *Sod* relates to the secrets (*Kabbalah*). These four levels together are known by the acronym PaRDeS, which is derived by taking the first letter of each level. Talmudic discourses are known for their opposing views, debates, and divided viewpoints. The Light of the Creator is infinite; therefore, every opinion is contained within the Light. Two people might have conflicting viewpoints, but according to Kabbalah, they can both be right. Life is a relative experience. We must always make an attempt to consider, or at least respect, the other person's perspective, no matter how right we think our view is. In our world, the ego usually causes divided opinions. Diverse viewpoints, however, are also rooted in the soul. If a soul is descended from the lineage of Abraham, it will have more mercy in its nature, which shapes its perspective in one direction. If a soul is descended from the lineage of Isaac, it will be imbued with more judgment, thereby influencing its perspective in another direction. Both souls can be right, relative to their perspectives.

Meditate here to elevate, *Netzach, Hod, Yesod* of *Asiyah* into *Chesed, Gevurah, Tiferet*; and then to elevate *Malchut* into *Netzach, Hod, Yesod*; and then to elevate the Sparks of Light that are in the *klipa* into *Malchut*.
We say this section here because it is the only chapter in the entire *Mishnah* where all the opinions are in agreement, and is why this chapter is called: "*Halacha Pesuka*," meaning unargumental law. Now, while the worlds are elevated, we need the power of peace, not of disagreement.

"May we compensate for the bull-offerings with our lips?" (Hosea 14:3) And as it was also said: "And he shall slaughter it on the northern side of the Altar before the Lord. Aaron's sons, the Kohens, shall sprinkle its blood upon the Altar, all around." (Leviticus 1:11) And: "This is the law regarding the burnt-offering, the meal-offering, the sin-offering, the guilt-offering, the inauguration-offering, and the peace-offering." (Leviticus 1:11)

FIRST MISHNAH

By saying this *Mishnah*, the Internal aspect of *Netzach* of *Asiyah* rises and becomes External to the External part of *Chesed* of *Asiyah*.

kodshei קָדְשֵׁי ◆zevachim זְבָחִים shel שֶׁל mekoman מְקוֹמָן ezehu אֵיזֶהוּ

par פַּר ◆batzafon בַּצָּפוֹן shechitatan שְׁחִיטָתָן kodashim קָדָשִׁים

hakipurim הַכִּפּוּרִים יום, אל יהוה, זֶן, נגד, מזבח, ע"ה yom יוֹם shel שֶׁל vesa'ir וְשָׂעִיר

bichlei בִּכְלֵי daman דָּמָן vekibul וְקִבּוּל batzafon בַּצָּפוֹן shechitatan שְׁחִיטָתָן

al עַל hazaya הַזָּיָה ta'un טָעוּן vedaman וְדָמָן ◆batzafon בַּצָּפוֹן sharet שָׁרֵת

ve'al וְעַל haparochet הַפָּרֹכֶת ve'al וְעַל habadim הַבַּדִּים ben בֵּין

mizbach מִזְבֵּחַ נגד, זֶן, אל יהוה matana מַתָּנָה נתה, קס"א קנ"א קמ"ג ◆וזהו hazahav הַזָּהָב

hadam הַדָּם shiyerei שִׁיֵּרִי ◆me'akevet מְעַכֶּבֶת mehen מֵהֶן achat אַחַת

ma'aravi מַעֲרָבִי ההע yesod יְסוֹד al עַל shofech שׁוֹפֵךְ יהה haya הָיָה

shel שֶׁל mizbe'ach מִזְבֵּחַ נגד, זֶן, אל יהוה hachitzon הַחִיצוֹן ◆im אִם יוהך,

מ"א אותיות דפשוט, דמילוי ודמילוי דמילוי דאהיה ע"ה lo לֹא natan נָתַן lo לֹא ◆ikev עִכֵּב

SECOND MISHNAH

By saying this *Mishnah*, the Internal aspect of *Hod* of *Asiyah* rises and becomes External to the External part of *Gevurah* of *Asiyah*.

hanisrafim הַנִּשְׂרָפִים us'irim וּשְׂעִירִים hanisrafim הַנִּשְׂרָפִים parim פָּרִים

daman דָּמָן vekibul וְקִבּוּל ◆batzafon בַּצָּפוֹן shechitatan שְׁחִיטָתָן

ta'un טָעוּן vedaman וְדָמָן ◆batzafon בַּצָּפוֹן sharet שָׁרֵת bichlei בִּכְלֵי

אל יהוה, זֶן, נגד mizbach מִזְבֵּחַ ve'al וְעַל haparochet הַפָּרֹכֶת al עַל hazaya הַזָּיָה

achat אַחַת קמ"ג קנ"א קס"א, נתה, matana מַתָּנָה ◆וזהו hazahav הַזָּהָב

THE POWER OF PEACE - FIRST MISHNAH

Where is the location of sacrifices? The most holy are slaughtered on the North side. The bull and male goat of Yom Kippur are slaughtered on the North side; their blood is received in service vessels on the North side. Their blood is required to be sprinkled between the poles, on the curtain, and on the Golden Altar. The absence of one of them hinders. He pours the leftover blood on the western foundation of the outer Altar; if he does not pour, he did not hinder.

SECOND MISHNAH

Bulls and male goats that are to be burned
are slaughtered on the North side. Their blood is received in service vessels on the North side. Their blood requires sprinkling upon the curtain and upon the Golden Altar. The absence of one

מֵהֶן mehen שׁוֹפֵךְ shofech עַל al יְסוֹד yesod מֵעֲרָבִי ma'aravi שֶׁל shel

מִזְבֵּחַ mizbe'ach הַחִיצוֹן hachitzon, אִם im נָתַן natan לֹא lo עִכֵּב ikev.

אֵלּוּ elu וְאֵלּוּ va'elu נִשְׂרָפִין nisrafin בְּבֵית bevet הַדֶּשֶׁן hadeshen:

מֵעַכֶּבֶת me'akevet שִׁירֵי shiyrei הַדָּם hadam הָיָה haya

THIRD MISHNAH

By saying this *Mishnah*, the Internal aspect of *Yesod* of *Asiyah* rises and becomes External to the External part of *Tiferet* of *Asiyah*. Here, we complete *Chesed, Gevurah, Tiferet* of *Asiyah*.

וְחַטֹּאת chatot הַצִּבּוּר hatzibur וְהַיָּחִיד vehayachid אֵלּוּ elu הֵן hen

וְחַטֹּאת chatot הַצִּבּוּר hatzibur: שְׂעִירֵי se'irei רָאשֵׁי rashei

חֳדָשִׁים chodashim וְשֶׁל veshel מוֹעֲדוֹת mo'adot שְׁחִיטָתָן shechitatan

בַּצָּפוֹן batzafon וְקִבּוּל vekibul דָּמָן daman בִּכְלֵי bichlei שָׁרֵת sharet

בַּצָּפוֹן batzafon וְדָמָן vedaman טָעוּן ta'un אַרְבַּע arba מַתָּנוֹת matanot

עַל al אַרְבַּע arba קְרָנוֹת keranot כֵּיצַד keitzad עָלָה ala

בַּכֶּבֶשׁ bakevesh וּפָנָה ufana לַסּוֹבֵב lasovev וּבָא uva לוֹ lo

לְקֶרֶן lekeren דְּרוֹמִית deromit מִזְרָחִית mizrachit מִזְרָחִית mizrachit

צְפוֹנִית tzefonit צְפוֹנִית tzefonit מַעֲרָבִית ma'aravit מַעֲרָבִית ma'aravit

שׁוֹפֵךְ shofech עַל al יְסוֹד yesod הַדְּרוֹמִי haderomi

וְנֶאֱכָלִין vene'echalin לִפְנִים lifnim מִן min הַקְּלָעִים hakela'im

לְזִכְרֵי lezichrei כְּהֻנָּה chehuna בְּכָל bechol מַאֲכָל ma'achal

לְיוֹם leyom וְלַיְלָה valayla עַד ad וַחֲצוֹת chatzot:

שׁוֹפֵךְ shofech עַל al יְסוֹד yesod הַדְּרוֹמִי deromit שִׁירֵי shiyrei הַדָּם hadam הָיָה haya

---

of them hinders. He pours the leftover blood upon the Western foundation of the outer Altar; if he did not pour, he did not hinder. These and the preceding offerings are burned in ash repositories.

THIRD *MISHNAH*

The communal and the personal sin-offerings are the communal sin-offerings: The male goats of Rosh Chodesh and of the festivals: these are slaughtered on the North side. And their blood is received in service vessels in the North side. Their blood requires four poured portions upon the four corners of the Altar. How: He ascends the ramp, then turns to the Surrounding ledge; then goes to the Southeastern corner, the Northeastern, the Northwestern, and the Southwestern corner. He pours the leftover blood on the Southern foundation. These are eaten within the curtains by the males of the Kohens, in every meal for one day and one night, until midnight.

FOURTH MISHNAH - THE OLAH (BURNT) OFFERING

You say this Mishnah for the entirety of Asiyah.

ha'ola הָעוֹלָה   kodesh קֹדֶשׁ   kodashim קָדָשִׁים   shechitata שְׁחִיטָתָהּ

batzafon בַּצָּפוֹן   vekibul וְקִבּוּל   dama דָּמָהּ   bichlei בִּכְלֵי

sharet שָׁרֵת   batzafon בַּצָּפוֹן   vedama וְדָמָהּ   ta'un טָעוּן   shetei שְׁתֵּי

matanot מַתָּנוֹת   shehen שֶׁהֵן   arba אַרְבַּע   ute'una וּטְעוּנָה

hefshet הֶפְשֵׁט   venitu'ach וְנִתּוּחַ   vechalil וְכָלִיל   la'ishim לָאִשִּׁים

FIFTH MISHNAH - THE ASHAM (GUILT) OFFERINGS

By saying this Mishnah, the Internal aspect of the Right Column of Malchut of Asiyah rises and becomes External to the External aspect of Netzach of Asiyah.

zivchei זִבְחֵי   shalmei שַׁלְמֵי   tzibur צִבּוּר   va'ashamot וַאֲשָׁמוֹת   elu אֵלוּ

hen הֵן   ashamot אֲשָׁמוֹת   asham אָשָׁם   gezelot גְּזֵלוֹת   asham אָשָׁם

me'ilot מְעִילוֹת   asham אָשָׁם   shifcha שִׁפְחָה   charufa וַחֲרוּפָה   asham אָשָׁם

nazir נָזִיר   asham אָשָׁם   metzora מְצוֹרָע   asham אָשָׁם   taluy תָּלוּי

shechitatan שְׁחִיטָתָן   batzafon בַּצָּפוֹן   vekibul וְקִבּוּל   daman דָּמָן

bichlei בִּכְלֵי   sharet שָׁרֵת   batzafon בַּצָּפוֹן   vedaman וְדָמָן

ta'un טָעוּן   shetei שְׁתֵּי   matanot מַתָּנוֹת   shehen שֶׁהֵן   arba אַרְבַּע

vene'echalin וְנֶאֱכָלִין   lifnim לִפְנִים   min מִן   hakela'im הַקְּלָעִים

lezichrei לְזִכְרֵי   chehuna כְּהֻנָּה   bechol בְּכָל, לכב ,ב"ך   ma'achal מַאֲכָל

leyom לְיוֹם ע"ה נגד, מזבוח, זך, אל יהוה   valayla וְלַיְלָה מלה   ad עַד   chatzot וְצוֹת

FOURTH MISHNAH - THE OLAH (BURNT) OFFERING

The burnt-offering belongs to the most holy.

It is slaughtered in the north and its blood is received in service vessels in the North. Its blood requires two four-part portions. It requires flaying, dismemberment, and complete consumption by fire.

FIFTH MISHNAH - THE ASHAM (GUILT) OFFERINGS

The communal peace-offerings and guilt-offerings. These are the guilt-offerings: The guilt-offerings for thefts, for misuses of sacred objects, for being with a married maid servant, of the Nazir, of a leper, and of a doubtful transgression. These are slaughtered on the North side and their blood is received in service vessels on the North side. Their blood requires two four-part portions. They are eaten within the curtains by the male Kohens, in every meal for one day and for one night, until midnight.

SIXTH MISHNAH - THE TODA (THANKS) OFFERINGS

> By saying this *Mishnah*, the Internal aspect of the Left Column of *Malchut* of *Asiyah* rises and becomes External to the External aspect of *Hod* of *Asiyah*.

הַתּוֹדָה hatoda וְאֵיל ve'el נָזִיר nazir קָדָשִׁים kodashim קָלִים kalim◆

שְׁחִיטָתָן shechitatan בְּכָל bechol ב״ן, לכב מָקוֹם makom בְּעֲזָרָה ba'azara

וְדָמָן vedaman טָעוּן ta'un שְׁתֵּי shetei מַתָּנוֹת matanot שֶׁהֵן shehen

אַרְבַּע arba◆ וְנֶאֱכָלִין vene'echalin בְּכָל bechol ב״ן, לכב הָעִיר ha'ir

בְּכָל bechol ב״ן, לכב אָדָם adam מ״ה לְכָל lechol יה אדני עָרֵי, סנדלפון, סֶזְוְזֶר,

מַאֲכָל ma'achal לְיוֹם leyom ע״ב נגד, מזבח, זן, אל יהוה עַד ad מלה וְלַיְלָה valayla

וְחָצוֹת chatzot◆ הַמּוּרָם hamuram מֵהֶם mehem כַּיּוֹצֵא kayotze בָּהֶם vahem

אֶלָּא ela שֶׁהַמּוּרָם shehamuram נֶאֱכָל ne'echal לַכֹּהֲנִים lakohanim

לִנְשֵׁיהֶם linshehem וְלִבְנֵיהֶם velivnehem וּלְעַבְדֵיהֶם ul'avdehem:

SEVENTH MISHNAH - THE SHELAMIM (PEACE) OFFERINGS

> By saying this *Mishnah*, the Internal aspect of the Central Column of *Malchut* of *Asiyah* rises and becomes External to the External aspect of *Yesod* of *Asiyah*.

שְׁלָמִים shelamim קָדָשִׁים kodashim קָלִים kalim◆ שְׁחִיטָתָן shechitatan

בְּכָל bechol ב״ן, לכב מָקוֹם makom בְּעֲזָרָה ba'azara◆ וְדָמָן vedaman

טָעוּן ta'un שְׁתֵּי shetei מַתָּנוֹת matanot שֶׁהֵן shehen אַרְבַּע arba◆

וְנֶאֱכָלִין vene'echalin בְּכָל bechol ב״ן, לכב הָעִיר ha'ir סֶזְוְזֶר, סנדלפון, עָרֵי

לְכָל lechol יה אדני אָדָם adam מ״ה בְּכָל bechol ב״ן, לכב מַאֲכָל ma'achal

לִשְׁנֵי lishnei יָמִים yamim נלך וְלַיְלָה velayla מלה אֶוָד echad אהבה, דאגה◆

SIXTH MISHNAH - THE TODA (THANKS) OFFERINGS

The thanks-offering and the Nazir's ram are of minor sanctity. They are slaughtered anywhere in the courtyard. Their blood requires two four-part portions. They are eaten throughout the city by any person, in every meal for one day and for one night until midnight. That part which is set aside is treated in the same manner, except that this portion is eaten by the Kohens, their wives, their sons, and their slaves.

SEVENTH MISHNAH - THE SHELAMIM (PEACE) OFFERINGS

The peace-offerings are of lesser sanctity.
They are slaughtered anywhere in the courtyard. Their blood requires two four-part portions. They are eaten throughout the city by any person, in every meal, for two days and one night.

hamuram הַמּוּרָם   mehem מֵהֶם   kayotze כָּיוֹצֵא   vahem בָּהֶם

ela אֶלָּא   shehamuram שֶׁהַמּוּרָם   ne'echal נֶאֱכָל   lakohanim לַכֹּהֲנִים

linshehem לִנְשֵׁיהֶם   velivnehem וְלִבְנֵיהֶם   ul'avdehem וּלְעַבְדֵיהֶם׃

THE FINAL MISHNAH

With this final *Mishnah*, we have the power to elevate the entire world of *Asiyah*. Any souls, or Light, that are trapped inside the *klipot* are also elevated by this verse. Because this specific section contains no debate or opposing views, it creates a thread of unity; it is only through this unity that we have the ability to elevate to the World of Formation (*Yetzirah*).

By saying this *Mishnah*, the Internal aspect (which was in the *klipa*) rises and becomes External to the External aspect of *Malchut* of *Asiyah*. And with this, you complete all of *Asiyah*.

habechor הַבְּכוֹר   vehama'aser וְהַמַּעֲשֵׂר   vehapesach וְהַפֶּסַח   kodashim קָדָשִׁים

kalim קָלִים ◆   shechitatan שְׁחִיטָתָן   bechol בְּכָל   makom מָקוֹם

ba'azara בָּעֲזָרָה   vedaman וְדָמָן   ta'un טָעוּן   matana מַתָּנָה

echat אֶחָת ◆   uvilvad וּבִלְבַד   sheyiten שֶׁיִּתֵּן   keneged כְּנֶגֶד

hayesod הַיְסוֹד   shina שִׁנָה ◆   va'achilatan בַּאֲכִילָתָן ◆   habechor הַבְּכוֹר

ne'echal נֶאֱכָל   lakohanim לַכֹּהֲנִים   vehama'aser וְהַמַּעֲשֵׂר   lechol לְכָל

ha'ir הָעִיר   bechol בְּכָל   vene'echalin וְנֶאֱכָלִין ◆   adam אָדָם

lishnei לִשְׁנֵי   ma'achal מַאֲכָל   bechol בְּכָל

yamim יָמִים   hapesach הַפֶּסַח ◆   echad אֶחָד   velayla וְלַיְלָה

ve'eno וְאֵינוֹ ◆   valayla בַּלַּיְלָה   ela אֶלָּא   ne'echal נֶאֱכָל   eno אֵינוֹ

ne'echal נֶאֱכָל   ve'eno וְאֵינוֹ ◆   chatzot וְחָצוֹת   ad עַד   ela אֶלָּא   ne'echal נֶאֱכָל

tzali צָלִי׃   ela אֶלָּא   ne'echal נֶאֱכָל   ve'eno וְאֵינוֹ ◆   limnuyav לִמְנוּיָו   ela אֶלָּא

That part which is set aside is treated
in the same manner, except that this portion is eaten by the Kohens, their wives, their sons, and their slaves.

THE FINAL MISHNAH

The firstborn animal, the tithes of cattle, and the Pesach-offering are of minor sanctity. They are slaughtered anywhere in the courtyard. Their blood requires one poured portion, provided that this is poured against the base of the Altar. They differ in the way that they are eaten: The firstborn animal may be eaten by the Kohen, and the tithe may be eaten by anyone. They are eaten throughout the city, in any meal for two days and one night. The Pesach-offering may be eaten only during that night, only until midnight, and may only be eaten by those who contributed to it. It may only be eaten roasted.

RIBI YISHMAEL

Ribi Yishmael acts as a link in the chain of *Sefirot*. It connects us to 13 *Sefirot*—ten in the World of Action (*Asiyah*) and three in the next level up, the World of Formation (*Yetzirah*). It is good to count the 13 *Sefirot* of *Asiyah* with the fingers of the right hand.

Ribi רִבִּי Yishmael יִשְׁמָעֵאל omer אוֹמֵר, bish'losh בְּשָׁלֹשׁ esre עֶשְׂרֵה

midot מִדּוֹת hatorah הַתּוֹרָה nidreshet נִדְרֶשֶׁת (1 mikal מִקַּל נּםם

vachomer וָחֹמֶר (2 migezera מִגְּזֵרָה shava שָׁוָה (3 mibinyan מִבִּנְיַן av אָב

vechatuv וְכָתוּב echad אֶחָד אהבה, דאגה. umibinyan וּמִבִּנְיַן av אָב

ushenei וּשְׁנֵי chetuvim כְּתוּבִים (4 mikelal מִכְּלָל ufrat וּפְרָט

(5 miperat מִפְּרָט uchlal וּכְלָל (6 kelal כְּלָל ufrat וּפְרָט uchlal וּכְלָל ei אִי

Ata אַתָּה dan דָּן ela אֶלָּא ke'en כְּעֵין haperat הַפְּרָט (7 mikelal מִכְּלָל

shehu שֶׁהוּא tzarich צָרִיךְ lifrat לִפְרָט umiperat וּמִפְּרָט shehu שֶׁהוּא

tzarich צָרִיךְ lichlal לִכְלָל (8 vechol וְכָל יָלִי davar דָּבָר ראה

shehaya שֶׁהָיָה יהה bichlal בִּכְלָל veyatza וְיָצָא min מִן hakelal הַכְּלָל

lelamed לְלַמֵּד lo לֹא lelamed לְלַמֵּד al עַל atzmo עַצְמוֹ yatza יָצָא

ela אֶלָּא lelamed לְלַמֵּד al עַל hakelal הַכְּלָל kulo כֻּלּוֹ yatza יָצָא:

(9 vechol וְכָל יָלִי davar דָּבָר ראה shehaya שֶׁהָיָה יהה bichlal בִּכְלָל.

veyatza וְיָצָא lit'on לִטְעוֹן ta'un טָעוּן acher אַחֵר shehu שֶׁהוּא

che'inyano כְּעִנְיָנוּ. yatza יָצָא lehakel לְהָקֵל velo וְלֹא lehachmir לְהַחֲמִיר:

RIBI YISHMAEL

"Rabbi Yishmael says: By thirteen attributes is the Torah taught: 1) From lenient law and from strict law. 2) From similarity of words. 3) From a general principle derived from one verse and from a general principle derived from two verses. 4) From a general statement followed by a specific statement. 5) From a specific statement followed by a generality. 6) From a general statement, followed by a specific statement, followed by a generally: then you may only infer what is similar to the specification. 7) From a general statement that requires a specific statement that, in turn, requires a general statement to explain it. 8) Anything that was part of a general statement which was then singled out from the general statement, to teach something. It was not to teach about itself that it was singled out, but to teach about the entire general statement. 9) Anything that was part of a general statement, which was later singled out to discuss another claim to its context. It was singled out in order to be more lenient and not more stringent.

10) וְכָל ילי vechol דָבָר davar ראה shehaya שֶׁהָיָה יהה bichlal בִּכְלָל

veyatza וְיָצָא lit'on לִטְעוֹן ta'un טָעוּן acher אַחֵר shelo שֶׁלֹּא

che'inyano כְּעִנְיָנוֹ yatza יָצָא lehakel לְהָקֵל ul'hachmir וּלְהַחֲמִיר:

11) וְכָל ילי vechol דָבָר davar ראה shehaya שֶׁהָיָה יהה bichlal בִּכְלָל

veyatza וְיָצָא lidon לִדּוֹן bedavar בְּדָבָר ראה chadash וְחָדָשׁ י"ב הויות, קס"א קנ"א

ei אִי Ata אַתָּה yachol יָכוֹל lehachaziro לְהַחֲזִירוֹ lichlalo לִכְלָלוֹ lichlalo לִכְלָלוֹ ad עַד

sheyachazirenu שֶׁיַּחֲזִירֶנּוּ hakatuv הַכָּתוּב lichlalo לִכְלָלוֹ beferush בְּפֵירוּשׁ:

12) וְדָבָר vedavar ראה halamed הַלָּמֵד me'inyano מֵעִנְיָנוֹ vedavar וְדָבָר ראה

halamed הַלָּמֵד misofo מִסּוֹפוֹ: 13) וְכֵן vechan (וּכְאָן) shenei שְׁנֵי

chetuvim כְּתוּבִים hamach'chishim הַמַּכְחִישִׁים ze זֶה et אֶת ze זֶה

ad עַד sheyavo שֶׁיָּבֹא hakatuv הַכָּתוּב hashelishi הַשְּׁלִישִׁי

veyachri'a וְיַכְרִיעַ benehem בֵּינֵיהֶם:

Yehuda יְהוּדָה ven בֶּן Tema תֵימָא omer אוֹמֵר: hevei הֱוֵי az עַז

kanamer כַּנָּמֵר vekal וְקַל נמם (שהם ה' גבורות) kanesher כַּנֶּשֶׁר veratz וְרָץ

katzevi כַּצְּבִי vegibor וְגִבּוֹר ka'ari כָּאֲרִי la'asot לַעֲשׂוֹת retzon רְצוֹן

avicha אָבִיךָ ע"ה אל שדי ע"ה, קס"א ע"ב ברִיבוע, ע"ב מהטע ע"ה, shebashamayim שֶׁבַּשָּׁמַיִם

hu הוּא haya הָיָה יהה omer אוֹמֵר: az עַז panim פָּנִים י"פ טל, י"פ כוזו

laGehinom לַגֵּיהִנָּם uvoshet וּבֹשֶׁת panim פָּנִים leGan לְגַן Eden עֵדֶן:

---

10) *Anything that was part of a general statement and was later singled out in order to discuss another claim out of its context. It was singled out in order to be more lenient and not more stringent. 11) Anything that was part of a general statement and was singled out in order to discuss a new concept, you cannot return it to its general context, unless the text returns it, explicitly, to its general context. 12) A matter that is learned from its context and a matter that is derived from its end. 13) And also from two verses that contradict each other, until a third one comes along and reconciles them.* (Torat Kohanim Portion of Vayikra.)

Yehuda Ben Tema says: Be courageous like a tiger and light as an eagle and run like a deer and be strong like a lion to thus fulfill the will of Your Father in Heaven. He used to frequently say: An insolent person goes to Hell and a modest person to the Garden of Eden. (Avot Ch. 5)

YEHI RATZON

Even though, according to Kabbalah, the Temple still exists in the spiritual reality of the Endless World, its physical structure is missing, leaving our physical world incomplete. This prayer helps set in motion and accelerate the eventual reconstruction of the physical Temple.

ע"ה   עדי אל   ע"ה,   מהש   ע"ה,   ע"ב   בריבוע   וקס"א   יהי **יְהִי**   ratzon **רָצוֹן**

ילה   Elohenu **אֱלֹהֵינוּ**   Adonai **יְהֹוָאדְנִיאהדונהי**   מ"ה ב"ן   ס"ג   milfanecha **מִלְפָנֶיךָ**

avotenu **אֲבוֹתֵינוּ**   ילה   ;   דמב   ע"ב,   מילוי   ;   לכב   velohei **וֵאלֹהֵי**

hamikdash **הַמִּקְדָּשׁ**   ראה   ב"פ   bet **בֵּית**   shetivne **שֶׁתִּבְנֶה**

chelkenu **וְחֶלְקֵנוּ**   veten **וְתֵן**   ◆veyamenu **בְיָמֵינוּ**   bim'hera **בִּמְהֵרָה**

retzonach **רְצוֹנֶךָ**   chukei **וְחֻקֵּי**   la'asot **לַעֲשׂוֹת**   betoratach **בְּתוֹרָתֶךָ**

shalem **שָׁלֵם**   בוכו   belevav **בְּלֵבָב**   אל אדני   פוי,   ul'ovdach **וּלְעָבְדְךָ**

You should be careful not to speak or even to pause too long here, and you should proceed to *Hodu* right after the *Kaddish*.

KADDISH AL YISRAEL

TEN DIMENSIONS AND FIVE WORLDS - Kabbalah explains that a spiritual infrastructure exists, consisting of five basic worlds—*Adam Kadmon* (Primordial Man), *Atzilut* (Emanation), *Beriah* (Creation), *Yetzirah* (Formation), and *Asiyah* (Action)—and ten dimensions—*Keter, Chochmah, Binah, Chesed, Gevurah, Tiferet, Netzach, Hod, Yesod* and *Malchut*—that make up the spiritual infrastructure. Six of these dimensions, (*Chesed, Gevurah, Tiferet, Netzach, Hod* and *Yesod*), are further enfolded into a unified realm called *Zeir Anpin* (see chart on pg 75). Each of the five worlds corresponds to a dimension: *Adam Kadmon = Keter; Atzilut = Chochmah; Beriah = Binah; Yetzirah = Zeir Anpin;* and *Asiyah = Malchut.* Each *Sefirah* acts as a curtain, diminishing the intensity of Light emanating from the Endless World. By the time the Light reaches the lowest level (our world, *Malchut*), it is concealed from our perception. This gives us the opportunity to perform our spiritual work in an arena where we can utilize free will to develop our Godlike, proactive nature. Only through hard work and challenging situations do we fully earn and appreciate fulfillment. To maneuver through these five worlds, we need a spiritual vehicle or elevator that can carry us upward and downward throughout the course of our prayers. The *Kaddish* is that vehicle. It connects us, realm by realm, to worlds that are directly above or directly below us. By connecting the five worlds, the *Kaddish* is also the conduit through which the Light flows to us.

Kaddish, in general, means to elevate the worlds in the secret of the Column. There is one column that connects the worlds to each other and stands in the middle of each palace. And by this column, each palace rises to the upper one and becomes one with it (as is mentioned in the *Zohar*). This column is the *Kaddish*. The secret of *Kaddish Al Yisrael* is that it elevates us from the World of *Asiyah* (ב"ן) to the World of *Yetzirah* (מ"ה).

YEHI RATZON

May it be Your will, Lord, our God and the God of our forefathers,
that You shall build the Temple speedily in our days. And that You may place our lot
in Your Torah, so that we may fulfill the laws of Your desires and worship You wholeheartedly.

יִתְגַּדֵּל yitgadal וְיִתְקַדֵּשׁ veyitkadash עַדִי וּמִלּוּי עַדִי ; י"א אוֹתִיּוֹת כְּמִנְיַן ו"ה

שְׁמֵיהּ shemei (שֵׁם י"ה דְּע"ב) רַבָּא raba קנ"א ב"ן, יהוה אלהים יהוה אדני,

מִלּוּי קס"א וס"ג, מ"ה בָּרָבוּעַ וע"ב ע"ה ; ר"ת = ו"פ אלהים ; ס"ת = ג"פ יב"ק: אָמֵן amen אידהנויה.

בְּעָלְמָא be'alma דִּי di בְּרָא vera כִּרְעוּתֵיהּ chir'utei.

וְיַמְלִיךְ veyamlich מַלְכוּתֵיהּ malchutei. וְיַצְמַח veyatzmach

פּוּרְקָנֵיהּ purkanei. וִיקָרֵב vikarev מְשִׁיחֵיהּ meshichei: אָמֵן amen אידהנויה.

בְּחַיֵּיכוֹן bechayechon וּבְיוֹמֵיכוֹן uvyomeichon וּבְחַיֵּי uvchayei

דְּכָל dechol יְלִי בֵּית bet ב"פ ראה יִשְׂרָאֵל Yisrael בַּעֲגָלָא ba'agala

וּבִזְמַן uvizman קָרִיב kariv וְאִמְרוּ ve'imru אָמֵן amen: אָמֵן amen אידהנויה.

The congregation and the chazan say the following:

מִלּוּי דְּמִלּוּי דס"ג (יוד ויו דלת הי יוד ואו אלף ואו הי יוד): 28 words (until *be'alma*) meditate:

מִלּוּי דְּמִלּוּי דמ"ה (יוד ואו דלת הא אלף ואו אלף ואו הא אלף): 28 letters (until *almaya*) meditate:

יְהֵא yehe שְׁמֵיהּ shemei (שֵׁם י"ה דס"ג) רַבָּא raba קנ"א ב"ן,

מְבָרַךְ mevarach, יהוה אלהים יהוה אדני, מִלּוּי קס"א וס"ג, מ"ה בָּרָבוּעַ וע"ב ע"ה

לְעָלַם le'alam לְעָלְמֵי le'almei עָלְמַיָּא almaya. יִתְבָּרַךְ yitbarach.

Seven words with six letters each (שֵׁם בֶּן מ"ב) meditate:

יהוה ★ יוד הי ויו הי ★ מִלּוּי דְּמִלּוּי דס"ג (יוד ויו דלת הי יוד ואו אלף ואו הי יוד)

Also, seven times the letter *Vav* (שֵׁם בֶּן מ"ב) meditate:

יהוה ★ יוד הי ואו הי ★ מִלּוּי דְּמִלּוּי דמ"ה (יוד ואו דלת הא אלף ואו אלף ואו הא אלף).

וְיִשְׁתַּבַּח veyishtabach י"פ ע"ב יהוה אל אבג יתץ.

וְיִתְפָּאַר veyitpa'ar הי נו יה קרע שטן. וְיִתְרֹמַם veyitromam וה כוזו נגד יכש.

וְיִתְנַשֵּׂא veyitnase בּמוכסז בטר צתג. וְיִתְהַדָּר veyit'hadar כוזו יה וזקב טנע.

וְיִתְעַלֶּה veyit'ale וה יוד ה יגל פזק. וְיִתְהַלָּל veyit'halal א ואו הא שקו צית.

שְׁמֵיהּ shemei (שֵׁם י"ה דמ"ה) דְּקוּדְשָׁא dekudsha בְּרִיךְ verich הוּא hu:

אָמֵן amen אידהנויה.

KADDISH AL YISRAEL

May His great Name be more exalted and sanctified. (Amen) In the world that He created according to His will, and may His Kingdom reign. And may He cause His redemption to sprout and may He bring the Mashiach closer. (Amen) In your lifetimes and in your days and in the lifetime of all the House of Israel, speedily and in the near future, and you shall say Amen. (Amen) May His great Name be blessed forever and for all eternity. Blessed and lauded, and glorified, and exalted, and extolled, and honored, and uplifted, and praised be the Name of the Holy Blessed One. (Amen)

le'ela לְעֵלָא min מִן kol כָּל יְלֵי birchata בִּרְכָתָא shirata שִׁירָתָא

tishbechata תֻּשְׁבְּחָתָא venechamata וְנֶחֱמָתָא da'amiran דַּאֲמִירָן

be'alma בְּעָלְמָא ve'imru וְאִמְרוּ amen אָמֵן : amen אָמֵן אידהנויה.

al עַל Yisrael יִשְׂרָאֵל ve'al וְעַל rabanan רַבָּנָן ve'al וְעַל

talmidehon תַּלְמִידֵיהוֹן ve'al וְעַל kol כָּל יְלֵי ; עמם talmidei תַּלְמִידֵי

talmidehon תַּלְמִידֵיהוֹן de'askin דְּעָסְקִין be'orayta בְּאוֹרַיְתָא

kadishta קַדִּשְׁתָּא di דִּי ve'atra בְּאַתְרָא haden הָדֵין vedi וְדִי

vechol בְּכָל ב״ן, לכב atar אָתָר ve'atar וְאָתָר yehe יְהֵא

lana לָנָא ul'hon וּלְהוֹן ul'chon וּלְכוֹן china חִנָּא vechisda וְחִסְדָּא

verachamei וְרַחֲמֵי min מִן kadam קָדָם marei מָארֵי shemaya שְׁמַיָּא

ve'ar'a וְאַרְעָא ve'imru וְאִמְרוּ amen אָמֵן : amen אָמֵן אידהנויה.

yehe יְהֵא shelama שְׁלָמָא raba רַבָּא קנ״א ב״ן, יהוה אלהים יהוה אדני, מילוי קס״א וס״ג,

min מִן shemaya שְׁמַיָּא chayim וְחַיִּים אהיה אהיה יהוה, בינה ע״ה מ״ה ברבוע וע״ב ע״ה

vesava וְשָׂבַע vishu'a וִישׁוּעָה venechama וְנֶחָמָה veshezava וְשֵׁיזָבָא

urfu'a וּרְפוּאָה ug'ula וּגְאֻלָּה uslicha וּסְלִיחָה vechapara וְכַפָּרָה

verevach וְרֶיוַח vehatzala וְהַצָּלָה lanu לָנוּ אלהים, אהיה אדני, אהיה ulchol וּלְכָל יה אדני

amo עַמּוֹ Yisrael יִשְׂרָאֵל ve'imru וְאִמְרוּ amen אָמֵן : amen אָמֵן אידהנויה.

Take three steps backwards and say:

ose עוֹשֶׂה shalom שָׁלוֹם bimromav בִּמְרוֹמָיו ע״ב, ריבוע יהוה. hu הוּא

berachamav בְּרַחֲמָיו ר״ת ש״ע נהורין ya'ase יַעֲשֶׂה shalom שָׁלוֹם alenu עָלֵינוּ

ve'al וְעַל kol כָּל יְלֵי ; עמם amo עַמּוֹ Yisrael יִשְׂרָאֵל ve'imru וְאִמְרוּ amen אָמֵן :

amen אָמֵן אידהנויה.

Above all blessings, songs, praises, and words of consolation that may be said in the world, and you shall say, Amen. (Amen) Upon Israel, His Sages, their disciples, and all the students of their disciples who occupy themselves with the Holy Torah, in this place and in each and every location, may there be for us, for them, and for all, grace, kindness, and compassion from the Master of the Heavens and Earth, and you shall say Amen. (Amen) May there be abundant peace from Heaven, life, contentment, salvation, consolation, deliverance, healing, redemption, pardon, atonement, comfort, and relief for us and for His entire Nation, Israel, and you shall say, Amen. (Amen) He, Who makes peace in His High Places, with His compassion He shall make peace for us and for His entire Nation, Israel. And you shall say, Amen. (Amen)

OLAM ASIYAH - יוד הה וו הה – אל אדני

HODU, EL NEKAMOT AND AROMIMCHA

The power of the *Kaddish* lies in its ability to elevate us to the Upper Worlds. But the initial launch from our physical world – *Asiyah* - requires an additional thrust. The ancient sages gave us three prayers, *Hodu*, *El Nekamot* and *Aromimcha*, for this purpose. This initial launch stage occurs in the World of Action (*Asiyah*).

HODU

Our *klipot's* sole nourishment comes from our world (*Malchut* or *Asiyah*), and consequently, the *klipot* try to prevent our world of *Malchut*, the World of Action (*Asiyah*), from rising to the World of Formation (*Yetzirah*), because that movement would disconnect them from their only source of Light. *Hodu* cuts off the *klipot's* oxygen supply, helping us break away from the *klipot's* gravitational pull.

We say *Hodu* to empower *Malchut* of *Yetzirah*, which is included in *Hechal Kodesh HaKodashim* of *Asiyah* in order to break the power of the *klipot* that prevents *Asiyah* from rising to *Yetzirah*. From *Hodu* to *baruch Elohim* (pg.125), there are 295 words which is the numerical value of *Elohim* spelled out with *Hei* (אלף למד הה יוד מם). And therefore, you should not add or omit any of the words. This prayer praises the sun on its trail when it comes to shine upon the world. So is *Yisrael* praising God with the sun, as it says: "You should be seen together with the sun" (Psalms 72:5).

הוֹדוּ hodu אהיה לַיהֹוָאדנילאהדונהי ladonai קִרְאוּ kir'u בִּשְׁמוֹ vishmo מהש ע"ה,

הוֹדִיעוּ hodi'u לאו אל שדי ע"ה, וקס"א בריבוע ע"ב בָּעַמִּים va'amim

עֲלִילֹתָיו alilotav: שִׁירוּ shiru לוֹ lo זַמְּרוּ zameru לוֹ lo שִׂיחוּ sichu

בְּכָל bechol לכב ב"ן, נִפְלְאוֹתָיו nifle'otav: הִתְהַלְלוּ hit'halelu בְּשֵׁם beshem

קָדְשׁוֹ kodsho יִשְׂמַח yismach משיח לֵב lev מְבַקְשֵׁי mevakshei

יְהֹוָאדנילאהדונהי Adonai: דִּרְשׁוּ dirshu יְהֹוָאדנילאהדונהי Adonai וְעֻזּוֹ ve'uzo

בַּקְשׁוּ bakeshu פָנָיו fanav תָּמִיד tamid ע"ה קס"א קנ"א ק"א קמ"ג:

זִכְרוּ zichru נִפְלְאֹתָיו nifle'otav אֲשֶׁר asher עָשָׂה asa מֹפְתָיו moftav

וּמִשְׁפְּטֵי umishpetei פִּיהוּ fihu: זֶרַע zera יִשְׂרָאֵל Yisrael

עַבְדּוֹ avdo בְּנֵי benei יַעֲקֹב Yaakov י' הויות, יאהדונהי אידהנויה

בְּחִירָיו bechirav: הוּא hu יְהֹוָאדנילאהדונהי Adonai אֱלֹהֵינוּ Elohenu יכה

בְּכָל bechol לכב ב"ן, הָאָרֶץ ha'aretz אלהים דההין ע"ה מִשְׁפָּטָיו mishpatav:

HODU, EL NEKAMOT AND AROMIMCHA
HODU

"Be grateful to the Lord Call out His Name and make His deeds known among nations. Sing to Him, chant to Him, and speak of all His wonders. Be proud of His Holy Name. The heart of those who seek the Lord and His power shall rejoice. Constantly seek His presence. Remember the wonders that He has performed, His miracles, and the law that He uttered. You are the seed of Israel, His servant, and the sons of Jacob, His Chosen Ones. He is the Lord, our God. His judgments cover the whole Earth.

רְאֵה davar דָּבָר berito בְּרִיתוֹ ס"ג וי' אותיות דס"ג ריבוע le'olam לְעוֹלָם zichru זִכְרוּ

asher אֲשֶׁר dor דּוֹר le'elef לָאֶלֶף tziva צִוָּה המספר אֶלֶף = אלף למד עיין דלת יוד ע"ה

(אברהם) רמ"ח נתיבות החוכמה, ול"ב רי"ו אל, וז"פ Avraham אַבְרָהָם et אֶת karat כָּרַת

ב"ן ד"פ leYitzchak לְיִצְחָק ush'vu'ato וּשְׁבוּעָתוֹ אותיות פשוטות וט"ו עסמ"ב

lechok לְחֹק יאהדונהי איהוויה היווית, ו leYaakov לְיַעֲקֹב vaya'amideha וַיַּעֲמִידֶהָ

lecha לָךְ lemor לֵאמֹר olam עוֹלָם berit בְּרִית leYisrael לְיִשְׂרָאֵל

nachalatchem נַחֲלַתְכֶם chevel וְחֶבֶל Kena'an כְּנַעַן eretz אֶרֶץ eten אֶתֵּן

kim'at כִּמְעַט mispar מִסְפָּר metei מְתֵי bih'yotchem בִּהְיוֹתְכֶם

el אֶל migoi מִגּוֹי ניצוצות קדושה vayit'halchu וַיִּתְהַלְּכוּ ba בָּהּ vegarim וְגָרִים

lo לֹא acher אַחֵר am עַם el אֶל umimamlacha וּמִמַּמְלָכָה goi גּוֹי

vayochach וַיּוֹכַח ר"ת ללה, אדני le'oshkam לְעָשְׁקָם le'ish לְאִישׁ hini'ach הִנִּיחַ

bimshichai בִּמְשִׁיחָי tige'u תִּגְּעוּ al אֶל melachim מְלָכִים alehem עֲלֵיהֶם

ladonai לַיהוָה(אהדונהי) shiru שִׁירוּ tare'u תָּרֵעוּ al אֶל uvinvi'ai וּבִנְבִיאַי

miyom מִיּוֹם baseru בַּשְּׂרוּ אלהים דההין ע"ה ha'aretz הָאָרֶץ kol כָּל

yeshu'ato יְשׁוּעָתוֹ yom יוֹם ע"ה נגד, מזבוח, זן, אל יהוה el אֶל ע"ה נגד, מזבוח, זן, אל יהוה

et אֶת (properly enunciate the letter *Alef* in the word "et") vagoyim בַּגּוֹיִם saperu סַפְּרוּ

nifle'otav נִפְלְאֹתָיו ha'amim הָעַמִּים לכב ב"ן, bechol בְּכָל kevodo כְּבוֹדוֹ

Adonai יְהוָה(ואדני)יאהדונהי להו ; עם ד' אותיות = מבה, יזל, אום gadol גָּדוֹל ki כִּי

al עַל hu הוּא venora וְנוֹרָא me'od מְאֹד ס"ת ללה, אדני um'hulal וּמְהֻלָּל

kol כָּל ki כִּי אהיה אדני Elohim אֱלֹהִים ; עמם kol כָּל

(pause here) elilim אֱלִילִים ha'amim הָעַמִּים ; ילה דמב מילוי ע"ב, elohei אֱלֹהֵי

Remember His Covenant always. That which He concluded with Abraham, vowed to Isaac, established for Jacob as a statute, and for Israel as an eternal Covenant: To you I give the land of Canaan, the share of your heritage, where you were only a few and were lost strangers in it. They wandered from one nation to another and from one kingdom to another. Yet He did not allow any one to harm them; He admonished kings because of them: Do not touch My anointed ones and do not cause distress to My prophets. Sing to the Lord all of Earth and proclaim daily His salvation. Relate His glory among the nations and His wonders among all peoples: For the Lord is great and most praised; He is awesome above and beyond all deities. For the gods of all nations are only deities

הוד hod :asa עָשָׂה shamayim שָׁמַיִם vadonai

:bimkomo בִּמְקֹמוֹ vechedva וְחֶדְוָה oz עֹז lefanav לְפָנָיו vehadar וְהָדָר

mishpechot מִשְׁפְּחוֹת ladonai לַיהוה havu הָבוּ

kavod כָּבוֹד ladonai לַיהוה havu הָבוּ amim עַמִּים

kevod כָּבוֹד ladonai לַיהוה :va'oz וָעֹז havu הָבוּ

shemo שְׂמוֹ

lefanav לְפָנָיו uvo'u וּבֹאוּ mincha מִנְחָה se'u שְׂאוּ

behadrat בְּהַדְרַת ladonai לַיהוה hishtachavu הִשְׁתַּחֲווּ

kodesh קֹדֶשׁ

ha'aretz הָאָרֶץ kol כָּל milfanav מִלְּפָנָיו chilu וְחִילוּ

:timot תִּמּוֹט bal בַּל tevel תֵּבֵל tikon תִּכּוֹן af אַף

hashamayim הַשָּׁמַיִם yismechu יִשְׂמְחוּ vetagel וְתָגֵל

ha'aretz הָאָרֶץ

malach מָלָךְ Adonai יהוה vagoyim בַגּוֹיִם veyomru וְיֹאמְרוּ

umlo'o וּמְלֹאוֹ hayam הַיָּם yir'am יִרְעַם

vechol וְכֹל hasade הַשָּׂדֶה ya'alotz יַעֲלֹץ

haya'ar הַיָּעַר atzei עֲצֵי yeranenu יְרַנְּנוּ az אָז :bo בּוֹ asher אֲשֶׁר

va בָא ki כִּי Adonai יהוה milifnei מִלִּפְנֵי

hodu הוֹדוּ :ha'aretz הָאָרֶץ אֶת et lishpot לִשְׁפֹּט

ki כִּי ladonai לַיהוה ki כִּי tov טוֹב ki כִּי

:le'olam לְעוֹלָם chasdo וְחַסְדּוֹ

---

and the Lord made the Heavens. Majesty and magnificence are His presence; power and joy are His place. Render the Lord you families of nations, render the Lord honor and power. Render the Lord honor befitting His Name, bring a gift and come before Him with splendor of holiness. Tremble before Him, all dwellers of Earth, so that the world will be built and will not collapse. Heaven will rejoice and the Earth will be happy. Let the nations say: the Lord reigns! Let the sea and all therein roar; let the field and all therein exult. Then shall the forest sing before the Lord, because He has come to judge the Earth. Be grateful to the Lord for He is good; for His kindness goes on forever.

וְאִמְרוּ (ve'imru) הוֹשִׁיעֵנוּ (hoshi'enu) אֱלֹהֵי (Elohei) מילוי ע"ב, דמב ; ילה

יִשְׁעֵנוּ (yish'enu) וְקַבְּצֵנוּ (vekabtzenu) וְהַצִּילֵנוּ (vehatzilenu) מִן (min)

הַגּוֹיִם (hagoyim) לְהוֹדוֹת (lehodot) לְשֵׁם (leshem) קָדְשֶׁךָ (kodshecha)

לְהִשְׁתַּבֵּחַ (lehishtabe'ach) בִּתְהִלָּתֶךָ: (bit'hilatecha) בָּרוּךְ (baruch)

יְהֹוָה (Adonai) אֱלֹהֵי (Elohei) מילוי ע"ב, דמב ; ילה יִשְׂרָאֵל (Yisrael)

יהוה אלהי ישראל = תרי"ג (מצוות) ; ס"ת = אדני הָעוֹלָם (ha'olam) מִן (min) וְעַד (ve'ad)

הָעֹלָם (ha'olam) וַיֹּאמְרוּ (vayomru) כָּל (chol) ילי הָעָם (ha'am) אָמֵן (amen) יאהדונהי

רוֹמְמוּ (romemu) לַיהֹוָה: (ladonai) אדני ללה, וְהַלֵּל (vehalel)

יְהֹוָה (Adonai) אֱלֹהֵינוּ (Elohenu) ילה וְהִשְׁתַּחֲווּ (vehishtachavu)

לַהֲדֹם (lahadom) רַגְלָיו (raglav) קָדוֹשׁ (kadosh) הוּא: (hu) רוֹמְמוּ (romemu)

יְהֹוָה (Adonai) אֱלֹהֵינוּ (Elohenu) ילה וְהִשְׁתַּחֲווּ (vehishtachavu)

לְהַר (lehar) קָדְשׁוֹ (kodsho) כִּי (ki) קָדוֹשׁ (kadosh) יְהֹוָה (Adonai)

אֱלֹהֵינוּ (Elohenu) ילה: וְהוּא (vehu) רַחוּם (rachum) יְכַפֵּר (yechaper) ר"ת רי"ו

עָוֹן (avon) (Abba of the klipa) וְלֹא (velo) יַשְׁחִית (yashchit) (Ima of the klipa)

וְהִרְבָּה (vehirba) לְהָשִׁיב (lehashiv) אַפּוֹ (apo) (Zeir of the klipa) וְלֹא (velo)

יָעִיר (ya'ir) כָּל (kol) ילי חֲמָתוֹ: (chamato) (Nukva of the klipa) אַתָּה (Ata)

יְהֹוָה (Adonai) לֹא (lo) תִכְלָא (tichla) רַחֲמֶיךָ (rachamecha) מִמֶּנִּי (mimeni)

וְחַסְדְּךָ (chasdecha) ר"ת = אברהם, וח"פ אל, רי"ו ול"ב נתיבות החכמה, רמ"ח (אברים), עסמ"ב וט"ו

וַאֲמִתְּךָ (va'amitecha) תָּמִיד (tamid) ע"ה קס"א קנ"א קמ"ג אותיות פשוטות יִצְּרוּנִי: (yitzeruni)

זְכֹר (zechor) ע"ב קס"א, יהי אור ע"ה (סוד המשכת העל פע מן ד' שמות הנקרא זכור)

רַחֲמֶיךָ (rachamecha) יְהֹוָה (Adonai) וַחֲסָדֶיךָ (vachasadecha) כִּי (ki)

And say: Save us, God of our salvation; gather us and save us from all nations, to give thanks to Your Holy Name, and to be glorified in saying Your praise. Blessed is the Lord, the God of Israel, from this world to the world to come! The whole nation says 'Amen' and gives praise to the Lord." (I Chronicles 16:8-36) "Exult the Lord, our God, and prostrate yourselves at His footrest, for He is sacred." (Psalms 99:5) "Exult the Lord, our God, and prostrate yourselves at His holy Mountain, for the Lord, our God, is Holy." (Psalms 99:9) "He is merciful, forgives iniquities, and does not destroy. He frequently contains His anger and does not release all His wrath." (Psalms 78:38) "And You, Lord, do not withhold Your mercy from me. May Your kindness and truth always protect me." (Psalms 40:12) "Remember Your mercy and kindness, Lord,

מֵעוֹלָם me'olam הֵמָּה hema ‹עמם› ; תְּנוּ tenu עֹז oz לֵאלֹהִים lelohim אהיה אדני ; ילה

עַל־ al יִשְׂרָאֵל Yisrael גַּאֲוָתוֹ ga'avato וְעֻזּוֹ ve'uzo בַּשְּׁחָקִים bashechakim:

נוֹרָא nora אֱלֹהִים Elohim אהיה אדני ; ילה ; מִמִּקְדָּשֶׁיךָ mimikdashecha

אֵל El יא"י ‹מילוי דס"ג› יִשְׂרָאֵל Yisrael אל ישראל = כ"ב הויות ‹כ"א דתפילין וא' דטלית›

הוּא hu נֹתֵן noten עֹז oz ‹שׁר אבגיתץ›, וְתַעֲצֻמוֹת veta'atzumot לָעָם la'am ‹עלם›

בָּרוּךְ baruch אֱלֹהִים Elohim אהיה אדני ; ילה ; ס"ת מילוי עֹדִי ‹ין לת וד› ; ברוך אלהים = עֹדִי:

EL NEKAMOT

The Name Yud, Hei, Vav, and Hei appear in this connection eleven times. The power of eleven removes the dominance of the klipot. There are ten Sefirot between our world and the Endless World. The eleventh connection is designed to give the klipot their nourishment so they won't try to rob us of ours. When we initiate this giving of Light, we gain control over the klipot. Additional support is available to us by virtue of ten spiritual giants who lived and died so they could assist us. These ten righteous souls were the incarnation of the ten brothers who sold Joseph (son of the biblical Patriarch Jacob), into slavery. In their last incarnation, Joseph's brothers were brutally murdered, but they possessed the power to leave the confines of their physical bodies so they suffered no pain. By reflecting on their actions, we can get an additional surge of power to help us lift off from the physical world.

From here until the Aromimcha, the Holy Name: יהוה appears eleven times in order to sort the klipot that are attached to the 11 curtains. When you say El Nekamot, you should meditate that God should avenge (Nekama - but the deeper meaning is to elevate, which comes from the same root - Lehakim) the deaths of the Ten Martyrs. When we recite El Nekamot it gives the Ten Martyrs' souls strength to be able to collect the sparks of the souls that are captured inside the klipa of Asiyah.

אֵל El יא"י ‹מילוי דס"ג› נְקָמוֹת nekamot יְהֹוָה‹אדני›‹אהדונהי› Adonai ר"ת אני

אֵל El יא"י ‹מילוי דס"ג› נְקָמוֹת nekamot מנק ; ר"ת = יב"ק, אלהים יהוה, אהיה אדני יהוה

הוֹפִיעַ hofi'a: הִנָּשֵׂא hinase שֹׁפֵט shofet הָאָרֶץ ha'aretz אלהים דההין ע"ה

הָשֵׁב hashev ר"ת = ע"ה ; עֹדִי ; גְּמוּל gemul עַל־ al גֵּאִים ge'im:

---

for they are eternal." (Psalms 25:6)
"Give power to God, for His majesty is over Israel and His power is in the Heavens. God, You are awesome in Your Temples, God of Israel. He gives powers and might to the nation, blessed is God." (Psalms 68:35-36)
EL NEKAMOT
"You are the God of retributions, Lord.
God of retributions appear. Arise, Judge of the world. Repay the arrogant with their due." (Psalms 94:1-2)

עַמֶּךָ amecha · עַל al · הַיְשׁוּעָה hayeshu'a · לַיהֹוָהאדנייאהדונהי ladonai

בִּרְכָתֶךָ virchatecha · סֶלָה sela · יְהֹוָהאדנייאהדונהי Adonai · צְבָאוֹת Tzeva'ot · פני שכינה

עִמָּנוּ imanu · מִשְׂגָּב misgav · לָנוּ lanu · אֱלֹהֵי Elohei · מילוי אדני

יַעֲקֹב Ya'akov · סֶלָה sela · יְהֹוָהאדנייאהדונהי Adonai

צְבָאוֹת Tzeva'ot · אַשְׁרֵי ashrei · אָדָם adam

בָּךְ bach · בֹּטֵחַ bote'ach

יְהֹוָהאדנייאהדונהי Adonai · הוֹשִׁיעָה hoshi'a · הַמֶּלֶךְ hamelech

יַעֲנֵנוּ ya'anenu · בְיוֹם veyom · קָרְאֵנוּ kore'nu

הוֹשִׁיעָה hoshi'a

אֶת־ et · עַמֶּךָ amecha · וּבָרֵךְ uvarech · אֶת־ et

נַחֲלָתֶךָ nachalatecha · וּרְעֵם ur'em · וְנַשְּׂאֵם venas'em · עַד־ ad · הָעוֹלָם ha'olam

נַפְשֵׁנוּ nafshenu · (properly enunciate the letter *Chet* in the word "chiketa") · וְכְּתָה chiketa

לַיהֹוָהאדנייאהדונהי ladonai (יוד הה וו הה)

עֶזְרֵנוּ ezrenu · וּמָגִנֵּנוּ umaginenu · הוּא hu · כִּי־ ki · בֹּו vo · יִשְׂמַח yismach

לִבֵּנוּ libenu · כִּי ki · בְשֵׁם veshem · קָדְשׁוֹ kodsho · בָטַחְנוּ vatachnu · יְהִי־ yehi

וְחַסְדְּךָ chasdecha · יְהֹוָהאדנייאהדונהי Adonai · עָלֵינוּ alenu · כַּאֲשֶׁר ka'asher

יִחַלְנוּ yichalnu · לָךְ lach · הַרְאֵנוּ har'enu · יְהֹוָהאדנייאהדונהי Adonai

וְחַסְדְּךָ chasdecha · וְיֶשְׁעֲךָ veyesh'acha · תִּתֶּן titen · לָנוּ lanu

---

"Salvation belongs to the Lord and Your blessing is upon Your Nation, Selah." (Psalms 3:9) "The Lord of Hosts is with us, and our strength is the God of Jacob, Selah." (Psalms 46:12) "The Lord of Hosts, joyful is the man that trusts in You." (Psalms 84:13) "Lord, redeem us. The King shall answer us upon the day we call Him." (Psalms 20:10) "Redeem Your Nation and bless Your inheritance, provide for them and uplift them forever." (Psalms 28:9) "Our soul has awaited Lord. He is our help and our shield. God, in Him our heart rejoices because we have trusted in His Holy Name. Lord, may Your kindness be upon us for we have placed our trust in You." (Psalms 33:20-22) "Show us Your kindness, Lord, and grant us Your salvation." (Psalms 85:8)

ufdenu וּפְדֵנוּ אֱלֹהִים, אֱהְיֶה אֲדֹנָי lanu לָּנוּ ezrata עֶזְרָתָה (מִקְוֶה) קנ"א kuma קוּמָה

Adonai יְהֹוָהאדנִיאהדונהי anochi אָנֹכִי chasdecha וְחַסְדְּךָ lema'an לְמַעַן

mitz'rayim מִצְרָיִם me'eretz מֵאֶרֶץ hama'alcha הַמַּעַלְךָ יהה Elohecha אֱלֹהֶיךָ

ashrei אַשְׁרֵי va'amal'ehu וַאֲמַלְאֵהוּ picha פִּיךָ harchev הַרְחֶב מצר

ha'am הָעָם shekacha שֶׁכָּכָה מֹשֶׁה, מהע', ע"ב בריבוע וקס"א, אל שדי, ד"פ אלהים ע"ה

lo לוֹ ashrei אַשְׁרֵי ha'am הָעָם ר"ת לאה sheAdonai שֶׁיְהֹוָהאדנִיאהדונהי

Elohav אֱלֹהָיו יהה va'ani וַאֲנִי אני bechasdecha בְּחַסְדְּךָ vatachti בָטַחְתִּי

yagel יָגֵל לההו libi לִבִּי bishu'atecha בִּישׁוּעָתֶךָ ר"ת = ב"ן ashira אָשִׁירָה

ladonai לַיהֹוָהאדנִיאהדונהי ki כִּי gamal גָּמַל alai עָלִי ס"ת יליכ

AROMIMCHA

When we do negative actions, we give our Light to the *klipa* – especially those in *Asiyah* - thereby preventing *Asiyah* from elevating. Because of this spiritual heaviness, we need to get rid of the *klipa* so *Asiyah* will be able to ascend to the World of Formation. Whereas the prayer *Hodu* disconnects us from the *klipa*, *Aromimcha* helps to retrieve and elevate the sparks of Light that are still trapped inside the *klipa*. When we separate these sparks of Light from the *klipa*, the *klipa* loses all its power and let go of *Asiyah*. The word *aromimcha* means "praise" but also "raise up," in reference to the lifting up of the sparks from the *klipa*. *Aromimcha* contain 92 words, which connects us to the power of the word "*Amen*" (equals 91 plus 1 for the word itself).

In this Psalm there are ten times the Name: יהוה which correspond to the Ten *Sefirot*. And there are 92 words, which is the numerical value of יהוה אדני (plus 1 for the word itself). *Aromimcha* is comprised of words of gratitude of the souls and the sparks of *Asiyah* that were saved and rose from the *klipot* of *Asiyah*, to become *Mayin Nukvin*. These souls thank God for raising them from *She'ol*.

aromimcha אֲרוֹמִמְךָ

(Keter) Adonai יְהֹוָהאדנִיאהדונהי עִנְיַן נִצוֹצֵי הַקְּדוֹשָׁה הָעוֹלִים וְיוֹצְאִים מִקְּלִיפוֹת דְעֲשִׂיָה הַנִקְרָא נֶפֶשׁ

ki כִּי dilitani דִלִּיתָנִי velo וְלֹא simach'ta שִׂמַּחְתָּ oyvai אֹיְבַי li לִי

"Arise and help us! Redeem us for the sake of Your kindness!" (Psalms 44:27) "I am the Lord, your God, Who took you out of the land of Egypt. Open your mouth wide and I shall fill it." (Psalms 81:11) "Joyful is the nation for whom all this is true; happy is the nation that the Lord is their God." (Psalms 144:15) "And I have trusted in Your kindness, therefore my heart shall rejoice in Your salvation. I shall sing for the Lord, for He has rewarded me." (Psalms 13:6)

AROMIMCHA

"I exalt You, Lord, for having uplifted me and did not rejoice my enemies on my account.

shivati שִׁוַּעְתִּי ילה ; דמב מילוי ע"ב, Elohai אֱלֹהַי (Chochmah) Adonai יהוהאדניאהדונהי

אֵלֶיךָ elecha וַתִּרְפָּאֵנִי vatirpa'eni: (Binah) Adonai יהוהאדניאהדונהי

הֶעֱלִיתָ he'elita מִן־ min שְׁאוֹל she'ol (elevation of the souls from Asiyah) nafshi נַפְשִׁי

זַמְּרוּ vor בּוֹר (כתיב: מיורדי) miyordi מִיָּרְדִי יל ס"ת chiyitani וְחִיִּיתַנִי zameru

אֲהיה vehodu וְהוֹדוּ chasidav וַחֲסִידָיו (Chesed) ladonai לַיהוהאדניאהדונהי

אלהים עם שיבכל ה' אותיות ג"פ rega רָגַע כִּי ki kodsho קָדְשׁוֹ: lezecher לְזֵכֶר

אדני ריבוע = דחוזיים ; ועם ס אלהים, אהיה אדני = אלהים = ס"ת be'apo בְּאַפּוֹ

עין דלת יוד = ברצונו וחיים באפו רגע כי בינה יהוה אהיה אהיה birtzono בִּרְצוֹנוֹ chayim וְחַיִּים

יהוה, אלהינו יהוה אותיות מספר כנגד) י"ד ר"ת bechi בְּכִי yalin יָלִין ba'erev בָּעֶרֶב

= רנה ולבקר בכי ילין בערב rina רִנָּה velaboker וְלַבֹּקֶר (כוזו במוכסז כוזו האותיות מספר וכן

בַּל־ bal veshalvi בְשַׁלְוִי amarti אָמַרְתִּי אני va'ani וַאֲנִי: הפנים שר מטטרון

(Gevurah) Adonai יהוהאדניאהדונהי אותיות וי' ס"ג ריבוע le'olam לְעוֹלָם emot אֶמּוֹט

oz עֹז lehareri לְהַרְרִי he'emadeta הֶעֱמַדְתָּה birtzoncha בִּרְצוֹנְךָ

nivhal: נִבְהָל hayiti הָיִיתִי ב"ן מ"ה ס"ג fanecha פָּנֶיךָ histarta הִסְתַּרְתָּ

ve'el וְאֶל ekra אֶקְרָא (Tiferet) Adonai יהוהאדניאהדונהי elecha אֵלֶיךָ

betza בֶּצַע מ"ה ma מַה־ etchanan: אֶתְחַנָּן (Netzach) Adonai יהוהאדניאהדונהי

hayodcha הַיוֹדְךָ shachat שַׁחַת יל ס"ת el אֶל berideti בְּרִדְתִּי bedami בְּדָמִי

(מזוזת) סופיות אותיות וה' (= אכא) פשוטות אותיות כ"ב ,ייז hayagid הֲיַגִּיד afar עָפָר

vechoneni וְחָנֵּנִי (Hod) Adonai יהוהאדניאהדונהי shema שְׁמַע amitecha: אֲמִתֶּךָ

מוחין: li לִי ozer עֹזֵר heyeh יהה הֱיֵה (Yesod) Adonai יהוהאדניואהדונהי

Lord, my God, I cried out to You, and You healed me. Lord, You raised my spirit from She'ol (Hell), and kept me alive when I sunk into the pit. Sing to the Lord, you, His pious ones, and give thanks to His Holy Name. For there is quietude in His anger and there is life in His will. In the evening, one may lie down crying yet be singing in the morning. When I was tranquil, I said that I shall never fall. Lord, You supported my mountain with strength; when You hid Your ountenance, I was frightened. It is to You, Lord, that I call, and to the Lord that I plead. What gain is there in spilling my blood; to be lowered into my grave? Does the dust give thanks to You, does it proclaim Your Truth? Lord, hear me and be gracious to me. Lord, be my helper.

הָפַכְתָּ hafachta מִסְפְּדִי mispedi לְמָחוֹל lemachol לִי li ס״ת יל׳

פִּתַּחְתָּ pitachta שַׂקִּי saki וַתְּאַזְּרֵנִי vate'azreni שִׂמְחָה simcha

לְמַעַן lema'an יְזַמֶּרְךָ yezamercha כָבוֹד chavod וְלֹא velo יִדֹּם yidom (pause)

לְהֹ (אדני יאהדונהי) Adonai (Malchut) ר״ת = אלהים, אהיה, אלהים אהיה אדני אֱלֹהָי Elohai

אוֹדֶךָּ odeka מילוי ע״ב, דמב ; ילה ; לְעוֹלָם le'olam ריבוע ס״ג וי׳ אותיות דס״ג

Recite this prayer between *Rosh Hashanah* and *Yom Kippur*.

YUD, HEI, VAV, AND HEI IS ELOHIM

Yud, Hei, Vav, and *Hei* corresponds to the Upper Worlds. *Elohim* refers both to the concept of judgment and to the physical world. During the ten days between *Rosh Hashanah* and *Yom Kippur*, the Upper and Lower Worlds are joined. This prayer helps us to transform any judgments decreed against us into mercy. It is important to understand that when life appears to be judging us harshly, there is always a reason.

יְהֹ(אדני יאהדונהי) Adonai הוּא hu הָאֱלֹהִים haElohim אהיה אדני ; ילה ;

יהוה הוא האלהים = ע״ו ע״ג ; ר״ת יהה.

יְהֹ(אדני יאהדונהי) Adonai הוּא hu הָאֱלֹהִים haElohim אהיה אדני ; ילה ;

יהוה הוא האלהים = ע״ו ע״ג ; ר״ת יהה.

Recite this verse twice.

ADONAI MELECH

This prayer transcends the concept of time, space, and motion, as well as the illusions of the five senses. The phrase "The Lord is King, the Lord has reigned, the Lord shall reign forever and for eternity" unifies past, present, and future, into one whole, so that when we recite *Adonai Melech* (The Lord is King) with the consciousness of transformation, we can correct mistakes we made in the past, while creating a better future and accomplishing it in the present. When we live in the present, we can correct the past and affect our future.

Angels are distinct energy forces that act as a transportation system for our prayers. This connection is so powerful that even the angels remain and sing along with us, instead of just carrying our words and thoughts to the Upper Worlds.

You have turned my mourning into a celebration for me.
You have undone my sackcloth and have girded me with joy. So that grace shall
sing for You and never be silenced, Lord, my God, I shall forever thank You." (Psalms 30:2-13)

YUD, HEI, VAV, AND HEI IS ELOHIM
The Lord is the God!
The Lord is the God! (I Kings 18:39)

According to the Book of *Hechalot*: "There is one angel that stands every morning in the middle of heaven, and sings the verses of '*Adonai Melech*,' and all the troops in the Upper Worlds sing with him all the way until *Barechu*." Because the angels sing *Adonai Melech* while standing, so do we.

Say this verse while standing.

חכמה – חסד Adonai יְהֹוָהאדניאהדונהי melech מֶלֶךְ Adonai יְהֹוָהאדניאהדונהי malach מָלַךְ בינה – גבורה ז

דעת – תפארת Adonai יְהֹוָהאדניאהדונהי | yimloch יִמְלֹךְ (מֶלֶךְ מָלַךְ יִמְלֹךְ = מנֹזֹפֹךְ, סנֹדלפֹוֹן, עֹרֹי) ו ן

יהוה le'olam לְעֹלָם ריבוע דס"ג ו' אותיות דס"ג ; ר"ת ייל וָעֶד va'ed ✧ דעת – תפארת

נצח Adonai יְהֹוָהאדניאהדונהי melech מֶלֶךְ Adonai יְהֹוָהאדניאהדונהי malach מָלַךְ הוד ז

יסוד Adonai יְהֹוָהאדניאהדונהי | yimloch יִמְלֹךְ (מֶלֶךְ מָלַךְ יִמְלֹךְ = מנֹזֹפֹךְ, סנֹדלפֹוֹן, עֹרֹי) ו ן

יהוה le'olam לְעֹלָם ריבוע דס"ג ו' אותיות דס"ג ; ר"ת ייל וָעֶד va'ed ✧ יסוד

vehaya וְהָיָה יהוה יהוה ; יהה Adonai יְהֹוָהאדניאהדונהי lemelech לְמֶלֶךְ

al עַל kol כָּל ילי ; עמם ha'aretz הָאָרֶץ אלהים דההין ע"ה bayom בַּיֹּום ע"ה

hahu הַהוּא זן, אל יהוה ע"ה yih'ye יִהְיֶה יי Adonai יְהֹוָהאדניאהדונהי

echad אֶחָד אהבה, דאגה ushmo וּשְׁמֹו מהע ע"ה, ע"ב בריבוע וקס"א, אל עֹדֹי ע"ה

echad אֶחָד אהבה, דאגה (בֹסוֹד אבא ואמא ואריך אנפֹין דעולם העשֹיֹה) ✧

ADONAI MELECH

The Lord is King, the Lord has reigned, the Lord shall reign forever and for eternity.
The Lord is King, the Lord has reigned, the Lord shall reign forever and for eternity.
"And the Lord has always been King over the whole earth.
And upon that day, the Lord shall be One and His Name One." (Zecharyah 14:9)

OLAM ASIYAH - יוד הה וו הה – אל אדני

HOSHI'ENU

| hoshi'enu הוֹשִׁיעֵנוּ   Adonai יְהֹוָֹאדִנִיאהדונהי   Elohenu אֱלֹהֵינוּ   ילה

vekabetzenu וְקַבְּצֵנוּ   min מִן   hagoyim הַגּוֹיִם   lehodot לְהוֹדוֹת

leshem לְשֵׁם   kodshecha קָדְשֶׁךָ   lehishtabe'ach לְהִשְׁתַּבֵּחַ

bit'hilatecha בִּתְהִלָּתֶךָ:

baruch בָּרוּךְ   Adonai יְהֹוָֹאדִנִיאהדונהי | Elohei אֱלֹהֵי   מילוי ע"ב, דמב ; ילה

Yisrael יִשְׂרָאֵל   ס"ת =   אדני ; יהוה אלהי ישראל = תרי"ג   (מצוות)

min מִן   ha'olam הָעוֹלָם   ve'ad וְעַד   ha'olam הָעוֹלָם

ve'amar וְאָמַר   kol כָּל   ילי   ha'am הָעָם   amen אָמֵן   יאהדונהי

haleluya הַלְלוּיָה   אלהים, אהיה אדני ; ללה:

kol כָּל   ילי   haneshama הַנְּשָׁמָה   tehalel תְּהַלֵּל   ר"ת כהת, משיוו בן דוד ע"ה

Yah יָהּ   haleluya הַלְלוּיָה   אלהים, אהיה אדני ; ללה:

LAMNATZE'ACH

By meditating upon the *Magen David* (Shield of David), we harness the power, strength, and valor of King David so that we can defeat our personal enemies. Our real enemies are not found in the outside world, regardless of what our ego tells us. Our real enemy is our *Desire to Receive for the Self Alone*. When we defeat the enemy within, external enemies suddenly disappear from our lives.

God revealed this Psalm to King David by Divine Inspiration. It was written on a golden plate made in the shape of the *Menorah* (shown on pg. 133). God also showed it to Moses. King David carried this Psalm written and engraved on the gold plate on his shield, the Shield of David. When King David went to war, he would meditate on the secrets of the *Menorah* and the seven sentences of this Psalm engraved in it, and his enemies would literally fall in defeat before him. By meditating upon it (reading the letters without turning the image upside down), we harness that power (*Midbar Kdemot*, by the Chida and also in *Menorat Zahav*, by Rav Zusha.)

HOSHI'ENU

"Save us, Lord, our God, and gather us from amongst the nations to give thanks to Your Holy Name and be glorified in Your praise. Blessed is the Lord, the God of Israel, from this world to the World to Come, and the whole nation said: Amen, Praise the Lord." (Psalms 106:47-48) *"Every soul will praise the Lord, Praise the Lord!"* (Psalms 150:6)

לַמְנַצֵּחַ lamnatze'ach   בִּנְגִינֹת binginot   מִזְמוֹר mizmor   שִׁיר shir:

אֱלֹהִים Elohim   אהיה אדני ; ילה   יְחָנֵּנוּ yechonenu   וִיבָרְכֵנוּ vivarchenu

יָאֵר ya'er   כף ויו זין ויו פָּנָיו panav   אִתָּנוּ itanu ר"ת פאי, אמן (יאהדונהי)   סֶלָה sela:

לָדַעַת lada'at   ר"ת סאל, אמן (יאהדונהי)   בָּאָרֶץ ba'aretz   דַּרְכֶּךָ darkecha

בְּכָל bechol   ב"ן,   לכב   גּוֹיִם goyim   יְשׁוּעָתֶךָ yeshu'atecha:

יוֹדוּךָ yoducha   עַמִּים amim   אֱלֹהִים Elohim   אהיה אדני ; ילה   יוֹדוּךָ yoducha

עַמִּים amim   כֻּלָּם kulam: יִשְׂמְחוּ yismechu   וִירַנְּנוּ viranenu

לְאֻמִּים le'umim   ר"ת ע"ה = איההיוהה   כִּי ki   תִשְׁפֹּט tishpot   עַמִּים amim

מִישֹׁר mishor   וּלְאֻמִּים ul'umim   בָּאָרֶץ ba'aretz   תַּנְחֵם tanchem   סֶלָה sela:

יוֹדוּךָ yoducha   עַמִּים amim   אֱלֹהִים Elohim   אהיה אדני ; ילה   יוֹדוּךָ yoducha

עַמִּים amim   כֻּלָּם kulam: ר"ת יודוך יעמוזו יודוך ארץ = יא"י   (מילוי דס"ג)

ארץ נָתְנָה natna   eretz   ריבוע יהוה = ע"ב, ירברכנו לדעת אלהים ר"ת ועם   נתה, קס"א קנ"א קמ"ג

יְבוּלָהּ yevula   ר"ת אני   יְבָרְכֵנוּ yevarchenu   אֱלֹהִים Elohim   אהיה אדני ; ילה

אֱלֹהֵינוּ Elohenu   ילה: יְבָרְכֵנוּ yevarchenu   אֱלֹהִים Elohim   אהיה אדני ; ילה

וְיִירְאוּ veyir'u   אוֹתוֹ oto   כָּל kol   ילי   אַפְסֵי afsei   אָרֶץ aretz:

LAMNATZE'ACH

"For the Leader; with string-music: A Psalm, a Song. God be gracious unto us, and bless us; may He cause His face to shine toward us; Selah. That Your way may be known upon earth, Your salvation among all nations. Let the people give thanks to You, God; let the people give thanks to You, all of them. Let the nations be glad and sing for joy; for You will judge the people with equity, and lead the nations upon earth. Selah Let the people give thanks to You, God; let the people give thanks to You, all of them. The earth has yielded her increase; may God, our own God, bless us. May God bless us; and let all the ends of the earth fear Him." (Psalms 67)

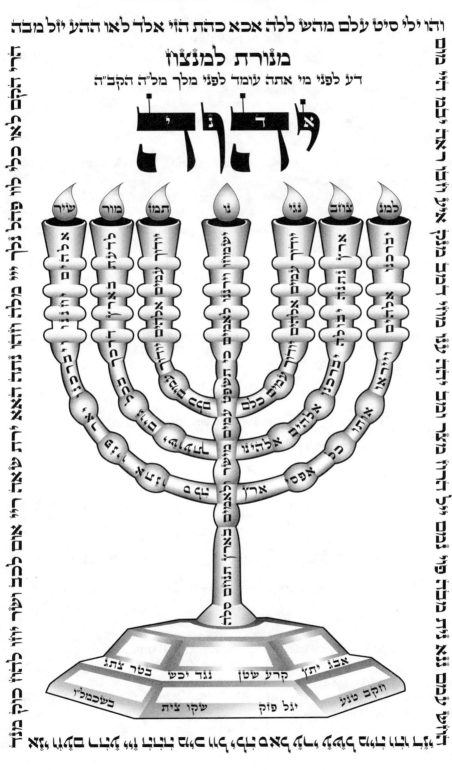

SHACHARIT – MORNING PRAYER
יוד הא ואו הא – אל יהוה - OLAM YETZIRAH

THE WORLD OF FORMATION (*YETZIRAH*)
BARUCH SHE'AMAR

From here ("*Baruch She'amar*") until "*Chei Ha'olamim*" (pg. 163) you are in the World of *Yetzirah*.

When saying *Baruch She'amar* you should stand and hold the two front *Tzitziot* and meditate to create equality between *Asiyah* and *Yetzirah* since the purification of *Yetzirah* is done by the *Talit*. Thirteen times the word "*Baruch*" corresponding to the Thirteen Attributes of *Yetzirah*.

(1) אל   **(Keter)** baruch בָּרוּךְ she'amar שֶׁאָמַר vehaya וְהָיָה יהיה

Olam Asiyah is now equal to *Olam Yetzirah* – בְּעֶשָׂיָה ◆ha'olam הָעוֹלָם

(2) רוֹוֹם   **(Chochmah)** baruch בָּרוּךְ ◆hu הוּא

(3) וווֹגֹן   **(Binah)** baruch בָּרוּךְ omer אוֹמֵר ◆ve'ose וְעֹשֶׂה

(4) ארך   baruch בָּרוּךְ gozer גּוֹזֵר ◆umkayem וּמְקַיֵּם

(5) אפים   baruch בָּרוּךְ ose עֹשֶׂה ◆vereshit בְּרֵאשִׁית

(6) ורב וֹחֶסד   baruch בָּרוּךְ merachem מְרַוֵם אברהם, וֹז"פ אל, רי"ו ול"ב נתיבות החכמה, al עַל ha'aretz הָאָרֶץ רמ"וז (אברים), עסמ"ב וט"ז אותיות פשוטות אלהים דהדין ע"ה

(7) ואמת   baruch בָּרוּךְ merachem מְרַוֵם אברהם, וֹז"פ אל, רי"ו ול"ב נתיבות החכמה, al עַל ◆haberiyot הַבְּרִיּוֹת רמ"וז (אברים), עסמ"ב וט"ז אותיות פשוטות

(8) נצר וֹחֶסד   baruch בָּרוּךְ meshalem מְשַׁלֵּם sachar שָׂכָר ב"ן י"פ tov טוֹב והו ◆lire'av לִירֵאָיו

(9) לאלפים   baruch בָּרוּךְ chai וָזי la'ad לְעַד ב"פ ב"ן vekayam וְקַיָּם ◆lanetzach לָנֶצַו

(10)נשׂא עון   baruch בָּרוּךְ pode פּוֹדֶה ◆umatzil וּמַצִּיל

(11)ופשׂע   baruch בָּרוּךְ shemo שְׁמוֹ מהע ע"ה, ע"ב ברביע וקס"א ע"ה, אל עדי ע"ה◆

THE WORLD OF FORMATION (*YETZIRAH*) - BARUCH SHE'AMAR

1) Blessed is the One Who spoke and the world came into being.
2) Blessed be He. 3) Blessed is the One Who says and does.
4) Blessed is the One Who decrees and fulfills. 5) Blessed is the One Who instigates Creation.
6) Blessed is the One Who is compassionate to the world. 7) Blessed is the One Who is compassionate to all creatures. 8) Blessed is the One Who repays well those who fear Him. 9) Blessed is the One Who lives forever and exists for eternity. 10) Blessed is the One Who redeems and saves. 11) Blessed is His Name.

(12) וזטאה baruch בָּרוּךְ Ata אַתָּה Adonai יְהֹוָה(אדני)(אהדונהי)

Elohenu אֱלֹהֵינוּ ילה melech מֶלֶךְ ha'olam הָעוֹלָם

haEl הָאֵל לאה ; יא"י (מילוי) דס"ג av אָב

harachman הָרַחֲמָן hamehulal הַמְהֻלָּל befe בְּפֶה פ"י

(מנין התיבות בברוך שאמר – בסוד "כתם טהור פו") amo עַמּוֹ◆

meshubach מְשֻׁבָּח umfo'ar וּמְפֹאָר bilshon בִּלְשׁוֹן

chasidav חֲסִידָיו va'avadav◆ וַעֲבָדָיו uvshirei וּבְשִׁירֵי

David דָּוִד avdach עַבְדְּךָ פוי, אל אדני nehalelach נְהַלֶּלְךָ

Adonai יְהֹוָה(אדני)(אהדונהי) Elohenu אֱלֹהֵינוּ ילה bishvachot בִּשְׁבָחוֹת

uvizmirot וּבִזְמִירוֹת◆ ungadelach וּנְגַדֶּלְךָ unshabchach וּנְשַׁבֵּחֲךָ

unfa'arach וּנְפָאֶרְךָ venamlichach וְנַמְלִיכְךָ venazkir וְנַזְכִּיר

shimcha שִׁמְךָ malkenu מַלְכֵּנוּ Elohenu אֱלֹהֵינוּ ילה

yachid יָחִיד chei וְחֵי (לפי הארי"ז"ל, וַחַי לפי הרש"ש) ha'olamim הָעוֹלָמִים◆ melech מֶלֶךְ meshubach מְשֻׁבָּח

um'fo'ar וּמְפֹאָר adei עֲדֵי ad עַד

shemo שְׁמוֹ מהטע ע"ה, ע"ב בריבוע וקס"א ע"ה, אל שדי ע"ה

hagadol הַגָּדוֹל להו ; עם ד' אותיות = מבה, יזל, אום◆

baruch בָּרוּךְ Ata אַתָּה Adonai יְהֹוָה(אדני)(יְהֹוָה(אדני))(אהדונהי) (13) ונקה

melech מֶלֶךְ mehulal מְהֻלָּל batishbachot בַּתִּשְׁבָּחוֹת:

---

12) Blessed are You, Lord, our God, the King of the world. The God, the compassionate Father, Who is lauded by the mouths of His Nation and Who is praised and glorified by the tongues of His righteous and His servants. With the songs of David, Your servant, We shall laud You, Lord, our God. With praises and songs, we shall exult and praise You, glorify You, and proclaim You, King. We shall mention Your Name our King, our God, Unique One and life of the worlds; the King Who is praised and glorified. And forever is His Name great. 13) Blessed are You, Lord, the King Who is extolled with praises.

MIZMOR LETODA

The essence of this prayer is appreciation for the unseen miracles that occur in our life. There are 42 words in this prayer, connecting us to the *Ana Beko'ach*, the 42-Letter Name of God. Each word connects to one of the 42 letters.

Mizmor LeToda is the *tikkun* of *Yetzirah* in *Yetzirah* and corresponds to *Abba* and *Ima* of *Yetzirah*.

(The Ari says to say this psalm while sitting down)

hari'u הָרִיעוּ   letoda לְתוֹדָה   (מ"ב תיבות – שם בן מ"ב)   mizmor מִזְמוֹר

ילי kol כָּל   ladonai לַיהוָֹהאדנייאהדונהי   יהוה אלף למד ע"ה ס"ת ; אלהים דיודין

ivdu עִבְדוּ   ha'aretz הָאָרֶץ   אלהים דההין ע"ה ; ר"ת הלכה ; ס"ת ע"ה כוק, ריבוע אדני

et אֶת   Adonai יְהוָֹהאדנייאהדונהי   besimcha בְּשִׂמְחָה   ר"ת = אהבה, אוד, דאגה

bo'u בֹּאוּ   lefanav לְפָנָיו   עשל   birnana בִּרְנָנָה: de'u דְּעוּ   ki כִּי

hu הוּא   Adonai יְהוָֹהאדנייאהדונהי   hu הוּא   Elohim אֱלֹהִים   אהיה אדני ; ילה

asanu עָשָׂנוּ   velo וְלוֹ   (כתיב: ולא)   anachnu אֲנַחְנוּ   amo עַמּוֹ   vetzon וְצֹאן

mar'ito מַרְעִיתוֹ:   bo'u בֹּאוּ   she'arav שְׁעָרָיו   betoda בְּתוֹדָה

chatzerotav חֲצֵרֹתָיו   bit'hila בִּתְהִלָּה   ע"ה אמת, אהיה פעמים אהיה ; ז"פ ס"ג

hodu הוֹדוּ   אהיה   lo לוֹ   barchu בָּרְכוּ   יהוה ריבוע יהוה ריבוע מ"ה

shemo שְׁמוֹ:   מהש   ע"ה, ע"ב   בריבוע   וקס"א   ע"ה, אל   עודי   ע"ה:

MIZMOR LETODA
"A song of thanks giving:
Sing joyfully to the Lord, all of the Earth. Serve the Lord with happiness. Come before Him with song. Know that the Lord is God. He made us and we are His. We are His nation, the flock of His pasture. Come to His gates with gratitude and to His courtyards with praise. Give thanks to Him; bless His Name.

ki **כִּי** tov וְהוּ ; כִּי טוֹב = יהוה אהיה, אום, מבה, יזל **לְהֹוּ**אדניאיאהדונהי Adonai

le'olam **לְעוֹלָם** רִיבוּעַ ס"ג ו'י אותיות דס"ג **וְחַסְדּוֹ** chasdo ג' הויות, מזלא (להמשיך

ve'ad **וְעַד** dor **דֹר** vador **וָדֹר** רי"ו, גבורה **אֱמוּנָתוֹ** emunato

הארה ממזלא עילאה)

YEHI CHEVOD

We find 18 verses in this connection, with 18 times the power of *Yud, Hei, Vav,* and *Hei.* The significance of 18 is found within the power of the *Mezuzah.* The kabbalists teach that the *Mezuzah,* which contains a piece of parchment bearing the Aramaic letters *Shin, Dalet, Yud* שד"י, or *Shaddai* - a powerful Name of God that brings us protection from negative forces, should be placed at each doorway. A doorway or entranceway is the beginning, or seed level of a room. Negative forces cling to all entryways, infecting the seed with negativity. The *Mezuzah* not only cancels this negative force but also transforms the negative energy into positive energy.

Another secret of *Shin, Dalet, Yud* is its a connection to another 72 Name of God, one that gives us the ability to eradicate all forms of negativity: The next letter after *Shin* ש in the Aramaic alphabet is *Tav* ת. The next letter to *Dalet* ד is *Hei* ה. The next letter after *Yud* י is *Kaf* כ. Placed side by side and in reverse order, these letters spell *Kaf, Hei, Tav* כהת. This three-letter sequence has the power to defuse negative energy, and was used to destroy the evil *Haman* in Persia during Purim, 2500 years ago.

When you say the 18 verses of *Yehi Chevod*, you should meditate on the 18 letters of the six combinations of the Name *Shaddai* שד"י that exist in the central Vessels of *Zeir Anpin* of *Yetzirah*, and also meditate on the 18 times the Name: יהוה appears in this section, because they are equal to the two letters *Tet* ט in the Name of the Angel Ma-tat-ron מטטרו"ן (**Do not pronounce**) which is in *Zeir Anpin* of *Yetzirah*. You should meditate that the *Tet* (9) corresponds to *Tikkunei Dikna* of *Zeir Anpin* of *Yetzirah* (nine of Direct Light and nine of Returning Light).

The numerical value of the acronym of the 18 verses of *Yehi Chevod* adds up to 686. The numerical value of the last letter of each of the 18 verses is 602, plus 18 (*Yesod – Chai - וז"י*) adds up to 620. The number of words in *Yehi Chevod* is 138 (with the *Kolel*). You should also meditate to draw קס"א, קמ"ג, קנ"א with ע"ב, ס"ג, מ"ה, ב"ן (which adds up to 686 – with the *Kolel* - and is equal to the numerical value of the word *Porat*), to *"Ben Porat Yosef "* which is *Yesod – Chai* (18) *Almin*. Thereby creating the *Keter* (620) of *Nukva* (which is called: *Chakal* וזק"ל, which adds up to 138).The *Keter* itself will be built later by the 22 letters of the *Ashrei.*

Because the Lord is good,
His kindness is eternal, and His faithfulness is for each and every generation." (Psalms 100)

(Keter—עׂ) yehi יְהִי chevod כְּבוֹד Adonai יְהֹוָאדנׂיאהדונׂהי (אַרך)

; yismach יִשְׂמַח le'olam לְעוֹלָם

bema'asav בְּמַעֲשָׂיו Adonai יְהֹוָאדנׂיאהדונׂהי (אפים)

yehi יְהִי (ד—Keter)

= mevorach מְבֹרָךְ (ורב וחסד) Adonai יְהֹוָאדנׂיאהדונׂהי shem שֵׁם

עוֹלָם olam וְעַד ve'ad מֵעַתָּה me'ata

(Chochmah—י) מִמִּזְרַח mimizrach שֶׁמֶשׁ shemesh עַד ad

מְבוֹאוֹ mevo'o מְהֻלָּל mehulal שֵׁם shem Adonai יְהֹוָאדנׂיאהדונׂהי (נשׂא עון)

goyim גּוֹיִם כָּל kol עַל al רָם ram (Chochmah—עׂ)

יְהֹוָאדנׂיאהדונׂהי Adonai (ופשע) עַל al הַשָּׁמַיִם hashamayim ;

shimcha שִׁמְךָ (ונקה) Adonai יְהֹוָאדנׂיאהדונׂהי (Binah—י) כְּבוֹדוֹ kevodo:

le'olam לְעוֹלָם Adonai יְהֹוָאדנׂיאהדונׂהי (פוקד)

zichrecha זִכְרְךָ ledor לְדֹר vador וָדֹר:

(ד—Binah) Adonai יְהֹוָאדנׂיאהדונׂהי (עַל עוֹלְשׂים) bashamayim בַּשָּׁמַיִם

hechin הֵכִין kis'o כִּסְאוֹ umalchuto וּמַלְכוּתוֹ bakol בַּכֹּל

hashamayim הַשָּׁמַיִם yismechu יִשְׂמְחוּ (ד—Chesed) mashala מָשָׁלָה:

ha'aretz הָאָרֶץ vetagel וְתָגֵל

vagoyim בַּגּוֹיִם veyomru וְיֹאמְרוּ

Adonai יְהֹוָאדנׂיאהדונׂהי (וְעַל רבעים) malach מָלָךְ:

YEHI CHEVOD

"May the glory of the Lord last forever. May the Lord rejoice in His works." (Psalms 104:31) "May the Name of the Lord be blessed from now and for all eternity. From the sun's rising until its setting the Lord's Name is praised. The Lord is high above all nations. His glory is above the heavens." (Psalms 113:2-4) "Lord, Your Name is forever. Lord, Your fame is for every generation." (Psalms 135:13) "The Lord established His Throne in the heavens, and His kingdom rules over everything." (Psalms 103:19) "Let the heavens rejoice and let the earth be glad and let them proclaim among the nations: The Lord has reigned. (I Chronicles 16:31)

melech מֶלֶךְ (ארך) Adonai יְהֹוָאדֹנָיאהדונֹהי (Chesed–ש')

יְהֹוָאדֹנָיאהדונֹהי Adonai (ורב וֹסד) | malach מָלָךְ (אפים) Adonai יְהֹוָאדֹנָיאהדונֹהי

יִמְלֹךְ le'olam לְעֹלָם ריבוע ס"ג וי' אותיות דס"ג yimloch מלך מלך ימלך = מזְזְר, סנדלפון, ערי

melech מֶלֶךְ (נושא עון) Adonai יְהֹוָאדֹנָיאהדונֹהי (Gevurah–י') :va'ed וָעֶד ר"ת ייל

goyim גוים avdu אָבְדוּ אדני ריבוע כוק, = ר"ת va'ed וָעֶד olam עֹולָם

(ופשע) Adonai יְהֹוָאדֹנָיאהדונֹהי (Gevurah–ד') בֹ:נֹ = ס"ת me'artzo מֵאַרְצֹו

machshevot מוֹזְשְׁבֹות heni הֵנִיא goyim גוים atzat עֲצַת hefir הֵפִיר

belev בְּלֶב machashavot מוֹזְשְׁבֹות rabot רַבֹּות (Tiferet–י') :amim עַמִּים

hee הִיא (ונֹקה) Adonai יְהֹוָאדֹנָיאהדונֹהי va'atzat וַעֲצַת ish אִישׁ

(פוקד) Adonai יְהֹוָאדֹנָיאהדונֹהי atzat עֲצַת (Tiferet–ש') כ"א הויות: takum תָּקוּם

machshevot מוֹזְשְׁבֹות ta'amod תַּעֲמֹד ריבוע ס"ג וי' אותיות דס"ג le'olam לְעֹולָם

hu הוּא ki כִּי (Netzach–י') רי"ו: vador וְדֹר ledor לְדֹר libo לִבֹּו

:vaya'amod וַיַּעֲמֹד tziva צִוָּה hu הוּא vayehi וַיְהִי amar אָמַר

(עולשים) Adonai יְהֹוָאדֹנָיאהדונֹהי (על) vachar בָּזֹור ki כִּי (Netzach–ש')

:lo לֹו lemoshav לְמוֹשָׁב חֹבֹו iva אִוָּה קנאה, ר' הויות, יוסף, beTziyon בְּצִיֹּון

Yah יָה lo לֹו bachar בָּזֹור אידהנויה, יאהדונהי הויות, ז' Yaakov יַעֲקֹב ki כִּי (Hod–ד')

yitosh יִטֹּשׁ lo לֹא ki כִּי (Hod–י') :lisgulato לִסְגֻלָּתֹו Yisrael יִשְׂרָאֵל

lo לֹא venachalato וְנַזֲלָתֹו amo עַמֹּו (רבעים על) Adonai יְהֹוָאדֹנָיאהדונֹהי

:ya'azov יַעֲזֹב (Yesod–ד') vehu וְהוּא rachum רַזֹום yechaper יְכַפֵּר ר"ת רי"ו

"The Lord reigns, the Lord has reigned. The Lord shall reign forever and ever. The Lord is King forever and ever. Nations have perished from His land." (Psalms 10:16) "The Lord has disrupted the conspiracy of peoples and thwarted the plans of nations." (Psalms 33:10) "Many are the thoughts in the heart of man, but it is the purpose of the Lord that takes place." (Proverbs 19:21) "The purpose of the Lord shall endure forever and the thoughts of His Heart, for all generations." (Psalms 33:11) "Because He said and it came to be, He commanded and it was established." (Psalms 33:9) "For the Lord chose Zion as His desired dwelling place." (Psalms 132:13) "For God chose Jacob for Himself and Israel as His treasure." (Psalms 135:4) "For the Lord shall not forsake His people nor shall He abandon His heritage." (Psalms 94:14) "And He is merciful, forgives

(Ima of the klipa) yashchit יַשְׁחִית velo וְלֹא־ (Abba of the klipa) avon עָוֹן

(Zeir of the klipa) apo אַפּוֹ lehashiv לְהָשִׁיב vehirba וְהִרְבָּה

‬:(Nukva of the klipa) chamato וַחֲמָתוֹ יל׳ kol כָּל־ ya'ir יָעִיר velo וְלֹא־

(ע׳-יסוד) נהורין ‬ וע׳׳ע יהוה hoshi'a הוֹשִׁיעָה Adonai לַיהֹוָאַדְנָיאהדונהי

וביום עם׳ה נצר, מזבח, זן אל יהוה veyom בְּיוֹם ya'anenu יַעֲנֵנוּ ר׳׳ת יהה hamelech הַמֶּלֶךְ

kor'enu קָרְאֵנוּ ר׳׳ת יב׳׳ק, אלהים יהוה, אהיה אדני יהוה; ס׳׳ת ב׳׳ן ועם כ׳ דהמלך = ע׳׳ב:

Then without any interruption you should immediately start the two verses of *Ashrei* to make *Keter* to *Nukva* from the 22 letters of *Ashrei* (as mentioned before *Yehi Chevod*).

THE ASHREI

Twenty-one of the twenty-two letters of the Aramaic alphabet are encoded in the *Ashrei* in their correct order from *Alef* to *Tav*. King David, the author, left out the Aramaic letter *Nun* from this prayer, because *Nun* is the first letter in the Aramaic word *nefilah*, which means "falling." Falling refers to a spiritual decline, as in falling into the *klipa*. Feelings of doubt, depression, worry, and uncertainty are consequences of spiritual falling. Because the Aramaic letters are the actual instruments of Creation, this prayer helps to inject order and the power of Creation into our lives, without the energy of falling.

In this Psalm there are ten times the Name: יהוה for the Ten *Sefirot*. This Psalm is written according to the order of the *Alef Bet*, but the letter *Nun* is omitted to prevent falling.

ב׳׳פ ראה vetecha בֵיתֶךָ yoshvei יוֹשְׁבֵי (סוד הכתר) ashrei אַשְׁרֵי

ha'am הָעָם ashrei אַשְׁרֵי :sela סֶלָה yehalelucha יְהַלְלוּךָ od עוֹד

lo לֹ ד׳׳ה אלהים ע׳׳ה mehsah, mosheh, ע׳׳ב בריבוע וקס׳׳א, אל עדי, ד׳׳פ shekacha שֶׁכָּכָה

(Keter) she'Adonai שֶׁיְהֹוָאַדְנָיאהדונהי לאה ר׳׳ת ha'am הָעָם ashrei אַשְׁרֵי

leDavid לְדָוִד ז׳׳פ ס׳׳ג אהיה פעמים אהיה, ע׳׳ה אמת, tehila תְהִלָּה ילה: Elohav אֱלֹהָיו

va'avarcha וַאֲבָרְכָה hamelech הַמֶּלֶךְ Elohai אֱלוֹהַי aromimcha אֲרוֹמִמְךָ

:va'ed וָעֶד דס׳׳ג ו׳ אותיות דס׳׳ג ריבוע le'olam לְעוֹלָם shimcha שִׁמְךָ

---

iniquity, and does not destroy; He frequently diverts His anger and does not arouse all His Wrath." (Psalms 70:38) "Lord save us. The King shall answer on the day that we call Him." (Psalms 20:10)

THE ASHREI

"Joyful are those who dwell in Your House, they shall praise You, Selah." (Psalms 84:5) *"Joyful is the nation that this is theirs and joyful the nation that the Lord is their God."* (Psalms 145:15) *"A Praise of David:* א *I shall exalt You, my God, the King, and I shall bless Your Name forever and for eternity.*

יהוה אל זן מזבוֹח, נגד ע"ה yom **יוֹם** לכב ב"ן, bechol **בְּכֹל**

shimcha **שִׁמְךָ** יהוה מ"ה va'ahalela **וַאֲהַלְלָה** avarcheka **אֲבָרְכֶךָ**

va'ed **וָעֶד** דס"ג אותיות וי' דס"ג ריבוע le'olam **לְעוֹלָם**

אום יזל, מבה, = אותיות ד' עם ; להוה gadol **גָּדוֹל**

ללה אדני, umhulal **וּמְהֻלָּל** *(Chochmah)* Adonai **יְהוָֹאדנִיאהדונהי**

cheker **וְחֵקֶר** en **אֵין** והו veligdulato **וְלִגְדֻלָּתוֹ** me'od **מְאֹד**

דלים ר"ת ma'asecha **מַעֲשֶׂיךָ** yeshabach **יְשַׁבַּח** ledor **לְדוֹר** dor **דּוֹר**

אותיות סופיות סן|זן|ך' והל (=אכא) כ"ב אותיות פשוטות יזן, yagidu **יַגִּידוּ** ugvurotecha **וּגְבוּרֹתֶיךָ**

vedivrei **וְדִבְרֵי** hodecha **הוֹדֶךָ** kevod **כְּבוֹד** hadar **הֲדַר**

אדני אהיה אלהים, ר"ת nifle'otecha **נִפְלְאֹתֶיךָ**

פז' טהור כתם (בסוד) = פ"ז הפסוק ר"ת asicha **אָשִׂיחָה**

ugdulatcha **וּגְדֻלָּתְךָ** yomeru **יֹאמֵרוּ** no'rotecha **נוֹרְאֹתֶיךָ** ve'ezuz **וֶעֱזוּז**

(מילוי דס"ג) יא"י = ס"ת asaperena **אֲסַפְּרֶנָּה** ריבוע יהוה ע"ב, = ר"ת (וּגְדֻלֹתָיך : כתיב)

yabi'u **יַבִּיעוּ** לאו tuvcha **טוּבְךָ** rav **רַב** zecher **זֵכֶר**

רי"ו יהוה = ר"ת הפסוק ; לכב יבמ, ב"ן, = ס"ת yeranenu **יְרַנֵּנוּ** vetzidkatcha **וְצִדְקָתְךָ**

(Binah) Adonai **יְהוָֹאדנִיאהדונהי** verachum **וְרַחוּם** chanun **חַנּוּן**

יהוה = ר"ת ב"ן ס"ג = ס"ת apayim **אַפַּיִם** erech **אֶרֶךְ** עאל = יהוה ורחום חנון

יהוה ריבוע ע"ב, chased **וְחֶסֶד** (וּגְדֹל : כתיב) ugdal **וּגְדָל**

ב *I shall bless You every day and I shall praise Your Name forever and for eternity.*
ג *The Lord is great and exceedingly praised. His greatness is unfathomable.*
ד *One generation and the next shall praise Your deeds and tell of Your might.*
ה *The brilliance of Your splendid glory and the wonders of Your acts, I shall speak of.*
ו *They shall speak of the might of Your awesome acts and I shall tell of Your greatness.*
ז *They shall express the remembrance of Your abundant goodness, and Your righteousness they shall joyfully proclaim.* ח *The Lord is merciful and compassionate, slow to anger and great in kindness.*

SHACHARIT – MORNING PRAYER
OLAM YETZIRAH – אל יהוה – הא וֹאוּ הא – יוד הא

lakol **לכֹל** (Chesed) Adonai לַיְהֹוָ֑ ואהדונהי והו **טוֹב**-tov

al **עַל**-verachamav **וְרַחֲמָיו** (מילוי דס"ג) ל"ז ; ס"ת ; אדני יה

kol **כָּל** ילי ; עמם ; ר"ת ריבוע ב"ן ע"ה ma'asav **מַעֲשָׂיו** ס"ת ע"ב, ריבוע יהוה

ma'asecha **מַעֲשֶׂיךָ** kol **כָּל** ילי (Gevurah) Adonai לַיְהֹוָ ואהדונהי yoducha **יוֹדוּךָ**

vachasidecha **וַחֲסִידֶיךָ** ר"ת אלהים, אהיה אדני **יְבָרְכוּכָה** yevarchucha ס"ת = מ"ה:

kevod **כְּבוֹד** malchutcha **מַלְכוּתְךָ** yomeru **יֹאמֵרוּ** ugvuratcha **וּגְבוּרָתְךָ**

yedaberu **יְדַבֵּרוּ** ר"ת הפסוק = אלהים, אהיה אדני ; ס"ת = ב"ן, יבמ, לכב:

lehodi'a **לְהוֹדִיעַ** livnei **לִבְנֵי** ha'adam **הָאָדָם** ר"ת ללה, אדני

gevurotav **גְּבוּרֹתָיו** uchvod **וּכְבוֹד** hadar **הֲדַר**

malchuto **מַלְכוּתוֹ** ר"ת מ"ה וס"ת = רי"ו ; ר"ת הפסוק ע"ה = ק"כ צירופי אלהים:

malchutcha **מַלְכוּתְךָ** malchut **מַלְכוּת** kol **כָּל**-ילי olamim **עֹלָמִים**

umemshaltecha **וּמֶמְשַׁלְתְּךָ** bechol **בְּכָל** ב"ן, לכב dor **דּוֹר** vador **וָדֹר** רי"ו:

somech **סוֹמֵךְ** ריבוע אדני Adonai יְהֹוָ ואהדניאאהדונהי (Tiferet)

hanoflim **הַנֹּפְלִים** (יאהדונהי) אמן סאל, ר"ת לכל אדני סומך ; אדני יה lechol **לְכֹל**

vezokef **וְזוֹקֵף** lechol **לְכֹל** יה אדני hakefufim **הַכְּפוּפִים** נמם:

enei **עֵינֵי** ריבוע דמ"ה chol **כָּל** ילי elecha **אֵלֶיךָ** yesaberu **יְשַׂבֵּרוּ** veAta **וְאַתָּה**

noten **נוֹתֵן** אבגיתץ, ושׂר lahem **לָהֶם** et **אֶת**-ochlam **אָכְלָם** be'ito **בְּעִתּוֹ**:

ט The Lord is good to all, His compassion extends over all His acts.
י All that You have made shall thank You, God, and Your pious ones shall bless You.
כ They shall speak of the glory of Your Kingdom and talk of Your mighty deeds.
ל His mighty deeds He makes known to man and the glory of His splendid Kingdom.
מ Yours is the Kingdom of all worlds and Your reign extends to each and every generation.
ס The Lord supports all those who fell and holds upright all those who are bent over.
ע The eyes of all look hopefully towards You, and You give them their food at its proper time.

POTE'ACH ET YADECHA

We connect to the letters *Pei, Alef,* and *Yud* by opening our hands and holding our palms skyward. Our consciousness is focused on receiving sustenance and financial prosperity from the Light through our actions of tithing and sharing, our *Desire to Receive for the Sake of Sharing.* In doing so, we also acknowledge that the sustenance we receive comes from a higher source and is not of our own doing. According to the sages, if we do not meditate on this idea at this juncture, we must repeat the prayer.

פתחו (שע"ו נהורין למ"ה ולס"ה)

פותחו את ידך ר"ת פאי	יוד הי ויו הי יוד הי ויו הי (וז' וזיוורתי)
גימ' יאהדונהי זו"ן	אלף למד אלף למד (ע"ע)
וחכמה דו"א ו"ק	יוד הא ואו הא (לו"א)
יסוד דנוק'	אדני (ולנוקבא)

פּוֹתֵחַ pote'ach **אֶת** et yadecha **יָדֶךָ** ר"ת פאי וס"ת וזהך עם ג' אותיות = **דִּיקָרְנוֹסָא**

ובאתב"ש הוא סאל, פאי, אמן, יאהדונהי ; ועוד יכוין שם וזהך בעילוב יהוה – **יְוֹהַתּוּכָה**

מצפץ מצפץ מווזין דפנים דאווזר אלהים אלהים
להמעיר פ"ו אורות לכל מילוי דכל

ואוזר דפרצופי נה"י וזג"ת	וזהך	אוזר דפרצופי נה"י וזג"ת
דיצירה דרוזל הנקראת לאה		דפרצופ וזג"ת דיצירה דו"א
לף מד י וד ם		לף מד י וד ם
אלף למד הי יוד מם	סאל יאהדונהי	אלף למד הי יוד מם

וּמַשְׂבִּיעַ umasbi'a וזהך עם ג' אותיות = **דִּיקָרְנוֹסָא**

ובא"ת ב"ע הוא סאל, אמן, יאהדונהי ; ועוד יכוין שם וזהך בעילוב יהוה – **יְוֹהַתּוּכָה**

מצפץ מצפץ מווזין דפנים דאווזר אלהים אלהים
להמעיר פ"ו אורות לכל מילוי דכל

ואוזר דפרצופי נה"י וזג"ת	וזהך	אוזר דפרצופי נה"י וזג"ת
דיצירה דרוזל הנקראת לאה		דפרצופ נה"י דיצירה דו"א
לף מד י וד ם		לף מד י וד ם
אלף למד הי יוד מם		אלף למד הי יוד מם

לְכָל lechol יה אדני (להמעיר מווזין ד–יה אל הנוקבא שהיא אדני)

וָֹי chai כל וזי = אהיה אהיה יהוה, בינה ע"ה, וזיים

רָצוֹן ratzon מהע ע"ה, ע"ב בריבוע וקס"א ע"ה, אל שדי ע"ה ; ר"ת רוזל שהיא המלכות הצריכה לעופע

יוד יוד הי יוד הי ויו יוד הי ויו הי יסוד דאבא
אלף הי יוד הי יסוד דאימא
להמתיק רוזל וב' דמעין שׁךְ פר

Also meditate to draw abundance and sustenance and blessing to all the worlds from the *ratzon* mentioned above. You should meditate and focus on this verse because it is the essence of prosperity, and that God is intervening and sustaining and supporting all of Creation.

POTE'ACH ET YADECHA

פ   *Open   Your   Hands   and   satisfy   every   living   thing   with   desire.*

OLAM YETZIRAH - יוד הא ואו הא – אל יהוה

לכב, ב"ן   bechol **בְּכָל** (Yesod) Adonai יוד הא ואו אדני יאהדונהי tzadik **צַדִּיק**

יבמ, ב"ן   ma'asav **מַעֲשָׂיו** לכב, ב"ן bechol **בְּכָל** vechasid **וְחָסִיד** derachav **דְּרָכָיו**

אדני   יה   lechol **לְכָל** (Malchut) Adonai יהוה אדני יאהדונהי karov **קָרוֹב**

asher **אֲשֶׁר**   אדני   יה   lechol **לְכָל** kor'av **קֹרְאָיו**

ס"ג   ז"פ אהיה, פעמים אהיה ve'emet **בֶּאֱמֶת** yikra'uhu **יִקְרָאֻהוּ**

ya'ase **יַעֲשֶׂה** yere'av **יְרֵאָיו** retzon **רְצוֹן**

veyoshi'em **וְיוֹשִׁיעֵם** yishma **יִשְׁמַע** shav'atam **שַׁוְעָתָם** ve'et **וְאֶת**

(Netzach) Adonai יהוה אדני יאהדונהי shomer **שׁוֹמֵר**

אכא   ר"ת   ohavav **אֹהֲבָיו** kol **כָּל** et **אֶת**

yashmid **יַשְׁמִיד** haresha'im **הָרְשָׁעִים** kol **כָּל** ve'et **וְאֶת**

pi **פִּי** yedaber **יְדַבֵּר** (Hod) Adonai יהוה אדני יאהדונהי tehilat **תְּהִלַּת**

vivarech **וִיבָרֵךְ** kol **כָּל** basar **בָּשָׂר**

me'ata **מֵעַתָּה** ya **יָהּ** nevarech **נְבָרֵךְ** va'anachnu **וַאֲנַחְנוּ** va'ed **וָעֶד**

haleluya **הַלְלוּיָהּ** olam **עוֹלָם** ve'ad **וְעַד**

THE FIVE PSALMS

At the beginning and end of each Psalm, we find the word *Haleluyah*, meaning "Praise the Lord." As Kabbalah always says, God does not need our praise. The word is a code; these ten *Haleuyahs* link us to the Ten *Sefirot*. They help us ascend to the top of the World of Formation, *Yetzirah*.

צ   *The Lord is righteous in all His ways and virtuous in all His deeds.*
ק   *The Lord is close to all who call Him, and only to those who call Him truthfully.*
ר   *He shall fulfill the will of those who fear Him; He hears their wailing and saves them.*
ש   *The Lord protects all who love Him and He destroys the wicked.*
ת   *My lips utter the praise of the Lord and all flesh shall bless His Holy Name, forever and for eternity."*
(Psalms 145) "And we shall bless the Lord forever and for eternity. Praise the Lord!" (Psalms 115:18)

OLAM YETZIRAH - אל יהוה – הא ואו הא יוד

> Ten times *Haleluyah* is the *tikkun* of the Ten *Sefirot* of *Beriah* in *Yetzirah*

THE FIRST PSALM – MALCHUT AND YESOD

This first Psalm contains *Yud*, *Hei*, *Vav*, and *Hei*, the Tetragrammaton (יהוה), nine times. This nine is linked to the upper nine *Sefirot*, from *Yesod* to *Keter*. The energy of our realm, the World of *Malchut*, is receiving. Like the moon, *Malchut* has no Light of its own and draws its Light from the upper nine dimensions through our spiritual actions of transformation.

(*Malchut of Yetzirah*) haleluya הַלְלוּיָהּ אהיה אדני ; ללה , אלהים, אהיה ארֹני haleli הַלְלִי

nafshi נַפְשִׁי et אֶת- Adonai יְהֹוָהִאַהרֹנִהֹי (*Keter*) ahalela אֲהַלְלָה מ"ה יהוה

(*Chochmah*) Adonai יְהֹוָהִאַהרֹנִהֹיאַ bechayai בְּחַיָּי azamra אֲזַמְּרָה

be'odi בְּעוֹדִי מילוי ע"ב, דמב ; ילה : ר"ת וס"ת הפסוק = אמן (יאהרונהי) lelohai לֵאלֹהַי

adam אָדָם beven בְּבֶן- vindivim בִנְדִיבִים tivtechu תִבְטְחוּ al אַל-

yashuv יָשֻׁב rucho רוּחוֹ tetze תֵצֵא teshu'a תְּשׁוּעָה lo לוֹ she'en שֶׁאֵין

hahu הַהוּא אל יהוה , זן מזבח, נגד, ע"ה bayom בַּיּוֹם le'admato לְאַדְמָתוֹ

avdu אָבְדוּ (מילוי דס"ג) יא"י sheEl שֶׁאֵל ashrei אַשְׁרֵי eshtonotav עֶשְׁתֹּנֹתָיו

be'ezro בְּעֶזְרוֹ אידהנויה , יאהדונהי , הויות Ya'akov יַעֲקֹב sivro שִׂבְרוֹ

al עַל (*Binah*) Adonai יְהֹוָהִאַהרֹנִהֹיאַ Elohav אֱלֹהָיו ילה ose עֹשֶׂה

shamayim שָׁמַיִם י"פ טל, י"פ כוזו et אֶת- va'aretz וָאָרֶץ hayam הַיָּם ילי

ve'et וְאֶת- kol כָּל- asher אֲשֶׁר- ילי bam בָּם עם בן מ"ב hashomer הַשֹׁמֵר

emet אֱמֶת אהיה פעמים אהיה, ז"פ ס"ג le'olam לְעוֹלָם ריבוע ס"ג ו' אותיות דס"ג

ose עֹשֶׂה mishpat מִשְׁפָּט ע"ה ה"פ אלהים la'ashukim לַעֲשׁוּקִים noten נֹתֵן

lechem לֶחֶם ג הויות lare'evim לָרְעֵבִים Adonai יְהֹוָהִאַהרֹנִהֹי

(*Chesed*) matir מַתִּיר asurim אֲסוּרִים Adonai יְהֹוָהִאַהרֹנִהֹי (*Gevurah*)

poke'ach פֹּקֵחַ ivrim עִוְרִים מ"ה קמ"ג Adonai יְהֹוָהִאַהרֹנִהֹיאַ (*Tiferet*) zokef זֹקֵף

kefufim כְּפוּפִים Adonai יְהֹוָהִאַהרֹנִהֹיאַ (*Netzach*) ohev אֹהֵב tzadikim צַדִּיקִים

THE FIVE PSALMS - THE FIRST PSALM

"Praise the Lord! My soul praises the Lord! I shall praise the Lord while I am still alive; I shall play melodies to my God while I exist. Do not place your trust in nobles; not in a man who has no means of salvation. His breath leaves him and he returns to his earth. Upon that day, his plans perish. Fortunate is the one whom the God of Jacob comes to his aid, and who rests his hope on the Lord, his God. He creates the heavens and the earth, the sea, and all that they contain. The One Who guards truth forever; Who acts justly toward the oppressed; Who gives bread to the hungry. The Lord releases those who are imprisoned. The Lord gives sight to the blind. The Lord stands upright those who are bent over. The Lord loves the righteous.

עדי = ר"ת gerim גֵּרִים אֶת־ et shomer שֹׁמֵר (Hod) Adonai יְהֹו(אדניליאהדונהי)

ve'almana וְאַלְמָנָה (מראה) ויפה תואר יפה יוסף (ויהי) יוסף yatom יָתוֹם

resha'im רְשָׁעִים ע"ב קס"א ,יב"ק ב"פ vederech וְדֶרֶךְ ר"ת = יהוה ye'oded יְעוֹדֵד

(Yesod) Adonai יהוהו(אדנילי)אהדונהי yimloch יִמְלֹךְ רי"ו ,ר"ת ye'avet יְעַוֵּת

Tziyon צִיּוֹן ילה Elohayich אֱלֹהַיִךְ ו"י דס"ג אותיות , ס"ג ריבוע le'olam לְעוֹלָם

יוסף, ו' הויות, קנאה, ד ledor לְדֹר vador וָדֹר רי"ו ; ר"ת אצלו (רמז שמלכות אצל ז"א

ללה: ; אדני אהיה , אלהים haleluya הַלְלוּיָהּ (Yesod of Yetzirah) (כנגדה היוה שאין אע"פ

THE SECOND PSALM – THE NEXT 2 SEFIROT

The power of this Psalm helps us balance our acts of judgment and mercy towards other people.

This Psalm contains the Name: יהוה five times, which corresponds to the five *Chasadim* (mercy) through which the five *Gevurot* (judgment) are sweetened. This Psalm contains 139 words (with the *Kolel*) which adds up to the numerical value of *ko'ach* (strength), and *Yabok* (יב"ק = יהוה + אלהים - a code for sweetening judgment).

כי טאב = ; כי והו ; tov טוֹב ki כִּי־ ללה ; אדני אהיה , אלהים haleluya הַלְלוּיָהּ

ki כִּי־ (Hod) ילה Elohenu אֱלֹהֵינוּ zamera זַמְּרָה (Yesod) יזל , מבה ,אום ,אהיה יהוה

ס"ג: ז"פ ,אהיה פעמים אהיה ,אמת ע"ה tehila תְּהִלָּה nava נָאוָה (Netzach) na'im נָעִים

(First Chesed) Adonai יְהֹו(אדניליאהדונהי) Yerushalayim יְרוּשָׁלַיִם ס"ג bone בּוֹנֵה

yechanes יְכַנֵּס: Yisrael יִשְׂרָאֵל יהוה ריבוע ,ע"ב , nidchei נִדְחֵי

אדני , ללה ר"ת lev לֵב lishvurei לִשְׁבוּרֵי harofe הָרֹפֵא

The Lord watches over the converts and gives encouragement to the orphan and the widow, But He twists the way of the wicked. The Lord shall reign forever, your God, for each and every generation, Zion. Praise the Lord!" (Psalms 146)

THE SECOND PSALM

"Praise the Lord! For it is good to play melodies to our God, for it is pleasant and beautiful to praise Him. The Lord builds Jerusalem. He shall gather the scattered of Israel. He is healer of the brokenhearted

OLAM YETZIRAH - אל יהוה – הא ואו הא יוד

UMECHABESH LE'ATZVOTAM

According to the *Zohar*, this verse releases the energy of immortality, hastening its arrival. By releasing the energy of immortality into our spiritual atmosphere, we are helping to empower medical researchers, biologists, geneticists, and all other scientists in their quest to find the secrets to longevity, anti-aging, and the regeneration of human cells and organs.

le'atzvotam לְעַצְבוֹתָם׃ umechabesh וּמְחַבֵּשׁ

lechulam לְכֻלָּם lakochavim לַכּוֹכָבִים mispar מִסְפָּר mone מוֹנֶה

shemot שֵׁמוֹת yikra יִקְרָא׃ gadol גָּדוֹל

verav וְרַב־ ko'ach כֹּחַ adonenu אֲדוֹנֵינוּ

anavim עֲנָוִים me'oded מְעוֹדֵד mispar מִסְפָּר׃ en אֵין litvunato לִתְבוּנָתוֹ

resha'im רְשָׁעִים mashpil מַשְׁפִּיל (Second Chesed) Adonai יְהוָה

(Third Chesed) ladonai לַיהוָה enu עֲנוּ aretz אָרֶץ׃ adei עֲדֵי־

vechinor בְּכִנּוֹר׃ lelohenu לֵאלֹהֵינוּ zameru זַמְּרוּ betoda בְּתוֹדָה

be'avim בְּעָבִים shamayim שָׁמַיִם ham'chase הַמְכַסֶּה

hamatzmi'ach הַמַּצְמִיחַ matar מָטָר la'aretz לָאָרֶץ hamechin הַמֵּכִין

livhema לִבְהֵמָה noten נוֹתֵן chatzir וְחָצִיר׃ harim הָרִים

yikra'u יִקְרָאוּ׃ asher אֲשֶׁר orev עֹרֵב livnei לִבְנֵי lachma לַחְמָה

yechpatz יֶחְפָּץ hasus הַסּוּס vigvurat בִּגְבוּרַת lo לֹא

yirtze יִרְצֶה׃ (Netzach and Hod) ha'ish הָאִישׁ veshokei בְּשׁוֹקֵי lo לֹא־

UMECHABESH LE'ATZVOTAM

And He tends to their grief. He sets the numbers of stars and calls them by their names. Our Master is great and exceedingly powerful. His understanding is limitless. The Lord gives strength to the humble, and lowers the wicked down to earth. Raise your voices to the Lord with gratitude. Play melodies with a harp to our God. He covers the heavens with clouds. He prepares rain for the earth; He causes mountains to grow grass. He provides the beasts with food and for the young ravens that call out. He does not desire the strength of the horse nor does He want the thighs of man.

yere'av יְרֵאָיו et אֶת־ (Fourth Chesed) Adonai יְהֹוָה rotze רוֹצֶה

et אֶת־ מלא, הויות, ג' lechasdo לְחַסְדּוֹ יִיי ham'yachalim הַמְיַחֲלִים

et אֶת־ Yerushalayim יְרוּשָׁלַיִם shabechi שַׁבְּחִי (להמשיך הארה ממלא עילאה)

Elohayich אֱלֹהָיִךְ ילה haleli הַלְלִי (Fifth Chesed) Adonai יְהֹוָה

berichei בְּרִיזֵי פהל chizak וְזֵּזַק ki כִּי־ הויות, ר' יוסף, קנאה Tziyon צִיּוֹן

bekirbech בְּקִרְבֵּךְ banayich בָּנַיִךְ berach בֵּרַךְ she'arayich שְׁעָרָיִךְ

chitim וְחִטִּים chelev וְחֵלֶב shalom שָׁלוֹם gevulech גְּבוּלֵךְ hasam הַשָּׂם־

aretz אֶרֶץ ר"ת האא imrato אִמְרָתוֹ hashole'ach הַשֹּׁלֵחַ yasbi'ech יַשְׂבִּיעֵךְ

devaro דְּבָרוֹ ראה: yarutz יָרוּץ mehera מְהֵרָה ad עַד־

katzamer כַּצֶּמֶר מצר sheleg שֶׁלֶג ועוד, יתן, אבג אלף אלף אלף דג' אהיה hanoten הַנֹּתֵן

karcho קָרְחוֹ mashlich מַשְׁלִיךְ yefazer יְפַזֵּר ka'efer כָּאֵפֶר kefor כְּפוֹר

ya'amod יַעֲמֹד ילי mi מִי karato קָרָתוֹ lifnei לִפְנֵי chefitim כְּפִתִּים

rucho רוּחוֹ yashev יַשֵּׁב veyamsem וְיַמְסֵם ראה devaro דְּבָרוֹ yishlach יִשְׁלַח

devarav דְּבָרָיו ראה (כתיב: דברו) magid מַגִּיד mayim מָיִם yizelu יִזְּלוּ

umishpatav וּמִשְׁפָּטָיו chukav וְחֻקָּיו הויות, יאהדונהי אידהנויה ו' leYaakov לְיַעֲקֹב

lechol לְכָל־ יה אדני chen כֵּן asa עָשָׂה lo לֹא (Hod) leYisrael לְיִשְׂרָאֵל

goy גּוֹי וּמִשְׁפָּטִים bal בַּל־ ל"ב נתיבות הקדושה וכנגדם ב"ל בס"א (בלעם ובלק) umishpatim

haleluya הַלְלוּיָהּ (Hod) yeda'um יְדָעוּם ר"ת = סמאל ; אהיה אדני ; ללה: אלהים, אהיה

The Lord only wants those who fear Him and those who place their hopes in His kindness. Praise the Lord, Jerusalem, and laud your God, Zion, for He has strengthened the bolts of your gates and blessed your children within. He sets peace at your borders. He satiates you with the best of wheat. He sends out His messages to the earth and His words travel very fast. He sends down snow as if it was wool and He scatters frost as if ash. He tosses His hail as if crumbs of bread. Who can stand up to His cold? He sends forth His word and melts it. He makes His wind blow and His waters to flow. He teaches His words to Jacob; His statutes and laws to Israel. He has not done so for any other nation. He informed them not of the laws. Praise the Lord!" (Psalms 147)

THE THIRD PSALM (DAILY HALEL) – TIFERET AND GEVURAH

In this Psalm, we offer thanks to the Creator, but what we are actually doing is acknowledging that we are not really entitled to anything - that our gifts in this life far outweigh our efforts. This does not come from the standpoint of having low self-worth, but rather from a combined sense of humility and appreciation for everything we receive in life.

You should be very careful with this Psalm and say it slowly with genuine deep meditation because here the sages said: "My part should be with those who say the *Halel* everyday." There are 14 verses for the word *yad* (hand) whose numerical value is 14, connecting us to *Yad Rama* (Central Column) and *Yad Chazaka* (Left Column).

(Asiyah) halelu הַלְלוּ ; ללה אהיה ארני, אלהים haleluya הַלְלוּיָה (Tiferet of Yetzirah)

hashamayim הַשָּׁמַיִם min מִן־ ר"ת אהיה Adonai יְהוָֹה et אֶת־

:bameromim בַּמְּרוֹמִים (Yetzirah) haleluhu הַלְלוּהוּ ; ר"ת מ"ה ; ר"ת מ"ה י"פ טל, י"פ כוזו

haleluhu הַלְלוּהוּ mal'achav מַלְאָכָיו ילי chol כָּל (Beriah) haleluhu הַלְלוּהוּ

:ס"ת ס"ג = אהיה ; ס"ת הפסוק = מ"ה ; ר"ת הפסוק = ע"ב ס"ג מ"ה tzeva'av צְבָאָו ילי kol כָּל (Atzilut)

ילי kol כָּל haleluhu הַלְלוּהוּ veyare'ach וְיָרֵחַ shemesh שֶׁמֶשׁ haleluhu הַלְלוּהוּ

shemei שְׁמֵי haleluhu הַלְלוּהוּ :סוף אין רז, or אוֹר kochvei כּוֹכְבֵי

me'al מֵעַל asher אֲשֶׁר vehamayim וְהַמַּיִם י"פ טל, י"פ כוזו hashamayim הַשָּׁמַיִם

et אֶת־ yehalelu יְהַלְלוּ :ר"ת מ"ה ; י"פ טל, י"פ כוזו hashamayim הַשָּׁמַיִם עולם

:venivra'u וְנִבְרָאוּ tziva צִוָּה hu הוּא ki כִּי Adonai יְהוָֹה shem שֵׁם

vaya'amidem וַיַּעֲמִידֵם ב"פ בן le'olam לְעוֹלָם :ריבוע ס"ג ו' אותיות דס"ג la'ad לָעַד

chok חֹק־ natan נָתַן velo וְלֹא ס"ת קנ"א (אלף הה יוד הה, מקוה), ארני אלהים

:ya'avor יַעֲבוֹר רפ"ח (להעלות רפ"ח ניצוצות שנפלו לקליפה דמשם באים התחלואים)

THE THIRD PSALM

"Praise the Lord! Praise the Lord from the Heavens; praise Him in the high places; praise Him, all His angels; praise Him, all His Hosts. Praise Him, sun and moon; praise Him, all stars of Light; praise Him, the Highest Heavens, and the water that is above the Heavens. They praise the Name of the Lord, for He commanded and they were created. And He erected them forever and ever; He set laws that cannot be transgressed.

הַלְלוּ halelu אֶת־ et יְהוָֹה/אהדונהי Adonai מִן min הָאָרֶץ ha'aretz אלהים דההין ע"ה

תַּנִּינִים taninim וְכָל־ vechol יוֹ תְּהֹמוֹת tehomot: אֵשׁ esh וּבָרָד uvarad

שֶׁלֶג sheleg אלף אלף דני אלף אהיה וְקִיטוֹר vekitor רוּחַ ru'ach סְעָרָה se'ara

עֹשָׂה osa דְבָרוֹ devaro ראה: הֶהָרִים heharim וְכָל־ vechol יוֹ גְּבָעוֹת geva'ot

עֵץ etz פְּרִי peri וְכָל־ vechol יוֹ אֲרָזִים arazim: הַחַיָּה hachaya וְכָל־ vechol יוֹ

בְּהֵמָה behema רֶמֶשׂ remes בן וְצִפּוֹר vetzipor כָּנָף kanaf ע"ה קנ"א, אדני אלהים:

מַלְכֵי malchei אֶרֶץ eretz וְכָל־ vechol יוֹ לְאֻמִּים le'umim שָׂרִים sarim

וְכָל־ vechol יוֹ שֹׁפְטֵי shoftei אָרֶץ aretz: בַּחוּרִים bachurim וְגַם־ vegam

בְּתוּלֹת betulot זְקֵנִים zekenim עִם־ im נְעָרִים ne'arim: יְהַלְלוּ yehalelu

אֶת־ et שֵׁם shem יְהוָֹה/אהדונהי Adonai כִּי־ ki נִשְׂגָּב nisgav

שְׁמוֹ shemo מהש"ע ע"ה, ע"ב בריבוע וקס"א ע"ה, אל עדי ע"ה לְבַדּוֹ levado שם בן מ"ב

הוֹדוֹ hodo אהיה עַל־ al אֶרֶץ eretz וְשָׁמָיִם veshamayim יוֹ טל, יוֹ כוֹזו:

וַיָּרֶם vayarem קֶרֶן keren לְעַמּוֹ le'amo תְּהִלָּה tehila ע"ה אמת, אהיה פעמים אהיה, זוֹ ס"ג

לְכֹל lechol יה אדני לַחֲסִידָיו chasidav לִבְנֵי livnei יִשְׂרָאֵל Yisrael

עַם־ am קְרֹבוֹ kerovo *(Gevurah of Yetzirah)* הַלְלוּיָהּ haleluya אלהים, אהיה אדני ; ללה:

THE FOURTH PSALM (SHIRU) - CHESED

This Psalm is comprised of nine verses referring to nine "skies" that separate the Upper Worlds from the Lower World. This idea of separation is a direct reference to the concept of time and its relationship to Cause and Effect. Through these verses, we manipulate time and shorten the distance between Cause and Effect.

To allow us to express our uniquely human trait of free will, time is inserted into the Cause and Effect process. This space gives Satan, our ego, and our limiting selfish thoughts the opportunity to challenge us. Satan makes us believe that we get away with our negative actions. He makes us believe that life is unfair and that good behavior goes unrewarded. Changing ourselves and our belief systems becomes more challenging. Now that we are approaching the end of days, the Final Correction, we can shorten the separation between Cause and Effect and reap the rewards of our positive behavior much more quickly. Likewise, our negative actions will produce a much quicker payback. The result in both situations is accelerated change on our part.

Praise the Lord from the Earth. Great fish and depths, fire and hail, snow and steam, and stormy wind do His bidding. The mountains and the hills, fruit trees and all the cedars, wild beasts and all cattle, creeping things and winged birds; Kings of the Earth and all nations, princes and all the judges of the Earth; Young men and maidens, old along with the young: they all praise the Name of the Lord, for His Name alone is powerful; His splendor is over the Earth and Heavens. And He praises the word of His nation, a praise for all His pious ones, for the children of Israel, the nation that is close to Him. Praise the Lord!" (Psalm 148)

There are 61 words in this Psalm like the numerical value of the Names: *Alef Gimel Lamed Alef* (אגלא) (35, also equals to *Alef Lamed Dalet* אלד) plus יהוה (26), to give us protection from Evil Eye.

(Chesed of Yetzirah) haleluya הַלְלוּיָה ; ללה אלהים, אהיה אדני shiru שִׁירוּ

ladonai ליהוה shir שִׁיר chadash וְדָשׁ י"ב הויות, קס"א קנ"א

tehilato תְּהִלָּתוֹ bik'hal בִּקְהַל chasidim וַחֲסִידִים: yismach יִשְׂמַח מעשיו

Yisrael יִשְׂרָאֵל be'osav בְּעֹשָׂיו benei בְּנֵי Tziyon צִיּוֹן יוסף, ו' הויות, קנאה

yagilu יָגִילוּ vemalkam בְמַלְכָּם: yehalelu יְהַלְלוּ shemo שְׁמוֹ מהשע ע"ה,

vechinor וְכִנּוֹר betof בְתֹף vemachol בְמָחוֹל ע"ה אל שדי ע"ה, vemalkam

yezameru יְזַמְּרוּ lo לוֹ: ki כִּי rotze רוֹצֶה Adonai ליהוה

be'amo בְעַמּוֹ ר"ת = ע"ב ס"ג מ"ה ב"ן, הברכה (למתק את ז' המלכים עמתו) ; ס"ת יהוה

yefa'er יְפָאֵר anavim עֲנָוִים bishu'a בִּישׁוּעָה פוי, אל אדני ; ר"ת הפסוק = שדי:

yalezu יַעְלְזוּ ג"פ אם (אותיות דפשוטו, דמילוי ודמילוי דמילוי דג"פ אהיה) chasidim וַחֲסִידִים

bechavod בְכָבוֹד בוכו, ובאאהב"ע הוא עם שלשפ"ק המבמתק את ג' אם דלעיל (והוא עולה למנין

yeranenu יְרַנְּנוּ al עַל mishkevotam מִשְׁכְּבוֹתָם: עסמ"ב קס"א קנ"א קמ"ג וג"פ אם הג"ל

romemot רוֹמְמוֹת El אֵל יא"י (מילוי) דס"ג bigronam בִגְרוֹנָם

vecherev וְחֶרֶב רי"ו pifiyot פִּיפִיּוֹת beyadam בְיָדָם: la'asot לַעֲשׂוֹת ר"ת = קנ"א ב"ן, מילוי יהוה אלהים אדני, קס"א וס"ג, מ"ה ברבוע וע"ב ע"ה

nekama נְקָמָה מנק bagoyim בַּגּוֹיִם tochechot תּוֹכֵחוֹת bale'umim בַּלְאֻמִּים:

lesor לֶאְסֹר malchehem מַלְכֵיהֶם bezikim בְּזִקִּים venichbedehem וְנִכְבְּדֵיהֶם

la'asot לַעֲשׂוֹת: bechavlei בְּכַבְלֵי varzel בַרְזֶל ר"ת בלהה רחל זלפה לאה:

bahem בָהֶם mishpat מִשְׁפָּט ע"ה ה"פ אלהים katuv כָּתוּב hadar הָדָר hu הוּא

lechol לְכָל יה אדני chasidav וַחֲסִידָיו haleluya הַלְלוּיָה alohim, אהיה אדני ; ללה:

THE FOURTH PSALM

"Praise the Lord! Sing to the Lord a new song. His praise is in the gathering of the pious. Israel shall rejoice with its Maker, the children of Zion shall exult with their King. They shall praise His Name with dance. With drum and harp they shall play melodies to Him. For the Lord favors His nation; He glorifies the humble with redemption. The pious shall be merry with His Glory and shall joyously sing upon their beds. The high praises of God are in their thoughts and a double-edged sword is in their hands to bring vengeance upon the nations, retributions upon the peoples, to bind their kings in chains, and their nobles in iron shackles, to administer to them justice that is written. Glory for all His pious ones, Praise the Lord!" (Psalms 149)

THE FIFTH PSALM (HALELU EL) – THE THREE UPPER SEFIROT

The six verses found here connect us to Ma-tat-ron (**do not pronounce**), the highest of all the angels. The Aramaic word for Ma-tat-ron contains six letters—*Mem, Tet, Tet, Reish, Vav,* final *Nun.* Each verse in this connection helps form the name. Because Ma-tat-ron controls all the angels in the spiritual world, he can help give us control over our physical world and assist us in accomplishing our spiritual work.

This Psalm has six verses for the six letters of the Angel מטטרו״ן (**do not pronounce**) of *Yetzirah* to raise *Asiyah* in it. The Angel סנדלפו״ן (**do not pronounce**) has seven letters and for this reason we repeat the sixth verse to complete the seventh. Also we say this Psalm to connect to the three Upper *Sefirot* of *Yetzirah*. It includes all the Ten *Sefirot* of *Yetzirah* with the secret of the Ten *Haleluyas*.

אל (יא"א מילוי דס"ג) אותיות בפסוק (Keter) haleluya הַלְלוּיָהּ אלהים, אהיה אדני ; ללה

bekodsho בְּקָדְשׁוֹ (דס"ג) (מילוי) יא"י El אֵל halelu- הַלְלוּ

(Chochmah) haleluhu הַלְלוּהוּ birki'a בִּרְקִיעַ uzo עֻזּוֹ ס"ת = ע"ב ב"ן :

(Binah) haleluhu הַלְלוּהוּ vigvurotav בִגְבוּרֹתָיו (Chesed) haleluhu הַלְלוּהוּ

kerov כְּרֹב gudlo גֻּדְלֹו: (Gevurah) haleluhu הַלְלוּהוּ beteka בְּתֵקַע

shofar שׁוֹפָר (Tiferet) haleluhu הַלְלוּהוּ benevel בְּנֵבֶל vechinor וְכִנּוֹר:

(Netzach) haleluhu הַלְלוּהוּ betof בְּתֹף umachol וּבְמָחוֹל (Hod) haleluhu הַלְלוּהוּ

beminim בְּמִנִּים ve'ugav וְעֻגָב: (Yesod) haleluhu הַלְלוּהוּ vetziltzelei בְצִלְצְלֵי

shama שָׁמַע (Malchut) haleluhu הַלְלוּהוּ betziltzelei בְצִלְצְלֵי teru'a תְרוּעָה:

kol כֹּל haneshamah הַנְּשָׁמָה tehalel תְּהַלֵּל ר"ת כהת, משיוז בן דוד ע"ה

Yah יָהּ haleluya הַלְלוּיָהּ אלהים, אהיה אדני ; ללה:

kol כֹּל haneshamah הַנְּשָׁמָה tehalel תְּהַלֵּל ר"ת כהת, משיוז בן דוד ע"ה

Yah יָהּ haleluya הַלְלוּיָהּ אלהים, אהיה אדני ; ללה:

THE FIFTH PSALM

"Praise the Lord! Praise Him in His Sanctuary; praise Him in the firmaments of His might; praise Him by His valorous deeds; praise Him according to His bountiful greatness; praise Him with blowing the Shofar; praise Him with lyre and harp; praise Him with drum and dance; praise Him with instruments and pipe; Praise Him with the sound of cymbals; praise Him with reverberating sounds. All the souls praise God. Praise Him! All the souls praise God. Praise Him!" (Psalms 150)

OLAM YETZIRAH - אל יהוה – יוד הא ואו הא

BARUCH

Each of these four verses is a conduit to the four letters in *Yud, Hei, Vav,* and *Hei* (יהוה), helping us make the jump to the upper part of the World of Formation – *Atzilut of Yetzirah.*

י

א"ס אותיות ו"י דס"ג ריבוע le'olam לְעוֹלָם Adonai יְהֹוָאדניליאתדונהי baruch בָּרוּךְ

לאו: ר"ת ; יאהדונהי ve'amen וְאָמֵן יאהדונהי amen אָמֵן

ה

קנאה הויות, ו' יוסף, miTziyon מִצִּיּוֹן Adonai יְהֹוָאדניליאתדונהי baruch בָּרוּךְ

ללה: ; אדני אהיה אלהים, haleluya הַלְלוּיָהּ Yerushalayim יְרוּשָׁלַיִם shochen שֹׁכֵן

ו

ילה ; אדני אהיה Elohim אֱלֹהִים Adonai יְהֹוָאדניליאתדונהי baruch בָּרוּךְ

Yisrael יִשְׂרָאֵל ילה ; דמב דע"ב, מילוי Elohei אֱלֹהֵי

מ"ב: בן שם levado לְבַדּוֹ nifla'ot נִפְלָאוֹת ose עֹשֵׂה

ה

א"ס אותיות ו"י דס"ג ריבוע le'olam לְעוֹלָם kevodo כְּבוֹדוֹ shem שֵׁם uvaruch וּבָרוּךְ

ילי kol כָּל־ et אֶת־ chevodo כְבוֹדוֹ veyimale וְיִמָּלֵא

יאהדונהי: ve'amen וְאָמֵן יאהדונהי amen אָמֵן ע"ה דההן אלהים ha'aretz הָאָרֶץ

BARUCH

"Blessed is the Lord forever, Amen and Amen." (Psalms 89:53) "Blessed is the Lord from Zion, He Who dwells in Jerusalem. Praise the Lord!" (Psalms 135:21) "Blessed is the Lord, our God, the God of Israel, Who alone performs wonders. And blessed is the Name of His glory, forever. May His glory fill the entire world, Amen and Amen." (Psalms 72:18-19)

OLAM YETZIRAH - יוד הא ואו הא – אל יהוה

VAY'VARECH DAVID - THE HIGHEST POINT OF THE WORLD OF FORMATION (YETZIRAH)

The kabbalists teach us that there are two prerequisites for activating the power of a prayer:
1) Understanding the inner significance of the prayer, and
2) Certainty that the prayer will produce the Light and energy that it is designed to generate.

This next prayer imbues us with the power of certainty. *Vadai* ודאי (certainty) is created by the first letter of each of the first four words of this prayer. Everyone who recites this prayer arouses an intense feeling of certainty in their life. If we are not certain that the prayer will work, it won't. Satan's job is to fill us with uncertainty every chance he gets, even as we read these words. This prayer combats our doubts and uncertainties, and fills us with conviction and certitude.

> *Tikkun* of *Atzilut* of *Yetzirah*.
> Until the Song of the Sea we have ten times the Name: יהוה, five for *Chasadim* and five for *Gevurot*.

Stand when reciting "vayvarech David."

David דָּוִיד (למתק את ז' המלכים שמתו) ע"ב ס"ג מ"ה ב"ן, הברכה vay'varech וַיְבָרֶךְ		
et אֶת־ (בשם זה עלה משה למרום) ר"ת ודאי (=אהיה) Adonai לַיהֹוָהואהדונהי (First Chesed)		
hakahal הַקָּהָל יל kol כָּל רביע מ"ה le'enei לְעֵינֵי (והוא מגן ממלאכי וזבלה)		
Ata אַתָּה baruch בָּרוּךְ אדני = ר"ת David דָּוִיד vayomer וַיֹּאמֶר		
Elohei אֱלֹהֵי מילוי ע"ב, רמב ; ילה (Second Chesed) Adonai יְהֹוָהואהדונהי		
me'olam מֵעוֹלָם avinu אָבִינוּ (מצוות) תרי"ג = ישראל אלהי יהוה Yisrael יִשְׂרָאֵל		
(Third Chesed) Adonai לַיהֹוָהואהדונהי lecha לְךָ :olam עוֹלָם ve'ad וְעַד		
vehatiferet וְהַתִּפְאֶרֶת רי"ו vehagevura וְהַגְּבוּרָה hagedula הַגְּדֻלָּה		
ילי chol כָּל ki כִּי יההה vehahod וְהַהוֹד vehanetzach וְהַנֵּצַח		
lecha לְךָ uva'aretz וּבָאָרֶץ כוזו י"פ טל, י"פ bashamayim בַּשָּׁמַיִם		
hamamlacha הַמַּמְלָכָה (Fourth Chesed) Adonai יְהֹוָהואהדונהי		
יורדין ואלהים אלהים רביע lerosh לְרֹאשׁ ארני יה lechol לְכֹל vehamitnase וְהַמִּתְנַשֵּׂא		
ע"ה: milfanecha מִלְּפָנֶיךָ לאו vehakavod וְהַכָּבוֹד veha'osher וְהָעֹשֶׁר ס"ג מ"ה ב"ן		

VAY'VARECH DAVID

"Then David blessed the Lord before the eyes of the whole congregation. David said: Blessed are You, Lord, the God of Israel, our Father, forever until eternity. Yours, Lord, are the greatness, the power, the glory, the victory, and the splendor. Everything in the Heavens and Earth is Yours. Yours, Lord, is the kingship; You are over all those who ascend to lead. The riches and honors are before You;

VEATA MOSHEL BAKOL

The giving of charity also helps to arouse certainty. In this prayer, we take three coins and place them in the hand of a fellow congregant or in a charity box (as explained in the following paragraph by the Ari).

You first place two coins in a fellow's hand or charity box, followed by the last one. The first coin corresponds to *Leah* and represents the letter *Yud* ', the second coin corresponds to *Malchut* of *Binah* which is in the head of *Zeir Anpin* (which *Leah* comes from) and represents the first letter *Hei* ה. The third coin corresponds to *Rachel*, the lower *Nukva*, and represents the letter *Vav* ', and the hand or charity box represents the final *Hei* ה, the World of *Malchut*.

ב"ן, לכב ; ר"ת ומב   bakol **בַּכֹּל**   moshel **מוֹשֵׁל**   veAta **וְאַתָּה**

(אהיה) ר"ת בוכו ; רי"ו   ugvura **וּגְבוּרָה**   ko'ach **כֹּחַ**   uvyadcha **וּבְיָדְךָ**

אדני יה   lakol **לַכֹּל**   פהל   ulchazek **וּלְחַזֵּק**   legadel **לְגַדֵּל**   uvyadcha **וּבְיָדְךָ**

מאמרים כל יום   ילה   modim **מוֹדִים**   כנגד מאה ברכות שתיקן דוד   Elohenu **אֱלֹהֵינוּ**   ve'ata **וְעַתָּה**

leshem **לְשֵׁם**   um'halelim **וּמְהַלְלִים**   lach **לָךְ**   anachnu **אֲנַחְנוּ**

shem **שֵׁם**   יהוה ריבוע יהוה ריבוע מ"ה   vivarchu **וִיבָרְכוּ**   tifartecha **תִּפְאַרְתֶּךָ**

עמם ; ילי   kol **כָּל**   al **עַל**   umromam **וּמְרוֹמֲמִם**   ב"ן, לכב   kevodecha **כְּבוֹדֶךָ**

ס"ג, ו"פ   ע"ה אמת, אהיה, אהיה פעמים   ut'hila **וּתְהִלָּה**   beracha **בְּרָכָה**

levadecha **לְבַדֶּךָ**   (Fifth Chesed)   Adonai יאהדונהיאהדונהי   hu **הוּא**   Ata **אַתָּה**

shemei **שְׁמֵי**   י"פ טל, י"פ כוזו   hashamayim **הַשָּׁמַיִם**   et **אֶת**   asita **עָשִׂיתָ**   ata **אַתָּה**

tzeva'am **צְבָאָם**   ילי   vechol **וְכָל**   י"פ טל, י"פ כוזו   hashamayim **הַשָּׁמַיִם**

פהל   aleha **עָלֶיהָ**   asher **אֲשֶׁר**   ילי   vechol **וְכָל**   אלהים דההין ע"ה   ha'aretz **הָאָרֶץ**

bahem **בָּהֶם**   asher **אֲשֶׁר**   ילי   vechol **וְכָל**   גלך   hayamim **הַיַּמִּים**

utzva **וּצְבָא**   kulam **כֻּלָּם**   et **אֶת**   ס"ג   mechaye **מְחַיֶּה**   veAta **וְאַתָּה**

ר"ת מלה   mishtachavim **מִשְׁתַּחֲוִים**   lecha **לְךָ**   י"פ טל, י"פ כוזו   hashamayim **הַשָּׁמַיִם**

VEATA MOSHEL BAKOL
You rule over everything.

In Your Hand are powers and might. And it is in Your Hand to make great and to give strength to all. Now, our God, we are grateful to You and praise the Name of Your splendors." (1 Chronicles 29:10-13) "And they shall bless the Name of Your glory, which is exalted above all blessing and praise. It is You, alone, Who is the Lord. You made the Heavens, the highest Heavens and all their hosts, the Earth and all that is upon it, the seas and all that they contain, and You sustain life in them all. And the hosts of the Heavens prostrate themselves before You.

אַתָּה Ata — הוּא hu — יְהֹוָה Adonai — *(First Gevurah)* — הָאֱלֹהִים haElohim

אֲשֶׁר asher — בָּחַרְתָּ bacharta — (stand until here)

בְּאַבְרָם beAvram — וְהוֹצֵאתוֹ vehotzeto — מֵאוּר meUr — כַּשְׂדִּים Kasdim

וְשַׂמְתָּ vesamta — שְׁמוֹ shemo

אַבְרָהָם Avraham

וּמָצָאתָ umatzata — אֶת et — לְבָבוֹ levavo — נֶאֱמָן ne'eman — לְפָנֶיךָ lefanecha

וְכָרוֹת vecharot — עִמּוֹ imo — הַבְּרִית haberit — לָתֵת latet — אֶת et

אֶרֶץ eretz — הַכְּנַעֲנִי haKena'ani — הַחִתִּי haChiti — הָאֱמֹרִי haEmori

וְהַפְּרִזִּי vehaPerizi — וְהַיְבוּסִי vehaYevusi — וְהַגִּרְגָּשִׁי vehaGirgashi — לָתֵת latet

לְזַרְעוֹ lezar'o — וַתָּקֶם vatakem — אֶת et — דְּבָרֶיךָ devarecha — כִּי ki

צַדִּיק tzadik — אָתָּה Ata — וַתֵּרֶא vatere — אֶת et — עֳנִי oni

אֲבֹתֵינוּ avotenu — בְּמִצְרָיִם beMitzrayim — וְאֶת ve'et — זַעֲקָתָם za'akatam

שָׁמַעְתָּ shamata — עַל al — יַם Yam — סוּף Suf — וַתִּתֵּן vatiten

אֹתֹת otot — וּמֹפְתִים umoftim — בְּפַרְעֹה beFar'oh — וּבְכָל uvchol

עֲבָדָיו avadav — וּבְכָל uvchol — עַם am — אַרְצוֹ artzo — כִּי ki — יָדַעְתָּ yadata

כִּי ki — הֵזִידוּ hezidu — עֲלֵיהֶם alehem — וַתַּעַשׂ vata'as — לְךָ lecha — שֵׁם shem

כְּהַיּוֹם kehayom — הַזֶּה haze — וְהַיָּם vehayam

בָּקַעְתָּ bakata — לִפְנֵיהֶם lifnehem — וַיַּעַבְרוּ vaya'avru — בְתוֹךְ vetoch

הַיָּם hayam — בַּיַּבָּשָׁה bayabasha — וְאֶת ve'et — רֹדְפֵיהֶם rodfehem

הִשְׁלַכְתָּ hishlachta — בִמְצוֹלֹת vimtzolot — כְּמוֹ kemo

אֶבֶן even — בְּמַיִם bemayim — עַזִּים azim

It is You, Lord, the God, Who chose Abram and brought him out of Ur of the Chaldeans and made his name Abraham. You found his heart faithful before You, and You established the Covenant with him to give the land of the Canaanite, the Hittite, the Amorite, the Perizzite, the Jebusite, and the Girgashite - to give it to his descendants. You have kept Your promise, for You are righteous. You saw the afflictions of our forefathers in Egypt and You heard their cries at the Sea of Reeds. You performed signs and wonders against Pharaoh, all his servants, and all the people of his land, for You knew that they had sinned willfully against our forefathers. You thereby made for Yourself a Name as it is to this day. You then split the sea before them so that they crossed mid-sea, on dry land; their pursuers You cast into the depths, like a stone in turbulent waters." (Nechamiah 9:5-11)

VAYOSHA

When said with enormous happiness, "*vayosha*" has the power to remove negativity and make our *tikkun* process much easier. The *tikkun* process refers to the personal corrections that each person has come into this world to make. The corrections we must make are based on our negative, reactive behavior from this life and from past lives. *Tikkun* can include areas of finance, relationships, and health among others. We can identify our *tikkun* in all areas of our life by noticing where we experience the most difficulties.

bayom בַּיּוֹם   (*Second   Gevurah*)   Adonai יְהֹוָה(אדני יאהדונהי)   vayosha וַיּוֹשַׁע

Yisrael יִשְׂרָאֵל   et אֶת־   hahu הַהוּא   ע"ה גגד, מזבוז, זן, אל יהוה ; ר"ת = וז"י

vayar וַיַּרְא (יאהדונהי) אמן = ר"ת ; מצר Mitzrayim מִצְרַיִם   miyad מִיַּד

al עַל   met מֵת   מצר Mitzrayim מִצְרַיִם   et אֶת־   Yisrael יִשְׂרָאֵל

et אֶת־   Yisrael יִשְׂרָאֵל   vayar וַיַּרְא   ילי: hayam הַיָּם   sefat שְׂפַת

asa עָשָׂה   asher אֲשֶׁר   אהיה ר"ת   hagedola הַגְּדֹלָה   וזהו hayad הַיָּד

מצר   beMitzrayim בְּמִצְרַיִם   (*Third   Gevurah*)   Adonai יְהֹוָה(אדני יאהדונהי)

(*Fourth   Gevurah*)   Adonai יְהֹוָה(אדני יאהדונהי)   et אֶת־   ha'am הָעָם   vayir'u וַיִּירְאוּ

איוב ; ר"ת   (*Fifth   Gevurah*)   badonai בַּיהֹוָה(אדני יאהדונהי)   vaya'aminu וַיַּאֲמִינוּ

avdo: עַבְדּוֹ   ע"ה מהע, ע"ב בריבוע וקס"א, אל שדי, ד"פ אלהים ע"ה   uvMoshe וּבְמֹשֶׁה

THE 72 NAMES OF GOD

This chart shows the 72 Names of God. Moses used these sequences and formulas to connect to the true laws of nature—miracles and wonders—and remove all the obstacles that prevent mankind from connecting to them. This is how the Red Sea was split (Exodus 14:19-21). The splitting of the Red Sea is an expression of connection to the 99 Percent Realm where miracles are the norm. Simply by scanning these configurations of letters, we connect to our true nature and power. We become more proactive and move closer to the true purpose of our soul.

VAYOSHA

"And on that day, the Lord saved Israel from the hand of Egypt, and Israel saw the Egyptians dead at the seashore. Israel beheld the great Hand that the Lord had wrought against Egypt; and the people feared the Lord; they believed in the Lord and in Moses, His servant." (Exodus 14:30-31)

To scan: Begin at upper right (A-1) and scan each row right to left, ending in lower left (I-8).

8	7	6	5	4	3	2	1	
כהת	אכא	ללה	מהש	עלם	סיט	ילי	והו	A
הקם	הרי	מבה	יזל	ההע	לאו	אלד	הזי	B
וזהו	מלה	ייי	נלך	פהל	לוו	כלי	לאו	C
ושר	לכב	אום	ריי	שאה	ירת	האא	נתה	D
ייז	רהע	וזעם	אני	מנד	כוק	להוו	יוז	E
מיה	עעל	ערי	סאל	ילה	וול	מיכ	ההה	F
פוי	מבה	נית	נגא	עמם	הזעו	דני	והו	G
מוזי	ענו	יהה	ומב	מצר	הרוז	ייל	נמם	H
מום	היי	יבמ	ראה	וזבו	איע	מנק	דמב	I

SONG OF THE SEA - AZ YASHIR MOSHE

Moses and the Israelites sang this song after the splitting of the Red Sea. It is the song of the soul. Unfortunately, we lose touch with our soul when we are caught up in the material world. This prayer helps to awaken the memory and power of the original song that resides in the depths of our soul; because when we are connected to our soul, we can achieve anything.

Eighteen times the Name of God (יהוה or אדני) for the eighteen blessings of the Worlds of *Yetzirah*. You should meditate that these eighteen are the numerical value of the two letters *Tet* ט in Ma-tat-ron (**do not pronounce**) which is in *Zeir Anpin* of *Yetzirah*, as well as meditate on the nine *tikkuns* of *Zeir Anpin* of *Yetzirah*, nine of Direct Light and nine of Returning Light. (The same way we meditated in *Yehi Chevod* on pg. 137) You should also imagine that you crossed the Red Sea on that day. Saying it with happiness will cleanse all of our transgressions.

az אָז yashir יָשִׁיר Moshe מֹשֶׁה uvnei וּבְנֵי Yisrael יִשְׂרָאֵל et אֶת hashira הַשִּׁירָה hazot הַזֹּאת ladonai לַיהוה vayomru וַיֹּאמְרוּ lemor לֵאמֹר ashira אָשִׁירָה ladonai לַיהוה ki כִּי ga'o גָּאֹה ga'a גָּאָה sus סוּס verochvo וְרֹכְבוֹ rama רָמָה vayam בַיָּם vezimrat וְזִמְרָת Yah יָהּ vayehi וַיְהִי li לִי lishu'a לִישׁוּעָה ze זֶה Eli אֵלִי ve'anvehu וְאַנְוֵהוּ (Meditate on the Holy Name: יהואל) Elohei אֱלֹהֵי avi אָבִי va'aromemenhu וַאֲרֹמְמֶנְהוּ

SONG OF THE SEA - AZ YASHIR MOSHE

"Moses and the Children of Israel sang this song to the Lord: I sing to the Lord because He became most exalted and flung the horse and its rider into the sea. My strength and my praise are God; He became my salvation. This is my God and I shall glorify Him, the God of my father; and I shall exalt Him.

milchama מִלְחָמָה ish אִישׁ (ורב וֹסד) Adonai יְהֹוָהאדניאיאהדונהי

Adonai יְהֹוָהאדניאיאהדונהי shemo שְׁמֹו (נשׂא עון) מהטע ע"ה, ע"ב ברריבוע וקס"א ע"ה, אל עדי ע"ה:

markevot מַרְכְּבֹת Par'oh פַּרְעֹה vechelo וְחֵילֹו yara יָרָה vayam בַיָּם יל'

umivchar וּמִבְחַר shalishav שָׁלִשָׁיו tube'u טֻבְּעוּ veYam בְיַם־ יל' סוּף Suf:

tehomot תְּהֹמֹת yechasyumu יְכַסְיֻמוּ yardu יָרְדוּ vimtzolot בִמְצוֹלֹת

kemo כְּמֹו־ aven אָבֶן ר"ת = אהיה yemincha יְמִינְךָ Adonai יְהֹוָהאדניאיאהדונהי

ne'edari נֶאְדָּרִי bako'ach בַּכֹּחַ ר"ת = ע"ב, ריבוע יהוה וס"ת = יגל (ופשע)

yemincha יְמִינְךָ Adonai יְהֹוָהאדניאיאהדונהי (ונקה) tir'atz תִּרְעַץ oyev אֹויֵב

te'shalach תְּשַׁלַּח יפ אהיה uvrov וּבְרֹב (בזמנא דמלכא משיווא:) ge'oncha גְּאֹונְךָ

taharos תַּהֲרֹס kamecha קָמֶיךָ (ביומי גוג ומגוג) charoncha חֲרֹנְךָ yochlemo יֹאכְלֵמֹו kakash כַּקַשׁ (בעת תחיית המתים:)

apecha אַפֶּיךָ ne'ermu נֶעֶרְמוּ mayim בַּיִם ר"ת אמן (יאהדונהי) uvru'ach וּבְרוּחַ

nitzevu נִצְּבוּ chemo כְּמֹו־ ned נֵד ר"ת ק"כ צירופי אלהים nozlim נֹזְלִים

kaf'u קָפְאוּ tehomot תְּהֹמֹת belev בְּלֶב־ yam יָם יל': amar אָמַר oyev אֹויֵב

erdof אֶרְדֹּף asig אַשִּׂיג achalek אֲחַלֵּק shalal שָׁלָל timla'emo תִּמְלָאֵמֹו

nafshi נַפְשִׁי arik אָרִיק charbi וְחַרְבִּי רי torishemo תֹּורִישֵׁמֹו yadi יָדִי:

nashafta נָשַׁפְתָּ veruchacha בְרוּחֲךָ ר"ת ב"ן kisamo כִּסָּמֹו yam יָם יל'

tzalelu צָלְלוּ ka'oferet כַּעֹופֶרֶת bemayim בְּמַיִם adirim אַדִּירִים הרי ; ר"ת קמ"ג:

The Lord is the Master of war – The Lord is His Name. The chariots of Pharaoh and his army, He cast into the sea and his select officers were sunk into the Sea of Reeds. The deep waters covered them and they sunk into the depths like a stone. Your right, Lord, is immensely powerful; Your right, Lord, smashes the enemy. With Your great ingenuity, You demolish those who rise against You. You send forth Your wrath and it consumes them like straw. And with the wing of Your anger, the waters were filled up; the flowing waters stood like a wall and the deep waters froze in the heart of the sea. The enemy said: I shall pursue, overtake, and divide the spoils. I shall satisfy my desires with them. I shall unsheathe my sword and my hand shall impoverish them. You blew with Your wind and the sea covered them. They sank like lead in the mighty waters.

(פוקד) Adonai אהדונהי יאהדונהי‎ יְהֹוָה ba'elim בָּאֵלִם chamocha כָּמֹכָה יֵלי mi מִי

ne'edar נֶאְדָּר kamocha כָּמֹכָה יֵלי mi מִי ; ס״ת מ״ה, ריבוע יהוה, ע״ב = ר״ת

tehilot תְּהִלֹת nora נוֹרָא bakodesh בַּקֹּדֶשׁ ר״ת = יבק, אלהים יהוה, אהיה אדני יהוה

tivla'emo תִּבְלָעֵמוֹ yemincha יְמִינְךָ natita נָטִיתָ fele פֶּלֶא ose עֹשֵׂה

am עַם־ vechasdecha בְחַסְדְּךָ ר״ת ב״ן nachita נָחִיתָ aretz אָרֶץ (זו מ״ות) r״ת גית

neve נֶוֵה el אֶל־ ve'ozcha בְעָזְּךָ nehalta נֵהַלְתָּ ga'alta גָּאַלְתָּ zu זוּ

kodshecha קָדְשֶׁךָ ר״ת קנ״א ב״ן, יהוה אלהים אדני, מילוי קס״א וס״ג, מ״ה ברבוע וע״ב ע״ה

achaz אָחַז ומב chil וָחִיל yirgazun יִרְגָּזוּן amim עַמִּים sham'u שָׁמְעוּ

nivhalu נִבְהֲלוּ az אָז (כוזות ישמעאל) Pelashet פְּלָשֶׁת yoshvei יֹשְׁבֵי

Mo'av מוֹאָב elei אֵילֵי (כוזות עשו) Edom אֱדוֹם alufei אַלּוּפֵי

yochazemo יֹאחֲזֵמוֹ ra'ad רַעַד (כוזות שאר כל השרים שהם נכנעים תוותיהם)

Chena'an כְּנָעַן yoshvei יֹשְׁבֵי יֵלי kol כֹּל namogu נָמֹגוּ

tipol תִּפֹּל alehem עֲלֵיהֶם emata אֵימָתָה vafachad וָפַחַד ר״ת שם קדוש תעא״ו

bigdol בִּגְדֹל zero'acha זְרוֹעֲךָ yidemu יִדְּמוּ ka'aven כָּאָבֶן ר״ת = טל (יוד הא ואו)

ad עַד ya'avor יַעֲבֹר amecha עַמְּךָ Adonai יאהדונהי יְהֹוָה (על שלשים)

ad עַד ya'avor יַעֲבֹר am עַם־ zu זוּ kanita קָנִיתָ tevi'emo תְּבִיאֵמוֹ

vetita'emo וְתִטָּעֵמוֹ behar בְּהַר nachalatcha נַחֲלָתְךָ ר״ת ב״ן machon מָכוֹן

leshivtecha לְשִׁבְתְּךָ pa'alta פָּעַלְתָּ Adonai יאהדונהי יְהֹוָה (ועל רבעים) ר״ת

mikedash מִקְּדָשׁ Adonai אֲדֹנָי (ארך) konenu כּוֹנֲנוּ yadecha יָדֶיךָ ע״ה = קס״א

Who among the deities is like You, Lord; Who is like You, awesome in holiness, tremendous in praise, and Who works wonders! You stretched out Your right and the earth swallowed them. With Your kindness, You governed this nation that You redeemed. You led them with Your strength to Your holy Sanctuary. Nations heard and trembled. Terror seized the dwellers of Philistia. Then the leaders of Edom were frightened. The mighty ones of Moab were panic-stricken and the dwellers of Canaan withered away. Dread and fear fell upon them, by the greatness of Your arm. They became still, like stones, until Your nation crossed over, the Lord, until the nation that You adopted crossed over Bring them and settle them in the mountains of Your heritage, in that place of Your dwelling which You have made, Lord. Your Hands established the Temple of the Lord.

OLAM YETZIRAH - יוד הא ואו הא – אל יהוה

A 72 Name of God is encoded in this connection: *Yud, Yud, Lamed* יי״ל. This formula gives us the power of certainty and us the ability to let go, especially in the face of adversity. When things are going well, most of us find it easy to accept the idea of a Creator and a Cause and Effect principle at work in our universe. But when we face a sudden obstacle or stressful situation, we just as readily doubt the existence of a Creator and the teachings of Kabbalah. The kabbalists teach us that absolutely everything is a test. If we can maintain certainty in the Light when adversity strikes, we will pass the test and the Light will work for us 100% of the time. Satan's mission is to flood our minds with uncertainty. The *Yud, Yud, Lamed* wipes out all uncertainties, giving us the strength to recognize and pass our tests. A test will produce negative consequences only if we fail to recognize that the hardship is a test—and if we doubt the existence of the Creator.

le'olam לְעֹלָם yimloch יִמְלֹךְ | (אפים) Adonai יְהֹוָה (אדני־יאהדונהי) |

| (ורב וֹסד) Adonai יְהֹוָה (אדני־יאהדונהי) va'ed וָעֶד ; ר״ת ייל ; אותיות דס״ג ו׳ ריבוע ס״ג |

va'ed וָעֶד ; ר״ת ייל ; אותיות דס״ג ו׳ ריבוע ס״ג le'olam לְעֹלָם yimloch יִמְלֹךְ

ka'em קָאִים malchutei מַלְכוּתֵיהּ (נשא עון) Adonai יְהֹוָה (אדני־יאהדונהי)

sus סוֹס va בָא ki כִּי almaya עָלְמַיָּא ul'almei וּלְעָלְמֵי le'alam לְעָלַם

bayam בַּיָּם ילי uvfarashav וּבְפָרָשָׁיו berichbo בְּרִכְבּוֹ Par'oh פַּרְעֹה אדני, כוך

mei בֵּי et אֶת־ alehem עֲלֵהֶם (ופשיע) Adonai יְהֹוָה (אדני־יאהדונהי) vayashev וַיָּשֶׁב

vayabasha בַיַּבָּשָׁה halchu הָלְכוּ Yisrael יִשְׂרָאֵל uvnei וּבְנֵי ילי hayam הַיָּם ילי

(ונקה) ladonai לַיהֹוָה (אדני־יאהדונהי) ki כִּי ילי: hayam הַיָּם betoch בְּתוֹךְ

umoshel וּמֹשֵׁל (רמז למלכות שהיא הכלה) כלה ר״ת hamelucha הַמְּלוּכָה

Tziyon צִיּוֹן behar בְּהַר moshi'im מוֹשִׁעִים ve'alu וְעָלוּ bagoyim בַּגּוֹיִם

vehayta וְהָיְתָה Esav עֵשָׂו har הַר et אֶת־ lishpot לִשְׁפֹּט יוסף, ר׳ הויות, קנאה

vehaya וְהָיָה hamelucha הַמְּלוּכָה (פוקד) ladonai לַיהֹוָה (אדני־יאהדונהי) ; יהוה ; יהה

kol כָּל ילי ; עמם al עַל־ lemelech לְמֶלֶךְ (על שלשים) Adonai יְהֹוָה (אדני־יאהדונהי)

hahu הַהוּא bayom בַּיּוֹם ha'aretz הָאָרֶץ אלהים דההן ע״ה, נצר, מזבוֹח, זן אל יהוה ע״ה

echad אֶחָד אהבה, דאגה (ועל רבעים) Adonai יְהֹוָה (אדני־יאהדונהי) יי yihye יִהְיֶה

echad אֶחָד אהבה, דאגה ushmo וּשְׁמוֹ מהש ע״ה, ע״ב בריבוע וקס״א ע״ה, אל עדי ע״ה

The Lord shall reign forever and for eternity. The Lord shall reign forever and for eternity."
(Exodus 15:1-18) Lord your kingdom will reign forever and eternity. "For when Pharaoh's horses, chariots, and cavalry came into the sea, Lord turned the water upon them; and the Children of Israel walked upon the dry land within the sea." (Exodus 15:19) "For the Kingdom belongs to the Lord and He rules over the nations." (Psalms 22:29) "And deliverers shall ascend Mount Zion to seek retribution from Mount Esav, and then the entire universe shall recognize the Kingship of the Lord." (Obadiah 1:21) "And the Lord shall then be King over the whole earth and upon that day the Lord shall be One and His Name One." (Zechariah 14:9)

SHACHARIT – MORNING PRAYER
OLAM YETZIRAH - יוד הא ואו הא – אל יהוה

YISHTABACH

Now that we have split the Red Sea, our next level of connection is the World of Creation (*Beriah*). The first word, *Yishtabach* ישתבח has a numerical value of 720, or ten times the 72 Names of God (10 x 72). By reciting *Yishtabach*, we receive the power of King Solomon, that of wisdom. Solomon שלמה is encoded in the next group of words and letters as shown below. Also, the first letters of each of the last five lines of this prayer spell out the name Abraham. Abraham denotes the power of sharing. We use the power of Solomon and Abraham—wisdom and sharing—to help us make the jump to the World of Creation.

The praise of *Yishtabach* is immense and awesome. It consists of 13 praises for the 13 Attributes of *Beriah* and the 13 *Sefirot* of *Yetzirah*. You should say the words slowly and gently and count them with the fingers of your right hand. Be careful not to stop between counting the 13 for any reason. And if you have to stop for any reason, you should go back and count them again from the beginning ("*ki lecha na'e*") in order to say them in one breath as mentioned in the *Zohar*.

malkenu מַלְכֵּנוּ ב"פ ב"ן   la'ad לָעַד   shimcha שִׁמְךָ י"פ ע"ב   yishtabach יִשְׁתַּבַּח

(*King Solomon*) hamelech הַמֶּלֶךְ (מילוי דס"ג) יא"י ; לאה   haEl הָאֵל

vehakadosh וְהַקָּדוֹשׁ ; עם ד' אותיות = מבה, יזל, אום   hagadol הַגָּדוֹל לההו ;

na'e נָאֶה lecha לְךָ ki כִּי   uva'aretz וּבָאָרֶץ י"פ כוזו, י"פ טל   bashamayim בַּשָּׁמַיִם

Adonai אֲדֹנָי Elohenu אֱלֹהֵינוּ ילה velohei וֵאלֹהֵי לכב ; מילוי ע"ב, דמב ; ילה   יְהֹוָה(אדנ"יאהדונה"י)

avotenu אֲבוֹתֵינוּ   le'olam לְעוֹלָם ריבוע ס"ג וי' אותיות דס"ג   va'ed וָעֶד

1) shir שִׁיר (אל)   2) ushvacha וּשְׁבָחָה (רוזום)   3) halel הַלֵּל (ווזון) ללה, אדני

4) vezimra וְזִמְרָה (ארך)   5) oz עֹז (אפים)   6) umemshala וּמֶמְשָׁלָה (ורב וחסד)

7) netzach נֶצַח (ואמת)   8) gedula גְּדֻלָּה (נצר וחסד)   9) gevura גְּבוּרָה

10) tehila תְּהִלָּה (נשא עון) ע"ה אמת, אהיה פעמים אהיה, ז"פ ס"ג (לאלפים) רי"ו

11) vetif'eret וְתִפְאֶרֶת (ופשע)   12) kedusha קְדֻשָׁה (וחטאה)

13) umalchut וּמַלְכוּת (ונקה)   berachot בְּרָכוֹת   vehoda'ot וְהוֹדָאוֹת

YISHTABACH

May Your Name be praised forever, our King, the God, the great and holy King, Who is in the Heavens and on the Earth. For to You are befitting, Lord, our God and the God of our forefathers, 1) song 2) and praise 3) exultation 4) and melody 5) power 6) and dominion 7) eternity 8) greatness 9) valor 10) praise 11) and glory 12) holiness 13) and sovereignty. Blessings and thanksgiving

לְשִׁמְךָ leshimcha הַגָּדוֹל hagadol לְהוֹ ; עם ד' אותיות = מבה, יזל, אום
וְהַקָּדוֹשׁ vehakadosh ♦ וּמֵעוֹלָם ume'olam וְעַד ve'ad עוֹלָם olam

אַתָּה Ata אֵל El יא"י (מילוי דס"ג)♦ בָּרוּךְ baruch אַתָּה Ata

יְהוָֹה(אדנ"י)(יה"ה)(אדנ"י)יאהדונהי Adonai מֶלֶךְ melech גָּדוֹל gadol לְהוֹ ; עם ד' אותיות =
מבה, יזל, אום אֵל El יא"י (מילוי דס"ג)♦ בְּתִשְׁבָּחוֹת batishbachot וּמְהֻלָּל umehulal

הַהוֹדָאוֹת hahoda'ot ♦ אֲדוֹן adon אני ♦ הַנִּפְלָאוֹת hanifla'ot ♦ בּוֹרֵא bore

כָּל kol ילי ♦ הַנְּשָׁמוֹת haneshamot רִבּוֹן ribon יהוה ע"ב ס"ג מ"ה ב"ן ♦ כָּל kol ילי

הַמַּעֲשִׂים hama'asim ♦ הַבּוֹחֵר habocher בְּשִׁירֵי beshirei זִמְרָה zimra ♦

מֶלֶךְ melech (Abraham) אֵל El יא"י (מילוי) דס"ג

וְחַי chei (לפי האריז"ל, וַי לפי הרש"ש) הָעוֹלָמִים ha'olamim : אָמֵן amen יאהדונהי ♦

---

to Your great and Holy Name from this world to the World to Come. You are God. Blessed are You, Lord, King, Who is great and lauded with praise. God of thanksgiving. Master of the wonders. Creator of the souls. Master of all deeds. One Who chooses melodious songs of praise. The King, the God Who gives life to all the worlds, Amen.

Binah בינה

שִׁיר shir הַמַּעֲלוֹת hama'alot

מִמַּעֲמַקִּים mima'amakim קְרָאתִיךָ keraticha יְהֹוָ(אדניאהדונהי) Adonai׃

Chesed חסד

אֲדֹנָי Adonai ללה שִׁמְעָה shim'a בְקוֹלִי vekoli תִּהְיֶינָה tihyena

אָזְנֶיךָ oznecha יוד הי ואו הה קַשֻׁבוֹת kashuvot לְקוֹל lekol תַּחֲנוּנָי tachanunai׃

Gevurah גבורה

אִם־ im יוהך, מ"א אותיות דפשוטו, דמילוי ודמילוי דמילוי דאהיה ע"ה עֲוֹנוֹת avonot

תִּשְׁמָר־ tishmor יָה Yah אֲדֹנָי Adonai ללה מִי mi יֹלי יַעֲמֹד ya'amod׃

Tiferet תפארת

כִּי־ ki עִמְּךָ imecha הַסְּלִיחָה haselicha לְמַעַן lema'an תִּוָּרֵא tivare׃

Netzach נצח

קִוִּיתִי kiviti יְהֹוָ(אדניאהדונהי) Adonai קִוְּתָה kiveta נַפְשִׁי nafshi

וְלִדְבָרוֹ velidvaro הוֹחָלְתִּי hochalti׃

Hod הוד

נַפְשִׁי nafshi לַאדֹנָי ladonai ללה מִשֹּׁמְרִים mishomrim לַבֹּקֶר laboker

שֹׁמְרִים shomrim לַבֹּקֶר laboker׃

Yesod יסוד

יוֹחֵל yachel יִשְׂרָאֵל Yisrael אֶל־ el יְהֹוָ(אדניאהדונהי) Adonai

כִּי־ ki עִם־ im יְהֹוָ(אדניאהדונהי) Adonai הַחֶסֶד hachesed ע"ב, רביע יהוה

וְהַרְבֵּה veharbe עִמּוֹ imo פְּדוּת fedut׃

Malchut מלכות

וְהוּא vehu יִפְדֶּה yifde אֶת־ et יִשְׂרָאֵל Yisrael

מִכֹּל mikol יֹלי עֲוֹנֹתָיו avonotav׃

SHIR HAMA'ALOT

"A Song of Ascents: From the depths I have called out to You, Lord. Lord, hear my voice. Let Your ears be attentive to the sound of my pleading. If You preserve iniquities, Almighty, who could survive? For forgiveness is Yours, so that You may be feared. I hoped for the Lord. My spirit hoped and I await His words. My soul yearns for the Lord among those who long for the morning. Israel places his hope in the Lord because kindness belongs to the Lord, and with Him redemptions abound. And He shall redeem Israel from all his sins." (Psalms 130)

HALF KADDISH

The secret of this half *Kaddish* is that it elevates us from *Yetzirah* (מ"ה) to *Beriah* (ס"ג).

יִתְגַּדַּל yitgadal וְיִתְקַדֵּשׁ veyitkadash ש"די ומילוי ש"די ; י"א אותיות כמנין ו"ה

שְׁמֵיהּ shemei (שם י"ה דע"ב) רַבָּא raba קנ"א ב"ן, יהוה אלהים יהוה אדני,

אָמֵן amen אידהנויה. מילוי קס"א וס"ג, מ"ה ברבוע וע"ב ע"ה ; ר"ת = ו"פ אלהים ; ס"ת = ג"פ יב"ק:

בְּעָלְמָא be'alma דִּי di בְּרָא vera כִרְעוּתֵיהּ chir'utei.

וְיַמְלִיךְ veyamlich מַלְכוּתֵיהּ mal'chutei. וְיַצְמַח veyatzmach

פּוּרְקָנֵיהּ purkanei. וִיקָרֵב vikarev מְשִׁיחֵיהּ meshichei: אָמֵן amen אידהנויה.

וּבְחַיֵּי uvchayei וּבְיוֹמֵיכוֹן uvyomechon בְּחַיֵּיכוֹן bechayechon

דְּכָל dechol ילי בֵּית bet ב"פ ראה יִשְׂרָאֵל Yisrael בַּעֲגָלָא ba'agala

וּבִזְמַן uvizman קָרִיב kariv וְאִמְרוּ ve'imru אָמֵן amen: אָמֵן amen אידהנויה.

The congregation and the *chazan* say the following:

28 words (until *be'alma*) meditate: מילוי דמילוי דע"ב (יוד ויו דלת הי יוד ויו יוד ויו הי הי יוד)
28 letters (until *almaya*) meditate: מילוי דמילוי דס"ג (יוד ויו דלת הי יוד ואו אלף ואו הי יוד)

יְהֵא yehe שְׁמֵיהּ shemei (שם י"ה דס"ג) רַבָּא raba קנ"א ב"ן,

מְבָרַךְ mevarach יהוה אלהים יהוה אדני, מילוי קס"א וס"ג, מ"ה ברבוע וע"ב ע"ה

יִתְבָּרַךְ yitbarach. לְעָלְמֵי le'almei עָלְמַיָּא almaya. לְעָלַם le'alam לְעָלַם לְעוֹלָם

Seven words with six letters each (שם בן מ"ה) meditate:
יהוה + יוד הי ויו הי + מילוי דמילוי דע"ב (יוד ויו דלת הי יוד ויו יוד ויו הי הי יוד)
Also, seven times the letter *Vav* (שם בן מ"ה) meditate:
יהוה + יוד הי ואו הי + מילוי דמילוי דס"ג (יוד ויו דלת הי יוד ואו אלף ואו הי יוד).

וְיִשְׁתַּבַּח veyishtabach י"פ ע"ב יהוה אל אבג יתץ.

וְיִתְפָּאַר veyitpa'ar הי גו יה קרע שטן. וְיִתְרֹמַם veyitromam וה כווו נגד יכש.

וְיִתְנַשֵּׂא veyitnase במוכסז בטר צתג. וְיִתְהַדָּר veyit'hadar כווו יה וזקב טנע.

וְיִתְעַלֶּה veyit'ale וה יוד ה יגל פזק. וְיִתְהַלָּל veyit'halal א ואו הא שקו צית.

שְׁמֵיהּ shemei (שם י"ה דמ"ה) דְּקוּדְשָׁא dekudsha בְּרִיךְ verich הוּא hu:

אָמֵן amen אידהנויה.

HALF KADDISH

May His great Name be more exalted and sanctified. (Amen) In the world that He created according to His will, and may His Kingdom reign. And may He cause His redemption to sprout and may He bring the Mashiach closer. (Amen) In your lifetimes and in your days and in the lifetime of all the House of Israel, speedily and in the near future, and you should say, Amen. (Amen) May His great Name be blessed forever and for all eternity blessed and lauded, and glorified and exalted, and extolled and honored, and uplifted and praised be, the Name of the Holy Blessed One. (Amen) le'ela לְעֵלָּא   min מִן בֵן   kol כָּל יְלי   birchata בִּרְכָתָא   shirata שִׁירָתָא

tishbechata תֻּשְׁבְּחָתָא   venechamata וְנֶחָמָתָא   da'amiran דַּאֲמִירָן

be'alma בְּעָלְמָא   ve'imru וְאִמְרוּ   amen אָמֵן   amen אָמֵן אידהנויה

BARCHU

When we enter the World of Creation *(Beriah)*, we recite the *Barchu* (you should bless). This powerful connection brings back the part of our soul that left us while we slept. Even if a person remains awake, a part of his soul still leaves during the night. There are five words in the *Barchu* that connect us to the five parts of our soul. Each part of the soul is connected to one of the five worlds.

The chazan says:

barchu בָּרְכוּ יהוה ריבוע יהוה ריבוע מ"ה   et אֶת   יְהֹוִאהדונהי Adonai

hamevorach הַמְבוֹרָךְ ס"ת כהת, משיח בן דוד ע"ה

While the chazan says the verse "barchu", the congregation says "yishtabach" as follows
(The chazan will say "yishtabach" as the congregation replies "baruch" as below):

yishtabach יִשְׁתַּבַּח י"פ ע"ב   veyitpa'ar וְיִתְפָּאַר   shemo שְׁמוֹ מהש ע"ה, ע"ב ברריבוע וקס"א ע"ה

melech מֶלֶךְ   malchei מַלְכֵי   hamelachim הַמְּלָכִים אל שדי ע"ה shel שֶׁל

baruch בָּרוּךְ   shehu שֶׁהוּא   hu הוּא   hakadosh הַקָּדוֹשׁ   rishon רִאשׁוֹן   vehu וְהוּא

acharon אַחֲרוֹן   umibal'adav וּמִבַּלְעָדָיו   en אֵין   Elohim אֱלֹהִים אהיה אדני ; ילה

yehi יְהִי   shem שֵׁם   Adonai יְהֹוִאהדונהי   mevorach מְבֹרָךְ ר"ת ריבוע ע"ב וריבוע ס"ג

me'ata מֵעַתָּה   ve'ad וְעַד ילב: olam עוֹלָם   umromam וּמְרוֹמַם   al עַל

kol כָּל ; עמם ילי   beracha בְּרָכָה   ut'hila וּתְהִלָּה ע"ה אמת, אהיה פעמים אהיה, ד"פ ס"ג:

When we reply "*baruch Adonai hamevorach le'olam va'ed*" we receive the five parts of the soul (*Nefesh, Ruach, Neshamah, Chayah* and *Yechidah*) that left us during the last night's sleep.

First the congregation replies the following, and then the chazan repeats it:

Neshamah   *Ruach*   *Nefesh*

baruch בָּרוּךְ   Adonai יְהֹוִאהדונהי   hamevorach הַמְבוֹרָךְ

Yechidah   *Chayah*

le'olam לְעוֹלָם ריבוע ס"ג ו' אותיות דס"ג   va'ed וְעֶד:

Above all blessings,
songs, praises, and words of consolation that may be said in the world, and you shall say, Amen. (Amen)

BARCHU

Bless the Lord, the Blessed One.
Praised and exalted is the Name of the King of all Kings, the Holy Blessed One, Who is first and Who is last and without Whom, there is no God. Let the Name of the Lord be blessed from now till all eternity, above all blessings and praise. Blessed be the Lord, the Blessed One, forever and for eternity.

OLAM BERIAH - יוד הי ואו הי – אל שדי

THE WORLD OF CREATION – *BERIAH*

The beginning verse states: *yotzer or uvore choshech* (forms light and creates darkness).
This refers to the concept of Light and darkness, good and evil. A 50/50 split between
good and evil gives us the free will to choose either Light or darkness.

From here ("*yotzer or*") until "*ga'al Yisrael*" (pg. 188) you are in the World of *Beriah*.

Hechal Livnat Hasapir (the Sapphire Stone Chamber) - *Yesod* of *Zeir Anpin* in *Beriah*.
In the following paragraph there are sixty words which correspond to the sixty mighty ones
(they protect the *Malchut* of *Atzilut* when it ascends to *Beriah*). The minister in this *Hechal* is the
angel *Adarhani-el* אדרהניאל (do not pronounce this name) and the spirit of this *Hechal* is יאהדונהי.

יכה Elohenu אֱלֹהֵינוּ	Adonai יְהֹוָה / אדני יאהדונהי	Ata אַתָּה	baruch בָּרוּךְ
סוף אין רז, or אוֹר	yotzer יוֹצֵר	ha'olam הָעוֹלָם	melech מֶלֶךְ

(You should touch and kiss the *Hand Tefilin* - as the purity of the World of *Beriah* was created by it)

shalom שָׁלוֹם ose עֹשֶׂה ◆ שך נצוצות של וי המלכים. choshech וְחֹשֶׁךְ uvore וּבוֹרֵא
la'aretz לָאָרֶץ hame'ir הַמֵּאִיר : יליו hakol הַכֹּל et אֶת uvore וּבוֹרֵא
◆ יי"פ מצפצ, אלהים דיודין, י"פ berachamim בְּרַחֲמִים פהל aleha עָלֶיהָ veladarim וְלַדָּרִים
קנ"א קס"א הויות, י"ב mechadesh מְחַדֵּשׁ (שהוא החוסד אור גנוז בו) uvtuvo וּבְטוּבוֹ
קמ"ג קנ"א קס"א ע"ה tamid תָּמִיד ע"ה יהוה אל זז, מזלוח, נגד ע"ה yom יוֹם לכב ב"ן bechol בְּכָל
מ"ה ma מַה : מ"ב ר"ת vereshit בְּרֵאשִׁית ma'ase מַעֲשֵׂה
kulam כֻּלָּם Adonai יְהֹוָה / אדני יאהדונהי ma'asecha מַעֲשֶׂיךָ rabu רַבּוּ
asita עָשִׂיתָ (מצוות) תרי"ג = במילוי bechochmah בְּחָכְמָה

All the actions come (as potential of potential) from *Abba* which encloses the Endless Light,
and done (as actual of potential) by *Ima* which encloses *Abba* - *Abba* says and *Ima* does.

‡kinyanecha קִנְיָנֶךָ ע"ה דההין אלהים ha'aretz הָאָרֶץ mal'a מָלְאָה
מ"ב בן שם levado לְבַדּוֹ hameromam הַמְרוֹמָם hamelech הַמֶּלֶךְ
hameshubach הַמְשֻׁבָּח (יאהדונהי) אמן = ע"ה מאו ; לבדו ומב me'az מֵאָז
‡olam עוֹלָם mimot מִימוֹת vehamitnase וְהַמִּתְנַשֵּׂא vehamefo'ar וְהַמְּפֹאָר

THE WORLD OF CREATION

*Blessed are You, Lord, our God, King of the Universe, Who forms Light and creates darkness,
makes peace, and creates everything. (Isaiah 45:7) He Who shines upon the Earth and upon those who
inhabit it, with compassion. And with His goodness, He renews, every day and always, the works
of Creation. How manifold are Your works, Lord! "You have made them all with wisdom, and the world
is filled with Your possessions." (Psalms 104:24) You are the King, and You alone are the exalted
One from the beginning; You, Who is praised, glorified, and exalted from the beginning of time.*

berachamecha בְּרַחֲמֶיךָ   olam עוֹלָם ; דמב , ע"ב מילוי   Elohei אֱלֹהֵי

rachem רַחֵם harabim הָרַבִּים אברהם, וה"פ אל, רי"ו ול"ב נתיבות החוכמה, רמ"ח (אברהם),

◆uzenu עֻזֵּנוּ אני   adon אָדוֹן   ◆alenu עָלֵינוּ פשוטות אותיות ט"ו עסמ"ב

◆misgabenu מִשְׂגַּבֵּנוּ ע"ה   ההין   אלהים   tzur צוּר

◆yish'enu יִשְׁעֵנוּ ג"פ אל (ייא"י מילוי דס"ג) ; ר"ת מיכאל גבריאל נוריאל   magen מָגֵן

◆ba'adenu בַּעֲדֵנוּ: מעשה, מהוע, ע"ב בריבוע וקס"א, אל שדי, ד"פ אלהים ע"ה misgav מִשְׂגָּב

EL BARUCH

The first letter of each word in this prayer follows the order of the 22 letters of the Aramaic alphabet. These 22 letters connect us to the metaphysical building blocks of the universe, providing us with an opportunity to take control over our world and over our destiny.

Hechal Etzem Hashamayim (the Heaven's Embodiment Chamber) - *Hod* of *Zeir Anpin* in *Beriah*. In this *Hechal* there are *Seraphim* with wings that are called *Chashmalim* and here is the secret of *chashmal* (electricity). אורפניאל — *Or-pnei-el* (do not pronounce this name - The Light of God's face) is the angel that ministers this *Hechal*. And this *Hechal* is called אלהים צבאות - *Elohim Tzeva'ot*, which is called *Hod* (Elohim Tzeva'ot with its ten letters adds up to 595, which is *Etzem Hashamayim*).

El אֵל (מילוי דס"ג) ייא"י ; עם ד' אותיות = מובה, יזל, אום לתוו   baruch בָּרוּךְ   gedol גָּדוֹל

de'a דֵּעָה הֵכִין   hechin הֵכִין   ufa'al וּפָעַל   zahorei זָהֳרֵי   chama חַמָּה tov טוֹב והו

yatzar יָצַר   kavod כָּבוֹד   lishmo לִשְׁמוֹ מהוע ע"ה, ע"ב בריבוע וקס"א ע"ה, אל שדי ע"ה

me'orot מְאוֹרוֹת   natan נָתַן   sevivot סְבִיבוֹת   uzo עֻזּוֹ

pinot פִּנּוֹת   tziv'ot צִבְאוֹת   kedoshim קְדוֹשִׁים   romemei רוֹמְמֵי

Shadai שַׁדַּי   tamid תָּמִיד ע"ה   קס"א קנ"א קמ"ג (ג) מילואי אהיה)

mesaprim מְסַפְּרִים,   kevod כְּבוֹד   El אֵל ייא"י (מילוי דס"ג) ;

ukdushato וּקְדֻשָּׁתוֹ: (Da'at of Nukva) ס"ג = אל (מיכאל = נֹגַא) ; כבוד אל = ס"ג   ר"ת מכאל

God of the World, take pity over us with Your plentiful compassions, Master of our strength, Rock of our stronghold. Shield of our redemption, Who is our stronghold.

EL BARUCH

God, blessed and great in knowledge, He prepared and generated the splendor of the sun. The good One, Who created glory for His Name, He set luminaries around His power. The heads of His Holy hosts, who exalt the Almighty, constantly relate the glory of God and His holiness.

ילה   Elohenu **אֱלֹהֵינוּ**   Adonai יְהוָֹאדיֹהאהדוהי   titbarach **תִּתְבָּרַךְ**

ve'al **וְעַל**   עולם mima'al **מִמַּעַל**   כוזו י"פ טל, י"פ   bashamayim **בַּשָּׁמַיִם**

kol **כָּל**   al **עַל**   mitachat **מִתַּחַת**   אלהים דההן ע"ה   ha'aretz **הָאָרֶץ**   עמם ; ילי

me'orei **מְאוֹרֵי**   ve'al **וְעַל** ◆ yadecha **יָדֶיךָ**   ma'asei **מַעֲשֵׂי**   shevach **שֶׁבַח**

yefa'arucha **יְפָאֲרוּךָ**   hema **הֵמָּה**   sheyatzarta **שֶׁיָּצַרְתָּ**   אין סוף   or **אוֹר** or רו,

sela **סֶלָה׃**

TITBARACH LANETZACH

The last Name of the 72 Names of God—*Mem, Vav, final Mem* מום appears in this connection.
This Name means "blemish" or "imperfection." If we are on this planet, we still have at least
one imperfection, if not countless more. This connection helps us to correct these blemishes.

malkenu **מַלְכֵּנוּ**   tzurenu **צוּרֵנוּ**   lanetzach **לָנֶצַח**   titbarach **תִּתְבָּרַךְ**

yishtabach **יִשְׁתַּבַּח**   kedoshim **קְדוֹשִׁים**   bore **בּוֹרֵא**   vego'alenu **וְגֹאֲלֵנוּ**

la'ad **לָעַד**   shimcha **שִׁמְךָ**   אהיה אדני יהוה אלהים יב"ק, ר"ת ; ע"ב י"פ   בן ב"פ

va'asher **וַאֲשֶׁר**   meshartim **מְשָׁרְתִים**   yotzer **יוֹצֵר**   malkenu **מַלְכֵּנוּ**

omdim **עוֹמְדִים**   kulam **כֻּלָּם**   אלהים מום, ר"ת   meshartav **מְשָׁרְתָיו**

olam **עוֹלָם**   berum **בְּרוּם**   הויות = י'   עומדים כלם ; ריבוע יהוה ר"ת ע"ב,

umashmi'im **וּמַשְׁמִיעִים**   (עצמם האהיה כולל לא) כוללים ג' עם ג קמ"א קנ"א קס"א = ע"ה עולם ברום

beyir'a **בְּיִרְאָה**   רי"ו   yachad **יַחַד**   bekol **בְּקוֹל**,   divrei **דִּבְרֵי**   ראה

Elohim **אֱלֹהִים**   chayim **וְחַיִּים** ילה ; אדני אהיה   בינה ע"ה יהוה אהיה אהיה   umelech **וּמֶלֶךְ**

olam **עוֹלָם** ◆ kulam **כֻּלָּם**   ahuvim **אֲהוּבִים** ◆ kulam **כֻּלָּם**   berurim **בְּרוּרִים** ◆

kulam **כֻּלָּם**   giborim **גִּבּוֹרִים** ר"ת אבג ◆ kulam **כֻּלָּם**   kedoshim **קְדוֹשִׁים** ◆

May You be blessed, Lord, our God in Heavens Above and upon the Earth Below, and upon all Your magnificent handiwork and upon all the luminaries that You have made. They shall glorify You, Selah.

TITBARACH LANETZACH

May You be eternally blessed, our Rock, our King, and our Redeemer, Creator of the holy angels. May Your Name be praised forever, our King, Who forms ministering angels. And Whose ministering angels stand in the heights of the world and loudly proclaim, with reverence and in unison, the words of the living God and the King of the Universe. They are all-beloved. They are all-pure. They are all-powerful. They are all-holy.

יהוה   ריבוע   ע"ב   ר"ת   be'ema   בְּאֵימָה   osim   עוֹשִׂים   kulam   כֻּלָם

ע"ב ע"ה   אל שדי   ע"ה וקס"א   ע"ב ברריבוע   מהש ע"ה   רי"ו   retzon   רָצוֹן   uvyir'a   וּבְיִרְאָה

et   אֶת   potchim   פּוֹתְחִים   vechulam   וְכֻלָם   konehem   קוֹנֵיהֶם

beshira   בְּשִׁירָה   uvtahora   וּבְטָהֳרָה   bikdusha   בִּקְדֻשָׁה   pihem   פִּיהֶם

◆umshabechin   וּמְשַׁבְּחִין   ◆umvarchin   וּמְבָרְכִין   uvzimra   וּבְזִמְרָה

◆uma'aritzin   וּמַעֲרִיצִין   ◆umakdishin   וּמַקְדִּישִׁין   ◆umfa'arin   וּמְפָאֲרִין

ר"ת ז' ווין בסוד שם בן מ"ב ; ס"ת = מצפ"צ, אלהים דיודין, י"פ יי"י ◆   umamlichin   וּמַמְלִיכִין

ET SHEM

The word *reshut* רשות is found inside this connection. *Reshut* has the same numerical value (906) as the initials of the words comprising the last sentence in the *Ana Beko'ach* (*Shav'atenu Kabel Ushma Tza'akatenu Yode'a Ta'alumot*) - שקוי צית. This specific sequence correlates to our physical world, *Malchut*.

hamelech   הַמֶּלֶךְ   (מילוי דס"ג יא"י)   אל   לאה   haEl   הָאֵל   shem   שֵׁם   et   אֶת

vehanora   וְהַנּוֹרָא   hagibor   הַגִּבּוֹר   לתהו ; עם ד' אותיות = מבה, יזל, אום   hagadol   הַגָּדוֹל

ר"ת = יהוה   kadosh   קָדוֹשׁ   ◆hu   הוּא   vechulam   וְכֻלָם   mekabelim   מְקַבְּלִים

ze   זֶה   י"פ טל, י"פ כוז'   shamayim   שָׁמַיִם   malchut   מַלְכוּת   ol   עוֹל   alehem   עֲלֵיהֶם

◆laze   לָזֶה   ze   זֶה   שקוי צית   reshut   רְשׁוּת   venotnim   וְנוֹתְנִים   ◆mize   מִזֶּה

◆ru'ach   רוּחַ   benachat   בְּנַחַת   leyotzram   לְיוֹצְרָם   lehakdish   לְהַקְדִּישׁ

◆uvin'ima   וּבִנְעִימָה   בשפה ברורה ע"ה = לשון הקודש   verura   בְּרוּרָה   besafa   בְּשָׂפָה

דאגה   אהבה,   ke'echad   כְּאֶחָד   kulam   כֻּלָם   kedusha   קְדֻשָׁה

רי"ו   beyir'a   בְּיִרְאָה   ve'omrim   וְאוֹמְרִים   ◆be'ema   בְּאֵימָה   onim   עוֹנִים

They all execute, with reverence and with awe, the will of their Maker. They all open their mouths with holiness and with purity, and give song and melody. They bless, praise, glorify, sanctify, revere, and enthrone.

ET SHEM

The Name of God, the King, the great, powerful and awesome One, for He is Holy. They all accept upon themselves the yoke of the Heavenly Kingdom, one from another. And they give leave to one another and they consent to sanctify their Creator. And in a calm spirit, with a clear expression, and pleasantly, they proclaim sanctity, with reverence. And they all say in unison and in awe:

KADOSH, KADOSH, KADOSH

This phrase translates into "Holy, Holy, Holy," but it does not refer to what we normally consider the word "holy" to mean (sacred, blessed, or sanctified). Rather, it signifies the concept of *whole* or "wholly", as in the quantum wholeness of reality that is unified and interconnected. Repeating the word "holy" three times also connects us to the Right (positive), Left (negative), and Central Columns (neutral). This prayer instills within us the awareness that although we may have imperfections, we still have the Divine Spark of Light within us. Our soul is part of God.

Before reciting *Kadosh* three times, kiss the Hand *Tefilin* and sit down.
It is good to recite this verse according to its intonations (*te'amim*).

(Central) kadosh קָדוֹשׁ **(Left)** kadosh קָדוֹשׁ **(Right)** | kadosh קָדוֹשׁ

שכינה פָּנֵי Tzeva'ot צְבָאוֹת Adonai יְהוָ(אדני יאהדונהי)

kevodo כְּבוֹדוֹ: אלהים דההין ע"ה ha'aretz הָאָרֶץ ילי chol כָּל melo מְלֹא

hakodesh הַקֹּדֶשׁ vechayot וְחַיּוֹת veha'ofanim וְהָאוֹפַנִּים

אום יזל, מזה, = אותיות ד' עם ; להו gadol גָּדוֹל bera'ash בְּרַעַשׁ

haserafim הַשְּׂרָפִים le'umat לְעֻמַּת mitnase'im מִתְנַשְּׂאִים

ve'omrim וְאוֹמְרִים: meshabchim מְשַׁבְּחִים le'umatam לְעֻמָּתָם

יוד הי ואו הה = יהוה ; כבוד יהוה Adonai יְהוָ(אדני יאהדונהי): kevod כְּבוֹד baruch בָּרוּךְ

שמתו) המלכים י' את (למתק) הברכה, עסמ"ב, mimekomo מִמְּקוֹמוֹ

ר"ת = ע"ב, ריבוע יהוה ; ר"ת מ"ק, י"פ האא:

LAEL BARUCH

Hechal Nogah (the Brightness Chamber) - *Netzach* of *Zeir Anpin* in *Beriah*.
In this *Hechal* there are Holy animals and the minister in charge in this *Hechal* is *Nogah* which adds up to 63 (יוד הי ואו הי) with the *Kolel*, which is *Netzach* of *Beriah* that is called: יְהוָה צְבָאוֹת.

yitenu יִתְּנוּ ne'imot נְעִימוֹת baruch בָּרוּךְ (דס"ג) (מילוי) יא"י laEl לָאֵל

vekayam וְקַיָּם chai וְחַי (דס"ג) (מילוי) יא"י El אַל lamelech לַמֶּלֶךְ

yashmi'u יַשְׁמִיעוּ vetishbachot וְתִשְׁבָּחוֹת yomeru יֹאמְרוּ zemirot זְמִירוֹת

KADOSH, KADOSH, KADOSH
"Holy, Holy, Holy
Is the Lord of Hosts. The world is full with His glory." (Isaiah 6:3)
"The Offanim and all the Holy Beasts soar with thunderous voice toward the Seraphs who stand opposite them, and give praise and say: Blessed is the glory of the Lord from His place." (Ezekiel 3:12)

LAEL BARUCH
To the blessed God, they give their melodies.
To the King, the living and everlasting God, they shall sing hymns and proclaim praises.

SEVEN VERSES

Each of these seven verses connects to a different heavenly body. Four thousand years ago, Abraham the Patriarch revealed that there were seven key heavenly bodies that could be seen with the naked eye - the sun, the moon, Mars, Mercury, Saturn, Venus and Jupiter. These are the ones with a direct influence over our physical world and they correspond to the seven lower *Sefirot*. According to Abraham, the upper three dimensions (*Sefirot*) do not directly influence our world.

ki כִּי **הוּא** hu **לְבַדּוֹ** levado מ"ב

(Keter) **מָרוֹם** marom (Chochmah) **וְקָדוֹשׁ** vekadosh•

corresponding to the seven planets – כנגד ז' כוכבי לכת:

כפרתבגד	(Sun)	gevurot **גְּבוּרוֹת**	po'el **פּוֹעֵל**	(*Binah*)
תבגדכפר	(Moon)	chadashot **וַחֲדָשׁוֹת**	ose **עוֹשֶׂה**	(*Chesed*)
דכפרתבגֹ	(Mars)	milchamot **מִלְחָמוֹת**	ba'al **בַּעַל**	(*Gevurah*)
רתבגדכפ	(Mercury)	tzedakot **צְדָקוֹת**	zore'a **זוֹרֵעַ**	(*Tiferet*)
בגֹדכפרת	(Saturn)	yeshu'ot **יְשׁוּעוֹת**	matzmi'ach **מַצְמִיחַ**	(*Netzach*)
פרתבגֹדכ	(Venus)	refu'ot **רְפוּאוֹת**	bore **בּוֹרֵא**	(*Hod*)
גֹדכפרתב	(Jupiter)	tehilot **תְּהִלּוֹת**	nora **נוֹרָא**	(*Yesod*)

(*Malchut*) **אֲדוֹן** adon אֲנִי **הַנִּפְלָאוֹת** hanifla'ot•

MA'ASE BERESHEET

Be aware at all times that every new day is a renewal of all of Creation. Too often, we live life either in the past or the future, letting the present slip away. Real spiritual growth occurs in the present. This prayer helps to instill this consciousness within us. In the present, we proactively deal with the effects we have created in the past and through our actions, we plant seeds for our future. If we miss the opportunities that the present offers us, we will find ourselves on a reactive wheel with no control over our lives.

Hechal Zechut (the Merit Chamber) - *Gevurah* of *Zeir Anpin* in *Beriah*.
In this *Hechal* are the *Sanhedrin* (Court of the Sages – who are the prosecuting attorneys) and the one in charge in this *Hechal* is called: אל יהֹו. This is the secret of the verse: "Velohai (ואלהֹי – "And my God" – the same letters as *Eliyahu*) *letzur machsi* (is my shelter)." And this is *Eliyahu* the Prophet who teaches the merits of Israel (defending attorney).

SEVEN VERSES

(Keter) *For He above is lofty* (Cochmah) *and holy.*

(Binah)	*He performs mighty deeds.*	(Sun)	(Chesed)	*Makes new things.*	(Moon)
(Gevurah)	*Master of wars.*	(Mars)	(Tiferet)	*Sows righteousness.*	(Mercury)
(Netzach)	*Brings about salvation.*	(Saturn)	(Hod)	*Creates remedies.*	(Venus)
(Yesod)	*Awesome in praises.*	(Jupiter)	(Malchut)	*He, in His goodness.*	

בכב ,ב"ן bechol בְּכָל betuvo בְּטוּבוֹ י"ב הויות, קס"א קנ"א hamechadesh הַמְּחַדֵּשׁ

קמ"ג קס"א קנ"א ע"ה tamid תָּמִיד אל יהוה ,זן ,מזבוח ,נגד ע"ה yom יוֹם

‡ka'amur כָּאָמוּר מ"ב ר"ת vereshit בְּרֵאשִׁית ma'ase מַעֲשֵׂה

ki כִּי gedolim גְּדֹלִים סוף אין ,רו orim אוֹרִים le'ose לַעֲשֵׂה

‡נגה = ר"ת ; מזלא ,הויות ג chasdo וְחַסְדּוֹ אותיות דס"ג ו"י ס"ג ריבוע le'olam לְעוֹלָם

‡hame'orot הַמְּאוֹרוֹת yotzer יוֹצֵר Adonai יְהֹוָאדְנִילִיאהדונהי Ata אַתָּה baruch בָּרוּךְ

AHAVAT OLAM

The purpose of this prayer is to inspire within us a love for the world and for other people.

Hechal Ahavah (the Love Chamber) - *Chesed* of *Zeir Anpin* in *Beriah*.

In this *Hechal* the minister in charge is called *El Shadai* אל שׁדי, from the word *Shadayim* (chest). And in this *Hechal* we find the secret of the embrace of *Yaakov* and *Leah*, which is the secret of *Chesed* that prepares them for the purpose of the *Amidah*; there we find the secret of the *Zivug* (the Unificiation).

יהוה ריבוע ,ע"ב ר"ת ahavtanu אֲהַבְתָּנוּ olam עוֹלָם ahavat אַהֲבַת

gedola גְּדוֹלָה chemla וְחֶמְלָה ילה Elohenu אֱלֹהֵינוּ Adonai יְהֹוָאדְנִילִיאהדונהי

malkenu מַלְכֵּנוּ avinu אָבִינוּ ◆alenu עָלֵינוּ chamalta וְחָמַלְתָּ vitera וִיתֵרָה

אום ,זל ,מבה = אותיות ד' עם ; לתנו hagadol הַגָּדוֹל shimcha שִׁמְךָ ba'avur בַּעֲבוּר

vach בָּךְ shebatchu שֶׁבָּטְחוּ avotenu אֲבוֹתֵינוּ uva'avur וּבַעֲבוּר

ע"ה בינה יהוה אהיה אהיה chayim וְחַיִּים chukei וְחֻקֵּי vatelamdemo וּתְלַמְּדֵמוֹ

◆shalem שָׁלֵם בוכו belevav בְּלֵבָב retzoncha רְצוֹנְךָ la'asot לַעֲשׂוֹת

◆harachaman הָרַחֲמָן av אָב avinu אָבִינוּ techonenu תְּחָנֵּנוּ ken כֵּן

MA'ASE BERESHEET

Renews, every day and forever, the work of Creation as it is stated: "To the One Who makes the great luminaries, for His kindness is forever." (Psalms 136:7) Blessed are You, Lord, Maker of luminaries.

AHAVAT OLAM

You have loved us an eternal love, Lord, our God. Great and abundant compassion You have bestowed upon us. our Father, our King, for the sake of Your great Name and for the sake of our forefathers who trusted in You. Teach life-giving precepts so we may fulfill Your will, wholeheartedly, so shall you be gracious to us, our Father, merciful Father.

SHACHARIT – MORNING PRAYER
יוד הֹי ואו הֹי – אל שׁדֹי - OLAM BERIAH

הַמְרַחֵם hamerachem — אברהם, וח"פ אל, רי"ו ול"ב נתיבות החוכמה, רמ"ח (אברים,)

רַחֵם rachem — עסמ"ב וט"ז אותיות פשוטות אברהם, וח"פ אל, רי"ו ול"ב נתיבות החוכמה, רמ"ח (אברים,)

נָא na עָלֵינוּ alenu וְתֵן veten בְּלִבֵּנוּ belibenu — עסמ"ב וט"ז אותיות פשוטות

בִּינָה vina — ע"ה אהיה אהיה יהוה, וחיים — לְהָבִין lehavin◆ לְהַשְׂכִּיל lehaskil◆

לִשְׁמוֹעַ lishmo'a◆ לִלְמוֹד lilmod וּלְלַמֵּד ulelamed◆ לִשְׁמוֹר lishmor

וְלַעֲשׂוֹת vela'asot וּלְקַיֵּם ulkayem אֶת־ et כָּל־ kol יבלי דִּבְרֵי divrei ראה

תַּלְמוּד talmud תּוֹרָתֶךָ toratecha בְּאַהֲבָה be'ahava אוזר, דאגה, וְהָאֵר veha'er

עֵינֵינוּ enenu ריבוע מ"ה בְּתוֹרָתֶךָ betoratecha◆ וְדַבֵּק vedabek

לִבֵּנוּ libenu בְּמִצְוֹתֶיךָ vemitzvotecha◆ וְיַחֵד veyached לְבָבֵנוּ levavenu

לְאַהֲבָה le'ahava אוזר, דאגה וּלְיִרְאָה ulyir'a רי"ו אֶת־ et שְׁמֶךָ shemecha◆

וְלֹא velo נֵבוֹשׁ nevosh וְלֹא velo נִכָּלֵם nikalem וְלֹא velo נִכָּשֵׁל nikashel

לְעוֹלָם le'olam ריבוע ס"ג ו' אותיות דס"ג וָעֶד va'ed◆ כִּי ki בְּשֵׁם veshem

קָדְשֶׁךָ kodshecha הַגָּדוֹל hagadol להו ; עם ד' אותיות = מבה, יזל, אום

וְהַנּוֹרָא vehanora בָּטָחְנוּ vatachnu◆ נָגִילָה nagila וְנִשְׂמְחָה venismecha

בִּישׁוּעָתֶךָ vishu'atecha◆ וְרַחֲמֶיךָ verachamecha יְהֹוָה Adonai אלדניאהדונהי

אֱלֹהֵינוּ Elohenu ילה וַחֲסָדֶיךָ vachasadecha הָרַבִּים harabim

אַל al יַעַזְבוּנוּ ya'azvunu נֶצַח netzach סֶלָה sela וָעֶד va'ed◆

Gather the four corners of the *Talit* in your left hand and hold them against your heart until after reciting the words *"la'ad ule'olmei olamim"* on pg. 184.

מַהֵר maher וְהָבֵא vehave עָלֵינוּ alenu בְּרָכָה beracha

וְשָׁלוֹם veshalom מְהֵרָה mehera מֵאַרְבַּע me'arba כַּנְפוֹת kanfot

הָאָרֶץ ha'aretz אלהים דההין ע"ה ; ר"ת = אדני◆

Be merciful to us, merciful One. Place understanding in our hearts so we may understand, discern, hear, study, teach, keep, do, and fulfill all the words of the teachings of Your Torah in love. Enlighten our eyes with Your Torah. Bond our hearts with Your commandments. Unify our hearts to love and fear Your Name; then we shall be neither ashamed nor humiliated; nor shall we fail ever and for all eternity. Because we have placed our trust in Your great and awesome Name. May we rejoice and be happy in Your salvation. May Your compassion never leave us, Lord, our God, nor Your many kindnesses, Selah, forever. Hurry and bring upon us blessing and peace, speedily, from the four corners of the Earth.

וּשְׁבוֹר ushvor עֹל ol הַגּוֹים hagoyim מֵעַל me'al עלם צַוָּארֵנוּ tzavarenu

וְהוֹלִיכֵנוּ veholichenu מְהֵרָה mehera קוֹמְמִיּוּת komemiyut לְאַרְצֵנוּ le'artzenu♦

כִּי ki אֵל El ייא"י (מילוי דס"ג) פּוֹעֵל po'el יְשׁוּעוֹת yeshu'ot אַתָּה Ata ר"ת פאי, אמן

וּבָנוּ uvanu (יאהדונהי) בָּחַרְתָּ vacharta מִכָּל mikol ילי עַם am וְלָשׁוֹן velashon♦

VEKERAVTANU MALKENU

Saying *Vekeravtanu Malkenu* reminds us of and gives us a direct connection to Mount Sinai and the energy of immortality.

וְקֵרַבְתָּנוּ vekeravtanu מַלְכֵּנוּ malkenu

LESHIMCHA HAGADOL

This phrase gives us the power to remove all doubt and uncertainty from our lives.

Without the power of certainty, all our prayers are rendered ineffective. The kabbalists explain that uncertainty is the seed of all evil in the world: about us, about the existence of God, about our destiny and about our ability to overcome challenges. Because our consciousness creates our reality, our uncertainty inevitably leads to chaos. When we destroy our doubt, all that can remain is positivity and certainty in the Light. The word *Amalek* עֲמָלֵק has the same numerical value as the Aramaic word for "uncertainty" and "doubt", סָפֵק (240). *Amalek* refers to the doubts and uncertainties that infect us, causing disunity and hatred among people. A story in the Bible recounts how God ordered the Israelites to go and slaughter all the men, women, and children of the nation of *Amalek*. The *Zohar* explains that in this passage is a code for the key to destroying our doubt. God was really telling the Israelites to slaughter the uncertainty within them.

לְשִׁמְךָ leshimcha הַגָּדוֹל hagadol להו ; עם ד' אותיות = מבה, יזל, אום

BE'AHAVA LEHODOT LACH

We are now gaining the strength to refrain from any kind of evil speech or gossip about other people.

Spiritualy, evil speech is considered one of the most serious negative actions a person can commit— even more serious than murder. With murder, say the sages, one person only dies once. When we gossip about someone spiritually, three people die – the speaker, the listener and whoever is spoken of. And not only that, every time the gossip spreads from one person to another we kill that person again. Speech has tremendous power. When we speak ill of others, not only do we hurt and damage their lives, but the harm spills over into the person listening to the gossip, as well as into our own lives. The *Talmud* teaches that the destruction of the Temple occurred because of evil speech and hatred between people. If we do not refrain from speaking ill about our fellow man, others will not be able to refrain from speaking ill of us. The kabbalists teach us that evil speech is one of the spiritual causes of the most negative force in our physical world, *hatred for no reason*.

בְּאַהֲבָה be'ahava אוזר, דאגה לְהוֹדוֹת lehodot לָךְ lach

Break the yoke of the nations from our necks and quickly lead us, proudly upright, to our land. For You are God, Who works salvation. You chose us from among all nations and tongues.

VEKERAVTANU MALKENU - *And brought us close, our King,*
LESHIMCHA HAGADOL - *To Your great Name*
BE'AHAVA LEHODOT LACH - *To lovingly express our gratitude,*

‏יוד הי ואו הי – אל עידי‎ - OLAM BERIAH

ul'yachedcha ‏וּלְיַחֶדְךָ‎   ul'ahava ‏וּלְאַהֲבָה‎   אוֹד, דאגה ‏אֶת־‎ et   shimcha ‏שְׁמֶךָ:‎

‏ר"ת הברכה עולה למנין ל"ב נתיבות החכמה‎

baruch ‏בָּרוּךְ‎ Ata ‏אַתָּה‎ ‏יְהֹוָ[אלהינו]אהדונהי‎ Adonai

habocher ‏הַבּוֹחֵר‎ be'amo ‏בְּעַמּוֹ‎ Yisrael ‏יִשְׂרָאֵל‎ be'ahava ‏בְּאַהֲבָה‎ אוֹד, דאגה

‏ר"ת שם קדוש ביב (באתב"ש עמש):‎

THE SHEMA

The *Shema* is one of the most powerful tools to draw the energy of healing to our lives. The true power of the *Shema* is unleashed when we meditate upon others who need healing energy while reciting it. The first verse of the *Shema* channels the energy of *Zeir Anpin,* or the Upper Worlds.

The second verse refers to our world, the World of *Malchut.*

There are a total of 248 words in this prayer, and these 248 words transmit healing energy to the 248 parts of the human body and its soul. The first paragraph of the *Shema* is built of 42 words, connecting us to the 42-Letter Name of God in the *Ana Beko'ach.* The second paragraph is composed of 72 words that connect us to The 72 Names of God. The third paragraph contains 50 words that link us to The 50 Gates of Binah, which helps us rise above the 50 Gates of Negativity. The final paragraph of the *Shema* has 72 words, which also connects us to The 72 Names of God, but through a different letter combination than that which is used in the second paragraph.

1) In order to receive the Light of the *Shema,* you have to accept upon yourself the precept of: "Love your neighbor as yourself," and see yourself together with all the souls that are part of the original Adam.

2) You need to meditate to connect to the precept of the Reading of *Shema* twice a day.

3) Before saying the *Shema* you should cover your eyes with the right hand (while saying the words "*Shema Yisrael ... le'olam va'ed*",) and hold the four *tzitziot* with the left hand and place them on your heart.

4) You should read the *Shema* with deep meditation, saying it with the intonations. It is necessary to be careful with the pronunciation of all the letters. Every word that ends with the same letter that the next word begins with must be pronounced on its own and not lead into the next word e.g. *bechol levavcha.* *Bechol* ends with a *Lamed* and *levavcha* begins with a *Lamed.* Each of these words must be pronounced separately so that both *Lameds* are heard. And therefore we add a special symbol (˙) on top of each place.

First, meditate in general, on the first *Yichud* of the four *Yichuds* of the Name: ‏יהוה‎, and in particular, to awaken the letter ‏ה‎, and then to connect it with the letter ‏ו‎. Then connect the letter ‏י‎ and the letter ‏ה‎ together in the following order: *Hei* (‏ה‎), *Hei-Vav* (‏ה"ו‎), then *Yud-Hei* (‏ה"י‎), which adds up to 31, the secret of ‏אי"א‎ of the Name ‏ס"ג‎. It is good to meditate on this *Yichud* before reciting any *Shema* because it acts as a replacement for the times that you may have missed reading the *Shema.* This *Yichud* has the same ability to create a Supernal connection like the reading of the *Shema* - to raise *Zeir* and *Nukva* together for the *Zivug* of *Abba* and *Ima.*

---

to unify You, and to love Your Name.
Blessed are You, Lord, Who has chosen His Nation Israel, with love.

Shema – שְׁמַע

The reason for saying here the *Shema* is to awaken the *Mochin* (brains/energy) for *Ze'ir Anpin*. We need to do so in *Beriah*, because in *Atzilut* we are not able to do that anymore.

General Meditation: שֹׁמַע — to draw the energy from the seven lower *Sefirot* of *Ima* to the *Nukva*, which enables the *Nukva* to elevate the *Mayin Nukvin* (awakening from Below).

Particular Meditation: שֹׁדֹי ‎ + יהוה = שֹׁם and five times the letters י and ה of ב"ן = ע [The letter *Hei* (ה) is formed by the letters *Dalet* (ד) and *Yud* (י), so in ב"ן we have four times the letter ה plus another time the letters י and ה from יוד of ב"ן.]. Also the three letters ו (18) that are left from ב"ן, plus ב"ן itself (52) equals ע (70).

Yisrael – יִשְׂרָאֵל

General Meditation: שֹׁיר אֵל — to draw energy from *Chesed* and *Gevurah* of *Abba* to *Zeir Anpin*, to do his action in the secret of *Mayin Duchrin* (awakening from Above).

Particular Meditation: (the rearranged letters of the word *Yisrael*) – שׁר אֵלִי

,'ש = (י"ה פעמים ה"י) י"ה דאלהים דמוֹח וחכמה בהכאה

,ר = (י"ד פעמים ה"ה) י"ה דאלהים דמוֹח בינה בהכאה

.אֵל"י = (י"ה) י"ה דאלהים דמוֹח דחֹסדים דדעת (י"ו" ה"א), וי"ה דאלהים דמוֹח דגבורות דדעת

Also meditate to draw the Surrounding Light of *Abba* of *Katnut* into *Zeir Anpin*.

Adonai Elohenu Adonai - יהוה אלהינו יהוה

General Meditation: to draw energy to *Abba*, *Ima* and *Da'at* from *Arich Anpin*,

Particular Meditation: ע"ב (יוֹד הֹי ויו הֹי) קֹס"א (אלף הֹי יוֹד הֹי) ע"ב (יוֹד הֹי וֹי הֹי).

Echad – אֶחָד
(The secret of the complete *Yichud-Unification*)

The letters *Alef* א and *Chet* ח from *Echad* אֶחָד are *Zeir Anpin* and the letter *Dalet* ד is *Nukva*. **You should meditate** to devote your soul for the sanctification of the Holy Name, thereby elevating your *Nefesh*, *Ruach*, *Neshamah* and *Neshamah* of *Neshamah* with *Zeir Anpin* and *Nukva* (using the Names: ע"ב and ס"ג) to *Abba* and *Ima* as the secret of *Mayin Nukvin*, and by that energy, *Abba* and *Ima* will be unified in the secret of the Name: יאההויהה. **Also meditate** to draw out the Inner Six Edges of *Gadlut* of *Ima* into *Zeir Anpin*. The Drop, which is ע"ב, is drawn out from the external of *Atik*, and descends to *Yesod* of *Ima*, where it becomes: ע"ב ס"ג מ"ה ב"ן, and the four spelled out אהיה (אלף הֹי יוֹד הֹי, אלף הֹי יוֹד הֹי, אלף הֹא יוֹד הֹא, אלף הֹה יוֹד הֹה) become Her clothing. **As a result**, *Zeir Anpin* now has four spelled out יה"ו (יוֹד הֹי וֹיו, יוֹד הֹי ואו, יוֹד הֹא ואו, יוֹד הֹה וֹו), four spelled out אה"י (אלף הֹי יוֹד, אלף הֹי יוֹד, אלף הֹא יוֹד, אלף הֹה יוֹד) and the Inner Six Edges of *Gadlut* of *Ima*. **Also meditate** on the Name: אל"ף הֹ"י וֹי"ו הֹ"י, which is the entire *Mochin* in the secret of *Da'at*. **And also meditate** (according to the Ramchal) on the four spelled out *Alef* (אלף=111) of the Name: אהי"ה that is equal to the word *Midat* (444), making the *Keter* for *Leah*.

Baruch Shem - בָּרוּךְ שֵׁם כְּבוֹד מַלְכוּתוֹ לְעוֹלָם וָעֶד

Baruch Shem Kevod – *Chochmah*, *Binah*, *Da'at* of *Leah*;

Malchuto – Her *Keter*; **Le'olam** – the rest of Her *Partzuf*;

Va'ed – the four הֹיה (4 times 20 equal to *Va'ed*=80) will make the *Keter* for *Rachel* .

And the four spelled out הֹיה (הֹי יוֹד הֹי, הֹי יוֹד הֹי, הֹא יוֹד הֹא, הֹה יוֹד הֹה) will make the rest of Her body.

Adonai יְהֹוָה(אֲדֹנָיאַהדוני) Yisrael יִשְׂרָאֵל ע' רבתי shema שְׁמַע

echad אֶחָד | Adonai יְהֹוָה(אֲדֹנָיאַהדוני) ילה Elohenu אֱלֹהֵינוּ ד' רבתי ; אהבה, דאגה:

malchuto, מַלְכוּתוֹ kevod כְּבוֹד shem שֵׁם baruch בָּרוּךְ יחו אותיות (Whisper :)

va'ed:וָעֶד le'olam לְעוֹלָם ריבוע דס"ג ו' אותיות דס"ג

<hr>

Yud, Chochmah, head — 42 words corresponding to the Holy 42-Letter Name of God.

ב   א

et אֵת (ה' אהבת על מ"ע לקיים יכוין ;) ב"פ אין סוף ,ב"פ רז ,ב"פ אור ve'ahavta וְאָהַבְתָּ

ג

יְהֹוָה(אֲדֹנָיאַהדוני) Adonai אֱלֹהֶיךָ Elohecha ילה ; ס"ת כהת, משיחו בן דוד ע"ה

ר   ק   צ   ת

nafshecha נַפְשֶׁךָ לכב ,ב"ן uvchol וּבְכָל levavcha לְבָבְךָ לכב ,ב"ן bechol בְּכָל

ב   ט   ש   ע

hadevarim הַדְּבָרִים vehayu וְהָיוּ me'odecha:מְאֹדֶךָ לכב ,ב"ן uvchol וּבְכָל

כ   י   ד   ג

hayom הַיּוֹם metzavecha מְצַוְּךָ anochi אָנֹכִי asher אֲשֶׁר ha'ele הָאֵלֶּה

ט   ב   ע

veshinantam וְשִׁנַּנְתָּם levavecha:לְבָבֶךָ al עַל (pause here) ע"ה נגד, מזבח, זן, אל יהוה

ש   ת   צ

beshivtecha בְּשִׁבְתְּךָ מ"ב bam בָּם vedibarta וְדִבַּרְתָּ levanecha לְבָנֶיךָ

ב   ק   ח

vaderech בַּדֶּרֶךְ uvlechtecha וּבְלֶכְתְּךָ ראה ב"פ bevetecha בְּבֵיתֶךָ

ג   ט

uvkumecha:וּבְקוּמֶךָ uvshochbecha וּבְשָׁכְבְּךָ קס"א ס"ג ,יב"ק ,ב"פ

ל   ג   י   ע

(You should touch the Hand *Tefilin*) yadecha יָדֶךָ al עַל le'ot לְאוֹת ukshartam וּקְשַׁרְתָּם

<hr>

THE SHEMA
"Hear Israel, the Lord our God. The Lord is One." (Deuteronomy 6:4)
"Blessed is the glorious Name, His Kingdom is forever and for eternity." (Pesachim 56a)
"And you shall love the Lord, your God, with all your heart and with all your soul and with all that you possess. Let those words that I command you today be upon your heart. And you shall teach them to your children and you shall speak of them while you sit in your home and while you walk on your way and when you lie down and when you rise. You shall bind them as a sign upon your hand

שׁ ק י פ

(You should touch the Head *Tefilin*) enecha עֵינֶיךָ ben בֵּין letotafot לְטֹטָפֹת vehayu וְהָיוּ

ו ק

al עַל uchtavtam וּכְתַבְתָּם מ"ה: ריבוע ; קס"א ע"ה

ת צ '

uvish'arecha וּבִשְׁעָרֶיךָ ב"פ ראה betecha בֵּיתֶךָ (וו מות) נית mezuzot מְזֻזֹת

VEHAYA IM SHAMO'A

Hei, Binah, **arms and body** — 72 words corresponding to the 72 Names of God.

יבי והו

vehaya וְהָיָה יהוה ; יהה im אִם יוה"ך, מ"א אותיות דפשוטי, דמילוי ודמילוי דמילוי דאהיה ע"ה

אכא ללה מהע עלם סיט

asher אֲשֶׁר mitzvotai מִצְוֹתַי el אֶל tishme'u תִּשְׁמְעוּ shamo'a שָׁמֹעַ

לאו אלד הזי כהת

anochi אָנֹכִי metzave מְצַוֶּה etchem אֶתְכֶם hayom הַיּוֹם ע"ה נגד, מזבח, זן, אל יהוה

מבה יזל הזע

Adonai יְהֹוָ‏‎ et אֶת‏ דאגה, אוזר, le'ahava לְאַהֲבָה (pause here)

הקם הרי

ul'ovdo וּלְעָבְדוֹ (enunciate the letter *Ayin* in the word "*ul'ovdo*") ילה Elohechem אֱלֹהֵיכֶם

לוו כלי לאו

לכב ב"ן, uvchol וּבְכָל levavchem לְבַבְכֶם לכב ב"ן, bechol בְּכָל

מלה ייי נלך פהל

artzechem אַרְצְכֶם metar מְטַר venatati וְנָתַתִּי nafshechem נַפְשְׁכֶם:

שׁאה ירת האא נתה וההו

deganecha דְגָנֶךָ ve'asafta וְאָסַפְתָּ umalkosh וּמַלְקוֹשׁ yore יוֹרֶה be'ito בְּעִתּוֹ

ושׁר לכב אום ר"יי

esev עֵשֶׂב ע"ב שׁמות venatati וְנָתַתִּי veyitz'harecha וְיִצְהָרֶךָ: vetiroshcha וְתִירֹשְׁךָ

---

and they shall be as frontlets between your eyes.

And you shall write them upon the doorposts of your house and your gates." (Deuteronomy 6:5-9)

VEHAYA IM SHAMO'A

"And it shall come to be that if you shall listen to My commandments that I am commanding you with today to love the Lord, your God, and to serve Him with all your heart and with all your soul, then I shall send rain upon your land in its proper time, both early rain and late rain. You shall then gather your grain and your wine and your oil. And I shall give grass

SHACHARIT – MORNING PRAYER
יוד ה"י ואו ה"י – אל שדי - OLAM BERIAH

180

מנד	כוק	להון	ייוו
׃vesavata וְשָׂבָעְתָּ	ve'achalta וְאָכַלְתָּ	livhemtecha לִבְהֶמְתֶּךָ	besadcha בְּשָׂדְךָ

ההה	ייז	רהע	ווֹעֹם	אני
levavchem לְבַבְכֶם	yifte יִפְתֶּה	pen פֶּן	lachem לָכֶם	hishamru הִשָּׁמְרוּ

סאל	ילה	ווֹל	מיכ
acherim אֲחֵרִים	elohim° אֱלֹהִים	va'avadetem° וַעֲבַדְתֶּם	vesartem וְסַרְתֶּם

עשׁל			מויה
׃lahem לָהֶם	vehishtachavitem וְהִשְׁתַּחֲוִיתֶם	(הקליפות) (העומד) נגד	משה

הוושׁ	ודי	והו	מויה
bachem בָּכֶם	Adonai יְהֹוָאדֹנָיֵאֱהֹוִֹנָהִי	af אַף	(pause here)	vechara וְחָרָה

מבה	נית	גֹּוֹא	עמם
velo וְלֹא	כוזו י"פ טל, י"פ השמים הַשָּׁמַיִם	et אֶת	ve'atzar וְעָצַר

דמב	מצר	הרוֹ	ייל	נמם	פוי
ב"פ כהת titen תִתֵּן	lo לֹא	veha'adama וְהָאֲדָמָה	matar מָטָר	yihye יִהְיֶה

דמב	מוזי	עֹגֹו	ומב
עלם me'al מֵעַל	mehera מְהֵרָה	va'avadetem° וַאֲבַדְתֶּם	yevula יְבוּלָהּ et אֶת

איע			ראה
asher אֲשֶׁר	hatova הַטֹּבָה	ע"ה דההין אלהים	ha'aretz הָאָרֶץ

היי			ראה
Vav, Zeir Anpin	׃lachem לָכֶם	אבג יתץ, וסר noten נֹתֵן	Adonai יְהֹוָאדֹנָיֵאֱהֹוִֹנָהִי

א		מום
et אֶת	**stomach** – 50 words corresponding to the 50 Gates of *Binah*	vesamtem° וְשַׂמְתֶּם

ה	א	ה	י	ה
ve'al וְעַל־	levavchem לְבַבְכֶם	al עַל־	ele אֵלֶּה	ראה devarai דְּבָרַי

ה	א	ה	י
ר"ת לאו le'ot לְאוֹת	otam אֹתָם	ukshartem° וּקְשַׁרְתֶּם	nafshechem נַפְשְׁכֶם

---

in your field for your cattle. And you shall eat and you shall be satiated. Be careful lest your heart be seduced and you may turn away and serve alien deities and prostrate yourself before them. And the wrath of the Lord shall be upon you and He shall stop the Heavens and there shall be no more rain and the earth shall not give forth its crop. And you shall quickly perish from the good land that the Lord has given you. And you shall place those words of Mine upon your heart and upon your soul and you shall bind them as a sign

עַל־ al יֶדְכֶם yedchem (You should touch the Hand *Tefilin*) וְהָיוּ vehayu

לְטוֹטָפֹת letotafot בֵּין ben עֵינֵיכֶם enechem ריבוע מ"ה ✦(You should touch the Head *Tefilin*)

וְלִמַּדְתֶּם velimadetem אֹתָם otam אֶת־ et בְּנֵיכֶם benechem

לְדַבֵּר ledaber בָּם bam ראה שׁם בֶן מ"ב בְּשִׁבְתְּךָ beshivtecha

בְּבֵיתֶךָ bevetecha ב"פ יב"ק ראה וּבְלֶכְתְּךָ uvlechtecha בַדֶּרֶךְ vaderech ב"פ יב"ק, ס"ג קס"א

וּבְשָׁכְבְּךָ uvshochbecha וּבְקוּמֶךָ uvkumecha✦ וּכְתַבְתָּם uchtavtam עַל־ al

לְמַעַן lema'an✦ וּבִשְׁעָרֶיךָ uvish'arecha בֵּיתֶךָ betecha ב"פ ראה מְזֻזוֹת mezuzot

יִרְבּוּ yirbu יְמֵיכֶם yemechem ר"ת ייל וִימֵי vimei ייל בְּנֵיכֶם venechem

עַל al הָאֲדָמָה ha'adama אֲשֶׁר asher (enunciate the letter *Ayin* in the word "*nishba*")

נִשְׁבַּע nishba יכוין לשבועות המבול יְהוָהאהדונהיאהדונהי Adonai

לַאֲבֹתֵיכֶם la'avotechem לָתֵת latet לָהֶם lahem כִּימֵי kimei

הַשָּׁמַיִם hashamayim ט"פ טל, י"פ כוזו עַל al הָאָרֶץ ha'aretz אלהים דההין ע"ה:

---

upon your hands and they shall be as frontlets between your eyes. And you shall teach them to your children and speak of them while you sit at home and while you walk on your way and when you lie down and when you rise. You shall write them upon the doorposts of your house and upon your gates. This is so that your days shall be numerous and so shall the days of your children upon the Earth that the Lord had sworn to your fathers to give them as the days of the Heavens upon the Earth." (Deuteronomy 11:13-21)

VAYOMER

Hei, Malchut, legs and reproductive organs,
72 words corresponding to the 72 Names of God in direct order (according to the Ramchal).

עֹאם מֹשֶׁה Moshe   סבט אֶל־ el   יי"י יְהֹוָה Adonai   ווו וַיֹּאמֶר vayomer

אָנָא אֶל־ el   ליה ראה דַּבֵּר daber   מבט לֵאמֹר׃ lemor   מהט, ע"ב בריבוע וקס"א, אל שׁדי, ד"פ אלהים ע"ה

הבוע וְעָשׂוּ ve'asu   להו אֲלֵהֶם alehem   אוד וְאָמַרְתָּ ve'amarta   הוי יִשְׂרָאֵל Yisrael   כמת בְּנֵי benei

לוו בִּגְדֵיהֶם vigdehem   הבם כַּנְפֵי kanfei   הי עַל־ al   מרה צִיצִת tzitzit   יצל לָהֶם lahem

נמר צִיצִת tzitzit   פעל עַל־ al   ליו וְנָתְנוּ venatnu   כבי לְדֹרֹתָם ledorotam

וזהו techelet תְּכֵלֶת׃   מנה petil פְּתִיל   ע"ה קנ"א, אדני אלהים   נהה hakanaf הַכָּנָף

רלי oto אֹתוֹ   שׂאה ur'item וּרְאִיתֶם   ירת letzitzit לְצִיצִת   השׂא lachem לָכֶם   נהה vehaya וְהָיָה

You should pass the tzitziot over the eyes and kiss them, then repeat this procedure.

Adonai יְהֹוָה   ייו mitzvot מִצְוֺת   לב kol כָּל־   והר et אֶת־   אום uzchartem וּזְכַרְתֶּם

רהע acharei אַחֲרֵי   וזם taturu תָתוּרוּ   אני velo וְלֹא־   מנד otam אֹתָם   כעק va'asitem וַעֲשִׂיתֶם

מ"ה enechem עֵינֵיכֶם   ve'acharei וְאַחֲרֵי   השׂה levavchem לְבַבְכֶם

You should pass the Tzitziot over the eyes and then kiss them.

Doing so (kissing the *tzitzit* and passing it over the eyes), is a great support and assistance for the soul to be protected from any transgression. And you should meditate on the precept: "not to follow negative sexual thoughts of the heart and the sights of the eyes for prostitution."

VAYOMER

"And the Lord spoke to Moses and said: Speak to the Children of Israel and say to them that they should make for themselves Tzitzit, on the corners of their garments, throughout all their generations. And they must place upon the Tzitzit, of each corner, a blue strand. And this shall be to you as a Tzitzit: you shall see it and remember the commandments of the Lord and fulfill them. And you shall not stray after your hearts and your eyes,

אֲשֶׁר asher אַתֶּם atem זֹנִים° zonim אֹחֲרֵיהֶם° acharehem לְמַעַן lema'an

תִּזְכְּרוּ tizkeru וַעֲשִׂיתֶם° va'asitem אֶת־ et כָּל־ kol מִצְוֹתָי mitzvotai

וִהְיִיתֶם vihyitem קְדֹשִׁים kedoshim לֵאלֹהֵיכֶם° lelohechem

אֲנִי° ani יְהֹוָה Adonai אֱלֹהֵיכֶם Elohechem אֲשֶׁר asher

הוֹצֵאתִי hotzeti אֶתְכֶם° etchem מֵאֶרֶץ me'eretz מִצְרַיִם Mitzrayim

You should meditate to remember the exodus from *Mitzrayim* (Egypt).

לִהְיוֹת lihyot לָכֶם lachem לֵאלֹהִים° lelohim

אֲנִי° ani יְהֹוָה Adonai אֱלֹהֵיכֶם Elohechem

Be careful to complete this paragraph together with the *chazan* and the congregation, and say the word *"emet"* out loud. The *chazan* should say the word *"emet"* in silence.

אֱמֶת emet אהיה פעמים אהיה, ז"פ ס"ג• יוד ה"י ויו

The congregation should be silent, listen and hear the words *"Adonai Elohechem emet"* spoken by the *chazan*. If you did not complete the paragraph together with the *chazan* you should repeat the last three words on your own. With these three words the *Shema* is completed.

יְהֹוָה Adonai אֱלֹהֵיכֶם° Elohechem

אֱמֶת° emet אהיה פעמים אהיה, ז"פ ס"ג•

VEYATZIV

Before the *Amidah*, or *Shmoneh Esre*, signifying the World of Emanation (*Atzilut*), we come across various connections. The Aramaic word *Emet* אמת appears four times on two occasions. The Ari says that the four appearances of the word *emet*, occuring on two occasions, for a total of eight times, refers to the four Exiles and to the four Redemptions of the Israelites that have occurred in history. This word means "truth." When a small degree of untruthfulness lies in our hearts, it is difficult to succeed in our spiritual work. This prayer has the power to remove all falsehoods and open our hearts to truth.

---

after which you adulterate. This is so that you shall remember to fulfill all My commandments and thereby be holy before your God. I am the Lord, your God, Who brought you out of the land of Egypt to be your God. I, the Lord, your God, Is true." (Numbers 15:37-41) the Lord, your God, is true!

OLAM BERIAH - אל שדי – יוד ה"י ואו ה"י

We find another code in the word *Emet* אמת:

In Aramaic, this word begins with the letter *Alef* א, the first letter of the alphabet. The second letter in *Emet* is *Mem* מ, the middle of the alphabet. The last letter in *Emet* is *Tav* ת, the last letter of the alphabet. A person of truth has the power of the entire alphabet, which, in essence, is the power of the entire universe.

Hechal Ratzon (the Desire Chamber) - *Tiferet* of *Zeir Anpin* in *Beriah*.
The word *Ratzon* has the same numerical value as the word *shemo* (His Name – both equal 346), as Its Name is the clothing of *Sefirat Tiferet*.

א' על אמת וי"ה ווין = אמן (יאהדונהי) •veyatziv וְיַצִּיב •venachon וְנָכוֹן •vekayam וְקַיָם

•veyashar וְיָשָׁר •vene'eman וְנֶאֱמָן •ve'ahuv וְאָהוּב vechaviv וְחָבִיב הֹוֶּ

•venechmad וְנֶחְמָד •vena'im וְנָעִים •venora וְנוֹרָא ve'adir וְאַדִּיר הֹרִי

•umtukan וּמְתוּקָן •umkubal וּמְקֻבָּל vetov וְטוֹב והֹו •veyafe וְיָפֶה

ראה hadavar הַדָּבָר הרי יהוה הדבר ור"ת, יה, עצמן הויין גימ' ט"ו יכוון

הֹוֶּה haze והֹו alenu עָלֵינוּ ריבוע ס"ג וי' אותיות דס"ג le'olam לְעוֹלָם va'ed וְעֶד:

יוד הי ואו emet אֱמֶת אהיה פעמים אהיה, ז"פ ס"ג מילוי ע"ב, דמב; ילה Elohei אֱלֹהֵי

Ya'akov יַעֲקֹב אלהים דההין ע"ה tzur צוּר •malkenu מַלְכֵּנוּ olam עוֹלָם

ו' הויות, יאהדונהי אידהנויה magen מָגֵן ג"ף אל (יא"י מילוי דס"ג) ; ר"ת מיכאל גבריאל נוריאל

kayam קַיָם hu הוּא רי"ו vador וָדוֹר ledor לְדוֹר •yish'enu יִשְׁעֵנוּ

vechis'o וְכִסְאוֹ kayam קַיָם ע"ה אל שדי ע"ה, אל"ב בריבוע וקס"א ע"ה, ע"ב מהש ע"ה, ushmo וּשְׁמוֹ

ר"ת לוו ; ב"פ ב"ן la'ad לְעַד ve'emunato וְאֱמוּנָתוֹ umalchuto וּמַלְכוּתוֹ nachon נָכוֹן

ע"ה בינה יהוה, אהיה chayim וְחַיִּים udvarav וּדְבָרָיו kayemet קַיֶּמֶת:

la'ad לְעַד venechemadim וְנֶחְמָדִים vene'emanim וְנֶאֱמָנִים vekayamim וְקַיָמִים

ב"פ ב"ן (kiss the *Tzitziot*, pass them over the eyes then release) ul'olmei וּלְעוֹלְמֵי •olamim עוֹלָמִים

VEYATZIV

And He is established, and correct, and lasting, and straightforward, and trustworthy, and beloved, and dear, and desirable, and pleasant, and awesome, and powerful and proper, and accepted, and good, and beautiful. This is to us, forever and ever. It is true that the God of the World is our King, the Rock of Jacob and the Shield of our salvation. For every generation He endures and His Name endures. His Throne is established; His sovereignty and His faithfulness endure forever. His words are alive, enduring, trustworthy and pleasant for all eternity.

עַל al ‎•avotenu אֲבוֹתֵינוּ alenu עָלֵינוּ ve'al וְעַל ve'al וְעַל banenu בָּנֵינוּ ve'al וְעַל

דוֹרוֹתֵינוּ dorotenu ve'al וְעַל kol כָּל־ ; עמם ילי dorot דוֹרוֹת zera זֶרַע

יִשְׂרָאֵל Yisrael ‎avadecha עֲבָדֶיךָ: al עַל harishonim הָרִאשׁוֹנִים ve'al וְעַל

הָאַחֲרוֹנִים ha'acharonim davar דָּבָר tov טוֹב ראה והו vekayam• וְקַיָּם:

וְחֹק chok uve'emuna וּבֶאֱמוּנָה‎• אהיה פעמים אהיה, ז"פ ס"ג be'emet בֶּאֱמֶת יוד הא ואו

וְלֹא velo יַעֲבוֹר ya'avor רפ"ח (להעלות רפ"ח ניצוצות שנפלו לקליפה דמשם באים התחלואים)‎•

שֶׁאַתָּה sheAta יוד הה וו emet אֱמֶת אהיה פעמים אהיה, ז"פ ס"ג

הוּא hu Adonai יְהֹוָהאהדונהיאתהדונהי Elohenu אֱלֹהֵינוּ ילה

וֵאלֹהֵי velohei לכב ; מילוי ע"ב, דמב ; ילה ‎•avotenu אֲבוֹתֵינוּ‎•

מַלְכֵּנוּ malkenu melech מֶלֶךְ avotenu אֲבוֹתֵינוּ go'alenu גֹּאֲלֵנוּ

גֹּאֵל go'el ‎•avotenu אֲבוֹתֵינוּ‎• yotzrenu יוֹצְרֵנוּ tzur צוּר אלהים דההין ע"ה

יְשׁוּעָתֵנוּ ‎•yeshu'atenu podenu פּוֹדֵנוּ וּמַצִּילֵנוּ umatzilenu ר"ת = אלהים, אהיה אדני

MEM, HEI, SHIN

The letters *Mem* מ, *Hei* ה, and *Shin* ש unleash the force of healing.

When we close our eyes and visualize these three letters emitting rays of Light, we awaken healing energy from the Upper Worlds and from within ourselves. We can meditate to bathe our entire body in a flood of white Light and to send this energy to others in need of healing. These letters, rearranged, spell out the name of Moses משה = מהש, who reached the highest level of connection to the Light of the Creator.

מֵעוֹלָם me'olam הוּא hu שִׁמְךָ shemecha

ר"ת מהש, מושה, ע"ב לריבוע וקס"א, אל שדי

אֱלֹהִים Elohim אהיה אדני ילה ; זוּלָתֶךָ zulatcha סֶלָה sela: ‎•
וְאֵין ve'en לָנוּ lanu Elohim אלהים, אהיה אדני od עוֹד

This is upon us and upon our sons and upon our future generations and upon all the future generations of the descendants of Israel, Your servants. Upon the earlier and upon the later ones, this is a good and an everlasting thing. With truth and with faith, this is an unbreakable decree. It is true that You are the Lord, our God and the God of our fathers, our King and the King of our fathers, our Redeemer and the Redeemer of our fathers, our Maker and the Rock of our salvation. Our Redeemer and Rescuer.

MEM HEI SHIN

Your Name is of eternity, and we have no other God but You. Selah.

EZRAT

Ayin, Alef, and *Alef,* עאא, the first letters of the first three words of this prayer, have a numerical value of 72. The number 72 is also a code for the concept of mercy and the *Sefirah* of *Chesed.* We learn from this connection that we were meant to live our lives with genuine mercy for others in order to activate the power of the 72 Names of God. If, for some reason, we are not generating results from our prayers, it is only for one reason: we are not treating the people in our life with true mercy. Kabbalah teaches us that even if we are justified in our anger and our refusal to forgive, we must have mercy in our hearts and in our actions towards both our friends and our enemies.

Ata **אַתָּה** avotenu **אֲבוֹתֵינוּ** מיכאל מלכיאל עננדיאל, יהוה פעמים יהוה ע"ה ezrat **עֶזְרַת**

hu **הוּא** me'olam **מֵעוֹלָם** magen **מָגֵן** ג"פ אל (יא"י מילוי דס"ג) ; ר"ת = ע"ב, ריבוע יהוה

umoshi'a **וּמוֹשִׁיעַ** ר"ת מיכאל גבריאל נוריאל lahem **לָהֶם** velivnehem **וְלִבְנֵיהֶם**

acharehem **אַחֲרֵיהֶם** bechol **בְּכָל** ב"ן, לכב dor **דּוֹר** vador **וָדוֹר** רי"ו

berum **בְּרוּם** olam **עוֹלָם** ר"ת ע"ב, ריבוע יהוה ; ברום עולם ע"ה = קס"א קנ"א קמ"ג

umishpatecha **וּמִשְׁפָּטֶיךָ** moshavecha **מוֹשָׁבֶךָ** (לא כולל האהיה עצמם) עם ג' כוללים

vetzidkatecha **וְצִדְקָתֶךָ** ad **עַד** afsei **אַפְסֵי** aretz **אֶרֶץ**

ahiyah emet **אֱמֶת** ahiyah פעמים ahiyah, ז"פ ס"ג ashrei **אַשְׁרֵי**

lemitzvotecha **לְמִצְוֹתֶיךָ** sheyishma **שֶׁיִּשְׁמַע** ish **אִישׁ**

vetoratcha **וְתוֹרָתְךָ** udvarcha **וּדְבָרְךָ** yasim **יָשִׂים** al **עַל** libo **לִבּוֹ**

ahiyah emet **אֱמֶת** ahiyah פעמים ahiyah, ז"פ ס"ג sheAta **שֶׁאַתָּה** hu **הוּא**

adon **אָדוֹן** ani le'amecha **לְעַמֶּךָ** umelech **וּמֶלֶךְ** gibor **גִּבּוֹר**

lariv **לָרִיב** rivam **רִיבָם** le'avot **לָאָבוֹת** uvanim **וּבָנִים**

EZRAT

You have always been the aid for our forefathers, a shield and a savior for them and their children after them in every generation. In the heights of the world is Your abode and Your laws and justice extend to the ends of the Earth. It is true that a man who abides by Your commandments is joyful while he sets Your Torah and Your teachings upon his heart. It is true that You are a Master of Your people and a valorous King, Who fights for their cause, be it the fathers or the sons.

rishon רִאשׁוֹן hu הוּא Ata אַתָּה ס"ג, ז"פ אהיה פעמים אהיה, emet אֱמֶת אהיה

en אֵין umibal'adecha וּמִבַּלְעָדֶיךָ •acharon אַחֲרוֹן hu הוּא veAta וְאַתָּה

lanu לָנוּ אלהים, אהיה אדני go'el גּוֹאֵל melech מֶלֶךְ umoshi'a וּמוֹשִׁיעַ:

miMitzrayim מִמִּצְרַיִם מצר אהיה פעמים אהיה, ז"פ ס"ג emet אֱמֶת אהיה

mibet מִבֵּית •ילה Elohenu אֱלֹהֵינוּ Adonai יְהֹוָה ge'altanu גְּאַלְתָּנוּ

bechorehem בְּכוֹרֵיהֶם ב"פ ראה kol כָּל יל •peditanu פְּדִיתָנוּ avadim עֲבָדִים

•ga'alta גָּאַלְתָּ Yisrael יִשְׂרָאֵל uvchorcha וּבְכוֹרְךָ haragta הָרַגְתָּ

vezedim וְזֵדִים •bakata בָּקַעְתָּ lahem לָהֶם Suf סוּף יל veYam וְיַם

vayechasu וַיְכַסּוּ •ילי yam יָם avru עָבְרוּ vididim וִידִידִים •tibata טִבַּעְתָּ

lo לֹא mehem מֵהֶם דאגה, אהבה, echad אֶחָד tzarehem צָרֵיהֶם mayim מַיִם

ahuvim אֲהוּבִים shibechu שִׁבְּחוּ zot זֹאת al עַל :notar נוֹתָר

yedidim יְדִידִים venatnu וְנָתְנוּ (מילוי דס"ג) laEl לָאֵל veromemu וְרוֹמְמוּ

berachot בְּרָכוֹת vetishbachot וְתִשְׁבָּחוֹת shirot שִׁירוֹת zemirot זְמִירוֹת

•vekayam וְקַיָּם chai וַי (מילוי דס"ג) El אֵל lamelech לַמֶּלֶךְ vehoda'ot וְהוֹדָאוֹת

•venora וְנוֹרָא לתו; עם ד' אותיות = מבה, יזל, אום gadol גָּדוֹל venisa וְנִשָּׂא ram רָם

magbiha מַגְבִּיהַּ •aretz אָרֶץ adei עֲדֵי ge'im גֵּאִים mashpil מַשְׁפִּיל

•asirim אֲסִירִים motzi מוֹצִיא •marom מָרוֹם ad עַד shefalim שְׁפָלִים

ha'one הָעוֹנֶה dalim דַּלִּים ozer עוֹזֵר •anavim עֲנָוִים pode פּוֹדֶה

•elav אֵלָיו shave'am שַׁוְּעָם be'et בְּעֵת Yisrael יִשְׂרָאֵל le'amo לְעַמּוֹ

Ozer Dalim: poverty removes the transgressions of a person and through that the Creator gives mercy to His creation. And therefore you should meditate to make yourself poor in the eyes of the *Shechinah* and be concerned that the *Shechinah* is in exile together with the Children of Israel.

It is true that You are first and You are last and apart from You we have no King Who redeems and saves. It is true that You have redeemed us from Egypt, Lord, our God, and from a house of slaves did You redeem us. You killed all their firstborn and You saved Your firstborn Israel. You split the Sea of Reeds for them. And You drowned the tyrants while Your beloved crossed the sea. The waters then covered their enemies and not one of them was spared. For this, the beloved ones praised and exalted God. And the dear ones offered melodies, songs, lyrics and praises, blessings and thanks to the King, to the living and lasting God. Who is Supernal and uplifted, powerful and awesome and Who degrades the arrogant to the ground; Who raises the meek to great heights; Who frees the imprisoned, redeems the humble and helps the needy; He, Who answers the Children of Israel when they cry out to Him.

TEHILOT

We now begin to elevate to the World of Emanation (*Atzilut*). Accordingly, we rise and stand to ignite the engines of our soul. To prepare ourselves for this launch, we must eliminate any hatred or ill feelings that we harbor for others from our minds.

Hechal Kodesh HaKodashim (the Holy of Holies Chamber) – of *Zeir Anpin* in *Beriah*.

go'alam גּוֹאֲלָם   elyon עֶלְיוֹן   (מילוי דס"ג)   יא"י   laEl לָאֵל   tehilot תְּהִלּוֹת

בָּרוּךְ baruch   הוּא hu   umvorach וּמְבוֹרָךְ •   מֹשֶׁה Moshe   מהעו, ע"ב בריבוע וקס"א,

לְךָ lecha   עָנוּ anu   שִׁירָה shira   בְּשִׂמְחָה besimcha   רַבָּה raba   וְאָמְרוּ ve'amru

כֻּלָּם chulam: בְּי mi   יל   כָּמֹכָה chamocha   בָּאֵלִם ba'elim

כָּמֹכָה mi בְּי יל   Adonai יְהֹוָה(אדני)אהדונהי   ; ר"ת = ע"ב, ריבוע יהוה ; ס"ת מ"ה ; נּוֹרָא nora

נֶאְדָּר ne'edar   בַּקֹּדֶשׁ bakodesh   ר"ת = יב"ק, אלהים יהוה, אהיה אדני יהוה   nora נּוֹרָא

תְּהִלֹּת tehilot   עֹשֵׂה ose   פֶלֶא fele: שִׁירָה shira   וְחֲדָשָׁה chadasha

שִׁבְּחוּ shibechu   גְאוּלִים ge'ulim   לְשִׁמְךָ leshimcha   הַגָּדוֹל hagadol   לֹהוּ ; עם ד'

עַל al   שְׂפַת sefat   הַיָּם hayam   יוֹד יל   יָחַד yachad   כֻּלָּם kulam   אותיות = מבה, יזל, אום

הוֹדוּ hodu   אהיה   וְהִמְלִיכוּ vehimlichu   וְאָמְרוּ ve'amru   יְהֹוָה(אדני)אהדונהי: Adonai |

יִמְלֹךְ yimloch   לְעֹלָם le'olam   ריבוע ס"ג וי' אותיות דס"ג ; ר"ת ייל   וָעֶד va'ed:

וְנֶאֱמַר vene'emar   גֹּאֲלֵנוּ go'alenu   יְהֹוָה(אדני)אהדונהי Adonai   צְבָאוֹת Tzeva'ot   פני שכינה

שְׁמוֹ shemo   מהעו ע"ה, ע"ב בריבוע וקס"א, אל שדי ע"ה   קְדוֹשׁ kedosh   יִשְׂרָאֵל Yisrael:

בָּרוּךְ baruch   אַתָּה Ata   יְהֹוָה(אדני)אהדונהי Adonai   גָּאַל ga'al   כתר   יִשְׂרָאֵל Yisrael:

You should kiss the Head *Tefilin* because the purification of *Atzilut* is done with it.
Begin the *Amidah* immediately without any interruption, not even one breath. Doing so prevents separation between *Yesod* (awakened by the words "*ga'al Yisrael*") and *Malchut* (awakened by the word "*Adonai*"). Your reward is great. You receive protection from negativity and from making mistakes. This action also helps to correct the transgression of spilling one's seed.

TEHILOT

Praises to the Supreme God, Who is their redeemer. Blessed is He Who is blessed. Moses and the Children of Israel raised their voice in song to You, with great joy, and they all said: "Who is like You among the deities, Lord? Who is like You, mighty in holiness, awesome in praises, and Who works wonders?" (Exodus 15:11) With a new song did the redeemed praise Your great Name by the seashore. All of them in unison gave thanks and accepted Your sovereignty and they said, "the Lord shall reign forever and ever." (Exodus 15:18) And it is said: "Our redeemer, the Lord of hosts is His Name, the holy One of Israel." (Isaiah 47:4) Blessed are You, Lord, Who redeemed Israel.

THE AMIDAH

The *Amidah* is our connection to the World of Emanation (*Atzilut*). Before we begin this prayer, we take a moment to arouse the feeling of emptiness (exile) within us. In this way, we awaken our yearning for a connection to the Light of the Creator. Kabbalah explains that the Light, or the *Shechinah*, is also in exile. The Light wants to share infinitely with us, but cannot until we rid ourselves of our reactive nature and complete our spiritual transformation. By becoming conscious of our emptiness, we create a Vessel to be filled by the Light of the *Amidah* to come into.

When we begin the connection, we take three steps backward, signifying our leaving this physical world. Then we take three steps forward to begin the *Amidah*. The three steps are:
1. Stepping into the land of Israel – to enter the first spiritual circle.
2. Stepping into the city of Jerusalem – to enter the second spiritual circle.
3. Stepping inside the Holy of Holies – to enter the innermost circle.

Before we recite the first verse of the *Amidah*, we ask: "*God, open my lips and let my mouth speak,*" thereby asking the Light to speak for us so that we can receive what we need and not just what we want. All too often, what we want from life is not necessarily the desire of the soul, which is what we actually need to fulfill us. By asking the Light to speak through us, we ensure that our connection will bring us genuine fulfillment and opportunities for spiritual growth and change.

THE STRUCTURE OF THE AMIDAH

The *Amidah* is like a rocket that carries us into the world of Emanation, *Atzilut*. The first three blessings act as the rocket engines and connect us to the three upper points of the *Magen David* (Shield of David -see pg. 39-40), as well as to Abraham (*Chesed*), Isaac (*Gevurah*[A]), and Jacob (*Tiferet*).

The middle thirteen blessings form the body of the rocket and are our requests for the world at large. We ask for world peace, prosperity, good health and well-being for all the people of the planet.

The last three blessings are the small engines that fire to return us back to Earth and connect us to the lower three points of the Magen David, and to Moses (Netzach, Aaron (Hod), and Joseph (Yesod).

We need the help of Abraham, Isaac, Jacob, Moses, Aaron, and Joseph who are the instruments that assist us to make a strong connection to the World of Emanation (*Atzilut*).

[A.] The physical body is the full expression of the reactive behavior known as *the Desire to Receive for the Self Alone*. We come to this world to nullify our *Desire to Receive for the Self Alone* and transform ourselves into beings that *Desire to Receive for the Sake of Sharing*. When humanity has completely eradicated the reactive aspect of the *Desire to Receive* and transformed themselves, the age of Messiah (*Mashiach*) will be upon us. Our world will be flooded with the Infinite Light of fulfillment. However, for sharing to occur there needs to be a recipient or receiver. The spiritual process known as the Resurrection of the Dead must occur to awaken the infinite Desire to Receive, so that we may become Vessels to receive all the Light that will radiate in our world at the time of Messiah. Put simply, the Vessel to receive this Infinite Light is made manifest through the physical body.

yagid יַּגִיד ufi וּפִי tiftach תִּפְתָּח sefatai שְׂפָתַי (pause here) כלה Adonai אֲדֹנָי

ייו (כ"ב אותיות פשוטות [=אכא] וה' אותיות סופיות סזחזף) ס"ת = בוכו: tehilatecha תְּהִלָּתֶךָ

THE FIRST BLESSING - INVOKES THE SHIELD OF ABRAHAM.

Abraham is the channel of the Right Column energy of positivity, sharing, and mercy. Sharing actions can protect us from all forms of negativity.

Chesed that becomes Chochmah

In this section there are 42 words, the secret of the 42-Letter Name of God and therefore it begins with the letter *Bet* (2) and ends with the letter *Mem* (40).

Bend your knees at 'baruch', bow at 'Ata' and straighten up at 'Adonai'.

המלכות לה' (אותיות הא"ב המסמלות את השפע המגיע) א–ת Ata אַתָּה baruch בָּרוּךְ

ילה Elohenu אֱלֹהֵינוּ (יא) Adonai אדני/אהדונהי יְהֹוָה

avotenu אֲבוֹתֵינוּ ילה ; דמב ע"ב, מילוי ; לכב velohei וֵאלֹהֵי

אותיות פשוטות וט"ז עסמ"ב (אברים), רמ"וז הוזכמה, נתיבות ול"ב רי"ו אל, וז"פ (Chochmah) Avraham אַבְרָהָם ילה ; דמב ע"ב, מילוי Elohei אֱלֹהֵי

ד"פ בן (Binah) Yitzchak יִצְחָק ילה ; דמב ע"ב, מילוי Elohei אֱלֹהֵי

איהנויה יאהדונהי הויות, ו' (Da'at) Yaakov יַעֲקֹב ילה ; דמב ע"ב, מילוי ; לכב velohei וֵאלֹהֵי

לההו = גדול ; סיט = הגדול האל האל הגדול (מילוי דס"ג) יא"י ; לאה hagadol הַגָּדוֹל haEl הָאֵל

vehanora וְהַנּוֹרָא ההה ר"ת hagibor הַגִּבּוֹר אום = מבה, יזל, עם ד' אותיות =

THE AMIDAH
"My Lord, open my lips, and my mouth shall relate Your praise." (Psalms 51:17)
THE FIRST BLESSING
Blessed are You, Lord, our God and God of our forefathers:
the God of Abraham, the God of Isaac, and the God of Jacob. The great, mighty and awesome God.

עֶלְיוֹן elyon•   יהוה רִיבּוּעַ ע"ב, ר"ת ;   (מילוי דס"ג) יי"א   אֵל El

גּוֹמֵל gomel   וְחֲסָדִים chasadim   טוֹבִים tovim•   קוֹנֵה kone   הַכֹּל hakol

וְזוֹכֵר vezocher   וְחַסְדֵי chasdei   אָבוֹת avot•   וּמֵבִיא umevi

גּוֹאֵל go'el   לִבְנֵי livnei   בְנֵיהֶם venehem   לְמַעַן lema'an

שְׁמוֹ shemo   בְּאַהֲבָה be'ahava אוֹזֵר, דאג"ה:

When saying the word *"be'ahava"* you should meditate to devote your soul to sanctify the Holy Name and accept upon yourself the four forms of death.

During the days between *Rosh Hashanah* and *Yom Kippur* we say the prayer of *"zochrenu"*:

זָכְרֵנוּ zochrenu   לְחַיִּים lechayim אהיה אהיה יהוה, בינה ע"ה.

מֶלֶךְ melech   וְחָפֵץ chafetz   בַּחַיִּים bachayim אהיה אהיה יהוה, בינה ע"ה.

כָּתְבֵנוּ kotvenu   בְּסֵפֶר besefer   וְחַיִּים chayim אהיה אהיה יהוה, בינה ע"ה.

לְמַעַנָךְ lema'anach   אֱלֹהִים Elohim   וְחַיִּים chayim אהיה אהיה יהוה, בינה ע"ה.

If you forget to say *"zochrenu"* and realize this before the end of the blessing (*"baruch Ata Adonai"*), you should return and say *"zochreno"* and continue as usual. But if you realize this only after the end of the blessing, you should continue and you may add *"zochrenu"* in *"shome'a tefila"* or at the end of *"Elohai netzor."*

מֶלֶךְ melech   עוֹזֵר ozer   וּמוֹשִׁיעַ umoshi'a   וּמָגֵן umagen

ג"פ אל (יי"י מילוי דס"ג) ; ר"ת מיכאל גבריאל נוריאל:

Bend your knees at *'baruch'*, bow at *'Ata'* and straighten up at *'Adonai'*.

בָּרוּךְ baruch   אַתָּה Ata   יְהֹוָה Adonai (הד)

(During the three weeks of *Ben HaMetzarim* meditate on the Holy Name: טדהד)

מָגֵן magen   אַבְרָהָם Avraham ג"פ אל (יי"י מילוי דס"ג) ; ר"ת מיכאל גבריאל נוריאל

ח"פ אל, רי"ו ול"ב נתיבות החוכמה, רמ"ח (אברים), עסמ"ב וט"ז אותיות פעוטות:

The Supernal God, Who bestows beneficial kindness and creates everything. Who recalls the kindness of the forefathers and brings a Redeemer to their descendants for the sake of His Name, lovingly.

During the days between *Rosh Hashanah* and *Yom Kippur*:
Remember us for life, King, Who desires life, and inscribe us in the Book of Life, for Your sake, Living God.

King, Helper, Savior and Shield. Blessed are You, Lord, the shield of Abraham.

OLAM ATZILUT - יוֹד הֵי וָיו הֵי

THE SECOND BLESSING

THE ENERGY OF ISAAC IGNITES THE POWER FOR THE RESURRECTION OF THE DEAD.

Whereas Abraham represents the power of sharing, Isaac represents the Left Column energy of judgment. Judgment shortens the *Tikkun* process and paves the way for our eventual resurrection (footnote A - pg. 189).

Gevurah that becomes *Binah*.

In this section there are 49 words corresponding to the 49 gates of the Pure System in *Binah*.

Ata **אַתָּה** gibor **גִּבּוֹר** le'olam **לְעוֹלָם** ריבוע ס"ג וי' אותיות דס"ג Adonai **אֲדֹנָי** ללה

(ר"ת אֲגְלָא והוא שם גדול ואמיץ, ובו היה יהודה מתגבר על אויביו. ע"ה אלד, בוכו).

mechaye **מְחַיֵּה** ס"ג metim **מֵתִים** Ata **אַתָּה** rav **רַב** lehoshi'a **לְהוֹשִׁיעַ**.

During the winter (*starting on Simchat Torah*):   **During the summer** (*starting on Pesach*):

mashiv **מַשִּׁיב** haru'ach **הָרוּחַ** ר"ת מ"ה   morid **מוֹרִיד**   hatal **הַטָּל**

umorid **וּמוֹרִיד** hageshem **הַגֶּשֶׁם**   יוד הא ואו, כוזו, מספר אותיות דמילואי עסמ"ב ;

שובל [וי"ע (= י"פ אל) ול"ב נתיבות החוכמה] ע"ה: ר"ת מ"ה (יוד הא ואו הא):

If you mistakenly say "*morid hatal*", and realize this before the end of the blessing ("*baruch Ata Adonai*"), you should return to the beginning of the blessing ("*Ata gibor*") and continue as usual. But if you only realize this after the end of the blessing, you should continue and not go back.   If you mistakenly say "*Mashiv haru'ach*", and realize this before the end of the blessing ("*baruch Ata Adonai*"), you should return to the beginning of the blessing ("*Ata gibor*") and continue as usual. But if you only realize this after the end of the blessing, you should start the *Amidah* from the beginning.

mechalkel **מְכַלְכֵּל** chayim **וְחַיִּים** אהיה אהיה יהוה, בינה ע"ה, אהיה יהוה bechesed **בְּחֶסֶד**

mechaye **מְחַיֵּה** ס"ג metim **מֵתִים** berachamim **בְּרַחֲמִים**

rabim **רַבִּים** י"פ יִיי י"פ, אלהים דההין, מצפצ, רבוע יהוה somech **סוֹמֵךְ** (טלא דעתיק). ע"ב

noflim **נוֹפְלִים** (ו"ן). verofe **וְרוֹפֵא** אדני ריבוע כוק, (אכדטם) cholim **חוֹלִים**

umatir **וּמַתִּיר** ד' אותיות. asurim **אֲסוּרִים** umekayem **וּמְקַיֵּם** חולה = מ"ה וד'

emunato **אֱמוּנָתוֹ** lishenei **לִישֵׁנֵי** afar **עָפָר**. mi **מִי** בי' ילי chamocha **כָּמוֹךָ**

(you should enunciate the letter *Ayin* in the word "*ba'al*") ba'al **בַּעַל** gevurot **גְּבוּרוֹת**

dome **דוֹמֶה** lach **לָךְ**. melech **מֶלֶךְ** memit **מֵמִית** umi **וּמִי** ילי

umchaye **וּמְחַיֵּה** ס"ג (יוד הי ואו הי) umatzmi'ach **וּמַצְמִיחַ** yeshu'a **יְשׁוּעָה**.

THE SECOND BLESSING

You are mighty forever, Lord. You resurrect the dead and are very capable of redeeming.

During the winter: During the summer:

Who causes wind to blow and rain to fall.   *Who causes dew to fall.*

You sustain life with kindness and resurrect the dead with great compassion. You support those who have fallen, heal the sick, release the imprisoned, and fulfill Your faithful words to those who are asleep in the dust. Who is like You, Master of might, and Who can compare to You, King, Who causes death, Who gives life, and Who sprouts salvation?

SHACHARIT – MORNING PRAYER
OLAM ATZILUT - יוד הי ויו הי

During the days between *Rosh Hashanah* and *Yom Kippur* we say the prayer of "*mi chamocha*":

zocher זוֹכֵר harachman הָרַחֲמָן av אָב chamocha כָּמוֹךָ mi מִי יִלִי

yetzurav יְצוּרָיו בְּרַחֲמִים berachamim מצפ״צ, אלהים דיורק, י״פ ייי

לְחַיִּים lechayim אהיה אהיה יהוה, בינה ע״ה.

If you forget to say "mi chamocha" and realize this before the end of the blessing ("baruch Ata Adonai"), you should return and say "mi chamocha" and continue as usual. But if you only realize this after the end of the blessing, you should continue as usual.

---

metim מֵתִים   lehachayot לְהַחֲיוֹת   Ata אַתָּה   vene'eman וְנֶאֱמָן

Adonai יְהֹוָה(יְהוָֹאֱלֹהִים)יאהדונהי Ata אַתָּה baruch בָּרוּךְ

(During the three weeks of *Ben HaMetzarim* meditate on the Holy Name: כוז)

hametim הַמֵּתִים (יוד הי ואו הי) ס״ג mechaye מְחַיֶּה   ר״ת מ״ה וס״ת מ״ה.

NAKDISHACH – THE KEDUSHA

The congregation recites this prayer together.

Lifting a heavy chest filled with vast treasures is impossible if you use just a single string: The string will snap because it is too weak. However, if we unite and combine numerous strings, we will eventually build a rope. A rope can easily lift the treasure chest. By combining and uniting the congregation's prayers, we become a united force, capable of pulling down the most valuable spiritual treasures. Furthermore, this unity helps people who are not well-versed or knowledgeable in the connections. By uniting and meditating as one soul, we all receive the benefit because of the power of unity, regardless of our knowledge and understanding. This prayer occurs in between the second and third blessings. It signifies the Central Column that unites the Left and Right Columns.

In this prayer the angels speak to each other, saying: "*Kadosh, Kadosh, Kadosh*" ("Holy, Holy, Holy"). When we recite these three words, we stand with our feet stand together as one. With each utterance of *Kadosh*, we jump a little higher in the air. Jumping is an act of restriction and it defies the force of gravity. Spiritually, gravity has the energy of the Desire to Receive for the Self Alone. It is the reactive force of our planet, always pulling everything toward itself.

Saying the *Kedusha* (holiness) we meditate to bring the holiness of the Creator among us. As it says: "*Venikdashti betoch Benei Israel*" (God is hallowed among the children of Israel). You should meditate on the letters *Gimel* ג and *Yud* י from the Name: אבגיתץ (the initials of the first verse of the *Ana Beko'ach*), which helps spiritual remembering.

During the days between *Rosh Hashanah* and *Yom Kippur*:
Who is like You, merciful Father, Who recalls His created with mercy for life?

And You are faithful to resurrecting the dead. Blessed are You, Lord, Who resurrects the dead.

נַקְדִּישָׁך nakdishach וְנַעֲרִיצָך vena'aritzach•

כְּנוֹעַם keno'am שִׂיחַ si'ach שִׂיוַֹ שִׂיָחַ האא י"פ מוכ, סוֹד sod שַׂרְפֵּי sarfei

קֹדֶשׁ kodesh הַמְשַׁלְּשִׁים hameshaleshim לְך lecha קְדֻשָׁה kedusha•

וְכֵן vechen כָּתוּב katuv עַל al יַד yad נְבִיאָך nevi'ach• וְקָרָא vekara

זֶה ze אֶל el זֶה ze י"ב פרקין דיעקב מאירים לי"ב פרקין דרחל וְאָמַר ve'amar:

קָדוֹשׁ kadosh | קָדוֹשׁ kadosh קָדוֹשׁ kadosh (סוד ג' רישין דעתיקא קדישא)

יְהֹוָאדֹנָיאהדונהי Adonai צְבָאוֹת Tzeva'ot פני שכינה מִלֹּא melo כָּל chol ילי

הָאָרֶץ ha'aretz אלהים דההין ע"ה כְּבוֹדוֹ kevodo:

לְעֻמָּתָם le'umatam מְשַׁבְּחִים meshabechim וְאוֹמְרִים ve'omrim:

(או"א) בָּרוּך baruch כְּבוֹד־ kevod לְיְהֹוָאדֹנָיאהדונהי Adonai ; כבוד ה' = יוד הי ואו הה

מִמְּקוֹמוֹ mimekomo עסמ"ב, הברכה (למתק את ז' המלכים עמותו) ; ר"ת ע"ב, ריבוע יהוה ; ר"ת מוכ:

וּבְדִבְרֵי uvdivrei קָדְשְׁך kodshach כָּתוּב katuv לֵאמֹר lemor:

(זו"ן) יִמְלֹך yimloch קדוש ברוך מלך ר"ת יב"ק, אלהים יהוה, אהיה אדני יהוה

יְהֹוָאדֹנָיאהדונהי Adonai לְעוֹלָם le'olam ריבוע ס"ג וי אותיות דס"ג אֱלֹהַיִך Elohayich ילה

צִיּוֹן Tziyon יוסף, ו הויות, קנאה לְדֹר ledor וָדֹר vador רי"ו ; ר"ת אצלו (מלכות אצל ז"א - ו)

הַלְלוּיָה haleluya אלהים, אהיה אדני ; ללה:

THE THIRD BLESSING

This blessing connects us to Jacob, the Central Column and the power of restriction. Jacob is our channel for connecting mercy with judgment. By restricting our reactive behavior, we are blocking our Desire to Receive for the Self Alone. Jacob also gives us the power to balance our acts of mercy and judgment toward other people in our lives.

NAKDISHACH

We sanctify You and we revere You,

according to the pleasant words of the counsel of the Holy Angels, who recite Holy before You three times, as it is written by Your Prophet: "And each called to the other and said: Holy, Holy, Holy, Is the Lord of Hosts, the entire world is filled with His glory." (Isaiah 6:3) Facing them they give praise and say: "Blessed is the glory of the Lord from His Place." (Ezekiel 3:12) And in Your Holy Words, it is written as follows: "The Lord, your God, shall reign forever, for each and for every generation. Zion, Praise the Lord!" (Psalms 146:10)

Tiferet that becomes *Da'at* (14 words).

אַתָּה Ata קָדוֹשׁ kadosh וְשִׁמְךָ veshimcha קָדוֹשׁ kadosh ר"ת = אור, רז, אין סוף♦

וּקְדוֹשִׁים ukdoshim בְּכָל bechol יוֹם yom ע"ה נגד, מזבח, זן, אל יהוה ב"ן, לכב:

יְהַלְלוּךָ yehalelucha סֶלָה sela:

בָּרוּךְ baruch אַתָּה Ata יְהֹוָה Adonai

(During the three weeks of *Ben HaMetzarim* meditate on the Holy Name: מצפצ)

הָאֵל haEl לאה; יא"י (מילוי דס"ג) הַקָּדוֹשׁ hakadosh י"פ מ"ה (יוד הא ואו הא):

Meditate here on the Name: יאהדונהי, as it can help to remove anger.

> During the days between *Rosh Hashanah* and *Yom Kippur* instead of "*haEl hakadosh*" we say:
>
> הַמֶּלֶךְ hamelech הַקָּדוֹשׁ hakadosh:
>
> If you mistakenly say "*haEl hakadosh*" and you realize this within three seconds, you should immediately say "*hamelech hakadosh*" and continue as usual. But if you have already started the next blessing you should start the *Amidah* from the beginning.

THIRTEEN MIDDLE BLESSINGS

There are thirteen blessings in the middle of the *Amidah* that connect us to the Thirteen Attributes of *Atzilut*.

The next nine blessings help to correct *Zeir Anpin* and *Malchut* of *Atzilut* from the aspect of *Malchut*.

THE FIRST (FOURTH) BLESSING

This blessing helps us transform information into knowledge by helping us internalize everything that we learn.

Chochmah

In this blessing there are 17 words, the same numerical value as the word *tov* (good) in the secret of *Etz HaDa'at Tov vaRa*, (Tree of Knowledge Good and Evil), where we connect only to the *Tov*.

אַתָּה Ata וֹנֵן chonen לָאָדָם le'adam מ"ה דַּעַת da'at♦

וּמְלַמֵּד umlamed לֶאֱנוֹשׁ le'enosh בִּינָה bina ע"ה אהיה אהיה יהוה, וזיים♦

וְחָנֵּנוּ vechonenu מֵאִתְּךָ me'itecha וְחָכְמָה chochma במילוי = תרי"ג (מצוות)

בִּינָה bina ע"ה אהיה אהיה יהוה, וזיים וְדָעַת vada'at ר"ת וזבו:

בָּרוּךְ baruch אַתָּה Ata יְהֹוָה Adonai וֹנֵן chonen הַדָּעַת hada'at:

THE THIRD BLESSING

You are holy, and Your Name is holy, and the Holy Ones praise You every day, for you are God, the Holy King Selah. Blessed are You, Lord, the Holy God

> During the days between *Rosh Hashanah* and *Yom Kippur*: The Holy King.

THIRTEEN MIDDLE BLESSINGS - THE FIRST (FOURTH) BLESSING

You graciously grant knowledge to man and understanding to humanity. Graciously grant us, from Yourself, wisdom, understanding, and knowledge. Blessed are You, Lord, Who graciously grants knowledge.

THE SECOND (FIFTH) BLESSING

This blessing keeps us in the Light. Everyone at one time or another succumbs to the doubt and uncertainty that the Satan constantly implants in us. If we make the unfortunate mistake of stepping back and falling away from the Light, we do not want the Creator to mirror our actions and step away from us. Instead, we want Him to catch us. In the box below there are certain lines that we can recite and meditate on for others who may be stepping back. The war against the Satan is the oldest war known to man. And the only way to defeat the Satan is to unite, share, help and pray for each other.

Binah

In this blessing there are 15 words, as the powerful action of *Teshuva* (repentance) raises 15 levels on the way to *Kise Hakavod* (the Throne of Honor). It goes through seven *Reki'im* (firmaments), seven *Avirim* (air), and another firmament on top of the Holy Animals (together this adds up to 15). Also, there are 15 words in the two main verses of Isaiah the Prophet and King David that speaks of *Teshuva* (*Isaiah 55:7; Psalms 32:5*). The number 15 is also the secret of the Name: יה.

הֲשִׁיבֵנוּ hashivenu אָבִינוּ avinu לְתוֹרָתֶךָ letoratecha (וסד שיבה – יְהֹוָהִאֲדֹנָיאהדונהי)

וְקָרְבֵנוּ vekarvenu מַלְכֵּנוּ malkenu לַעֲבוֹדָתֶךָ la'avodatecha

וְהַחֲזִירֵנוּ vehachazirenu בִּתְשׁוּבָה bitshuva שְׁלֵמָה shelema

לְפָנֶיךָ lefanecha ס"ג מ"ה ב"ן

If you want to pray for another and help them in their spiritual process say:

יְהִי yehi רָצוֹן ratzon מהט ע"ה, ע"ב, בריבוע וקס"א ע"ה, אל עודי ע"ה

מִלְפָנֶיךָ milfanecha ס"ג מ"ה ב"ן יְהֹוָהִאֲדֹנָיאהדונהי Adonai אֱלֹהַי Elohai מילוי ע"ב, דמב ;ילה

וֵאלֹהַי velohei ; מילוי ע"ב, לכב ; אֲבוֹתַי avotai ילה ; דמב , שֶׁתַּחְתּוֹר shetachtor

וְתִירָה chatira מִתְּוחַת mitachat כִּסֵּא kise כְּבוֹדֶךָ kevodecha וּתְקַבֵּל utkabel

בִּתְשׁוּבָה bitshuva אֶת et (the person's name and his/her father's name) כִּי ki יְמִינְךָ yemincha

יְהֹוָהִאֲדֹנָיאהדונהי Adonai פְּשׁוּטָה peshuta לְקַבֵּל lekabel שָׁבִים shavim

---

בָּרוּךְ baruch אַתָּה Ata יְהֹוָהִאֲדֹנָיאהדונהי Adonai

הָרוֹצֶה harotze בִּתְשׁוּבָה bitshuva

THE SECOND (FIFTH) BLESSING

Bring us back, our Father, to Your Torah,
and bring us close, our King, to Your service, and cause us to return with perfect repentance before You.

May it be pleasing before You, Lord, my God and God of my forefathers, that You shall dig deep beneath the Throne of Your glory and accept as repentant (the person's name and his/her father's name) because Your Right Hand, Lord, extends outwards to receive those who repent.

Blessed are You, Lord, Who desires repentance.

THE THIRD (SIXTH) BLESSING

This blessing helps us achieve true forgiveness. We have the power to cleanse ourselves of our negative behavior and hurtful actions toward others through forgiveness. This blessing does not mean we plead for forgiveness and our slate is wiped clean. Forgiveness refers to the methodologies for washing away the residue that comes from our iniquities. There are two ways to wash away the residue: physical and spiritual. We collect physical residue when we are in denial of our misdeeds and the laws of cause and effect. We cleanse ourselves when we experience any kind of pain, whether it is financial, emotional, or physical. If we choose to cleanse spiritually, we forgo the physical cleansing. We do so by arousing the pain in ourselves that we caused to others. We feel the other person; and with a truthful heart, recite this prayer experiencing the hurt and heartache we inflicted on others. This form of spiritual cleansing prevents us from having to cleanse physically.

Chesed

In this blessing there are 21 words which is the numerical value of the Holy Name: אהיה.

סְלַח selach יהוה ע"ב lanu לָנוּ אלהים, אהיה אדני ר"ת סאל, אמן (יאהדונהי) avinu אָבִינוּ

כִּי ki וְחָטָאנוּ chatanu◆ מְחוֹל mechol לָנוּ lanu אלהים, אהיה אדני ; מחול לנו ע"ה =

קס"א ו' אותיות יוא"י (מילוי דס"ג) El אֵל כִּי ki ◆פָשָׁעְנוּ fashanu כִּי ki malkenu מַלְכֵּנוּ

Ata אַתָּה baruch בָּרוּךְ Ata אַתָּה יהוה ע"ב vesalach וְסָלַח ותו tov טוֹב

lislo'ach לִסְלוֹחַ hamarbe הַמַרְבֶּה chanun חַנּוּן Adonai יְהֹוָה(אדני)(יאהדונהי)

THE FOURTH (SEVENTH) BLESSING

This blessing helps us achieve redemption after we are spiritually cleansed.

Gevurah

רְאֵה re'e ראה נָא na בְעָנְיֵנוּ ve'onyenu ר"ת רנ"ב (אברים באשה, כנגד הגבורה)

לְגָאֳלֵנוּ lega'olenu וּמַהֵר umaher רִיבֵנוּ rivenu◆ וְרִיבָה veriva

שְׁמֶךָ shemecha לְמַעַן lema'an שְׁלֵמָה shelema מ"ה ge'ula גְאֻלָּה

Ata אַתָּה פהל chazak וְחָזָק go'el גֹּאֵל (מילוי דס"ג) יוא"י El אֵל כִּי ki

Yisrael יִשְׂרָאֵל go'el גֹּאֵל Adonai יְהֹוָה(אדני)(יאהדונהי) Ata אַתָּה baruch בָּרוּךְ

THE THIRD (SIXTH) BLESSING
Forgive us, our Father, for we have transgressed. Pardon us, our King, for we have sinned, because You are a good and forgiving God. Blessed are You, Lord, Who is gracious and forgives magnanimously.
THE FOURTH (SEVENTH) BLESSING
Behold our poverty and take up our fight; hurry to redeem us with a complete redemption for the sake of Your Name, because You are a powerful and a redeeming God. Blessed are You, Lord, Who redeems Israel.

THE BLESSING FOR A FAST DAY

This blessing is recited by the *chazan* on fast days, during the repetition of the *Amidah*. If the *chazan* forgets to say it here and realizes this before the end of the next blessing ("*baruch Ata Adonai*"), he should return and say "*anenu avinu*" and continue as usual. But if the *chazan* only realized this after the end of the next blessing, he should continue and he may add this blessing in "*shome'a tefila*".

אֵל יהוה זֹ, מזבח, נגד, ע"ה **beyom** בְּיוֹם **anenu** עֲנֵנוּ **avinu** אָבִינוּ **anenu** עֲנֵנוּ

אלהים דההין **vetzara** בְּצָרָה **ki** כִּי והי **haze** הַזֶּה **hata'anit** הַתַּעֲנִית **tzom** צוֹם

lerish'enu לְרִשְׁעֵנוּ **tefen** תֵּפֶן **al** אַל ◆**anachnu** אֲנַחְנוּ **gedola** גְדוֹלָה

◆**mibakashatenu** מִבַּקָּשָׁתֵנוּ **malkenu** מַלְכֵּנוּ **tit'alam** תִּתְעַלָּם **ve'al** וְאַל

terem טֶרֶם ◆**leshav'atenu** לְשַׁוְעָתֵנוּ **karov** קָרוֹב **na** נָא יהה **heye** הֱיֵה

ראה **nedaber** נְדַבֵּר ◆**ta'ane** תַעֲנֶה **Ata** אַתָּה **elecha** אֵלֶיךָ **nikra** נִקְרָא

:**shene'emar** שֶׁנֶּאֱמַר ראה **kadavar** כַּדָּבָר **tishma** תִּשְׁמַע **veAta** וְאַתָּה

e'ene אֶעֱנֶה אני **va'ani** וַאֲנִי **yikra'u** יִקְרָאוּ **terem** טֶרֶם יהוה ; יהה **vehaya** וְהָיָה

:**eshma** אֶשְׁמָע אני **va'ani** וַאֲנִי **medabrim** מְדַבְּרִים **hem** הֵם **od** עוֹד

ve'one וְעוֹנֶה **umatzil** וּמַצִּיל **pode** פּוֹדֶה **Adonai** יְהֹוָאהּדּונּהּי **Ata** אַתָּה **ki** כִּי

עסמ"ב וט"ז (אברים) רמ"ח נתיבות החוכמה, ל"ב רי"ו אל, וז"פ אברהם, **umrachem** וּמְרַחֵם

אלהים דההין **tzara** צָרָה **et** עֵת לכב ב"ן, **bechol** בְּכֹל אותיות פשוטות עסמ"ב וט"ז **Adonai** יְהֹוָאהּדּונּהּי **Ata** אַתָּה **baruch** בָּרוּךְ :**vetzuka** וְצוּקָה **ha'one** הָעוֹנֶה

(continue "*refa'enu*") :**tzara** צָרָה **be'et** בְּעֵת **Yisrael** יִשְׂרָאֵל **le'amo** לְעַמּוֹ

THE FIFTH (EIGHTH) BLESSING

This blessing gives us the power to heal every part of our body. All healing originates from the Light of the Creator. Accepting and understanding this truth opens us to receive this Light. We should also think of sharing this healing energy with others.

THE BLESSING FOR A FAST DAY

Answer us, our Father, answer us on this day of fasting because we are in great distress. Do not pay heed to our wickedness, and, our King, do not ignore our pleas. Please come close to our cries and answer us even before we call out to You. We shall speak and You shall hear us, as it is said: 'And it shall be that before they call, I shall answer, and while they speak, I shall hear.' (Isaiah 65:24) For You, Lord, redeem, save, respond, and show compassion in every time of trouble and distress. Blessed are You, Lord, who responds to His Nation Israel, in time of trouble.

Tiferet

רְפָאֵנוּ refa'enu   יְהֹוָה Adonai   וְנֵרָפֵא venerafe   ר״ת   רי״ו

הוֹשִׁיעֵנוּ hoshi'enu   וְנִוָּשֵׁעָה venivashe'a   כִּי ki   תְהִלָּתֵנוּ tehilatenu

אַתָּה Ata   ר״ת = ב״פ רי״ו   וְהַעֲלֵה veha'ale   אֲרוּכָה arucha   וּמַרְפֵּא umarpe

לְכָל־ lechol   יה   אדני   תַּחֲלוּאֵינוּ tachalu'enu   וּלְכָל־ ulchol   יה   אדני

מַכְאוֹבֵינוּ mach'ovenu   וּלְכָל־ ulchol   אדני   מַכּוֹתֵינוּ makotenu

---

To pray for healing for yourself and/or others add the following, in the parentheses below, insert the names:

יְהִי yehi   רָצוֹן ratzon   מהע ע״ה   בריבוע   ע״ב   ע״ה, וקס״א   אל   שדי   ע״ה

מִלְפָנֶיךָ milfanecha   ס״ג מ״ה ב״ן   יְהֹוָה Adonai   אֱלֹהַי Elohai   מילוי ע״ב, דמב ; ילה

וֵאלֹהֵי velohei   אֲבוֹתַי avotai   ילה ; דמב ; מילוי ע״ב ; לכב   שֶׁתִּרְפָּאֵנִי shetirpa'eni

(וְתִרְפָּא) vetirpa (insert the person's name)   בֶּן ben (Women: בַּת bat) (insert their mother's name)

רְפוּאָה refu'a   שְׁלֵמָה shelema   רְפוּאַת refu'at   הַנֶּפֶשׁ hanefesh

וּרְפוּאַת urfu'at   הַגּוּף haguf, (פהל)   כְּדֵי kedei   שֶׁאֶהְיֶה she'ehye   וְחָזָק chazak   פהל

(Women: וְחָזָקָה chazaka) (פהל)   בִּבְרִיאוּת bivri'ut,   וְאַמִּיץ ve'amitz

(Women: וְאַמִּצַת ve'amitzat)   כּוֹחַ ko'ach,   בְּמָאתַיִם bematayim   וְאַרְבָּעִים ve'arba'im

וּשְׁמוֹנָה ushmona (אברים) רמ״ח, וז״ף אל, רי״ו ול״ב נתיבות החכמה, עסמ״ב וט״ו אותיות פשוטות

(Women: בְּמָאתַיִם bematayim   וַחֲמִשִּׁים vechamishim   וּשְׁנַיִם ushnayim)

אֵבָרִים evarim   וּשְׁלֹשׁ ushlosh   מֵאוֹת me'ot   המספר = ע״י = אלהים דיודין

וְשִׁשִּׁים veshishim   המספר = מילוי היו׳ (ו') וְשִׁשָּׁה vachamisha   גִּידִים gidim   שֶׁל shel

נִשְׁמָתִי nishmati   וְגוּפִי vegufi, לְקִיּוּם lekiyum   תוֹרָתְךָ toratcha   הַקְּדוֹשָׁה hakedosha.

כִּי ki   אֵל El   (מילוי דס״ג) יא״י   רוֹפֵא rofe   רַחֲמָן rachaman   וְנֶאֱמָן vene'eman

אַתָּה :Ata   בָּרוּךְ baruch   אַתָּה Ata   יְהֹוָה Adonai   רוֹפֵא rofe

חוֹלֵי cholei   זוֹכֶה = מ״ה = (יוד הא ואו הא) וד׳ אותיות   עַמּוֹ amo   יִשְׂרָאֵל Yisrael

ר״ת רפ״ח (להעלות הניצוצות שנפלו לקליפה דמעם באים התחלואים):

THE FIFTH (EIGHTH) BLESSING

Heal us, Lord, and we shall heal. Save us and we shall be saved.
For You are our praise. Bring cure and healing to all our ailments, to all our pains, and to all our wounds.

May it be pleasing before You, Lord, my God and God of my forefathers, that You would heal me (and the person's name and their mother's name) completely with healing of the spirit and healing of the body, so that I shall be strong in health and vigorous in my strength in all 248 (a woman says: 252) organs and 365 sinews of my soul and my body, so that I shall be able to keep Your Holy Torah.

Because You are a healing,
compassionate, and trustworthy God, blessed are You, Lord, Who heals the sick of His People, Israel.

SHACHARIT – MORNING PRAYER
יוֹד הֵי וָיו הֵי - OLAM ATZILUT

THE SIXTH (NINTH) BLESSING

This blessing draws sustenance and prosperity for the entire globe and provides us with personal sustenance. We would like all of our years to be filled with dew and rain, the sustaining lifeblood of our world.

Netzach

During the summer (starting on the first day of *Pesach*) **the following is said:**

If you mistakenly say *"barech alenu"* instead of *"barchenu"*, and realize this before the end of the *Amidah* (*"yihyu leratzon"* – the second one), then you should return and say *"barchenu"* and continue as usual. If you realize this later, you should start the *Amidah* from the beginning.

bechol בְּכָל יל: Elohenu אֱלֹהֵינוּ Adonai יְהֹוָ״אדנ״יאהדונ״הי barchenu בָּרְכֵנוּ

ב"ן, לכב ma'asei מַעֲשֵׂי yadenu יָדֵינוּ uvarech וּבָרֵךְ shenatenu שְׁנָתֵנוּ

ע"ה שֹדי אל, ע"ה betalelei בְּטַלְלֵי ratzon רָצוֹן מהש״ ע"ה, ע"ב בריבוע וקס"א ע"ה, ב"ן

utehi וּתְהִי וז״ים) יהוה, אהיה (וע״ה אהיה בינה undava וּנְדָבָה beracha בְּרָכָה

vesava וְשָׂבַע ע"ה בינה יהוה, אהיה אהיה chayim וְחַיִּים acharita אַחֲרִיתָהּ

livracha לִבְרָכָה hatovot הַטּוֹבוֹת kashanim כַּשָּׁנִים veshalom וְשָׁלוֹם

If you want to pray for sustenance you can add:

milfanecha מִלְפָנֶיךָ ע"ה אל, שׁדי אל, ע"ה וקס"א בריבוע ע"ב ע"ה, מהש ratzon רָצוֹן yehi יְהִי

velohei וֵאלֹהֵי ב"ן מ"ה ס"ג יל: Elohenu אֱלֹהֵינוּ Adonai יְהֹוָ״אדנ״יאהדונ״הי

li לִי כהת ב"פ shetiten שֶׁתִּתֵּן avotenu אֲבוֹתֵינוּ יל: דמב, ע"ב, מילוי לכב

hayom הַיּוֹם shulchani שׁוּלְחָנִי al עַל hasemuchim הַסְּמוּכִים אדני יה ulchol וּלְכָל

velo וְלֹא בוכו bechavod בְּכָבוֹד umzonotehem וּמְזוֹנוֹתֵיהֶם mezonotai מְזוֹנוֹתַי ז, מזבוח, נגד ע"ה yom יוֹם לכב ב"ן, מזבוח, נגד ז, אל יהוה, אל יהוה yom, uvchol וּבְכָל

bizchut בִּזְכוּת be'isur בָּאִיסוּר velo וְלֹא beheter בְּהֶיתֵר bevizui בְּבִזּוּי

אום יזל, מבה = אותיות ד' עם ; לה״ו hagadol הַגָּדוֹל shimcha שִׁמְךָ

(יאהדונ״הי אמן, סאל בואתב״ע – אותיות ג' עם וחתך דִיקְרְנוֹסָא :Do not pronounce this name)

THE SIXTH (NINTH) BLESSING

During the summer:

Bless us, Lord, our God, in all our endeavors, and bless our years with the dews of good will, blessing, and benevolence. May its conclusion be life, contentment, and peace, as with other years for blessing,

May it be pleasing before You, Lord, my God and God of my forefathers, that You would provide for me and for my household, today and everyday, mine and their nourishment, with dignity and not with shame, in a permissible but not a forbidden manner, by virtue of your great name

hayotze הַיּוֹצֵא ‏:mipasuk מִפָּסוּק vaharikoti וַהֲרִיקֹתִי lachem לָכֶם

beracha בְּרָכָה ad-עַד beli בְּלִי dai דַּי ‏:umipasuk וּמִפָּסוּק nesa נְשָׂא

alenu עָלֵינוּ or אוֹר or רוֹ, אֵין סוֹף panecha פָּנֶיךָ ס"ג מ"ה ב"ן יְהֹוָאדֹנֵיאהדונהי Adonai

ve'al וְאַל tatzrichenu תַּצְרִיכֵנוּ lidei לִידֵי matnot מַתְּנֹות basar בָּשָׂר

vadam וָדָם ki כִּי im אִם יוֹהך, מ"א אותיות אהיה בפשוטו וּמִילוּאו וּמִילוּי דְמִילוּאו וּמִילוּי דְמִילוּאו ע"ה

miyadcha מִיָּדְךָ hamele'a הַמְּלֵאָה ume'otzar וּמֵאוֹצַר matnat מַתְּנַת chinam וְחִנָּם

techalkelni תְּכַלְכְּלֵנִי vetashpi'eni וְתַשְׁפִּיעֵנִי amen אָמֵן יאהדונהי ‏•sela סֶלָה

ki כִּי El אֵל יא"י (במילוי) (דס"ג) tov טוֹב והו umetiv וּמֵטִיב

Ata אַתָּה umvarech וּמְבָרֵךְ ‏:hashanim הַשָּׁנִים baruch בָּרוּךְ

Ata אַתָּה Adonai יְהֹוָאדֹנֵיאהדונהי mevarech מְבָרֵךְ ‏:hashanim הַשָּׁנִים

During the winter (starting on the 7th of *Cheshvan*, two weeks after *Sukkot*) **the following is said:** If you mistakenly say "*barchenu*" instead of "*barech alenu*", and realize this before the end of the blessing ("*baruch Ata Adonai*"), you should return to say "*barech alenu*" and continue as usual. If you only realize this after, you should say "*Veten tal umatar livracha*" in "*shome'a tefila*". If you only relize this after you have already started "*retze*" you should start the *Amidah* from the beginning.

barech בָּרֵךְ alenu עָלֵינוּ Adonai יְהֹוָאדֹנֵיאהדונהי Elohenu אֱלֹהֵינוּ יל"ה

et אֶת hashana הַשָּׁנָה ‏•hazot הַזֹּאת ve'et וְאֶת kol כֹּל ילי

minei מִינֵי tevu'ata תְּבוּאָתָהּ letova לְטוֹבָה אכא‏• veten וְתֵן

tal טַל יוֹד הֵא וָאו, כוֹזו umatar וּמָטָר livracha לִבְרָכָה al עַל kol כָּל ילי ; עמם

penei פָּנֵי וְחָכְמָה בִּינָה ‏•ha'adama הָאֲדָמָה verave וְרַוֵּה penei פָּנֵי וְחָכְמָה בִּינָה ‏•

tevel תֵּבֵל ב"פ רי"ו vesaba וְשַׂבַּע et אֶת ha'olam הָעוֹלָם

kulo כֻּלּוֹ mituvach מִטּוּבֶךָ לאו‏• umale וּמַלֵּא yadenu יָדֵינוּ

mibirchotecha מִבִּרְכוֹתֶיךָ ume'osher וּמֵעֹשֶׁר mat'not מַתְּנֹות ‏•yadecha יָדֶיךָ

---

that comes from the verse: "pour down for you blessing until there be no room to suffice for it" (Malachi 3:10) and from the verse: "Raise up over us the light of Your countenance, Lord" (Psalms 4:7), and we will not require the gifts of flesh and blood, but only from your hand which is full, and from the treasure of the free gift you shall support and nurish me. Amen. Sela.

for You are a good
and a beneficent God and You bless the years. Blessed are You, Lord, Who blesses the years.
During the winter:
Bless us, Lord, our God, this year and all its kinds of crops for good. And give dew and rain for blessing over the entire face of the Earth. Quench the thirst of the face of the Earth and satiate the entire world from Your bounty. Fill our hands with Your blessings and from the wealth of gifts of Your Hands.

If you want to pray for sustenance you can add:

milfanecha מִלְּפָנֶיךָ ratzon רָצוֹן מהש ע"ה, ע"ב בריבוע וקס"א ע"ה, אל שדי ע"ה yehi יְהִי

velohei וֵאלֹהֵי ילה Elohenu אֱלֹהֵינוּ Adonai יְהֹוָ־אֲדֹנָי־אהדונהי מ"ה ב"ן ס"ג

li לִי ב"פ כהת shetiten שֶׁתִּתֵּן ילה ; דמב, ע"ב, מילוי ; avotenu אֲבוֹתֵינוּ לכב

hayom הַיּוֹם shulchani שׁוּלְחָנִי יה אדני al עַל hasmuchim הַסְּמוּכִים ulchol וּלְכָל

velo וְלֹא בוכו bechavod בְּכָבוֹד umzonotehem וּמְזוֹנוֹתֵיהֶם mezonotai מְזוֹנוֹתַי

bizchut בִּזְכוּת be'isur בְּאִיסוּר velo וְלֹא beheter בְּהֶיתֵּר bevizuy בְּבִזּוּי

(Do not pronounce this name) דִּיקַרְנוֹסָא וזהר עם ג' אותיות – ובאתב"ש סאל, אמן, יאהדונהי)

lachem לָכֶם vaharikoti וַהֲרִיקֹתִי mipasuk מִפָּסוּק hayotze הַיּוֹצֵא

nesa נְסָה umipasuk וּמִפָּסוּק dai דַּי beli בְּלִי ad עַד beracha בְּרָכָה

Adonai יְהֹוָ־אֲדֹנָי־אהדונהי ס"ג מ"ה ב"ן panecha פָּנֶיךָ אין סוף רז, or אוֹר alenu עָלֵינוּ

basar בָּשָׂר matnot מַתְּנוֹת lidei לִידֵי tatzrichenu תַּצְרִיכֵנוּ ve'al וְאַל

chinam חִנָּם matnat מַתְּנַת ume'otzar וּמֵאוֹצָר hamele'a הַמְּלֵאָה miyadcha מִיָּדְךָ

sela סֶלָה amen אָמֵן יאהדונהי vetashpi'eni וְתַשְׁפִּיעֵנִי techalkelni תְּכַלְכְּלֵנִי

---

davar דָּבָר ילי mikol מִכָּל zo זוֹ shana שָׁנָה vehatzila וְהַצִּילָה shomra שָׁמְרָה

ra רָע umikol וּמִכָּל mashchit מַשְׁחִית minei מִינֵי ילי umikol וּמִכָּל ראה

tikva תִּקְוָה la לָהּ va'ase וַעֲשֵׂה pura'nut פּוּרְעָנוּת minei מִינֵי

verachem וְרַחֵם chus חוּס ra'os וְחוּס shalom שָׁלוֹם ve'acharit וְאַחֲרִית tova טוֹבָה אכא

aleha עָלֶיהָ פהל אותיות פשוטות וט"ז עסמ"ב (אברים), רמ"ח הזכמה נתיבות ול"ב רי"ו אל, וז"פ אברהם,

uferoteha וּפֵירוֹתֶיהָ tevu'ata תְּבוּאָתָה עמם ; kol כָּל ילי ve'al וְעַל

May it be pleasing before You, Lord, my God and God of my forefathers, that You would provide for me and for my household, today and everyday, mine and their nourishment, with dignity and not with shame, in a permissible but not a forbidden manner, by virtue of your great name that comes from the verse: "pour down for you blessing until there be no room to suffice for it" (Malachi 3:10) and from the verse: "Raise up over us the light of Your countenance, Lord" (Psalm 4:7), and we will not require the gifts of flesh and blood, but only from your hand which is full, from the treasure of the free gift you shall support and nurish me. Amen. Sela.

Protect and save this year from all evil

and from all manner of destruction and from all manner of tribulation. Make for it a good hope and a peaceful ending. Take pity and have mercy upon it and upon all its crops and fruits;

וּבָרְכָה uvarcha בְּגִשְׁמֵי begishmei רָצוֹן ratzon מַהֵט ע"ה, ע"ב בְּרִיבוּעַ וקס"א ע"ה,

וּתְהִי utehi בְּרָכָה beracha וּנְדָבָה undava בִּינָה (וע"ה אהיה אהיה יהוה, וזיים) אל שדי ע"ה

וּתְהִי utehi אַחֲרִיתָהּ acharita וְחַיִּים chayim אהיה אהיה יהוה, בינה ע"ה

וְשָׂבַע vesava וְשָׁלוֹם ◆veshalom כְּשָׁנִים kashanim הַטּוֹבוֹת hatovot

לְבִרְכָה ◆livracha כִּי ki אֵל El יא"י (מילוי דס"ג) טוֹב tov והו ◆ umetiv וּמֵטִיב

אַתָּה Ata וּמְבָרֵךְ umvarech הַשָּׁנִים hashanim‡ בָּרוּךְ baruch

אַתָּה Ata יְהֹואדנִיאהדונהי Adonai מְבָרֵךְ mevarech הַשָּׁנִים hashanim‡

THE SEVENTH (TENTH) BLESSING

This blessing gives us the power to positively influence all of humanity. Kabbalah teaches that each individual affects the whole. We affect the world, and the rest of the world affects us, even though we cannot perceive this relationship with our five senses. We call this relationship quantum consciousness.

Hod

תְּקַע teka ב"פ סזווך וי' אותיות בְּשׁוֹפָר beshofar גָּדוֹל gadol להו ; עם ד' אותיות = אותיות

לְקַבֵּץ lekabetz נֵס nes וְשָׂא vesa מ"ה אדני ◆ lecherutenu לְחֵרוּתֵנוּ מבה, יכל, אום

מֵאַרְבַּע me'arba יוֹד yachad וְקַבְּצֵנוּ vekabetzenu ◆ galuyotenu גָּלֻיּוֹתֵנוּ

כַּנְפוֹת kanfot וּבוּ (בסגולתו להוציא ניצוצות מן הקליפות) ויכוין וֹבֻן עם נקודותיו = ע"ב, ריבוע יהוה

הָאָרֶץ ha'aretz אלהים דההין ע"ה ; ר"ת = אדני ◆ le'artzenu לְאַרְצֵנוּ

The following is recited throughout the entire year, and especially during the time of the *Shovavim*:

The first six portions of the Book of Exodus—*Shemot, Va'era, Bo, Beshalach, Yitro, Mishpatim,* (*Terumah Tetzave*)—tell us the story of the Israelites exodus from Egypt and signify the beginning of a unique cosmic opening that lasts for six weeks (8 weeks during a leap year), each year. The word *shovavim* means "irresponsible," as in the verse, "Return, irresponsible children says the Lord," (Jeremiah 3:14) and is an acronym comprised of the first initial of each of the six weekly portions: The kabbalists teach us that the story of Exodus is a code and that during these six/eight weeks there is a window of time for personal redemption. The Ari explains that the fall of Adam corrupted almost everything in our physical world, resulting in human pain and suffering. During the time of the Exodus, Moses and the Israelites corrected the most important aspects of this corruption. The following meditation helps us to release and redeem all the remaining sparks of Light we have lost through our irresponsible actions (especially sexual misconduct):

---

bless it with rains of goodwill, blessing, and benevolence. And may its end be life, contentment, and peace, for You are a good and a beneficent God and You bless the years. Blessed are You, Lord, Who blesses the years.

THE SEVENTH (TENTH) BLESSING

Blow a great Shofar for our freedom and
raise a banner to gather our exiles, and gather us speedily from all four corners of the Earth to our Land.

milfanecha מִלְּפָנֶיךָ מהש״ע ע״ה, ע״ב בריבוע וקס״א ע״ה, אל שדי ע״ה ratzon רָצוֹן yehi יְהִי

ס״ג מ״ה ב״ן יְהֹוֶהֶאֲדֹנָיֵאלֹהֵיֵ Elohai אֱלֹהַי Adonai אֲדֹנָי ; ילה

tipa טִיפָּה ילי shekol שֶׁכָּל avotai אֲבוֹתַי ילה ; מילוי ע״ב, דמב ; לכב velohei וֵאלֹהַי

levatala לְבַטָּלָה mimeni מִמֶּנִּי sheyatza שֶׁיָּצָא keri קֶרִי shel שֶׁל vetipa וְטִיפָּה

shelo שֶׁלֹּא uvifrat וּבִפְרָט bichlal בִּכְלָל Yisrael יִשְׂרָאֵל ילי umikol וּמִכָּל

beratzon בְּרָצוֹן ben בֵּין be'ones בְּאוֹנֶס ben בֵּין mitzva מִצְוָה bimkom בִּמְקוֹם

ben בֵּין beshogeg בְּשׁוֹגֵג ben בֵּין מהש״ע ע״ה, ע״ב בריבוע וקס״א ע״ה, אל שדי ע״ה ben בֵּין

bema'ase בְּמַעֲשֶׂה uven וּבֵין behirhur בְּהִרְהוּר ben בֵּין, bemezid בְּמֵזִיד,

acher אַחֵר begilgul בְּגִלְגּוּל ben בֵּין ze זֶה begilgul בְּגִלְגּוּל ben בֵּין

hakelipot הַקְּלִיפּוֹת shetaki שֶׁתָּקִיא, bakelipot בַּקְּלִיפּוֹת venivla וְנִבְלַע

bizechut בִּזְכוּת ba בָּהּ shenivle'u שֶׁנִּבְלְעוּ keri קֶרִי hanitzotzot הַנִּיצוֹצוֹת

hayotze הַיּוֹצֵא עם ד' אותיות = מבה, יזל, אום ; להו hagadol הַגָּדוֹל shimcha שִׁמְךָ

ר״ת חובו ו-ילי vayki'enu וַיְקִאֶנּוּ ומב bala בָּלַע chayil וְחַיִל :mipasuk מִפָּסוּק

uvizechut וּבִזְכוּת El אֵל ייא״י (מילוי דס״ג) ; ס״ת ויל וּבִזְכוּת yorishenu יוֹרִשֶׁנּוּ mibitno מִבִּטְנוֹ

יוֹזְהֲבֹוָה אום ,יזל ,מבה = אותיות 'ד עם ; להו hagadol הַגָּדוֹל shimcha שִׁמְךָ

limkom לִמְקוֹם shetachazirem שֶׁתַּחֲזִירֵם (יוֹזְהֲבֹוָה) :during the Shovavim)

ase עֲשֵׂה מ״ה ; ריבוע קס״א ע״ה be'enecha בְּעֵינֶיךָ ויהו vehatov וְהַטּוֹב kedusha קְדוּשָׁה

You should meditate to correct the thought that caused the loss of the sparks of Light. Also meditate on the Names that control our thoughts for each of the six days of the week as follow:

Sunday	יְהוָה	וְשֵׁם: דמרגלא אהיה מן א	על צבא כף ואו זין ואו טפטפיה	.Beriah
Monday	יְהֹוָה	וְשֵׁם: דמרגלא אהיה מן ה	על מגן כף ואו זין ואו טפטפיה	.Yetzirah
Tuesday	מצפץ	וְשֵׁם: דמרגלא אהיה מן י	צוה פוזד כף ואו זין ואו טפטפיה	.Asiyah
Wednesday	אל	וְשֵׁם: דמרגלא יהו מן י	צוה פוזד כף ואו זין ואו טפטפיה	.Asiyah
Thursday	אלהים	וְשֵׁם: דמרגלא יהו מן ה	על מגן כף ואו זין ואו טפטפיה	.Yetzirah
Friday	מצפץ	וְשֵׁם: דמרגלא יהו מן ו	על צבא כף ואו זין ואו טפטפיה	.Beriah

Each of these Names (עַל צבא, כף ואו זין ואו, טפטפיה) adds up to 193, which is the same numerical value as the word *zokef* (raise). These Names raise the Holy Spark from the *Chitzoniyim*. Also, when you say the words "*mekabetz nidchei*" (in the continuation of the blessing), which add up to 304 — the same numerical value of *Shin*, *Dalet* (demon), meditate to collect all the lost sparks and cancel out the power of the negative forces.

May it be pleasing before You, Lord, my God and God of my forefathers, that every single drop of keri that came out of me for vain, and from all of Yisrael in general, and especially not as a cause of precept, if it was coerced or willfully, with intention or without, by passing thought or by an action, in this lifetime or in previous, and it was swallowed by the klipa, that the klipa will vomit all the sparks of keri that was swollen by it, by virtue of your great name that comes from the verse:"He swallowed up wealth and vomited it out, and from his belly God will cast it." (Job 20:15), and by the virtue of your great name you will return them to the holy place, and do what is good in Your eyes.

בָּרוּךְ baruch אַתָּה Ata יְהֹוָהֵאֱדֹנָיאֱהֱדֹנָהי Adonai ; יכוין חֹבי בעֹילוב יהֹה כֹזֹה: יְוֹהֵבֵוֹהָ

מְקַבֵּץ mekabetz ע"ב ס"ג מ"ה ב"ֹ, הברכה (למֹתֹק) את ז' המֹלכֹים עֹמֹתֹו)

נִדְוֹזֵי nidchei ע"ב, ריבֹיעֹ יהֹה עַמּוֹ amo חֹבֹי יִשְׂרָאֵל Yisrael:

THE EIGHTH (ELEVENTH) BLESSING

This blessing helps us to balance judgment with mercy. As mercy is time, we can use it to change ourselves before judgment occurs.

Yesod

הָשִׁיבָה hashiva שׁוֹפְטֵינוּ shoftenu כְּבָרִאשׁוֹנָה kevarishona●

וְיוֹעֲצֵינוּ veyo'atzenu כְּבַתְּוֹזִלָּה kevatechila ר"ת עֹב"ה (דֹיֹנֹים זכֹרֹים עֹבֹיֹסֹוֹד) ויהֹוה (הֹמֹמֹתֹקֹם)●

וְהָסֵר vehaser מִמֶּנּוּ mimenu יָגוֹן yagon (סֹמֹאל) וַאֲנוּזֹה va'anacha (לֹיֹלֹיֹת)●

וּמְלוֹךְ umloch עָלֵינוּ aleinu מְהֵרָה mehera אַתָּה Ata

יְהֹוָהֵאֱדֹנָיאֱהֱדֹנָהי Adonai לְבַדְּךָ levadcha● בְּוֶזֶסֶד bechesed ע"ב, ריבֹיעֹ יהֹה

וּבְרַוֲזֶמִים uvrachamim מֹצֹפֹצ, אֹלֹהֹים דֹיֹוֹדֹין, י"פֹ יֹיֹי ; לֹהֹמֹתֹיֹק בֹרֹוֹזֹמֹים דֹיֹנֹי צֹדֹק וֹמֹעֹפֹטֹ

בְּצֶדֶק betzedek וּבְמִשְׁפָּט uvmishpat ע"ה = ה"פֹ אֹלֹהֹים: בָּרוּךְ baruch אַתָּה Ata

יְוֹהֵוֹוֹאֱדֹנָיאֱהֱדֹנָהי Adonai מֶלֶךְ melech אוֹהֵב ohev מֹמֹתֹיֹק דֹיֹנֹי

צְדָקָה tzedaka ע"ה ריבֹיעֹ אֹלֹהֹים וּמִשְׁפָּט umishpat ע"ה ה"פֹ אֹלֹהֹים:

During the days between *Rosh Hashanah* and *Yom Kippur* instead of "*melech ohev tzedaka umishpat*" we say:

הַמֶּלֶךְ hamelech הַמִּשְׁפָּט hamishpat ע"ה ה"פֹ אֹלֹהֹים:

If you mistakenly say "*melech ohev...*" and realize this within three seconds, you should say "*hamelech hamishpat*" and continue as usual. But if you have already begun the next blessing you should not go back.

THE NINTH (TWELFTH) BLESSING

This blessing helps us remove all forms of negativity, whether it comes from people, situations or even the negative energy of the Angel of Death [(**do not pronounce these names**) *Sa-ma-el* (male aspect) and*Li-li-th* (female aspect), which are encoded here], by using the Holy Name: *Shadai* עֹד"י, which is encoded mathematically into the last four words of this blessing and also appears inside a *Mezuzah* for the same purpose.

Blessed are You, Lord, Who gathers the displaced of His Nation, Israel.
THE EIGHTH (ELEVENTH) BLESSING
Restore our judges, as at first, and our mentors, as in the beginning. Remove from us sorrow and moaning. Reign over us soon, You alone, Lord, with kindness and compassion, with righteousness and justice. Blessed are You, Lord, the King Who loves righteousness and justice.

During the days between *Rosh Hashanah* and *Yom Kippur*: *The King the judgment.*

Keter

tikva תִּקְוָה tehi תְּהִי al אַל velamalshinim וְלַמַּלְשִׁינִים laminim לַמִּינִים

vechol וְכָל ילי hazedim הַזֵּדִים kerega כְּרֶגַע ג"פ אלהים עם ט"ו אותיות פשוטות

yovedu יֹאבֵדוּ vechol וְכָל ילי oyvecha אוֹיְבֶיךָ (סמאל)

yikaretu יִכָּרֵתוּ mehera מְהֵרָה (לילית) son'echa שׂוֹנְאֶיךָ ילי vechol וְכָל

te'aker תְּעַקֵּר mehera מְהֵרָה harish'a הָרִשְׁעָה umalchut וּמַלְכוּת

bimhera בִּמְהֵרָה vetachni'em וְתַכְנִיעֵם utchalem וּתְכַלֵּם utshaber וּתְשַׁבֵּר

Adonai יְהֹוָה(יֱהֹוִה)יאהדונהי Ata אַתָּה baruch בָּרוּךְ veyamenu בְּיָמֵינוּ:

shover שׁוֹבֵר oyvim אוֹיְבִים umachni'a וּמַכְנִיעַ zedim זֵדִים ר"ת = עֹדִי:

Malchut of the World of Atzilut ends here.
The next four blessings help to correct *Zeir Anpin* and *Malchut* of *Atzilut* from the aspect of *Zeir Anpin*.

THE TENTH (THIRTEENTH) BLESSING

This blessing surrounds us with total positivity to help us always be at the right place at the right time. It also helps attract only positive people into our lives.

Yesod

hachasidim הַחֲסִידִים ve'al וְעַל צדיק יסוד עולם hatzadikim הַצַּדִּיקִים al עַל

Yisrael יִשְׂרָאֵל ב"פ ראה bet בֵּית amecha עַמְּךָ she'erit שְׁאֵרִית ve'al וְעַל

sofrehem סוֹפְרֵיהֶם ב"פ ראה bet בֵּית peletat פְּלֵיטַת ve'al וְעַל

yehemu יֶהֱמוּ ve'alenu וְעָלֵינוּ hatzedek הַצֶּדֶק gerei גֵּרֵי ve'al וְעַל

Elohenu אֱלֹהֵינוּ ילה Adonai יְהֹוָה(יֱהֹוִה)יאהדונהי rachamecha רַחֲמֶיךָ na נָא

lechol לְכֹל ה ארני tov טוֹב ב"ן י"פ sachar שָׂכָר veten וְתֵן

habotchim הַבּוֹטְחִים beshimcha בְּשִׁמְךָ be'emet בֶּאֱמֶת אהיה פעמים אהיה, ז"פ ס"ג:

THE NINTH (TWELFTH) BLESSING
For the heretics and for the slanderers, let there be no hope.
Let all the wicked perish in an instant. And may all Your foes and all Your haters be speedily cut down. And as for the evil government, may You quickly uproot and smash it, and may You destroy and humble it, speedily in our days. Blessed are You, Lord, Who smashes foes and humbles the wicked.

THE TENTH (THIRTEENTH) BLESSING
On the righteous, on the pious, on the remnants of the House of Israel, on the remnants of their writers' academies, on the righteous converts, and on us, may Your compassion be stirred, Lord, our God. And give good reward to all those who truly trust in Your Name

וְשִׂים vesim וְחֶלְקֵנוּ chelkenu עִמָּהֶם imahem וּלְעוֹלָם ul'olam וְשִׂים רִיבּוּעַ ס״ג וי׳ אותיות דס״ג

לֹא lo נֵבוֹשׁ nevosh כִּי ki בְּךָ vecha בָּטַחְנוּ batachnu♦

וְעַל ve'al וְחַסְדְּךָ chasdecha הַגָּדוֹל hagadol ; לְהוֹ = עם ד׳ אותיות = מבה׳, יזל, אום

בֶּאֱמֶת be'emet אהיה פעמים אהיה ז״פ ס״ג נִשְׁעַנּוּ nish'anenu✦

בָּרוּךְ baruch אַתָּה Ata יְהֹוִוּ־אדני־יאהדונהי Adonai מִשְׁעָן mish'an

וּמִבְטָח umivtach לַצַּדִּיקִים latzadikim ר״ת יבול (כל מי שׁנִיבמול נקרא צדיק)✦

THE ELEVENTH (FOURTEENTH) BLESSING

This blessing connects us to the power of Jerusalem, to the building of the Temple, and to the preparation for the *Mashiach*.

Hod

תִּשְׁכּוֹן tishkon בְּתוֹךְ betoch יְרוּשָׁלַיִם Yerushalayim עִירְךָ ircha

כַּאֲשֶׁר ka'asher דִּבַּרְתָּ dibarta ראה וְכִסֵּא vechise דָּוִד David

עַבְדְּךָ avdecha פוי, אל אדני מְהֵרָה mehera בְּתוֹכָהּ vetocha תָּכִין tachin

Meditate here that *Mashiach Ben Yosef* shall not be killed by the wicked *Armilos* (**Do not pronounce**).

וּבְנֵה uvne אוֹתָהּ ota בִּנְיַן binyan עוֹלָם olam בִּמְהֵרָה bimhera

בְּיָמֵינוּ veyamenu✦ בָּרוּךְ baruch אַתָּה Ata יְהֹוִוּ־אדני־יאהדונהי Adonai

בּוֹנֵה bone ס״ג יְרוּשָׁלַיִם Yerushalayim✦

THE TWELFTH (FIFTEENTH) BLESSING

This blessing helps us achieve a personal state of *Mashiach* by transforming our reactive nature into becoming proactive. Just as there is a global *Mashiach*, each person has a personal *Mashiach* within. When enough people achieve their transformation, the way will be paved for the appearance of the global *Mashiach*.

---

and place our lot with them. And may we never be embarrassed, for it is in You that we place our trust; it is upon Your great compassion that we truly rely. Blessed are You, Lord, the support and security of the righteous.

THE ELEVENTH (FOURTEENTH) BLESSING

May You dwell in Jerusalem, Your City,
as You have promised. And may You establish the throne of David, Your servant, speedily within it and build it as an eternal structure, speedily in our days Blessed are You, Lord, Who builds Jerusalem.

SHACHARIT – MORNING PRAYER
OLAM ATZILUT - יוֹד הֵי וִיו הֵי

Netzach

This blessing contains 20 words, which is the same number of words in *"Ki nicham Adonai Tziyon nicham kol chorvoteha…" (Isaiah 51:3),* a verse that speaks about the Final Redemption.

David דָּוִד אֲדֹנָי יהוה אֶהְיֶה יהוה tzemach צֶמַח et אֶת

vekarno וְקַרְנוֹ tatzmia'ch תַּצְמִיחַ mehera מְהֵרָה פוי, אל אדני avdecha עַבְדְּךָ

lishu'atcha לִישׁוּעָתְךָ ki כִּי ◆bishu'atecha בִּישׁוּעָתְךָ tarum תָּרוּם

kivinu קִוִּינוּ kol כָּל ילי hayom הַיּוֹם ע"ה נגד, מזבוח, ז, אל יהוה

You should meditate and ask here for the Final Redemption to occur right away.

Adonai יהו אדני אהיה יאהדונהי Ata אַתָּה baruch בָּרוּךְ

matzmi'ach מַצְמִיחַ keren קֶרֶן yeshu'a יְשׁוּעָה◆

THE THIRTEENTH (SIXTEENTH) BLESSING

This blessing is the most important of all blessings, because here we acknowledge all of our reactive behavior. We make reference to our wrongful actions in general, and we also specify a particular incident. The section inside the box provides us with an opportunity to ask the Light for personal sustenance. The Ari states that throughout this prayer, even on fast days, we have a personal angel accompanying us. If we meditate upon this angel, all our prayers must be answered. The Thirteenth Blessing is one above the twelve zodiac signs, and it raises us above the influence of the stars and planets.

Tiferet

(יוֹד הֵה וָו הֵה) Adonai יהו אדני אהיה יאהדונהי kolenu קוֹלֵנוּ shema שְׁמַע

rachem רוֹם harachaman הָרַחֲמָן av אָב ◆(אבג יתץ) ילה Elohenu אֱלֹהֵינוּ

alenu עָלֵינוּ אברהם, וז"פ אל, רי"ו ול"ב נתיבות הוזכמה, רמ"וז (אברים), עסמ"ב וט"ו אותיות פשוטות

(קרע שטן) מצפצ, אלהים דיורין, י"פ ייי berachamim בְּרַחֲמִים vekabel וְקַבֵּל

et אֶת ע"ה שׁדי אל ע"ה, וקס"א ע"ב בריבוע ע"ב, ע"ה מהש uvratzon וּבְרָצוֹן

(מילוי) דס"ג יאי El אֵל ki כִּי (נגד) יכש◆ tefilatenu תְּפִלָּתֵנוּ

(בטר צתג)◆ Ata אַתָּה vetachanunim וְתַחֲנוּנִים tefilot תְּפִלּוֹת shome'a שׁוֹמֵעַ

THE TWELFTH (FIFTEENTH) BLESSING

The offspring of David, Your servant, may You speedily cause to sprout.
And may You raise their worth with Your salvation, because it is for Your salvation that we have hoped all day long. Blessed are You, Lord, Who sprouts out the worth of the salvation.

THE THIRTEENTH (SIXTEENTH) BLESSING

Hear our voice, Lord, our God. Merciful Father, have mercy over us.
Accept our prayer with compassion and favor, because You are God, Who hears prayers and supplications.

It is good for you to be aware, acknowledge and confess your prior negative actions and to ask for your livelihood here:

aviti עָוִיתִי chatati וְחָטָאתִי ,olam עוֹלָם shel שֶׁל ribono רִבּוֹנוֹ

וּפָשַׁעְתִּי ratzon רָצוֹן yehi יְהִי לְפָנֶיךָ lefanecha ufashati

shetimchol שֶׁתִּמְחוֹל milfanecha מִלְפָנֶיךָ

וְתִסְלַח vetislach utchaper וּתְכַפֵּר li לִי al עַל kol כָּל

veshepashati וְשֶׁפָשַׁעְתִּי veshe'aviti וְשֶׁעָוִיתִי shechatati שֶׁחָטָאתִי ma מַה

לְפָנֶיךָ lefanecha miyom מִיוֹם

שֶׁנִּבְרֵאתִי shenivreti hayom הַיוֹם ad עַד haze הֶזֶה

(mention here a specific negative action or behavior you have and ask for forgivness) uvifrat וּבִפְרָט

וִיהִי vihi ratzon רָצוֹן

מִלְפָנֶיךָ milfanecha Adonai יְהֹוָה Elohenu אֱלֹהֵינוּ

shetazmin שֶׁתַזְמִין avotenu אֲבוֹתֵינוּ velohei וֵאלֹהֵי

פַּרְנָסָתֵנוּ parnasatenu umzonotenu וּמְזוֹנוֹתֵינוּ li לִי ulchol וּלְכָל

anshei אַנְשֵׁי veti בֵיתִי hayom הַיוֹם

uvchol וּבְכָל yom יוֹם

vayom וְיוֹם berevach בְּרֵיוַוח velo וְלֹא

,vetzimtzum בְּצִמְצוּם velo וְלֹא bechavod בְּכָבוֹד ,bevizui בְּבִזוּי

benachat בְּנַחַת velo וְלֹא ,vetza'ar בְּצַעַר velo וְלֹא etztarech אֶצְטָרֵךְ

lematenot לְמַתְנוֹת basar בָּשָׂר vadam וְדָם velo וְלֹא ,lehalva'atam לְהַלְוָאָתָם

vehapetucha וְהַפְּתוּחָה harchava הָרְוָחָה miyadcha מִיָּדְךָ ela אֶלָּא

hagadol הַגָּדוֹל shimcha שִׁמְךָ uvizchut וּבִזְכוּת vehamele'a וְהַמְלֵאָה

דִּיקַרְנוֹסָא :Do not pronounce this Name)

:haparnasa הַפַּרְנָסָה al עַל hamemune הַמְמוּנֶה)

Master of the World!

I have transgressed. I have committed iniquity and I have sinned before You. May it be Your will that You would pardon, forgive and excuse all my transgressions, and all the iniquities that I have committed, and all the sins that I have sinned before You, ever since the day I was created and until this day (and especially...). May it be pleasing before You, Lord, our God and God of my forefathers, that You would provide for my livelihood and sustenance, and that of my household, today and each and every day, with abundance and not with meagerness; with dignity and not with shame; with comfort and not with suffering; and that I may not require the gifts of flesh and blood, nor their loans, but only from Your Hand, which is generous, open, and full, and by virtue of Your great Name, which is responsible for livelihood.

וּמִלְפָנֶיךָ umilfanecha   ס״ג   מ״ה   ב״ן   מַלְכֵּנוּ malkenu

רֵיקָם rekam   אַל־ al   תְּשִׁיבֵנוּ te'shivenu   (וזקב טוע)

וְחָנֵנוּ chonenu   וַעֲנֵנוּ va'anenu   וּשְׁמַע ushma   תְּפִלָתֵנוּ׃tefilatenu

---

THE BLESSING FOR A FAST DAY
This blessing is recited by individuals on fast days, during the silent *Amidah*.

עֲנֵנוּ anenu   אָבִינוּ avinu   עֲנֵנוּ anenu   בְּיוֹם beyom   ע״ה נגד, מזבח, זן, אל יהוה צוֹם tzom

הַתַעֲנִית hata'anit   הַזֶה haze   והו כִּי ki   בְּצָרָה vetzara   אלהים דההין גְּדוֹלָה gedola

אֲנַחְנוּ anachnu   אַל־ al   תֵּפֶן tefen   לְרִשְׁעֵנוּ lerish'enu

וְאַל־ ve'al   תִּתְעַלַּם tit'alam   מַלְכֵּנוּ malkenu   מִבַּקָשָׁתֵנוּ mibakashatenu

הֱיֵה heye   יהה   נָא na   קָרוֹב karov   לְשַׁוְעָתֵנוּ leshav'atenu

טֶרֶם terem   נִקְרָא nikra   אֵלֶיךָ elecha   אַתָה Ata   תַעֲנֶה ta'ane

נְדַבֵּר nedaber   ראה   וְאַתָה veAta   תִּשְׁמַע tishma   כַּדָבָר kadavar   ראה

שֶׁנֶאֱמַר׃shene'emar   וְהָיָה vehaya   יהה ; יהוה   טֶרֶם־ terem   יִקְרָאוּ yikra'u

וַאֲנִי va'ani   אני   אֶעֱנֶה e'ene   עוֹד od   הֵם hem   מְדַבְּרִים medabrim

וַאֲנִי va'ani   אני   אֶשְׁמַע׃eshma   כִּי ki   אַתָה Ata   יְהֹוֹ(אדני)יאהדונהי Adonai

פּוֹדֶה pode   וּמַצִיל umatzil   וְעוֹנֶה ve'one   וּמְרַחֵם umrachem   אברהם,

בְּכָל bechol   ב״ן, לכב צֵת et   צָרָה tzara   אלהים דההין וְצוּקָה׃vetzuka   (continue "ki Ata")

כִּי ki   אַתָה Ata   שׁוֹמֵעַ shome'a   תְּפִלַת tefilat   כָּל־ kol   ילי   פֶה pe

(פֶה דו״א) מילה ; וע״ה אלהים, אהיה אדני (יגל פוק)

בָּרוּךְ baruch   אַתָה Ata   יְהֹוֹ(אדני)(יהוה)יאהדונהי Adonai

---

You should meditate here on the Holy Name: אראריתּ״א

Rav Chaim Vital says: "I have found in the books of the kabbalists that the prayer of a person, who meditates on this Name in the blessing *shome'a tefila*, will never go unanswered."

שׁוֹמֵעַ shome'a   תְּפִלָה tefila   (שׁוֹקוֹ צִית) אתב״ש אוכצ, ב״ן אדני וניקודה ע״ה = יוד הי וו הה׃

And from before You,
our King, do not turn us away empty-handed but be gracious, answer us, and hear our prayer.

THE BLESSING FOR A FAST DAY
Answer us, our Father,
answer us on this day of fasting because we are in great distress. Do not pay heed to our wickedness and, our King, do not ignore our plea. Please come close to our cries and answer us even before we call out to You. We shall speak and You shall hear us, as it is said: And it shall be that before they call, I shall answer, and while they speak, I shall hear. (Isaiah 65:24) For You, Lord, redeem, save, respond, and show compassion in every time of trouble and distress.

Because You hear the prayer of every mouth. Blessed are You, Lord, Who hears prayers.

OLAM ATZILUT - יוד הי ויו הי

THE FINAL THREE BLESSINGS

Through the merit of Moses, Aaron and Joseph, who are our channels for the final three blessings, we are able to bring down all the spiritual energy that we aroused with our prayers and blessings.

THE SEVENTEENTH BLESSING

During this blessing, referring to Moses, we should always meditate to try to know exactly what God wants from us in our life, as signified by the phrase, "Let it be the will of God." We ask God to guide us toward the work we came to Earth to do. The Creator cannot just accept the work that we want to do; we must carry out the work we were destined to do.

Netzach

You have made requests (of daily needs) to God. Now, after asking for your needs to be met, you should praise the Creator in the last three blessings. This is like a person who has received what he needs from his Master and departs from Him. You should say "*retze*" and meditate for the Supernal Desire (*Keter*) that is called *metzach haratzon* (the Forehead of the Desire).

רְצֵה retze אלף למד הה יוד מם

Meditate here to transform misfortune and tragedy (צרה) into desire and acceptance (רצה).

(**During the three weeks of** *Ben HaMetzarim*, meditate here on these Holy Names: אלהים דההין ארני, שין ע"ה, טדהד כוו מצפצ - with these Names we transform צרה into רצה).

יְהֹוָה Adonai Elohenu אֱלֹהֵינוּ ילה be'amecha בְּעַמְּךָ Yisrael יִשְׂרָאֵל

velitfilatam וְלִתְפִלָּתָם she'e שְׁעֵה vehashev וְהָשֵׁב ha'avoda הָעֲבוֹדָה

lidvir לִדְבִיר betecha בֵּיתֶךָ ve'ishei וְאִשֵּׁי Yisrael יִשְׂרָאֵל

utfilatam וּתְפִלָּתָם mehera מְהֵרָה be'ahava בְּאַהֲבָה

tekabel תְּקַבֵּל beratzon בְּרָצוֹן

ut'hi וּתְהִי leratzon לְרָצוֹן tamid תָּמִיד avodat עֲבוֹדַת Yisrael יִשְׂרָאֵל amecha עַמֶּךָ

THE FINAL THREE BLESSINGS
THE SEVENTEENTH BLESSING
Find favor, Lord, our God,
in Your People, Israel, and turn to their prayer.
Restore the service to the inner sanctuary of Your Temple. Accept the offerings of Israel and their prayer with favor, speedily, and with love. May the service of Your People Israel always be favorable to You.

FOR *ROSH CHODESH*, *PESACH*, AND *SUKKOT* :

During these events, there is an extra surge of spiritual energy in our midst. These additional blessings are
our antenna for drawing this extra power into our lives.

If you mistakenly forgot to say "*ya'ale veyavo*," and realize this before the end of the blessing
("*baruch Ata Adonai*"), you should return to say "*ya'ale veyavo*" and continue as usual.
If you realize this after the end of the blessing ("*hamachazir shechinato leTziyon*") but before you start
the next blessing ("*modim*") you should say "*ya'ale veyavo*" there and continue as usual.
If you only realize this after you have started the next blessing ("*modim*") but before the second
"*yih'yu leratzon*" (on pg. 223) you should return to "*retze*" (pg. 211) and continue from there.
If you realize this after (the second "*yih'yu leratzon*") you should start the *Amidah* from the beginning.

avotenu אֲבוֹתֵינוּ ילה ; רמב ע"ב, מילוי ; לכב velohei וֵאלֹהֵי ילה Elohenu אֱלֹהֵינוּ

veyeratze וְיֵרָצֶה רי"ו veyera'e וְיֵרָאֶה veyagi'a וְיַגִּיעַ veyavo וְיָבֹא ya'ale יַעֲלֶה

(ו ע"פ) ו ר"ת מ"ב veyizacher וְיִזָּכֵר veyipaked וְיִפָּקֵד veyishama וְיִשָּׁמַע

avotenu‏◆ אֲבוֹתֵינוּ ונ'ע"ב קס"א ע"ב vezichron וְזִכְרוֹן zichronenu זִכְרוֹנֵנוּ

irach◆ עִירָךְ Yerushalayim יְרוּשָׁלַיִם ונ'ע"ב קס"א ע"ב zichron זִכְרוֹן

David דָוִד ben בֶּן mashi'ach מְשִׁיחַ ונ'ע"ב קס"א ע"ב vezichron וְזִכְרוֹן

ע"ה כהת ; בן דוד = אדני ע"ה = אדנ"י avdach עַבְדָּךְ פוי, אל אדנ"י vezichron וְזִכְרוֹן◆ ע"ב קס"א ונ'ע"ב

Yisrael יִשְׂרָאֵל ראה ב"פ bet בֵּית amecha עַמְּךָ ילי kol כָּל

◆אכא letova לְטוֹבָה lifleta לִפְלֵיטָה ב"ן מ"ה ס"ג lefanecha לְפָנֶיךָ

יהוה ריבוע ע"ב, lechesed לְחֶסֶד מוזי בריבוע, דמ"ה מילוי lechen לְחֵן

ע"ה. בינה יהוה, אהיה אהיה lechayim לְחַיִּים ulrachamim◆ וּלְרַחֲמִים

אל יהוה: זן, מזבוז, נגד ע"ה beyom בְּיוֹם ulshalom◆ וּלְשָׁלוֹם tovim טוֹבִים

FOR *ROSH CHODESH*, *PESACH*, AND *SUKKOT* :
Our God and God of our forefathers,
may it rise, come, arrive, appear, find favor, be heard, be considered, and be remembered, our remembrance and
the remembrance of our forefathers: the remembrance of Jerusalem, Your City, and the remembrance of Mashiach,
Son of David, Your servant, and the remembrance of Your entire Nation, the House of Israel, before You
for deliverance, for good, for grace, kindness, and compassion, for a good life, and for peace on the day of:

On *Rosh Chodesh*:

רִבּוּעַ אלהים ואלהים דיודין ע"ה Rosh **רֹאשׁ**

י"ב הוּיוֹת, קס"א קנ"א ; ראש וזדע ע"ה = שין דלת יוד **הַזֶּה** haze הַחֹדֶשׁ haChodesh וְהוּ.

On mid-holiday of *Pesach*:

וְהוּ haze הַזֶּה haMatzot הַמַּצּוֹת chag וְזֶה

בְּיוֹם beyom ע"ה נגד, מזבח, זן, אל יהוה מִקְרָא mikra קֹדֶשׁ kodesh הַזֶּה haze וְהוּ.

On mid-holiday of *Sukkot*:

וְהוּ haze הַזֶּה haSukkot הַסֻּכּוֹת chag וְזֶה

בְּיוֹם beyom ע"ה נגד, מזבח, זן, אל יהוה מִקְרָא mikra קֹדֶשׁ kodesh הַזֶּה haze וְהוּ.

(אברים), רמ"ח נתיבות החכמה, רי"י ול"ב אל, וֹ"פ אברהם, lerachem לְרַחֵם

ulhoshi'enu וּלְהוֹשִׁיעֵנוּ alenu עָלֵינוּ bo בּוֹ פעוטות אותיות וט"ז עסמ"ב

bo בּוֹ ילה Elohenu אֱלֹהֵינוּ Adonai יְהֹוָהאדיאהדונהי zochrenu זָכְרֵנוּ

livracha לִבְרָכָה vo בּוֹ ufokdenu וּפָקְדֵנוּ אכא. letova לְטוֹבָה

vehoshi'enu וְהוֹשִׁיעֵנוּ vo בּוֹ לְחַיִּים lechayim אהיה יהוה, אהיה בינה ע"ה

verachamim וְרַחֲמִים yeshu'a יְשׁוּעָה bidvar בִּדְבַר ראה tovim טוֹבִים.

chus וְחָנֵּנוּ vechonenu וַחֲמוֹל vachamol וְרַחֵם verachem אברהם, וֹ"פ אל,

alenu עָלֵינוּ פעוטות אותיות וט"ז עסמ"ב, רמ"ח (אברים), החכמה נתיבות ול"ב רי"י

vehoshi'enu וְהוֹשִׁיעֵנוּ ki כִּי elecha אֵלֶיךָ enenu עֵינֵינוּ ריבוע מ"ה. ki כִּי

Ata אָתָּה verachum וְרַחוּם chanun וְחַנּוּן melech מֶלֶךְ (מילוי דס"ג) El אֵל יא"י:

veAta וְאַתָּה verachamecha בְּרַחֲמֶיךָ harabim הָרַבִּים tachpotz תַּחְפֹּץ.

banu בָּנוּ vetirtzenu וְתִרְצֵנוּ vetechezena וְתֶחֱזֶינָה enenu עֵינֵינוּ ריבוע מ"ה

beshuvcha בְּשׁוּבְךָ leTziyon לְצִיּוֹן יוסף, ר הויות, קנאה berachamim בְּרַחֲמִים

baruch בָּרוּךְ Ata אַתָּה יְהֹוָהאדיאהדונהי Adonai י"פ ייי, דיודין אלהים מצפצ.

hamachazir הַמַּחֲזִיר shechinato שְׁכִינָתוֹ leTziyon לְצִיּוֹן יוסף, ר הויות, קנאה:

On *Rosh Chodesh*: *This Rosh Chodesh.*
On mid-holiday of *Pesach*: *This festival of Matzot, on this holy day of convocation.*
On mid-holiday of *Sukkot*: *This festival of Sukkot, on this holy day of convocation.*
To take pity on us and to save us.
Remember us, Lord, our God, on this day, for good; consider us on it for blessing; and deliver us on it for a good life, with the words of deliverance and mercy. Take pity and be gracious to us, have mercy and be compassionate with us, and save us, for our eyes turn to You, because You are God, the King Who is gracious and compassionate.

And You in Your great compassion take delight in us and are pleased with us. May our eyes witness Your return to Zion with compassion. Blessed are You, Lord, Who returns His Shechinah to Zion.

SHACHARIT – MORNING PRAYER

OLAM ATZILUT - יוֹד הֹי וִיו הֹי

THE EIGHTEENTH BLESSING

This blessing is our thank you. Kabbalistically, the biggest 'thank you' we can give the Creator is to do exactly what we are supposed to do in terms of our spiritual work.

Hod

Bow your entire body at 'modim' and straighten up at 'Adonai'.

lach לָךְ anachnu אֲנַחְנוּ מאה ברכות שׁתיקן דוד לאמרם כל יום modim מוֹדִים

שָׁאַתָּה sheAta הוּא hu יְהֹוָהאדיאאהדונהי Adonai (וּ) אֱלֹהֵינוּ Elohenu יָלַה

וֵאלֹהֵי velohei לְעוֹלָם le'olam אֲבוֹתֵינוּ avotenu יָלַה ; מִילוּי עַ"ב, דמב ; לְכַב

צוּר tzur צוּרֵנוּ tzurenu וָעֵד va'ed דס"ג וַ"וֹ אוֹתיוֹת רִיבּוּעַ ס"ג אֱלֹהִים דההֹין עַ"ה

וַחַיֵּינוּ chayenu וּמָגֵן umagen ג"פ אל (יֹא"י מִילוּי דס"ג) ; ר"ת מיכאל גבריאל נוּריאל

יִשְׁעֵנוּ yish'enu אַתָּה Ata הוּא hu כְּדוֹר ledor וָדוֹר vador רִ"יוֹ נוֹדֶה node

לָךְ lecha וּנְסַפֵּר unsaper תְּהִלָּתֶךָ tehilatecha עַל al וַחַיֵּינוּ chayenu

הַמְּסוּרִים hamesurim בְּיָדֶךָ beyadecha וְעַל ve'al נִשְׁמוֹתֵינוּ nishmotenu

הַפְּקוּדוֹת hapekudot לָךְ lach וְעַל ve'al נִסֶּיךָ nisecha שֶׁבְּכָל shebechol

עִמָּנוּ imanu יוֹם yom עַ"ה נגד, מזבח, ז, אל יהוה רִיבּוּעַ ס"ג, קס"א עַ"ה וד' אוֹתיוֹת לְכַב, ב"ן

וְעַל ve'al נִפְלְאוֹתֶיךָ nifle'otecha וְטוֹבוֹתֶיךָ vetovotecha שֶׁבְּכָל shebechol

הַטּוֹב hatov עֵת et וְצָהֳרָיִם vetzahorayim וָבֹקֶר vavoker עֶרֶב erev עֵת לְכַב, ב"ן

הַמְרַחֵם hamerachem רַחֲמֶיךָ rachamecha כָּלוּ chalu לֹא lo כִּי ki וְהֹו

לֹא lo כִּי ki אברהם, וח"פ אל, רִי"ו ול"ב נתיבות החוכמה, רמ"ח (אברים), עסמ"ב וטי"ז אוֹתיוֹת פּעוֹטוֹת

וָחֲסָדֶיךָ chasadecha תַּמּוּ tamu כִּי ki מֵעוֹלָם me'olam קִוִּינוּ kivinu לָךְ lach

---

THE EIGHTEENTH BLESSING

We give thanks to You, for it is You, Lord, Who is our God and God of our forefathers, forever and for all eternity. You are our Rock, the Rock of our lives, and the Shield of our salvation. From one generation to another, we shall give thanks to You and we shall tell of Your praise. For our lives that are entrusted in Your hands, for our souls that are in Your care, for Your miracles that are with us every day, and for Your wonders and Your favors that are with us at all times: evening, morning and afternoon. You are the good One, for Your compassion has never ceased. You are the compassionate One, for Your kindness has never ended, for we have always placed our hope in You.

MODIM DERABANAN

This prayer is recited by the congregation in the repetition when the chazan *says "modim."*

In this section there are 44 words which is the same numerical value as the Name:
ריבוע אהיה (א אה אהי אהיה).

lach לָךְ anachnu אֲנַחְנוּ מאה ברכות שׂתיקן דוד לאמרם כל יום modim מוֹדִים

יל׳ה Elohenu אֱלֹהֵינוּ Adonai יְהֹוָה הוּא hu הוּא sheAta שָׁאַתָּה

avotenu אֲבוֹתֵינוּ יל׳ה ; ד׳מב ע״ב, מילוי ; לכב velohei וֵאלֹהֵי

yotzrenu יוֹצְרֵנוּ ◆basar בָּשָׂר ילי chol כָּל ; ד׳מב ע״ב, מילוי Elohei אֱלֹהֵי

vehoda'ot וְהוֹדָאוֹת berachot בְּרָכוֹת ◆bereshit בְּרֵאשִׁית yotzer יוֹצֵר

אום ,יזל ,מבה = אותיות ד׳ עם ; להוו hagadol הַגָּדוֹל leshimcha לְשִׁמְךָ

◆vekiyamtanu וְקִיַּמְתָּנוּ shehecheyitanu שֶׁהֶחֱיִיתָנוּ al עַל vehakadosh וְהַקָּדוֹשׁ

vete'esof וְתֶאֱסוֹף ◆utchonenu וּתְחָנֵּנוּ techayenu תְּחַיֵּינוּ ken כֵּן

lishmor לִשְׁמֹר ◆kodshecha קָדְשֶׁךָ lechatzrot לְחַצְרוֹת galuyoteinu גָּלֻיּוֹתֵינוּ

ul'ovdecha וּלְעָבְדְּךָ ◆retzoncha רְצוֹנְךָ vela'asot וְלַעֲשׂוֹת chukecha חֻקֶּיךָ

she'anachnu שֶׁאֲנַחְנוּ al עַל ◆shalem שָׁלֵם בוכי belevav בְּלֵבָב פוי, אל אדני

hahoda'ot הַהוֹדָאוֹת: יא״י (מילוי דס״ג) El אֵל baruch בָּרוּךְ ◆lach לָךְ modim מוֹדִים

FOR CHANUKAH AND PURIM

Chanukah and *Purim* generate an added dimension of the energy of miracles. This blessing helps us harness this energy, thereby drawing miracles into our lives whenever they are truly needed.

◆hapurkan הַפֻּרְקָן ve'al וְעַל hanisim הַנִּסִּים ve'al וְעַל

hateshu'ot הַתְּשׁוּעוֹת ve'al וְעַל ◆hagevurot הַגְּבוּרוֹת ve'al וְעַל

hanechamot הַנֶּחָמוֹת ve'al וְעַל hanifla'ot הַנִּפְלָאוֹת ve'al וְעַל

hahem הָהֵם גלך bayamim בַּיָּמִים la'avotenu לַאֲבוֹתֵינוּ she'asita שֶׁעָשִׂיתָ

bazeman בַּזְּמַן haze הַזֶּה והו:

MODIM DERABANAN

We give thanks to You, for it is You Lord,
our God and God of our forefathers, the God of all flesh, our Maker and the Former of all Creation. Blessings and thanks to Your great and Holy Name for giving us life and for preserving us. So may You continue to give us life, be gracious to us, and gather our exiles to the courtyards of Your Sanctuary, so that we may keep Your laws, fulfill Your will, and serve You wholeheartedly. For this, we thank You. Bless the God of thanksgiving.

FOR CHANUKAH AND PURIM

And also for the miracles, deliverance, the mighty acts, the salvation, wonders,
and comforting deeds that You performed for our forefathers, in those days and at this time.

FOR CHANUKAH:

בִּימֵי bimei   מַתִּתְיָה Matitya   בֶּן ven   יוֹחָנָן Yochanan   כֹּהֵן kohen   מלה

גָּדוֹל gadol [לחו׳ ; עם ד׳ אותיות = מבה, יזל, אום]   וַחַשְׁמוֹנָאִי Chashmonai   וּבָנָיו uvanav

כְּשֶׁעָמְדָה keshe'amda   מַלְכוּת malchut   יָוָן Yavan   הָרְשָׁעָה harsha'a   עַל al

עַמְּךָ amecha   יִשְׂרָאֵל Yisrael   לְשַׁכְּחָם leshakecham   תּוֹרָתָךְ toratach

וּלְהַעֲבִירָם ulha'aviram   מֵחֻקֵּי mechukei   רְצוֹנָךְ retzonach◦   וְאַתָּה veAta

בְּרַחֲמֶיךָ verachamecha   הָרַבִּים harabim   עָמַדְתָּ amadeta   לָהֶם lahem

בְּעֵת be'et   צָרָתָם tzaratam◦   רַבְתָּ ravta   אֶת et   רִיבָם rivam◦   דַּנְתָּ danta

אֶת et   דִּינָם dinam◦   נָקַמְתָּ nakamta   מנק אֶת et   נִקְמָתָם nikmatam◦ מנק׳

מָסַרְתָּ masarta   גִּבּוֹרִים giborim   בְּיַד beyad   וְחַלָּשִׁים chalashim◦   וְרַבִּים verabim

בְּיַד beyad   מְעַטִּים me'atim◦   וּרְשָׁעִים ursha'im   בְּיַד beyad   צַדִּיקִים tzadikim◦

וּטְמֵאִים utme'im   בְּיַד beyad   טְהוֹרִים tehorim◦   וְזֵדִים vezedim   בְּיַד beyad

עוֹסְקֵי oskei   תוֹרָתֶךָ toratecha◦   לְךָ lecha   עָשִׂיתָ asita   שֵׁם shem

גָּדוֹל gadol [לחו׳ ; עם ד׳ אותיות = מבה, יזל, אום]   וְקָדוֹשׁ vekadosh   בְּעוֹלָמָךְ be'olamach◦

וּלְעַמְּךָ ul'amecha   יִשְׂרָאֵל Yisrael   עָשִׂיתָ asita   תְּשׁוּעָה teshu'a   גְדוֹלָה gedola

וּפֻרְקָן ufurkan   כְּהַיּוֹם kehayom [ע״ה נגד, מזבוז, זן, אל יהוה]   הַזֶּה haze וחו׳

וְאַחַר ve'achar   כָּךְ kach   בָּאוּ ba'u   בָנֶיךָ vanecha   לִדְבִיר lidvir רי״

בֵּיתֶךָ betecha   וּפִנּוּ ufinu [ב״פ ראה]   אֶת et   הֵיכָלֶךָ hechalecha◦   וְטִהֲרוּ vetiharu

אֶת et   מִקְדָּשֶׁךָ mikdashecha◦   וְהִדְלִיקוּ vehidliku   נֵרוֹת nerot

בְּחַצְרוֹת bechatzrot   קָדְשֶׁךָ kodshecha◦   וְקָבְעוּ vekav'u   שְׁמוֹנַת shemonat

יְמֵי yemei   חֲנֻכָּה Chanukah   אֵלּוּ elu   בְּהַלֵּל behalel [אדני, לכל]   וּבְהוֹדָאָה uvhoda'a◦

וְעָשִׂיתָ ve'asita   עִמָּהֶם imahem   נִסִּים nisim   וְנִפְלָאוֹת venifla'ot   וְנוֹדֶה venode

לְשִׁמְךָ leshimcha   הַגָּדוֹל hagadol [לחו׳ ; עם ד׳ אותיות = מבה, יזל, אום]   סֶלָה sela:

FOR CHANUKAH

In the days of Mattatiyahu, the son of Yochanan, the High Priest, the Hasmonean, and his sons, when the evil Greek Empire rose up against Your Nation, Israel, to force them to forget Your Torah and to force them away from the laws of Your desire, You, with Your compassion, stood up for them in their time of trouble. You fought their battles, sought justice for them, avenged them, and delivered the strong into the hands of the weak, the many into the hands of the few, the wicked into the hands of the righteous, the defiled into the hands of the pure, and the tyrants into the hands of those who occupy themselves with Your Torah. For Yourself, You made a Holy Name in Your world, and for Your People, Israel, You carried out a great salvation and deliverance on this day. Then Your Children came into the Sanctuary of Your House, they cleansed Your Palace, they purified Your Temple, they lit candles in the courtyards of Your Holy Domain, and they established these eight days of Chanukah for praise and thanksgiving. And You performed for them miracles and wonders. For that, we are grateful to Your Great Name. Selah.

FOR PURIM:

בִּימֵי bimei מָרְדְּכַי Mardechai וְאֶסְתֵּר veEster עִם הָאוֹתִיּוֹת = מִילּוּי אֲדֹנָי

בְּשׁוּשַׁן beShushan הַבִּירָה habira· כְּשֶׁעָמַד keshe'amad עֲלֵיהֶם alehem

הָמָן Haman הָרָשָׁע harasha· בִּקֵּשׁ bikesh לְהַשְׁמִיד lehashmid לַהֲרוֹג laharog

וּלְאַבֵּד ul'abed אֶת et כָּל kol הַיְּהוּדִים hayehudim מִנַּעַר mina'ar וְעַד ve'ad

זָקֵן zaken טַף taf וְנָשִׁים venashim בְּיוֹם beyom

בִּשְׁלֹשָׁה bishlosha עָשָׂר asar לְחֹדֶשׁ lechodesh

שְׁנֵים shenem עָשָׂר asar הוּא hu וְחֹדֶשׁ chodesh

אֲדָר adar וּשְׁלָלָם ushlalam לָבוֹז lavoz· וְאַתָּה veAta בְּרַחֲמֶיךָ verachamecha

הָרַבִּים harabim הֵפַרְתָּ hefarta אֶת et עֲצָתוֹ atzato וְקִלְקַלְתָּ vekilkalta

אֶת et מַחֲשַׁבְתּוֹ machashavto· וַהֲשֵׁבוֹתָ vahashevota לוֹ lo גְּמוּלוֹ gemulo

בְּרֹאשׁוֹ berosho· וְתָלוּ vetalu אוֹתוֹ oto וְאֶת ve'et בָּנָיו banav עַל al הָעֵץ ha'etz·

וְעָשִׂיתָ ve'asita עִמָּהֶם imahem נִסִּים nisim וְנִפְלָאוֹת venifla'ot וְנוֹדֶה venode

לְשִׁמְךָ leshimcha הַגָּדוֹל hagadol לָהֶם ; עִם ד' אוֹתִיּוֹת = מַבַּה, יַ"ל, אוּם סֶלָה sela·

וְעַל ve'al כֻּלָּם kulam יִתְבָּרַךְ yitbarach וְיִתְרוֹמַם veyitromam

וְיִתְנַשֵּׂא veyitnase תָּמִיד tamid שִׁמְךָ shimcha

מַלְכֵּנוּ malkenu לְעוֹלָם le'olam וָעֶד va'ed·

וְכֹל vechol הַחַיִּים hachayim יוֹדוּךָ yoducha סֶלָה sela·

During the days between *Rosh Hashanah* and *Yom Kippur* we say the prayer of "*uchtov*":

וּכְתוֹב uchtov לְחַיִּים lechayim כָּל kol בְּנֵי benei בְּרִיתֶךָ veritecha:

If you forget to say "*uchtov*" and realize this before the end of the blessing ("*baruch Ata Adonai*"), you should return and say "*uchtov*" and continue as usual. But if you only realize this after the end of the blessing, you should continue and you may add "*uchtov*" in the end of "*Elohai netzor*".

FOR PURIM:

In the days of Mardechai and Esther, in Shushan, the capital, when the evil Haman rose up against them, he sought to destroy, slay, and annihilate all the Jews, young and old, children and women, in one day, on the thirteenth day of the twelfth month, which is the month of Adar, and to take their spoils. But You, in Your great compassion, ruined his plan, foiled his design, and turned his due upon his own head. They hanged him and his sons upon the gallows. And You performed for them [Israel] miracles and wonders. We give thanks to Your great Name. Selah.

And for all those things, may Your Name be always blessed,
exalted and extolled, our King, forever and ever, and all the living shall thank You, Selah.

During the days between *Rosh Hashanah* and *Yom Kippur*:
And write down for a good life all the members of Your Covenant.

וִיהַלְלוּ vihalelu וִיבָרְכוּ vivarchu יְהֹוָה רִיבּוּעַ יְהֹוָה רִיבּוּעַ מ״ה אָת et

שִׁמְךָ shimcha הַגָּדוֹל hagadol לְהוּ׳ ; עִם ד׳ אוֹתיות = מבּה, יכל, אוֹם בָּאֱמֶת be'emet

לְעוֹלָם le'olam רִיבּוּעַ ס״ג ו׳ אוֹתיות דס״ג ; ז״פ ס״ג אהיה פעמים אהיה, כִּי טוֹב ki טוֹב tov ; והי׳

הָאֵל haEl (מילוי דס״ג) יא״י ; לאה, יכל, אוֹם, מבּה, אהיה = יהוה כי טוב יְשׁוּעָתֵנוּ yeshu'atenu

וְעֶזְרָתֵנוּ ve'ezratenu סֶלָה sela• הָאֵל haEl לאה ; יא״י (מילוי דס״ג) הַטּוֹב hatov :והי׳

Bend your knees at 'baruch', bow at 'Ata' and straighten up at 'Adonai'.

בָּרוּךְ baruch אַתָּה Ata יְהֹוָֹאדֹנָיאהדונהי Adonai (הי) הַטּוֹב hatov והי׳

שִׁמְךָ shimcha וּלְךָ ulcha נָאֶה na'e לְהוֹדוֹת lehodot ס״ת כהת, מש״יוה בן דוד ע״ה:

BLESSING OF THE *KOHANIM*

During the repetition we say the blessing of the *Kohanim*. The Kohen is a channel for the Right Column energy of sharing and therefore also for healing. Because the Light revealed through this blessing is stronger than we can handle, we cover our eyes to prevent looking directly at this awesome healing Light.

If there is no Kohen present, the chazan should say:

אֱלֹהֵינוּ Elohenu וֵאלֹהֵי velohei ילה ; מילוי ע״ב, דמב ; ילה לכב אֲבוֹתֵינוּ avotenu,

בָּרְכֵנוּ barchenu בַּבְּרָכָה baberacha הַמְשֻׁלֶּשֶׁת hameshuleshet בַּתּוֹרָה batora

הַכְּתוּבָה haketuva עַל al יְדֵי yedei מֹשֶׁה Moshe מהע, ע״ב בריבוע וקס״א, אל שדי, עַבְדֶּךָ avdecha פוי, אל אדני הָאֲמוּרָה ha'amura מִפִּי mipi אַהֲרֹן Aharon ד״פ אלהים ע״ה

וּבָנָיו uvanav כֹּהֲנִים kohanim עַם am קְדוֹשֶׁךָ kedoshecha, כָּאָמוּר ka'amur:

Then the chazan will continue from "yevarechecha Adonai…" until "veyasem lecha Shalom" (on the next page).

After the congregation answers Amen, the chazan will say "Kohanim". Then the Kohanim will recite the following in silence:

יְהִי yehi רָצוֹן ratzon מהע ע״ה, ע״ב בריבוע וקס״א ע״ה, אל שדי ע״ה מִלְּפָנֶיךָ milfanecha

יְהֹוָֹאדֹנָיאהדונהי Adonai אֱלֹהֵינוּ Elohenu ילה וֵאלֹהֵי velohei ס״ג מ״ה ב״ן

אֲבוֹתֵינוּ avotenu, ילה ; מילוי ע״ב, דמב ; ילה לכב שֶׁתִּהְיֶה shetihye בְּרָכָה beracha זוֹ zo

שֶׁצִּוִּיתָנוּ shetzivitanu לְבָרֵךְ levarech אֶת et עַמְּךָ amecha יִשְׂרָאֵל Yisrael

בְּרָכָה beracha שְׁלֵמָה shelema וְלֹא velo יִהְיֶה yihye ... בָּהּ ba

מִכְשׁוֹל michshol וְעָוֹן ve'avon מֵעַתָּה me'ata וְעַד ve'ad עוֹלָם olam:

And they shall praise and bless Your Great Name,

sincerely and forever, for It is good, the God of our salvation and our help, Selah, the good God. Blessed are You, Lord, whose Name is good, and to You it is befitting to give thanks.

BLESSING OF THE *KOHANIM*

Our God and the God of our forefathers, bless us with the triple blessing written in the Torah by Moses, Your servant, and said by Aaron and his sons the Kohanim, Your Holy People, as it says:

May it be your will Lord, our God and the God of our forefathers, that this blessing with which You commanded us to bless Your People, Israel, be a perfect blessing, and may it not contain any hindrance or iniquity from now until eternity.

The *Kohanim* say the following blessing facing the Ark and when they reach the word "*vetzivanu*," they should turn clockwise and face the congregation and continue the blessing. If there is only one *Kohen*, the *chazan* should not call him but instead the *Kohen* should say the following blessing right away.

ילה‎ Elohenu אֱלֹהֵינוּ‎ Adonai יְהֹוָאהדוֹנָהי‎ Ata אַתָּה‎ baruch בָּרוּךְ‎

kideshanu קִדְּשָׁנוּ‎ asher אֲשֶׁר‎ ha'olam הָעוֹלָם‎ melech מֶלֶךְ‎

vetzivanu וְצִוָּנוּ‎ Aharon אַהֲרֹן‎ shel שֶׁל‎ bikdushato בִּקְדֻשָּׁתוֹ‎

אוֹד, דאה‎ be'ahava בְּאַהֲבָה‎ Yisrael יִשְׂרָאֵל‎ amo עַמּוֹ‎ et אֶת‎ levarech לְבָרֵךְ‎

The *chazan* prompts the *Kohanim* by reciting one word at a time (even if there is only one *Kohen* present). And the congregation answers: "*Amen*" (or "*ken yehi ratzon*" in case the *chazan* reciting it) after each verse.

The initials of the three verses give us the Holy Name: יי׳.
In this section, there are 15 words, which are equal to the numerical value of the Holy Name: ההה‎

(Right – *Chesed*)

veyishmerecha וְיִשְׁמְרֶךָ‎ Adonai יְהֹוָאהדוֹנָהי‎ yevarechecha יְבָרֶכְךָ‎

ר"ת = יהוה ; וס"ת = מ"ה:‎

(Left - *Gevurah*)

elecha אֵלֶיךָ‎ panav פָּנָיו‎ | Adonai יְהֹוָאהדוֹנָהי‎ ya'er יָאֵר‎ כף ויו זין ויו יוד‎

vichuneka וִיחֻנֶּךָּ‎ מנד ; יהה אותיות בפסוק:‎

(Central – *Tiferet*)

elecha אֵלֶיךָ‎ panav פָּנָיו‎ | Adonai יְהֹוָאהדוֹנָהי‎ yisa יִשָּׂא‎

veyasem וְיָשֵׂם‎ lecha לְךָ‎ shalom שָׁלוֹם‎ האא תיבות בפסוק:‎

(*Malchut*)

Yisrael יִשְׂרָאֵל‎ benei בְּנֵי‎ al עַל‎ shemi שְׁמִי‎ et אֶת‎ vesamu וְשָׂמוּ)‎

va'ani וַאֲנִי‎ אני‎ avarchem אֲבָרְכֵם‎:)

The *Kohanim* add in silence:

ha'olamim הָעוֹלָמִים‎ ribon רִבּוֹן‎ יהוה ע"ב ס"ג מ"ה ב"ן‎

Ata אַתָּה‎ ase עֲשֵׂה‎ alenu עָלֵינוּ‎ shegazarta שֶׁגָּזַרְתָּ‎ מ"ה‎ ma מַה‎ asinu עָשִׂינוּ‎

mime'on מִמְּעוֹן‎ hashkifa הַשְׁקִיפָה‎ shehivtachtanu שֶׁהִבְטַחְתָּנוּ:‎ מ"ה‎ ma מַה‎

hashamayim הַשָּׁמַיִם‎ min מִן‎ kodshecha קָדְשְׁךָ‎ י"פ טל, י"פ כוזו ; ר"ת מ"ה‎

Yisrael יִשְׂרָאֵל:‎ et אֶת‎ amecha עַמְּךָ‎ et אֶת‎ uvarech וּבָרֵךְ‎

Blessed are You, Lord, our God, King of the universe,
Who has sanctified us with the sanctity of Aaron, and has commanded us to bless His People, Israel, with love.
(Right) May the Lord bless you and protect you. (Amen)
(Left) May the Lord shine His Countenance upon you and be gracious to you. (Amen).
(Central) May the Lord lift His Face towards you and give you peace. (Amen)
(And they shall place My Name upon the Children of Israel and I shall bless them). (Numbers 6:24-27)
Master of the world, we have done what you have decreed for us. Now, You do as you promised us:
"Gaze down from your holy abode, from the heaven, and bless your people, Yisrael" (Devarim 26,15)

In this section there are 22 words, which is the numerical value of the Holy Name: אכא
You should medidtate on the following when the *chazan* says the first word of each verse:

Yevarechecha (first verse): אֵל נָא קָרֵב תְּשׁוּעַת בְּצִפִּיר (ר״ת אוּנְקְתָם)

Ya'er (second verse): פּוֹדְךָ סָר תּוֹצִיאֵם בְּמֵאֵסָר (ר״ת פָּסְתָם)

Yisa (third verse): פְּדֵה סוֹעִים פַּתּוּחַ סוּמִים יְשַׁעֵר בְּצִפִּים (ר״ת פַּסְפַּסִים)

malchuto מַלְכוּתוֹ *kevod* כְּבוֹד *shem* שֵׁם *baruch* בָּרוּךְ (whisper: יזו אותיות בפסוק) דְּלֵה יוּקְשִׁים וְקַבֵּץ נְפוּצִים סָמוּךְ לה׳ בְּמַפַּלְתָּם (ר״ת דִּיוּנָסִים)

va'ed וָעֶד (ריבוע ס״ג וי׳ אותיות דס״ג) *le'olam* לְעוֹלָם:

If you had a bad dream that is causing you distress, say the following while the *Kohanim* say their blessing:

ribono רִבּוֹנוֹ *shel* שֶׁל *olam* עוֹלָם *ani* אֲנִי *shelcha* שֶׁלְּךָ *vechalomotai* וַחֲלוֹמוֹתַי

shelcha. שֶׁלְּךָ *chalom* חֲלוֹם *chalamti* וְחָלַמְתִּי *ve'eni* וְאֵינִי *yode'a* יוֹדֵעַ *ma* מַה (מ״ה)

hu. הוּא *ben* בֵּין *shechalamti* שֶׁחָלַמְתִּי *ani* אֲנִי *le'atzmi* לְעַצְמִי *uven* וּבֵין

shechalmu שֶׁחָלְמוּ *li* לִי *acherim* אֲחֵרִים *uven* וּבֵין *she'ani* שֶׁאֲנִי *chalamti* וְחָלַמְתִּי

al עַל *acherim* אֲחֵרִים *im* אִם (יוהך, מ״א אותיות אהיה בפשוטו במילואו ובמילוי דמילואו ע״ה)

tovim טוֹבִים *hem* הֵם *chazkem* וְחַזְּקֵם *ve'amtzem* וְאַמְּצֵם *kachalomotav* כַּחֲלוֹמוֹתָיו

shel שֶׁל *Yosef* יוֹסֵף (קנאה, ר׳ הויות, ציון מ״א אותיות אהיה) *ve'im* וְאִם (יוהך, מ״א אותיות אהיה) *hatzadik* הַצַּדִּיק

tzerichim צְרִיכִים (בפשוטו במילואו ובמילוי דמילואו ע״ה) *refu'a* רְפוּאָה *refa'em* רְפָאֵם

kemei כְּמֵי *mara* מָרָה *al* עַל *yedei* יְדֵי *Moshe* מֹשֶׁה (מהע, ע״ב ברבוע וקס״א, אל שדי)

rabenu רַבֵּנוּ *alav* עָלָיו *hashalom* הַשָּׁלוֹם *uchmei* וּכְמֵי (ד״פ אלהים ע״ה)

Yericho יְרִיחוֹ *al* עַל *yedei* יְדֵי *Elisha* אֱלִישָׁע *ucheMiryam* וּכְמִרְיָם

mitzarata מִצָּרַעְתָּהּ *ucheNa'aman* וּכְנַעֲמָן *mitzarato* מִצָּרַעְתּוֹ *ucheChizkiyahu* וּכְחִזְקִיָּהוּ

mecholyo. מֵחָלְיוֹ *uchshem* וּכְשֵׁם *shehafachta* שֶׁהָפַכְתָּ *kilelat* קִלְלַת *Bil'am* בִּלְעָם

harasha הָרָשָׁע *livracha* לִבְרָכָה *ken* כֵּן *hafoch* הֲפוֹךְ *kol* כָּל *chalomotai* וַחֲלוֹמוֹתַי

alai עָלַי *ve'al* וְעַל *kol* כָּל *Yisrael* יִשְׂרָאֵל *letova* לְטוֹבָה אכא

velivracha וְלִבְרָכָה *vetirtzeni* וְתִרְצֵנִי *berachamecha* בְּרַחֲמֶיךָ *harabim.* הָרַבִּים

yihyu יִהְיוּ (מ״ב אותיות בפסוק) אל (יא״י מילוי דס״ג) *leratzon* לְרָצוֹן (מהע ע״ה, ע״ב ברבוע וקס״א)

imrei אִמְרֵי *fi* פִי (ר״ת אלף = אלף למד דלת שין דלת יוד ה״ה) *vehegyon* וְהֶגְיוֹן

libi לִבִּי *lefanecha* לְפָנֶיךָ (ס״ג מ״ה בן) יאהדונהי *Adonai* *tzuri* צוּרִי *vego'ali.* וְגֹאֲלִי

Master of the World! I am Yours and my dreams are Yours. I had a dream, but I do not know its meaning: whether I had dreamt about myself, or whether others dreamt about me, or whether I had dreamt about others. If they [my dreams] are good, then strengthen them and invigorate them, like the dreams of Joseph, the righteous one. If they require healing, then remedy them like the waters of Marah at the hands of Moses, our master, may peace be upon him, like the waters of Jericho at the hands of Elisha and like Miriam from her leprosy, like Na'aman from his leprosy, and like Chizkiyahu from his illness. And just as You have converted the curse of the wicked Bilaam into blessings, so, too, change my dreams, for my sake and for the sake of all Israel, into good and into blessing. Favor me with Your bountiful compassions. "May the utterances of my mouth and the thoughts oef my heart find favor before You, Lord, my Rock and my Redeemer." (Psalms 19:15)

THE FINAL BLESSING

We are emanating the energy of peace to the entire world. We also make it our intent to use our mouths only for good. Kabbalistically, the power of words and speech is unimaginable. We hope to use that power wisely, which is perhaps one of the most difficult tasks we have to carry out.

Yesod

sim עָשִׂים   shalom שָׂלוֹם

(During the three weeks of *Ben HaMetzarim*, meditate here on these Holy Names:

עֵין ראשׁוֹנָה (ע"ה = טדהד כוו מצפצ) ממתקת את העֵין העֶניה (= אלהֵים דההֵן אדנֵי) ;

וכֵן עֵים שׁלום ע"ה = ו העֹלמות (טדהד כוו מצפצ אלהֵים אדנֵי יהוה) אדנֵי טדהד כוו מצפצ ואלהֵים דההֵן)

chen חֵן   chayim וְחַיִּים   uvracha וּבְרָכָה   tova טוֹבָה

tzedaka צְדָקָה   vachesed וָחֶסֶד

ve'al וְעַל   alenu עָלֵינוּ   verachamim וְרַחֲמִים

kulanu כֻּלָּנוּ   avinu אָבִינוּ   uvarchenu וּבָרְכֵנוּ   amecha עַמֶּךָ   Yisrael יִשְׂרָאֵל

ki כִּי   panecha פָּנֶיךָ   be'or בְּאוֹר   ke'echad כְּאֶחָד

ve'or בְּאוֹר   lanu לָנוּ   natata נָתַתָּ   panecha פָּנֶיךָ

vechayim וְחַיִּים   torah תּוֹרָה   Elohenu אֱלֹהֵינוּ   Adonai יְהֹוָה

vachesed וָחֶסֶד   ahava אַהֲבָה

beracha בְּרָכָה   verachamim וְרַחֲמִים   tzedaka צְדָקָה

be'enecha בְּעֵינֶיךָ   vetov וְטוֹב   veshalom וְשָׁלוֹם

amecha עַמֶּךָ   kol כָּל   et אֶת   ulvarech וּלְבָרֵךְ   levarchenu לְבָרְכֵנוּ

veshalom וְשָׁלוֹם   oz עֹז   berov בְּרֹב   Yisrael יִשְׂרָאֵל

THE FINAL BLESSING

Place peace, goodness, blessing, life, grace, kindness, righteousness, and mercy upon us and upon all of Israel, Your People. Bless us all as one, our Father, with the Light of Your Countenance, because it is with the Light of Your Countenance that You, Lord, our God, have given us Torah and life, love and kindness, righteousness and mercy, blessing and peace. May it be good in Your Eyes to bless us and to bless Your entire Nation, Israel, with abundant power and with peace.

During the days between *Rosh Hashanah* and *Yom Kippur* we say the prayer of "*uvsefer chayim*":

ע"ה	בינה	יהוה, אהיה	אהיה	chayim וְחַיִּים	uvsefer וּבְסֵפֶר
אכא	tova טוֹבָה	ufarnasa וּפַרְנָסָה	veshalom וְשָׁלוֹם	beracha בְּרָכָה
◆tovot טוֹבוֹת	ugzerot וּגְזֵרוֹת	venechama וְנֶחָמָה	vishu'a וִישׁוּעָה
ב"ן מ"ה ס"ג	lefanecha לְפָנֶיךָ	venikatev וְנִכָּתֵב	nizacher נִזָּכֵר
Yisrael יִשְׂרָאֵל	amecha עַמְּךָ	ילי vechol וְכֹל	anachnu אֲנַחְנוּ
ulshalom וּלְשָׁלוֹם:	tovim טוֹבִים	ע"ה, בינה יהוה, אהיה אהיה	lechayim לְחַיִּים

If you forgot to say "*uvsefer chayim*" and realize this before the end of the blessing ("*baruch Ata Adonai*"), you should return and say "*uvsefer chayim*" and continue as usual. But if you realize this only after the end of the blessing, you should continue and you may add "*uvsefer chayim*" in the end of "*Elohai netzor*".

Adonai יְהֹוִהּוּוּהּוֹאדניאהדונהי Ata אַתָּה baruch בָּרוּךְ

Yisrael יִשְׂרָאֵל amo עַמּוֹ et אֶת hamevarech הַמְבָרֵךְ

amen אָמֵן יאהדונהי ◆bashalom בְּשָׁלוֹם (יב"ק) = אלהים (אילההויהם) ר"ת

YIH'YU LERATZON

There are 42 letters in the verse in the secret of *Ana Beko'ach*.

yih'yu יִהְיוּ אל (ייא"י מילוי דס"ג) leratzon לְרָצוֹן מהע ע"ה, ע"ב ברבוע וקס"א ע"ה, אל שדי ע"ה

imrei אִמְרֵי fi פִי ר"ת אֶלֶף = אלף למד עין דלת יוד ע"ה vehegyon וְהֶגְיוֹן libi לִבִּי

lefanecha לְפָנֶיךָ ס"ג מ"ה ב"ן Adonai יְהֹוִהּוֹאדניאהדונהי tzuri צוּרִי vego'ali וְגֹאֲלִי:

ELOHAI NETZOR

You should kiss the Head *Tefilin* here.

Elohai אֱלֹהַי מילוי ע"ב, דמב; ילה netzor נְצוֹר leshoni לְשׁוֹנִי mera מֵרָע◆

vesiftotai וְשִׂפְתוֹתַי midaber מִדַּבֵּר ראה mirma מִרְמָה◆ וְלִבְמְקַלְלַי velimkalelai

nafshi נַפְשִׁי tidom תִדּוֹם◆ venafshi וְנַפְשִׁי ke'afar כֶּעָפָר

lakol לַכֹּל יה אדני tih'ye תִהְיֶה◆ petach פְּתַח libi לִבִּי betoratecha בְּתוֹרָתֶךָ◆

During the days between *Rosh Hashanah* and *Yom Kippur*:

And in the Book of Life, for blessing, peace, good livelihood, salvation, consolation, and good decrees, may we all be remembered and be inscribed before You: we and Your entire Nation, Israel, for good life and for peace.

Blessed are You, Lord, Who blesses His Nation, Israel, with peace, Amen.

YIH'YU LERATZON

"May the utterances of my mouth and the thoughts of my heart find favor before You, Lord, my Rock and my Redeemer." (Psalms 19:15)

ELOHAI NETZOR

My God, guard my tongue from evil and my lips from speaking deceit. To those who curse me, let my spirit remain silent, and let my spirit be as dust for everyone. Open my heart to Your Torah

וְאַחֲרֵי ve'acharei בְּמִצְוֹתֶיךָ mitzvotecha תִרְדּוֹף tirdof נַפְשִׁי nafshi•

וְכָל־ vechol יְלֵי הַקָּמִים hakamim עָלַי alai לְרָעָה lera'a רָעָע• מְהֵרָה mehera

הָפֵר hafer עֲצָתָם atzatam וְקַלְקֵל vekalkel מַחְשְׁבוֹתָם machshevotam•

עֲשֵׂה ase לְמַעַן lema'an שְׁמֶךָ shemach• עֲשֵׂה ase לְמַעַן lema'an

יְמִינֶךָ yeminach• עֲשֵׂה ase לְמַעַן lema'an תוֹרָתֶךָ toratach• עֲשֵׂה ase

לְמַעַן lema'an קְדֻשָּׁתֶךָ kedushatach• ר"ת הפסוק = מ"ה יהוה לְמַעַן lema'an

יֵחָלְצוּן yechaltzun יְדִידֶיךָ yedidecha ר"ת ילי יהוה הוֹשִׁיעָה hoshi'a יהוה וע"ע נוהרין

יְמִינְךָ yemincha וַעֲנֵנִי va'aneni (כתיב: וענני) ר"ת אל (ייא"י מילוי דס"ג) יְמִינֶךָ•

Before we recite the next verse ("*yih'yu leratzon*") we have an opportunity to strengthen our connection to our soul using our name. Each person has a verse in the *Torah* that connects to their name. Either their name is in the verse, or the first and last letters of the name correspond to the first or last letters of a verse. For example, the name Yehuda begins with a *Yud* and ends with a *Hei*. Before we end the *Amidah*, we state that our name will always be remembered when our soul leaves this world.

YIH'YU LERATZON (THE SECOND)
There are 42 letters in the verse in the secret of *Ana Beko'ach*.

יִהְיוּ yih'yu אל (ייא"י מילוי דס"ג) לְרָצוֹן leratzon מהוע ע"ה, ע"ב בריבוע וקס"א ע"ה, אל שדי ע"ה

אִמְרֵי־ imrei פִּי fi ר"ת אֱלֶף = אלף למד עין דלת יוד ע"ה וְהֶגְיוֹן vehegyon לִבִּי libi

לְפָנֶיךָ lefanecha ס"ג מ"ה ב"ן יְהֹוָאדֹנָהיאהדונהי Adonai צוּרִי tzuri וְגֹאֲלִי vego'ali•

OSE SHALOM
We now take three steps backward to draw the Light of the World of Emanation (*Atzilut*) into our life. These steps are to move away from the World of *Atzilut* through the three Worlds of *Beriah*, *Yetzirah* and *Asiyah*.

We bow to the Left, Right and Centre, because we have learned that Nebuchadnezzar took three steps in honor of God and thereby merited to become a king (who later destroyed the Holy Temple). We should meditate that by taking these three steps backwards, the destroyed Holy Temple shall be rebuilt once again.

---

and let my heart pursue Your commandments. All those who rise against me to do me harm, speedily nullify their plans and disturb their thoughts. Do so for the sake of Your Name. Do so for the sake of Your Right. Do so for the sake of Your Torah. Do so for the sake of Your Holiness, "So that Your loved ones may be saved. Redeem Your right and answer me." (Psalms 60:7)

YIH'YU LERATZON (THE SECOND)
"May the utterances of my mouth and the thoughts of my heart find favor before You, Lord, my Rock and my Redeemer." (Psalms 19:15)

You take three steps backward;

ose עֹשֶׂה שָׁלוֹם shalom

(**During the days between** *Rosh Hashanah* **and** *Yom Kippur* **instead of** "*shalom*" **we say:**

Left

You turn to the left and say:

הַשָׁלוֹם hashalom ספריאל המלאך הווחם לחיים)

בִּמְרוֹמָיו bimromav ר"ת ע"ב, ריבוע יהוה

הוּא hu יַעֲשֶׂה verachamav בְּרַחֲמָיו ya'ase

Right

You turn to the right and say:

שָׁלוֹם shalom עָלֵינוּ alenu ר"ת ש"ע נהורין

Center

You face the center and say:

וְעַל ve'al כָּל kol; יּלי עַמּוֹ amo עמם; יִשְׂרָאֵל Yisrael

וְאִמְרוּ ve'imru אָמֵן amen: יאהדונהי

יְהִי yehi רָצוֹן ratzon מהש ע"ה, ע"ב, בריבוע וקס"א ע"ה, ע"ה עדי אל ע"ה

מִלְפָנֶיךָ milfanecha ס"ג מ"ה ב"ן יָהֹדֿוֻנָהִיֵאהדונהי Adonai אֲדֹנָי Elohenu אֱלֹהֵינוּ ילה

וֵאלֹהֵי velohei יּלה; ע"ב, דמב; לכב מילוי avotenu אֲבוֹתֵינוּ, שֶׁתִּבְנֶה shetivne

בֵּית bet ב"פ ראה הַמִקְדָּשׁ hamikdash בִּמְהֵרָה bimhera בְּיָמֵינוּ veyamenu

וְתֵן veten וְזַלְקֵנוּ chelkenu בְּתוֹרָתֶךָ betoratach לַעֲשׂוֹת la'asot וְחֻקֵּי chukei

רְצוֹנֶךָ retzonach וּלְעָבְדָךְ ul'ovdach פוי, אל אדני בְּלֵבָב belevav שָׁלֵם shalem בכו

You take three steps forward.

On regular days we say here "*yehi shem*" followed by half *Kaddish* on pg. 228.
During the days between *Rosh Hashanah* **and** *Yom Kippur* we say here "*Avinu Malkenu*" (pg. 225-227).
On *Rosh Chodesh* **or on** *Chanukah* we say here "*Halel*" (on pg. 446).

OSE SHALOM

He, Who makes peace (During the days between *Rosh Hashanah* and *Yom Kippur*: *The peace*) *in His high places, He, in His compassion, shall make peace upon us And upon His entire nation, Israel, and you shall say, Amen.*

May it be pleasing before You,
Lord, our God and God of our forefathers, that You shall rebuild the Temple speedily, in our days, and place our lot in Your Torah, so that we may fulfill the laws of Your desire and serve You wholeheartedly.

AVINU MALKENU

Between Rosh Hashanah and Yom Kippur, we recite the prayer of "Avinu Malkenu."

We ask for specific things from the Creator because if we don't ask, we cannot receive even what we deserve.

אָבִינוּ Avinu (יְהֹוָה) מַלְכֵּנוּ Malkenu (יְהֹוָה)

rachem רַחֵם ב"ן מ"ה ס"ג lefanecha לְפָנֶיךָ chatanu וְחָטָאנוּ

alenu עָלֵינוּ אותיות פשוטות, עסמ"ב וט"ו (אברים), רמ"ח נתיבות החכמה, רי"ו ול"ב אל, וח"פ אברהם,

אָבִינוּ Avinu (יְהֹוָה) מַלְכֵּנוּ Malkenu (יְהֹוָה)

ata אָתָּה ela אֶלָּא melech מֶלֶךְ אדני אהיה אלהים, lanu לָנוּ en אֵין

אָבִינוּ Avinu (יְהֹוָה) מַלְכֵּנוּ Malkenu (יְהֹוָה)

shemecha שְׁמֶךָ lema'an לְמַעַן אותיות וד' ע"ה קס"א ס"ג, ריבוע imanu עִמָּנוּ ase עֲשֵׂה

אָבִינוּ Avinu (יְהֹוָה) מַלְכֵּנוּ Malkenu (יְהֹוָה)

אכא tova טוֹבָה shana שָׁנָה alenu עָלֵינוּ קנ"א קס"א, הויות י"ב chadesh וְדֵּשׁ

אָבִינוּ Avinu (יְהֹוָה) מַלְכֵּנוּ Malkenu (יְהֹוָה)

veraot וְרָעוֹת kashot קָשׁוֹת gezerot גְּזֵרוֹת kol כָּל־ ילי me'alenu מֵעָלֵינוּ batel בַּטֵּל

אָבִינוּ Avinu (יְהֹוָה) מַלְכֵּנוּ Malkenu (יְהֹוָה)

son'enu שׂוֹנְאֵינוּ mach'shevot מַחְשְׁבוֹת batel בַּטֵּל

אָבִינוּ Avinu (יְהֹוָה) מַלְכֵּנוּ Malkenu (יְהֹוָה)

oyveinu אוֹיְבֵינוּ atzat עֲצַת hafer הָפֵר

אָבִינוּ Avinu (יְהֹוָה) מַלְכֵּנוּ Malkenu (יְהֹוָה)

me'alenu מֵעָלֵינוּ umastin וּמַשְׂטִין tzar צַר ילי kol כָּל־ kale כַּלֵּה

אָבִינוּ Avinu (יְהֹוָה) מַלְכֵּנוּ Malkenu (יְהֹוָה)

vera'av וְרָעָב רהע vera'a וְרָעָה רי"י vecherev וְחֶרֶב dever דֶּבֶר kale כַּלֵּה

veyetzer וְיֵצֶר (נגף) umagefa וּמַגֵּפָה umashchit וּמַשְׁחִית uviza וּבִזָּה ushvi וּשְׁבִי

veritecha בְּרִיתֶךָ mibnei מִבְּנֵי ra'im רָעִים vechola'im וְחֳלָאִים hara הָרָע

אָבִינוּ Avinu (יְהֹוָה) מַלְכֵּנוּ Malkenu (יְהֹוָה)

אדני יה lechol לְכָל־ shelema שְׁלֵמָה refu'a רְפוּאָה shelach שְׁלַח

amecha עַמֶּךָ העם אותיות וד' מ"ה = חולה cholei וְחוֹלֵי

AVINU MALKENU

Our Father, our King, we have sinned before You, have mercy over us.
Our Father, our King, we have no other king but You. Our Father, our King, deal with us for the sake of Your Name.
Our Father, our King, renew a good year for us. Our Father, our King, nullify from us all hard and evil decrees.
Our Father, our King, nullify the thoughts of our haters. Our Father, our King, thwart the plans of our enemies.
Our Father, our King, annihilate any oppressor and accuser from over us. Our Father, our King, annihilate pestilence,
sword, evil, famine, captivity, plunder, ruin, plague, evil inclination and terrible diseases from the members of Your Covenant.
Our Father, our King, send complete healing to all the sick among Your nation.

אָבִינוּ Avinu (יְהֹוָה) מַלְכֵּנוּ Malkenu (יְהֹוָה)

מְנַע mena מַגֵּפָה magefa (נֶגֶף) מִנַּחֲלָתֶךָ minachalatecha:

אָבִינוּ Avinu (יְהֹוָה) מַלְכֵּנוּ Malkenu (יְהֹוָה)

זְכוֹר zachur ע"ב קס"א, יהי אור ע"ה כִּי ki עָפָר afar אֲנָחְנוּ anachnu:

אָבִינוּ Avinu (יְהֹוָה) מַלְכֵּנוּ Malkenu (יְהֹוָה)

מְחוֹל mechol וּסְלַח uslach יהוה ע"ב לְכָל lechol יה אדני עֲווֹנוֹתֵינוּ avonotenu:

אָבִינוּ Avinu (יְהֹוָה) מַלְכֵּנוּ Malkenu (יְהֹוָה)

קְרַע kera יכוין בעם קרע שטן רוֹעַ ro'a גְּזַר gezar דִּינֵנוּ dinenu:

אָבִינוּ Avinu (יְהֹוָה) מַלְכֵּנוּ Malkenu (יְהֹוָה)

מְחוֹק mechok בְּרַחֲמֶיךָ berachamecha הָרַבִּים harabim

כָּל־ kol יבי שִׁטְרֵי shitrei וְחוֹבוֹתֵינוּ chovoteinu:

אָבִינוּ Avinu (יְהֹוָה) מַלְכֵּנוּ Malkenu (יְהֹוָה)

מְחֵה meche וְהַעֲבֵר veha'aver פְּשָׁעֵינוּ pesha'enu

מִנֶּגֶד mineged ז"ך, מזבוח, אל יהוה ע"ה עֵינֶיךָ enecha קס"א ע"ה ריבוע מ"ה:

אָבִינוּ Avinu (יְהֹוָה) מַלְכֵּנוּ Malkenu (יְהֹוָה)

כָּתְבֵנוּ kotvenu בְּסֵפֶר besefer וְחַיִּים chayim אהיה אהיה יהוה, בינה ע"ה טוֹבִים tovim:

אָבִינוּ Avinu (יְהֹוָה) מַלְכֵּנוּ Malkenu (יְהֹוָה)

כָּתְבֵנוּ kotvenu בְּסֵפֶר besefer צַדִּיקִים tzadikim וַחֲסִידִים vachasidim:

אָבִינוּ Avinu (יְהֹוָה) מַלְכֵּנוּ Malkenu (יְהֹוָה)

כָּתְבֵנוּ kotvenu בְּסֵפֶר besefer יְשָׁרִים yesharim וּתְמִימִים utmimim:

אָבִינוּ Avinu (יְהֹוָה) מַלְכֵּנוּ Malkenu (יְהֹוָה)

כָּתְבֵנוּ kotvenu בְּסֵפֶר besefer פַּרְנָסָה parnasa וְכַלְכָּלָה vechalkala טוֹבָה tova אכא:

יְהִי yehi רָצוֹן ratzon מהטע ע"ה, ע"ב בריבוע וקס"א ע"ה, אל שדי ע"ה

מִלְּפָנֶיךָ milfanecha ס"ג מ"ה ב"ן יְהוֹאדֹנָהי Adonai אֱלֹהֵינוּ Elohenu ילה

וֵאלֹהֵי velohei מילוי ע"ב, דמב ; ילה אֲבוֹתֵינוּ avotenu שֶׁתִּתֵּן shetiten ב"פ כהת

לָנוּ lanu אלהים, אהיה אדני וּלְכָל ulechol יה אדני בְּנֵי benei בֵּיתֵנוּ betenu

וּלְכָל ulechol יה אדני הַסְּמוּכִים hasemuchim עַל al שֻׁלְחָנֵנוּ shulchanenu

הַיּוֹם hayom ע"ה נגד, ז"ך, מזבוח, אל יהוה ב"ן, לכב וּבְכָל uvechol yom יוֹם

וְיוֹם veyom ויום אל יהוה ע"ה נגד, ז"ך, מזבוח, אל יהוה

mezonotenu מְזוֹנוֹתֵינוּ bechavod בְּכָבוֹד בּוֹכוּ bizchut בְּזֹכוּת shimcha שִׁמְךָ

hagadol הַגָּדוֹל לְהוּ ; עִם ד' אותיות = מבה, יֹל, אום (Do not pronounce דִּיקְרְנוֹסָא

al עַל הַפַּרְנָסָה :haparnasa hamemune הַמְמוּנֶה (יאהדונהי, אמן, סאל) ובאתב"ע אותיות ג' עם וחזר

Avinu אָבִינוּ (יְהֹוָה) Malkenu מַלְכֵּנוּ (יְהֹוָה)

kotvenu כָּתְבֵנוּ besefer בְּסֵפֶר mechila מְחִילָה uslicha וּסְלִיחָה vechapara וְכַפָּרָה:

Avinu אָבִינוּ (יְהֹוָה) Malkenu מַלְכֵּנוּ (יְהֹוָה)

kotvenu כָּתְבֵנוּ besefer בְּסֵפֶר ge'ula גְּאוּלָה vishua וִישׁוּעָה:

Avinu אָבִינוּ (יְהֹוָה) Malkenu מַלְכֵּנוּ (יְהֹוָה) zochrenu זָכְרֵנוּ

bezichron בְּזִכָּרוֹן tov טוֹב וה"ו ע"ב קס"א ע"ב וע"ד milfanecha מִלְּפָנֶיךָ ס"ג מ"ה ב"ן:

Avinu אָבִינוּ (יְהֹוָה) Malkenu מַלְכֵּנוּ (יְהֹוָה)

hatzmach הַצְמַח lanu לָנוּ אלהים, אהיה אדני yeshu'a יְשׁוּעָה bekarov בְּקָרוֹב:

Avinu אָבִינוּ (יְהֹוָה) Malkenu מַלְכֵּנוּ (יְהֹוָה)

harem הָרֵם keren קֶרֶן Yisrael יִשְׂרָאֵל amecha עַמֶּךָ:

Avinu אָבִינוּ (יְהֹוָה) Malkenu מַלְכֵּנוּ (יְהֹוָה)

veharem וְהָרֵם keren קֶרֶן meshichecha מְשִׁיחֶךָ:

Avinu אָבִינוּ (יְהֹוָה) Malkenu מַלְכֵּנוּ (יְהֹוָה) chonenu וְחָנֵנוּ va'anenu וַעֲנֵנוּ:

Avinu אָבִינוּ (יְהֹוָה) Malkenu מַלְכֵּנוּ (יְהֹוָה)

hachazirenu הַחֲזִירֵנוּ biteshuva בִּתְשׁוּבָה shelema שְׁלֵמָה lefanecha לְפָנֶיךָ ס"ג מ"ה ב"ן:

Avinu אָבִינוּ (יְהֹוָה) Malkenu מַלְכֵּנוּ (יְהֹוָה)

shema שְׁמַע kolenu קוֹלֵנוּ chus וְחוּס verachem וְרַחֵם אברהם, וז"פ אל, רי"ו ול"ב נתיבות החכמה, רמ"ח (אברים), עסמ"ב וט"ז אותיות פשוטות alenu עָלֵינוּ:

Avinu אָבִינוּ (יְהֹוָה) Malkenu מַלְכֵּנוּ (יְהֹוָה)

ase עֲשֵׂה lema'anach לְמַעֲנָךְ im אִם יוהך, מ"א אותיות אהיה בפשוטו, במילואו ובמילוי דמילואו ע"ה lo לֹא lema'anenu לְמַעֲנֵנוּ:

Avinu אָבִינוּ (יְהֹוָה) Malkenu מַלְכֵּנוּ (יְהֹוָה)

kabel קַבֵּל berachamim בְּרַחֲמִים מצפצ, אלהים דיודין, י"פ ייי uvratzon וּבְרָצוֹן et אֶת מהש ע"ה, ע"ב ברבוע וקס"א, אל שדי ע"ה tefilatenu תְּפִלָּתֵנוּ:

Avinu אָבִינוּ (יְהֹוָה) Malkenu מַלְכֵּנוּ (יְהֹוָה)

al אַל te'shivenu תְּשִׁיבֵנוּ rekam רֵיקָם milfanecha מִלְּפָנֶיךָ ס"ג מ"ה ב"ן:

---

our nourishment, with grace and by virtue of Your great Name, which is responsible for livelihood. Our Father, our King, write us in the book of forgiveness, pardon and atonement.
Our Father, our King, write us in the book of redemption and salvation. Our Father, our King, remember us favorably before You. Our Father, our King, sprout salvation for us soon. Our Father, our King, raise the worth of Israel, Your nation. Our Father, our King, raise the worth of Your Mashiach. Our Father, our King, be gracious to us and save us. Our Father, our King, cause our return with complete redemption before You. Our Father, our King, hear our voice. Take pity and be compassionate with us. Our Father, our King, do so for Your sake, if not for our sake. Our Father, our King, compassionately and willingly accept our prayer. Our Father, our King, do not turn us away from You empty-handed.

YEHI SHEM

יְהִי yehi שֵׁם shem יְהֹוָה Adonai מְבֹרָךְ mevorach ר"ת ריבוע ע"ב וריבוע ס"ג

יהוה מברך = רפ"ח (להעלות רפ"ח נִיצוֹצוֹת שנפלו לקליפה דמשם באים התחלואים) מֵעַתָּה me'ata

וְעַד ve'ad עוֹלָם olam יכ: מִמִזְרַח mimizrach שֶׁמֶשׁ shemesh עַד ad

מְבוֹאוֹ mevo'o מְהֻלָּל mehulal שֵׁם shem יְהֹוָה Adonai ר"ת קדוש

רָם ram עַל al כָּל kol יכ; עמם גּוֹיִם goyim יְהֹוָה Adonai עַל al

הַשָּׁמַיִם hashamayim י"פ טל, י"פ כוזו; ר"ת וחשמל כְּבוֹדוֹ kevodo:

יְהֹוָה Adonai אֲדֹנֵינוּ adonenu מַה ma מ"ה אַדִּיר adir הרי

שִׁמְךָ shimcha ב"ן, לכב; ומב הָאָרֶץ ha'aretz בְּכָל bechol ב"ן, ומב אלהים דההין ע"ה:

HALF KADDISH

This *Kaddish* draws the Light from the World of *Atzilut* (ע"ב) into the World of *Beriah* (ס"ג).

יִתְגַּדַּל yitgadal וְיִתְקַדַּשׁ veyitkadash שֹׁדִי ומילוי שֹׁדִי; י"א אותיות כמנין ו"ה

שְׁמֵיהּ shemei (שֵׁם י"ה דע"ב) רַבָּא raba קנ"א ב"ן, יהוה אלהים יהוה אדני,

אמן amen אֱמֶן: יב"ק: ס"ת = ג"פ יב"ק; ר"ת = ו"פ אלהים; מ"ה ברבוע וע"ב ע"ה; מילוי קס"א וס"ג, אידהנויה.

בְּעָלְמָא be'alma דִּי di בְּרָא vera כִרְעוּתֵיהּ chir'utei

וְיַמְלִיךְ veyamlich מַלְכוּתֵיהּ malchutei וְיַצְמַח veyatzmach

פּוּרְקָנֵיהּ purkanei וִיקָרֵב vikarev מְשִׁיחֵיהּ meshichei: אֱמֶן amen אידהנויה:

בְּחַיֵּיכוֹן bechayechon וּבְיוֹמֵיכוֹן uvyomechon וּבְחַיֵּי uvchayei

דְּכָל dechol בֵּית bet יכ ב"פ ראה יִשְׂרָאֵל Yisrael בַּעֲגָלָא ba'agala

וּבִזְמַן uvizman קָרִיב kariv וְאִמְרוּ ve'imru אֲמֵן amen: אֱמֶן amen אידהנויה:

YEHI SHEM

"May the Name of the Lord be blessed from now till all eternity. From sunrise till sundown, may the Name of the Lord be praised and elevated. Above all nations is the Lord. His glory is above the Heavens." (Psalms 113:2-4) "The Lord, our Master, how tremendous is Your Name in all the Earth." (Psalms 8:10)

HALF KADDISH

May His great Name be more exalted and sanctified. (Amen) In the world that He created according to His will, and may His Kingdom reign. And may He cause His redemption to sprout and may He bring the Mashiach closer. (Amen) In your lifetimes and in your days and in the lifetime of all the House of Israel, speedily and in the near future, and you shall say, Amen. (Amen)

The congregation and the *chazan* say the following:

28 words (until *be'alma*) – meditate:

(מילוי דמילוי דע״ב (יוד ויו דלת הי יוד ויו יוד ויו הי יוד)

28 letters (until *almaya*) - meditate:

(מילוי דמילוי דע״ב (יוד ויו דלת הי יוד ויו יוד ויו הי יוד)

קנ״א ב״ן, raba רַבָּא (שם י״ה דס״ג) shemei שְׁמֵיהּ yehe יְהֵא

מברך ע״ה ע״ב מילוי קס״א וס״ג, מ״ה ברבוע וע״ג, מילוי אדני, יהוה אלהים יהוה mevarach מְבָרַךְ,

yitbarach יִתְבָּרַךְ• almaya עָלְמַיָּא• le'almei לְעָלְמֵי le'alam לְעָלַם

Seven words with six letters each (שם בן מ״ב) meditate:

יהוה ← יוד הי ויו הי ← מילוי דמילוי דע״ב (יוד ויו דלת הי יוד ויו יוד ויו הי יוד)

Also, seven times the letter *Vav* (שם בן מ״ב) meditate:

יהוה ← יוד הי ויו הי ← מילוי דמילוי דע״ב (יוד ויו דלת הי יוד ויו יוד ויו הי יוד)

וְיִשְׁתַּבַּח veyishtabach י״פ ע״ב יהוה אל אבג יתץ•

וְיִתְפָּאַר הי גו יה קרע שטן• וְיִתְרֹמַם veyitromam וה כוזו נגד יכש• veyitpa'ar

וְיִתְנַשֵּׂא במוכסז בטר צתג• וְיִתְהַדָּר veyit'hadar כוזו יה וזקב טנע• veyitnase

וְיִתְעַלֶּה וה יוד ה יגל פזק• וְיִתְהַלָּל veyit'halal א ואו הא שקו צית• veyit'ale

הוּא hu• verich בְּרִיךְ dekudsha דְּקוּדְשָׁא (שם י״ה דמ״ה) shemei שְׁמֵיהּ

אָמֵן amen אידהנויה•

לְעֵלָּא le'ela• min מִן kol כָּל ילי birchata בִּרְכָתָא• shirata שִׁירָתָא•

da'amiran דַּאֲמִירָן venechamata וְנֶחָמָתָא• tishbechata תֻּשְׁבְּחָתָא

amen אידהנויה• amen אָמֵן• amen אָמֵן ve'imru וְאִמְרוּ be'alma בְּעָלְמָא

May His great Name be blessed forever and for all eternity.
Blessed and lauded, and glorified, and exalted, and extolled, and honored, and uplifted, and praised be the Name of the Holy Blessed One. (Amen) Above all blessings, songs, praises, and words of consolation that may be said in the world, and you shall say, Amen. (Amen)

SHACHARIT – MORNING PRAYER
THE ORDER OF THE TORAH READING

We read the *Torah* on Monday, Thursday, *Rosh Chodesh*, *Chanukah* and *Purim*.

It is said that one should never go more than three days without making a connection to the Torah. Going for more than three days without connecting to the Torah will result in a complete disconnection from the Light of the Creator. We connect to the Torah on Shabbat (Saturdays), Mondays and Thursdays to nourish our spiritual umbilical chord to the Light.

אָל (מילוי דס״ג) יא״י El chesed וְחֶסֶד verav וְרַב apayim אַפַּיִם erech אֶרֶךְ (דס״ג) ע״ב, ריבוע יהוה

tochichenu תוֹכִיחֵנוּ be'apcha בְּאַפְּךָ al אַל (אהיה פעמים אהיה, ז״פ ס״ג). ve'emet וֶאֱמֶת

amecha עַמְּךָ Yisrael יִשְׂרָאֵל al עַל Adonai יְהֹוָאדנִיאהדונהי chusa חוּסָה

adon אֲדוֹן אני lecha לְךָ chatanu חָטָאנוּ. וְטָאנוּ ra רָע יּלי mikol מִכָּל vehoshi'enu וְהוֹשִׁיעֵנוּ

selach סְלַח יהוה ע״ב (מילוי דס״ג) na נָא. kerov כְּרוֹב rachamecha רַחֲמֶיךָ El אֵל יא״י (מילוי דס״ג):

אֵל יא״י (מילוי דס״ג) El rachamim רַחֲמִים umale וּמְלֵא apayim אַפַּיִם erech אֶרֶךְ (דס״ג)

al אַל taster תַּסְתֵּר panecha פָּנֶיךָ ב״פ מצר מ״ה ב״ן ס״ג mimenu מִמֶּנוּ. chusa חוּסָה

amecha עַמְּךָ Yisrael יִשְׂרָאֵל she'erit שְׁאֵרִית al עַל Adonai יְהֹוָאדנִיאהדונהי

adon אֲדוֹן אני lecha לְךָ. chatanu חָטָאנוּ. וְטָאנוּ ra רָע יּלי mikol מִכָּל vehatzilenu וְהַצִּילֵנוּ

selach סְלַח יהוה ע״ב (מילוי דס״ג) na נָא. kerov כְּרוֹב rachamecha רַחֲמֶיךָ El אֵל יא״י (מילוי דס״ג):

On the days we do not recite *Tachanun*, we begin here:

imanu עִמָּנוּ ילה Elohenu אֱלֹהֵינוּ Adonai יְהֹוָאדנִיאהדונהי yehi יְהִי

im עִם יהה haya הָיָה ka'asher כַּאֲשֶׁר ו ד' אותיות ע״ה קס״א ס״ג, ריבוע

yiteshenu יִטְּשֵׁנוּ ve'al וְאַל ya'azvenu יַעַזְבֵנוּ al אַל avotenu אֲבֹתֵינוּ

hoshi'a הוֹשִׁיעָה יהוה ועו״ע נהורין ס״ת כהת, משיח בן דוד ע״ה amecha עַמֶּךָ et אֶת

venase'em וְנַשְּׂאֵם ure'em וּרְעֵם nachalatecha נַחֲלָתֶךָ et אֶת uvarech וּבָרֵךְ

avdecha עַבְדְּךָ David דָּוִד ba'avur בַּעֲבוּר ha'olam הָעוֹלָם ad עַד

meshichecha מְשִׁיחֶךָ penei פָּנֵי וזכמה בינה tashev תָּשֵׁב al אַל פוי, אל אדני

le'amo לְעַמּוֹ torah תּוֹרָה shenatan שֶׁנָּתַן hamakom הַמָּקוֹם baruch בָּרוּךְ

ha'am הָעָם ashrei אַשְׁרֵי hu הוּא baruch בָּרוּךְ Yisrael יִשְׂרָאֵל

lo לוֹ מהע, משה, ע״ב בריבוע וקס״א, אל עודי, ד״פ אלהים ע״ה shekacha שֶׁכָּכָה

ashrei אַשְׁרֵי ha'am הָעָם ר״ת לאה שֶׁיְהֹוָאדנִיאהדונהי sheAdonai Elohav אֱלֹהָיו ילה:

God, Who is slow to anger and Who abounds in kindness and truth. Do not admonish us with Your anger. Take pity, Lord, on Israel, Your Nation, and save us from evil. We have sinned against You, our Master. God, forgive us in accordance with Your abounding compassion. God, Who is slow to anger and Who abounds in kindness, do not conceal Your Countenance from us. Take pity, Lord, on the remnant of Israel, Your Nation, and save us from all evil. We have sinned against You, our Master. Please forgive us according to Your abounding compassion, God.

"May the Lord, our God, be with us as He was with our forefathers. May He not abandon or forsake us." (I Kings 8:57) *"Save Your People and bless Your Heritage. Lead them and uplift them forever."* (Psalms 28:9) *"For the sake of David, Your servant, do not turn Your Countenance away from Your anointed one."* (Psalms 132:10) *Blessed is the Omnipresent, Who gave the Torah to His People, Israel. Blessed is He.* *"Joyful is the nation that this is theirs and joyful the nation that the Lord is their God."* (Psalms 144:15)

OPENING OF THE ARK

Drawing the Light of *Chochmah*.

Rabbi Shimon Bar Yochai says: "While the Ark is open, we should prepare ourselves with awe. Everyone should arouse an inner sense of wonder, as if we are actually standing on Mount Sinai, trembling as we behold the overwhelming expression of Light. Silent we stand, focused solely on the opportunity of hearing each sacred word of the scroll. When we take out the Torah in public to read, all the Gates of Mercy in Heaven are open, and we awaken a love from above."

Moshe מֹשֶׁה vayomer וַיֹּאמֶר ha'aron הָאָרֹן binso'a בִּנְסֹעַ vayhi וַיְהִי

(מקוה) קנ"א kuma קוּמָה ע"ה אלהים ד"פ עֹדִי, אֶל וְקֹסְ"א, בְּרִיבוּעַ ע"ב, מהטע, |

veyanusu וְיָנֻסוּ oyvecha אֹיְבֶיךָ veyafutzu וְיָפֻצוּ Adonai יְהוָֹה

ki כִּי ב"ן: מ"ה ס"ג mipanecha מִפָּנֶיךָ mesan'echa מְשַׂנְאֶיךָ

ראה udvar וּדְבַר torah תוֹרָה tetze תֵּצֵא קֹנאה, היוית, ר יוסף, miTziyon מִצִּיּוֹן

shenatan שֶׁנָּתַן baruch בָּרוּךְ mirushalaim מִירוּשָׁלָם: Adonai יְהוָֹה

bikdushato בִּקְדֻשָּׁתוֹ◆ Yisrael יִשְׂרָאֵל le'amo לְעַמּוֹ torah תוֹרָה

BERICH SHEMEI

This section is taken directly from the *Zohar* and appears in its original Aramaic. The *Berich Shemei* works like a time machine that literally transports our soul to Mount Sinai, when Moses received the tablets. By revisiting the exact time and place of the revelation, we are able to draw down aspects of the original Light through the reading of the Torah. The *Berich Shemei* contains 130 words. Adam was separated from his wife, Eve, for 130 years during which time he sinned. Each word in the prayer helps to correct one of those years. Each of us was included in the soul of Adam. We are Adam. Adam is merely the code name of the unified soul that includes every human being who has and will ever walk this planet.

berich בְּרִיךְ alma עָלְמָא demarei דְּמָארֵי shemei שְׁמֵיהּ berich בְּרִיךְ

im עִם re'utach רְעוּתָךְ yehe יְהֵא ve'atrach וְאַתְרָךְ◆ kitrach כִּתְרָךְ

yeminach יְמִינָךְ ufurkan וּפוּרְקָן le'alam לְעָלַם◆ Yisrael יִשְׂרָאֵל amach עַמָּךְ

mikdashach מִקְדְּשָׁךְ◆ בּ"פ ראה bevet בְּבֵית le'amach לְעַמָּךְ achzei אַחֲזֵי

OPENING OF THE ARK

"When the Ark traveled forward, Moses would say: Arise, Lord. Let Your enemies be scattered and let those who hate You flee before You." (Numbers 10:35) *"Because out of Zion shall the Torah emerge, and the Word of the Lord from Jerusalem."* (Isaiah 2:3) *Blessed is He Who gave the Torah to His Nation, Israel, due to His Holiness.*

BERICH SHEMEI

Blessed is the Name

of the Master of the World. Blessed are Your Crown and Your Location. May Your desire be with Your Nation, Israel, forever. The redemption of Your Right may You show to Your Nation in Your Temple.

ulkabel וּלְקַבֵּל • nehorach נְהוֹרָךְ mituv מִטּוּב lana לָנָא le'amtuye לְאַמְטוּיֵי

ra'ava רַעֲוָא yehe יְהֵא • berachamin בְּרַחֲמִין tzelotana צְלוֹתָנָא

• betivu בְּטִיבוּ chayin וְחַיִּין lan כָּן detorich דְּתוֹרִיךְ kodamach קֳדָמָךְ

pekida פְּקִידָא פוי, אל אדני avdach עַבְדָּךְ ב"ן ana אֲנָא velehevei וְלֶהֱוֵי

בְּגוֹ bego צַדִּיקַיָּא tzadikaya אברהם, וח"פ אל, רי"ו ול"ב נחובות lemircham לְמִרְחַם • tzadikaya

yati יָתִי ulmintar וּלְמִנְטַר alai עֲלֵי עסמ"ב וט"ז אותיות פשוטות (אברים), רמ"ח הוחכמה,

• Yisrael יִשְׂרָאֵל le'amach לְעַמָּךְ vedi וְדִי dili דִּילִי kal כָּל veyat וְיָת

umfarnes וּמְפַרְנֵס lechola לְכֹלָּא גָּר, מזבח, אל יהוה zan זָן hu הוּא ant אַנְתְּ

ant אַנְתְּ • kola כֹּלָּא al עַל shalit שַׁלִּיט hu הוּא ant אַנְתְּ • lechola לְכֹלָּא

umalchuta וּמַלְכוּתָא malchaya מַלְכַיָּא al עַל deshalit דְּשַׁלִּיט hu הוּא

dekudsha דְּקוּדְשָׁא avda עַבְדָּא ב"ן ana אֲנָא • hee הִיא dilach דִּילָךְ

kame קַמֵּהּ umin וּמִן kame קַמֵּהּ desagidna דְּסָגִידְנָא hu הוּא berich בְּרִיךְ

• ve'idan וְעִידָן idan עִידָן ב"ן, לכב bechol בְּכֹל orayte אוֹרַיְתֵהּ dikar דִּיקַר

al עַל vela וְלָא • rachitzna רָחִיצְנָא enash אֱנָשׁ al עַל la לָא

be'elaha בֵּאלָהָא ela אֶלָּא • samichna סָמִיכְנָא ילה elahin אֱלָהִין bar בַּר

• keshot קְשׁוֹט elaha אֱלָהָא dehu דְּהוּא • dishmaya דִּשְׁמַיָּא

• keshot קְשׁוֹט unvi'ohi וּנְבִיאוֹהִי keshot קְשׁוֹט ve'orayte וְאוֹרַיְתֵהּ

• ukshot וּקְשׁוֹט tavevan טָבְוָן lemebad לְמֶעְבַּד umasgei וּמַסְגֵּי

yakira יַקִּירָא velishme וְלִשְׁמֵהּ rachitz רָחִיץ ב"ן ana אֲנָא bei בֵּהּ

• tushbechan תֻּשְׁבְּחָן emar אֲמַר ב"ן ana אֲנָא kadisha קַדִּישָׁא

May You fill us with the best of Your enlightenment, and may You receive our prayers with mercy. May it be pleasing before You to lengthen our lives with good. And I, Your servant, shall be remembered together with the righteous ones. Have mercy on me and protect me, and all that I have, and all that belongs to Your Nation, Israel. You are the One Who nourishes all and provides all with their livelihood. You are the One Who controls everything. You have control over kings, and their kingdoms are Yours. I am the servant of the Holy Blessed One, as I prostrate myself before Him and before the glory of His Torah, at each and every moment. I put not my trust in any man, and I have no faith in the sons of the gods. My trust and faith are only in the God in Heaven, Who is the true God; His Torah is true; His prophets are true; and He abundantly performs compassion and truth. In Him, I trust and I say praises to His Holy and precious Name.

liba'i לְבָּאִי detiftach דְּתִתְפְּתַּח kodamach קֳדָמָךְ ra'ava רַעֲוָא yehe יְהֵא

dichrin דִּכְרִין benin בְּנִין li לִי vetihav (וְתִיהַב) ✦be'oraytach בְּאוֹרַיְתָךְ

mish'alin מִשְׁאֲלִין vetashlim וְתַשְׁלִים (✦re'utach רְעוּתָךְ) de'avdin דְעָבְדִין

Yisrael יִשְׂרָאֵל amach עַמָּךְ יִלִי dechol דְּכָל veliba וְלִבָּא deliba'i דְלִבָּאִי

יאהדונהי amen אָמֵן velishlam וְלִשְׁלָם ulchayin וּלְחַיִּין letav לְטַב

TAKING OUT THE TORAH FROM THE ARK

The *Torah* is taken out to give us all a chance to make a personal connection with it, either by kissing or touching it. Sometimes, people rush to make their connection, pushing, crowding, and shoving others aside as they try to touch the scroll. Spiritually, these actions reflect energy opposite to that of the *Torah*. The *Torah* connection is not just physical. Connections to the *Torah* are made by way of a spiritual state of mind, which includes tolerance and care for others. One cannot be in the right spiritual frame of mind if he is rude to another individual.

Before the Torah is carried to the bimah (podium), the chazan says:

uneromema וּנְרוֹמְמָה iti אִתִּי ladonai לַיְהֹוָואדנייאהדונהי gadelu גַּדְּלוּ

מהש ע"ה, ע"ב ברביבוע וקס"א ע"ה, אל עדי ע"ה ✦yachdav יַחְדָּו shemo שְׁמוֹ

Then the congregation says the following while the Torah is carried to the bimah:

רי"ו vehagevura וְהַגְּבוּרָה hagedula הַגְּדֻלָּה Adonai יְהֹוָואדנייאהדונהי lecha לְךָ

ki כִּי הההה vehahod וְהַהוֹד vehanetzach וְהַנֵּצַח vehatiferet וְהַתִּפְאֶרֶת

lecha לְךָ uva'aretz וּבָאָרֶץ י"פ טל, י"פ כוזו bashamayim בַּשָּׁמַיִם יִלִי chol כָּל

vehamitnase וְהַמִּתְנַשֵּׂא hamamlacha הַמַּמְלָכָה Adonai יְהֹוָואדנייאהדונהי

romemu רוֹמְמוּ ריבוע אלהים ואלהים ואלהים דיודין ע"ה lerosh לְרֹאשׁ יה אדני lechol לְכָל

vehishtachavu וְהִשְׁתַּחֲווּ יִלְה Elohenu אֱלֹהֵינוּ Adonai יְהֹוָואדנייאהדונהי

romemu רוֹמְמוּ ✦hu הוּא kadosh קָדוֹשׁ raglav רַגְלָיו lahadom לַהֲדֹם

lehar לְהַר vehishtachavu וְהִשְׁתַּחֲווּ יִלְה Elohenu אֱלֹהֵינוּ Adonai יְהֹוָואדנייאהדונהי

✦Elohenu אֱלֹהֵינוּ Adonai יְהֹוָואדנייאהדונהי kadosh קָדוֹשׁ ki כִּי kodsho קָדְשׁוֹ יִלְה

May it be pleasing before You that You shall open my heart with Your Torah (and that You may give me male sons, who shall fulfill Your desire). And may You fulfill the requests of my heart and the heart of Your entire Nation, Israel, for good, for life, and for peace. Amen.

TAKING OUT THE TORAH FROM THE ARK

"Proclaim the Lord's greatness with me and let us exalt His Name together." (Psalms 34:4) "Yours, Lord, is the greatness, the strength, the splendor, the triumph, and the glory, and everything in the Heavens and the Earth. Yours, Lord, is the Kingdom and the sovereignty over every leader." (I Chronicles 29:11) "Exalt the Lord, our God, and prostrate yourselves at His footstool, is holy. Exalt the Lord, our God, and prostrate yourselves at His holy mountain because the Lord, our God, is holy." (Psalms 99:9)

Some add this section:

en אֵין קָדוֹשׁ kadosh כ׳הוּאהדניאהדנוהי kadonai ki כִּי en אֵין biltecha בִּלְתֶּךָ

ילי mi מִי bi בִּי ki כִּי: ילה kelohenu כֵּאלֹהֵינוּ tzur צוּר ve'en וְאֵין

tzur צוּר ילי umi וּמִי Adonai יְהוָׂאדניאהדנוהי mibal'adei מִבַּלְעָדֶי Eloha אֱלוֹהַ

lanu לָנוּ tziva צִוָּה torah תּוֹרָה Elohenu אֱלֹהֵינוּ zulati זוּלָתִי

Moshe מֹשֶׁה morasha מוֹרָשָׁה etz עֵץ

Yaakov יַעֲקֹב kehilat קְהִלַּת morasha

hee הִיא chayim חַיִּים lamachazikim לַמַּחֲזִיקִים

deracheha דְּרָכֶיהָ me'ushar מְאֻשָּׁר vetomcheha וְתֹמְכֶיהָ ba בָּהּ

shalom שָׁלוֹם netivoteha נְתִיבוֹתֶיהָ vechol וְכָל no'am נֹעַם darchei דַּרְכֵי

lamo לָמוֹ ve'en וְאֵין toratecha תוֹרָתֶךָ le'ohavei לְאֹהֲבֵי rav רָב shalom שָׁלוֹם

yiten יִתֵּן le'amo לְעַמּוֹ oz עֹז Adonai יְהוָאדניאהדנוהי michshol מִכְשׁוֹל:

yevarech יְבָרֵךְ Adonai יְהוָאדניאהדנוהי

et אֶת amo עַמּוֹ vashalom בַשָׁלוֹם

ki כִּי shem שֵׁם Adonai יְהוָאדניאהדנוהי ekra אֶקְרָא havu הָבוּ

oz עֹז tenu תְּנוּ hakol הַכֹּל lelohenu לֵאלֹהֵינוּ godel גֹּדֶל

latorah לַתּוֹרָה: chavod כָּבוֹד utnu וּתְנוּ lelohim לֵאלֹהִים

RAISING THE TORAH

After the scroll is placed on the *bimah* (the podium), a person is called up to raise the Torah for the congregation to see the specific section we will be reading from the Torah Scroll. As we raise the Torah, we meditate to also raise our level of consciousness. We should look at the parchment to try to see the first letter of that week's reading. We should also attempt to find the first letter of our Hebrew name within the text. You can use the *Talit* to help yourself focus (if you don't have a Talit you can use your finger).

"There is none as holy as the Lord, because there is none other beside You. There is no Rock like our God." (I Samuel 2:2) "For Who is God beside the Lord? Who is a Rock, other than our God?" (Psalms 18:32) "The Torah that Moses commanded us with is a heritage for the congregation of Jacob." (Deuteronomy 33:4) "It is a tree of life to those who hold on to it, and those who support it are happy." (Proverb 3:18) "Its ways are the way of pleasantness and all its paths lead to peace." (Proverbs 3:17) "Abundance of peace for those who love Your Torah and for them there is no obstacle." (Psalms 119:165) "The Lord give might to his people, The Lord will bless his nation with peace." (Psalms 29:11) "When I call out the Name of the Lord, proclaim greatness to our God." (Dutoronomy 32:3) "All should attribute power to God and give honor to the Torah." (Psalms 68:35)

Moshe מֹשֶׁה   sam שָׂם   asher אֲשֶׁר   hatorah הַתּוֹרָה   vezot וְזֹאת

Yisrael יִשְׂרָאֵל׃   benei בְּנֵי   lifnei לִפְנֵי   מהע, ע"ב בר"בוע וקס"א, אל שדי, ד"פ אלהים ע"ה

El אֵל (מילוי דס"ג) יא"י   אל שדי = משה, מהע, ע"ב בריבוע וקס"א, ד"פ אלהים ע"ה   Shadai שַׁדַּי

emet אֱמֶת   אהיה פעמים אהיה, ז"פ ס"ג   uMoshe וּמֹשֶׁה   מהע, ע"ב בריבוע וקס"א, אל שדי,

vetorato וְתוֹרָתוֹ   ז"פ ס"ג   אהיה פעמים אהיה,   emet אֱמֶת   ד"פ אלהים ע"ה

tziva צִוָּה   torah תּוֹרָה   ס"ג׃   ז"פ   אהיה פעמים אהיה,   emet אֱמֶת

lanu לָנוּ   אלהים, אהיה אדני אהיה, ע"ב בריבוע וקס"א, אל שדי, ד"פ אלהים ע"ה   Moshe מֹשֶׁה

morasha מוֹרָשָׁה׃   kehilat קְהִלַּת   Yaakov יַעֲקֹב   ז הויות, יאהדונהי אידהנויה׃

haEl הָאֵל   יא"י (מילוי דס"ג)   tamim תָּמִים   darko דַּרְכּוֹ   imrat אִמְרַת

Adonai יְהֹוָהאדנייאהדונהי   tzerufa צְרוּפָה   magen מָגֵן   ג"פ אל (יא"י מילוי דס"ג)

bo בּוֹ   hachosim הַחוֹסִים   יה אדני   lechol לְכֹל   hu הוּא   ר"ת מיכאל גבריאל נוריאל

THE READING

To maximize the power of the connection, we must think to share all the energy we're receiving with everyone else. We should become channels for sharing spiritual Light. If we think only about ourselves, it is like blowing a fuse. No current will flow, even though the plug is connected into the socket.

On Mondays and Thursdays, we read the first part of the portion that will be read on the upcoming *Shabbat*, to help us maintain a link to the Light that will be revealed on *Shabbat*.

Three people are called up to the *Torah* on a weekday. Each one acts as channel for one *Sfirah*. On Monday, they correspond to *Chesed*, *Gevurah* and *Tiferet*, and on Thursday, to *Netzach*, *Hod* and *Yesod*. On *Chanukah* and *Purim* three people are called up and they represent the sefirot: *Chesed*, *Gevurah* and *Tiferet*. On *Rosh Chodesh* or *Chol Hamo'ed* four people are called up to the *Torah*, they correspond to *Sfirot* of *Chesed*, *Gevurah*, *Tif'eret* and *Malchut*.

When you are called up (the *ole*) to recite the blessing before the *Torah* reading, you must visually connect with the letters of the *Torah* to ignite the power of his words. A blessing is recited before and after each of the readings. The first blessing is equivalent to plugging a wire (our soul) into a wall socket (the *Torah*). The last blessing draws the spiritual current to us to bring the Light into our lives.

RAISING THE TORAH

"And this is the Torah that Moses placed before the Children of Israel." (Deuteronomy 4:44)
God is true and Moses is true and His Torah is true. "The Torah, which Moses commanded us with, is a heritage for the Congregation of Jacob." (Deuteronomy 33:4) "God! His ways are perfect. Lord's statement is pure. He is the Shield for all who take refuge in Him" (II Samuel 22:31)

SHACHARIT – MORNING PRAYER
THE ORDER OF THE TORAH READING

The chazan says:

בֵּית bet ב"פ ראה אַהֲרֹן Aharon בָּרְכוּ barchu יהוה ריבוע יהוה ריבוע מ"ה אֶת et

ה' Hashem הַמְבֹרָך hamevorach, כֹּהֵן kohen קָרָב kerav מלה וְכַהֵן vechahen מלה.

The one who goes up to the Torah ("the ole"), holds the Scroll with both his hands, and says:

יְהֹוָאדְנִיאהדוּנְהי Adonai עִמָּכֶם imachem:

The congregation replies:

יְבָרֶכְךָ yevarchecha ה' Hashem:

The ole continues:

(ויכוין "ברכו את ה' המבורך" – מ"ב ור"ך שׂהם עמאל ויִמין):

רַבָּנָן rabanan: בָּרְכוּ barchu יהוה ריבוע יהוה ריבוע מ"ה אֶת et

יְהֹוָאדְנִיאהדוּנְהי Adonai הַמְבֹרָך hamevorach ס"ת כהת, מעיזו בן דוד ע"ה.

The congregation then replies:

Nefesh	Ruach	Neshamah
בָּרוּך baruch	יְהֹוָאדְנִיאהדוּנְהי Adonai	הַמְבֹרָך hamevorach
Chayah		Yechidah
לְעוֹלָם le'olam	ריבוע ס"ג וי' אותיות דס"ג	וָעֶד va'ed:

The ole repeats this line after the congregation:

Nefesh	Ruach	Neshamah
בָּרוּך baruch	יְהֹוָאדְנִיאהדוּנְהי Adonai	הַמְבֹרָך hamevorach
Chayah		Yechidah
לְעוֹלָם le'olam	ריבוע ס"ג וי' אותיות דס"ג	וָעֶד va'ed:

And then says the following blessing:

בָּרוּך baruch אַתָּה Ata יְהֹוָאדְנִיאהדוּנְהי Adonai אֱלֹהֵינוּ Elohenu ילה

מֶלֶך melech הָעוֹלָם ha'olam אֲשֶׁר asher בָּחַר bachar בָּנוּ banu

מִכָּל mikol ילי הָעַמִּים ha'amim וְנָתַן venatan לָנוּ lanu אלהים, אהיה אדני

אֶת et תּוֹרָתוֹ torato. בָּרוּך baruch אַתָּה Ata יְהֹוָאדְנִיאהדוּנְהי Adonai

נוֹתֵן noten אבג יתץ, ועד הַתּוֹרָה hatorah.

THE READING

(The House of Aaron, bless the Lord, the Blessed One. Kohen, come close and stand and do your priestly duty.)
May the Lord be with you! May the Lord bless you!
Masters, Bless the Lord, the Blessed One. Blessed is the Lord, the Blessed One, forever and for eternity.
Blessed are You, Lord, our God, the King of the World,
Who chose us from among the nations and gave us His Torah. Blessed are You, Lord, Who gives the Torah.

After the reading, the ole says the following blessing:

יִלֹה Elohenu אֱלֹהֵינוּ Adonai יְהֹוָאֲדֹנָיֶאהֲדֹונָהי Ata אַתָּה baruch בָּרוּךְ

אהיה אדני, אלהים, אהיה lanu לָנוּ natan נָתַן asher אֲשֶׁר ha'olam הָעוֹלָם melech מֶלֶךְ

ז"פ ס"ג, אהיה פעמים אהיה emet אֱמֶת torat תּוֹרַת־ torato תּוֹרָתוֹ et אֶת

baruch בָּרוּךְ ‏◆betochenu בְּתוֹכֵנוּ nata נָטַע olam עוֹלָם vechayei וְחַיֵּי

◆hatorah הַתּוֹרָה אבג יתץ, ושר noten נוֹתֵן Adonai יְהֹוָאֲדֹנָיֶאהֲדֹונָהי Ata אַתָּה

BLESSING OF HAGOMEL

We recite this blessing after we have flown in an airplane or experienced any kind of accident or near-accident in a car. We were occupying a specific space that was charged with a potential for danger, and this blessing closes that space. We also received additional Light of protection while we occupied that space. *Hagomel* (Eng. 'rewarding') enlarges our vessel, so we can receive that extra Light in a balanced way.

בוכו levav לֵבָב ב"ן, לכב bechol בְּכָל־ Adonai יְהֹוָאֲדֹנָיֶאהֲדֹונָהי ode אוֹדֶה

סיט ve'eda וְעֵדָה yesharim יְשָׁרִים מיכ, י"פ האא besod בְּסוֹד

יִלֹה Elohenu אֱלֹהֵינוּ Adonai יְהֹוָאֲדֹנָיֶאהֲדֹונָהי Ata אַתָּה baruch בָּרוּךְ

lechayavim לַחַיָּבִים hagomel הַגּוֹמֵל ha'olam הָעוֹלָם melech מֶלֶךְ

◆והו tuv טוֹב ילי kol כָּל shegemalani שֶׁגְּמָלַנִי ,tovot טוֹבוֹת

The congregation answers Amen:

יאהדונהי amen אָמֵן

And then the congregation recites:

◆והו tuv טוֹב ילי kol כָּל shegemalach שֶׁגְּמָלְךָ מילוי דס"ג ; יא"י לאה: haEl הָאֵל

◆sela סֶלָה והו tuv טוֹב ילי kol כָּל yigmolcha יִגְמָלְךָ hu הוּא

Then he recites silently:

◆אל עודי ע"ה, אל ע"ה, ע"ב בריבוע וקס"א ע"ה ratzon רָצוֹן מהע ע"ה, yehi יְהִי ken כֵּן יאהדונהי amen אָמֵן

FATHER'S BLESSING FOR HIS BARMITZVAH SON

When a young man of 13 goes up to the Torah for the first time his father says the following:

‏◆shelaze שֶׁלָּזֶה me'onsho מֵעָנְשׁוֹ shepetarani שֶׁפְּטָרַנִי baruch בָּרוּךְ

---

*Blessed are You, Lord, our God, King of the World, Who gave us His Torah,
the Torah of truth, and implanted within us eternal life. Blessed are You, Lord, Who gives the Torah.*

BLESSING OF HAGOMEL

*"I give thank to the Lord whole heartedly, in the conceal of the upright and congregation." (Psalms 111:1)
Blessed are You, Lord, our God, King of the World, Who gives goodness to the guilty, Who bestows upon me all that is good. The God, Who bestows upon you all the best, he will bestow upon you all the best,
Selah.*

Amen, so shall it be desired.

FATHER'S BLESSING FOR HIS BARMITZVAH SON

Blessed is the One Who has dismissed me from the punishment of this boy.

SHACHARIT – MORNING PRAYER
THE ORDER OF THE TORAH READING

HALF KADDISH

This *Kaddish* draws the Light from the World of *Atzilut* (ע"ב) into the World of *Beriah* (ס"ג).

יִתְגַּדַּל yitgadal וְיִתְקַדַּשׁ veyitkadash שְׁדֵי וּמִילוּי שְׁדֵי ; י"א אוֹתִיּוֹת כְּמִנְיַן ר"ה

שְׁמֵיהּ shemei (שֵׁם י"ה דֵּע"ב) רַבָּא raba קֵנ"א ב"ן, יהוה אלהים יהוה אדני,

אָמֵן amen אידהנויה. מִילוּי קְס"א וס"ג, מ"ה בְּרָבוּעַ וְע"ב ע"ה ; ר"ת = ו"פ אלהים ; ס"ת = ג"פ יב"ק:

בְּעָלְמָא be'alma דִּי di דִּי vera בְּרָא chir'utei כִרְעוּתֵיהּ.

וְיַמְלִיךְ veyamlich מַלְכוּתֵיהּ mal'chutei. וְיַצְמַח veyatzmach

פּוּרְקָנֵהּ purkanei. וִיקָרֵב vikarev מְשִׁיחֵיהּ meshichei: אָמֵן amen אידהנויה.

בְּחַיֵּיכוֹן bechayechon וּבְיוֹמֵיכוֹן uvyomechon וּבְחַיֵּי uvchayei

דְּכָל dechol יְלִי בֵּית bet ב"פ ראה Yisrael יִשְׂרָאֵל בַּעֲגָלָא ba'agala

וּבִזְמַן uvizman קָרִיב kariv וְאִמְרוּ ve'imru אָמֵן amen: אָמֵן amen אידהנויה.

The congregation and the chazan say the following:

28 words (until *be'alma*) – meditate: מִילוּי דְּמִילוּי דֵּע"ב (יוד ויו דלת הי יוד ויו יוד ויו הי יוד)
28 letters (until *almaya*) – meditate: מִילוּי דְּמִילוּי דֵּע"ב (יוד ויו דלת הי יוד ויו יוד ויו הי יוד)

יְהֵא yehe שְׁמֵיהּ shemei (שֵׁם י"ה דס"ג) רַבָּא raba קֵנ"א ב"ן,

מְבָרַךְ mevarach יהוה אלהים אדני, מִילוּי קְס"א וס"ג, מ"ה בְּרָבוּעַ וְע"ב ע"ה

לְעָלַם le'alam לְעָלְמֵי le'almei עָלְמַיָּא almaya. יִתְבָּרַךְ yitbarach.

Seven words with six letters each (שֵׁם בֶּן מ"ב) meditate:
יהוה ~ יוד הי ויו הי ~ מִילוּי דְּמִילוּי דֵּע"ב (יוד ויו דלת הי יוד ויו יוד ויו הי יוד)
Also, seven times the letter *Vav* (שֵׁם בֶּן מ"ב) meditate:
יהוה ~ יוד הי ויו הי ~ מִילוּי דְּמִילוּי דֵּע"ב (יוד ויו דלת הי יוד ויו יוד ויו הי יוד)

וְיִשְׁתַּבַּח veyishtabach י"פ ע"ב יהוה אל אבג יתץ.

וְיִתְפָּאַר veyitpa'ar הי גו יה קְרַע שְׂטָן וְיִתְרוֹמַם veyitromam וה כוזו נגד יכש.

וְיִתְנַשֵּׂא veyitnase בְּמוּכְסַז בְּטַר צְתַג וְיִתְהַדָּר veyit'hadar כוזו יה וזקב טנע.

וְיִתְעַלֶּה veyit'ale וה יוד ה יגל פזק. וְיִתְהַלָּל veyit'halal א ואו הא שׁקו צית.

שְׁמֵיהּ shemei (שֵׁם י"ה דמ"ה) דְּקוּדְשָׁא dekudsha בְּרִיךְ verich הוּא hu:

אָמֵן amen אידהנויה.

HALF KADDISH

May His great Name be more exalted and sanctified. (Amen) In the world that He created according to His will, and may His kingdom reign. And may He cause His redemption to sprout and may He bring the Mashiach closer. (Amen) In your lifetimes and in your days and in the lifetime of all the House of Israel, speedily and in the near future, and you should say, Amen. (Amen) May His great Name be blessed forever and for all eternity blessed and lauded, and glorified and exalted, And extolled and honored, and uplifted and praised, be the Name of the Holy Blessed One. (Amen)

shirata שִׁירָתָא ◆birchata בִּרְכָתָא י“לי kol כָּל min מִן le'ela לְעֵלָּא

da'amiran דַאֲמִירָן ◆venechamata וְנֶחָמָתָא tishbechata תֻּשְׁבְּחָתָא

amen אָמֵן אידהנויה ◆amen אָמֵן ve'imru וְאִמְרוּ be'alma בְּעָלְמָא

RETURNING THE TORAH TO THE ARK

Placing the Torah in the Ark is similar to depositing money in a bank. For example, anytime we want to draw out funds, we have a cash reserve waiting for us at our local bank. The Ark is our bank of Light. All the spiritual energy that we've generated is now on reserve waiting for us to draw upon it throughout our week.

Before the Torah is carried back to the ark, the chazan says:

nisgav נִשְׂגָּב ki כִּי Adonai יְהֹוָה shem שֵׁם et אֶת yehalelu יְהַלְלוּ

levado לְבַדּוֹ מ"ב מוהש ע"ה, ע"ב בריבוע וקס"א וע"ה, אל עדי ע"ה shemo שְׁמוֹ

Then the congregation says while carrrying the Torah back to the Ark:

veshamayim וְשָׁמַיִם י"פ טל, י"פ כוזו eretz אֶרֶץ al עַל אהיה hodo הוֹדוֹ

tehila תְהִלָּה ע"ה אמת, אהיה פעמים אהיה le'amo לְעַמּוֹ keren קֶרֶן vayerem וַיָּרֶם

Yisrael יִשְׂרָאֵל livnei לִבְנֵי chasidav וְחֲסִידָיו יה אדני lechol לְכָל י"פ ס"ג

haleluya הַלְלוּיָהּ אלהים, אהיה אדני ; ללה kerovo קְרֹבוֹ am עַם

Then the chazan says:

haElohim הָאֱלֹהִים אהיה אדני ; ילה ; ר"ת יהה hu הוּא Adonai יְהֹוָה

haElohim הָאֱלֹהִים hu הוּא Adonai יְהֹוָה ועולה למנין עזו עם ג' כוללים bashamayim בַּשָּׁמַיִם י"פ טל, י"פ כוזו אהיה אדני ; ילה ; ר"ת יהה ועולה למנין עזו עם ג' כוללים

mitachat מִתַּחַת ע"ה אלהים דההין ha'aretz הָאָרֶץ ve'al וְעַל עלם mima'al מִמַּעַל

vaElohim בָאֱלֹהִים kamocha כָּמוֹךָ en אֵין od עוֹד en אֵין

kema'asecha כְּמַעֲשֶׂיךָ ve'en וְאֵין ללה Adonai אֲדֹנָי ילה ; אהיה אדני

Adonai יְהֹוָה הושע shuva שׁוּבָה yomar יֹאמַר uvnucho וּבְנֻחֹה

hashivenu הֲשִׁיבֵנוּ Yisrael יִשְׂרָאֵל alfei אַלְפֵי rivevot רִבְבוֹת

venashuva וְנָשׁוּבָה (כתיב: ונשוב) elecha אֵלֶיךָ Adonai יְהֹוָה

kekedem כְּקֶדֶם yamenu יָמֵינוּ קנ"א קס"א הויות, י"ב chadesh וְחַדֵּשׁ

Above all blessings,
songs, praises, and words of consolation that may be said in the world, and you shall say, Amen. (Amen)

RETURNING THE TORAH TO THE ARK

"Praise be the name of the Lord, His name alone is exalted His glory on heaven and earth. He raised funds to his nation, praise to his Chassidim, people of Israel his close nation, praise the Lord." (Psalms 148:13-14) "The Lord is the God! The Lord is the God! In the Heavens above and on the Earth below, there is no other." (Deuteronomy 4:39) "There is none like You among the gods, Lord, and there is nothing like Your handiwork." (Psalms 86:8) "And when the Ark rested, Moses would say, Return, Lord, to the tens of thousands of Israel." (Numbers 10:36) "Bring us back, Lord, and we shall return. Renew our days as of old." (Lamentataion 5:21)

From here ("*Ashrei*") until "*Bet Yaakov*" (pg. 253) you are in the World of *Beriah* (Creation).

THE ASHREI

Twenty-one of the twenty-two letters of the Aramaic alphabet are encoded in the *Ashrei* in their correct order from *Alef* to *Tav*. King David, the author, left out the Aramaic letter *Nun* from this prayer, because *Nun* is the first letter in the Aramaic word *nefilah*, which means "falling." Falling refers to a spiritual decline, as in falling into the *klipa*. Feelings of doubt, depression, worry, and uncertainty are consequences of spiritual falling. Because the Aramaic letters are the actual instruments of Creation, this prayer helps to inject order and the power of Creation into our lives, without the energy of falling.

In this Psalm there are ten times the Name: יהוה for the Ten *Sefirot*. This Psalm is written according to the order of the *Alef Bet*, but the letter *Nun* is omitted to prevent falling.

ראה ב"פ vetecha בֵּיתֶךָ yoshvei יוֹשְׁבֵי (סוד הכתר) ashrei אַשְׁרֵי

ha'am הָעָם ashrei אַשְׁרֵי sela סֶלָה: yehalelucha יְהַלְלוּךָ od עוֹד

lo לוֹ ע"ה אלהים ד"פ א, אל עׁדׁי וקס"א ע"ב בריבוע מ'שׁ'ע', משה, מהׁש', shekacha שֶׁכָּכָה

(Keter) she'Adonai שֶׁיהוׁהׁ אדניׁ לאה ר"ת ha'am הָעָם ashrei אַשְׁרֵי

leDavid לְדָוִד ז"פ ס"ג, אהיה פעמים אהיה, ע"ה אמת, יׁלׁהׁ: tehila תְּהִלָּה Elohav אֱלֹהָיו

va'avarcha וַאֲבָרְכָה hamelech הַמֶּלֶךְ Elohai אֱלֹהַי aromimcha אֲרוֹמִמְךָ

va'ed וָעֶד: אותיות ו'י' דס"ג ריבוע ע"ג le'olam לְעוֹלָם shimcha שִׁמְךָ

יהוה אל חן נגד, מזבוח, ע"ה לכב ב"ן, bechol בְּכָל

shimcha שִׁמְךָ יהוה מ"ה va'ahalela וַאֲהַלְלָה avarcheka אֲבָרְכֶךָ

va'ed וָעֶד: דס"ג אותיות ו'י' ריבוע דס"ג le'olam לְעוֹלָם

אום יׁזׁלׁ, מבה = אותיות ד' עם ; לׁהׁו gadol גָּדוֹל

ללה אדניׁ, umhulal וּמְהֻלָּל (Chochmah) Adonai יהוׁהׁ אדניׁ אהיׁהׁ

cheker חֵקֶר: en אֵין וׁהׁו veligdulato וְלִגְדֻלָּתוֹ me'od מְאֹד

THE ASHREI

"Joyful are those who dwell in Your House, they shall praise You, Selah." (Psalms 84:5)
"Joyful is the nation that this is theirs and joyful the nation that the Lord is their God." (Psalms 144:15)
"A praise of David.

א   I shall exalt You, my God, the King, and I shall bless Your Name forever and for eternity.

ב   I shall bless You every day and I shall praise Your Name forever and for eternity.

ג   The Lord is great and exceedingly praised. His greatness is unfathomable.

ר"ת דלים   מַעֲשֶׂיךָ ma'asecha   יְשַׁבַּח yeshabach   לְדוֹר ledor   דוֹר dor

וּגְבוּרֹתֶיךָ ugvurotecha   יוד, כ"ב אותיות פשוטות (=אכא) וה' אותיות סופיות בּוֹמֶנְצֶפֵּ"ךְ:   יַגִּידוּ yagidu

וְדִבְרֵי vedivrei   הוֹדֶךָ hodecha   כָּבוֹד kevod   הָדָר hadar

אֲדֹנָי   אהיה   אלהים,   ר"ת   נִפְלְאֹתֶיךָ nifle'otecha

אֲשִׂיחָה asicha   ר"ת   הַפָּסוּק   =   פ"ז   (בסוד   כתם   טהור   פז):

וְגֻדֻלָּתְךָ ugdulatcha   יֹאמֵרוּ yomeru   נוֹרְאֹתֶיךָ nor'otecha   וֶעֱזוּז ve'ezuz

(כתיב: וּגְדֻלּוֹתֶיךָ) ר"ת = ע"ב, ריבוע יהוה   ס"ת = י"א (מילוי דס"ג):   אֲסַפְּרֶנָּה asaprena

יַבִּיעוּ yabi'u   לאו   טוּבְךָ tuvcha   רַב rav   זֵכֶר zecher

וְצִדְקָתְךָ vetzidkatcha   ס"ת = ב"ן, יבם, לכב ; ר"ת הַפָּסוּק = רי"ו יהוה: יְרַנֵּנוּ yeranenu

(Binah)   Adonai לְהֵוֹ[אדני]יָהדֹוֹנָהי   וְרַחוּם verachum   חַנּוּן chanun

ר"ת = יהוה   אַפַּיִם apayim   ס"ת = ס"ג ב"ן = ע"על   erech אֶרֶךְ   חנון ורחום יהוה

ריבוע יהוה: ע"ב,   chased וָחֶסֶד   (כתיב: וְגָדוֹל)   ugdal וּגְדָל־

לַכֹּל lakol   (Chesed)   Adonai לְהֵוֹ[אדני]יָהדֹוֹנָהי   והו   tov טוֹב־

עַל־ al   וְרַחֲמָיו verachamav   (מילוי דס"ג)   ל"ז ;   ס"ת   אֲדֹנָי   יה

כָּל kol   ילי ; עמם ;   ר"ת ריבוע ב"ן ע"ה   מַעֲשָׂיו ma'asav   ס"ת ע"ב, ריבוע יהוה:

ד   *One generation and the next shall praise Your deeds and tell of Your might.*

ה   *The brilliance of Your splendid glory and the wonders of Your acts, I shall speak of.*

ו   *They shall speak of the might of Your awesome acts and I shall tell of Your greatness.*

ז   *They shall express the remembrance of Your abundant goodness, and Your righteousness they shall joyfully proclaim.* ח *The Lord is merciful and compassionate, slow to anger and great in kindness.*

ט   *The Lord is good to all, His compassion extends over all His acts.*

ma'asecha **בְּעֲשֶׂיךָ** ילי kol **כָּל** (*Gevurah*) Adonai להואהדיאהדונהי yoducha **יוֹדוּךָ**

ס"ת = מ"ה: yevarchucha **יְבָרְכוּכָה** vachasidecha ר"ת אלהים, אהיה אדני **וַחֲסִידֶיךָ**

ugvuratcha **וּגְבוּרָתְךָ** yomeru **יֹאמֵרוּ** malchutcha **מַלְכוּתְךָ** kevod **כְּבוֹד**

ר"ת הפסוק = אלהים, אהיה אדני ; ס"ת = ב"ן, יבמ, לכב: yedaberu **יְדַבֵּרוּ**

אדני ללה, ר"ת ha'adam **הָאָדָם** livnei **לִבְנֵי** lehodi'a **לְהוֹדִיעַ**

hadar **הֲדַר** uchvod **וּכְבוֹד** gevurotav **גְּבוּרֹתָיו**

ר"ת מ"ה וס"ת = רי"ו ; ר"ת הפסוק ע"ה = ק"כ צירופי אלהים: malchuto **מַלְכוּתוֹ**

olamim **עֹלָמִים** ילי kol **כָּל** malchut **מַלְכוּת** malchutcha **מַלְכוּתְךָ**

רי"ו: vador **וָדֹר** dor **דֹר** ב"ן, לכב bechol **בְּכָל** umemshaltecha **וּמֶמְשַׁלְתְּךָ**

(*Tiferet*) Adonai להואהדיאהדונהי אדני ריבוע somech **סוֹמֵךְ**

hanoflim **הַנֹּפְלִים** (יאהדונהי) סומך אדני לכל ר"ת סאל, אמן יה אדני lechol **לְכָל**

נמם: hakefufim **הַכְּפוּפִים** אדני יה lechol **לְכָל** vezokef **וְזוֹקֵף**

enei **עֵינֵי** ריבוע דמ"ה chol **כָּל** ילי elecha **אֵלֶיךָ** yesaberu **יְשַׂבֵּרוּ** veAta **וְאַתָּה**

be'ito: **בְּעִתּוֹ** ochlam **אָכְלָם** et **אֶת** lahem **לָהֶם** אבגיתצ, וער noten **נוֹתֵן**

<table>
<tr><td>י</td><td>*All that You have made shall thank You, Lord, and Your pious ones shall bless You.*</td></tr>
<tr><td>כ</td><td>*They shall speak of the glory of Your Kingdom and talk of Your mighty deeds.*</td></tr>
<tr><td>ל</td><td>*His mighty deeds He makes known to man and the glory of His splendid Kingdom.*</td></tr>
<tr><td>מ</td><td>*Yours is the Kingdom of all worlds and Your reign extends to each and every generation.*</td></tr>
<tr><td>ס</td><td>*The Lord supports all those who fell and holds upright all those who are bent over.*</td></tr>
<tr><td>ע</td><td>*The eyes of all look hopefully towards You, and You give them their food at its proper time.*</td></tr>
</table>

DRAWING LIGHT TO BERIAH - אל שדי – יוד הי ואו הי

POTE'ACH ET YADECHA

We connect to the letters *Pei, Alef,* and *Yud* by opening our hands and holding our palms skyward. Our consciousness is focused on receiving sustenance and financial prosperity from the Light through our actions of personal tithing and sharing, our *Desire to Receive for the Sake of Sharing.* In doing so, we also acknowledge that the sustenance we receive comes from a higher source and is not of our own doing. According to the sages, if we do not meditate on this idea at this juncture, we must repeat the prayer.

פתוֹ (שע"ח נהורין לב"ה ולס"ה)

פותחו את ידרך ר"ת פאי	יוד הי ויו הי יוד הי ויו הי (ו' וזיוורתי)
ג'ימ' יאהדונהי ז"ן	אלף למד אלף למד (ע"ע)
וחכמה ח"א ו"ק	יוד הא ואו הא (ל"א)
יסוד דנוק'	אדני (ולנוקבא)

פ**וֹתֵוּ** et **אֶת** pote'ach **יָדֶךְ** yadecha ר"ת פאי וס"ת וחתך עם ג' אותיות = דִּיקָרְנוֹסָא

ובאתב"ע הוא סאל, פאי, אמן, יאהדונהי ; ועוד יכוין שם וחתך בשילוב יהוה – יוֹזְהַתוּכַה

Drawing abundance and sustenance from *Chochmah* of *Zeir Anpin*

יוד הי ויו הי יוד הי ויו דלת הי ויו יוד הי ויו הי יוד

וחתך סאל יאהדונהי

וּמַשְׂבִּיעַ umasbi'a וחתך עם ג' אותיות = דִּיקָרְנוֹסָא

ובא"ת ב"ע הוא סאל, אמן, יאהדונהי ; ועוד יכוין שם וחתך בשילוב יהוה – יוֹזְהַתוּכַה

Drawing abundance and sustenance from *Chochmah* of *Zeir Anpin*

יוד הי ויו הי יוד הי ויו דלת הי ויו יוד הי ויו הי יוד

לְכָל־ lechol יה אדני (להמשיך מווזן ד-יה אל הנוקבא שהיא אדני)

וְחַי chai כל וחי = אהיה אהיה יהוה, בינה ע"ה, וזיים

רָצוֹן ratzon מוהע ע"ה, ע"ב בריבוע וקס"א ע"ה, אל שדי ע"ה

ר"ת רוחל שהיא המלכות הצריכה לשפע

יוד יוד הי יוד הי ויו יוד הי ויו הי יוד הי ויו הי יסוד דאבא

אלף הי יוד הי יסוד דאימא

להמתיק רוחל וב' דמעין שך פר

Also meditate to draw abundance and sustenance and blessing to all the worlds from the *ratzon* mentioned above. You should meditate and focus on this verse because it is the essence of prosperity, and that God is intervening and sustaining and supporting all of Creation.

POTE'ACH ET YADECHA

פ *Open* *Your* *Hands* *and* *satisfy* *every* *living* *thing* *with* *desire.*

ב"ן, לכב	bechol בְּכֹל	(Yesod)	Adonai יְהוָֹוּהַהּהּהָוֹהֵיאהדונהי	tzadik צַדִּיק
ma'asav מַעֲשָׂיו יבמ, ב"ן:	bechol בְּכֹל ב"ן, לכב	vechasid וְחָסִיד	derachav דְּרָכָיו	
ארני יה	lechol לְכֹל	(Malchut)	Adonai יְהוָֹאֲדֹנָיאהדונהי	karov קָרוֹב
asher אֲשֶׁר	ארני יה		lechol לְכֹל	kor'av קֹרְאָיו
ז"פ ס"ג:	אהיה פעמים אהיה	ve'emet בֶּאֱמֶת		yikra'uhu יִקְרָאֻהוּ
ya'ase יַעֲשֶׂה	yere'av יְרֵאָיו מהש ע"ה, ע"ב ברבוע וקס"א ע"ה, אל שׁדי ע"ה	retzon רְצוֹן		
veyoshi'em וְיוֹשִׁיעֵם	yishma יִשְׁמַע	shav'atam שַׁוְעָתָם	ve'et וְאֶת ר"ת רי	
(Netzach)	Adonai יְהוָֹאֲדֹנָיאהדונהי	שׁבתפילין הויות כ"א	shomer שׁוֹמֵר
אכא	ר"ת	ohavav אֹהֲבָיו	kol כָּל ילי	et אֶת
yashmid יַשְׁמִיד:	haresha'im הָרְשָׁעִים	kol כָּל ילי	ve'et וְאֶת
pi פִּי ראה	yedaber יְדַבֶּר	(Hod)	Adonai יְהוָֹאֲדֹנָיאהדונהי	tehilat תְּהִלַּת
vivarech וִיבָרֵךְ ע"ב ס"ג מ"ה ב"ן, הברכה (למתק את ז' המלכים עומתו) kol כָּל ילי	basar בָּשָׂר	shem שֵׁם	kodsho קָדְשׁוֹ	le'olam לְעוֹלָם ריבוע ס"ג וי' אותיות דס"ג
me'ata מֵעַתָּה	Yah יָהּ	nevarech נְבָרֵךְ	va'anachnu וַאֲנַחְנוּ	va'ed וָעֶד:
ללה:	; ארני אהיה, אלהים	haleluya הַלְלוּיָהּ	olam עוֹלָם	ve'ad וְעַד:

LAMNATZE'ACH

During the death anniversary of a Righteous Sage, *Rosh Chodesh*, or any special holiday connection, we do not recite *Lamnatze'ach* because its purpose is to help us in times of trouble. Because extra energy is available during *Rosh Chodesh* and special holidays, there is no need to recite it.

Raising *Mayin Nukvin* (awakening from Below) in the aspect of *Neshamah*.
In this Psalm, there are 70 words, which correspond to the 70 voices of the *Ayalah* (doe).

צ   *The Lord is righteous in all His ways and virtuous in all His deeds.*

ק   *The Lord is close to all who call Him, only to those who call Him truthfully.*

ר   *He shall fulfill the will of those who fear Him; He hears their wailing and saves them.*

ש   *The Lord protects all who love Him and He destroys the wicked.*

ת   *My lips utter the praise of the Lord and all flesh shall bless His holy Name, forever and for eternity."*
(Psalms 145) "And we shall bless the Lord forever and for eternity. Praise the Lord!" (Psalms 115:18)

לַמְנַצֵּחַ lamnatze'ach מִזְמוֹר mizmor לְדָוִד: leDavid לַעַנְךָ ya'ancha

צָרָה tzara בְּיוֹם beyom אֲדֹנָי Adonai ע"ה נגד, מזבח, זן אל יהוה אלהים דההין יַעַנְךָ יְהֹוָאדנילאהדונהי

שֵׁם shem אֱלֹהֵי Elohei יְשַׂגֶּבְךָ yesagevcha שם = יב"ק, אלהים יהוה, אהיה אדני יהוה אֱלֹהֵי

יַעֲקֹב Yaakov ו הויות, יאהדונהי אידהנויה ; ס"ת = ב"ן : יִשְׁלַח yishlach מילוי ע"ב, דמב ; ילה

עֶזְרְךָ ezrecha מִקֹּדֶשׁ mikodesh וּמִצִּיּוֹן umiTziyon יוסף, ו הויות, קנאה

יִסְעָדֶךָ yis'adeka : יִזְכֹּר yizkor כָּל־ kol ילי ; ר"ת וס"ת = י' הויות

מִנְחֹתֶךָ minchotecha וְעוֹלָתְךָ ve'olatcha יְדַשְּׁנֶה yedashne סֶלָה sela ס"ת הפסוק =

יִתֶּן yiten לְךָ lecha כִלְבָבֶךָ chilvavecha וְכָל־ vechol ילי ; סזהזר, סנדלפון, ערי:

בִּישׁוּעָתֶךָ bishu'atecha נְרַנְּנָה neranena יְמַלֵּא yemale : עֲצָתְךָ atzatcha ר"ת יהוה

נִדְגֹּל nidgol יְלה אֱלֹהֵינוּ Elohenu אדני = ס"ת uvshem וּבְשֵׁם־ ר"ת ב"ן

יִמַלֵּא yemale כָּל־ kol ילי Adonai יְהֹוָאדנילאהדונהי (יאהדונהי) = אמן ; ר"ת וס"ת =

מִשְׁאֲלוֹתֶיךָ mishalotecha : עַתָּה ata יָדַעְתִּי yadati כִּי ki הוֹשִׁיעַ hoshi'a

בִּמְשֹׁמֵי mishmei יַעֲנֵהוּ ya'anehu meshicho מְשִׁיחוֹ ר"ת מיה Adonai יְהֹוָאדנילאהדונהי

קָדְשׁוֹ kodsho בִּגְבֻרוֹת bigvurot יֵשַׁע yesha ר"ת יב"ק, אלהים יהוה, אהיה אדני יהוה

Meditate here to be protected from *Gog uMagog* (Armageddon) war יְמִינוֹ: yemino

אֵלֶּה ele בָרֶכֶב varechev וְאֵלֶּה ve'ele ר"ת וס"ת = אהיה ; ועם ר"ת וס"ת בסוסים = ס"ג

בַּסּוּסִים vasusim וַאֲנַחְנוּ va'anachnu בְּשֵׁם־ beshem Adonai יְהֹוָאדנילאהדונהי

אֱלֹהֵינוּ Elohenu ילה : נַזְכִּיר nazkir הֵמָּה hema כָּרְעוּ kar'u וְנָפָלוּ venafalu

וַאֲנַחְנוּ va'anachnu קַמְנוּ kamnu וַנִּתְעוֹדָד vanit'odad ר"ת יב"ק, אלהים יהוה, אהיה

הַמֶּלֶךְ hamelech Adonai יְהֹוָאדנילאהדונהי : הוֹשִׁיעָה hoshi'a יהוה ועי"ע נהורין אדני יהוה:

לַעֲנֵנוּ ya'anenu בְּיוֹם־ beyom יהוה = veyom ע"ה נגד, מזבח, זן אל יהוה

קָרְאֵנוּ kor'enu ר"ת יב"ק, אלהים יהוה, אהיה אדני יהוה אלהים ועם אות כף דהמלך = ע"ב:

LAMNATZE'ACH

"To the chief musician, a Psalm of David: May the Lord answer you on your day of distress. May the Name of the God of Jacob strengthen you. May He send you help from His Sanctuary and may He send you support from Zion. May He remember all your meal-offerings and abound your burnt-offerings, Selah. May He grant you as your heart desires, and may He fulfill your every plan. May we rejoice with your deliverance and raise a banner to the Name of our God. The Lord, shall fulfill all your requests. I now know that the Lord has delivered His anointed one. He answers him from His holy heavens, with the mighty deliverance of His right. Some trust in chariots, others in horses, but we shall call the Name of the Lord, our God. They were forced to kneel and they fell, but we rose and were encouraged. Lord, save us! The King shall answer us on the day we call Him." (Psalms 20)

SHACHARIT – MORNING PRAYER

DRAWING LIGHT TO BERIAH - יוד הֹי ואו הֹי – אל שׁדי

UVA LETZIYON

This prayer is our connection to redemption. The prayer starts, "And a redeemer should come to *Zion*." The redeemer is a reference to the *Mashiach*. Kabbalistically, the *Mashiach* is not a righteous person who will come and save us and bring about *world peace*. *Mashiach* is a state of spirituality and consciousness that every individual can achieve. No one is coming to save us and do the work for us. We must each achieve our own level of spiritual growth and fulfillment, our personal *Mashiach*, and when a critical mass of people have reached this state, the global *Mashiach* will appear for humanity.

fesha פֶשַׁע ulshavei וּלְשָׁבֵי go'el גֹּאֵל גֹּאֵל קֹנֶה, רֹ הויות, יוסף leTziyon לְצִיּוֹן uva וּבָא

beYaakov בְּיַעֲקֹב וֹ הויות, יאהדונהי אידהנויה ne'um נְאֻם יְהֹוָאֲדֹנָיאהדונהי Adonai:

va'ani וַאֲנִי אֲנִי ר"ת גוף בניו (שירדו לחיצונים בעון הוצאת ז"ל, ויחזרו לגוף אוצר הנשמות, ויבוא גואל) zot זֹאת beriti בְּרִיתִי otam אוֹתָם amar אָמַר יְהֹוָאֲדֹנָיאהדונהי Adonai

ruchi רוּחִי asher אֲשֶׁר alecha עָלֶיךָ udvarai וּדְבָרַי asher אֲשֶׁר

samti שַׂמְתִּי beficha בְּפִיךָ lo לֹא yamushu יָמֻשׁוּ mipicha מִפִּיךָ

umipi וּמִפִּי zar'acha זַרְעֲךָ zera זֶרַע umipi וּמִפִּי zar'acha זַרְעֲךָ

amar אָמַר יְהֹוָאֲדֹנָיאהדונהי Adonai me'ata מֵעַתָּה ve'ad וְעַד olam עוֹלָם:

On *Tish'a Be'av* and in a mourning house we skip from "*uva leTziyon*" (the above paragraph) and start here.

veAta וְאַתָּה kadosh קָדוֹשׁ yoshev יוֹשֵׁב tehilot תְּהִלּוֹת Yisrael יִשְׂרָאֵל:

vekara וְקָרָא ze זֶה el אֶל ze זֶה י"ב פרקין דיעקב מאירין לי"ב פרקין דרחל

ve'amar וְאָמַר kadosh קָדוֹשׁ | (Chesed) kadosh קָדוֹשׁ (Gevurah)

kadosh קָדוֹשׁ (Tiferet) יְהֹוָאֲדֹנָיאהדונהי Adonai Tzeva'ot צְבָאוֹת פני שכינה

melo מְלֹא chol כָּל ha'aretz הָאָרֶץ ילי אלהים דההן ע"ה kevodo כְּבוֹדוֹ:

umkabelin וּמְקַבְּלִין den דֵּין min מִן den דֵּין ve'amrin וְאָמְרִין◆

kadish קַדִּישׁ ב"פ אור, רז, ב"פ ב"פ א"ס bishmei בִּשְׁמֵי

meroma מְרוֹמָא ila'a עִלָּאָה bet בֵּית ב"פ ראה shechinte שְׁכִינְתֵּהּ◆

UVA LETZIYON

"A redeemer shall come to Zion and to those who shall turn away from sin from amongst [the House of] Jacob, so says the Lord. And as for Me, this is My Covenant with them, says the Lord. My spirit, which is upon you, and My words, that I have put in your mouth, shall not depart from your mouths, the mouths of your children, or the mouths of your children's children, says the Lord, from now and forever." (Isaiah 59:20-21) "And You are holy and await the praises of Israel. And one called to the other and said: Holy, Holy, Holy is the Lord of Hosts, the whole earth is filled with His glory." (Isaiah 6:3) And they receive consent from one another and say: Holy in the Highest Heavens is the abode of His Shechinah.

ovad עוֹבַד ara אַרְעָא al עַל־ ב״פ א״ס, ב״פ רז, ב״פ אור, ב״פ kadish קָדִישׁ

le'alam לְעָלַם gevurte גְּבוּרְתֵהּ ב״פ א״ס, ב״פ רז, ב״פ אור, ב״פ kadish קָדִישׁ

Tzeva'ot צְבָאוֹת Adonai יְהֹוָאדֹנָיאהדונהי almaya עָלְמַיָא ule'almei וּלְעָלְמֵי

yekare יְקָרֵהּ ziv זִיו ar'a אַרְעָא ילי chol כָּל malya מַלְיָא פני שכינה

kol קוֹל acharai אֹחֲרַי va'eshma וָאֶשְׁמַע ru'ach רוּחַ vatisa'eni וַתִּשָּׂאֵנִי

baruch בָּרוּךְ אום, יזל, מזבה, = אותיות ד״ה עם ; לתו gadol גָּדוֹל ra'ash רַעַשׁ

mimekomo מִמְּקוֹמוֹ Adonai יְהֹוָאדֹנָיאהדונהי כבוד יהוה = יוד הי ואו הי kevod כְּבוֹד

עסמ״ב, הברכה (למתק את ז' המלכים שמותו) ; ר״ת = ע״ב, ריבוע יהוה ; ר״ת מ״ח, י״פ האא

kal כָּל batrai בַּתְרַי ushma'it וּשְׁמָעִית rucha רוּחָא untalatni וּנְטָלַתְנִי

ve'amrin וְאָמְרִין dim'shabechin דִּמְשַׁבְּחִין sagi שַׂגִּיא zi'a זִיע גמם (ה' גבורות)

me'atar מֵאֲתַר dadonai דַּיהֹוָאדֹנָיאהדונהי yekara יְקָרָא berich בְּרִיךְ

yimloch יִמְלֹךְ | Adonai יְהֹוָאדֹנָיאהדונהי shechinte שְׁכִינְתֵּהּ bet בֵּית ב״פ ראה

Adonai יְהֹוָאדֹנָיאהדונהי va'ed וָעֶד ; ר״ת ייל אותיות דס״ג ; ו' אותיות ס״ג ריבוע le'olam לְעָלָם

ule'almei וּלְעָלְמֵי le'alam לְעָלַם ka'im קָאֵם malchute מַלְכוּתֵהּ

לה ; דמב, ע״ב מילוי Elohei אֱלֹהֵי Adonai יְהֹוָאדֹנָיאהדונהי almaya עָלְמַיָא

אבים פשוטות אותיות וטו״ז (אברים), עסמ״ב רמו״ח (החכמה, נתיבות ול״ב רי״ו, אל, ח״פ וז Avraham אַבְרָהָם

avotenu אֲבֹתֵינוּ veYisrael וְיִשְׂרָאֵל בן ד״פ Yitzchak יִצְחָק

דס״ג אותיות ו' ס״ג ריבוע le'olam לְעוֹלָם zot זֹאת shomrah שָׁמְרָה

בוכו levav לְבַב mach'shevot מַחְשְׁבוֹת leyetzer לְיֵצֶר

elecha אֵלֶיךָ levavam לְבָבָם vehachen וְהָכֵן amecha עַמֶּךָ

Holy, upon the Earth, is the work of His valor. Holy, forever and for all eternity, is the Lord of Hosts, the entire Earth is filled with the splendor of His glory. "And a wind carried me and from behind me I heard a great thunderous voice giving praise: Blessed is the glory of the Lord from His abode." (Ezikiel 3:12) And saying: Blessed is the glory of the Lord from the place of residence of His Shechinah. "The Lord shall reign forever and ever" (Exodus 15:18) The Lord, His Kingdom is established forever and for eternity. "The Lord, God of Abraham, Isaac, and Israel - our forefathers - safeguard this forever for the sake of the thoughts in the hearts of Your Nation, and direct their hearts toward You!" (I Chronicles 29:18)

וְהוּא vehu רַחוּם rachum יְכַפֵּר yechaper עָוֹן avon ר״ת רי״ו (Abba of the klipa)

וְלֹא velo יַשְׁחִית yashchit (Ima of the klipa) וְהִרְבָּה vehirba לְהָשִׁיב lehashiv

אַפּוֹ apo (Zeir of the klipa) וְלֹא velo יָעִיר ya'ir כָּל kol ילי וַחֲמָתוֹ chamato

:(Nukva of the klipa) כִּי ki אַתָּה Ata אֲדֹנָי Adonai כלה טוֹב tov והו

וְסַלָּח vesalach (Yitzchak) וְרַב verav יהוה ע״ב, ריבוע יהוה חֶסֶד chesed (Avraham)

לְכֹל lechol יה אדני קֹרְאֶיךָ kor'echa (Yaakov) צִדְקָתְךָ tzidkat'cha צֶדֶק tzedek

לְעוֹלָם le'olam ריבוע ס״ג וי׳ אותיות דס״ג וְתוֹרָתְךָ vetorat'cha אֱמֶת emet

אהיה פעמים אהיה, ז״פ ס״ג: תִּתֵּן titen אֱמֶת emet אהיה פעמים אהיה, ז״פ ס״ג

לְיַעֲקֹב leYaakov י׳ הויות, יאהדונהי וְחֶסֶד chesed ע״ב, ריבוע יהוה

לְאַבְרָהָם leAvraham וז״פ אל, רי״ו ול״ב נתיבות החכמה, רמ״ח (אברים), עסמ״ב וט״ו אותיות פשוטות

אֲשֶׁר asher נִשְׁבַּעְתָּ nishbata לַאֲבֹתֵינוּ la'avotenu מִימֵי mimei קֶדֶם kedem:

בָּרוּךְ baruch אֲדֹנָי Adonai לכה יום yom ע״ה נגד, מזבח, זן אל יהוה יום yom

יַעֲמָס ya'amos ר״ת יי לָנוּ lanu אלהים, אהיה אדני ; ר״ת ייל ע״ה נגד, מזבח, זן אל יהוה

הָאֵל haEl לאה ; אל (יי״א מילוי דס״ג) ; ר״ת ילה יְשׁוּעָתֵנוּ yeshu'atenu סֶלָה sela:

יְהֹוָאֲדֹנָהִ״יַ Adonai צְבָאוֹת Tzeva'ot פני שכינה עִמָּנוּ imanu

מִשְׂגָּב misgav מהע״ה, ע״ב בריבוע וקס״א, אל שׁדּי, ד״פ אלהים ע״ה ריבוע ס״ג, קס״א ע״ה וד׳ אותיות

לָנוּ lanu אלהים, אהיה אדני Elohei אֱלֹהֵי מילוי ע״ב, דמב ; ילה יַעֲקֹב Yaakov

יְהֹוָאֲדֹנָהִ״יַ Adonai צְבָאוֹת Tzeva'ot סֶלָה sela: י׳ הויות, יאהדונהי אידהנויה פני שכינה

אַשְׁרֵי ashrei אָדָם adam מ״ה ; יהוה צבאות אשרי אדם = תפארת בּוֹטֵחַ bote'ach

בָּךְ bach אדם בוטח בך = אמן ; בוטח בך (יאהדונהי) ע״ה ; מילוי ע״ב ע״ה:

"And He is merciful and forgives iniquities and shall not destroy, and He frequently thwarts His wrath and will never arouse all His anger." (Psalms 78:38) "Because You, Lord, are good and forgiving and abound in kindness to all who call to You." (Psalms 86:5) "Your righteousness is an everlasting justice, and Your Torah is true." (Psalms 119:142) "You give truth to Jacob and kindness to Abraham, as You have vowed to our forefathers since the earliest days." (Michah 7:20) "Blessed is the Lord, Who heaps burdens upon us each and every day, the God of our salvation. Selah." (Psalms 68:20) "The Lord of Hosts is with us; the God of Jacob is our strength. Selah." (Psalms 46:12) "Lord of Hosts, joyful is the man who trusts in You." (Psalms 84:13)

ר"ת יהה hamelech הַמֶּלֶךְ יהוה וע"ע נהורין hoshi'a הוֹשִׁיעָה Adonai אדני אהיה

kor'enu קָרְאֵנוּ בְּיוֹם- veyom ע"ה גגר, מזבח, זך, אל יהוה ya'anenu יַעֲנֵנוּ

ר"ת יב"ק, אלהים, אהיה אדני יהוה וס"ת ב"ן ועם אות כ' דהמלך = ע"ב:

BARUCH ELOHENU

Reciting the next verse ("baruch Elohenu") with genuine happiness and a trusting heart will generate extra Light in our lives and our *tikkun* process will be much easier. Meditate to devote your soul to sanctify the Holy Name (*Kedushat HaShem*).

lichvodo לִכְבוֹדוֹ shebera'anu שֶׁבְּרָאָנוּ ילה Elohenu אֱלֹהֵינוּ baruch בָּרוּךְ

vehivdilanu וְהִבְדִּילָנוּ min מִן hato'im הַתּוֹעִים (connecting to the right information)

venatan וְנָתַן lanu לָנוּ אלהים, אהיה אדני, אהיה torat תּוֹרַת emet אֱמֶת אהיה פעמים אהיה, ז"פ ס"ג

vechayei וְחַיֵּי olam עוֹלָם nata נָטַע betochenu בְּתוֹכֵנוּ. hu הוּא yiftach יִפְתַּח

libenu לִבֵּנוּ betorato בְּתוֹרָתוֹ. veyasim וְיָשִׂים belibenu בְּלִבֵּנוּ ahavato אַהֲבָתוֹ

veyir'ato וְיִרְאָתוֹ la'asot לַעֲשׂוֹת retzono רְצוֹנוֹ ule'ovdo וּלְעָבְדוֹ

belevav בְּלֵבָב בוכו shalem שָׁלֵם. lo לֹא niga נִיגַע larik לָרִיק

(Meditate here to be protected from night emission, so that the spiritual effort will not go to negativity [*Rik* and *Behala*]. Also meditate to have righteous children following the way of the Light)

velo וְלֹא neled נֵלֵד labehala לַבֶּהָלָה. yehi יְהִי ratzon רָצוֹן מהש ע"ה,

Adonai אדני אהיה ע"ב בריבוע וקס"א מ"ה ב"ן milfanecha מִלְּפָנֶיךָ ס"ג מ"ה ע"ה, אל שדי ע"ה,

avotenu אֲבוֹתֵינוּ velohei וֵאלֹהֵי ילה מילוי ע"ב, רמב ; לכב Elohenu אֱלֹהֵינוּ ילה

shenishmor שֶׁנִּשְׁמֹר chukecha חֻקֶּיךָ umitzvotecha וּמִצְוֹתֶיךָ

ba'olam בָּעוֹלָם haze הַזֶּה והו. venizke וְנִזְכֶּה venichye וְנִחְיֶה venirash וְנִירַשׁ

tova טוֹבָה אבא uvracha וּבְרָכָה lechayei לְחַיֵּי ha'olam הָעוֹלָם ha'olam הַבָּא.

"Lord, save us. The King shall answer us on the day when we call him." (Psalms 20:10)

BARUCH ELOHENU

Blessed is our God, Who created us for the sake of His glory, Who separated us from those who have been led astray, Who gave us the Torah of truth, and Who implanted within us eternal life. May He open our hearts with His Torah, and place within our hearts love for Him and fear of Him, to fulfill His will and to serve Him wholeheartedly. May we not toil in vain, and may we not give birth to panic. May it be Your will, Lord, our God and God of our forefathers, that we should keep Your statutes and Your commandments in this world, and may we merit, live, and attain goodness and blessing for the life in the World to Come.

לְמַעַן lema'an | יְזַמֶּרְךָ yezamercha | כָבוֹד chavod | וְלֹא velo | יִדֹם yidom

אֱלֹהַי Elohai ר"ת = אלהים, אהיה אדני מילוי ע"ב, דמב ; ילה | יְהֹוָואֲדֹנָיאהדונהי Adonai

אוֹדֶךָּ odeka ריבוע ס"ג ו' אותיות דס"ג | יְהֹוָואֲדֹנָיאהדונהי Adonai | לְעוֹלָם le'olam

וְחָפֵץ chafetz | לְמַעַן lema'an | צִדְקוֹ tzidko | יַגְדִּיל yagdil | תוֹרָה torah ר"ת צית

וְיָאַדִיר veya'adir ר"ת = אבגיתץ, ושר | וְיִבְטְוֹוּ veyivtechu | בְךָ vecha | יוֹדְעֵי yod'ei

שְׁמֶךָ shemecha | כִּי ki ר"ת יכש | לֹא lo | עָזַבְתָּ azavta | דֹרְשֶׁיךָ dorshecha

יְהֹוָואֲדֹנָיאהדונהי Adonai ס"ת כהת, משיחו בן דוד ע"ה | יְהֹוָואֲדֹנָיאהדונהי Adonai

אֲדֹנֵינוּ adonenu | מָה ma מ"ה | אַדִּיר adir הרי מ"ה | שִׁמְךָ shimcha | בְּכָל bechol ב"ן, לכב ; ומב

הָאָרֶץ ha'aretz אלהים דההן ע"ה | וְיַחֲזֵק chizku ע"ה | וְיַאֲמֵץ veya'ametz

לְבַבְכֶם levavchem | כָּל kol ילי | הַמְיַחֲלִים hameyachalim | לַיהֹוָואֲדֹנָיאהדונהי ladonai

KADDISH TITKABAL

This *Kaddish* draws the Light from the World of *Beriah* (ס"ג) into the World of *Yetzirah* (מ"ה).

יִתְגַּדַּל yitgadal | וְיִתְקַדַּשׁ veyitkadash עֹדִי ומילוי עֹדִי ; י"א אותיות כמנין ו"ה

שְׁמֵיהּ shemei (שם י"ה דע"ב) | רַבָּא raba קֹנָא ב"ן, יהוה אלהים יהוה אדני,

אָמֵן amen אידהנויה. מילוי קס"א וס"ג, מ"ה ברבוע וע"ב ע"ה ; ר"ת = ו"פ אלהים ; ס"ת = ג"פ יב"ק

בְּעָלְמָא be'alma | דִּי di | בְרָא vera | כִרְעוּתֵיהּ chir'utei

וְיַמְלִיךְ veyamlich | מַלְכוּתֵיהּ mal'chutei | וְיַצְמַח veyatzmach

פּוּרְקָנֵיהּ purkanei | וִיקָרֵב vikarev | מְשִׁיחֵיהּ meshichei | אָמֵן amen אידהנויה.

"So that glory should make melodies to You and not be silent, Lord, my God, I shall forever thank You."
(Psalms 30:13) "Lord desires righteousness: He makes the Torah great and powerful." (Isaiah 42:21)
"And they shall place their trust in You, all those who know Your Name, for You have not abandoned
those who seek You, Lord." (Psalms 9:11) "Lord, our Master, how mighty is Your Name throughout
the world." (Psalms 8:2) Be strong and your hearts be courageous, all you, who place your hope in the Lord.

KADDISH TITKABAL

May His great Name be more exalted and sanctified. (Amen)
In the world that He created according to His will, and may His kingdom reign.
And may He cause His redemption to sprout and may He bring the Mashiach closer. (Amen)

DRAWING LIGHT TO BERIAH - יוֹד הֵי וָאו הֵי – אֵל שַׁדַּי

bechayechon בְּחַיֵּיכוֹן — uvyomechon וּבְיוֹמֵיכוֹן — uvchayei וּבְחַיֵּי

dechol דְּכָל ילי — bet בֵּית ב"פ ראה — Yisrael יִשְׂרָאֵל — ba'agala בַּעֲגָלָא

uvizman וּבִזְמַן — kariv קָרִיב — ve'imru וְאִמְרוּ — amen אָמֵן — amen אָמֵן אידהנויה.

The congregation and the *chazan* say the following:

28 words (until *be'alma*) – meditate:

מילוי דמילוי דע"ב (יוד ויו דלת הי יוד ויו ויו יוד הי הי יוד)

28 letters (until *almaya*) - meditate:

מילוי דמילוי דס"ג (יוד ויו דלת הי יוד ואו אלף ואו הי יוד).

yehe יְהֵא — shemei שְׁמֵיה (שם י"ה דס"ג) — raba רַבָּא (קנ"א ב"ן)

mevarach מְבָרֵךְ ע"ב מ"ה ברבוע ס"ג מילוי קס"א וס"ג, אדני, מילוי אלהים יהוה

le'alam לְעָלַם — le'almei לְעָלְמֵי — almaya עָלְמַיָּא — yitbarach יִתְבָּרֵךְ

Seven words with six letters each (שם בן מ"ב) – meditate:

יהוה + יוד הי ויו הי + מילוי דמילוי דע"ב (יוד ויו דלת הי יוד ויו ויו יוד הי הי יוד)

Also, seven times the letter Vav (שם בן מ"ב) – meditate:

יהוה + יוד הי ואו הי + מילוי דמילוי דס"ג (יוד ויו דלת הי יוד ואו אלף ואו הי יוד).

veyishtabach וְיִשְׁתַּבַּח י"פ ע"ב יהוה אל אבג יתץ.

veyitpa'ar וְיִתְפָּאַר הי נו יה קרע שטן — veyitromam וְיִתְרוֹמַם וה כוזו נגד יכש.

veyitnase וְיִתְנַשֵּׂא במוכסז בטר צתג — veyit'hadar וְיִתְהַדָּר כוזו יה וזקב טנע.

veyit'ale וְיִתְעַלֶּה וה יוד ה יגל פזק — veyit'halal וְיִתְהַלָּל א ואו הא שקו צית.

shemei שְׁמֵיה (שם י"ה דמ"ה) — dekudsha דְּקוּדְשָׁא — verich בְּרִיךְ — hu הוּא

amen אָמֵן אידהנויה.

le'ela לְעֵלָּא — min מִן — kol כָּל יל — birchata בְּרְכָתָא — shirata שִׁירָתָא

tishbechata תֻּשְׁבְּחָתָא — venechamata וְנֶחָמָתָא — da'amiran דַּאֲמִירָן

be'alma בְּעָלְמָא — ve'imru וְאִמְרוּ — amen אָמֵן — amen אָמֵן אידהנויה.

In your lifetimes and in your days and in the lifetime of all the House of Israel, speedily and in the near future, and you shall say, Amen. (Amen) May His great Name be blessed forever and for all eternity. Blessed and lauded, and glorified, and exalted, and extolled, and honored, and uplifted, and praised be the Name of the Holy Blessed One (Amen) Above all blessings, songs, praises, and words of consolation that may be said in the world, and you shall say, Amen. (Amen)

וּבָעוּתָנָא uva'utana   צְלוֹתָנָא tzelotana   תִּתְקַבַּל titkabal

ילי   דְּכָל dechol   וּבָעוּתְהוֹן uva'utehon   צְלוֹתְהוֹן tzelotehon   עִם im

אֲבוּנָא avuna   קָדָם kadam   יִשְׂרָאֵל Yisrael   ב"פ ראה   בֵּית bet

אידהנויה.   אָמֵן amen   אָמֵן amen: וְאִמְרוּ ve'imru   דְּבִשְׁמַיָּא devishmaya

קנ"א ב"ן, יהוה אלהים יהוה אדני, מילוי קס"א וס"ג,   רַבָּא raba   שְׁלָמָא shelama   יְהֵא yehe

מ"ה ברבוע וע"ב ע"ה   אהיה אהיה יהוה, בינה ע"ה   וְחַיִּים chayim   שְׁמַיָּא shemaya   מִן min

וְשֵׁיזָבָא veshezava   וְנֶחָמָה venechama   וִישׁוּעָה vishu'a   וְסָבָע vesava

וְכַפָּרָה vechapara   וּסְלִיחָה uslicha   וּגְאֻלָּה ug'ula   וּרְפוּאָה urfu'a

יה אדני   וּלְכָל ulchol   לָנוּ lanu   אלהים, אהיה אדני   וְהַצָּלָה vehatzala   וְרֵיוַח verevach

אידהנויה.   אָמֵן amen   אָמֵן amen: וְאִמְרוּ ve'imru   יִשְׂרָאֵל Yisrael   עַמּוֹ amo

Take three steps backwards and say:

שָׁלוֹם shalom   עֹשֶׂה ose

(During the days between *Rosh Hashanah* and *Yom Kippur* instead of "shalom" we say:

הַשָּׁלוֹם hashalom ספריאל המלאך החותם לחיים)

בְּרַחֲמָיו berachamav   הוּא hu   יהוה   ריבוע   ע"ב,   bimromav בִּמְרוֹמָיו

נהורין.   alenu עָלֵינוּ   ר"ת   ש"ע   shalom שָׁלוֹם   ya'ase יַעֲשֶׂה

אָמֵן amen: וְאִמְרוּ ve'imru   יִשְׂרָאֵל Yisrael   עַמּוֹ amo   עמם ; ילי   כָּל kol   וְעַל ve'al

אָמֵן amen אידהנויה.

May our prayers and pleas be accepted, together with the prayers and pleas of the entire House of Israel, before our Father in Heaven, and you say, Amen. (Amen) May there be abundant peace from heaven. Life, contentment, salvation, consolation, deliverance, healing, redemption, pardon, atonement, comfort, and relief. For us and for His entire nation, Israel, and you shall say, Amen. (Amen) He, Who makes peace (During the days between *Rosh Hashanah* and *Yom Kippur*: The peace) *in His high places, He, in His compassion, shall make peace upon us And upon His entire nation, Israel, and you shall say, Amen. (Amen)*

From here ("*Bet Yaakov*") until "*Kave*" (pg. 270) you are in the World of *Yetzirah* (Formation).

BET YAAKOV

In this prayer we are reminded that there is only one God and that we should not serve other gods. Today, other gods come in the form of addictions to money, career, or other people's perception of us, to name a few. When we allow the trapping of the material word to give sway over us, we are serving other gods. God's nature is proactive and sharing. When we live our lives in a proactive, sharing manner, we bring God's Light into our lives.

אידהנויה יאהדונהי הויות, ו ראה ב"פ bet בֵּית Yaakov יַעֲקֹב

לְכוּ lechu וְנֵלְכָה venelcha בְּאוֹר be'or רז, אין סוף יְהֹוָ Adonai:

כִּי ki כָּל kol יל הָעַמִּים ha'amim יֵלְכוּ yelchu אִישׁ ish בְּשֵׁם beshem

אֱלֹהָיו elohav ילה וַאֲנַחְנוּ va'anachnu נֵלֵךְ nelech בְּשֵׁם beshem

יְהֹוָ Adonai אֱלֹהֵינוּ Elohenu ילה לְעוֹלָם le'olam

וָעֶד va'ed: יְהִי yehi יְהֹוָ Adonai אֱלֹהֵינוּ Elohenu ילה עִמָּנוּ imanu

כַּאֲשֶׁר ka'asher הָיָה haya עִם im

אֲבֹתֵינוּ avotenu אַל al יַעַזְבֵנוּ ya'azvenu וְאַל ve'al יִטְּשֵׁנוּ yiteshenu:

לְהַטּוֹת lehatot לְבָבֵנוּ levavenu אֵלָיו elav לָלֶכֶת lalechet בְּכָל bechol

דְּרָכָיו derachav וְלִשְׁמֹר velishmor מִצְוֹתָיו mitzvotav וְחֻקָּיו vechukav

וּמִשְׁפָּטָיו umishpatav אֲשֶׁר asher צִוָּה tziva אֶת et אֲבֹתֵינוּ avotenu:

וְיִהְיוּ veyihyu דְבָרַי devarai אֵלֶּה ele אֲשֶׁר asher

הִתְחַנַּנְתִּי hitchananti לִפְנֵי lifnei יְהֹוָ Adonai קְרֹבִים kerovim

אֶל el יְהֹוָ Adonai אֱלֹהֵינוּ Elohenu ילה יוֹמָם yomam

וְלַיְלָה valayla מלה לַעֲשׂוֹת la'asot | מִשְׁפַּט mishpat

עַבְדּוֹ avdo וּמִשְׁפַּט umishpat עַמּוֹ amo יִשְׂרָאֵל Yisrael

דְּבַר devar רָאה יוֹם yom בְּיוֹמוֹ beyomo:

BET YAAKOV

"The House of Jacob come, let us walk by the Light of the Lord." (Isaiah 2:5) "For all the nations shall each walk in the name of his god, but we shall walk in the Name of the Lord, our God, forever and ever." (Michah 4:5) "May the Lord, our God, be with us as He was with our forefathers. May He not abandon or forsake us, so we may bend our hearts to Him, walk in all His ways, keep His commandments, His statutes, and His laws, as He commanded our forefathers. Let those words, which I have pleaded before the Lord, be near the Lord, our God, day and night, to provide for the needs of His servant and the needs of His nation, Israel.

DRAWING LIGHT TO YETZIRAH - אל יהוה – הא ואו הא יוד

amei עַמֵּי   ילי   kol כָּל־   da'at דַּעַת   lema'an לְמַעַן

hu הוּא   Adonai יְהֹוָאדֹנָהּיֶאֱהְדֹוִנָהּי   ki כִּי   ע"ה דההן   אלהים   ha'aretz הָאָרֶץ

od עוֹד׃   en אֵין   haElohim הָאֱלֹהִים   אהיה אדני ; ילה ף ר"ת יהה ועולה למנין ענו עג"כ

SHIR HAMA'ALOT

The 57 words in this paragraph correspond to the numeric value of *Nun* נ, *Gimel* ג, *Dalet* ד, in the *Ana Becho'ach*, the 42-Letters Name of God. This number is also the value of the word *Zan* זן which is the Hebrew word for sustenance. It is important to recite this prayer as a single unit without any distraction between words. The unity of the prayer is the spark that ignites the power of sustenance.

Adonai יְהֹוָאדֹנָהּיֶאֱהְדֹוִנָהּי   lulei לוּלֵי   leDavid לְדָוִד   hama'alot הַמַּעֲלוֹת   shir שִׁיר

na נָא   yomar יֹאמַר־   אהיה אדני   אלהים,   lanu לָנוּ   יהה   shehaya שֶׁהָיָה

יהה shehaya שֶׁהָיָה   ר"ת ילי ; Adonai יְהֹוָאדֹנָהּיֶאֱהְדֹוִנָהּי   lulei לוּלֵי   Yisrael יִשְׂרָאֵל׃

(אדם בליעל ס"מ) adam אָדָם   alenu עָלֵינוּ   bekum בְּקוּם   אלהים, אהיה אדני   lanu לָנוּ

bacharot בָּחֳרוֹת   bela'unu בְּלָעוּנוּ   בינה ע"ה אהיה אהיה יהוה,   chayim וָחַיִּים   azai אֲזַי

shetafunu שְׁטָפוּנוּ   hamayim הַמַּיִם   azai אֲזַי   banu בָנוּ׃   (נוקבא דס"מ) apam אַפָּם

azai אֲזַי   nafshenu נַפְשֵׁנוּ׃   al עַל־   avar עָבַר   nachla נַחְלָה   (ליליח וכח דלהון)

hazedonim הַזֵּידוֹנִים׃   hamayim הַמַּיִם   nafshenu נַפְשֵׁנוּ   al עַל־   avar עָבַר

teref טָרֶף   netananu נְתָנָנוּ   shelo שֶׁלֹּא   Adonai יְהֹוָאדֹנָהּיֶאֱהְדֹוִנָהּי   baruch בָּרוּךְ

nimleta נִמְלְטָה   ketzipor כְּצִפּוֹר   nafshenu נַפְשֵׁנוּ   leshinehem לְשִׁנֵּיהֶם׃

nishbar נִשְׁבָּר   hapach הַפַּח   yokshim יוֹקְשִׁים   mipach מִפַּח

beshem בְּשֵׁם   ezrenu עֶזְרֵנוּ   nimlatnu נִמְלָטְנוּ׃   va'anachnu וַאֲנַחְנוּ

va'aretz וָאָרֶץ׃   י"פ טל, י"פ כוזו   shamayim שָׁמַיִם   ose עֹשֵׂה   Adonai יְהֹוָאדֹנָהּיֶאֱהְדֹוִנָהּי

All the nations of the earth shall know that the Lord is the God and there is none other." (I Kings 8:57-60)

SHIR HAMA'ALOT

"A Song of David: If it was not for the Lord, Who was there for us, let Israel now say: If it was not for the Lord, Who was there for us when men rose against us, then they would have swallowed us alive, when their anger raged against us. The waters would have flooded us, and the stream engulfed us. The evil waters would have engulfed us. Blessed is the Lord, Who did not allow us to be prey to their teeth. Our soul escaped like a bird from the snare of the trappers. The snare broke and we escaped. Our help is the Name of the Lord, Who forms the Heavens and the Earth." (Psalms 124)

SHIR SHEL YOM

The next six Psalms connect us to the six days of the week and to the six days of Creation. Each day we say the Psalm that corresponds to the unique expression of the spiritual Light of that day. Connecting to the original seed level of the six days of Creation gives us the power to alter our destiny.

SUNDAY - CHESED - ABRAHAM

Meditate that on Sunday, *Chesed* of *Atzilut* is illuminating יְהֹוָה

Also meditate on the Name: אבגיתץ which includes all the Names of *Ana Beko'ach*.

And on the Name: יְהֹוָה

(Tetragrammaton with the vowels of the initials of the verse: "בראשית ברא אלהים את")

אל יהוה ,זן ,מזבח ,נגד ע״ה hayom הַיּוֹם yom יוֹם אל יהוה זן ,מזבח ,נגד ע״ה

echad אוֹד אהבה ,דאגה beShabbat בְּשַׁבָּת kodesh קוֹדֶשׁ hashir הַשִּׁיר

shehayu שֶׁהָיוּ haleviyim הַלְוִיִם omrim אוֹמְרִים al עַל haduchan :הַדּוּכָן

leDavid לְדָוִד mizmor מִזְמוֹר (pause)

ladonai לַיהוה ha'aretz הָאָרֶץ אלהים דההין ע״ה umelo'a וּמְלוֹאָהּ

tevel תֵּבֵל veyoshvei וְיוֹשְׁבֵי va בָהּ: ki כִּי hu הוּא

al עַל yamim יַמִּים yesada יְסָדָהּ ve'al וְעַל neharot נְהָרוֹת

yechoneneha יְכוֹנְנֶהָ mi מִי: ya'ale יַעֲלֶה

vehar וְהַר Adonai יהוה umi וּמִי yakum יָקוּם

bimkom בִּמְקוֹם kodsho קָדְשׁוֹ

SHIR SHEL YOM
SUNDAY - CHESED - ABRAHAM

Today is day one of the counting to the Holy Shabbat.
The song the Levites used to recite on the rostrum.
"A Psalm to David:
The earth and all it contains belong to the Lord,
as the habitation and all who dwell in it. He founded it upon the seas and established it upon the rivers. Who shall ascend the mountain of the Lord and who shall stand in His holy place?

נְקִי neki ע"ה קס"א ע"ה קנ"א, אדני אלהים (מזרע לבטלה) כַּפַּיִם chapayim

וּבַר־ uvar יצוחק, ד"פ ב"ן ; בר לבב = ע"ב ס"ג מ"ה ב"ן, לֵבָב levav בוכו ;

lashav לַשָּׁוְא nasa נָשָׂא lo לֹא־ asher אֲשֶׁר הברכה (למתק את ז' המלכים עמתו)

נַפְשִׁי nafshi (כתיב: נפשו) velo וְלֹא nishba נִשְׁבַּע lemirma לְמִרְמָה:

Adonai יְהֹוָ֖הִאדנייאהדונהי ב"ן ר"ת יבמ, me'et מֵאֵת veracha בְרָכָה yisa יִשָּׂא

וּצְדָקָה utz'daka ע"ה ריבוע אלהים ; יהה מילוי ע"ב, דמב ; ילה meElohei מֵאֱלֹהֵי

yish'o יִשְׁעוֹ שכינה ע"ה ; ס"ת יהוה: ze זֶה dor דּוֹר dorshav דֹּרְשָׁיו

(כתיב: דרשו) mevakshei מְבַקְשֵׁי fanecha פָנֶיךָ ס"ג מ"ה ב"ן

Yaakov יַעֲקֹב ז' הויות, יאהדונהי אידהנויה sela סֶלָה: su שְׂאוּ se'u שְׁעָרִים she'arim כתר

רָאשֵׁיכֶם rashechem vehinase'u וְהִנָּשְׂאוּ ו' שהוא זעיר אנפין וה' שהיא מלכות - נשאו

פִּתְחֵי pitchei olam עוֹלָם melech מֶלֶךְ veyavo וְיָבוֹא hakavod הַכָּבוֹד לאו:

mi מִי ילי ze זֶה melech מֶלֶךְ ר"ת = פ"ו בסוד כתם טהור פז

הַכָּבוֹד hakavod לאו יְהֹוָ֖הִאדנייאהדונהי Adonai ; כבוד יהוה = יוד הי ואו הה izuz עִזּוּז

וְגִבּוֹר vegibor Adonai יְהֹוָ֖הִאדנייאהדונהי gibor גִּבּוֹר milchama מִלְחָמָה:

שְׂאוּ se'u שְׁעָרִים she'arim כתר רָאשֵׁיכֶם rashechem

use'u וּשְׂאוּ ר' עילאה שהוא ת"ת נשא pitchei פִּתְחֵי

olam עוֹלָם veyavo וְיָבוֹא melech מֶלֶךְ hakavod הַכָּבוֹד לאו:

mi מִי ילי hu הוּא ze זֶה melech מֶלֶךְ hakavod הַכָּבוֹד לאו

יְהֹוָ֖הִאדנייאהדונהי Adonai ; כבוד יהוה = יוד הי ואו הה Tzevaot צְבָאוֹת פני שכינה

hu הוּא melech מֶלֶךְ hakavod הַכָּבוֹד לאו sela סֶלָה:

On *Chanukah* continue on pg. 265 – "*mizmor shir chanukat habayit*". On any other day continue "*hoshi'enu*" on pg. 267.

He whose hands are clean, whose heart is pure, and who neither has sworn in vain by his soul nor vowed falsely. He shall receive a blessing from the Lord and charity from the God of his salvation. This is the generation of those who seek Him, who seek your countenance, Jacob, Selah! Raise up your hand gates, and become uplifted, you portals of the world, and let the glorious King in. Who is the glorious King? It is the Lord, Who is powerful and valiant. The Lord, Who is mighty in war. Raise up your heads gates, and lift up your eternal portals and let the glorious King in. Who is the glorious King? It is the Lord of Hosts. He is the glorious King, Selah." (Psalms 24) [Save us]

MONDAY - GEVURAH - ISAAC

Meditate that on Monday, *Gevurah* of *Atzilut* is illuminating יהוה

Also meditate on the Name: קרעשטן and on the Name: יהוה

(Tetragrammaton with the vowels of the initials of the verse: "ויאמר אלהים יהי רקיע")

In this Psalm there are 15 verses, which correspond to the Holy Name: יה

אל יהוה זן, מזבח, נגר ע"ה yom יוֹם אל יהוה זן, מזבח, נגר ע"ה hayom הַיּוֹם

hashir הַשִּׁיר kodesh קוֹדֶשׁ beShabbat בְּשַׁבָּת sheni שֵׁנִי

haduchan: הַדּוּכָן al עַל omrim אוֹמְרִים haleviyim הַלְוִיִם shehayu שֶׁהָיוּ

להם gadol גָּדוֹל Korach: קֹרַח livnei לִבְנֵי mizmor מִזְמוֹר shir שִׁיר עִיר

עם ד' אותיות = מובה, יזל, אום Adonai אהדונהי יאהדונהי יְהוָה (אדני) umhulal וּמְהֻלָּל ס"ת ללה, אדני

יֵלה Elohenu אֱלֹהֵינוּ ערי בזהֶר, סנדלפון, me'od מְאֹד be'ir בְּעִיר

ילי kol כָּל mesos מְשׂוֹשׂ nof נוֹף yefe יְפֵה kodsho: קָדְשׁוֹ har הַר

קנאה הויות, ר יוסף, Tziyon צִיּוֹן har הַר ע"ה אלהים דהדהין ha'aretz הָאָרֶץ

rav: רַב melech מֶלֶךְ kiryat קִרְיַת tzafon צָפוֹן yarketei יַרְכְּתֵי

noda נוֹדַע be'armenoteha בְּאַרְמְנוֹתֶיהָ אהיה אדני; ילה Elohim אֱלֹהִים

ki כִּי: lemisgav לְמִשְׂגָּב מושה, מהע, ע"ב בריבוע וקס"א, אל שדי, ד"פ אלהים ע"ה:

yachdav: יַחְדָּו avru עָבְרוּ no'adu נוֹעֲדוּ hamelachim הַמְּלָכִים hine הִנֵּה

nechpazu: נֶחְפָּזוּ nivhalu נִבְהֲלוּ tamahu תָּמָהוּ ken כֵּן rau רָאוּ hema הֵמָּה

kayoleda: כַּיּוֹלֵדָה ומב chil וְחִיל sham שָׁם achazatam אֲחָזָתַם re'ada רְעָדָה

Tarshish: תַּרְשִׁישׁ oniyot אֳנִיּוֹת teshaber תְּשַׁבֵּר kadim קָדִים beru'ach בְּרוּחַ

MONDAY - GVURAH - ISAAC

Today is the second day of the counting to the Holy Shabbat.
The song the Levites used to recite upon the rostrum.
"A song and a Psalms of the sons of Korach:
The lord is great and exceedingly praised in the city of our God,
His holy mountain - a beautiful scene and a source of joy for the entire land, Mount Zion, at the northern side, the city of a great King. God is known in her palaces as powerful. Behold, the kings have gathered and set out together. They saw and were astonished. They panicked and quickly fled. A tremble took hold of them; fright like that of a woman in labor. With an easterly wind, You smashed the ships of Tarshish.

ka'asher כַּאֲשֶׁר   shamanu שָׁמַעְנוּ   ken כֵּן   ra'inu רָאִינוּ

be'ir בְּעִיר בֹּזְחֹזֶף, סנּדלפֿון, ערי   Adonai יְהֹוָה(אֲדֹנָיאהדונהי)   Tzeva'ot צְבָאוֹת פני שכינה

be'ir בְּעִיר בֹּזְחֹזֶף, סנּדלפֿון, ערי   Elohenu אֱלֹהֵינוּ ילה   Elohim אֱלֹהִים אהיה אדני ; ילה

yechoneneha יְכוֹנְנֶהָ עם התיבה וע"ה קמ"ג   ad עַד־   olam עוֹלָם   sela סֶלָה׃

diminu דִּמִּינוּ   Elohim אֱלֹהִים אהיה אדני ; ילה   chasdecha וַֽחַסְדֶּךָ   bekerev בְּקֶרֶב

hechalecha הֵיכָלֶךָ׃   keshimcha כְּשִׁמְךָ   Elohim אֱלֹהִים אהיה אדני ; ילה

ken כֵּן   tehilatcha תְּהִלָּתְךָ   al עַל־   katzvei קַצְוֵי   eretz אֶרֶץ   tzedek צֶדֶק

mal'a מָלְאָה   yeminecha יְמִינֶךָ׃   yismach יִשְׂמַח משיח   har הַר־

Tziyon צִיּוֹן יוסף, ו' הויות, קנאה   tagelna תָּגֵלְנָה   benot בְּנוֹת   Yehuda יְהוּדָה

lema'an לְמַעַן   mishpatecha מִשְׁפָּטֶיךָ׃   sobu סֹבּוּ   Tziyon צִיּוֹן יוסף, ו' הויות, קנאה

vehakifuha וְהַקִּיפֽוּהָ   sifru סִפְרוּ   migdaleha מִגְדָּלֶיהָ׃   shitu שִׁיתוּ

libchem לִבְּכֶם   lechela לְחֵילָה   pasegu פַּסְּגוּ   armenoteha אַרְמְנוֹתֶיהָ

lema'an לְמַעַן   tesaperu תְּסַפְּרוּ   ledor לְדוֹר   acharon אַחֲרוֹן׃

ki כִּי   ze זֶה   Elohim אֱלֹהִים אהיה אדני ; ילה   Elohenu אֱלֹהֵינוּ ילה

olam עוֹלָם   va'ed וָעֶד   hu הוּא   yenahagenu יְנַהֲגֵנוּ   al עַל־   mut מוּת׃

On *Chanukah* continue on pg. 265 – "*mizmor shir chanukat habayit*". On any other day continue "*hoshi'enu*" on pg. 267.

TUESDAY – TIFERET - JACOB

Meditate that on Tuesday, *Tiferet* of *Atzilut* is illuminating יְהֹוָה

Also meditate on the Name: נגדיכש and on the Name: יְהֹוָה

(Tetragrammaton with the vowels of the initials of the verse: "וַיֹּאמֶר אֱלֹהִים יִקָּווּ הַמַּיִם")

As we have heard, so we have seen in the city of the Lord of Hosts, in the city of our God. May God establish it forever, Selah! God, we had hoped for Your kindness in the midst of Your Sanctuary. As is Your Name, God, so is Your praise in all corners of the earth. Righteousness fills Your right hand. Mount Zion shall rejoice and the daughters of Judah shall delight, for the sake of Your judgments. Surround Zion and walk around her. Count her towers. Set Your Heart to Her walls and raise her walls, so that You may relate to the next generation. For this is the Lord, our God, for all eternity He shall lead us forever." (Psalms 48) [Save us]

הַיּוֹם hayom — ע"ה נגד, מזבח, זן, אל יהוה — yom יוֹם — ע"ה נגד, מזבח, זן, אל יהוה

שְׁלִישִׁי shelishi — בְּשַׁבָּת beShabbat — קוֹדֶשׁ kodesh — הַשִּׁיר hashir

שֶׁהָיוּ shehayu — הַלְוִיִּם haleviyim — אוֹמְרִים omrim — עַל al — הַדּוּכָן haduchan

מִזְמוֹר mizmor — לְאָסָף leAsaf — אֱלֹהִים Elohim

נִצָּב nitzav — בַּעֲדַת ba'adat — אֵל El — בְּקֶרֶב bekerev

אֱלֹהִים Elohim — יִשְׁפֹּט yishpot — עַד ad — מָתַי matai

תִּשְׁפְּטוּ tishpetu — עָוֶל avel — וּפְנֵי ufnei — רְשָׁעִים resha'im

תִּשְׂאוּ tis'u — סֶלָה sela — שִׁפְטוּ shiftu — דַל dal — וְיָתוֹם veyatom

עָנִי ani — וָרָשׁ varash — הַצְדִּיקוּ hatz'diku — פַּלְּטוּ paltu — דַל dal

וְאֶבְיוֹן ve'evyon — מִיַּד miyad — רְשָׁעִים resha'im — הַצִּילוּ hatzilu

לֹא lo — יָדְעוּ yad'u — וְלֹא velo — יָבִינוּ yavinu — בַּחֲשֵׁכָה bachashecha

יִתְהַלָּכוּ yit'halachu — יִמּוֹטוּ yimotu — כָּל kol — מוֹסְדֵי mosdei — אָרֶץ aretz

אֲנִי ani — אָמַרְתִּי amarti — אֱלֹהִים Elohim — אַתֶּם atem

עֶלְיוֹן elyon — וּבְנֵי uvnei — כֻּלְּכֶם kulchem — אָכֵן achen — כְּאָדָם ke'adam

תְּמוּתוּן temutun — וּכְאַחַד uche'achad — הַשָּׂרִים hasarim

תִּפֹּלוּ tipolu — קוּמָה kuma — אֱלֹהִים Elohim

שָׁפְטָה shofta — הָאָרֶץ ha'aretz — כִּי ki

אַתָּה Ata — תִנְחַל tinchal — בְּכָל bechol — הַגּוֹיִם hagoyim

On Chanukah continue on pg. 265 – "mizmor shir chanukat habayit". On any other day continue "hoshi'enu" on pg. 267.

TUESDAY - TIFERET - JACOB

Today is the third day of the counting to the Holy Shabbat.
The song the Levites used to recite upon the rostrum.

"A Psalms of Asaf:

God is present in the supernal assembly. Amidst judges, He judges. Until when shall you judge dishonestly and show favor to the wicked? Selah! Judge the destitute and the orphan. Rule in favor of the poor and the needy. Rescue the destitute and the wretched. Deliver them from the hands of the wicked, who do not know or understand that they walk in darkness; they cause the foundations of the earth to collapse. I had said that you are like angels and are all sons of the supernal, yet, you shall die like Adam and shall fall like one of the princes. Rise, God, and judge the world for You shall bequeath upon all the nations." *(Psalms 82)* *[Save us]*

SHACHARIT – MORNING PRAYER
DRAWING LIGHT TO YETZIRAH - יוד הא ואו הא – אל יהוה

WEDNESDAY - NETZACH - MOSES

Meditate that on Wednesday, *Netzach* of *Atzilut* is illuminating יְהֹוָה
Also meditate on the Name: בְּטַרְצַתַג and on the Name: יְהֹוָה
(Tetragrammaton with the vowels of the initials of the verse: "וַיֹּאמֶר אֱלֹהִים יְהִי מְאוֹרֹת")

הַיּוֹם hayom ז"ן, נגד, מזבח, ע"ה — אל יהוה, ז"ן, מזבח, נגר ע"ה — yom יוֹם אל יהוה, ז"ן, מזבח, נגר, אל יהוה

רְבִיעִי revi'i בְּשַׁבָּת beShabbat קוֹדֶשׁ kodesh הַשִּׁיר hashir

שֶׁהָיוּ shehayu הַלְוִיִּם haleviyim אוֹמְרִים omrim עַל al הַדּוּכָן haduchan:

אֵל El יא"י (מילוי דס"ג) נְקָמוֹת nekamot יְהֹוָ‎ Adonai ; ר"ת אני

אֵל El יא"י (מילוי דס"ג) נְקָמוֹת nekamot ר"ת = יב"ק, אלהים יהוה, אהיה אדנ"י יהוה

הוֹפִיעַ :hofi'a הִנָּשֵׂא hinase שֹׁפֵט shofet הָאָרֶץ ha'aretz אלהים דההין ע"ה

הָשֵׁב hashev ר"ת = שׂדי ע"ה גְּמוּל gemul עַל al גֵּאִים :ge'im עַד ad

מָתַי matai עַד ad Adonai יְהֹוָ‎ רְשָׁעִים resha'im מָתַי matai

רְשָׁעִים resha'im יַעֲלֹזוּ ya'alozu ג"פ אמ: יַבִּיעוּ yabi'u יְדַבְּרוּ yedaberu

עָתָק atak יִתְאַמְּרוּ yit'amru כָּל kol יל פֹּעֲלֵי po'alei אָוֶן :aven עַמְּךָ amecha

יְהֹוָ‎ Adonai יְדַכְּאוּ yedake'u וְנַחֲלָתְךָ venachalatcha יְעַנּוּ :ye'anu

אַלְמָנָה almana וְגֵר veger יַהֲרֹגוּ yaharogu וִיתוֹמִים vitomim יְרַצֵּחוּ :yeratzechu

וַיֹּאמְרוּ vayomru לֹא lo יִרְאֶה yir'e רי"ו יָהּ Yah וְלֹא velo יָבִין yavin

אֱלֹהֵי Elohei מילוי ע"ב, רמב ; יָלֵ‎ יַעֲקֹב Yaakov ו' הויות, יאהדונהי איהדונהי: בִּינוּ binu

בֹּעֲרִים bo'arim בָּעָם ba'am וּכְסִילִים uchsilim מָתַי matai תַּשְׂכִּילוּ :taskilu

---

WEDNESDAY - NETZACH - MOSES

Today is the fourth day of the counting to the Holy Shabbat.
The song that the Levites used to recite upon the rostrum.

"The God of retribution is the Lord. God of retribution, appear! Arise, You judge of the earth! Repay the arrogant their due. How long shall the wicked, Lord, how long shall the wicked rejoice? They express themselves and speak with arrogance. All the evil-doers are proud; Lord, they debase Your Nation and they torture Your Children. They kill widow and convert; they murder orphans. And they say: The Lord does not see, and the God of Jacob does not understand. You should understand, you imbeciles among the people, and you fools: when shall you become wise?

hanota הַנֹּטַע | ozen אֹזֶן | יוד הי ואו הי דה דה | halo הֲלֹא | yishma יִשְׁמַע

im אִם- | יוהך, מ"א אותיות דפעוטת, דמילוי ודמילוי דמילוי דאהיה ע"ה | yotzer יֹצֵר

ayin עַיִן | רבוע מ"ה | halo הֲלֹא | yabit יַבִּיט: | hayoser הַיֹּצֵר | goyim גּוֹיִם

halo הֲלֹא | yochi'ach יוֹכִיחַ | hamelamed הַמְלַמֵּד | adam אָדָם | מ"ה | da'at דָּעַת:

Adonai יְהוָֹה | yode'a יֹדֵעַ | machshevot מַחְשְׁבוֹת | adam אָדָם | מ"ה

ki כִּי- | hema הֵמָּה | havel הָבֶל | מילוי דס"ג | ashrei אַשְׁרֵי | hagever הַגֶּבֶר

asher אֲשֶׁר- | teyasrenu תְּיַסְּרֶנּוּ | Yah יָּהּ | umitorat'cha וּמִתּוֹרָתְךָ

telamedenu תְלַמְּדֶנּוּ: | lehashkit לְהַשְׁקִיט | lo לוֹ | mimei מִימֵי | ra רָע | ad עַד

yikare יִכָּרֶה | larasha לָרָשָׁע | shachat שָׁחַת: | ki כִּי | lo לֹא- | yitosh יִטֹּשׁ

Adonai יְהוָֹה | amo עַמּוֹ | venachalato וְנַחֲלָתוֹ | lo לֹא | ya'azov יַעֲזֹב:

ki כִּי- | ad עַד- | tzedek צֶדֶק | yashuv יָשׁוּב | mishpat מִשְׁפָּט | ע"ה ה"פ אלהים

ve'acharav וְאַחֲרָיו | kol כָּל- | ילי | yishrei יִשְׁרֵי | ילי | lev לֵב: | mi מִי- | ילי

yakum יָקוּם | li לִי | im אִם- | mere'im מְרֵעִים | ילי | mi מִי- | yityatzev יִתְיַצֵּב

li לִי | im אִם- | po'alei פֹּעֲלֵי | aven אָוֶן: | lulei לוּלֵי | Adonai יְהוָֹה

ezrata עֶזְרָתָה | li לִי | kim'at כִּמְעַט | shachna שָׁכְנָה | duma דוּמָה | nafshi נַפְשִׁי:

im אִם | יוהך, מ"א אותיות דפעוטת, דמילוי ודמילוי דמילוי דאהיה ע"ה | amarti אָמַרְתִּי | ר"ת = ב"ן

mata מָטָה | ragli רַגְלִי | chasdecha וַסְדְּךָ | Adonai יְהוָֹה

yis'adeni יִסְעָדֵנִי: | שדי | berov בְּרֹב | sar'apai שַׂרְעַפַּי | י"פ אהיה | bekirbi בְּקִרְבִּי

tanchumecha תַּנְחוּמֶיךָ | yesha'ashe'u יְשַׁעַשְׁעוּ | nafshi נַפְשִׁי: | ר"ת נית (ו מות)

Can the One Who implanted the ear, not hear? Can the One Who formed the eye, not behold? Shall the One Who punishes nations, not admonish? He Who teaches man knowledge! Lord knows the thoughts of man, that they are in vain. Fortunate is the man whom You chastise, Lord, and from Your Torah, You teach him, so that he would be secure against bad times, until a deep abyss is dug for the wicked. The Lord does not forsake His Nation or abandon His Heritage, for until justice is done, the judgment shall last. Following Him are all who are upright at heart. Who shall rise for me against evil-doers? Who shall stand by me against the workers of iniquity? Was it not for the Lord Who had helped me, then my soul would have dwelt in Hell. If I said that my foot slipped, Your kindness, Lord, would support me. When many depressing thoughts were within me, Your consoling words would cheer my soul.

DRAWING LIGHT TO YETZIRAH - יוד הא ואו הא – אל יהוה

הַיְחָבְרְךָ hayechovrecha כִּסֵּא kise הַוּוֹת havot יֵצֶר yotzer עָמָל amal

עֲלֵי־ alei וֹק chok: יְגוֹדוּ yagodu עַל־ al נֶפֶשׁ nefesh צַדִּיק tzadik

וְדָם vedam נָקִי naki ע"ה קס"א וְירַשִׁיעוּ yarshi'u: וִיְהִי vayehi

יְהֹוָ אדני יאהדונהי Adonai לִי li לְמִשְׂגָּב lemisgav מושה, מהע, ע"ב בריבוע וקס"א,

לְצוּר letzur אלהים דההין ע"ה מָעוּזִי machsi הרזו: וַיָּשֶׁב vayashev אל שדי, ד"פ אלהים ע"ה מילוי ע"ב, דמב ; ילה וָאֱלֹהַי velohai (אליהו הנביא) לכב ; מילוי ע"ב, דמב, דמב ; ילה

עֲלֵיהֶם alehem אֶת־ et אוֹנָם onam וּבְרָעָתָם uvra'atam יַצְמִיתֵם yatzmitem

יַצְמִיתֵם yatzmitem יְהֹוָ אדני יאהדונהי Adonai אֱלֹהֵינוּ Elohenu ילה:

On *Chanukah* continue on pg. 265 – "*mizmor shir chanukat habayit*". On any other day continue "*hoshi'enu*" on pg. 267.

THURSDAY - HOD - AARON

Meditate that on Thursday, *Hod* of *Atzilut* is illuminating יְהֹוָ

Also meditate on the Name: וֹזָקְבְּטַנֵע and on the Name: יְהֹוָ

(Tetragrammaton with the vowels of the initials of the verse: "וַיֹּאמֶר אֱלֹהִים יִשְׁרְצוּ הַמַּיִם")

In this Psalm there are 126 words corresponding to the Holy Name: ריבוע אדני (א אר אדני אדני) = כוק

הַיּוֹם hayom ע"ה נגד, מזבוח, זן, אל יהוה יוֹם yom אל יהוה זן, מזבוח, נגד, ע"ה וְהַמִּישִׁי chamishi בְּשַׁבָּת beShabbat קוֹדֶשׁ kodesh הַשִּׁיר hashir

שֶׁהָיוּ shehayu הַלְוִיִּם haleviyim אוֹמְרִים omrim עַל־ al הַדּוּכָן haduchan:

לַמְנַצֵּחַ lamnatze'ach עַל־ al הַגִּתִּית hagitit לְאָסָף leAsaf: הַרְנִינוּ harninu

לֵאלֹהִים lelohim אהיה אדני ; ילה עוּזֵנוּ uzenu הָרִיעוּ hari'u אלהים דאלפין

לֵאלֹהֵי lelohei מילוי ע"ב, דמב ; ילה יַעֲקֹב Yaakov ו' הויות, יאהדונהי אידהנויה ; ר"ת ילה:

Can a throne of evil be linked with You by one who fashions injustice into law? They gather against the life of the righteous, and they condemn innocent blood. But the Lord became my strength, and my God was the Rock of my refuge. He shall turn their evil acts against them and shall strike them down with their wickedness. The Lord, our God, shall strike them down." (Psalms 94)[Save us]

THURSDAY - HOD - AARON

Today is the fifth day of the counting to the Holy Shabbat.
The song the Levites used to recite upon the rostrum.
"To the Chief musician, set for the Gittit, by Asaf:
Sing with joy to the God of our strength. Hail loudly the God of Jacob.

שְׂאוּ se'u זִמְרָה zimra וּתְנוּ utnu תֹף tof כִּנּוֹר kinor נָעִים na'im

עִם im נָבֶל navel תִּקְעוּ tik'u בַחֹדֶשׁ vachodesh

שׁוֹפָר shofar בַּכֶּסֶה bakese לְיוֹם leyom וַיִּגֶּנוּ chagenu

כִּי ki חֹק chok לְיִשְׂרָאֵל leYisrael הוּא hu מִשְׁפָּט mishpat

לֵאלֹהֵי lelohei יַעֲקֹב Yaakov

עֵדוּת edut בִּיהוֹסֵף bihosef שָׂמוֹ samo בְּצֵאתוֹ betzeto עַל al אֶרֶץ eretz

מִצְרַיִם Mitzrayim שְׂפַת sefat לֹא lo יָדַעְתִּי yadati אֶשְׁמָע eshma

הֲסִירוֹתִי hasiroti מִסֵּבֶל misevel שִׁכְמוֹ shichmo כַּפָּיו kapav מִדּוּד midud

קָרָאתָ karata בַּצָּרָה batzara תַעֲבֹרְנָה ta'avorna

וָאֲחַלְּצֶךָ va'achaletzeka אֶעֶנְךָ e'encha בְּסֵתֶר beseter רַעַם ra'am

אֶבְחָנְךָ evchoncha עַל al בֵּי mei מְרִיבָה meriva סֶלָה sela

שְׁמַע shema עַמִּי ami וְאָעִידָה ve'a'ida בָּךְ bach יִשְׂרָאֵל Yisrael

אִם im תִּשְׁמַע tishma לִי li

לֹא lo יִהְיֶה yihye בְךָ vecha אֵל el זָר zar

וְלֹא velo תִשְׁתַּחֲוֶה tishtachave לְאֵל le'el נֵכָר nechar אָנֹכִי anochi

יְהוָה Adonai אֱלֹהֶיךָ Elohecha הַמַּעַלְךָ hama'alcha

מֵאֶרֶץ me'eretz מִצְרַיִם Mitzrayim הַרְחֶב harchev פִּיךָ picha

וָאֲמַלְאֵהוּ va'amal'ehu וְלֹא velo שָׁמַע shama עַמִּי ami לְקוֹלִי lekoli

וְיִשְׂרָאֵל veYisrael לֹא lo אָבָה ava לִי li וָאֲשַׁלְּחֵהוּ va'ashalechehu

בִּשְׁרִירוּת bishrirut לִבָּם libam יֵלְכוּ yelchu בְּמוֹעֲצוֹתֵיהֶם bemo'atzotehem

---

Take to singing and beat the drum, a pleasant harp together with the lyre. Blow the Shofar at the renewal of the month upon the concealment of the moon for our day of festival. Because it is a statute for Israel, a judgment day for the God of Jacob. Vestments were put on Joseph when he went out over the land for Egypt, where he heard a language that he never knew. I removed the load from his shoulder; his hands I withdrew from the pots. In trouble you have called and I rescued you. I answer your secret call with thunder. I tested you at the waters of Mrivah. Selah. My People listen and I shall warn you: Israel, if you would only listen to Me. There shall not be among you a foreign deity, nor should you bow to an alien god. I am the Lord, your God, Who brought you out of the land of Egypt. Open your mouth wide and I shall fill it. My People did not heed My words. Israel did not obey Me. I banished them to the folly of their hearts. They walked in their evil counsel.

lu לּו ami עַמִּי shome'a שֹׁמֵעַ li לִי Yisrael יִשְׂרָאֵל bidrachai בִּדְרָכַי

yehalechu יְהַלֵּכוּ: kim'at כִּמְעַט oyvehem אוֹיְבֵיהֶם achni'a אַכְנִיעַ

ve'al וְעַל tzarehem צָרֵיהֶם ashiv אָשִׁיב yadi יָדִי: mesan'ei מְשַׂנְאַי

Adonai יְהֹוָה yechachashu יְכַחֲשׁוּ lo לוֹ vihi וִיהִי itam עִתָּם

le'olam לְעוֹלָם רִיבוּע דס"ג וי אותיות דס"ג: vaya'achilehu וַיַּאֲכִילֵהוּ

mechelev מֵחֵלֶב chita חִטָּה אכא umitzur וּמִצּוּר אלהים דההן ע"ה

devash דְּבַשׁ עו' י"ד דעופר (ועם י"ד האווזן הרי ע"ך דינין הגדולות) asbi'eka אַשְׂבִּיעֶךָ:

On Chanukah continue on pg. 265 – "mizmor shir chanukat habayit". On any other day continue "hoshi'enu" on pg. 267.

FRIDAY - YESOD - JOSEPH

Meditate that on Friday, *Yesod* of *Atzilut* is illuminating יְהֹוִוהוּ
Also meditate on the Name: יִגְלפְזְק and on the Name: יְהֹוָה
(Tetragrammaton with the vowels of the initials of the verse: "וַיֹּאמֶר אֱלֹהִים תּוֹצֵא הָאָרֶץ")
In this Psalm there are 45 words, corresponding to the Holy Name: מ"ה (יוד הֵא וָאו הֵא)

hayom הַיּוֹם ע"ה נגד, מזבח, זן, אל יהוה ע"ה yom יוֹם אל יהוה זן, מזבח, נגד, ע"ה זן, אל יהוה

hashishi הַשִּׁשִּׁי beShabbat בְּשַׁבָּת kodesh קֹדֶשׁ hashir הַשִּׁיר

shehayu שֶׁהָיוּ haleviyim הַלְוִיִּם omrim אוֹמְרִים al עַל haduchan הַדּוּכָן:

Adonai יְהֹוָה malach מָלָךְ ge'ut גֵּאוּת lavesh לָבֵשׁ lavesh לָבֵשׁ

Adonai יְהֹוָה oz עֹז hit'azar הִתְאַזָּר af אַף-ר"ת = אלהים, אהיה אדני

tikon תִּכּוֹן tevel תֵּבֵל ב"פ רי"ו ב"פ bal בַּל timot תִּמּוֹט: nachon נָכוֹן kis'acha כִּסְאֲךָ

me'az מֵאָז ומב me'olam מֵעוֹלָם Ata אָתָּה ר"ת הפסוק קנ"א, אדני אלהים:

If My Nation would listen to Me, and Israel would walk in My ways, I would completely subdue their enemies and would turn My Hand against their oppressors. The haters of the Lord deny Him, but Israel's time shall be forever. I shall feed him from the best of the wheat and satiate you with honey drawn from rocks." (Psalms 81) [Save us]

FRIDAY - YESOD - JOSEPH

Today is the sixth day of the counting to the Holy Shabbat.
The song the Levites used to recite upon the rostrum.
"The Lord reigns. He clothes Himself with pride.
The Lord clothes Himself and girds Himself with might. He also established the world firmly, so that it would not collapse. Your Throne has been established. Ever since that time, You have been forever.

נָשְׂאוּ ר"ת = קין nas'u נָשְׂאוּ Adonai יְהֹוָ(אדני־אהדונהי) neharot נְהָרוֹת nas'u נָשְׂאוּ

נְהָרוֹת dochyam דָּכְיָם ר"ת דני: neharot נְהָרוֹת yis'u יִשְׂאוּ kolam קוֹלָם neharot נְהָרוֹת

מִקֹּלוֹת adirim אַדִּירִים הרי rabim רַבִּים mayim מַיִם mikolot מִקֹּלוֹת

מִשְׁבְּרֵי adir אַדִּיר הרי אמי ר"ת ; ילי yam יָם mishbelei מִשְׁבְּרֵי

בַּמָּרוֹם edotecha עֵדֹתֶיךָ אבי: ר"ת ; Adonai יְהֹוָ(אדני־אהדונהי) bamarom בַּמָּרוֹם

נֶאֶמְנוּ levetcha לְבֵיתֶךָ ב"פ ראה ר"ת = קין me'od מְאֹד ne'emnu נֶאֶמְנוּ

נָאֲוָה le'orech לְאֹרֶךְ: Adonai יְהֹוָ(אדני־אהדונהי) kodesh קֹדֶשׁ na'avah נָאֲוָה

לְיָמִים: yamim נלך ; ר"ת ילי ; ס"ת = אדני ; יהוה ; לאורך ימים = ע"ע נהורין עם י"ג אותיות:

On *Chanukah* continue below with "*mizmor shir chanukat habayit.*" On any other day continue with "*hoshi'enu*" on pg. 267.

SPECIAL PSALM FOR *CHANUKAH*

In this Psalm there are ten times the Name: יהוה which correspond to the Ten *Sefirot*. Also there are 92 words, which is the numerical value of יהוה אדני (plus 1 in general).

מִזְמוֹר mizmor שִׁיר shir וְזֻנְכַּת chanukat הַבַּיִת habayit לְדָוִד: leDavid

אֲרוֹמִמְךָ aromimcha נצוצי הקדושה העולים ויוצאים מקליפות דעשיה הנקרא נפשי

יְהֹוָ(אדני־אהדונהי) Adonai (*Keter*) כִּי ki דִּלִּיתָנִי dilitani וְלֹא־ velo שִׂמַּחְתָּ simachta

אֹיְבַי oyvai לִי li: יְהֹוָ(אדני־אהדונהי) Adonai (*Chochmah*) אֱלֹהָי Elohai מילוי ע"ב, דמב ; ילה

שִׁוַּעְתִּי shivati אֵלֶיךָ elecha וַתִּרְפָּאֵנִי: vatirpa'eni יְהֹוָ(אדני־אהדונהי) Adonai (*Binah*)

הֶעֱלִיתָ he'elita מִן min שְׁאוֹל she'ol נַפְשִׁי nafshi (העלאת הנשמות מעשיה)

וְחִיִּיתַנִי chiyitani ס"ת ילי מִיָּרְדִי־ miyordi (כתיב: מיורדי) בּוֹר vor:

The rivers have lifted, Lord, the rivers have raised their voices. The rivers shall raise their powerful waves. More than the roaring of many waters and the powerful waves of the sea, You are mighty in the High Places, Lord. Your testimonies are extremely trustworthy. Your House is the Holy Sanctuary. The Lord shall be for the length of days." (Psalms 93) [Save us]

SPECIAL PSALM FOR *CHANUKAH*

"A Psalm, a Song for the Inauguration of the Temple, by David:
I exalt You, Lord, for having uplifted me and did not let my enemies rejoice on my account. Lord, my God, I cried out to You and You healed me. Lord, You raised my spirit from Sheol and kept me alive when I sank into the pit.

זַמְּרוּ zameru לַיהוה ladonai (Chesed) חֲסִידָיו chasidav וְהוֹדוּ vehodu אהיה

לְזֵכֶר lezecher קָדְשׁוֹ kodsho: כִּי ki רֶגַע rega ג"פ אלהים עם ט"ו אותיות עוב"ג אלהים

בְּאַפּוֹ be'apo ס"ת = אלהים, אהיה אדני ; ועם ם דוויים = ריבוע אדני וְחַיִּים chayim

בִּרְצוֹנוֹ birtzono בינה ע"ה אהיה אהיה יהוה כי רגע באפו וחיים ברצונו = עין דלת יוד

בָּעֶרֶב ba'erev יָלִין yalin בְּכִי bechi ר"ת י"ד כנגד אותיות עב-יהוה אלהינו יהוה,

וְלַבֹּקֶר velaboker רִנָּה rina בערב ילין בכי ולבקר רנה = מטטרון שר הפנים: ובה-כוזו במוכסז כוזו

וַאֲנִי va'ani אני אָמַרְתִּי amarti בְשַׁלְוִי veshalvi בַּל bal אֶמּוֹט emot

לְעוֹלָם le'olam ריבוע ס"ג וי' אותיות דס"ג Adonai יהוה (Gevurah)

בִּרְצוֹנְךָ birtzoncha הֶעֱמַדְתָּה he'emadeta לְהַרְרִי lehareri עֹז oz

הִסְתַּרְתָּ histarta פָנֶיךָ fanecha ס"ג מ"ה ב"ן הָיִיתִי hayiti נִבְהָל nivhal:

אֵלֶיךָ elecha Adonai יהוה (Tiferet) אֶקְרָא ekra

וְאֶל ve'el Adonai יהוה (Netzach) אֶתְחַנָּן etchanan: מַה ma מ"ה

בֶּצַע betza בְדָמִי bedami בְּרִדְתִּי bereideti אֶל el ס"ת ילי שַׁחַת shachat

הֲיוֹדְךָ hayodcha עָפָר afar הֲיַגִּיד hayagid יוד (כ"ב אותיות [אכא] וה' אותיות סוזוזר)

אֲמִתֶּךָ amitecha: שְׁמַע shema Adonai יהוה (Hod) וְחָנֵּנִי vechoneni

Adonai יהוה (Yesod) הֱיֵה heye יהה עֹזֵר ozer לִי li מ"וי:

הָפַכְתָּ hafachta מִסְפְּדִי mispedi לְמָחוֹל lemachol לִי li ס"ת ילי

פִּתַּחְתָּ pitachta שַׂקִּי saki וַתְּאַזְּרֵנִי vate'azreni שִׂמְחָה simcha:

לְמַעַן lema'an יְזַמֶּרְךָ yezamercha כָבוֹד chavod וְלֹא velo

יִדֹּם yidom (pause here) Adonai יהוה (Malchut) ר"ת = אלהים, אהיה אדני

אֱלֹהַי Elohai מילוי ע"ב, דמב ; ילה לְעוֹלָם le'olam ריבוע ס"ג וי' אותיות דס"ג אוֹדֶךָּ odeka:

Sing to the Lord, you, His pious ones, and give thanks to His Holy Name. For there is quietude in His anger, and there is life in His will. In the evening, one may lie down crying, yet be singing in the morning. When I was tranquil, I said that I shall never fall. Lord, you supported my mountain with Your strength; when You hid Your Countenance, I was frightened. It is to You, Lord, that I call, and to the Lord that I plead. What gain is there in spilling my blood, to be lowered into my grave? Does the dust give thanks to You? Does it proclaim Your truth? Lord, hear me and be gracious to me. Lord, be my helper. You have turned my mourning into a celebration for me. You have undone my sackcloth and have girded me with joy. So that grace shall sing for You and never be silenced, Lord, my God, I shall forever thank You." (Psalms 30)

DRAWING LIGHT TO YETZIRAH - אל יהוה – הא ואו הא יוד

HOSHI'ENU

Receiving extra energy for the day

After reciting the daily Psalms, the following is said:

ילה hoshi'enu הוֹשִׁיעֵנוּ Adonai יְהֹוָ֒ואדני֒יאהדונהי Elohenu אֱלֹהֵינוּ

leshem לְשֵׁם lehodot לְהוֹדוֹת hagoyim הַגּוֹיִם min מִן vekabetzenu וְקַבְּצֵנוּ

‡bit'hilatecha בִּתְהִלָּתֶךָ lehishtabe'ach לְהִשְׁתַּבֵּחַ kodshecha קָדְשֶׁךָ

ילה ; דמב ,ע"ב מילוי Elohei אֱלֹהֵי Adonai יְהֹוָ֒ואדני֒יאהדונהי baruch בָּרוּךְ

ha'olam הָעוֹלָם min מִן (מצוות) תרי"ג = ישראל אלהי יהוה ; אדני = ס"ת Yisrael יִשְׂרָאֵל

ha'am הָעָם ילי kol כָּל ve'amar וְאָמַר ha'olam הָעוֹלָם ve'ad וְעַד

לכה‡ ; אדני אהיה אלהים, haleluya הַלְלוּיָהּ יאהדונהי amen אָמֵן

קנאה הויות, ר' יוסף, miTziyon מִצִּיּוֹן Adonai יְהֹוָ֒ואדני֒יאהדונהי baruch בָּרוּךְ

לכה‡ ; אדני אהיה אלהים, haleluya הַלְלוּיָהּ Yerushalayim יְרוּשָׁלַיִם shochen שֹׁכֵן

ילה ; אדני אהיה Elohim אֱלֹהִים Adonai יְהֹוָ֒ואדני֒יאהדונהי baruch בָּרוּךְ

nifla'ot נִפְלָאוֹת ose עֹשֵׂה Yisrael יִשְׂרָאֵל ; ילה דמב ,ע"ב מילוי Elohei אֱלֹהֵי

le'olam לְעוֹלָם kevodo כְּבוֹדוֹ shem שֵׁם uvaruch וּבָרוּךְ: מ"ב levado לְבַדּוֹ

ילי kol כָּל et אֶת־ chevodo כְּבוֹדוֹ veyimale וְיִמָּלֵא ג רביוע ס"ג ו' אותיות דס"ג

יאהדונהי‡ ve'amen וְאָמֵן: יאהדונהי amen אָמֵן ע"ה דההין אלהים ha'aretz הָאָרֶץ

On **Rosh Chodesh** say Half Kaddish (pg. 458), take off the *Tefilin,* and then recite the *Musaf* (pg. 460).

HOSHI'ENU

"Save us, Lord, our God, and gather us from among the nations to give thanks to Your Holy Name and to find ourselves glorified in Your praise. Blessed is the Lord, God of Israel, from this world to the Next World, and all the people shall say: Amen! Praise the Lord!" (Psalms 106:47-48) "Blessed is the Lord from Zion. He Who dwells in Jerusalem. Praise the Lord!" (Psalms 135:21) Blessed is the Lord, our God, God of Israel, Who alone does wonders. And blessed is the Name of His glory forever. And His glory shall fill the entire world. Amen and Amen.

KADDISH YEHE SHELAMA

This *Kaddish* draws Light from the World of *Yetzirah* (מ"ה) into the World of *Asiyah* (ב"ן).

שדי ומילוי שדי ; י"א אותיות כמנין ו"ה	veyitkadash וְיִתְקַדַּשׁ	yitgadal יִתְגַּדַּל
קנ"א ב"ן, יהוה אלהים יהוה אדני,	raba רַבָּא (שם י"ה דע"ב)	shemei שְׁמֵיהּ
מילוי קס"א וס"ג, מ"ה ברבוע וע"ב ע"ה ; ר"ת = ו"פ אלהים ; ס"ת = ג"פ יב"ק:	amen אָמֵן אידהנויה.	
chir'utei כִרְעוּתֵיהּ	vera בְרָא	di דִּי	be'alma בְּעָלְמָא
veyatzmach וְיַצְמַח	malchutei מַלְכוּתֵיהּ	veyamlich וְיַמְלִיךְ
amen אָמֵן אידהנויה.	meshichei מְשִׁיחֵיהּ	vikarev וִיקָרֵב	purkanei פֻּרְקָנֵיהּ
uvchayei וּבְחַיֵּי	uvyomechon וּבְיוֹמֵיכוֹן	bechayechon בְּחַיֵּיכוֹן
ba'agala בַּעֲגָלָא	Yisrael יִשְׂרָאֵל	bet בֵּית	dechol דְּכָל
amen אָמֵן אידהנויה.	amen אָמֵן:	ve'imru וְאִמְרוּ	kariv קָרִיב	uvizman וּבִזְמַן

The congregation and the *chazan* say the following:

28 words (until *be'alma*) – meditate:
(מילוי דמילוי דס"ג (יוד ויו דלת הי יוד ואו אלף ואו הי יוד

28 letters (until *almaya*) - meditate:
מילוי דמילוי דמ"ה (יוד ואו דלת הא אלף ואו אלף ואו הא אלף).

ב"ן,	קנ"א	raba רַבָּא	דס"ג	י"ה (שם	shemei שְׁמֵיהּ	yehe יְהֵא
יהוה אלהים יהוה אדני, מילוי קס"א וס"ג, מ"ה ברבוע וע"ב ע"ה		mevarach מְבָרַךְ,
yitbarach יִתְבָּרַךְ	almaya עָלְמַיָּא	le'almei לְעָלְמֵי	le'alam לְעָלַם

Seven words with six letters each (שם בן מ"ב) – meditate:
; יהוה ← יוד הי ואו הי ← מילוי דמילוי דס"ג (יוד ויו דלת הי יוד ואו אלף ואו הי יוד)

Also, seven times the letter Vav (שם בן מ"ב) – meditate:
יהוה ← יוד הא ואו הא ← מילוי דמילוי דמ"ה (יוד ואו דלת הא אלף ואו אלף ואו הא אלף).

KADDISH YEHE SHELAMA

May His great Name be more exalted and sanctified. (Amen)
In the world that He created according to His will, and may His kingdom reign. And may
He cause His redemption to sprout and may He bring the Mashiach closer. (Amen) In your lifetimes
and in your days and in the lifetime of all the House of Israel, speedily and in the near future,
and you shall say, Amen. (Amen) May His great Name be blessed forever and for all eternity. Blessed

וְיִשְׁתַּבַּח veyishtabach י"פ ע"ב יהוה אל אבג יתץ

וְיִתְפָּאַר veyitpa'ar הי נו יה קרע שטן ‧ וְיִתְרֹמַם veyitromam וה כוזו נגד יכש

וְיִתְנַשֵּׂא veyitnase במוכסז בטר צתג ‧ וְיִתְהַדָּר veyit'hadar כוזו יה וזקב טנע

וְיִתְעַלֶּה veyit'ale וה יוד ה יגל פזק ‧ וְיִתְהַלָּל veyit'halal א ואו הא שקו צית

שְׁמֵיהּ shemei (שם י"ה דמ"ה) דְּקוּדְשָׁא dekudsha בְּרִיךְ verich הוּא hu:

אָמֵן amen אידהנויה‧

לְעֵלָּא le'ela מִן min כָּל kol יֵלי בִּרְכָתָא birchata‧ שִׁירָתָא shirata‧

תֻּשְׁבְּחָתָא tishbechata וְנֶחָמָתָא venechamata‧ דַּאֲמִירָן da'amiran

בְּעָלְמָא be'alma וְאִמְרוּ ve'imru אָמֵן amen‧ אָמֵן amen אידהנויה‧

יְהֵא yehe שְׁלָמָא shelama רַבָּא raba קנ"א ב"ן, יהוה אלהים יהוה אדני, מילוי קס"א וס"ג, מ"ה ברבוע וע"ב ע"ה

מִן min שְׁמַיָּא shemaya‧ וְחַיִּים chayim אהיה אהיה יהוה, בינה ע"ה

וְשָׂבָע vesava וִישׁוּעָה vishu'a וְנֶחָמָה venechama וְשֵׁיזָבָא veshezava

וּרְפוּאָה urefu'a וּגְאֻלָּה uge'ula וּסְלִיחָה uslicha וְכַפָּרָה vechapara

וְרֵיוַח verevach וּלְכָל ulchol יה אדני וְהַצָּלָה vehatzala‧ לָנוּ lanu אלהים, אהיה אדני

עַמּוֹ amo יִשְׂרָאֵל Yisrael וְאִמְרוּ ve'imru אָמֵן amen‧ אָמֵן amen אידהנויה‧

Take three steps backwards and say:

עוֹשֶׂה ose שָׁלוֹם shalom בִּמְרוֹמָיו bimromav ע"ב, ריבוע יהוה הוּא hu‧

בְּרַחֲמָיו berachamav יַעֲשֶׂה ya'ase שָׁלוֹם shalom עָלֵינוּ alenu ר"ת ש"ע נהורין

וְעַל ve'al כָּל kol יֵלי ; עמם amo עַמּוֹ Yisrael יִשְׂרָאֵל ve'imru וְאִמְרוּ אָמֵן amen:

אָמֵן amen אידהנויה‧

---

and lauded, and glorified, and exalted, and extolled, and honored, and uplifted, and praised be the Name of the Holy Blessed One. (Amen) Above all blessings, songs, praises, and words of consolation that may be said in the world, and you shall say, Amen. (Amen) May there be abundant peace from heaven, life, contentment, salvation, consolation, deliverance, healing, redemption, pardon, atonement, comfort, and relief. For us and for His entire nation, Israel, and you shall say, Amen. (Amen) He, Who makes peace in His high places, with His compassion He shall make peace for us and for His entire nation, Israel. And you shall say, Amen. (Amen)

KAVE

We now connect to the World of Action, *Asiyah*. Something remarkable happens during this prayer. We have finished all our morning spiritual connections, and now would like to retain all this energy that we have worked so hard for by sealing and secure it up. *Kave* takes us back up through the Upper Words of Action (*Asiyah*), Formation (*Yetzirah*), Creation (*Beriah*) and Emanation (*Atzilut*) to a realm known as *Arich Anpin* (Long Face). From this realm we still elevate higher, passed the realms of Atik (Ancient), and *Adam Kadmon* (Primordial Man) until we travel into the realm of the Light of Endless Word. This journey retraces our steps through the Upper Words ensuring that we leave no openings behind for negativity to enter.

At this point, the Satan wants to prevent us from closing these openings, so he bombards us with a feeling of impatience that the prayers will be over soon. His goal is to lower our guard and weaken our concentration during this final stage so that we leave an opening for him to enter and sabotage our efforts and taint our Light with negative energy.

פהל   chazak וֵזַק   Adonai יְהֹוָואדניאהדונהי   el אֶל־   kave קַוֵּה

וְיַאֲמֵץ veya'ametz   לִבֶּךָ libecha   וְקַוֵּה vekave   אֶל־ el   יְהֹוָואדניאהדונהי Adonai:

אֵין en   קָדוֹשׁ kadosh   כַּיְהֹוָואדניאהדונהי kadonai   כִּי ki   אֵין en   בִּלְתֶּךָ biltecha

כִּי ki   כֵּאלֹהֵינוּ kelohenu ילה: צוּר tzur אלהים דההין ע"ה   וְאֵין ve'en

בְּמִי mi ילי   אֱלוֹהַ Eloha שם בן מ"ב   מִבַּלְעֲדֵי mibal'adei   יְהֹוָואדניאהדונהי Adonai

וּבְמִי umi ילי   צוּר tzur אלהים דההין ע"ה   זוּלָתִי zulati   אֱלֹהֵינוּ Elohenu ילה:

Connection to *Olam Asiyah* (Action).

נוקבא.	ילה	kelohenu כֵּאלֹהֵינוּ	הה	en אֵין
ז"א.		kadonenu כַּאדוֹנֵנוּ	וו	en אֵין
אמא.		kemalkenu כְּמַלְכֵּנוּ	הה	en אֵין
אבא:		kemoshi'enu כְּמוֹשִׁיעֵנוּ	יוד	en אֵין

KAVE

"Place hope in the Lord. Make your heart strong and courageous, and place your hope in the Lord." (Psalms 27:14). "There is none as holy as the Lord, for there is none besides You and there is no Rock to compare with our God." (1 Samuel 2:2) "For who is God besides the Lord, and who is a rock besides our God?" (Psalms 18:32)

There is none like our God.

There is none like our Master. There is none like our King. There is none like our Redeemer.

DRAWING LIGHT TO ASIYAH - יוד הה וו הה – אל אדנ"י

Connection to *Olam Yetzirah* (Formation).

נוקבא.	ילה	chelohenu כֵּאלהֵינוּ	הא	mi מִי יל'
ז"א.		chadonenu כַּאדונֵנוּ	ואו	mi מִי יל'
אמא.		chemalkenu כְּמַלְכֵּנוּ	הא	mi מִי יל'
אבא:		chemoshi'enu כְּמוֹשִׁיעֵנוּ	יוד	mi מִי יל'

Connection to *Olam Beriah* (Creation).

אין, מי, נודה ר"ת אמן = יאהדונה"י – וחיבור ז"א ומלכות.

נוקבא.	ילה	lelohenu לֵאלהֵינוּ	ה'	node נוֹדֶה
ז"א.		ladonenu לַאדונֵנוּ	ואו	node נוֹדֶה
אמא.		lemalkenu לְמַלְכֵּנוּ	ה'	node נוֹדֶה
אבא:		lemoshi'enu לְמוֹשִׁיעֵנוּ	יוד	node נוֹדֶה

Connection to *Olam Atzilut* (Emanation).

נוקבא.	ילה	Elohenu אֱלהֵינוּ	ה'	baruch בָּרוּךְ
ז"א.		adonenu אֲדונֵנוּ	ו'י	baruch בָּרוּךְ
אמא.		malkenu מַלְכֵּנוּ	ה'	baruch בָּרוּךְ
אבא:		moshi'enu מוֹשִׁיעֵנוּ	יוד	baruch בָּרוּךְ

Connection to the hidden Worlds above *Atzilut*,
Connection to *Keter* of *Arich Anpin* (Long Face).

אַתָּה Ata הוּא hu אֱלהֵינוּ Elohenu יל'ה.

Connection to the head of *Atik* (Ancient).

אַתָּה Ata הוּא hu אֲדונֵנוּ adonenu.

Connection to *Adam Kadmon* (Primordial Man).

אַתָּה Ata הוּא hu מַלְכֵּנוּ malkenu.

Connection to the Endless Light, which is enclosed by *Adam Kadmon*.

אַתָּה Ata הוּא hu מוֹשִׁיעֵנוּ moshi'enu:

Who is like our God? Who is like our Master? Who is like our King? Who is like our Redeemer?
We shall give thanks to our God, we shall give thanks to our Master, we shall give thanks to our King,
we shall give thanks to our Redeemer. Blessed is our God. Blessed is our Master. Blessed is our King.
Blessed is our Redeemer. You are our God. You are our Master. You are our King. You are our Redeemer.

אַתָּה Ata *Keneset Yisrael (Congregation of Yisrael)* תּוֹשִׁיעֵנוּ toshi'enu

אַתָּה Ata תָקוּם takum תְּרַחֵם terachem כ"א הויות שבתפילין ג"פ רי"ו ; אברהם, וז"פ אל,

רי"ו ול"ב נתיבות החכמה, רמ"ח (אברים), עסמ"ב וט"ז אותיות פשוטות צִיּוֹן Tziyon יוסף, ו' הויות, קָנָאה

כִּי ki עֵת et לְחֶנְנָהּ lechenena כִּי ki בָא va מוֹעֵד mo'ed:

(Some say here "The *Ketoret* portion", on pg. 98-104)

TANA DEVEI ELIYAHU

It is said that people who learn the *Torah* bring peace. Because each Hebrew letter is imbued with mystical forces, reciting words that speak about bringing peace arouses the energy of peace within the world. The Hebrew word *Shalom* inspires feelings of peace and harmony within us. If we cannot develop peace within ourselves, we cannot share peace with others, for one cannot share what he doesn't have. To conclude this connection we say that God will bless us with peace.

תָּנָא tana דְּבֵי devei אֵלִיָּהוּ Eliyahu לכב: kol כָּל kol הַשּׁוֹנֶה hashone

הֲלָכוֹת halachot בְּכָל bechol יוֹם yom ע"ה נגד, מזבח, ז, אל יהוה

מוּבְטָח muvtach לוֹ lo שֶׁהוּא shehu בֶּן ben הָעוֹלָם ha'olam

הַבָּא haba. שֶׁנֶּאֱמַר shene'emar: הֲלִיכוֹת halichot עוֹלָם olam לוֹ lo.

אַל al תִּקְרֵי tikrei הֲלִיכוֹת halichot אֶלָּא ela הֲלָכוֹת halachot:

אָמַר amar רִבִּי Ribi אֶלְעָזָר Elazar אָמַר amar רִבִּי Ribi וַחֲנִינָא Chanina:

תַּלְמִידֵי talmidei חֲכָמִים chachamim מַרְבִּים marbim שָׁלוֹם shalom

בָּעוֹלָם ba'olam. שֶׁנֶּאֱמַר shene'emar: וְכָל vechol בָּנַיִךְ banayich

לִמּוּדֵי limudei יְהֹוָה Adonai וְרַב verav שְׁלוֹם shelom בָּנַיִךְ banayich:

אַל al תִּקְרֵי tikrei בָּנַיִךְ banayich אֶלָּא ela בּוֹנַיִךְ bonayich: יְהִי yehi

שָׁלוֹם shalom בְּחֵילֵךְ bechelech שַׁלְוָה shalva בְּאַרְמְנוֹתָיִךְ be'armenotayich:

You shall redeem us. You shall rise
and be merciful to Zion, for the time for favor has come and it is the appointed time. (Psalms 102:14)

TANA DEVEI ELIYAHU

"It was taught in the learning House of Eliyahu that one who studies law rulings, every day, is assured to be present in the World to Come." (Megillah 28b) It was said: "The ways of the world are His." (Chavakuk 3:6) Do not read it 'ways' but 'law rulings'. Rabbi Elazar said that Rabbi Chanina had said that learned scholars increase the peace in the world. (Brachot 64a; Yvamot 122b; Kritut 28b; Tamid 32b) As it is said: "And all your children are the students of God." (Isaiah 54:13) Do not read it 'your children' but 'your builders.' May there be peace in your chambers and serenity in your palaces.

לְמַעַן lema'an אַחַי achai וְרֵעָי vere'ai אֲדַבְּרָה adabra נָא na

שָׁלוֹם shalom בָּךְ bach: לְמַעַן lema'an בֵּית־ bet ב״פ ראה

יְהֹוָה Adonai אֱלֹהֵינוּ Elohenu ילה אֲבַקְשָׁה avaksha

טוֹב tov וו וְרָאֵה ure'e ראה בָנִים vanim לְבָנֶיךָ levanecha

שָׁלוֹם shalom עַל־ al יִשְׂרָאֵל Yisrael: שָׁלוֹם shalom רָב rav

לְאֹהֲבֵי le'ohavei תוֹרָתֶךָ toratecha וְאֵין ve'en לָמוֹ lamo מִכְשׁוֹל michshol:

עֹז oz Adonai יְהֹוָה לְעַמּוֹ le'amo יִתֵּן yiten יְהֹוָה Adonai

יְבָרֵךְ yevarech ע״ב ס״ג מ״ה ב״ן, (למתק הברכה, המלכים את ז' שמדתו)

אֶת־ et עַמּוֹ amo בַּשָּׁלוֹם vashalom ר״ת ע״ב, ריבוע יהוה:

KADDISH AL YISRAEL

This *Kaddish* helps elevate all souls in the secret of the Resurrection of Death. According to the Ari – If a person lost a parent he should say this *Kaddish* through the whole first year, even on *Shabbat* and holidays. Because, besides that the *Kaddish* helps a soul to be saved form the spiritual cleansing of *Gehenom*, this *Kaddish* also helps to elevate a soul from one spiritual level to the upper one and to enter to the Garden of Eden.

יִתְגַּדַּל yitgadal וְיִתְקַדַּשׁ veyitkadash עׄדׄ ומילוי עׄדׄי ; י״א אותיות כמנין ו״ה

שְׁמֵיה shemei (שׄם יׄהׄ דעׄבׄ) רַבָּא raba קנׄא בׄן, יהוה אלהים יהוה אדני,

מילוי קסׄא וסׄג, מׄה ברבוע ועׄב עׄה ; רׄת = וׄפ אלהים ; סׄת = גׄפ יבׄק: אָמֵן amen אידהנויה

בְּעָלְמָא be'alma דִּי di בְּרָא vera כִרְעוּתֵיה chir'utei

וְיַמְלִיךְ veyamlich מַלְכוּתֵיה malchutei וְיַצְמַח veyatzmach

פּוּרְקָנֵיה purkanei וִיקָרֵב vikarev מְשִׁיחֵיה meshichei: אָמֵן amen אידהנויה

"For the sake of my brothers and my friends, I shall seek peace concerning you. For the sake of the House of the Lord, our God, I shall seek well for you." *(Psalms 122:7-9)* "May you witness children for your children and peace for Israel." *(Psalms 128:6)* "There is abundance of peace for those who love Your Torah and for them, there is no obstacle." *(Psalms 128:6)* "May the Lord give strength to His people may the Lord bless His nation with peace." *(Psalms 29:11)*

KADDISH AL YISRAEL

May His great Name be more exalted and sanctified. (Amen)
In the world that He created according to His will, and may His Kingdom reign.
And may He cause His redemption to sprout and may He bring the Mashiach closer. (Amen)

uvchayei וּבְחַיֵּי   uvyomechon וּבְיוֹמֵיכוֹן   bechayechon בְּחַיֵּיכוֹן

ba'agala בַּעֲגָלָא   Yisrael יִשְׂרָאֵל   ב"פ ראה   bet בֵּית ילי   dechol דְּכָל

uvizman וּבִזְמַן   kariv קָרִיב   ve'imru וְאִמְרוּ   amen אָמֵן :amen   amen אָמֵן אידהנויה.

The congregation and the chazan say the following:

> **28 words (until be'alma),**
> **and 28 letters (until almaya)**

yehe יְהֵא   shemei שְׁמֵיהּ   (שם י"ה דס"ג)   raba רַבָּא   קנ"א ב"ן,

לְעָלַם le'alam יהוה אלהים יהוה אדני, מילוי קס"א וס"ג, מ"ה ברבוע וע"ב ע"ה   mevarach מְבָרַךְ,

le'alam לְעָלַם   le'almei לְעָלְמֵי   almaya עָלְמַיָּא.   yitbarach יִתְבָּרַךְ.

> **Seven words with six letters each (שם בן מ"ב),**
> **And also, seven times the letter Vav (שם בן מ"ב).**

veyishtabach וְיִשְׁתַּבַּח יפ ע"ב יהוה אל אבג יתץ.

veyitpa'ar וְיִתְפָּאַר הי גו יה קרע שטן   veyitromam וְיִתְרוֹמַם וה כוזו נגד יכש.

veyit'hadar וְיִתְהַדָּר במוכסז בטר צתג   veyitnase וְיִתְנַשֵּׂא כוזו יה וזקב טנע.

veyit'halal וְיִתְהַלָּל א ואו הא שקו צית.   veyit'ale וְיִתְעַלֶּה וה יוד ה יגל פזק.

shemei שְׁמֵיהּ (שם י"ה דמ"ה)   dekudsha דְּקוּדְשָׁא   verich בְּרִיךְ   hu הוּא:

amen אָמֵן אידהנויה.

le'ela לְעֵלָּא   min מִן   kol כָּל ילי   birchata בִּרְכָתָא.   shirata שִׁירָתָא.

da'amiran דַּאֲמִירָן   venechamata וְנֶחָמָתָא.   tishbechata תֻּשְׁבְּחָתָא

be'alma בְּעָלְמָא   ve'imru וְאִמְרוּ   amen אָמֵן: amen אָמֵן אידהנויה.

In your lifetimes and in your days and in the lifetime of all the House of Israel,
speedily and in the near future, and you shall say, Amen. (Amen) May His great Name be blessed forever and for all eternity. Blessed and lauded, and glorified, and exalted, and extolled, and honored, and uplifted, and praised be the Name of the Holy Blessed One. (Amen) Above all blessings, songs, praises, and words of consolation that may be said in the world, and you shall say, Amen. (Amen)

al עַל   Yisrael יִשְׂרָאֵל   ve'al וְעַל   rabanan רַבָּנָן   ve'al וְעַל

talmidehon תַּלְמִידֵיהוֹן   ve'al וְעַל   kol כָּל   ; יל עמם   talmidei תַּלְמִידֵי

talmidehon תַּלְמִידֵיהוֹן   de'askin דְּעָסְקִין   be'oraita בְּאוֹרַיְתָא

kadishta קַדִּשְׁתָּא   di דִּי   ve'atra בְּאַתְרָא   haden הָדֵין   vedi וְדִי

vechol בְּכָל   לכב ב"ן   atar אֲתַר   ve'atar וְאֲתַר   yehe יְהֵא

lana לָנָא   ul'hon וּלְהוֹן   ul'chon וּלְכוֹן   china וְחִנָּא   vechisda וְחִסְדָּא

verachamei וְרַחֲמֵי   min מִן   kadam קֳדָם   marei מָארֵי   shemaya שְׁמַיָּא

ve'ara וְאַרְעָא   ve'imru וְאִמְרוּ   amen אָמֵן   amen אָמֵן אידהנויה.

yehe יְהֵא   shelama שְׁלָמָא   raba רַבָּא   קנ"א ב"ן, יהוה אלהים יהוה אדני, מילוי קס"א וס"ג,

min מִן   shemaya שְׁמַיָּא   chayim וְחַיִּים   אהיה אהיה יהוה, בינה ע"ה   מ"ה ברבוע וע"ב ע"ה

vesava וְשָׂבַע   vishu'a וִישׁוּעָה   venechama וְנֶחָמָה   veshezava וְשֵׁיזָבָא

urefu'a וּרְפוּאָה   uge'ula וּגְאֻלָּה   uslicha וּסְלִיחָה   vechapara וְכַפָּרָה

verevach וְרֵיוַח   vehatzala וְהַצָּלָה   lanu לָנוּ   אלהים, אהיה אדני   ulchol וּלְכָל   יה אדני

amo עַמּוֹ   Yisrael יִשְׂרָאֵל   ve'imru וְאִמְרוּ   amen אָמֵן   amen אָמֵן אידהנויה.

Take three steps backwards and say:

ose עוֹשֶׂה   shalom שָׁלוֹם   bimromav בִּמְרוֹמָיו   ע"ב, ריבוע יהוה   hu הוּא

berachamav בְּרַחֲמָיו   ya'ase יַעֲשֶׂה   shalom שָׁלוֹם   alenu עָלֵינוּ   ר"ת ע"ד נֹהורין   בְּרַחֲמָיו

ve'al וְעַל   kol כָּל   ; יל עמם   amo עַמּוֹ   Yisrael יִשְׂרָאֵל   ve'imru וְאִמְרוּ   amen אָמֵן

amen אָמֵן אידהנויה.

Upon Israel, His Sages, Their disciples, and all the students of their disciples who occupy themselves with the Holy Torah, in this place and in each and every location, may there be for us, for them, and for all, grace, kindness, and compassion from the Master of the Heavens and earth, and you shall say Amen. (Amen) May there be abundant peace from Heaven, life, contentment, salvation, consolation, deliverance, healing, redemption, pardon, atonement, comfort, and relief for us and for His entire Nation, Israel, and you shall say, Amen. (Amen) He, Who makes peace in His High Places, with His compassion He shall make peace for us And for His entire Nation, Israel. And you shall say, Amen. (Amen)

SHACHARIT – MORNING PRAYER
DRAWING SURROUNDING LIGHT

BARCHU

The *chazan* (or a person who said the *Kaddish Al Yisrael*) says:

רַבָּנָן rabanan   יהוה ריבוע מ״ה   יהוה ריבוע יהוה   barchu בָּרְכוּ   אֶת et

יְהֹוָאֲדֹנָיאהדונהי Adonai   ס״ת כהת, משיוז בן דוד ע״ה: hamevorach הַמְבוֹרָךְ

First the congregation replies with the following and then the *chazan* (or a person who said the *Kaddish Al Yisrael*) repeats it:

Neshamah	*Ruach*	*Nefesh*
hamevorach הַמְבוֹרָךְ	יְהֹוָאֲדֹנָיאהדונהי Adonai	baruch בָּרוּךְ

Yechidah					*Chayah*
וָעֶד: va'ed	דס״ג	אותיות	ו״י	ס״ג ריבוע	le'olam לְעוֹלָם

ALENU

Alenu is a cosmic sealing agent. It cements and secures all of our prayers, protecting them from any negative forces such as the *klipot*. All prayers prior to *Alenu* drew down what the kabbalists call Inner Light. *Alenu*, however, attracts Surrounding Light, which envelops our prayers with a protective force-field to block out the *klipot*.

Drawing Surrounding Light to *Atzilut*.

ועור, יתן, אבג = עליו לעשבח עלינו leshabe'ach לְשַׁבֵּחַ דס״ג ריבוע alenu עָלֵינוּ

אֲדֹנָי, כלה, ר״ת hakol הַכֹּל ע״ה ס״ת ; אני la'adon לַאֲדוֹן

Drawing Surrounding Light to *Beriah*.

ר״ת גלב (בא״ך ב״י יג״ל) bereshit בְּרֵאשִׁית leyotzer לְיוֹצֵר gedula גְּדֻלָּה latet לָתֵת

Drawing Surrounding Light to *Yetzirah*.
---

ha'aratzot הָאֲרָצוֹת   kegoyei כְּגוֹיֵי   asanu עָשָׂנוּ   shelo שֶׁלֹּא

Drawing Surrounding Light to *Asiyah*.
---

ha'adama הָאֲדָמָה   kemishpechot כְּמִשְׁפְּחוֹת   samanu שָׂמָנוּ   velo וְלֹא

BARCHU

Masters: Bless the Lord, the Blessed One.
Blessed be the Lord, the Blessed One, forever and for eternity.

ALENU

It is incumbent upon us to give praise to the Master of all and to attribute greatness to the Molder of Creation, for He did not make us like the nations of the lands. He did not place us like the families of the earth

שֶׁלֹּא shelo שָׂם sam וְחֶלְקֵנוּ chelkenu כָּהֶם kahem וְגֹרָלֵנוּ vegoralenu

כְּכָל kechol הֲמוֹנָם hamonam◆ שֶׁהֵם shehem מִשְׁתַּחֲוִים mishtachavim

לַהֶבֶל lahevel וָרִיק varik וּמִתְפַּלְלִים umitpalelim אֶל el אֶל el

לֹא lo יוֹשִׁיעַ Yoshi'a◆ (pause here, and when you say "va'anachnu mishtachavim" bow your entire body)

וַאֲנַחְנוּ va'anachnu מִשְׁתַּחֲוִים mishtachavim לִפְנֵי lifnei מֶלֶךְ melech

מַלְכֵי malchei הַמְּלָכִים hamelachim הַקָּדוֹשׁ hakadosh בָּרוּךְ baruch

הוּא hu◆ שֶׁהוּא shehu note נוֹטֶה shamayim שָׁמַיִם י"פ טל, י"פ כוזו ; ר"ת = י"פ אדנ"י

וּמוֹשַׁב umoshav אָרֶץ aretz◆ וְיוֹסֵד veyosed דו"א שׂבי' ספירות שׂל נוקבא

יְקָרוֹ yekaro בַּשָּׁמַיִם bashamayim י"פ טל, י"פ כוזו mima'al מִמַּעַל◆ עלם◆

וּשְׁכִינַת ush'chinat עֻזּוֹ uzo בְּגָבְהֵי begovhei מְרוֹמִים meromim◆

הוּא hu אֱלֹהֵינוּ Elohenu ילה וְאֵין ve'en עוֹד od אַחֵר acher◆

אֱמֶת emet אהיה פעמים אהיה, ז"פ ס"ג מַלְכֵּנוּ malkenu וְאֶפֶס ve'efes

זוּלָתוֹ zulato◆ כַּכָּתוּב kakatuv בַּתּוֹרָה batorah❖ וְיָדַעְתָּ veyadata

הַיּוֹם hayom ע"ה נגד, מזבוז, זז, אל יהוה וַהֲשֵׁבֹתָ vahashevota אֶל el

לְבָבֶךָ levavecha ר"ת לאו כִּי ki יְהוָֹהַדני יאהדונהי Adonai הוּא hu

הָאֱלֹהִים haElohim אהיה אדנ"י ; ילה ; ר"ת יהה וכן עולה למנצן עתו עג"כ

בַּשָּׁמַיִם bashamayim י"פ טל, י"פ כוזו מִמַּעַל mima'al עלם ;

ע"ה רמז לאור פנימי המתחיל מלמעלה וְעַל ve'al הָאָרֶץ ha'aretz אלהים דההין

מִתָּחַת mitachat רמז לאור המתחיל מלמטה מקיף אֵין en עוֹד od❖

He did not make our lot like theirs and our destiny like that of their multitudes, for they prostrate themselves to futility and emptiness and they pray to a deity that does not help. But we prostrate ourselves before the King of all Kings, the Holy Blessed One. It is He Who spreads the Heavens and establishes the earth. The Seat of His glory is in the Heaven above and the Divine Presence of His power is in the Highest of Heights. He is our God and there is no other. Our King is true and there is none beside Him. As it is written in the Torah: "And you shall know today and you shall take it to your heart that it is the Lord Who is God in the Heavens above and upon the Earth below, and there is none other". (Deuteronomy 4:39)

עַל al כֵּן ken נְקַוֶּה nekave לְךָ lach יְהֹוָה Adonai אֱלֹהֵינוּ Elohenu

לִרְאוֹת lir'ot מְהֵרָה mehera בְּתִפְאֶרֶת betiferet עֻזֶּךָ uzach

לְהַעֲבִיר leha'avir גִּלּוּלִים gilulim מִן min הָאָרֶץ ha'aretz

וְהָאֱלִילִים veha'elilim כָּרוֹת karot יִכָּרֵתוּן yikaretun לְתַקֵּן letaken

עוֹלָם olam בְּמַלְכוּת bemalchut שַׁדַּי Shadai וְכָל vechol בְּנֵי benei

בָשָׂר vasar יִקְרְאוּ yikre'u בִשְׁמֶךָ vishmecha לְהַפְנוֹת lehafnot אֵלֶיךָ elecha

כָּל kol רִשְׁעֵי rish'ei אָרֶץ aretz יַכִּירוּ yakiru וְיֵדְעוּ veyed'u כָּל kol

יוֹשְׁבֵי yoshvei תֵבֵל tevel כִּי ki לְךָ lecha תִּכְרַע tichra כָּל kol

בֶּרֶךְ berech תִּשָּׁבַע tishava כָּל kol לָשׁוֹן lashon לְפָנֶיךָ lefanecha

יְהֹוָה Adonai אֱלֹהֵינוּ Elohenu יִכְרְעוּ yichre'u וְיִפֹּלוּ veyipolu

וְלִכְבוֹד velichvod שִׁמְךָ shimcha יְקָר yekar יִתֵּנוּ yitenu וִיקַבְּלוּ vikabelu

כֻלָּם chulam אֶת et עֹל ol מַלְכוּתֶךָ malchutecha וְתִמְלֹךְ vetimloch

עֲלֵיהֶם alehem מְהֵרָה mehera לְעוֹלָם le'olam וָעֶד va'ed

כִּי ki הַמַּלְכוּת hamalchut שֶׁלְּךָ shelcha הִיא hee וּלְעוֹלְמֵי ul'olmei

עַד ad תִּמְלֹךְ timloch בְּכָבוֹד bechavod כַּכָּתוּב kakatuv

בְּתוֹרָתֶךָ betoratach יְהֹוָה Adonai | יִמְלֹךְ yimloch לְעֹלָם le'olam

וָעֶד va'ed וְנֶאֱמַר vene'emar וְהָיָה vehaya

יְהֹוָה Adonai לְמֶלֶךְ lemelech עַל al כָּל kol הָאָרֶץ ha'aretz

בַּיּוֹם bayom הַהוּא hahu יִהְיֶה yih'ye יְהֹוָה Adonai אֶחָד echad וּשְׁמוֹ ushmo

אֶחָד echad

Consequently, we place our hope in You, Lord, our God, that we shall speedily see the glory of Your might, when You remove the idols from the earth and the deities shall be completely destroyed to correct the world with the kingdom of the Almighty. And all mankind shall then call out Your Name and You shall turn back to Yourself all the wicked ones of the earth. Then all the inhabitants of the world shall recognize and know that, for You, every knee bends and every tongue vows. Before You, Lord, our God, they shall kneel and fall and shall give honor to Your glorious Name. And they shall all accept the yoke of Your Kingdom and You shall reign over them, forever and ever. Because the kingdom is Yours. and forever and for eternity, You shall reign gloriously. As it is written in the Torah: "The Lord shall reign forever and ever," (Exodus 15:18) and it is also stated: "The Lord shall be King over the whole world and, on that day, the Lord shall be One and His Name One." (Zechariah 14:9)

VAYOMER

There is a specific angel that carries each prayer we make to the Upper Worlds. By reciting this additional prayer after *Alenu* we ensure that our prayers elevate into the Upper Worlds. There are four Yuds יייי within the verse "I am your God, your healer," which according to the Ari, ignite the power of healing.

וַיֹּאמֶר vayomer אִם־ im יוֹהֵך, מ"א אותיות דפשוטו, דמילוי ודמילוי דמילוי דאהיה ע"ה

תִּשְׁמַע shamo'a תִּשְׁמַע tishma לְקוֹל lekol | יְהוָֹה Adonai

אֱלֹהֶיךָ Elohecha וְהַיָּשָׁר vehayashar בְּעֵינָיו be'enav מ"ה

תַּעֲשֶׂה ta'ase וְהַאֲזַנְתָּ veha'azanta לְמִצְוֹתָיו lemitzvotav וְשָׁמַרְתָּ veshamarta

כָּל־ kol וְזִקָּיו chukav כָּל־ kol הַמַּחֲלָה hamachala

אֲשֶׁר־ asher שַׂמְתִּי samti בְמִצְרַיִם veMitzrayim לֹא־ lo אָשִׂים asim

עָלֶיךָ alecha כִּי ki אֲנִי ani יְהוָֹה Adonai

Corresponds to the four *Yuds* in the Holy Name: (יוד הי ויו הי ע"ב)

רֹפְאֶךָ rofecha ר"ת איר

עֵץ־ etz וְחַיִּים chayim אהיה אהיה יהוה, בינה ע"ה הִיא hee

לַמַּחֲזִיקִים lamachazikim ר"ת להוד בָּהּ ba וְתֹמְכֶיהָ vetomcheha

מְאֻשָּׁר me'ushar דְּרָכֶיהָ deracheha דַרְכֵי darchei נֹעַם no'am וְכָל vechol

נְתִיבוֹתֶיהָ netivoteha שָׁלוֹם shalom מִגְדָּל migdal עֹז oz שֵׁם shem

יְהוָֹה Adonai בּוֹ bo יָרוּץ yarutz צַדִּיק tzadik וְנִשְׂגָּב venisgav

מבטע	עוי	מביע
יצד	ווה	גרג
היי	זדו	דצב
ונק	סוה	לקה

כִּי ki בִּי vi מ"ב יִרְבּוּ yirbu יָמֶיךָ yamecha וְיוֹסִיפוּ veyosifu לְךָ lecha

שְׁנוֹת shenot וְחַיִּים chayim אהיה אהיה יהוה, בינה ע"ה

VAYOMER

"And God said: If you shall listen to the voice of the Lord, your God, and do that which is upright in His eyes, and if you carefully heed His commandments and keep all His statutes, then all the illnesses that I had set upon Egypt, I shall not set upon you, for I am the Lord, your healer." (Exodus 15:26) "It is a Tree of Life for those who hold on to it, and those who support it are joyful." (Proverbs 3:18) "Its ways are ways of pleasantness and all its pathways are of peace." (Proverbs 3:17) "The Name of the Lord is a tower of strength. In it, a righteous person runs and is strengthened." (Proverbs 18:10) "For through Me, your days shall be increased, and years of life shall be added to you." (Proverbs 9:11)

YEHI RATZON

The following connection helps us to make sure our prayers are accepted.
It also helps us to remove jealousy and envy from within.

ע"ה אל עודי ע"ה, ע"א וקס"א, ברריבוע ע"ב, ע"ה, מהשע ratzon רָצוֹן yehi יְהִי

Elohai אֱלֹהַי Adonai יְהֹוָאדנִיאהדונהי ב"ן מ"ה ס"ג milefanecha מִלְפָנֶיךָ

avotai, אֲבוֹתַי ; ילה ; דמב דע"ב, מולוי ; לכב ; דמב ע"ב, מילוי velohei וֵאלֹהַי ; ילה דמב, ע"ב, מילוי

halacha הֲלָכָה ראה bidvar בִּדְבַר nikashel נִכָּשֵׁל shelo שֶׁלֹּא

velo וְלֹא tahor טָהוֹר יֵ"פ אכא tame טָמֵא al עַל nomar נֹאמַר velo וְלֹא

isur אִיסוּר al עַל velo וְלֹא tame, טָמֵא אכא יֵ"פ tahor טָהוֹר al עַל

velo וְלֹא isur, אִיסוּר mutar מוּתָר al עַל velo וְלֹא mutar מוּתָר

halacha הֲלָכָה ראה bidvar בִּדְבַר chaverai וַחֲבֵרַי yikashlu יִכָּשְׁלוּ

ekashel אֶכָּשֵׁל velo וְלֹא bahem. בָּהֶם ani אֲנִי ve'esmach וְאֶשְׂמַח

ki כִּי bi, בִּי hem הֵם veyismechu וְיִשְׂמְחוּ vo בּוֹ ani אֲנִי

(מצוות) תרי"ג = במילוי chochmah וְחָכְמָה yiten יִתֵּן Adonai יְהֹוָאדנִיאהדונהי

enai עֵינַי gal גַּל utvuna. וּתְבוּנָה da'at דַּעַת mipiv מִפִּיו

mitoratecha: מִתּוֹרָתֶךָ nifla'ot נִפְלָאוֹת ve'abita וְאַבִּיטָה מ"ה ריבוע

LeDavid

During the months of *Elul* and *Tishrei* (until after *Hoshana Raba*), known as times of judgment, we say this additional prayer. The purpose of this psalm is to arouse the Thirteen Attributes of mercy in our life. Mercy helps sweeten the judgment that appears through *Elul*, *Rosh Hashanah*, *Yom Kippur*, and *Sukkot*.

veyish'i וְיִשְׁעִי אין סוף רז, (אל) ori אוֹרִי Adonai יְהֹוָאדנִיאהדונהי | leDavid לְדָוִד

chayai חַיַּי ma'oz מָעוֹז (רוזם) Adonai יְהֹוָאדנִיאהדונהי ira אִירָא ילי mimi מִמִּי

mere'im מֵרֵעִים alai עָלַי bikrov בִּקְרֹב efchad: אֶפְחָד ילי mimi מִמִּי

ייי י"פ דיודין, אלהים מצפצ, tzarai צָרַי besari בְּשָׂרִי et- אֶת- le'echol לֶאֱכֹל

venafalu: וְנָפָלוּ chashlu כָּשְׁלוּ hema הֵמָּה li לִי ve'oyvai וְאֹיְבַי

YEHI RATZON
May it be Your will,

Lord, my God and God of my forefathers, that we may not err in a matter of halachah, and that we may not impure pure or pure impure, or that we may not call forbidden permitted or permitted forbidden. That my colleagues may not err in a matter of halachah and that I may rejoice in them, and that no offence may occur through me, and that my colleagues may rejoice in me. Because from his mouth Lord gives wisdom and understanding "open my eyes, so that I will see wonders from your Torah" (Psalms 119:18)

LeDavid
"By David. The Lord is my Light and my salvation, whom shall I fear? The Lord is the fortress of my life, whom shall I dread? When evil people approach me to consume my flesh, those enemies who oppress me shall stumble and fall.

אִם־ im יוהך, מ"א אותיות דפשוט, דמילוי ודמילוי דמילוי דאהיה ע"ה תַּחֲנֶה tachane עָלַי alai

מַחֲנֶה machane im אִם־ יוהך, מ"א אותיות דפשוט, דמילוי lo לֹא־ yira יִירָא libi לִבִּי

milchama מִלְחָמָה alai עָלַי takum תָּקוּם כ"א הויות שבתפילין ע"ה דאהיה דמילוי ודמילוי דמילוי

bezot בְּזֹאת ani אֲנִי vote'ach בּוֹטֵחַ׃ achat אַחַת sha'alti שָׁאַלְתִּי

me'et מֵאֵת־ Adonai יְהֹוָאֲדֹנָהִי (וזון) ota אוֹתָהּ avakesh אֲבַקֵּשׁ

shivti שִׁבְתִּי bevet בְּבֵית ב"פ ראה Adonai יְהֹוָאֲדֹנָהִי (ארך) kol כָּל־ ילי

chayai חַיַּי vayemei וִיְמֵי lachazot לַחֲזוֹת ben'oam בְּנֹעַם Adonai יְהֹוָאֲדֹנָהִי (אפים)

ulvaker וּלְבַקֵּר behechalo בְּהֵיכָלוֹ׃ ki כִּי yitzpeneni יִצְפְּנֵנִי besuko בְּסֻכֹּה

beyom בְּיוֹם ע"ה נגד, מזבוח, זן, אל יהוה ra'a רָעָה רהע yastireni יַסְתִּרֵנִי beseter בְּסֵתֶר

aholo אָהֳלוֹ ב"פ מצר betzur בְּצוּר אלהים דההין ע"ה yeromemeni יְרוֹמְמֵנִי׃

ve'ata וְעַתָּה yarum יָרוּם roshi רֹאשִׁי al עַל ר"ת ערי oyvai אֹיְבַי

sevivotai סְבִיבוֹתַי ve'ezbecha וְאֶזְבְּחָה ve'aholo בְאָהֳלוֹ zivchei זִבְחֵי

teru'a תְרוּעָה ashira אָשִׁירָה va'azamra וַאֲזַמְּרָה ladonai לַיהֹוָאֲדֹנָהִי (ורב וחסד)׃

shema שְׁמַע־ Adonai יְהֹוָאֲדֹנָהִי (ואמת) koli קוֹלִי ekra אֶקְרָא

vechoneni וְחָנֵּנִי va'aneni וַעֲנֵנִי׃ lecha לְךָ amar אָמַר libi לִבִּי bakeshu בַּקְּשׁוּ

fanai פָנָי חוכמה בינה דעה Adonai יְהֹוָאֲדֹנָהִי ס"ג מ"ה ב"ן et אֶת־ panecha פָּנֶיךָ (נצר וחסד)

avakesh אֲבַקֵּשׁ ס"ג מ"ה ב"ן panecha פָּנֶיךָ ב"פ מצר taster תַּסְתֵּר al אַל־ avakesh אֲבַקֵּשׁ׃

mimeni מִמֶּנִּי al אַל־ tat תֵּט־ be'af בְּאַף avdecha עַבְדֶּךָ פוי, אל אדני

ezrati עֶזְרָתִי hayita הָיִיתָ al אַל־ titesheni תִּטְּשֵׁנִי ve'al וְאַל־ ta'azveni תַּעַזְבֵנִי

Elohei אֱלֹהֵי מילוי ע"ב, דמב ; ילה yish'i יִשְׁעִי׃ ki כִּי־ avi אָבִי

horeni הוֹרֵנִי Adonai יְהֹוָאֲדֹנָהִי (נשא) עון) darkecha דַּרְכֶּךָ

uncheni וּנְחֵנִי be'orach בְּאֹרַח mishor מִישׁוֹר lema'an לְמַעַן shorerai שׁוֹרְרָי׃

If an army encampment shall besiege me, my heart shall not fear. If war is waged against me, then it is in this that I place my trust. I ask one thing of the Lord and it is that which I require: that I may dwell in the house of the Lord all the days of my life, to behold the pleasantness of the Lord and to dwell in His Sanctuary. He shall conceal me in His Tabernacle on the day of evil; He shall conceal me within the covering of His Tent and lift me up with strength. And now, my head shall be lifted above my enemies who surround me and I shall slaughter, in His Tent, offerings accompanied by song. I shall sing and play melodies to the Lord. Lord, hear my voice when I call. Favor me and answer me. My heart said on Your behalf: Seek My Countenance, and Your Countenance I shall seek, Lord. Do not conceal Your Countenance from me. Do not turn Your servant away in Your anger. You have always been my Help. Do not forsake or abandon me, God of my salvation. Though my father and mother have abandoned me, the Lord has gathered me. Lord, teach me Your ways and lead me on the straight path despite those who want my downfall.

אַל־ al titeneni תִּתְּנֵנִי benefesh בְּנֶפֶשׁ tzarai צָרָי mitzpatz, alohim diyudin, y"p ווי

כִּי ki kamu קָמוּ vi בִ֑י edei עֵדִי sheker שֶׁקֶר vife'ach וִיפֵחַ chamas: וְחָמָס

לוּלֵא lule bina בינה ; v'a"h ehyeh ehyeh yhvh, vzeh he'emanti הֶאֱמַנְתִּי lir'ot לִרְאוֹת lir'ot

בְּטוּב betuv v'hu ; r"t hevel (l'mitak or vchozer a"m l'taken ayin hevel shotta br'iyah)

יְהֹוָה adni yahdonhi (v'pesha) Adonai be'eretz בְּאֶרֶץ chayim וְ֝חַיִּ֗ים ehyeh ehyeh yhvh, bina a"h:

קַוֵּה kave el אֶל Adonai יְהֹוָה adni yahdonhi (v'chta'ah) Adonai chazak וַחֲזֹק (v'chta'ah) p'hl

וְ֝יַאֲמֵץ veya'ametz libecha לִבֶּךָ vekave וְ֝קַוֵּה el אֶל יְהֹוָה adni yahdonhi Adonai (v'nukah):

RABBENU TAM TEFILIN (ACCORDING TO RAV SHABTAI OF RASHKOV)

RABBENU TAM HAND TEFILIN

> Meditate that the *Rabbenu Tam* Hand *Tefilin* is the secret of the illumination of:
> *Netzach* and *Hod* of *Abba* in *Netzach* and *Hod* of *Zeir Anpin* as it becomes *Mochin* to *Nukva.*

והנה תפילין אלו הם דאבא לעיר אנפין והם כ"א אזכרות עיבור א' אההי

ודי פרשיות שבתוכו יהיו והם די הויות ע"ב ס"ג מ"ה ב"ן ולבושם קס"א קס"א קנ"א קמ"ג כזה:

לבושין
Levushin (clothing)

אלף הי יוד הי. אלף הי יוד הי.

אלף הא יוד הא. אלף הה יוד הה.

מוחין
Mochin (brains)

יוד הי ויו הי. יוד הי ואו הי.

יוד הא ואו הא. יוד הה וו הה.

הח"ג הוא אלף הי ויו הי

והבית הוא אלף דלת נון יוד

והנה אהיה יהוה אדני עולים למנין יב"ק (סוד מעבר יב"ק).

RABBENU TAM HEAD TEFILIN

> Meditate that the *Rabbenu Tam* Head *Tefilin* is the secret of the illumination of:
> *Netzach* and *Hod* of *Abba* in the Head of *Zeir Anpin.*

וכ"א אזכרות הם עיבור א' אההי

עיבור א' ודי פרשיות הם יההו

והם סוד די יהוה ולבושים די אהיה כנ"ל.

ודי בתים הם אההי עיבור ב'

הנה אהיה יההו אהיה עולים למנין וזיים (סוד וזי מלך).

והנה יב"ק (של יד) ו- וזיים (של ראש) עולים למנין

ע"ב (יוד הי ויו הי) + ס"ג (יוד הי ואו הי) + מ"ה (יוד הא ואו הא)

Then scan the meditation of the Small *Shema* (pg. 90-91) and then say the first portion of *Shema* (pg. 178-179).

Do not surrender me to the will of my foes, for false witnesses have risen up against me who talk of violence. Were it not that I had faith in seeing the goodness of the Lord in the land of the living! Place your hope in the Lord to be strong and courageous, and trust in the Lord." (Psalms 27)

BLESSING FOR SUSTENANCE

Kabbalah teaches us that blessed business is an outcome of our proactive actions and our connection to the Light. Too often, when it comes to money we forget that the source for our sustenance is the Light and we fall into doubt and uncertainty. The following prayer helps us to keep our connection with the Light all day long, especially in our business.

hu הוּא · berich בְּרִיךְ · kudsha קוּדְשָׁא · yichud יִוּוּד · leshem לְשֵׁם

ush'chintei וּשְׁכִינְתֵּיהּ (יאהדונהי) · bid'chilu בִּדְחִילוּ (יאהדונהי) · ur'chimu וּרְחִימוּ

ur'chimu וּרְחִימוּ · ud'chilu וּדְחִילוּ (איההיוהה) · leyachada לְיַחֲדָא · shem שֵׁם (יהוה)

yud יו"ד · kei קֵי · bevav בְּוָא"ו · kei קֵי · beyichuda בְּיִחוּדָא · shelim שְׁלִים (יהוה)

beshem בְּשֵׁם · kol כָּל יל' · Yisrael יִשְׂרָאֵל · hareni הֲרֵינִי · matchil מַתְחִיל

bimlacha בִּמְלָאכָה · zu זוּ · oh אוֹ · holech הוֹלֵךְ · le'esek לְעֵסֶק · ze זֶה · oh אוֹ

masa מַשָּׂא · umatan וּבְמַתָּן · ze זֶה · yehi יְהִי · ratzon רָצוֹן

milfanecha מִלְפָנֶיךָ · Adonai יְהֹוָה · Elohenu אֱלֹהֵינוּ

shetishlach שֶׁתִּשְׁלַח · avotenu אֲבוֹתֵינוּ · velohei וֵאלֹהֵי

hatzlacha הַצְלָוחָה · vechol בְּכָל · ma'ase מַעֲשֶׂה · yadai יָדַי

utfarneseni וּתְפַרְנְסֵנִי · bechavod בְּכָבוֹד · shelo שֶׁלֹּא · etztarech אֶצְטָרֵךְ

lidei לִידֵי · matnot מַתְנֹת · basar בָּשָׂר · vadam וָדָם · velo וְלֹא · lidei לִידֵי

halva'atam הַלְוָאָתָם · im אִם · ki כִּי

leyadcha לְיָדְךָ · vesheyihye וְשֶׁיִהְיֶה · li לִי · penai פְּנַאי · le'ovdecha לְעָבְדְּךָ

beyir'a בְּיִרְאָה · ki כִּי · Ata אַתָּה · El אֵל · tov טוֹב · lakol לַכֹּל

umechin וּמֵכִין · mazon מָזוֹן · lechol לְכֹל · beriyotecha בְּרִיּוֹתֶיךָ

dichtiv דִכְתִיב: · noten נֹתֵן · lechem לֶחֶם · lechol לְכֹל

basar בָּשָׂר · ki כִּי · le'olam לְעוֹלָם

chasdo וְחַסְדּוֹ

BLESSING FOR SUSTENANCE

For the sake of unification between The Holy Blessed One and His Shechinah, with fear and love, and with love and fear, in order to unify the Name Yud-Kei and Vav-Kei in perfect unity, and in the name of all Israel, I am hereby start this activity, or this business, or this negotiation. May it be pleasing before You, the Lord, my God and God of my forefathers, that You send success in all my handwork, and You will sustain me with dignity, so I will not need people's largesse and not their loan, but only Your hand. So I will be leisure to worship you with awe. Because You are good God for everyone and prepare food to all of Yours creation. As it says: "He gives nourishment to all flesh, for his kindness endures forever" (Psalm 136:25)

SHACHARIT – MORNING PRAYER
DRAWING SURROUNDING LIGHT

פּוֹתֵחַ pote'ach אֶת et יָדֶךָ yadecha ר"ת פאי וס"ת וחתך (עם ג' אותיות = דִיקַרְנֹוסָא ובאתב"ש

הוא סאל, פאי, יאהדונהי ; ועוד יכוין עם וחתך בעילוב יהוה כזה: יְוֹדֵהֵוֹאֵוּכֵֹה המסוגל לפרנסה)

וּמַשְׂבִּיעַ umasbi'a וחתך (עם ג' אותיות = דִיקַרְנֹוסָא ובא"ת ב"ש הוא סאל, פאי, אמן, יאהדונהי;

ועוד יכוין עם וחתך בעילוב יהוה כזה: יְוֹדֵהֵוֹאֵוּכֵֹה שהוא מסוגל לפרנסה) לְכֹל lechol יה אדני וְזִי chai

כל וזי = אהיה אהיה יהוה, בינה ע"ה, וחיים ע"ה, ע"ב בריבוע וקס"א ע"ה, אל עדוי ע"ה;

רָצוֹן ratzon מהיא ע"ה, בינה ע"ה ר"ת רוזל שהיא המלכות הצריכה לשפע: וְתַמְצִיא vetamtzi לִי li al עַל al יְדֵי yedei

מְלָאכָה melacha זו zu עֵסֶק esek oh אוֹ ze זֶה, מַשָׂא masa oh אוֹ וּמַתָּן umatan

זֶה ze כְּדֵי kedei שֶׁאוּכַל she'uchal לְפַרְנֵס lefarnes בְּנֵי benei בֵּיתִי beti,

לֶחֶם lechem לֶאֱכוֹל le'echol וּבֶגֶד uveged לִלְבֹּשׁ lilbosh וְיִשְׁמַע ushma

תְּפִלָּתִי tefilati כִּי ki אַתָּה Ata שׁוֹמֵעַ shome'a תְּפִלַּת tefilat עַמְּךָ amecha

בָּרוּךְ baruch יִשְׂרָאֵל Yisrael בְּרַחֲמִים berachamim אֱלֹהִים, י"פ ייי

אַתָּה Ata שׁוֹמֵעַ shome'a תְּפִלָּה tefila

There is an additional connection that helps us keep the Light in our consciousness the entire day. Before we close our prayer book and leave, we recite this prayer to keep the angels with us all day.

יְהֹוָ֨ Adonai נְחֵנִי necheni בְּצִדְקָתֶךָ vetzidkatecha לְמַעַן lema'an

שׁוֹרְרָי shorerai הַיָשָׁר hayshar (כתיב: הוֹשֵׁר) לְפָנַי lefanai דַּרְכֶּךָ darkecha:

וְיַעֲקֹב veYaakov הָלַךְ halach לְדַרְכּוֹ ledarko

וַיִּפְגְּעוּ vayifge'u בּוֹ vo מַלְאֲכֵי mal'achei אֱלֹהִים Elohim

וַיֹּאמֶר vayomer יַעֲקֹב Yaakov כַּאֲשֶׁר ka'asher

רָאָם ra'am מַחֲנֵה machane אֱלֹהִים Elohim זֶה ze וַיִּקְרָא vayikra

שֵׁם shem הַמָּקוֹם hamakom הַהוּא hahu מַחֲנָיִם Machanayim:

"Open Your Hands and give fulfillment to every living creature's desire." (Psalms 145:16)
And You will deliver me by this activity, or this business, or this negotiation, so I can sustain my family and my household with bread to eat and clothing to wear, and hear my prayer, for You hear the prayer of your people Yisrael with compassion. Bless are You, who hears prayers.

"Lord, instruct me with Your righteousness, and against my foes lead me in Your ways." (Psalms 5:9)
"And Jacob went on his way, and the angels of God met him. And Jacob, when he saw them, said: This is the camp of God. And he called that place Machanayim." (Genesis 32:2-3)

The purpose of the *Minchah* prayer is not simply to make a connection to the Light of the Creator, it is to quiet the energy of judgment in the world. The best time to do this is when the energy of judgment appears in its greatest number and intensity. Kabbalist Rav Isaac Luria (the Ari), would only recite *Minchah* when the sun was setting. He understood that the numerical value of the word *Minchah* (103) is also the number of sub-worlds (within the five major worlds), controlled by the Left Column energy of judgment.

The sin of the golden calf occurred during the time of *Minchah*, consequently becoming the seed that helped infuse the world with judgment in the late afternoon. Isaac the Patriarch is our channel to overcome judgment. Isaac came to this world to create a path that would lead us to sweetening the judgment in our lives. We can choose to either continue creating difficult paths for ourselves or we can follow the path of sweetening judgment paved by Isaac.

> After midday until the sun sets is a time of harsh judgment.
> For this reason we bring *menucha* (rest) to the judgment by the prayer of *Minchah*.

LESHEM YICHUD

hu הוּא berich בְּרִיךְ kudsha קוּדְשָׁא yichud יִחוּד leshem לְשֵׁם

ur'chimu וּרְחִימוּ bid'chilu בִּדְחִילוּ (יְאהֹדוֹנַהִי) ush'chintei וּשְׁכִינְתֵּיה

leyachda לְיַחֲדָא (אֵיהֹהֵיוּהֵה) ud'chilu וּדְחִילוּ ur'chimu וּרְחִימוּ (יְאהֹהֵיוּהֵה)

beyichuda בְּיִחוּדָא kei קֵי bevav בְּוָא"ו kei קֵי yud יוֹ"ד shem שֵׁם

,Yisrael יִשְׂרָאֵל kol כָּל beshem בְּשֵׁם (יְהֹוָה) shelim שְׁלִים

tefilat תְּפִלַּת lehitpalel לְהִתְפַּלֵּל ba'im בָּאִים anachnu אֲנַחְנוּ hine הִנֵּה

avinu אָבִינוּ Yitzchak יִצְחָק shetiken שֶׁתִּקֵּן mincha מִנְחָה

hamitzvot הַמִּצְוֹת kol כָּל im עִם hashalom הַשָּׁלוֹם alav עָלָיו

shorsha שׁוֹרְשָׁה et אֶת letaken לְתַקֵּן ba בָּה hakelulot הַכְּלוּלוֹת

ru'ach רוּחַ nachat נַחַת la'asot לַעֲשׂוֹת elyon עֶלְיוֹן bemakom בְּמָקוֹם

retzon רְצוֹן vela'asot וְלַעֲשׂוֹת leyotzrenu לְיוֹצְרֵנוּ

Adonai אֲדֹנָי no'am נֹעַם vihi וִיהִי bor'enu בּוֹרְאֵנוּ

yadenu יָדֵינוּ uma'ase וּמַעֲשֵׂה alenu עָלֵינוּ Elohenu אֱלֹהֵינוּ

konenehu כּוֹנְנֵהוּ yadenu יָדֵינוּ uma'ase וּמַעֲשֵׂה alenu עָלֵינוּ konena כּוֹנְנָה

THE MINCHAH (AFTERNOON) PRAYER - LESHEM YICHUD

For the sake of unification of The Holy Blessed One and His Shechinah, with fear and love and with love and fear, in order to unify The Name Yud-Kei and Vav-Kei in perfect unity, and in the name of Israel, we have hereby come to recite the prayer of Minchah, established by Isaac, our forefather, may peace be upon him, With all its commandments, to correct its root in the supernal place, to bring satisfaction to our Maker, and to fulfill the wish of our Creator. "And may the pleasantness of the Lord, our God, be upon us and may He establish the work of our hands for us and may the work of our hands establish Him." (Psalms 90:17)

THE SACRIFICES – KORBANOT - THE TAMID - (DAILY) OFFERING

וַיְדַבֵּר vaydaber ראה יְהֹוָ֙הִיֵאהדונהי Adonai אֶל־ el מֹשֶׁה Moshe

מ'הע, ע''ב ברריבוע וקס''א, פוי, אל עדי צַו tzav אֶת־ et בְּנֵי benei

יִשְׂרָאֵל Yisrael וְאָמַרְתָּ ve'amarta אֲלֵהֶם alehem אֶת־ et קָרְבָּנִי korbani

לַחְמִי lachmi לְאִשַּׁי le'ishai רֵיחַ re'ach נִיחֹחִי nichochi תִּשְׁמְרוּ tishmeru

לְהַקְרִיב lehakriv לִי li בְּמוֹעֲדוֹ bemo'ado: וְאָמַרְתָּ ve'amarta לָהֶם lahem

זֶה ze הָאִשֶּׁה ha'ishe אֲשֶׁר asher תַּקְרִיבוּ takrivu לַיהֹוָ֙הִיֵאהדונהי ladonai

כְּבָשִׂים kevasim בְּנֵי benei שָׁנָה shana תְמִימִם temimim שְׁנַיִם shenayim

לַיּוֹם layom עֹלָה ola ר''ת נגר, מזבח, ז, אל יהוה עה קס''א קנ''א קמ''ג: תָּמִיד tamid

אֶת־ et הַכֶּבֶשׂ hakeves אֶחָד echad אהבה, דאה תַּעֲשֶׂה ta'ase בַבֹּקֶר vaboker

וְאֵת ve'et הַכֶּבֶשׂ hakeves הַשֵּׁנִי hasheni תַּעֲשֶׂה ta'ase בֵּין ben

הָעַרְבָּיִם ha'arbayim: וְעֲשִׂירִית va'asirit הָאֵיפָה ha'efa סֹלֶת solet

בְּשֶׁמֶן beshemen בְּלוּלָה belula עה ב''ה ב''פ ב''ן לְמִנְחָה lemincha

כָּתִית katit רְבִיעִת revi'it הַהִין hahin: עֹלַת olat ושר, אבויתץ

(Meditate here to surrender the *klipa* named *Tola* using the Name: אבגיתץ)

תָּמִיד tamid קמ''ג קנ''א קס''א עה הָעֲשֻׂיָה ha'asuya

בְּהַר behar סִינַי Sinai נממ, ה' הויות (ה' גבורות) לְרֵיחַ lere'ach נִיחֹחַ nicho'ach

אִשֶּׁה ishe לַיהֹוָ֙הִיֵאהדונהי ladonai: וְנִסְכּוֹ venisko רְבִיעִת revi'it

הַהִין hahin לַכֶּבֶשׂ lakeves הָאֶחָד ha'echad אהבה, דאה בַּקֹּדֶשׁ bakodesh

הַסֵּךְ hasech נֶסֶךְ nesech שֵׁכָר shechar י''פ ב''ן לַיהֹוָ֙הִיֵאהדונהי ladonai:

THE SACRIFICES – KORBANOT - THE TAMID – (DAILY) OFFERING

"And the Lord spoke to Moses and said, Command the Children of Israel and say to them, My offering, the bread of My fire-offering, My pleasing fragrance, you shall take care to sacrifice to Me at its specified time. And you shall say to them: This is the fire-offering that you shall sacrifice to God, perfect one-year-old sheep, two per day, as a regular daily offering; one sheep you shall do in the morning and the second sheep you shall do in the late afternoon. And one tenth of ephah of fine flour, for a meal-offering, mixed with one quarter of a hin of pressed oil. This is a regular burnt-offering that is made at Mount Sinai as a pleasing fragrance and as a fire-offering before the Lord. Its libation is one quarter of a hin for the one sheep in the Sanctuary, pour a libation of old wine before the Lord.

ben בֵּין ta'ase תַּעֲשֶׂה hasheni הַשֵּׁנִי hakeves הַכֶּבֶשׂ ve'et וְאֵת

uchnisko וּכְנִסְכּוֹ haboker הַבֹּקֶר keminchat כְּמִנְחַת ha'arbayim הָעַרְבַּיִם

(elevation to *Beriah*) re'ach רֵיחַ (elevation to *Yetzirah*) ishe אִשֵּׁה ta'ase תַּעֲשֶׂה

✦(elevation to the Endless World) ladonai לַיהוֹוָאהדונהי (elevation to *Atzilut*) nicho'ach נִיחֹוַ

THE INCENSE

These verses from the *Torah* and the *Talmud* speak about the 11 herbs and spices that were used in the Temple. These herbs and spices were used for one purpose: to help us remove the force of death from every area of our lives. This is one of the few prayers whose sole goal is the eradication of death. The *Zohar* teaches us that whoever has judgment pursuing him needs to connect to this incense. The 11 herbs and spices connect to 11 Lights that sustain the *klipot* (shells of negativity). When we uproot the 11 Lights from the *klipot* through the power of the incense, the *klipot* lose their life-force and die. In addition to bringing the 11 spices to the Temple, the people brought resin, wine, and other items with metaphysical properties to help battle the Angel of Death.

It says in the *Zohar*: "Come and see, whoever is pursued by judgment is in need of incense and must repent before his master, for incense helps judgment to disappear from him." The 11 herbs and spices correspond to the 11 holy illuminations that revive the *klipa*. By elevating them, the *klipa* will die. Through these 11 herbs, the *klipot* are pushed away and the energy-point that was giving them life is removed. And since the Pure Side and its livelihood disappear, the *klipot* is left with no life. Thus the secret of the incense is that it cleanses the force of plague and cancels it. The incense kills the Angel of Death and takes away his power to kill.

Elohenu אֱלֹהֵינוּ Adonai יְהוֹוָאהדונהי hu הוּא Ata אַתָּה

lefanecha לְפָנֶיךָ avotenu אֲבוֹתֵינוּ shehiktiru שֶׁהִקְטִירוּ

ketoret קְטֹרֶת et אֶת

hasamim הַסַּמִּים

kayam קָיָם hamikdash הַמִּקְדָּשׁ shebet שֶׁבֵּית bizman בִּזְמָן

Moshe מֹשֶׁה yad יַד al עַל otam אוֹתָם tzivita צִוִּיתָ ka'asher כַּאֲשֶׁר

✦betoratach בְּתוֹרָתֶךָ kakatuv כַּכָּתוּב nevia'ch נְבִיאֶךָ

The second sheep you shall do in the afternoon like the meal-offering of the morning; its libation you shall do as a fire-offering of a fragrance which is pleasing to the Lord." (Numbers 28:1-8)

THE INCENSE

It is You, Lord, our God, before whom our forefathers burned the incense spices, during the time when the Temple existed, as You had commanded them through Moses, Your Prophet, and as it is written in Your Torah:

THE PORTION OF THE INCENSE

To raise the *Sefirot* from all of *Nogah* of *Atzilut*, *Beriah*, *Yetzirah* and *Asiyah*.

וַיֹּאמֶר vayomer יְהֹוָה Adonai אֶל־ el מֹשֶׁה Moshe

קַח־ kach לְךָ lecha סַמִּים samim (Tiferet, Netzach) מֵהֹע, ע"ב בריבוע וקס"א, אל עדי

נָטָף nataf | (Hod) וּשְׁחֵלֶת ushchelet (Yesod) וְחֶלְבְּנָה vechelbena ע"ה קנ"א, אדני אלהים

סַמִּים samim (Keter, Chochmah, Binah, Chesed, Gevurah) אל אדני פוי, ע"ה (Malchut)

וּלְבֹנָה ulvona זַכָּה zaka (Surrounding Light) בַּד bad בְּבַד bevad ע"ה קנ"א, אדני אלהים

וְעָשִׂיתָ ve'asita אֹתָהּ ota קְטֹרֶת ketoret י"א פעמים אדני (הנברים) יְהְיֶה yih'ye ייי׃

רֹקַח rokach (מצוות) תרי"ג = ד' באתב"ש הק' – קטרת; (י"א הסממנים) מַעֲשֵׂה ma'ase

רוֹקֵחַ roke'ach עדי מְמֻלָּח memulach טָהוֹר tahor י"פ אכא קֹדֶשׁ kodesh

וְשָׁחַקְתָּ veshachakta מִמֶּנָּה mimena ס"ת רוזע בכוזו לגרע החיצונים ויועיל לוכירה׃

הָדֵק hadek וְנָתַתָּה venatata מִמֶּנָּה mimena לִפְנֵי lifnei הָעֵדֻת ha'edut

בְּאֹהֶל be'ohel מוֹעֵד mo'ed אֲשֶׁר asher אוּעֵד iva'ed לְךָ lecha שָׁמָּה shama

קֹדֶשׁ kodesh קָדָשִׁים kadashim תִּהְיֶה tihye לָכֶם lachem ◆ וְנֶאֱמַר vene'emar׃

וְהִקְטִיר vehiktir עָלָיו alav אַהֲרֹן Aharon קְטֹרֶת ketoret י"א פעמים אדני

(מצוות) תרי"ג = ד' באתב"ש הק' ; (י"א הסממנים) מהקליפות (הנברים) סַמִּים samim

בַּבֹּקֶר baboker בַּבֹּקֶר baboker ע"ה קנ"א, אדני אלהים בְּהֵיטִיבוֹ behetivo

אֶת־ et הַנֵּרֹת hanerot יַקְטִירֶנָּה yaktirena׃ וּבְהַעֲלֹת uveha'alot

אַהֲרֹן Aharon אֶת־ et הַנֵּרֹת hanerot בֵּין ben הָעַרְבַּיִם ha'arbayim

קְטֹרֶת ketoret י"א אדני פעמים יַקְטִירֶנָּה yaktirena ר"ת אהבה, דאנה, אוזד

תָּמִיד tamid (מצוות) תרי"ג = ד' באתב"ש הק' ; קטרת (י"א הסממנים) מהקליפות (הנברים)

לִפְנֵי lifnei יְהֹוָה Adonai ע"ה קס"א קנ"א קמ"ג לְדֹרֹתֵיכֶם ledorotechem׃

THE PORTION OF THE INCENSE

"And the Lord said to Moses: Take for yourself spices, balsam sap, onycha, galbanum, and pure frankincense, each of equal weight. You shall prepare it as an incense compound: the work of a spice-mixer, well-blended, pure, and holy. You shall grind some of it fine and place it before the Testimony in the Tabernacle of Meeting, in which I shall meet with you. It shall be the Holy of Holies unto you." (Exodus 30:34-36) *And God also said: "Aaron shall burn upon the Altar incense spices early each morning when he prepares the candles. And when Aaron raises the candles at sundown, he shall burn the incense spices as a continual incense-offering before God throughout all your generations."* (Exodus 30:7-8)

THE WORKINGS OF THE INCENSE

The filling of the incense has two purposes: First, to remove the *klipot* in order to stop them from going up along with the elevation of the Worlds, and second, to draw Light to *Asiyah*. So meditate to raise the sparks of Light from all of the *Nogah* of *Azilut*, *Beriah*, *Yetzirah* and *Asiyah*.

Count the incense using your right hand, one by one, and don't skip even one, as it is said: "If one omits one of all the ingredients, he is liable to receive the penalty of death." And therefore, you should be careful not to skip any of them, because reciting this paragraph is a substitute for the actual burning of the incense.

אֲדֹנָי פְּעָמִים י"א haketoret הַקְּטֹרֶת pitum פִּטּוּם rabanan רַבָּנָן tanu תָּנוּ
(מִצְוֹת) תרי"ג = ד' באתב"ע הֵק' – קְטֹרֶת הַסַּמָּנִים י"א עַ"י מֵהַקְּלִיפוֹת הַנִּבְרָרִים)

(ו' מַרְגְּלָאִין דְּשַׁבָּת) מֻצְפָּץ אֱלֹהִים אֵל אֲדֹנָי יָה מֻצְפָּץ יְהוָֹה יֶהֱוֶה = הַקְּטֹרֶת פִּטּוּם

דְּיוֹדִין אֱלֹהִים ,ע = הַמִּסְפָּר me'ot מֵאוֹת shelosh שְׁלֹש ◆ketzad כֵּיצַד

hayu הָיוּ manim מָנִים ushmona וּשְׁמוֹנָה (יְן) = בְּמִלּוּי הֵעַ' מִלּוּי = הַמִּסְפָּר veshishim וְשִׁשִּׁים וְשִׁשִּׁים

דְּיוֹדִין אֱלֹהִים ,ע = הַמִּסְפָּר me'ot מֵאוֹת shelosh שְׁלֹש ◆va בָּהּ veshishim וְשִׁשִּׁים

yemot יְמוֹת keminyan כְּמִנְיַן vachamisha וְוֲמִשָׁה (יְן) = הֵעַ' בְּמִלּוּי = הַמִּסְפָּר

לְכב ,ב"ן bechol בְּכָל אֲדֹנָי אֵל ,פוי ,עַ"ה mane מָנֶה hachama הַחַמָּה

baboker בַּבֹּקֶר machatzito מַוֲצִיתוֹ ◆ יהוה אֵל ,זְן ,מוֹזְחוֹ ,נְגֵר עַ"ה yom יוֹם

manim מָנִים ushlosha וּשְׁלֹשָׁה ◆ba'erev בָּעֶרֶב umachatzito וּמַוֲצִיתוֹ

מלה kohen כֹּהֵן machnis מַכְנִיס shemehem שֶׁמֵּהֶם קְנַ"א וּקְמַ"ג ,קְנַ"א ,קֵסַ"א yeterim יְתֵרִים

mehem מֵהֶם venotel וְנוֹטֵל אוֹם ,יְזֵל ,מבה = אוֹתִיּוֹת ד' עַם ; לָהוּ gadol גָּדוֹל

hakipurim הַכִּפּוּרִים chofnav וְזָפְנָיו melo מְלֹא יהוה אֵל ,זְן ,מוֹזְחוֹ ,נְגֵר עַ"ה beyom בְּיוֹם

be'erev בָּעֶרֶב lamachteshet לַמַּכְתֶּשֶׁת machaziran מַוֲזִירָן

דְּאָגָה ,אֲהֲבָה ve'achad וְאֶוָד ◆hadaka הַדַּדָּקָה min מִן daka דַּדָּקָה mitzvat מִצְוֹת מְוַזֵּרָן

hen הֵן ve'elu וְאֵלּוּ ◆va בָּהּ hayu הָיוּ samanim סַמָּנִים asar עֶשֶׂר

THE WORKINGS OF THE INCENSE

Our Sages have taught: How was the compounding of the incense done? Three hundred and sixty-eight portions were contained therein. These corresponded to the number of days in the solar year, one portion for each day: Half of it in the morning and half at sundown. As for the remaining three portions, the High Priest, on Yom Kippur, filled both his hands with them. On the Eve of Yom Kippur, he would take them back to the mortar to fulfill the requirement that they should be very finely ground. Each portion contained eleven spices:

(1 הַצֳּרִי haTzori (Keter) מצפצ, אלהים דיודין, י"פ יוי 2. וְהַצִּפֹּרֶן vehaTziporen (Yesod)

יהוה אדני אהיה שדי ע"ה (Malchut) vehaChelbena וְהַחֶלְבְּנָה 3. ♦ ע"ה פוי, אל אדני ♦

(4 וְהַלְּבוֹנָה vehaLevona (Surounding Light) – שהוא אור לבן והוא יוזידי הנקרא אדון יוזיד

מִשְׁקָל mishkal שִׁבְעִים shiv'im שִׁבְעִים shiv'im מָנֶה mane ע"ה פוי, אל אדני ♦

(5 מוֹר Mor (Chesed)♦ רהע (Gevurah) – וּקְצִיעָה uKtzi'ah 6) "כי מצפון תפתוח הרעה",

(7 וְשִׁבֹּלֶת veShibolet נֵרְדְּ Nerd (Tiferet)♦ ♦ צפון רווח סוד והגבורה

(8 וְכַרְכֹּם veCharkom (Netzach) סנדלפון, עריֹ, בזכור, ♦ מִשְׁקָל mishkal שִׁשָּׁה shisha

עָשָׂר asar שִׁשָּׁה shisha עָשָׂר asar מָנֶה mane ע"ה פוי, אל אדני ♦ 9) קֹשְׁטְ Kosht

(Chochmah) שְׁנַיִם sheneim עָשָׂר asar 10. קְלוּפָה Kilufa (Binah) שְׁלֹשָׁה shelosha♦

(11 קִנָּמוֹן Kinamon (Hod) ר"ת ג"פ ק' (בסוד קדוש קדוש קדוש) תִּשְׁעָה tish'ah♦

בּוֹרִית borit כַּרְשִׁינָא karshina תִּשְׁעָה tish'ah קַבִּין kabin♦ יַיִן yen מיכ, י"פ האא

קַפְרִיסִין Kafrisin סְאִין se'in תְּלַת telat וְקַבִּין vekabin תְּלָתָא telata אהיה קבין

וְאִם ve'im לֹא lo מָצָא matza יוהך, מ"א אותיות דפשוטו, דמילוי ודמילוי דמילוי דאהיה ע"ה

יַיִן yen מיכ, י"פ האא קַפְרִיסִין Kafrisin מֵבִיא mevi וְחֲמַר chamar וְיָוָר chivar

עָתִיק atik♦ מֶלַח melach סְדוֹמִית Sedomit רוֹבַע rova♦ מַעֲלֶה ma'ale

עָשָׁן ashan כֹּל kol יְלי שֶׁהוּא shehu♦ רִבִּי Ribi נָתָן Natan הַבַּבְלִי haBavli

אוֹמֵר omer: אַף af כִּפַּת kipat הַיַּרְדֵּן haYarden י' הווית וד' אותיות כָּל kol יְלי

נָתַן natan ע"ה דמילוי ודמילוי דמילוי, דמילוי, מ"א אותיות דפשוטו, יוהך im אִם♦ shehi שֶׁהִיא

פְּסָלָה pesala♦ גדלות דינין ש"ך = (האווז) וי"ד (דעושפר) שו devash דְּבַשׁ ba בָּה

וְאִם ve'im יוהך, מ"א אותיות דפשוטו, דמילוי ודמילוי דמילוי דאהיה ע"ה וְחֲסַר chiser

אוֹת achat מִכָּל mikol יְלי סַמְמָנֶיהָ samemaneha וְחַיָּיב chayav מִיתָה mita:

---

1) Balsam. 2) Onycha. 3) Galbanum. 4) Frankincense; the weight of seventy portions each. 5) Myrrh.
6) Cassia. 7) Spikenard. 8) And Saffron; the weight of sixteen portions each. 9) Twelve portions of Costus.
10) Three of aromatic Bark 11) Nine of Cinnamon. Further, nine kavs of Lye of Carsina. And
three kavs and three se'ehs of Cyprus wine. And if one should not find any Cyprus wine, he should bring an
old white wine. And a quarter of the salt of Sodom. And a small measure of a smoke raising herb.
Rabbi Natan, the Babylonian, advised also, a small amount of Jordan resin. If he added to it
honey, he would make it defective. If he omits even one of all its herbs, he would be liable to death.

רַבָּן Raban שִׁמְעוֹן Shimon בֶּן ben גַּמְלִיאֵל Gamli'el אוֹמֵר omer:

הַצֳּרִי haTzori מצפצ, אלהים דיודין, י"פ יי', אֵינוֹ eno אֶלָּא ela שְׂרָף seraf

הַנּוֹטֵף hanotef מֵעֲצֵי me'atzei הַקְּטָף haketaf בּוֹרִית borit

כַּרְשִׁינָא karshina לְמָה lema הִיא hee בָּאָה va'a כְּדֵי kedei

לְשַׁפּוֹת leshapot בָּהּ ba אֶת et הַצִּפֹּרֶן haTziporen יהוה אדני אהיה שדי

כְּדֵי kedei שֶׁתְּהֵא shetehe נָאָה na'a יַיִן yen ע' (כנגד ע' אומות העולם התלויים בסמאל)

קַפְרִיסִין Kafrisin לְמָה lema הוּא hu בָּא va כְּדֵי kedei מ"כ, י"פ האא

לִשְׁרוֹת lishrot בּוֹ bo אֶת et הַצִּפֹּרֶן haTziporen יהוה אדני אהיה שדי

כְּדֵי kedei שֶׁתְּהֵא shetehe עַזָּה aza וַהֲלֹא vahalo מֵי mei יל רַגְלַיִם raglayim

יָפִין yafin לָהּ la אֶלָּא ela שֶׁאֵין she'en מַכְנִיסִין machnisin מֵי mei יל

רַגְלַיִם raglayim בַּמִּקְדָּשׁ bamikdash מִפְּנֵי mipenei הַכָּבוֹד hakavod לאו:

תַּנְיָא tanya רִבִּי Ribi נָתָן Natan אוֹמֵר omer: כְּשֶׁהוּא keshehu

שׁוֹחֵק shochek אוֹמֵר omer הָדֵק hadek הֵיטֵב hetev הֵיטֵב hetev

הָדֵק hadek מִפְּנֵי mipenei שֶׁהַקּוֹל shehakol יָפֶה yafe לַבְּשָׂמִים labesamim

פִּטְּמָהּ pitema לַחֲצָאִין lachatza'in כְּשֵׁרָה keshera לְשָׁלִישׁ leshalish

וְלִרְבִיעַ ulravi'a לֹא lo שָׁמָעְנוּ shamanu אָמַר amar רִבִּי Ribi

יְהוּדָה Yehuda: זֶה ze הַכְּלָל hakelal אִם im יוהך, מ"א אותיות דפעוט, דמילוי

כְּמִדָּתָהּ kemidata כְּשֵׁרָה keshera לַחֲצָאִין lachatza'in ודמילוי דמילוי דאהיה ע"ה

וְאִם ve'im יוהך, מ"א אותיות דפעוט, דמילוי ודמילוי דמילוי דאהיה ע"ה וְחִסֵּר chiser

אַחַת achat מִכָּל mikol יל סַמְמָנֶיהָ samemaneha וְחַיָּב chayav ויי"ב מִיתָה mita:

Rabban Shimon ben Gamliel says: The balsam was a sap that only seeped from the balsam trees. For what purpose was the lye of Carsina added? In order to rub the Onycha with it to make it pleasant looking. For what purpose was the Cyprus wine added? In order to steep in it the Onycha. Urine is more appropriate for this, but urine is not brought into the Temple out of respect. It was taught that Rabbi Natan said: When he ground, he said: 'Grind it fine, grind it fine.' This is because voice is beneficial to the spices. If he compounds half the amount it is still valid, yet regarding a third or a quarter, we have no information. Rabbi Yehuda said: This is the general rule: If it is in its correct proportions, then half is valid. Yet if he omits one of all its spices, he is liable to death.

tanei תָּנֵי — Var בַּר — Kapara: קַפָּרָא — achat אַוַׂזת — leshishim לְשִׁשִּׁים — o אוׂ

leshiv'im לְשִׁבְעִים — shana שָׁנָה — hayta הָיְתָה — va'a בָּאָה — shel שֶׁל

shirayim שִׁירַיִם — lachatza'in לַחֲצָאִין — ve'od וְעוׂד — tanei תָּנֵי — Var בַּר

Kapara: קַפָּרָא — ilu אִלּוּ — haya הָיָה (יהה) — noten נוׂתֵן (אבגיתך, ועיר) — ba בָּהּ

kortov קׂרְטוׂב — shel שֶׁל — devash דְּבַשׁ — (דעׂיר) וי"ד (האווז) = ש"ך דינין דגדלות

en אֵין — adam אָדָם (מ"ה) — yachol יָכוׂל — la'amod לַעֲמוׂד — mipenei מִפְּנֵי

devash דְּבַשׁ — ba בָּהּ — me'arvin מְעָרְבִין — en אֵין — velama וְלָמָּה — recha רֵיחָהּ•

shehatorah שֶׁהַתּוׂרָה — mipenei מִפְּנֵי — (דעׂיר) וי"ד (האווז) = ש"ך דינין דגדלות (דעׂיר)

amra: אָמְרָה — ki כִּי — chol כָּל־ (ילי) — se'or שְׂאׂר (ג' מווזין דאלהים דקטנות)

vechol וְכָל־ (ילי) (א' כללות שם אלהים; ר' = ריבוע אלהים) — devash דְּבַשׁ (ילי)

mimenu מִמֶּנּוּ — taktiru תַּקְטִירוּ — lo לׂא־ — (דעׂיר) וי"ד (האווז) = ש"ך דינין דגדלות

ishe אִשֶּׁה — ladonai לַיהוׂה/אדני (שוכן הם בוחינת דינין דקטנות ורגדלות לכן נאסרה הקרבתן)

Right

imanu עִמָּנוּ (שכינה) פני — Tzeva'ot צְבָאוׂת — Adonai יהוה/אדני

misgav מִשְׂגָּב (ריבוע דס"ג, קס"א ע"ה ור' אותיות משׂה, מהׂש, ע"ב ברבוע וקס"א, אל שדי,

lanu לָנוּ (אלהים, אהיה אדני אלׂהים ע"ה) — Elohei אֱלׂהֵי (מילוי ע"ב, דמב; יׂלה)

Yaakov יַעֲקׂב (י' היוׂת, יאהדונהי אידהנויה) — sela סֶלָה:

Left

ashrei אַשְׁרֵי (שוכנה) פני — Tzeva'ot צְבָאוׂת — Adonai (אדני/אהדונהי) יהוה

adam אָדָם (מ"ה) ; יהוה צבאות אשרי אדם = תפארת — bote'ach בָּטוּחַ

bach בָּךְ: (אדם בוטוׂח בך (יאהדונהי) ע"ה) ; אמן = בוטח בך = מילוי ע"ב ע"ה:

Bar Kappara taught that once every sixty or seventy years the leftovers would accumulate to half the measure. Bar Kappara also taught that if one would add to it a Kortov of honey, no man would withstand its smell. Why is honey not mixed with it? Because the Torah had stipulated: Because any leaven or honey, you must not burn any of it as burnt-offering to the Lord. (Kritut 6; Yerushalmi, Yoma: ch.4)
(Right) "The Lord of Hosts is with us, our strength is the God of Jacob, Selah." (Psalms 46:12)
(Left) "The Lord of Hosts, joyful is one who trusts in You." (Psalms 84:13)

Central

יְהֹוֶאֱדנִיאֱהרונהי hamelech הַמֶּלֶךְ יהוה וע״ע נהורין hoshi'a הוֹשִׁיעָה Adonai יהוה וע״ע נהורין

לַעֲנֵנוּ אֵל, זֹ, נֶגֶר, מזבוח, ע״ה veyom בְיוֹם ya'anenu

קׇרְאֵנוּ ר״ת יב״ק, אלהים יהוה, אהיה יהוה, אהיה אדני יהוה ; ס״ת = ב״ן ועם כף דהמלך = ע״ב: kor'enu

ladonai לַיהֹוֶאֱדנִיאֱהרונהי ve'arva וְעָרְבָה

virushalaim וְירוּשָׁלִַם Yehuda יְהוּדָה minchat מִנְחַת

kadmoniyot קַדְמֹנִיּוֹת uch'shanim וּכְשָׁנִים olam עוֹלָם kimei כִּימֵי

ANA BEKO'ACH (to learn more about the *Ana Beko'ach* go to pg. 106)

The *Ana Beko'ach* is perhaps the most powerful prayer in the entire universe. Second-century Kabbalist Rav Nachunya ben HaKana was the first sage to reveal this combination of 42 letters, which encompass the power of creation.

Chesed, Sunday *(Alef Bet Gimel Yud Tav Tzadik)* אבג יתץ

◆yeminecha יְמִינֶךְ gedulat גְּדוּלַת ◆beko'ach בְּכֹחַ ana אָנָּא

❖tzerura צְרוּרָה tatir תַּתִּיר

Gevurah, Monday *(Kuf Resh Ayin Shin Tet Nun)* קרע שטן

◆sagvenu שַׂגְּבֵנוּ amecha עַמֶּךְ ◆rinat רִנַּת kabel קַבֵּל

❖nora נוֹרָא taharenu טַהֲרֵנוּ

(Central) *"Lord save us. The King shall answer us the day we call."* (Psalms 20:10) *"May the Lord find the offering of Yehuda and Jerusalem pleasing as He had always done and as in the years of old."* (Malachi 3:4)

ANA BEKO'ACH
Chesed, Sunday אבג יתץ
We beseech You, with the power of Your great right, undo this entanglement.
Gevurah, Monday קרע שטן
Accept the singing of Your Nation. Strengthen and purify us, Awesome One.

Tiferet, Tuesday (Nun Gimel Dalet Yud Kaf Shin) נֶּד יכש

na נָא	•gibor גִּבּוֹר	dorshei דוֹרְשֵׁי	•yichudecha יִחוּדְךָ
		kevavat כְּבָבַת	‡shomrem שָׁמְרֵם

Netzach, Wednesday (Bet Tet Resh Tzadik Tav Gimel) בטר צתג

barchem בָּרְכֵם	•taharem טַהֲרֵם	rachamei רַחֲמֵי	•tzidkatecha צִדְקָתְךָ
	tamid תָּמִיד		‡gomlem גָּמְלֵם

Hod, Thursday (Chet Kuf Bet Tet Nun Ayin) חקב טנע

chasin חֲסִין	•kadosh קָדוֹשׁ	berov בְּרוֹב	•tuvcha טוּבְךָ
	nahel נַהֵל		‡adatecha עֲדָתֶךָ

Yesod, Friday (Yud Gimel Lamed Pei Zayin Kuf) יגל פזק

yachid יָחִיד	•ge'e גֵּאֶה	le'amecha לְעַמְּךָ	•pene פְּנֵה
	zochrei זוֹכְרֵי		‡kedushatecha קְדֻשָּׁתֶךָ

Malchut, Saturday (Shin Kuf Vav Tzadik Yud Tav) שקו צית

shav'atenu שַׁוְעָתֵנוּ	•kabel קַבֵּל	ushma וּשְׁמַע	•tza'akatenu צַעֲקָתֵנוּ
	yode'a יוֹדֵעַ		‡ta'alumot תַּעֲלוּמוֹת

BARUCH SHEM KEVOD
Whispering this final verse brings all the Light from the Upper Worlds into our physical existence.

(Whisper): יוזו אותיות | baruch בָּרוּךְ | shem שֵׁם | kevod כְּבוֹד | malchuto מַלְכוּתוֹ

va'ed וָעֶד‡ | le'olam לְעוֹלָם | רִבּוּעַ ס"ג ו' אותיות דס"ג

Tiferet, Tuesday נֶּד יכש
Please, Mighty One, those who seek Your unity, guard them like the pupil of the eye.

Netzach, Wednesday בטר צתג
Bless them. Purify them. Your compassionate righteousness always grant them.

Hod, Thursday חקב טנע
Invincible and Mighty One, with the abundance of Your goodness, govern Your congregation.

Yesod, Friday יגל פזק
Sole and proud One, turn to Your people, those who remember Your sanctity.

Malchut, Saturday שקו צית
Accept our cry and hear our wail, You that knows all that is hidden.

BARUCH SHEM KEVOD
"Blessed is the Name of Glory. His Kingdom is forever and for eternity." (Pesachim 56a)

THE ASHREI

Twenty-one of the twenty-two letters of the Aramaic alphabet are encoded in the *Ashrei* in their correct order from *Alef* to *Tav*. King David, the author, left out the Aramaic letter *Nun* from this prayer, because *Nun* is the first letter in the Aramaic word *nefilah*, which means "falling." Falling refers to a spiritual decline, as in falling into the *klipa*. Feelings of doubt, depression, worry, and uncertainty are consequences of spiritual falling. Because the Aramaic letters are the actual instruments of Creation, this prayer helps to inject order and the power of Creation into our lives, without the energy of falling.

In this Psalm there are ten times the Name: יהוה for the Ten *Sefirot*. This Psalm is written according to the order of the *Alef Bet*, but the letter *Nun* is omitted to prevent falling.

אַשְׁרֵי ashrei (סוֹד הַכֶּתֶר) yoshvei יוֹשְׁבֵי vetecha בֵיתֶךָ ב"פ ראה

עוֹד od yehalelucha יְהַלְלוּךָ סֶלָה sela: ashrei אַשְׁרֵי ha'am הָעָם

שֶׁכָּכָה shekacha מהש, ע"ב בריבוע וקס"א, אל שדי, ד"פ אלהים ע"ה לוֹ lo

אַשְׁרֵי ashrei הָעָם ha'am ר"ת לאה עָם֑יֹהֹוּ֥ she'Adonai leDavid (Keter)

אֱלֹהָיו Elohav ילה: תְהִלָּה tehila ע"ה אמת, אהיה פעמים אהיה, ז"פ ס"ג aromimcha אֲרוֹמִמְךָ Elohai אֱלוֹהַי hamelech הַמֶּלֶךְ va'avarcha וַאֲבָרְכָה

שִׁמְךָ shimcha לְעוֹלָם le'olam ריבוע דס"ג וי' אותיות דס"ג וָעֶד va'ed:

בְּכָל bechol ב"ן, לכב yom יוֹם ע"ה גגד, מזבח, זן אל יהוה

אֲבָרְכֶךָ avarcheka וַאֲהַלְלָה va'ahalela מ"ה יהוה שִׁמְךָ shimcha

לְעוֹלָם le'olam ריבוע דס"ג וי' אותיות דס"ג וָעֶד va'ed:

גָּדוֹל gadol להו ; עם ד' אותיות = מבה, יזל, אום

יֱהֹוָה Adonai (Chochmah) וּמְהֻלָּל umhulal אדני, ללה

מְאֹד me'od וְלִגְדֻלָתוֹ veligdulato יהו אֵין en חֵקֶר cheker:

THE ASHREI

"Joyful are those who dwell in Your House, they shall praise You, Selah." (Psalms 84:5) *"Joyful is the nation that this is theirs and joyful the nation that the Lord is their God."* (Psalms 145:15) *"A praise of David:*

א *I shall exalt You, my God, the King, and I shall bless Your Name forever and for eternity.*

ב *I shall bless You every day and I shall praise Your Name forever and for eternity.*

ג *The Lord is great and exceedingly praised. His greatness is unfathomable.*

דּוֹר dor לְדוֹר ledor יְשַׁבַּח yeshabach מַעֲשֶׂיךָ ma'asecha ר"ת דלים

וּגְבוּרֹתֶיךָ ugvurotecha יַגִּידוּ yagidu יי"ז, כ"ב אותיות פשוטות (=אבא) וה' אותיות סופיות בזֹחֶר:

הֲדַר hadar כְּבוֹד kevod הוֹדֶךָ hodecha וְדִבְרֵי vedivrei

נִפְלְאֹתֶיךָ nifle'otecha ר"ת אלהים, אהיה אדני

אָשִׂיחָה asicha ר"ת הפסוק פ"ז = (בסוד כתם טהור פז):

וֶעֱזוּז ve'ezuz נוֹרְאֹתֶיךָ no'rotecha יֹאמֵרוּ yomeru וּגְדֻלָּתְךָ ugdulatcha

אֲסַפְּרֶנָּה asaperena ס"ת = יא"י (מילוי דס"ג): ר"ת = ע"ב, ריבוע יהוה (כתיב: וגדלותיך)

זֵכֶר zecher רַב rav טוּבְךָ tuvcha לאו יַבִּיעוּ yabi'u

וְצִדְקָתְךָ vetzidkatcha יְרַנֵּנוּ yeranenu ס"ת = ב"ן, יבם, לכב ; ר"ת הפסוק = רי"ו יהוה:

חַנּוּן chanun וְרַחוּם verachum יְהֹוָה Adonai (Binah)

אֶרֶךְ erech ס"ת = ס"ג ב"ן = עֹיֹל = ר"ת אַפַּיִם apayim ר"ת = יהוה חנון ורחום יהוה

וּגְדָל ugdal (כתיב: וגדול) וְחֶסֶד chased ע"ב, ריבוע יהוה:

טוֹב tov והו (Chesed) Adonai יְהֹוָה לַכֹּל lakol

עַל al וְרַחֲמָיו verachamav (מילוי דס"ג) ל"ז ; ס"ת ; אדני יה

כֹּל kol מַעֲשָׂיו ma'asav ס"ת ע"ב, ריבוע יהוה: ר"ת ריבוע ב"ן ע"ה ; עמם ; ילי

ד *One generation and the next shall praise Your deeds and tell of Your might.*

ה *The brilliance of Your splendid glory and the wonders of Your acts, I shall speak of.*

ו *They shall speak of the might of Your awesome acts and I shall tell of Your greatness.*

ז *They shall express the remembrance of Your abundant goodness, and Your righteousness they shall joyfully proclaim.* ח *The Lord is merciful and compassionate, slow to anger and great in kindness.*

ט *The Lord is good to all, His compassion extends over all His acts.*

יוֹדוּךָ yoducha לַ‏יהוה‏ אדני‏ אהיה‏ דונהי (Gevurah) Adonai כָּל־ kol ילי מַעֲשֶׂיךָ ma'asecha

וַחֲסִידֶיךָ vachasidecha ר"ת אלהים, אהיה אדני לִבְרֲכוּכָה yevarchucha ס"ת = מ"ה:

כְּבוֹד kevod מַלְכוּתְךָ malchutcha יֹאמֵרוּ yomeru וּגְבוּרָתְךָ ugvuratcha

יְדַבֵּרוּ yedaberu ר"ת הפסוק = אלהים, אהיה אדני ; ס"ת = ב"ן, יבמ, לכב:

לְהוֹדִיעַ lehodi'a לִבְנֵי livnei הָאָדָם ha'adam ר"ת ללה, אדני

גְּבוּרֹתָיו gevurotav וּכְבוֹד uchvod הֲדַר hadar

מַלְכוּתוֹ malchuto ר"ת מ"ה וס"ת = רי"ו ; ר"ת הפסוק ע"ה = ק"כ צירופי אלהים:

מַלְכוּתְךָ malchutcha מַלְכוּת malchut כָּל־ kol ילי עֹלָמִים olamim

וּמֶמְשַׁלְתְּךָ umemshaltecha בְּכָל־ bechol ב"ן, לכב dor דּוֹר vador וָדֹר רי"ו:

סוֹמֵךְ somech ריבוע אדני Adonai לַ‏יהוה‏ אדני‏ אהיה‏ דונהי (Tiferet)

לְכָל־ lechol יה אדני ; סומך אדני לכל ר"ת סאל, אמן (יאהדונהי) הַנֹּפְלִים hanoflim נוממ:

וְזוֹקֵף vezokef לְכָל־ lechol יה אדני הַכְּפוּפִים hakefufim נוממ:

עֵינֵי enei ריבוע דמ"ה כֹל chol ילי אֵלֶיךָ elecha יְשַׂבֵּרוּ yesaberu וְאַתָּה veAta

נוֹתֵן noten אבגיתצ, ושר לָהֶם lahem אֶת־ et אָכְלָם ochlam בְּעִתּוֹ be'ito:

י *All that You have made shall thank You, Lord, and Your pious ones shall bless You.*
כ *They shall speak of the glory of Your Kingdom and talk of Your mighty deeds.*
ל *His mighty deeds He makes known to man and the glory of His splendid Kingdom.*
מ *Yours is the Kingdom of all worlds and Your reign extends to each and every generation.*
ס *The Lord supports all those who fell and holds upright all those who are bent over.*
ע *The eyes of all look hopefully towards You, and You give them their food at its proper time.*

POTE'ACH ET YADECHA

We connect to the letters *Pei, Alef,* and *Yud* by opening our hands and holding our palms skyward. Our consciousness is focused on receiving sustenance and financial prosperity from the Light through our actions of tithing and sharing, our *Desire to Receive for the Sake of Sharing.* In doing so, we also acknowledge that the sustenance we receive comes from a higher source and is not of our own doing. According to the sages, if we do not meditate on this idea at this juncture, we must repeat the prayer.

פתחו (שׁע"ן נהורין לבמ"ה ולס"ה)

פותחו את ידך ר"ת פאי	יוד הי ויו הי יוד הי ויו הי (ו' וזוורתי)
גימ' יאהדונהי זו"ן	אלף למד אלף למד (שׁע"ן)
וחכמה דו"א ו"ק	יוד הא ואו הא (כלי"א)
יסוד דנוק'	אדני (ולנוקבא)

פּוֹתֵחַ pote'ach **אֶת** et **יָדֶךָ** yadecha ר"ת פאי וס"ת וחתך עם ג' אותיות = **דִּיקָרְנוֹסָא**

ובאתב"ש הוא סאל, פאי, אמן, יאהדונהי ; ועוד יכוין שׁם וחתך בשׁילוב יהוה – **יְוֹהַהַתֻכָה**

אלף למד הי יוד מם אלף למד הי יוד מם מוזין דפנים דאוזר אלהים אלהים
להמשׁיך פ"ו אורות לכל מילוי דכל

ואוזר דפרצופי נה"י וזג"ת		אוזר דפרצופי נה"י וזג"ת
דיצירה דרוזל הנקראת לאה	וחתך	דפרצוף וזג"ת דיצירה דו"א
לף מד י וד ם		לף מד י וד ם
אלף למד הי יוד מם	סאל יאהדונהי	אלף למד הי יוד מם

וּמַשְׂבִּיעַ umasbi'a וחתך עם ג' אותיות = **דִּיקָרְנוֹסָא**

ובא"ת ב"ש הוא סאל, אמן, יאהדונהי ; ועוד יכוין שׁם וחתך בשׁילוב יהוה – **יְוֹהַהַתֻכָה**

אלף למד הי יוד מם אלף למד הי יוד מם מוזין דפנים דאוזר אלהים אלהים
להמשׁיך פ"ו אורות לכל מילוי דכל

ואוזר דפרצופי נה"י וזג"ת		אוזר דפרצופי נה"י וזג"ת
דיצירה דרוזל הנקראת לאה	וחתך	דפרצוף נה"י דיצירה דו"א
לף מד י וד ם		לף מד י וד ם
אלף למד הי יוד מם		אלף למד הי יוד מם

לְכָל lechol יה אדני (להמשׁיך מוזין ד–יה אל הנוקבא שׁהיא אדני)

וַי chai כל וזי = אהיה אהיה יהוה, בינה ע"ה, וזיים

רָצוֹן ratzon מהשׁע ע"ה, ע"ב בר־ביבוע וקס"א ע"ה, אל שׁדי ע"ה ; ר"ת רוזל שׁהיא המלכות הצריכה לשׁפע

יוד יוד הי יוד הי ויו הי יוד הי ויו הי יסוד דאבא
אלף הי יוד הי יסוד דאימא
להמתיק רוזל וב' דמעין שׁך פר

We should also meditate to draw abundance and sustenance and blessing to all the worlds from the *ratzon* mentioned above. We should meditate and focus on this verse because it is the essence of prosperity, and meditate that God is intervening and sustaining and supporting all of Creation.

POTE'ACH ET YADECHA

פ *Open* *Your* *Hands* *and* *satisfy* *every* *living* *thing* *with* *desire.*

צַדִּיק tzadik יְהוָֹוּוּאדנּיויאהדונהי Adonai (Yesod) בְּכֹל bechol ב"ן, לכב

דְּרָכָיו derachav וְחָסִיד vechasid בְּכֹל bechol ב"ן, לכב בְּמַעֲשָׂיו ma'asav יבמ, ב"ן:

קָרוֹב karov יְהוָֹוּאדנּיויאהדונהי Adonai (Malchut) לְכָל lechol יה אדני

קֹרְאָיו kor'av לְכֹל lechol יה אדני אֲשֶׁר asher

יִקְרָאֻהוּ yikra'uhu בֶּאֱמֶת ve'emet אהיה פעמים אהיה, ז"פ ס"ג:

רָצוֹן retzon מהש"ע ע"ה, ע"ב ברבוע וקס"א ע"ה, אל שדי ע"ה יְרֵאָיו yere'av יַעֲשֶׂה ya'ase

וְאֶת ve'et שַׁוְעָתָם shav'atam יִשְׁמַע yishma וְיוֹשִׁיעֵם veyoshi'em: ר"ת רוי

שׁוֹמֵר shomer כ"א הויות עובתפילין Adonai יְהוָֹוּאדנּיויאהדונהי (Netzach)

אֶת et כָּל kol ילי אֹהֲבָיו ohavav ר"ת אכא

וְאֶת ve'et כָּל kol ילי הָרְשָׁעִים haresha'im יַשְׁמִיד yashmid:

תְּהִלַּת tehilat יְהוָֹוּאדנּיויאהדונהי Adonai (Hod) יְדַבֶּר yedaber ראה פִּי pi

וִיבָרֵךְ vivarech ע"ב ס"ג מ"ה ב"ן, הברכה (למתק את ז' המלכים שמותו) כָּל kol ילי

בָּשָׂר basar שֵׁם shem קָדְשׁוֹ kodsho לְעוֹלָם le'olam ריבוע ס"ג וי' אותיות דס"ג

וְעֶד va'ed: נְבָרֵךְ nevarech יָהּ Yah מֵעַתָּה me'ata וַאֲנַחְנוּ va'anachnu

וְעַד ve'ad עוֹלָם olam הַלְלוּיָהּ haleluya אלהים, אהיה אדני ; ללה:

On fast days the *chazan* will recite the Half *Kaddish* (pg.300), a *Torah* Scroll is taken out of the Ark (pg.230) and we read the portion of "*Vayechal Moshe*" (pg. 522). Three men are called for the reading. After the reading the *Torah* Scroll is returned to the Ark (without *Kaddish* - pg. 239) and we continue as below.

צ *The Lord is righteous in all His ways and virtuous in all His deeds.*

ק *The Lord is close to all who call Him, and only to those who call Him truthfully.*

ר *He shall fulfill the will of those who fear Him; He hears their wailing and saves them.*

ש *The Lord protects all who love Him and He destroys the wicked.*

ת *My lips utter the praise of the Lord and all flesh shall bless His Holy Name, forever and for eternity."*

(Psalms 145) *"And we shall bless the Lord forever and for eternity. Praise the Lord!"* (Psalms 115:18)

ר"ת הפסוק = נפעל רווח נשמה וזיה יוזידה ע"ה

תִּכּוֹן tikon תְּפִלָּתִי tefilati קְטֹרֶת ketoret י"א פעמים אדני לְפָנֶיךָ lefanecha ס"ג מ"ה ב"ן

מַשְׂאַת mas'at כַּפַּי kapai מִנְחַת־ minchat עֶרֶב arev הַקְשִׁיבָה hakshiva

לְקוֹל lekol שַׁוְעִי shave'i מַלְכִּי malki וֵאלֹהָי velohai לכב ; מילוי ע"ב, דמ"ב ; ילה

כִּי־ ki אֵלֶיךָ elecha אֶתְפַּלָל etpalal:

HALF KADDISH

יִתְגַּדַּל yitgadal וְיִתְקַדַּשׁ veyitkadash שדי ומילוי שדי ; י"א אותיות כמנין ו"ה

שְׁמֵיהּ shemei (שם י"ה דע"ב) רַבָּא raba קנ"א ב"ן, יהוה אלהים יהוה אדני,

מילוי קס"א וס"ג, מ"ה ברבוע וע"ב מ"ה ; ר"ת = ו"פ אלהים ; ס"ת = ג"פ יב"ק: אָמֵן amen אידהנויה.

בְּעָלְמָא be'alma דִּי di בְּרָא vera כִּרְעוּתֵיהּ kir'utei

וְיַמְלִיךְ veyamlich מַלְכוּתֵיהּ malchutei וְיַצְמַח veyatzmach

פּוּרְקָנֵיהּ purkanei וִיקָרֵב vikarev מְשִׁיחֵיהּ meshichei אָמֵן amen אידהנויה.

בְּחַיֵּיכוֹן bechayechon וּבְיוֹמֵיכוֹן uvyomechon וּבְחַיֵּי uvchayei

דְכָל dechol יל בֵּית bet ב"פ ראה יִשְׂרָאֵל Yisrael בַּעֲגָלָא ba'agala

וּבִזְמַן uvizman קָרִיב kariv וְאִמְרוּ ve'imru אָמֵן amen: אָמֵן amen אידהנויה.

The congregation and the *chazan* say the following:

> מילוי דבמילוי דע"ב (יוד ויו דלת הי יוד ויו יוד ויו הי יוד)
> **28 words (until *be'alma*) – meditate:**
> מילוי דבמילוי דע"ב (יוד ויו דלת הי יוד ויו יוד ויו הי יוד)
> **28 letters (until *almaya*) – meditate:**

יְהֵא yehe שְׁמֵיהּ shemei (שם י"ה דס"ג) רַבָּא raba קנ"א ב"ן,

יהוה אלהים אדני, מילוי קס"א וס"ג, מ"ה ברבוע וע"ב מ"ה ע"ב מְבָרַךְ mevarach,

לְעָלַם le'alam לְעָלְמֵי le'almei עָלְמַיָּא almaya יִתְבָּרַךְ yitbarach

---

"Let my prayer be set before You
as the incense offering, the lifting up of my hand as the afternoon meal offering." (Psalms 141:2)
"Listen to the sound of my outcry, my King, My God for it is to You I am praying." (Psalms 5:3)

HALF KADDISH

May His great Name be more exalted and sanctified. (Amen)
In the world that He created according to His will, and may His kingdom reign.
And may He cause His redemption to sprout and may He bring the Mashiach closer. (Amen) In your
lifetimes and in your days and in the lifetime of all the House of Israel, speedily and in the near future,
and you should say, Amen. (Amen) May His great Name be blessed forever and for all eternity blessed

Seven words with six letters each (שם בן מ"ב) meditate:

יהוה – יוד הי ויו הי – מילוי דמילוי דע"ב (יוד ויו דלת הי יוד ויו יוד ויו הי הי יוד)

Also, seven times the letter Vav (שם בן מ"ב) meditate:

יהוה – יוד הי ויו הי – מילוי דמילוי דע"ב (יוד ויו דלת הי יוד ויו יוד ויו הי הי יוד).

וְיִשְׁתַּבַּח veyishtabach יְ"פ ע"ב יהוה אל אבג יתץ.

וְיִתְפָּאַר veyitpa'ar הי גו יה קרע שטן. וְיִתְרַבַם veyitromam וה כוזו נגד יכש.

וְיִתְנַשֵּׂא veyitnase במוכסז בטר צתג. וְיִתְהַדָּר veyit'hadar כוזו יה וזקב טנע.

וְיִתְעַלֶּה veyit'ale וה יוד ה יגל פזק. וְיִתְהַלָּל veyit'halal א ואו הא שקו צית.

שְׁמֵיהּ shemei (שם י"ה דמ"ה) דְּקוּדְשָׁא dekudsha בְּרִיךְ berich הוּא hu:

אָמֵן amen אידהנויה.

לְעֵלָּא le'ela מִן min כָּל kol ילי מִן מִן בִּרְכָתָא birchata. שִׁירָתָא shirata.

תֻּשְׁבְּחָתָא tishbechata וְנֶחָמָתָא venechamata. דַּאֲמִירָן da'amiran

בְּעָלְמָא be'alma וְאָמְרוּ ve'imru אָמֵן amen: אָמֵן amen אידהנויה.

THE AMIDAH (to learn more about the *Amidah* go to pg. 189)

When we begin the connection, we take three steps backward, signifying our leaving this physical world. Then we take three steps forward to begin the *Amidah*. The three steps are:

1. Stepping into the land of Israel – to enter the first spiritual circle.
2. Stepping into the city of Jerusalem – to enter the second spiritual circle.
3. Stepping inside the Holy of Holies – to enter the innermost circle.

Before we recite the first verse of the *Amidah*, we ask: "God, open my lips and let my mouth speak," thereby asking the Light to speak for us so that we can receive what we need and not just what we want. All too often, what we want from life is not necessarily the desire of the soul, which is what we actually need to fulfill us. By asking the Light to speak through us, we ensure that our connection will bring us genuine fulfillment and opportunities for spiritual growth and change.

---

and lauded, and glorified and exalted, And extolled and honored,
and uplifted and praised, be the Name of the Holy Blessed One. (Amen) Above all blessings,
songs, praises, and words of consolation that may be said in the world, and you shall say, Amen. (Amen)

yagid יַגִּיד   ufi וּפִי   tiftach תִּפְתָּח   sefatai שְׂפָתַי   (pause here)   לכה   Adonai אֲדֹנָי

ייו (כ"ב אותיות פשוטות [=אכא] וה' אותיות סופיות מנצפ"ך)   tehilatecha תְּהִלָּתֶךָ   ס"ת = בוכו:

THE FIRST BLESSING - INVOKES THE SHIELD OF ABRAHAM.

Abraham is the channel of the Right Column energy of positivity, sharing, and mercy. Sharing actions can protect us from all forms of negativity.

Chesed that becomes Chochmah

In this section there are 42 words, the secret of the 42-Letter Name of God and therefore it begins with the letter *Bet* (2) and ends with the letter *Mem* (40).

Bend your knees at 'baruch', bow at 'Ata' and straighten up at 'Adonai'.

המלכות כה' המגיע העושפע את הבמסמלות (אותיות הא"ב) א–ת   Ata אַתָּה   baruch בָּרוּךְ

יכה   Elohenu אֱלֹהֵינוּ   (יא)   Adonai יְהֹוָה אהדונהי יאהדונהי

◆avotenu אֲבוֹתֵינוּ   יכה ; דמב , ע"ב , מילוי ; לכב   velohei וֵאלֹהֵי

(Chochmah) Avraham אַבְרָהָם   יכה ; דמב , ע"ב , מילוי   Elohei אֱלֹהֵי

פשוטות אותיות וט"ז (אברים), עסמ"ב רמ"ח, הוכמה נתיבות ול"ב רי"ו, אל, וו"פ

ב"ן ד"פ   (Binah) Yitzchak יִצְחָק   יכה ; דמב , ע"ב , מילוי   Elohei אֱלֹהֵי

איהדנויה יאהדונהי , הויות ו' (Da'at) Yaakov יַעֲקֹב ; יכה ; דמב , ע"ב מילוי ; לכב   velohei וֵאלֹהֵי

לההו = גדול ; סיט = הגדול האל הָאֵל הגדול (מילוי דס"ג) ; יא"י לאה   hagadol הַגָּדוֹל   haEl הָאֵל

◆vehanora וְהַנּוֹרָא   ההה ר"ת   hagibor הַגִּבּוֹר   אום , יזל , מבה = אותיות ד' עם

THE AMIDAH

"My Lord, open my lips, and my mouth shall relate Your praise." (Psalms 51:17)

THE FIRST BLESSING

Blessed are You, Lord, our God and God of our forefathers:
the God of Abraham, the God of Isaac, and the God of Jacob. The great, mighty and awesome God.

אֵל El (מילוי דס"ג) יי"א ר"ת ע"ב, ריבוע יהוה עֶלְיוֹן elyon◆

גּוֹמֵל gomel וְחֲסָדִים chasadim ◆טוֹבִים tovim קוֹנֶה kone הַכֹּל hakol

וְזוֹכֵר vezocher וְחַסְדֵי chasdei ◆אָבוֹת avot וּמֵבִיא umevi

גּוֹאֵל go'el לִבְנֵי livnei בְּנֵיהֶם venehem לְמַעַן lema'an

שְׁמוֹ shemo מהש"ע ע"ה, ע"ב בריבוע וקס"א ע"ה, אל שדי ע"ה בְּאַהֲבָה be'ahava אוזר, דאגה:

When saying the word *"be'ahava"* you should meditate to devote your soul to sanctify the Holy Name and accept upon yourself the four forms of death.

During the days between *Rosh Hashanah* and *Yom Kippur* we say the prayer of *"zochrenu"*:

זָכְרֵנוּ zochrenu לְחַיִּים lechayim אהיה אהיה יהוה, בינה ע"ה.

מֶלֶךְ melech וְחָפֵץ chafetz בַּחַיִּים bachayim אהיה אהיה יהוה, בינה ע"ה.

כָּתְבֵנוּ kotvenu בְּסֵפֶר besefer וְחַיִּים chayim אהיה אהיה יהוה, בינה ע"ה.

לְמַעַנָךְ lema'anach אֱלֹהִים Elohim אהיה אדני ; יל"ה אדני וְחַיִּים chayim אהיה אהיה יהוה, בינה ע"ה.

If you forget to say *"zochrenu"* and realize this before the end of the blessing (*"baruch Ata Adonai"*), you should return and say *"zochreno"* and continue as usual. But if you realize this only after the end of the blessing, you should continue and you may add *"zochrenu"* in *"shome'a tefila"* or at the end of *"Elohai netzor."*

וּמָגֵן umagen וּמוֹשִׁיעַ umoshi'a עוֹזֵר ozer מֶלֶךְ melech

ג"פ אל (יי"א מילוי דס"ג) ; ר"ת מיכאל גַּבריאל נוריאל:

Bend your knees at *'baruch'*, bow at *'Ata'* and straighten up at *'Adonai'*.

בָּרוּךְ baruch אַתָּה Ata יְהֹוָה(יְהֹוָאדֱנִי)יאהדונהי Adonai (הד)

(During the three weeks of *Ben HaMetzarim* meditate on the Holy Name: טדהד)

מָגֵן magen ג"פ אל (יי"א מילוי דס"ג) ; ר"ת מיכאל גַּבריאל נוריאל אַבְרָהָם Avraham

ו" פ אל, רי"ו ול"ב נתיבות החוכמה, רמ"ח (אברים), עסמ"ב וט"ו אותיות פשוטות:

The Supernal God, Who bestows beneficial kindness and creates everything. Who recalls the kindness of the forefathers and brings a Redeemer to their descendants for the sake of His Name, lovingly.

During the days between *Rosh Hashanah* and *Yom Kippur*:
Remember us for life, King, Who desires life, and inscribe us in the Book of Life, for Your sake, Living God.

King, Helper, Savior and Shield. Blessed are You, Lord, the shield of Abraham.

THE SECOND BLESSING

THE ENERGY OF ISAAC IGNITES THE POWER FOR THE RESURRECTION OF THE DEAD.

Whereas Abraham represents the power of sharing, Isaac represents the Left Column energy of judgment. Judgment shortens the *Tikkun* process and paves the way for our eventual resurrection (footnote A - pg. 189).

Gevurah that becomes *Binah*.

In this section there are 49 words corresponding to the 49 gates of the Pure System in *Binah*.

Ata אַתָּה gibor גִּבּוֹר le'olam לְעוֹלָם רִיבּוּע ס"ג וי' אותיות דס"ג Adonai אֲדֹנָי לכה

(ר"ת אַגְלָא והוא שם גָּדוֹל ואמיץ, ובו היה יהודה מתגבר על אויביו. ע"ה אלד, בוכו).

mechaye מְחַיֵּה ס"ג metim מֵתִים Ata אַתָּה. rav רַב lehoshi'a לְהוֹשִׁיעַ.

During the winter (*starting on Simchat Torah*):

mashiv מַשִּׁיב haru'ach הָרוּחַ ר"ת מ"ה

umorid וּמוֹרִיד hageshem הַגֶּשֶׁם

עוֹבִיל [י"ע (= י"פ אל) ול"ב נתיבות החוכמה] ע"ה:

If you mistakenly say "*morid hatal*", and realize this before the end of the blessing ("*baruch Ata Adonai*"), you should return to the beginning of the blessing ("*Ata gibor*") and continue as usual. But if you only realize this after the end of the blessing, you should continue and not go back.

During the summer (*starting on Pesach*):

morid מוֹרִיד hatal הַטָּל

יוד הא ואו, כוזו, מספר אותיות דמילואי עסמ"ב ;

ר"ת מ"ה א"ל (יוד הא ואו הא:)

If you mistakenly say "*Mashiv haru'ach*", and realize this before the end of the blessing ("*baruch Ata Adonai*"), you should return to the beginning of the blessing ("*Ata gibor*") and continue as usual. But if you only realize this after the end of the blessing, you should start the *Amidah* from the beginning.

mechalkel מְכַלְכֵּל chayim חַיִּים אהיה אהיה יהוה, בינה ע"ה bechesed בְּחֶסֶד

עב, ריבוע יהוה. mechaye מְחַיֵּה ס"ג metim מֵתִים berachamim בְּרַחֲמִים

(במוכסד) מצפצ, אלהים דההין, י"פ יי' rabim רַבִּים (טלא דעתיק). somech סוֹמֵךְ

(אכדטם) כוק, ריבוע אדני noflim נוֹפְלִים (ז"ך). verofe וְרוֹפֵא cholim חוֹלִים

וזולה = מ"ה וד' אותיות. umatir וּמַתִּיר asurim אֲסוּרִים. umekayem וּמְקַיֵּם

emunato אֱמוּנָתוֹ lishenei לִישֵׁנֵי afar עָפָר. mi מִי ילי chamocha כָּמוֹךָ

(you should enunciate the letter *Ayin* in the word "*ba'al*") ba'al בַּעַל gevurot גְּבוּרוֹת

umi וּמִי ילי dome דּוֹמֶה lach לָךְ. melech מֶלֶךְ memit מֵמִית

umchaye וּמְחַיֵּה ס"ג (יוד הי ואו הי) umatzmi'ach וּמַצְמִיחַ yeshu'a יְשׁוּעָה:

THE SECOND BLESSING

You are mighty forever, Lord. You resurrect the dead and are very capable of redeeming.

During the winter:	During the summer:
Who causes wind to blow and rain to fall.	*Who causes dew to fall.*

You sustain life with kindness and resurrect the dead with great compassion. You support those who have fallen, heal the sick, release the imprisoned, and fulfill Your faithful words to those who are asleep in the dust. Who is like You, Master of might, and Who can compare to You, King, Who causes death, Who gives life, and Who sprouts salvation?

During the days between *Rosh Hashanah* and *Yom Kippur* we say the prayer of "*mi chamocha*":

מִי mi יְלִ כָּמוֹךָ chamocha אָב av הָרַחֲמָן harachman זוֹכֵר zocher

יְצוּרָיו yetzurav בְּרַחֲמִים berachamim מצפצ, אלהים דיודין, י"פ יייי

לְוֹיִּים lechayim אהיה אהיה יהוה, בינה ע"ה.

If you forget to say "*mi chamocha*" and realize this before the end of the blessing ("*baruch Ata Adonai*"), you should return and say "*mi chamocha*" and continue as usual. But if you only realize this after the end of the blessing, you should continue as usual.

וְנֶאֱמָן vene'eman אַתָּה Ata לְהַחֲיוֹת lehachayot מֵתִים metim:

בָּרוּךְ baruch אַתָּה Ata יְ־ְ־ָ(יְהֹאֲדֹנִי)יאהדונהי Adonai

(During the three weeks of *Ben HaMetzarim* meditate on the Holy Name: כוזו)

מְוַזְּיָה mechaye ס"ג (יוד הי ואו הי) הַמֵּתִים hametim ר"ת מ"ה וס"ת מ"ה:

NAKDISHACH – THE KEDUSHA

The congregation recites this prayer together.

Lifting a heavy chest filled with vast treasures is impossible if you use just a single string: The string will snap because it is too weak. However, if we unite and combine numerous strings, we will eventually build a rope. A rope can easily lift the treasure chest. By combining and uniting the congregation's prayers, we become a united force, capable of pulling down the most valuable spiritual treasures. Furthermore, this unity helps people who are not well-versed or knowledgeable in the connections. By uniting and meditating as one soul, we all receive the benefit because of the power of unity, regardless of our knowledge and understanding. This prayer occurs in between the second and third blessings. It signifies the Central Column that unites the Left and Right Columns.

In this prayer the angels speak to each other, saying: "Kadosh, Kadosh, Kadosh" ("Holy, Holy, Holy"). When we recite these three words, we stand with our feet stand together as one. With each utterance of *Kadosh*, we jump a little higher in the air. Jumping is an act of restriction and it defies the force of gravity. Spiritually, gravity has the energy of the Desire to Receive for the Self Alone. It is the reactive force of our planet, always pulling everything toward itself.

Saying the *Kedusha* (holiness) we meditate to bring the holiness of the Creator among us. As it says: "*Venikdashti betoch Benei Israel*" (God is hallowed among the children of Israel). You should meditate on the letters *Alef* א and *Bet* ב from the Name: אבגיתץ (the initials of the first verse of the *Ana Beko'ach*), which helps spiritual remembering.

During the days between *Rosh Hashanah* and *Yom Kippur*:
Who is like You, merciful Father, Who recalls His created with mercy for life?

And You are faithful to resurrecting the dead. Blessed are You, Lord, Who resurrects the dead.

נַקְדִּישָׁךְ nakdishach וְנַעֲרִיצָךְ vena'aritzach◆

כְּנֹעַם keno'am שִׂיחַ si'ach סוֹד sod מלכ, י"פ האא שַׂרְפֵי sarfei

קֹדֶשׁ kodesh הַמְשַׁלְּשִׁים hameshaleshim לְךָ lecha קְדֻשָּׁה kedusha◆

וְכֵן vechen כָּתוּב katuv עַל al יַד yad נְבִיאָךְ nevi'ach◆ וְקָרָא vekara

זֶה ze אֶל el זֶה ze י"ב פרקין דיעקב מאירים לי"ב פרקין דרחל וְאָמַר ve'amar:

קָדוֹשׁ kadosh | קָדוֹשׁ kadosh קָדוֹשׁ kadosh (סוד ג' רישין דעתיקא קדישא)

יְהֹוָאֲדֹנָי Adonai צְבָאוֹת Tzeva'ot פני שכינה מְלֹא melo כָּל chol יל"י

הָאָרֶץ ha'aretz אלהים דההין ע"ה כְּבוֹדוֹ kevodo:

לְעֻמָּתָם le'umatam מְשַׁבְּחִים meshabechim וְאוֹמְרִים ve'omrim:

בָּרוּךְ baruch כְּבוֹד kevod יְהֹוָאֲדֹנָי Adonai ; כבוד ה' = יוד ה' ואו הה (או"א)

מִמְּקוֹמוֹ mimekomo עסמ"ב, הברכה (למתק את ז' המלכים עמתו) ; ר"ת ע"ב, ריבוע יהוה ; ר"ת מיכ:

וּבְדִבְרֵי uvdivrei קָדְשָׁךְ kodshach כָּתוּב katuv לֵאמֹר lemor:

יִמְלֹךְ yimloch קָדוֹשׁ בָּרוּךְ ר"ת יב"ק, אלהים יהוה, אהיה אדני יהוה (זו"ן)

יְהֹוָאֲדֹנָי Adonai לְעוֹלָם le'olam ריבוע ס"ג ו' אותיות דס"ג אֱלֹהַיִךְ Elohayich ילה

צִיּוֹן Tziyon יוסף, ו' הויות, קנאה לְדֹר ledor וָדֹר vador רי"ו ; ר"ת אצלו (מלכות אצל ז"א - ו)

הַלְלוּיָהּ haleluya אלהים, אהיה אדני ; ללה:

THE THIRD BLESSING

This blessing connects us to Jacob, the Central Column and the power of restriction. Jacob is our channel for connecting mercy with judgment. By restricting our reactive behavior, we are blocking our Desire to Receive for the Self Alone. Jacob also gives us the power to balance our acts of mercy and judgment toward other people in our lives.

NAKDISHACH

We sanctify You and we revere You,
according to the pleasant words of the counsel of the Holy Angels, who recite Holy before You three times,
as it is written by Your Prophet: "And each called to the other and said: Holy, Holy, Holy, Is the Lord of Hosts,
the entire world is filled with His glory." (Isaiah 6:3) Facing them they give praise and say:
"Blessed is the glory of the Lord from His Place." (Ezekiel 3:12) And in Your Holy Words, it is written as follows:
"The Lord, your God, shall reign forever, for each and for every generation. Zion, Praise the Lord!" (Psalms 146:10)

Tiferet that becomes *Da'at* (14 words).

אַתָּה Ata קָדוֹשׁ kadosh וְשִׁמְךָ veshimcha קָדוֹשׁ kadosh ר"ת = אור, רז, אין סוף

וּקְדוֹשִׁים ukdoshim בְּכָל bechol יוֹם yom ב"ק, לכב ע"ה נגד, מזבוז, זן, אל יהוה

יְהַלְלוּךָ yehalelucha סֶלָה sela

בָּרוּךְ baruch אַתָּה Ata יְהֹוָה Adonai

(During the three weeks of *Ben HaMetzarim* meditate on the Holy Name: מצפצ)

הָאֵל haEl הַקָּדוֹשׁ hakadosh י"פ מ"ה (יוד הא ואו הא)

Meditate here on the Name: אהדונהי, as it can help to remove anger.

> **During the days between *Rosh Hashanah* and *Yom Kippur* instead of "*haEl hakadosh*" we say:**
>
> הַמֶּלֶךְ hamelech הַקָּדוֹשׁ hakadosh
>
> If you mistakenly say "*haEl hakadosh*" and you realize this within three seconds, you should immediately say "*hamelech hakadosh*" and continue as usual. But if you have already started the next blessing you should start the *Amidah* from the beginning.

THIRTEEN MIDDLE BLESSINGS

There are thirteen blessings in the middle of the *Amidah* that connect us to the Thirteen Attributes.

THE FIRST (FOURTH) BLESSING

This blessing helps us transform information into knowledge by helping us internalize everything that we learn.

Chochmah

In this blessing there are 17 words, the same numerical value as the word *tov* (good) in the secret of *Etz HaDa'at Tov vaRa*, (Tree of Knowledge Good and Evil), where we connect only to the *Tov*.

אַתָּה Ata חוֹנֵן chonen לְאָדָם le'adam דַּעַת da'at מ"ה

וּמְלַמֵּד umlamed לֶאֱנוֹשׁ le'enosh בִּינָה bina ע"ה אהיה אהיה יהוה, וחיים

וְחָנֵנוּ vechonenu מֵאִתְּךָ me'itecha חָכְמָה chochma במילוי = תרי"ג (מצוות)

בִּינָה bina ע"ה אהיה אהיה יהוה, וחיים וְדַעַת vada'at ר"ת וזבו

בָּרוּךְ baruch אַתָּה Ata יְהֹוָה Adonai חוֹנֵן chonen הַדַּעַת hada'at

THE THIRD BLESSING

You are holy, and Your Name is holy, and the Holy Ones praise You every day, for you are God, the Holy King Selah. Blessed are You, Lord, the Holy God

> During the days between *Rosh Hashanah* and *Yom Kippur*: *The Holy King.*

THIRTEEN MIDDLE BLESSINGS - THE FIRST (FOURTH) BLESSING

You graciously grant knowledge to man and understanding to humanity. Graciously grant us, from Yourself, wisdom, understanding, and knowledge. Blessed are You, Lord, Who graciously grants knowledge.

THE SECOND (FIFTH) BLESSING

This blessing keeps us in the Light. Everyone at one time or another succumbs to the doubt and uncertainty that the Satan constantly implants in us. If we make the unfortunate mistake of stepping back and falling away from the Light, we do not want the Creator to mirror our actions and step away from us. Instead, we want Him to catch us. In the box below there are certain lines that we can recite and meditate on for others who may be stepping back. The war against the Satan is the oldest war known to man. And the only way to defeat the Satan is to unite, share, help and pray for each other.

> ### Binah
>
> In this blessing there are 15 words, as the powerful action of *Teshuva* (repentance) raises 15 levels on the way to *Kise Hakavod* (the Throne of Honor). It goes through seven *Reki'im* (firmaments), seven *Avirim* (air), and another firmament on top of the Holy Animals (together this adds up to 15). Also, there are 15 words in the two main verses of Isaiah the Prophet and King David that speak of *Teshuva* (*Isaiah 55:7*; *Psalms 32:5*). The number 15 is also the secret of the Name: יה.

letoratecha לְתוֹרָתֶךָ (וֹסד שׁוֹבה – יְהֹוִאֲהדִֹיאהדונהי)◆   avinu אָבִינוּ   hashivenu הַשִׁיבֵנוּ

◆la'avodatecha לַעֲבוֹדָתֶךָ   malkenu מַלְכֵּנוּ   vekarvenu וְקָרְבֵנוּ

shelema שְׁלֵמָה   bitshuva בִּתְשׁוּבָה   vehachazirenu וְהַחֲזִירֵנוּ

lefanecha לְפָנֶיךָ ס"ג מ"ה ב"ן:◆

If you want to pray for another and help them in their spiritual process say:

ע"ה   שַׂדַי   אַל   ע"ה,   וקס"א   בריבוע   ע"ב,   ע"ה   מהשׁ   ratzon רָצוֹן   yehi יְהִי

מִלְפָנֶיךָ ס"ג מ"ה ב"ן יְהֹוָאֲהדִֹיאהדונהי   Adonai אֲדֹנָי   Elohai אֱלֹהַי מילוי ע"ב, דמב;ילה   milfanecha מִלְפָנֶיךָ

shetachtor שֶׁתַּחְתּוֹר   avotai אֲבוֹתַי   ; ילה דמב ; ע"ב, מילוי ; לכב   velohei וֵאלֹהֵי

utkabel וּתְקַבֵּל   kevodecha כְּבוֹדֶךָ   kise כִּסֵא   mitachat מִתַּחַת   chatira חֲתִירָה

yemincha יְמִינְךָ   ki כִּי (*the person's name and his/her father's name*)   et אֶת   bitshuva בִּתְשׁוּבָה

◆shavim שָׁבִים   lekabel לְקַבֵּל   peshuta פְּשׁוּטָה   Adonai יְהֹוָאֲהדִֹיאהדונהי

Adonai יְהֹוָאֲהדִֹיאהדונהי   Ata אַתָּה   baruch בָּרוּךְ

bitshuva בִּתְשׁוּבָה: harotze הָרוֹצֶה

THE SECOND (FIFTH) BLESSING

Bring us back, our Father, to Your Torah,
and bring us close, our King, to Your service, and cause us to return with perfect repentance before You.

> *May it be pleasing before You, Lord, my God and God of my forefathers, that You shall dig deep beneath the Throne of Your glory and accept as repentant (the person's name and his/her father's name) because Your Right Hand, Lord, extends outwards to receive those who repent.*

Blessed are You, Lord, Who desires repentance.

THE THIRD (SIXTH) BLESSING

This blessing helps us achieve true forgiveness. We have the power to cleanse ourselves of our negative behavior and hurtful actions toward others through forgiveness. This blessing does not mean we plead for forgiveness and our slate is wiped clean. Forgiveness refers to the methodologies for washing away the residue that comes from our iniquities. There are two ways to wash away the residue: physical and spiritual. We collect physical residue when we are in denial of our misdeeds and the laws of cause and effect. We cleanse ourselves when we experience any kind of pain, whether it is financial, emotional, or physical. If we choose to cleanse spiritually, we forgo the physical cleansing. We do so by arousing the pain in ourselves that we caused to others. We feel the other person; and with a truthful heart, recite this prayer experiencing the hurt and heartache we inflicted on others. This form of spiritual cleansing prevents us from having to cleanse physically.

Chesed

In this blessing there are 21 words which is the numerical value of the Holy Name: אהיה.

סְלַח selach ע״ב יהוה lanu לָנוּ אלהים, אהיה אדני avinu אָבִינוּ ר״ת סאל, אמן (יאהדונהי)

כִּי ki lanu לָנוּ אלהים, אהיה אדני ; מוזל לנו ע״ה = mechol מִוזֹל chatanu וְחָטָאנוּ

אֵל El ki כִּי fashanu פָּשַׁעְנוּ ki כִּי malkenu מַלְכֵּנוּ קס״א ו״י אותיות יא״י (מילוי דס״ג) טוֹב tov והו vesalach וְסָלַח ע״ב יהוה Ata אַתָּה baruch בָּרוּךְ Ata אַתָּה

יְהוָהאדניאהדונהי Adonai וְחַנּוּן chanun הַמַּרְבֶּה hamarbe לִסְלוֹחַ lislo'ach

THE FOURTH (SEVENTH) BLESSING

This blessing helps us achieve redemption after we are spiritually cleansed.

Gevurah

רְאֵה re'e ראה נָא na בְעָנְיֵנוּ ve'onyenu ר״ת רנ״ב (אברים באשה, כנגד הגבורה)

וְרִיבָה veriva רִיבֵנוּ rivenu וּמַהֵר umaher לְגָאֳלֵנוּ lega'olenu

גְאֻלָּה ge'ula מ״ה shelema שְׁלֵמָה לְמַעַן lema'an שְׁמֶךָ shemecha

כִּי ki אֵל El יא״י (מילוי דס״ג) go'el גּוֹאֵל chazak וְחָזָק פהל Ata אַתָּה

בָּרוּךְ baruch אַתָּה Ata יְהוָהאדניאהדונהי Adonai גּוֹאֵל go'el יִשְׂרָאֵל Yisrael

---

THE THIRD (SIXTH) BLESSING

Forgive us, our Father, for we have transgressed. Pardon us, our King, for we have sinned, because You are a good and forgiving God. Blessed are You, Lord, Who is gracious and forgives magnanimously.

THE FOURTH (SEVENTH) BLESSING

Behold our poverty and take up our fight; hurry to redeem us with a complete redemption for the sake of Your Name, because You are a powerful and a redeeming God. Blessed are You, Lord, Who redeems Israel.

THE BLESSING FOR A FAST DAY

This blessing is recited by the *chazan* on fast days, during the repetition of the *Amidah*. If the *chazan* forgets to say it here and realizes this before the end of the next blessing ("*baruch Ata Adonai*"), he should return and say "*anenu avinu*" and continue as usual. But if the *chazan* only realized this after the end of the next blessing, he should continue and he may add this blessing in "*shome'a tefila*".

יהוה אל ,זז ,מזבוח ,נגד ע"ה beyom בְּיוֹם anenu עֲנֵנוּ avinu אָבִינוּ anenu עֲנֵנוּ

דההין אלהים בְּצָרָה vetzara כִּי ki והו haze הֲזֶה hata'anit הַתַּעֲנִית tzom צוֹם

lerish'enu לְרִשְׁעֵנוּ tefen תֵּפֶן al- אַל- anachnu אֲנַחְנוּ gedola גְדוֹלָה

mibakashatenu מִבַּקָּשָׁתֵנוּ malkenu מַלְכֵּנוּ tit'alam תִּתְעַלָּם ve'al וְאַל-

terem טֶרֶם leshav'atenu לְשַׁוְעָתֵנוּ karov קָרוֹב na נָא יהה heye הֱיֵה

ראה nedaber נְדַבֵּר ta'ane תַעֲנֶה Ata אַתָּה elecha אֵלֶיךָ nikra נִקְרָא

shene'emar שֶׁנֶּאֱמַר ראה kadavar כַּדָּבָר tishma תִּשְׁמַע veAta וְאַתָּה

e'ene אֶעֱנֶה אני va'ani וַאֲנִי yikra'u יִקְרָאוּ terem טֶרֶם- יהוה ; vehaya וְהָיָה

eshma אֶשְׁמָע אני va'ani וַאֲנִי medabrim מְדַבְּרִים hem הֵם od עוֹד

ve'one וְעוֹנֶה umatzil וּמַצִּיל pode פּוֹדֶה Adonai יְהֹוָהאהדונהי Ata אַתָּה ki כִּי

(אברים) רמ"ז ,הוֹכמה נתיבות ל"ב ,רי"ו ,אל וז"פ ,אברהם umrachem וּמְרַחֵם

דההין אלהים צָרָה tzara et עֵת לכב ,ב"ז bechol בְּכָל עסמ"ב וט"ז אותיות פשוטות

ha'one הָעוֹנֶה Adonai יְהֹוָהאהדונהי Ata אַתָּה baruch בָּרוּךְ vetzuka וְצוּקָה

(continue "*refa'enu*") tzara צָרָה be'et בְּעֵת Yisrael יִשְׂרָאֵל le'amo לְעַמּוֹ

THE FIFTH (EIGHTH) BLESSING

This blessing gives us the power to heal every part of our body. All healing originates from the Light of the Creator. Accepting and understanding this truth opens us to receive this Light. We should also think of sharing this healing energy with others.

THE BLESSING FOR A FAST DAY

Answer us, our Father, answer us on this day of fasting because we are in great distress. Do not pay heed to our wickedness, and, our King, do not ignore our pleas. Please come close to our cries and answer us even before we call out to You. We shall speak and You shall hear us, as it is said: 'And it shall be that before they call, I shall answer, and while they speak, I shall hear.' (Isaiah 65:24) For You, Lord, redeem, save, respond, and show compassion in every time of trouble and distress. Blessed are You, Lord, who responds to His Nation Israel, in time of trouble.

Tiferet

רְפָאֵנוּ refa'enu יְהֹוָה Adonai וְנֵרָפֵא venerafe ר״ת רי״ו

הוֹשִׁיעֵנוּ hoshi'enu וְנִוָּשֵׁעָה venivashe'a כִּי ki תְהִלָּתֵנוּ tehilatenu

אַתָּה Ata ר״ת = ב״פ רי״ו וְהַעֲלֵה veha'ale אֲרוּכָה arucha וּמַרְפֵּא umarpe

לְכָל lechol יה אדני תַחֲלוּאֵינוּ tachalu'enu וּלְכָל ulchol אדני יה

מַכְאוֹבֵינוּ mach'ovenu וּלְכָל ulchol אדני יה מַכּוֹתֵינוּ makotenu

---

To pray for healing for yourself and/or others add the following, in the parentheses below, insert the names:

יְהִי yehi רָצוֹן ratzon מהש ע״ה, ע״ב, ע״ב, בריבוע וקס״א ע״ה, אל שדי ע״ה ע״ה

מִלְפָנֶיךָ milfanecha יְהֹוָה Adonai אֱלֹהַי Elohai ס״ג מ״ה ב״ן מילוי ע״ב, דמב ; ילה

וֵאלֹהֵי velohei אֲבוֹתַי avotai ילה ; מילוי ע״ב, דמב לכב ; שֶׁתִּרְפָּאֵנִי shetirpa'eni

vetirpa (וְתִרְפָּא) (insert the person's name) בֶּן ben (Women: בַּת bat) (insert their mother's name)

רְפוּאָה refu'a שְׁלֵמָה shelema רְפוּאַת refu'at הַנֶּפֶשׁ hanefesh

וּרְפוּאַת urfu'at הַגּוּף haguf, כְּדֵי kedei שֶׁאֶהְיֶה she'ehye חָזָק chazak פהל

(Women: וַחֲזָקָה chazaka פהל), בִּבְרִיאוּת bivri'ut, וְאַמִּיץ ve'amitz

(Women: וְאַמִּיצַת ve'amitzat) כֹּחַ ko'ach בְּמָאתַיִם bematayim וְאַרְבָּעִים ve'arba'im

(Women: בְּמָאתַיִם bematayim וַחֲמִשִּׁים vechamishim) פשוטות רמ״ח (אברים), אברהם, ו״ק אל, ח״פ ל״ו ל״ב נתיבות החכמה, עסמ״ב וט״ז אותיות ushmona וּשְׁמוֹנָה

(ushnayim וּשְׁנַיִם) אֵבָרִים evarim וּשְׁלֹשׁ ushlosh מֵאוֹת me'ot המספר = ע = שי אלהים דיודין

וְשִׁשִּׁים veshishim (יֵין) וַחֲמִשָּׁה vachamisha המספר = מילוי הע׳ (ין) גִּידִים gidim שֶׁל shel

נִשְׁמָתִי nishmati וְגוּפִי vegufi, לְקִיּוּם lekiyum תּוֹרָתְךָ toratcha הַקְּדוֹשָׁה hakedosha.

כִּי ki אֵל El יא״י (מילוי דס״ג) רוֹפֵא rofe רַחֲמָן rachaman וְנֶאֱמָן vene'eman

אַתָּה Ata :Ata בָּרוּךְ baruch אַתָּה Ata יְהֹוָה Adonai רוֹפֵא rofe

חוֹלֵי cholei חולה = מ״ה (יוד הא ואו הא) וד׳ אותיות עַמּוֹ amo יִשְׂרָאֵל Yisrael

ר״ת רפ״ח (להעלות הניצוצות שנפלו לקליפה דמשם באים התחלואים):

THE FIFTH (EIGHTH) BLESSING
Heal us, Lord, and we shall heal. Save us and we shall be saved.
For You are our praise. Bring cure and healing to all our ailments, to all our pains, and to all our wounds.

May it be pleasing before You, Lord, my God and God of my forefathers, that You would heal me (and the person's name and their mother's name) completely with healing of the spirit and healing of the body, so that I shall be strong in health and vigorous in my strength in all 248 (a woman says: 252) organs and 365 sinews of my soul and my body, so that I shall be able to keep Your Holy Torah.

Because You are a healing,
compassionate, and trustworthy God, blessed are You, Lord, Who heals the sick of His People, Israel.

THE SIXTH (NINTH) BLESSING

This blessing draws sustenance and prosperity for the entire globe and provides us with personal sustenance. We would like all of our years to be filled with dew and rain, the sustaining lifeblood of our world.

Netzach

During the summer (starting on the first day of *Pesach*) **the following is said:**
If you mistakenly say "*barech alenu*" instead of "*barchenu*", and realize this before the end of the *Amidah* ("*yihyu leratzon*" – the second one), then you should return and say "*barchenu*" and continue as usual. If you realize this later, you should start the *Amidah* from the beginning.

bechol בְּכֹל ילה Elohenu אֱלֹהֵינוּ Adonai יְהֹוֹאַדְנִיְאָהְדּוֹנָהִי barchenu בָּרְכֵנוּ

shenatenu שְׁנָתֵנוּ uvarech וּבָרֵךְ ♦yadenu יָדֵינוּ ma'asei מַעֲשֵׂי ב״ן, לכב

betalelei בְּטַלְלֵי ratzon רָצוֹן מהש ע״ה, ע״ב בריבוע וקס״א ע״ה, אל עדי ע״ה

utehi וּתְהִי♦ בינה (וע״ה אהיה אהיה יהוה, וויים) undava וּנְדָבָה beracha בְּרָכָה

vesava וְשָׂבַע ע״ה, בינה אהיה אהיה יהוה, chayim וְחַיִּים acharita אַחֲרִיתָהּ

♦livracha לִבְרָכָה hatovot הַטּוֹבוֹת kashanim כַּשָּׁנִים veshalom וְשָׁלוֹם

If you want to pray for sustenance you can add:

milfanecha מִלְפָנֶיךָ ratzon רָצוֹן מהש ע״ה, ע״ב בריבוע וקס״א ע״ה, אל עדי ע״ה yehi יְהִי

velohei וֵאלֹהֵי ילה Elohenu אֱלֹהֵינוּ Adonai יְהֹוֹאַדְנִיְאָהְדּוֹנָהִי ס״ג מ״ה ב״ן

li לִי ב״פ כהת shetiten שֶׁתִּתֵּן avotenu אֲבוֹתֵינוּ ילה ; מילוי ע״ב, דמב לכב

hayom הַיּוֹם shulchani שׁוּלְחָנִי al עַל hasemuchim הַסְּמוּכִים יה אדני ulchol וּלְכֹל

velo וְלֹא bichavod בִּכְבוֹד umzonotehem וּמְזוֹנוֹתֵיהֶם mezonotai מְזוֹנוֹתַי
yom יוֹם לכב ב״ן, אל יהוה uvchol וּבְכֹל ע״ה גגד, מזבח, זן, מזבח, זן, אל יהוה

bizchut בִּזְכוּת be'isur בְּאִיסוּר velo וְלֹא beheter בְּהֶיתֵר bevizui בְּבִזּוּי

shimcha שִׁמְךָ hagadol הַגָּדוֹל להו ; עם ד׳ אותיות = מבה, יזל, אום

(**Do not pronounce this name**: דְּיִקַרְנוֹסָא וחזר עם ג׳ אותיות – ובאתב״ש סאל, אמן, יאהדונהי)

THE SIXTH (NINTH) BLESSING

During the summer:

Bless us, Lord, our God, in all our endeavors, and bless our years with the dews of good will, blessing, and benevolence. May its conclusion be life, contentment, and peace, as with other years for blessing,

May it be pleasing before You, Lord, my God and God of my forefathers, that You would provide for me and for my household, today and everyday, mine and their nourishment, with dignity and not with shame, in a permissible but not a forbidden manner, by virtue of your great name

הַיּוֹצֵא hayotze מִפָּסוּק: mipasuk וַהֲרִיקֹתִי vaharikoti לָכֶם lachem

בְּרָכָה beracha עַד ad בְּלִי beli דַי dai וּמִפָּסוּק: umipasuk נְשָׂא nesa

עָלֵינוּ alenu אוֹר or רז, אין סוף מ"ה ב"ן ס"ג פָּנֶיךָ panecha יְהֹוָ(אדני)אהדונהי Adonai

וְאַל ve'al תַּצְרִיכֵנוּ tatzrichenu לִידֵי lidei מַתְּנוֹת matnot בָּשָׂר basar

וָדָם vadam כִּי ki אִם im יוהך, מ"א אותיות אהיה בפשוטו ומילואו ומילוי דמילואו דמילואו ע"ה

מִיָּדְךָ miyadcha הַמְּלֵאָה hamele'a וּמֵאוֹצַר ume'otzar בִּמַתְּנַת matnat וְזֹּם chinam

תְּכַלְכְּלֵנִי techalkelni וְתַשְׂפִּיעֵנִי vetashpi'eni אָמֵן amen יאהדונהי סֶלָה sela.

כִּי ki אֵל El יי"י (מילוי) דס"ג טוֹב tov והו umetiv וּמֵטִיב

אַתָּה Ata וּמְבָרֵךְ umvarech הַשָּׁנִים: hashanim בָּרוּךְ baruch

אַתָּה Ata יְהֹוָ(אדני)אהדונהי Adonai מְבָרֵךְ mevarech הַשָּׁנִים: hashanim

During the winter (starting on the 7th of *Cheshvan*, two weeks after *Sukkot*) **the following is said:**
If you mistakenly say "*barchenu*" instead of "*barech alenu*", and realize this before the end of the blessing ("*baruch Ata Adonai*"), you should return to say "*barech alenu*" and continue as usual. If you only realize this after, you should say "*Veten tal umatar livracha*" in "*shome'a tefila*". If you only relize this after you have already started "*retze*" you should start the *Amidah* from the beginning

בָּרֵךְ barech עָלֵינוּ alenu יְהֹוָ(אדני)אהדונהי Adonai אֱלֹהֵינוּ Elohenu ילה

אֶת et הַשָּׁנָה hashana הַזֹּאת hazot. וְאֶת ve'et כָּל־ kol ילי

מִינֵי minei תְּבוּאָתָהּ tevu'ata לְטוֹבָה letova. וְתֵן veten אכא

טַל tal יוד הא ואו, כוזו וּמָטָר umatar לִבְרָכָה livracha עַל al כָּל־ kol ילי ; עמם

פְּנֵי penei וחכמה ורי"ו וְרַוֵּה verave הָאֲדָמָה ha'adama. בינה פְּנֵי penei בינה

תֵּבֵל tevel ב"פ ורי"ו וְשַׂבַּע vesaba אֶת et הָעוֹלָם ha'olam

כֻּלּוֹ kulo מִטּוּבָךְ mituvach לאו. וּמַלֵּא umale יָדֵינוּ yadenu

מִבִּרְכוֹתֶיךָ mibirchotecha וּמֵעשֶׁר ume'osher מַתְּנוֹת mat'not יָדֶיךָ yadecha.

---

that comes from the verse: "pour down for you blessing until there be no room to suffice for it" (Malachi 3:10) and from the verse: "Raise up over us the light of Your countenance, Lord" (Psalms 4:7), and we will not require the gifts of flesh and blood, but only from your hand which is full, and from the treasure of the free gift you shall support and nurish me. Amen. Sela.

for You are a good
and a beneficent God and You bless the years. Blessed are You, Lord, Who blesses the years.
During the winter:
Bless us, Lord, our God, this year and all its kinds of crops for good. And give dew and rain for blessing over the entire face of the Earth. Quench the thirst of the face of the Earth and satiate the entire world from Your bounty. Fill our hands with Your blessings and from the wealth of gifts of Your Hands.

If you want to pray for sustenance you can add:

milfanecha מִלְפָנֶיךָ מהשע ע"ה, ע"ב בריבוע וקס"א ע"ה, אל שדי ע"ה ratzon רָצוֹן yehi יְהִי

velohei וֵאלֹהֵי ילה Elohenu אֱלֹהֵינוּ ס"ג מ"ה ב"ן Adonai יְהֹוֶאדֶנִילֶיאֲהדֹנִהי

li לִי ב"פ כהת shetiten שֶׁתִּתֵּן avotenu אֲבוֹתֵינוּ ; דמב ע"ב, מילוי ; ילה

hayom הַיוֹם shulchani שׁוּלְחָנִי al עַל hasmuchim הַסְּמוּכִים יה אדני ulchol וּלְכָל

yom יוֹם ע"ה נגד, מזבוח, זן, אל יהוה uvchol וּבְכָל ב"ן, לכב יום ע"ה נגד, מזבוח, זן, אל יהוה

velo וְלֹא בוכו bechavod בְּכָבוֹד umzonotehem וּמְזוֹנוֹתֵיהֶם mezonotai מְזוֹנוֹתַי

bizchut בִּזְכוּת be'isur בָּאִסוּר velo וְלֹא beheter בְּהֶיתֵּר bevizuy בְּבִזּוּי

shimcha שִׁמְךָ ; עם ד' אותיות = מבה, יזל, אום hagadol הַגָּדוֹל להו

(Do not pronounce this name: דִּיקַרְנוֹסָא וזהך עם ג' אותיות – ובאתב"ע סאל, אמן, יאהדונהי)

hayotze הַיוֹצֵא mipasuk:מִפָּסוּק vaharikoti וַהֲרִיקוֹתִי lachem לָכֶם

nesa נְסָה umipasuk:וּמִפָּסוּק dai דַּי beli בְּלִי ad עַד beracha בְּרָכָה

Adonai יְהֹוֶאדֶנִילֶיאֲהדֹנִהי ס"ג מ"ה ב"ן panecha פָנֶיךָ רז, אין סוף or אוֹר or alenu עָלֵינוּ

basar בָשָׂר matnot מַתְנוֹת lidei לִידֵי tatzrichenu תַּצְרִיכֵנוּ ve'al וְאַל

vadam וְדָם ki כִּי im אִם יוהך, מ"א אותיות אהיה בפשוטו ומילואו ומילוי דמילואו ע"ה

chinam חִנָּם matnat מַתְנַת ume'otzar וּמֵאוֹצַר hamele'a הַמְּלֵאָה miyadcha מִיָּדְךָ

sela.סֶלָה יאהדונהי amen אָמֵן vetashpi'eni וְתַשְׁפִּיעֵנִי techalkelni תְּכַלְכְּלֵנִי

---

davar דָבָר ילי mikol מִכָּל zo זוֹ shana שָׁנָה vehatzila וְהַצִּילָה shomra שָׁמְרָה

umikol וּמִכָּל ילי mashchit מַשְׁחִית minei מִינֵי ילי umikol וּמִכָּל ra• רָע ראה

tikva תִּקְוָה la לָהּ va'ase וַעֲשֵׂה pura'nut• פּוּרְעָנוּת minei מִינֵי

verachem וְרַחֵם chus חוּס אכא shalom• שָׁלוֹם ve'acharit וְאַחֲרִית tova טוֹבָה

aleha עָלֶיהָ פהל אברהם, וו"פ אל, רי"ו ול"ב נתיבות החוכמה, רמ"וז (אברים), עסמ"ב וט"וז אותיות פשוטות

uferoteha• וּפֵירוֹתֶיהָ tevu'ata תְּבוּאָתָהּ עמם ; ילי kol כָּל ve'al וְעַל

May it be pleasing before You, Lord, my God and God of my forefathers, that You would provide for me and for my household, today and everyday, mine and their nourishment, with dignity and not with shame, in a permissible but not a forbidden manner, by virtue of your great name that comes from the verse: "pour down for you blessing until there be no room to suffice for it" (Malachi 3:10) and from the verse: "Raise up over us the light of Your countenance, Lord" (Psalm 4:7), and we will not require the gifts of flesh and blood, but only from your hand which is full, from the treasure of the free gift you shall support and nourish me. Amen. Sela.

Protect and save this year from all evil
and from all manner of destruction and from all manner of tribulation. Make for it a good hope and a peaceful ending. Take pity and have mercy upon it and upon all its crops and fruits;

וּבְרָכָה uvarcha begishmei בְּגִשְׁמֵי ratzon רָצוֹן מהט ע"ה, ע"ב בריבוע וקס"א ע"ה,

אל טדי ע"ה (וע"ה אהיה אהיה יהוה, וזיים) beracha בְּרָכָה undava וּנְדָבָה בינה (וע"ה אהיה אהיה יהוה, וזיים)

וּתְהִי utehi acharita אוֹחֲרִיתָהּ chayim וְחַיִּים אהיה אהיה יהוה, בינה ע"ה

וְשָׂבַע vesava veshalom וְשָׁלוֹם kashanim כְּשָׁנִים הַטּוֹבוֹת hatovot

לִבְרָכָה livracha ki כִּי El אֵל יא"י (מילוי דס"ג) tov טוֹב והו umetiv וּמֵטִיב

אַתָּה Ata umvarech וּמְבָרֵךְ hashanim הַשָּׁנִים בָּרוּךְ baruch

אַתָּה Ata Adonai יְהֹוָאדֹנִיאהדונהי mevarech מְבָרֵךְ hashanim הַשָּׁנִים

THE SEVENTH (TENTH) BLESSING

This blessing gives us the power to positively influence all of humanity. Kabbalah teaches that each individual affects the whole. We affect the world, and the rest of the world affects us, even though we cannot perceive this relationship with our five senses. We call this relationship quantum consciousness.

Hod

תְּקַע teka ב"פ בזוֹזְרך וי' אותיות = beshofar בְּשׁוֹפָר gadol גָּדוֹל לָהוֹ ; עם ד' אותיות =

גָּלְיוֹתֵינוּ lecherutenu לְחֵרוּתֵנוּ vesa וְשָׂא nes נֵס אדני מ"ה lekabetz לְקַבֵּץ מבה, יזל, אום

מֵאַרְבַּע me'arba yachad יוַֹד vekabetzenu וְקַבְּצֵנוּ galuyotenu גָּלְיוֹתֵינוּ

כַּנְפוֹת kanfot וֹבוֹ (בסגולתו להוציא ניצוצות מן הקליפות) ויכוון וֹזֶבְן עם נקודותיו = ע"ב, ריבוע יהוה

הָאָרֶץ ha'aretz אלהים דההין ע"ה ; ר"ת = אדני = לְאַרְצֵנוּ le'artzenu

---

The following is recited throughout the entire year, and especially during the time of the *Shovavim*:

The first six portions of the Book of Exodus—*Shemot, Va'era, Bo, Beshalach, Yitro, Mishpatim,* (*Terumah Tetzave*)—tell us the story of the Israelites exodus from Egypt and signify the beginning of a unique cosmic opening that lasts for six weeks (8 weeks during a leap year), each year. The word *shovavim* means "irresponsible," as in the verse, "Return, irresponsible children says the Lord," (Jeremiah 3:14) and is an acronym comprised of the first initial of each of the six weekly portions: The kabbalists teach us that the story of Exodus is a code and that during these six/eight weeks there is a window of time for personal redemption. The Ari explains that the fall of Adam corrupted almost everything in our physical world, resulting in human pain and suffering. During the time of the Exodus, Moses and the Israelites corrected the most important aspects of this corruption. The following meditation helps us to release and redeem all the remaining sparks of Light we have lost through our irresponsible actions (especially sexual misconduct):

---

bless it with rains of goodwill, blessing, and benevolence. And may its end be life, contentment, and peace, for You are a good and a beneficent God and You bless the years. Blessed are You, Lord, Who blesses the years.

THE SEVENTH (TENTH) BLESSING

Blow a great Shofar for our freedom and
raise a banner to gather our exiles, and gather us speedily from all four corners of the Earth to our Land.

yehi יְהִי ratzon רָצוֹן מהע ע"ה, ע"ב בריבוע וקס"א ע"ה, אל שדי ע"ה milfanecha מִלְפָנֶיךָ

Adonai יְהֹוָ־הִאהדונהי Elohai אֱלֹהַי מילוי ע"ב, דמב ; ילה ; ס"ג מ"ה ב"ן

velohei וֵאלֹהַי shekol שֶׁכׇּל avotai אֲבוֹתַי מילוי ע"ב, דמב ; ילה ; tipa טִיפָּה לכב ; מילוי ע"ב, דמב

shelo שֶׁלֹּא uvifrat וּבִפְרָט bichlal בִּכְלָל Yisrael יִשְׂרָאֵל ילי umikol וּמִכׇּל
vetipa וְטִיפָּה shel שֶׁל keri קְרִי sheyatza שֶׁיָּצָא mimeni מִמֶּנִּי levatala לְבַטָּלָה

beratzon בְּרָצוֹן ben בֵּין be'ones בְּאוֹנֶס ben בֵּין mitzva מִצְוָה bimkom בִּמְקוֹם

ben בֵּין beshogeg בְּשׁוֹגֵג ben בֵּין מהע ע"ה, ע"ב בריבוע וקס"א ע"ה, אל שדי ע"ה

acher אַחֵר begilgul בְּגִלְגּוּל ben בֵּין ze זֶה begilgul בְּגִלְגּוּל ben בֵּין
bema'ase בְּמַעֲשֶׂה, uven וּבֵין behirhur בְּהִרְהוּר ben בֵּין, bemezid בְּמֵזִיד

hakelipot הַקְּלִיפוֹת shetaki שֶׁתָּקִיא, bakelipot בַּקְּלִיפוֹת venivla וְנִבְלַע

bizechut בִּזְכוּת ba בָּהּ shenivle'u שֶׁנִּבְלְעוּ keri קְרִי hanitzotzot הַנִּיצוֹצוֹת

hayotze הַיּוֹצֵא shimcha שִׁמְךָ hagadol הַגָּדוֹל להו ; עם ד' אותיות = מבה, יל, אום

vayki'enu וַיְקִאֶנּוּ bala בָּלַע chayil חַיִל ומב vezil וֵזִיל ר"ת וחבו ו-יל"י mipasuk מִפָּסוּק

uvizechut וּבִזְכוּת yorishenu יֹרִשֶׁנּוּ El אֵל ייא"י (מילוי דס"ג) ; ס"ת וזל mibitno מִבִּטְנוֹ

shimcha שִׁמְךָ hagadol הַגָּדוֹל להו ; עם ד' אותיות = מבה, יל, אום יְזַהֲבֶוָה

limkom לִמְקוֹם shetachazirem שֶׁתַּחֲזִירֵם (יְזַהֲבֶוָה during the Shovavim)

ase עֲשֵׂה ריבוע מ"ה ; קס"א ע"ה be'enecha בְּעֵינֶיךָ וֹהו vehatov וְהַטּוֹב kedusha קְדוּשָׁה.

You should meditate to correct the thought that caused the loss of the sparks of Light.
Also meditate on the Names that control our thoughts for each of the six days of the week as follow:

Day						.World
Sunday	יְהֹוָה	ושם: דמרגלא אהיה מן א ואו זין ואו טפטפיה כף צבא עַל				.Beriah
Monday	יְהֹוָה	ושם: דמרגלא אהיה מן ה ואו זין ואו טפטפיה כף מגן עַל				.Yetzirah
Tuesday	מצפץ	ושם: דמרגלא אהיה מן י ואו זין ואו טפטפיה כף פוזד צוה				.Asiyah
Wednesday	אל	ושם: דמרגלא יהו מן י ואו זין ואו טפטפיה כף פוזד צוה				.Asiyah
Thursday	אלהים	ושם: דמרגלא יהו מן ה ואו זין ואו טפטפיה כף מגן עַל				.Yetzirah
Friday	מצפץ	ושם: דמרגלא יהו מן ו ואו זין ואו טפטפיה כף צבא עַל				.Beriah

Each of these Names (עַל צבא, כף ואו זין ואו, טפטפיה) adds up to 193, which is the same
numerical value as the word *zokef* (raise). These Names raise the Holy Spark from the *Chitzoniyim*.
Also, when you say the words "*mekabetz nidchei*" (in the continuation of the blessing),
which adds up to 304 — the same numerical value of *Shin*, *Dalet* (demon),
you should meditate to collect all the lost sparks and cancel out the power of the negative forces.

---

*May it be pleasing before You, Lord, my God and God of my forefathers, that every single drop of keri that came out
of me for vain, and from all of Yisrael in general, and especially not as a cause of precept, if it was coerced or willfully,
with intention or without, by passing thought or by an action, in this lifetime or in previous, and it was swallowed by
the klipa, that the klipa will vomit all the sparks of keri that was swollen by it, by virtue of your great name that
comes from the verse:"He swallowed up wealth and vomited it out, and from his belly God will cast it." (Job 20:15),
and by the virtue of your great name you will return them to the holy place, and do what is good in Your eyes.*

בָּרוּךְ baruch אַתָּה Ata יְהוָֹואֲדֹנָיאהדונהי Adonai ; יכוין חוֹבו בעילוב יהוה כזה: יְוָֹהֲבֻוֹֹה

מְקַבֵּץ mekabetz ע"ב ס"ג מ"ה ב"ן, הַבְּרָכָה (למתק) אֶת ז' הַמְּלכים שֹמַתוּ)

נִדְחֵי nidchei ע"ב, רִיבוּע יהוה amo עַמֹּו חֹבו :Yisrael יִשְׂרָאֵל

THE EIGHTH (ELEVENTH) BLESSING

This blessing helps us to balance judgment with mercy. As mercy is time, we can use it to change ourselves before judgment occurs.

Yesod

הָשִׁיבָה hashiva שׁוֹפְטֵינוּ shoftenu כְּבָרִאשׁוֹנָה kevarishona◆

וְיוֹעֲצֵינוּ veyo'atzenu כְּבַתְּחִלָּה kevatechila ר"ת עכ"ד (דינים זכרים עובדיסור) ויהוה (המבמתקם)◆

וְהָסֵר vehaser מִמֶּנּוּ mimenu יָגוֹן yagon (סמאל) וַאֲנָחָה va'anacha (לילית)◆

וּמְלוֹךְ umloch עָלֵינוּ aleinu מְהֵרָה mehera אַתָּה Ata

יְהוָֹואֲדֹנָיאהדונהי Adonai לְבַדְּךָ levadcha◆ בְּחֶסֶד bechesed ע"ב, רִיבוּע יהוה

וּבְרַחֲמִים uvrachamim מצפצ, אלהים דיודין, י"פ יי"י ; להממתיק ברוזמים דיני צדק ומשפט

בְּצֶדֶק betzedek וּבְמִשְׁפָּט uvmishpat ע"ה = ה"פ אלהים: בָּרוּךְ baruch אַתָּה Ata

יְהוָֹואֲדֹנָיאהדונהי Adonai מֶלֶךְ melech אוֹהֵב ohev ממתיק דיני

צְדָקָה tzedaka ע"ה רִיבוּע אלהים וּבְמִשְׁפָּט umishpat ה"פ ע"ה אלהים:

During the days between *Rosh Hashanah* and *Yom Kippur* instead of "*melech ohev tzedaka umishpat*" we say:

הַמֶּלֶךְ hamelech הַמִּשְׁפָּט hamishpat ע"ה ה"פ אלהים:

If you mistakenly say "*melech ohev...*" and realize this within three seconds, you should say "*hamelech hamishpat*" and continue as usual. But if you have already begun the next blessing you should not go back.

THE NINTH (TWELFTH) BLESSING

This blessing helps us remove all forms of negativity, whether it comes from people, situations or even the negative energy of the Angel of Death [(**do not pronounce these names**) *Sa-ma-el* (male aspect) and *Li-li-th* (female aspect), which are encoded here], by using the Holy Name: *Shadai* שדי, which is encoded mathematically into the last four words of this blessing and also appears inside a *Mezuzah* for the same purpose.

Blessed are You, Lord, Who gathers the displaced of His Nation, Israel.
THE EIGHTH (ELEVENTH) BLESSING
Restore our judges, as at first, and our mentors, as in the beginning. Remove from us sorrow and moaning. Reign over us soon, You alone, Lord, with kindness and compassion, with righteousness and justice. Blessed are You, Lord, the King Who loves righteousness and justice.

During the days between *Rosh Hashanah* and *Yom Kippur*: *The King the judgment.*

Keter

לַמִּינִים laminim וְלַמַּלְשִׁינִים velamalshinim אַל al תְּהִי tehi תִקְוָה tikva

וְכָל vechol יל"י הַזֵּדִים hazedim כְּרֶגַע kerega ג"פ אלהים עם ט"ו אותיות פשוטות

יאבֵדוּ yovedu וְכָל־ vechol יל"י אוֹיְבֶיךָ oyvecha (סמאל)

וְכָל־ vechol יל"י שׂוֹנְאֶיךָ son'echa (לילית) מְהֵרָה mehera יִכָּרֵתוּ yikaretu

וּמַלְכוּת umalchut הָרִשְׁעָה harish'a מְהֵרָה mehera תְעַקֵּר te'aker

וּתְשַׁבֵּר utshaber וּתְכַלֵּם utchalem וְתַכְנִיעֵם vetachni'em בִּמְהֵרָה bimhera

בְיָמֵינוּ veyamenu בָּרוּךְ baruch אַתָּה Ata יְהֹוָה(יֱהֹוִה)(אֲדֹנָי)יֱאֱהֹדֹנָהִי Adonai

שׁוֹבֵר shover אוֹיְבִים oyvim וּמַכְנִיעַ umachni'a זֵדִים zedim ר"ת = שׁדי:

THE TENTH (THIRTEENTH) BLESSING
This blessing surrounds us with total positivity to help us always be at the right place at the right time. It also helps attract only positive people into our lives.

Yesod

עַל al הַצַּדִּיקִים hatzadikim צַדִּיק יְסוֹד עוֹלָם וְעַל ve'al הַחֲסִידִים hachasidim

וְעַל ve'al שְׁאֵרִית she'erit עַמְּךָ amecha בֵּית bet ב"פ ראה יִשְׂרָאֵל Yisrael

וְעַל ve'al פְּלֵיטַת peletat בֵּית bet ב"פ ראה סוֹפְרֵיהֶם sofrehem

וְעַל ve'al גֵּרֵי gerei הַצֶּדֶק hatzedek וְעָלֵינוּ ve'alenu יֶהֱמוּ yehemu

נָא na רַחֲמֶיךָ rachamecha יְהֹוָהֹיֱאֱהֹדֹנָהִיאַהֲדֹנָהִי Adonai אֱלֹהֵינוּ Elohenu ילה

וְתֵן veten שָׂכָר sachar ב"ן י"פ טוֹב tov והו לְכָל־ lechol יה אֲדֹנָי

הַבּוֹטְחִים habotchim בְּשִׁמְךָ beshimcha בֶּאֱמֶת be'emet אֶהְיֶה פַעֲמַיִם אֶהְיֶה, ז"פ ס"ג.

THE NINTH (TWELFTH) BLESSING
For the heretics and for the slanderers, let there be no hope.
Let all the wicked perish in an instant. And may all Your foes and all Your haters be speedily cut down. And as for the evil government, may You quickly uproot and smash it, and may You destroy and humble it, speedily in our days. Blessed are You, Lord, Who smashes foes and humbles the wicked.

THE TENTH (THIRTEENTH) BLESSING
On the righteous, on the pious, on the remnants of the House of Israel, on the remnants of their writers' academies, on the righteous converts, and on us, may Your compassion be stirred, Lord, our God. And give good reward to all those who truly trust in Your Name.

וְשִׂים vesim וְחֶלְקֵנוּ chelkenu עִמָּהֶם imahem וּלְעוֹלָם ul'olam רִיבּוּעַ ס״ג ו״י אותיות דס״ג

לֹא lo נֵבוֹשׁ nevosh כִּי ki בְּךְ vecha בְּטָחְנוּ batachnu◆

וְעַל ve'al וְחַסְדְּךְ chasdecha הַגָּדוֹל hagadol לְהוּ ; עם ד׳ אותיות = מבה, יזל, אום

בֶּאֱמֶת be'emet אהיה פעמים אהיה, ז״פ ס״ג נִשְׁעָנֶנוּ nish'anenu‡

בָּרוּךְ baruch אַתָּה Ata יְהֹוֹוּוּ‫אַדֹנָי‬ Adonai מִשְׁעָן mish'an

וּמִבְטָח umivtach לַצַּדִּיקִים latzadikim ר״ת ימול (כל מי שנימול נקרא צדיק)‡

THE ELEVENTH (FOURTEENTH) BLESSING

This blessing connects us to the power of Jerusalem, to the building of the Temple, and to the preparation for the *Mashiach*.

Hod

תִּשְׁכּוֹן tishkon בְּתוֹךְ betoch יְרוּשָׁלַיִם Yerushalayim עִירְךְ ircha

כַּאֲשֶׁר ka'asher דִּבַּרְתָּ dibarta ראה וְכִסֵּא vechise דָּוִד David

עַבְדְּךְ avdecha פוי, אל אדני מְהֵרָה mehera בְּתוֹכָהּ vetocha תָּכִין tachin

Meditate here that *Mashiach Ben Yosef* shall not be killed by the wicked *Armilos* **(Do not pronounce)**.

וּבְנֵה uvne אוֹתָהּ ota בִּנְיַן binyan עוֹלָם olam

בִּמְהֵרָה bimhera בְיָמֵינוּ veyamenu‡

---

according to the Ari on Minchah of Tisha B'Av we make this additional connection:

CONNECTION FOR THE NINTH OF AV

The ninth day of Av (*Tisha B'Av*) has the potential to be the most destructive, negative day of the year. Both ancient Temples in Jerusalem were destroyed on this day, five hundred years apart. Historically, many other traumatic events have also taken place on this day. Yet, according to the sages, *Tisha B'Av* is also the day when the *Mashiach* will be born. In Kabbalah we learn that where you find the greatest negativity, there is also the potential to reveal the greatest positive Light through spiritual transformation. The time of *Minchah* (afternoon) of *Tisha B'Av* is the best time to confront the destructive energy prevalent on this day. Reciting this blessing helps us bring about the building of the final Temple in Jerusalem instead of connecting us to the destructive forces of the day. We all have a brick to contribute in the building of the Temple and as we transform and rebuild ourselves spiritually, we rebuild our brick in the final Temple. When enough of us have rebuilt our spiritual bricks, the physical Temple will reappear.

---

and place our lot with them. And may we never be embarrassed, for it is in You that we place our trust; it is upon Your great compassion that we truly rely. Blessed are You, Lord, the support and security of the righteous.

THE ELEVENTH (FOURTEENTH) BLESSING

May You dwell in Jerusalem, Your city, as You have promised. And may You establish the throne of David, Your servant, speedily within it and build it as an eternal structure, speedily in our days

nachem נַחֵם Adonai יְהֹוָאדֹנָיאַהדֹונָהי Elohenu אֱלֹהֵינוּ et אֶת אֲבֵלֵי avelei

Tziyon צִיּוֹן יוסף, ו' הויית, קנאה, ve'et וְאֶת avelei אֲבֵלֵי יְרוּשָׁלַיִם ,Yerushalayim

ve'et וְאֶת ha'ir הָעִיר בֶּחָזֶק, סגדלפון, עֵרִי הַחֲרֵבָה hachareva הַוֲרֵבָה vehabezuya וְהַבְּזוּיָה

vehashomema וְהַשּׁוֹמֵמָה mibli מִבְּלִי vaneha בָּנֶיהָ hee הִיא yoshevet יוֹשֶׁבֶת,

verosha וְרֹאשָׁה chafuy וְחָפוּי ke'isha כְּאִשָּׁה akara עֲקָרָה shelo שֶׁלֹּא yalada יָלָדָה.

amecha עַמְּךָ Yisrael יִשְׂרָאֵל ligyonim לִגְיוֹנִים vayval'uha וַיְבַלְּעוּהָ vayirashuha וַיִּירָשׁוּהָ, vayatilu וַיַּטִּילוּ et אֶת

bemerer בְּמֵרֶר vayahargu וַיַּהַרְגוּ, lecharev לְחָרֶב vezadon בְּזָדוֹן

tivke תִּבְכֶּה, virushalayim וִירוּשָׁלַיִם titen תִּתֵּן kola קוֹלָהּ, libi לִבִּי libi לִבִּי al עַל elyon עֶלְיוֹן chasidei וְחֲסִידֵי Tziyon צִיּוֹן ken כֵּן al עַל

ki כִּי. harugehem הֲרוּגֵיהֶם al עַל me'ai מֵעַי me'ai מֵעַי, chalelehem וְחַלְלֵיהֶם

Ata אַתָּה uva'esh וּבָאֵשׁ, hitzata הִצַּתָּהּ ba'esh בְּאֵשׁ Adonai יְהֹוָאדֹנָיאַהדֹונָהי Ata אַתָּה

la לָהּ ehye אֶהְיֶה va'ani וַאֲנִי: kakatuv כַּכָּתוּב, livnota לִבְנוֹתָהּ atid עָתִיד

קמ"ג קנ"א קס"א ע"ה chomat חוֹמַת Adonai יְהֹוָאדֹנָיאַהדֹונָהי ne'um נְאֻם

vetocha בְּתוֹכָהּ ehye אֶהְיֶה ulchavod וּלְכָבוֹד saviv סָבִיב esh אֵשׁ

Tziyon צִיּוֹן menachem מְנַחֵם Adonai יְהֹוָאדֹנָיאַהדֹונָהי Ata אַתָּה baruch בָּרוּךְ

continue "et tzemach David": Yerushalayim יְרוּשָׁלַיִם vevinyan בְּבִנְיַן קנאה, ו' הויית, יוסף

baruch בָּרוּךְ Ata אַתָּה Adonai יְהֹוָאדֹנָיאַהדֹונָהי

bone בּוֹנֶה Yerushalayim יְרוּשָׁלַיִם:

THE TWELFTH (FIFTEENTH) BLESSING

This blessing helps us achieve a personal state of *Mashiach* by transforming our reactive nature into becoming proactive. Just as there is a global *Mashiach*, each person has a personal *Mashiach* within. When enough people achieve their transformation, the way will be paved for the appearance of the global *Mashiach*.

CONNECTION FOR THE NINTH OF AV

Console, Lord, the mourners of Zion, the mourners of Jerusalem and, also the city that was destroyed, debased and laid desolate. She sits without her sons and with her head covered, like a barren woman who has never given birth. Legions have devoured and have possessed her and they have put Your people, Israel, to the sword. They have willfully murdered the supreme pious ones. Therefore, let Zion weep bitterly and let Jerusalem make her voice be heard. My heart! My heart! For their slain ones. My insides! My insides! For their murdered ones. For You, Lord, have burned her down with fire, and with fire You are destined to rebuild her, as it is written: I shall be for her, so did the Lord proclaim, a wall of fire all around and, for glory, shall I be within her. Blessed are You, Lord, Who consoles Zion with he rebuilding of Jerusalem.

Blessed are You, Lord, Who builds Jerusalem.

Netzach

This blessing contains 20 words, which is the same number of words in *"Ki nicham Adonai Tzion nicham kol chorvoteha..."* (Isaiah 51:3), a verse that speaks about the Final Redemption.

אֶת et   צֶמַח tzemach   יהוה   אהיה   יהוה   אדני   דָּוִד David

עַבְדְּךָ avdecha   פוי, אל אדני   מְהֵרָה mehera   תַצְמִיחַ tatzmia'ch   וְקַרְנוֹ vekarno

תָרוּם tarum   בִּישׁוּעָתֶךָ bishu'atecha◆   כִּי ki   לִישׁוּעָתְךָ lishu'atcha

קִוִּינוּ kivinu   כָּל kol ילי   הַיּוֹם hayom ע"ה   נגד, מזבוח, זן, אל יהוה

You should meditate and ask here for the Final Redemption to occur right away.

בָּרוּך baruch   אַתָּה Ata   יְהֹוִ(אדניאהדונהי) Adonai

מַצְמִיחַ matzmi'ach   קֶרֶן keren   יְשׁוּעָה yeshu'a◆

THE THIRTEENTH (SIXTEENTH) BLESSING

This blessing is the most important of all blessings, because here we acknowledge all of our reactive behavior. We make reference to our wrongful actions in general, and we also specify a particular incident. The section inside the box provides us with an opportunity to ask the Light for personal sustenance. The Ari states that throughout this prayer, even on fast days, we have a personal angel accompanying us. If we meditate upon this angel, all our prayers must be answered. The Thirteenth Blessing is one above the twelve zodiac signs, and it raises us above the influence of the stars and planets.

Tiferet

שְׁמַע shema   קוֹלֵנוּ kolenu   יְהֹו(אדניאהדונהי) Adonai   (יוד הֹה וו הֹה)

אֱלֹהֵינוּ Elohenu ילה   (אבג יתץ)◆   אָב av   הָרַחֲמָן harachaman   רַחֵם rachem

עָלֵינוּ alenu   אברהם, וז"פ אל, רי"ו ול"ב נתיבות החוכמה, רמ"ח (אברים), עסמ"ב וט"ז אותיות פשוטות

וְקַבֵּל vekabel   בְּרַחֲמִים berachamim   מצפצ, אלהים דיודין, י"פ ייי (קרע שׂטן)◆

אֶת et ע"ה אל שדי ע"ה   וּבְרָצוֹן uvratzon   מהש ע"ה, ע"ב בריבוע וקס"א וקס"א ע"ה

תְּפִלָּתֵנוּ tefilatenu   (נגד יכש)◆   כִּי ki   אָל El   ייא"י (מילוי דס"ג)

שׁוֹמֵעַ shome'a   תְּפִלּוֹת tefilot   וְתַחֲנוּנִים vetachanunim   אַתָּה Ata (בטר צתג)◆

THE TWELFTH (FIFTEENTH) BLESSING

The offspring of David, Your servant, may You speedily cause to sprout.
And may You raise their worth with Your salvation, because it is for Your salvation that we have hoped all day long. Blessed are You, Lord, Who sprouts out the worth of the salvation.

THE THIRTEENTH (SIXTEENTH) BLESSING

Hear our voice, Lord, our God. Merciful Father, have mercy over us.
Accept our prayer with compassion and favor, because You are God, Who hears prayers and supplications.

It is good for you to be aware, acknowledge and confess your prior negative actions and to ask for your livelihood here:

רִבּוֹנוֹ ribono שֶׁל shel עוֹלָם ,olam וְחָטָאתִי chatati עָוִיתִי aviti

וּפָשַׁעְתִּי ufashati לְפָנֶיךָ lefanecha ס"ג מ"ה ב"ן yehi יְהִי ratzon רָצוֹן מהש ע"ה,

שֶׁתִּמְחוֹל shetimchol ס"ג מ"ה ב"ן milfanecha מִלְּפָנֶיךָ אל עדי ע"ה, וקס"א ברבוע ע"ב,

וְתִסְלַח vetislach יהוה ע"ב וּתְכַפֵּר utchaper עַל al לִי li כָּל kol יל"י ; עמם

מַה ma מ"ה שֶׁחָטָאתִי shechatati וְשֶׁעָוִיתִי veshe'aviti וְשֶׁפָּשַׁעְתִּי veshepashati

לְפָנֶיךָ lefanecha ס"ג מ"ה ב"ן מִיּוֹם miyom ע"ה נגד, מזבח, זן, אל יהוה

שֶׁנִּבְרֵאתִי shenivreti עַד ad הַיּוֹם hayom ע"ה נגד, מזבח, זן, אל יהוה הַזֶּה haze והו

וּבִפְרָט uvifrat (mention here a specific negative action or behavior you have and ask for forgivness)

וִיהִי vihi רָצוֹן ratzon מהש ע"ה, ע"ב ברבוע וקס"א ע"ה, אל עדי ע"ה

מִלְּפָנֶיךָ milfanecha ס"ג מ"ה ב"ן יְהֹוָ֑אֲדֹנָי Adonai אֱלֹהֵינוּ Elohenu ילה

וֵאלֹהֵי velohei מילוי ע"ב, דמב ; ילה אֲבוֹתֵינוּ avotenu שֶׁתַּזְמִין shetazmin

פַּרְנָסָתֵנוּ parnasatenu וּמְזוֹנוֹתֵינוּ umzonotenu לִי li וּלְכָל ulchol יה אדני

אַנְשֵׁי anshei בֵּיתִי veti ב"פ ראה הַיּוֹם hayom ע"ה נגד, מזבח, זן, אל יהוה

וּבְכָל uvchol ב"ן, לכב יוֹם yom ע"ה נגד, מזבח, זן, אל יהוה

וָיוֹם vayom ע"ה נגד, מזבח, זן, אל יהוה בְּרֶיוַוח berevach וְלֹא velo

בְּצִמְצוּם ,vetzimtzum בְּכָבוֹד bechavod וֹכּו וְלֹא velo בְּבִזּוּי ,bevizui

בְּנַחַת benachat וְלֹא velo בְּצַעַר ,vetza'ar וְלֹא velo אֶצְטָרֵךְ etztarech

לְמַתְּנוֹת lematenot בָּשָׂר basar וָדָם vadam וְלֹא velo לְהַלְוָאָתָם ,lehalva'atam

אֶלָּא ela מִיָּדְךָ miyadcha הָרְוָחָה harchava וְהַפְּתוּחָה vehapetucha

וְהַמְּלֵאָה vehamele'a וּבִזְכוּת uvizchut שִׁמְךָ shimcha הַגָּדוֹל hagadol

דִּיקַרְנוֹסָא (Do not pronounce this Name): וזהר עם ג' אותיות, עם ד' אותיות = מבה, יזל, אום להו

הַמְּמֻנֶּה hamemune (יאהדונהי, אמן, סאל = ובאתב"ע) עַל al הַפַּרְנָסָה haparnasa:

Master of the World!

I have transgressed. I have committed iniquity and I have sinned before You. May it be Your will that You would pardon, forgive and excuse all my transgressions, and all the iniquities that I have committed, and all the sins that I have sinned before You, ever since the day I was created and until this day (and especially...). May it be pleasing before You, Lord, our God and God of my forefathers, that You would provide for my livelihood and sustenance, and that of my household, today and each and every day, with abundance and not with meagerness; with dignity and not with shame; with comfort and not with suffering; and that I may not require the gifts of flesh and blood, nor their loans, but only from Your Hand, which is generous, open, and full, and by virtue of Your great Name, which is responsible for livelihood.

malkenu מַלְכֵּנוּ   בְּ"ן   מ"ה   ס"ג   umilfanecha וּמִלְּפָנֶיךָ

רֵיקָם (וזקב טוע) rekam   al- אַל-   teshivenu תְּשִׁיבֵנוּ

וְחָנֵּנוּ chonenu   va'anenu וַעֲנֵנוּ   ushma וּשְׁמַע   tefilatenu תְּפִלָּתֵנוּ:

THE BLESSING FOR A FAST DAY
This blessing is recited by individuals on fast days, during the silent *Amidah*.

עֲנֵנוּ anenu אָבִינוּ avinu עֲנֵנוּ anenu בְּיוֹם beyom ע"ה נגר, מזבח, זן, אל יהו

צוֹם tzom הַתַּעֲנִית hata'anit הַזֶּה haze והו כִּי ki בְּצָרָה vetzara vetzara אלהים דההין

וְאַל- ve'al לְרִשְׁעֵנוּ lerish'enu תֵּפֶן tefen אַל- al ◦anachnu אֲנַחְנוּ gedola גְדוֹלָה

תִּתְעַלָּם tit'alam מַלְכֵּנוּ malkenu ◦mibakashatenu מִבַּקָּשָׁתֵנוּ◦ הֱיֵה heye יהה

אֵלֶיךָ elecha נִקְרָא nikra טֶרֶם terem ◦leshav'atenu לְשַׁוְעָתֵנוּ◦ karov קָרוֹב na נָא

תִּשְׁמַע tishma וְאַתָּה veAta רְאֵה nedaber נְדַבֵּר◦ ta'ane תַּעֲנֶה Ata אַתָּה

יהוה ; יהה vehaya וְהָיָה shene'emar שֶׁנֶּאֱמַר: רְאֵה kadavar כַּדָּבָר

הֵם hem od עוֹד e'ene אֶעֱנֶה אני va'ani וַאֲנִי yikra'u יִקְרָאוּ terem טֶרֶם-

Ata אַתָּה ki כִּי :eshma אֶשְׁמָע אני va'ani וַאֲנִי medaberim מְדַבְּרִים

umrachem וּמְרַחֵם ve'one וְעוֹנֶה umatzil וּמַצִּיל pode פּוֹדֶה Adonai יהואדהינויאהדונהי

(continue "*ki Ata*") vetzuka וְצוּקָה: tzara צָרָה et עֵת בכל bechol בְּכָל

pe פֶּה ילי kol כָּל- tefilat תְּפִלַּת shome'a שׁוֹמֵעַ Ata אַתָּה ki כִּי

(פה דו"א) מילה ; וע"ה אלהים, אהיה אדני (יגל פזק)

Adonai יהואדהינוי(יהואדהה)יאהדונהי Ata אַתָּה baruch בָּרוּךְ

You should meditate here on the Holy Name: **ארארית"א**

Rav Chaim Vital says: "I have found in the books of the kabbalists that the preyer of a person, who meditates on this Name in the blessing *shome'a tefila*, will never go unanswered."

שׁוֹמֵעַ shome'a תְּפִלָּה tefila (שקו צית)

אתב"ע אוכצ, ב"ן אדני וניקודה ע"ה = יוד הי וו ההי:

---

*And from before You,
our King, do not turn us away empty-handed but be gracious, answer us, and hear our prayer.*

THE BLESSING FOR A FAST DAY
Answer us, our Father,

answer us on this day of fasting because we are in great distress. Do not pay heed to our wickedness and, our King, do not ignore our plea. Please come close to our cries and answer us even before we call out to You. We shall speak and You shall hear us, as it is said: And it shall be that before they call, I shall answer, and while they speak, I shall hear. (Isaiah 65:24) For You, Lord, redeem, save, respond, and show compassion in every time of trouble and distress.

Because You hear the prayer of every mouth. Blessed are You, Lord, Who hears prayers.

THE FINAL THREE BLESSINGS

Through the merit of Moses, Aaron and Joseph, who are our channels for the final three blessings, we are able to bring down all the spiritual energy that we aroused with our prayers and blessings.

THE SEVENTEENTH BLESSING

During this blessing, referring to Moses, we should always meditate to try to know exactly what God wants from us in our life, as signified by the phrase, "Let it be the will of God." We ask God to guide us toward the work we came to Earth to do. The Creator cannot just accept the work that we want to do; we must carry out the work we were destined to do.

Netzach

You have made requests (of daily needs) to God. Now, after asking for your needs to be met, you should praise the Creator in the last three blessings. This is like a person who has received what he needs from his Master and departs from Him. You should say "*retze*" and meditate for the Supernal Desire (*Keter*) that is called *metzach haratzon* (the Forehead of the Desire).

רְצֵה retze אלף למד הה יוד מם

Meditate here to transform misfortune and tragedy (צרה) into desire and acceptance (רצה).

(During the three weeks of *Ben HaMetzarim*, meditate here on these Holy Names:
אלהים ההין אדני, שין ע"ה, טדהד כוו מצפצ - with these Names we transform צרה into רצה).

Yisrael יִשְׂרָאֵל	be'amecha בְּעַמְּךָ ילה	Elohenu אֱלֹהֵינוּ	Adonai יְהֹוָאדְנֹיאהדונהי
ha'avoda הָעֲבוֹדָה	vehashev וְהָשֵׁב	she'e שְׁעֵה	velitfilatam וְלִתְפִלָּתָם
Yisrael יִשְׂרָאֵל	ve'ishei וְאִשֵּׁי ב"פ ראה	betecha בֵּיתֶךָ רי"ו	lidvir לִדְבִיר
אוזר, דאגה	be'ahava בְּאַהֲבָה	mehera מְהֵרָה	utfilatam וּתְפִלָּתָם
beratzon בְּרָצוֹן מהש ע"ה, ע"ב בריבוע וקס"א וקס"א ע"ה, אל שדי ע"ה	tekabel תְּקַבֵּל		
leratzon לְרָצוֹן מהש ע"ה, ע"ב בריבוע וקס"א ע"ה, אל שדי ע"ה	ut'hi וּתְהִי		
amecha עַמֶּךָ	Yisrael יִשְׂרָאֵל	avodat עֲבוֹדַת ע"ה קס"א קנ"א קמ"ג	tamid תָּמִיד

THE FINAL THREE BLESSINGS
THE SEVENTEENTH BLESSING

Find favor, Lord, our God,
in Your People, Israel, and turn to their prayer.

Restore the service to the inner sanctuary of Your Temple. Accept the offerings of Israel and their prayer with favor, speedily, and with love. May the service of Your People Israel always be favorable to You.

MINCHAH – AFTERNOON PRAYER
SWEETENING HARSH JUDGMENT

FOR *ROSH CHODESH*, *PESACH*, AND *SUKKOT*:

During these events, there is an extra surge of spiritual energy in our midst. These additional blessings are our antenna for drawing this extra power into our lives.

> If you mistakenly forgot to say "*ya'ale veyavo*," and realize this before the end of the blessing ("*baruch Ata Adonai*"), you should return to say "*ya'ale veyavo*" and continue as usual. If you realize this after the end of the blessing ("*hamachazir shechinato leTziyon*") but before you start the next blessing ("*modim*") you should say "*ya'ale veyavo*" there and continue as usual. If you only realize this after you have started the next blessing ("*modim*") but before the second "*yih'yu leratzon*" (on pg. 333) you should return to "*retze*" (pg. 324) and continue from there. If you realize this after (the second "*yih'yu leratzon*") you should start the *Amidah* from the beginning.

אֱלֹהֵינוּ Elheinu ילה ; מילוי ע"ב,= דמב ; ילה וֵאלֹהֵי velohei לכב ; ע"ב,= דמב ; ילה אֲבוֹתֵינוּ avotenu

יַעֲלֶה ya'ale וְיָבֹא veyavo וְיַגִּיעַ veyagi'a וְיֵרָאֶה veyera'e רי"ו veyeratze וְיֵרָצֶה

וְיִשָּׁמַע veyishama וְיִפָּקֵד veyipaked וְיִזָּכֵר veyizacher ר"ת מ"ב (י"פ ו')

זִכְרוֹנֵנוּ zichronenu וְזִכְרוֹן vezichron ע"ב קס"א ונט"ב אֲבוֹתֵינוּ avotenu♦

זִכְרוֹן zichron ע"ב קס"א ונט"ב יְרוּשָׁלַיִם Yerushalayim עִירָךְ irach♦

וְזִכְרוֹן vezichron ע"ב קס"א ונט"ב מְשִׁיחַ Mashi'ach בֶּן ben דָּוִד David

וְזִכְרוֹן vezichron ע"ב קס"א ונט"ב avdach עַבְדָּךְ אדני ע"ה = ארני ע"ה ; בן דוד ; ע"ה כהת

כָּל kol ילי עַמְּךָ amecha בֵּית bet ב"פ ראה יִשְׂרָאֵל Yisrael

לְפָנֶיךָ lefanecha ס"ג מ"ה ב"ן לִפְלֵיטָה lifleta לְטוֹבָה letova אכא♦

לְחֵן lechen מילוי דמ"ה בריבוע, מוזי לְחֶסֶד lechesed ע"ב, ריבוע יהוה

וּלְרַחֲמִים ulrachamim♦ לְחַיִּים lechayim אהיה אהיה יהוה, בינה ע"ה♦

טוֹבִים tovim וּלְשָׁלוֹם ulshalom♦ בְּיוֹם beyom ע"ה נגד, מזבוז, זן, אל יהוה:

FOR *ROSH CHODESH*, *PESACH*, AND *SUKKOT*:
Our God and God of our forefathers,

may it rise, come, arrive, appear, find favor, be heard, be considered, and be remembered, our remembrance and the remembrance of our forefathers: the remembrance of Jerusalem, Your City, and the remembrance of Mashiach, Son of David, Your servant, and the remembrance of Your entire Nation, the House of Israel, before You for deliverance, for good, for grace, kindness, and compassion, for a good life, and for peace on the day of:

On Rosh Chodesh:

ראש rosh ריבוע אלהים ואלהים דיורין ע"ה

הַחֹדֶשׁ hachodesh י"ב הויות, קס"א קנ"א ; ראש וזדע ע"ה = עין דלת יוד הֹזֶה haze והו•

On mid-holiday of Pesach:

וַזג chag הַמַצות hamatzot הֹזֶה haze והו

בְּיוֹם beyom ע"ה נגד, מזבוז, זן, אל יהוה kodesh קֹדֶשׁ mikra מִקְרָא haze הֹזֶה haze והו•

On mid-holiday of Sukkot:

וַזג chag הַסֻכות hasukot הֹזֶה haze והו

בְּיוֹם beyom ע"ה נגד, מזבוז, זן, אל יהוה kodesh קֹדֶשׁ mikra מִקְרָא haze הֹזֶה haze והו•

לְרַחֵם lerachem אברהם, ח"פ אל, רי"ו ול"ב נתיבות הוזכמה, רמ"וז (אברים),

עסמ"ב וט"ז אותיות פשוטות alenu עָלֵינוּ bo בּוֹ ulhoshi'enu וּלְהוֹשִׁיעֵנוּ•

zochrenu זָכְרֵנוּ Adonai יְהֹוָה Elohenu אֱלֹהֵינוּ ילה bo בּוֹ

letova לְטוֹבָה אכא• ufokdenu וּפָקְדֵנוּ vo בּוֹ livracha לִבְרָכָה•

vehoshi'enu וְהוֹשִׁיעֵנוּ vo בּוֹ lechayim לְחַיִּים אהיה יהוה אהיה בינה ע"ה

tovim טוֹבִים• bidvar בְּדְבַר ראה yeshu'a יְשׁוּעָה verachamim וְרַחֲמִים•

chus וְחוּס vechonenu וְחָנֵּנוּ vachamol וַחֲמוֹל verachem וְרַחֵם אברהם, ח"פ אל,

alenu עָלֵינוּ• אותיות וט"ז (אברים), רמ"וז הוזכמה נתיבות ול"ב רי"ו

vehoshi'enu וְהוֹשִׁיעֵנוּ ki כִּי elecha אֵלֶיךָ enenu עֵינֵינוּ ki כִּי ריבוע מ"ה•

El אל יא"י (מילוי הס"ג) melech מֶלֶךְ chanun וְחַנּוּן verachum וְרַחוּם Ata אָתָּה:

veAta וְאַתָּה verachamecha בְּרַחֲמֶיךָ harabim הָרַבִּים• tachpotz תַּחְפּוֹץ

banu בָּנוּ vetirtzenu וְתִרְצֵנוּ vetechezena וְתֶחֱזֶינָה enenu עֵינֵינוּ ריבוע מ"ה

beshuvcha בְּשׁוּבְךָ leTziyon לְצִיּוֹן יוסף, ו הויות, קנאה berachamim בְּרַחֲמִים

baruch בָּרוּךְ Ata אַתָּה יְהֹוָה Adonai מצפצ, אלהים דיורין, י"פ יי"י:

hamachazir הַמַּחֲזִיר שְׁכִינָתוֹ shechinato leTziyon לְצִיּוֹן יוסף, ו הויות, קנאה:

On Rosh Chodesh: This Rosh Chodesh.
On mid-holiday of Pesach: This festival of Matzot, on this holy day of convocation.
On mid-holiday of Sukkot: This festival of Sukkot, on this holy day of convocation.
To take pity on us and to save us.
Remember us, Lord, our God, on this day, for good; consider us on it for blessing; and deliver us on it for a good life, with the words of deliverance and mercy. Take pity and be gracious to us, have mercy and be compassionate with us, and save us, for our eyes turn to You, because You are God, the King Who is gracious and compassionate.

And You in Your great compassion take delight in us and are pleased with us. May our eyes witness Your return to Zion with compassion. Blessed are You, Lord, Who returns His Shechinah to Zion.

THE EIGHTEENTH BLESSING

This blessing is our thank you. Kabbalistically, the biggest 'thank you' we can give the Creator is to do exactly what we are supposed to do in terms of our spiritual work.

Hod

Bow your entire body at '*modim*' and straighten up at '*Adonai*'.

lach כְּךָ anachnu אֲנַוְנוּ מאה ברכות עתיקן דוד לאמרם כל יום modim מוֹדִים

שָׁאַתָּה sheAta הוּא hu יְהֹוָהֹאדנֹיאהדונֹהי Adonai (וג) אֱלֹהֵינוּ Elohenu ילה

וֵאלֹהֵי velohei לכב ; מילוי ע"ב, דמב ; ילה avotenu אֲבוֹתֵינוּ le'olam לְעוֹלָם

רבוע ס"ג וי' אותיות דס"ג tzur צוּר tzurenu צוּרֵנוּ va'ed וָעֶד אלהים דההן ע"ה

וְחַיֵּינוּ chayenu וּמָגֵן umagen ג"פ אל (ייא"י מילוי דס"ג) ; ר"ת מיכאל גבריאל נוריאל

node נוֹדֶה ר"ו vador וָדוֹר ledor לְדוֹר hu הוּא Ata אַתָּה yish'enu יִשְׁעֵנוּ

chayenu וְחַיֵּינוּ al עַל tehilatecha תְּהִלָּתֶךָ unsaper וּנְסַפֵּר lecha לְךָ

nishmotenu נִשְׁמוֹתֵינוּ ve'al וְעַל beyadecha בְּיָדֶךָ hamesurim הַמְּסוּרִים

shebechol שֶׁבְּכָל nisecha נִסֶּיךָ ve'al וְעַל lach לָךְ hapekudot הַפְּקוּדוֹת

ב"ן, לכב yom יוֹם ע"ה נגד, מזבוח, ז', אל יהוה ריבוע ס"ג, קס"א ע"ה וד' אותיות imanu עִמָּנוּ

ve'al וְעַל vetovotecha וְטוֹבוֹתֶיךָ nifle'otecha נִפְלְאוֹתֶיךָ shebechol שֶׁבְּכָל

hatov הַטּוֹב vetzahorayim וְצָהֳרָיִם vavoker וָבֹקֶר erev עֶרֶב et עֵת ב"ן, לכב

hamerachem הַמְּרַחֵם rachamecha רַחֲמֶיךָ chalu כָלוּ lo לֹא ki כִּי והו

lo לֹא ki כִּי אברהם, וח"פ אל, רי"ו ול"ב נתיבות החוכמה, רמ"ח (אברים), עסמ"ב וט"ז אותיות פשוטות

lach לָךְ kivinu קִוִּינוּ me'olam מֵעוֹלָם ki כִּי chasadecha חֲסָדֶיךָ tamu תַמּוּ וַחֲסָדֶיךָ

THE EIGHTEENTH BLESSING

We give thanks to You, for it is You, Lord, Who is our God and God of our forefathers, forever and for all eternity. You are our Rock, the Rock of our lives, and the Shield of our salvation. From one generation to another, we shall give thanks to You and we shall tell of Your praise. For our lives that are entrusted in Your hands, for our souls that are in Your care, for Your miracles that are with us every day, and for Your wonders and Your favors that are with us at all times: evening, morning and afternoon. You are the good One, for Your compassion has never ceased. You are the compassionate One, for Your kindness has never ended, for we have always placed our hope in You.

MODIM DERABANAN

This prayer is recited by the congregation in the repetition when the chazan says "modim."

In this section there are 44 words which is the same numerical value as the Name: רִבּוּעַ אֲהֹיָה (א אה אהי אהיה).

מוֹדִים modim sheAta שָׁאַתָּה hu הוּא Adonai יְהֹוָה anachnu אֲנַחְנוּ lach לָךְ

וֵאלֹהֵי velohei Elohei אֱלֹהֵי Elohenu אֱלֹהֵינוּ Elohenu avotenu אֲבוֹתֵינוּ

yotzer יוֹצֵר bereshit בְּרֵאשִׁית berachot בְּרָכוֹת vehoda'ot וְהוֹדָאוֹת chol כָּל basar בָּשָׂר yotzrenu יוֹצְרֵנוּ

leshimcha לְשִׁמְךָ hagadol הַגָּדוֹל vehakadosh וְהַקָּדוֹשׁ al עַל shehecheyitanu שֶׁהֶחֱיִיתָנוּ vekiyamtanu וְקִיַּמְתָּנוּ

ken כֵּן techayenu תְּחַיֵּינוּ utchonenu וּתְחָנֵּנוּ vete'esof וְתֶאֱסוֹף

galuyotenu גָּלֻיּוֹתֵינוּ lechatzrot לְחַצְרוֹת kodshecha קָדְשֶׁךָ lishmor לִשְׁמוֹר

chukecha חֻקֶּיךָ vela'asot וְלַעֲשׂוֹת retzoncha רְצוֹנְךָ ul'ovdecha וּלְעָבְדְּךָ

belevav בְּלֵבָב shalem שָׁלֵם al עַל she'anachnu שֶׁאֲנַחְנוּ

modim מוֹדִים lach לָךְ baruch בָּרוּךְ El אֵל hahoda'ot הַהוֹדָאוֹת

FOR CHANUKAH AND PURIM

Chanukah and Purim generate an added dimension of the energy of miracles. This blessing helps us harness this energy, thereby drawing miracles into our lives whenever they are truly needed.

ve'al וְעַל hanisim הַנִּסִּים ve'al וְעַל hapurkan הַפֻּרְקָן

ve'al וְעַל hagevurot הַגְּבוּרוֹת ve'al וְעַל hateshu'ot הַתְּשׁוּעוֹת

ve'al וְעַל hanifla'ot הַנִּפְלָאוֹת ve'al וְעַל hanechamot הַנֶּחָמוֹת

she'asita שֶׁעָשִׂיתָ la'avotenu לַאֲבוֹתֵינוּ bayamim בַּיָּמִים hahem הָהֵם

bazeman בַּזְּמַן haze הַזֶּה

MODIM DERABANAN

We give thanks to You, for it is You Lord, our God and God of our forefathers, the God of all flesh, our Maker and the Former of all Creation. Blessings and thanks to Your great and Holy Name for giving us life and for preserving us. So may You continue to give us life, be gracious to us, and gather our exiles to the courtyards of Your Sanctuary, so that we may keep Your laws, fulfill Your will, and serve You wholeheartedly. For this, we thank You. Bless the God of thanksgiving.

FOR CHANUKAH AND PURIM

And also for the miracles, deliverance, the mighty acts, the salvation, wonders, and comforting deeds that You performed for our forefathers, in those days and at this time.

FOR CHANUKAH:

בִּימֵי bimei מַתִּתְיָה Matitya בֶּן ven יוֹחָנָן Yochanan כֹּהֵן kohen מלה

גָּדוֹל gadol לההו ; עם ד' אותיות = מבה, יזל, אום וְחַשְׁמוֹנַאי Chashmonai וּבָנָיו uvanav

כְּשֶׁעָמְדָה keshe'amda מַלְכוּת malchut יָוָן Yavan הָרְשָׁעָה harsha'a עַל al

עַמְּךָ amecha יִשְׂרָאֵל Yisrael לְשַׁכְּחָם leshakecham תּוֹרָתֶךָ toratach

וּלְהַעֲבִירָם ulha'aviram מֵחֻקֵּי mechukei רְצוֹנֶךָ retzonach ♦ וְאַתָּה veAta

בְּרַחֲמֶיךָ verachamecha הָרַבִּים harabim עָמַדְתָּ amadeta לָהֶם lahem

בְּעֵת be'et צָרָתָם tzaratam ♦ רַבְתָּ ravta אֶת et רִיבָם rivam ♦ דַּנְתָּ danta

אֶת et דִּינָם dinam ♦ נָקַמְתָּ nakamta מנק אֶת et נִקְמָתָם nikmatam מנק ♦

מָסַרְתָּ masarta גִּבּוֹרִים giborim בְּיַד beyad וְחַלָּשִׁים chalashim ♦ וְרַבִּים verabim

בְּיַד beyad מְעַטִּים me'atim ♦ וּרְשָׁעִים ursha'im בְּיַד beyad צַדִּיקִים tzadikim ♦

וּטְמֵאִים utme'im בְּיַד beyad טְהוֹרִים tehorim ♦ וְזֵדִים vezedim בְּיַד beyad

עוֹסְקֵי oskei תוֹרָתֶךָ toratecha ♦ לְךָ lecha עָשִׂיתָ asita שֵׁם shem

גָּדוֹל gadol לההו ; עם ד' אותיות = מבה, יזל, אום וְקָדוֹשׁ vekadosh בְּעוֹלָמֶךָ be'olamach ♦

וּלְעַמְּךָ ul'amecha יִשְׂרָאֵל Yisrael עָשִׂיתָ asita תְּשׁוּעָה teshu'a גְדוֹלָה gedola

וּפֻרְקָן ufurkan עה נגד, מזבוח, יז, אל יהוה כְּהַיּוֹם kehayom הַזֶּה haze והו ♦

וְאַחַר ve'achar כָּךְ kach בָּאוּ ba'u בָנֶיךָ vanecha לִדְבִיר lidvir רי״ו

בֵּיתֶךָ betecha ב״פ ראה וּפִנּוּ ufinu אֶת et הֵיכָלֶךָ hechalecha ♦ וְטִהֲרוּ vetiharu

אֶת et מִקְדָּשֶׁךָ mikdashecha ♦ וְהִדְלִיקוּ vehidliku נֵרוֹת nerot

בְּחַצְרוֹת bechatzrot קָדְשֶׁךָ kodshecha ♦ וְקָבְעוּ vekav'u שְׁמוֹנַת shemonat

יְמֵי yemei וְחֲנֻכָּה Chanukah אֵלּוּ elu בְּהַלֵּל behalel אדני, לכה, וּבְהוֹדָאָה uvhoda'a ♦

וְעָשִׂיתָ ve'asita עִמָּהֶם imahem נִסִּים nisim וְנִפְלָאוֹת venifla'ot וְנוֹדֶה venode

לְשִׁמְךָ leshimcha הַגָּדוֹל hagadol לההו ; עם ד' אותיות = מבה, יזל, אום סֶלָה sela:

FOR CHANUKAH

In the days of Mattatiyahu, the son of Yochanan, the High Priest, the Hasmonean, and his sons, when the evil Greek Empire rose up against Your Nation, Israel, to force them to forget Your Torah and to force them away from the laws of Your desire, You, with Your compassion, stood up for them in their time of trouble. You fought their battles, sought justice for them, avenged them, and delivered the strong into the hands of the weak, the many into the hands of the few, the wicked into the hands of the righteous, the defiled into the hands of the pure, and the tyrants into the hands of those who occupy themselves with Your Torah. For Yourself, You made a Holy Name in Your world, and for Your People, Israel, You carried out a great salvation and deliverance on this day. Then Your Children came into the Sanctuary of Your House, they cleansed Your Palace, they purified Your Temple, they lit candles in the courtyards of Your Holy Domain, and they established these eight days of Chanukah for praise and thanksgiving. And You performed for them miracles and wonders. For that, we are grateful to Your Great Name. Selah.

FOR PURIM:

מִילוּי אדֹנָי = הָאוֹתִיוֹת עִם וְאֶסְתֵּר veEster מָרְדְּכַי Mardechai בִּימֵי bimei

עֲלֵיהֶם alehem כְּשֶׁעָמַד keshe'amad הַבִּירָה habira בְּשׁוּשַׁן beShushan

לַהֲרֹג laharog לְהַשְׁמִיד lehashmid בִּקֵּשׁ bikesh הָרָשָׁע harasha הָמָן Haman

וּלְאַבֵּד ul'abed אֵת et כָּל kol הַיְּהוּדִים hayehudim מִנַּעַר mina'ar וְעַד ve'ad

אַל יהוה זָּ, מִזְבּוֹ, גֹּדֶר, ע"ה beyom בְּיוֹם venashim וְנָשִׁים taf טַף zaken זָקֵן

לְחֹדֶשׁ lechodesh עָשָׂר asar בִּשְׁלשָׁה bishlosha אַהְבָה, דְּאָגָה echad אֶחָד

קֹ"א הֱיוֹת, קס"א קֹ"א chodesh וֹדֶשׁ hu הוּא עָשָׂר asar שְׁנֵים shenem י"ב הֱיוֹת, קס"א קֹ"א

verachamecha בְּרַחֲמֶיךָ veAta וְאַתָּה lavoz לָבוֹז ushlalam וּשְׁלָלָם adar אֲדָר

vekilkalta וְקִלְקַלְתָּ atzato עֲצָתוֹ et אֵת hefarta הֵפַרְתָּ harabim הָרַבִּים

gemulo גְּמוּלוֹ lo לוֹ vahashevota וַהֲשֵׁבוֹתָ machashavto מַחֲשַׁבְתּוֹ et אֵת

ha'etz הָעֵץ al עַל banav בָּנָיו ve'et וְאֶת oto אוֹתוֹ vetalu וְתָלוּ berosho בְּרֹאשׁוֹ

venode וְנוֹדֶה venifla'ot וְנִפְלָאוֹת nisim נִסִּים imahem עִמָּהֶם ve'asita וְעָשִׂיתָ

אוֹם, יזל, מִבָה = הָאוֹתִיוֹת עִם ; לְהוּ sela סֶלָה hagadol הַגָּדוֹל leshimcha לְשִׁמְךָ

---

veyitromam וְיִתְרוֹמַם yitbarach יִתְבָּרַךְ kulam כֻּלָּם ve'al וְעַל

shimcha שִׁמְךָ קמ"ג קנ"א קס"א ע"ה tamid תָּמִיד veyitnase וְיִתְנַשֵּׂא

va'ed וָעֶד דס"ג אוֹתִיוֹת וי ס"ג רִיבּוּעַ le'olam לְעוֹלָם malkenu מַלְכֵּנוּ

sela סֶלָה yoducha יוֹדוּךָ בִּינָה ע"ה אֶהְיֶה אֲהֵיה יהוה hachayim הַחַיִּים vechol וְכָל

During the days between *Rosh Hashanah* and *Yom Kippur* we say the prayer of "*uchtov*":

tovim טוֹבִים בִּינָה ע"ה אֶהְיֶה אֲהֵיה יהוה lechayim לְחַיִּים uchtov וּכְתוֹב

veritecha בְּרִיתֶךָ benei בְּנֵי kol כָּל

If you forget to say "*uchtov*" and realize this before the end of the blessing ("*baruch Ata Adonai*"), you should return and say "*uchtov*" and continue as usual. But if you only realize this after the end of the blessing, you should continue and you may add "*uchtov*" in the end of "*Elohai netzor*".

FOR PURIM:

In the days of Mardechai and Esther, in Shushan, the capital, when the evil Haman rose up against them, he sought to destroy, slay, and annihilate all the Jews, young and old, children and women, in one day, on the thirteenth day of the twelfth month, which is the month of Adar, and to take their spoils. But You, in Your great compassion, ruined his plan, foiled his design, and turned his due upon his own head. They hanged him and his sons upon the gallows. And You performed for them [Israel] miracles and wonders. We give thanks to Your great Name. Selah.

And for all those things, may Your Name be always blessed,
exalted and extolled, our King, forever and ever, and all the living shall thank You, Selah.

During the days between *Rosh Hashanah* and *Yom Kippur*:
And write down for a good life all the members of Your Covenant.

et אֶת־ מ״ה ריבוע יהוה ריבוע יהוה vivarchu וִיבָרְכוּ vihalelu וִיהַלְלוּ

be'emet בֶּאֱמֶת אום יזל, = מבה ; עם ד׳ אותיות = להו׳ hagadol הַגָּדוֹל shimcha שִׁמְךָ

וְהוּ ; tov טוֹב ki כִּי le'olam לְעוֹלָם ריבוע ס״ג ו׳ אותיות דס״ג, ז״פ ס״ג, אהיה פעמים אהיה

yeshu'atenu יְשׁוּעָתֵנוּ לאה ; יא״י (מילוי דס״ג) haEl הָאֵל. יזל, מבה, אום, אהיה = יהוה = טוב כי

והו hatov הַטּוֹב (מילוי דס״ג) haEl הָאֵל sela. סֶלָה ve'ezratenu וְעֶזְרָתֵנוּ

Bend your knees at 'baruch', bow at 'Ata' and straighten up at 'Adonai'.

והו hatov הַטּוֹב (הִי) Adonai יְהוָֹה Ata אַתָּה baruch בָּרוּךְ

שמי דוד ע״ה ס״ת כהת, משיוח בן lehodot לְהוֹדוֹת na'e נָאֶה ulcha וּלְךָ shimcha שִׁמְךָ

On fast days we say here the "blessing of the Kohanim" (see pg. 218).

THE FINAL BLESSING

We are emanating the energy of peace to the entire world. We also make it our intent to use our mouths only for good. Kabbalistically, the power of words and speech is unimaginable. We hope to use that power wisely, which is perhaps one of the most difficult tasks we have to carry out.

Yesod

shalom שָׁלוֹם sim שִׂים

(During the three weeks of Ben HaMetzarim, meditate here on these Holy Names:

עין ראשונה (ע״ה = טדהד כוזו מצפצ) ממתקת את העין השניה (= אלהים דההן אדני) ;
וכן שים שלום ע״ה = ו׳ השמות (טדהד כוזו מצפצ אלהים אדני יהוה) אדני טדהד כוזו מצפצ אלהים ואלהים דההן)

chen וְחֵן אכא chayim וְחַיִּים אהיה אהיה יהוה, בינה ע״ה uvracha וּבְרָכָה tova טוֹבָה

tzedaka צְדָקָה ע״ב, ריבוע יהוה ע״ה ריבוע אלהים vachesed וָחֶסֶד מילוי דמ״ה בריבוע, מוזי

עמם ; ילי kol כָּל־ ve'al וְעַל־ alenu עָלֵינוּ verachamim וְרַחֲמִים

kulanu כֻּלָּנוּ avinu אָבִינוּ uvarchenu וּבָרְכֵנוּ amecha עַמְּךָ Yisrael יִשְׂרָאֵל

ki כִּי panecha פָּנֶיךָ ס״ג מ״ה ב״ן רז, א״ס be'or בְּאוֹר אהבה, דאה ke'echad כְּאֶחָד

אדני אהיה אלהים, lanu לָנוּ natata נָתַתָּ ס״ג מ״ה ב״ן panecha פָּנֶיךָ רז, א״ס ve'or וְאוֹר

vechayim וְחַיִּים tora תוֹרָה ילה Elohenu אֱלֹהֵינוּ Adonai יְהוָֹה

אהיה אהיה יהוה, בינה ע״ה vachesed וָחֶסֶד ע״ב, ריבוע יהוה. ahava אַהֲבָה אוזר, דאה

And they shall praise and bless Your Great Name,
sincerely and forever, for It is good, the God of our salvation and our help, Selah, the good God.
Blessed are You, Lord, whose Name is good, and to You it is befitting to give thanks.

THE FINAL BLESSING

Place peace, goodness, blessing, life, grace, kindness, righteousness, and mercy upon us and upon all of Israel,
Your People. Bless us all as one, our Father, with the Light of Your Countenance, because it is with the
Light of Your Countenance that You, Lord, our God, have given us Torah and life, love and kindness,

beracha בְּרָכָה ◆verachamim וְרַחֲמִים אלהים ריבוע ע"ה tzedaka צְדָקָה

ע"ה קס"א ; ריבוע מ"ה be'enecha בְּעֵינֶיךָ והו vetov וְטוֹב ◆veshalom וְשָׁלוֹם

amecha עַמְּךָ ילי kol כָּל et אֶת ulvarech וּלְבָרֵךְ levarchenu לְבָרְכֵנוּ

‡veshalom וְשָׁלוֹם oz עֹז אהיה י"פ berov בְּרֹב Yisrael יִשְׂרָאֵל

During the days between _Rosh Hashanah_ and _Yom Kippur_ we say the prayer of "_uvsefer chayim_":

ע"ה בינה יהוה, אהיה אהיה chayim וְחַיִּים uvsefer וּבְסֵפֶר

אכא tova טוֹבָה ufarnasa וּפַרְנָסָה veshalom וְשָׁלוֹם beracha בְּרָכָה

◆tovot טוֹבוֹת ugzerot וּגְזֵרוֹת venechama וְנֶחָמָה vishu'a וִישׁוּעָה

ב"ן ס"ג מ"ה lefanecha לְפָנֶיךָ venikatev וְנִכָּתֵב nizacher נִזָּכֵר

Yisrael יִשְׂרָאֵל amecha עַמְּךָ ילי vechol וְכָל anachnu אֲנַחְנוּ

‡ulshalom וּלְשָׁלוֹם tovim טוֹבִים ע"ה בינה יהוה, אהיה אהיה lechayim לְחַיִּים

If you forgot to say "_uvesefer chayim_" and realize this before the end of the blessing ("_baruch Ata Adonai_"),
you should return and say "_uvesefer chayim_" and continue as usual. But if you realize this only after the end
of the blessing, you should continue and you may add "_uvesefer chayim_" in the end of "_Elohai netzor_".

Adonai יוהוו·אדני·יאהדונהי Ata אַתָּה baruch בָּרוּךְ

Yisrael יִשְׂרָאֵל amo עַמּוֹ et אֶת hamevarech הַמְבָרֵךְ

ר"ת = אלהים (אילההויהם) = יב"ק ◆bashalom בַּשָׁלוֹם amen אָמֵן יאהדונהי◆

YIH'YU LERATZON

There are 42 letters in the verse in the secret of _Ana Beko'ach_.

מהלע ע"ה, ע"ב בר··וע וקס"א ע"ה, אל שדי ע"ה אל (יא"י מילוי דס"ג) leratzon לְרָצוֹן yih'yu יִהְיוּ

libi לִבִּי vehegyon וְהֶגְיוֹן אלף למד שׁין דלת יוד ע"ה = ר"ת אלף פ"י fi פִּי imrei אִמְרֵי

‡vego'ali וְגֹאֲלִי tzuri צוּרִי Adonai יהו·אדני·יאהדונהי ס"ג מ"ה ב"ן lefanecha לְפָנֶיךָ

_righteousness and mercy, blessing and peace. May it be good in Your Eyes
to bless us and to bless Your entire Nation, Israel, with abundant power and with peace._

During the days between _Rosh Hashanah_ and _Yom Kippur_:
_And in the Book of Life, for blessing, peace, good livelihood, salvation, consolation, and good decrees, may we all be
remembered and be inscribed before You: we and Your entire Nation, Israel, for good life and for peace._

Blessed are You, Lord, Who blesses His Nation, Israel, with peace, Amen.

YIH'YU LERATZON

_"May the utterances of my mouth
and the thoughts of my heart find favor before You, Lord, my Rock and my Redeemer." (Psalms 19:15)_

ELOHAI NETZOR

אֱלֹהַי Elohai מילוי ע"ב, דמב ; ילה נְצוֹר netzor לְשׁוֹנִי leshoni מֵרָע mera◆

וְשִׂפְתוֹתַי vesiftotai מִדַּבֵּר midaber ראה בִּרְמָה mirma◆ וְלִמְקַלְלַי velimkalelai

נַפְשִׁי nafshi תִדּוֹם tidom◆ וְנַפְשִׁי venafshi כֶּעָפָר ke'afar

לַכֹּל lakol יה אדני תִּהְיֶה tihye◆ פְּתַח petach לִבִּי libi בְּתוֹרָתֶךָ betoratecha◆

וְאַחֲרֵי ve'acharei מִצְוֹתֶיךָ mitzvotecha תִּרְדּוֹף tirdof נַפְשִׁי nafshi◆

וְכֹל vechol ילי הַקָּמִים hakamim עָלַי alai לְרָעָה lera'a רהע◆ מְהֵרָה mehera

הָפֵר hafer עֲצָתָם atzatam וְקַלְקֵל vekalkel מַחְשְׁבוֹתָם machshevotam◆

עֲשֵׂה ase לְמַעַן lema'an שְׁמֶךָ shemach◆ עֲשֵׂה ase לְמַעַן lema'an

יְמִינֶךָ yeminach◆ עֲשֵׂה ase לְמַעַן lema'an תּוֹרָתֶךָ toratach◆ עֲשֵׂה ase

לְמַעַן lema'an קְדֻשָּׁתֶךָ kedushatach◆ ר"ת הפסוק = מ"ה יהוה לְמַעַן lema'an

יֵחָלְצוּן yechaltzun יְדִידֶיךָ yedidecha ר"ת ילי הוֹשִׁיעָה hoshi'a יהוה וע"ע נהורין

יְמִינְךָ yemincha וַעֲנֵנִי va'aneni ר"ת (כתיב: וַעֲנֵנוּ) אל ר"ת (יא"י מילוי דס"ג)◆

Before we recite the next verse ("*yih'yu leratzon*") we have an opportunity to strengthen our connection to our soul using our name. Each person has a verse in the *Torah* that connects to their name. Either their name is in the verse, or the first and last letters of the name correspond to the first or last letters of a verse. For example, the name Yehuda begins with a *Yud* and ends with a *Hei*. Before we end the *Amidah*, we state that our name will always be remembered when our soul leaves this world.

YIH'YU LERATZON (THE SECOND)
There are 42 letters in the verse in the secret of *Ana Beko'ach*.

יִהְיוּ yih'yu (יא"י מילוי דס"ג) אל לְרָצוֹן leratzon מהש ע"ה, ע"ב בריבוע וקס"א ע"ה, אל שדי ע"ה

אִמְרֵי imrei פִי fi ר"ת פּ אֶלֶף = אלף למד מם דלת עין יוד ע"ה וְהֶגְיוֹן vehegyon לִבִּי libi

לְפָנֶיךָ lefanecha ס"ג מ"ה ב"ן יְהֹוָהאדניאהדונהי Adonai צוּרִי tzuri וְגֹאֲלִי vego'ali◆

ELOHAI NETZOR
My God, guard my tongue from evil and my lips from speaking deceit. To those who curse me, let my spirit remain silent, and let my spirit be as dust for everyone. Open my heart to Your Torah and let my heart pursue Your commandments. All those who rise against me to do me harm, speedily nullify their plans and disturb their thoughts. Do so for the sake of Your Name. Do so for the sake of Your Right. Do so for the sake of Your Torah. Do so for the sake of Your Holiness, "So that Your loved ones may be saved. Redeem Your right and answer me." (Psalms 60:7)

YIH'YU LERATZON (THE SECOND)
"May the utterances of my mouth and the thoughts of my heart find favor before You, Lord, my Rock and my Redeemer." (Psalms 19:15)

OSE SHALOM

We now take three steps backward to draw the Light of the Upper Worlds into our life. We bow to the Left, Right, and Center, and we should meditate that by taking these three steps backwards, that the Holy Temple that was destroyed should be built once again.

You take three steps backward;

עוֹשֶׂה ose שָׁלוֹם shalom

(**During the days between** *Rosh Hashanah* **and** *Yom Kippur* **instead of** *"shalom"* **we say:**)

Left
You turn to the left and say:

הַשָׁלוֹם hashalom ספריאל המלאך הוזתם לחיים)

בִּמְרוֹמָיו bimromav ר"ת ע"ב, ריבוע יהוה

Right
You turn to the right and say:

הוּא hu בְּרַחֲמָיו verachamav יַעֲשֶׂה ya'ase

שָׁלוֹם shalom עָלֵינוּ aleinu ר"ת ש"ע נהורין

Center
You face the center and say:

וְעַל ve'al כָּל־ kol יַלי ; עַמוֹ amo יִשְׂרָאֵל Yisrael

וְאִמְרוּ ve'imru אָמֵן amen יאהדונהי:

יְהִי yehi רָצוֹן ratzon מהש ע"ה, ע"ב, בריבוע וקס"א ע"ה, אל שדי ע"ה ע"ה

מִלְפָנֶיךָ milfaneicha ס"ג מ"ה ב"ן יְהֹוָאדניאהדונהי Adonai אֱלֹהֵינוּ eloheinu ילה

וֵאלֹהֵי velohei לכב ; מילוי ע"ב, דמב ; ילה אֲבוֹתֵינוּ avoteinu, שֶׁתִבְנֶה shetivne

בֵּית bet ב"פ ראה הַמִקְדָּשׁ hamikdash בִּמְהֵרָה bimhera בִּמְהֵרָה veyameinu

וְתֵן veten וְזַלְקֵנוּ chelkenu בְּתוֹרָתֶךָ betoratach לַעֲשׂוֹת la'asot וְזֻקֵּי chukei

רְצוֹנֶךָ retzonach וּלְעָבְדֶךָ ul'ovdach פוי, אל אדני בְּלֵבָב belevav בובי שָׁלֵם shalem

You take three steps forward.

On regular days we say *"yehi shem"* followed by *Kaddish Titkabal* on pg. 336.
During the days between *Rosh Hashanah* **and** *Yom Kippur* we say here *"Avinu Malkenu"*
(pg. 225-227) and then continue as usual *("yehi shem"* followed by *Kaddish Titkabal* on pg. 336).

OSE SHALOM

He, Who makes peace (During the days between *Rosh Hashanah* and *Yom Kippur: The peace*) *in His high places, He, in His compassion, shall make peace upon us And upon His entire nation, Israel, and you shall say, Amen.*

May it be pleasing before You,
Lord, our God and God of our forefathers, that You shall rebuild the Temple speedily, in our days, and place our lot in Your Torah, so that we may fulfill the laws of Your desire and serve You wholeheartedly.

THE ORDER OF PARTICIPATING IN A PERSONAL FAST

If, for some reason, you would like to take upon yourself to fast for spiritual cleansing or repentance you need to commit to it the day before during *Minchah* and before the end of the *Amidah* of *Minchah*. If you have forgotten to commit then, you can still commit later even after the sun has set, as long as you have not begun the *Arvit* connection.

רבּוֹן ribon יהוה הָעוֹלָמִים עסמ"ב ha'olamim, הֲרֵינִי hareni לְפָנֶיךָ lefanecha ס"ג מ"ה ב"ן

עַל al תְּנַאי tenai בְּתַעֲנִית beta'anit נְדָבָה nedava לְמָחָר lemachar מֵעֲלוֹת me'alot

הַשַּׁחַר hashachar עַד ad אַוזֹר achar תְּפִלַּת tefilat עַרְבִית arvit. וְאִם ve'im לֹא lo

אוּכַל uchal אוֹ oh לֹא lo אֶרְצֶה ertze כְּשֶׁאוֹמַר keshe'omar מִזְמוֹר mizmor

לְדָוִד leDavid ה' Hashem רֹעִי Ro'i אוּכַל uchal לְהַפְסִיק lehafsik וְלֹא velo

יִהְיֶה yih'ye בִּי bi שׁוּם shum עָוֹן avon. אֲבָל aval, יְהִי yehi רָצוֹן ratzon מהש"ע ע"ה,

אֱלֹהַי Elohai מילוי דע"ב, דמב ; מילוי דע"ב, דמב ; ילה אֲבוֹתַי avotai,

שֶׁתִּתֵּן shetitan ב"פ כהת בִּי bi כּוֹחַ ko'ach וּבְרִיאוּת uvri'ut וְאֶזְכֶּה ve'ezke אוזר, דאוה

לְהִתְעַנּוֹת lehit'anot לְמָחָר lemachar וּתְקַבְּלֵנִי utkabeleni בְּאַהֲבָה be'ahava

וּבְרָצוֹן uvratzon מהש"ע ע"ה, ע"ב בריבוע וקס"א ע"ה, אל שדי ע"ה, וּתְזַכֵּנִי utzakeni

לָשׁוּב lashuv בִּתְשׁוּבָה bitshuva שְׁלֵמָה shelema וְתַעֲנֶה veta'ane עֲתִירָתִי atirati

וְתִשְׁמַע vetishma תְּפִלָּתִי tefilati. כִּי ki אַתָּה Ata שׁוֹמֵעַ shome'a תְּפִלָּה tefila:

In the *Minchah* of the day of the fast, after "lemnatze'ach binginot" (Psalms 67) you should say "tefilah le'ani" (Psalms 86).
And in *Arvit*, after the fast day, you should say (before taking three steps at the end of the *Amidah*):

רבּוֹן ribon יהוה עסמ"ב הָעוֹלָמִים ha'olamim, גָּלוּי galui וְיָדוּעַ veyadu'a

לְפָנֶיךָ lefanecha ס"ג מ"ה ב"ן בִּזְמַן bizman שֶׁבֵּית shabat הַמִּקְדָּשׁ hamikdash

קָיָם kayam, אָדָם adam וֹזוֹטֵא chote וּמַקְרִיב umakriv קָרְבָּן korban וְאֵין ve'en

מַקְרִיבִין makrivin מִמֶּנּוּ mimenu אֶלָּא ela חֶלְבּוֹ chelbo וְדָמוֹ vedamo

וּמִתְכַּפֵּר umitkaper לוֹ lo, וְעַכְשָׁיו ve'ach'shav יָשַׁבְתִּי yashavti בְּתַעֲנִית beta'anit

וְנִתְמַעֵט venitma'et חֶלְבִּי chelbi וְדָמִי vedami. יְהִי yehi רָצוֹן ratzon מהש"ע ע"ה, ע"ב

וְזֹלְבִּי chelbi שֶׁיְּהֵא sheyehe ע"ב בריבוע וקס"א ע"ה, אל שדי ע"ה ב"ן מִלְּפָנֶיךָ milefanecha

שֶׁנִּתְמַעֵט shenitma'et וְדָמִי vedami כְּאִלּוּ ke'ilu הִקְרַבְתִּיו hikravtiv לְפָנֶיךָ lefanecha

עַל al גַּבֵּי gabei הַמִּזְבֵּחַ hamizbe'ach נגד, זן, אל יהוה ס"ג מ"ה ב"ן וְתִירְצֵנִי vetirtzeni:

THE ORDER OF PARTICIPATING IN A PERSONAL FAST

Master of the Worlds, I hereby taking it upon myself to be before you, conditionally, in a state of deliberate fast tomorrow, from dawn until after Arvit connection. And if I will be unable or not wish to complete the fast then when I recite: "Mizmor Ledavid etc. (psalms 23)" I will be enable to end my fast and it shal not be considered sinful for me. However, May it be pleasing before You, Lord, my God, and the God of my forefathers, that You grant me the strength and the health that I may succeed in fasting tomorrow and that you accept me with love and kindness. And grant me the merit to repent perfectly and respond to my request and hear my prayer for you hear prayer.

Master of the Worlds, it is revealed well and known before you that during the time that the Holy Temple stood, a person who sinned would offer a sacrifice from which were offered only the fat and blood and it would atone for his sin. I have fasted now and have thereby diminished my fat and blood. May it be pleasing before You, that my diminished fat and blood be considered as if I had offered them upon the alter and may you favor me.

YEHI SHEM

יְהִי yehi שֵׁם shem לְהֹוָה Adonai מְבֹרָךְ mevorach ר"ת ריבוע ע"ב וריבוע ס"ג

יהוה מברך = רפ"ח (להעלות רפ"ח ניצוצות שנפלו לקליפה דמשם באים התולדים) מֵעַתָּה me'ata

וְעַד ve'ad עוֹלָם olam יכל׃ בְּמִזְרַח mimizrach שֶׁמֶשׁ shemesh עַד ad

מְבוֹאוֹ mevo'o מְהֻלָּל mehulal שֵׁם shem יְהֹוָה Adonai׃ ר"ת קדוש

רָם ram עַל al כָּל kol יכל ; עמם גּוֹיִם goyim יְהֹוָה Adonai עַל al

הַשָּׁמַיִם hashamayim יפ טל, י"פ כוזו ; ר"ת וזשמל כְּבוֹדוֹ kevodo׃

יְהֹוָה Adonai אֲדֹנֵינוּ adonenu מָה ma מ"ה אַדִּיר adir הרי

שִׁמְךָ shimcha בְּכָל bechol ב"ן, לכב ; ומב הָאָרֶץ ha'aretz אלהים דההין ע"ה׃

KADDISH TITKABAL

יִתְגַּדַּל yitgadal וְיִתְקַדַּשׁ veyitkadash שדי ומילוי שדי ; י"א אותיות כמנין ו"ה

שְׁמֵהּ shemei (שם י"ה דע"ב) רַבָּא raba קנ"א ב"ן, יהוה אלהים יהוה אדני,

אמן amen אידהנויה. מילוי קס"א וס"ג, מ"ה ברבוע וע"ב ע"ה ; ר"ת = ו"פ אלהים ; ס"ת = ג"פ יב"ק.

בְּעָלְמָא be'alma דִי di בְּרָא vera כִרְעוּתֵיהּ chir'utei.

וְיַמְלִיךְ veyamlich מַלְכוּתֵיהּ malchutei. וְיַצְמַח veyatzmach

פּוּרְקָנֵיהּ purkanei. וִיקָרֵב vikarev מְשִׁיחֵיהּ meshichei׃ אמן amen אידהנויה.

בְּחַיֵּיכוֹן bechayechon וּבְיוֹמֵיכוֹן uvyomechon וּבְחַיֵּי uvchayei

דְכָל dechol יכל בֵּית bet ב"פ ראה יִשְׂרָאֵל Yisrael בַּעֲגָלָא ba'agala

וּבִזְמַן uvizman קָרִיב kariv וְאִמְרוּ ve'imru אָמֵן amen׃ אָמֵן amen אידהנויה.

YEHI SHEM
"May the Name of the Lord be blessed from now till all eternity. From sunrise till sundown, may the Name of the Lord be praised and elevated. Above all nations is the Lord. His glory is above the Heavens." (Psalms 113:2-4) "The Lord, our Master, how tremendous is Your Name in all the Earth." (Psalms 8:10)

KADDISH TITKABAL
May His great Name be more exalted and sanctified. (Amen) In the world that He created according to His will, and may His Kingdom reign. And may He cause His redemption to sprout and may He bring the Mashiach closer. (Amen) In your lifetimes and in your days and in the lifetime of all the House of Israel, speedily and in the near future, and you shall say, Amen. (Amen)

The congregation and the *chazan* say the following:

28 words (until be'alma) – meditate:

מילוי דמילוי דע"ב (יוד ויו דלת הי יוד ויו יוד הי יוד)

28 letters (until almaya) - meditate:

מילוי דמילוי דע"ב (יוד ויו דלת הי יוד ויו יוד ויו יוד הי יוד)

ב"ן, קנ"א raba **רַבָּא** דס"ג) י"ה (שם shemei **שְׁמֵיהּ** yehe **יְהֵא**

mevarach, **מְבָרַךְ** ע"ב מ"ה ברבוע וע"ב קס"א מילוי אדני, יהוה אלהים יהוה

yitbarach **יִתְבָּרַךְ** almaya **עָלְמַיָּא** le'almei **לְעָלְמֵי** le'alam **לְעָלַם**

Seven words with six letters each (שם בן מ"ב) – meditate:

יהוה + יוד הי ויו הי + מילוי דמילוי דע"ב (יוד ויו דלת הי יוד ויו יוד הי יוד)

Also, seven times the letter Vav (שם בן מ"ב) – meditate:

יהוה + יוד הי ויו הי + מילוי דמילוי דע"ב (יוד ויו דלת הי יוד ויו יוד הי יוד).

י"פ ע"ב יהוה אל אבג יתץ. veyishtabach **וְיִשְׁתַּבַּח**

הי נו יה קרע שטן veyitromam **וְיִתְרוֹמַם** וה כוזו נגד יכש. veyitpa'ar **וְיִתְפָּאַר**

כוזו יה וזקב טנע. veyit'hadar **וְיִתְהַדָּר** במוכסז בטר צתג. veyitnase **וְיִתְנַשֵּׂא**

א ואו הא שקו צית. veyit'halal **וְיִתְהַלָּל** וה יוד ה יגל פזק. veyit'ale **וְיִתְעַלֶּה**

hu **הוּא:** verich **בְּרִיךְ** dekudsha **דְּקֻדְשָׁא** דמ"ה) י"ה (שם shemei **שְׁמֵיהּ**

אידהנויה. amen **אָמֵן**

shirata **שִׁירָתָא** birchata **בִּרְכָתָא** ילי kol **כָּל** min **מִן** le'ela **לְעֵלָּא**

da'amiran **דַּאֲמִירָן** venechamata **וְנֶחָמָתָא** tishbechata **תֻּשְׁבְּחָתָא**

אידהנויה. amen **אָמֵן** amen **אָמֵן:** ve'imru **וְאִמְרוּ** be'alma **בְּעָלְמָא**

uva'utana **וּבָעוּתָנָא** tzelotana **צְלוֹתָנָא** titkabal **תִּתְקַבֵּל**

ילי dechol **דְּכָל** uva'utehon **וּבָעוּתְהוֹן** tzelotehon **צְלוֹתְהוֹן** im **עִם**

avuna **אֲבוּנָא** kadam **קֳדָם** Yisrael **יִשְׂרָאֵל** ב"פ ראה beit **בֵּית**

אידהנויה. amen **אָמֵן** amen **אָמֵן:** ve'imru **וְאִמְרוּ** devishmaya **דְּבִשְׁמַיָּא**

May His great Name be blessed forever and for all eternity. Blessed and lauded, and glorified, and exalted, and extolled, and honored, and uplifted, and praised be the Name of the Holy Blessed One. (Amen) Above all blessings, songs, praises, and words of consolation that may be said in the world, and you shall say, Amen. (Amen) May our prayers and pleas be accepted, together with the prayers and pleas of the entire House of Israel, before our Father in Heaven, and you say, Amen. (Amen)

יְהֵא yehe שְׁלָמָא shelama רַבָּא raba קָנ"א ב"ן, יהוה אלהים יהוה אדני, מילוי קס"א וס"ג,

מִן min שְׁמַיָּא shemaya וְחַיִּים chayim מ"ה ברבוע וע"ב ע"ה אהיה אהיה יהוה, בינה ע"ה

וְשֵׁיזָבָא vesheizava וְנֶחָמָה venechama וִישׁוּעָה vishu'a וְשֵׂבַע vesava

וּרְפוּאָה urfu'a וּגְאֻלָּה ug'ula וּסְלִיחָה uslicha וְכַפָּרָה vechapara

וְרֵיוַוח verevach וְהַצָּלָה vehatzala לָנוּ lanu אלהים, אהיה אדני יה אדני וּלְכָל ulchol

עַמּוֹ amo יִשְׂרָאֵל Yisrael וְאִמְרוּ ve'imru אָמֵן amen אָמֵן amen אידהנויה.

Take three steps backwards and say:

עוֹשֶׂה ose שָׁלוֹם shalom

(**During the days between** *Rosh Hashanah* and *Yom Kippur* instead of "*shalom*" we say:

הַשָּׁלוֹם hashalom ספריאל המלאך החותם לחיים)

בִּמְרוֹמָיו bimromav ע"ב, ריבוע יהוה הוּא hu בְּרַחֲמָיו berachamav

יַעֲשֶׂה ya'ase שָׁלוֹם shalom עָלֵינוּ alenu ר"ת ס"ע נהורין

וְעַל ve'al כָּל kol ילי ; עמם עַמּוֹ amo יִשְׂרָאֵל Yisrael וְאִמְרוּ ve'imru אָמֵן amen:

אָמֵן amen אידהנויה.

LAMNATZE'ACH

By meditating upon the *Magen David* (Shield of David), we harness the power, strength, and valor of King David so that we can defeat our personal enemies. Our real enemies are not found in the outside world, regardless of what our ego tells us. Our real enemy is our *Desire to Receive for the Self Alone*. When we defeat the enemy within, external enemies suddenly disappear from our lives.

God revealed this Psalm to King David by Divine Inspiration. It was written on a golden plate made in the shape of the *Menorah* (shown on pg. 340). God also showed it to Moses. King David carried this Psalm written and engraved on the gold plate on his shield, the Shield of David. When King David went to war, he would meditate on the secrets of the *Menorah* and the seven sentences of this Psalm engraved in it, and his enemies would literally fall in defeat before him. By meditating upon it (reading the letters without turning the image upside down), we harness that power (*Midbar Kdemot*, by the Chida and also in *Menorat Zahav*, by Rav Zusha.)

May there be abundant peace from heaven. Life, contentment, salvation, consolation, deliverance, healing, redemption, pardon, atonement, comfort, and relief. For us and for His entire nation, Israel, and you shall say, Amen. (Amen) He, Who makes peace (During the days between *Rosh Hashanah* and *Yom Kippur*: *The peace*) *in His high places, He, in His compassion, shall make peace upon us And upon His entire nation, Israel, and you shall say, Amen. (Amen)*

לַמְנַצֵּחַ lamnatze'ach בִּנְגִינֹת binginot מִזְמוֹר mizmor שִׁיר shir:

אֱלֹהִים Elohim אהיה אדני ; ילה ; יְחָנֵּנוּ yechonenu וִיבָרְכֵנוּ vivarchenu

יָאֵר ya'er כף ויו זין ויו פָּנָיו panav איתנו ר"ת פאי, אמן (יאהדונהי) אִתָּנוּ itanu סֶלָה sela:

לָדַעַת lada'at ר"ת סאל, אמן (יאהדונהי) בָּאָרֶץ ba'aretz דַּרְכֶּךָ darkecha

בְּכָל bechol ב"ן, לכב גוֹיִם goyim יְשׁוּעָתֶךָ yeshu'atecha:

יוֹדוּךָ yoducha עַמִּים amim אֱלֹהִים Elohim אהיה אדני ; ילה יוֹדוּךָ yoducha

עַמִּים amim כֻּלָּם kulam: יִשְׂמְחוּ yismechu וִירַנְּנוּ viranenu

לְאֻמִּים le'umim ר"ת ע"ה = איההויהה כִּי ki תִשְׁפֹּט tishpot עַמִּים amim

מִישׁוֹר mishor וּלְאֻמִּים ul'umim בָּאָרֶץ ba'aretz תַּנְחֵם tanchem סֶלָה sela:

יוֹדוּךָ yoducha עַמִּים amim אֱלֹהִים Elohim אהיה אדני ; ילה יוֹדוּךָ yoducha

עַמִּים amim כֻּלָּם kulam: ר"ת יודוך ישמחו יודוך ארץ = יא"י (מילוי דס"ג)

ועם ר"ת אלהים לדעת יברכנו = ע"ב, ריבוע יהוה נתה, קס"א קנ"א קמ"ג אָרֶץ eretz נָתְנָה natna

יְבוּלָהּ yevula ר"ת אני יְבָרְכֵנוּ yevarchenu אֱלֹהִים Elohim אהיה אדני ; ילה

אֱלֹהֵינוּ eloheinu ילה: יְבָרְכֵנוּ yevarchenu אֱלֹהִים Elohim אהיה אדני ; ילה

וְיִירְאוּ veyir'u אוֹתוֹ oto כָּל kol ילי אַפְסֵי afsei אָרֶץ aretz:

LAMNATZE'ACH

*"For the Leader; with string-music: A Psalm, a Song. God be gracious unto us, and bless us;
may He cause His face to shine toward us; Selah. That Your way may be known upon earth,
Your salvation among all nations. Let the people give thanks to You, God; let the people give thanks
to You, all of them. Let the nations be glad and sing for joy; for You will judge the people with equity,
and lead the nations upon earth. Selah Let the people give thanks to You, God; let the people
give thanks to You, all of them. The earth has yielded her increase; may God, our own God,
bless us. May God bless us; and let all the ends of the earth fear Him." (Psalms 67)*

MINCHAH - AFTERNOON PRAYER
SWEETENING HARSH JUDGMENT

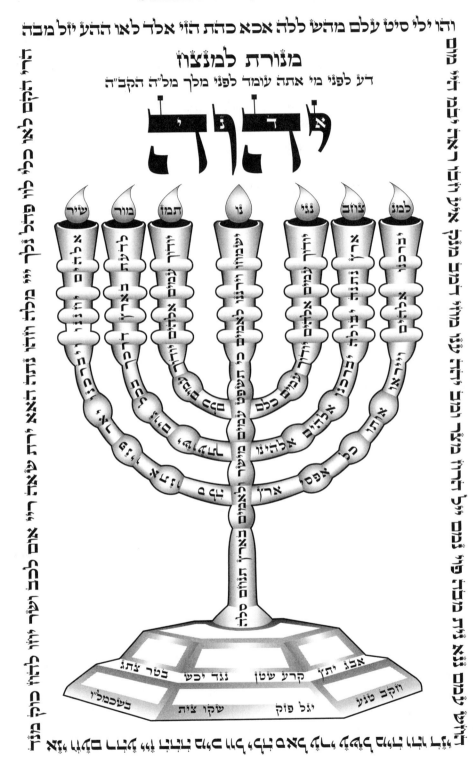

On Friday afternoon the following is recited instead of "*lamnatze'ach binginot*":

לְבֵשׁ lavesh לָבֵשׁ lavesh גֵּאוּת ge'ut מָלָךְ malach יְהֹוָאדנָיאהדונהי Adonai

עֹז oz הִתְאַזָּר hit'azar אַף־ af = ר״ת = אלהים, אהיה אדני יְהֹוָאדנָיאהדונהי Adonai

תִּכּוֹן tikon תֵבֵל tevel בַּל־ bal = ב״פ רי״ו תִּמּוֹט timot נָכוֹן nachon כִּסְאֲךָ kis'acha

מֵאָז me'az ומב מֵעוֹלָם me'olam אַתָּה Ata ר״ת הפסוק קנ״א, אדני אלהים: נָשְׂאוּ nas'u

נְהָרוֹת neharot קין = ר״ת nas'u נָשְׂאוּ Adonai יְהֹוָאדנָיאהדונהי נְהָרוֹת neharot

קוֹלָם kolam יִשְׂאוּ yis'u נְהָרוֹת neharot דָּכְיָם dochyam ר״ת דני:

מִקֹּלוֹת mikolot מַיִם mayim רַבִּים rabim אַדִּירִים adirim הרי

מִשְׁבְּרֵי־ mishberei יָם yam לי ; ר״ת אמי אַדִּיר adir הרי

בַּמָּרוֹם bamarom Adonai יְהֹוָאדנָיאהדונהי ; ר״ת אבי: עֵדֹתֶיךָ edoteicha

נֶאֶמְנוּ ne'emnu מְאֹד me'od ר״ת = קין לְבֵיתְךָ leveitcha ב״פ ראה

נָאֲוָה־ na'avah קֹדֶשׁ kodesh יְהֹוָאדנָיאהדונהי Adonai לְאֹרֶךְ le'orech

לְיָמִים yamim נלך ; ר״ת ילי ; ס״ת = אדני ; יהוה לאורך ימים = ע״ע נהורין עם י״ג אותיות:

KADDISH YEHE SHELAMA

יִתְגַּדַּל yitgadal וְיִתְקַדַּשׁ veyitkadash שׁדי ומילוי שׁדי ; י״א אותיות כמנין ו״ה

שְׁמֵיהּ shemei (עׂם י״ה דע״ב) רַבָּא raba קנ״א ב״ן, יהוה אלהים יהוה אדני,

אָמֵן amen אידהנויה. מילוי קס״א וס״ג, מ״ה ברבוע וע״ב ע״ה ; ר״ת = ו״פ אלהים ; ס״ת = ג״פ יב״ק:

בְּעָלְמָא be'alma דִּי di בְּרָא vera כִּרְעוּתֵיהּ chir'utei

וְיַמְלִיךְ veyamlich מַלְכוּתֵיהּ malchutei וְיַצְמַח veyatzmach

פּוּרְקָנֵיהּ purkanei וִיקָרֵב vikarev מְשִׁיחֵיהּ meshichei אָמֵן amen אידהנויה.

"The Lord has reigned. He clothed Himself with pride. The Lord clothed Himself and girded Himself with might. He also established the world firmly, so that it would not collapse. Your Throne has been established. Ever since then, You have been forever. The rivers have lifted, Lord, the rivers have raised their voices. The rivers shall raise their powerful waves. More than the roars of many waters, and the powerful waves of the sea, You are immense in the high places, Lord. Your testimonies are extremely trustworthy. Your house is the holy sanctuary. The Lord shall be for the length of days." (Psalms 93)

KADDISH YEHE SHELAMA

May His great Name be more exalted and sanctified. (Amen)
In the world that He created according to His will, and may His kingdom reign.
And may He cause His redemption to sprout and may He bring the Mashiach closer. (Amen)

בְּחַיֵּיכוֹן bechayechon וּבְיוֹמֵיכוֹן uvyomechon וּבְחַיֵּי uvchayei

דְכָל dechol יְלִי בֵּית bet ב"פ ראה בֵּית יִשְׂרָאֵל Yisrael בַּעֲגָלָא ba'agala

וּבִזְמַן uvizman קָרִיב kariv וְאִמְרוּ ve'imru אָמֵן amen אָמֵן amen אידהנויה.

The congregation and the *chazan* say the following:

---

28 words (until *be'alma*) – meditate:
מילוי דמילוי דס"ג (יוד ויו דלת הי יוד ואו אלף ואו הי יוד)
28 letters (until *almaya*) - meditate:
מילוי דמילוי דמ"ה (יוד ואו דלת הא אלף ואו אלף ואו הא אלף).

יְהֵא yehe שְׁמֵיהּ shemei (שם י"ה דס"ג) רַבָּא raba קנ"א ב"ן,

מְבָרַךְ mevarach, יהוה אלהים יהוה אדני, מילוי קס"א וס"ג, מ"ה ברבוע וע"ב ע"ה

לְעָלַם le'alam לְעָלְמֵי le'almei עָלְמַיָּא almaya יִתְבָּרַךְ yitbarach

---

Seven words with six letters each (שם בן מ"ב) – meditate:
יהוה ← יוד הי ואו הי ← מילוי דמילוי דס"ג (יוד ויו דלת הי יוד ואו הי יוד) ;
Also, seven times the letter Vav (שם בן מ"ב) – meditate:
יהוה ← יוד הא ואו הא ← מילוי דמילוי דמ"ה (יוד ואו דלת הא אלף ואו אלף ואו הא אלף).

וְיִשְׁתַּבַּח veyishtabach י"פ ע"ב יהוה אל אבג יתץ.

וְיִתְפָּאַר veyitpa'ar הי גו יה קרע שטן. וְיִתְרַמַם veyitromam וה כוזו נגד יכש.

וְיִתְנַשֵּׂא veyitnase במוכסז בטר צתג. וְיִתְהַדָּר veyit'hadar כוזו יה וזקב טנע.

וְיִתְעַלֶּה veyit'ale וה יוד ה יגל פזק. וְיִתְהַלָּל veyit'halal א ואו הא שקו צית.

שְׁמֵיהּ shemei (שם י"ה דמ"ה) דְקוּדְשָׁא dekudsha בְּרִיךְ verich הוּא hu:

אָמֵן amen אידהנויה.

לְעֵלָּא le'ela מִן min כָּל kol יְלִי בִּרְכָתָא birchata שִׁירָתָא shirata

תֻּשְׁבְּחָתָא tishbechata וְנֶחָמָתָא venechamata דַּאֲמִירָן da'amiran

בְּעָלְמָא be'alma וְאִמְרוּ ve'imru אָמֵן amen אָמֵן amen אידהנויה.

In your lifetimes and in your days and in the lifetime of all the House of Israel, speedily and in the near future, and you shall say, Amen. (Amen) May His great Name be blessed forever and for all eternity. Blessed and lauded, and glorified, and exalted, and extolled, and honored, and uplifted, and praised be the Name of the Holy Blessed One. (Amen) Above all blessings, songs, praises, and words of consolation that may be said in the world, and you shall say, Amen. (Amen)

יְהֵא yehe שְׁלָמָא shelama רַבָּא raba קס"א ב"ן, יהוה אלהים יהוה אדני, מילוי קס"א וס"ג,

מ"ה ברביע וע"ב ע"ה, אהיה אהיה יהוה, בינה ע"ה מִן min שְׁמַיָּא shemaya◆ וְחַיִּים chayim

וְשֵׂבַע vesava וִישׁוּעָה vishu'a וְנֶחָמָה venechama וְשֵׁיזָבָא veshezava

וּרְפוּאָה urefu'a וּגְאֻלָּה uge'ula וּסְלִיחָה uslicha וְכַפָּרָה vechapara

וְרֵיוַח verevach וְהַצָּלָה◆ vehatzala לָנוּ lanu אלהים, אהיה אדני וּלְכָל ulchol יה אדני

עַמּוֹ amo יִשְׂרָאֵל Yisrael וְאָמְרוּ ve'imru אָמֵן amen: אָמֵן amen אידהנויה.

Take three steps backwards and say:

עוֹשֶׂה ose שָׁלוֹם shalom בִּמְרוֹמָיו bimromav ע"ב, ריבוע יהוה. הוּא hu

בְּרַחֲמָיו berachamav יַעֲשֶׂה ya'ase שָׁלוֹם shalom עָלֵינוּ alenu ר"ת ע"ע נהורין◆

וְעַל ve'al כָּל kol ילי ; עמם amo עַמּוֹ Yisrael יִשְׂרָאֵל ve'imru וְאָמְרוּ amen: אָמֵן

אָמֵן amen אידהנויה◆

ALENU

Alenu is a cosmic sealing agent. It cements and secures all of our prayers, protecting them from any negative forces such as the *klipot*. All prayers prior to *Alenu* drew down what the kabbalists call Inner Light. *Alenu*, however, attracts Surrounding Light, which envelops our prayers with a protective force-field to block out the *klipot*.

Drawing Surrounding Light in order to be protected from the *klipot* (negative side).

עָלֵינוּ alenu ריבוע דס"ג לְשַׁבֵּחַ leshabe'ach עלינו לשבוח = אבג יתץ, ושר

לַאֲדוֹן la'adon אני ; ס"ת ס"ג ע"ה הַכֹּל hakol ר"ת ללה, אדני

לָתֵת latet גְּדֻלָּה gedula לְיוֹצֵר leyotzer בְּרֵאשִׁית bereshit ר"ת גלב (באר"ך ב"י יג"ל)

שֶׁלֹּא shelo עָשָׂנוּ asanu כְּגוֹיֵי kegoyei הָאֲרָצוֹת ha'aratzot

וְלֹא velo שָׂמָנוּ samanu כְּמִשְׁפְּחוֹת kemishpechot הָאֲדָמָה ha'adama

---

May there be abundant peace from heaven, life, contentment, salvation, consolation, deliverance, healing, redemption, pardon, atonement, comfort, and relief. For us and for His entire nation, Israel, and you shall say, Amen. (Amen) He, Who makes peace in His high places, with His compassion He shall make peace for us and for His entire nation, Israel. And you shall say, Amen. (Amen)

ALENU

It is incumbent upon us to give praise to the Master of all and to attribute greatness to the Molder of Creation, for He did not make us like the nations of the lands. He did not place us like the families of the earth

שֶׁלֹּא shelo · שָׂם sam · וְחֶלְקֵנוּ chelkenu · כָּהֶם kahem · וְגוֹרָלֵנוּ vegoralenu

כְּכָל kechol · הֲמוֹנָם hamonam · שֶׁהֵם shehem · מִשְׁתַּחֲוִים mishtachavim

לַהֶבֶל lahevel · וָרִיק varik · וּמִתְפַּלְלִים umitpalelim · אֶל el · אֵל el

לֹא lo · יוֹשִׁיעַ Yoshi'a ·
(pause here, and when you say "va'anachnu mishtachavim" bow your entire body)

וַאֲנַחְנוּ va'anachnu · מִשְׁתַּחֲוִים mishtachavim · לִפְנֵי lifnei · מֶלֶךְ melech

מַלְכֵי malchei · הַמְּלָכִים hamelachim · הַקָּדוֹשׁ hakadosh · בָּרוּךְ baruch

הוּא hu · שֶׁהוּא shehu · נוֹטֶה note · שָׁמַיִם shamayim

וּמוֹשַׁב umoshav · אֶרֶץ aretz · וְיוֹסֵד veyosed

יְקָרוֹ yekaro · בַּשָּׁמַיִם bashamayim · מִמַּעַל mima'al

וּשְׁכִינַת ush'chinat · עֻזּוֹ uzo · בְּגָבְהֵי begovhei · מְרוֹמִים meromim

הוּא hu · אֱלֹהֵינוּ eloheinu · וְאֵין ve'ein · עוֹד od · אַחֵר acher

אֱמֶת emet · מַלְכֵּנוּ malkenu · וְאֶפֶס ve'efes

זוּלָתוֹ zulato · כַּכָּתוּב kakatuv · בַּתּוֹרָה batorah · וְיָדַעְתָּ veyadata

הַיּוֹם hayom · וַהֲשֵׁבֹתָ vahashevota · אֶל el

לְבָבֶךָ lvavecha · כִּי ki · יְהֹוָה Adonai · הוּא hu

הָאֱלֹהִים haElohim · בַּשָּׁמַיִם bashamayim · מִמַּעַל mima'al

וְעַל ve'al · הָאָרֶץ ha'aretz · מִתַּחַת mitachat

מִתָּחַת mitachat · אֵין en · עוֹד od

He did not make our lot like theirs and our destiny like that of their multitudes, for they prostrate themselves to futility and emptiness and they pray to a deity that does not help. But we prostrate ourselves before the King of all Kings, the Holy Blessed One. It is He Who spreads the Heavens and establishes the earth. The Seat of His glory is in the Heaven above and the Divine Presence of His power is in the Highest of Heights. He is our God and there is no other. Our King is true and there is none beside Him. As it is written in the Torah: "And you shall know today and you shall take it to your heart that it is the Lord Who is God in the Heavens above and upon the Earth below, and there is none other". (Deuteronomy 4:39)

עַל al כֵּן ken נְקַוֶּה nekave לְךָ lach יהוה Adonai אֱלֹהֵינוּ Elohenu

לִרְאוֹת lir'ot מְהֵרָה mehera בְּתִפְאֶרֶת betiferet עֻזָּךְ uzach

לְהַעֲבִיר leha'avir גִּלּוּלִים gilulim מִן min הָאָרֶץ ha'aretz

וְהָאֱלִילִים veha'elilim כָּרוֹת karot יִכָּרֵתוּן yikaretun לְתַקֵּן letaken

עוֹלָם olam בְּמַלְכוּת bemalchut שַׁדַּי Shadai וְכָל vechol בְּנֵי benei

בָשָׂר vasar יִקְרְאוּ yikre'u בִשְׁמֶךָ vishmecha לְהַפְנוֹת lehafnot אֵלֶיךָ eleicha

כָּל kol רִשְׁעֵי rish'ei אָרֶץ aretz יַכִּירוּ yakiru וְיֵדְעוּ veyed'u כָּל kol

יוֹשְׁבֵי yoshvei תֵבֵל tevel כִּי ki לְךָ lecha תִּכְרַע tichra כָּל kol

בֶּרֶךְ berech תִּשָּׁבַע tishava כָּל kol לָשׁוֹן lashon לְפָנֶיךָ lefanecha

יהוה Adonai אֱלֹהֵינוּ Elohenu יִכְרְעוּ yichre'u וְיִפֹּלוּ veyipolu

וְלִכְבוֹד velichvod שִׁמְךָ shimcha יְקָר yekar יִתֵּנוּ yitenu וִיקַבְּלוּ vikabelu

כֻלָּם chulam אֶת et עוֹל ol מַלְכוּתֶךָ malchutecha וְתִמְלֹךְ vetimloch

עֲלֵיהֶם alehem מְהֵרָה mehera לְעוֹלָם le'olam וָעֶד va'ed

כִּי ki הַמַּלְכוּת hamalchut שֶׁלְּךָ shelcha הִיא hee וּלְעוֹלְמֵי ul'olmei

עַד ad תִּמְלֹךְ timloch בְּכָבוֹד bechavod כַּכָּתוּב kakatuv

בְּתוֹרָתֶךָ betoratach יהוה Adonai יִמְלֹךְ yimloch לְעֹלָם le'olam

וָעֶד va'ed וְנֶאֱמַר vene'emar וְהָיָה vehaya

יהוה Adonai לְמֶלֶךְ lemelech עַל al כָּל kol

הָאָרֶץ ha'aretz בַּיּוֹם bayom

הַהוּא hahu יִהְיֶה yih'ye יהוה Adonai אֶחָד echad

וּשְׁמוֹ ushmo אֶחָד echad

Consequently, we place our hope in You, Lord, our God, that we shall speedily see the glory of Your might, when You remove the idols from the earth and the deities shall be completely destroyed to correct the world with the kingdom of the Almighty. And all mankind shall then call out Your Name and You shall turn back to Yourself all the wicked ones of the earth. Then all the inhabitants of the world shall recognize and know that, for You, every knee bends and every tongue vows. Before You, Lord, our God, they shall kneel and fall and shall give honor to Your glorious Name. And they shall all accept the yoke of Your Kingdom and You shall reign over them, forever and ever. Because the kingdom is Yours. and forever and for eternity, You shall reign gloriously. As it is written in the Torah: "The Lord shall reign forever and ever," (Exodus 15:18) and it is also stated: "The Lord shall be King over the whole world and, on that day, the Lord shall be One and His Name One." (Zechariah 14:9)

In the evening prayer of *Arvit*, we connect to Jacob the Patriarch, who is the channel for Central Column energy. He helps us connect the two energies of Judgment and Mercy in a balanced way. It is said that the whole world was created only for Jacob, who embodies truth: "Give truth to Jacob" (*Michah 7:20*). To activate the power of our prayer, and specifically the power of the prayer of *Arvit*, we must be truthful with others and, most importantly, with ourselves.

LeShem Yichud

לְשֵׁם leshem   יִוזוּד yichud   קוּדְשָׁא kudsha   בְּרִיךְ berich   הוּא hu

וּשְׁכִינְתֵּיה ush'chintei (יאהדונהי)   בִּדְוזִילוּ bid'chilu   וּרְוזִימוּ ur'chimu

(יאההויהה)   וּרְוזִימוּ ur'chimu   וּדְוזִילוּ ud'chilu (איההיוהה)   לְיַוזְדָּא leyachda

בְּיִוזוּדָא beyichuda   קֵי kei   בְּוא"ו bevav   קֵי kei   יו"ד yud   שֵׁם shem

שְׁלִים shelim (יהוה)   בְּשֵׁם beshem   כָּל kol   ילי   יִשְׂרָאֵל, Yisrael,

הִנֵּה hine   אֲנַוזְנוּ anachnu   בָּאִים ba'im   לְהִתְפַּלֵּל lehitpalel   תְּפִלַת tefilat

עַרְבִית arvit   שֶׁתִּקֵן shetiken   יַעֲקֹב Yaakov י הויה, יאהדונהי אידהנויה   אָבִינוּ avinu

עָלָיו alav   הַשָּׁלוֹם hashalom   עִם im   כָּל kol ילי   הַמִּצְווֹת hamitzvot

הַכְּלוּלוֹת hakelulot   בָּהּ ba   לְתַקֵּן letaken   אֶת et   שׁוֹרְשָׁהּ shorsha

בִּמְקוֹם bemakom   עֶלְיוֹן elyon   לַעֲשׂוֹת la'asot   נַוַזת nachat   רוּוַז ru'ach

לְיוֹצְרֵנוּ leyotzrenu   וְלַעֲשׂוֹת vela'asot   רָצוֹן retzon מהע ע"ה, ע"ב בריבוע וקס"א ע"ה,

אֵל שדי ע"ה   בּוֹרְאֵנוּ bor'enu.   וִיהִי vihi   נֹעַם no'am   אֲדֹנָי Adonai ללה

אֱלֹהֵינוּ Elohenu ילה   עָלֵינוּ alenu   וּמַעֲשֵׂה uma'ase   יָדֵינוּ yadenu

כּוֹנְנָה konena   עָלֵינוּ alenu   וּמַעֲשֵׂה uma'ase   יָדֵינוּ yadenu   כּוֹנְנֵהוּ konenehu:

THE ARVIT (EVENING) PRAYER
LESHEM YICHUD

For the sake of unification of The Holy Blessed One and His Shechinah, with fear and love and with love and fear, in order to unify The Name Yud-Kei and Vav-Kei in perfect unity, and in the name of Israel, we have hereby come to recite the prayer of Arvit, established by Jacob, our forefather, may peace be upon him, With all its commandments, to correct its root in the supernal place, to bring satisfaction to our Maker, and to fulfill the wish of our Creator. "And may the pleasantness of the Lord, our God, be upon us and may He establish the work of our hands for us and may the work of our hands establish Him." (Psalms 90:17)

Right

יְהֹוָ Adonai אֲדֹנָיאהדונהי צְבָאוֹת Tzeva'ot שׁכינה פְּנֵי imanu עִמָּנוּ

ריבוע ס"ג, קס"א וד' אותיות מ.ש.ה, מ.ה.ע, ריבוע ע"ב וקס"א, אל שדי, misgav מִשְׂגָּב

ד"פ אלהים ע"ה Elohei אֱלֹהֵי אדני אהיה אלהים, lanu לָנוּ מילוי ע"ב, דמב ; ילה

Yaakov יַעֲקֹב י' הויות, יאהדונהי אידהנויה sela סֶלָה:

Left

יְהֹוָ Adonai אֲדֹנָיאהדונהי צְבָאוֹת Tzeva'ot שׁכינה פְּנֵי ashrei אַשְׁרֵי

adam אָדָם מ"ה ; ה' צבאות אשרי אדם = תפארת bote'ach בֹּטֵחַ

בָּךְ bach אדם בוטח בך = אמן (יאהדונהי) ע"ה ; בוטח בך = מילוי ע"ב ע"ה:

Central

יְהֹוָ Adonai אֲדֹנָיאהדונהי hoshi'a הוֹשִׁיעָה יהוה וע"ע נהורין ר"ת יהה hamelech הַמֶּלֶךְ

kor'enu קָרְאֵנוּ ע"ה נגד, מזבוד, זן, אל יהוה veyom בְּיוֹם ya'anenu יַעֲנֵנוּ

ר"ת יב"ק, אלהים יהוה, אהיה אדני יהוה ; ס"ת = ב"ן ועם אות כ' דהמלך = ע"ב:

HALF KADDISH

יִתְגַּדַּל yitgadal וְיִתְקַדֵּשׁ veyitkadash שדי ומילוי שדי ; י"א אותיות כמנין ו"ה

שְׁמֵהּ shemei raba רַבָּא (שם י"ה דע"ב) קנ"א ב"ן, יהוה אלהים יהוה אדני,

מילוי קס"א וס"ג, מ"ה ברבוע וע"ב ע"ה ; ר"ת = ו"פ אלהים ; ס"ת = ג"פ יב"ק: amen אָמֵן אידהנויה.

בְּעָלְמָא be'alma di דִּי vera בְּרָא chir'utei כִרְעוּתֵהּ.

veyamlich וְיַמְלִיךְ mal'chutei מַלְכוּתֵהּ. veyatzmach וְיַצְמַח

פּוּרְקָנֵהּ purkanei. vikarev וִיקָרֵב meshichei מְשִׁיחֵהּ: amen אָמֵן אידהנויה.

"The Lord of Hosts, joyful is one who trusts in You." (Psalms 84:13)
"The Lord of Hosts is with us. The God of Jacob is a refuge for us, Selah.
Lord redeem us. The King shall answer us on the day we call Him." (Psalms 20:10)

HALF KADDISH
May His great Name be more exalted and sanctified. (Amen)
In the world that He created according to His will, and may His Kingdom reign.
And may He cause His redemption to sprout and may He bring the Mashiach closer. (Amen)

בְּחַיֵּיכוֹן bechayechon   וּבְיוֹמֵיכוֹן uvyomechon   וּבְחַיֵּיי uvchayei

דְכָל dechol   יל"י   בֵּית bet   ב"פ ראה   יִשְׂרָאֵל Yisrael   בַּעֲגָלָא ba'agala

וּבִזְמַן uvizman   קָרִיב kariv   וְאִמְרוּ ve'imru   אָמֵן amen   אָמֵן amen איד'הנויה

The congregation and the *chazan* say the following:

28 words (until *be'alma*) – meditate:
מילוי דמילוי דע"ב (יוד ויו דלת הי יוד ויו יוד ויו הי יוד)
28 letters (until *almaya*) – meditate:
מילוי דמילוי דס"ג (יוד ויו דלת הי יוד ואו אלף ואו הי יוד)

יְהֵא yehe   שְׁמֵיהּ shemei   (שם י"ה דס"ג)   רַבָּא raba   קנ"א ב"ן,

מְבָרַךְ mevarach   ע"ה ע"ב ברבוע וע"ב מ"ה וס"ג, מילוי קס"א ארני, יהוה אלהים יהוה

לְעָלַם le'alam   לְעָלְמֵי le'almei   עָלְמַיָּא almaya   יִתְבָּרַךְ yitbarach

Seven words with six letters each (שם בן מ"ב) – meditate:
יהוה ← יוד הי ויו הי ← מילוי דמילוי דע"ב (יוד ויו דלת הי יוד ויו יוד ויו הי יוד)
Also, seven times the letter Vav (שם בן מ"ב) – meditate:
יהוה ← יוד הי ואו הי ← מילוי דמילוי דס"ג (יוד ויו דלת הי יוד ואו אלף ואו הי יוד).

וְיִשְׁתַּבַּח veyishtabach   יפ ע"ב יהוה אל אבג יתץ

וְיִתְפָּאַר veyitpa'ar   הי גו יה קרע שטן   וְיִתְרַמַם veyitromam   וה כוו נגד יכש

וְיִתְנַשֵּׂא veyitnase   במוכסז בטר צתג   וְיִתְהַדָּר veyit'hadar   כוו יה וזקב טנע

וְיִתְעַלֶּה veyit'ale   וה יוד ה יגל פזק   וְיִתְהַלָּל veyit'halal   א ואו הא עקו צית

שְׁמֵיהּ shemei   (שם י"ה דמ"ה)   דְּקֻדְשָׁא dekudsha   בְּרִיךְ verich   הוּא hu

אָמֵן amen איד'הנויה

לְעֵלָּא le'ela   מִן min   כָּל kol   יל"י   בִּרְכָתָא birchata   שִׁירָתָא shirata

תֻּשְׁבְּחָתָא tishbechata   וְנֶחֱמָתָא venechamata   דַּאֲמִירָן da'amiran

בְּעָלְמָא be'alma   וְאִמְרוּ ve'imru   אָמֵן amen   אָמֵן amen איד'הנויה

In your lifetimes and in your days and in the lifetime of all the House of Israel, speedily and in the near future, and you should say, Amen. (Amen) May His great Name be blessed forever and for all eternity blessed and lauded, and glorified and exalted, and extolled and honored, and uplifted and praised be, the Name of the Holy Blessed One. (Amen) Above all blessings, songs, praises, and words of consolation that may be said in the world, and you shall say, Amen. (Amen)

VEHU RACHUM

"*Vehu Rachum*" contains thirteen words. The number thirteen denotes the Thirteen Attributes of Mercy, which, in this instance, we recite to cool down the fires of hell for all who reside there.

There are 13 words corresponding to the 13 Atributes of Mercy of *Arich Anpin*.

(*Abba of the klipa*) avon עָוֹן ר״ת רי״ו yechaper יְכַפֵּר rachum רַחוּם vehu וְהוּא

lehashiv לְהָשִׁיב vehirba וְהִרְבָּה (*Ima of the klipa*) yashchit יַשְׁחִית velo וְלֹא

chamato וַחֲמָתוֹ ילי kol כָּל ya'ir יָעִיר velo וְלֹא (*Zeir of the klipa*) apo אַפּוֹ

יהוה ועי״ע נהורין hoshi'a הוֹשִׁיעָה Adonai יְהֹוָה :(*Nukva of the klipa*)

זה אל יהוה מזבח, נגד, ע״ה veyom בְיוֹם ya'anenu יַעֲנֵנוּ ר״ת יהה hamelech הַמֶּלֶךְ

ע״ב = דהמלך כ׳ ועם ב״ן ס״ת ; אהיה אדני יהוה, אהיה אלהים יהוה, ר״ת יב״ק, kor'enu קָרְאֵנוּ

BARCHU

The *chazan* says:

Adonai יְהֹוָה et אֵת מ״ה ריבוע יהוה ריבוע יהוה barchu בָּרְכוּ

:ע״ה דוד בן משיחו כהת, ס״ת hamevorach הַמְבוֹרָךְ

First the congregation replies the following, and then the *chazan* repeats it:

Neshamah   *Ruach*   *Nefesh*

hamevorach הַמְבוֹרָךְ Adonai יְהֹוָה baruch בָּרוּךְ

Yechidah   *Chayah*

:va'ed וָעֶד אותיות דס״ג וי׳ ס״ג ריבוע le'olam לְעוֹלָם

VEHU RACHUM
And He is merciful,
forgives iniquity, and does not destroy; He frequently diverts His anger and does not arouse all His wrath."
(Psalms 70:38) *"Lord save us. The King shall answer on the day that we call Him." (Psalms 20:10)*
BARCHU
Bless the Lord, the Blessed One.
Blessed be the Lord, the Blessed One, forever and for eternity.

HaMa'ariv Aravim – First Chamber – Livnat Hasapir

In the time of *Arvit*, we have an opportunity to connect to four different "Chambers" in the House of the King - Chamber of Sapphire Stone (*Livnat Hasapir*), Chamber of Love (*Ahavah*), Chamber of Desire (*Ratzon*), and the Chamber of Holy of Holies (*Kodesh HaKodeshim*). Each Chamber connects us to another level in the spiritual plane. The blessing connecting us to the First Chamber, *Livnat Hasapir*, contains 53 words, which is also the numerical value of the word gan גַּן, meaning "garden," therefore connecting us to the Garden of Eden of our world.

Hechal Livnat Hasapir (the Sapphire Stone Chamber) of *Nukva* in *Beriah*.

baruch בָּרוּךְ Ata אַתָּה Adonai יְהֹוָאדֹנָיאהדונהי Elohenu אֱלֹהֵינוּ יכה

melech מֶלֶךְ ha'olam הָעוֹלָם asher אֲשֶׁר bidvaro בִּדְבָרוֹ ma'ariv מַעֲרִיב

aravim עֲרָבִים bechochmah בְּחָכְמָה (*Atzulut*) = בְּמִילוּי תרי"ג (מצוות)•

pote'ach פּוֹתֵחַ she'arim שְׁעָרִים כתר bitvuna בִּתְבוּנָה *(Beriah)*•

meshane מְשַׁנֶּה (*Yetzirah*) itim עִתִּים umachalif וּמַחֲלִיף et אֶת

hazemanim הַזְּמַנִּים (*Asiyah*) umsader וּמְסַדֵּר et אֶת hakochavim הַכּוֹכָבִים

•(*The Seven Planets*) bemishmerotehem בְּמִשְׁמְרוֹתֵיהֶם baraki'a בָּרָקִיעַ

kirtzono כִּרְצוֹנוֹ• bore בּוֹרֵא yomam יוֹמָם valayla וָלַיְלָה מלה• golel גּוֹלֵל

or אוֹר, אֵין סוֹף רוֹ, שֶׁךְ נִצוֹצוֹת שֶׁל וֹ' הַמְלֵכִים mipenei מִפְּנֵי choshech וְשֶׁךְ

vechoshech וְוֹשֶׁךְ שֶׁךְ נִצוֹצוֹת שֶׁל וֹ' הַמְלֵכִים mipenei מִפְּנֵי or אוֹר, רוֹ, אֵין סוֹף•

hama'avir הַמַּעֲבִיר yom יוֹם ע"ה נֶגֶד, מִזְבֵּחַ, זַ, אֵל יְהֹוה umevi וּמֵבִיא layla לַיְלָה

umavdil וּמַבְדִּיל ben בֵּין yom יוֹם ע"ה נֶגֶד, מִזְבֵּחַ, זַ, אֵל יְהֹוה uven וּבֵין

layla לַיְלָה מלה• Adonai יְהֹוָאדֹנָיאהדונהי Tzeva'ot צְבָאוֹת פְּנֵי שְׁכִינָה shemo שְׁמוֹ

baruch בָּרוּךְ מוֹהַשׁ ע"ה, ע"ב בְּרִבּוּעַ וקס"א ע"ה, אֵל שַׁדֵּי ע"ה, Adonai יְהֹוָאדֹנָיאהדונהי•

Ata אַתָּה Adonai יְהֹוָאדֹנָיאהדונהי hama'ariv הַמַּעֲרִיב aravim עֲרָבִים:

HaMa'ariv Aravim – First Chamber – Livnat Hasapir

Blessed are You, Lord, our God, King of the universe,
Who brings with His words evenings with wisdom. He opens gates with understanding. He changes the seasons and varies the times and arranges the stars in their constellations in the sky, according to His will. He creates day and night and rolls Light away from before darkness, and darkness from before Light. He is the One Who causes the day to pass and brings on night and separates between day and night. Lord of Hosts, His Name is the Lord. Blessed are You, Lord, who brings on evenings.

AHAVAT OLAM – SECOND CHAMBER - LOVE

This blessing connects us to the Second Chamber, *Ahavah* (Love) and its purpose is to inspire us with a renewed love for others and for the world.

Hechal Ahavah (the Love Chamber) of *Nukva* in *Beriah*.
The following paragraph has 50 words corresponding to the 50 Gates of *Binah*.

amecha עַמְּךָ Yisrael יִשְׂרָאֵל ב״פ ראה bet בֵּית olam עוֹלָם ahavat אַהֲבַת

chukim וְחֻקִּים (*Beriah*) umitzvot וּמִצְוֹת (*Atzilut*) torah תּוֹרָה ◆ahavta אָהַבְתָּ

◆limadeta לִמַּדְתָּ otanu אוֹתָנוּ (*Asiyah*) umishpatim וּמִשְׁפָּטִים (*Yetzirah*)

Elohenu אֱלֹהֵינוּ Adonai יְהֹוָה ken כֵּן al עַל

bechukecha בְּחֻקֶּיךָ nasi'ach נָשִׂיחַ uvkumenu וּבְקוּמֵנוּ beshochvenu בְּשָׁכְבֵנוּ

talmud תַּלְמוּד bedivrei בְּדִבְרֵי vena'aloz וְנַעֲלוֹז venismach וְנִשְׂמַח

vechukotecha וְחֻקּוֹתֶיךָ umitzvotecha וּמִצְוֹתֶיךָ toratecha תּוֹרָתֶךָ

hem הֵם ki כִּי ◆va'ed וָעֶד le'olam לְעוֹלָם

nehge נֶהְגֶּה uvahem וּבָהֶם yamenu יָמֵינוּ ve'orech וְאֹרֶךְ chayenu וְחַיֵּינוּ

tasur תָּסוּר lo לֹא ve'ahavatcha וְאַהֲבָתְךָ ◆ valayla וְלַיְלָה yomam יוֹמָם

Ata אַתָּה baruch בָּרוּךְ ◆le'olamim לְעוֹלָמִים mimenu מִמֶּנּוּ

Yisrael יִשְׂרָאֵל amo עַמּוֹ et אֶת ohev אוֹהֵב Adonai יְהֹוָה

THE SHEMA (to learn more about the *Shema* go to pg. 176)

The *Shema* is one of the most powerful tools to draw the energy of healing to our lives. The true power of the *Shema* is unleashed when we recite this prayer while meditating on others who need healing energy.

1) In order to receive the Light of the *Shema*, you have to accept upon yourself the precept of: "Love your neighbor as yourself," and see yourself united with all the souls that comprise the Original Adam.
2) You need to meditate to connect to the precept of the Reciting of *Shema* twice a day.
3) Before saying the *Shema* you should cover your eyes with your right hand (saying the words "*Shema Yisrael … le'olam va'ed*".) And you should read the *Shema* with deep meditation, chanting it with the intonations. It is necessary to be careful with the pronunciation of all the letters.

AHAVAT OLAM – SECOND CHAMBER - LOVE

With eternal love, You have loved Your Nation, the House of Israel.
Torah, commandments, statutes, and laws, You have taught us. Therefore, Lord, our God, when we lie down and when we rise up, we shall discuss Your statutes and we shall rejoice and exult in the words of the teachings of Your Torah, Your commandments, and Your statutes, forever and ever. They are our lifetimes and the length of our days; with them we shall direct ourselves day and night. And Your love, You shall never remove from us. Blessed are You, Lord, Who loves His Nation, Israel.

First, meditate in general, on the first *Yichud* of the four *Yichuds* of the Name: יהוה, and in particular, to awaken the letter ה, and then to connect it with the letter ו. Then connect the letter י and the letter ה together in the following order: *Hei* (ה), *Hei-Vav* (ה"ו), then *Yud-Hei* (י"ה), which adds up to 31, the secret of יא"י of the Name ס"ג. It is good to meditate on this *Yichud* before reciting any *Shema* because it acts as a replacement for the times that you may have missed reading the *Shema*. This *Yichud* has the same ability to create a Supernal connection like the reading of the *Shema* - to raise *Zeir* and *Nukva* together for the *Zivug* of *Abba* and *Ima*.

Shema – שׁמע

General Meditation: שם ע — to draw the energy from the seven lower *Sefirot* of *Ima* to the *Nukva*, which enables the *Nukva* to elevate the *Mayin Nukvin* (awakening from Below).
Particular Meditation: שם = יהוה + שׁדי and five times the letters י and ה of ב"ן = ע [The letter *Hei* (ה) is formed by the letters *Dalet* (ד) and *Yud* (י), so in ב"ן we have four times the letter ה plus another time the letters י and ד from יוד of ב"ן.]. Also the three letters ו (18) - that are left from ב"ן, plus ב"ן itself (52) equals ע (70).

Yisrael – יׁשׂראל

General Meditation: שׁיר אל — to draw energy from *Chesed* and *Gevurah* of *Abba* to *Zeir Anpin*, to do his action in the secret of *Mayin Duchrin* (awakening from Above).
Particular Meditation: (the rearranged letters of the word *Yisrael*) – שׁר אלי
אלהים דיודין (אלף למד הי יוד מם) = ע'י,
רבוע אלהים (א אל אלה אלהי אלהים) = ר'י,
מ"א אותיות רבוע אלהים במילואו (אלף אלף למד אלף למד הי אלף למד הי יוד אלף אלף למד הי יוד מם) = אל"י.
Also meditate to draw the Inner *Mochin* of *Abba* of *Katnut* into *Zeir Anpin*.

Adonai Elohenu Adonai - יהוה אלהינו יהוה

General Meditation: to draw energy to *Abba*, *Ima* and *Da'at* from *Arich Anpin*,
Particular Meditation: ע"ב (יוד הי ויו הי) קס"א (אלף הי יוד הי) ע"ב (יוד הי וי הי).

Echad – אוׄד
(The secret of the complete *Yichud-Unification*)

The letters *Alef* א and *Chet* ח from *Echad* אחד are *Zeir Anpin* and the letter *Dalet* ד is *Nukva*. **You should meditate** to devote your soul for the sanctification of the Holy Name, thereby elevating your *Nefesh*, *Ruach*, *Neshamah* and *Neshamah* of *Neshamah* with *Zeir Anpin* and *Nukva* (using the Names: ע"ב and ס"ג) to *Abba* and *Ima* as the secret of *Mayin Nukvin*, and by that energy, *Abba* and *Ima* will be unified in the secret of the Name: יאהבותיה. **Also meditate** to draw out the Inner Six Edges of *Gadlut* of *Ima* into *Zeir Anpin*. The Drop, which is ע"ב, is drawn out from the external of *Arich Anpin,* and descends to *Yesod* of *Ima*, where it becomes: ע"ב ס"ג מ"ה ב"ן, and the four spelled out אהיה (אלף הי יוד הי, אלף הי יוד הי, אלף הא יוד הא, אלף הה יוד הה) become Her clothing. As a result, *Zeir Anpin* now has four spelled out יה"ו (יוד הי ויו, יוד הי ואו, יוד הא ואו, יוד הה וו), four spelled out אה"י (אלף הי יוד, אלף הי יוד, אלף הא יוד, אלף הה יוד) and the Inner Six Edges of *Gadlut* of *Ima*. **Also meditate** on the Name: אל"ף ה"י וי"ו ה"י, which is the entire *Mochin* in the secret of *Da'at*. **And also meditate** (according to the Ramchal) on the four spelled out *Alef* (אלף=111) of the Name: אהי"ה that is equal to the word *Midat* (444), making the *Keter* for *Leah*.

Baruch Shem - ברוך שם כבוד מלכותו לעולם ועׄד
Baruch Shem Kevod — *Chochmah*, *Binah*, *Da'at* of *Leah*;
Malchuto — Her *Keter*; *Le'olam* — the rest of Her *Partzuf*;
Va'ed — the four היה (4 times 20 equal to *Va'ed*=80) will make the *Keter* for *Rachel* .
And the four spelled out היה (הי יוד הי, הי יוד הי, הא יוד הא, הה יוד הה) will make the rest of Her body.

שְׁמַע shema ע׳ רבתי יִשְׂרָאֵל Yisrael יְהֹוָ֥הּאדני־אהדונהי Adonai

אֱלֹהֵינוּ Elohenu ילה ד׳ רבתי יְהֹוָ֥הּאדני־אהדונהי Adonai | אֶחָ֑ד echad ד׳ רבתי ; אהבה, דאגה׃

(Whisper :) יוזו אותיות בָּרוּךְ baruch שֵׁם shem כְּבוֹד kevod מַלְכוּתוֹ malchuto,

לְעוֹלָם le'olam רביע דס״ג ו״י אותיות דס״ג וָעֶֽד va'ed׃

Yud, Chochmah, head — 42 words corresponding to the Holy 42-Letter Name of God.

א		ב

אֵת et (ה׳ של אהבת מ״ע לקיים יכוין ;) סוף אין ב״פ ,רז ב״פ ,אור ב״פ ve'ahavta וְאָהַבְתָּ֕

ג		י

ע״ה דוד בן משיוו ,כהת ס״ת ; ילה Elohecha אֱלֹהֶ֑יךָ Adonai יְהֹוָ֥הּאדני־אהדונהי

ת		ק		ר

בְּכָל־ bechol לכב ,ב״ן uvchol וּבְכָל־ levavcha לְבָבְךָ֥ לכב ,ב״ן nafshecha נַפְשְׁךָ֖ לכב ,ב״ן

ע		ע		ט		ז

uvchol וּבְכָל־ לכב ,ב״ן me'odecha מְאֹדֶֽךָ vehayu וְהָיֽוּ hadevarim הַדְּבָרִ֣ים

ז		ד		ז		כ

ha'ele הָאֵ֗לֶּה asher אֲשֶׁ֨ר anochi אָנֹכִ֧י metzavecha מְצַוְּךָ֛ hayom הַיּ֖וֹם

ר		ע		ב		ט

(pause here) על יהוה אל ,זן ,מזבוז ,גגר ע״ה al עַל־ levavecha לְבָבֶֽךָ׃ veshinantam וְשִׁנַּנְתָּ֣ם

ר		צ		ת		ג

levanecha לְבָנֶ֔יךָ vedibarta וְדִבַּרְתָּ֖ bam בָּ֑ם מ״ב beshivtecha בְּשִׁבְתְּךָ֤

ו		ב		ק		ב

bevetecha בְּבֵיתֶ֨ךָ֙ ב״פ ראה uvlechtecha וּבְלֶכְתְּךָ֣ vaderech בַדֶּ֔רֶךְ

ל		ט		ב

uvkumecha וּבְקוּמֶֽךָ׃ uvshochbecha וּֽבְשָׁכְבְּךָ֖ קס״א ס״ג יב״ק ב״פ

ל		ג		ע

yadecha יָדֶ֑ךָ al עַל־ le'ot לְא֖וֹת ukshartam וּקְשַׁרְתָּ֥ם

THE SHEMA

"Hear Israel, the Lord our God. The Lord is One." (Deuteronomy 6:4)

"Blessed is the glorious Name, His Kingdom is forever and for eternity." (Pesachim 56a)

"And you shall love the Lord, your God, with all your heart and with all your soul and with all that you possess. Let those words that I command you today be upon your heart. And you shall teach them to your children and you shall speak of them while you sit in your home and while you walk on your way and when you lie down and when you rise. You shall bind them as a sign upon your hand

עֵינֶיךָ enecha   בֵּין ben   לְטֹטָפֹת letotafot   וְהָיוּ vehayu

עַל al   וּכְתַבְתָּם uchtavtam   מ"ה: רִיבוּעַ ; קס"א ע"ה

מְזוּזוֹת mezuzot (זז מות) נית   בֵּיתֶךָ betecha ב"פ ראה   וּבִשְׁעָרֶיךָ: uvish'arecha

VEHAYA IM SHAMO'A

Hei, Binah, **arms and body** — 72 words corresponding to the 72 Names of God.

וְהָיָה vehaya יהוה ; יהוה אם im יה"ך, מ"א אותיות דפשוט, דמילוי ודמילוי דמילוי דאהיה ע"ה

שְׁמֹעַ shamo'a   תִּשְׁמְעוּ tishme'u   אֶל el   מִצְוֹתַי mitzvotai   אֲשֶׁר asher

אָנֹכִי anochi   מְצַוֶּה metzave   אֶתְכֶם etchem   הַיּוֹם hayom ע"ה נגד, מזבוח, זז, אל יהוה

לְאַהֲבָה le'ahava (pause here)   אֶת et   יְהֹוָה Adonai

אֱלֹהֵיכֶם Elohechem ילה (enunciate the letter *Ayin* in the word *"ul'ovdo"*)   וּלְעָבְדוֹ ul'ovdo

בְּכָל bechol   לְבַבְכֶם levavchem   וּבְכָל uvchol ב"ף, לכב

נַפְשְׁכֶם: nafshechem   וְנָתַתִּי venatati   מְטַר metar   אַרְצְכֶם artzechem

בְּעִתּוֹ be'ito   יוֹרֶה yore   וּמַלְקוֹשׁ umalkosh   וְאָסַפְתָּ ve'asafta   דְגָנֶךָ deganecha

וְתִירֹשְׁךָ vetiroshcha   וְיִצְהָרֶךָ: veyitz'harecha   וְנָתַתִּי venatati   עֵשֶׂב esev ע"ב שמות

---

and they shall be as frontlets between your eyes.
And you shall write them upon the doorposts of your house and your gates." (Deuteronomy 6:5-9)

VEHAYA IM SHAMO'A

"And it shall come to be that if you shall listen to My commandments that I am commanding you with today to love the Lord, your God, and to serve Him with all your heart and with all your soul, then I shall send rain upon your land in its proper time, both early rain and late rain. You shall then gather your grain and your wine and your oil. And I shall give grass

besadcha בְּשָׂדְךָ — livhemtecha לִבְהֶמְתֶּךָ — ve'achalta וְאָכַלְתָּ — vesavata וְשָׂבָעְתָּ:

hishamru הִשָּׁמְרוּ — lachem לָכֶם — pen פֶּן־ — yifte יִפְתֶּה — levavchem לְבַבְכֶם

vesartem וְסַרְתֶּם — va'avadetem וַעֲבַדְתֶּם — elohim אֱלֹהִים — acherim אֲחֵרִים

vehishtachavitem וְהִשְׁתַּחֲוִיתֶם — (הַקְּלִיפוֹת) — lahem לָהֶם:

vechara וְחָרָה — (pause here) — af אַף־ — Adonai יְהֹוָה/אֲדֹנָי — bachem בָּכֶם

ve'atzar וְעָצַר — et אֶת־ — hashamayim הַשָּׁמַיִם — velo וְלֹא־

yihye יִהְיֶה — matar מָטָר — veha'adama וְהָאֲדָמָה — lo לֹא — titen תִתֵּן

et אֶת־ — yevula יְבוּלָהּ — va'avadetem וַאֲבַדְתֶּם — mehera מְהֵרָה — me'al מֵעַל

ha'aretz הָאָרֶץ — hatova הַטֹּבָה — asher אֲשֶׁר

Adonai יְהֹוָה/אֲדֹנָי — noten נֹתֵן — lachem לָכֶם:

Vav, Zeir Anpin

stomach — 50 words corresponding to the 50 Gates of *Binah* — vesamtem וְשַׂמְתֶּם

et אֶת־ — devarai דְּבָרַי — ele אֵלֶּה — al עַל־ — levavchem לְבַבְכֶם

ve'al וְעַל־ — nafshechem נַפְשְׁכֶם — ukshartem וּקְשַׁרְתֶּם — otam אֹתָם

---

in your field for your cattle. And you shall eat and you shall be satiated. Be careful lest your heart be seduced and you may turn away and serve alien deities and prostrate yourself before them. And the wrath of the Lord shall be upon you and He shall stop the Heavens and there shall be no more rain and the earth shall not give forth its crop. And you shall quickly perish from the good land that the Lord has given you. And you shall place those words of Mine upon your heart and upon your soul and you shall bind them

לְאוֹת le'ot | ר"ת | לאו | עַל־ al | יֶדְכֶם yedchem | וְהָיוּ vehayu

לְטוֹטָפֹת letotafot | בֵּין ben | עֵינֵיכֶם enechem | ריבוע | מ"ה:

וְלִמַּדְתֶּם velimadetem | אֹתָם otam | אֶת־ et | בְּנֵיכֶם benechem

לְדַבֵּר ledaber | ראה | בָּם bam | שׂים | בן | מ"ב | בְּשִׁבְתְּךָ beshivtecha

בְּבֵיתֶךָ bevetecha | ב"פ ראה | וּבְלֶכְתְּךָ uvlechtecha | בַדֶּרֶךְ vaderech | ב"פ יב"ק, ס"ג קס"א

וּבְשָׁכְבְּךָ uvshochbecha | וּבְקוּמֶךָ uvkumecha | וּכְתַבְתָּם uchtavtam | עַל־ al

מְזוּזוֹת mezuzot | בֵּיתֶךָ betecha | ב"פ ראה | וּבִשְׁעָרֶיךָ uvish'arecha | לְמַעַן lema'an

יִרְבּוּ yirbu | יְמֵיכֶם yemechem | ר"ת | ייל | וִימֵי vimei | בְּנֵיכֶם venechem

עַל al | הָאֲדָמָה ha'adama | אֲשֶׁר asher | (enunciate the letter *Ayin* in the word "*nishba*")

נִשְׁבַּע nishba | יכוין | לשבועת | המבול | יְהֹוָה Adonai

לַאֲבֹתֵיכֶם la'avotechem | לָתֵת latet | לָהֶם lahem | כִּימֵי kimei

הַשָּׁמַיִם hashamayim | י"פ טל, י"פ כוזו | עַל־ al | הָאָרֶץ ha'aretz | אלהים דההין ע"ה:

---

as a sign upon your hands and they shall be as frontlets between your eyes. And you shall teach them to your children and speak of them while you sit at home and while you walk on your way and when you lie down and when you rise. You shall write them upon the doorposts of your house and upon your gates. This is so that your days shall be numerous and so shall the days of your children upon the Earth that the Lord had sworn to your fathers to give them as the days of the Heavens upon the Earth." (Deuteronomy 11:13-21)

VAYOMER

Hei, *Malchut,* legs and reproductive organs,

72 words corresponding to the 72 Names of God in direct order (according to the Ramchal).

עאם	סבט	ייי	ווו
Moshe מֹשֶׁה	el אֶל־	Adonai יְהֹוָה	vayomer וַיֹּאמֶר

אנא	ליה	מבטע	
el אֶל־	ראה daber דַּבֵּר	lemor לֵאמֹר	מהטע, ע"ב בריבוע וקס"א, אל עדי, ד"פ אלהים ע"ה

הטע	להו	אנד	הוי	כמת
ve'asu וְעָשׂוּ	alehem אֲלֵהֶם	ve'amarta וְאָמַרְתָּ	Yisrael יִשְׂרָאֵל	benei בְּנֵי

לוו	הטם	היי	מרה	יצל
vigdehem בִּגְדֵיהֶם	kanfei כַּנְפֵי	al עַל־	tzitzit צִיצִת	lahem לָהֶם

נמך	פֹל	ליו	כבי
tzitzit צִיצִת	al עַל־	venatnu וְנָתְנוּ	ledorotam לְדֹרֹתָם

וזהו	מנה		
techelet תְּכֵלֶת:	י"פ ב"ן petil פְּתִיל	ע"ה קנ"א, אדני אלהים	hakanaf הַכָּנָף

רלי	שאה	ירת	השא	גיה
oto אֹתוֹ	ur'item וּרְאִיתֶם	letzitzit לְצִיצִת	lachem לָכֶם יהה ; יהוה	vehaya וְהָיָה

לההו	ייו	והר	ליב	אום
Adonai יְהֹוָה	mitzvot מִצְוֹת	kol כָּל־ ילי	et אֶת־	uzchartem וּזְכַרְתֶּם

רהע	וזם	אני	מנד	כעק
acharei אַחֲרֵי	taturu תָתוּרוּ	velo וְלֹא־	otam אֹתָם	va'asitem וַעֲשִׂיתֶם

מכב	העה	יוזז
enechem עֵינֵיכֶם מ"ה ריבוע	ve'acharei וְאַחֲרֵי	levavchem לְבַבְכֶם

You should meditate on the precept:
"not to follow negative sexual thoughts of the heart and the sights of the eyes for prostitution."

VAYOMER

"And the Lord spoke to Moses and said,
Speak to the Children of Israel and say to them that they should make for themselves Tzitzit,
on the corners of their garments, throughout all their generations. And they must place upon the Tzitzit,
of each corner, a blue strand. And this shall be to you as a Tzitzit: you shall see it and remember
the commandments of the Lord and fulfill them. And you shall not stray after your hearts and your eyes,

אֲשֶׁר asher אַתֶּם atem זֹנִים zonim אַחֲרֵיהֶם acharehem לְמַעַן lema'an

תִּזְכְּרוּ tizkeru וַעֲשִׂיתֶם va'asitem אֶת et כָּל kol מִצְוֺתָי mitzvotai

וִהְיִיתֶם vihyitem קְדֹשִׁים kedoshim לֵאלֹהֵיכֶם lelohechem

אָנִי ani יְהֹוָה Adonai אֱלֹהֵיכֶם Elohechem אֲשֶׁר asher

הוֹצֵאתִי hotzeti אֶתְכֶם etchem מֵאֶרֶץ me'eretz מִצְרַיִם Mitzrayim

---

You should meditate to remember the exodus from *Mitzrayim* (Egypt).

לִהְיוֹת lihyot לָכֶם lachem לֵאלֹהִים lelohim אֱהֶיה ; אֲדֹנָי

אָנִי ani יְהֹוָה Adonai אֱלֹהֵיכֶם Elohechem

Be careful to complete this paragraph together with the *chazan* and the congregation, and say the word "*emet*" out loud. The *chazan* should say the word "*emet*" in silence.

אֱמֶת emet אהיה פעמים אהיה, ז"פ ס"ג

The congregation should be silent, listen and hear the words "*Adonai Elohechem emet*" spoken by the *chazan*. If you did not complete the paragraph together with the *chazan* you should repeat the last three words on your own. With these three words the *Shema* is completed.

יְהֹוָה Adonai אֱלֹהֵיכֶם Elohechem

אֱמֶת emet אהיה פעמים אהיה, ז"פ ס"ג

---

after which you adulterate. This is so that you shall remember to fulfill all My commandments and thereby be holy before your God. I am the Lord, your God, Who brought you out of the land of Egypt to be your God. I, the Lord, your God, Is true." (Numbers 15:37-41) the Lord, your God, is true!

VE'EMUNA – THIRD CHAMBER – RATZON

Ve'emuna connects us to the Third Chamber in the House of the King: *Ratzon,* or desire. Before we can connect to any form of spiritual energy, we need to feel a want or desire. Desire is the vessel that draws spiritual Light. A small desire draws a small amount of Light. A large desire draws a large amount.

Hechal Ratzon (the Desire Chamber) of *Nukva* in *Beriah.*

וֶאֱמוּנָה ve'emuna (בוֹויעת לילה) כָּל kol ילי זֹאת zot וְקַיָּם vekayam עָלֵינוּ alenu,

כִּי ki הוּא hu יְהֹוָה Adonai ילה אֱלֹהֵינוּ Elohenu וְאֵין ve'en

זוּלָתוֹ zulato. וַאֲנַחְנוּ va'anachnu יִשְׂרָאֵל Yisrael עַמּוֹ amo.

הַפּוֹדֵנוּ hapodenu מִיַּד miyad מְלָכִים melachim. הַגּוֹאֲלֵנוּ hago'alenu

מַלְכֵּנוּ malkenu מִכַּף mikaf כָּל kol יל עָרִיצִים aritzim.

הָאֵל haEl לאה ; יא"י (מילוי דס"ג) הַנִּפְרָע hanifra לָנוּ lanu אלהים, אהיה אדני

מִצָּרֵנוּ mitzarenu. הַמְשַׁלֵּם hameshalem גְּמוּל gemul לְכָל lechol יה אדני

אוֹיְבֵי oyvei נַפְשֵׁנוּ nafshenu: הַשָּׂם hasam נַפְשֵׁנוּ nafshenu

בַּחַיִּים bachayim אהיה אהיה יהוה, בינה ע"ה וְלֹא־ velo נָתַן natan לַמּוֹט lamot

רַגְלֵנוּ raglenu. הַמַּדְרִיכֵנוּ hamadrichenu עַל al בָּמוֹת bamot

אוֹיְבֵינוּ oyvenu; עמם יל כָּל kol עַל al קַרְנֵנוּ karnenu וַיָּרֶם vayarem

שׂוֹנְאֵינוּ son'enu. הָאֵל haEl לאה ; יא"י (מילוי דס"ג) הָעוֹשֶׂה ha'ose

לָנוּ lanu אלהים, אהיה אדני נִסִּים nisim וּנְקָמָה unkama בְּפַרְעֹה beFar'o.

בְּאוֹתוֹת be'otot וּבְמוֹפְתִים uvmoftim בְּאַדְמַת be'admat בְּנֵי benei

וְ... Cham. הַמַּכֶּה hamake בְּעֶבְרָתוֹ ve'evrato כָּל kol יל

בְּכוֹרֵי bechorei מִצְרָיִם Mitzrayim מצר. וַיּוֹצִיא vayotzi אֵת et

עַמּוֹ amo יִשְׂרָאֵל Yisrael מִתּוֹכָם mitocham לְחֵרוּת lecherut עוֹלָם olam.

VE'EMUNA – THIRD CHAMBER - RATZON

And trustworthy. All this and He are set upon us because He is the Lord, our God, and there is none other. And we are Israel, His Nation. He redeems us from the hands of kings. He is our King, Who delivers us from the reach of tyrants; The God, Who avenges us against our enemies. He pays our mortal enemies their due. He Who keeps us alive and does not allow our feet to falter; He Who lets us walk upon the plains of our foes. He Who raises our worth over all our enemies. He is God, Who wrought for us retribution against Pharaoh, with signs and wonders, in the land of the children of Cham. He Who struck down with His anger at the first-born of Egypt, and brought out His Nation, Israel, from amongst them to everlasting freedom.

הַמַּעֲבִיר hama'avir בָּנָיו banav

בֵּין ben גִּזְרֵי gizrei יָם yam ילי סוּף Suf ◆ וְאֶת ve'et רוֹדְפֵיהֶם rodfehem

וְאֶת ve'et שׂוֹנְאֵיהֶם son'ehem בִּתְהוֹמוֹת bitehomot טִבַּע tiba ◆ רָאוּ ra'u

בָנִים vanim אֶת et גְּבוּרָתוֹ gevurato שִׁבְּחוּ shibechu וְהוֹדוּ vehodu אהיה

וּמַלְכוּתוֹ umalchuto ◆ לִשְׁמוֹ lishmo

קִבְּלוּ kibelu בְּרָצוֹן beratzon

מֹשֶׁה Moshe ◆ עֲלֵיהֶם alehem

עָנוּ anu לְךָ lecha יִשְׂרָאֵל Yisrael וּבְנֵי uvnei

כֻּלָּם chulam: וְאָמְרוּ ve'amru רַבָּה raba בְּשִׂמְחָה besimcha שִׁירָה shira

יהוה Adonai בָּאֵלִם ba'elim כָּמֹכָה chamocha ילי מִי mi

נֶאְדָּר nedar כָּמֹכָה kamocha ילי מִי mi

תְהִלֹת tehilot נוֹרָא nora בַּקֹּדֶשׁ bakodesh

יהוה Adonai מַלְכוּתְךָ malchutcha פֶלֶא fele: עֹשֵׂה ose

אֱלֹהֵינוּ Elohenu ילה רָאוּ ra'u בָנֶיךָ vanecha עַל־ al הַיָּם hayam ילי

יוד yachad כֻּלָּם kulam הוֹדוּ hodu אהיה וְהִמְלִיכוּ vehimlichu

לְעֹלָם le'olam יִמְלֹךְ yimloch יהוה Adonai | וְאָמְרוּ ve'amru:

פָּדָה fada כִּי ki וְנֶאֱמַר vene'emar: וָעֶד va'ed ◆

יהוה Adonai אֶת et יַעֲקֹב Yaakov

בָּרוּךְ baruch מִמֶּנּוּ mimenu: חָזָק chazak מִיַּד miyad וּגְאָלוֹ ug'alo

יִשְׂרָאֵל Yisrael: גָּאַל ga'al יהוה Adonai אַתָּה Ata

He Who caused His Children to pass between the sections of the Sea of Reeds, while their pursuers and their enemies, He drowned in the depths. The Children saw His might and they praised and gave thanks to His Name; they accepted His sovereignty over them willingly. Moses and the Children of Israel raised their voices in song to Him, with great joy, and they all said, as one "Who is like You among the gods, Lord? Who is like You, awesome in holiness, tremendous in praise and Who works wonders?" (Exodus 15:11) Our Children saw Your Kingdom, Lord, our God, upon the sea, and they all in unison gave thanks to You and accepted Your sovereignty and said: "The Lord shall reign forever and ever." (Exodus 15:18) And it is stated: "For the Lord has delivered Jacob and redeemed him from the hand of one that is stronger than he." (Jeremiah 31:10) Blessed are You, Lord, Who redeemed Israel.

HASHKIVENU – FOURTH CHAMBER – HOLY OF HOLIES

The Fourth Chamber is *Kodesh HaKodeshim,* the Holy of Holies, which is our link to the next level that we reach through the *Amidah.*

Hechal Kodesh HaKodashim (the Holy of Holies Chamber) of *Nukva* in *Beriah.*

לאה ר"ת leshalom לְשָׁלוֹם avinu אָבִינוּ hashkivenu הַשְׁכִּיבֵנוּ

אהיה אהיה יהוה, בינה ע"ה lechayim לְחַיִּים malkenu מַלְכֵּנוּ veha'amidenu וְהַעֲמִידֵנוּ

alenu עָלֵינוּ ufros וּפְרוֹשׂ ulshalom וּלְשָׁלוֹם tovim טוֹבִים

סֻכַּת sukat סוכה = סאל, אמן (יאהדונהי) shelomecha שְׁלוֹמֶךָ vetakenenu וְתַקְּנֵנוּ

ס"ג מ"ה ב"ן milfanecha מִלְּפָנֶיךָ אכא tova טוֹבָה be'etza בְּעֵצָה malkenu מַלְכֵּנוּ

shemecha שְׁמֶךָ lema'an לְמַעַן mehera מְהֵרָה vehoshi'enu וְהוֹשִׁיעֵנוּ

makat מַכַּת me'alenu מֵעָלֵינוּ vehaser וְהָסֵר ba'adenu בַּעֲדֵנוּ vehagen וְהָגֵן

מ"ה עם ד' אותיות choli וְחוֹלִי = וזולה cherev וְחֶרֶב dever דֶּבֶר oyev אוֹיֵב

veyagon וְיָגוֹן ra'av רָעָב רהע ra'a רָעָה אלהים דההין tzara צָרָה

vehaser וְהָסֵר shevor שְׁבוֹר umagefa וּמַגֵּפָה umashchit וּמַשְׁחִית

uvtzel וּבְצֵל ume'acharenu וּמֵאַחֲרֵינוּ milfanenu מִלְּפָנֵינוּ hasatan הַשָּׂטָן

tzetenu צֵאתֵנוּ ushmor וּשְׁמוֹר tastirenu תַּסְתִּירֵנוּ kenafecha כְּנָפֶיךָ

tovim טוֹבִים אהיה יהוה, בינה ע"ה lechayim לְחַיִּים uvo'enu וּבוֹאֵנוּ

יא"י El אֵל ki כִּי olam עוֹלָם ve'ad וָעַד me'ata מֵעַתָּה ulshalom וּלְשָׁלוֹם

(מילוי דס"ג) shomrenu שׁוֹמְרֵנוּ כ"א הויות שובתפילין umatzilenu וּמַצִּילֵנוּ Ata אַתָּה

מלה layla לַיְלָה umipachad וּמִפַּחַד ra רַע רָע ראה davar דָּבָר ילי mikol מִכָּל

כ"א הויות שובתפילין shomer שׁוֹמֵר Adonai יְהֹוָה אדניאיאהדונהי Ata אַתָּה baruch בָּרוּךְ

יאהדונהי amen אָמֵן ב"ן ב"פ la'ad לָעַד Yisrael יִשְׂרָאֵל amo עַמּוֹ et אֶת

HASHKIVENU – FOURTH CHAMBER – HOLY OF HOLIES

Lay us down in peace, Father, and stand us up, our King, for good life and for peace. Spread over us Your protection of peace. Set us straight with good counsel from You and save us speedily for the sake of Your Name. And remove from us the blow of our enemy, pestilence, sword, illness, distress, evil, famine, sorrow, ruin, and plague. Destroy and remove Satan from before us and from behind us. Hide us in the shade of Your Wings and watch over our goings and our comings, for a good life and for peace, from now and until eternity. For You, God, are our Guardian and our Rescuer from all evil things and from the terror of the night. Blessed are You, Lord, Who guards His Nation, Israel, forever. Amen!

ARVIT – EVENING PRAYER
SWEETENING SOFT JUDGMENT

HALF KADDISH

יִתְגַּדַּל veyitkadash וְיִתְקַדַּשׁ עוֹדִי וּמִילוּי עוֹדִי ; י"א אוֹתִיוֹת כְּמִנְיַן ו"ה

שְׁמֵיהּ shemei (שֵׁם י"ה דע"ב) רַבָּא raba קנ"א ב"ן, יהוה אלהים יהוה אדני,

מִילוּי קס"א וס"ג, מ"ה בְּרִבּוּעַ וע"ב ע"ה ; ר"ת = ו"פ אלהים ; ס"ת = ג"פ יב"ק: אָמֵן amen אִידַהֲנוּיֵהּ.

כִּרְעוּתֵיהּ chir'utei בְּרָא vera דִּי di בְּעָלְמָא be'alma

וְיַצְמַח veyatzmach מַלְכוּתֵיהּ malchutei וְיַמְלִיךְ veyamlich

פּוּרְקָנֵיהּ purkanei מְשִׁיחֵיהּ meshichei: וִיקָרֵב vikarev אָמֵן amen אִידַהֲנוּיֵהּ.

וּבְחַיֵּי uvchayei וּבְיוֹמֵיכוֹן uvyomechon בְּחַיֵּיכוֹן bechayechon

בַּעֲגָלָא ba'agala יִשְׂרָאֵל Yisrael ב"פ ראה בֵּית bet יב"י דְּכָל dechol

וּבִזְמַן uvizman קָרִיב kariv וְאִמְרוּ ve'imru אָמֵן amen: אָמֵן amen אִידַהֲנוּיֵהּ.

The congregation and the *chazan* say the following:

28 words (until *be'alma*) – meditate: (יוד ויו דלת הי יוד ויו יוד ויו הי יוד) מילוי דמילוי דע"ב
28 letters (until *almaya*) - meditate: (יוד ויו דלת הי יוד ויו יוד ויו הי יוד) מילוי דמילוי דע"ב

יְהֵא yehe שְׁמֵיהּ shemei (שֵׁם י"ה דס"ג) רַבָּא raba קנ"א ב"ן,

מְבָרַךְ mevarach יהוה אלהים יהוה אדני, מילוי קס"א וס"ג, מ"ה בְּרִבּוּעַ וע"ב ע"ה

יִתְבָּרַךְ yitbarach עָלְמַיָּא almaya לְעָלְמֵי le'almei לְעָלַם le'alam

---

HALF KADDISH
May His great Name be more exalted and sanctified. (Amen)
In the world that He created according to His will, and may His kingdom reign. And may He cause His redemption to sprout and may He bring the Mashiach closer. (Amen) In your lifetimes and in your days and in the lifetime of all the House of Israel, speedily and in the near future, and you should say, Amen. (Amen) May His great Name be blessed forever and for all eternity blessed

Seven words with six letters each (שֵׁם בֶּן מ"ב) – meditate:

יהוה ▪ יוד הי ויו הי ▪ מילוי דמילוי דע"ב (יוד ויו דלת הי יוד ויו הי ויו הי יוד)

Also, seven times the letter Vav (שֵׁם בֶּן מ"ב) – meditate:

יהוה ▪ יוד הי ויו הי ▪ מילוי דמילוי דע"ב (יוד ויו דלת הי יוד ויו הי ויו הי יוד).

veyishtabach וְיִשְׁתַּבַּח י"פ ע"ב יהוה אל אבג יתץ.

veyitpa'ar וְיִתְפָּאַר הי גו יה קרע שטן. וְיִתְרַמֵּם veyitromam וה כוזו נגד יכש.

veyitnase וְיִתְנַשֵּׂא במוכסז בטר צתג. וְיִתְהַדָּר veyit'hadar כוזו יה וזקב טנע.

veyit'ale וְיִתְעַלֶּה וה' יוד ה יגל פזק. וְיִתְהַלָּל veyit'halal א ואו הא שקו צית.

shemei שְׁמֵיהּ (שֵׁם י"ה דמ"ה) דְּקוּדְשָׁא dekudsha בְּרִיךְ verich הוּא hu:

אָמֵן amen אידהנויה.

le'ela לְעֵלָּא min מִן kol כָּל יל' birchata בִּרְכָתָא shirata שִׁירָתָא.

be'alma בְּעָלְמָא ve'imru וְאָמְרוּ amen אָמֵן: amen אָמֵן אידהנויה. tishbechata תֻּשְׁבְּחָתָא venechamata וְנֶחֱמָתָא da'amiran דַּאֲמִירָן.

THE AMIDAH (to learn more about the *Amidah* go to pg. 189)

When we begin the connection, we take three steps backward, signifying our leaving this physical world. Then we take three steps forward to begin the *Amidah*. The three steps are:

1. Stepping into the land of Israel – to enter the first spiritual circle.
2. Stepping into the city of Jerusalem – to enter the second spiritual circle.
3. Stepping inside the Holy of Holies – to enter the innermost circle.

Before we recite the first verse of the *Amidah*, we ask: "*God, open my lips and let my mouth speak,*" thereby asking the Light to speak for us so that we can receive what we need and not just what we want. All too often, what we want from life is not necessarily the desire of the soul, which is what we actually need to fulfill us. By asking the Light to speak through us, we ensure that our connection will bring us genuine fulfillment and opportunities for spiritual growth and change.

and lauded, and glorified and exalted, And extolled and honored,
and uplifted and praised, be the Name of the Holy Blessed One. (Amen) Above all blessings,
songs, praises, and words of consolation that may be said in the world, and you shall say, Amen. (Amen)

yagid יַגִּיד ufi וּפִי tiftach תִּפְתָּח sefatai שְׂפָתַי (pause here) ללה Adonai אֲדֹנָי

ייו (כ"ב אותיות פשוטות [=אכא] וה' אותיות סופיות מזוזר) tehilatecha תְּהִלָּתֶךָ ס"ת = בוכו:

THE FIRST BLESSING - INVOKES THE SHIELD OF ABRAHAM.

Abraham is the channel of the Right Column energy of positivity, sharing, and mercy. Sharing actions can protect us from all forms of negativity.

Chesed that becomes *Chochmah*

In this section there are 42 words, the secret of the 42-Letter Name of God and therefore it begins with the letter *Bet* (2) and ends with the letter *Mem* (40).

Bend your knees at *'baruch'*, bow at *'Ata'* and straighten up at *'Adonai'*.

המלכות לה' (אותיות הא"ב המסמלות את השפע המגיע) א–ת Ata אַתָּה baruch בָּרוּךְ

ילה   Elohenu אֱלֹהֵינוּ   (יא)   Adonai יְהֹוָ֒ה

avotenu אֲבוֹתֵינוּ ילה ; דמב ע"ב, מילוי ; לכב velohei וֵאלֹהֵי

(Chochmah) Avraham אַבְרָהָם ילה ; דמב ע"ב, מילוי Elohei אֱלֹהֵי
וו"פ אל, רי"ו ול"ב נתיבות החוכמה, רמ"ח (אברים), עסמ"ב, וט"ז אותיות פשוטות

ד"פ ב"ן (Binah) Yitzchak יִצְחָק ילה ; דמב ע"ב, מילוי Elohei אֱלֹהֵי

הויות, יאהדונהי אידהנויה ד' (Da'at) Yaakov יַעֲקֹב ילה ; דמב ; ע"ב מילוי ; לכב velohei וֵאלֹהֵי

לההו = גדול ; סיט = האל הגדול hagadol הַגָּדוֹל (מילוי דס"ג) ייא"י ; לאה haEl הָאֵל

vehanora וְהַנּוֹרָא ר"ת ההה hagibor הַגִּבּוֹר אום ,יזל מבה = אותיות ד' עם

THE AMIDAH

"My Lord, open my lips, and my mouth shall relate Your praise." (Psalms 51:17)

THE FIRST BLESSING

Blessed are You, Lord, our God and God of our forefathers:
the God of Abraham, the God of Isaac, and the God of Jacob. The great, mighty and awesome God.

אֵל El יא"י (מילוי דס"ג) ; ר"ת ע"ב, ; ר"ת ע"ב, ריבוע יהוה עֶלְיוֹן elyon

גּוֹמֵל gomel וַחֲסָדִים chasadim טוֹבִים tovim קוֹנֶה kone הַכֹּל hakol

וְזוֹכֵר vezocher חַסְדֵי chasdei אָבוֹת avot וּמֵבִיא umevi

גּוֹאֵל go'el לִבְנֵי livnei בְנֵיהֶם venehem לְמַעַן lema'an

שְׁמוֹ shemo מהש ע"ה, ע"ב בריבוע וקס"א ע"ה, אל שדי ע"ה בְּאַהֲבָה be'ahava אוזר, ראגה

When saying the word *"be'ahava"* you should meditate to devote your soul to sanctify the Holy Name and accept upon yourself the four forms of death.

During the days between *Rosh Hashanah* and *Yom Kippur* we say the prayer of "zochrenu":

זָכְרֵנוּ zochrenu לְחַיִּים lechayim אהיה אהיה יהוה, בינה ע"ה.

מֶלֶךְ melech וְחָפֵץ chafetz בַּחַיִּים bachayim אהיה אהיה יהוה, בינה ע"ה.

כָּתְבֵנוּ kotvenu בְּסֵפֶר besefer וְחַיִּים chayim אהיה אהיה יהוה, בינה ע"ה.

לְמַעֲנָךְ lema'anach אֱלֹהִים Elohim אהיה אדני ; ילה וְחַיִּים chayim אהיה אהיה יהוה, בינה ע"ה.

If you forget to say "zochrenu" and realize this before the end of the blessing ("baruch Ata Adonai"), you should return and say "zochrenu" and continue as usual. But if you realize this only after the end of the blessing, you should continue and you may add "zochrenu" in "shome'a tefila" or at the end of "Elohai netzor."

מֶלֶךְ melech עוֹזֵר ozer וּמוֹשִׁיעַ umoshi'a וּמָגֵן umagen

ג"פ אל (יא"י מילוי דס"ג) ; ר"ת ביכאל גבריאל נוריאל

Bend your knees at 'baruch', bow at 'Ata' and straighten up at 'Adonai'.

בָּרוּךְ baruch אַתָּה Ata יְהֹוָה (אהיה)(יהוה)יאהדונהי Adonai (הד)

(During the three weeks of *Ben HaMetzarim* meditate on the Holy Name: טרהד)

מָגֵן magen ג"פ אל (יא"י מילוי דס"ג) ; ר"ת ביכאל גבריאל נוריאל אַבְרָהָם Avraham

וז"פ אל, רי"ו ול"ב נתיבות החוכמה, רמ"ח (אברים), עסמ"ב ומ"ז אותיות פשוטות:

The Supernal God, Who bestows beneficial kindness and creates everything. Who recalls the kindness of the forefathers and brings a Redeemer to their descendants for the sake of His Name, lovingly.

During the days between *Rosh Hashanah* and *Yom Kippur*:
Remember us for life, King, Who desires life, and inscribe us in the Book of Life, for Your sake, Living God.

King, Helper, Savior and Shield. Blessed are You, Lord, the shield of Abraham.

THE SECOND BLESSING

THE ENERGY OF ISAAC IGNITES THE POWER FOR THE RESURRECTION OF THE DEAD.

Whereas Abraham represents the power of sharing, Isaac represents the Left Column energy of judgment. Judgment shortens the *Tikkun* process and paves the way for our eventual resurrection (footnote A - pg. 189).

Gevurah that becomes *Binah*.

In this section there are 49 words corresponding to the 49 gates of the Pure System in *Binah*.

ללה Adonai אֲדֹנָי רִיבּוֹעַ ס"ג ו' אותיות דס"ג le'olam לְעוֹלָם gibor גִּבּוֹר Ata אַתָּה

(ר"ת אגלא והוא שם גדול ואמיץ, ובו היה יהודה מתגבר על אויביו. ע"ה אלד, בוכו).

◆lehoshi'a לְהוֹשִׁיעַ rav רַב ◆Ata אַתָּה metim מֵתִים ס"ג mechaye מְחַיֶּה

During the winter (starting on Simchat Torah):

מ"ה ר"ת haru'ach הָרוּחַ mashiv מַשִּׁיב

hageshem הַגֶּשֶׁם umorid וּמוֹרִיד

שׁבִּיל [י"ע (= י"ף אל) ול"ב נתיבות החכמה] ע"ה:

If you mistakenly say "*morid hatal*", and realize this before the end of the blessing ("*baruch Ata Adonai*"), you should return to the beginning of the blessing ("*Ata gibor*") and continue as usual. But if you only realize this after the end of the blessing, you should continue and not go back.

During the summer (starting on Pesach):

hatal הַטָּל morid מוֹרִיד

יוד הא ואו, כזו, מספר אותיות דמילואי עסמ"ב ;
ר"ת מ"ה (יוד הא ואו הא):

If you mistakenly say "*Mashiv haru'ach*", and realize this before the end of the blessing ("*baruch Ata Adonai*"), you should return to the beginning of the blessing ("*Ata gibor*") and continue as usual. But if you only realize this after the end of the blessing, you should start the *Amidah* from the beginning.

bechesed בְּחֶסֶד אהיה אהיה יהוה, בינה ע"ה chayim וְחַיִּים mechalkel מְכַלְכֵּל

berachamim בְּרַחֲמִים metim מֵתִים ס"ג mechaye מְחַיֶּה ◆ יהוה, ריבּוע ע"ב,

somech סוֹמֵךְ (טלא דעתיק) rabim רַבִּים י"פ יי אלהים ההוין, מצפצ (בּמוכסז)

cholim חוֹלִים verofe וְרוֹפֵא (זו"ן) ◆ noflim נוֹפְלִים אדני ריבּוע כוכ, (אכדטם)

umekayem וּמְקַיֵּם ◆asurim אֲסוּרִים umatir וּמַתִּיר ◆ אותיות וד' מ"ה = וחזלה

chamocha כָּמוֹךָ ילי mi מִי ◆afar עָפָר lishenei לִישֵׁנֵי emunato אֱמוּנָתוֹ

gevurot גְּבוּרוֹת ba'al בַּעַל (you should enunciate the letter *Ayin* in the word "*ba'al*")

memit מֵמִית melech מֶלֶךְ ◆lach לָךְ dome דוֹמֶה ילי umi וּמִי

‡yeshu'a יְשׁוּעָה umatzmi'ach וּמַצְמִיחַ (יוד הי ואו הי) ס"ג umchaye וּמְחַיֶּה

THE SECOND BLESSING

You are mighty forever, Lord. You resurrect the dead and are very capable of redeeming.

During the winter:	During the summer:
Who causes wind to blow and rain to fall.	*Who causes dew to fall.*

You sustain life with kindness and resurrect the dead with great compassion. You support those who have fallen, heal the sick, release the imprisoned, and fulfill Your faithful words to those who are asleep in the dust. Who is like You, Master of might, and Who can compare to You, King, Who causes death, Who gives life, and Who sprouts salvation?

During the days between *Rosh Hashanah* and *Yom Kippur* we say the prayer of "*mi chamocha*":

מִי יִלי **מִי** mi chamocha **כָּמוֹךָ** av **אָב** harachman **הָרַחֲמָן** zocher **זוֹכֵר**

יְצוּרָיו yetzurav **בְּרַחֲמִים** berachamim מצפצ, אלהים דיודין, י"פ ייי

לְחַיִּים lechayim אהיה אהיה יהוה, בינה ע"ה.

If you forget to say "*mi chamocha*" and realize this before the end of the blessing
("*baruch Ata Adonai*"), you should return and say "*mi chamocha*" and continue as usual.
But if you only realize this after the end of the blessing, you should continue as usual.

וְנֶאֱמָן vene'eman **אַתָּה** Ata **לְהַחֲיוֹת** lehachayot **מֵתִים** metim

בָּרוּך baruch **אַתָּה** Ata יְהֹוָה(יֱהֹוֱִאֲדֹנָי)יאהדונהי Adonai

מְחַיֵּה mechaye ס"ג (יוד הי ואו הי) **הַמֵּתִים** hametim ר"ת מ"ה וס"ת מ"ה:

THE THIRD BLESSING

This blessing connects us to Jacob, the Central Column and the power of restriction. Jacob is our channel for connecting mercy with judgment. By restricting our reactive behavior, we are blocking our Desire to Receive for the Self Alone. Jacob also gives us the power to balance our acts of mercy and judgment toward other people in our lives.

Tiferet that becomes *Da'at* (14 words).

אַתָּה Ata kadosh **קָדוֹשׁ** veshimcha **וְשִׁמְךָ** kadosh **קָדוֹשׁ** ר"ת = אור, רז, אין סוף.

וּקְדוֹשִׁים ukdoshim bechol **בְּכָל** ב"ף, לכב yom **יוֹם** ע"ה נגד, מזבוח, זן, אל יהוה

יְהַלְלוּךָ yehalelucha **סֶלָה** sela:

בָּרוּך baruch **אַתָּה** Ata יְהֹוָה(יֱהֹוֱִאֲדֹנָי)יאהדונהי Adonai

הָאֵל haEl י"פ מ"ה (יוד הא ואו הא): hakadosh **הַקָּדוֹשׁ** ס"ג (מילוי דס"ג) ; יא"י לאה:

Meditate here on the Name: **יאהדונהי**, as it can help to remove anger.

During the days between *Rosh Hashanah* and *Yom Kippur* instead of "*haEl hakadosh*" we say:

הַמֶּלֶך hamelech **הַקָּדוֹשׁ** hakadosh:

If you mistakenly say "*haEl hakadosh*" and you realize this within three seconds,
you should immediately say "*hamelech hakadosh*" and continue as usual.
But if you have already started the next blessing you should start the *Amidah* from the beginning.

During the days between *Rosh Hashanah* and *Yom Kippur*:
Who is like You, merciful Father, Who recalls His created with mercy for life?

And You are faithful to resurrecting the dead. Blessed are You, Lord, Who resurrects the dead.

THE THIRD BLESSING

You are holy, and Your Name is holy, and the Holy Ones praise You every day,
for you are God, the Holy King Selah. Blessed are You, Lord, the Holy God.

During the days between *Rosh Hashanah* and *Yom Kippur*: *The Holy King.*

THIRTEEN MIDDLE BLESSINGS

There are thirteen blessings in the middle of the *Amidah* that connect us to the Thirteen Attributes.

THE FIRST (FOURTH) BLESSING

This blessing helps us transform information into knowledge by helping us internalize everything that we learn.

Chochmah

In this blessing there are 17 words, the same numerical value as the word *tov* (good) in the secret of *Etz HaDa'at Tov vaRa*, (Tree of Knowledge Good and Evil), where we connect only to the *Tov*.

אַתָּה Ata　וֹזֵן chonen　לְאָדָם le'adam　מ"ה　דַּעַת da'at◆

וּמְלַמֵּד umlamed　לֶאֱנוֹשׁ le'enosh　בִּינָה bina　ע"ה　אהיה אהיה יהוה, וזיים◆

On Saturday night (*Motza'ei Shabbat*) we add the following:

אַתָּה ata　וֹזֵנְתָּנוּ chonantanu　יְהֹוָאדֹנִיאהדֹנֹהי Adonai　אֱלֹהֵינוּ Elohenu　ילה

מַדָּע mada　וְהַשְׂכֵּל vehaskel，אַתָּה Ata　אָמַרְתָּ amarta　לְהַבְדִּיל lehavdil

בֵּין ben　קוֹדֶשׁ kodesh　לְחוֹל lechol　וּבֵין uven　אוֹר or，רֹז，א"ס

לְחוֹשֶׁךְ lechoshech　וּבֵין uven　יִשְׂרָאֵל Yisrael　לָעַמִּים la'amim，

וּבֵין uven　יוֹם yom　ע"ה נגד, מזבוז, זך, אל יהוה　הַשְּׁבִיעִי hashevi'i　לְשֵׁשֶׁת lesheshet

יְמֵי yemei　הַמַּעֲשֶׂה hama'ase◆　כְּשֵׁם keshem　שֶׁהִבְדַּלְתָּנוּ shehivdaltanu

יְהֹוָאדֹנִיאהדֹנֹהי Adonai　אֱלֹהֵינוּ Elohenu　ילה　מֵעַמֵּי me'amei

הָאֲרָצוֹת ha'aratzot　וּמִמִּשְׁפְּחוֹת umimishpechot　הָאֲדָמָה ha'adama，

כָּךְ kach　פְּדֵנוּ pedenu　וְהַצִּילֵנוּ vehatzilenu　מִשָּׂטָן misatan　רָע ra

וּמִכָּל umikol　ילי　רָע ra，וּמִפֶּגַע umipega　גְּזֵרוֹת gezerot　קָשׁוֹת kashot

וְרָעוֹת vera'ot　הַבָּאוֹת גֵּשָׁוֹת hamitrageshot　לָבֹא lavo　בָּעוֹלָם ba'olam：

וְוֹזֵנּוּ vechonenu　מֵאִתְּךָ me'itecha　וְזְכְמָה chochma　במילוי = תרי"ג (מצוות)

בִּינָה bina　ע"ה אהיה אהיה יהוה, וזיים　וְדַעַת vada'at　ר"ת　וזבו:

בָּרוּךְ baruch　אַתָּה Ata　יְהֹוָאדֹנִיאהדֹנֹהי Adonai　וֹזֵן chonen　הַדַּעַת hada'at:

THIRTEEN MIDDLE BLESSINGS - THE FIRST (FOURTH) BLESSING

You graciously grant knowledge to man and understanding to humanity.

You have graciously granted us, Lord our God, knowledge and intelligence.
You commanded us to separate between the holy and non-holy, between Light and darkness, between Israel and the nations and between the seventh day and the six days of creation. Just as You separated us, Lord our God, from the nations of the lands and from the families of earth, so may You redeem us and rescue us from any evil adversary, from any mishap, and from all types of harsh and evil decrees which enthusiastically come to the world.

Graciously grant us, from Yourself,
wisdom, understanding, and knowledge. Blessed are You, Lord, Who graciously grants knowledge.

THE SECOND (FIFTH) BLESSING

This blessing keeps us in the Light. Everyone at one time or another succumbs to the doubt and uncertainty that the Satan constantly implants in us. If we make the unfortunate mistake of stepping back and falling away from the Light, we do not want the Creator to mirror our actions and step away from us. Instead, we want Him to catch us. In the box below there are certain lines that we can recite and meditate on for others who may be stepping back. The war against the Satan is the oldest war known to man. And the only way to defeat the Satan is to unite, share, help and pray for each other.

Binah

In this blessing there are 15 words, as the powerful action of *Teshuva* (repentance) raises 15 levels on the way to *Kise Hakavod* (the Throne of Honor). It goes through seven *Reki'im* (firmaments), seven *Avirim* (air), and another firmament on top of the Holy Animals (together this adds up to 15). Also, there are 15 words in the two main verses of Isaiah the Prophet and King David that speak of *Teshuva* (*Isaiah 55:7; Psalms 32:5*). The number 15 is also the secret of the Name: יה.

הֲשִׁיבֵנוּ hashivenu אָבִינוּ avinu לְתוֹרָתֶךָ letoratecha (וּסֵד טובה – יְהוָֹאדֹנָיאהדונהי)

וְקָרְבֵנוּ vekarvenu מַלְכֵּנוּ malkenu לַעֲבוֹדָתֶךָ la'avodatecha

וְהַחֲזִירֵנוּ vehachazirenu בִּתְשׁוּבָה bitshuva שְׁלֵמָה shelema

לְפָנֶיךָ lefanecha ס"ג מ"ה ב"ן

If you want to pray for another and help them in their spiritual process say:

יְהִי yehi רָצוֹן ratzon מהשע ע"ה, ע"ב בריבוע וקס"א ע"ה, אל עודי ע"ה

מִלְּפָנֶיךָ milfanecha ס"ג מ"ה ב"ן יְהוָֹאדֹנָיאהדונהי Adonai אֱלֹהַי Elohai מילוי ע"ב, דמב;ילה

וֵאלֹהֵי velohei אֲבוֹתַי avotai שֶׁתַּחְתּוֹר shetachtor

וְחָתִירָה chatira מִתַּחַת mitachat כִּסֵּא kise כְּבוֹדֶךָ kevodecha וּתְקַבֵּל utkabel

בִּתְשׁוּבָה bitshuva אֶת et (the person's name and his/her father's name) כִּי ki יְמִינְךָ yemincha

יְהוָֹאדֹנָיאהדונהי Adonai פְּשׁוּטָה peshuta לְקַבֵּל lekabel עָבִים shavim

בָּרוּךְ baruch אַתָּה Ata יְהוָֹאדֹנָיאהדונהי Adonai

הָרוֹצֶה harotze בִּתְשׁוּבָה bitshuva

THE SECOND (FIFTH) BLESSING

Bring us back, our Father, to Your Torah,
and bring us close, our King, to Your service, and cause us to return with perfect repentance before You.

May it be pleasing before You, Lord, my God and God of my forefathers, that You shall dig deep beneath the Throne of Your glory and accept as repentant (the person's name and his/her father's name) because Your Right Hand, Lord, extends outwards to receive those who repent.

Blessed are You, Lord, Who desires repentance.

THE THIRD (SIXTH) BLESSING

This blessing helps us achieve true forgiveness. We have the power to cleanse ourselves of our negative behavior and hurtful actions toward others through forgiveness. This blessing does not mean we plead for forgiveness and our slate is wiped clean. Forgiveness refers to the methodologies for washing away the residue that comes from our iniquities. There are two ways to wash away the residue: physical and spiritual. We collect physical residue when we are in denial of our misdeeds and the laws of cause and effect. We cleanse ourselves when we experience any kind of pain, whether it is financial, emotional, or physical. If we choose to cleanse spiritually, we forgo the physical cleansing. We do so by arousing the pain in ourselves that we caused to others. We feel the other person; and with a truthful heart, recite this prayer experiencing the hurt and heartache we inflicted on others. This form of spiritual cleansing prevents us from having to cleanse physically.

Chesed

In this blessing there are 21 words which is the numerical value of the Holy Name: אהיה.

סְלַח selach יהוה ע"ב לָנוּ lanu אלהים, אהיה אדני אָבִינוּ avinu ר"ת סאל, אמן (יאהדונהי)

כִּי ki וְטָאנוּ chatanu מָחוֹל mechol לָנוּ lanu אלהים, אהיה אדני ; מחול לנו ע"ה =

אֵל El כִּי ki פָּשַׁעְנוּ fashanu כִּי ki מַלְכֵּנוּ malkenu קס"א ו' אותיות יא"י (מילוי דס"ג)

טוֹב tov וְהוּ וְסָלַח vesalach יהוה ע"ב אַתָּה Ata: בָּרוּך baruch אַתָּה Ata

יהוה Adonai וְנוּן chanun הַמַּרְבֶּה hamarbe לִסְלוֹחַ lislo'ach:

THE FOURTH (SEVENTH) BLESSING
This blessing helps us achieve redemption after we are spiritually cleansed.

Gevurah

רְאֵה re'e ראה נָא na בְעָנְיֵנוּ ve'onyenu ר"ת רנ"ב (אברים באשה, כנגד הגבורה)

וְרִיבָה veriva רִיבֵנוּ rivenu וּמַהֵר umaher לְגָאֳלֵנוּ lega'olenu

גְאֻלָּה ge'ula מ"ה shelema שְׁלֵמָה לְמַעַן lema'an שְׁמֶךָ shemecha

כִּי ki אֵל El יא"י (מילוי דס"ג) גּוֹאֵל go'el וְחָזָק chazak פהל אַתָּה Ata:

בָּרוּך baruch אַתָּה Ata יהוה Adonai גּוֹאֵל go'el יִשְׂרָאֵל Yisrael:

THE FIFTH (EIGHTH) BLESSING
This blessing gives us the power to heal every part of our body. All healing originates from the Light of the Creator. Accepting and understanding this truth opens us to receive this Light. We should also think of sharing this healing energy with others.

THE THIRD (SIXTH) BLESSING
Forgive us, our Father, for we have transgressed. Pardon us, our King, for we have sinned, because You are a good and forgiving God. Blessed are You, Lord, Who is gracious and forgives magnanimously.

THE FOURTH (SEVENTH) BLESSING
Behold our poverty and take up our fight; hurry to redeem us with a complete redemption for the sake of Your Name, because You are a powerful and a redeeming God. Blessed are You, Lord, Who redeems Israel.

Tiferet

רְפָאֵנוּ refa'enu יְהֹוָ Adonai וְנֵרָפֵא venerafe ר"ת רי"ו.

הוֹשִׁיעֵנוּ hoshi'enu וְנִוָּשֵׁעָה venivashe'a כִּי ki תְּהִלָּתֵנוּ tehilatenu

אַתָּה Ata ר"ת = ב"פ רי"ו. וְהַעֲלֵה veha'ale אֲרוּכָה arucha וּמַרְפֵּא umarpe

לְכָל lechol תַּחֲלוּאֵינוּ tachalu'enu וּלְכָל ulchol

מַכְאוֹבֵינוּ mach'ovenu וּלְכָל ulchol מַכּוֹתֵינוּ makotenu

---

To pray for healing for yourself and/or others add the following, in the parentheses below, insert the names:

יְהִי yehi רָצוֹן ratzon מֵהַע ע"ה, ע"ב בְּרִיבוּעַ וְקַסָ"א ע"א ע"ה, אַל עֹדִי ע"ה

מִלְּפָנֶיךָ milfanecha ס"ג מ"ה ב"ן יְהֹוָ Adonai אֱלֹהַי Elohai מילוי ע"ב, דמב ; ילה

וֵאלֹהֵי velohei לכב ; מילוי ע"ב, דמב ; ילה אֲבוֹתַי avotai שֶׁתִּרְפָּאֵנִי shetirpa'eni

(וְתִרְפָּא vetirpa (insert the person's name) בֶּן ben :Women) בַּת bat) (insert their mother's name)

רְפוּאָה refu'a שְׁלֵמָה shelema רְפוּאַת refu'at הַנֶּפֶשׁ hanefesh

וּרְפוּאַת urfu'at הַגּוּף haguf, כְּדֵי kedei שֶׁאֶהְיֶה she'ehye חָזָק chazak פהל

:Women) וַחֲזָקָה chazaka (פהל) בִּבְרִיאוּת bivri'ut, וְאַמִּיץ ve'amitz

:Women) וְאַמִיצַת ve'amitzat) כֹּחַ ko'ach בְּמָאתַיִם bematayim וְאַרְבָּעִים ve'arba'im

וּשְׁמוֹנָה ushmona רמ"ח (אברים), אברהם, וז"פ אל, רי"ו ול"ב נתיבות החכמה, עסמ"ב וט"ו אותיות

פשוטות (ushnayim וּשְׁנַיִם vechamishim וַחֲמִשִׁים bematayim בְּמָאתַיִם (Women:

אֵבָרִים evarim וּשְׁלֹשׁ ushlosh מֵאוֹת me'ot המספר = ש"י = אלהים דיודין

וְשִׁשִּׁים veshishim המספר = מילוי הע' (יף) וַחֲמִשָּׁה vachamisha גִּידִים gidim שֶׁל shel

נִשְׁמָתִי nishmati וְגוּפִי vegufi, לְקִיּוּם lekiyum תּוֹרָתְךָ toratcha הַקְּדוֹשָׁה hakedosha.

כִּי ki אֵל El יי"א (מילוי דס"ג) רוֹפֵא rofe רַחֲמָן rachaman וְנֶאֱמָן vene'eman

אַתָּה :Ata בָּרוּךְ baruch אַתָּה Ata יְהֹוָ Adonai רוֹפֵא rofe

חוֹלֵי cholei חוֹלה = מ"ה (יוד הא ואו הא) וד' אותיות עַמּוֹ amo יִשְׂרָאֵל Yisrael

ר"ת רפ"ח (להעלות הניצוצות שנפלו לקליפה דמשם באים התחלואים):

THE FIFTH (EIGHTH) BLESSING

Heal us, Lord, and we shall heal. Save us and we shall be saved.
For You are our praise. Bring cure and healing to all our ailments, to all our pains, and to all our wounds.

May it be pleasing before You, Lord, my God and God of my forefathers, that You would heal me (and the person's name and their mother's name) completely with healing of the spirit and healing of the body, so that I shall be strong in health and vigorous in my strength in all 248 (a woman says: 252) organs and 365 sinews of my soul and my body, so that I shall be able to keep Your Holy Torah.

Because You are a healing,
compassionate, and trustworthy God, blessed are You, Lord, Who heals the sick of His People, Israel.

THE SIXTH (NINTH) BLESSING

This blessing draws sustenance and prosperity for the entire globe and provides us with personal sustenance. We would like all of our years to be filled with dew and rain, the sustaining lifeblood of our world.

Netzach

During the summer (starting on the first day of *Pesach*) **the following is said:**

If you mistakenly say *"barech alenu"* instead of *"barchenu"*, and realize this before the end of the *Amidah* (*"yihyu leratzon"* – the second one), then you should return and say *"barchenu"* and continue as usual. If you realize this later, you should start the *Amidah* from the beginning.

barchenu בָּרְכֵנוּ Adonai יְהֹוָה(אדני-יאהדונהי) Elohenu אֱלֹהֵינוּ יל'ה bechol בְּכָל

ma'asei מַעֲשֵׂי לכב ב"ן yadenu יָדֵינוּ ◆ uvarech וּבָרֵךְ shenatenu שְׁנָתֵנוּ

betalelei בְּטַלְלֵי ratzon רָצוֹן מהש ע"ה, ע"ב בריבוע וקס"א ע"ה, אל שדי ע"ה ע"ה

beracha בְּרָכָה undava וּנְדָבָה (וע"ה אהיה אהיה יהוה, וזיים) ◆ utehi וּתְהִי

acharita אַחֲרִיתָהּ chayim וְחַיִּים בינה ע"ה, בינה אהיה אהיה יהוה, vesava וְשָׂבַע

veshalom וְשָׁלוֹם kashanim כְּשָׁנִים hatovot הַטּוֹבוֹת livracha לִבְרָכָה ◆

If you want to pray for sustenance you can add:

yehi יְהִי ratzon רָצוֹן מהש ע"ה, ע"ב בריבוע וקס"א ע"ה, אל שדי ע"ה milfanecha מִלְפָנֶיךָ ס"ג מ"ה ב"ן

Adonai יְהֹוָה(אדני-יאהדונהי) Elohenu אֱלֹהֵינוּ יל'ה velohei וֵאלֹהֵי

avotenu אֲבוֹתֵינוּ יל'ה ; ע"ב, דמב shetiten שֶׁתִּתֵּן ב"פ כהת li לִי לכב ; מילוי ע"ב,

ulchol וּלְכָל yh אדני hasemuchim הַסְּמוּכִים al עַל shulchani שֻׁלְחָנִי hayom הַיּוֹם

mezonotai מְזוֹנוֹתַי umzonotehem וּמְזוֹנוֹתֵיהֶם bechavod בְּכָבוֹד בוכו velo וְלֹא ע"ה נגד, מזלוח, זן, אל יהוה uvchol וּבְכָל yom יוֹם ע"ה נגד, מזלוח, זן ב"ן, לכב

shimcha שִׁמְךָ hagadol הַגָּדוֹל להו ; עם ד' אותיות = מבה, יזל, אום bivizui בְּבִזּוּי beter בְּהֶתֵּר velo וְלֹא be'isur בְּאִיסוּר bizchut בִּזְכוּת

(:Do not pronounce this name) דִּיקַרְנוֹסָא וזהר עם ג' אותיות – ובאתב"ש סאל, אמן, יאהדונהי

THE SIXTH (NINTH) BLESSING

During the summer:

Bless us, Lord, our God, in all our endeavors, and bless our years with the dews of good will, blessing, and benevolence. May its conclusion be life, contentment, and peace, as with other years for blessing.

May it be pleasing before You, Lord, my God and God of my forefathers, that You would provide for me and for my household, today and everyday, mine and their nourishment, with dignity and not with shame, in a permissible but not a forbidden manner, by virtue of your great name

lachem לָכֶם vaharikoti וַהֲרִיקֹתִי :mipasuk מִפָּסוּק hayotze הַיּוֹצֵא

nesa נְסָה :umipasuk וּמִפָּסוּק dai דַּי beli בְּלִי ad עַד beracha בְּרָכָה

Adonai יְהֹוָה panecha פָּנֶיךָ or אוֹר alenu עָלֵינוּ

basar בָּשָׂר matnot מַתְּנוֹת lidei לִידֵי tatzrichenu תַּצְרִיכֵנוּ ve'al וְאַל

vadam וְדָם ki כִּי im אִם

chinam חִנָּם matnat מַתְּנַת ume'otzar וּמֵאוֹצָר hamele'a הַמְּלֵאָה miyadcha מִיָּדְךָ

techalkelni תְּכַלְכְּלֵנִי vetashpi'eni וְתַשְׂפִּיעֵנִי amen אָמֵן :sela סֶלָה.

ki כִּי El אֵל tov טוֹב umetiv וּמֵטִיב

Ata אַתָּה umvarech וּמְבָרֵךְ :hashanim הַשָּׁנִים baruch בָּרוּךְ

Ata אַתָּה Adonai יְהֹוָה mevarech מְבָרֵךְ :hashanim הַשָּׁנִים

During the winter (starting on the 7th of *Cheshvan*, two weeks after *Sukkot*) **the following is said:**
If you mistakenly say "*barchenu*" instead of "*barech alenu*", and realize this before the end
of the blessing ("*baruch Ata Adonai*"), you should return to say "*barech alenu*" and continue as usual.
If you only realize this after, you should say "*Veten tal umatar livracha*" in "*shome'a tefila*".
If you only relize this after you have already started "*retze*" you should start the *Amidah* from the beginning.

barech בָּרֵךְ alenu עָלֵינוּ Adonai יְהֹוָה Elohenu אֱלֹהֵינוּ

et אֶת hashana הַשָּׁנָה hazot הַזֹּאת ve'et וְאֶת kol כָּל

minei מִינֵי tevu'ata תְבוּאָתָהּ letova לְטוֹבָה veten וְתֵן

tal טַל umatar וּמָטָר livracha לִבְרָכָה al עַל kol כָּל

penei פְּנֵי ha'adama הָאֲדָמָה verave וְרַוֵּה penei פְּנֵי

tevel תֵּבֵל vesaba וְשַׂבַּע et אֶת ha'olam הָעוֹלָם

kulo כֻּלּוֹ mituvach מִטּוּבָךְ umale וּמַלֵּא yadenu יָדֵינוּ

mibirchotecha מִבִּרְכוֹתֶיךָ ume'osher וּמֵעֹשֶׁר mat'not מַתְּנוֹת yadecha יָדֶיךָ

---

that comes from the verse: "*pour down for you blessing until there be no room to suffice for it*" (Malachi 3:10)
and from the verse: "*Raise up over us the light of Your countenance, Lord*" (Psalms 4:7),
and we will not require the gifts of flesh and blood, but only from your hand which is full,
and from the treasure of the free gift you shall support and nurish me. Amen. Sela.

for You are a good
and a beneficent God and You bless the years. Blessed are You, Lord, Who blesses the years.
During the winter:
Bless us, Lord, our God, this year and all its kinds of crops for good. And give dew and rain for blessing
over the entire face of the Earth. Quench the thirst of the face of the Earth and satiate the entire world
from Your bounty. Fill our hands with Your blessings and from the wealth of gifts of Your Hands.

If you want to pray for sustenance you can add:

יְהִי yehi ע"ה עדי אל, וקס"א וקריבוע ע"ב, מהש ע"ה רָצוֹן ratzon מִלְפָנֶיךָ milfanecha

אֱלֹהֵינוּ Elohenu יְהֹוָאדֹנָיאהדונהי Adonai ילה ב"ן מ"ה ס"ג וֵאלֹהֵי velohei

אֲבוֹתֵינוּ avotenu רמב, ע"ב, מילוי ; כהת ב"פ שֶׁתִּתֵּן shetiten לִי li

עַל al הַסְּמוּכִים hasmuchim אדני יה עוֹלְוֹזֵנִי ulchol הַיּוֹם hayom shulchani

וּבְכָל uvchol אל יהוה, זן, מזבוח, נגד ע"ה לכב, ב"ן יוֹם yom וְבְכָל uvchol הַיּוֹם shulchani

מְזוֹנוֹתַי mezonotai וּמְזוֹנוֹתֵיהֶם umzonotehem בְּכָבוֹד bechavod בוכו וְלֹא velo

שִׁמְךָ shimcha הַגָּדוֹל hagadol להו ; עם ד' אותיות = מבה, יזל, אום בִּזְכוּת bizchut בְּאִיסוּר be'isur וְלֹא velo בְּהֵיתֵר beheter בְּבִזּוּי bevizuy

(Do not pronounce this name) דִּיקְרָנוֹסָא זחך עם ג' אותיות – ובאתבש"ע סאל, אמן, יאהדונהי

הַיּוֹצֵא hayotze מִפָּסוּק mipasuk וַהֲרִיקוֹתִי vaharikoti לָכֶם lachem

בְּרָכָה beracha עַד ad בְּלִי beli דַּי dai וּמִפָּסוּק umipasuk נְשָׂא nesa

עָלֵינוּ alenu אוֹר or רז, אין סוף ס"ג מ"ה ב"ן פָּנֶיךָ panecha יְהֹוָאדֹנָיאהדונהי Adonai

וְאַל ve'al תַּצְרִיכֵנוּ tatzrichenu לִידֵי lidei מַתְּנוֹת matnot בָּשָׂר basar

וָדָם vadam כִּי ki אִם im יוהך, מ"א אותיות אהיה בפשוטו ומילואו ומילוי דמילואו ע"ה

מִיָּדְךָ miyadcha הַמְּלֵאָה hamele'a וּמֵאוֹצָר ume'otzar מַתְּנַת matnat וְזָן chinam

תְכַלְכְּלֵנִי techalkelni וְתַשְׁפִּיעֵנִי vetashpi'eni אָמֵן amen יאהדונהי סֶלָה sela.

שָׁמְרָה shomra וְהַצִּילָה vehatzila זוֹ zo שָׁנָה shana ילי דָבָר davar מִכָּל mikol

וּמִכָּל umikol ילי מִינֵי minei מַשְׁחִית mashchit וּמִכָּל umikol רָע ra. ראה

מִינֵי minei פּוּרְעָנוּת pura'nut וַעֲשֵׂה va'ase כָּה la תִּקְוָה tikva

טוֹבָה tova אכא וְאַחֲרִית ve'acharit שָׁלוֹם shalom. וְזוּם chus וְרַחֵם verachem

עָלֶיהָ aleha פהל אברהם, וז"פ אל, רי"ו ול"ב נתיבות החכמה, רמ"ח (אברים), עסמ"ב וט"ז אותיות פשוטות

וְעַל ve'al כָּל kol ילי ; עמם תְּבוּאָתָהּ tevu'ata וּפֵירוֹתֶיהָ uferoteha.

,ה"ע א"סקו עובירב ב"ע ,ה"ע השמ ratzon רָצוֹן begishmei בְּגִשְׁמֵי uvarcha וּבָרְכָהּ

(םייזו ,הוהי היהא ה"עו) הנּיב undava וּנְדָבָה beracha בְּרָכָה ה"ע ידש לא

ה"ע הנּיב ,הוהי היהא chayim וְחַיִּים acharita אַחֲרִיתָהּ utehi וּתְהִי

hatovot הַטּוֹבוֹת kashanim כַּשָּׁנִים veshalom וְשָׁלוֹם vesava וְשָׂבַע◆

umetiv וּמֵטִיב והּ tov טוֹב (ג"ס ימילוּמ) י"אי El אֵל ki כִּי livracha לִבְרָכָה◆

baruch בָּרוּךְ hashanim הַשָּׁנִים◆ umvarech וּמְבָרֵךְ Ata אַתָּה

hashanim הַשָּׁנִים◆ mevarech מְבָרֵךְ Adonai יְהֹוָאֲדֹנָיֵאֲהֹדֹנָהֹי Ata אַתָּה

THE SEVENTH (TENTH) BLESSING

This blessing gives us the power to positively influence all of humanity. Kabbalah teaches that each individual affects the whole. We affect the world, and the rest of the world affects us, even though we cannot perceive this relationship with our five senses. We call this relationship quantum consciousness.

Hod

אותיות 'וי סוזרך פ"ב teka תְּקַע = אותיות 'ד םע ; להוّ gadol גָּדוֹל beshofar בְּשׁוֹפָר

lekabetz לְקַבֵּץ אדני מ"ה nes נֵס vesa וְשָׂא◆ lecherutenu לְחֵרוּתֵנוּ אום ,לזי ,הבמ

me'arba מֵאַרְבַּע yachad יַחַד vekabetzenu וְקַבְּצֵנוּ galuyotenu גָּלֻיּוֹתֵינוּ◆

יהוה עוביר ,ב"ע = ויתודוּקנ םע וֹבֵזְו ןיכיו (תופילקה ןמ תוצוצינ איצוהל ותלוגסב) וֹבוּ kanfot כַּנְפוֹת

le'artzenu לְאַרְצֵנוּ◆ אדני = ת"ר ; ה"ע ןיהדה םיהלא ha'aretz הָאָרֶץ

The following is recited throughout the entire year, and especially during the time of the *Shovavim*:

The first six portions of the Book of Exodus—*Shemot, Va'era, Bo, Beshalach, Yitro, Mishpatim,* (*Terumah Tetzave*)—tell us the story of the Israelites exodus from Egypt and signify the beginning of a unique cosmic opening that lasts for six weeks (8 weeks during a leap year), each year. The word *shovavim* means "irresponsible," as in the verse, "Return, irresponsible children says the Lord," (Jeremiah 3:14) and is an acronym comprised of the first initial of each of the six weekly portions: The kabbalists teach us that the story of Exodus is a code and that during these six/eight weeks there is a window of time for personal redemption. The Ari explains that the fall of Adam corrupted almost everything in our physical world, resulting in human pain and suffering. During the time of the Exodus, Moses and the Israelites corrected the most important aspects of this corruption. The following meditation helps us to release and redeem all the remaining sparks of Light we have lost through our irresponsible actions (especially sexual misconduct):

---

bless it with rains of goodwill, blessing, and benevolence. And may its end be life, contentment, and peace, for You are a good and a beneficent God and You bless the years. Blessed are You, Lord, Who blesses the years.

THE SEVENTH (TENTH) BLESSING

Blow a great Shofar for our freedom and
raise a banner to gather our exiles, and gather us speedily from all four corners of the Earth to our Land.

יְהִי yehi רָצוֹן ratzon מהש ע"ה, ע"ב בריבוע וקס"א ע"א ע"ה, אל שדי ע"ה מִלְפָנֶיךָ milfanecha

ס"ג מ"ה ב"ן יְהֹוָואֲדֹהִיאַהדֹוּנַהִי Adonai אֱלֹהַי Elohai מילוי ע"ב, דמב ; ילה אֱלֹהַי

וֵאלֹהֵי velohei avotai אֲבוֹתַי ; ילה ; מילוי ע"ב, דמב ; לכב shekol שֶׁכָל yali טִיפָּה tipa

וְטִיפָּה vetipa shel שֶׁל keri קְרִי sheyatza שֶׁיָצָא mimeni מִמֶּנִי levatala לִבַטָלָה

וּמִכָל umikol yali Yisrael יִשְׂרָאֵל bichlal בִכְלָל uvifrat וּבִפְרָט shelo שֶׁלֹא

בִמָקוֹם bimkom mitzva מִצְוָה ben בֵין be'ones בְאוֹנֶס ben בֵין be'ratzon בְרָצוֹן

בֵין ben beshogeg בְשׁוֹגֵג מהש ע"ה, ע"ב בריבוע וקס"א ע"א, אל שדי ע"ה ben בֵין

בְמֵזִיד bemezid, ben בֵין בְהִרְהוּר behirhur uven וּבֵין בְמַעֲשֶׂה bema'ase,

בֵין ben begilgul בְגִלְגוּל ze זֶה בֵין ben begilgul בְגִלְגוּל acher אַחֵר

וְנִבְלַע venivla בַקְלִיפוֹת bakelipot, shetaki שֶׁתָקְיָא hakelipot הַקְלִיפוֹת

הַנִּיצוֹצוֹת hanitzotzot keri קְרִי shenivle'u שֶׁנִבְלְעוּ ba בָה bizechut בִזְכוּת

שִׁמְךָ shimcha hagadol הַגָדוֹל ; עם ד' אותיות = מבה, יכל, אום hayotze הַיוֹצֵא

מִפָסוּק mipasuk ר"ת וזבו ו-ילי chayil וְחַיִל ומב bala בְלַע vayki'enu וַיְקִאֶנוּ

מִבִּטְנוֹ mibitno yorishenu יֹרִשֶׁנּוּ El אֵל יא"י (מילוי דס"ג) ; ס"ת וכ uvizechut וּבִזְכוּת

שִׁמְךָ shimcha hagadol הַגָדוֹל ; עם ד' אותיות = מבה, יכל, אום יוֹהֲבֵוֵה

לִמְקוֹם limkom shetachazirem שֶׁתַחֲזִירֵם (יוֹהֲבֵוֵה during the Shovavim)

קְדוּשָׁה kedusha וְהַטוֹב vehatov וכו be'enecha בְעֵינֶיךָ .ase עֲשֵׂה

You should meditate to correct the thought that caused the loss of the sparks of Light. Also meditate on the Names that control our thoughts for each of the six days of the week as follow:

Sunday	יְהֹוָה	עם: ועם דמרגלא אהיה מן א מן טפטפיה ואו זין ואו כף צבא עֹל	Beriah.
Monday	יְהֹוָה	עם: ועם דמרגלא אהיה מן ה מן טפטפיה ואו זין ואו כף מגן עֹל	Yetzirah.
Tuesday	מצפץ	עם: ועם דמרגלא אהיה מן י מן טפטפיה ואו זין ואו כף פודד צוה	Asiyah.
Wednesday	אל	עם: ועם דמרגלא יהו מן י מן טפטפיה ואו זין ואו כף פודד צוה	Asiyah.
Thursday	אלהים	עם: ועם דמרגלא יהו מן ה מן טפטפיה ואו זין ואו כף מגן עֹל	Yetzirah.
Friday	מצפץ	עם: ועם דמרגלא יהו מן ו מן טפטפיה ואו זין ואו כף צבא עֹל	Beriah.

Each of these Names (עֹל צבא, כף ואו זין ואו, טפטפיה) adds up to 193, which is the same numerical value as the word zokef (raise). These Names raise the Holy Spark from the Chitzoniyim. Also, when you say the words "mekabetz nidchei" (in the continuation of the blessing), which adds up to 304 — the same numerical value of Shin, Dalet (demon), you should meditate to collect all the lost sparks and cancel out the power of the negative forces.

May it be pleasing before You, Lord, my God and God of my forefathers, that every single drop of keri that came out of me for vain, and from all of Yisrael in general, and especially not as a cause of precept, if it was coerced or willfully, with intention or without, by passing thought or by an action, in this lifetime or in previous, and it was swallowed by the klipa, that the klipa will vomit all the sparks of keri that was swollen by it, by virtue of your great name that comes from the verse:"He swallowed up wealth and vomited it out, and from his belly God will cast it." (Job 20:15), and by the virtue of your great name you will return them to the holy place, and do what is good in Your eyes.

בָּרוּךְ baruch אַתָּה Ata יְהֹוָה Adonai ; יכוין וזו בשילוב יהוה כזה: יְזֶהֹבֶוֶה

מְקַבֵּץ mekabetz ע"ב ס"ג מ"ה ב"ן, הברכה (למתק את המלכים שמתו)

נִדְחֵי nidchei ע"ב, ריבוע יהוה עַמּוֹ amo וזו יִשְׂרָאֵל Yisrael:

THE EIGHTH (ELEVENTH) BLESSING

This blessing helps us to balance judgment with mercy. As mercy is time, we can use it to change ourselves before judgment occurs.

Yesod

הָשִׁיבָה hashiva שׁוֹפְטֵינוּ shoftenu כְּבָרִאשׁוֹנָה kevarishona◆

וְיוֹעֲצֵינוּ veyo'atzenu כְּבַתְּחִלָּה kevatechila ר"ת שכ"ה (דינים זכרים עביסוד) וידוה (הממתקם)◆

וְהָסֵר vehaser מִמֶּנּוּ mimenu יָגוֹן yagon (סמאל) וַאֲנָחָה va'anacha (לילית)◆

וּמְלוֹךְ umloch עָלֵינוּ aleinu מְהֵרָה mehera אַתָּה Ata

יְהֹוָה Adonai לְבַדֶּךָ levadcha◆ בְּחֶסֶד bechesed ע"ב, ריבוע יהוה

וּבְרַחֲמִים uvrachamim מצפ"ץ, אלהים דיודין, י"פ יי' ; להמתיק ברחמים דיני צדק ומשפט

בְּצֶדֶק betzedek וּבְמִשְׁפָּט uvmishpat ע"ה = ה"פ אלהים: בָּרוּךְ baruch אַתָּה Ata

יְהֹוָה Adonai מֶלֶךְ melech אוֹהֵב ohev ממתיק דיני

צְדָקָה tzedaka ע"ה ריבוע אלהים וּמִשְׁפָּט umishpat ע"ה ה"פ אלהים:

During the days between *Rosh Hashanah* and *Yom Kippur* instead of "*melech ohev tzedaka umishpat*" we say:

הַמֶּלֶךְ hamelech הַמִּשְׁפָּט hamishpat ע"ה ה"פ אלהים:

If you mistakenly say "*melech ohev...*" and realize this within three seconds, you should say "*hamelech hamishpat*" and continue as usual. But if you have already begun the next blessing you should not go back.

THE NINTH (TWELFTH) BLESSING

This blessing helps us remove all forms of negativity, whether it comes from people, situations or even the negative energy of the Angel of Death [(do not pronounce these names) *Sa-ma-el* (male aspect) and *Li-li-th* (female aspect), which are encoded here], by using the Holy Name: *Shadai* עי"ד, which is encoded mathematically into the last four words of this blessing and also appears inside a *Mezuzah* for the same purpose.

Blessed are You, Lord, Who gathers the displaced of His Nation, Israel.
THE EIGHTH (ELEVENTH) BLESSING
Restore our judges, as at first, and our mentors, as in the beginning. Remove from us sorrow and moaning. Reign over us soon, You alone, Lord, with kindness and compassion, with righteousness and justice. Blessed are You, Lord, the King Who loves righteousness and justice.

During the days between *Rosh Hashanah* and *Yom Kippur*: *The King the judgment.*

Keter

לַמִּינִים laminim וְלַמַּלְשִׁינִים velamalshinim אַל al תְּהִי tehi תִקְוָה tikva

וְכֹל vechol הַזֵּדִים hazedim כְּרֶגַע kerega ג"פ אלהים עם ט"ו אותיות פשוטות

וְכֹל vechol אוֹיְבֶיךָ oyvecha (סמאל) יֹאבֵדוּ yovedu

וְכֹל vechol שׂוֹנְאֶיךָ son'echa (לילית) מְהֵרָה mehera יִכָּרֵתוּ yikaretu

וּמַלְכוּת umalchut הָרִשְׁעָה harish'a מְהֵרָה mehera תְעַקֵּר te'aker

וּתְשַׁבֵּר utshaber וּתְכַלֵּם utchalem וְתַכְנִיעֵם vetachni'em בִּמְהֵרָה bimhera

בְּיָמֵינוּ veyamenu בָּרוּךְ baruch אַתָּה Ata יְהֹוָה Adonai

שׁוֹבֵר shover אוֹיְבִים oyvim וּמַכְנִיעַ umachni'a זֵדִים zedim

THE TENTH (THIRTEENTH) BLESSING

This blessing surrounds us with total positivity to help us always be at the right place at the right time. It also helps attract only positive people into our lives.

Yesod

עַל al הַצַּדִּיקִים hatzadikim צדיק יסוד עולם וְעַל ve'al הַחֲסִידִים hachasidim

וְעַל ve'al שְׁאֵרִית she'erit עַמְּךָ amecha בֵּית bet ב"פ ראה יִשְׂרָאֵל Yisrael

וְעַל ve'al פְּלֵיטַת peletat בֵּית bet ב"פ ראה סוֹפְרֵיהֶם sofrehem

וְעַל ve'al גֵּרֵי gerei הַצֶּדֶק hatzedek וְעָלֵינוּ ve'alenu יֶהֱמוּ yehemu

נָא na רַחֲמֶיךָ rachamecha יְהֹוָה Adonai אֱלֹהֵינוּ Elohenu יה

וְתֵן veten שָׂכָר sachar טוֹב tov לְכֹל lechol

הַבּוֹטְחִים habotchim בְּשִׁמְךָ beshimcha בֶּאֱמֶת be'emet

THE NINTH (TWELFTH) BLESSING

For the heretics and for the slanderers, let there be no hope.
Let all the wicked perish in an instant. And may all Your foes and all Your haters be speedily cut down. And as for the evil government, may You quickly uproot and smash it, and may You destroy and humble it, speedily in our days. Blessed are You, Lord, Who smashes foes and humbles the wicked.

THE TENTH (THIRTEENTH) BLESSING

On the righteous, on the pious, on the remnants of the House of Israel, on the remnants of their writers' academies, on the righteous converts, and on us, may Your compassion be stirred, Lord, our God. And give good reward to all those who truly trust in Your Name.

וְשִׂים vesim וְחֶלְקֵנוּ chelkenu עִמָהֶם imahem וּלְעוֹלָם ul'olam ריבוע ס"ג ו' אותיות דס"ג

לֹא lo נֵבוֹשׁ nevosh כִּי ki בָּךְ vecha בָּטָחְנוּ batachnu

וְעַל ve'al וְחַסְדְּךָ chasdecha הַגָּדוֹל hagadol לָהֶן ; עם ד' אותיות = מבה, יזל, אום

בֶּאֱמֶת be'emet אֶהְיֶה פעמים אהיה, ז"פ ס"ג נִשְׁעָנְנוּ nish'anenu

בָּרוּךְ baruch אַתָּה Ata יהוה Adonai מִשְׁעָן mish'an

וּמִבְטָח umivtach לַצַדִיקִים latzadikim ר"ת ימול (כל מי שנימול נקרא צדיק)

THE ELEVENTH (FOURTEENTH) BLESSING

This blessing connects us to the power of Jerusalem, to the building of the Temple, and to the preparation for the *Mashiach*.

Hod

תִּשְׁכּוֹן tishkon בְּתוֹךְ betoch יְרוּשָׁלַיִם Yerushalayim עִירְךָ ircha

כַּאֲשֶׁר ka'asher דִּבַּרְתָּ dibarta ראה וְכִסֵּא vechise דָּוִד David

עַבְדְּךָ avdecha פני, אל אדני מְהֵרָה mehera בְּתוֹכָהּ vetocha תָּכִין tachin

Meditate here that Mashiach Ben Yosef shall not be killed by the wicked Armilos **(Do not pronounce)**.

וּבְנֵה uvne אוֹתָהּ ota בִּנְיַן binyan עוֹלָם olam בִּמְהֵרָה bimhera

בְּיָמֵינוּ veyamenu בָּרוּךְ baruch אַתָּה Ata יהוה Adonai

בּוֹנֵה bone ס"ג יְרוּשָׁלַיִם Yerushalayim

THE TWELFTH (FIFTEENTH) BLESSING

This blessing helps us achieve a personal state of *Mashiach* by transforming our reactive nature into becoming proactive. Just as there is a global *Mashiach*, each person has a personal *Mashiach* within. When enough people achieve their transformation, the way will be paved for the appearance of the global *Mashiach*.

---

and place our lot with them. And may we never be embarrassed, for it is in You that we place our trust; it is upon Your great compassion that we truly rely. Blessed are You, Lord, the support and security of the righteous.

THE ELEVENTH (FOURTEENTH) BLESSING

May You dwell in Jerusalem, Your City,
as You have promised. And may You establish the throne of David, Your servant, speedily within it and build it as an eternal structure, speedily in our days Blessed are You, Lord, Who builds Jerusalem.

Netzach

This blessing contains 20 words, which is the same number of words in *"Ki nicham Adonai Tziyon nicham kol chorvoteha..."* (Isaiah 51:3), a verse that speaks about the Final Redemption.

David דָּוִד   אדני   יהוה אהיה יהוה   tzemach צֶמַח   et אֶת

vekarno וְקַרְנוֹ tatzmia'ch תַצְמִיחַ mehera מְהֵרָה פוי, אל אדני avdecha עַבְדְּךָ

lishu'atcha לִישׁוּעָתְךָ ki כִּי ♦bishu'atecha בִּישׁוּעָתֶךָ tarum תָּרוּם

יהוה אל זֹ, נגד, מזבוח, ע"ה hayom הַיּוֹם ילי kol כָּל־ kivinu קִוִּינוּ

You should meditate and ask here for the Final Redemption to occur right away.

Adonai יְהֹוָהאהדינהי Ata אַתָּה baruch בָּרוּךְ

yeshu'a יְשׁוּעָה keren קֶרֶן matzmi'ach מַצְמִיחַ

THE THIRTEENTH (SIXTEENTH) BLESSING

This blessing is the most important of all blessings, because here we acknowledge all of our reactive behavior. We make reference to our wrongful actions in general, and we also specify a particular incident. The section inside the box provides us with an opportunity to ask the Light for personal sustenance. The Ari states that throughout this prayer, even on fast days, we have a personal angel accompanying us. If we meditate upon this angel, all our prayers must be answered. The Thirteenth Blessing is one above the twelve zodiac signs, and it raises us above the influence of the stars and planets.

Tiferet

(יוד הה וו הה) Adonai יְהֹוָהאהדינהי kolenu קוֹלֵנוּ shema שְׁמַע

alenu עָלֵינוּ av אָב (אבג יתץ) ילה Elohenu אֱלֹהֵינוּ harachaman הָרַחֲמָן rachem רַחֵם

(קרע שטן) מצפצ, אלהים דיודין, י"פ ייי berachamim בְּרַחֲמִים vekabel וְקַבֵּל

et אֶת ע"ה אל שדי ע"ה, ע"ב בריבוע וקס"א ע"ה, מהט ע"ה, uvratzon וּבְרָצוֹן

(דס"ג) (מילוי) ייא"י El אֵל ki כִּי (נגד יכש') tefilatenu תְּפִלָּתֵנוּ

(בטר צתג) Ata אַתָּה vetachanunim וְתַחֲנוּנִים tefilot תְּפִלּוֹת shome'a שׁוֹמֵעַ

THE TWELFTH (FIFTEENTH) BLESSING

The offspring of David, Your servant, may You speedily cause to sprout.
And may You raise their worth with Your salvation, because it is for Your salvation that we have hoped all day long. Blessed are You, Lord, Who sprouts out the worth of the salvation.

THE THIRTEENTH (SIXTEENTH) BLESSING

Hear our voice, Lord, our God. Merciful Father, have mercy over us.
Accept our prayer with compassion and favor, because You are God, Who hears prayers and supplications.

It is good for you to be aware, acknowledge and confess your prior negative actions and to ask for your livelihood here:

רִבּוֹנוֹ ribono שֶׁל shel עוֹלָם olam, וְחָטָאתִי chatati עָוִיתִי aviti

וּפָשַׁעְתִּי ufashati לְפָנֶיךָ lefanecha יְהִי yehi רָצוֹן ratzon

שֶׁתִּמְחוֹל shetimchol מִלְפָנֶיךָ milfanecha

וְתִסְלַח vetislach וּתְכַפֵּר utchaper לִי li עַל al כָּל kol

מַה ma שֶׁחָטָאתִי shechatati וְשֶׁעָוִיתִי veshe'aviti וְשֶׁפָּשַׁעְתִּי veshepashati

לְפָנֶיךָ lefanecha מִיּוֹם miyom

שֶׁנִּבְרֵאתִי shenivreti עַד ad הַיּוֹם hayom הַזֶּה haze

וּבִפְרָט uvifrat (mention here a specific negative action or behavior you have and ask for forgivness)

וִיהִי vihi רָצוֹן ratzon

מִלְפָנֶיךָ milfanecha אֲדֹנָי Adonai אֱלֹהֵינוּ Elohenu

וֵאלֹהֵי velohei אֲבוֹתֵינוּ avotenu שֶׁתַּזְמִין shetazmin

פַּרְנָסָתֵנוּ parnasatenu וּמְזוֹנוֹתֵינוּ umzonotenu לִי li וּלְכָל ulchol

אַנְשֵׁי anshei בֵּיתִי veti הַיּוֹם hayom

וּבְכָל uvchol יוֹם yom

וָיוֹם vayom בְּרֵיוַוח berevach וְלֹא velo

וְצִמְצוּם vetzimtzum, בְּכָבוֹד bechavod וְלֹא velo בְּבִזּוּי bevizui,

בְּנַחַת benachat וְלֹא velo בְּצַעַר vetza'ar, וְלֹא velo אֶצְטָרֵךְ etztarech

לְמַתְּנוֹת lematenot בָּשָׂר basar וָדָם vadam וְלֹא velo לְהַלְוָאתָם lehalva'atam,

אֶלָּא ela מִיָּדְךָ miyadcha הָרְחָבָה harchava וְהַפְּתוּחָה vehapetucha

וְהַמְּלֵאָה vehamele'a וּבִזְכוּת uvizchut שִׁמְךָ shimcha הַגָּדוֹל hagadol

דִּיקַרְנוֹסָא (Do not pronounce this Name)

הַמְמוּנֶּה hamemune עַל al הַפַּרְנָסָה haparnasa

Master of the World!
I have transgressed. I have committed iniquity and I have sinned before You. May it be Your will that You would pardon, forgive and excuse all my transgressions, and all the iniquities that I have committed, and all the sins that I have sinned before You, ever since the day I was created and until this day (and especially…). May it be pleasing before You, Lord, our God and God of my forefathers, that You would provide for my livelihood and sustenance, and that of my household, today and each and every day, with abundance and not with meagerness; with dignity and not with shame; with comfort and not with suffering; and that I may not require the gifts of flesh and blood, nor their loans, but only from Your Hand, which is generous, open, and full, and by virtue of Your great Name, which is responsible for livelihood.

malkenu מַלְכֵּנוּ ב״ן מ״ה ס״ג umilfanecha וּמִלְּפָנֶיךָ

(וזקב טנע) te'shivenu תְּשִׁיבֵנוּ al אַל- rekam רֵיקָם

tefilatenu תְּפִלָּתֵנוּ׃ ushma וּשְׁמַע va'anenu וַעֲנֵנוּ chonenu וְחָנֵּנוּ

THE BLESSING FOR A FAST DAY
This blessing is recited by individuals on fast days, during the silent *Amidah*.

tzom צוֹם אל יהוה ז״, מזבו, ע״ה נגד, beyom בְּיוֹם anenu עֲנֵנוּ avinu אָבִינוּ anenu עֲנֵנוּ

gedola גְּדוֹלָה אלהים דההין vetzara בְצָרָה ki כִּי יהו haze הַזֶּה hata'anit הַתַּעֲנִית

lerish'enu לְרִשְׁעֵנוּ tefen תֵּפֶן al אַל- anachnu אֲנַחְנוּ.

mibakashatenu מִבַּקָּשָׁתֵנוּ. malkenu מַלְכֵּנוּ tit'alam תִּתְעַלַּם ve'al וְאַל-

leshav'atenu לְשַׁוְעָתֵנוּ. karov קָרוֹב na נָא heye הֱיֵה יהה

ta'ane תַעֲנֶה. Ata אַתָּה elecha אֵלֶיךָ nikra נִקְרָא terem טֶרֶם

kadavar כַּדָּבָר ראה tishma תִּשְׁמַע veAta וְאַתָּה ראה nedaber נְדַבֵּר

yikra'u יִקְרָאוּ terem טֶרֶם- יהוה ; vehaya וְהָיָה יהה shene'emar שֶׁנֶּאֱמַר׃

medabrim מְדַבְּרִים hem הֵם od עוֹד e'ene אֶעֱנֶה אני va'ani וַאֲנִי

Adonai יְהֹוָ(אדני)אהדונהי Ata אַתָּה ki כִּי eshma אֶשְׁמָע אני va'ani וַאֲנִי

umrachem וּמְרַחֵם אברהם, ve'one וְעוֹנֶה umatzil וּמַצִּיל pode פּוֹדֶה

(continue "ki Ata") vetzuka וְצוּקָה׃ אלהים דההין tzara צָרָה et עֵת לכב ב״ן, bechol בְּכָל וז״פ אל, רי״ו ול״ב נתיבות החכמה, רמ״ח (אברים), עסמ״ב וט״ז אותיות פשוטות

pe פֶּה ילי kol כָּל- tefilat תְּפִלַּת shome'a שׁוֹמֵעַ Ata אַתָּה ki כִּי

(פה דו״א) מילה ; וע״ה אלהים, אהיה אדני (יגל פזק)

Adonai יְהֹוָ(אדני)(יהו(אדני)אהדונהי Ata אַתָּה baruch בָּרוּךְ

You should meditate here on the Holy Name: אראר״ית

Rav Chaim Vital says: "I have found in the books of the kabbalists that the prayer of a person, who meditates on this Name in the blessing *shome'a tefila*, will never go unanswered."

---

shome'a שׁוֹמֵעַ tefila תְּפִלָּה (שׂקו צית) אתב״ש אוכצ, ב״ן אדני וניקודה ע״ה = יוד הי וו הה׃

And from before You,
our King, do not turn us away empty-handed but be gracious, answer us, and hear our prayer.

THE BLESSING FOR A FAST DAY
Answer us, our Father,
answer us on this day of fasting because we are in great distress. Do not pay heed to our wickedness and, our King, do not ignore our plea. Please come close to our cries and answer us even before we call out to You. We shall speak and You shall hear us, as it is said: And it shall be that before they call, I shall answer, and while they speak, I shall hear. (Isaiah 65:24) For You, Lord, redeem, save, respond, and show compassion in every time of trouble and distress.

Because You hear the prayer of every mouth. Blessed are You, Lord, Who hears prayers.

THE FINAL THREE BLESSINGS

Through the merit of Moses, Aaron and Joseph, who are our channels for the final three blessings, we are able to bring down all the spiritual energy that we aroused with our prayers and blessings.

THE SEVENTEENTH BLESSING

During this blessing, referring to Moses, we should always meditate to try to know exactly what God wants from us in our life, as signified by the phrase, "Let it be the will of God." We ask God to guide us toward the work we came to Earth to do. The Creator cannot just accept the work that we want to do; we must carry out the work we were destined to do.

Netzach

You have made requests (of daily needs) to God. Now, after asking for your needs to be met, you should praise the Creator in the last three blessings. This is like a person who has received what he needs from his Master and departs from Him. You should say *"retze"* and meditate for the Supernal Desire (*Keter*) that is called *metzach haratzon* (the Forehead of the Desire).

רְצֵה retze אלף למד הה יוד מם

Meditate here to transform misfortune and tragedy (צָרָה) into desire and acceptance (רצה).

(During the three weeks of *Ben HaMetzarim*, meditate here on these Holy Names:
אלהים דההין ארני, עין ע״ה, טדהד כוזו מצפצ - with these Names we transform צָרָה into רצה).

Yisrael יִשְׂרָאֵל	be'amecha בְּעַמְּךָ ילה	Elohenu אֱלֹהֵינוּ	Adonai יהוה אדניאהדונהי
ha'avoda הָעֲבוֹדָה	vehashev וְהָשֵׁב	she'e שְׁעֵה ◆	velitfilatam וְלִתְפִלָּתָם
Yisrael יִשְׂרָאֵל	ve'ishei וְאִשֵׁי ◆ ראה ב״פ	betecha בֵּיתֶךָ רי״י	lidvir לִדְבִיר
דאגה אוזר,	be'ahava בְּאַהֲבָה	mehera מְהֵרָה	utfilatam וּתְפִלָּתָם
ע״ה אל שדי ע״ה ◆	beratzon בְּרָצוֹן מוהש ע״ה, ע״ב בריבוע וקס״א ע״ה,	tekabel תְּקַבֵּל	
ע״ה אל שדי ע״ה	leratzon לְרָצוֹן מוהש ע״ה, ע״ב בריבוע וקס״א ע״ה,	ut'hi וּתְהִי	
amecha עַמְּךָ ‡	Yisrael יִשְׂרָאֵל	avodat עֲבוֹדַת קמ״ג	tamid תָּמִיד ע״ה קס״א קנ״א

THE FINAL THREE BLESSINGS
THE SEVENTEENTH BLESSING
Find favor, Lord, our God,
in Your People, Israel, and turn to their prayer.
Restore the service to the inner sanctuary of Your Temple. Accept the offerings of Israel and their prayer
with favor, speedily, and with love. May the service of Your People Israel always be favorable to You.

FOR *ROSH CHODESH*, *PESACH*, AND *SUKKOT* :

During these events, there is an extra surge of spiritual energy in our midst. These additional blessings are our antenna for drawing this extra power into our lives.

If you mistakenly forgot to say "*ya'ale veyavo*", and realize this before the end of the blessing ("*baruch Ata Adonai*"), you should return to say "*ya'ale veyavo*" and continue as usual. If you realize this after the end of the blessing ("*hamachazir shechinato leTziyon*") but before you start the next blessing ("*modim*") you should say "*ya'ale veyavo*" there and continue as usual. If you only realize this after you have started the next blessing ("*modim*") but before the second "*yih'yu leratzon*" (on pg. 393) you should return to "*retze*" (pg. 383) and continue from there. If you realize this after (the second "*yih'yu leratzon*") you should start the *Amidah* from the beginning. **On *Erev* (eve) of *Rosh Chodesh*** – if you mistakenly forgot to say "*ya'ale veyavo*", and realize this before the end of the blessing ("*baruch Ata Adonai*"), you should return to say "*ya'ale veyavo*" and continue as usual. Otherwise you continue your prayer and not return back.

avotenu אֲבוֹתֵינוּ ילה ; דמב , ע״ב מילוי ; לכב velohei וֵאלֹהֵי ילה Elohenu אֱלֹהֵינוּ

veyeratze וְיֵרָצֶה רי"ו veyera'e וְיֵרָאֶה veyagi'a וְיַגִּיעַ veyavo וְיָבֹא ya'ale יַעֲלֶה

(ר פ״ז) מ"ב ר"ת veyizacher וְיִזָּכֵר veyipaked וְיִפָּקֵד veyishama וְיִשָּׁמַע

avotenu אֲבוֹתֵינוּ וגע"ב קס"א ע"ב vezichron וְזִכְרוֹן zichronenu זִכְרוֹנֵנוּ

irach עִירָךְ Yerushalayim יְרוּשָׁלַיִם וגע"ב קס"א ע"ב zichron זִכְרוֹן

David דָּוִד ben בֶּן mashi'ach מְשִׁיחַ וגע"ב קס"א ע"ב vezichron וְזִכְרוֹן

ע"ה כהת ; בן דוד = אדני ע"ה avdach עַבְדְּךָ פוי, אל אדני vezichron וְזִכְרוֹן ע"ב קס"א וגע"ב

Yisrael יִשְׂרָאֵל ראה ב"פ bet בֵּית amecha עַמְּךָ ילי kol כָּל

אכא letova לְטוֹבָה lifleta לִפְלֵיטָה ב"ן מ"ה ס"ג lefanecha לְפָנֶיךָ

יהוה ריבוע ,ע"ב lechesed לְחֶסֶד מוזי ,בריבוע דמ"ה מילוי lechen לְחֵן

ע"ה. בינה יהוה, אהיה אהיה lechayim לְחַיִּים ulrachamim וּלְרַחֲמִים

אל יהוה: ,זן מזבוז ,נגד ע"ה beyom בְּיוֹם ulshalom וּלְשָׁלוֹם tovim טוֹבִים

FOR ROSH CHODESH, PESACH, AND SUKKOT :
Our God and God of our forefathers,

may it rise, come, arrive, appear, find favor, be heard, be considered, and be remembered, our remembrance and the remembrance of our forefathers: the remembrance of Jerusalem, Your City, and the remembrance of Mashiach, Son of David, Your servant, and the remembrance of Your entire Nation, the House of Israel, before You for deliverance, for good, for grace, kindness, and compassion, for a good life, and for peace on the day of:

On Rosh Chodesh:

רִבּוּעַ אלהים ואלהים דיודין ע"ה Rosh **רֹאשׁ**

haChodesh **הַחֹדֶשׁ** י"ב הויות, קס"א קנ"א ; ראש וחדש ע"ה = שין דלת יוד haze **הַזֶּה** והו.

On mid-holiday of Pesach:

haMatzot **הַמַּצּוֹת** chag **וְחַג** הַזֶּה **haze** והו

beyom **בְּיוֹם** ע"ה נגד, מזבח, זן, אל יהוה mikra **מִקְרָא** kodesh **קֹדֶשׁ** haze **הַזֶּה** והו.

On mid-holiday of Sukkot:

haSukkot **הַסֻּכּוֹת** chag **וְחַג** הַזֶּה **haze** והו

beyom **בְּיוֹם** ע"ה נגד, מזבח, זן, אל יהוה mikra **מִקְרָא** kodesh **קֹדֶשׁ** haze **הַזֶּה** והו.

lerachem **לְרַחֵם** אברהם, ח"פ אל, רי"ו ול"ב נתיבות החוכמה, רמ"ח (אברים), alenu **עָלֵינוּ** bo **בּוֹ** אותיות פעוטות עסמ"ב וט"ז ulhoshi'enu **וּלְהוֹשִׁיעֵנוּ**.

zochrenu **זָכְרֵנוּ** Adonai **יְהֹוָה**אדני אהיה Elohenu **אֱלֹהֵינוּ** ילה bo **בּוֹ**

letova **לְטוֹבָה** אכא ufokdenu **וּפָקְדֵנוּ** vo **בּוֹ** livracha **לִבְרָכָה**.

vehoshi'enu **וְהוֹשִׁיעֵנוּ** vo **בּוֹ** lechayim **לְחַיִּים** אהיה אהיה יהוה, בינה ע"ה.

tovim טוֹבִים. bidvar **בִּדְבַר** ראה yeshu'a **יְשׁוּעָה** verachamim **וְרַחֲמִים**.

chus **חוּס** vechonenu **וְחָנֵּנוּ** vachamol **וַחֲמוֹל** verachem **וְרַחֵם** אברהם, ח"פ אל, רי"ו ול"ב נתיבות החוכמה, רמ"ח (אברים), עסמ"ב וט"ז אותיות פעוטות alenu **עָלֵינוּ**.

vehoshi'enu **וְהוֹשִׁיעֵנוּ** ki **כִּי** elecha **אֵלֶיךָ** enenu **עֵינֵינוּ** ריבוע מ"ה ki **כִּי**.

El **אֵל** יא"י (מילוי דס"ג) melech **מֶלֶךְ** chanun **וְחַנּוּן** verachum **וְרַחוּם** Ata **אָתָּה**:

veAta **וְאַתָּה** verachamecha **בְּרַחֲמֶךָ** harabim **הָרַבִּים** tachpotz **תַּחְפֹּץ**

banu **בָּנוּ** vetirtzenu **וְתִרְצֵנוּ** vetechezena **וְתֶחֱזֶינָה** enenu **עֵינֵינוּ** ריבוע מ"ה

beshuvcha **בְּשׁוּבְךָ** leTziyon **לְצִיּוֹן** יוסף, ו' הויות, קנאה berachamim **בְּרַחֲמִים**

baruch **בָּרוּךְ** Ata **אַתָּה** יהוה אדני Adonai **יְהֹוָה**אדני ❖ יא"פ, יפ ייי, מצפצ, אלהים דיודין

hamachazir **הַמַּחֲזִיר** shechinato **שְׁכִינָתוֹ** leTziyon **לְצִיּוֹן** יוסף, ו' הויות, קנאה:

On Rosh Chodesh: This Rosh Chodesh.
On mid-holiday of Pesach: This festival of Matzot, on this holy day of convocation.
On mid-holiday of Sukkot: This festival of Sukkot, on this holy day of convocation.
To take pity on us and to save us.
Remember us, Lord, our God, on this day, for good; consider us on it for blessing; and deliver us on it for a good life, with the words of deliverance and mercy. Take pity and be gracious to us, have mercy and be compassionate with us, and save us, for our eyes turn to You, because You are God, the King Who is gracious and compassionate.

And You in Your great compassion take delight in us and are pleased with us. May our eyes witness Your return to Zion with compassion. Blessed are You, Lord, Who returns His Shechinah to Zion.

ARVIT – EVENING PRAYER
SWEETENING SOFT JUDGMENT

THE EIGHTEENTH BLESSING

This blessing is our thank you. Kabbalistically, the biggest 'thank you' we can give the Creator is to do exactly what we are supposed to do in terms of our spiritual work.

Hod

Bow your entire body at 'modim' and straighten up at 'Adonai'.

lach לָךְ anachnu אֲנַחְנוּ מאה ברכות שׂתיקן דוד לאמרם כל יום modim מוֹדִים

שָׁאַתָּה sheAta hu הוּא Adonai יְהוָֹה(אדניאהדונהי) (וו) Elohenu אֱלֹהֵינוּ ילה

וֵאלֹהֵי velohei ; לכב ; מילוי ע"ב, דמב ; ילה avotenu אֲבוֹתֵינוּ le'olam לְעוֹלָם

ריבוע ס"ג וי' אותיות דס"ג va'ed וָעֶד tzur צוּר tzurenu צוּרֵנוּ אלהים דההין ע"ה

וּמָגֵן umagen (ג"פ אל ("יא"י מילוי דס"ג) ; ר"ת מיכאל גבריאל נוריאל chayenu חַיֵּינוּ

node נוֹדֶה רי"ו vador וָדוֹר ledor לְדוֹר hu הוּא Ata אַתָּה yish'enu יִשְׁעֵנוּ

chayenu וְזֵּיינוּ al עַל tehilatecha תְּהִלָּתֶךָ unsaper וּנְסַפֵּר lecha לָךְ

nishmotenu נִשְׁמוֹתֵינוּ ve'al וְעַל beyadecha בְּיָדֶךָ hamesurim הַמְּסוּרִים

shebechol שֶׁבְּכָל nisecha נִסֶּיךָ ve'al וְעַל lach לָךְ hapekudot הַפְּקוּדוֹת

ב"ן, לכב יוֹם yom ע"ה נגד, מזבוז, ז, אל יהוה ריבוע ס"ג, קס"א ע"ה וד' אותיות imanu עִמָּנוּ

ve'al וְעַל vetovotecha וְטוֹבוֹתֶיךָ nifle'otecha נִפְלְאוֹתֶיךָ shebechol שֶׁבְּכָל

ב"ן, לכב עֵת et erev עֶרֶב vavoker וָבֹקֶר vetzahorayim וְצָהֳרַיִם hatov הַטּוֹב

hamerachem הַמְרַחֵם rachamecha רַחֲמֶיךָ chalu כָּלוּ lo לֹא ki כִּי והו

lo לֹא ki כִּי אברהם, וז"פ אל, רי"ו ול"ב נתיבות החוכמה, רמ"ח (אברים), עסמ"ב וט"ז אותיות פעוטות

tamu תַמּוּ chasadecha וַחֲסָדֶיךָ ki כִּי me'olam מֵעוֹלָם kivinu קִוִּינוּ lach לָךְ:

THE EIGHTEENTH BLESSING

We give thanks to You, for it is You, Lord, Who is our God and God of our forefathers, forever and for all eternity. You are our Rock, the Rock of our lives, and the Shield of our salvation. From one generation to another, we shall give thanks to You and we shall tell of Your praise. For our lives that are entrusted in Your hands, for our souls that are in Your care, for Your miracles that are with us every day, and for Your wonders and Your favors that are with us at all times: evening, morning and afternoon. You are the good One, for Your compassion has never ceased. You are the compassionate One, for Your kindness has never ended, for we have always placed our hope in You.

FOR CHANUKAH AND PURIM

Chanukah and *Purim* generate an added dimension of the energy of miracles. This blessing helps us harness this energy, thereby drawing miracles into our lives whenever they are truly needed.

וְעַל ve'al הַנִּסִים hanisim וְעַל ve'al הַפֻּרְקָן hapurkan•

וְעַל ve'al הַגְּבוּרוֹת hagevurot• וְעַל ve'al הַתְּשׁוּעוֹת hateshu'ot

וְעַל ve'al הַנִּפְלָאוֹת hanifla'ot וְעַל ve'al הַנֶּחָמוֹת hanechamot

שֶׁעָשִׂיתָ she'asita לַאֲבוֹתֵינוּ la'avotenu בַּיָּמִים bayamim נלך הָהֵם hahem

בַּזְּמַן bazeman הַזֶּה haze והו׃

FOR CHANUKAH:

בִּימֵי bimei מַתִּתְיָה Matitya בֶּן ven יוֹחָנָן Yochanan כֹּהֵן kohen מלה

גָּדוֹל gadol להו ; עם ד׳ אותיות = מבה, יזל, אום וַחַשְׁמוֹנָאִי Chashmonai וּבָנָיו uvanav

כְּשֶׁעָמְדָה keshe'amda מַלְכוּת malchut יָוָן Yavan הָרְשָׁעָה harsha'a עַל al

עַמְּךָ amecha יִשְׂרָאֵל Yisrael לְשַׁכְּחָם leshakecham תּוֹרָתֶךְ toratach

וּלְהַעֲבִירָם ulha'aviram מֵחֻקֵּי mechukei רְצוֹנָךְ retzonach• וְאַתָּה veAta

בְּרַחֲמֶיךָ verachamecha הָרַבִּים harabim עָמַדְתָּ amadeta לָהֶם lahem

בְּעֵת be'et צָרָתָם tzaratam• רַבְתָּ ravta אֶת et רִיבָם rivam• דַּנְתָּ danta

אֶת et דִּינָם dinam• נָקַמְתָּ nakamta מנק אֶת et נִקְמָתָם nikmatam מנק•

מָסַרְתָּ masarta גִּבּוֹרִים giborim בְּיַד beyad וְחַלָּשִׁים chalashim• וְרַבִּים verabim

בְּיַד beyad מְעַטִּים me'atim• וּרְשָׁעִים ursha'im בְּיַד beyad צַדִּיקִים tzadikim•

וּטְמֵאִים utme'im בְּיַד beyad טְהוֹרִים tehorim• וְזֵדִים vezedim בְּיַד beyad

עוֹסְקֵי oskei תוֹרָתֶךָ toratecha• לְךָ lecha עָשִׂיתָ asita שֵׁם shem

גָּדוֹל gadol להו ; עם ד׳ אותיות = מבה, יזל, אום וְקָדוֹשׁ vekadosh בְּעוֹלָמָךְ be'olamach•

וּלְעַמְּךָ ul'amecha יִשְׂרָאֵל Yisrael עָשִׂיתָ asita תְּשׁוּעָה teshu'a גְּדוֹלָה gedola

וּפֻרְקָן ufurkan כְּהַיּוֹם kehayom ע״ה נגד, מזבוח, זן, אל יהוה הָזֶה haze והו•

FOR CHANUKAH AND PURIM

*And also for the miracles, deliverance, the mighty acts, the salvation, wonders,
and comforting deeds that You performed for our forefathers, in those days and at this time.*

FOR CHANUKAH

In the days of Mattatiyahu, the son of Yochanan, the High Priest, the Hasmonean, and his sons, when the evil Greek Empire rose up against Your Nation, Israel, to force them to forget Your Torah and to force them away from the laws of Your desire, You, with Your compassion, stood up for them in their time of trouble. You fought their battles, sought justice for them, avenged them, and delivered the strong into the hands of the weak, the many into the hands of the few, the wicked into the hands of the righteous, the defiled into the hands of the pure, and the tyrants into the hands of those who occupy themselves with Your Torah. For Yourself, You made a Holy Name in Your world, and for Your People, Israel, You carried out a great salvation and deliverance on this day.

רי״ו lidvir לִדְבִיר vanecha בָנֶיךָ ba'u בָּאוּ kach כָךְ ve'achar וְאַחַר

vetiharu וְטִהֲרוּ hechalecha הֵיכָלֶךָ et אֶת־ ufinu וּפִנּוּ ב״פ ראה betecha בֵּיתֶךָ

nerot נֵרוֹת vehidliku וְהִדְלִיקוּ mikdashecha מִקְדָּשֶׁךָ et אֶת

shemonat שְׁמוֹנַת vekav'u וְקָבְעוּ kodshecha קָדְשֶׁךָ bechatzrot בְּחַצְרוֹת

yemei יְמֵי Chanukah וַחֲנֻכָּה elu אֵלּוּ behalel בְּהַלֵּל אדני, לכה ובהודאה uvhoda'a

ve'asita וְעָשִׂיתָ venifla'ot וְנִפְלָאוֹת nisim נִסִים imahem עִמָּהֶם venode וְנוֹדֶה

leshimcha לְשִׁמְךָ hagadol הַגָּדוֹל להו ; עם ד׳ אותיות = מבה, יזל, אום sela סֶלָה:

FOR PURIM:

bimei בִּימֵי Mardechai מָרְדְּכַי veEster וְאֶסְתֵּר עם האותיות = מילוי אדני

alehem עֲלֵיהֶם keshe'amad כְּשֶׁעָמַד habira הַבִּירָה beShushan בְּשׁוּשָׁן

laharog לַהֲרֹג lehashmid לְהַשְׁמִיד bikesh בִּקֵּשׁ harasha הָרָשָׁע Haman הָמָן

ve'ad וְעַד mina'ar מִנַּעַר hayehudim הַיְּהוּדִים kol כָּל et אֶת ul'abed וּלְאַבֵּד

zaken זָקֵן taf טַף venashim וְנָשִׁים beyom בְּיוֹם ע״ה נגד, מזבח, זן, אל יהוה

lechodesh לְחֹדֶשׁ asar עָשָׂר bishlosha בִּשְׁלוֹשָׁה echad אֶחָד אהבה, דאגה

chodesh וְחֹדֶשׁ hu הוּא asar עָשָׂר shenem שְׁנֵים י״ב היות, קס״א קנ״א, קס״א קנ״א

verachamecha בְּרַחֲמֶיךָ veAta וְאַתָּה lavoz לָבוֹז ushlalam וּשְׁלָלָם adar אֲדָר

vekilkalta וְקִלְקַלְתָּ atzato עֲצָתוֹ et אֶת hefarta הֵפַרְתָּ harabim הָרַבִּים

gemulo גְּמוּלוֹ lo לוֹ vahashevota וַהֲשֵׁבוֹתָ machashavto מַחֲשַׁבְתּוֹ et אֶת

ha'etz הָעֵץ al עַל banav בָּנָיו ve'et וְאֶת oto אוֹתוֹ vetalu וְתָלוּ berosho בְּרֹאשׁוֹ

ve'asita וְעָשִׂיתָ venifla'ot וְנִפְלָאוֹת nisim נִסִים imahem עִמָּהֶם venode וְנוֹדֶה

leshimcha לְשִׁמְךָ hagadol הַגָּדוֹל להו ; עם ד׳ אותיות = מבה, יזל, אום sela סֶלָה:

Then Your Children came into the Sanctuary of Your House, they cleansed Your Palace, they purified Your Temple, they lit candles in the courtyards of Your Holy Domain, and they established these eight days of Chanukah for praise and thanksgiving. And You performed for them miracles and wonders. For that, we are grateful to Your Great Name. Selah!

FOR PURIM:

In the days of Mardechai and Esther, in Shushan, the capital, when the evil Haman rose up against them, he sought to destroy, slay, and annihilate all the Jews, young and old, children and women, in one day, on the thirteenth day of the twelfth month, which is the month of Adar, and to take their spoils. But You, in Your great compassion, ruined his plan, foiled his design, and turned his due upon his own head. They hanged him and his sons upon the gallows. And You performed for them [Israel] miracles and wonders. We give thanks to Your great Name. Selah!

veyitromam וְיִתְרוֹמָם yitbarach יִתְבָּרַךְ kulam כֻּלָּם ve'al וְעַל

shimcha שִׁמְךָ קמ"ג קנ"א קס"א ע"ה tamid תָּמִיד veyitnase וְיִתְנַשֵּׂא

va'ed וָעֶד דס"ג וי' אותיות ריבוע ס"ג le'olam לְעוֹלָם malkenu מַלְכֵּנוּ

sela סֶלָה: yoducha יוֹדוּךָ אהיה אהיה יהוה, בינה ע"ה hachayim הַחַיִּים יל vechol וְכָל־

During the days between *Rosh Hashanah* and *Yom Kippur* we say the prayer of "uchtov":

tovim טוֹבִים אהיה אהיה יהוה, בינה ע"ה lechayim לְחַיִּים uchtov וּכְתֹב

veritecha בְּרִיתֶךָ: benei בְּנֵי יל kol כָּל־

If you forget to say "*uchtov*" and realize this before the end of the blessing ("*baruch Ata Adonai*"), you should return and say "*uchtov*" and continue as usual. But if you only realize this after the end of the blessing, you should continue and you may add "*uchtov*" in the end of "*Elohai netzor*".

---

et אֶת־ מ"ה ריבוע יהוה יהוה ריבוע יהוה vivarchu וִיבָרְכוּ vihalelu וִיהַלְלוּ

be'emet בֶּאֱמֶת שמה, יזל, אום = אותיות ד' עם ; להו hagadol הַגָּדוֹל shimcha שִׁמְךָ

tov טוֹב והו ; אהיה פעמים אהיה, ז"פ ס"ג le'olam לְעוֹלָם ריבוע ס"ג וי' אותיות דס"ג ki כִּי

yeshu'atenu יְשׁוּעָתֵנוּ יא"י (מילוי דס"ג) ; לאה יא"י ; יזל, מבה, אום, אהיה יהוה = טוב כי haEl הָאֵל

hatov הַטּוֹב והו (מילוי דס"ג) יא"י ; לאה haEl הָאֵל sela סֶלָה ve'ezratenu וְעֶזְרָתֵנוּ

*Bend your knees at '*baruch*', bow at '*Ata*' and straighten up at '*Adonai*'.*

hatov הַטּוֹב (הי) והו Adonai יֱהֹוָ֥הֱאֲדֹנָֽיאֲדֹנָֽי Ata אַתָּה baruch בָּרוּךְ

shimcha שִׁמְךָ ס"ת כהת, משיח בן דוד ע"ה: lehodot לְהוֹדוֹת na'e נָאֶה ulcha וּלְךָ

And for all those things, may Your Name be always blessed,
exalted and extolled, our King, forever and ever, and all the living shall thank You, Selah.

During the days between *Rosh Hashanah* and *Yom Kippur*:
And write down for a good life all the members of Your Covenant.

And they shall praise and bless Your Great Name,
sincerely and forever, for It is good, the God of our salvation and our help, Selah,
the good God. Blessed are You, Lord, whose Name is good, and to You it is befitting to give thanks.

THE FINAL BLESSING

We are emanating the energy of peace to the entire world. We also make it our intent to use our mouths only for good. Kabbalistically, the power of words and speech is unimaginable. We hope to use that power wisely, which is perhaps one of the most difficult tasks we have to carry out.

Yesod

shalom שָׂלוֹם sim שִׂים

(During the three weeks of Ben HaMetzarim, meditate here on these Holy Names:
שׁין ראשׁונה (ע"ה = טרהד כוזו מצפצ) ממתקת את העין העליונה (= אלהים דההין אדני) ;
וכן שׂים שׁלום ע"ה = ו' השׁמות (טרהד כוזו מצפצ אלהים אדני יהוה) אדני טרהד כוזו מצפצ אלהים ואלהים דההין)

chen וְחֵן tova טוֹבָה אכא chayim וְחַיִּים uvracha וּבְרָכָה chayim אהיה אהיה יהוה, בינה ע"ה

tzedaka צְדָקָה ע"ב, ריבוע יהוה vachesed וָחֶסֶד מילוי דמ"ה בריבוע, מוז"ו ע"ה ריבוע אלהים

verachamim וְרַחֲמִים alenu עָלֵינוּ ve'al וְעַל kol כָּל yli עמם

Yisrael יִשְׂרָאֵל amecha עַמֶּךְ uvarchenu וּבָרְכֵנוּ avinu אָבִינוּ kulanu כֻּלָּנוּ

ki כִּי ke'echad כְּאֶחָד be'or בְּאוֹר ר, א"ס אהבה, דאגה panecha פָּנֶיךָ ס"ג מ"ה בן

ve'or בְּאוֹר ר, א"ס panecha פָּנֶיךָ ס"ג מ"ה בן natata נָתַתָּ lanu לָנוּ אלהים, אהיה אדני

Adonai יְהֹוָאֲדֹנָיאיאהדונהי Elohenu אֱלֹהֵינוּ ילה torah תּוֹרָה vechayim וְחַיִּים

ahava אַהֲבָה אוזר, דאגה אהיה אהיה יהוה, בינה ע"ה vachesed וָחֶסֶד ע"ב, ריבוע יהוה

tzedaka צְדָקָה ע"ה ריבוע אלהים verachamim וְרַחֲמִים beracha בְּרָכָה

veshalom וְשָׁלוֹם vetov וְטוֹב והו be'enecha בְּעֵינֶיךָ ע"ה קס"א ; ריבוע מ"ה

levarchenu לְבָרְכֵנוּ ulvarech וּלְבָרֵךְ et אֵת kol כָּל yli amecha עַמֶּךְ

Yisrael יִשְׂרָאֵל berov בְּרוֹב י"פ אהיה oz עֹז veshalom וְשָׁלוֹם

THE FINAL BLESSING

Place peace, goodness, blessing, life, grace, kindness, righteousness, and mercy upon us and upon all of Israel, Your People. Bless us all as one, our Father, with the Light of Your Countenance, because it is with the Light of Your Countenance that You, Lord, our God, have given us Torah and life, love and kindness, righteousness and mercy, blessing and peace. May it be good in Your Eyes to bless us and to bless Your entire Nation, Israel, with abundant power and with peace.

During the days between *Rosh Hashanah* and *Yom Kippur* we say the prayer of "*uvsefer chayim*":

ע"ה בִּינָה יהוה, אֶהְיֶה אֶהְיֶה chayim וְחַיִּים uvsefer וּבְסֵפֶר

אכא tova טוֹבָה ufarnasa וּפַרְנָסָה veshalom וְשָׁלוֹם beracha בְּרָכָה

tovot טוֹבוֹת ugzerot וּגְזֵרוֹת venechama וְנֶחָמָה vishu'a וִישׁוּעָה

ב"ן מ"ה ס"ג lefanecha לְפָנֶיךָ venikatev וְנִכָּתֵב nizacher נִזָּכֵר

Yisrael יִשְׂרָאֵל amecha עַמְּךָ ילי vechol וְכָל anachnu אֲנַחְנוּ

:ulshalom וּלְשָׁלוֹם tovim טוֹבִים ע"ה בִּינָה יהוה, אֶהְיֶה אֶהְיֶה lechayim לְחַיִּים

If you forgot to say "*uvesefer chayim*" and realize this before the end of the blessing ("*baruch Ata Adonai*"), you should return and say "*uvesefer chayim*" and continue as usual. But if you realize this only after the end of the blessing, you should continue and you may add "*uvesefer chayim*" in the end of "*Elohai netzor*".

Adonai יֻדֹוּוָוִדֹאֱלֹהֵיִיאַהֲדוֹנַהִי Ata אַתָּה baruch בָּרוּךְ

Yisrael יִשְׂרָאֵל amo עַמּוֹ et אֵת hamevarech הַמְבָרֵךְ

:amen אָמֵן ◆bashalom בְּשָׁלוֹם (יב"ק) = (אֱלֹהֵיהֶם) = אלהים = ר"ת

YIH'YU LERATZON

There are 42 letters in the verse in the secret of *Ana Beko'ach*.

ע"ה leratzon לְרָצוֹן (יא"י מילוי דס"ג) אל yih'yu יִהְיוּ

libi לִבִּי vehegyon וְהֶגְיוֹן fi פִי imrei אִמְרֵי

:vego'ali וְגֹאֲלִי tzuri צוּרִי Adonai יֻדֹוּוָוִדֹ lefanecha לְפָנֶיךָ

During the days between *Rosh Hashanah* and *Yom Kippur*:
And in the Book of Life, for blessing, peace, good livelihood, salvation, consolation, and good decrees, may we all be remembered and be inscribed before You: we and Your entire Nation, Israel, for good life and for peace.

Blessed are You, Lord, Who blesses His Nation, Israel, with peace, Amen.

YIH'YU LERATZON
"May the utterances of my mouth and the thoughts of my heart find favor before You, Lord, my Rock and my Redeemer." (Psalms 19:15)

ELOHAI NETZOR

Elohai אֱלֹהַי מילוי ע"ב, דמב ; ילה netzor נְצוֹר leshoni לְשׁוֹנִי mera מֵרָע◆

vesiftotai וְשִׂפְתוֹתַי midaber מִדַּבֵּר ראה mirma מִרְמָה◆ velimkalelai וְלִמְקַלְלַי

nafshi נַפְשִׁי tidom תִדוֹם◆ venafshi וְנַפְשִׁי ke'afar כֶּעָפָר

lakol לַכֹּל tih'ye תִהְיֶה יה אדני petach פְּתַח libi לִבִּי betoratecha בְּתוֹרָתֶךְ◆

ve'acharei וְאַחֲרֵי mitzvotecha מִצְוֹתֶיךָ tirdof תִרְדּוֹף nafshi נַפְשִׁי◆

vechol וְכָל־ ילי hakamim הַקָּמִים alai עָלַי lera'a לְרָעָה רהע◆ mehera מְהֵרָה◆

hafer הָפֵר atzatam עֲצָתָם vekalkel וְקַלְקֵל machshevotam מַחְשְׁבוֹתָם◆

ase עֲשֵׂה lema'an לְמַעַן shemach שְׁמָךְ◆ ase עֲשֵׂה lema'an לְמַעַן

yeminach יְמִינָךְ◆ ase עֲשֵׂה lema'an לְמַעַן toratach תוֹרָתָךְ◆ ase עֲשֵׂה

lema'an לְמַעַן kedushatach קְדוּשָׁתָךְ◆ ר"ת הפסוק = מ"ה יהוה lema'an לְמַעַן

yechaltzun יֵחָלְצוּן yedidecha יְדִידֶיךָ ר"ת ילי hoshi'a הוֹשִׁיעָה יהוה וט"ע נהורין

yemincha יְמִינְךָ va'aneni וַעֲנֵנִי (כתיב: וַעֲנֵנוּ) ר"ת אל (יא"י מילוי דס"ג):

Before we recite the next verse ("*yih'yu leratzon*") we have an opportunity to strengthen our connection to our soul using our name. Each person has a verse in the *Torah* that connects to their name. Either their name is in the verse, or the first and last letters of the name correspond to the first or last letters of a verse. For example, the name Yehuda begins with a *Yud* and ends with a *Hei*. Before we end the *Amidah*, we state that our name will always be remembered when our soul leaves this world.

ELOHAI NETZOR

My God, guard my tongue from evil and my lips from speaking deceit. To those who curse me, let my spirit remain silent, and let my spirit be as dust for everyone. Open my heart to Your Torah and let my heart pursue Your commandments. All those who rise against me to do me harm, speedily nullify their plans and disturb their thoughts. Do so for the sake of Your Name. Do so for the sake of Your Right. Do so for the sake of Your Torah. Do so for the sake of Your Holiness, "So that Your loved ones may be saved. Redeem Your right and answer me." (Psalms 60:7)

YIH'YU LERATZON (THE SECOND)

There are 42 letters in the verse in the secret of *Ana Beko'ach*.

יִהְיוּ yih'yu אל (ייא"י מילוי דס"ג) leratzon לְרָצוֹן מהטע ע"ה, ע"ב ברבוע וקס"א ע"ה, אל שדי ע"ה

imrei אִמְרֵי fi פִי ר"ת אלף = אלף למד מם דלת עין דלת יוד ע"ה vehegyon וְהֶגְיוֹן libi לִבִּי

lefanecha לְפָנֶיךָ Adonai יְהֹוָה ס"ג מ"ה ב"ן tzuri צוּרִי vego'ali וְגֹאֲלִי:

OSE SHALOM

You take three steps backward;

ose עוֹשֶׂה shalom שָׁלוֹם

Left
You turn to the left and say:

(During the days between *Rosh Hashanah* and *Yom Kippur* instead of "*shalom*" we say:

hashalom הַשָּׁלוֹם ספריאל המלאך הוותם לוזיים)

bimromav בִּמְרוֹמָיו ר"ת ע"ב, ריבוע יהוה

Right
You turn to the right and say:

hu הוּא verachamav בְּרַחֲמָיו ya'ase יַעֲשֶׂה

shalom שָׁלוֹם alenu עָלֵינוּ ר"ת ע"ע נהורין

Center
You face the center and say:

ve'al וְעַל kol כָּל־ עמם amo עַמּוֹ Yisrael יִשְׂרָאֵל

ve'imru וְאִמְרוּ amen אָמֵן יאהדונהי:

yehi יְהִי ratzon רָצוֹן מהטע ע"ה, ע"ב ברבוע וקס"א ע"ה, אל שדי ע"ה

milfanecha מִלְּפָנֶיךָ Adonai יְהֹוָה ס"ג מ"ה ב"ן Elohenu אֱלֹהֵינוּ ילה

velohei וֵאלֹהֵי avotenu אֲבוֹתֵינוּ shetivne שֶׁתִּבְנֶה

bet בֵּית hamikdash הַמִּקְדָּשׁ bimhera בִּמְהֵרָה veyamenu בְיָמֵינוּ

veten וְתֵן chelkenu וְחֶלְקֵנוּ betoratach בְּתוֹרָתֶךָ la'asot לַעֲשׂוֹת chukei וְחֻקֵי

retzonach רְצוֹנֶךָ ul'ovdach וּלְעָבְדְךָ belevav בְּלֵבָב shalem שָׁלֵם.

You take three steps forward.

YIH'YU LERATZON (THE SECOND)
"May the utterances of my mouth and the thoughts of my heart find favor before You, Lord, my Rock and my Redeemer." (Psalms 19:15)

OSE SHALOM
He, Who makes peace (During the days between *Rosh Hashanah* and *Yom Kippur*: *The peace*) *in His high places, He, in His compassion, shall make peace upon us And upon His entire nation, Israel, and you shall say, Amen.*

May it be pleasing before You,
Lord, our God and God of our forefathers, that You shall rebuild the Temple speedily, in our days, and place our lot in Your Torah, so that we may fulfill the laws of Your desire and serve You wholeheartedly.

KADDISH TITKABAL

יִתְגַּדַּל yitgadal וְיִתְקַדַּשׁ veyitkadash שְׁדִי וּמִילוּי שְׁדִי ; י"א אותיות כמנין ו"ה

שְׁמֵיהּ shemei (שם י"ה דע"ב) רַבָּא raba קנ"א ב"ן, יהוה אלהים יהוה אדני,

מילוי קס"א וס"ג, מ"ה ברבוע וע"ב ע"ה ; ר"ת = ו"פ אלהים ; ס"ת = ג"פ יב"ק אָמֵן amen אידהנויה.

בְּעָלְמָא be'alma דִּי di בְרָא vera כִּרְעוּתֵיהּ chir'utei.

וְיַמְלִיךְ veyamlich מַלְכוּתֵיהּ malchutei. וְיַצְמַח veyatzmach

פּוּרְקָנֵיהּ purkanei. אָמֵן amen אידהנויה וִיקָרֵב vikarev מְשִׁיחֵיהּ meshichei.

בְּחַיֵּיכוֹן bechayechon וּבְיוֹמֵיכוֹן uvyomechon וּבְחַיֵּי uvchayei

דְכָל dechol בֵּית bet ב"פ ראה יִשְׂרָאֵל Yisrael בַּעֲגָלָא ba'agala

וּבִזְמַן uvizman קָרִיב kariv וְאִמְרוּ ve'imru אָמֵן amen. אָמֵן amen אידהנויה.

The congregation and the *chazan* say the following:

28 words (until *be'alma*) – meditate: מילוי דמילוי דע"ב (יוד ויו דלת הי יוד ויו יוד ויו הי יוד)

28 letters (until *almaya*) – meditate: מילוי דמילוי דע"ב (יוד ויו דלת הי יוד ויו יוד ויו הי יוד)

יְהֵא yehe שְׁמֵיהּ shemei (שם י"ה דס"ג) רַבָּא raba קנ"א ב"ן,

מְבָרַךְ mevarach יהוה אלהים יהוה אדני, מילוי קס"א וס"ג, מ"ה ברבוע וע"ב ע"ה

לְעָלַם le'alam לְעָלְמֵי le'almei עָלְמַיָּא almaya. יִתְבָּרַךְ yitbarach.

Seven words with six letters each (שם בן מ"ב) – meditate:
יהוה + יוד הי ויו הי + מילוי דמילוי דע"ב (יוד ויו דלת הי יוד ויו יוד ויו הי יוד)

Also, seven times the letter Vav (שם בן מ"ב) – meditate:
יהוה + יוד הי ויו הי + מילוי דמילוי דע"ב (יוד ויו דלת הי יוד ויו יוד ויו הי יוד).

וְיִשְׁתַּבַּח veyishtabach י"פ ע"ב יהוה אל אבג יתץ.

וְיִתְפָּאַר veyitpa'ar הי גו יה קרע שטן. וְיִתְרַמֵּם veyitromam וה כוזו נגד יכש.

וְיִתְנַשֵּׂא veyitnase במוכסז בטר צתג. וְיִתְהַדָּר veyit'hadar כוזו יה וזקב טנע.

וְיִתְעַלֶּה veyit'ale וה יוד ה יגל פזק. וְיִתְהַלָּל veyit'halal א ואו הא שקו צית.

שְׁמֵיהּ shemei (שם י"ה דמ"ה) דְּקוּדְשָׁא dekudsha בְּרִיךְ verich הוּא hu.

אָמֵן amen אידהנויה.

KADDISH TITKABAL

May His great Name be more exalted and sanctified. (Amen) In the world that He created according to His will, and may His Kingdom reign. And may He cause His redemption to sprout and may He bring the Mashiach closer. (Amen) In your lifetimes and in your days and in the lifetime of all the House of Israel, speedily and in the near future, and you shall say, Amen. (Amen) May His great Name be blessed forever and for all eternity. Blessed and lauded, and glorified, and exalted, and extolled, and honored, and uplifted, and praised be the Name of the Holy Blessed One. (Amen)

לְעֵלָּא le'ela · מִן min · כָּל kol · יל׳ · בִּרְכָתָא birchata · שִׁירָתָא shirata

תֻּשְׁבְּחָתָא tishbechata · וְנֶחָמָתָא venechamata · דַּאֲמִירָן da'amiran

בְּעָלְמָא be'alma · וְאִמְרוּ ve'imru · אָמֵן amen · אָמֵן amen אידהנויה.

תִּתְקַבֵּל titkabal · צְלוֹתָנָא tzelotana · וּבָעוּתָנָא uva'utana

עִם im · צְלוֹתְהוֹן tzelotehon · וּבָעוּתְהוֹן uva'utehon · דְּכָל dechol יל׳

בֵּית bet ב״פ ראה · יִשְׂרָאֵל Yisrael · קֳדָם kadam · אֲבוּנָא avuna

דְּבִשְׁמַיָּא devishmaya · וְאִמְרוּ ve'imru · אָמֵן amen · אָמֵן amen אידהנויה·

יְהֵא yehe · שְׁלָמָא shelama · רַבָּא raba קנ״א ב״ן, יהוה אלהים יהוה אדני, מילוי קס״א וס״ג,

מִן min ע״ב ע״ה · שְׁמַיָּא shemaya · שֶׁמַיָּא — וְחַיִּים chayim אהיה אהיה יהוה, בינה יהוה ע״ה מ״ה ברבוע וע״ב ע״ה

וְשָׂבָע vesava · וִישׁוּעָה vishu'a · וְנֶחָמָה venechama · וְשֵׁיזָבָא veshezava

וּרְפוּאָה urfu'a · וּגְאֻלָּה ug'ula · וּסְלִיחָה uslicha · וְכַפָּרָה vechapara

וְרֶיוַח verevach · וְהַצָּלָה vehatzala · לָנוּ lanu אלהים, אהיה אדני · וּלְכָל ulchol יה אדני

עַמּוֹ amo · יִשְׂרָאֵל Yisrael · וְאִמְרוּ ve'imru · אָמֵן amen · אָמֵן amen אידהנויה.

Take three steps backwards and say:

עוֹשֶׂה ose שָׁלוֹם shalom

(During the days between *Rosh Hashanah* and *Yom Kippur* instead of "*shalom*" we say:

הַשָּׁלוֹם hashalom ספריאל המלאך החותם לחיים)

בִּמְרוֹמָיו bimromav ע״ב, ריבוע יהוה· · הוּא hu · בְּרַחֲמָיו berachamav

יַעֲשֶׂה ya'ase · שָׁלוֹם shalom · עָלֵינוּ alenu ר״ת ע״ע נהורין·

וְעַל ve'al · כָּל kol יל׳ ; עמם · עַמּוֹ amo · יִשְׂרָאֵל Yisrael וְאִמְרוּ ve'imru · אָמֵן amen·

אָמֵן amen אידהנויה·

Above all blessings, songs, praises, and words of consolation that may be said in the world, and you shall say, Amen. (Amen) May our prayers and pleas be accepted, together with the prayers and pleas of the entire House of Israel, before our Father in Heaven, and you say, Amen. (Amen) May there be abundant peace from heaven. Life, contentment, salvation, consolation, deliverance, healing, redemption, pardon, atonement, comfort, and relief. For us and for His entire nation, Israel, and you shall say, Amen. (Amen) He, Who makes peace (During the days between *Rosh Hashanah* and *Yom Kippur*: *The peace*) *in His high places, He, in His compassion, shall make peace upon us And upon His entire nation, Israel, and you shall say, Amen. (Amen)*

SHIR LAMA'ALOT

שִׁיר shir לַמַּעֲלוֹת lama'alot אֶשָּׂא esa עֵינַי enai רִיבוּע מ"ה

אֶל־ el הֶהָרִים heharim מֵאַיִן me'ayin יָבֹא yavo עֶזְרִי ezri:

עֶזְרִי ezri מֵעִם me'im יְהֹוָה Adonai עֹשֵׂה ose שָׁמַיִם shamayim

וָאָרֶץ va'aretz: אַל־ al יִתֵּן yiten לַמּוֹט lamot רַגְלֶךָ raglecha י"פ טל, י"פ כוו

אַל־ al יָנוּם yanum שֹׁמְרֶךָ shomrecha: הִנֵּה hine לֹא lo יָנוּם yanum

וְלֹא velo יִישָׁן yishan ע"ע נהורין דא"א שׁוֹמֵר shomer כ"א ההויות שבתפילין

יִשְׂרָאֵל Yisrael: יְהֹוָה Adonai שֹׁמְרֶךָ shomrecha

יְהֹוָה Adonai צִלְּךָ tzilecha עַל־ al יַד yad יְמִינֶךָ yeminecha הי:

יוֹמָם yomam הַשֶּׁמֶשׁ hashemesh לֹא־ lo יַכֶּכָּה yakeka ר"ת ילה

וְיָרֵחַ veyare'ach בַּלָּיְלָה balayla מלה: יְהֹוָה Adonai

יִשְׁמָרְךָ yishmorcha מִכָּל־ mikol ילי רָע ra יִשְׁמֹר yishmor

אֶת־ et נַפְשֶׁךָ nafshecha מיכ: יְהֹוָה Adonai יִשְׁמֹר yishmor

צֵאתְךָ tzetcha וּבוֹאֶךָ uvo'echa מֵעַתָּה me'ata וְעַד־ ve'ad עוֹלָם olam וול:

KADDISH YEHE SHELAMA

יִתְגַּדַּל yitgadal וְיִתְקַדַּשׁ veyitkadash שׁדי ומילוי שׁדי ; י"א אותיות כמנין ו"ה

שְׁמֵיהּ shemei (שם י"ה דע"ב) רַבָּא raba קנ"א ב"ן, יהוה אלהים יהוה אדני,

אָמֵן amen אידהנויה: מילוי קס"א וס"ג, מ"ה ברבוע וע"ב ע"ה ; ר"ת = ו"פ אלהים ; ס"ת = ג"פ יב"ק:

בְּעָלְמָא be'alma דִּי di בְּרָא vera כִרְעוּתֵיהּ chir'utei:

וְיַמְלִיךְ veyamlich מַלְכוּתֵיהּ malchutei: וְיַצְמַח veyatzmach

פּוּרְקָנֵיהּ purkanei: וִיקָרֵב vikarev מְשִׁיחֵיהּ meshichei: אָמֵן amen אידהנויה:

SHIR LAMA'ALOT

"A Song of Ascents: I lift up my eyes to the mountains; from where will my help come? My help is from the Lord, Creator of the Heavens and the Earth. He will not allow your legs to falter. Your Guardian shall not sleep. Behold: the Guardian of Israel shall neither slumber nor sleep. The Lord is your Guardian. The Lord is your protective shade at your right hand. During the day, the sun shall not harm you, nor shall the moon, at night. The Lord shall protect you from all evil, He will guard your soul. He shall guard you when you leave and when you come, from now and for eternity." (Psalms 121)

KADDISH YEHE SHELAMA

May His great Name be more exalted and sanctified. (Amen)
In the world that He created according to His will, and may His kingdom reign.
And may He cause His redemption to sprout and may He bring the Mashiach closer. (Amen)

בְּחַיֵּיכוֹן bechayechon וּבְיוֹמֵיכוֹן uvyomechon וּבְחַיֵּי uvchayei

דְכָל dechol יְלי בֵּית bet בְּ"פ ראה בֵּית bet יִשְׂרָאֵל Yisrael בַּעֲגָלָא ba'agala

וּבִזְמַן uvizman קָרִיב kariv וְאָמְרוּ ve'imru אָמֵן amen :אָמֵן amen אידהנויה. amen

The congregation and the *chazan* say the following:

---

28 words (until *be'alma*) – meditate:

מילוי דמילוי דס"ג (יוד ויו דלת הי יוד ואו אלף ואו הי יוד)

28 letters (until *almaya*) - meditate:

מילוי דמילוי דמ"ה (יוד ואו דלת הא אלף הא ואו אלף ואו הא אלף).

יְהֵא yehe שְׁמֵיהּ shemei (שם י"ה דס"ג) רַבָּא raba קנ"א ב"ן,

מְבָרַךְ mevarach ע"ה מ"ה ברבוע ועה"ב וס"ג, קס"א מילוי, אדנ"י, יהוה אלהים יהוה

לְעָלַם le'alam לְעָלְמֵי le'almei עָלְמַיָּא almaya יִתְבָּרַךְ yitbarach

---

Seven words with six letters each (שם בן מ"ב) – meditate:

יהוה + יוד הי ואו הי + מילוי דמילוי דס"ג (יוד ויו דלת הי יוד ואו אלף ואו הי יוד) ;

Also, seven times the letter Vav (שם בן מ"ב) – meditate:

יהוה + יוד הא ואו הא + מילוי דמילוי דמ"ה (יוד ואו דלת הא אלף הא ואו אלף ואו הא אלף).

וְיִשְׁתַּבַּח veyishtabach י"פ ע"ב יהוה אל אבג יתץ.

וְיִתְפָּאַר veyitpa'ar הי גו יה קרע שטן. וְיִתְרַמַם veyitromam וה כוזו נגד יכש.

וְיִתְנַשֵּׂא veyitnase במוכסז בטר צתג. וְיִתְהַדָּר veyit'hadar כוזו יה וזקב טנע.

וְיִתְעַלֶּה veyit'ale וה יוד ה יגל פזק. וְיִתְהַלָּל veyit'halal א ואו הא שקו צית.

שְׁמֵיהּ shemei (שם י"ה דמ"ה) דְּקוּדְשָׁא dekudsha בְּרִיךְ verich הוּא: hu

אָמֵן amen אידהנויה.

לְעֵלָא le'ela מִן min כָּל kol יְלי בִּרְכָתָא birchata שִׁירָתָא shirata

תֻּשְׁבְּחָתָא tishbechata וְנֶחָמָתָא venechamata דַּאֲמִירָן da'amiran

בְּעָלְמָא be'alma וְאָמְרוּ ve'imru אָמֵן amen :amen אָמֵן amen אידהנויה.

In your lifetimes and in your days and in the lifetime of all the House of Israel, speedily and in the near future, and you shall say, Amen. (Amen) May His great Name be blessed forever and for all eternity. Blessed and lauded, and glorified, and exalted, and extolled, and honored, and uplifted, and praised be the Name of the Holy Blessed One. (Amen) Above all blessings, songs, praises, and words of consolation that may be said in the world, and you shall say, Amen. (Amen)

יְהֵא yehe שְׁלָמָא shelama רַבָּא raba קנ"א ב"ן, יהוה אלהים יהוה אדני, מילוי קס"א וס"ג,

מ"ה ברבוע וע"ב ע"ה אהיה אהיה יהוה, בינה ע"ה chayim וְחַיִּים • shemaya שְׁמַיָּא min מִן

vesava וְשָׂבָע vishu'a וְישׁוּעָה venechama וְנֶחָמָה veshezava וְשֵׁיזָבָא

urefu'a וּרְפוּאָה uge'ula וּגְאֻלָּה uslicha וּסְלִיחָה vechapara וְכַפָּרָה

verevach וְרֵיוַח lanu לָנוּ אלהים, אהיה אדני יה אדני vehatzala וְהַצָּלָה ulchol וּלְכָל יה אדני

amo עַמּוֹ Yisrael יִשְׂרָאֵל ve'imru וְאִמְרוּ amen אָמֵן: amen אָמֵן אידהנויה.

Take three steps backwards and say:

ose עוֹשֶׂה shalom שָׁלוֹם bimromav בִּמְרוֹמָיו ע"ב, ריבוע יהוה. hu הוּא

berachamav בְּרַחֲמָיו ya'ase יַעֲשֶׂה shalom שָׁלוֹם alenu עָלֵינוּ ר"ת ס"ע נהורין•

ve'al וְעַל kol כָּל יל'; עמם ילי amo עַמּוֹ Yisrael יִשְׂרָאֵל ve'imru וְאִמְרוּ amen אָמֵן:

amen אָמֵן אידהנויה•

BARCHU

The chazan *(or a person who said the* Kaddish Yehe Shelama*) says:*

rabanan רַבָּנָן: barchu בָּרְכוּ יהוה ריבוע יהוה ריבוע מ"ה et אֶת

Adonai יְהֹוָאדֹנִיאהדונהי hamevorach הַמְּבוֹרָךְ ס"ת כהת, משיזו בן דוד ע"ה:

First the congregation replies with the following,
and then the chazan *(or a person who said the "*Kaddish Yehe Shelama*") repeats it:*

Neshamah	*Ruach*	*Nefesh*
hamevorach הַמְּבוֹרָךְ	Adonai יְהֹוָאדֹנִיאהדונהי	baruch בָּרוּךְ

Yechidah	*Chayah*	
va'ed וָעֶד:	le'olam לְעוֹלָם ריבוע ס"ג ו' אותיות דס"ג	

May there be abundant peace from heaven, life, contentment, salvation, consolation, deliverance, healing, redemption, pardon, atonement, comfort, and relief. For us and for His entire nation, Israel, and you shall say, Amen. (Amen) He, Who makes peace in His high places, with His compassion He shall make peace for us and for His entire nation, Israel. And you shall say, Amen. (Amen)

BARCHU
Masters: Bless the Lord, the Blessed One.
Blessed be the Lord, the Blessed One, forever and for eternity.

ALENU

Alenu is a cosmic sealing agent. It cements and secures all of our prayers, protecting them from any negative forces such as the *klipot*. All prayers prior to *Alenu* drew down what the kabbalists call Inner Light. *Alenu*, however, attracts Surrounding Light, which envelops our prayers with a protective force-field to block out the *klipot*.

Drawing Surrounding Light in order to be protected from the *klipot* (negative side).

ושר יתן, אבג = לשבוח עלינו   leshabe'ach לְשַׁבֵּחַ   ריבוע דס"ג   alenu עָלֵינוּ

אדני, ללה, ר"ת   hakol הַכֹּל   ע"ה   ס"ג   ;   אני   la'adon לַאֲדוֹן

(כאך ב"י יג"ל) ר"ת גלב bereshit בְּרֵאשִׁית   leyotzer לְיוֹצֵר   gedula גְּדֻלָּה   latet לָתֵת

ha'aratzot הָאֲרָצוֹת   kegoyei כְּגוֹיֵי   asanu עָשָׂנוּ   shelo שֶׁלֹּא

ha'adama הָאֲדָמָה   kemishpechot כְּמִשְׁפְּחוֹת   samanu שָׂמָנוּ   velo וְלֹא

vegoralenu וְגוֹרָלֵנוּ   kahem כָּהֶם   chelkenu וְחֶלְקֵנוּ   sam שָׂם   shelo שֶׁלֹּא

mishtachavim מִשְׁתַּחֲוִים   shehem שֶׁהֵם   hamonam ◆הֲמוֹנָם   kechol כְּכָל

el אֵל   el אֵל   umitpalelim וּמִתְפַּלְלִים   varik וָרִיק   lahevel לְהֶבֶל

(pause here, and when you say *"va'anachnu mishtachavim"* bow your entire body) ◆Yoshi'a יוֹשִׁיעַ   lo לֹא

melech מֶלֶךְ   lifnei לִפְנֵי   mishtachavim מִשְׁתַּחֲוִים   va'anachnu וַאֲנַחְנוּ

baruch בָּרוּךְ   hakadosh הַקָּדוֹשׁ   hamelachim הַמְּלָכִים   malchei מַלְכֵי

י"פ טל, י"פ כוזו ; ר"ת = י"פ אדני   shamayim שָׁמַיִם   note נוֹטֶה   shehu שֶׁהוּא   hu◆ הוּא

umoshav וּמוֹשַׁב   aretz◆ אָרֶץ   veyosed וְיוֹסֵד   עובי ספירות עול נוקבא דו"א   hu שֶׁהוּא

עלם◆ mima'al מִמַּעַל   י"פ טל, י"פ כוזו   bashamayim בַּשָּׁמַיִם   yekaro יְקָרוֹ

meromim◆ מְרוֹמִים   begovhei בְּגָבְהֵי   uzo עֻזּוֹ   ush'chinat וּשְׁכִינַת

acher◆ אַחֵר   od עוֹד   ve'en וְאֵין   ילה   Elohenu אֱלֹהֵינוּ   hu הוּא

ALENU

It is incumbent upon us to give praise to the Master of all and to attribute greatness to the Molder of Creation, for He did not make us like the nations of the lands. He did not place us like the families of the earth He did not make our lot like theirs and our destiny like that of their multitudes, for they prostrate themselves to futility and emptiness and they pray to a deity that does not help. But we prostrate ourselves before the King of all Kings, the Holy Blessed One. It is He Who spreads the Heavens and establishes the earth. The Seat of His glory is in the Heaven above and the Divine Presence of His power is in the Highest of Heights. He is our God and there is no other.

וְאֶפֶס ve'efes   מַלְכֵּנוּ malkenu   ס״ג ז״פ,   אֶהְיֶה, פְּעָמִים אֶהְיֶה   emet אֱמֶת

וְיָדַעְתָּ veyadata   בַּתּוֹרָה: batorah   כַּכָּתוּב kakatuv   zulato זוּלָתוֹ

אֶל el   וַהֲשֵׁבֹתָ vahashevota   אֶל יהוה נֶגֶד, מִצְוֹת, זַ, ע״ה   hayom הַיּוֹם

הוּא hu   יְהֹוָה Adonai   כִּי ki   לָאו ר״ת   levavecha לְבָבֶךָ

אֶהְיֶה אַדֹנִי ; יְלֹה ; ר״ת יהה וְכֵן עוֹלֶה לְמִנְיַן עֲנוּ עֲג״ב   haElohim הָאֱלֹהִים

מִבַּעַל mima'al   כֹּחוֹ י״פ טַל, י״פ   bashamayim בַּשָּׁמַיִם   ; עֹלֶם ;

הָאָרֶץ ha'aretz   וְעַל ve'al   מִלְמַעְלָה הַמִּתֹחֵיל פְּנִימִי לְאוֹר רָמַז   אֱלֹהִים דְהַהֵין ע״ה ve'al

עוֹד: od   אֵין en   מִלְמַטָּה הַמִּתֹחֵיל מִקֹף לְאוֹר רָמַז   mitachat מִתַּחַת

עַל al   כֵּן ken   נְקַוֶּה nekave   לְךָ lach   יְהֹוָה Adonai

בְּתִפְאֶרֶת betiferet   מְהֵרָה mehera   לִרְאוֹת lir'ot   יְלֹה   Elohenu אֱלֹהֵינוּ

מִן min   גִּלּוּלִים gilulim   לְהַעֲבִיר leha'avir   ס״ת כהת, מָשִׁיחוֹ בֶּן דָּוִד ע״ה   uzach עוּזֶּךָ

כָּרוֹת karot   וְהָאֱלִילִים veha'elilim   אֱלֹהִים דְהַהֵין ע״ה   ha'aretz הָאָרֶץ

בְּמַלְכוּת bemalchut   עוֹלָם olam   לְתַקֵּן letaken   yikaretun יִכָּרֵתוּן

יִקְרְאוּ yikre'u   בָּשָׂר vasar   בְּנֵי benei   יְלִי   וְכָל vechol   Shadai שַׁדַּי

רִשְׁעֵי rish'ei   יְלִי כָּל kol   אֵלֶיךָ elecha   לְהַפְנוֹת lehafnot   vishmecha בְּשִׁמְךָ

יוֹשְׁבֵי yoshvei   יְלִי כָּל kol   וְיֵדְעוּ veyed'u   יַכִּירוּ yakiru   aretz אֶרֶץ

בֶּרֶךְ berech   יְלִי כָּל kol   תִּכְרַע tichra   לְךָ lecha   כִּי ki   ב״פ רי״ו.   tevel תֵּבֵל

---

*Our King is true and there is none beside Him. As it is written in the Torah:
"And you shall know today and you shall take it to your heart that it is the Lord Who is God in
the Heavens above and upon the earth below, and there is none other". (Deuteronomy 4:39)
Consequently, we place our hope in You, Lord, our God, that we shall speedily see the glory
of Your might, when You remove the idols from the earth and the deities shall be completely
destroyed to correct the world with the kingdom of the Almighty. And all mankind shall then
call out Your Name and You shall turn back to Yourself all the wicked ones of the earth.
Then all the inhabitants of the world shall recognize and know that, for You, every knee bends*

תִּשָּׁבַע tishava כָּל kol ילי לָשׁוֹן lashon ♦ lefanecha לְפָנֶיךָ ס"ג מ"ה ב"ן

יְהֹוָה Adonai אֱלֹהֵינוּ Elohenu ילה יִכְרְעוּ yichre'u וְיִפֹּלוּ veyipolu

וְלִכְבוֹד velichvod שִׁמְךָ shimcha יְקָר yekar יִתֵּנוּ yitenu ♦ וִיקַבְּלוּ vikabelu

כֻלָּם chulam אֶת et עוֹל ol אֶת מַלְכוּתְךָ malchutecha ♦ וְתִמְלוֹךְ vetimloch

עֲלֵיהֶם alehem מְהֵרָה mehera לְעוֹלָם le'olam רִיבוּע ס"ג וי' אותיות דס"ג וָעֶד va'ed ♦

כִּי ki הַמַּלְכוּת hamalchut שֶׁלְּךָ shelcha הִיא hee ♦ וּלְעוֹלְמֵי ul'olmei

עַד ad תִּמְלוֹךְ timloch בְּכָבוֹד bechavod בוכו ♦ כַּכָּתוּב kakatuv

בְּתוֹרָתֶךָ betoratach: יְהֹוָה Adonai | יִמְלֹךְ yimloch לְעֹלָם le'olam

רִיבוּע ס"ג וי' אותיות דס"ג וְהָיָה vehaya יהוה; יהה וְנֶאֱמַר vene'emar: וָעֶד va'ed ♦ רִיבוע יל ; ר"ת יל דס"ג

יְהֹוָה Adonai לְמֶלֶךְ lemelech עַל al כָּל kol ילי; עמם

הָאָרֶץ ha'aretz אלהים דההין ע"ה אלהים גגד, מזבוח, ז"ן, אל יהוה בַּיּוֹם bayom ע"ה ע"ה הַהוּא hahu

יִהְיֶה yihye יְהֹוָה Adonai אֶחָד echad אהבה, דאגה וּשְׁמוֹ ushmo מהש"

עֲ"ה, דאגה אֶחָד echad ע"ה עֹדי, אל ע"ה, וקס"א בריבוע ע"ב, ע"ה:

If you prayed alone recite the following before you start Arvit *and before* "Alenu" *instead of* "Barchu":

אָמַר amar רַבִּי Rabi עֲקִיבָא Akiva וְחַיָּה chaya אַחַת achat עוֹמֶדֶת omedet

בָּרָקִיעַ baraki'a וּשְׁמָהּ ushma יִשְׂרָאֵל Yisrael וַחֲקוּק vechakuk עַל al

בְּאֶמְצַע be'emtza עוֹמֶדֶת omedet יִשְׂרָאֵל Yisrael ♦ מִצְחָהּ mitzcha

הָרָקִיעַ haraki'a יהוה ריבוע יהוה וריבוע מ"ה בָּרְכוּ barchu וְאוֹמֶרֶת ve'omeret: אֶת et

וְכָל vechol הַמְבוֹרָךְ hamevorach ס"ת כהת, משיח בן דוד ע"ה יְהֹוָה Adonai

גְּדוּדֵי gedudei מַעְלָה mala עוֹנִים onim: בָּרוּךְ baruch יְהֹוָה Adonai ילי

הַמְבוֹרָךְ hamevorach לְעוֹלָם le'olam רִיבוּע ס"ג וי' אותיות דס"ג וָעֶד va'ed ♦

---

and every tongue vows. Before You, Lord, our God, they shall kneel and fall and shall give honor to Your glorious Name. And they shall all accept the yoke of Your Kingdom and You shall reign over them, forever and ever. Because the kingdom is Yours. and forever and for eternity, You shall reign gloriously. As it is written in the Torah: "The Lord shall reign forever and ever," (Exodus 15:18) *and it is also stated: "The Lord shall be King over the whole world and, on that day, the Lord shall be One and His Name One."* (Zechariah 14:9)

Rabbi Akiva said: Standing in Heaven, there is one animal named Israel, and Israel is engraved on her forehead, and she is standing in mid-Heaven saying: Bless the Lord, the Blessed One, and all of Heaven's armies are answering: Blessed be the Lord, the Blessed One, forever and for eternity.

THE OMER

The 49 days between *Pesach* (the Israelites exodus from Egypt) and *Shavuot* (receiving the Ten Utterances at Mount Sinai) are known as the *Omer*. The Aramaic letters we recite, during the 49 days when we count the Omer, are the DNA forces we tap into to correct and prepare us for the enormous revelation of Light of Immortality on Shavuot.

The sages explain that the Ten Plagues that facilitated the Israelites release from bondage (slavery) in Egypt were, in reality, ten surges of Light that destroyed ten levels of darkness and negativity. The term "slavery" does not describe the Israelites enslavement by the Egyptians, but rather concerns the Israelites' slavery to their own Desire to Receive for the Self Alone. Unlike any case of physical slavery, throughout the Exodus, the freed Israelites constantly complained to Moses to let them go back to Egypt.

This kind of slavery exists today. All of us, to one degree or another, are slaves to our desires and egos. We would much rather remain immersed in our egos—Egypt—than surrender our pride for the sake of spiritual growth. The Israelites of the Exodus were in no position to reveal the tremendous Light that helped to free them. These ten surges of Light were a gift from the Creator. The 49 days that it took for the Israelites to travel from Egypt to Mount Sinai was a time for them to earn this Light of freedom, with inner correction and spiritual cleansing. Today, the process of the Counting the Omer during these 49 days assists us in our work of spiritual transformation and correction, preparing us for the Light of Immortality we receive on *Shavuot*.

When God infused our world with the Light of Immortality on Mount Sinai, with the giving of the two Tablets, this Light was so powerful that it literally stamped out darkness, decay and even death, far beyond the scope of our present comprehension. When the Israelites built the golden calf—the instrument they used to receive direct Light without earning it through their own efforts—their capacity to receive the totality of the Light of Immortality was reduced. Consequently, the Light of Immortality vanished and death was reinstated.

Each year, Shavuot is our opportunity to connect to and draw down the totality of the Light of Immortality revealed at Mount Sinai some 3400 years ago, and bring about the removal of death from our world forever. Each year, with the number of people who apply the wisdom and the technology of Kabbalah in their lives increasing, more of the Light of Immortality is revealed in our world. Remarkably, medical science is moving a step closer to discovering the potentiality of immortality. We can greatly accelerate this process through unity, sharing, and having a greater awareness of the Kabbalah and becoming a more active participant in the Shavuot connection.

SPARKS OF LIGHT

Kabbalah teaches that there are 50 Gates of Impurity (Negativity). If we should ever reach the 50th Gate of Impurity, our individual war against Satan would be lost. When we count the Omer, we raise the sparks of Light that are trapped in our own personal 49 Gates of Impurity.

Adam consisted of 613 parts. When Adam's soul shattered, these 613 parts fragmented into countless pieces—all the souls who have ever or will ever walk this Earth. The action of raising our personal sparks from the Gates of Impurity, not only affects us, but also all the people who are connected to our soul and the rest of humanity in a positive way.

Our physical and spiritual actions have a ripple effect on all of humanity and enhancing this ripple effect with the Light of Immortality should be the intent of our meditation while we Count the Omer.

SEVEN WEEKS (SEFIROT) X SEVEN DAYS = 49 DAYS OF THE OMER

The 49 days of the Omer are broken down into seven weeks. Each of the seven weeks corresponds to one of the seven *Sefirot* (*Chesed* to *Malchut*) that influence our world.

The first week of the Omer corresponds to *Chesed*. The first day also corresponds to *Chesed*; therefore, the first day of the first week connects to *Chesed* of *Chesed*. On the second day of the first week, it would be *Gevurah* of *Chesed*. During the second week, we reach the *Sefira* of *Gevurah*; therefore, on the first day of the second week, it would be *Chesed* of *Gevurah*, and so on.

According to the lunar month, a day is measured from sunset to sunset. So, for example, if the 16th of Nissan (the first day of the Omer) falls on a Sunday, we will start counting the Omer on the preceding Saturday night. Then on Sunday evening we will count the second day of the Omer, and so on.

It is written in the *Torah*: **"From the day after the Sabbath, the day you brought the sheaf of the wave offering** (*Omer hatenufah*) **count off seven full weeks."** (*Leviticus 23:15*).

And the *Zohar* says **"And you should count... for you, for yourselves"** as it is written, **"And she would count for her seven days..."** (*Leviticus 15:28*). In the same way that she counted for herself, you count for yourself. The *Zohar* explains the secret of the Counting of the *Omer* with the secret of counting seven "clean" weeks. After the impurity stops, and in the exile of Egypt, the *klipot* were sucking energy from the Pure/Holy System and the Impure System controlled the Children of *Yisrael* from Above and Below. And the Children of *Yisrael* were then in the 49th Gate of Impurity.

On the first day of *Pesach*, the impurity stopped and they needed to count seven clean (*nekiyim*) weeks. And therefore it is written 'for you', for yourselves and as the other verse says: **"And she will count for her seven days..."** 'her' means for herself. Also the coming out of Egypt was possible by the awakening of Above (*It'aruta dile'ela*) and God wanted the Children of *Yisrael* to "work on their own" from the time of the coming out of Egypt until the giving of the *Torah*, and build their Vessel during the 49 days in such a way as awakening of Below (*It'aruta Diletata*).

COUNTING OF THE OMER
LESHEM YICHUD

We recite *LeShem Yichud* and accepting the precept: "Love thy neighbor as thyself." According to the Ari, this action creates unity and connects us to the prayers of all people on the planet.

לְשֵׁם leshem יְחוּד yichud קוּדְשָׁא kudsha בְּרִיךְ berich הוּא hu

וּשְׁכִינְתֵּיהּ ush'chintei (יאהדונהי) בִּדְחִילוּ bid'chilu וּרְחִימוּ ur'chimu

וּרְחִימוּ ur'chimu וּדְחִילוּ ud'chilu (איההיותה), לְיַחֲדָא leyachda

שֵׁם shem יוּ"ד yud קֵי kei בְּוָא"ו bevav קֵי kei בְּיִחוּדָא beyichuda

שְׁלִים shelim (יהוה) beshem כָּל kol יִשְׂרָאֵל Yisrael, הִנֵּה hine

אֲנַחְנוּ anachnu בָּאִים ba'im לְקַיֵּם lekayem מִצְוַת mitzvat סְפִירַת sefirat

הָעוֹמֶר ha'omer "פ אל. לַעֲשׂוֹת la'asot נַחַת- nachat רוּחַ ru'ach

לְיוֹצְרֵנוּ leyotzrenu וְלַעֲשׂוֹת vela'asot רָצוֹן retzon מהש ע"ה, ע"ב בריבוע וקס"א ע"ה,

אל שדי ע"ה בּוֹרְאֵנוּ bore'nu. וִיהִי vihi נֹעַם no'am אֲדֹנָי Adonai ללה

אֱלֹהֵינוּ Elohenu ילה עָלֵינוּ alenu וּמַעֲשֵׂה uma'ase יָדֵינוּ yadenu

כּוֹנְנָה konena עָלֵינוּ alenu וּמַעֲשֵׂה uma'ase יָדֵינוּ yadenu כּוֹנְנֵהוּ konenehu:

SURROUNDING LIGHT – OR MAKIF

Surrounding Light - *Or Makif* - is our potential Light, it is the force that pushes and motivates us to explore spirituality and the meaning of our existence. Surrounding Light also refers to the amount of Light that each of us came here to reveal. The more Surrounding Light we reveal, the more momentum we gather toward greater spiritual actions. We can also tap into Surrounding Light through reciting blessings. Each day of the *Omer*, we choose the appropriate blessing, which connect us to the Surrounding Light followed by the Inner Light (*Or Penimi* – our actual Light - see more on pg. 414), and both Lights together will help materialize all the Light in our world.

בָּרוּךְ baruch אַתָּה Ata יְהֹוָ֨אדְהָיאהדונהי Adonai (יוד הא ואו הא)

אֱלֹהֵינוּ Elohenu ילה מֶלֶךְ melech הָעוֹלָם ha'olam אֲשֶׁר asher

קִדְּשָׁנוּ kideshanu בְּמִצְוֹתָיו bemitzvotav וְצִוָּנוּ vetzivanu עַל al

סְפִירַת sefirat הָעוֹמֶר ha'omer "פ אל ; ר"ת אדני:

COUNTING OF THE OMER - LESHEM YICHUD

For the sake of unification between the Holy Blessed One and His Shechinah, with fear and love and with love and fear, in order to unify the Name Yud-Kei and Vav-Kei in perfect unity, and in the name of all Israel, we have hereby come to fulfill the commandment of the counting of the Omer. In order to give pleasure to our Maker and to fulfill the wish of our Creator. "And may the pleasantness of the Lord, our God, be upon us and may He establish the work of our hands for us and may the work of our hands establish Him." (Psalms 90:17)

SURROUNDING LIGHT – OR MAKIF

Blessed are You, Lord, our God, King of the world,
Who has sanctified us with His commandments and obliged us with the counting of the Omer.

חסד – שבוע א' - CHESED – FIRST WEEK

הַיּוֹם hayom ע"ה נגד, מזבוח, זן, אל יהוה

יום / Date	ספירה / Sefira	תיבה / Word	אות / Letter	מ"ב / From Ana Beko'ach
ט"ז בניסן / 16th of Nissan	וחסד שבחסד / Chesed of Chesed	אלהים / Elohim	י / Yud	אנא / Ana
ע"ה נגד, מזבוח, זן, אל יהוה yom יוֹם	echad אוֹד אהבה, דאגה / echad	la'omer לְעוֹמֶר	ל"פ אל:	
י"ז בניסן / 17th of Nissan	גבורה שבחסד / Gevurah of Chesed	יחוֹנֵנוּ / yechonenu	ש / Shin	בכח / Beko'ach
shenei שְׁנֵי	ימים yamim יָמִים	נלך	la'omer לְעוֹמֶר	אל: ל"פ
י"ח בניסן / 18th of Nissan	תפארת שבחסד / Tiferet of Chesed	ויברכנו / vivarchenu	מ / Mem	גדולת / Gedulat
shelosha שְׁלֹשָׁה	ימים yamim יָמִים	נלך	la'omer לְעוֹמֶר	אל: ל"פ
י"ט בניסן / 19th of Nissan	נצח שבחסד / Netzach of Chesed	יאר / ya'er	ח / Chet	ימינך / Yeminecha
arba'a אַרְבָּעָה	ימים yamim יָמִים	נלך	la'omer לְעוֹמֶר	אל: ל"פ
כ' בניסן / 20th of Nissan	הוד שבחסד / Hod of Chesed	פָּנָיו / panav	ו / Vav	תתיר / Tatir
chamisha וַחֲמִישָׁה	ימים yamim יָמִים	נלך	la'omer לְעוֹמֶר	אל: ל"פ
כ"א בניסן / 21st of Nissan	יסוד שבחסד / Yesod of Chesed	אתנו / itanu	ו / Vav	צרורה / Tzerura
shisha שִׁשָּׁה	ימים yamim יָמִים	נלך	la'omer לְעוֹמֶר	אל: ל"פ
כ"ב בניסן / 22nd of Nissan	מלכות שבחסד / Malchut of Chesed	סלה / sela	י / Yud	אבגית"ץ / Alef Bet Gimel Yud Tav Tzadik
shiv'a שִׁבְעָה	ימים yamim יָמִים	נלך	la'omer לְעוֹמֶר	אל ל"פ
shehem שֶׁהֵם	shavu'a שָׁבוּעַ	echad אוֹד אהבה, / echad	דאגה:	

CHESED - FIRST WEEK

Today	One	day	of	the	Omer.
Today	Two	days	of	the	Omer.
Today	Three	days	of	the	Omer.
Today	Four	days	of	the	Omer.
Today	Five	days	of	the	Omer.
Today	Six	days	of	the	Omer.
Today	Seven days of the Omer which are one week.				

גבורה – שבוע ב' – Gevurah - Second Week

הַיּוֹם hayom ע״ה נגד, מזבח, זן, אל יהוה

יום / Date	ספירה / Sefira	תיבה / Word	אות / Letter	מ״ב / From Ana Beko'ach
כ״ג בניסן / 23rd of Nissan	חסד שבגבורה / Chesed of Gevurah	לדעת / lada'at	ר / Resh	קבל / Kabel

שְׁמוֹנָה shemona לְעוֹמֶר la'omer יְמִים yamim נלך, י״פ, אל

שֶׁהֵם shehem אֶחָד echad שָׁבוּעַ shavu'a אהבה, דאגה

וְיוֹם veyom ע״ה נגד, זן, אל יהוה אֶחָד echad אהבה, דאגה:

| כ״ד בניסן / 24th of Nissan | גבורה שבגבורה / Gevurah of Gevurah | בארץ / ba'aretz | נ / Nun | רנת / Rinat |

תִּשְׁעָה tish'a יְמִים yamim נלך לְעוֹמֶר la'omer י״פ אל שֶׁהֵם shehem

שָׁבוּעַ shavu'a אֶחָד echad אהבה, דאגה וּשְׁנֵי ushnei יְמִים yamim נלך:

| כ״ה בניסן / 25th of Nissan | תפארת שבגבורה / Tiferet of Gevurah | דרכך / darkecha | נ / Nun | עמך / Amecha |

עֲשָׂרָה asara יְמִים yamim נלך לְעוֹמֶר la'omer י״פ אל שֶׁהֵם shehem

שָׁבוּעַ shavu'a אֶחָד echad אהבה, דאגה וּשְׁלֹשָׁה ushlosha יְמִים yamim נלך:

| כ״ו בניסן / 26th of Nissan | נצח שבגבורה / Netzach of Gevurah | בכל / bechol | ו / Vav | שגבנו / Sagvenu |

אֶחָד achad אהבה, דאגה yom יוֹם asar עָשָׂר ע״ה נגד, מזבח, זן, אל יהוה

לְעוֹמֶר la'omer י״פ אל שֶׁהֵם shehem שָׁבוּעַ shavu'a אֶחָד echad אהבה, דאגה

וְאַרְבָּעָה ve'arba'a יְמִים yamim נלך:

| כ״ז בניסן / 27th of Nissan | הוד שבגבורה / Hod of Gevurah | גוים / goyim | ל / Lamed | טהרנו / Taharenu |

שְׁנֵים shenem la'omer שֶׁהֵם shehem asar עָשָׂר yom יוֹם ע״ה נגד, מזבח, זן, אל יהוה

לְעוֹמֶר la'omer י״פ אל שֶׁהֵם shehem שָׁבוּעַ shavu'a אֶחָד echad אהבה, דאגה

וַחֲמִשָּׁה vachamisha יְמִים yamim נלך:

GEVURAH - SECOND WEEK

Today	Eight days of the Omer which are one week and one day.
Today	Nine days of the Omer which are one week and two days.
Today	Ten days of the Omer which are one week and three days.
Today	Eleven days of the Omer which are one week and four days.
Today	Twelve days of the Omer which are one week and five days.

כ"ח בניסן	יסוד שבגבורה	ישועתך	א	נורא
28th of Nissan	Yesod of Gevurah	yeshu'atecha	Alef	Nora

שְׁלֹשָׁה shelosha עָשָׂר asar יוֹם yom — ע"ה נגד, מזבח, זן, אל יהוה

לְעוֹמֶר la'omer י"פ אל שֶׁהֵם shehem שָׁבוּעַ shavu'a אֶחָד echad — אהבה, דאגה

וְשִׁשָּׁה veshisha יָמִים yamim נלך:

כ"ט בניסן	מלכות שבגבורה	יודוך	מ	קרע שטן
29th of Nissan	Malchut of Gevurah	yoducha	Mem	Kuf Resh Ayin Sin Tet Nun

אַרְבָּעָה arba'a עָשָׂר asar יוֹם yom — ע"ה נגד, מזבח, זן, אל יהוה

לְעוֹמֶר la'omer י"פ אל שֶׁהֵם shehem שְׁנֵי shenei שָׁבוּעוֹת shavu'ot:

Tiferet – Third Week – שבוע ג' – תפארת

הַיּוֹם hayom — ע"ה נגד, מזבח, זן, אל יהוה

יום Date	ספירה Sefira	תיבה Word	אות Letter	מ"ב From Ana Beko'ach
ל' בניסן 30th of Nissan	וחסד שבתפארת Chesed of Tiferet	עמים amim	י Yud	נא Na

וַחֲמִשָּׁה chamisha עָשָׂר asar יוֹם yom — ע"ה נגד, מזבח, זן, אל יהוה

שָׁבוּעוֹת shavu'ot שְׁנֵי shenei שֶׁהֵם shehem אל י"פ la'omer לְעוֹמֶר

וְיוֹם veyom — ע"ה נגד, מזבח, זן, אל יהוה אֶחָד echad אהבה, דאגה:

א' באייר	גבורה שבתפארת	אלהים	ם	גבור
1st of Iyar	Gevurah of Tiferet	Elohim	Mem	Gibor

שִׁשָּׁה shisha עָשָׂר asar יוֹם yom — ע"ה נגד, מזבח, זן, אל יהוה

שָׁבוּעוֹת shavu'ot שְׁנֵי shenei שֶׁהֵם shehem אל י"פ la'omer לְעוֹמֶר

וּשְׁנֵי ushnei יָמִים yamim נלך:

Today — *Thirteen days of the Omer which are one week and six days.*

Today — *Fourteen days of the Omer which are two weeks.*

TIFERET – THIRD WEEK

Today — *Fifteen days of the Omer which are two weeks and one day.*

Today — *Sixteen days of the Omer which are two weeks and two days.*

ב' באייר — 2nd of Iyar | **תפארת שבתפארת** — Tiferet of Tiferet | **יודוך** — yoducha | **כ** — Kaf | **דורשי** — Dorshei

שִׁבְעָה shiva עָשָׂר asar יוֹם yom   כ   נגד, מצוה, זו, אל יהוה ע"ה

לָעוֹמֶר la'omer אל י"פ שֶׁהֵם shehem שְׁנֵי shenei שָׁבוּעוֹת shavu'ot

וּשְׁלֹשָׁה ushlosha יָמִים yamim נכלך:

ג' באייר — 3rd of Iyar | **נצח שבתפארת** — Netzach of Tiferet | **עמים** — amim | **י** — Yud | **יוזדרך** — Yichudecha

שְׁמוֹנָה shemona עָשָׂר asar יוֹם yom   נגד, מצוה, זו, אל יהוה ע"ה

לָעוֹמֶר la'omer אל י"פ שֶׁהֵם shehem שְׁנֵי shenei שָׁבוּעוֹת shavu'ot

וְאַרְבָּעָה ve'arba'a יָמִים yamim נכלך:

ד' באייר — 4th of Iyar | **הוד שבתפארת** — Hod of Tiferet | **כלם** — kulam | **ת** — Tav | **כבבת** — Kevavat

תִּשְׁעָה tish'a עָשָׂר asar יוֹם yom   נגד, מצוה, זו, אל יהוה ע"ה

לָעוֹמֶר la'omer י"פ אל שֶׁהֵם shehem שְׁנֵי shenei שָׁבוּעוֹת shavu'ot

וַחֲמִשָּׁה vachamisha יָמִים yamim נכלך:

ה' באייר — 5th of Iyar | **יסוד שבתפארת** — Yesod of Tiferet | **ישמחו** — yismechu | **ש** — Shin | **שומרם** — Shomrem

עֶשְׂרִים esrim יוֹם yom   נגד, מצוה, זו, אל יהוה ע"ה י"פ אל   לָעוֹמֶר la'omer

שֶׁהֵם shehem שְׁנֵי shenei שָׁבוּעוֹת shavu'ot וְשִׁשָּׁה veshisha יָמִים yamim נכלך:

ו' באייר — 6th of Iyar | **מלכות שבתפארת** — Malchut of Tiferet | **ויראנו** — viranenu | **פ** — Pe | **נגד יכעש** — Nun Gimel Dalet Yud Kaf Shin

אָוֶד echad אהבה, דאגה, נגד, מצוה, זו, אל יהוה ע"ה יוֹם yom וְעֶשְׂרִים ve'esrim

לָעוֹמֶר la'omer י"פ אל שֶׁהֵם shehem שְׁלֹשָׁה shelosha שָׁבוּעוֹת shavu'ot:

Today	Seventeen days of the Omer which are two weeks and three days.
Today	Eighteen days of the Omer which are two weeks and four days.
Today	Nineteen days of the Omer which are two weeks and five days.
Today	Twenty days of the Omer which are two weeks and six days.
Today	Twenty one days of the Omer which are three weeks.

Netzach – Fourth Week - נצח – שבוע ד'

הַיּוֹם hayom ע"ה נגד, מזבוז, זן, אל יהוה

מ"ב / From Ana Beko'ach	אות / Letter	תיבה / Word	ספירה / Sefira	יום / Date
ברכם Barchem	ו Vav	לאמים le'umim	וחסד שבנצח Chesed of Netzach	ז' באייר 7th of Iyar

שְׁנַיִם shenayim וְעֶשְׂרִים ve'esrim יוֹם yom ע"ה נגד, מזבוז, זן, אל יהוה

לָעוֹמֶר la'omer אל ל"פ שֶׁהֵם shehem שְׁלֹשָׁה shelosha shelosha שָׁבוּעוֹת shavu'ot

וְיוֹם veyom ע"ה נגד, זן, מזבוז, אל יהוה אָחָד echad אהבה, דאגה

| טהרם Taharem | ט Tet | כי ki | גבורה שבנצח Gevurah of Netzach | ח' באייר 8th of Iyar |

שְׁלֹשָׁה shelosha וְעֶשְׂרִים ve'esrim יוֹם yom ע"ה נגד, מזבוז, זן, אל יהוה

לָעוֹמֶר la'omer אל ל"פ שֶׁהֵם shehem שְׁלֹשָׁה shelosha shelosha שָׁבוּעוֹת shavu'ot

וּשְׁנֵי ushnei יָמִים yamim נלך:

| רחמי Rachamei | ע Ayin | תשפוט tishpot | תפארת שבנצח Tiferet of Netzach | ט' באייר 9th of Iyar |

אַרְבָּעָה arba'a וְעֶשְׂרִים ve'esrim יוֹם yom ע"ה נגד, מזבוז, זן, אל יהוה

לָעוֹמֶר la'omer אל ל"פ שֶׁהֵם shehem שְׁלֹשָׁה shelosha shelosha שָׁבוּעוֹת shavu'ot

וּשְׁלֹשָׁה ushlosha יָמִים yamim נלך:

| צדקתך Tzidkatecha | מ Mem | עמים amim | נצח שבנצח Netzach of Netzach | י' באייר 10th of Iyar |

וַחֲמִשָּׁה chamisha וְעֶשְׂרִים ve'esrim יוֹם yom ע"ה נגד, מזבוז, זן, אל יהוה

לָעוֹמֶר la'omer אל ל"פ שֶׁהֵם shehem שְׁלֹשָׁה shelosha shelosha שָׁבוּעוֹת shavu'ot

וְאַרְבָּעָה ve'arba'a יָמִים yamim נלך:

NETZACH - FOURTH WEEK

Today	Twenty two days of the Omer which are three weeks and one day.
Today	Twenty three days of the Omer which are three weeks and two days.
Today	Twenty four days of the Omer which are three weeks and three days.
Today	Twenty five days of the Omer which are three weeks and four days.

Day (11th of Iyar)

תמיד	י	מישור	הוד שבנצח	י"א באייר
Tamid	Yud	mishor	Hod of Netzach	11th of Iyar

שִׁשָּׁה shisha וְעֶשְׂרִים ve'esrim יוֹם yom ע"ה נגד, מזבח, זן, אל יהוה

לָעוֹמֶר la'omer י"פ אל שֶׁהֵם shehem שְׁלֹשָׁה shelosha שָׁבוּעוֹת shavu'ot

וַחֲמִשָּׁה vachamisha יָמִים yamim וכו':

Day (12th of Iyar)

גמלם	מ	ולאמים	יסוד שבנצח	י"ב באייר
Gomlem	Mem	ul'umim	Yesod of Netzach	12th of Iyar

שִׁבְעָה shiv'a וְעֶשְׂרִים ve'esrim יוֹם yom ע"ה נגד, מזבח, זן, אל יהוה

לָעוֹמֶר la'omer י"פ אל שֶׁהֵם shehem שְׁלֹשָׁה shelosha שָׁבוּעוֹת shavu'ot

וְשִׁשָּׁה veshisha יָמִים yamim וכו':

Day (13th of Iyar)

בטר צתג	מ	בארץ	מלכות שבנצח	י"ג באייר
Bet Tet Resh Tzadik Tav Gimel	Mem	ba'aretz	Malchut of Netzach	13th of Iyar

שְׁמוֹנָה shemona וְעֶשְׂרִים ve'esrim יוֹם yom ע"ה נגד, מזבח, זן, אל יהוה

לָעוֹמֶר la'omer י"פ אל שֶׁהֵם shehem אַרְבָּעָה arba'a שָׁבוּעוֹת shavu'ot:

Hod – Fifth Week - הוֹד – שָׁבוּעַ ה'

הַיּוֹם hayom ע"ה נגד, מזבח, זן, אל יהוה

יום	ספירה	תיבה	אות	מ"ב
Date	Sefira	Word	Letter	From Ana Beko'ach
י"ד באייר	חסד שבהוד	תנחם	י	חסין
14th of Iyar	Chesed of Hod	tanchem	Yud	Chasin

תִּשְׁעָה tish'a וְעֶשְׂרִים ve'esrim יוֹם yom ע"ה נגד, מזבח, זן, אל יהוה

לָעוֹמֶר la'omer י"פ אל שֶׁהֵם shehem אַרְבָּעָה arba'a שָׁבוּעוֹת shavu'ot

וְיוֹם veyom ע"ה נגד, מזבח, זן, אל יהוה אֶחָד echad אהבה, דאגה:

Today   *Twenty six days of the Omer which are three weeks and five days.*

Today   *Twenty seven days of the Omer which are three weeks and six days.*

Today   *Twenty eight days of the Omer which are four weeks.*

HOD - FIFTH WEEK

Today   *Twenty nine days of the Omer which are four weeks and one day.*

COUNTING OF THE OMER

15th of Iyar	Gevurah of Hod	sela	Shin	Kadosh

שְׁלֹשִׁים sheloshim ... yom יוֹם ... נגד, מזבח, זך, אל יהוה

לָעוֹמֶר la'omer ... י"פ אל ... שֶׁהֵם shehem ... אַרְבָּעָה arba'a ... שָׁבוּעוֹת shavu'ot

וּשְׁנֵי ushnei ... לְמִים yamim וכו':

16th of Iyar	Tiferet of Hod	yoducha	Vav	Berov

אֶחָד echad אהבה, דאגה, ... יוֹם yom ... וּשְׁלֹשִׁים ushloshim עְ"ה נגד, מזבח, זך, אל יהוה

לָעוֹמֶר la'omer ... י"פ אל ... שֶׁהֵם shehem ... אַרְבָּעָה arba'a ... שָׁבוּעוֹת shavu'ot

וּשְׁלֹשָׁה ushlosha ... לְמִים yamim וכו':

17th of Iyar	Netzach of Hod	amim	Resh	Tuvcha

שְׁנַיִם shenayim וּשְׁלֹשִׁים ushloshim ... יוֹם yom ... נגד, מזבח, זך, אל יהוה

לָעוֹמֶר la'omer ... י"פ אל ... שֶׁהֵם shehem ... אַרְבָּעָה arba'a ... שָׁבוּעוֹת shavu'ot

וְאַרְבָּעָה ve'arba'a ... לְמִים yamim וכו':

18th of Iyar	Hod of Hod	Elohim	Vav	Nahel

שְׁלֹשָׁה shelosha וּשְׁלֹשִׁים ushloshim ... יוֹם yom ... נגד, מזבח, זך, אל יהוה

לָעוֹמֶר la'omer ... י"פ אל ... שֶׁהֵם shehem ... אַרְבָּעָה arba'a ... שָׁבוּעוֹת shavu'ot

וַחֲמִשָּׁה vachamisha ... לְמִים yamim וכו':

19th of Iyar	Yesod of Hod	yoducha	Lamed	Adatecha

אַרְבָּעָה arba'a וּשְׁלֹשִׁים ushloshim ... יוֹם yom ... נגד, מזבח, זך, אל יהוה

לָעוֹמֶר la'omer ... י"פ אל ... שֶׁהֵם shehem ... אַרְבָּעָה arba'a ... שָׁבוּעוֹת shavu'ot

וְשִׁשָּׁה veshisha ... לְמִים yamim וכו':

Today	Thirty days of the Omer which are four weeks and two days.
Today	Thirty one days of the Omer which are four weeks and three days.
Today	Thirty two days of the Omer which are four weeks and four days.
Today	Thirty three days of the Omer which are four weeks and five days.
Today	Thirty four days of the Omer which are four weeks and six days.

וֹקֵב טֹנֵע Chet Kuf Bet Tet Nun Ayin	א Alef	עמים amim	מלכות שבהוד Malchut of Hod	כ' באייר 20th of Iyar

וַחֲמִשָּׁה chamisha וּשְׁלשִׁים ushloshim יוֹם yom ע"ה נגד, מזבוז, זן, אל יהוה

לָעֹמֶר la'omer ײפ אל שֶׁהֵם shehem וְזֶמִשָּׁה chamisha שָׁבוּעוֹת shavu'ot:

Yesod – Sixth Week – יסוד – שבוע ו'

הַיּוֹם hayom ע"ה נגד, מזבוז, זן, אל יהוה

מ"ב From Ana Beko'ach	אות Letter	תיבה Word	ספירה Sefira	יום Date
יָחִיד Yachid	מ Mem	כלם kulam	חֶסֶד שֶׁבִּיסוֹד Chesed of Yesod	כ"א באייר 21st of Iyar

שִׁשָּׁה shisha וּשְׁלשִׁים ushloshim יוֹם yom ע"ה נגד, מזבוז, זן, אל יהוה

לָעֹמֶר la'omer ײפ אל שֶׁהֵם shehem וְזֶמִשָּׁה chamisha שָׁבוּעוֹת shavu'ot

וְיוֹם veyom ע"ה נגד, מזבוז, זן, אל יהוה אֶחָד echad אהבה, דאגה:

גֵאֶה Ge'e	י Yud	ארץ eretz	גְבוּרָה שֶׁבִּיסוֹד Gevurah of Yesod	כ"ב באייר 22nd of Iyar

שִׁבְעָה shiv'a וּשְׁלשִׁים ushloshim יוֹם yom ע"ה נגד, מזבוז, זן, אל יהוה

לָעֹמֶר la'omer ײפ אל שֶׁהֵם shehem וְזֶמִשָּׁה chamisha שָׁבוּעוֹת shavu'ot

וּשְׁנֵי ushnei יָמִים yamim נלך:

לְעַמֶּךָ Le'amecha	ם Mem	נתנה natna	תִּפְאֶרֶת שֶׁבִּיסוֹד Tiferet of Yesod	כ"ג באייר 23rd of Iyar

שְׁמוֹנָה shemona וּשְׁלשִׁים ushloshim יוֹם yom ע"ה נגד, מזבוז, זן, אל יהוה

לָעֹמֶר la'omer ײפ אל שֶׁהֵם shehem וְזֶמִשָּׁה chamisha שָׁבוּעוֹת shavu'ot

וּשְׁלשָׁה ushlosha יָמִים yamim נלך:

פְּנֵה Pene	ב Bet	יבולה yevula	נֶצַח שֶׁבִּיסוֹד Netzach of Yesod	כ"ד באייר 24th of Iyar

תִּשְׁעָה tish'a וּשְׁלשִׁים ushloshim יוֹם yom ע"ה נגד, מזבוז, זן, אל יהוה

לָעֹמֶר la'omer ײפ אל שֶׁהֵם shehem וְזֶמִשָּׁה chamisha שָׁבוּעוֹת shavu'ot

וְאַרְבָּעָה ve'arba'a יָמִים yamim נלך:

Today   Thirty five days of the Omer which are five weeks.

YESOD - SIXTH WEEK

Today   Thirty six days of the Omer which are five weeks and one day.

Today   Thirty seven days of the Omer which are five weeks and two days.

Today   Thirty eight days of the Omer which are five weeks and three days.

Today   Thirty nine days of the Omer which are five weeks and four days.

כ"ה באייר	הוד שביסוד	יברכנו	א	זוכרי
25th of Iyar	Hod of Yesod	yevarchenu	Alef	Zochrei

אַרְבָּעִים arbaim — יוֹם yom — ע"ה — נגד, מזבוח, זן, אל יהוה

לְעוֹמֶר la'omer — י"פ אל — שֶׁהֵם shehem — וְזֵמִשָׁה chamisha — שָׁבוּעוֹת shavu'ot

וַוְזֵמִשָׁה vachamisha — יָמִים yamim וגו׳:

כ"ו באייר	יסוד שביסוד	אלהים	ר	קדושתך
26th of Iyar	Yesod of Yesod	Elohim	Resh	Kedushatcha

אֶחָד echad — אהבה, דאגה — ע"ה יום — וְאַרְבָּעִים ve'arbaim — נגד, מזבוח, זן, אל יהוה — יוֹם yom

לְעוֹמֶר la'omer — י"פ אל — שֶׁהֵם shehem — וְזֵמִשָׁה chamisha — שָׁבוּעוֹת shavu'ot

וְשִׁשָׁה veshisha — יָמִים yamim וגו׳:

כ"ז באייר	מלכות שביסוד	אלהינו	צ	יגל פזק
27th of Iyar	Malchut of Yesod	Elohenu	Tzadik	Yud Gimel Lamed Pei Zayin Kuf

שְׁנַיִם shenayim — וְאַרְבָּעִים ve'arbaim — יוֹם yom — נגד, מזבוח, זן, אל יהוה

לְעוֹמֶר la'omer — י"פ אל — שֶׁהֵם shehem — עֲשָׂה shisha — שָׁבוּעוֹת shavu'ot:

Malchut – Seventh Week - שבוע ז' – מלכות

הַיּוֹם hayom — ע"ה נגד, מזבוח, זן, אל יהוה

יום	ספירה	תיבה	אות	מ"ב
Date	Sefira	Word	Letter	From Ana Beko'ach
כ"ח באייר	וזסד שבמלכות	יברכנו	ת	שוועתנו
28st of Iyar	Chesed of Malchut	yevarchenu	Tav	Shav'atenu

שְׁלֹשָׁה shelosha — וְאַרְבָּעִים ve'arbaim — יוֹם yom — ע"ה נגד, מזבוח, זן, אל יהוה

לְעוֹמֶר la'omer — י"פ אל — שֶׁהֵם shehem — עֲשָׂה shisha — שָׁבוּעוֹת shavu'ot

וְיוֹם veyom — ע"ה נגד, מזבוח, זן, אל יהוה — אֶחָד echad — אהבה, דאגה:

כ"ט באייר	גבורה שבמלכות	אלהים	נ	קבל
29nd of Iyar	Gevurah of Malchut	Elohim	Nun	Kabel

אַרְבָּעָה arba'a — וְאַרְבָּעִים ve'arbaim — יוֹם yom — ע"ה נגד, מזבוח, זן, אל יהוה

לְעוֹמֶר la'omer — י"פ אל — שֶׁהֵם shehem — עֲשָׂה shisha — שָׁבוּעוֹת shavu'ot

וּשְׁנֵי ushnei — יָמִים yamim וגו׳:

Today	Forty days of the Omer which are five weeks and five days.
Today	Forty one days of the Omer which are five weeks and six days.
Today	Forty two days of the Omer which are six weeks.

MALCHUT - SEVENTH WEEK

Today	Forty three days of the Omer which are six weeks and one day.
Today	Forty four days of the Omer which are six weeks and two days.

1st of Sivan (א' בסיון) — Tiferet of Malchut (תפארת שבמלכות) — veyir'u (וייראו) — Chet (חו) — Ushma (ושמע)

חֲמִשָׁה chamisha — וְאַרְבָּעִים ve'arbaim — יוֹם yom — [ע"ה נגד, מזבוז, זו, אל יהוה] — וַחֲמִשָׁה
לָעוֹמֶר la'omer — אל [י"פ] — שֶׁהֵם shehem — עֲשָׂה shisha — שָׁבוּעוֹת shavu'ot — לְעוֹמֶר
וּשְׁלֹשָׁה ushlosha — יָמִים yamim — נכל:

2nd of Sivan (ב' בסיון) — Netzach of Malchut (נצח שבמלכות) — oto (אותו) — Mem (מ) — Tza'akatenu (צעקתנו)

שִׁשָׁה shisha — וְאַרְבָּעִים ve'arbaim — יוֹם yom — [ע"ה נגד, מזבוז, זו, אל יהוה]
לָעוֹמֶר la'omer — אל [י"פ] — שֶׁהֵם shehem — עֲשָׂה shisha — שָׁבוּעוֹת shavu'ot
וְאַרְבָּעָה ve'arba'a — יָמִים yamim — נכל:

3rd of Sivan (ג' בסיון) — Hod of Malchut (הוד שבמלכות) — kol (כל) — Samech (ס) — Yode'a (יודע)

שִׁבְעָה shiv'a — וְאַרְבָּעִים ve'arbaim — יוֹם yom — [ע"ה נגד, מזבוז, זו, אל יהוה]
לָעוֹמֶר la'omer — אל [י"פ] — שֶׁהֵם shehem — עֲשָׂה shisha — שָׁבוּעוֹת shavu'ot
וַחֲמִשָׁה vachamisha — יָמִים yamim — נכל:

4th of Sivan (ד' בסיון) — Yesod of Malchut (יסוד שבמלכות) — afsei (אפסי) — Lamed (ל) — Ta'alumot (תעלומות)

שְׁמוֹנָה shemona — וְאַרְבָּעִים ve'arbaim — יוֹם yom — [ע"ה נגד, מזבוז, זו, אל יהוה]
לָעוֹמֶר la'omer — אל [י"פ] — שֶׁהֵם shehem — עֲשָׂה shisha — שָׁבוּעוֹת shavu'ot
וְשִׁשָׁה veshisha — יָמִים yamim — נכל:

5th of Sivan (ה' בסיון) — Malchut of Malchut (מלכות שבמלכות) — aretz (ארץ) — Hei (ה) — Shin Kuf Vav Tzadik Yud Tav (שקו צית)

תִּשְׁעָה tish'a — וְאַרְבָּעִים ve'arbaim — יוֹם yom — [ע"ה נגד, מזבוז, זו, אל יהוה]
לָעוֹמֶר la'omer — אל [י"פ] — שֶׁהֵם shehem — שִׁבְעָה shiv'a — שָׁבוּעוֹת shavu'ot:

INNER LIGHT – OR PENIMI

Inner Light refers to the life-force that breathes us into existence. It is the fuel that sustains and animates us. For example, whereas the blessing over wine embodies Surrounding Light, the action of drinking the wine connects us to Inner Light.

Today	Forty five days of the Omer which are six weeks and three days.
Today	Forty six days of the Omer which are six weeks and four days.
Today	Forty seven days of the Omer which are six weeks and five days.
Today	Forty eight days of the Omer which are six weeks and six days.
Today	Forty nine days of the Omer which are seven weeks.

harachaman הָרַחֲמָן

hu הוּא yachazir יַחֲזִיר avodat עֲבוֹדַת bet בֵּית ב"פ ראה hamikdash הַמִּקְדָּשׁ

limkoma לִמְקוֹמָהּ bimhera בִּמְהֵרָה veyamenu בְיָמֵינוּ amen אָמֵן (יאהדונהי)

LAMNATZE'ACH (to learn more about the *Menorah* go to pg. 39-40)

The Psalm of *Lamnatze'ach* consists of 49 words, and its middle verse ("*Yismechu*") consists of 49 letters. Each word and each letter corresponds to one day of the *Omer*. By meditating on the related word and letter (see charts - pg. 420-426) we connect with the Light, which helps us achieve the spiritual cleansing during this time.

lam'natze'ach לַמְנַצֵּחַ binginot בִּנְגִינֹת mizmor מִזְמוֹר shir שִׁיר

Elohim אֱלֹהִים אהיה אדני ; ילה yechonenu יְחָנֵּנוּ vivarchenu וִיבָרְכֵנוּ

ya'er יָאֵר כף ויו זין ויו panav פָּנָיו itanu אִתָּנוּ ר"ת פאי, אמן (יאהדונהי) sela סֶלָה

lada'at לָדַעַת ר"ת סאל, אמן (יאהדונהי) ba'aretz בָּאָרֶץ darkecha דַּרְכֶּךָ

bechol בְּכָל ב"ן, לכב goyim גּוֹיִם yeshu'atecha יְשׁוּעָתֶךָ

yoducha יוֹדוּךָ amim עַמִּים Elohim אֱלֹהִים אהיה אדני ; ילה

yoducha יוֹדוּךָ amim עַמִּים kulam כֻּלָּם yismechu יִשְׂמְחוּ viranenu וִירַנְּנוּ

le'umim לְאֻמִּים ר"ת ע"ה = איההיוהה ki כִּי tishpot תִשְׁפֹּט amim עַמִּים

mishor מִישֹׁר ul'umim וּלְאֻמִּים ba'aretz בָּאָרֶץ tanchem תַּנְחֵם sela סֶלָה

yoducha יוֹדוּךָ amim עַמִּים Elohim אֱלֹהִים אהיה אדני ; ילה yoducha יוֹדוּךָ

amim עַמִּים kulam כֻּלָּם ר"ת יודוך ישמוזו יודוך ארץ = יי" י (מילוי דס"ג)

eretz אֶרֶץ natna נָתְנָה נתה, קס"א קנ"א קמ"ג ועם ר"ת אלהים לדעת יברכנו = ע"ב, ריבוע יהוה

yevula יְבוּלָהּ ר"ת אני yevarchenu יְבָרְכֵנוּ Elohim אֱלֹהִים אהיה אדני ; ילה

Elohenu אֱלֹהֵינוּ ילה: yevarchenu יְבָרְכֵנוּ Elohim אֱלֹהִים אהיה אדני ; ילה

veyir'u וְיִירְאוּ oto אוֹתוֹ kol כָּל ילי afsei אַפְסֵי aretz אָרֶץ

INNER LIGHT – OR PENIMI

The merciful One, He will return the service of the Temple to its place, speedily and in our days. Amen.

LAMNATZE'ACH

"*For the Musician, a melodious Psalm and a Song: May God give us favor and bless us. May He shine His Countenance upon us, Selah! To make known Your ways to the world and Your salvation among the nations. The nations shall give thanks to You, God. All the nations shall give thanks to You. The peoples shall rejoice and sing because You judge nations with fairness, and You guide peoples on earth. Selah. The nations shall give thanks to You, God. All nations shall give thanks to You. The earth has given its yield. May the Lord, our God, bless us. May God bless us and may all fear Him from all the ends of the earth.*" (Psalms 67)

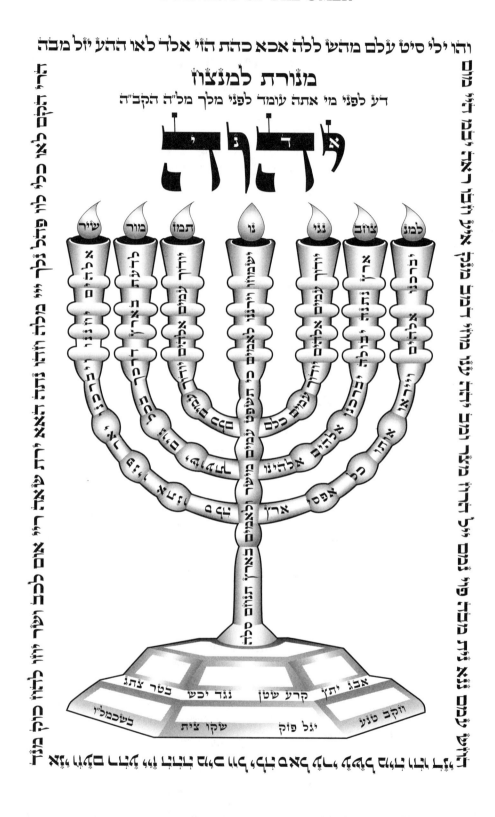

ANA BEKO'ACH (to learn more about the *Ana Beko'ach* go to pg. 106)

The *Ana Beko'ach* is perhaps the most powerful prayer in the entire universe. Second-century Kabbalist Rav Nachunya ben HaKana was the first sage to reveal this combination of 42 letters, which encompass the power of creation.

Chesed, Sunday *(Alef Bet Gimel Yud Tav Tzadik)* אבג יתץ

◆yeminecha לִימִינֶךָ　gedulat גְּדוּלַּת　◆beko'ach בְּכֹחַ　ana אָנָּא

◆tzerura צְרוּרָה　tatir תַּתִּיר

Gevurah, Monday *(Kuf Resh Ayin Shin Tet Nun)* קְרַע שָׂטָן

◆sagvenu שַׂגְּבֵנוּ　amecha עַמְּךָ　◆rinat רִנַּת　kabel קַבֵּל

◆nora נוֹרָא　taharenu טַהֲרֵנוּ

Tiferet, Tuesday *(Nun Gimel Dalet Yud Kaf Shin)* נגד יכש

◆yichudecha יִחוּדְךָ　dorshei דוֹרְשֵׁי　◆gibor גִּבּוֹר　na נָא

◆shomrem שָׁמְרֵם　kevavat כְּבָבַת

Netzach, Wednesday *(Bet Tet Resh Tzadik Tav Gimel)* בטר צתג

◆tzidkatecha צִדְקָתְךָ　rachamei רַחֲמֵי　◆taharem טַהֲרֵם　barchem בָּרְכֵם

◆gomlem גָּמְלֵם　tamid תָּמִיד

ANA BEKO'ACH

Chesed, Sunday אבג יתץ

We beseech You, with the power of Your great right, undo this entanglement.

Gevurah, Monday קְרַע שָׂטָן

Accept the singing of Your Nation. Strengthen and purify us, Awesome One.

Tiferet, Tuesday נגד יכש

Please, Mighty One, those who seek Your unity, guard them like the pupil of the eye.

Netzach, Wednesday בטר צתג

Bless them. Purify them. Your compassionate righteousness always grant them.

Hod, Thursday *(Chet Kuf Bet Tet Nun Ayin)* חקב טנע

chasin וְזָסִין   kadosh קָדוֹשׁ   berov בְּרוֹב   tuvcha טוּבְךָ

nahel נַהֵל   adatecha עֲדָתֶךָ

Yesod, Friday *(Yud Gimel Lamed Pei Zayin Kuf)* יגל פזק

yachid יָחִיד   ge'e גֵּאֶה   le'amecha לְעַמְּךָ   pene פְּנֵה

zochrei זוֹכְרֵי   kedushatecha קְדוּשָׁתֶךָ

Malchut, Saturday *(Shin Kuf Vav Tzadik Yud Tav)* שקו צית

shav'atenu שַׁוְעָתֵנוּ   kabel קַבֵּל   ushma וּשְׁמַע   tza'akatenu צַעֲקָתֵנוּ

yode'a יוֹדֵעַ   ta'alumot תַּעֲלוּמוֹת

BARUCH SHEM KEVOD

Whispering this final verse brings all the Light from the Upper Worlds into our physical existence.

(Whisper): יוזו אותיות   baruch בָּרוּךְ   shem שֵׁם   kevod כְּבוֹד   malchuto מַלְכוּתוֹ

va'ed וָעֶד   אותיות דס"ג וי'   ריבוע ס"ג   le'olam לְעוֹלָם

RIBONO SHEL OLAM

ribono רִבּוֹנוֹ   shel שֶׁל   olam עוֹלָם   ata אַתָּה   tzivitanu צִוִּיתָנוּ   al עַל

avdecha עַבְדֶּךָ   ד"פ אלהים ע"ה, אל שדי, ע"ב ברבוע וקס"א, ע"ב בריבוע מהטע,   Moshe מֹשֶׁה   yedei יְדֵי

kedei כְּדֵי   ha'omer הָעוֹמֶר   sefirat סְפִירַת   lispor לִסְפּוֹר   י"פ אל אדני, אל

letaharenu לְטַהֲרֵנוּ   miklipotenu מִקְלִפּוֹתֵנוּ   umitum'atenu וּמִטּוּמְאָתֵינוּ

Hod, Thursday חקב טנע
Invincible and Mighty One, with the abundance of Your goodness, govern Your congregation.
Yesod, Friday יגל פזק
Sole and proud One, turn to Your people, those who remember Your sanctity.
Malchut, Saturday שקו צית
Accept our cry and hear our wail, You that knows all that is hidden.
BARUCH SHEM KEVOD
"Blessed is the Name of Glory. His Kingdom is forever and for eternity." (Pesachim 56a)
RIBONO SHEL OLAM
Master of the World, You have commanded us through Moses, Your servant,
to enumerate the counting of the Omer, in order to purify us from our Klipot and our defilements.

כְּמוֹ kemo שֶׁכָּתַבְתָּ shekatavta בְּתוֹרָתֶךָ betoratach:

וּסְפַרְתֶּם usfartem לָכֶם lachem מִמָּחֳרַת mimachorat הַשַּׁבָּת haShabbat

מִיּוֹם miyom ע"ה נגד, מזבח, ז, אל יהוה הֲבִיאֲכֶם havi'achem אֶת־ et

עֹמֶר omer י"פ אל הַתְּנוּפָה hatenufa שֶׁבַע sheva שַׁבָּתוֹת shabbatot

תְּמִימֹת temimot תִּהְיֶינָה tih'yena: עַד ad מִמָּחֳרַת mimachorat

הַשַּׁבָּת haShabbat הַשְּׁבִיעִת hashevi'it תִּסְפְּרוּ tisperu וַחֲמִשִּׁים chamishim

יוֹם yom ע"ה נגד, מזבח, ז, אל יהוה כְּדֵי kedei שֶׁיִּטַּהֲרוּ sheyitaharu

נַפְשׁוֹת nafshot עַמְּךָ amecha יִשְׂרָאֵל Yisrael מִזּוּהֲמָתָם mizohamatam♦

וּבְכֵן uvchen ע"ב, ריבוע יהוה

יְהִי yehi רָצוֹן ratzon מהש ע"ה, ע"ב ברבוע וקס"א ע"ה, אל שדי ע"ה

מִלְפָנֶיךָ milfanecha ס"ג מ"ה ב"ן יְהֹוָ[ה] אדני ואהדונהי Adonai אֱלֹהֵינוּ Elohenu יל"ה

וֵאלֹהֵי velohei לכב ; מילוי דע"ב, דמב ; יל"ה אֲבוֹתֵינוּ avotenu,

שֶׁבִּזְכוּת shebizchut סְפִירַת sefirat הָעוֹמֶר ha'omer י"פ אל

שֶׁסָּפַרְתִּי shesafarti הַיּוֹם hayom ע"ה נגד, מזבח, ז, אל יהוה יְתֻקַּן yetukan

מַה ma מ"ה (יוד הא ואו הא) שֶׁפָּגַמְתִּי shepagamti בִּסְפִירָה bisfira

> You should mention the Name of the *Sefira* for tonight and meditate on it.
> You should also scan the meditations from the Ari and the Rashash in the charts on the next pages.

וְאֶטְהֵר ve'etaher וְאֶתְקַדֵּשׁ ve'etkadesh בִּקְדֻשָׁה bikdusha

שֶׁל shel מַעְלָה ma'ala אָמֵן amen יאהדונהי סֶלָה sela:

This is as it is written in Your Torah: And you shall count for yourselves, from the day following the Shabbat, from the day on which you bring the portion of your wave-offering, seven complete weeks, until the day following the seventh week. You shall count fifty days, so that the spirits of your Nation, Israel, shall be purified from their defilement. (Leviticus 23:15-16) Therefore, may it be pleasing before You, Lord, our God and God of our forefathers, that by virtue of the counting of the Omer that I have counted today, the flaw that I have caused in the Sefira of (mention the name of the Sefira that corresponds to that evening) will be corrected and I shall be purified and sanctified with supernal sanctity. Amen. Selah.

1st week – *Mochin are entering Chochmah of Zeir Anpin*

דהזה – ונכנסין מוחין לבחינת החכמה אל הז"א, וימשכו אליו ע"י א"א ויקבלו כח מה' גבורות דאימא

Day Of The Omer	Day of the week	אהיה EHKH	מ"ה Mah	ב"ן Ban	מ"ה דב"ן 42 Mah of Ban	ב"ן דמ"ה 42 Ban of Mah	אנא בכח Ana Beko'ach	במנורה The Menorah	פסוק אמצעי Central verse	מלכים 7 Kings	מוחין The Mochin	המוחין באים מן: Mochin coming from:	אדם (מ"ה דס"ג) Adam (Mah of Sag)	הויה YKVK	כוונת המוחין Mochin Meditation
1	1st	א	י	י	י	י	אנא	אלהים	א	הבל ודן	Gadlut A Abba	Inner Netzach of Israel Saba		יהוה	
2	2nd	ה	י	י	ה	ה	בכח	ייאי	ב	חתב ודן	Gadlut A Ima	Inner Netzach of Tevunah		יהוה	
3	3rd	י	י	ה	י	ה	גדלת	מנצפך	ג	חמש ודן	Katnut B Abba & Ima	Outer Chesed of Supernal Abba & Ima		יהוה	אלהים
4	4th	ה	י	ה	י	ה	ימינך	נגד	ד	דרור ודן	Gadlut B Ima	Inner Chesed of Supernal Ima		יהוה	
5	5th	א	י	ה	י	י	תתיר	פלא	ה	שאבל ודן	Katnut A Abba & Ima	Outer Netzach of Israel Saba & Tevunah		יהוה	
6	6th	ה	י	ה	י	י	צרורה	אזר	ו	בעל חנן ודן	Reshimo of Gadlut B Abba	Inner Chesed of Supernal Abba		יהוה	
7	7th	י	יה	יה	יה	יה	קבל	עלץ	ז	הדר ומן	Gadlut B Abba	Inner Chesed of Supernal Abba		יהוה	

Each night - from the first night to the sixth night of the week - you should meditate to elevate 45 sparks of a total of 320 sparks:

On the seventh night - of each week - you should meditate to elevate 50 sparks of a total of 320 sparks

2nd week — *Mochin* are entering *Binah* of *Zeir Anpin*

שבוע שני – המוחין נכנסים לבינה דז"א, וחסד ב' לז"א וגבורה ב' לנוקבא – יְהוָה

Day Of The Omer	Day of the week	אהיה EHKH	מ"ה Mah	ב"ן Ban	מ"ב דמ"ה 42 of Mah	מ"ב דב"ן 42 of Ban	אנא בכח Ana Beko'ach	למנצח בנגינות The Menorah	פסוק ישמחו Central verse	ז' מלכים 7 Kings	מוחין The Mochin	המוחין באים מ: Mochin coming from:	אדם (מ"ה דס"ג) Adam (Mah of Sag)	הויה YKVK	כוונת המוחין Mochin Meditation
8	1st	ה	הא	ההה	ד	ד	קבל	לדעת	ר	בלע דיוכב	Gadlut A Abba	Inner Hod of Israel Saba	000 יודהיוא	יְהֹוָה	יוד הי ואו הי
9	2nd	א	יוד	יוד	ה	ה	רנת	בארץ	ג	יוכב דיוכב	Gadlut A Ima	Inner Hod of Tevunah	000ההיוידה00	יְהֹוָה	יוד הי ואו הי
10	3rd	ה	הא	ההה	א	ה	עמך	דרכך	ג	וחשם דיוכב	Katnut B Abba & Ima	Outer Gevurah of Supernal Abba & Ima	0000000000וואהדה000000000	יְהֹוָה	א"ם ג"ל
11	4th	י	ואו	וו	ו	ו	שגבנו	בכל	ו	הדד דיוכב	Gadlut B Ima	Inner Gevurah of Supernal Ima	ורדהיואוה0	יְהֹוָה	יוד הי ואו הי
12	5th	ה	הא	ההה	א	ו	טהרנו	גוים	ל	עמלה דיוכב	Katnut A Abba & Ima	Outer Hod of Israel Saba & Tevunah	ויודההי0000000	יְהֹוָה	אלף למד ההה יוד מם
13	6th	א	יוד	יוד	ו	ה	נורא	ישועתך	א	שאול דיוכב	Reshimo of Gadlut B Abba	Inner Gevurah of Supernal Abba	00000היווהד0000	יְהֹוָוהֹי	יוד הי ואו הי
14	7th	ה	הא	ההה	דהא ואו	דההה והה	קרע שטן	יודוך	מ	בעל חנן דיוכב	Gadlut B Abba	Inner Gevurah of Supernal Abba	00ההיואוהי	יְהֹוָה	יוד הי ואו הי

Each night - from the first night to the sixth night of the week - you should meditate to elevate 45 sparks of a total of 320 sparks:

בשעת הלילות יכוין להעלות מ"ה ניצוצין מכל ש"ך: 1) ס"ג 2) דְי"ן 3) מ"ה 4) ל"ב נתיבות 5) עד"י 6) א"ל יהו"ה

On the seventh night – of each week - you should meditate to elevate 50 sparks of a total of 320 sparks

ובלילה השביעי יכוין להעלות נ' ניצוצין מעשׂה ש"ך הנ"ל

3rd week – Mochin are entering Chasadim of Da'at of Zeir Anpin

הויה – אהיה, מ"ה ב"ן, מ"ב, ב"ן, אנא בכח, המנורה, פסוק מרכזי, ז' מלכים, המוחין, המוחין באים מן, אדם, הויה, כוונת המוחין

Day Of The Omer	Day of the week	אהיה EHKH	מ"ה ב"ן Mah Ban	מ"ב Mah of 42	ב"ן Ban of 42	אנא בכח Ana Beko'ach	המנורה The Menorah	פסוק מרכזי Central verse	ז' מלכים 7 Kings	המוחין The Mochin	המוחין באים מן: Mochin coming from:	אדם (מ"ה דס"ג) Adam (Mah of Sag)	הויה YKVK	כוונת המוחין Mochin Meditation
15	1st						עשתי	י	בלע והדר	Gadlut A Abba	Inner Yesod of Israel Saba			
16	2nd						אלהים	ט	יובב והדר	Gadlut A Ima	Inner Yesod of Tevunah			
17	3rd						יהוה	ן	חשם והדר	Katnut B Abba & Ima	Outer Tiferet of Supernal Abba & Ima			
18	4th						מלך	י	הדד והדר	Gadlut B Ima	Inner Tiferet of Supernal Ima			
19	5th						ישמלה	ה	שמלה והדר	Katnut A Abba & Ima	Outer Yesod of Israel Saba & Tevunah			
20	6th						תירש	ב	שאול והדר	Reshimo of Gadlut B Abba	Inner Tiferet of Supernal Abba			
21	7th						יציב	ם	בעל חנן והדר	Gadlut B Abba	Inner Tiferet of Supernal Abba			

Each night - from the first night to the sixth night of the week - you should meditate to elevate 45 sparks of a total of 320 sparks:

On the seventh night – of each week - you should meditate to elevate 50 sparks of a total of 320 sparks

4ᵗʰ week – *Mochin are entering Gevurot of Da'at of Zeir Anpin*

Day Of The Omer	Day of the week	EHKH	Mah Ban	Mah of Mah 42	Mah of Ban 42	Ana Beko'ach	The Menorah	Central verse	7 Kings	The Mochin	Mochin coming from:	Adam (Mah of Sag)	YKVK	Mochin Meditation
22	1st									Gadlut A Abba	Inner Yesod of Israel Saba			
23	2nd									Gadlut A Ima	Inner Yesod of Tevunah			
24	3rd									Katnut B Abba & Ima	Outer Tiferet of Supernal Abba & Ima			
25	4th									Gadlut B Ima	Inner Tiferet of Supernal Ima			
26	5th									Katnut A Abba & Ima	Outer Yesod of Israel Saba & Tevunah			
27	6th									Reshimo of Gadlut B Abba	Inner Tiferet of Supernal Abba			
28	7th									Gadlut B Abba	Inner Tiferet of Supernal Abba			

Each night - from the first night to the sixth night of the week - you should meditate to elevate 45 sparks of a total of 320 sparks:

On the seventh night — of each week — you should meditate to elevate 50 sparks of a total of 320 sparks

5th week – *Mochin are entering Chesed of Zeir Anpin*

דעת – אבהקית ח' דהוד חב"ד לד ה' דלו לבו לד חא"ד לז לד ה' דהד מוחין דחסדים נכנסים לחסד דז"א – המוחין הם בחי'

Day Of The Omer	Day of the week	EHKH אהיה	Mah מ"ה	Ban ב"ן	Mah of 42 מ"ה 42	Ban of Ban 42 ב"ן 42	Ana Beko'ach אנא בכח	The Menorah המנורה למנצח	Central verse פסוק המרכזי	7 Kings ז' מלכים	The Mochin המוחין	Mochin coming from: המוחין באים מ:	Adam (Mah of Sag) אדם (מ"ה דס"ג)	YKVK הוי'	Mochin Meditation כוונת המוחין
29	1st	א	מ"ה	ב"ן	א	ה	יתץ	הטים	י	בלע וימלוך	Gadlut A Abba	Inner Netzach of Israel Saba	000אדם000	הוי'	י ה ו ה
30	2nd	ה	מ"ה	ב"ן	א	ד	קרע	קרע	ט	יובב וימלוך	Gadlut A Ima	Inner Netzach of Tevunah	00אדם000	הוי'	י ה ו ה
31	3rd	י	מ"ה	ב"ן	ל	ד	נגד	יכין	ח	חשם וימלוך	Katnut B Abba & Ima	Outer Chesed of Supernal Abba & Ima	000000000אדם000000000	הוי'	אלהים
32	4th	ה	מ"ה	ב"ן	ח	ד	בטר	חמל	ז	הדד וימלוך	Gadlut B Ima	Inner Chesed of Supernal Ima	0אדם00	הוי'	י ה ו ה
33	5th	א	מ"ה	ב"ן	ד	ד	חקב	אכל	ו	שמלה וימלוך	Katnut A Abba & Ima	Outer Netzach of Israel Saba & Tevunah	0אדם000000000	הוי'	אלבם לב קר ן י ה ם
34	6th	ה	מ"ה	ב"ן	א	ה	תנע	ותיקם	ל	שאול וימלוך	Reshimo of Gadlut B Abba	Inner Chesed of Supernal Abba	00אדם00	הוי'	י ה ו ה
35	7th	י	מ"ה	ב"ן	אאל תוא	וה	יגל פזק	במב	א	בעל חנן וימלוך	Gadlut B Abba	Inner Chesed of Supernal Abba	אדם00	הוי'	י ה ו ה

Each night - from the first night to the sixth night of the week - you should meditate to elevate 45 sparks of a total of 320 sparks:

On the seventh night - of each week - you should meditate to elevate 50 sparks of a total of 320 sparks

6th week – *Mochin are entering Gevurah of Zeir Anpin*

Day Of The Omer	Day of the week	EHKH אהיה	Mah מ"ה	Ban ב"ן	מ"ב מ"ה of Mah 42	מ"ב ב"ן of Ban 42	Ana Beko'ach	The Menorah למנצח בנגינות	Central verse פסוק אמצעי	7 Kings ז' מלכים	The Mochin מוחין	Mochin coming from: למוחין באים מן	Adam (Mah of Sag) אדם (מ"ה דס"ג)	YKVK הויה	Mochin Meditation כוונת המוחין
36	1st									בלע דאלקים	Gadlut A Abba	Inner Hod of Israel Saba			
37	2nd									יובב דאלקים	Gadlut A Ima	Inner Hod of Tevunah			
38	3rd									חשם באלקים	Katnut B Abba & Ima	Outer Gevurah of Supernal Abba & Ima			
39	4th									הדד דאלקים	Gadlut B Ima	Inner Gevurah of Supernal Ima			
40	5th									שמלה דאלקים	Katnut A Abba & Ima	Outer Hod of Israel Saba & Tevunah			
41	6th									שאול דאלקים	Reshimo Gadlut B Abba	Inner Gevurah of Supernal Abba			
42	7th									בעל חנן דאלקים	Gadlut B Abba	Inner Gevurah of Supernal Abba			

Each night - from the first night to the sixth night of the week - you should meditate to elevate 45 sparks of a total of 320 sparks:

On the seventh night – of each week - you should meditate to elevate 50 sparks of a total of 320 sparks

7th week – *Mochin* are entering *Tiferet* and *Malchut of Zeir Anpin*

Day Of The Omer	Day of the week	EHKH אהיה	Mah מ"ה	Ban ב"ן	42 of Mah of Ban	Ana Beko'ach	The Menorah	Central verse	7 Kings	The Mochin	Mochin coming from:	Adam (Mah of Sag)	YKVK	Mochin Meditation
43	1st	אהיה	מ"ה	ב"ן	ו	שקוצית	בהלך	ד	בלע וכל	Gadlut A Abba	Inner Hod of Israel Saba		הוי"ה	
44	2nd	אהיה	מ"ה	ב"ן	ה	קרע	אלהים	ו	יובב וכל	Gadlut A Ima	Inner Hod of Tevunah		הוי"ה	
45	3rd	אהיה	מ"ה	ב"ן	א	בטרצתג	דרויא	ה	חשם וכל	Katnut B Abba & Ima	Outer Gevurah of Supernal Abba & Ima		הוי"ה	
46	4th	אהיה	מ"ה	ב"ן	א	נגדיכש	ארני	ם	הדד וכל	Gadlut B Ima	Inner Gevurah of Supernal Ima		הוי"ה	
47	5th	אהיה	מ"ה	ב"ן	ל	שקוצית	כס	ס	שמלה וכל	Katnut A Abba & Ima	Outer Hod of Israel Saba & Tevunah		הוי"ה	
48	6th	אהיה	מ"ה	ב"ן	ה	חקבטנע	אפם	ל	שאול וכל	Reshimo of Gadlut B Abba	Inner Gevurah of Supernal Abba		הוי"ה	
49	7th	אהיה	מ"ה	ב"ן	אלף	שקו רית	אינו	ד	בעל וכל	Gadlut B Abba	Inner Gevurah of Supernal Abba		הוי"ה	

Each night - from the first night to the sixth night of the week - you should meditate to elevate 45 sparks of a total of 320 sparks:

On the seventh night - of each week - you should meditate to elevate 50 sparks of a total of 320 sparks

READING OF THE SHEMA AT BEDTIME

After enduring the rigors and adversity associated with the day, the soul is drained. Each night, our soul ascends to the Upper Realms for recharging and rejuvenation. Even if we remain awake, a part of soul departs when the sun has set and the stars have begun to appear in the heavens, which is why we feel more tired as the night unfolds. The more negative we are, the more drained we feel when this part of our soul leaves our body. Each night, there is an actual force that induces us to sleep to allow our soul to vacate our body. We recite the Bedtime *Shema* to attach an umbilical chord to our soul so that is will return and fill the space it has left behind.

LeShem Yichud

leshem לְשֵׁם   yichud יִחוּד   kudsha קוּדְשָׁא   berich בְּרִיךְ   hu הוּא

ush'chintei וּשְׁכִינְתֵּיהּ (יאההויהה)   bid'chilu בִּדְחִילוּ (יאהדונהי)   ur'chimu וּרְחִימוּ

ur'chimu וּרְחִימוּ   ud'chilu וּדְחִילוּ (איההויהה)   leyachda לְיַחֲדָא   shem שֵׁם

yud יו"ד   kei קֵי   bevav בְּוָא"ו   kei קֵי   beyichuda בְּיִחוּדָא   shelim שְׁלִים (יהוה)

beshem בְּשֵׁם   kol כָּל י"לי   Yisrael יִשְׂרָאֵל,   hareni הֲרֵינִי   mekabel מְקַבֵּל

alai עָלַי   Elahuto אֱלָהוּתוֹ   yitbarach יִתְבָּרַךְ   ve'ahavato וְאַהֲבָתוֹ

veyir'ato וְיִרְאָתוֹ   vehareni וְהָרֵינִי   yare יָרֵא   mimenu מִמֶּנּוּ   begin בְּגִין

de'ihu דְאִיהוּ   rav רָב   veshalit וְשַׁלִּיט   al עַל   kula כּוּלָא,   vechula וְכוּלָא

kamei קָמֵיהּ   kela כְּלָא,   vehareni וְהָרֵינִי   mamlicho מַמְלִיכוֹ   al עַל   kol כָּל

יל"י ; עמם   ever אֶבֶר   ve'ever וְאֶבֶר   vegid וְגִיד   vagid וְגִיד   meramach מֶרְמַ"ח

evarim אֲבָרִים אותיות פשוטות וט"ז (אברהם), עסמ"ב רמ"ח (אברים), נתיבות החכמה ול"ב רי"ו ול"ו אל"פ, וז"פ אברהם,

veshasa וְשַׁסָּ"ה   gidim גִּידִים   shel שֶׁל   gufi גּוּפִּי   venafshi וְנַפְשִׁי,   ruchi רוּחִי

venishmati וְנִשְׁמָתִי   malchut מַלְכוּת   gemura גְּמוּרָה   ushlema וּשְׁלֵמָה,

vahareni וַהֲרֵינִי   eved עֶבֶד   leHashem לְהַשֵׁם   yitbarach יִתְבָּרַךְ,   vehu וְהוּא

berachamav בְּרַחֲמָיו בובו   yezakeni יְזַכֵּנִי   le'ovdo לְעָבְדוֹ   belevav בְּלֵבָב   שָׁלֵם

shalem שָׁלֵם   venefesh וְנֶפֶשׁ   chafetza וַחֲפֵצָה   amen אָמֵן   יאהדונהי

ken כֵּן   yehi יְהִי   ratzon רָצוֹן   מהש ע"ה, ע"ב בריבוע וקס"א, ע"ב ברבוע וקס"א ע"ה, אל שדי ע"ה:

READING OF THE SHEMA AT BEDTIME - LeShem Yichud

For the sake of unification between the Holy Blessed One and His Shechinah, with fear and love and with love and fear, in order to unify the Name Yud, Kei and Vav, Kei in perfect unity, and in the name of all Israel, I hereby accept upon myself His divinity, blessed be He, and the love of Him and the fear of Him. And I hereby fear Him for being great, He Who reigns over everything. Before Him, everything is insignificant. I hereby accept His Sovereignty over each and every organ and each and every sinew of the 248 (a woman says 252) organs and 365 sinews of my body, with lower spirit, my Neshamah and soul as a complete and perfect sovereignty. And I hereby declare myself a servant of the Lord, blessed be He. May He, in His mercy, allow me the privilege of serving Him wholeheartedly and with a willing spirit. Amen, so may it be His will.

RIBONO SHEL OLAM

Before we recite this prayer, we should reflect on our day and search for any negativity that we may have caused others, or that others may have caused us. If a person goes to sleep harboring any ill feeling toward another person, this feeling will prevent both souls from elevating to the Upper Worlds during the night. In this prayer, we ask for forgiveness from those people to whom we caused pain. We acknowledge that this forgiveness applies to everything that occurred, whether intentional or accidental, through words or through physical activity, in this lifetime or in past lifetimes. The concept of forgiving others has nothing to do with the person we are forgiving. Spiritually, forgiveness is about letting go of our anger and resentments. Kabbalistically, the people who hurt us in life are merely messengers. We should never blame the messenger. All our prior actions, positive or negative, are subject to a boomerang effect and will eventually return to us through the deeds of others.

mochel מוֹחֵל   hareni הֲרֵינִי   olam עוֹלָם   shel שֶׁל   Ribono רִבּוֹנוֹ

shehich'is שֶׁהִכְעִיס   mi מִי   lechol לְכָל   vesole'ach וְסוֹלֵחַ

ben בֵּין • kenegdi כְּנֶגְדִּי   shechata שֶׁחָטָא   oh אוֹ   oti אוֹתִי   vehiknit וְהִקְנִיט

bichvodi בִּכְבוֹדִי   ben בֵּין   bemamoni בְּמָמוֹנִי   ben בֵּין   begufi בְּגוּפִי

be'ones בְּאוֹנֶס   ben בֵּין • li לִי   asher אֲשֶׁר   bechol בְּכָל   ben בֵּין

beratzon בְּרָצוֹן   ben בֵּין

bedibur בְּדִבּוּר   ben בֵּין   bemezid בְּמֵזִיד   ben בֵּין   beshogeg בְּשׁוֹגֵג   ben בֵּין

ben בֵּין   ze זֶה   begilgul בְּגִלְגּוּל   ben בֵּין • bema'ase בְּמַעֲשֶׂה   ben בֵּין

Yisrael יִשְׂרָאֵל   bar בַּר   lechol לְכָל   acher אַחֵר   begilgul בְּגִלְגּוּל

• besibati בְּסִבָּתִי   adam אָדָם   shum שׁוּם   ye'anesh יֵעָנֵשׁ   velo וְלֹא

milfanecha מִלְפָנֶיךָ   ratzon רָצוֹן   yehi יְהִי

velohei וֵאלֹהֵי   Elohai אֱלֹהַי   Adonai יְהֹוָה

• od עוֹד   echeta אֶחֱטָא   shelo שֶׁלֹא   avotai אֲבוֹתַי

lefanecha לְפָנֶיךָ   shechatati שֶׁחָטָאתִי   uma וּמַה

aval אֲבָל   harabim הָרַבִּים   berachamecha בְּרַחֲמֶיךָ   mechok מְחוֹק

• ra'im רָעִים   vechola'im וְחֳלָאִים   yisurin יִסּוּרִין   yedei יְדֵי   al עַל   lo לֹא

RIBONO SHEL OLAM

Master of the World, I hereby forgive and pardon anyone who has angered or has irritated me or has sinned against me, whether against my body, my money, my honor, or anything else that is mine; whether by force or willingly, whether by mistake or wantonly, whether through speech or action; whether in this incarnation or any past lifetime, or from any of the Children of Israel, and may no one be punished on my behalf. May it be Your will, Lord, my God and God of my fathers, that I will not sin again. And any sin that I have already committed before You, erase with Your bountiful compassion, but not by means of suffering or evil illnesses.

מ״ב אותיות בפסוק

יִהְיוּ yih'yu ייא״י (מילוי דס״ג) מהע ע״ה, ע״ב בריבוע וקס״א ע״ה, אל שדי ע״ה לְרָצוֹן leratzon

אִמְרֵי imrei פִּי fi ר״ת אֶלֶף = אלף למד שׁין דלת יוד ע״ה וְהֶגְיוֹן vehegyon לִבִּי libi

לְפָנֶיךָ lefanecha ס״ג מ״ה ב״ן יְהֹוָאדנהיאהדונהי Adonai צוּרִי tzuri וְגֹאֲלִי vego'ali:

HAMAPIL

This blessing ensures that our soul safely departs during sleep and returns to our body upon awakening. It is the lifeline between the body and the soul.

If you go to sleep **before midnight**, you say the entire blessing (from *"baruch Ata"* to *"bichvodo"*).
If you go to sleep **after midnight**, you skip the words *"Adonai Eloheinu melech ha'olam"* at the beginning of the blessing, and the words *"Ata Adonai"* at the end of the blessing.

בָּרוּךְ baruch אַתָּה Ata יְהֹוָאדנהיאהדונהי Adonai אֱלֹהֵינוּ Elohenu ילה

מֶלֶךְ melech הָעוֹלָם ha'olam הַמַפִּיל hamapil וְחֶבְלֵי chevlei

שֵׁנָה shena עַל al עֵינַי enai ריבוע דמ״ה וּתְנוּמָה utnuma עַל al

עַפְעַפָּי afapai וּמֵאִיר ume'ir לְאִישׁוֹן le'ishon בַּת bat עַיִן ayin ריבוע דמ״ה:

יְהִי yehi רָצוֹן ratzon מהע ע״ה, ע״ב בריבוע וקס״א ע״ה, אל שדי ע״ה

מִלְפָנֶיךָ milfanecha ס״ג מ״ה ב״ן יְהֹוָאדנהיאהדונהי Adonai אֱלֹהַי Elohai

אֲבוֹתַי avotai ילה ; דמב מילוי דע״ב, לכב ; מילוי דע״ב, דמב ; ילה וֵאלֹהֵי velohei

שֶׁתַּשְׁכִּיבֵנִי shetashkiveni לְשָׁלוֹם leshalom וְתַעֲמִידֵנִי veta'amideni

לְחַיִּים lechayim אהיה אהיה יהוה, בינה ע״ה טוֹבִים tovim וּלְשָׁלוֹם ulshalom

וְתֵן veten וְחֶלְקִי chelki בְּתוֹרָתֶךָ betoratecha וְתַרְגִּילֵנִי vetargileni

לִדְבַר lidvar ראה מִצְוָה mitzva וְאַל ve'al תַּרְגִּילֵנִי targileni

לִדְבַר lidvar ראה עֲבֵרָה avera◆ וְאַל ve'al תְּבִיאֵנִי tevi'eni לִידֵי lidei

וְחֵטְא chet וְלֹא velo לִידֵי lidei נִסָּיוֹן nisayon וְלֹא velo לִידֵי lidei

בִּזָּיוֹן vizayon◆ וְיִשְׁלֹט veyishlot בִּי bi יֵצֶר yetzer הַטּוֹב hatov והו

וְאַל ve'al יִשְׁלֹט yishlot בִּי bi יֵצֶר yetzer הָרָע hara◆

"May the utterances of my mouth and the thoughts of my heart be favorable before You, Lord, my Rock and my Redeemer." (Psalms 19:15)

HAMAPIL

Blessed are You, Lord, Our God, King of the world, Who causes the bonds of sleep to fall upon my eyes and slumber upon my lids, and Who brings the light of sight to the pupil of my eye. May it be pleasing before You, Lord, my God and God of my fathers, that You may lay me down in peace and make me rise to a good life and to peace, and that You may give me my portion in Your Torah and accustom me to observe the commandments and not accustom me to transgressions. Do not lead me to sins, to trials, or to shame. Let the good inclination govern me and do not allow the evil inclination to control me.

vetatzileni וְתַצִּילֵנִי miyetzer מִיֵּצֶר hara הָרָע umechola'im וּמֵחֳלָאִים

ra'im רָעִים ve'al וְאַל yavhiluni יְבַהֲלוּנִי chalomot וְחֲלוֹמוֹת

ra'im רָעִים vehirhurim וְהִרְהוּרִים ra'im רָעִים utehe וּתְהֵא

mitati מִטָּתִי shelema שְׁלֵמָה lefanecha לְפָנֶיךָ ס״ג מ״ה ב״ן vehaer וְהָאֵר

enai עֵינַי רִבּוּעַ דמ״ה pen פֶּן ishan אִישַׁן ◆hamavet הַמָּוֶת

baruch בָּרוּךְ Ata אַתָּה יְהֹוָה אדנ״י אהדונ״הי Adonai hame'ir הַמֵּאִיר

la'olam לְעוֹלָם רִבּוּעַ דס״ג ו״י אותיות דס״ג kulo כֻּלּוֹ ‡bichvodo בִּכְבוֹדוֹ

THE SHEMA (to learn more about the *Shema* go to pg. 176)

The *Shema* is one of the most powerful tools to draw the energy of healing to our lives. The true power of the *Shema* is unleashed when we recite this prayer while meditating on others who need healing energy.

1) In order to receive the Light of the *Shema*, you have to accept upon yourself the precept of: "Love your neighbor as yourself," and see yourself united with all the souls that comprise the Original Adam.

2) Before saying the *Shema* you should cover your eyes with your right hand, then say the words "*Shema Yisrael … le'olam va'ed.*" And you should read the *Shema* with deep meditation, chanting it with the intonations. It is necessary to be careful with the pronunciation of all the letters.

First, meditate in general, on the first *Yichud* of the four *Yichuds* of the Name: יהוה, and in particular, to awaken the letter ה, and then to connect it with the letter ו. Then connect the letter י and the letter ה together in the following order: *Hei* (ה), *Hei-Vav* (ה״ו), then *Yud-Hei* (י״ה), which adds up to 31, the secret of יא״י of the Name ס״ג. It is good to meditate on this *Yichud* before reciting any *Shema* because it acts as a replacement for the times that you may have missed reading the *Shema*. This *Yichud* has the same ability to create a Supernal connection like the reading of the *Shema* - to raise *Zeir* and *Nukva* together for the *Zivug* of *Abba* and *Ima*.

Shema – שׁמע

General Meditation: שׂם ע — to draw the energy from the seven lower *Sefirot* of *Ima* to the *Nukva*, which enables the *Nukva* to elevate the *Mayin Nukvin* (awakening from Below).

Particular Meditation: שׂם = יהוה ↓ עד״י and five times the letters י and ד of ב״ן = ע [The letter *Hei* (ה) is formed by the letters *Dalet* (ד) and *Yud* (י), so in ב״ן we have four times the letter ה plus another time the letters י and ד from יו״ד of ב״ן.]. Also the three letters ו (18) that are left from ב״ן, plus ב״ן itself (52) equals ע (70).

And save me from the evil inclination and from evil illnesses. Do not let bad dreams or evil thoughts frighten me. Let my bed be complete before You. Enlighten my eyes lest I sleep a sleep of death. Blessed are You, Lord, Who illuminates the whole world with His glory.

Yisrael – יִשְׂרָאֵל

General Meditation: שִׁיר אֵל — to draw energy from *Chesed* and *Gevurah* of *Abba* to *Zeir Anpin*, to do his action in the secret of *Mayin Duchrin* (awakening from Above).

Particular Meditation: (the rearranged letters of the word *Yisrael*) – שִׁר אֵלִי –

ריבוע המילוי דקס"א (אלף, לף י, לף י יוד, לף י יוד י) = שׁר,

בּ"א אותיות של פּעוֹטוֹ, מילוי וּמילוי דמילוי דקס"א = אֵלִ"י

(אֱהִיה, אלף הי יוד הי, אלף למד פּי הי יוד יוד ויו דלת הי יוד)

Also meditate to draw the Surrounding *Mochin* of *Ima* of *Katnut* into *Zeir Anpin*.

Adonai Elohenu Adonai – יְהוָה אֱלֹהֵינוּ יְהוָה

General Meditation: to draw energy to *Abba*, *Ima* and *Da'at* from *Arich Anpin*,

Particular Meditation: ע"ב (יוד הי ויו הי) קְס"א (אלף הי יוד הי) ע"ב (יוד הי וי הי).

Also meditate three times ע"ב (72) which equal רי"ו (216).

Then to draw the רי"ו to *Ima* in order to make Her as a vessel

(רי"ו equals וֹרֶב – sword – that kills all the *klipot* that become bodies to the lost sparks of Light).

Echad – אֶחָד

(The secret of the complete Yichud-Unification)

The letters *Alef* א and *Chet* ח from *Echad* אֶחָד is *Zeir Anpin* and the letter *Dalet* ד is *Nukva*. **You should meditate** to devote your soul for the sanctification of the Holy Name, thereby elevating your *Nefesh*, *Ruach*, *Neshamah* and *Neshamah* of *Neshamah* with *Zeir Anpin* and *Nukva* (using the Names: ע"ב and ס"ג) to *Abba* and *Ima* as the secret of *Mayin Nukvin*, and by that energy, *Abba* and *Ima* will be unified in the secret of the Name: יאההויה"ה. **Also meditate** to draw out the inner and surrounding of *Abba* of *Katnut* and the inner six edges of *Gadlut* of *Ima* into *Zeir Anpin*. The Drop, which is ע"ב, is drawn out from the external of *Abba*, and descends to *Yesod* of *Ima*, where it becomes: ע"ב ס"ג מ"ה ב"ן, and the four spelled out אהיה (אלף הי יוד הי, אלף הי יוד הי, אלף הא יוד הא, אלף הה יוד הה) become her clothing. As a result, *Zeir Anpin* now has four spelled out יהו"ה (יוד הי ויו, יוד הי ואו, יוד הא ואו, יוד הה וו), four spelled out אדנ"י (אלף הי יוד, אלף הי יוד, אלף הא יוד, אלף הה יוד) and the Inner Six Edges of *Gadlut* of *Ima*. **Also meditate** on the Name: אל"ף ה"י ו"י ה"י, which is the entire *Mochin* in the secret of *Da'at*.

Baruch Shem – בָּרוּךְ שֵׁם כְּבוֹד מַלְכוּתוֹ לְעוֹלָם וָעֶד

Its secret is to make a vessel for the *Malchut*, using one רי"ו which is drawn from *Zeir Anpin* (its secret is: רי"ו = י יה יהו יהוה, יוד יוד הה יוד הה וו יוד הה וו הה)

Baruch Shem Kevod — *Chochmah*, *Binah*, *Da'at* of *Zeir Anpin* (the root of the above mentioned רי"ו), are giving illumination to *Nukva* in Her skull (which later becomes — מלכותו — His kingdom); *Malchuto* — the above mention illumination;

Now meditate to deposit your soul as it will become as *Mayin Nukvin* (awakning from Below), so *Zeir Anpin* and *Nukva* can be integrated and the רי"ו is given to Her so She becomes a vessel. **Le'olam Va'ed** — לְעוֹלָם וָעֶד equal רי"ו — You should be aware to mention the final *Mem* (ם) only after the word *va'ed*. As in the begining we need to draw the רי"ו (=le'ola va'ed לְעוֹלָ וָעֶד) and only then the vessel can be illuminated which is the final *Mem* (ם — the womb - the embryo creation space). **Also meditate** to elevate all the sparks from the *klipot* and to eradicate their bodies using the two above mentioned רי"ו (which are two swords) so the sparks become the secret of the vessel, and it will fulfill the lack that was created by wasting male energy without a female vessel.

שְׁמַע shema 🔯 ע׳ רבתי יִשְׂרָאֵל Yisrael יְהֹוָֹהֵאדְנָיֵאהדונהי Adonai

אֱלֹהֵינוּ Elohenu ילה יְהֹוָֹהֵאדְנָיֵאהדונהי Adonai | אֶחָד echad ד׳ רבתי ; אהבה, דאגה.

(: Whisper) יוצו אותיות בָּרוּךְ baruch שֵׁם shem כְּבוֹד kevod מַלְכוּתוֹ malchuto,

לְעוֹלָם le'olam רביע דס״ג וי׳ אותיות דס״ג וָעֶד va'ed:

Yud, Chochmah, head — 42 words corresponding to the Holy 42-Letter Name of God.

ב   א

אֵת et (יכוין לקיים מ״ע עול אהבת ה) ; ב״פ אין סוף, ב״פ רז, ב״פ אור וְאָהַבְתָּ ve'ahavta

י   ג

ע״ה דוד בן משיחו כהת, ס״ת ; ילה Elohecha אֱלֹהֶיךָ Adonai יְהֹוָֹהֵאדְנָיֵאהדונהי

ר   ק   צ   ת

נַפְשֶׁךָ nafshecha לבב, ב״ן וּבְכָל־ uvchol לבב, ב״ן לְבָבְךָ levavcha לבב, ב״ן בְּכָל־ bechol

ז   ט   ש   ע

הַדְּבָרִים hadevarim וְהָיוּ vehayu מְאֹדֶךָ: me'odecha לבב, ב״ן וּבְכָל־ uvchol

כ   י   ד   ה

הַיּוֹם hayom מְצַוְּךָ metzavecha אָנֹכִי anochi אֲשֶׁר asher הָאֵלֶּה ha'ele

ט   ב   י

וְשִׁנַּנְתָּם veshinantam לְבָבֶךָ: levavecha עַל־ al (pause here) ע״ה נגד, מזבח, ז, אל יהוה

ג   ת   צ   ר

בְּשִׁבְתְּךָ beshivtecha מ״ב בָּם bam וְדִבַּרְתָּ vedibarta לְבָנֶיךָ levanecha

ב   ק   ו

בַּדֶּרֶךְ vaderech וּבְלֶכְתְּךָ uvlechtecha ראה ב״פ בְּבֵיתֶךָ bevetecha

נ   ט

וּבְקוּמֶךָ: uvkumecha וּבְשָׁכְבְּךָ uvshochbecha קס״א ס״ג, יב״ק, ב״פ

ל   ג   י   ע

יָדֶךָ yadecha עַל־ al לְאוֹת le'ot וּקְשַׁרְתָּם ukshartam

THE SHEMA

"Hear Israel, the Lord our God. The Lord is One." (Deuteronomy 6:4)

"Blessed is the glorious Name, His Kingdom is forever and for eternity." (Pesachim 56a)

"And you shall love the Lord, your God, with all your heart and with all your soul and with all that you possess. Let those words that I command you today be upon your heart. And you shall teach them to your children and you shall speak of them while you sit in your home and while you walk on your way and when you lie down and when you rise. You shall bind them as a sign upon your hand

וְהָיוּ vehayu   לְטֹטָפֹת letotafot   בֵּין ben   עֵינֶיךָ enecha

ע"ה   קס"א   ;   ריבוע   מ"ה: וּכְתַבְתָּם uchtavtam   עַל al

מְזֻזוֹת mezuzot נית (זו מות)   בֵּיתֶךָ betecha ב"פ ראה   וּבִשְׁעָרֶיךָ: uvish'arecha

VEHAYA IM SHAMO'A

Hei, Binah, **arms and body** — 72 words corresponding to the 72 Names of God.

וְהָיָה vehaya יהוה ; יהה im אִם יוה"ך, מ"א אותיות דפשוט, דמילוי ודמילוי דמילוי דאהיה ע"ה

שָׁמֹעַ shamo'a   תִּשְׁמְעוּ tishme'u   אֶל el   מִצְוֹתַי mitzvotai   אֲשֶׁר asher

אָנֹכִי anochi   מְצַוֶּה metzave   אֶתְכֶם etchem   הַיּוֹם hayom ע"ה נגד, מזבח, זן, אל יהוה

Adonai יְהֹוָה (אדני/אהדונהי)   אֶת et   דאגה, אוזר, le'ahava לְאַהֲבָה (pause here)

ul'ovdo וּלְעָבְדוֹ (enunciate the letter *Ayin* in the word "*ul'ovdo*") Elohechem אֱלֹהֵיכֶם

בְּכָל bechol ב"ן, לכב   לְבַבְכֶם levavchem לכב   וּבְכָל uvchol ב"ן, לכב

נַפְשְׁכֶם: nafshechem   וְנָתַתִּי venatati   מְטַר metar   אַרְצְכֶם artzechem

בְּעִתּוֹ be'ito   יוֹרֶה yore   וּמַלְקוֹשׁ umalkosh   וְאָסַפְתָּ ve'asafta   דְּגָנֶךָ deganecha

וְתִירֹשְׁךָ vetiroshcha   וְיִצְהָרֶךָ: veyitz'harecha   וְנָתַתִּי venatati   עֵשֶׂב esev ע"ב שמות

and they shall be as frontlets between your eyes.
And you shall write them upon the doorposts of your house and your gates." (Deuteronomy 6:5-9)

VEHAYA IM SHAMO'A

"And it shall come to be that if you shall listen to My commandments that I am commanding you with today to love the Lord, your God, and to serve Him with all your heart and with all your soul, then I shall send rain upon your land in its proper time, both early rain and late rain. You shall then gather your grain and your wine and your oil. And I shall give grass

בְּשָׂדְךָ besadcha   לִבְהֶמְתֶּךָ livhemtecha   וְאָכַלְתָּ ve'achalta   וְשָׂבָעְתָּ vesavata:

הִשָּׁמְרוּ hishamru   לָכֶם lachem   פֶּן pen   יִפְתֶּה yifte   לְבַבְכֶם levavchem

וְסַרְתֶּם vesartem   וַעֲבַדְתֶּם va'avadetem   אֱלֹהִים elohim   אֲחֵרִים acherim

(הָעוֹמֵד גֶגֶד הַקְלִיפּוֹת)   וְהִשְׁתַּחֲוִיתֶם vehishtachavitem   לָהֶם lahem:

וְחָרָה vechara   (pause here)   אַף af   יְהֹוָה Adonai   בָּכֶם bachem

וְעָצַר ve'atzar   אֶת et   הַשָּׁמַיִם hashamayim   וְלֹא velo

יִהְיֶה yihye   מָטָר matar   וְהָאֲדָמָה veha'adama   לֹא lo   תִתֵּן titen

אֶת et   יְבוּלָהּ yevula   וַאֲבַדְתֶּם va'avadetem   מְהֵרָה mehera   מֵעַל me'al

הָאָרֶץ ha'aretz   הַטֹּבָה hatova   אֲשֶׁר asher

יְהֹוָה Adonai   נֹתֵן noten   לָכֶם lachem: *Vav, Zeir Anpin*

stomach — 50 words corresponding to the 50 Gates of *Binah*   וְשַׂמְתֶּם vesamtem

אֶת et   דְּבָרַי devarai   אֵלֶּה ele   עַל al   לְבַבְכֶם levavchem

וְעַל ve'al   נַפְשְׁכֶם nafshechem   וּקְשַׁרְתֶּם ukshartem   אֹתָם otam

---

in your field for your cattle. And you shall eat and you shall be satiated. Be careful lest your heart be seduced and you may turn away and serve alien deities and prostrate yourself before them. And the wrath of the Lord shall be upon you and He shall stop the Heavens and there shall be no more rain and the earth shall not give forth its crop. And you shall quickly perish from the good land that the Lord has given you. And you shall place those words of Mine upon your heart and upon your soul and you shall bind them

אות

לְאוֹת le'ot ר"ת לאו עַל־ al יֶדְכֶם yedchem וְהָיוּ vehayu

ה

לְטוֹטָפֹת letotafot בֵּין ben עֵינֵיכֶם enechem ריבוע מ"ה:

ה

וְלִמַּדְתֶּם velimadetem אֹתָם otam אֶת־ et בְּנֵיכֶם benechem

ה

לְדַבֵּר ledaber ראה בָּם bam שׁם בּן מ"ב בְּשִׁבְתְּךָ beshivtecha

ה

בְּבֵיתֶךָ bevetecha ב"פ ראה וּבְלֶכְתְּךָ uvlechtecha בַדֶּרֶךְ vaderech ב"פ יב"ק, ס"ג קס"א בְּבֵיתֶךָ

ה

uvshochbecha וּבְקוּמֶךָ uvkumecha: וּכְתַבְתָּם uchtavtam עַל־ al

ה

מְזוּזוֹת mezuzot בֵּיתֶךָ betecha ב"פ ראה וּבִשְׁעָרֶיךָ uvish'arecha: לְמַעַן lema'an

ה

יִרְבּוּ yirbu יְמֵיכֶם yemechem ר"ת ייל וִימֵי vimei בְּנֵיכֶם venechem

אהיה

עַל al הָאֲדָמָה ha'adama אֲשֶׁר asher (enunciate the letter _Ayin_ in the word "_nishba_")

אהיה

נִשְׁבַּע nishba יכוין לשבועת המבול יְהֹוָ֒ה/אֲדֹנָי/אֱלֹהִים Adonai

אהיה

לַאֲבֹתֵיכֶם la'avotechem לָתֵת latet לָהֶם lahem כִּימֵי kimei

אהיה

הַשָּׁמַיִם hashamayim יֹ"פ טל, יֹ"פ כוזו עַל־ al הָאָרֶץ ha'aretz אלהים דההין ע"ה:

---

as a sign upon your hands and they shall be as frontlets between your eyes. And you shall teach them to your children and speak of them while you sit at home and while you walk on your way and when you lie down and when you rise. You shall write them upon the doorposts of your house and upon your gates. This is so that your days shall be numerous and so shall the days of your children upon the Earth that the Lord had sworn to your fathers to give them as the days of the Heavens upon the Earth." (Deuteronomy 11:13-21)

VAYOMER

Hei, Malchut, legs and reproductive organs,

72 words corresponding to the 72 Names of God in direct order (according to the Ramchal).

עאם	סבט	ייי	ווו
Moshe מֹשֶׁה	el אֶל־	Adonai יְהֹוָה	vayomer וַיֹּאמֶר

אוא	ליה	מבע	
el אֶל־ ראה daber דַבֵּר		lemor לֵאמֹר	מהלע, ע"ב ברבוע וקס"א, אל עדי, ד"פ אלהים ע"ה

הבע	לחו	אנד	הוי	כמת
ve'asu וְעָשׂוּ	alehem אֲלֵהֶם	ve'amarta וְאָמַרְתָּ	Yisrael יִשְׂרָאֵל	benei בְּנֵי

לוו	הממ	היי	מרה	יצל
vigdehem בִּגְדֵיהֶם	kanfei כַּנְפֵי	al עַל־	tzitzit צִיצִת	lahem לָהֶם

נמך	פול	לוו	כבי
tzitzit צִיצִת	al עַל־	venatnu וְנָתְנוּ	ledorotam לְדֹרֹתָם

וזהו	מנה	יוזי
techelet תְּכֵלֶת	petil פְּתִיל	hakanaf הַכָּנָף
	ע"ה קנ"א, אדני אלהים	

רלי	שאה	ירת	השא	נזה
oto אֹתוֹ	ur'item וּרְאִיתֶם	letzitzit לְצִיצִת	lachem לָכֶם	vehaya וְהָיָה

לחו	יוו	והר	לב	אום
Adonai יְהֹוָה	mitzvot מִצְוֹת	kol כָּל־	et אֶת־	uzchartem וּזְכַרְתֶּם

רהע	וום	אני	מגד	כעק
acharei אַחֲרֵי	taturu תָתוּרוּ	velo וְלֹא	otam אֹתָם	va'asitem וַעֲשִׂיתֶם

מכך	העוה	יוז
enechem עֵינֵיכֶם	ve'acharei וְאַחֲרֵי	levavchem לְבַבְכֶם

You should meditate on the precept:
"not to follow negative sexual thoughts of the heart and the sights of the eyes for prostitution."

VAYOMER

"And the Lord spoke to Moses and said,
Speak to the Children of Israel and say to them that they should make for themselves Tzitzit,
on the corners of their garments, throughout all their generations. And they must place upon the Tzitzit,
of each corner, a blue strand. And this shall be to you as a Tzitzit: you shall see it and remember
the commandments of the Lord and fulfill them. And you shall not stray after your hearts and your eyes,

אֲשֶׁר־ asher אַתֶּם atem זֹנִים zonim אַחֲרֵיהֶם acharehem לְמַעַן lema'an

תִּזְכְּרוּ tizkeru וַעֲשִׂיתֶם va'asitem אֶת־ et כָּל־ kol מִצְוֹתָי mitzvotai

וִהְיִיתֶם vihyitem קְדֹשִׁים kedoshim לֵאלֹהֵיכֶם lelohechem

אֲנִי ani יְהֹוָה Adonai אֱלֹהֵיכֶם Elohechem אֲשֶׁר asher

הוֹצֵאתִי hotzeti אֶתְכֶם etchem מֵאֶרֶץ me'eretz מִצְרַיִם Mitzrayim

You should meditate to remember the exodus from *Mitzrayim* (Egypt).

לִהְיוֹת lihyot לָכֶם lachem לֵאלֹהִים lelohim ;

אֲנִי ani יְהֹוָה Adonai אֱלֹהֵיכֶם Elohechem

אֱמֶת emet אהיה פעמים אהיה, ז"פ ס"ג

You should repeat the last three words in order to complete 248 words.

יְהֹוָה Adonai אֱלֹהֵיכֶם Elohechem אֱמֶת emet אהיה פעמים אהיה, ז"פ ס"ג

YA'ALZU

Every negative act we perform produces negative angels that surround us each and every day. These negative entities are often the unseen cause of all those things that go wrong in our lives. These verses help remove the negative angels and their destructive influence.

וַחֲסִידִים Chasidim ג"פ אם אותיות דפשוט, דמילוי ודמילוי דמילוי דג"פ אהיה ya'lezu יַעְלְזוּ

בְכָבוֹד bechavod בוכו, ובאתב"ש הוא עם שלעופ"ק הממתק את ג' אם דלעיל

(והוא עולה למנין עסמ"ב קס"א קנ"א קמ"ג וג"פ אם הנ"ל)

יְרַנְּנוּ yeranenu עַל־ al מִשְׁכְּבוֹתָם mishkevotam

---

after which you adulterate. This is so that you shall remember to fulfill all My commandments and thereby be holy before your God. I am the Lord, your God, Who brought you out of the land of Egypt to be your God. I, the Lord, your God, Is true." (Numbers 15:37-41) the Lord, your God, is true!

YA'ALZU
The pious shall exult in glory and sing joyously upon their beds.

רוֹמְמוֹת romemot אֵל El (מילוי דס"ג) יא"י בִּגְרוֹנָם bigronam

ר"ת קנ"א ב"ן, יהוה אלהים יהוה אדני, מילוי קס"א וס"ג, מ"ה ברבוע וע"ב ע"ה

וְחֶרֶב vecherev רי"ו פִּיפִיּוֹת pifiyot בְּיָדָם beyadam:

HINE MITATO SHELISHLOMO

The kabbalists teach us that sleep is 1/60th of death. It is important to ask ourselves: "Did I do enough spiritual change in my life today? Am I happy if this should be my last day?"

The next verse contains 20 words; they are recited three times (20 x 3 = 60) to correspond to the 1/60th of death that occurs when we sleep.

Meditate that by going to sleep you elevate your soul, as you depart now from the world.

הִנֵּה hine מִטָּתוֹ mitato שֶׁלִּשְׁלֹמֹה shelishlomo ר"ת מהע,

ע"ב ברבוע וקס"א, אל עדי, ד"פ אלהים ע"ה שִׁשִּׁים shishim גִּבֹּרִים giborim

סָבִיב saviv לָהּ la מִגִּבֹּרֵי migiborei יִשְׂרָאֵל Yisrael: כֻּלָּם kulam

אֲחֻזֵי achuzei חֶרֶב cherev מְלֻמְּדֵי melumedei מִלְחָמָה milchama אִישׁ ish

וְחַרְבּוֹ charbo רי"ו עַל al יְרֵכוֹ yerecho מִפַּחַד mipachad בַּלֵּילוֹת balelot:

BLESSING OF THE KOHANIM

There are 60 letters in the Blessing of the *Kohanim*.
The initials of the three verses give us the Holy Name: יי.
In this section, there are 15 words, which are equal to the numerical value of the Holy Name: יהה.

(Right – *Chesed*) יְבָרֶכְךָ yevarechecha יְהֹוָואדנייאהדונהי Adonai

וְיִשְׁמְרֶךָ veyishmerecha ר"ת = יהוה ; וס"ת = מ"ה:

(Left - *Gevurah*) יָאֵר ya'er יְהֹוָואדנייאהדונהי Adonai | פָּנָיו panav

אֵלֶיךָ elecha וִיחֻנֶּךָּ vichuneka מנצ"ד ; יהה אותיות בפסוק:

(Central – *Tiferet*) יִשָּׂא yisa יְהֹוָואדנייאהדונהי Adonai | פָּנָיו panav אֵלֶיךָ elecha

וְיָשֵׂם veyasem לְךָ lecha שָׁלוֹם shalom האא תיבות בפסוק:

High praises of God in their throats and a double edged sword in their hands. (Psalms 149:5-6)

HINE MITATO SHELISHLOMO

Behold the bed of Solomon:
sixty mighty men surround it from among the mighty ones of Israel. They are all armed with swords and trained in battle, each with his sword ready by his side through fear of the nights. (Song of Songs 3:7-8)

BLESSING OF THE KOHANIM

(Right) *May the Lord bless you and protect you.*
(Left) *May the Lord shine His Countenance upon you and be gracious to you.*
(Central) *May the Lord turn His Face towards you and give you peace. (Numbers 6:24-26)*

YOSHEV BESETER ELYON

There are 60 words here, which help our soul to be elevated without the negative aspect of death.

yoshev יֹשֵׁב beseter בְּסֵתֶר elyon עֶלְיוֹן betzel בְּצֵל Shadai שַׁדַּי

yitlonan יִתְלוֹנָן omar אֹמַר ladonai לַיהֹוָה machsi מַחְסִי

umtzudati וּמְצוּדָתִי Elohai אֱלֹהַי evtach אֶבְטַח bo בּוֹ ki כִּי hu הוּא yatzilcha יַצִּילְךָ

mipach מִפַּח yakush יָקוּשׁ midever מִדֶּבֶר havot הַוּוֹת

be'evrato בְּאֶבְרָתוֹ yasech יָסֶךְ lach לָךְ vetachat וְתַחַת kenafav כְּנָפָיו

techse תֶּחְסֶה tzina צִנָּה vesochera וְסֹחֵרָה amito אֲמִתּוֹ lo לֹא tira תִירָא

mipachad מִפַּחַד layla לָיְלָה mechetz מֵחֵץ ya'uf יָעוּף yomam יוֹמָם

midever מִדֶּבֶר ba'ofel בָּאֹפֶל yahaloch יַהֲלֹךְ miketev מִקֶּטֶב

yashud יָשׁוּד tzahorayim צָהֳרָיִם yipol יִפֹּל mitzidcha מִצִּדְּךָ

elef אֶלֶף urvava וּרְבָבָה miminecha מִימִינֶךָ

elecha אֵלֶיךָ lo לֹא yigash יִגָּשׁ rak רַק be'enecha בְּעֵינֶיךָ

tabit תַּבִּיט veshilumat וְשִׁלֻּמַת resha'im רְשָׁעִים tir'e תִּרְאֶה

ki כִּי Ata אַתָּה Adonai יְהֹוָה machsi מַחְסִי

VIDUI – AWARENESS AND ACKNOWLEDGMENT

The next two sections ("ashamnu..." and "yehi ratzon..." on pg. 440-441) are to be said only on weekdays, not on *Shabbat* or holidays.

All our wrongful actions leave a residue on our body. Reciting and connecting with *Vidui* and *"Yehi Ratzon"* cleanses away all these negative remnants, working like the fast on Yom Kippur.

While reciting the *Vidui*, you should strike your chest with the right hand to shake the *Chasadim* (mercy) and the *Gevurot* (judgment) so they can grow up for the sake of the *Zivug* (unification). Even if you know that you didn't commit one of the below-mentioned negative actions, you should still say the *Vidui*. Because we are all act as guarantors to each other. The *Vidui* is said in plural because the *Vidui* is about other lifetimes and other people who are connected to your soul's root.

YOSHEV BESETER ELYON

One who finds refuge in the supreme One and dwells in the shade of Shaddai, I say of Lord: He is my Refuge and my Fortress, my God in Whom I put my trust. He shall rescue you from the snare of the trap and from destructive pestilence. He shall cover you with His Pinion and you shall find refuge under His Wings. His Truth is a shield and armor. You shall not fear the terrors of the night, the arrow that flies by day, the pestilence that moves in the darkness, or the destruction that strikes at noon. A thousand will fall at your side and ten thousand at your right, yet they will not approach you. You shall merely look with your eyes and see the retribution of the wicked, because You, the Lord, are my Refuge. (Psalms 91:1-9)

The 22 letters are the numerical value of the Holy Name: אכא.

יכה   Elohenu אֱלֹהֵינוּ   Adonai יְהֹוָה/אֲדֹנָי/אֲהֹוִי   ב"ן   ana אָנָּא   velohei וֵאלֹהֵי   לכב ; מילוי ע"ב, דמב ; יכה   avotenu אֲבוֹתֵינוּ.   tavo תָּבֹא

tit'alam תִּתְעַלַּם   ve'al וְאַל   tefilatenu תְּפִלָּתֵנוּ   ס"ג מ"ה ב"ן   lefanecha לְפָנֶיךָ

anachnu אֲנַחְנוּ   she'en שֶׁאֵין   mit'chinatenu מִתְּחִנָּתֵנוּ.   malkenu מַלְכֵּנוּ

oref עֹרֶף   ukshei וּקְשֵׁי   fanim פָּנִים   ע"ה אֲדֹנָי אֲהֹיֵ, אֱהֹיֶה, אֱלֹהִים ע"ה   azei עַזֵּי

Adonai יְהֹוָה/אֲדֹנָי/אֲהֹוִי   ב"ן   מ"ה ס"ג   lefanecha לְפָנֶיךָ   lomar לוֹמַר

יכה ; דמב ; מילוי ע"ב, לכב   velohei וֵאלֹהֵי   יכה Elohenu אֱלֹהֵינוּ

velo וְלֹא־   anachnu אֲנַחְנוּ   tzadikim צַדִּיקִים   avotenu אֲבוֹתֵינוּ

pashanu פָּשַׁעְנוּ.   avinu עָוִינוּ.   chatanu וְחָטָאנוּ.   aval אֲבָל   chatanu חָטָאנוּ.

anachnu אֲנַחְנוּ   va'avotenu וַאֲבוֹתֵינוּ   ve'anshei וְאַנְשֵׁי   vetenu בֵיתֵנוּ   ב"פ ראה:

dofi דֹּפִי   dibarnu דִּבַּרְנוּ   gazalnu גָזַלְנוּ.   bagadnu בָּגַדְנוּ.   ashamnu אָשַׁמְנוּ

zadnu זַדְנוּ.   vehirshanu וְהִרְשַׁעְנוּ.   he'evinu הֶעֱוִינוּ.   hara הָרַע   velashon וְלָשׁוֹן

ya'atznu יָעַצְנוּ.   umirma וּמִרְמָה   sheker שֶׁקֶר   tafalnu טָפַלְנוּ.   chamasnu חָמַסְנוּ

latznu לַצְנוּ.   ka'asnu כָּעַסְנוּ.   kizavnu כִּזַּבְנוּ.   ra'ot רָעוֹת   etzot עֵצוֹת

ni'atznu נִאַצְנוּ.   devarecha דְּבָרֶיךָ.   marinu מָרִינוּ   maradnu מָרַדְנוּ.

pagamnu פָּגַמְנוּ.   pashanu פָּשַׁעְנוּ.   avinu עָוִינוּ.   sararnu סָרַרְנוּ   ni'afnu נִאַפְנוּ.

oref עֹרֶף   kishinu קִשִּׁינוּ.   va'em וָאֵם   av אָב   tzi'arnu צִעַרְנוּ   tzararnu צָרַרְנוּ.

VIDUI

We beseech You, Lord, our God and the God of our fathers. May our prayer come before You and may Our King not ignore our plea. For we are not arrogant and stiff necked to say before You Lord, our God and the God of our fathers that we are righteous and we did not sin. For we have sinned, we have committed iniquity, we have transgressed, we and our fathers and the people of our household.

א We are guilty, ב we betrayed, ג we stole, ד we spoke gossip and evil speech, ה we caused iniquity, ו we convicted, ז we were wanton, ח we robbed, ט we accused falsely and deceitfully, י we gave bad advice, כ we lied, ך we have anger, ל we mocked, מ we revolted, ם we rebelled Your commandments, נ we gave contempt, ן we committed adultery, ס we have been perverted, ע we caused wickedness,פ we transgressed, ף we damaged, צ we have oppressed, ץ we gave sorrow to our mother and father, ק we were stubborn,

רְשַׁעְנוּ rashanu. שִׁחַתְנוּ shichatnu. תִּעַבְנוּ ti'avnu. תָּעִינוּ ta'inu. תָּעִינוּ וְהִתְעַתָּעְנוּ veti'atanu

וְסַרְנוּ vesarnu מִמִּצְוֹתֶיךָ mimitzvotecha וּמִמִּשְׁפָּטֶיךָ umimishpatecha

הַטּוֹבִים hatovim וְלֹא velo שָׁוָה shava לָנוּ lanu אלהים, אהיה אדני.

וְאַתָּה veAta צַדִּיק tzadik עַל al כָּל kol יל; עמם הַבָּא haba עָלֵינוּ alenu כִּי ki

אֱמֶת emet אהיה פעמים אהיה, ז"פ ס"ג עָשִׂיתָ asita וַאֲנַחְנוּ va'anachnu הִרְשָׁעְנוּ hirsha'nu

:Meditate to ensure that your negative actions are part of the past and are not part of your present anymore

יְהִי רָצוֹן מהע"ה, ע"ב בריבוע וקס"א ע"ה, אל עדי ע"ה קס"א ע"ה מ"ה בן יהו אלהי אהדונהי
אלהֵינוּ ילה ואלהֵי לכב; מילוי דע"ב, רמב; ילה אֲבוֹתֵינוּ שֶׁאִם וְחָטָאתִי לְפָנֶיךָ ס"ג מ"ה בן
וּפָגַמְתִּי בָּאוֹת (י) שֶׁל שִׁמְךָ (יהוה) וּבָאוֹת (א) שֶׁל (אדני) יְהִיֶה יי נוֹשׂוֹב לְפָנֶיךָ ס"ג מ"ה בן
כְּאִלּוּ נִסְקַלְתִּי בְּבֵית ב"פ ראה דִּין עַל יְדֵי אוֹת (א) שֶׁל שֵׁם (אדני). וְאִם וְחָטָאתִי לְפָנֶיךָ
ס"ג מ"ה בן וּפָגַמְתִּי בָּאוֹת (ה) רִאשׁוֹנָה שֶׁל שִׁמְךָ (יהוה) וּבָאוֹת (ד) שֶׁל (אדני) יְהִיֶה יי
נוֹשׂוֹב לְפָנֶיךָ ס"ג מ"ה בן כְּאִלּוּ נִשְׂרַפְתִּי בְּבֵית ב"פ ראה דִּין עַל יְדֵי אוֹת (ד) שֶׁל
שֵׁם (אדני). וְאִם וְחָטָאתִי לְפָנֶיךָ ס"ג מ"ה בן וּפָגַמְתִּי בָּאוֹת (ו) שֶׁל שִׁמְךָ (יהוה) וּבָאוֹת (נ)
שֶׁל (אדני) יְהִיֶה יי נוֹשׂוֹב לְפָנֶיךָ ס"ג מ"ה בן כְּאִלּוּ נֶהֱרַגְתִּי בַּסַּיִף בְּבֵית ב"פ ראה דִּין עַל
יְדֵי אוֹת (נ) שֶׁל שֵׁם (אדני). וְאִם וְחָטָאתִי לְפָנֶיךָ ס"ג מ"ה בן וּפָגַמְתִּי בָּאוֹת (ה) אַחֲרוֹנָה שֶׁל
שִׁמְךָ (יהוה) וּבָאוֹת (י) שֶׁל (אדני) יְהִיֶה יי נוֹשׂוֹב לְפָנֶיךָ ס"ג מ"ה בן כְּאִלּוּ נֶחֱנַקְתִּי בְּבֵית
ב"פ ראה דִּין עַל יְדֵי אוֹת (י) שֶׁל שֵׁם (אדני) (ויחשוב בעצמו כאילו מת על ידי בית דין)

ANA BEKO'ACH (to learn more about the *Ana Beko'ach* go to pg. 106)

Recite the line that corresponds to each particular night, the start of the next day, three times.

Chesed, Sunday *(Alef Bet Gimel Yud Tav Tzadik)* אבג יתץ

| ◆yeminecha לְיְמִינֶךָ | gedulat גְּדוּלַת | ◆beko'ach בְּכֹחַ | ana אָנָּא |

| :tzerura צְרוּרָה | | tatir תַּתִּיר | |

Gevurah, Monday *(Kuf Resh Ayin Shin Tet Nun)* קרע שטן

| ◆sagvenu שַׂגְּבֵנוּ | amecha עַמְּךָ | ◆rinat רִנַּת | kabel קַבֵּל |

| :nora נוֹרָא | | taharenu טַהֲרֵנוּ | |

ר we have been wicked, ש we have corrupted, ת we committed abominations,
we have gone astray from Your commandments and good laws, and it has not benefited us. For You
are righteous regarding whatever has befallen us, for You have acted truthfully and we caused wickedness.

ANA BEKO'ACH

Chesed, Sunday אבג יתץ

We beseech You, with the power of Your great right, undo this entanglement.

Gevurah, Monday קרע שטן

Accept the singing of Your Nation. Strengthen and purify us, Awesome One.

Tiferet, Tuesday *(Nun Gimel Dalet Yud Kaf Shin)* נֶּגֶד יכ"ש

na נָא   •gibor גִּבּוֹר   dorshei דּוֹרְשֵׁי   •yichudecha יִוּוּדְךָ

kevavat כְּבָבַת   ‡shomrem שָׁמְרֵם

Netzach, Wednesday *(Bet Tet Resh Tzadik Tav Gimel)* בטר צת"ג

barchem בָּרְכֵם   •taharem טַהֲרֵם   rachamei רַחֲמֵי   •tzidkatecha צִדְקָתְךָ

tamid תָּמִיד   ‡gomlem גָּמְלֵם

Hod, Thursday *(Chet Kuf Bet Tet Nun Ayin)* חקב טנ"ע

chasin וְזָסִין   •kadosh קָדוֹשׁ   berov בְּרוֹב   •tuvcha טוּבְךָ

nahel נַהֵל   ‡adatecha עֲדָתְךָ

Yesod, Friday *(Yud Gimel Lamed Pei Zayin Kuf)* יגל פז"ק

yachid יָוִיד   •ge'e גֵּאֶה   le'amecha לְעַמְּךָ   •pene פְּנֵה

zochrei זוֹכְרֵי   ‡kedushatecha קְדוּשָׁתְךָ

Malchut, Saturday *(Shin Kuf Vav Tzadik Yud Tav)* שקו צי"ת

shav'atenu שַׁוְעָתֵנוּ   •kabel קַבֵּל   ushma וּשְׁמַע   •tza'akatenu צַעֲקָתֵנוּ

yode'a יוֹדֵעַ   ‡ta'alumot תַּעֲלוּמוֹת

BARUCH SHEM KEVOD

Whispering this final verse brings all the Light from the Upper Worlds into our physical existence.

malchuto מַלְכוּתוֹ   kevod כְּבוֹד   shem שֵׁם   baruch בָּרוּךְ   (Whisper): יב"ו אותיות

‡va'ed וָעֶד   le'olam לְעוֹלָם   ריבוע ס"ג ו"י אותיות דס"ג

Tiferet, Tuesday נגד יכ"ש

Please, Mighty One, those who seek Your unity, guard them like the pupil of the eye.

Netzach, Wednesday בטר צת"ג

Bless them. Purify them. Your compassionate righteousness always grant them.

Hod, Thursday חקב טנ"ע

Invincible and Mighty One, with the abundance of Your goodness, govern Your congregation.

Yesod, Friday יגל פז"ק

Sole and proud One, turn to Your people, those who remember Your sanctity.

Malchut, Saturday שקו צי"ת

Accept our cry and hear our wail, You that knows all that is hidden.

BARUCH SHEM KEVOD

"Blessed is the Name of Glory. His Kingdom is forever and for eternity." (Pesachim 56a)

NAFSHI IVITICHA

According to Kabbalah, death occurs for two reasons:

1) A person has accumulated so much negativity in this lifetime that he faces no possibility of transforming the nature of his current incarnation. The process of death acts as a cleansing agent that destroys the reactive nature of the body. The soul then returns in a new body to begin its spiritual work again.

2) The Ari says death also occurs when a person has attained a certain level of spirituality. He leaves this world to reincarnate and begin work toward the next level of spiritual growth.

This verse helps us to cleanse and eliminate the reactive nature of our body so that we need not go through the process of death. It allows us to continue working toward higher spiritual levels in our current incarnation.

מלה balayla בְּלַיְלָה iviticha אִוִּיתִךָ nafshi נַפְשִׁי

ashachareka אֲשַׁחֲרֶךָ שדי vekirbi בְקִרְבִּי ruchi רוּחִי af אַף־

la'aretz לָאָרֶץ mishpatecha מִשְׁפָּטֶיךָ ka'asher כַּאֲשֶׁר ki כִּי

רי"ו ב"פ tevel תֵּבֵל yoshvei יֹשְׁבֵי lamdu לָמְדוּ tzedek צֶדֶק

LAMNATZE'ACH

The Ari teaches that this Psalm helps to enhance and stimulate our memory. It also helps the soul achieve its full potential in terms of motivating us to accomplish all the spiritual work that we came to this world to do.

elav אֵלָיו bevo בְּבוֹא leDavid לְדָוִד mizmor מִזְמוֹר lamnatze'ach לַמְנַצֵּחַ

el אֵל ba בָּא ka'asher כַּאֲשֶׁר hanavi הַנָּבִיא Natan נָתָן

ילה ; אדני אהיה Elohim אֱלֹהִים choneni וְחָנֵּנִי Batshava בַּת־שָׁבַע

meche מְחֵה rachamecha רַחֲמֶיךָ kerov כְּרֹב kechasdecha כְּחַסְדְּךָ

kabeseni כַּבְּסֵנִי (כתיב : הַרְבֵּה) herev הֶרֶב fesha'ai פְשָׁעָי

fesha'ai פְשָׁעַי ki כִּי tahareni טַהֲרֵנִי umechatati וּמֵחַטָּאתִי me'avoni מֵעֲוֺנִי

ani אני אֲנִי eda אֵדָע vechatati וְחַטָּאתִי negdi נֶגְדִּי גֶגֶד, מזבוח, זז, אל יהוה

chatati וְחַטָּאתִי levadecha לְבַדְּךָ lecha לְךָ ע"ה קס"א קנ"א קמ"ג tamid תָּמִיד

lema'an לְמַעַן asiti עָשִׂיתִי ע"ה קס"ה ; ריבוע דמ"ה קס"א be'enecha בְּעֵינֶיךָ vehara וְהָרַע

veshoftecha בְשָׁפְטֶךָ tizke תִּזְכֶּה bedovrecha בְּדָבְרְךָ titzdak תִּצְדַּק

NAFSHI IVITICHA

"With my soul I have desired You at night, and with my spirit within me, I will seek You early in the morning. For when Your judgments are in the earth, the inhabitants of the world will learn righteousness." (Isaiah 26:9)

LAMNATZE'ACH

"To the Chief Musician, a Psalm of David, when Nathan, the prophet, came to him after he (David) had come upon Bathsheba: Have mercy upon me, God, and according to Your compassion and the multitude of Your mercies, wipe away my transgressions. Wash away my iniquities and purify me from my sins, because I acknowledge my sins and my transgressions are before me, always. I have sinned before You alone and I have done this evil before Your eyes; You are justified when you speak and are clear in Your judgment.

הֵן hen   בְּעָווׂן be'avon   וְזׂוּלַלְתִּי cholalti   וּבְחֵטְא uvchet   יֶחֱמַתְנִי yechematni

אִמִּי imi   הֵן hen   אֱמֶת emet   אהיה פעמים אהיה, ז״פ ס״ג   וְזׂפַצְתָּ chafatzta

בַּטֻחוׂת vatuchot   וּבְסָתֻם uvsatum   וְחָכְמָה chochmah   במילוי = תרי״ג (מצוות)

תּוׂדִיעֵנִי todi'eni   תְּחַטְּאֵנִי techateni   בְאֵזוׂב ve'ezov   וְאֶטְהָר ve'ethar

תְּכַבְּסֵנִי techabseni   וּמִשֶּׁלֶג umisheleg   אלף אלף אלף (רי״ג אהיה)   אַלְבִּין albin

תַּשְׁמִיעֵנִי tashmi'eni   שָׂשׂוׂן sason   וְשִׂמְחָה vesimcha   תָּגֵלְנָה tagelna

עֲצָמוׂת atzamot   דִּכִּיתָ dikita   הַסְתֵּר haster   ב״פ מצר פָּנֶיךָ panecha   ס״ג מ״ה ב״ן

מֵחֲטָאַי mechata'ai   וְכָל vechol   עֲוׂנׂתַי avonotai   מׂוׂזה meche

לֵב lev   טָהוׂר tahor   י״פ אכא   בְּרָא bera   קנ״א ב״ן,

יהוה אלהים יהוה אדני, מילוי קס״א וס״ג, מ״ה ברבוע וע״ב ע״ה ; לב טהור ברא = קס״א קנ״א קמ״ג

לִי li   אֱלׂהִים Elohim   אהיה אדני ; ילה ; לי אלהים = ריבוע אדני   וְרוּחַ veru'ach

נָכוׂן nachon   חַדֵּשׁ chadesh   י״ב הויות, קס״א קנ״א   בְּקִרְבִּי bekirbi   שדי״ אַל al

תַּשְׁלִיכֵנִי tashlicheni   מִלְּפָנֶיךָ milfanecha   ס״ג מ״ה ב״ן   וְרוּחַ veru'ach

קָדְשְׁךָ kodshecha   אַל al   תִּקַּח tikach   מִמֶּנִּי mimeni   הָשִׁיבָה hashiva

לִי li   שְׂשׂוׂן seson   יִשְׁעֶךָ yishecha   וְרוּחַ veru'ach   נְדִיבָה nediva

תִּסְמְכֵנִי tismecheni   אֲלַמְּדָה alameda   פּׂשְׁעִים fosh'im   דְּרָכֶיךָ derachecha

וְחַטָּאִים vechata'im   אֵלֶיךָ elecha   יָשׁוּבוּ yashuvu   הַצִּילֵנִי hatzileni

מִדָּמִים midamim   אֱלׂהִים Elohim   אהיה אדני ; ילה   אֱלׂהֵי Elohei   מילוי דע״ב, דמב ; ילה

תְּשׁוּעָתִי te'shuati   תְּרַנֵּן teranen   לְשׁוׂנִי leshoni   צִדְקָתֶךָ tzidkatecha

אֲדׂנָי Adonai   ללה   שְׂפָתַי sefatai   תִּפְתָּח tiftach   וּפִי ufi   יַגִּיד yagid   (כ״ב אותיות

תְּהִלָּתֶךָ tehilatecha   ס״ת בוכו׃   כִּי ki   לׂא lo   תַחְפּׂץ tachpotz   (=אכא) וה אותיות מזוזך

זֶבַח zevach   וְאֶתֵּנָה ve'etena   נתה, קס״א קנ״א קמ״ג   עוׂלָה ola   לׂא lo   תִרְצֶה tirtze

---

I was born in iniquity and my mother conceived me in sin. You desire truth and You shall inform me of the most concealed of wisdom. Purge me with hyssop and I shall be clean. Wash me and I shall be whiter than snow. Make me hear joy and gladness, so that the bones which You have broken may rejoice. Hide Your Face from my sins and wipe away all my iniquities. Create for me a pure heart and renew the correct spirit within me. Do not cast me away from Your Presence and do not withhold Your Holy Spirit from me. Restore to me the joy of Your salvation and uphold me with Your free spirit. Then I shall teach transgressors Your ways, and sinners will return to You. Save me from bloodguilt, God: You are the God of my salvation. My tongue shall sing Your praise. Lord, open my lips and my heart shall say Your praise. You do not desire sacrifices and You do not want the offerings that I give.

זִבְווֹ zivchei אֱלֹהִים Elohim ; רוּחַ ru'ach ; נִשְׁבָּרָה nishbara

venidke וְנִדְכֶּה nishbar נִשְׁבָּר lev לֵב

Elohim אֱלֹהִים ; לֹא lo תִבְזֶה tivze ;

Tziyon צִיּוֹן et אֶת virtzoncha בִרְצוֹנְךָ heitiva הֵיטִיבָה

Yerushalayim יְרוּשָׁלָיִם chomot וְחוֹמוֹת tivne תִבְנֶה

ola עוֹלָה tzedek צֶדֶק zivchei זִבְווֹ tachpotz תַחְפּוֹץ az אָז

farim פָרִים mizbachacha מִזְבַּחֲךָ al עַל ya'alu יַעֲלוּ az אָז vechalil וְכָלִיל

IM TISHKAV

These five verses act like a deposit on our soul, guaranteeing that it will return to us in the morning.

im אִם ; lo לֹא tishkav תִשְׁכַּב

ata אַתָּה shenatecha שְׁנָתֶךָ ve'arva וְעָרְבָה veshachavta וְשָׁכַבְתָּ tifchad תִפְחָד

seter סֵתֶר li לִי mitzar מִצַּר

todi'eni תּוֹדִיעֵנִי sela סֶלָה tesoveveni תְּסוֹבְבֵנִי falet פַלֵּט rane רָנֵּי titzreni תִּצְּרֵנִי

semachot שְׂמָחוֹת sova שֹׂבַע chayim וְחַיִּים orach אֹרַח

et אֶת panecha פָנֶךָ ne'imot נְעִמוֹת bimincha בִּימִינְךָ netzach נֶצַח

ata אַתָּה takum תָקוּם terachem תְּרַחֵם

Tziyon צִיּוֹן

ki כִּי et עֵת lechenena לְחֶנְנָה ki כִּי va בָא moed מוֹעֵד beyadcha בְּיָדְךָ

afkid אַפְקִיד ruchi רוּווֹ

oti אוֹתִי padita פָּדִיתָה Adonai לְהוֹ

El אֵל emet אֱמֶת

The sacrifices of God are a broken spirit and a broken and contrite heart. Do not despise, God. Improve Zion with Your good will and build the walls of Jerusalem. Then You shall be pleased with the sacrifices of righteousness: the burnt-offerings, and the whole-offerings. Then bullocks will be placed upon Your Altar." (Psalms 51)

IM TISHKAV

"If you lie down, you shall not fear. You shall lie down and your sleep shall be sweet." (Proverbs 3:24) "You are my refuge. You shall shield me away from trouble. You shall surround me with songs of deliverance." (Psalms 32:7) "Inform me about the path of life. In Your presence is fullness of joy. At Your Hand, there is pleasantness for eternity." (Psalms 16:11) "You shall rise to have mercy over Zion, for it is time for compassion. For the time has come." (Psalms 102:14) "In Your Hands, I entrust my spirit, for You will redeem me, Lord, true God." (Psalms 31:6)

THE HALEL

The *Halel* is recited on *Rosh Chodesh* (the first day of the lunar month), and for holidays. The word *Halel* has the same numerical value (65) as *Lamed, Lamed, Hei* ללה, the 72 Name of God for dreams. Sixty five is also the numerical value of both the word *hakeli* הכלי, which means the Vessel, and the Aramaic word אדני *Adonai*, the Name of God that corresponds to our physical world of *Malchut*. This blessing helps us lift off from this physical world to make our connections to *Rosh Chodesh* and holidays. *Rosh Chodesh* is the seed of the new month, so this blessing also helps us acquire control over the coming month. The seven parts of the *Halel* correspond to the seven *Sefirot* that directly influence our world.

The intention and meditation for Rosh Chodesh - In the beginning the crown of *Nukva* was equal to the crown of *Zeir Anpin*, and they were in a 'face to face' position. Then after *Nukva's* complaint She was told "Go and diminish yourself." Then She descended from the World of *Atzilut* to the World of *Beriah*. We learn that the women who did not give their gold to participate in the sin of the Golden Calf fixed the *Nukva* a little bit so She could rise and renew Herself every month. Her elevation in *Rosh Chodesh* happened in a few steps: 1) on the eve of *Rosh Chodesh* there is no elevation yet; 2) in *Shacharit* silent connection She ascends to *Netzach, Hod, Yesod* of *Zeir Anpin*; 3) in the repetition of *Shacharit* She ascends to *Chesed, Gevurah, Tiferet* of *Zeir Anpin*; 4) and in *Musaf* the *Nukva* rises up to *Keter* of *Zeir Anpin*.

During the week days, *Zeir Anpin* is in *Netzach* and *Nukva* is in *Hod*. During *Rosh Chodesh* the *Nukva* rises also to *Netzach* (in the *Shacharit* silent connection). Since the women cause this elevation, and the main rising in *Rosh Chodesh* is for the *Nukva*, whether it is in the night or the day, and the *Nukva* is the essence of women, therefore women are prohibited from certain actions during *Rosh Chodesh* but not the men. Also, when we say that the *Nukva* rises, it means that only Her head expands itself to the level above *Chesed, Gevurah, Tiferet* of *Zeir Anpin* up to His head − but the rest stays in its place of emanation. Therefore, there is no work prohibition on *Rosh Chodesh* as in holidays and *Shabbat* when *Zeir Anpin* and *Nukva* are elevated to *Abba* and *Ima*.

As it has been explained, in the beginning *Nukva* rises to *Netzach* of *Zeir Anpin*, we add in the *Amidah*, "*ya'ale veyavo*" in the blessing that connects to *Netzach* ("*Retze*"). However, on the eve of *Rosh Chodesh* the *Zivug* is with *Leah*, which represents the hidden *Nukva* (*Alma De'itkasya* - the Concealed World), if you did not say "*ya'ale veyavo*" in *Arvit*, you don't need to go back and say it. This is not so during the day connections, because the elevation is for *Rachel* and the *Zivug* is with Her (*Alma De'itgalya* - the Revealed World) so if you forgot to say it, you should go back and say it.

The intention and meditation for saying Halel on Rosh Chodesh:
During *Shabbat*, which is *Kodesh* (Holy), the aspect of *Abba* − total energy of mercy, does not expand further than the end of *Atzilut* to prevent Judgment (that exists below *Atzilut*) to enter. For this reason we don't say *Halel* or Thirteen Attributes (connection to sweeten judgment) on *Shabbat*, because on *Shabbat* there is no judgment.
During the holidays it's different − on the holidays the energy is in the level of *Ima* (Six Edges of *Ima* itself, a complete enlightment). Since *Ima* includes the roots of Judgment, therefore the Nukva is resting in in *Beriah* (like in a nest), we say *Halel* there to sweeten its judgment. And because the supervision on holidays is by the Six Edges of *Ima*, which is ס"ג (63 − the same numerical value as *Yom Tov* − holiday) and not by *Malchut* of *Ima*, which is the essence of the work, certain work and actions are prohibited on the holidays.
On *Rosh Chodesh*, *Nukva* receives its Light from *Malchut* of *Binah*, which is not considered an addition of enlightenment, and therefore we say *Halel* to sweeten its judgment (*Halel* has the same numerical value as אדני, which is *Malchut* of *Atzilut*), and with that She is sweetened like the Thirteen Attributes which also sweeten judgment. *Halel* is said instead of the Thirteen Attributes of Mercy.

You should meditate, while saying the verses of *"min hametzar"* for the Thirteen Attributes, which means - Nine *Tikunei Dikna* of *Zeir Anpin,* in order to have a *Zivug* for *Leah* instead of *"Vaya'avor".* And since there is no complete enlightenment like on the holidays (energy of the holidays is from the Six Edges of *Ima,* and *Rosh Chodesh* energy is from *Malchut* of *Ima*), there is no complete *Halel* in *Rosh Chodesh.* While the Nukva is diminished, the judgment increases, but by *Rosh Chodesh* She renews Herself and sweetens Her judgement which diminishes the grip of the *klipot* and the world is saved.

On days we don't complete the *Halel* (Rosh Chodesh, Chol Hamo'ed Pesach and Seventh Day of Pesach)
we bless *"likro et hahalel"*. On days that we complete the *Halel*, we bless *"ligmor et hahalel"*.

יכה Elohenu אֱלֹהֵינוּ Adonai יְהֹוָאדְנִיאהדונהי Ata אַתָּה baruch בָּרוּךְ

kideshanu קִדְּשָׁנוּ asher אֲשֶׁר haolam הָעוֹלָם melech מֶלֶךְ

(likro לִקְרוֹא) (ligmor לִגְמוֹר) vetzivanu וְצִוָּנוּ bemitzvotav בְּמִצְוֹתָיו

ללה, אדני ; ר"ת לאה: hahalel הַהַלֵּל et אֶת

CHESED – HALELUYA

"God lifts me up from dust." This verse signifies the ability for positive change to occur at any moment. The first step is letting go of our ego. If we tune out those whispers and maintain total certainty that the Light can dramatically alter our situation instantly, we will ignite the power of this connection.

In this Psalm there are 58 words which is the numerical value of the Holy Name: אל יהוה ע"ה.

avdei עַבְדֵי halelu הַלְלוּ ללה ; אדני אהיה אלהים, haleluya הַלְלוּיָה

Adonai:יְהֹוָאדְנִיאהדונהי shem שֵׁם et אֶת־ halelu הַלְלוּ Adonai יְהֹוָאדְנִיאהדונהי

ר"ת ריבוע ע"ב ריבוע ס"ג mevorach מְבֹרָךְ Adonai יְהֹוָאדְנִיאהדונהי shem שֵׁם yehi יְהִי

יהוה מברך = רפ"ח (להעלות רפ"ח ניצוצות שנפלו לקליפה דמשם באים התוללאים) me'ata מֵעַתָּה

ad עַד־ shemesh שֶׁמֶשׁ mimizrach מִמִּזְרַח יכה: olam עוֹלָם ve'ad וְעַד־

Adonai:יְהֹוָאדְנִיאהדונהי shem שֵׁם mehulal מְהֻלָּל mevo'o מְבוֹאוֹ ר"ת קדוש

Adonai יְהֹוָאדְנִיאהדונהי goyim גּוֹיִם עמם ; יכי kol כָּל־ al עַל־ ram רָם

kevodo:כְּבוֹדוֹ וֹשמל ; ר"ת כוזו י"פ טל, י"פ hashamayim הַשָּׁמַיִם al עַל

THE HALEL
Blessed are You, Lord, our God, King of the world,
Who has sanctified us with His commandments and obliged us   (to complete)   (to read)   The Halel.
CHESED – HALELUYA
"Praise the Lord, You servants of the Lord. Praise the Name of the Lord. May the Name of the Lord be blessed from now and forever. From the rising of the sun until its setting, God's Name is praised. God is high above all nations, His glory is above the Heavens.

יּלה   Elohenu **אֱלֹהֵינוּ**   kadonai **כַּיְהֹוָהֵ֑{אֲדֹנָיַאהַדֹוֹנָהִי}**   יּלי   mi **מִי**

lir'ot **לִרְאוֹת**   hamashpili **הַמַּשְׁפִּילִי**   lashavet **לָשָׁבֶת:**   hamagbihi **הַמַּגְבִּיהִי**

uva'aretz **וּבָאָרֶץ:**   כוזו   י"פ   טל,   י"פ   bashamayim **בַּשָּׁמַיִם**

yarim **יָרִים**   me'ashpot **מֵאַשְׁפֹּת**   dal **דָּל**   me'afar **מֵעָפָר**   mekimi **מְקִימִי**

im **עִם**   nedivim **נְדִיבִים**   im **עִם־**   lehoshivi **לְהוֹשִׁיבִי**   evyon **אֶבְיוֹן:**

habayit **הַבָּיִת**   akeret **עֲקֶרֶת**   moshivi **מוֹשִׁיבִי:**   amo **עַמּוֹ**   nedivei **נְדִיבֵי**

ב"פ ראה ; עקרת הבית היא רחל **אֵם־** em   יוֹהךְ, מ"א אותיות דפשוט, דמילוי ודמילוי דמילוי דמילוי דאהיה ע"ה

habanim **הַבָּנִים**   semecha **שְׂמֵחָה**   haleluya **הַלְלוּיָהּ:**   אלהים, אהיה אדני ; ללה:

GEVURAH - BETZET YISRAEL

"Yehuda was holy," refers to the head of the Tribe of Yehuda, a man named Nachshon ben Aminadav. Nachshon was the first person to demonstrate complete certainty when he entered the Red Sea during the Exodus. He overcame his reactive fears and doubts and continued into the water until it reached his nostrils, whereupon it rushed into his throat and began choking him. At that precise moment, Satan attempted to bombard him with fear and uncertainty. Even when miracles are supposed to happen, the slightest doubt can prevent them from occurring. But Nachshon ben Aminadav didn't waver. A split second later, he was breathing fresh air as the waters of the Red Sea climbed toward the Heavens.

In this Psalm there are 52 words which correspond to the Holy Name: (בוזינת נוקבא) יוד הה וו הה.

ב"פ ראה   bet **בֵּית**   מצר   miMitzrayim **מִמִּצְרָיִם**   Yisrael **יִשְׂרָאֵל**   betzet **בְּצֵאת**

hayta **הָיְתָה**   lo'ez **לֹעֵז:**   me'am **מֵעַם**   י   הויות, יאהדונהי אידהנויה   Yaakov **יַעֲקֹב**

mamshelotav **מַמְשְׁלוֹתָיו:**   Yisrael **יִשְׂרָאֵל**   lekadsho **לְקָדְשׁוֹ**   Yehuda **יְהוּדָה**

יּלי   ר"ד אותיות   הויות   י   haYarden **הַיַּרְדֵּן**   vayanos **וַיָּנֹס**   ra'a ראה   ra'a **רָאָה**   יּלי   hayam **הַיָּם**

che'elim **כְּאֵילִים**   rakdu **רָקְדוּ**   heharim **הֶהָרִים**   le'achor **לְאָחוֹר:**   yisov **יִסֹּב**

יּלי   hayam **הַיָּם**   lecha **לְּךָ**   מ"ה   ma **מַה**   tzon **צֹאן:**   kivnei **כִּבְנֵי**   geva'ot **גְּבָעוֹת**

le'achor **לְאָחוֹר:**   tisov **תִּסֹּב**   י   הויות ור' אותיות   haYarden **הַיַּרְדֵּן**   tanus **תָנוּס**   ki **כִּי**

Who is like the Lord, our God, Who dwells so high, Who looks down upon the Heavens and the earth? He raises the poor from the dust and uplifts the pauper from the trash heap. He seats them together with the noblemen, with the nobility of His Nation. He seats the mistress of the house, the mother of the children, happily. Praise the Lord!" (Psalms 113)

GEVURAH - BETZET YISRAEL

"When Israel left Egypt, and the House of Jacob from among a foreign nation, Judah then became sanctified to Him and Israel was His Dominion. The sea saw and fled, the Jordan turned backward. The mountains skipped like rams, and the hills like young lambs. What ails you sea, that you flee? Jordan, that you turn backward?

geva'ot גְּבָעוֹת   che'elim כְּאֵילִים   tirkedu תִּרְקְדוּ   heharim הֶהָרִים

aretz אֶרֶץ   chuli וְוּלִי אני   adon אָדוֹן   milifnei מִלִּפְנֵי   tzon צֹאן   kivnei כִּבְנֵי

milifnei מִלִּפְנֵי   Eloha אֱלוֹהַּ   שם בן מ"ב   Yaakov יַעֲקֹב   ו הויות, יאהדונהי אידהנויה

hahofchi הַהֹפְכִי   hatzur הַצּוּר   אלהים דההין ע"ה   agam אֲגַם־   ריבוע אהיה = דם

mayim בַּיִם (ומהפכו למים)   mayim בַּיִם   chalamish וְחַלָּמִישׁ   lema'yno לְמַעְיְנוֹ־מָיִם

This section is omitted on *Rosh Chodesh, Chol Hamo'ed* of *Pesach* and Seventh Day of *Pesach*

TIFERET - LO LANU

Rav Yehuda Ashlag reminds us that despite whatever we are able to achieve spiritually on our own, we still can never truly earn or merit the Light that glimmers within us. Our physical body may not deserve anything in this world, but the Creator gave us the spark of Light that sustains our soul and is our essence. This spark of Light is known by the code word *Name*, from the verse: *"Do it for Your Name!"* In reality, we are asking the Creator to give us Light for the God-like part of us—our soul. To ensure that we receive the Creator's Light with this prayer, we must mirror our request through actions. We do that when we recognize the spark of Light within others. Even our worst enemy is imbued with a spark of the Light of God. The more we recognize this, the more blessings and good fortune we receive in our own life.

lanu לָנוּ   lo לֹא   Adonai יְהוָֹואדנים־יאהדונהי ארני   אהיה   אלהים   lanu לָנוּ   lo לֹא

kavod כָּבוֹד   ten תֵּן   leshimcha לְשִׁמְךָ   ki כִּי־ ארני אהיה אלהים

lama לָמָּה   amitecha אֲמִתֶּךָ   al עַל   chasdecha וַחַסְדְּךָ   al עַל־

Elohehem אֱלֹהֵיהֶם ילה   na נָא   aye אַיֵּה־   hagoyim הַגּוֹיִם   yomru יֹאמְרוּ

kol כֹּל ילי   "פ טל, "פ כוזו "פ   vashamayim בַּשָּׁמָיִם ילה   velohenu וֵאלֹהֵינוּ

kesef כֶּסֶף   atzabehem עֲצַבֵּיהֶם   asa עָשָׂה   chafetz וָפֵץ   asher אֲשֶׁר

pe פֶּה־ מילה ; ע"ה   adam אָדָם מ"ה   yedei יְדֵי   ma'ase מַעֲשֵׂה   vezahav וְזָהָב

lahem לָהֶם אלהים, אהיה ארני   enayim עֵינַיִם ריבוע דמ"ה   velo וְלֹא   yedaberu יְדַבְּרוּ

lahem לָהֶם   oznayim אָזְנַיִם יוד הי ואו הה   yir'u יִרְאוּ   velo וְלֹא   lahem לָהֶם

yerichun יְרִיוּזוֹן   velo וְלֹא   lahem לָהֶם   af אַף   yishma'u יִשְׁמְעוּ   velo וְלֹא

Mountains, that you skip like rams? Hills, like young lambs? Before the Lord tremble, Earth, before the God of Jacob, Who turns the rock into a lake of water, the flint into a flowing fountain." (Psalms 113)

TIFERET - LO LANU

Not for our sake, Lord, not for our sake, but for the sake of Your Name give glory, for the sake of Your kindness and Your Truth. Why should the nations say: Where is their God? Our God is in the Heavens. He formed all that He desired. Their idols are of silver and gold, the work of the hands of man. They have mouths but cannot speak. They have eyes but cannot see. They have noses but cannot smell.

raglehem רַגְלֵיהֶם   yemishun יְמִישׁוּן   velo וְלֹא   yedehem יְדֵיהֶם

bigronam בִּגְרוֹנָם: yehgu יֶהְגּוּ   lo לֹא־   yehalechu יְהַלֵּכוּ   velo וְלֹא

osehem עֹשֵׂיהֶם   (דס"ג)   (מילוי)   ייא"י   yih'yu יִהְיוּ   kemohem כְּמוֹהֶם

Yisrael יִשְׂרָאֵל   bahem בָּהֶם: bote'ach בֹּטֵחַ   asher אֲשֶׁר־   ילי kol כֹּל

umaginam וּמָגִנָּם   ezram עֶזְרָם   badonai בַּיהֹוָאהדונהי   betach בְּטַח

bitchu בִּטְחוּ   Aharon אַהֲרֹן   ראה   ב"פ   bet בֵּית   hu הוּא:

yir'ei יִרְאֵי   hu הוּא   umaginam וּמָגִנָּם   ezram עֶזְרָם   badonai בַּיהֹוָאהדונהי

ezram עֶזְרָם   badonai בַּיהֹוָאהדונהי   bitchu בִּטְחוּ   Adonai יְהֹוָאהדונהי

hu הוּא: umaginam וּמָגִנָּם   (כ"ב אותיות פשוטות (=אכא) ועוד ה' אותיות סופצרך) יו"ד

NETZACH – ADONAI ZECHARANU

"*The Heavens were given to God, but the land was given to the people.*" The Creator separated from this world so that we could become creators and express the godliness that is part of all of us. This paragraph gives us the strength to become true creators in our own lives. A tiny candle glimmering on a blazing sunlit day contributes little. But even the darkness of a large stadium responds to the light of a single candle. In this realm of darkness in which we find ourselves, one candle takes on tremendous value and worth.

When our own actions are those of sharing and revealing Light, we achieve oneness with the Creator through similarity of form. This oneness enables us to become true creators in our own lives.

הברכה, עסמ"ב,   yevarech יְבָרֵךְ   zecharanu זְכָרָנוּ   Adonai יְהֹוָאהדונהי

(למתק את ז' המלכים שמתו) ; ר"ת ייז   yevarech יְבָרֵךְ עסמ"ב, הברכה (למתק את ז' המלכים שמתו)

הברכה, עסמ"ב,   yevarech יְבָרֵךְ   Yisrael יִשְׂרָאֵל   ראה ב"פ   bet בֵּית   et אֶת־

Aharon אַהֲרֹן: ראה ב"פ   bet בֵּית   et אֶת־   (למתק את ז' המלכים שמתו)

yir'ei יִרְאֵי   שמתו) המלכים ז' את (למתק   הברכה, עסמ"ב,   yevarech יְבָרֵךְ

hagedolim הַגְּדֹלִים: im עִם   haketanim הַקְּטַנִּים   ר"ת ייי   Adonai יְהֹוָאהדונהי

Their hands cannot touch, their legs cannot walk. They utter no sounds from their throats. May their makers be like them and whoever trusts in them. Israel, place your trust in the Lord. He is your Helper and Protector. House of Aaron, place your trust in the Lord. He is your Helper and Protector. Those who fear the Lord, place your trust in the Lord. He is your Helper and Protector." (Psalms 115:1-11)

NETZACH – ADONAI ZECHARANU

"The Lord Who remembers us, blesses. He blesses the House of Israel. He blesses the House of Aaron. He blesses those who fear the Lord, the small as well as the great.

yosef יֹסֵף	Adonai יְהֹוָ(אדני/אהדונהי)	alechem עֲלֵיכֶם	alechem עֲלֵיכֶם
ve'al וְעַל	:benechem בְּנֵיכֶם	beruchim בְּרוּכִים	atem אַתֶּם
ladonai לַיהֹוָ(אדני/אהדונהי)	ose עֹשֵׂה	shamayim שָׁמַיִם י"פ טל, י"פ כוזו	
:va'aretz וָאָרֶץ	hashamayim הַשָּׁמַיִם י"פ טל, י"פ כוזו, י"פ כוזו	shamayim שָׁמַיִם י"פ טל, י"פ כוזו	
natan נָתַן ע"ה דההין אלהים	veha'aretz וְהָאָרֶץ	ladonai לַיהֹוָ(אדני/אהדונהי)	
yehalelu יְהַלְלוּ	hametim הַמֵּתִים	lo לֹא מ"ה:	adam אָדָם	livnei לִבְנֵי
va'anachnu וַאֲנַחְנוּ	:duma דוּמָה	yordei יֹרְדֵי ילי	kol כָּל	velo וְלֹא	Yah יָהּ
olam עוֹלָם	ve'ad וְעַד	me'ata מֵעַתָּה	Yah יָהּ	nevarech נְבָרֵךְ

haleluya הַלְלוּיָהּ אלהים, אהיה אדני ; כלה:

This section is omitted on *Rosh Chodesh, Chol Hamo'ed* of *Pesach* and Seventh Day of *Pesach*

HOD– AHAVTI

Rav Elimelech, a great 18th century Kabbalist, teaches us that while we pray, Satan, our Opponent, often comes to us to say: "Why are you bothering to stand here and pray? You don't really want to change. It's too difficult. So why bother with all this complicated spiritual work? Given all the negative actions you have already performed, your personal situation is hopeless." This prayer shuts down Satan's negative and destructive influence and helps us understand that it doesn't matter what we did previously. From this moment forward, we can change and transform our nature if we really want to.

"God protects and saves the fools." The smartest men can make the biggest mistakes. If we think we really know it all, if our egos tell us that we are brilliant people, then we really are fools and the Light will never reach us. But those people who can admit that there is always something to learn are acknowledging that we are all fools, in a proactive manner. God will protect them and take them to even higher levels of fulfillment.

Adonai יְהֹוָ(אדני/אהדונהי)	yishma יִשְׁמַע	ki כִּי־	ahavti אָהַבְתִּי
hita הִטָּה	ki כִּי־	:tachanunai תַּחֲנוּנָי	koli קוֹלִי	et אֶת־
:ekra אֶקְרָא	uvyamai וּבְיָמַי	li לִי הה ואי הי יוד	ozno אָזְנוֹ
she'ol שְׁאוֹל	umtzarei וּמְצָרֵי	mavet מָוֶת	chevlei וְחֶבְלֵי	afafuni אֲפָפוּנִי
:emtza אֶמְצָא	veyagon וְיָגוֹן דההין אלהים	tzara צָרָה	metza'uni מְצָאוּנִי

May the Lord increase you more and more, you and your children. Blessed are you Lord, Creator of Heaven and Earth. The Heavens are the Heavens of the Lord, and the Earth He gave to mankind. The dead do not praise the Lord, nor do those who descend to the grave. But we will bless the Lord from now and forever. Praise the Lord." (Psalms 115:12-end)

HOD– AHAVTI

"I wanted that the Lord would listen to my voice and to my supplications and turn His Ear towards me and that all my days I would call upon Him. Pangs of death have surrounded me and the misery of the grave has found me. I found trouble and sorrow.

אבגיתץ ‏ וְשֵׁר, ‏ ekra אֶקְרָא ‏ Adonai יהו״אדני״אהדונהי ‏ uvshem וּבְשֵׁם

‏:nafshi נַפְשִׁי ‏ maleta מִלְּטָה ‏ Adonai יהו״אדני״אהדונהי ‏ ana אָנָּה

ילה velohenu וֵאלֹהֵינוּ ‏ vetzadik וְצַדִּיק ‏ Adonai יהו״אדני״אהדונהי ‏ chanun חַנּוּן

merachem מְרַחֵם ‏ אברהם, וז״פ אל, רי״ו ול״ב נתיבות החכמה, רמ״ח (אברים), עסמ״ב וט״ז אותיות ‏ מְרֻחָם

daloti דַּלּוֹתִי ‏ Adonai יהו״אדני״אהדונהי ‏ peta'im פְּתָאִים ‏ shomer שֹׁמֵר ‏ פשוטות:

limnuchaychi לִמְנוּחָיְכִי ‏ nafshi נַפְשִׁי ‏ shuvi שׁוּבִי ‏ yehoshi'a :יְהוֹשִׁיעַ ‏ veli וְלִי

ki כִּי ‏ :alaychi עָלָיְכִי ‏ gamal גָּמַל ‏ Adonai יהו״אדני״אהדונהי ‏ ki כִּי

מ״ה ריבוע eni עֵינִי ‏ et אֶת־ ‏ mimavet מִמָּוֶת ‏ nafshi נַפְשִׁי ‏ chilatzta וְכִלַּצְתָּ

‏:midechi מִדֶּחִי ‏ ragli רַגְלִי ‏ et אֶת־ ‏ dim'a דִּמְעָה ‏ min מִן־

be'artzot בְּאַרְצוֹת ‏ Adonai יהו״אדני״אהדונהי ‏ lifnei לִפְנֵי ‏ ethalech אֶתְהַלֵּךְ

ki כִּי ‏ he'emanti הֶאֱמַנְתִּי ‏ ע״ה בינה יהוה, אהיה אהיה מ״ה: ‏ hachayim הַחַיִּים

אני ani אֲנִי ‏ :me'od מְאֹד ‏ aniti עָנִיתִי ‏ אני ani אֲנִי ‏ ראה adaber אֲדַבֵּר

‏:kozev כֹּזֵב מ״ה ‏ ha'adam הָאָדָם ‏ ילי kol כָּל ‏ vechofzi בְחָפְזִי ‏ amarti אָמַרְתִּי

YESOD - MA ASHIV

In the following paragraph, we find the verse *Ana Hashem*, which acknowledges that the Creator is our only true spiritual master and asks the Creator to give us signs, teachers, directions, and pathways that will lead us to the Light.

ילי kol כָּל ‏ ladonai לַיהו״אדני״אהדונהי ‏ ashiv אָשִׁיב ‏ מ״ה ma מָה־

אדני אהיה אלהים, kos כּוֹס ‏ :alai עָלַי ‏ tagmulohi תַּגְמוּלוֹהִי

yeshu'ot יְשׁוּעוֹת ‏ במילוי (כף וו סמך) = עסמ״ב, הברכה (למתק את ז׳ המלכים שמתו)

‏:ekra אֶקְרָא ‏ Adonai יהו״אדני״אהדונהי ‏ uvshem וּבְשֵׁם ‏ esa אֶשָּׂא

Then I called the Name of the Lord: Please, God, rescue my soul. For our Lord is gracious and righteous; our Lord is merciful. The Lord watches over the simple people. I became destitute and He saved me. Return, my soul, to your peacefulness, for the Lord has dealt kindly with you. For You have salvaged my soul from death, my eyes from tears, and my feet from stumbling. I shall walk before the Lord in the land of the living. I believed even as I spoke, when I was greatly impoverished, and I said in my haste, all men are treacherous." (Psalms 116:1-11)

YESOD - MA ASHIV
"How can I repay the Lord
for all that He has bestowed upon me? I raise a cup of salvation and call out in the Name of the Lord.

negda נֶגְדָּה ashalem אֲשַׁלֵם ladonai לַיהֹוָה nedarai נְדָרַי

yakar יָקָר :amo עַמּוֹ lechol לְכָל־ na נָא

hamavta הַמָּוְתָה Adonai יְהֹוָה דמ״ה רִיבוּעַ be'enei בְּעֵינֵי

אני ani אֲנִי ki כִּי־ Adonai יְהֹוָה ana אָנָּה :lachasidav לַחֲסִידָיו

עַבְדְּךָ avdecha עַבְדְּךָ אֲנִי ani אֲנִי־ avdecha עַבְדְּךָ

lecha לְךָ :lemoserai לְמוֹסֵרָי pitachta פִּתַּחְתָּ amatecha אֲמָתֶךָ ben בֶּן־

Adonai יְהֹוָה uvshem וּבְשֵׁם toda תּוֹדָה zevach זֶבַח ezbach אֶזְבַּח

ashalem אֲשַׁלֵם ladonai לַיהֹוָה nedarai נְדָרַי :ekra אֶקְרָא

נֶגְדָּה negda na נָא lechol לְכָל־ :amo עַמּוֹ

betochechi בְּתוֹכֵכִי Adonai יְהֹוָה bet בֵּית bechatzrot בְּחַצְרוֹת

ירושלים Yerushalayim haleluya הַלְלוּיָהּ

MALCHUT - HALELU

"All the nations of the world should praise God." Each nation, according to Kabbalah, has its own path to the Light. But there is only one Creator who gives Light to all of us. For this reason, *"Love your neighbor as yourself"* applies to all the nations of the world. We must treat all people with dignity. There is war between nations and chaos in society only because of the lack of compassion and sensitivity between people.

goyim גּוֹיִם kol כָּל־ Adonai יְהֹוָה et אֶת־ halelu הַלְלוּ

gavar גָּבַר ki כִּי :ha'umim הָאֻמִּים kol כָּל־ shabechuhu שַׁבְּחוּהוּ

chasdo וְחַסְדּוֹ alenu עָלֵינוּ

Adonai יְהֹוָה ve'emet וֶאֱמֶת־

le'olam לְעוֹלָם haleluya הַלְלוּיָהּ

I shall pay my vows to Lord before all His People. It is difficult in the Eyes of the Lord, the death of His pious ones. Please, Lord, I am Your servant. I am Your servant, then a son of Your handmaid. You have untied my bonds. To You I shall sacrifice a thanksgiving-offering and call out in the Name of the Lord. I shall pay my vows to the Lord, before all His People, in the courtyards of the Lord, within Jerusalem. Praise the Lord." (Psalms 116:12-end)

MALCHUT - HALELU

"Praise the Lord, all you people, Exalt Him, all you people. For His kindness has overwhelmed us and the truth of the Lord is eternal, Praise the Lord." (Psalms 117)

MALCHUT – HODU

The next four verses connect us to the four spiritual worlds, represented by the four different combinations of the *Yud, Hei, Vav,* and *Hei.* Each of these different combinations of letters is a transformer that channels currents of spiritual energy from various levels of the *Ten Sfirot* to our physical realm. Spiritually speaking, some people are connected to the Highest Worlds, while others are connected to the Middle and Lower Realms. The only way for humanity to achieve true unity is for each of us to let go of our ego and accept the fact that no one is higher or lower than anyone else; only our connections are different.

The *Talmud* reinforces this concept. We learn that a mosquito is actually on a much higher spiritual level than a man who isn't pursuing his spiritual work. A mosquito comes into this world to bite. As we all know, the mosquito does his job quite effectively. We came here to achieve a spiritual transformation. We give too much importance to a person's physical status in this world. However, whether one is an executive or a factory worker – if they are both doing their spiritual work, they are on the same level according to the Creator. Some people are never happy with where they are. Part of their work is to appreciate that they are doing their spiritual work. They should realize that they're on the same spiritual level as not only the people they envy but also the people they consider to be on a lower level than themselves. They are all working on spiritual tranformation.

Chochmah (ע"ב – יוד הי ויו הי, קס"א –אלף הי יוד הי)

והו tov טוֹב ki כִּי־ ladonai לַיהוָֹהאֲדֹנָיֵיאהדונהי aheyh הֹודוּ hodu

כי טוב = יהוה אהיה, אום, מבה, יזל

chasdo וְחַסְדּוֹ אותיות דס"ג ו"י ס"ג ריבוע le'olam לְעוֹלָם ki כִּי

ג' הויות, מזלא (להמשיך הארה ממזלא עילאה) ; ר"ת = נגה:

Binah (ס"ג – יוד הי ואו הי, קס"א – אלף הי יוד הי)

Yisrael יִשְׂרָאֵל na נָא yomar יֹאמַר־

chasdo וְחַסְדּוֹ אותיות דס"ג ו"י ס"ג ריבוע le'olam לְעוֹלָם ki כִּי

ג' הויות, מזלא (להמשיך הארה ממזלא עילאה) ; ר"ת = נגה:

Zeir Anpin (מ"ה – יוד הא ואו הא, קמ"ג – אלף הא יוד הא)

Aharon אַהֲרֹן ב"פ ראה vet בֵּית־ na נָא yomru יֹאמְרוּ־

chasdo וְחַסְדּוֹ אותיות דס"ג ו"י ס"ג ריבוע le'olam לְעוֹלָם ki כִּי

ג' הויות, מזלא (להמשיך הארה ממזלא עילאה) ; ר"ת = נגה:

Malchut (ב"ן – יוד הה והו הה, קנ"א – אלף הה יוד הה)

Adonai יְהוָֹהאֲדֹנָיֵיאהדונהי yir'ei יִרְאֵי na נָא yomru יֹאמְרוּ־

chasdo וְחַסְדּוֹ אותיות דס"ג ו"י ס"ג ריבוע le'olam לְעוֹלָם ki כִּי

ג' הויות, מזלא (להמשיך הארה ממזלא עילאה) ; ר"ת = נגה:

MALCHUT – HODU

"Give thanks to the Lord for He is good, for His kindness is forever.
Let Israel say so now, for His kindness is forever.
Let the House of Aaron say so now, for His kindness is forever.
Let those who fear the Lord say so now, for His kindness is forever.

MIN HAMETZAR

"From the straits I called upon God." Unfortunately, most of us call upon the Creator when we are in dire straits. Kabbalah teaches that we also need to call upon the Creator during good times and recognize the Light's influence in all of our good fortune. *The Zohar* teaches us that if we create a spiritual opening within ourselves no wider than the eye of a needle, God will answer us and open the Supernal Gates for us. Whatever its size, this opening for spirituality must be a complete opening where there can be no doubt or uncertainty.

Yah יָהּ	karati קָרָאתִי	מֵצַר	hametzar הַמֵּצַר	min מִן	א׳ ארך
Yah יָהּ׃		vamerchav בַמֶּרְחָב	anani עָנָנִי		ב׳ אפים
ira אִירָא	lo לֹא	li לִי	Adonai יְהֹוָאדָנָיאהדונהי		ג׳ ורב חסד
adam אָדָם מ״ה׃	li לִי	ya'ase יַעֲשֶׂה	ma מַה־ מ״ה		ד׳ נשא עון
be'ozrai בְּעֹזְרָי	li לִי	Adonai יְהֹוָאדָנָיאהדונהי			ה׳ ופשע
veson'ai בְשֹׂנְאָי׃	er'e אֶרְאֶה אני	va'ani וַאֲנִי			ו׳ ונקה
badonai בַּיהֹוָאדָנָיאהדונהי	lachasot לַחֲסוֹת והו	tov טוֹב			ז׳ פוקד
ba'adam בָּאָדָם מ״ה׃		mibetoach מִבְּטֹחַ			ח׳ על שלשים
badonai בַּיהֹוָאדָנָיאהדונהי	lachasot לַחֲסוֹת והו	tov טוֹב			ט׳ ועל רבעים
goyim גוֹיִם ילי	kol כָּל־	bindivim בִּנְדִיבִים	mibetoa'ch מִבְּטֹחַ		
amilam אֲמִילַם׃	ki כִּי	Adonai יְהֹוָאדָנָיאהדונהי	beshem בְּשֵׁם	sevavuni סְבָבוּנִי	
Adonai יְהֹוָאדָנָיאהדונהי	beshem בְּשֵׁם	sevavuni סְבָבוּנִי	gam גַם־	sabuni סַבּוּנִי	
do'achu דֹעֲכוּ	chidvorim כִּדְבוֹרִים	sabuni סַבּוּנִי	amilam אֲמִילַם׃	ki כִּי	
Adonai יְהֹוָאדָנָיאהדונהי	beshem בְּשֵׁם	kotzim קוֹצִים	ke'esh כְּאֵשׁ		
linpol לִנְפֹּל	dechitani דְחִיתַנִי	dacho דָחֹה	amilam אֲמִילַם׃	ki כִּי	
עֲ״ה אַהיה אֲדֹנָי ע״ה אלהים ע״ה	ozi עֻזִּי	azarani עֲזָרָנִי׃	vadonai וַיהֹוָאדָנָיאהדונהי		
lishu'a לִישׁוּעָה׃	li לִי	vay'hi וַיְהִי־	Yah יָהּ	vezimrat וְזִמְרָת	

MIN HAMETZAR

Greatly from my distress I called out to the Lord. Patient Lord answered me in His expansiveness. The Lord is with me, I shall not fear those who bear iniquities. What can man do to me? And sins, the Lord shall come to my rescue and cleanses. And I shall look upon my enemies. It is good to take refuge in the Lord rather than to trust in man. It is better to take refuge in the Lord than to trust in noblemen. All the nations surrounded me. In the Name of the Lord, I shall cut them down. They surrounded me again and again. In the Name of the Lord, I shall cut them down. They surrounded me like bees, but are extinguished like a fire on thorns. With the Name of the Lord, I shall cut them down. They pushed me time and again to fall and the Lord came to my aid. The strength and cutting power of God were for me a salvation.

kol קוֹל rina רָנָּה vishua וִישׁוּעָה be'aholei בְּאָהֳלֵי tzadikim צַדִּיקִים

yemin יְמִין Adonai יְהֹוָה osa עֹשָׂה chayil וָזִיל ומב:

yemin יְמִין Adonai יְהֹוָה romema רוֹמֵמָה ר"ת רי yemin יְמִין

Adonai יְהֹוָה osa עֹשָׂה chayil וָזִיל lo לֹא amut אָמוּת

ki כִּי echye אֶחְיֶה va'asaper וַאֲסַפֵּר ma'asei מַעֲשֵׂי Yah יָהּ

yasor יַסֹּר yisrani יִסְּרַנִּי Yah יָהּ velamavet וְלַמָּוֶת lo לֹא

netanani נְתָנָנִי pitchu פִּתְחוּ li לִי sha'arei שַׁעֲרֵי tzedek צֶדֶק avo אָבֹא

vam בָם ode אוֹדֶה Yah יָהּ zeh זֶה hasha'ar הַשַּׁעַר

ladonai לַיהֹוָה tzadikim צַדִּיקִים yavo'u יָבֹאוּ vo בוֹ

ODCHA
We have four verses that connect us to the four letters of the Tetragrammaton. Each verse is recited twice.

Yud – Chochmah – י

odcha אוֹדְךָ ki כִּי anitani עֲנִיתָנִי vatehi וַתְּהִי li לִי lishua לִישׁוּעָה 2x

Hei – Binah – ה

even אֶבֶן ma'asu מָאֲסוּ habonim הַבּוֹנִים hayta הָיְתָה

lerosh לְרֹאשׁ pina פִּנָּה 2x

Vav – Zeir Anpin – ו

me'et מֵאֵת Adonai יְהֹוָה hayta הָיְתָה zot זֹאת

hee הִיא niflat נִפְלָאת be'enenu בְּעֵינֵינוּ 2x

Hei – Malchut – ה

ze זֶה hayom הַיּוֹם asa עָשָׂה Adonai יְהֹוָה

nagila נָגִילָה venismecha וְנִשְׂמְחָה vo בוֹ 2x

The sound of song and salvation is in the tents of the righteous. The right of the Lord does mighty things. The right of the Lord is raised. The right of the Lord does mighty things. I shall not die, but rather I shall live and tell of the deeds of God. God has chastised me again and again, but He has not surrendered me to death. Open for me the gates of righteousness. I will go through them and give thanks to God. This is the Gate of the Lord, the righteous may go through It.

ODCHA
I am grateful to You, for You have answered me and have become my salvation.
The stone that was rejected by the builders has become the main cornerstone.
This came about from the Lord, it is wondrous in our eyes.
The Lord has made this day let us be glad and rejoice in it.

ANA

These four verses offer us a different pathway to connect to the Light. The numeric equivalent of the word אנא (Ana) is 52, which is also the numerical value of the Name of God that connects to our physical realm of *Malchut*.

You should meditate that *Malchut*, which is: ב"ן, receives from *Chochmah* which is: ע"ב.

(יוד הי ויו הי) Adonai יְהֹוָ(אדנייאהדונהי) (יוד הה וו הה) ב"ן ana אָנָּא

na גָּא hoshi'a הוֹשִׁיעָה יהוה וע"ע נהורין

You should meditate that *Malchut*, which is: ב"ן, receives from *Binah* which is: ס"ג.

(יוד הי ואו הי) Adonai יְהֹוָ(אדנייאהדונהי) (יוד הה וו הה) ב"ן ana אָנָּא

na גָּא hoshi'a הוֹשִׁיעָה יהוה וע"ע נהורין

You should meditate that *Malchut*, which is ב"ן, receives from *Zeir Anpin* which is: מ"ה.

(יוד הא ואו הא) Adonai יְהֹוָ(אדנייאהדונהי) (יוד הה וו הה) ב"ן ana אָנָּא

na גָּא hatzlicha הַצְלִיחָה

Meditate that *Malchut*, which is ב"ן, receives from all the above mentioned: ע"ב, ס"ג, מ"ה.

Adonai יְהֹוָ(אדנייאהדונהי) (יוד הה וו הה) ב"ן ana אָנָּא

na גָּא hatzlicha הַצְלִיחָה (יוד הא ואו הא, יוד הי ואו הי, יוד הי ויו הי)

BARUCH HABA

We have four verses that connect us to the four letters of the Tetragrammaton. Each verse is recited twice.

Yud — Chochmah - י

Adonai יְהֹוָ(אדנייאהדונהי) beshem בְּשֵׁם haba הַבָּא baruch בָּרוּךְ

2x Adonai יְהֹוָ(אדנייאהדונהי) ב"פ ראה mibet מִבֵּית berachnuchem בֵּרַכְנוּכֶם

Hei — Binah - ה

ויו ויו זין כף ויו vaya'er וַיָּאֶר Adonai יְהֹוָ(אדנייאהדונהי) (מילוי דס"ג) יא"י El אֵל

ba'avotim בַּעֲבֹתִים chag וָֹג isru אִסְרוּ אדני אהיה, אלהים, lanu לָנוּ

2x אל יהוה זין, נגד, hamizbe'ach הַמִּזְבֵּוֹחַ karnot קַרְנוֹת ad עַד

Vav — Zeir Anpin - ו

ve'odeka וְאוֹדֶךָ Ata אַתָּה Eli אֵלִי

2x aromemeka אֲרוֹמְמֶךָ ילה ; דמב דע"ב, מילוי Elohai אֱלֹהַי

ANA

We beseech You, Lord, save us now. We beseech You, Lord, save us now.
We beseech You, Lord, give us success now. We beseech You, Lord, give us success now.

BARUCH HABA

Blessed is the one who comes in the Name of the Lord. We bless you from The House of the Lord. The Lord is God, He illuminates for us. Tie the holiday-offering with ropes till the corners of the Altar. You are my God and I thank You, my God, and I shall exalt You.

Hei – Malchut – ה

והו tov טוֹב ki כִּי־ ladonai לַיהֹוָה אהיה hodu הוֹדוּ
כי טוב = יהוה אהיה, אום, מבה, יזל

כִּי le'olam לְעוֹלָם ki אותיות ו"י ס"ג ריבוע דס"ג chasdo וְחַסְדּוֹ
ג' הויות, מזלא (להמשיך הארה ממזלא עילאה) ; ר"ת = נגה : 2x

This section is omitted on *Rosh Chodesh*, *Chol Hamo'ed* of *Pesach* and Seventh Day of *Pesach*

ילי kol כָּל ילה Elohenu אֱלֹהֵינוּ Adonai יְהֹוָה yehalelucha יְהַלְלוּךָ
osei עוֹשֵׂי vetzadikim וְצַדִּיקִים vachasidecha וַחֲסִידֶיךָ ma'asecha מַעֲשֶׂיךָ
kulam כֻּלָּם Yisrael יִשְׂרָאֵל ב"פ ראה bet בֵּית ve'amcha וְעַמְּךָ retzonecha רְצוֹנֶךָ
בּ"ן, לכבב vivarchu יהוה ריבוע יהוה vivarchu וִיבָרְכוּ yodu יוֹדוּ berina בְּרִנָּה מ"ה
na'im נָעִים ulshimcha וּלְשִׁמְךָ lehodot לְהוֹדוֹת tov טוֹב lecha לְךָ ki כִּי
ata אַתָּה olam עוֹלָם ve'ad וְעַד ume'olam וּמֵעוֹלָם lezamer לְזַמֵּר
Adonai יְהֹוָה Ata אַתָּה baruch בָּרוּךְ (מילוי דס"ג) El אֵל ייא"י
אָהדונהי amen אָמֵן batishbachot בַּתִּשְׁבָּחוֹת mehulal מְהֻלָּל melech מֶלֶךְ

Recite this verse three times to connect to the Light of protection.

וזי"פ אל, רי"ו ול"ב נתיבות החוכמה, רמ"ח (אברים), עסמ"ב וט"ז אותיות פשוטות veAvraham וְאַבְרָהָם
et אֶת berach בֵּרַךְ vadonai וַיהֹוָה זקן וי bayamim בַּיָּמִים ba בָּא zaken זָקֵן
וזי"פ אל, רי"ו ול"ב נתיבות החוכמה, רמ"ח (אברים), עסמ"ב וט"ז אותיות פשוטות Avraham אַבְרָהָם
בּ"ן, לכבב bakol בַּכֹּל

Meditate on the Name of the Angel (וּבְדִיָה) derived from the above mentioned verse.

ratzon רָצוֹן yehi יְהִי ken כֵּן viychayeni וִיחַיֵּנִי yishmereni יִשְׁמְרֵנִי
מהש"ע ע"ה, ע"ב בריבוע וקס"א ע"ה, אל שדי ע"ה milfanecha מִלְּפָנֶיךָ ס"ג מ"ה בּ"ן
umelech וּמֶלֶךְ אהיה אהיה יהוה, בינה ע"ה chayim וְחַיִּים ; ילה אדני Elohim אֱלֹהִים
amen אָמֵן chai וְזִי ילי kol כָּל nefesh נֶפֶשׁ beyado בְּיָדוֹ asher אֲשֶׁר olam עוֹלָם
יאהדונהי ratzon רָצוֹן מהש"ע ע"ה, ע"ב בריבוע וקס"א ע"ה, אל שדי ע"ה yehi יְהִי ken כֵּן

Be grateful to the Lord for He is good. For His kindness is forever." (Psalms 118)

All Your deeds and all Your pious ones shall praise You, Lord, our God, and the righteous ones who do Your will, as well as Your nation, the House of Israel. They shall all joyously give thanks, bless, praise and glorify the Name of Your glory, because to You it is good to give thanks, and to Your Name, it is pleasing to sing. And from this world until the next, You are God. Blessed are You, Lord, a King Who is extolled in praises. Amen.

"And Abraham was old, and ripe in age, and God has blessed Abraham with everything." (Genesis 24:1)
May He preserve me and enliven me. And may it so be pleasing before the God of life and the King of the world, in Whose Hands lie the spirit of all that lives. Amen, may it so be His pleasure.

KADDISH TITKABAL

יִתְגַּדַּל yitgadal וְיִתְקַדַּשׁ veyitkadash שׂדי ומילוי שׂדי ; י"א אותיות כמנין ו"ה

שְׁמֵהּ shemei (שם י"ה דע"ב) רַבָּא raba קנ"א ב"ן, יהוה אלהים יהוה אדני,

אָמֵן amen אידהנויה. מילוי קס"א וס"ג, מ"ה ברבוע ועו"ב ע"ה ; ר"ת = ו"פ אלהים ; ס"ת = ג"פ יב"ק

בְּעָלְמָא be'alma דִּי di בְּרָא vera כִּרְעוּתֵהּ chir'utei

וְיַמְלִיךְ veyamlich מַלְכוּתֵהּ mal'chutei וְיַצְמַח veyatzmach

פּוּרְקָנֵהּ purkanei וִיקָרֵב vikarev מְשִׁיחֵהּ meshichei אָמֵן amen אידהנויה.

בְּחַיֵּיכוֹן bechayechon וּבְיוֹמֵיכוֹן uvyomechon וּבְחַיֵּי uvchayei

דְכָל dechol בֵּית bet יִשְׂרָאֵל Yisrael בַּעֲגָלָא ba'agala

וּבִזְמַן uvizman קָרִיב kariv וְאִמְרוּ ve'imru אָמֵן amen אָמֵן amen אידהנויה.

The congregation and the *chazan* say the following:
28 words (until *be'alma*) and 28 letters (until *almaya*)

יְהֵא yehe שְׁמֵהּ shemei (שם י"ה דס"ג) רַבָּא raba קנ"א ב"ן,

מְבָרַךְ mevarach יהוה אלהים יהוה אדני, מ"ה ברבוע ועו"ב ע"ה וס"ג, מילוי קס"א

לְעָלַם le'alam לְעָלְמֵי le'almei עָלְמַיָּא almaya יִתְבָּרַךְ yitbarach

Seven words with six letters each (שם בן מ"ב) – and seven times the letter *Vav*

וְיִשְׁתַּבַּח veyishtabach י"פ ע"ב יהוה אל אבג יתץ.

וְיִתְפָּאַר veyitpa'ar הי גו יה קרע שׂטן. וְיִתְרוֹמַם veyitromam וה כוזו נגד יכש.

וְיִתְנַשֵּׂא veyitnase במוכסז בטר צתג. וְיִתְהַדָּר veyit'hadar כוזו יה וזקב טנע.

וְיִתְעַלֶּה veyit'ale א ואו הא שׂקו צית. וְיִתְהַלָּל veyit'halal וה יוד ה יגל פזק.

שְׁמֵהּ shemei (שם י"ה דמ"ה) דְּקוּדְשָׁא dekudsha בְּרִיךְ verich הוּא hu:

אָמֵן amen אידהנויה.

KADDISH TITKABAL
May His great Name be more exalted and sanctified. (Amen)
In the world that He created according to His will, and may His kingdom reign. And may He cause His redemption to sprout and may He bring the Mashiach closer. (Amen) In your lifetimes and in your days and in the lifetime of all the House of Israel, speedily and in the near future, and you shall say, Amen. (Amen) May His great Name be blessed forever and for all eternity. Blessed and lauded, and glorified, and exalted, and extolled, and honored, and uplifted, and praised be the Name of the Holy Blessed One (Amen)

le'ela לְעֵלָּא min מִן kol כָּל יְלֵי birchata בִּרְכָתָא shirata שִׁירָתָא

tishbechata תֻּשְׁבְּחָתָא venechamata וְנֶחֱמָתָא da'amiran דַּאֲמִירָן

be'alma בְּעָלְמָא ve'imru וְאִמְרוּ amen אָמֵן amen אָמֵן איהנויה.

On *Chanukah* you should stop here and continue on pg. 230.

titkabal תִּתְקַבַּל tzelotana צְלוֹתָנָא uva'utana וּבָעוּתָנָא

im עִם tzelotehon צְלוֹתְהוֹן uva'utehon וּבָעוּתְהוֹן dechol דְּכָל יְלֵי

bet בֵּית ראה ב"פ Yisrael יִשְׂרָאֵל kadam קֳדָם avuna אֲבוּנָא

devishmaya דְּבִשְׁמַיָּא ve'imru וְאִמְרוּ amen אָמֵן amen אָמֵן איהנויה.

yehe יְהֵא shelama שְׁלָמָא raba רַבָּא קנ"א ב"ן, יהוה אלהים יהוה אדני, מילוי קס"א וס"ג,

min מִן shemaya שְׁמַיָּא chayim וְחַיִּים אהיה אהיה יהוה, בונה ע"ה מ"ה ברבוע וע"ב ע"ה

vesava וְשָׂבָע vishu'a וִישׁוּעָה venechama וְנֶחָמָה veshezava וְשֵׁיזָבָא

urfu'a וּרְפוּאָה ug'ula וּגְאֻלָּה uslicha וּסְלִיחָה vechapara וְכַפָּרָה

verevach וְרֵיוַח vehatzala וְהַצָּלָה lanu לָנוּ אלהים, אהיה אדני ulchol וּלְכָל יה אדני

amo עַמּוֹ Yisrael יִשְׂרָאֵל ve'imru וְאִמְרוּ amen אָמֵן amen אָמֵן איהנויה.

Take three steps backwards and say:

ose עוֹשֶׂה shalom שָׁלוֹם

bimromav בִּמְרוֹמָיו ע"ב, ריבוע יהוה hu הוּא berachamav בְּרַחֲמָיו

ya'ase יַעֲשֶׂה shalom שָׁלוֹם alenu עָלֵינוּ ר"ת שי"ע נהורין.

ve'al וְעַל kol כָּל יְלֵי עמם; amo עַמּוֹ Yisrael יִשְׂרָאֵל ve'imru וְאִמְרוּ amen אָמֵן.

amen אָמֵן איהנויה.

On Rosh Chodesh- we read the *Torah* (opening of the Arc is on pg. 230 and the reading is on pg. 517). After the reading of the *Torah* we say Half *Kaddish* (pg. 239), *Yehalelu*, and we bring the *Torah* back to the Ark. Then we say *Ashrei* (pg. 240), *Uva-letzion* (skipping *Kaddish Titkabal* on pg. 252-253), *Bet Yaakov* (pg. 254), *Shir Hama'alot*, *Shir shel yom*, *Hoshi'einu*, Half *Kaddish*, taking off the *Tefilin* and then *Musaf*.

Above all blessings, songs, praises, and words of consolation that may be said in the world, and you shall say, Amen. (Amen) May our prayers and pleas be accepted, together with the prayers and pleas of the entire House of Israel, before our Father in Heaven, and you say, Amen. (Amen) May there be abundant peace from heaven. Life, contentment, salvation, consolation, deliverance, healing, redemption, pardon, atonement, comfort, and relief. For us and for His entire nation, Israel, and you shall say, Amen. (Amen) He, Who makes peace in His high places, With His compassion He shall make peace for us and for His entire nation, Israel. And you shall say, Amen. (Amen)

We take off the *Tefilin* before *Musaf* – up to *Musaf* we are elevated to *Chesed, Gevurah, Tiferet* of *Zeir Anpin* (as it is on regular days), and from here we start to ascend towards *Chochmah, Binah, Da'at* of *Zeir Anpin* (so the *Keter* of *Nukva* will be on the same level as the *Keter* of *Zeir Anpin*), and this is the addition (*Musaf*) that *Nukva* receives on *Rosh Chodesh*. And even though it does not ascend all the way up to *Atika*, with all that, the Light of *Atika* is revealed upon *Zeir Anpin*, and through the different stages of *Zeir Anpin* to *Nukva* and to us. This Light is higher than the Light that is revealed by the *Tefilin*, and therefore we need to take the *Tefilin* off and only then pray *Musaf* (this illumination stays only until after *Musaf* – which the *Musaf* is for the renewal of the moon).
In the Silent prayer – *Chochmah* of *Yaakov* and *Rachel* rise onto *Chesed* of *Israel Sava* and *Tevuna*.
In the repetition - *Chochmah* of *Yaakov* and *Rachel* rise onto *Chochmah* of *Israel Sava* and *Tevuna*.

yagid יַגִּיד ufi וּפִי tiftach תִּפְתָּח sefatai שְׂפָתַי (pause here) ללה Adonai אֲדֹנָי

יי׳ (כ"ב אותיות פשוטות [=אכא] וה' אותיות סופיות סזזזך) ס"ת = בוכו: tehilatecha תְּהִלָּתֶךָ

THE FIRST BLESSING - INVOKES THE SHIELD OF ABRAHAM.

Abraham is the channel of the Right Column energy of positivity, sharing, and mercy. Sharing actions can protect us from all forms of negativity.

Chesed that becomes Chochmah

In this section there are 42 words, the secret of the 42-Letter Name of God and therefore it begins with the letter *Bet* (2) and ends with the letter *Mem* (40).

Bend your knees at 'baruch', bow at 'Ata' and straighten up at 'Adonai'.

המלכות (לה' המגיע) את העשפע המסמלות (אותיות הא"ב א-ת) Ata אַתָּה baruch בָּרוּךְ

ילה Elohenu אֱלֹהֵינוּ (יא) Adonai יְאֲדֹנָיאהדונהי

avotenu אֲבוֹתֵינוּ ילה ; דמב ע"ב, מילוי ; לכב velohei וֵאלֹהֵי

(*Chochmah*) Avraham אַבְרָהָם ; ילה דמב ע"ב, מילוי Elohei אֱלֹהֵי
אותיות פשוטות וט"ז עסמ"ב (אברים), רמ"ח הזוכמה, נתיבות ול"ב רי"ו אל, וו"פ

ד"פ ב"ן (*Binah*) Yitzchak יִצְחָק ילה ; דמב ע"ב, מילוי Elohei אֱלֹהֵי

איהדונהי יאהדונהי הויות, ו (*Da'at*) Yaakov יַעֲקֹב ; ילה ; דמב מילוי ע"ב, לכב velohei וֵאלֹהֵי

THE AMIDAH OF MUSAF
"My Lord, open my lips, and my mouth shall relate Your praise." (Psalms 51:17)
THE FIRST BLESSING
Blessed are You, Lord,
our God and God of our forefathers: the God of Abraham, the God of Isaac, and the God of Jacob.

הָאֵל haEl ; יא"י (מילוי דס"ג) לאה ; האל הגדול hagadol הַגָּדוֹל = סיט = גָּדוֹל = להוו

וְהַנּוֹרָא vehanora♦ ר"ת ההה hagibor הַגִּבּוֹר עם ד' אותיות = מבה, יזל, אום

אֵל El יא"י (מילוי דס"ג) ; ר"ת ע"ב, ריבוע יהוה עֶלְיוֹן elyon♦

גּוֹמֵל gomel וְחֲסָדִים chasadim טוֹבִים tovim♦ קוֹנֵה kone הַכֹּל hakol יכי

וְזוֹכֵר vezocher וְחַסְדֵּי chasdei אָבוֹת avot♦ וּמֵבִיא umevi

גּוֹאֵל go'el לִבְנֵי livnei בְנֵיהֶם venehem לְמַעַן lema'an

שְׁמוֹ shemo מהע ע"ה, ע"ב בריבוע וקס"א וקס"א ע"ה, אל עדי ע"ה בְּאַהֲבָה be'ahava אוזר, דאגה:

When saying the word "be'ahava" you should meditate to devote your soul to sanctify the Holy Name and accept upon yourself the four forms of death.

מֶלֶךְ melech עוֹזֵר ozer וּמוֹשִׁיעַ umoshi'a וּמָגֵן umagen

ג"פ אל (יא"י מילוי דס"ג) ; ר"ת מיכאל גבריאל נוריאל:

Bend your knees at 'baruch', bow at 'Ata' and straighten up at 'Adonai'.

בָּרוּךְ baruch אַתָּה Ata יְהֹוָה(אדני)(יֱהֹוִאדֱנִי)יאהדונהי Adonai (הד)

(On *Rosh Chodesh Menachem Av* – **Leo**, meditate on the Holy Name: טדהד)

מָגֵן magen ג"פ אל (יא"י מילוי דס"ג) ; ר"ת מיכאל גבריאל נוריאל אַבְרָהָם Avraham

וז"פ אל, רי"ו ול"ב נתיבות החכמה, רמ"ח (אברים), עסמ"ב וט"ו אותיות פשוטות:

The God Who is great, valorous, and awesome. The Supernal God, Who bestows beneficial kindness and creates everything. Who recalls the kindness of the forefathers and brings a Redeemer to their descendants for the sake of His Name, lovingly. King, Helper, Savior and Shield. Blessed are You, Lord, the shield of Abraham.

THE SECOND BLESSING

THE ENERGY OF ISAAC IGNITES THE POWER FOR THE RESURRECTION OF THE DEAD.

Whereas Abraham represents the power of sharing, Isaac represents the Left Column energy of judgment. Judgment shortens the *Tikkun* process and paves the way for our eventual resurrection (footnote A - pg. 189).

Gevurah that becomes *Binah*.

In this section there are 49 words corresponding to the 49 gates of the Pure System in *Binah*.

ללה Adonai אֲדֹנָי ס"ג וי' אותיות דס"ג ריבוע ס"ג le'olam לְעוֹלָם gibor גִּבּוֹר Ata אַתָּה

(ר"ת אֲגְלָא והוא שם גָּדוֹל ואמיץ, ובו היה יהודה מתגבר על אויביו. ע"ה אלד, בוכו).

lehoshi'a לְהוֹשִׁיעַ rav רַב Ata אַתָּה metim מֵתִים ס"ג mechaye מְחַיֵּה

During the winter (starting on Simchat Torah):

haru'ach הָרוּחַ ר"ת מ"ה משי"ב mashiv מַשִּׁיב

hageshem הַגֶּשֶׁם umorid וּמוֹרִיד

שׂוֹבל [י"ע (= י"פ אל) ול"ב נתיבות החכמה] ע"ה:

If you mistakenly say *"morid hatal"*, and realize this before the end of the blessing (*"baruch Ata Adonai"*), you should return to the beginning of the blessing (*"Ata gibor"*) and continue as usual. But if you only realize this after the end of the blessing, you should continue and not go back.

During the summer (starting on Pesach):

hatal הַטָּל morid מוֹרִיד

יוד הא ואו, כוזו, מספר אותיות דמילוי עסמ"ב ;

ר"ת מ"ה (יוד הא ואו הא):

If you mistakenly say *"Mashiv haru'ach"*, and realize this before the end of the blessing (*"baruch Ata Adonai"*), you should return to the beginning of the blessing (*"Ata gibor"*) and continue as usual. But if you only realize this after the end of the blessing, you should start the *Amidah* from the beginning.

bechesed בְּחֶסֶד אהיה אהיה יהוה, בינה ע"ה chayim חַיִּים mechalkel מְכַלְכֵּל

berachamim בְּרַחֲמִים metim מֵתִים ס"ג mechaye מְחַיֵּה ע"ב, ריבוע יהוה.

somech סוֹמֵךְ (טלא דעתיק) rabim רַבִּים י"פ יי' אלהים דההין, מצפצ (במוכסז)

cholim חוֹלִים verofe וְרוֹפֵא (וז"ן) noflim נוֹפְלִים כוק, ריבוע אדני (אכדטם)

umekayem וּמְקַיֵּם asurim אֲסוּרִים umatir וּמַתִּיר ה אותיות. וזוכה = מ"ה וד'

chamocha כָּמוֹךָ יל מי מִי afar עָפָר lishenei לִישֵׁנֵי emunato אֱמוּנָתוֹ

gevurot גְּבוּרוֹת ba'al בַּעַל (you should enunciate the letter *Ayin* in the word "ba'al")

memit מֵמִית melech מֶלֶךְ lach לָךְ dome דוֹמֶה יל umi וּמִי

yeshu'a יְשׁוּעָה umatzmi'ach וּמַצְמִיחַ (יוד הי ואו הי) ס"ג umchaye וּמְחַיֵּה

THE SECOND BLESSING

You are mighty forever, Lord. You resurrect the dead and are very capable of redeeming.

During the winter:
Who causes wind to blow and rain to fall.

During the summer:
Who causes dew to fall.

You sustain life with kindness and resurrect the dead with great compassion. You support those who have fallen, heal the sick, release the imprisoned, and fulfill Your faithful words to those who are asleep in the dust. Who is like You, Master of might, and Who can compare to You, King, Who causes death, Who gives life, and Who sprouts salvation?

vene'eman וְנֶאֱמָן   Ata אַתָּה   lehachayot לְהַחֲיוֹת   metim מֵתִים:

baruch בָּרוּךְ   Ata אַתָּה יְהֹוָה(יֱהוֹוִהֵ)יאהדונהי   Adonai

(On *Rosh Chodesh Menachem Av* – Leo, meditate on the Holy Name: כוו).

mechaye מְחַיֵּה mechaye ס"ג (יוד הי ואו הי) הַמֵּתִים hametim ר"ת מ"ה וס"ת מ"ה:

KETER FOR MUSAF

This is one of the most powerful prayers to help us connect to the seed level of life before there was any differentiation between the cells of the body. Our meditations during this time increase the production of stem cells in our body.

Lifting a heavy chest filled with vast treasures is impossible if you use just a single string: The string will snap because it is too weak. However, if we unite and combine numerous strings, we will eventually build a rope. A rope can easily lift the treasure chest. By combining and uniting the congregation's prayers, we become a united force, capable of pulling down the most valuable spiritual treasures. Furthermore, this unity helps people who are not well-versed or knowledgeable in the connections. By uniting and meditating as one soul, we all receive the benefit because of the power of unity, regardless of our knowledge and understanding. This prayer occurs in between the second and third blessings. It signifies the Central Column that unites the Left and Right Columns.

In this prayer the angels speak to each other, saying: "*Kadosh, Kadosh, Kadosh*" ("Holy, Holy, Holy"). When we recite these three words, we stand with our feet stand together as one. With each utterance of *Kadosh*, we jump a little higher in the air. Jumping is an act of restriction and it defies the force of gravity. Spiritually, gravity has the energy of the Desire to Receive for the Self Alone. It is the reactive force of our planet, always pulling everything toward itself.

כֶּתֶר keter יהוה מלך יהוה מלך יהוה ימלוך לעולם ועד ובאתב"ש גאל יִתְּנוּ yitenu לְךָ lecha

יְהֹוָהיאהדונהי Adonai אֱלֹהֵינוּ Elohenu ילה (א' ונוק') מַלְאָכִים mal'achim

הֲמוֹנֵי hamonei מַעְלָה ma'la עִם im עַמְּךָ amecha יִשְׂרָאֵל Yisrael

קְבוּצֵי kevutzei מַטָּה mata (על ידי הצדיקים) יוד yachad כֻּלָּם kulam

קְדֻשָּׁה kedusha לְךָ lecha יְשַׁלֵּשׁוּ yeshaleshu כַּדָּבָר kadavar ראה

הָאָמוּר ha'amur עַל al יָד yad נְבִיאָךְ nevi'ach וְקָרָא vekara

זֶה ze אֶל el זֶה ze י"ב פרקין דיעקב מאירים לי"ב פרקין דרחל וְאָמַר ve'amar:

And You are faithful to resurrecting the dead. Blessed are You, Lord, Who resurrects the dead.

KETER FOR MUSAF

They shall give a crown to You, Lord, our God, those multitudes of angels above, together with Your People, Israel, who gather below. Together, they shall all declare holiness three times to You, as it is written by Your Prophet: And each called to the other and said:

קָדוֹשׁ | kadosh קָדוֹשׁ kadosh קָדוֹשׁ (סוֹד ג' רישין דעתיקא קדישא)

יְהֹוָה(אדני-יאהדונהי) Adonai צְבָאוֹת Tzeva'ot פני שכינה melo מְלֹא chol כָּל־ ילי

הָאָרֶץ ha'aretz אלהים דההין ע"ה: כְּבוֹדוֹ kevodo:

לְעֻמָּתָם le'umatam מְשַׁבְּחִים meshabechim וְאוֹמְרִים ve'omrim:

(או"א) בָּרוּךְ baruch כְּבוֹד־ kevod יְהֹוָה(אדני-יאהדונהי) Adonai ; כבוד ה' = יוד הי ואו הה

מִמְּקוֹמוֹ mimekomo עסמ"ב, הברכה (למתק את ז' המלכים עמתו) ;ר"ת ע"ב, ריבוע יהוה ;ר"ת מי:כ:

וּבְדִבְרֵי uvdivrei קָדְשְׁךָ kodshach כָּתוּב katuv לֵאמֹר lemor:

(וז"ן) יִמְלֹךְ yimloch קדוש ברוך ימלך ר"ת יב"ק, אלהים יהוה, אהיה אדני יהוה

יְהֹוָה(אדני-יאהדונהי) Adonai לְעוֹלָם le'olam ריבוע ס"ג ו' אותיות דס"ג אֱלֹהַיִךְ Elohayich ילה

צִיּוֹן Tziyon יוסף, ו' הויות, קנאה ledor לְדֹר vador וָדֹר רי"ו ;ר"ת אצלו (מלכות אצל ז"א – ו)

הַלְלוּיָהּ haleluya אלהים, אהיה אדני ; ללה:

THE THIRD BLESSING

This blessing connects us to Jacob, the Central Column and the power of restriction. Jacob is our channel for connecting mercy with judgment. By restricting our reactive behavior, we are blocking our Desire to Receive for the Self Alone. Jacob also gives us the power to balance our acts of mercy and judgment toward other people in our lives.

Tiferet **that becomes** *Da'at* (14 words).

אַתָּה Ata קָדוֹשׁ kadosh וְשִׁמְךָ veshimcha קָדוֹשׁ kadosh ר"ת = אור, רז, אין סוף

וּקְדוֹשִׁים ukdoshim בְּכָל־ bechol ב"ן, לכב יוֹם yom ע"ה נגד, מזבוח, זן, אל יהוה

יְהַלְלוּךָ yehalelucha סֶלָה sela:

בָּרוּךְ baruch אַתָּה Ata יְהֹוָה(אדני)(יאהדה)(יאהדונהי) Adonai

(On *Rosh Chodesh Menachem Av* – Leo, meditate on the Holy Name: מצפצ**)**

הָאֵל haEl הַקָּדוֹשׁ hakadosh יי"פ מ"ה (יוד הא ואו הא):יא"י (מילוי דס"ג) לאה ;

Meditate here on the Name: יאהדונהי, as it can help to remove anger.

"(Center) *Holy,* (Left) *Holy,* (Right) *Holy, is the Lord of Hosts, the entire world is filled with His glory."* (Isaiah 6:3) *The Offanim and all the Holy Beasts, who stand opposite them, give praise and say: "Blessed is the glory of the Lord from His Place." (Ezekiel 3:12) And in Your Holy Words, it is written as follows: "The Lord, your God, shall reign forever, for each and for every generation. Zion, praise the Lord!" (Psalms 146:10)*

THE THIRD BLESSING

You are holy, and Your Name is holy, and the Holy Ones praise You every day, for you are God, the Holy King Selah. Blessed are You, Lord, the Holy God.

THE FOURTH BLESSING

The middle of the *Musaf Amidah* is our additional connection to *Rosh Chodesh*. In this, the Ari's version of the *Musaf*, the first three letters of the first three words form the name of Rachel רחל. Rachel the Matriarch is the physical expression of *Malchut*, our physical universe. *Malchut*, like the moon, has no Light of its own, so this connection via the power of Rachel helps to pour Light into the empty vessel of *Malchut*.

ר"ת רחל le'amcha לְעַמְּךָ chodashim וְחֳדָשִׁים rashei רָאשֵׁי

Initial of *Rachel* (רחל) which She is elevated from *Beriah* to *Atzilut*.

toldotam תּוֹלְדוֹתָם יה אדני lechol לְכָל kapara כַּפָּרָה zeman זְמַן natata נָתַתָּ

bihyotam בִּהְיוֹתָם ס"ג מ"ה ב"ן lefanecha לְפָנֶיךָ makrivim מַקְרִיבִים

zivchei זִבְחֵי מהש ע"ה, ע"ב בריבוע וקס"א ע"א, אל שדי ע"ה ratzon רָצוֹן use'ir וּשְׂעִיר

chatat וְחַטַּאת lechaper לְכַפֵּר ba'adam בַּעֲדָם zikaron זִכָּרוֹן ע"ב קס"א ונע"ב miyad בְּיָד

lechulam לְכֻלָּם haya הָיָה יהה teshu'at תְּשׁוּעַת nafsham נַפְשָׁם miyad בְּיָד

sone שׂוֹנֵא נגד, זך, אל יהוה mizbe'ach מִזְבֵּחַ chadash וְחָדָשׁ י"ב הויות, קס"א קנ"א

beTziyon בְּצִיּוֹן יוסף, ו הויות, קנאה tachin תָּכִין ve'olat וְעוֹלַת אבג יתץ, ושר

rosh רֹאשׁ ריבוע אלהים ואלהים דיודין ע"ה chodesh וְחָדָשׁ י"ב הויות, קס"א קנ"א ;

izim עִזִּים use'ir וּשְׂעִיר alav עָלָיו na'ale נַעֲלֶה ראש וזרע ע"ה = שׁין דלת יוד

na'ase נַעֲשֶׂה מהש ע"ה, ע"ב בריבוע וקס"א ע"א, אל שדי ע"ה veratzon בְּרָצוֹן

nismach נִשְׂמַח hamikdash הַמִּקְדָּשׁ ב"פ ראה bet בֵּית uva'avodat וּבַעֲבוֹדַת

kulanu כֻּלָּנוּ פוי, אל אדני avdach עַבְדָּךְ David דָּוִד veshirei וְשִׁירֵי

lifnei לְפָנֵי ha'amurim הָאֲמוּרִים be'irach בְּעִירָךְ nishma נִשְׁמַע

lahem לָהֶם tavi תָּבִיא olam עוֹלָם ahavat אַהֲבַת mizbachach מִזְבְּחֶךָ

uvrit וּבְרִית avot אָבוֹת labanim לַבָּנִים tizkor תִּזְכּוֹר׃

THE FOURTH BLESSING

You have given the beginning of new moons to Your People. A time of atonement for all their generations, when they would offer before You sacrifices of favor and a goat for a sin-offering, to atone for them. It served as a reminder for them of the deliverance of their lives from the hands of their enemy. You shall establish a new Altar in Zion, that we may offer the burnt-offering of the new moon upon it. And may we prepare a he-goat with favor, and may we all rejoice in the service of the Temple. And the songs of David, Your servant, may we hear in Your City, the ones that are recited before Your Altar. Bring to them eternal love, and remember the Covenant of the Fathers for the children.

YEHI RATZON

יְהִי yehi רָצוֹן ratzon

אֱלֹהֵינוּ Elohenu יְהוָֹואדנילהי Adonai מִלְּפָנֶיךָ milfanecha

שֶׁתַּעֲלֵנוּ sheta'alenu אֲבוֹתֵינוּ avotenu וֵאלֹהֵי velohei

בְּשִׂמְחָה vesimcha לְאַרְצֵנוּ le'artzenu וְתִטָּעֵנוּ vetita'enu בִּגְבוּלֵנוּ bigvulenu

וְשָׁם vesham נַעֲשֶׂה na'ase לְפָנֶיךָ lefanecha

אֶת et קָרְבְּנוֹת karbenot וְחוֹבוֹתֵינוּ chovotenu תְּמִידִים temidim

כְּסִדְרָם kesidram וּמוּסָפִים umusafim כְּהִלְכָתָם kehilchatam אֶת et

מוּסְפֵי musfei יוֹם yom רֹאשׁ rosh

וְחֹדֶשׁ chodesh הַזֶּה haze

נַעֲשֶׂה na'ase וְנַקְרִיב venakriv לְפָנֶיךָ lefanecha בְּאַהֲבָה be'ahava

רְצוֹנֶךָ kimitzvat כְּמִצְוַת retzonach כְּמוֹ kemo שֶׁכָּתַבְתָּ shekatavta

עָלֵינוּ alenu בְּתוֹרָתֶךָ betoratach עַל al יְדֵי yedei מֹשֶׁה Moshe

עַבְדֶּךָ avdach כָּאָמוּר ka'amur

THE SACRIFICES

This prayer speaks of the sacrifices that were brought to the Temple to generate Light. In the absence of the Temple, the Aramaic letters that make up this prayer are the DNA forces behind the original sacrifices and act as a surrogate to help us tap the original power of the Temple.

וּבְרָאשֵׁי uvrashei וְחָדְשֵׁיכֶם chadshechem תַּקְרִיבוּ takrivu עֹלָה ola

לַיהוה ladonai פָּרִים parim בְּנֵי benei בָקָר vakar

שְׁנַיִם shenayim וְאַיִל ve'ayil אֶחָד echad כְּבָשִׂים kevasim

בְּנֵי benei שָׁנָה shana שִׁבְעָה shiv'a תְּמִימִם temimim

YEHI RATZON

May it be pleasing before You, Lord, our God and God of our fathers, that You may bring us up to Your Land with joy, and establish us within our borders, and there, we shall prepare before You our obligatory offerings: the Tamid-offerings in this order, and the Musaf offerings in their prescribed manner. The Musaf of this new moon, we shall prepare and offer before You with love, and according to the commandment of Your will as You wrote for us in Your Torah, through Moses, Your servant, and as it was stated:

THE SACRIFICES

*"And on your new moons, you shall offer a burnt-offering to the Lord:
two young bulls and one ram, seven one-year-old unblemished lambs,*

ראה.   kimdubar כְּמֻדְבָּר   veniskehem וְנִסְכֵּיהֶם   uminchatam וּמִנְחָתָם

esronim עֶשְׂרֹנִים   ushnei וּשְׁנֵי   lapar לַפָּר   esronim עֶשְׂרֹנִים   shelosha שְׁלֹשָׁה

veyayin וְיָיִן   lakeves לַכֶּבֶשׂ   ve'isaron וְעִשָּׂרוֹן   la'ayil לָאַיִל.

vesa'ir וְעָעִיר   kenisko כְּנִסְכּוֹ   ע' (כנגד ע' אומות העולם התלויים בסמאל, מוכ, י"פ האא

lechaper לְכַפֵּר   ushnei וּשְׁנֵי   temidim תְּמִידִים   kehilchatam כְּהִלְכָתָם:

ELOHENU

In this section, we find 12 specific blessings. These 12 blessings encapsulate the 12 months of the year into this one month.

avotenu אֲבוֹתֵינוּ   ילה ; מילוי דע"ב, דמב ; ילה   velohei וֵאלֹהֵי   ילה Elohenu אֱלֹהֵינוּ

hachodesh הַחֹדֶשׁ   et אֶת   alenu עָלֵינוּ   י"ב הויות, קס"א קנ"א   chadesh חַדֵּשׁ

velivracha וְלִבְרָכָה   אבא letova לְטוֹבָה   והו haze הַזֶּה   י"ב הויות, קס"א קנ"א

ulnechama וּלְנֶחָמָה   lishu'a לִישׁוּעָה   ulsimcha וּלְשִׂמְחָה   lesason לְשָׂשׂוֹן

lechayim לְחַיִּים   אהיה אהיה יהוה, בינה ע"ה   ulchalkala וּלְכַלְכָּלָה   lefarnasa לְפַרְנָסָה

chet חֵטְא   וְ limchilat לִמְחִילַת   ulshalom וּלְשָׁלוֹם   tovim טוֹבִים

(pesha פֶּשַׁע) ulchaparat וּלְכַפָּרַת :on leap year add)   avon עָוֹן   velislichat וְלִסְלִיחַת

chodesh חֹדֶשׁ   rosh רֹאשׁ   ריבוע אלהים ואלהים דיודין ע"ה   יי veyih'ye וְיִהְיֶה

vaketz מנק וְקֵץ   sof סוֹף   והו haze הַזֶּה   י"ב הויות, קס"א קנ"א ; ראש וזדע ע"ה = שׁין דלת יוד

lechol לְכָל   יה אדני צָרוֹתֵינוּ tzarotenu   techila תְּחִלָּה וְרֹאשׁ varosh ריבוע אלהים

ve'amcha בְּעַמְּךָ   ki כִּי   nafshenu נַפְשֵׁנוּ lefidyon לְפִדְיוֹן   ואלהים דיודין ע"ה

bacharta בָּחַרְתָּ   ha'umot הָאֻמּוֹת   יל mikol מִכָּל   Yisrael יִשְׂרָאֵל

kavata קָבַעְתָּ   lahem לָהֶם   chodashim וְחֳדָשִׁים   rashei רָאשֵׁי   vechukei וְחֻקֵּי

---

with their meal-offerings and their libations as was stated: three-tenths for each bull and two-tenths for each ram, and one-tenth for each lamb, and wine according to its libation, and a goat for atonement, and two Tamid-offerings, according to their prescribed law." (Numbers 28:11)

ELOHENU

Our God and God of our forefathers, renew this month for us for good and for blessing, for joy and for happiness, for salvation and for consolation, for livelihood and for sustenance, for good life and for peace, for forgiveness of transgression and for pardon of iniquity. (During a leap year add: and for atonement of sin). And may the beginning of this new moon be the last and the end of all our troubles, and the beginning and the outset of the redemption of our lives. Because You have chosen Your People, Israel, rom among all the nations, and the statutes of the new moon, You have established for them.

Adonai יְ‎הֹ‎וָ‎ה‏ Ata אַתָּה baruch בָּרוּךְ

MEDITATION OF THE MONTH

The following blessing is perhaps our most important connection on *Rosh Chodesh*. On the chart below, we have different sequences of the Holy Tetragrammaton corresponding to each month of the year. By scanning the appropriate sequence, we draw Light for the entire month to our entire body as well as to a specific area of our body. We also meditate on two specific letters of the month (see chart) that denote the respective planet and zodiac sign. This meditation helps us rise above astrological influences, giving us control over our destiny.

It is known from the writings of the Ari that: on every *Rosh Chodesh* at the end of the middle blessing of *Musaf*, you should meditate on the Tetragrammatron combination (26) that controls the particular month. This explains what the sages said: "Why the Children of Israel pray and are not answered. Because they do not know how to pray with the Name", as it is written: "I will extol him because he **knows** My Name." This statement is confusing but with the above explanation it is understood – it speaks about the one who does not know the intention of the Name that controls the month (12 times 26 has the same numerical value for the word "month" חֹדֶשׁ - And these combinations are as in *Hakdamat Tikunei HaZohar*). So in order for our prayers to be answered, meditate as follow:

Month-Zodiac / Planet	Sefirah	Body Part	Sequence
ה-Nissan-Aries / ד-Mars	Chesed	גולגלתא דנוקבא *Nukva's Skull*	יְשַׂמְּחוּ הַשָּׁמַיִם וְתָגֵל הָאָרֶץ אֲהָיָה יְהֹוָה
ו-Iyar-Taurus / פ-Venus	Gevurah	אזן ימין דנוקבא *Nukva's Right Ear*	יִתְהַלֵּל הַמִּתְהַלֵּל הַשֵׂכֵּל וְיָדֹעַ אֲהֹוָי יְהֹוָ
ז-Sivan-Gemini / ר-Mercury	Tiferet	אזן שמאל דנוקבא *Nukva's Left Ear*	לְדוֹדָתָיו וְלְצֵלַע הַמִּשְׁכָּן הַשֵּׁנִית אִיְהָה יֹוהָה
ח-Tammuz-Cancer / ת-Moon	Netzach	עין ימין דנוקבא *Nukva's Right Eye*	זֶה אֵינֶנּוּ שֹׁוֶה לֹי לֹי הְיָהֹא הֱיֶהִ
ט-Av-Leo / כ-Sun	Hod	עין שמאל דנוקבא *Nukva's Left Eye*	הִסַּכֵּת וּשְׁמַע יִשְׂרָאֵל הַיּוֹם הִיאָה הֹוִיָה
י-Elul-Virgo / ר-Mercury	Yesod	חוטמא דנוקבא *Nukva's Nose*	וּצְדָקָה תִּהְיֶה לָנוּ כָּל הֹהִיָא הֹהָוְי
כ-Tishrei-Libra / פ-Venus	Chesed	גולגלתא דז"א *Z"A's Skull*	וַיִּרְאוּ אוֹתָהּ שָׂרֵי פַרְעֹה יְהָאָה וְהָיֹה
ל-Cheshvan-Scorpio / ד-Mars	Gevurah	אזן ימין דז"א *Z"A's Right Ear*	וְדָבַשׁ הַיּוֹם הַזֶּה לְיהוָה יְהָוָא וְהֹוְי
מ-Kislev-Sagittarius / ג-Jupiter	Tiferet	אזן שמאל דז"א *Z"A's Left Ear*	וַיִּרָא יוֹעֵב הָאָרֶץ הַכְּנַעֲנִי יַאֲהֹה וְיֹהָה
נ-Tevet-Capricorn / ב-Saturn	Netzach	עין ימין דז"א *Z"A's Right Eye*	לַיהֹוֹה אַתִּי וּנְרוֹמְמָה שְׁמוֹ הָאֲהִי הָאֲהִי הָיֹהִן
ס-Shevat-Aquarius / ב-Saturn	Hod	עין שמאל דז"א *Z"A's Left Eye*	הֹאמֶר לְמֵירֹנוּ וְהָיָה הוּא הָאֵיָה הָיֹה
ק-Adar-Pisces / ג-Jupiter	Yesod	חוטמא דז"א *Z"A's Nose*	עִירֹה וְלַשׂוֹרֵקָה בְּנִי אֲתֹנוֹ הָהָאִי הָהֹאִי הֹהִין

On *Rosh Chodesh Adar*, you should meditate on all 12 sequences of יהוה and אהיה together. **On a leap year,** you should meditate on *Adar 1*, for the sequence that is relevant for *Adar*, and on second *Adar 2*, on all the sequences together.

chodashim חֳדָשִׁים verashei וְרָאשֵׁי Yisrael יִשְׂרָאֵל mekadesh מְקַדֵּשׁ

Blessed are You, Lord, Who sanctifies Israel and the beginning of the new moons.

THE FINAL THREE BLESSINGS

Through the merit of Moses, Aaron and Joseph, who are our channels for the final three blessings, we are able to bring down all the spiritual energy that we aroused with our prayers and blessings.

THE FIFTH BLESSING

During this blessing, referring to Moses, we should always meditate to try to know exactly what God wants from us in our life, as signified by the phrase, "Let it be the will of God." We ask God to guide us toward the work we came to Earth to do. The Creator cannot just accept the work that we want to do; we must carry out the work we were destined to do.

Netzach

Meditate for the Supernal Desire (*Keter*) that is called *metzach haratzon* (the Forehead of the Desire).

רְצֵה retze אלף למד הה יוד מם

Meditate here to transform misfortune and tragedy (צרה) into desire and acceptance (רצה).

(On *Rosh Chodesh Menachem Av* – Leo, meditate here on these Holy Names:

אלהים דההין ארני, שיז ע"ה, טדהד כוזו מצפצ - with these Names we transform צרה into רצה).

Yisrael יִשְׂרָאֵל	be'amecha בְּעַמְּךָ	Elohenu אֱלֹהֵינוּ	Adonai יְהֹוָאדֹנָיאהדונהי
ha'avoda הָעֲבוֹדָה	vehashev וְהָשֵׁב	she'e שְׁעֵה	velitfilatam וְלִתְפִלָּתָם
Yisrael יִשְׂרָאֵל	ve'ishei וְאִשֵּׁי	betecha בֵּיתֶךָ	lidvir לִדְבִיר
be'ahava בְּאַהֲבָה	mehera מְהֵרָה	utfilatam וּתְפִלָּתָם	
beratzon בְּרָצוֹן	tekabel תְּקַבֵּל		
leratzon לְרָצוֹן	ut'hi וּתְהִי		
amecha עַמְּךָ	Yisrael יִשְׂרָאֵל	avodat עֲבוֹדַת	tamid תָּמִיד
tachpotz תַּחְפֹּץ	harabim הָרַבִּים	verachamecha בְּרַחֲמֶיךָ	veAta וְאַתָּה
enenu עֵינֵינוּ	vetechezena וְתֶחֱזֶינָה	vetirtzenu וְתִרְצֵנוּ	banu בָּנוּ
berachamim בְּרַחֲמִים	leTziyon לְצִיּוֹן	beshuvcha בְּשׁוּבְךָ	
Adonai יְהֹוָאדֹנָיאהדונהי	Ata אַתָּה	baruch בָּרוּךְ	
leTziyon לְצִיּוֹן	shechinato שְׁכִינָתוֹ	hamachazir הַמַּחֲזִיר	

THE FINAL THREE BLESSINGS - THE FIFTH BLESSING

Find favor, Lord, our God, in Your People, Israel, and turn to their prayer.
Restore the service to the inner sanctuary of Your Temple. Accept the offerings of Israel and their prayer with favor, speedily, and with love. May the service of Your People Israel always be favorable to You.
And You in Your great compassion take delight in us and are pleased with us. May our eyes witness Your return to Zion with compassion. Blessed are You, Lord, Who returns His Shechinah to Zion.

THE SIXTH BLESSING

This blessing is our thank you. Kabbalistically, the biggest 'thank you' we can give the Creator is to do exactly what we are supposed to do in terms of our spiritual work.

Hod

Bow your entire body at 'modim' and straighten up at 'Adonai'.

מוֹדִים modim מאה ברכות עתיקן דוד לאמרים כל יום anachnu אֲנַחְנוּ lach לָךְ

שֶׁאַתָּה sheAta הוּא hu יְהֹוָה Adonai (וג) אֱלֹהֵינוּ Elohenu

וֵאלֹהֵי velohei לכב ; מילוי ע״ב, דמב ; אֲבוֹתֵינוּ avotenu לְעוֹלָם le'olam

וָעֶד va'ed ריבוע ס״ג וי׳ אותיות דס״ג צוּרֵנוּ tzurenu צוּר tzur

וּמָגֵן umagen ג״פ אל (ייא״י מילוי דס״ג) ; ר״ת מיכאל גבריאל נוריאל חַיֵּינוּ chayenu

אַתָּה Ata הוּא hu לְדֹר ledor וָדֹר vador רי״ו node נוֹדֶה yish'enu יִשְׁעֵנוּ

וּנְסַפֵּר unsaper תְּהִלָּתֶךָ tehilatecha עַל al chayenu וַיֵּינוּ lecha לְךָ

הַמְּסוּרִים hamesurim בְּיָדֶךָ beyadecha וְעַל ve'al נִשְׁמוֹתֵינוּ nishmotenu

הַפְּקוּדוֹת hapekudot לָךְ lach וְעַל ve'al נִסֶּיךָ nisecha shebechol שֶׁבְּכָל

עִמָּנוּ imanu ריבוע ס״ג, קס״א ע״ה וד׳ אותיות yom יוֹם ע״ה נגד, מזבח, זן, אל יהוה לכב, ב״ן

וְעַל ve'al נִפְלְאוֹתֶיךָ nifle'otecha וְטוֹבוֹתֶיךָ vetovotecha שֶׁבְּכָל shebechol

et עֵת לכב ,ב״ן עֶרֶב erev וָבֹקֶר vavoker וְצָהֳרַיִם vetzahorayim הַטּוֹב hatov

כִּי ki וְהוּ לֹא lo כָלוּ chalu רַחֲמֶיךָ rachamecha הַמְרַחֵם hamerachem

כִּי ki לֹא lo אברהם, וז״פ אל, רי״ו ול״ב נתיבות החכמה, רמ״ח (אברים), עסמ״ב וט״ז אותיות פשוטות

וַחֲסָדֶיךָ chasadecha כִּי ki מֵעוֹלָם me'olam קִוִּינוּ kivinu לָךְ lach תַּמּוּ tamu

---

THE SIXTH BLESSING

We give thanks to You, for it is You, Lord, Who is our God and God of our forefathers, forever and for all eternity. You are our Rock, the Rock of our lives, and the Shield of our salvation. From one generation to another, we shall give thanks to You and we shall tell of Your praise. For our lives that are entrusted in Your hands, for our souls that are in Your care, for Your miracles that are with us every day, and for Your wonders and Your favors that are with us at all times: evening, morning and afternoon. You are the good One, for Your compassion has never ceased. You are the compassionate One, for Your kindness has never ended, for we have always placed our hope in You.

MODIM DERABANAN

This prayer is recited by the congregation in the repetition when the chazan says "modim."

In this section there are 44 words which is the same numerical value as the Name:
רִבּוּעַ אֶהְיֶה (א אה אהי אהיה).

מוֹדִים modim   מֵאָה בְּרָכוֹת שֶׁתִּיקֵן דָּוִד כָּל יוֹם לְאָמְרָם   אֲנַֽחְנוּ anachnu   לָךְ lach

שֶׁאַתָּה sheAta   הוּא hu   יְהֹוָה Adonai   אֱלֹהֵֽינוּ Elohenu   ילה

וֵאלֹהֵי velohei   לכב;   מילוי ע"ב, דמב;   ילה;   אֲבוֹתֵֽינוּ avotenu

אֱלֹהֵי Elohei   מילוי ע"ב, דמב; ילה   כָּל chol   ילי בָּשָׂר basar   יוֹצְרֵֽנוּ yotzrenu

יוֹצֵר yotzer   בְּרֵאשִׁית bereshit   בְּרָכוֹת berachot   וְהוֹדָאוֹת vehoda'ot

לְשִׁמְךָ leshimcha   הַגָּדוֹל hagadol   לְהוּ; עם ד' אותיות = מבה, יזל, אום

וְהַקָּדוֹשׁ vehakadosh   עַל al   שֶׁהֶחֱיִיתָֽנוּ shehecheyitanu   וְקִיַּמְתָּֽנוּ vekiyamtanu

כֵּן ken   תְּחַיֵּֽנוּ techayenu   וּתְחָנֵּֽנוּ utchonenu   וְתֶאֱסוֹף vete'esof

גָּלֻיוֹתֵֽינוּ galuyoteinu   לְחַצְרוֹת lechatzrot   קָדְשֶֽׁךָ kodshecha   לִשְׁמֹר lishmor

חֻקֶּֽיךָ chukecha   וְלַעֲשׂוֹת vela'asot   רְצוֹנֶֽךָ retzoncha   וּלְעָבְדְּךָ ul'ovdecha

שֶׁאֲנַֽחְנוּ she'anachnu   עַל al   שָׁלֵם shalem   בֵּלְבָב belevav   she'anachnu

מוֹדִים modim   לָךְ lach   בָּרוּךְ baruch   אֵל El   הַהוֹדָאוֹת hahoda'ot

---

FOR CHANUKAH

Chanukah generates an added dimension of the energy of miracles. This blessing helps us harness this energy, thereby drawing miracles into our lives whenever they are truly needed.

וְעַל ve'al   הַנִּסִּים hanisim   וְעַל ve'al   הַפֻּרְקָן hapurkan

וְעַל ve'al   הַגְּבוּרוֹת hagevurot   וְעַל ve'al   הַתְּשׁוּעוֹת hateshu'ot

וְעַל ve'al   הַנִּפְלָאוֹת hanifla'ot   וְעַל ve'al   הַנֶּחָמוֹת hanechamot

שֶׁעָשִׂיתָ she'asita   לַאֲבוֹתֵֽינוּ la'avotenu   בַּיָּמִים bayamim   הָהֵם hahem

בַּזְּמַן bazeman   הַזֶּה haze

MODIM DERABANAN

*We give thanks to You, for it is You the Lord,
our God and God of our forefathers, the God of all flesh, our Maker and the Former of all Creation. Blessings and thanks to Your great and Holy Name for giving us life and for preserving us. So may You continue to give us life, be gracious to us, and gather our exiles to the courtyards of Your Sanctuary, so that we may keep Your laws, fulfill Your will, and serve You wholeheartedly. For this, we thank You. Bless the God of thanksgiving.*

FOR CHANUKAH

*And also for the miracles, deliverance, the mighty acts, the salvation, wonders,
and comforting deeds that You performed for our forefathers, in those days and at this time.*

MUSAF FOR ROSH CHODESH

473

FOR CHANUKAH:

בִּימֵי bimei מַתִּתְיָה Matitya בֶּן ven יוֹחָנָן Yochanan כֹּהֵן kohen גָּדוֹל gadol וַחַשְׁמוֹנַאי Chashmonai וּבָנָיו uvanav כְּשֶׁעָמְדָה keshe'amda מַלְכוּת malchut יָוָן Yavan הָרְשָׁעָה harsha'a עַל al עַמְּךָ amecha יִשְׂרָאֵל Yisrael לְשַׁכְּחָם leshakecham תּוֹרָתֶךָ toratach וּלְהַעֲבִירָם ulha'aviram מֵחֻקֵּי mechukei רְצוֹנֶךָ retzonach וְאַתָּה veAta בְּרַחֲמֶיךָ verachamecha הָרַבִּים harabim עָמַדְתָּ amadeta לָהֶם lahem בְּעֵת be'et צָרָתָם tzaratam רַבְתָּ ravta אֶת et רִיבָם rivam דַּנְתָּ danta אֶת et דִּינָם dinam נָקַמְתָּ nakamta אֶת et נִקְמָתָם nikmatam מָסַרְתָּ masarta גִּבּוֹרִים giborim בְּיַד beyad וְחַלָּשִׁים chalashim וְרַבִּים verabim בְּיַד beyad מְעַטִּים me'atim וּרְשָׁעִים ursha'im בְּיַד beyad צַדִּיקִים tzadikim וּטְמֵאִים utme'im בְּיַד beyad טְהוֹרִים tehorim וְזֵדִים vezedim בְּיַד beyad עוֹסְקֵי oskei תוֹרָתֶךָ toratecha לְךָ lecha עָשִׂיתָ asita שֵׁם shem גָּדוֹל gadol וְקָדוֹשׁ vekadosh בְּעוֹלָמֶךָ be'olamach וּלְעַמְּךָ ul'amecha יִשְׂרָאֵל Yisrael עָשִׂיתָ asita תְשׁוּעָה teshu'a גְדוֹלָה gedola וּפֻרְקָן ufurkan כְּהַיּוֹם kehayom הַזֶּה haze וְאַחַר ve'achar כָּךְ kach בָּאוּ ba'u בָנֶיךָ vanecha לִדְבִיר lidvir בֵּיתֶךָ betecha וּפִנּוּ ufinu אֶת et הֵיכָלֶךָ hechalecha וְטִהֲרוּ vetiharu אֶת et מִקְדָּשֶׁךָ mikdashecha וְהִדְלִיקוּ vehidliku נֵרוֹת nerot בְּחַצְרוֹת bechatzrot קָדְשֶׁךָ kodshecha וְקָבְעוּ vekav'u שְׁמוֹנַת shemonat יְמֵי yemei חֲנֻכָּה Chanukah אֵלוּ elu בְּהַלֵּל behalel וּבְהוֹדָאָה uvhoda'a וְעָשִׂיתָ ve'asita עִמָּהֶם imahem נִסִּים nisim וְנִפְלָאוֹת venifla'ot וְנוֹדֶה venode לְשִׁמְךָ leshimcha הַגָּדוֹל hagadol סֶלָה sela:

FOR CHANUKAH

In the days of Mattatiyahu, the son of Yochanan, the High Priest, the Hasmonean, and his sons, when the evil Greek Empire rose up against Your Nation, Israel, to force them to forget Your Torah and to force them away from the laws of Your desire, You, with Your compassion, stood up for them in their time of trouble. You fought their battles, sought justice for them, avenged them, and delivered the strong into the hands of the weak, the many into the hands of the few, the wicked into the hands of the righteous, the defiled into the hands of the pure, and the tyrants into the hands of those who occupy themselves with Your Torah. For Yourself, You made a Holy Name in Your world, and for Your People, Israel, You carried out a great salvation and deliverance on this day. Then Your Children came into the Sanctuary of Your House, they cleansed Your Palace, they purified Your Temple, they lit candles in the courtyards of Your Holy Domain, and they established these eight days of Chanukah for praise and thanksgiving. And You performed for them miracles and wonders. For that, we are grateful to Your Great Name. Selah

וְעַל ve'al — כֻּלָּם kulam — יִתְבָּרַךְ yitbarach — וְיִתְרוֹמֵם veyitromam

שִׁמְךָ shimcha — קמ״ג קנ״א קס״א ע״ה — תָּמִיד tamid — וְיִתְנַשֵּׂא veyitnase

וָעֶד va'ed — דס״ג וי׳ אותיות — רִבּוּע ס״ג — לְעוֹלָם le'olam — מַלְכֵּנוּ malkenu

סֶלָה sela — יוֹדוּךָ yoducha — אהיה אהיה יהוה, בינה ע״ה — הַחַיִּים hachayim — יל׳ — וְכָל vechol

אֵת־ et — יהוה רִבּוּע יהוה מ״ה — וִיבָרְכוּ vivarchu — וִיהַלְלוּ vihalelu

בֶּאֱמֶת be'emet — שִׁמְךָ shimcha — הַגָּדוֹל hagadol — לָהֶם ; עם ד' אותיות = מבה, יל, אום

כִּי טוֹב ki tov — לְעוֹלָם le'olam — רִבּוּע ס״ג וי׳ אותיות דס״ג — אהיה פעמים אהיה, ז״פ ס״ג, והו ;

יְשׁוּעָתֵנוּ yeshu'atenu — הָאֵל haEl — לאה ; יא״י (מילוי דס״ג) — כי טוב = יהוה אהיה, אום, מבה, יל׳

הַטּוֹב hatov — סֶלָה sela — הָאֵל haEl — ve'ezratenu וְעֶזְרָתֵנוּ — לאה ; יא״י (מילוי דס״ג) — והו

Bend your knees at 'baruch', bow at 'Ata' and straighten up at 'Adonai'.

הַטּוֹב hatov — (הִי) — יְהֹוָהאדנייאהדונהי Adonai — אַתָּה Ata — בָּרוּךְ baruch — והו

לְהוֹדוֹת lehodot — נָאֶה na'e — וּלְךָ ulcha — שִׁמְךָ shimcha — ס״ת כהת, משיח בן דוד ע״ה

For the blessing of the Kohanim – see pg. 218.

THE FINAL BLESSING

We are emanating the energy of peace to the entire world. We also make it our intent to use our mouths only for good. Kabbalistically, the power of words and speech is unimaginable. We hope to use that power wisely, which is perhaps one of the most difficult tasks we have to carry out.

Yesod

שָׂים sim — שָׁלוֹם shalom

(On *Rosh Chodesh Menachem Av* – Leo, meditate here on these Holy Names:
עִין ראשׁוֹנה (ע״ה = טדהד כוזו מצפצ) ממתקת את העין העניה (= אלהים דההין אדני) ;
וכן שים שלום ע״ה = ו' העצמות (טדהד כוזו מצפצ אלהים אדני יהוה) אדני טדהד כוזו מצפצ אלהים ואלהים דההין)

טוֹבָה tova — אבא — וּבְרָכָה uvracha — וְחַיִּים chayim — אהיה אהיה יהוה, בינה ע״ה

חֵן chen — מילוי דמ״ה — בריבוע, מזוי — וָחֶסֶד vachesed — ע״ב, רִבּוּע יהוה

צְדָקָה tzedaka — ע״ה — רִבּוּע — אלהים — וְרַחֲמִים verachamim

---

And for all those things, may Your Name be always blessed, exalted and exulted, our King, forever and ever, and all the living shall thank You, Selah. And they shall praise and bless Your great Name, sincerely and forever, for It is good, the God of our salvation and our help, Selah, the good God. Blessed are You, Lord, whose Name is good and to You it is befitting to give thanks.

THE FINAL BLESSING

Place peace, goodness, blessing, life, grace, kindness, righteousness, and mercy,

עָלֵינוּ alenu וְעַל־ ve'al כָּל־ kol ; יִלי עַמם ; יִשְׂרָאֵל Yisrael עַמֶּךָ amecha

וּבָרְכֵנוּ uvarchenu אָבִינוּ avinu כֻּלָּנוּ kulanu כְּאֶחָד ke'echad אהבה, דאגה

פָּנֶיךָ panecha ס״ג מ״ה ב״ן ki כִּי be'or בְּאוֹר ve'or רו, א״ס רו, א״ס

נָתַתָּ natata לָנוּ lanu אלהים, אהיה אהיה אדני ב״ן ס״ג מ״ה panecha פָּנֶיךָ

אֱלֹהֵינוּ Elohenu Adonai יְהֹוֵאדֹנָיאהדֹנָהֵ ילה torah תּוֹרָה vechayim וְחַיִּים

אַהֲבָה ahava אֹהד, דאגה אהיה יהוה, בינה ע״ה vachesed וָחֶסֶד ע״ב, ריבוע יהוה

צְדָקָה tzedaka ע״ה ריבוע אלהים ע״ה verachamim וְרַחֲמִים beracha בְּרָכָה

וְשָׁלוֹם veshalom ותו vetov וְטוֹב be'enecha בְּעֵינֶיךָ ע״ה קס״א ; ריבוע מ״ה

לְבָרְכֵנוּ levarchenu וּלְבָרֵךְ ulvarech אֶת et כָּל־ kol יִלי עַמְּךָ amecha

יִשְׂרָאֵל Yisrael בְּרוֹב־ berov י״פ אהיה oz עֹז veshalom וְשָׁלוֹם

בָּרוּךְ baruch אַתָּה Ata יְהֹוִוּהֹוֵאֲדֹנָיאהדֹנָהֵ Adonai

הַמְבָרֵךְ hamevarech אֶת et עַמּוֹ amo יִשְׂרָאֵל Yisrael

בַּשָׁלוֹם bashalom יב״ק = אלהים (אילהההויהם) ר״ת = אלהים אָמֵן amen יאהדונהי

YIH'YU LERATZON

There are 42 letters in the verse in the secret of *Ana Beko'ach*.

יִהְיוּ yih'yu אל (ייא״י מולוי דס״ג) מהשע ע״ה, ע״ב ברריבוע וקס״א ע״ה, אל שדי ע״ה leratzon לְרָצוֹן

אִמְרֵי imrei fi פִי ר״ת אָלֶף = אלף למד שין דלת יוד ע״ה vehegyon וְהֶגְיוֹן libi לִבִּי

לְפָנֶיךָ lefanecha ס״ג מ״ה ב״ן Adonai יְהֹוֵאֲדֹנָיאהדֹנָהֵ tzuri צוּרִי vego'ali וְגֹאֲלִי

---

upon us and upon all of Israel, Your People. Bless us all as one, our Father, with the Light of Your Countenance, because it is with the Light of Your Countenance that You, Lord, our God, have given us Torah and life, love and kindness, righteousness and mercy, blessing and peace. May it be good in Your Eyes to bless us and to bless Your entire Nation, Israel, with abundant power and with peace. Blessed are You, Lord Who blesses His nation, Israel, with peace, Amen.

YIH'YU LERATZON

"May the utterances of my mouth and the thoughts of my heart find favor before You, Lord, my Rock and my Redeemer." (Psalms 19:15)

ELOHAI NETZOR

אֱלֹהַי Elohai מילוי ע״ב, דמב ; יל״ה נְצוֹר netzor לְשׁוֹנִי leshoni מֵרָע mera•

וְשִׂפְתוֹתַי vesiftotai מִדַּבֵּר midaber ראה מִרְמָה mirma• וְלִמְקַלְלַי velimkalelai

נַפְשִׁי nafshi תִדֹּם tidom• וְנַפְשִׁי venafshi כֶּעָפָר ke'afar

לַכֹּל lakol יה אדני תִּהְיֶה tih'ye• פְּתַח petach לִבִּי libi בְּתוֹרָתֶךָ betoratecha•

וְאַחֲרֵי ve'acharei מִצְוֹתֶיךָ mitzvotecha תִּרְדּוֹף tirdof נַפְשִׁי nafshi•

וְכָל־ vechol הַקָּמִים hakamim עָלַי alai לְרָעָה lera'a מְהֵרָה mehera•

הָפֵר hafer עֲצָתָם atzatam וְקַלְקֵל vekalkel מַחְשְׁבוֹתָם machshevotam•

עֲשֵׂה ase לְמַעַן lema'an שְׁמֶךָ shemach• עֲשֵׂה ase לְמַעַן lema'an

יְמִינֶךָ yeminach• עֲשֵׂה ase לְמַעַן lema'an תּוֹרָתֶךָ toratach• עֲשֵׂה ase

לְמַעַן lema'an קְדֻשָּׁתֶךָ kedushatach• ר״ת הפסוק = מ״ה יהוה

לְמַעַן lema'an יְחָלְצוּן yechaltzun יְדִידֶיךָ yedidecha ר״ת ילי הוֹשִׁיעָה hoshi'a יהוה וש״ע נהורין

יְמִינְךָ yemincha וַעֲנֵנִי va'aneni (כתיב : וַעֲנֵנוּ) ר״ת אל (ייא״י מילוי דס״ג)

Before we recite the next verse ("*yih'yu leratzon*") we have an opportunity to strengthen our connection to our soul using our name. Each person has a verse in the *Torah* that connects to their name. Either their name is in the verse, or the first and last letters of the name correspond to the first or last letters of a verse. For example, the name Yehuda begins with a *Yud* and ends with a *Hei*. Before we end the *Amidah*, we state that our name will always be remembered when our soul leaves this world.

YIH'YU LERATZON (THE SECOND)
There are 42 letters in the verse in the secret *Ana Beko'ach*.

יִהְיוּ yih'yu (ייא״י מילוי דס״ג) אל לְרָצוֹן leratzon מהטע ע״ה, ע״ב ברביוע וקס״א ע״ה, אל שדי ע״ה

אִמְרֵי imrei פִּי fi ר״ת אָלֶף = אלף למד עיין דלת יוד ע״ה וְהֶגְיוֹן vehegyon לִבִּי libi

לְפָנֶיךָ lefanecha ס״ג מ״ה ב״ן יְהֹוָה Adonai צוּרִי tzuri וְגֹאֲלִי vego'ali

---

ELOHAI NETZOR
My God, guard my tongue from evil and my lips from speaking deceit. To those who curse me, let my spirit remain silent, and let my spirit be as dust for everyone. Open my heart to Your Torah and let my heart pursue Your commandments. All those who rise against me to do me harm, speedily nullify their plans and disturb their thoughts. Do so for the sake of Your Name. Do so for the sake of Your Right. Do so for the sake of Your Torah. Do so for the sake of Your Holiness, "So that Your loved ones may be saved. Redeem Your right and answer me." (Psalms 60:7)

YIH'YU LERATZON (THE SECOND)
"May the utterances of my mouth and the thoughts of my heart find favor before You, Lord, my Rock and my Redeemer." (Psalms 19:15)

OSE SHALOM

We now take three steps backward to draw the Light of the Upper Worlds into our life. We bow to the Left, Right, and Center, and we should meditate that by taking these three steps backwards, that the Holy Temple that was destroyed should be built once again.

You take three steps backward;

עוֹשֶׂה שָׁלוֹם ose shalom

Left

You turn to the left and say:

בִּמְרוֹמָיו bimromav ר"ת ע"ב, ריבוע יהוה

הוּא hu יַעֲשֶׂה verachamav בְּרַחֲמָיו ya'ase

Right

You turn to the right and say:

שָׁלוֹם shalom עָלֵינוּ alenu ר"ת ס"ע נהורין

Center

You face the center and say:

וְעַל ve'al כָּל kol יֵלי ; עמם עַמּוֹ amo יִשְׂרָאֵל Yisrael

וְאָמְרוּ ve'imru אָמֵן amen יאהדונהי:

יְהִי yehi רָצוֹן ratzon מהש ע"ה, ע"ב בריבוע וקס"א ע"ה, מהש ע"ה, אל שדי ע"ה

מִלְפָנֶיךָ milfanecha ס"ג מ"ה ב"ן יְהֹוָאדנּיאהדונהי Adonai אֱלֹהֵינוּ Elohenu ילה

וֵאלֹהֵי velohei ילה ; לכב מילוי ע"ב, דמב ; אֲבוֹתֵינוּ avotenu, שֶׁתִּבְנֶה shetivne

בֵּית bet ב"פ ראה הַמִּקְדָשׁ hamikdash בִּמְהֵרָה bimhera בְּיָמֵינוּ veyamenu

וְתֵן veten וְחֶלְקֵנוּ chelkenu בְּתוֹרָתֶךָ betoratach לַעֲשׂוֹת la'asot וְחֻקֵי chukei

רְצוֹנֶךָ retzonach וּלְעָבְדְךָ ul'ovdach פוי, אל אדני בְּלֵבָב belevav בוכו שָׁלֵם shalem.

You take three steps forward.

OSE SHALOM

He, Who makes peace in His high places, He,
in His compassion, shall make peace upon us And upon His entire nation, Israel, and you shall say, Amen.

May it be pleasing before You,
Lord, our God and God of our forefathers, that You shall rebuild the Temple speedily, in our days, and place our lot in Your Torah, so that we may fulfill the laws of Your desire and serve You wholeheartedly.

YEHI SHEM

יְהִי yehi שֵׁם shem יְהֹוָאֲדֹנָיאהדונהי Adonai ר״ת ריבוע ע״ב וריבוע ס״ג מְבֹרַךְ mevorach

יהוה מברך = רפ״ח (להעלות רפ״ח ניצוצות שנפלו לקליפה דמשם באים התחלואים) מֵעַתָּה me'ata

וְעַד־ ve'ad עוֹלָם olam יב״ל: מִמִּזְרַח mimizrach שֶׁמֶשׁ shemesh עַד־ ad

מְבוֹאוֹ mevo'o מְהֻלָּל mehulal שֵׁם shem יְהֹוָאֲדֹנָיאהדונהי Adonai: ר״ת קדוש

רָם ram גּוֹיִם goyim עמם ; יל״י כָּל־ kol עַל al יְהֹוָאֲדֹנָיאהדונהי Adonai עַל־ al

הַשָּׁמַיִם hashamayim ר״ת ; כוזו י״פ טל, י״פ וזעמל כְּבוֹדוֹ: kevodo

יְהֹוָאֲדֹנָיאהדונהי Adonai אֲדֹנֵינוּ adonenu בְּמָה־ ma מ״ה אַדִּיר adir הרי

שִׁמְךָ shimcha בְּכָל־ bechol ב״ן, לכב ; ומב הָאָרֶץ ha'aretz אלהים דההין ע״ה:

KADDISH TITKABAL

יִתְגַּדַּל yitgadal וְיִתְקַדַּשׁ veyitkadash שׁדי ומילוי שׁדי ; י״א אותיות כמנין ו״ה

שְׁמֵהּ shemei (שם י״ה דע״ב) רַבָּא raba קנ״א ב״ן, יהוה אלהים יהוה אדני,

אמן amen אידהנויה: אָמֵן מילוי קס״א וס״ג, מ״ה ברבוע וע״ב ע״ה ; ר״ת ; ו״פ אלהים ; ס״ת = ג״פ יב״ק:

בְּעָלְמָא be'alma דִי di בְּרָא vera כִרְעוּתֵיהּ chir'utei

וְיַמְלִיךְ veyamlich מַלְכוּתֵיהּ malchutei וְיַצְמַח veyatzmach

פּוּרְקָנֵיהּ purkanei וִיקָרֵב vikarev מְשִׁיחֵיהּ meshichei אָמֵן amen אידהנויה:

בְּחַיֵּיכוֹן bechayechon וּבְיוֹמֵיכוֹן uvyomechon וּבְחַיֵּי uvchayei

דְּכָל dechol יל״י בֵּית bet ב״פ ראה יִשְׂרָאֵל Yisrael בַּעֲגָלָא ba'agala

וּבִזְמַן uvizman קָרִיב kariv וְאִמְרוּ ve'imru אָמֵן amen: אָמֵן amen אידהנויה:

YEHI SHEM

"May the Name of the Lord be blessed from now till all eternity. From sunrise till sundown, may the Name of the Lord be praised and elevated. Above all nations is our Lord. His glory is above the Heavens." (Psalms 113:2-4) "Lord, our Master, how tremendous is Your Name in all the earth." (Psalms 8:10)

KADDISH TITKABAL

May His great Name be more exalted and sanctified. (Amen)
In the world that He created according to His will, and may His Kingdom reign. And may He cause His redemption to sprout and may He bring the Mashiach closer. (Amen) In your lifetimes and in your days and in the lifetime of all the House of Israel, speedily and in the near future, and you shall say, Amen. (Amen)

The congregation and the *chazan* say the following:

28 words (until be'alma) and 28 letters (until almaya)

יְהֵא yehe שְׁמֵיהּ shemei (שֵׁם י"ה דס"ג) רַבָּא raba קנ"א ב"א ב"ן

לְעָלַם le'alam מְבָרַךְ mevarach, ע"ה ע"ב וע"ב מ"ה קס"א וס"ג, מילוי אדני, יהוה יהוה אלהים

לְעָלַם le'alam לְעָלְמֵי le'almei עָלְמַיָּא almaya. יִתְבָּרַךְ yitbarach.

Seven words with six letters each (שֵׁם בֶּן מ"ב) and also, seven times the letter Vav (שֵׁם בֶּן מ"ב)

וְיִשְׁתַּבַּח veyishtabach י"פ ע"ב יהוה אל אבג יתץ.

וְיִתְפָּאַר veyitpa'ar הי גו יה קרע שטן. וְיִתְרומַם veyitromam וה כוזו נגד יכש.

וְיִתְנַשֵּׂא veyitnase במוכסז בטר צתג. וְיִתְהַדָּר veyit'hadar כוזו יה וזקב טנע.

וְיִתְעַלֶּה veyit'ale וה יוד ה יגל פזק. וְיִתְהַלָּל veyit'halal א ואו הא שקו צית.

שְׁמֵיהּ shemei (שֵׁם י"ה דמ"ה) דְּקֻדְשָׁא dekudsha בְּרִיךְ verich הוּא hu:

אָמֵן amen אידהנויה.

לְעֵלָּא le'ela מִן min כָּל kol יל"י מִן בִּרְכָתָא birchata שִׁירָתָא shirata.

תֻּשְׁבְּחָתָא tishbechata וְנֶחֱמָתָא venechamata. דַּאֲמִירָן da'amiran

בְּעָלְמָא be'alma וְאִמְרוּ ve'imru אָמֵן amen: אָמֵן amen אידהנויה.

תִּתְקַבֵּל titkabal צְלוֹתָנָא tzelotana וּבָעוּתָנָא uva'utana

עִם im צְלוֹתְהוֹן tzelotehon וּבָעוּתְהוֹן uva'utehon דְּכָל dechol יל"י

בֵּית bet ב"פ ראה יִשְׂרָאֵל Yisrael קֳדָם kadam אֲבוּנָא avuna

דְּבִשְׁמַיָּא devishmaya וְאִמְרוּ ve'imru אָמֵן amen: אָמֵן amen אידהנויה.

May His great Name be blessed forever and for all eternity. Blessed and lauded, and glorified, and exalted, and extolled, and honored, and uplifted, and praised be the Name of the Holy Blessed One. (Amen) Above all blessings, songs, praises, and words of consolation that may be said in the world, and you shall say, Amen. (Amen) May our prayers and pleas be accepted, together with the prayers and pleas of the entire House of Israel, before our Father in Heaven, and you say, Amen. (Amen) yehe יְהֵא shelama שְׁלָמָא raba רַבָּא קנ"א ב"ן, יהוה אלהים יהוה אדני, מילוי קס"א וס"ג,

min מִן שְׁמַיָּא shemaya• חַיִּים chayim אהיה אהיה יהוה, בינה ע"ה מ"ה ברבוע וע"ב ע"ה

vesava וְשָׂבָע vishu'a וִישׁוּעָה venechama וְנֶחָמָה veshezava וְשֵׁיזָבָא

urfu'a וּרְפוּאָה ug'ula וּגְאֻלָּה uslicha וּסְלִיחָה vechapara וְכַפָּרָה

verevach וְרֵיוַח vehatzala וְהַצָּלָה• lanu לָנוּ אלהים, אהיה אדני ulchol וּלְכָל יה אדני

amo עַמּוֹ Yisrael יִשְׂרָאֵל ve'imru וְאִמְרוּ amen אָמֵן• amen אָמֵן אידהנויה.

Take three steps backwards and say:

ose עֹשֶׂה shalom שָׁלוֹם bimromav בִּמְרוֹמָיו• ע"ב, ריבוע יהוה. hu הוּא

berachamav בְּרַחֲמָיו ya'ase יַעֲשֶׂה shalom שָׁלוֹם alenu עָלֵינוּ ר"ת ס"ע נהורין•

ve'al וְעַל kol כָּל ילי ; עמם amo עַמּוֹ Yisrael יִשְׂרָאֵל ve'imru וְאִמְרוּ amen אָמֵן:

BARCHI NAFSI

This Psalm gives us an additional burst of energy that is present on *Rosh Chodesh*.

barchi בָּרְכִי nafshi נַפְשִׁי et אֶת Adonai יְהֹוָה(אֲדֹנָיֵאֱלֹהֵנוֵּ) |

Adonai יְהֹוָה(אֲדֹנָיֵאֱלֹהֵנוֵּ) Elohai אֱלֹהַי מילוי דע"ב, דמב ; ילה גָּדַלְתָּ gadalta

me'od מְאֹד hod הוֹד ההה vehadar וְהָדָר לָבָשְׁתָּ lavashta:

ote עֹטֶה or אוֹר רז, or אֵין סוֹף kasalma כַּשַּׂלְמָה note נוֹטֶה

shamayim שָׁמַיִם כוזו י"פ טל, י"פ כ"ו kayeri'a כַּיְרִיעָה: hamekare הַמְקָרֶה

vamayim בַּמַּיִם aliyotav עֲלִיּוֹתָיו hasam הַשָּׂם־ avim עָבִים rechuvo רְכוּבוֹ

hamehalech הַמְהַלֵּךְ al עַל־ kanfei כַּנְפֵי־ ru'ach רוּחַ: ose עֹשֶׂה

mal'achav מַלְאָכָיו ruchot רוּחוֹת meshartav מְשָׁרְתָיו esh אֵשׁ lohet לֹהֵט:

May there be abundant peace from heaven. Life, contentment, salvation, consolation, deliverance, healing, redemption, pardon, atonement, comfort, and relief. For us and for His entire nation, Israel, and you shall say, Amen. (Amen) He, Who makes peace in His high places, With His compassion He shall make peace for us and for His entire nation, Israel. And you shall say, Amen. (Amen)

BARCHI NAFSHI

My soul, bless the Lord! Lord, my God, You have become extremely great. You cloth Yourself in splendor and majesty. You enwrap Yourself with Light like a garment and stretch out the Heavens like a curtain. He Who roofs His upper levels with water, Who makes clouds His chariots, and Who walks on the wings of winds, He makes His winds messengers and His flaming fires ministers.

יָסַד yasad אֶרֶץ eretz עַל־ al מְכוֹנֶיהָ mechoneha בַּל־ bal תִּמּוֹט timot

עוֹלָם olam וָעֶד va'ed תְּהוֹם tehom כַּלְּבוּשׁ kalevush כִּסִּיתוֹ kisito עַל al

הָרִים harim יַעֲמְדוּ ya'amdu מָיִם mayim מִן min גַּעֲרָתְךָ ga'aratcha

יְנוּסוּן yenusun מִן min קוֹל kol רַעַמְךָ ra'amcha יֵחָפֵזוּן yechafezun

יַעֲלוּ ya'alu הָרִים harim יֵרְדוּ yerdu בְקָעוֹת vekaot אֶל־ el מְקוֹם mekom

זֶה ze יָסַדְתָּ yasadeta לָהֶם lahem גְּבוּל־ gevul שַׂמְתָּ samta

בַּל bal יַעֲבֹרוּן ya'avorun בַּל־ bal יְשׁוּבוּן yeshuvun לְכַסּוֹת lechasot

הָאָרֶץ ha'aretz אלהים דההן ע"ה הַמְשַׁלֵּחַ hameshale'ach מַעְיָנִים ma'yanim

בַּנְּחָלִים banechalim בֵּין ben הָרִים harim יְהַלֵּכוּן yehalechun יַשְׁקוּ yashku

כָּל־ kol יל וְזַיתוֹ chayto שָׂדָי sadai יִשְׁבְּרוּ yishberu פְּרָאִים fera'im

צְמָאָם tzema'am עֲלֵיהֶם alehem עוֹף־ of הַשָּׁמַיִם hashamayim ל"פ טל, ל"פ כוזו

יִשְׁכּוֹן yishkon מִבֵּין miben עָפָאִים ofayim יִתְּנוּ yitenu קוֹל kol

מַשְׁקֶה mashke הָרִים harim מֵעֲלִיּוֹתָיו me'aliyotav מִפְּרִי miperi

מַעֲשֶׂיךָ ma'asecha תִּשְׂבַּע tisba הָאָרֶץ ha'aretz אלהים דההן ע"ה

מַצְמִיחַ matzmi'ach חָצִיר chatzir לַבְּהֵמָה labehema ע"ב שמות וְעֵשֶׂב ve'esev

לַעֲבֹדַת la'avodat הָאָדָם ha'adam מ"ה לְהוֹצִיא lehotzi לֶחֶם lechem ג' הויות

מִן־ min הָאָרֶץ ha'aretz אלהים דההן ע"ה ע' כנגד ע' אומות העולם התלויים וְיַיִן veyayin

אֱנוֹשׁ enosh בוכו לְבַב־ levav משיוו יְשַׂמַּח yesamach י"פ האא בסמאל), מ"כ, י"פ

לְהַצְהִיל lehatz'hil פָּנִים panim מִשָּׁמֶן mishamen וְלֶחֶם velechem ג' הויות

לְבַב־ levav בוכו אֱנוֹשׁ enosh יִסְעָד yis'ad יִשְׂבְּעוּ yisbe'u עֲצֵי atzei

יְהֹוָה Adonai אֲרָזֵי arzei לְבָנוֹן Levanon יל אֲשֶׁר asher נָטָע nata

---

He founded the earth upon its bases, so that it would never ever collapse. You covered the depths as with a garment, the waters stand over the mountains. They fled from Your roar, they rushed away from the sound of Your thunder. The mountains go up and the valleys go down to that place that You have established for them. You set boundaries for them that they would not cross, so that they will not return to cover the earth. You Who direct springs into streams and they flow between mountains. They give water to every beast in the field, and the wild animals quench their thirst. Upon them do the birds of the skies dwell. From between, they give forth song. You Who irrigate the mountains from Your High Places. From the fruit of what You have made is the earth satiated. You Who cause grasses to sprout for the animals and vegetation for the service of man, to bring bread out of the earth, and wine, which gladdens the heart of man, and bread, which sustains the heart of man. The trees of the Lord will be satiated, those cedars of Lebanon, which He had planted.

וַחֲסִידָה (chasida) יְקַנֵּנוּ (yekanenu) צִפֳּרִים (tziporim) שָׁם (sham) אֲשֶׁר (asher)

הַגְּבֹהִים (hagevohim) הָרִים (harim) ב"פ ראה: בֵּיתָהּ (beta) בְּרוֹשִׁים (beroshim)

לַשְׁפַנִּים (lashfanim): מַחְסֶה (machse) סְלָעִים (sela'im) לַיְּעֵלִים (laye'elim)

יָדַע (yada) שֶׁמֶשׁ (shemesh) לְמוֹעֲדִים (lemo'adim) יָרֵחַ (yare'ach) עָשָׂה (asa)

וַיְהִי (vihi) שך נצוצות על ו' המלכים חֹשֶׁךְ (choshech) תָּשֶׁת (tashet) מְבוֹאוֹ: (mevo'o)

יַעַר (ya'ar) ילי וְחַיְתוֹ (chayto) כָּל (kol) תִּרְמֹשׂ (tirmos) בּוֹ (bo) מלה לַיְלָה (layla)

לַטָּרֶף (lataref) שֹׁאֲגִים (sho'agim) הַכְּפִירִים (hakefirim): סנדלפון, ערי,

תִּזְרַח (tizrach) אָכְלָם: (ochlam) יא"י (מלוי דס"ג) מֵאֵל (meEl) וּלְבַקֵּשׁ (ulvakesh)

מְעוֹנֹתָם (me'onotam) וְאֶל (ve'el) יֵאָסֵפוּן (ye'asefun) הַשֶּׁמֶשׁ (hashemesh)

לְפָעֳלוֹ (lefa'olo) מ"ה אָדָם (adam) יֵצֵא (yetze) יִרְבָּצוּן: (yirbatzun)

רַבּוּ (rabu) מ"ה מַה (ma) עֶרֶב: (arev) עֲדֵי (adei) וְלַעֲבֹדָתוֹ (vela'avodato)

בְּחָכְמָה (bechochmah) כֻּלָּם (kulam) יְהֹוָה (Adonai) מַעֲשֶׂיךָ (ma'asecha)

ריה"ה אלהים דההין ע"ה הָאָרֶץ (ha'aretz) מָלְאָה (mal'a) עָשִׂיתָ (asita) (מצות) = תרי"ג במלוי

קִנְיָנֶךָ (kinyanecha): עם ד' אותיות – מובה, יזל, אום ; להם גָּדוֹל (gadol) ילי הַיָּם (hayam) זֶה (ze) kinyanecha

מִסְפָּר (mispar) וְאֵין (ve'en) רֶמֶשׂ (remes) שָׁם (sham) יָדָיִם (yadayim) וּרְחַב (urchav)

שָׁם (sham) גְּדֹלוֹת: (gedolot) עִם (im) קְטַנּוֹת (ketanot) חַיּוֹת (chayot) וְחַיּוֹת

יָצַרְתָּ (yatzarta) זֶה (ze) לִוְיָתָן (livyatan) יְהַלֵּכוּן (yehalechun) אֳנִיּוֹת (oniyot)

יְשַׂבֵּרוּן (yesaberun) אֵלֶיךָ (elecha) כֻּלָּם (kulam) בּוֹ: (bo) לְשַׂחֶק (lesachek)

לָהֶם (lahem) כהה ב"פ תִּתֵּן (titen) בְּעִתּוֹ: (be'ito) אָכְלָם (ochlam) לָתֵת (latet)

והו: טוֹב (tov) יִשְׂבְּעוּן (yisbe'un) יָדְךָ (yadcha) תִּפְתַּח (tiftach) יִלְקֹטוּן (yilkotun)

---

and in which the birds build their nests. The stork makes a dwelling in the cypress. The high mountains for wild goats, the rocks as refuge for hares. He made a moon for the festivals and a sun that knows its path. You set the darkness so that it would be night, when all the beasts of the forest walk about. The young lions roar for their prey and seek their food from God. The sun rises and they gather and they lay down in their lairs. Man goes out to his occupation and to his work until the evening. How numerous are Your works, Lord, You made them all with wisdom. The world is filled with Your possessions. The sea is great and expansive; therein are innumerable moving things, small living creatures together with the large. Ships journey there. You created the Leviathan to play in it. They all look hopefully to You to give them their food at its proper time. You give and they gather it. You open Your Hand and satiate with good.

tosef תֹסֵף	yibahelun יִבָּהֵלוּן		panecha פָּנֶיךָ	tastir תַּסְתִּיר
afaram עָפָרָם	ve'el וְאֶל		yigva'un יִגְוָעוּן	rucham רוּחָם
yibare'un יִבָּרֵאוּן	ruchacha רוּחֲךָ	te'shalach תְּשַׁלַּח		yeshuvun יְשׁוּבוּן
adama אֲדָמָה	penei פְּנֵי	utchadesh וּתְחַדֵּשׁ		
yehi יְהִי	chevod כְּבוֹד	Adonai יְהֹוָה		
le'olam לְעוֹלָם	yismach יִשְׂמַח			
bema'asav בְּמַעֲשָׂיו	Adonai יְהֹוָה			
la'aretz לָאָרֶץ	hamabit הַמַּבִּיט			
veye'eshanu וְיֶעְשָׁנוּ	beharim בֶּהָרִים	yiga יִגַּע		vatir'ad וַתִּרְעָד
azamera אֲזַמְּרָה	bechayai בְּחַיָּי	ladonai לַיהֹוָה		ashira אָשִׁירָה
alav עָלָיו	ye'erav יֶעֱרַב	be'odi בְּעוֹדִי		lelohai לֵאלֹהָי
badonai בַּיהֹוָה	esmach אֶשְׂמַח	anochi אָנֹכִי		sichi שִׂיחִי
yitamu יִתַּמּוּ	chata'im וְחַטָּאִים	min מִן	ha'aretz הָאָרֶץ	
nafshi נַפְשִׁי	barchi בָּרְכִי	enam אֵינָם	od עוֹד	ursha'im וּרְשָׁעִים
et אֶת	Adonai יְהֹוָה	haleluya הַלְלוּיָהּ		

Kaddish Yehe Shelama (on pg. 268) and the prayer is continued like regular days.

THE ORDER OF SHACHARIT FOR CHANUKAH

We pray *Shacharit* as on a regular day. We add "*al hanisim*" in *Amidah* (pg. 215). After *Amidah* we say *Halel* (pg. 446) and then *Half Kaddish* (pg. 459). We take out the *Torah* (pg. 230) and read from pg. 518 and on (according to the specific day). Then we say Half *Kaddish* (pg. 238) and so on as regular days (at the song of the day, we skip the words "*Hashir shehayu haleviyim omrim al haduchan.*" After the song of the day we say *Mizmor shir hanukat habayit* - pg. 265).

THE ORDER OF SHACHARIT FOR ROSH CHODESH TEVET THAT OCCURS DURING THE WEEK

We pray *Shacharit* as on a regular day. We add "*Yale yavo*" (pg. 212) and *Al hanisim*" (pg. 215) in *Amidah.*" After *Amidah* we say *Halel* (pg. 446) and then *Kaddish Titkabel* (pg. 459). We take out two *Torah* (pg. 230) and read for *Rosh Chodesh* (pg. 517) for three *Olim* and then for *Chanukah*, from the second *Torah*, from pg. 518 and on (according to the specific day) for the fourth *ole*. Then we say Half *Kaddish* (pg. 238) *Ashrei, Uva letzion*, skeep *Kaddish Titkabal*, and then *Beit Yaakov*, Song of the Day (skip the words "*Hashir shehayu haleviyim omrim al haduchan.*"), *Mizmor shir hanukat habayit* (pg. 265) and then *Hosi'enu*. Then Half *Kaddish* and *Musaf* of *Rosh Chodesh* (pg. 461), we add "*Al hanissim*" (pg. 472), *Kaddish Titkabel* and *Barchi Nafshi* (pg. 478-483). Then *Kaddish Yehe Shelema* (pg. 268) and we end the prayer like regular days.

THE ORDER OF SHACHARIT FOR PURIM

We pray *Shacharit* as on a regular day. We add "*Al hanisim*" in *Amidah* (pg. 215). After the *Amidah* we say Half *Kaddish* (pg. 228) and take out the *Torah* and read on pg. 521. Then Half *Kaddish* (pg. 238), *Ashrei, Uva letzion* until "*me'ata ve'ad olam.*" We read the *Megilat Esther*, and then we continue from "*veAta kadosh*" (pg. 246) and on like regular days.

When You hide Your Presence, they are terrified. You gather their souls and they die and they return to their dust. You send forth Your Breath and they are created, and You renew the face of the earth. May the glory of the Lord last forever. May the Lord rejoice with His works. He gazes upon the earth and it trembles. He touches the mountains and they smoke. I shall sing to the Lord as long as I live and play melodies to my God as long as I exist. May my utterances be sweet to Him, and let me rejoice in the Lord. The wicked will vanish from the earth and the wicked will be no more. Bless the Lord, my soul! Praise the Lord." (Psalms 104)

The next connection concerns the power of the Temple.

On the first day of the month of *Nissan* (Aries), the Temple was erected. The heads of the Twelve Tribes of Israel brought sacrifices to the inauguration of the Alter in the Temple. Every head of the tribe brought his offering on a specific day. On the first day of *Nissan* until the 13th day of *Nissan*, we read from the portion of Naso concerning the heads of the Tribe. Each day of *Nissan*, we read the section from the *Torah* Scroll that pertains to that particular day, without the blessings.

FOR THE FIRST DAY - *NISSAN* – ARIES – ה, MARS – ד (NASO: NUMBERS 7:1)

וַיְדַבֵּר יְהֹוָה (אֲדֹנָי אֱלֹהִים) אֶל־מֹשֶׁה לֵּאמֹר: דַּבֵּר אֶל־אַהֲרֹן וְאֶל־בָּנָיו לֵאמֹר

כֹּה תְבָרְכוּ אֶת־בְּנֵי יִשְׂרָאֵל אָמוֹר לָהֶם: יְבָרֶכְךָ יְהֹוָה (אֲדֹנָי אֱלֹהִים) וְיִשְׁמְרֶךָ:

יָאֵר יְהֹוָה (אֲדֹנָי אֱלֹהִים) פָּנָיו אֵלֶיךָ וִיחֻנֶּךָּ: יִשָּׂא יְהֹוָה (אֲדֹנָי אֱלֹהִים) פָּנָיו אֵלֶיךָ וְיָשֵׂם

לְךָ שָׁלוֹם: וְשָׂמוּ אֶת־שְׁמִי עַל־בְּנֵי יִשְׂרָאֵל וַאֲנִי אֲבָרֲכֵם: וַיְהִי בְּיוֹם כַּלּוֹת

מֹשֶׁה לְהָקִים אֶת־הַמִּשְׁכָּן וַיִּמְשַׁח אֹתוֹ וַיְקַדֵּשׁ אֹתוֹ וְאֶת־כָּל־כֵּלָיו

וְאֶת־הַמִּזְבֵּחַ וְאֶת־כָּל־כֵּלָיו וַיִּמְשָׁחֵם וַיְקַדֵּשׁ אֹתָם: וַיַּקְרִיבוּ נְשִׂיאֵי יִשְׂרָאֵל

רָאשֵׁי בֵּית אֲבֹתָם הֵם נְשִׂיאֵי הַמַּטֹּת הֵם הָעֹמְדִים עַל־הַפְּקֻדִים: וַיָּבִיאוּ

אֶת־קָרְבָּנָם לִפְנֵי יְהֹוָה (אֲדֹנָי אֱלֹהִים) שֵׁשׁ־עֶגְלֹת צָב וּשְׁנֵי עָשָׂר בָּקָר עֲגָלָה

עַל־שְׁנֵי הַנְּשִׂאִים וְשׁוֹר לְאֶחָד וַיַּקְרִיבוּ אוֹתָם לִפְנֵי הַמִּשְׁכָּן: וַיֹּאמֶר

יְהֹוָה (אֲדֹנָי אֱלֹהִים) אֶל־מֹשֶׁה לֵּאמֹר: קַח מֵאִתָּם וְהָיוּ לַעֲבֹד אֶת־עֲבֹדַת אֹהֶל

מוֹעֵד וְנָתַתָּה אוֹתָם אֶל־הַלְוִיִּם אִישׁ כְּפִי עֲבֹדָתוֹ: וַיִּקַּח מֹשֶׁה אֶת־הָעֲגָלֹת

וְאֶת־הַבָּקָר וַיִּתֵּן אוֹתָם אֶל־הַלְוִיִּם: אֵת | שְׁתֵּי הָעֲגָלוֹת וְאֵת אַרְבַּעַת

הַבָּקָר נָתַן לִבְנֵי גֵרְשׁוֹן כְּפִי עֲבֹדָתָם: וְאֵת | אַרְבַּע הָעֲגָלֹת וְאֵת שְׁמֹנַת

הַבָּקָר נָתַן לִבְנֵי מְרָרִי כְּפִי עֲבֹדָתָם בְּיַד אִיתָמָר בֶּן־אַהֲרֹן הַכֹּהֵן:

וְלִבְנֵי קְהָת לֹא נָתָן כִּי־עֲבֹדַת הַקֹּדֶשׁ עֲלֵהֶם בַּכָּתֵף יִשָּׂאוּ: וַיַּקְרִיבוּ

הַנְּשִׂאִים אֵת חֲנֻכַּת הַמִּזְבֵּחַ בְּיוֹם הִמָּשַׁח אֹתוֹ וַיַּקְרִיבוּ הַנְּשִׂיאִם

אֶת־קָרְבָּנָם לִפְנֵי הַמִּזְבֵּחַ: וַיֹּאמֶר יְהֹוָה (אֲדֹנָי אֱלֹהִים) אֶל־מֹשֶׁה נָשִׂיא אֶחָד לַיּוֹם

נָשִׂיא אֶחָד לַיּוֹם יַקְרִיבוּ אֶת־קָרְבָּנָם לַחֲנֻכַּת הַמִּזְבֵּחַ: וַיְהִי הַמַּקְרִיב בַּיּוֹם

הָרִאשׁוֹן אֶת־קָרְבָּנוֹ נַחְשׁוֹן בֶּן־עַמִּינָדָב לְמַטֵּה יְהוּדָה: וְקָרְבָּנוֹ קַעֲרַת־כֶּסֶף

אַחַת שְׁלֹשִׁים וּמֵאָה מִשְׁקָלָהּ מִזְרָק אֶחָד כֶּסֶף שִׁבְעִים שֶׁקֶל בְּשֶׁקֶל

הַקֹּדֶשׁ שְׁנֵיהֶם | מְלֵאִים סֹלֶת בְּלוּלָה בַשֶּׁמֶן לְמִנְחָה: כַּף אַחַת עֲשָׂרָה זָהָב

מְלֵאָה קְטֹרֶת: פַּר אֶחָד בֶּן־בָּקָר אַיִל אֶחָד כֶּבֶשׂ־אֶחָד בֶּן־שְׁנָתוֹ לְעֹלָה:

שְׂעִיר־עִזִּים אֶחָד לְחַטָּאת: וּלְזֶבַח הַשְּׁלָמִים בָּקָר שְׁנַיִם אֵילִם חֲמִשָּׁה

עַתּוּדִים חֲמִשָּׁה כְּבָשִׂים בְּנֵי־שָׁנָה חֲמִשָּׁה זֶה קָרְבַּן נַחְשׁוֹן בֶּן־עַמִּינָדָב:

FOR THE SECOND DAY – *IYAR* – TAURUS – וּ, VENUS – פ (NASO: NUMBERS 7:18)

בַּיּוֹם הַשֵּׁנִי הִקְרִיב נְתַנְאֵל בֶּן־צוּעָר נְשִׂיא יִשָּׂשכָר: הִקְרִב אֶת־קָרְבָּנוֹ
קַעֲרַת־כֶּסֶף אַחַת שְׁלֹשִׁים וּמֵאָה מִשְׁקָלָהּ מִזְרָק אֶחָד כֶּסֶף שִׁבְעִים שֶׁקֶל
בְּשֶׁקֶל הַקֹּדֶשׁ שְׁנֵיהֶם | מְלֵאִים סֹלֶת בְּלוּלָה בַשֶּׁמֶן לְמִנְחָה: כַּף אַחַת
עֲשָׂרָה זָהָב מְלֵאָה קְטֹרֶת: פַּר אֶחָד בֶּן־בָּקָר אַיִל אֶחָד כֶּבֶשׂ־אֶחָד בֶּן־
שְׁנָתוֹ לְעֹלָה: שְׂעִיר־עִזִּים אֶחָד לְחַטָּאת: וּלְזֶבַח הַשְּׁלָמִים בָּקָר שְׁנַיִם אֵילִם
וַחֲמִשָּׁה עַתּוּדִים וַחֲמִשָּׁה כְּבָשִׂים בְּנֵי־שָׁנָה וַחֲמִשָּׁה זֶה קָרְבַּן נְתַנְאֵל בֶּן־צוּעָר:

FOR THE THIRD DAY – *SIVAN* – GEMINI – וּ, MERCURY – ר (NASO: NUMBERS 7:24)

בַּיּוֹם הַשְּׁלִישִׁי נָשִׂיא לִבְנֵי זְבוּלֻן אֱלִיאָב בֶּן־חֵלֹן: קָרְבָּנוֹ קַעֲרַת־כֶּסֶף אַחַת
שְׁלֹשִׁים וּמֵאָה מִשְׁקָלָהּ מִזְרָק אֶחָד כֶּסֶף שִׁבְעִים שֶׁקֶל בְּשֶׁקֶל הַקֹּדֶשׁ
שְׁנֵיהֶם | מְלֵאִים סֹלֶת בְּלוּלָה בַשֶּׁמֶן לְמִנְחָה: כַּף אַחַת עֲשָׂרָה זָהָב מְלֵאָה
קְטֹרֶת: פַּר אֶחָד בֶּן־בָּקָר אַיִל אֶחָד כֶּבֶשׂ־אֶחָד בֶּן־שְׁנָתוֹ לְעֹלָה:
שְׂעִיר־עִזִּים אֶחָד לְחַטָּאת: וּלְזֶבַח הַשְּׁלָמִים בָּקָר שְׁנַיִם אֵילִם וַחֲמִשָּׁה
עַתּוּדִים וַחֲמִשָּׁה כְּבָשִׂים בְּנֵי־שָׁנָה וַחֲמִשָּׁה זֶה קָרְבַּן אֱלִיאָב בֶּן־חֵלֹן:

FOR THE FOURTH DAY – *TAMMUZ* – CANCER – וּ, MOON – ת (NASO: NUMBERS 7:30)

בַּיּוֹם הָרְבִיעִי נָשִׂיא לִבְנֵי רְאוּבֵן אֱלִיצוּר בֶּן־שְׁדֵיאוּר: קָרְבָּנוֹ קַעֲרַת־כֶּסֶף
אַחַת שְׁלֹשִׁים וּמֵאָה מִשְׁקָלָהּ מִזְרָק אֶחָד כֶּסֶף שִׁבְעִים שֶׁקֶל בְּשֶׁקֶל
הַקֹּדֶשׁ שְׁנֵיהֶם | מְלֵאִים סֹלֶת בְּלוּלָה בַשֶּׁמֶן לְמִנְחָה: כַּף אַחַת עֲשָׂרָה זָהָב
מְלֵאָה קְטֹרֶת: פַּר אֶחָד בֶּן־בָּקָר אַיִל אֶחָד כֶּבֶשׂ־אֶחָד בֶּן־שְׁנָתוֹ לְעֹלָה:
שְׂעִיר־עִזִּים אֶחָד לְחַטָּאת: וּלְזֶבַח הַשְּׁלָמִים בָּקָר שְׁנַיִם אֵילִם וַחֲמִשָּׁה
עַתּוּדִים וַחֲמִשָּׁה כְּבָשִׂים בְּנֵי־שָׁנָה וַחֲמִשָּׁה זֶה קָרְבַּן אֱלִיצוּר בֶּן־שְׁדֵיאוּר:

FOR THE FIFTH DAY – *AV* – LEO – ט, SUN – כ (NASO: NUMBERS 7:31)

בַּיּוֹם הַחֲמִישִׁי נָשִׂיא לִבְנֵי שִׁמְעוֹן שְׁלֻמִיאֵל בֶּן־צוּרִישַׁדָּי: קָרְבָּנוֹ קַעֲרַת־
כֶּסֶף אַחַת שְׁלֹשִׁים וּמֵאָה מִשְׁקָלָהּ מִזְרָק אֶחָד כֶּסֶף שִׁבְעִים שֶׁקֶל בְּשֶׁקֶל
הַקֹּדֶשׁ שְׁנֵיהֶם | מְלֵאִים סֹלֶת בְּלוּלָה בַשֶּׁמֶן לְמִנְחָה: כַּף אַחַת עֲשָׂרָה זָהָב
מְלֵאָה קְטֹרֶת: פַּר אֶחָד בֶּן־בָּקָר אַיִל אֶחָד כֶּבֶשׂ־אֶחָד בֶּן־שְׁנָתוֹ לְעֹלָה:
שְׂעִיר־עִזִּים אֶחָד לְחַטָּאת: וּלְזֶבַח הַשְּׁלָמִים בָּקָר שְׁנַיִם אֵילִם וַחֲמִשָּׁה
עַתּוּדִים וַחֲמִשָּׁה כְּבָשִׂים בְּנֵי־שָׁנָה וַחֲמִשָּׁה זֶה קָרְבַּן שְׁלֻמִיאֵל בֶּן־צוּרִישַׁדָּי:

FOR THE SIXTH DAY – *ELUL* – VIRGO – י, MERCURY - ר (NASO: NUMBERS 7:42)

בַּיּוֹם הַשִּׁשִּׁי נָשִׂיא לִבְנֵי גָד אֶלְיָסָף בֶּן־דְּעוּאֵל: קָרְבָּנוֹ קַעֲרַת־כֶּסֶף אַחַת
שְׁלֹשִׁים וּמֵאָה מִשְׁקָלָהּ מִזְרָק אֶחָד כֶּסֶף שִׁבְעִים שֶׁקֶל בְּשֶׁקֶל הַקֹּדֶשׁ
שְׁנֵיהֶם | מְלֵאִים סֹלֶת בְּלוּלָה בַשֶּׁמֶן לְמִנְחָה: כַּף אַחַת עֲשָׂרָה זָהָב מְלֵאָה
קְטֹרֶת: פַּר אֶחָד בֶּן־בָּקָר אַיִל אֶחָד כֶּבֶשׂ־אֶחָד בֶּן־שְׁנָתוֹ לְעֹלָה:
שְׂעִיר־עִזִּים אֶחָד לְחַטָּאת: וּלְזֶבַח הַשְּׁלָמִים בָּקָר שְׁנַיִם אֵילִם חֲמִשָּׁה
עַתֻּדִים חֲמִשָּׁה כְּבָשִׂים בְּנֵי־שָׁנָה חֲמִשָּׁה זֶה קָרְבַּן אֶלְיָסָף בֶּן־דְּעוּאֵל:

FOR THE SEVENTH DAY – *TISHREI* – LIBRA – ל, VENUS - פ (NASO: NUMBERS 7:48)

בַּיּוֹם הַשְּׁבִיעִי נָשִׂיא לִבְנֵי אֶפְרָיִם אֱלִישָׁמָע בֶּן־עַמִּיהוּד: קָרְבָּנוֹ קַעֲרַת־
כֶּסֶף אַחַת שְׁלֹשִׁים וּמֵאָה מִשְׁקָלָהּ מִזְרָק אֶחָד כֶּסֶף שִׁבְעִים שֶׁקֶל בְּשֶׁקֶל
הַקֹּדֶשׁ שְׁנֵיהֶם | מְלֵאִים סֹלֶת בְּלוּלָה בַשֶּׁמֶן לְמִנְחָה: כַּף אַחַת עֲשָׂרָה זָהָב
מְלֵאָה קְטֹרֶת: פַּר אֶחָד בֶּן־בָּקָר אַיִל אֶחָד כֶּבֶשׂ־אֶחָד בֶּן־שְׁנָתוֹ לְעֹלָה:
שְׂעִיר־עִזִּים אֶחָד לְחַטָּאת: וּלְזֶבַח הַשְּׁלָמִים בָּקָר שְׁנַיִם אֵילִם חֲמִשָּׁה
עַתֻּדִים חֲמִשָּׁה כְּבָשִׂים בְּנֵי־שָׁנָה חֲמִשָּׁה זֶה קָרְבַּן אֱלִישָׁמָע בֶּן־עַמִּיהוּד:

FOR THE EIGHTH DAY – *CHESHVAN* – SCORPIO – נ, MARS - ד (NASO: NUMBERS 7:54)

בַּיּוֹם הַשְּׁמִינִי נָשִׂיא לִבְנֵי מְנַשֶּׁה גַּמְלִיאֵל בֶּן־פְּדָהצוּר: קָרְבָּנוֹ קַעֲרַת־כֶּסֶף
אַחַת שְׁלֹשִׁים וּמֵאָה מִשְׁקָלָהּ מִזְרָק אֶחָד כֶּסֶף שִׁבְעִים שֶׁקֶל בְּשֶׁקֶל
הַקֹּדֶשׁ שְׁנֵיהֶם | מְלֵאִים סֹלֶת בְּלוּלָה בַשֶּׁמֶן לְמִנְחָה: כַּף אַחַת עֲשָׂרָה זָהָב
מְלֵאָה קְטֹרֶת: פַּר אֶחָד בֶּן־בָּקָר אַיִל אֶחָד כֶּבֶשׂ־אֶחָד בֶּן־שְׁנָתוֹ לְעֹלָה:
שְׂעִיר־עִזִּים אֶחָד לְחַטָּאת: וּלְזֶבַח הַשְּׁלָמִים בָּקָר שְׁנַיִם אֵילִם חֲמִשָּׁה
עַתֻּדִים חֲמִשָּׁה כְּבָשִׂים בְּנֵי־שָׁנָה חֲמִשָּׁה זֶה קָרְבַּן גַּמְלִיאֵל בֶּן־פְּדָהצוּר:

FOR THE NINTH DAY – *KISLEV* – SAGITTARIUS – ס, JUPITER - ג (NASO: NUMBERS 7:60)

בַּיּוֹם הַתְּשִׁיעִי נָשִׂיא לִבְנֵי בִנְיָמִן אֲבִידָן בֶּן־גִּדְעֹנִי: קָרְבָּנוֹ קַעֲרַת־כֶּסֶף
אַחַת שְׁלֹשִׁים וּמֵאָה מִשְׁקָלָהּ מִזְרָק אֶחָד כֶּסֶף שִׁבְעִים שֶׁקֶל בְּשֶׁקֶל
הַקֹּדֶשׁ שְׁנֵיהֶם | מְלֵאִים סֹלֶת בְּלוּלָה בַשֶּׁמֶן לְמִנְחָה: כַּף אַחַת עֲשָׂרָה זָהָב
מְלֵאָה קְטֹרֶת: פַּר אֶחָד בֶּן־בָּקָר אַיִל אֶחָד כֶּבֶשׂ־אֶחָד בֶּן־שְׁנָתוֹ לְעֹלָה:
שְׂעִיר־עִזִּים אֶחָד לְחַטָּאת: וּלְזֶבַח הַשְּׁלָמִים בָּקָר שְׁנַיִם אֵילִם חֲמִשָּׁה
עַתֻּדִים חֲמִשָּׁה כְּבָשִׂים בְּנֵי־שָׁנָה חֲמִשָּׁה זֶה קָרְבַּן אֲבִידָן בֶּן־גִּדְעֹנִי:

FOR THE TENTH DAY – *TEVET* – CAPRICORN – ע, SATURN - ב (NASO: NUMBERS 7:66)

בַּיּוֹם הָעֲשִׂירִי נָשִׂיא לִבְנֵי דָן אֲחִיעֶזֶר בֶּן־עַמִּישַׁדָּי: קׇרְבָּנֹו קַעֲרַת־כֶּסֶף אַחַת שְׁלֹשִׁים וּמֵאָה מִשְׁקָלָהּ מִזְרָק אֶחָד כֶּסֶף שִׁבְעִים שֶׁקֶל בְּשֶׁקֶל הַקֹּדֶשׁ שְׁנֵיהֶם | מְלֵאִים סֹלֶת בְּלוּלָה בַשֶּׁמֶן לְמִנְחָה: כַּף אַחַת עֲשָׂרָה זָהָב מְלֵאָה קְטֹרֶת: פַּר אֶחָד בֶּן־בָּקָר אַיִל אֶחָד כֶּבֶשׂ־אֶחָד בֶּן־שְׁנָתוֹ לְעֹלָה: שְׂעִיר־עִזִּים אֶחָד לְחַטָּאת: וּלְזֶבַח הַשְּׁלָמִים בָּקָר שְׁנַיִם אֵילִם חֲמִשָּׁה עַתֻּדִים חֲמִשָּׁה כְּבָשִׂים בְּנֵי־שָׁנָה חֲמִשָּׁה זֶה קׇרְבַּן אֲחִיעֶזֶר בֶּן־עַמִּישַׁדָּי:

FOR THE ELEVENTH DAY – *SHEVAT* – AQUARIUS – צ, SATURN - ב (NASO: NUMBERS 7:72)

בְּיוֹם עַשְׁתֵּי עָשָׂר יוֹם נָשִׂיא לִבְנֵי אָשֵׁר פַּגְעִיאֵל בֶּן־עׇכְרָן: קׇרְבָּנוֹ קַעֲרַת־ כֶּסֶף אַחַת שְׁלֹשִׁים וּמֵאָה מִשְׁקָלָהּ מִזְרָק אֶחָד כֶּסֶף שִׁבְעִים שֶׁקֶל בְּשֶׁקֶל הַקֹּדֶשׁ שְׁנֵיהֶם | מְלֵאִים סֹלֶת בְּלוּלָה בַשֶּׁמֶן לְמִנְחָה: כַּף אַחַת עֲשָׂרָה זָהָב מְלֵאָה קְטֹרֶת: פַּר אֶחָד בֶּן־בָּקָר אַיִל אֶחָד כֶּבֶשׂ־אֶחָד בֶּן־שְׁנָתוֹ לְעֹלָה: שְׂעִיר־עִזִּים אֶחָד לְחַטָּאת: וּלְזֶבַח הַשְּׁלָמִים בָּקָר שְׁנַיִם אֵילִם חֲמִשָּׁה עַתֻּדִים חֲמִשָּׁה כְּבָשִׂים בְּנֵי־שָׁנָה חֲמִשָּׁה זֶה קׇרְבַּן פַּגְעִיאֵל בֶּן־עׇכְרָן:

FOR THE TWELFTH DAY – *ADAR* – PISCES – ק, JUPITER - ג (NASO: NUMBERS 7:78)

בְּיוֹם שְׁנֵים עָשָׂר יוֹם נָשִׂיא לִבְנֵי נַפְתָּלִי אֲחִירַע בֶּן־עֵינָן: קׇרְבָּנוֹ קַעֲרַת־ כֶּסֶף אַחַת שְׁלֹשִׁים וּמֵאָה מִשְׁקָלָהּ מִזְרָק אֶחָד כֶּסֶף שִׁבְעִים שֶׁקֶל בְּשֶׁקֶל הַקֹּדֶשׁ שְׁנֵיהֶם | מְלֵאִים סֹלֶת בְּלוּלָה בַשֶּׁמֶן לְמִנְחָה: כַּף אַחַת עֲשָׂרָה זָהָב מְלֵאָה קְטֹרֶת: פַּר אֶחָד בֶּן־בָּקָר אַיִל אֶחָד כֶּבֶשׂ־אֶחָד בֶּן־שְׁנָתוֹ לְעֹלָה: שְׂעִיר־עִזִּים אֶחָד לְחַטָּאת: וּלְזֶבַח הַשְּׁלָמִים בָּקָר שְׁנַיִם אֵילִם חֲמִשָּׁה עַתֻּדִים חֲמִשָּׁה כְּבָשִׂים בְּנֵי־שָׁנָה חֲמִשָּׁה זֶה קׇרְבַּן אֲחִירַע בֶּן־עֵינָן:

FOR THE THIRTEENTH DAY (BEHA'ALOTECHA: NUMBERS 7:84)

וַיְדַבֵּר יְהֹוָה(אֲדֹנָי־אֱלֹהִים)אֲדֹנָי אֶל־מֹשֶׁה לֵּאמֹר: דַּבֵּר אֶל־אַהֲרֹן וְאָמַרְתָּ אֵלָיו בְּהַעֲלֹתְךָ אֶת־הַנֵּרֹת אֶל־מוּל פְּנֵי הַמְּנוֹרָה יָאִירוּ שִׁבְעַת הַנֵּרוֹת: וַיַּעַשׂ כֵּן אַהֲרֹן אֶל־מוּל פְּנֵי הַמְּנוֹרָה הֶעֱלָה נֵרֹתֶיהָ כַּאֲשֶׁר צִוָּה יְהֹוָה(אֲדֹנָי־אֱלֹהִים)אֲדֹנָי אֶת־מֹשֶׁה: וְזֶה מַעֲשֵׂה הַמְּנֹרָה מִקְשָׁה זָהָב עַד־יְרֵכָהּ עַד־פִּרְחָהּ מִקְשָׁה הִוא כַּמַּרְאֶה אֲשֶׁר הֶרְאָה יְהֹוָה(אֲדֹנָי־אֱלֹהִים)אֲדֹנָי אֶת־מֹשֶׁה כֵּן עָשָׂה אֶת־הַמְּנֹרָה:

ANA BEKO'ACH (for transaltion and explanation see more on pg. 106).

Chesed, Sunday *(Alef Bet Gimel Yud Tav Tzadik)* אבג יתץ

ana אָנָּא   beko'ach בְּכֹחַ◆   gedulat גְּדוּלַת   ◆yeminecha יְמִינְךָ

tatir תַּתִּיר   tzerura צְרוּרָה:

Gevurah, Monday *(Kuf Resh Ayin Shin Tet Nun)* קרע שטן

kabel קַבֵּל   rinat רִנַּת◆   amecha עַמְּךָ   ◆sagevenu שַׂגְּבֵנוּ

taharenu טַהֲרֵנוּ   nora נוֹרָא:

Tiferet, Tuesday *(Nun Gimel Dalet Yud Kaf Shin)* נגד יכש

na נָא   gibor גִּבּוֹר◆   dorshei דוֹרְשֵׁי   ◆yichudecha יִחוּדְךָ

kevavat כְּבָבַת   shomrem שָׁמְרֵם:

Netzach, Wednesday *(Bet Tet Resh Tzadik Tav Gimel)* בטר צתג

barchem בָּרְכֵם   taharem טַהֲרֵם◆   rachamei רַחֲמֵי   ◆tzidkatecha צִדְקָתְךָ

tamid תָּמִיד   gomlem גָּמְלֵם:

Hod, Thursday *(Chet Kuf Bet Tet Nun Ayin)* חקב טנע

chasin וְחֲסִין   kadosh קָדוֹשׁ◆   berov בְּרוֹב   ◆tuvcha טוּבְךָ

nahel נַהֵל   adatecha עֲדָתֶךָ:

Yesod, Friday *(Yud Gimel Lamed Pei Zayin Kuf)* יגל פזק

yachid יָחִיד   ge'e גֵּאֶה◆   le'amecha לְעַמְּךָ   ◆pene פְּנֵה

zochrei זוֹכְרֵי   kedushatecha קְדוּשָׁתֶךָ:

Malchut, Saturday *(Shin Kuf Vav Tzadik Yud Tav)* שקו צית

shav'atenu שַׁוְעָתֵנוּ   kabel קַבֵּל◆   ushma וּשְׁמַע   ◆tza'akatenu צַעֲקָתֵנוּ

yode'a יוֹדֵעַ   ta'alumot תַּעֲלוּמוֹת:

(Whisper) : יוֹזוֹ אותיות   baruch בָּרוּךְ   shem שֵׁם   kevod כְּבוֹד   malchuto מַלְכוּתוֹ

le'olam לְעוֹלָם ריבוע ס"ג ו' אותיות דס"ג   va'ed וָעֶד:

SHIR HAMA'ALOT (for transaltion and transliteration see on pg. 47).

שִׁיר הַמַּעֲלוֹת בְּשׁוּב יְהוָֹ֯אֱלֹהִים־אֲדֹנָי אֶת־שִׁיבַת צִיּוֹן יוֹסֵף, ר הוויה, קְנְאָה הָיִינוּ כְּחֹלְמִים:

אָז יִמָּלֵא שְׂחוֹק פִּינוּ וּלְשׁוֹנֵנוּ רִנָּה אָז יֹאמְרוּ בַגּוֹיִם הִגְדִּיל יְהוָֹ֯אֱלֹהִים־אֲדֹנָי לַעֲשׂוֹת

עִם־אֵלֶּה: הִגְדִּיל יְהוָֹ֯אֱלֹהִים־אֲדֹנָי לַעֲשׂוֹת עִמָּנוּ ריבוע דס"ג = קס"א ע"ה ו"ד אותיות הָיִינוּ שְׂמֵחִים:

שׁוּבָה הויע יְהוָֹ֯אֱלֹהִים־אֲדֹנָי אֶת־שְׁבִיתֵנוּ (כתיב שבותנו) כַּאֲפִיקִים בַּנֶּגֶב: הַזֹּרְעִים בְּדִמְעָה

בְּרִנָּה יִקְצֹרוּ: הָלוֹךְ יֵלֵךְ וּבָכֹה נֹשֵׂא מֶשֶׁךְ־הַזָּרַע בֹּא־יָבֹא בְרִנָּה נֹשֵׂא אֲלֻמֹּתָיו:

THE DAILY HALLEL (for transaltion and explanation see more on page 149).

Adonai יְ‑הֹוָ‑ה et אֶת‑ halelu הַלְלוּ ; לכה אדני, אהיה אלהים haleluya הַלְלוּיָה

haleluhu הַלְלוּהוּ ; ר"ת מ"ה יי"פ כוזו , יי"פ טל haleluhu הַלְלוּהוּ ; ר"ת אהיה min בִּן‑ hashamayim הַשָּׁמַיִם

mal'achav מַלְאָכָיו ילי chol כָּל‑ haleluhu הַלְלוּהוּ bameromim בַּמְּרוֹמִים׃

haleluhu הַלְלוּהוּ = הפסוק ס"ת ; מ"ה מ"ב ע"ב = הפסוק ר"ת tzeva'av צְבָאָו ילי kol כָּל‑ haleluhu הַלְלוּהוּ

haleluhu הַלְלוּהוּ veyare'ach וְיָרֵחַ shemesh שֶׁמֶשׁ haleluhu הַלְלוּהוּ׃ ס"ג אהיה

shemei שְׁמֵי haleluhu הַלְלוּהוּ׃ אין סוף , רו or אוֹר kochvei כּוֹכְבֵי ילי kol כָּל‑

עלם me'al מֵעַל asher אֲשֶׁר vehamayim וְהַמַּיִם כוזו יי"פ , טל יי"פ hashamayim הַשָּׁמָיִם

shem שֵׁם et אֶת‑ yehalelu יְהַלְלוּ׃ מ"ה ר"ת ; כוזו יי"פ , טל יי"פ hashamayim הַשָּׁמָיִם

venivra'u וְנִבְרָאוּ tziva צִוָּה hu הוּא ki כִּי Adonai יְ‑הֹוָ‑ה

אותיות ו' ס"ג ריבוע le'olam לְעוֹלָם ב"ן ב"פ la'ad לָעַד vaya'amidem וַיַּעֲמִידֵם

מקוה , הה יוד הה אלף) קנ"א ס"ת velo וְלֹא natan נָתַן chok חֹק‑ אלהים אדני ,

halelu הַלְלוּ׃ (התולאים באים דמעים לקליפה שנפלו נצוצות רפ"ח להעלות) רפ"ח ya'avor יַעֲבוֹר

taninim תַּנִּינִים ע"ה דההן אלהים ha'aretz הָאָרֶץ min בִּן‑ Adonai יְ‑הֹוָ‑ה et אֶת‑

אלף אלף אלף sheleg שֶׁלֶג uvarad וּבָרָד esh אֵשׁ tehomot תְּהֹמוֹת׃ ילי vechol וְכָל‑

devaro דְּבָרוֹ osa עֹשָׂה se'ara סְעָרָה ru'ach רוּחַ vekitor וְקִיטוֹר׃ אהיה הג

peri פְּרִי etz עֵץ geva'ot גְּבָעוֹת ילי vechol וְכָל‑ heharim הֶהָרִים

remes רֶמֶשׂ ב"ן behema בְּהֵמָה ילי vechol וְכָל‑ hachaya הַחַיָּה arazim אֲרָזִים׃

eretz אֶרֶץ malchei מַלְכֵי אלהים אדני , קנ"א ע"ה kanaf כָּנָף vetzipor וְצִפּוֹר

shoftei שֹׁפְטֵי ילי vechol וְכָל‑ sarim שָׂרִים le'umim לְאֻמִּים ילי vechol וְכָל‑

zekenim זְקֵנִים betulot בְּתוּלוֹת vegam וְגַם‑ bachurim בַּחוּרִים aretz אָרֶץ׃

Adonai יְ‑הֹוָ‑ה shem שֵׁם et אֶת‑ yehalelu יְהַלְלוּ׃ ne'arim נְעָרִים im עִם‑

אל שדי ע"ה קס"א ע"ה , ע"ב בריבוע ע"ב , מהש ע"ה shemo שְׁמוֹ nisgav נִשְׂגָּב ki כִּי

veshamayim וְשָׁמָיִם eretz אֶרֶץ al עַל‑ hodo הוֹדוֹ לשם בן מ"ב levado לְבַדּוֹ

אמת , ע"ה tehila תְּהִלָּה le'amo לְעַמּוֹ keren קֶרֶן vayarem וַיָּרֶם׃ כוזו יי"פ , טל יי"פ

livnei לִבְנֵי chasidav וְחֲסִידָיו אדני יה lechol לְכָל‑ ס"ג ז"פ , אהיה פעמים אהיה

Yisrael יִשְׂרָאֵל am עַם‑ kerovo קְרֹבוֹ haleluya הַלְלוּיָה אלהים , אהיה אדני ; לכה׃

THREE COINS

The most effective method to reveal all the Light that we have aroused is by sharing and behaving like the Light: Similarity of nature begets closeness in the spiritual realm. Being close to the Creator means having the Light in your life. Therefore, we give three coins as an act of sharing and charity. These three coins connect to Right, Left, and Central Columns, thereby completing the circuitry established by all of our prayers and actions of sharing.

BERESHEET

בְּרֵאשִׁית בָּרָא אֱלֹהִים אֵת הַשָּׁמַיִם וְאֵת הָאָרֶץ: וְהָאָרֶץ הָיְתָה תֹהוּ וָבֹהוּ וְחֹשֶׁךְ
עַל־פְּנֵי תְהוֹם וְרוּחַ אֱלֹהִים מְרַחֶפֶת עַל־פְּנֵי הַמָּיִם: וַיֹּאמֶר אֱלֹהִים יְהִי אוֹר וַיְהִי־אוֹר:
וַיַּרְא אֱלֹהִים אֶת־הָאוֹר כִּי־טוֹב וַיַּבְדֵּל אֱלֹהִים בֵּין הָאוֹר וּבֵין הַחֹשֶׁךְ:
וַיִּקְרָא אֱלֹהִים | לָאוֹר יוֹם וְלַחֹשֶׁךְ קָרָא לָיְלָה וַיְהִי־עֶרֶב וַיְהִי־בֹקֶר יוֹם אֶחָד: *Levi*
וַיֹּאמֶר אֱלֹהִים יְהִי רָקִיעַ בְּתוֹךְ הַמָּיִם וִיהִי מַבְדִּיל בֵּין מַיִם לָמָיִם: וַיַּעַשׂ אֱלֹהִים
אֶת־הָרָקִיעַ וַיַּבְדֵּל בֵּין הַמַּיִם אֲשֶׁר מִתַּחַת לָרָקִיעַ וּבֵין הַמַּיִם אֲשֶׁר מֵעַל לָרָקִיעַ
וַיְהִי־כֵן: וַיִּקְרָא אֱלֹהִים לָרָקִיעַ שָׁמָיִם וַיְהִי־עֶרֶב וַיְהִי־בֹקֶר יוֹם שֵׁנִי: *Yisrael*
וַיֹּאמֶר אֱלֹהִים יִקָּווּ הַמַּיִם מִתַּחַת הַשָּׁמַיִם אֶל־מָקוֹם אֶחָד וְתֵרָאֶה הַיַּבָּשָׁה וַיְהִי־כֵן:
וַיִּקְרָא אֱלֹהִים | לַיַּבָּשָׁה אֶרֶץ וּלְמִקְוֵה הַמַּיִם קָרָא יַמִּים וַיַּרְא אֱלֹהִים כִּי־טוֹב: וַיֹּאמֶר
אֱלֹהִים תַּדְשֵׁא הָאָרֶץ דֶּשֶׁא עֵשֶׂב מַזְרִיעַ זֶרַע עֵץ פְּרִי עֹשֶׂה פְּרִי לְמִינוֹ אֲשֶׁר זַרְעוֹ־בוֹ
עַל־הָאָרֶץ וַיְהִי־כֵן: וַתּוֹצֵא הָאָרֶץ דֶּשֶׁא עֵשֶׂב מַזְרִיעַ זֶרַע לְמִינֵהוּ וְעֵץ עֹשֶׂה־פְּרִי
אֲשֶׁר זַרְעוֹ־בוֹ לְמִינֵהוּ וַיַּרְא אֱלֹהִים כִּי־טוֹב: וַיְהִי־עֶרֶב וַיְהִי־בֹקֶר יוֹם שְׁלִישִׁי:

NO'ACH

אֵלֶּה תּוֹלְדֹת נֹחַ נֹחַ אִישׁ צַדִּיק תָּמִים הָיָה בְּדֹרֹתָיו אֶת־הָאֱלֹהִים הִתְהַלֶּךְ־נֹחַ: וַיּוֹלֶד נֹחַ
שְׁלֹשָׁה בָנִים אֶת־שֵׁם אֶת־חָם וְאֶת־יָפֶת: וַתִּשָּׁחֵת הָאָרֶץ לִפְנֵי הָאֱלֹהִים וַתִּמָּלֵא הָאָרֶץ
חָמָס: וַיַּרְא אֱלֹהִים אֶת־הָאָרֶץ וְהִנֵּה נִשְׁחָתָה כִּי־הִשְׁחִית כָּל־בָּשָׂר אֶת־דַּרְכּוֹ
עַל־הָאָרֶץ: וַיֹּאמֶר אֱלֹהִים לְנֹחַ קֵץ כָּל־בָּשָׂר בָּא לְפָנַי כִּי־מָלְאָה הָאָרֶץ חָמָס מִפְּנֵיהֶם
וְהִנְנִי מַשְׁחִיתָם אֶת־הָאָרֶץ: עֲשֵׂה לְךָ תֵּבַת עֲצֵי־גֹפֶר קִנִּים תַּעֲשֶׂה אֶת־הַתֵּבָה וְכָפַרְתָּ
אֹתָהּ מִבַּיִת וּמִחוּץ בַּכֹּפֶר: וְזֶה אֲשֶׁר תַּעֲשֶׂה אֹתָהּ שְׁלֹשׁ מֵאוֹת אַמָּה אֹרֶךְ הַתֵּבָה
חֲמִשִּׁים אַמָּה רָחְבָּהּ וּשְׁלֹשִׁים אַמָּה קוֹמָתָהּ: צֹהַר | תַּעֲשֶׂה לַתֵּבָה וְאֶל־אַמָּה
תְּכַלֶּנָּה מִלְמַעְלָה וּפֶתַח הַתֵּבָה בְּצִדָּהּ תָּשִׂים תַּחְתִּיִּם שְׁנִיִּם וּשְׁלִשִׁים תַּעֲשֶׂהָ:   *Levi*
וַאֲנִי הִנְנִי מֵבִיא אֶת־הַמַּבּוּל מַיִם עַל־הָאָרֶץ לְשַׁחֵת כָּל־בָּשָׂר אֲשֶׁר־בּוֹ
רוּחַ חַיִּים מִתַּחַת הַשָּׁמָיִם כֹּל אֲשֶׁר־בָּאָרֶץ יִגְוָע: וַהֲקִמֹתִי אֶת־בְּרִיתִי אִתָּךְ
וּבָאתָ אֶל־הַתֵּבָה אַתָּה וּבָנֶיךָ וְאִשְׁתְּךָ וּנְשֵׁי־בָנֶיךָ אִתָּךְ: וּמִכָּל־הָחַי מִכָּל־בָּשָׂר
שְׁנַיִם מִכֹּל תָּבִיא אֶל־הַתֵּבָה לְהַחֲיֹת אִתָּךְ זָכָר וּנְקֵבָה יִהְיוּ:   *Yisrael*
מֵהָעוֹף לְמִינֵהוּ וּמִן־הַבְּהֵמָה לְמִינָהּ מִכֹּל רֶמֶשׂ הָאֲדָמָה לְמִינֵהוּ שְׁנַיִם מִכֹּל
יָבֹאוּ אֵלֶיךָ לְהַחֲיוֹת: וְאַתָּה קַח־לְךָ מִכָּל־מַאֲכָל אֲשֶׁר יֵאָכֵל וְאָסַפְתָּ אֵלֶיךָ
וְהָיָה לְךָ וְלָהֶם לְאָכְלָה: וַיַּעַשׂ נֹחַ כְּכֹל אֲשֶׁר צִוָּה אֹתוֹ אֱלֹהִים כֵּן עָשָׂה:

LECH LECHA

וַיֹּאמֶר יְהוָֹה אֶל־אַבְרָם לֶךְ־לְךָ מֵאַרְצְךָ וּמִמּוֹלַדְתְּךָ וּמִבֵּית אָבִיךָ
אֶל־הָאָרֶץ אֲשֶׁר אַרְאֶךָּ: וְאֶעֶשְׂךָ לְגוֹי גָּדוֹל וַאֲבָרֶכְךָ וַאֲגַדְּלָה שְׁמֶךָ וֶהְיֵה בְּרָכָה:
וַאֲבָרֲכָה מְבָרְכֶיךָ וּמְקַלֶּלְךָ אָאֹר וְנִבְרְכוּ בְךָ כֹּל מִשְׁפְּחֹת הָאֲדָמָה: *Levi*

וַיֵּ֣לֶךְ אַבְרָ֗ם כַּאֲשֶׁ֨ר דִּבֶּ֤ר אֵלָיו֙ יְהֹוָ֔אֱלֹהִים֠אֲדֹנָי וַיֵּ֥לֶךְ אִתּ֖וֹ ל֑וֹט וְאַבְרָ֗ם בֶּן־חָמֵ֤שׁ
שָׁנִים֙ וְשִׁבְעִ֣ים שָׁנָ֔ה בְּצֵאת֖וֹ מֵחָרָֽן: וַיִּקַּ֣ח אַבְרָם֩ אֶת־שָׂרַ֨י אִשְׁתּ֜וֹ וְאֶת־ל֣וֹט
בֶּן־אָחִ֗יו וְאֶת־כָּל־רְכוּשָׁם֙ אֲשֶׁ֣ר רָכָ֔שׁוּ וְאֶת־הַנֶּ֖פֶשׁ אֲשֶׁר־עָשׂ֣וּ בְחָרָ֑ן וַיֵּצְא֗וּ
לָלֶ֨כֶת֙ אַ֣רְצָה כְּנַ֔עַן וַיָּבֹ֖אוּ אַ֣רְצָה כְּנָֽעַן: וַיַּעֲבֹ֤ר אַבְרָם֙ בָּאָ֔רֶץ עַ֚ד מְק֣וֹם שְׁכֶ֔ם עַ֖ד
אֵל֣וֹן מוֹרֶ֑ה וְהַֽכְּנַעֲנִ֖י אָ֥ז בָּאָֽרֶץ: _Yisrael_ וַיֵּרָ֤א יְהֹוָ֨אֱלֹהִים֠אֲדֹנָי אֶל־אַבְרָ֔ם וַיֹּ֕אמֶר
לְזַ֨רְעֲךָ֔ אֶתֵּ֖ן אֶת־הָאָ֣רֶץ הַזֹּ֑את וַיִּ֤בֶן שָׁם֙ מִזְבֵּ֔חַ לַיהֹוָ֨אֱלֹהִים֠אֲדֹנָי הַנִּרְאֶ֥ה אֵלָֽיו:
וַיַּעְתֵּ֨ק מִשָּׁ֜ם הָהָ֗רָה מִקֶּ֛דֶם לְבֵית־אֵ֖ל וַיֵּ֣ט אָֽהֳלֹ֑ה בֵּֽית־אֵ֤ל מִיָּם֙ וְהָעַ֣י מִקֶּ֔דֶם וַיִּֽבֶן־שָׁ֤ם
מִזְבֵּ֨חַ֙ לַֽיהֹוָ֨אֱלֹהִים֠אֲדֹנָי וַיִּקְרָ֖א בְּשֵׁ֥ם יְהֹוָ֨אֱלֹהִים֠אֲדֹנָי: וַיִּסַּ֣ע אַבְרָ֔ם הָל֥וֹךְ וְנָס֖וֹעַ הַנֶּֽגְבָּה:
וַיְהִ֥י רָעָ֖ב בָּאָ֑רֶץ וַיֵּ֨רֶד אַבְרָ֤ם מִצְרַ֨יְמָה֙ לָג֣וּר שָׁ֔ם כִּֽי־כָבֵ֥ד הָרָעָ֖ב בָּאָֽרֶץ:
וַיְהִ֕י כַּֽאֲשֶׁ֥ר הִקְרִ֖יב לָב֣וֹא מִצְרָ֑יְמָה וַיֹּ֨אמֶר֙ אֶל־שָׂרַ֣י אִשְׁתּ֔וֹ הִנֵּה־נָ֣א יָדַ֔עְתִּי
כִּ֛י אִשָּׁ֥ה יְפַת־מַרְאֶ֖ה אָֽתְּ: וְהָיָ֗ה כִּֽי־יִרְא֤וּ אֹתָךְ֙ הַמִּצְרִ֔ים וְאָמְר֖וּ אִשְׁתּ֣וֹ זֹ֑את וְהָרְג֥וּ
אֹתִ֖י וְאֹתָ֥ךְ יְחַיֽוּ: אִמְרִי־נָ֖א אֲחֹ֣תִי אָ֑תְּ לְמַ֨עַן֙ יִֽיטַב־לִ֣י בַעֲבוּרֵ֔ךְ וְחָיְתָ֥ה נַפְשִׁ֖י בִּגְלָלֵֽךְ:

VAYERA

וַיֵּרָ֤א אֵלָיו֙ יְהֹוָ֨אֱלֹהִים֠אֲדֹנָי בְּאֵלֹנֵ֖י מַמְרֵ֑א וְה֛וּא יֹשֵׁ֥ב פֶּֽתַח־הָאֹ֖הֶל כְּחֹ֥ם הַיּֽוֹם: וַיִּשָּׂ֤א
עֵינָיו֙ וַיַּ֔רְא וְהִנֵּה֙ שְׁלֹשָׁ֣ה אֲנָשִׁ֔ים נִצָּבִ֖ים עָלָ֑יו וַיַּ֗רְא וַיָּ֤רָץ לִקְרָאתָם֙ מִפֶּ֣תַח הָאֹ֔הֶל
וַיִּשְׁתַּ֖חוּ אָֽרְצָה: וַיֹּאמַ֑ר אֲדֹנָ֗י אִם־נָ֨א מָצָ֤אתִי חֵן֙ בְּעֵינֶ֔יךָ אַל־נָ֥א תַעֲבֹ֖ר מֵעַ֥ל עַבְדֶּֽךָ:
יֻקַּֽח־נָ֣א מְעַט־מַ֔יִם וְרַחֲצ֖וּ רַגְלֵיכֶ֑ם וְהִֽשָּׁעֲנ֖וּ תַּ֥חַת הָעֵֽץ: וְאֶקְחָ֨ה פַת־לֶ֜חֶם וְסַעֲד֤וּ לִבְּכֶם֙
אַחַ֣ר תַּעֲבֹ֔רוּ כִּֽי־עַל־כֵּ֥ן עֲבַרְתֶּ֖ם עַֽל־עַבְדְּכֶ֑ם וַיֹּ֣אמְר֔וּ כֵּ֥ן תַּעֲשֶׂ֖ה כַּאֲשֶׁ֥ר דִּבַּֽרְתָּ: _Levi_
וַיְמַהֵ֧ר אַבְרָהָ֛ם הָאֹ֖הֱלָה אֶל־שָׂרָ֑ה וַיֹּ֗אמֶר מַהֲרִ֞י שְׁלֹ֤שׁ סְאִים֙ קֶ֣מַח סֹ֔לֶת ל֖וּשִׁי
וַעֲשִׂ֥י עֻגֽוֹת: וְאֶל־הַבָּקָ֖ר רָ֣ץ אַבְרָהָ֑ם וַיִּקַּ֨ח בֶּן־בָּקָ֜ר רַ֤ךְ וָטוֹב֙ וַיִּתֵּ֣ן אֶל־הַנַּ֔עַר
וַיְמַהֵ֖ר לַעֲשׂ֥וֹת אֹתֽוֹ: וַיִּקַּ֨ח חֶמְאָ֜ה וְחָלָ֗ב וּבֶן־הַבָּקָר֙ אֲשֶׁ֣ר עָשָׂ֔ה וַיִּתֵּ֖ן לִפְנֵיהֶ֑ם וְהֽוּא־עֹמֵ֧ד
עֲלֵיהֶ֛ם תַּ֥חַת הָעֵ֖ץ וַיֹּאכֵֽלוּ: _Yisrael_ וַיֹּאמְר֣וּ אֵלָ֔יו אַיֵּ֖ה שָׂרָ֣ה אִשְׁתֶּ֑ךָ וַיֹּ֖אמֶר הִנֵּ֥ה בָאֹֽהֶל:
וַיֹּ֗אמֶר שׁ֣וֹב אָשׁ֤וּב אֵלֶ֨יךָ֙ כָּעֵ֣ת חַיָּ֔ה וְהִנֵּה־בֵ֖ן לְשָׂרָ֣ה אִשְׁתֶּ֑ךָ וְשָׂרָ֥ה שֹׁמַ֛עַת פֶּ֥תַח הָאֹ֖הֶל
וְה֥וּא אַחֲרָֽיו: וְאַבְרָהָ֤ם וְשָׂרָה֙ זְקֵנִ֔ים בָּאִ֖ים בַּיָּמִ֑ים חָדַל֙ לִהְי֣וֹת לְשָׂרָ֔ה אֹ֖רַח כַּנָּשִֽׁים:
וַתִּצְחַ֥ק שָׂרָ֖ה בְּקִרְבָּ֣הּ לֵאמֹ֑ר אַחֲרֵ֤י בְלֹתִי֙ הָֽיְתָה־לִּ֣י עֶדְנָ֔ה וַֽאדֹנִ֖י זָקֵֽן: וַיֹּ֥אמֶר
יְהֹוָ֨אֱלֹהִים֠אֲדֹנָי אֶל־אַבְרָהָ֑ם לָ֣מָּה זֶּה֩ צָחֲקָ֨ה שָׂרָ֜ה לֵאמֹ֗ר הַאַ֥ף אֻמְנָ֛ם אֵלֵ֖ד
וַאֲנִ֥י זָקַֽנְתִּי: הֲיִפָּלֵ֥א מֵֽיהֹוָ֨אֱלֹהִים֠אֲדֹנָי דָּבָ֑ר לַמּוֹעֵ֞ד אָשׁ֥וּב אֵלֶ֛יךָ כָּעֵ֥ת חַיָּ֖ה וּלְשָׂרָ֥ה בֵֽן:

CHAYEI SARAH

וַיִּהְיוּ֙ חַיֵּ֣י שָׂרָ֔ה מֵאָ֥ה שָׁנָ֛ה וְעֶשְׂרִ֥ים שָׁנָ֖ה וְשֶׁ֣בַע שָׁנִ֑ים שְׁנֵ֖י חַיֵּ֥י שָׂרָֽה: וַתָּ֣מָת שָׂרָ֗ה
בְּקִרְיַ֥ת אַרְבַּ֛ע הִ֥וא חֶבְר֖וֹן בְּאֶ֣רֶץ כְּנָ֑עַן וַיָּבֹא֙ אַבְרָהָ֔ם לִסְפֹּ֥ד לְשָׂרָ֖ה וְלִבְכֹּתָֽהּ: וַיָּ֨קָם֙
אַבְרָהָ֔ם מֵעַ֖ל פְּנֵ֣י מֵת֑וֹ וַיְדַבֵּ֥ר אֶל־בְּנֵי־חֵ֖ת לֵאמֹֽר: גֵּר־וְתוֹשָׁ֥ב אָנֹכִ֖י עִמָּכֶ֑ם תְּנ֨וּ לִ֤י
אֲחֻזַּת־קֶ֨בֶר֙ עִמָּכֶ֔ם וְאֶקְבְּרָ֥ה מֵתִ֖י מִלְּפָנָֽי: וַיַּעֲנ֧וּ בְנֵי־חֵ֛ת אֶת־אַבְרָהָ֖ם לֵאמֹ֥ר לֽוֹ: שְׁמָעֵ֣נוּ ׀
אֲדֹנִ֗י נְשִׂ֨יא אֱלֹהִ֤ים אַתָּה֙ בְּתוֹכֵ֔נוּ בְּמִבְחַ֣ר קְבָרֵ֔ינוּ קְבֹ֖ר אֶת־מֵתֶ֑ךָ אִ֣ישׁ מִמֶּ֔נּוּ אֶת־
Levi קִבְר֔וֹ לֹֽא־יִכְלֶ֥ה מִמְּךָ֖ מִקְּבֹ֥ר מֵתֶֽךָ: וַיָּ֧קָם אַבְרָהָ֛ם וַיִּשְׁתַּ֥חוּ לְעַם־הָאָ֖רֶץ לִבְנֵי־חֵֽת:

וַיְדַבֵּ֣ר אִתָּ֔ם לֵאמֹ֑ר אִם־יֵ֣שׁ אֶֽת־נַפְשְׁכֶ֗ם לִקְבֹּ֤ר אֶת־מֵתִי֙ מִלְּפָנַ֔י שְׁמָע֕וּנִי וּפִגְעוּ־לִ֖י
בְּעֶפְר֥וֹן בֶּן־צֹֽחַר: וְיִתֶּן־לִ֗י אֶת־מְעָרַ֤ת הַמַּכְפֵּלָה֙ אֲשֶׁר־ל֔וֹ אֲשֶׁ֖ר בִּקְצֵ֣ה שָׂדֵ֑הוּ בְּכֶ֨סֶף
מָלֵ֜א יִתְּנֶ֥נָּה לִ֛י בְּתֽוֹכְכֶ֖ם לַאֲחֻזַּת־קָֽבֶר: וְעֶפְר֥וֹן יֹשֵׁ֖ב בְּת֣וֹךְ בְּנֵי־חֵ֑ת וַיַּ֩עַן֩ עֶפְר֨וֹן הַֽחִתִּ֜י
אֶת־אַבְרָהָ֗ם בְּאָזְנֵ֤י בְנֵי־חֵת֙ לְכֹ֛ל בָּאֵ֥י שַֽׁעַר־עִיר֖וֹ לֵאמֹֽר: לֹֽא־אֲדֹנִ֣י שְׁמָעֵ֔נִי
הַשָּׂדֶה֙ נָתַ֣תִּי לָ֔ךְ וְהַמְּעָרָ֥ה אֲשֶׁר־בּ֖וֹ לְךָ֣ נְתַתִּ֑יהָ לְעֵינֵ֧י בְנֵֽי־עַמִּ֛י נְתַתִּ֥יהָ לָּ֖ךְ קְבֹ֥ר מֵתֶֽךָ:
וַיִּשְׁתַּ֨חוּ֙ אַבְרָהָ֔ם לִפְנֵ֖י עַ֥ם הָאָֽרֶץ: *Yisrael* וַיְדַבֵּ֨ר אֶל־עֶפְר֜וֹן בְּאָזְנֵ֤י עַם־הָאָ֙רֶץ֙ לֵאמֹ֔ר
אַ֛ךְ אִם־אַתָּ֥ה ל֖וּ שְׁמָעֵ֑נִי נָתַ֜תִּי כֶּ֤סֶף הַשָּׂדֶה֙ קַ֣ח מִמֶּ֔נִּי וְאֶקְבְּרָ֥ה אֶת־מֵתִ֖י שָֽׁמָּה:
וַיַּ֧עַן עֶפְר֛וֹן אֶת־אַבְרָהָ֖ם לֵאמֹ֥ר לֽוֹ: אֲדֹנִ֣י שְׁמָעֵ֔נִי אֶ֩רֶץ֩ אַרְבַּ֨ע מֵאֹ֧ת שֶֽׁקֶל־כֶּ֛סֶף בֵּינִ֥י
וּבֵֽינְךָ֖ מַה־הִ֑וא וְאֶת־מֵתְךָ֖ קְבֹֽר: וַיִּשְׁמַ֣ע אַבְרָהָם֮ אֶל־עֶפְרוֹן֒ וַיִּשְׁקֹ֤ל אַבְרָהָם֙ לְעֶפְרֹ֔ן
אֶת־הַכֶּ֕סֶף אֲשֶׁ֥ר דִּבֶּ֖ר בְּאָזְנֵ֣י בְנֵי־חֵ֑ת אַרְבַּ֤ע מֵאוֹת֙ שֶׁ֣קֶל כֶּ֔סֶף עֹבֵ֖ר לַסֹּחֵֽר:

TOLDOT

וְאֵ֛לֶּה תּוֹלְדֹ֥ת יִצְחָ֖ק בֶּן־אַבְרָהָ֑ם אַבְרָהָ֖ם הוֹלִ֥יד אֶת־יִצְחָֽק: וַיְהִ֤י יִצְחָק֙
בֶּן־אַרְבָּעִ֣ים שָׁנָ֔ה בְּקַחְתּ֣וֹ אֶת־רִבְקָ֗ה בַּת־בְּתוּאֵל֙ הָֽאֲרַמִּ֔י מִפַּדַּ֖ן אֲרָ֑ם
אֲח֛וֹת לָבָ֥ן הָאֲרַמִּ֖י ל֥וֹ לְאִשָּֽׁה: וַיֶּעְתַּ֨ר יִצְחָ֤ק לַֽיהֹוָ֙ה לְנֹ֣כַח אִשְׁתּ֔וֹ
כִּ֥י עֲקָרָ֖ה הִ֑וא וַיֵּעָ֤תֶר לוֹ֙ יְהֹוָ֔ה וַתַּ֖הַר רִבְקָ֥ה אִשְׁתּֽוֹ: וַיִּתְרֹֽצֲצ֤וּ הַבָּנִים֙ בְּקִרְבָּ֔הּ
Levi וַתֹּ֣אמֶר אִם־כֵּ֔ן לָ֥מָּה זֶּ֖ה אָנֹ֑כִי וַתֵּ֖לֶךְ לִדְרֹ֥שׁ אֶת־יְהֹוָֽה:
וַיֹּ֨אמֶר יְהֹוָ֜ה לָ֗הּ שְׁנֵ֤י גוֹיִם֙ (כתיב: גיים) בְּבִטְנֵ֔ךְ וּשְׁנֵ֣י לְאֻמִּ֔ים
מִמֵּעַ֖יִךְ יִפָּרֵ֑דוּ וּלְאֹם֙ מִלְאֹ֣ם יֶֽאֱמָ֔ץ וְרַ֖ב יַעֲבֹ֥ד צָעִֽיר: וַיִּמְלְא֥וּ יָמֶ֖יהָ לָלֶ֑דֶת
וְהִנֵּ֥ה תוֹמִ֖ם בְּבִטְנָֽהּ: וַיֵּצֵ֤א הָֽרִאשׁוֹן֙ אַדְמוֹנִ֔י כֻּלּ֖וֹ כְּאַדֶּ֣רֶת שֵׂעָ֑ר וַיִּקְרְא֥וּ שְׁמ֖וֹ עֵשָֽׂו:
וְאַֽחֲרֵי־כֵ֞ן יָצָ֣א אָחִ֗יו וְיָד֤וֹ אֹחֶ֙זֶת֙ בַּעֲקֵ֣ב עֵשָׂ֔ו וַיִּקְרָ֥א שְׁמ֖וֹ יַעֲקֹ֑ב וְיִצְחָ֛ק בֶּן־שִׁשִּׁ֥ים
שָׁנָ֖ה בְּלֶ֥דֶת אֹתָֽם: *Yisrael* וַֽיִּגְדְּלוּ֙ הַנְּעָרִ֔ים וַיְהִ֣י עֵשָׂ֗ו אִ֛ישׁ יֹדֵ֥עַ צַ֖יִד אִ֣ישׁ שָׂדֶ֑ה
וְיַעֲקֹב֙ אִ֣ישׁ תָּ֔ם יֹשֵׁ֖ב אֹהָלִֽים: וַיֶּאֱהַ֥ב יִצְחָ֛ק אֶת־עֵשָׂ֖ו כִּי־צַ֣יִד בְּפִ֑יו וְרִבְקָ֖ה אֹהֶ֥בֶת
אֶֽת־יַעֲקֹֽב: וַיָּ֥זֶד יַעֲקֹ֖ב נָזִ֑יד וַיָּבֹ֥א עֵשָׂ֛ו מִן־הַשָּׂדֶ֖ה וְה֥וּא עָיֵֽף: וַיֹּ֨אמֶר עֵשָׂ֜ו אֶֽל־יַעֲקֹ֗ב
הַלְעִיטֵ֤נִי נָא֙ מִן־הָאָדֹ֤ם הָאָדֹם֙ הַזֶּ֔ה כִּ֥י עָיֵ֖ף אָנֹ֑כִי עַל־כֵּ֥ן קָרָֽא־שְׁמ֖וֹ אֱדֽוֹם:
וַיֹּ֖אמֶר יַעֲקֹ֑ב מִכְרָ֥ה כַיּ֛וֹם אֶת־בְּכֹֽרָתְךָ֖ לִֽי: וַיֹּ֣אמֶר עֵשָׂ֔ו הִנֵּ֛ה אָנֹכִ֥י הוֹלֵ֖ךְ לָמ֑וּת
וְלָמָּה־זֶּ֥ה לִ֖י בְּכֹרָֽה: וַיֹּ֣אמֶר יַעֲקֹ֗ב הִשָּׁ֤בְעָה לִּי֙ כַּיּ֔וֹם וַיִּשָּׁבַ֖ע ל֑וֹ וַיִּמְכֹּ֥ר אֶת־בְּכֹרָת֖וֹ
לְיַעֲקֹֽב: וְיַעֲקֹ֞ב נָתַ֣ן לְעֵשָׂ֗ו לֶ֚חֶם וּנְזִ֣יד עֲדָשִׁ֔ים וַיֹּ֣אכַל וַיֵּ֔שְׁתְּ וַיָּ֖קׇם וַיֵּלַ֑ךְ וַיִּ֥בֶז עֵשָׂ֖ו
אֶת־הַבְּכֹרָֽה: וַיְהִ֤י רָעָב֙ בָּאָ֔רֶץ מִלְּבַד֙ הָרָעָ֣ב הָרִאשׁ֔וֹן אֲשֶׁ֥ר הָיָ֖ה בִּימֵ֣י אַבְרָהָ֑ם
וַיֵּ֧לֶךְ יִצְחָ֛ק אֶל־אֲבִימֶ֥לֶךְ מֶֽלֶךְ־פְּלִשְׁתִּ֖ים גְּרָֽרָה: וַיֵּרָ֤א אֵלָיו֙ יְהֹוָ֔ה וַיֹּ֖אמֶר
אַל־תֵּרֵ֣ד מִצְרָ֑יְמָה שְׁכֹ֣ן בָּאָ֔רֶץ אֲשֶׁ֖ר אֹמַ֥ר אֵלֶֽיךָ: גּ֚וּר בָּאָ֣רֶץ הַזֹּ֔את וְאֶֽהְיֶ֥ה עִמְּךָ֖
וַאֲבָרְכֶ֑ךָּ כִּֽי־לְךָ֣ וּֽלְזַרְעֲךָ֗ אֶתֵּן֙ אֶת־כׇּל־הָֽאֲרָצֹ֣ת הָאֵ֔ל וַהֲקִֽמֹתִי֙ אֶת־הַשְּׁבֻעָ֔ה
אֲשֶׁ֥ר נִשְׁבַּ֖עְתִּי לְאַבְרָהָ֣ם אָבִֽיךָ: וְהִרְבֵּיתִ֤י אֶֽת־זַרְעֲךָ֙ כְּכֽוֹכְבֵ֣י הַשָּׁמַ֔יִם
וְנָתַתִּ֣י לְזַרְעֲךָ֗ אֵ֚ת כׇּל־הָאֲרָצֹ֣ת הָאֵ֔ל וְהִתְבָּרְכ֣וּ בְזַרְעֲךָ֔ כֹּ֖ל גּוֹיֵ֥י הָאָֽרֶץ:
עֵ֕קֶב אֲשֶׁר־שָׁמַ֥ע אַבְרָהָ֖ם בְּקֹלִ֑י וַיִּשְׁמֹר֙ מִשְׁמַרְתִּ֔י מִצְוֺתַ֖י חֻקּוֹתַ֥י וְתוֹרֹתָֽי:

VAYETZE

וַיֵּצֵא יַעֲקֹב מִבְּאֵר שָׁבַע וַיֵּלֶךְ חָרָנָה: וַיִּפְגַּע בַּמָּקוֹם וַיָּלֶן שָׁם כִּי־בָא הַשֶּׁמֶשׁ
וַיִּקַּח מֵאַבְנֵי הַמָּקוֹם וַיָּשֶׂם מְרַאֲשֹׁתָיו וַיִּשְׁכַּב בַּמָּקוֹם הַהוּא: וַיַּחֲלֹם וְהִנֵּה סֻלָּם מֻצָּב
אַרְצָה וְרֹאשׁוֹ מַגִּיעַ הַשָּׁמָיְמָה וְהִנֵּה מַלְאֲכֵי אֱלֹהִים עֹלִים וְיֹרְדִים בּוֹ: *Levi*
וְהִנֵּה יְהֹוָֽהֲדֹנָי נִצָּב עָלָיו וַיֹּאמַר אֲנִי יְהֹוָֽהֲדֹנָי אֱלֹהֵי אַבְרָהָם אָבִיךָ וֵאלֹהֵי
יִצְחָק הָאָרֶץ אֲשֶׁר אַתָּה שֹׁכֵב עָלֶיהָ לְךָ אֶתְּנֶנָּה וּלְזַרְעֶךָ: וְהָיָה זַרְעֲךָ כַּעֲפַר הָאָרֶץ
וּפָרַצְתָּ יָמָּה וָקֵדְמָה וְצָפֹנָה וָנֶגְבָּה וְנִבְרְכוּ בְךָ כָּל־מִשְׁפְּחֹת הָאֲדָמָה וּבְזַרְעֶךָ: וְהִנֵּה
אָנֹכִי עִמָּךְ וּשְׁמַרְתִּיךָ בְּכֹל אֲשֶׁר־תֵּלֵךְ וַהֲשִׁבֹתִיךָ אֶל־הָאֲדָמָה הַזֹּאת כִּי לֹא אֶעֱזָבְךָ
עַד אֲשֶׁר אִם־עָשִׂיתִי אֵת אֲשֶׁר־דִּבַּרְתִּי לָךְ: וַיִּיקַץ יַעֲקֹב מִשְּׁנָתוֹ וַיֹּאמֶר אָכֵן יֵשׁ
יְהֹוָֽהֲדֹנָי בַּמָּקוֹם הַזֶּה וְאָנֹכִי לֹא יָדָעְתִּי: וַיִּירָא וַיֹּאמַר מַה־נּוֹרָא הַמָּקוֹם הַזֶּה אֵין
זֶה כִּי אִם־בֵּית אֱלֹהִים וְזֶה שַׁעַר הַשָּׁמָיִם: *Yisrael* וַיַּשְׁכֵּם יַעֲקֹב בַּבֹּקֶר וַיִּקַּח אֶת־
הָאֶבֶן אֲשֶׁר־שָׂם מְרַאֲשֹׁתָיו וַיָּשֶׂם אֹתָהּ מַצֵּבָה וַיִּצֹק שֶׁמֶן עַל־רֹאשָׁהּ: וַיִּקְרָא אֶת־שֵׁם־
הַמָּקוֹם הַהוּא בֵּית־אֵל וְאוּלָם לוּז שֵׁם־הָעִיר לָרִאשֹׁנָה: וַיִּדַּר יַעֲקֹב נֶדֶר לֵאמֹר
אִם־יִהְיֶה אֱלֹהִים עִמָּדִי וּשְׁמָרַנִי בַּדֶּרֶךְ הַזֶּה אֲשֶׁר אָנֹכִי הוֹלֵךְ וְנָתַן־לִי לֶחֶם לֶאֱכֹל
וּבֶגֶד לִלְבֹּשׁ: וְשַׁבְתִּי בְשָׁלוֹם אֶל־בֵּית אָבִי וְהָיָה יְהֹוָֽהֲדֹנָי לִי לֵאלֹהִים: וְהָאֶבֶן
הַזֹּאת אֲשֶׁר־שַׂמְתִּי מַצֵּבָה יִהְיֶה בֵּית אֱלֹהִים וְכֹל אֲשֶׁר תִּתֶּן־לִי עַשֵּׂר אֲעַשְּׂרֶנּוּ לָךְ:

VAYISHLACH

וַיִּשְׁלַח יַעֲקֹב מַלְאָכִים לְפָנָיו אֶל־עֵשָׂו אָחִיו אַרְצָה שֵׂעִיר שְׂדֵה אֱדוֹם: וַיְצַו אֹתָם
לֵאמֹר כֹּה תֹאמְרוּן לַאדֹנִי לְעֵשָׂו כֹּה אָמַר עַבְדְּךָ יַעֲקֹב עִם־לָבָן גַּרְתִּי וָאֵחַר עַד־עָתָּה:
וַיְהִי־לִי שׁוֹר וַחֲמוֹר צֹאן וְעֶבֶד וְשִׁפְחָה וָאֶשְׁלְחָה לְהַגִּיד לַאדֹנִי לִמְצֹא־חֵן בְּעֵינֶיךָ: *Levi*
וַיָּשֻׁבוּ הַמַּלְאָכִים אֶל־יַעֲקֹב לֵאמֹר בָּאנוּ אֶל־אָחִיךָ אֶל־עֵשָׂו וְגַם הֹלֵךְ
לִקְרָאתְךָ וְאַרְבַּע־מֵאוֹת אִישׁ עִמּוֹ: וַיִּירָא יַעֲקֹב מְאֹד וַיֵּצֶר לוֹ וַיַּחַץ
אֶת־הָעָם אֲשֶׁר־אִתּוֹ וְאֶת־הַצֹּאן וְאֶת־הַבָּקָר וְהַגְּמַלִּים לִשְׁנֵי מַחֲנוֹת: וַיֹּאמֶר אִם־יָבוֹא
עֵשָׂו אֶל־הַמַּחֲנֶה הָאַחַת וְהִכָּהוּ וְהָיָה הַמַּחֲנֶה הַנִּשְׁאָר לִפְלֵיטָה: *Yisrael*
וַיֹּאמֶר יַעֲקֹב אֱלֹהֵי אָבִי אַבְרָהָם וֵאלֹהֵי אָבִי יִצְחָק יְהֹוָֽהֲדֹנָי הָאֹמֵר אֵלַי
שׁוּב לְאַרְצְךָ וּלְמוֹלַדְתְּךָ וְאֵיטִיבָה עִמָּךְ: קָטֹנְתִּי מִכֹּל הַחֲסָדִים וּמִכָּל־הָאֱמֶת
אֲשֶׁר עָשִׂיתָ אֶת־עַבְדֶּךָ כִּי בְמַקְלִי עָבַרְתִּי אֶת־הַיַּרְדֵּן הַזֶּה וְעַתָּה הָיִיתִי לִשְׁנֵי מַחֲנוֹת:
הַצִּילֵנִי נָא מִיַּד אָחִי מִיַּד עֵשָׂו כִּי־יָרֵא אָנֹכִי אֹתוֹ פֶּן־יָבוֹא וְהִכַּנִי אֵם עַל־בָּנִים: וְאַתָּה
אָמַרְתָּ הֵיטֵב אֵיטִיב עִמָּךְ וְשַׂמְתִּי אֶת־זַרְעֲךָ כְּחוֹל הַיָּם אֲשֶׁר לֹא־יִסָּפֵר מֵרֹב:

VAYESHEV

וַיֵּשֶׁב יַעֲקֹב בְּאֶרֶץ מְגוּרֵי אָבִיו בְּאֶרֶץ כְּנָעַן: אֵלֶּה | תֹּלְדוֹת יַעֲקֹב
יוֹסֵף בֶּן־שְׁבַע־עֶשְׂרֵה שָׁנָה הָיָה רֹעֶה אֶת־אֶחָיו בַּצֹּאן וְהוּא נַעַר אֶת־בְּנֵי בִלְהָה
וְאֶת־בְּנֵי זִלְפָּה נְשֵׁי אָבִיו וַיָּבֵא יוֹסֵף אֶת־דִּבָּתָם רָעָה אֶל־אֲבִיהֶם:
וְיִשְׂרָאֵל אָהַב אֶת־יוֹסֵף מִכָּל־בָּנָיו כִּי־בֶן־זְקֻנִים הוּא לוֹ וְעָשָׂה לוֹ כְּתֹנֶת פַּסִּים: *Levi*

וַיִּרְאוּ אֶחָיו כִּי־אֹתוֹ אָהַב אֲבִיהֶם מִכָּל־אֶחָיו וַיִּשְׂנְאוּ אֹתוֹ וְלֹא יָכְלוּ דַּבְּרוֹ לְשָׁלֹם:
וַיַּחֲלֹם יוֹסֵף חֲלוֹם וַיַּגֵּד לְאֶחָיו וַיּוֹסִפוּ עוֹד שְׂנֹא אֹתוֹ: וַיֹּאמֶר אֲלֵיהֶם
שִׁמְעוּ־נָא הַחֲלוֹם הַזֶּה אֲשֶׁר חָלָמְתִּי: וְהִנֵּה אֲנַחְנוּ מְאַלְּמִים אֲלֻמִּים בְּתוֹךְ הַשָּׂדֶה
וְהִנֵּה קָמָה אֲלֻמָּתִי וְגַם־נִצָּבָה וְהִנֵּה תְסֻבֶּינָה אֲלֻמֹּתֵיכֶם וַתִּשְׁתַּחֲוֶיןָ לַאֲלֻמָּתִי: *Yisrael*
וַיֹּאמְרוּ לוֹ אֶחָיו הֲמָלֹךְ תִּמְלֹךְ עָלֵינוּ אִם־מָשׁוֹל תִּמְשֹׁל בָּנוּ וַיּוֹסִפוּ עוֹד שְׂנֹא אֹתוֹ
עַל־חֲלֹמֹתָיו וְעַל־דְּבָרָיו: וַיַּחֲלֹם עוֹד חֲלוֹם אַחֵר וַיְסַפֵּר אֹתוֹ לְאֶחָיו וַיֹּאמֶר הִנֵּה חָלַמְתִּי
חֲלוֹם עוֹד וְהִנֵּה הַשֶּׁמֶשׁ וְהַיָּרֵחַ וְאַחַד עָשָׂר כּוֹכָבִים מִשְׁתַּחֲוִים לִי: וַיְסַפֵּר אֶל־אָבִיו
וְאֶל־אֶחָיו וַיִּגְעַר־בּוֹ אָבִיו וַיֹּאמֶר לוֹ מָה הַחֲלוֹם הַזֶּה אֲשֶׁר חָלָמְתָּ הֲבוֹא נָבוֹא
אֲנִי וְאִמְּךָ וְאַחֶיךָ לְהִשְׁתַּחֲוֹת לְךָ אָרְצָה: וַיְקַנְאוּ־בוֹ אֶחָיו וְאָבִיו שָׁמַר אֶת־הַדָּבָר:

MIKETZ

וַיְהִי מִקֵּץ שְׁנָתַיִם יָמִים וּפַרְעֹה חֹלֵם וְהִנֵּה עֹמֵד עַל־הַיְאֹר: וְהִנֵּה מִן־הַיְאֹר
עֹלֹת שֶׁבַע פָּרוֹת יְפוֹת מַרְאֶה וּבְרִיאֹת בָּשָׂר וַתִּרְעֶינָה בָּאָחוּ: וְהִנֵּה שֶׁבַע פָּרוֹת אֲחֵרוֹת
עֹלוֹת אַחֲרֵיהֶן מִן־הַיְאֹר רָעוֹת מַרְאֶה וְדַקּוֹת בָּשָׂר וַתַּעֲמֹדְנָה אֵצֶל הַפָּרוֹת
עַל־שְׂפַת הַיְאֹר: וַתֹּאכַלְנָה הַפָּרוֹת רָעוֹת הַמַּרְאֶה וְדַקֹּת הַבָּשָׂר אֵת שֶׁבַע הַפָּרוֹת
יְפֹת הַמַּרְאֶה וְהַבְּרִיאֹת וַיִּיקַץ פַּרְעֹה: *Levi* וַיִּישָׁן וַיַּחֲלֹם שֵׁנִית וְהִנֵּה | שֶׁבַע שִׁבֳּלִים
עֹלוֹת בְּקָנֶה אֶחָד בְּרִיאוֹת וְטֹבוֹת: וְהִנֵּה שֶׁבַע שִׁבֳּלִים דַּקּוֹת וּשְׁדוּפֹת קָדִים
צֹמְחוֹת אַחֲרֵיהֶן: וַתִּבְלַעְנָה הַשִּׁבֳּלִים הַדַּקּוֹת אֵת שֶׁבַע הַשִּׁבֳּלִים הַבְּרִיאוֹת וְהַמְּלֵאוֹת
וַיִּיקַץ פַּרְעֹה וְהִנֵּה חֲלוֹם: *Yisrael* וַיְהִי בַבֹּקֶר וַתִּפָּעֶם רוּחוֹ וַיִּשְׁלַח וַיִּקְרָא
אֶת־כָּל־חַרְטֻמֵּי מִצְרַיִם וְאֶת־כָּל־חֲכָמֶיהָ וַיְסַפֵּר פַּרְעֹה לָהֶם אֶת־חֲלֹמוֹ וְאֵין־פּוֹתֵר
אוֹתָם לְפַרְעֹה: וַיְדַבֵּר שַׂר הַמַּשְׁקִים אֶת־פַּרְעֹה לֵאמֹר אֶת־חֲטָאַי אֲנִי מַזְכִּיר הַיּוֹם:
פַּרְעֹה קָצַף עַל־עֲבָדָיו וַיִּתֵּן אֹתִי בְּמִשְׁמַר בֵּית שַׂר הַטַּבָּחִים אֹתִי וְאֵת שַׂר הָאֹפִים:
וַנַּחַלְמָה חֲלוֹם בְּלַיְלָה אֶחָד אֲנִי וָהוּא אִישׁ כְּפִתְרוֹן חֲלֹמוֹ חָלָמְנוּ: וְשָׁם אִתָּנוּ
נַעַר עִבְרִי עֶבֶד לְשַׂר הַטַּבָּחִים וַנְּסַפֶּר־לוֹ וַיִּפְתָּר־לָנוּ אֶת־חֲלֹמֹתֵינוּ אִישׁ
כַּחֲלֹמוֹ פָּתָר: וַיְהִי כַּאֲשֶׁר פָּתַר־לָנוּ כֵּן הָיָה אֹתִי הֵשִׁיב עַל־כַּנִּי וְאֹתוֹ תָלָה:
וַיִּשְׁלַח פַּרְעֹה וַיִּקְרָא אֶת־יוֹסֵף וַיְרִיצֻהוּ מִן־הַבּוֹר וַיְגַלַּח וַיְחַלֵּף שִׂמְלֹתָיו וַיָּבֹא אֶל־פַּרְעֹה:

VAYIGASH

וַיִּגַּשׁ אֵלָיו יְהוּדָה וַיֹּאמֶר בִּי אֲדֹנִי יְדַבֶּר־נָא עַבְדְּךָ דָבָר בְּאָזְנֵי אֲדֹנִי וְאַל־יִחַר אַפְּךָ
בְּעַבְדֶּךָ כִּי כָמוֹךָ כְּפַרְעֹה: אֲדֹנִי שָׁאַל אֶת־עֲבָדָיו לֵאמֹר הֲיֵשׁ־לָכֶם אָב אוֹ־אָח:
וַנֹּאמֶר אֶל־אֲדֹנִי יֶשׁ־לָנוּ אָב זָקֵן וְיֶלֶד זְקֻנִים קָטָן וְאָחִיו מֵת וַיִּוָּתֵר הוּא לְבַדּוֹ
לְאִמּוֹ וְאָבִיו אֲהֵבוֹ: *Levi* וַתֹּאמֶר אֶל־עֲבָדֶיךָ הוֹרִדֻהוּ אֵלָי וְאָשִׂימָה עֵינִי עָלָיו:
וַנֹּאמֶר אֶל־אֲדֹנִי לֹא־יוּכַל הַנַּעַר לַעֲזֹב אֶת־אָבִיו וְעָזַב אֶת־אָבִיו וָמֵת:
וַתֹּאמֶר אֶל־עֲבָדֶיךָ אִם־לֹא יֵרֵד אֲחִיכֶם הַקָּטֹן אִתְּכֶם לֹא תֹסִפוּן לִרְאוֹת פָּנָי:
וַיְהִי כִּי עָלִינוּ אֶל־עַבְדְּךָ אָבִי וַנַּגֶּד־לוֹ אֵת דִּבְרֵי אֲדֹנִי: *Yisrael*

וַיֹּ֣אמֶר אָבִ֔ינוּ שֻׁ֖בוּ שִׁבְרוּ־לָ֥נוּ מְעַט־אֹֽכֶל: וַנֹּ֕אמֶר לֹ֥א נוּכַ֖ל לָרֶ֑דֶת אִם־יֵשׁ֩
אָחִ֨ינוּ הַקָּטֹ֤ן אִתָּ֙נוּ֙ וְיָרַ֔דְנוּ כִּי־לֹ֣א נוּכַ֗ל לִרְאוֹת֙ פְּנֵ֣י הָאִ֔ישׁ וְאָחִ֥ינוּ הַקָּטֹ֖ן
אֵינֶ֥נּוּ אִתָּֽנוּ: וַיֹּ֛אמֶר עַבְדְּךָ֥ אָבִ֖י אֵלֵ֑ינוּ אַתֶּ֣ם יְדַעְתֶּ֔ם כִּ֥י שְׁנַ֖יִם יָֽלְדָה־לִּ֥י אִשְׁתִּֽי:
וַיֵּצֵ֤א הָֽאֶחָד֙ מֵֽאִתִּ֔י וָֽאֹמַ֕ר אַ֖ךְ טָרֹ֣ף טֹרָ֑ף וְלֹ֥א רְאִיתִ֖יו עַד־הֵֽנָּה: וּלְקַחְתֶּ֧ם
גַּם־אֶת־זֶ֛ה מֵעִ֥ם פָּנַ֖י וְקָרָ֣הוּ אָס֑וֹן וְהֽוֹרַדְתֶּ֧ם אֶת־שֵֽׂיבָתִ֛י בְּרָעָ֖ה שְׁאֹֽלָה:
וְעַתָּ֞ה כְּבֹאִ֣י אֶל־עַבְדְּךָ֣ אָבִ֗י וְהַנַּ֙עַר֙ אֵינֶ֣נּוּ אִתָּ֔נוּ וְנַפְשׁ֖וֹ קְשׁוּרָ֥ה בְנַפְשֽׁוֹ:

VAYECHI

וַיְחִ֤י יַֽעֲקֹב֙ בְּאֶ֣רֶץ מִצְרַ֔יִם שְׁבַ֥ע עֶשְׂרֵ֖ה שָׁנָ֑ה וַיְהִ֤י יְמֵֽי־יַֽעֲקֹב֙ שְׁנֵ֣י חַיָּ֔יו שֶׁ֣בַע שָׁנִ֔ים
וְאַרְבָּעִ֥ים וּמְאַ֖ת שָׁנָֽה: וַיִּקְרְב֣וּ יְמֵֽי־יִשְׂרָאֵל֮ לָמוּת֒ וַיִּקְרָ֣א | לִבְנ֣וֹ לְיוֹסֵ֗ף
וַיֹּ֤אמֶר לוֹ֙ אִם־נָ֨א מָצָ֤אתִי חֵן֙ בְּעֵינֶ֔יךָ שִֽׂים־נָ֥א יָֽדְךָ֖ תַּ֣חַת יְרֵכִ֑י וְעָשִׂ֤יתָ עִמָּדִי֙
חֶ֣סֶד וֶֽאֱמֶ֔ת אַל־נָ֥א תִקְבְּרֵ֖נִי בְּמִצְרָֽיִם: וְשָֽׁכַבְתִּי֙ עִם־אֲבֹתַ֔י וּנְשָׂאתַ֙נִי֙ מִמִּצְרַ֔יִם
וּקְבַרְתַּ֖נִי בִּקְבֻֽרָתָ֑ם וַיֹּאמַ֕ר אָֽנֹכִ֖י אֶֽעֱשֶׂ֥ה כִדְבָרֶֽךָ: וַיֹּ֕אמֶר הִשָּֽׁבְעָ֖ה לִ֑י וַיִּשָּׁבַ֖ע ל֑וֹ
וַיִּשְׁתַּ֥חוּ יִשְׂרָאֵ֖ל עַל־רֹ֥אשׁ הַמִּטָּֽה: Levi   וַיְהִ֗י אַֽחֲרֵי֙ הַדְּבָרִ֣ים הָאֵ֔לֶּה וַיֹּ֣אמֶר לְיוֹסֵ֔ף
הִנֵּ֥ה אָבִ֖יךָ חֹלֶ֑ה וַיִּקַּ֞ח אֶת־שְׁנֵ֤י בָנָיו֙ עִמּ֔וֹ אֶת־מְנַשֶּׁ֖ה וְאֶת־אֶפְרָֽיִם: וַיַּגֵּ֣ד לְיַֽעֲקֹ֔ב
וַיֹּ֕אמֶר הִנֵּ֛ה בִּנְךָ֥ יוֹסֵ֖ף בָּ֣א אֵלֶ֑יךָ וַיִּתְחַזֵּק֙ יִשְׂרָאֵ֔ל וַיֵּ֖שֶׁב עַל־הַמִּטָּֽה: וַיֹּ֤אמֶר יַֽעֲקֹב֙
אֶל־יוֹסֵ֔ף אֵ֥ל שַׁדַּ֛י נִרְאָֽה־אֵלַ֥י בְּל֖וּז בְּאֶ֣רֶץ כְּנָ֑עַן וַיְבָ֖רֶךְ אֹתִֽי: Yisrael   וַיֹּ֣אמֶר אֵלַ֗י
הִנְנִ֤י מַפְרְךָ֙ וְהִרְבִּיתִ֔ךָ וּנְתַתִּ֖יךָ לִקְהַ֣ל עַמִּ֑ים וְנָ֨תַתִּ֜י אֶת־הָאָ֧רֶץ הַזֹּ֛את לְזַרְעֲךָ֥ אַֽחֲרֶ֖יךָ
אֲחֻזַּ֥ת עוֹלָֽם: וְעַתָּ֡ה שְׁנֵֽי־בָנֶ֩יךָ֩ הַנּֽוֹלָדִ֨ים לְךָ֜ בְּאֶ֣רֶץ מִצְרַ֗יִם עַד־בֹּאִ֥י אֵלֶ֛יךָ מִצְרַ֖יְמָה
לִי־הֵ֑ם אֶפְרַ֙יִם֙ וּמְנַשֶּׁ֔ה כִּרְאוּבֵ֥ן וְשִׁמְע֖וֹן יִֽהְיוּ־לִֽי: וּמֽוֹלַדְתְּךָ֛ אֲשֶׁר־הוֹלַ֥דְתָּ אַֽחֲרֵיהֶ֖ם
לְךָ֣ יִהְי֑וּ עַ֣ל שֵׁ֧ם אֲחֵיהֶ֛ם יִקָּֽרְא֖וּ בְּנַֽחֲלָתָֽם: וַֽאֲנִ֣י | בְּבֹאִ֣י מִפַּדָּ֗ן מֵ֩תָה֩ עָלַ֨י רָחֵ֜ל
בְּאֶ֤רֶץ כְּנַ֙עַן֙ בַּדֶּ֔רֶךְ בְּע֥וֹד כִּבְרַת־אֶ֖רֶץ לָבֹ֣א אֶפְרָ֑תָה וָֽאֶקְבְּרֶ֤הָ שָּׁם֙ בְּדֶ֣רֶךְ אֶפְרָ֔ת
הִ֖וא בֵּ֥ית לָֽחֶם: וַיַּ֥רְא יִשְׂרָאֵ֖ל אֶת־בְּנֵ֣י יוֹסֵ֑ף וַיֹּ֖אמֶר מִי־אֵֽלֶּה: וַיֹּ֤אמֶר יוֹסֵף֙
אֶל־אָבִ֔יו בָּנַ֣י הֵ֔ם אֲשֶׁר־נָֽתַן־לִ֥י אֱלֹהִ֖ים בָּזֶ֑ה וַיֹּאמַ֕ר קָֽחֶם־נָ֥א אֵלַ֖י וַֽאֲבָֽרֲכֵֽם:

SHEMOT

וְאֵ֗לֶּה שְׁמוֹת֙ בְּנֵ֣י יִשְׂרָאֵ֔ל הַבָּאִ֖ים מִצְרָ֑יְמָה אֵ֣ת יַֽעֲקֹ֔ב אִ֥ישׁ וּבֵית֖וֹ בָּֽאוּ:
רְאוּבֵ֣ן שִׁמְע֔וֹן לֵוִ֖י וִֽיהוּדָֽה: יִשָּׂשכָ֥ר זְבוּלֻ֖ן וּבִנְיָמִֽן: דָּ֥ן וְנַפְתָּלִ֖י גָּ֥ד וְאָשֵֽׁר: וַיְהִ֗י
כָּל־נֶ֛פֶשׁ יֹֽצְאֵ֥י יֶֽרֶךְ־יַֽעֲקֹ֖ב שִׁבְעִ֣ים נָ֑פֶשׁ וְיוֹסֵ֖ף הָיָ֥ה בְמִצְרָֽיִם: וַיָּ֤מָת יוֹסֵף֙ וְכָל־אֶחָ֔יו
וְכֹ֖ל הַדּ֥וֹר הַהֽוּא: וּבְנֵ֣י יִשְׂרָאֵ֗ל פָּר֧וּ וַֽיִּשְׁרְצ֛וּ וַיִּרְבּ֥וּ וַיַּֽעַצְמ֖וּ בִּמְאֹ֣ד מְאֹ֑ד וַתִּמָּלֵ֥א
הָאָ֖רֶץ אֹתָֽם: Levi   וַיָּ֥קָם מֶֽלֶךְ־חָדָ֖שׁ עַל־מִצְרָ֑יִם אֲשֶׁ֥ר לֹֽא־יָדַ֖ע אֶת־יוֹסֵֽף:
וַיֹּ֖אמֶר אֶל־עַמּ֑וֹ הִנֵּ֗ה עַ֚ם בְּנֵ֣י יִשְׂרָאֵ֔ל רַ֥ב וְעָצ֖וּם מִמֶּֽנּוּ: הָ֥בָה נִֽתְחַכְּמָ֖ה ל֑וֹ פֶּן־יִרְבֶּ֗ה
וְהָיָ֞ה כִּֽי־תִקְרֶ֤אנָה מִלְחָמָה֙ וְנוֹסַ֤ף גַּם־הוּא֙ עַל־שֹׂ֣נְאֵ֔ינוּ וְנִלְחַם־בָּ֖נוּ וְעָלָ֥ה מִן־הָאָֽרֶץ:
וַיָּשִׂ֤ימוּ עָלָיו֙ שָׂרֵ֣י מִסִּ֔ים לְמַ֥עַן עַנֹּת֖וֹ בְּסִבְלֹתָ֑ם וַיִּ֜בֶן עָרֵ֤י מִסְכְּנוֹת֙ לְפַרְעֹ֔ה אֶת־פִּתֹ֖ם
וְאֶת־רַֽעַמְסֵֽס: Yisrael   וְכַֽאֲשֶׁר֙ יְעַנּ֣וּ אֹת֔וֹ כֵּ֥ן יִרְבֶּ֖ה וְכֵ֣ן יִפְרֹ֑ץ וַיָּקֻ֕צוּ מִפְּנֵ֖י בְּנֵ֥י יִשְׂרָאֵֽל:

וַיַּעֲבִ֧דוּ מִצְרַ֛יִם אֶת־בְּנֵ֥י יִשְׂרָאֵ֖ל בְּפָֽרֶךְ: וַיְמָרְר֨וּ אֶת־חַיֵּיהֶ֜ם בַּעֲבֹדָ֣ה קָשָׁ֗ה בְּחֹ֙מֶר֙
וּבִלְבֵנִ֔ים וּבְכָל־עֲבֹדָ֖ה בַּשָּׂדֶ֑ה אֵ֚ת כָּל־עֲבֹ֣דָתָ֔ם אֲשֶׁר־עָבְד֥וּ בָהֶ֖ם בְּפָֽרֶךְ: וַיֹּ֙אמֶר֙ מֶ֣לֶךְ
מִצְרַ֔יִם לַֽמְיַלְּדֹ֖ת הָֽעִבְרִיֹּ֑ת אֲשֶׁ֨ר שֵׁ֤ם הָֽאַחַת֙ שִׁפְרָ֔ה וְשֵׁ֥ם הַשֵּׁנִ֖ית פּוּעָֽה: וַיֹּ֗אמֶר בְּיַלֶּדְכֶן֙
אֶת־הָֽעִבְרִיּ֔וֹת וּרְאִיתֶ֖ן עַל־הָאָבְנָ֑יִם אִם־בֵּ֥ן הוּא֙ וַהֲמִתֶּ֣ן אֹת֔וֹ וְאִם־בַּ֥ת הִ֖וא וָחָֽיָה: וַתִּירֶ֤אןָ
הַֽמְיַלְּדֹת֙ אֶת־הָ֣אֱלֹהִ֔ים וְלֹ֣א עָשׂ֔וּ כַּאֲשֶׁ֛ר דִּבֶּ֥ר אֲלֵיהֶ֖ן מֶ֣לֶךְ מִצְרָ֑יִם וַתְּחַיֶּ֖יןָ אֶת־הַיְלָדִֽים:

VA'ERA

וַיְדַבֵּ֥ר אֱלֹהִ֖ים אֶל־מֹשֶׁ֑ה וַיֹּ֥אמֶר אֵלָ֖יו אֲנִ֥י יְהֹוָ֖הֽאהדונהי: וָאֵרָ֗א אֶל־אַבְרָהָ֛ם אֶל־יִצְחָ֥ק
וְאֶֽל־יַעֲקֹ֖ב בְּאֵ֣ל שַׁדָּ֑י וּשְׁמִ֣י יְהֹוָ֖הֽאהדונהי לֹ֥א נוֹדַ֖עְתִּי לָהֶֽם: וְגַ֨ם הֲקִמֹ֤תִי אֶת־בְּרִיתִי֙
אִתָּ֔ם לָתֵ֥ת לָהֶ֖ם אֶת־אֶ֣רֶץ כְּנָ֑עַן אֵ֛ת אֶ֥רֶץ מְגֻרֵיהֶ֖ם אֲשֶׁר־גָּ֥רוּ בָֽהּ: וְגַ֣ם | אֲנִ֣י שָׁמַ֗עְתִּי
אֶֽת־נַאֲקַת֙ בְּנֵ֣י יִשְׂרָאֵ֔ל אֲשֶׁ֥ר מִצְרַ֖יִם מַעֲבִדִ֣ים אֹתָ֑ם וָאֶזְכֹּ֖ר אֶת־בְּרִיתִֽי: *Levi* לָכֵ֞ן אֱמֹ֥ר
לִבְנֵֽי־יִשְׂרָאֵל֮ אֲנִ֣י יְהֹוָהֽאהדונהי֒ וְהוֹצֵאתִ֣י אֶתְכֶ֗ם מִתַּ֙חַת֙ סִבְלֹ֣ת מִצְרַ֔יִם וְהִצַּלְתִּ֥י אֶתְכֶ֖ם
מֵעֲבֹֽדָתָ֑ם וְגָאַלְתִּ֤י אֶתְכֶם֙ בִּזְר֣וֹעַ נְטוּיָ֔ה וּבִשְׁפָטִ֖ים גְּדֹלִֽים: וְלָקַחְתִּ֨י אֶתְכֶ֥ם לִי֙ לְעָ֔ם
וְהָיִ֥יתִי לָכֶ֖ם לֵֽאלֹהִ֑ים וִֽידַעְתֶּ֗ם כִּ֣י אֲנִ֤י יְהֹוָ֙הֽאהדונהי֙ אֱלֹֽהֵיכֶ֔ם הַמּוֹצִ֣יא אֶתְכֶ֔ם מִתַּ֖חַת
סִבְל֥וֹת מִצְרָֽיִם: וְהֵבֵאתִ֤י אֶתְכֶם֙ אֶל־הָאָ֔רֶץ אֲשֶׁ֤ר נָשָׂ֙אתִי֙ אֶת־יָדִ֔י לָתֵ֣ת אֹתָ֔הּ לְאַבְרָהָ֥ם
לְיִצְחָ֖ק וּֽלְיַעֲקֹ֑ב וְנָתַתִּ֨י אֹתָ֥הּ לָכֶ֛ם מוֹרָשָׁ֖ה אֲנִ֥י יְהֹוָֽהֽאהדונהי: וַיְדַבֵּ֥ר מֹשֶׁ֛ה כֵּ֖ן אֶל־בְּנֵ֣י
יִשְׂרָאֵ֑ל וְלֹ֤א שָֽׁמְעוּ֙ אֶל־מֹשֶׁ֔ה מִקֹּ֣צֶר ר֔וּחַ וּמֵעֲבֹדָ֖ה קָשָֽׁה: *Yisrael* וַיְדַבֵּ֥ר יְהֹוָ֖הֽאהדונהי
אֶל־מֹשֶׁ֥ה לֵּאמֹֽר: בֹּ֣א דַבֵּ֔ר אֶל־פַּרְעֹ֖ה מֶ֣לֶךְ מִצְרָ֑יִם וִֽישַׁלַּ֥ח אֶת־בְּנֵֽי־יִשְׂרָאֵ֖ל מֵאַרְצֽוֹ:
וַיְדַבֵּ֣ר מֹשֶׁ֔ה לִפְנֵ֥י יְהֹוָ֖הֽאהדונהי לֵאמֹ֑ר הֵ֤ן בְּנֵֽי־יִשְׂרָאֵל֙ לֹֽא־שָׁמְע֣וּ אֵלַ֔י וְאֵיךְ֙ יִשְׁמָעֵ֣נִי
פַרְעֹ֔ה וַאֲנִ֖י עֲרַ֥ל שְׂפָתָֽיִם: וַיְדַבֵּ֣ר יְהֹוָ֔הֽאהדונהי אֶל־מֹשֶׁ֖ה וְאֶֽל־אַהֲרֹ֑ן וַיְצַוֵּם֙ אֶל־בְּנֵ֣י
יִשְׂרָאֵ֔ל וְאֶל־פַּרְעֹ֖ה מֶ֣לֶךְ מִצְרָ֑יִם לְהוֹצִ֥יא אֶת־בְּנֵֽי־יִשְׂרָאֵ֖ל מֵאֶ֥רֶץ מִצְרָֽיִם:

BO

וַיֹּ֤אמֶר יְהֹוָ֙הֽאהדונהי֙ אֶל־מֹשֶׁ֔ה בֹּ֖א אֶל־פַּרְעֹ֑ה כִּֽי־אֲנִ֞י הִכְבַּ֤דְתִּי אֶת־לִבּוֹ֙ וְאֶת־לֵ֣ב
עֲבָדָ֔יו לְמַ֗עַן שִׁתִ֛י אֹתֹתַ֥י אֵ֖לֶּה בְּקִרְבּֽוֹ: וּלְמַ֡עַן תְּסַפֵּר֩ בְּאָזְנֵ֨י בִנְךָ֜ וּבֶן־בִּנְךָ֗ אֵ֣ת אֲשֶׁ֤ר
הִתְעַלַּ֙לְתִּי֙ בְּמִצְרַ֔יִם וְאֶת־אֹֽתֹתַ֖י אֲשֶׁר־שַׂ֣מְתִּי בָ֑ם וִֽידַעְתֶּ֖ם כִּֽי־אֲנִ֥י יְהֹוָֽהֽאהדונהי: וַיָּבֹ֨א
מֹשֶׁ֤ה וְאַֽהֲרֹן֙ אֶל־פַּרְעֹ֔ה וַיֹּאמְר֣וּ אֵלָ֗יו כֹּֽה־אָמַ֤ר יְהֹוָ֙הֽאהדונהי֙ אֱלֹהֵ֣י הָֽעִבְרִ֔ים עַד־מָתַ֣י
מֵאַ֔נְתָּ לֵעָנֹ֖ת מִפָּנָ֑י שַׁלַּ֥ח עַמִּ֖י וְיַֽעַבְדֻֽנִי: *Levi* כִּ֣י אִם־מָאֵ֥ן אַתָּ֖ה לְשַׁלֵּ֣חַ אֶת־עַמִּ֑י הִנְנִ֨י
מֵבִ֥יא מָחָ֛ר אַרְבֶּ֖ה בִּגְבֻלֶֽךָ: וְכִסָּה֙ אֶת־עֵ֣ין הָאָ֔רֶץ וְלֹ֥א יוּכַ֖ל לִרְאֹ֣ת אֶת־הָאָ֑רֶץ וְאָכַ֣ל |
אֶת־יֶ֣תֶר הַפְּלֵטָ֗ה הַנִּשְׁאֶ֤רֶת לָכֶם֙ מִן־הַבָּרָ֔ד וְאָכַל֙ אֶת־כָּל־הָעֵ֔ץ הַצֹּמֵ֥חַ לָכֶ֖ם
מִן־הַשָּׂדֶֽה: וּמָלְא֨וּ בָתֶּ֜יךָ וּבָתֵּ֣י כָל־עֲבָדֶ֗יךָ וּבָתֵּ֣י כָל־מִצְרַ֔יִם אֲשֶׁ֨ר לֹֽא־רָא֤וּ אֲבֹתֶ֙יךָ֙
וַֽאֲב֣וֹת אֲבֹתֶ֔יךָ מִיּ֗וֹם הֱיוֹתָם֙ עַל־הָ֣אֲדָמָ֔ה עַ֖ד הַיּ֣וֹם הַזֶּ֑ה וַיִּ֥פֶן וַיֵּצֵ֖א מֵעִ֥ם פַּרְעֹֽה:
Yisrael וַיֹּֽאמְרוּ֩ עַבְדֵ֨י פַרְעֹ֜ה אֵלָ֗יו עַד־מָתַי֙ יִהְיֶ֨ה זֶ֥ה לָ֙נוּ֙ לְמוֹקֵ֔שׁ שַׁלַּח֙ אֶת־הָ֣אֲנָשִׁ֔ים
וְיַֽעַבְד֖וּ אֶת־יְהֹוָ֣הֽאהדונהי אֱלֹֽהֵיהֶ֑ם הֲטֶ֣רֶם תֵּדַ֔ע כִּ֥י אָבְדָ֖ה מִצְרָֽיִם: וַיּוּשַׁ֞ב אֶת־מֹשֶׁ֤ה
וְאֶֽת־אַהֲרֹן֙ אֶל־פַּרְעֹ֔ה וַיֹּ֣אמֶר אֲלֵהֶ֔ם לְכ֥וּ עִבְד֖וּ אֶת־יְהֹוָ֣הֽאהדונהי אֱלֹֽהֵיכֶ֑ם מִ֥י וָמִ֖י
הַהֹלְכִֽים: וַיֹּ֣אמֶר מֹשֶׁ֔ה בִּנְעָרֵ֥ינוּ וּבִזְקֵנֵ֖ינוּ נֵלֵ֑ךְ בְּבָנֵ֨ינוּ וּבִבְנוֹתֵ֜נוּ בְּצֹאנֵ֤נוּ וּבִבְקָרֵ֙נוּ֙ נֵלֵ֔ךְ
כִּ֥י חַג־יְהֹוָ֖הֽאהדונהי לָֽנוּ: וַיֹּ֣אמֶר אֲלֵהֶ֗ם יְהִ֨י כֵ֤ן יְהֹוָהֽ֙אהדונהי֙ עִמָּכֶ֔ם כַּאֲשֶׁ֛ר אֲשַׁלַּ֥ח
אֶתְכֶ֖ם וְאֶֽת־טַפְּכֶ֑ם רְא֕וּ כִּ֥י רָעָ֖ה נֶ֥גֶד פְּנֵיכֶֽם: לֹ֣א כֵ֗ן לְכֽוּ־נָ֤א הַגְּבָרִים֙ וְעִבְד֣וּ
אֶת־יְהֹוָ֔הֽאהדונהי כִּ֥י אֹתָ֖הּ אַתֶּ֣ם מְבַקְשִׁ֑ים וַיְגָ֣רֶשׁ אֹתָ֔ם מֵאֵ֖ת פְּנֵ֥י פַרְעֹֽה:

BESHALACH

וַיְהִ֗י בְּשַׁלַּ֣ח פַּרְעֹה֮ אֶת־הָעָם֒ וְלֹא־נָחָ֣ם אֱלֹהִ֗ים דֶּ֚רֶךְ אֶ֣רֶץ פְּלִשְׁתִּ֔ים כִּ֥י קָר֖וֹב ה֑וּא כִּ֣י ׀ אָמַ֣ר אֱלֹהִ֗ים פֶּֽן־יִנָּחֵ֥ם הָעָ֛ם בִּרְאֹתָ֥ם מִלְחָמָ֖ה וְשָׁ֥בוּ מִצְרָֽיְמָה: וַיַּסֵּ֨ב אֱלֹהִ֧ים ׀ אֶת־הָעָ֛ם דֶּ֥רֶךְ הַמִּדְבָּ֖ר יַם־ס֑וּף וַֽחֲמֻשִׁ֛ים עָל֥וּ בְנֵֽי־יִשְׂרָאֵ֖ל מֵאֶ֥רֶץ מִצְרָֽיִם: וַיִּקַּ֥ח מֹשֶׁ֛ה אֶת־עַצְמ֥וֹת יוֹסֵ֖ף עִמּ֑וֹ כִּי֩ הַשְׁבֵּ֨עַ הִשְׁבִּ֜יעַ אֶת־בְּנֵ֤י יִשְׂרָאֵל֙ לֵאמֹ֔ר פָּקֹ֨ד יִפְקֹ֤ד אֱלֹהִים֙ אֶתְכֶ֔ם וְהַֽעֲלִיתֶ֧ם אֶת־עַצְמֹתַ֛י מִזֶּ֖ה אִתְּכֶֽם: וַיִּסְע֖וּ מִסֻּכֹּ֑ת וַיַּֽחֲנ֣וּ בְאֵתָ֔ם בִּקְצֵ֖ה הַמִּדְבָּֽר: וַֽיהֹוָ֡הֽאֲדֹנָי הֹלֵךְ֩ לִפְנֵיהֶ֨ם יוֹמָ֜ם בְּעַמּ֤וּד עָנָן֙ לַנְחֹתָ֣ם הַדֶּ֔רֶךְ וְלַ֛יְלָה בְּעַמּ֥וּד אֵ֖שׁ לְהָאִ֣יר לָהֶ֑ם לָלֶ֖כֶת יוֹמָ֥ם וָלָֽיְלָה: לֹֽא־יָמִ֞ישׁ עַמּ֤וּד הֶֽעָנָן֙ יוֹמָ֔ם וְעַמּ֥וּד הָאֵ֖שׁ לָ֑יְלָה לִפְנֵ֖י הָעָֽם: *Levi* וַיְדַבֵּ֥ר יְהֹוָ֛הֽאֲדֹנָי אֶל־מֹשֶׁ֖ה לֵּאמֹֽר: דַּבֵּר֮ אֶל־בְּנֵ֣י יִשְׂרָאֵל֒ וְיָשֻׁ֗בוּ וְיַֽחֲנוּ֙ לִפְנֵי֙ פִּ֣י הַֽחִירֹ֔ת בֵּ֥ין מִגְדֹּ֖ל וּבֵ֣ין הַיָּ֑ם לִפְנֵי֙ בַּ֣עַל צְפֹ֔ן נִכְח֥וֹ תַֽחֲנ֖וּ עַל־הַיָּֽם: וְאָמַ֤ר פַּרְעֹה֙ לִבְנֵ֣י יִשְׂרָאֵ֔ל נְבֻכִ֥ים הֵ֖ם בָּאָ֑רֶץ סָגַ֥ר עֲלֵיהֶ֖ם הַמִּדְבָּֽר: וְחִזַּקְתִּ֣י אֶת־לֵֽב־פַּרְעֹה֮ וְרָדַ֣ף אַֽחֲרֵיהֶם֒ וְאִכָּֽבְדָ֤ה בְּפַרְעֹה֙ וּבְכָל־חֵיל֔וֹ וְיָֽדְע֥וּ מִצְרַ֖יִם כִּֽי־אֲנִ֣י יְהֹוָ֑הֽאֲדֹנָי וַיַּֽעֲשׂוּ־כֵֽן: *Yisrael* וַיֻּגַּד֙ לְמֶ֣לֶךְ מִצְרַ֔יִם כִּ֥י בָרַ֖ח הָעָ֑ם וַיֵּֽהָפֵ֡ךְ לְבַ֣ב פַּרְעֹ֨ה וַֽעֲבָדָ֜יו אֶל־הָעָ֗ם וַיֹּֽאמְרוּ֙ מַה־זֹּ֣את עָשִׂ֔ינוּ כִּֽי־שִׁלַּ֥חְנוּ אֶת־יִשְׂרָאֵ֖ל מֵֽעָבְדֵֽנוּ: וַיֶּאְסֹ֖ר אֶת־רִכְבּ֑וֹ וְאֶת־עַמּ֖וֹ לָקַ֥ח עִמּֽוֹ: וַיִּקַּ֗ח שֵֽׁשׁ־מֵא֥וֹת רֶ֨כֶב֙ בָּח֔וּר וְכֹ֖ל רֶ֣כֶב מִצְרָ֑יִם וְשָֽׁלִשִׁ֖ם עַל־כֻּלּֽוֹ: וַיְחַזֵּ֣ק יְהֹוָ֗הֽאֲדֹנָי אֶת־לֵ֤ב פַּרְעֹה֙ מֶ֣לֶךְ מִצְרַ֔יִם וַיִּרְדֹּ֕ף אַֽחֲרֵ֖י בְּנֵ֣י יִשְׂרָאֵ֑ל וּבְנֵ֣י יִשְׂרָאֵ֔ל יֹֽצְאִ֖ים בְּיָ֥ד רָמָֽה:

YITRO

וַיִּשְׁמַ֞ע יִתְר֨וֹ כֹהֵ֤ן מִדְיָן֙ חֹתֵ֣ן מֹשֶׁ֔ה אֵת֩ כָּל־אֲשֶׁ֨ר עָשָׂ֤ה אֱלֹהִים֙ לְמֹשֶׁ֔ה וּלְיִשְׂרָאֵ֖ל עַמּ֑וֹ כִּֽי־הוֹצִ֧יא יְהֹוָ֛הֽאֲדֹנָי אֶת־יִשְׂרָאֵ֖ל מִמִּצְרָֽיִם: וַיִּקַּ֗ח יִתְרוֹ֙ חֹתֵ֣ן מֹשֶׁ֔ה אֶת־צִפֹּרָ֖ה אֵ֣שֶׁת מֹשֶׁ֑ה אַחַ֖ר שִׁלּוּחֶֽיהָ: וְאֵ֖ת שְׁנֵ֣י בָנֶ֑יהָ אֲשֶׁ֨ר שֵׁ֤ם הָֽאֶחָד֙ גֵּֽרְשֹׁ֔ם כִּ֣י אָמַ֔ר גֵּ֣ר הָיִ֔יתִי בְּאֶ֖רֶץ נָכְרִיָּֽה: *Levi* וְשֵׁ֥ם הָֽאֶחָ֖ד אֱלִיעֶ֑זֶר כִּֽי־אֱלֹהֵ֤י אָבִי֙ בְּעֶזְרִ֔י וַיַּצִּלֵ֖נִי מֵחֶ֥רֶב פַּרְעֹֽה: וַיָּבֹ֞א יִתְר֨וֹ חֹתֵ֥ן מֹשֶׁ֛ה וּבָנָ֥יו וְאִשְׁתּ֖וֹ אֶל־מֹשֶׁ֑ה אֶל־הַמִּדְבָּ֗ר אֲשֶׁר־ה֛וּא חֹנֶ֥ה שָׁ֖ם הַ֥ר הָֽאֱלֹהִֽים: וַיֹּ֨אמֶר֙ אֶל־מֹשֶׁ֔ה אֲנִ֛י חֹתֶנְךָ֥ יִתְר֖וֹ בָּ֣א אֵלֶ֑יךָ וְאִ֨שְׁתְּךָ֔ וּשְׁנֵ֥י בָנֶ֖יהָ עִמָּֽהּ: וַיֵּצֵ֨א מֹשֶׁ֜ה לִקְרַ֣את חֹֽתְנ֗וֹ וַיִּשְׁתַּ֨חוּ֙ וַיִּשַּׁק־ל֔וֹ וַיִּשְׁאֲל֥וּ אִישׁ־לְרֵעֵ֖הוּ לְשָׁל֑וֹם וַיָּבֹ֖אוּ הָאֹֽהֱלָה: וַיְסַפֵּ֤ר מֹשֶׁה֙ לְחֹ֣תְנ֔וֹ אֵת֩ כָּל־אֲשֶׁ֨ר עָשָׂ֤ה יְהֹוָהֽ֙אֲדֹנָי לְפַרְעֹ֣ה וּלְמִצְרַ֔יִם עַ֖ל אוֹדֹ֣ת יִשְׂרָאֵ֑ל אֵ֤ת כָּל־הַתְּלָאָה֙ אֲשֶׁ֣ר מְצָאָ֣תַם בַּדֶּ֔רֶךְ וַיַּצִּלֵ֖ם יְהֹוָֽהֽ֑אֲדֹנָי *Yisrael* וַיִּ֣חַדְּ יִתְר֔וֹ עַ֥ל כָּל־הַטּוֹבָ֖ה אֲשֶׁר־עָשָׂ֣ה יְהֹוָ֛הֽאֲדֹנָי לְיִשְׂרָאֵ֑ל אֲשֶׁ֥ר הִצִּיל֖וֹ מִיַּ֥ד מִצְרָֽיִם: וַיֹּאמֶר֮ יִתְרוֹ֒ בָּר֣וּךְ יְהֹוָ֔הֽאֲדֹנָי אֲשֶׁ֨ר הִצִּ֥יל אֶתְכֶ֛ם מִיַּ֥ד מִצְרַ֖יִם וּמִיַּ֣ד פַּרְעֹ֑ה אֲשֶׁ֤ר הִצִּיל֙ אֶת־הָעָ֔ם מִתַּ֖חַת יַד־מִצְרָֽיִם: עַתָּ֣ה יָדַ֔עְתִּי כִּֽי־גָד֥וֹל יְהֹוָ֖הֽאֲדֹנָי מִכָּל־הָֽאֱלֹהִ֑ים כִּ֣י בַדָּבָ֔ר אֲשֶׁ֥ר זָד֖וּ עֲלֵיהֶֽם: וַיִּקַּ֞ח יִתְר֨וֹ חֹתֵ֤ן מֹשֶׁה֙ עֹלָ֣ה וּזְבָחִ֖ים לֵֽאלֹהִ֑ים וַיָּבֹ֨א אַֽהֲרֹ֜ן וְכֹ֣ל ׀ זִקְנֵ֣י יִשְׂרָאֵ֗ל לֶֽאֱכָל־לֶ֛חֶם עִם־חֹתֵ֥ן מֹשֶׁ֖ה לִפְנֵ֥י הָֽאֱלֹהִֽים:

MISHPATIM

וְאֵ֗לֶּה הַמִּשְׁפָּטִ֔ים אֲשֶׁ֥ר תָּשִׂ֖ים לִפְנֵיהֶֽם: כִּ֤י תִקְנֶה֙ עֶ֣בֶד עִבְרִ֔י שֵׁ֥שׁ שָׁנִ֖ים יַעֲבֹ֑ד
וּבַ֨שְּׁבִעִ֔ת יֵצֵ֥א לַֽחָפְשִׁ֖י חִנָּֽם: אִם־בְּגַפּ֣וֹ יָבֹ֔א בְּגַפּ֖וֹ יֵצֵ֑א אִם־בַּ֤עַל אִשָּׁה֙ ה֔וּא
וְיָצְאָ֥ה אִשְׁתּ֖וֹ עִמּֽוֹ: אִם־אֲדֹנָיו֙ יִתֶּן־ל֣וֹ אִשָּׁ֔ה וְיָלְדָה־ל֥וֹ בָנִ֖ים א֣וֹ בָנ֑וֹת
הָאִשָּׁ֣ה וִֽילָדֶ֗יהָ תִּהְיֶה֙ לַֽאדֹנֶ֔יהָ וְה֖וּא יֵצֵ֥א בְגַפּֽוֹ: וְאִם־אָמֹ֤ר יֹאמַר֙ הָעֶ֔בֶד
אָהַ֨בְתִּי֙ אֶת־אֲדֹנִ֔י אֶת־אִשְׁתִּ֖י וְאֶת־בָּנָ֑י לֹ֥א אֵצֵ֖א חָפְשִֽׁי: וְהִגִּישׁ֤וֹ אֲדֹנָיו֙ אֶל־הָ֣אֱלֹהִ֔ים
וְהִגִּישׁוֹ֙ אֶל־הַדֶּ֔לֶת א֖וֹ אֶל־הַמְּזוּזָ֑ה וְרָצַ֨ע אֲדֹנָ֤יו אֶת־אָזְנוֹ֙ בַּמַּרְצֵ֔עַ וַעֲבָד֖וֹ לְעֹלָֽם: _Levi_
וְכִֽי־יִמְכֹּ֥ר אִ֛ישׁ אֶת־בִּתּ֖וֹ לְאָמָ֑ה לֹ֥א תֵצֵ֖א כְּצֵ֥את הָעֲבָדִֽים: אִם־רָעָ֞ה בְּעֵינֵ֤י אֲדֹנֶ֨יהָ֙
אֲשֶׁר־ל֣וֹ (כתיב: לא) יְעָדָ֔הּ וְהֶפְדָּ֑הּ לְעַ֥ם נָכְרִ֛י לֹֽא־יִמְשֹׁ֥ל לְמָכְרָ֖הּ בְּבִגְדוֹ־בָֽהּ: וְאִם־לִבְנ֖וֹ
יִֽיעָדֶ֑נָּה כְּמִשְׁפַּ֥ט הַבָּנ֖וֹת יַעֲשֶׂה־לָּֽהּ: אִם־אַחֶ֖רֶת יִֽקַּֽח־ל֑וֹ שְׁאֵרָ֛הּ כְּסוּתָ֥הּ וְעֹנָתָ֖הּ
לֹ֥א יִגְרָֽע: וְאִ֨ם־שְׁלָשׁ־אֵ֔לֶּה לֹ֥א יַעֲשֶׂ֖ה לָ֑הּ וְיָצְאָ֥ה חִנָּ֖ם אֵ֥ין כָּֽסֶף: _Yisrael_ מַכֵּ֥ה אִ֛ישׁ וָמֵ֖ת
מ֣וֹת יוּמָֽת: וַאֲשֶׁר֙ לֹ֣א צָדָ֔ה וְהָאֱלֹהִ֖ים אִנָּ֣ה לְיָד֑וֹ וְשַׂמְתִּ֤י לְךָ֙ מָק֔וֹם אֲשֶׁ֥ר יָנ֖וּס שָֽׁמָּה:
וְכִֽי־יָזִ֥ד אִ֛ישׁ עַל־רֵעֵ֖הוּ לְהָרְג֣וֹ בְעָרְמָ֑ה מֵעִ֣ם מִזְבְּחִ֔י תִּקָּחֶ֖נּוּ לָמֽוּת: וּמַכֵּ֥ה אָבִ֛יו וְאִמּ֖וֹ
מ֥וֹת יוּמָֽת: וְגֹנֵ֨ב אִ֧ישׁ וּמְכָר֛וֹ וְנִמְצָ֥א בְיָד֖וֹ מ֥וֹת יוּמָֽת: וּמְקַלֵּ֥ל אָבִ֛יו וְאִמּ֖וֹ מ֥וֹת יוּמָֽת:
וְכִֽי־יְרִיבֻ֣ן אֲנָשִׁ֗ים וְהִכָּה־אִישׁ֙ אֶת־רֵעֵ֔הוּ בְּאֶ֖בֶן א֣וֹ בְאֶגְרֹ֑ף וְלֹ֥א יָמ֖וּת וְנָפַ֥ל לְמִשְׁכָּֽב:
אִם־יָק֞וּם וְהִתְהַלֵּ֥ךְ בַּח֛וּץ עַל־מִשְׁעַנְתּ֖וֹ וְנִקָּ֣ה הַמַּכֶּ֑ה רַ֥ק שִׁבְתּ֛וֹ יִתֵּ֖ן וְרַפֹּ֥א יְרַפֵּֽא:

TERUMAH

וַיְדַבֵּ֥ר יְהֹוָ֖ה אֶל־מֹשֶׁ֥ה לֵּאמֹֽר: דַּבֵּר֙ אֶל־בְּנֵ֣י יִשְׂרָאֵ֔ל וְיִקְחוּ־לִ֖י תְּרוּמָ֑ה
מֵאֵ֤ת כָּל־אִישׁ֙ אֲשֶׁ֣ר יִדְּבֶ֣נּוּ לִבּ֔וֹ תִּקְח֖וּ אֶת־תְּרוּמָתִֽי: וְזֹאת֙ הַתְּרוּמָ֔ה אֲשֶׁ֥ר תִּקְח֖וּ
מֵֽאִתָּ֑ם זָהָ֥ב וָכֶ֖סֶף וּנְחֹֽשֶׁת: וּתְכֵ֤לֶת וְאַרְגָּמָן֙ וְתוֹלַ֣עַת שָׁנִ֔י וְשֵׁ֖שׁ וְעִזִּֽים: וְעֹרֹ֨ת אֵילִ֧ם
מְאָדָּמִ֛ים וְעֹרֹ֥ת תְּחָשִׁ֖ים וַעֲצֵ֥י שִׁטִּֽים: _Levi_ שֶׁ֖מֶן לַמָּאֹ֑ר בְּשָׂמִים֙ לְשֶׁ֣מֶן הַמִּשְׁחָ֔ה
וְלִקְטֹ֖רֶת הַסַּמִּֽים: אַבְנֵי־שֹׁ֕הַם וְאַבְנֵ֖י מִלֻּאִ֑ים לָאֵפֹ֖ד וְלַחֹֽשֶׁן: וְעָ֥שׂוּ לִ֖י מִקְדָּ֑שׁ וְשָׁכַנְתִּ֖י
בְּתוֹכָֽם: כְּכֹ֗ל אֲשֶׁ֤ר אֲנִי֙ מַרְאֶ֣ה אוֹתְךָ֔ אֵ֚ת תַּבְנִ֣ית הַמִּשְׁכָּ֔ן וְאֵ֖ת תַּבְנִ֣ית כָּל־כֵּלָ֑יו וְכֵ֖ן
תַּעֲשֽׂוּ: _Yisrael_ וְעָשׂ֥וּ אֲר֖וֹן עֲצֵ֣י שִׁטִּ֑ים אַמָּתַ֨יִם וָחֵ֜צִי אָרְכּ֗וֹ וְאַמָּ֤ה וָחֵ֨צִי֙ רָחְבּ֔וֹ וְאַמָּ֥ה
וָחֵ֖צִי קֹֽמָת֑וֹ: וְצִפִּיתָ֤ אֹתוֹ֙ זָהָ֣ב טָה֔וֹר מִבַּ֥יִת וּמִח֖וּץ תְּצַפֶּ֑נּוּ וְעָשִׂ֧יתָ עָלָ֛יו זֵ֥ר זָהָ֖ב סָבִֽיב:
וְיָצַ֣קְתָּ לּ֗וֹ אַרְבַּע֙ טַבְּעֹ֣ת זָהָ֔ב וְנָ֣תַתָּ֔ה עַ֖ל אַרְבַּ֣ע פַּעֲמֹתָ֑יו וּשְׁתֵּ֣י טַבָּעֹ֗ת עַל־צַלְעוֹ֙ הָֽאֶחָ֔ת
וּשְׁתֵּי֙ טַבָּעֹ֔ת עַל־צַלְע֖וֹ הַשֵּׁנִֽית: וְעָשִׂ֥יתָ בַדֵּ֖י עֲצֵ֣י שִׁטִּ֑ים וְצִפִּיתָ֥ אֹתָ֖ם זָהָֽב:
וְהֵֽבֵאתָ֤ אֶת־הַבַּדִּים֙ בַּטַּבָּעֹ֔ת עַ֖ל צַלְעֹ֣ת הָאָרֹ֑ן לָשֵׂ֥את אֶת־הָאָרֹ֖ן בָּהֶֽם: בְּטַבְּעֹת֙
הָֽאָרֹ֔ן יִֽהְי֖וּ הַבַּדִּ֑ים לֹ֥א יָסֻ֖רוּ מִמֶּֽנּוּ: וְנָתַתָּ֖ אֶל־הָאָרֹ֑ן אֵ֚ת הָעֵדֻ֔ת אֲשֶׁ֥ר אֶתֵּ֖ן אֵלֶֽיךָ:

TETZAVE

וְאַתָּ֞ה תְּצַוֶּ֣ה ׀ אֶת־בְּנֵ֣י יִשְׂרָאֵ֗ל וְיִקְח֨וּ אֵלֶ֜יךָ שֶׁ֣מֶן זַ֥יִת זָ֛ךְ כָּתִ֖ית לַמָּא֑וֹר
לְהַעֲלֹ֥ת נֵ֖ר תָּמִֽיד: בְּאֹ֣הֶל מוֹעֵ֗ד מִח֣וּץ לַפָּרֹ֜כֶת אֲשֶׁ֣ר עַל־הָעֵדֻ֗ת יַעֲרֹ֨ךְ אֹת֜וֹ אַהֲרֹ֤ן
וּבָנָיו֙ מֵעֶ֣רֶב עַד־בֹּ֔קֶר לִפְנֵ֖י יְהֹוָ֑ה חֻקַּ֤ת עוֹלָם֙ לְדֹרֹתָ֔ם מֵאֵ֖ת בְּנֵ֥י יִשְׂרָאֵֽל:

וְאַתָּה הַקְרֵב אֵלֶיךָ אֶת־אַהֲרֹן אָחִיךָ וְאֶת־בָּנָיו אִתּוֹ מִתּוֹךְ בְּנֵי יִשְׂרָאֵל לְכַהֲנוֹ־לִי
אַהֲרֹן נָדָב וַאֲבִיהוּא אֶלְעָזָר וְאִיתָמָר בְּנֵי אַהֲרֹן: וְעָשִׂיתָ בִגְדֵי־קֹדֶשׁ לְאַהֲרֹן אָחִיךָ
לְכָבוֹד וּלְתִפְאָרֶת: וְאַתָּה תְּדַבֵּר אֶל־כָּל־חַכְמֵי־לֵב אֲשֶׁר מִלֵּאתִיו רוּחַ חָכְמָה וְעָשׂוּ
אֶת־בִּגְדֵי אַהֲרֹן לְקַדְּשׁוֹ לְכַהֲנוֹ־לִי: וְאֵלֶּה הַבְּגָדִים אֲשֶׁר יַעֲשׂוּ חֹשֶׁן וְאֵפוֹד וּמְעִיל
וּכְתֹנֶת תַּשְׁבֵּץ מִצְנֶפֶת וְאַבְנֵט וְעָשׂוּ בִגְדֵי־קֹדֶשׁ לְאַהֲרֹן אָחִיךָ וּלְבָנָיו לְכַהֲנוֹ־לִי:
Levi וְהֵם יִקְחוּ אֶת־הַזָּהָב וְאֶת־הַתְּכֵלֶת וְאֶת־הָאַרְגָּמָן וְאֶת־תּוֹלַעַת הַשָּׁנִי וְאֶת־הַשֵּׁשׁ:
וְעָשׂוּ אֶת־הָאֵפֹד זָהָב תְּכֵלֶת וְאַרְגָּמָן תּוֹלַעַת שָׁנִי וְשֵׁשׁ מָשְׁזָר מַעֲשֵׂה חֹשֵׁב:
שְׁתֵּי כְתֵפֹת חֹבְרֹת יִהְיֶה־לּוֹ אֶל־שְׁנֵי קְצוֹתָיו וְחֻבָּר: וְחֵשֶׁב אֲפֻדָּתוֹ אֲשֶׁר עָלָיו
כְּמַעֲשֵׂהוּ מִמֶּנּוּ יִהְיֶה זָהָב תְּכֵלֶת וְאַרְגָּמָן וְתוֹלַעַת שָׁנִי וְשֵׁשׁ מָשְׁזָר: וְלָקַחְתָּ אֶת־שְׁתֵּי
אַבְנֵי־שֹׁהַם וּפִתַּחְתָּ עֲלֵיהֶם שְׁמוֹת בְּנֵי יִשְׂרָאֵל: Yisrael שִׁשָּׁה מִשְּׁמֹתָם עַל הָאֶבֶן
הָאֶחָת וְאֶת־שְׁמוֹת הַשִּׁשָּׁה הַנּוֹתָרִים עַל־הָאֶבֶן הַשֵּׁנִית כְּתוֹלְדֹתָם: מַעֲשֵׂה חָרַשׁ אֶבֶן
פִּתּוּחֵי חֹתָם תְּפַתַּח אֶת־שְׁתֵּי הָאֲבָנִים עַל־שְׁמֹת בְּנֵי יִשְׂרָאֵל מֻסַבֹּת מִשְׁבְּצֹת
זָהָב תַּעֲשֶׂה אֹתָם: וְשַׂמְתָּ אֶת־שְׁתֵּי הָאֲבָנִים עַל כִּתְפֹת הָאֵפֹד אַבְנֵי זִכָּרֹן
לִבְנֵי יִשְׂרָאֵל וְנָשָׂא אַהֲרֹן אֶת־שְׁמוֹתָם לִפְנֵי יְ—ה—וֹ—ה—אדני—אלהים עַל־שְׁתֵּי כְתֵפָיו לְזִכָּרֹן:

KI TISA

וַיְדַבֵּר יְ—ה—וֹ—ה—אדני—אלהים אֶל־מֹשֶׁה לֵּאמֹר: כִּי תִשָּׂא אֶת־רֹאשׁ בְּנֵי־יִשְׂרָאֵל לִפְקֻדֵיהֶם
וְנָתְנוּ אִישׁ כֹּפֶר נַפְשׁוֹ לַיְ—ה—וֹ—ה—אדני—אלהים בִּפְקֹד אֹתָם וְלֹא־יִהְיֶה בָהֶם נֶגֶף בִּפְקֹד אֹתָם:
זֶה | יִתְּנוּ כָּל־הָעֹבֵר עַל־הַפְּקֻדִים מַחֲצִית הַשֶּׁקֶל בְּשֶׁקֶל הַקֹּדֶשׁ עֶשְׂרִים גֵּרָה הַשֶּׁקֶל
מַחֲצִית הַשֶּׁקֶל תְּרוּמָה לַיְ—ה—וֹ—ה—אדני—אלהים: Levi כֹּל הָעֹבֵר עַל־הַפְּקֻדִים מִבֶּן עֶשְׂרִים
שָׁנָה וָמָעְלָה יִתֵּן תְּרוּמַת יְ—ה—וֹ—ה—אדני—אלהים: הֶעָשִׁיר לֹא־יַרְבֶּה וְהַדַּל לֹא יַמְעִיט מִמַּחֲצִית
הַשָּׁקֶל לָתֵת אֶת־תְּרוּמַת יְ—ה—וֹ—ה—אדני—אלהים לְכַפֵּר עַל־נַפְשֹׁתֵיכֶם: וְלָקַחְתָּ אֶת־כֶּסֶף הַכִּפֻּרִים
מֵאֵת בְּנֵי יִשְׂרָאֵל וְנָתַתָּ אֹתוֹ עַל־עֲבֹדַת אֹהֶל מוֹעֵד וְהָיָה לִבְנֵי יִשְׂרָאֵל לְזִכָּרוֹן לִפְנֵי
יְ—ה—וֹ—ה—אדני—אלהים לְכַפֵּר עַל־נַפְשֹׁתֵיכֶם: Yisrael וַיְדַבֵּר יְ—ה—וֹ—ה—אדני—אלהים אֶל־מֹשֶׁה לֵּאמֹר:
וְעָשִׂיתָ כִּיּוֹר נְחֹשֶׁת וְכַנּוֹ נְחֹשֶׁת לְרָחְצָה וְנָתַתָּ אֹתוֹ בֵּין־אֹהֶל מוֹעֵד וּבֵין הַמִּזְבֵּחַ וְנָתַתָּ
שָׁמָּה מָיִם: וְרָחֲצוּ אַהֲרֹן וּבָנָיו מִמֶּנּוּ אֶת־יְדֵיהֶם וְאֶת־רַגְלֵיהֶם: בְּבֹאָם אֶל־אֹהֶל מוֹעֵד
יִרְחֲצוּ־מַיִם וְלֹא יָמֻתוּ אוֹ בְגִשְׁתָּם אֶל־הַמִּזְבֵּחַ לְשָׁרֵת לְהַקְטִיר אִשֶּׁה לַיְ—ה—וֹ—ה—אדני—אלהים:
וְרָחֲצוּ יְדֵיהֶם וְרַגְלֵיהֶם וְלֹא יָמֻתוּ וְהָיְתָה לָהֶם חָק־עוֹלָם לוֹ וּלְזַרְעוֹ לְדֹרֹתָם:

VAYAKHEL

וַיַּקְהֵל מֹשֶׁה אֶת־כָּל־עֲדַת בְּנֵי יִשְׂרָאֵל וַיֹּאמֶר אֲלֵהֶם אֵלֶּה הַדְּבָרִים
אֲשֶׁר־צִוָּה יְ—ה—וֹ—ה—אדני—אלהים לַעֲשֹׂת אֹתָם: שֵׁשֶׁת יָמִים תֵּעָשֶׂה מְלָאכָה
וּבַיּוֹם הַשְּׁבִיעִי יִהְיֶה לָכֶם קֹדֶשׁ שַׁבַּת שַׁבָּתוֹן לַיְ—ה—וֹ—ה—אדני—אלהים כָּל־הָעֹשֶׂה בוֹ
מְלָאכָה יוּמָת: Levi לֹא־תְבַעֲרוּ אֵשׁ בְּכֹל מֹשְׁבֹתֵיכֶם בְּיוֹם הַשַּׁבָּת:

וַיֹּאמֶר מֹשֶׁה אֶל־כָּל־עֲדַת בְּנֵי־יִשְׂרָאֵל לֵאמֹר זֶה הַדָּבָר אֲשֶׁר־צִוָּה יְהוָֹהאהדונהי
לֵאמֹר: קְחוּ מֵאִתְּכֶם תְּרוּמָה לַיהוָֹהאהדונהי כֹּל נְדִיב לִבּוֹ יְבִיאֶהָ אֵת תְּרוּמַת
יְהוָֹהאהדונהי זָהָב וָכֶסֶף וּנְחֹשֶׁת: וּתְכֵלֶת וְאַרְגָּמָן וְתוֹלַעַת שָׁנִי וְשֵׁשׁ וְעִזִּים: וְעֹרֹת
אֵילִם מְאָדָּמִים וְעֹרֹת תְּחָשִׁים וַעֲצֵי שִׁטִּים: וְשֶׁמֶן לַמָּאוֹר וּבְשָׂמִים לְשֶׁמֶן הַמִּשְׁחָה
וְלִקְטֹרֶת הַסַּמִּים: וְאַבְנֵי־שֹׁהַם וְאַבְנֵי מִלֻּאִים לָאֵפוֹד וְלַחֹשֶׁן: וְכָל־חֲכַם־לֵב בָּכֶם יָבֹאוּ
וְיַעֲשׂוּ אֵת כָּל־אֲשֶׁר צִוָּה יְהוָֹהאהדונהי *Yisrael* אֶת־הַמִּשְׁכָּן אֶת־אָהֳלוֹ וְאֶת־מִכְסֵהוּ
אֶת־קְרָסָיו וְאֶת־קְרָשָׁיו אֶת־בְּרִיחָו אֶת־עַמֻּדָיו וְאֶת־אֲדָנָיו: אֶת־הָאָרֹן וְאֶת־בַּדָּיו אֶת־
הַכַּפֹּרֶת וְאֵת פָּרֹכֶת הַמָּסָךְ: אֶת־הַשֻּׁלְחָן וְאֶת־בַּדָּיו וְאֶת־כָּל־כֵּלָיו וְאֵת לֶחֶם הַפָּנִים:
וְאֶת־מְנֹרַת הַמָּאוֹר וְאֶת־כֵּלֶיהָ וְאֶת־נֵרֹתֶיהָ וְאֵת שֶׁמֶן הַמָּאוֹר: וְאֶת־מִזְבַּח הַקְּטֹרֶת
וְאֶת־בַּדָּיו וְאֵת שֶׁמֶן הַמִּשְׁחָה וְאֵת קְטֹרֶת הַסַּמִּים וְאֶת־מָסַךְ הַפֶּתַח לְפֶתַח הַמִּשְׁכָּן:
אֵת | מִזְבַּח הָעֹלָה וְאֶת־מִכְבַּר הַנְּחֹשֶׁת אֲשֶׁר־לוֹ אֶת־בַּדָּיו וְאֶת־כָּל־כֵּלָיו אֶת־הַכִּיֹּר
וְאֶת־כַּנּוֹ: אֵת קַלְעֵי הֶחָצֵר אֶת־עַמֻּדָיו וְאֶת־אֲדָנֶיהָ וְאֵת מָסַךְ שַׁעַר הֶחָצֵר: אֶת־יִתְדֹת
הַמִּשְׁכָּן וְאֶת־יִתְדֹת הֶחָצֵר וְאֶת־מֵיתְרֵיהֶם: אֶת־בִּגְדֵי הַשְּׂרָד לְשָׁרֵת בַּקֹּדֶשׁ אֶת־בִּגְדֵי
הַקֹּדֶשׁ לְאַהֲרֹן הַכֹּהֵן וְאֶת־בִּגְדֵי בָנָיו לְכַהֵן: וַיֵּצְאוּ כָּל־עֲדַת בְּנֵי־יִשְׂרָאֵל מִלִּפְנֵי מֹשֶׁה:

PEKUDEI

אֵלֶּה פְקוּדֵי הַמִּשְׁכָּן מִשְׁכַּן הָעֵדֻת אֲשֶׁר פֻּקַּד עַל־פִּי מֹשֶׁה עֲבֹדַת הַלְוִיִּם
בְּיַד אִיתָמָר בֶּן־אַהֲרֹן הַכֹּהֵן: וּבְצַלְאֵל בֶּן־אוּרִי בֶן־חוּר לְמַטֵּה יְהוּדָה עָשָׂה
אֵת כָּל־אֲשֶׁר־צִוָּה יְהוָֹהאהדונהי אֶת־מֹשֶׁה: וְאִתּוֹ אָהֳלִיאָב בֶּן־אֲחִיסָמָךְ
לְמַטֵּה־דָן חָרָשׁ וְחֹשֵׁב וְרֹקֵם בַּתְּכֵלֶת וּבָאַרְגָּמָן וּבְתוֹלַעַת הַשָּׁנִי וּבַשֵּׁשׁ: *Levi*
כָּל־הַזָּהָב הֶעָשׂוּי לַמְּלָאכָה בְּכֹל מְלֶאכֶת הַקֹּדֶשׁ וַיְהִי | זְהַב הַתְּנוּפָה תֵּשַׁע וְעֶשְׂרִים
כִּכָּר וּשְׁבַע מֵאוֹת וּשְׁלֹשִׁים שֶׁקֶל בְּשֶׁקֶל הַקֹּדֶשׁ: וְכֶסֶף פְּקוּדֵי הָעֵדָה מְאַת כִּכָּר
וְאֶלֶף וּשְׁבַע מֵאוֹת וַחֲמִשָּׁה וְשִׁבְעִים שֶׁקֶל בְּשֶׁקֶל הַקֹּדֶשׁ: בֶּקַע לַגֻּלְגֹּלֶת מַחֲצִית
הַשֶּׁקֶל בְּשֶׁקֶל הַקֹּדֶשׁ לְכֹל הָעֹבֵר עַל־הַפְּקֻדִים מִבֶּן עֶשְׂרִים שָׁנָה וָמַעְלָה לְשֵׁשׁ־מֵאוֹת
אֶלֶף וּשְׁלֹשֶׁת אֲלָפִים וַחֲמֵשׁ מֵאוֹת וַחֲמִשִּׁים: וַיְהִי מְאַת כִּכַּר הַכֶּסֶף לָצֶקֶת אֵת אַדְנֵי
הַקֹּדֶשׁ וְאֵת אַדְנֵי הַפָּרֹכֶת מְאַת אֲדָנִים לִמְאַת הַכִּכָּר כִּכָּר לָאָדֶן: *Yisrael* וְאֶת־הָאֶלֶף
וּשְׁבַע הַמֵּאוֹת וַחֲמִשָּׁה וְשִׁבְעִים עָשָׂה וָוִים לָעַמּוּדִים וְצִפָּה רָאשֵׁיהֶם וְחִשַּׁק אֹתָם:
וּנְחֹשֶׁת הַתְּנוּפָה שִׁבְעִים כִּכָּר וְאַלְפַּיִם וְאַרְבַּע־מֵאוֹת שָׁקֶל: וַיַּעַשׂ בָּהּ אֶת־אַדְנֵי פֶּתַח
אֹהֶל מוֹעֵד וְאֵת מִזְבַּח הַנְּחֹשֶׁת וְאֶת־מִכְבַּר הַנְּחֹשֶׁת אֲשֶׁר־לוֹ וְאֵת כָּל־כְּלֵי הַמִּזְבֵּחַ:
וְאֶת־אַדְנֵי הֶחָצֵר סָבִיב וְאֶת־אַדְנֵי שַׁעַר הֶחָצֵר וְאֵת כָּל־יִתְדֹת הַמִּשְׁכָּן וְאֶת־כָּל־יִתְדֹת
הֶחָצֵר סָבִיב: וּמִן־הַתְּכֵלֶת וְהָאַרְגָּמָן וְתוֹלַעַת הַשָּׁנִי עָשׂוּ בִגְדֵי־שְׂרָד לְשָׁרֵת
בַּקֹּדֶשׁ וַיַּעֲשׂוּ אֶת־בִּגְדֵי הַקֹּדֶשׁ אֲשֶׁר לְאַהֲרֹן כַּאֲשֶׁר צִוָּה יְהוָֹהאהדונהי אֶת־מֹשֶׁה:

VAYIKRA

וַיִּקְרָ֖א אֶל־מֹשֶׁ֑ה וַיְדַבֵּ֤ר יְהֹוָֽאֲדֹנָי֙ אֵלָ֔יו מֵאֹ֥הֶל מוֹעֵ֖ד לֵאמֹֽר: דַּבֵּ֞ר אֶל־בְּנֵ֤י
יִשְׂרָאֵל֙ וְאָמַרְתָּ֣ אֲלֵהֶ֔ם אָדָ֗ם כִּֽי־יַקְרִ֥יב מִכֶּ֛ם קָרְבָּ֖ן לַֽיהֹוָֽאֲדֹנָי֑ מִן־הַבְּהֵמָ֗ה
מִן־הַבָּקָר֙ וּמִן־הַצֹּ֔אן תַּקְרִ֖יבוּ אֶת־קָרְבַּנְכֶֽם: אִם־עֹלָ֤ה קָרְבָּנוֹ֙ מִן־הַבָּקָ֔ר זָכָ֥ר תָּמִ֖ים
יַקְרִיבֶ֑נּוּ אֶל־פֶּ֜תַח אֹ֤הֶל מוֹעֵד֙ יַקְרִ֣יב אֹת֔וֹ לִרְצֹנ֖וֹ לִפְנֵ֥י יְהֹוָֽאֲדֹנָֽי: וְסָמַ֣ךְ יָד֔וֹ
עַ֖ל רֹ֣אשׁ הָֽעֹלָ֑ה וְנִרְצָ֥ה ל֖וֹ לְכַפֵּ֥ר עָלָֽיו: **Levi** וְשָׁחַ֛ט אֶת־בֶּ֥ן הַבָּקָ֖ר לִפְנֵ֣י יְהֹוָֽאֲדֹנָי֑
וְ֠הִקְרִ֠יבוּ בְּנֵ֨י אַֽהֲרֹ֤ן הַכֹּֽהֲנִים֙ אֶת־הַדָּ֔ם וְזָֽרְק֨וּ אֶת־הַדָּ֤ם עַל־הַמִּזְבֵּ֙חַ֙ סָבִ֔יב אֲשֶׁר־פֶּ֖תַח
אֹ֥הֶל מוֹעֵֽד: וְהִפְשִׁ֖יט אֶת־הָֽעֹלָ֑ה וְנִתַּ֥ח אֹתָ֖הּ לִנְתָחֶֽיהָ: וְ֠נָֽתְנ֠וּ בְּנֵ֨י אַֽהֲרֹ֧ן הַכֹּהֵ֛ן אֵ֖שׁ
עַל־הַמִּזְבֵּ֑חַ וְעָֽרְכ֥וּ עֵצִ֖ים עַל־הָאֵֽשׁ: וְעָֽרְכ֗וּ בְּנֵ֤י אַֽהֲרֹן֙ הַכֹּ֣הֲנִ֔ים אֵ֚ת הַנְּתָחִ֔ים אֶת־הָרֹ֖אשׁ
וְאֶת־הַפָּ֑דֶר עַל־הָֽעֵצִים֙ אֲשֶׁ֣ר עַל־הָאֵ֔שׁ אֲשֶׁ֖ר עַל־הַמִּזְבֵּֽחַ: וְקִרְבּ֥וֹ וּכְרָעָ֖יו יִרְחַ֣ץ בַּמָּ֑יִם
וְהִקְטִ֨יר הַכֹּהֵ֤ן אֶת־הַכֹּל֙ הַמִּזְבֵּ֔חָה עֹלָ֛ה אִשֵּׁ֥ה רֵֽיחַ־נִיח֖וֹחַ לַֽיהֹוָֽאֲדֹנָֽי: **Yisrael**
וְאִם־מִן־הַצֹּ֨אן קָרְבָּנ֜וֹ מִן־הַכְּשָׂבִ֛ים א֥וֹ מִן־הָֽעִזִּ֖ים לְעֹלָ֑ה זָכָ֥ר תָּמִ֖ים יַקְרִיבֶֽנּוּ: וְשָׁחַ֣ט
אֹת֠וֹ עַ֣ל יֶ֧רֶךְ הַמִּזְבֵּ֛חַ צָפֹ֖נָה לִפְנֵ֣י יְהֹוָֽאֲדֹנָי֑ וְזָֽרְק֡וּ בְּנֵי֩ אַֽהֲרֹ֨ן הַכֹּֽהֲנִ֧ים אֶת־דָּמ֛וֹ
עַל־הַמִּזְבֵּ֖חַ סָבִֽיב: וְנִתַּ֤ח אֹתוֹ֙ לִנְתָחָ֔יו וְאֶת־רֹאשׁ֖וֹ וְאֶת־פִּדְר֑וֹ וְעָרַ֤ךְ הַכֹּהֵן֙ אֹתָ֔ם
עַל־הָֽעֵצִים֙ אֲשֶׁ֣ר עַל־הָאֵ֔שׁ אֲשֶׁ֖ר עַל־הַמִּזְבֵּֽחַ: וְהַקֶּ֥רֶב וְהַכְּרָעַ֖יִם יִרְחַ֣ץ בַּמָּ֑יִם וְהִקְרִ֨יב
הַכֹּהֵ֤ן אֶת־הַכֹּל֙ וְהִקְטִ֣יר הַמִּזְבֵּ֔חָה עֹלָ֣ה ה֗וּא אִשֵּׁ֛ה רֵ֥יחַ נִיח֖וֹחַ לַֽיהֹוָֽאֲדֹנָֽי:

TZAV

וַיְדַבֵּ֥ר יְהֹוָֽאֲדֹנָ֖י אֶל־מֹשֶׁ֥ה לֵּאמֹֽר: צַ֤ו אֶֽת־אַֽהֲרֹן֙ וְאֶת־בָּנָ֣יו לֵאמֹ֔ר
זֹ֥את תּוֹרַ֖ת הָֽעֹלָ֑ה הִ֣וא הָֽעֹלָ֡ה עַל֩ מוֹקְדָ֨ה עַל־הַמִּזְבֵּ֤חַ כָּל־הַלַּ֙יְלָה֙ עַד־הַבֹּ֔קֶר
וְאֵ֥שׁ הַמִּזְבֵּ֖חַ תּ֥וּקַד בּֽוֹ: וְלָבַ֨שׁ הַכֹּהֵ֜ן מִדּ֣וֹ בַ֗ד וּמִכְנְסֵי־בַד֮ יִלְבַּ֣שׁ עַל־בְּשָׂרוֹ֒
וְהֵרִ֣ים אֶת־הַדֶּ֗שֶׁן אֲשֶׁ֨ר תֹּאכַ֥ל הָאֵ֛שׁ אֶת־הָֽעֹלָ֖ה עַל־הַמִּזְבֵּ֑חַ וְשָׂמ֕וֹ אֵ֖צֶל הַמִּזְבֵּֽחַ: **Levi**
וּפָשַׁט֙ אֶת־בְּגָדָ֔יו וְלָבַ֖שׁ בְּגָדִ֣ים אֲחֵרִ֑ים וְהוֹצִ֤יא אֶת־הַדֶּ֙שֶׁן֙ אֶל־מִח֣וּץ לַֽמַּחֲנֶ֔ה אֶל־מָק֖וֹם
טָהֽוֹר: וְהָאֵ֨שׁ עַל־הַמִּזְבֵּ֤חַ תּֽוּקַד־בּוֹ֙ לֹ֣א תִכְבֶּ֔ה וּבִעֵ֨ר עָלֶ֧יהָ הַכֹּהֵ֛ן עֵצִ֖ים בַּבֹּ֣קֶר בַּבֹּ֑קֶר
וְעָרַ֤ךְ עָלֶ֙יהָ֙ הָֽעֹלָ֔ה וְהִקְטִ֥יר עָלֶ֖יהָ חֶלְבֵ֣י הַשְּׁלָמִֽים: אֵ֗שׁ תָּמִ֛יד תּוּקַ֥ד עַל־הַמִּזְבֵּ֖חַ
לֹ֥א תִכְבֶּֽה: **Yisrael** וְזֹ֥את תּוֹרַ֖ת הַמִּנְחָ֑ה הַקְרֵ֨ב אֹתָ֤הּ בְּנֵֽי־אַֽהֲרֹן֙ לִפְנֵ֣י יְהֹוָֽאֲדֹנָ֔י
אֶל־פְּנֵ֖י הַמִּזְבֵּֽחַ: וְהֵרִ֨ים מִמֶּ֜נּוּ בְּקֻמְצ֗וֹ מִסֹּ֤לֶת הַמִּנְחָה֙ וּמִשַּׁמְנָ֔הּ וְאֵת֙ כָּל־הַלְּבֹנָ֔ה אֲשֶׁ֖ר
עַל־הַמִּנְחָ֑ה וְהִקְטִ֣יר הַמִּזְבֵּ֗חַ רֵ֧יחַ נִיחֹ֛חַ אַזְכָּֽרָתָ֖הּ לַֽיהֹוָֽאֲדֹנָֽי: וְהַנּוֹתֶ֙רֶת֙ מִמֶּ֔נָּה
יֹֽאכְל֖וּ אַֽהֲרֹ֣ן וּבָנָ֑יו מַצּ֤וֹת תֵּֽאָכֵל֙ בְּמָק֣וֹם קָדֹ֔שׁ בַּֽחֲצַ֥ר אֹֽהֶל־מוֹעֵ֖ד יֹֽאכְלֽוּהָ: לֹ֤א תֵֽאָפֶה֙
חָמֵ֔ץ חֶלְקָ֛ם נָתַ֥תִּי אֹתָ֖הּ מֵֽאִשָּׁ֑י קֹ֤דֶשׁ קָֽדָשִׁים֙ הִ֔וא כַּֽחַטָּ֖את וְכָֽאָשָֽׁם: כָּל־זָכָ֞ר בִּבְנֵ֤י
אַֽהֲרֹן֙ יֹֽאכְלֶ֔נָּה חָק־עוֹלָם֙ לְדֹרֹ֣תֵיכֶ֔ם מֵֽאִשֵּׁ֖י יְהֹוָֽאֲדֹנָ֑י כֹּ֛ל אֲשֶׁר־יִגַּ֥ע בָּהֶ֖ם יִקְדָּֽשׁ:

SHEMINI

וַֽיְהִי֙ בַּיּ֣וֹם הַשְּׁמִינִ֔י קָרָ֣א מֹשֶׁ֔ה לְאַֽהֲרֹ֖ן וּלְבָנָ֑יו וּלְזִקְנֵ֖י יִשְׂרָאֵֽל: וַיֹּ֣אמֶר אֶֽל־אַֽהֲרֹ֗ן קַח־לְ֠ךָ֠
עֵ֣גֶל בֶּן־בָּקָ֧ר לְחַטָּ֛את וְאַ֥יִל לְעֹלָ֖ה תְּמִימִ֑ם וְהַקְרֵ֖ב לִפְנֵ֥י יְהֹוָֽאֲדֹנָֽי: וְאֶל־בְּנֵ֤י
יִשְׂרָאֵל֙ תְּדַבֵּ֣ר לֵאמֹ֔ר קְח֤וּ שְׂעִֽיר־עִזִּים֙ לְחַטָּ֔את וְעֵ֣גֶל וָכֶ֛בֶשׂ בְּנֵֽי־שָׁנָ֥ה תְּמִימִ֖ם לְעֹלָֽה:

וְעוֹר וָאַיִל לִשְׁלָמִים לִזְבֹּחַ לִפְנֵי יְהֹוָאהדֹנָהִי וּמִנְחָה בְלוּלָה בַשָּׁמֶן כִּי הַיּוֹם
יְהֹוָאהדֹנָהִי נִרְאָה אֲלֵיכֶם: וַיִּקְחוּ אֵת אֲשֶׁר צִוָּה מֹשֶׁה אֶל־פְּנֵי אֹהֶל מוֹעֵד וַיִּקְרְבוּ
כָּל־הָעֵדָה וַיַּעַמְדוּ לִפְנֵי יְהֹוָאהדֹנָהִי: וַיֹּאמֶר מֹשֶׁה זֶה הַדָּבָר אֲשֶׁר־צִוָּה
יְהֹוָאהדֹנָהִי תַּעֲשׂוּ וְיֵרָא אֲלֵיכֶם כְּבוֹד יְהֹוָאהדֹנָהִי: _Levi_ וַיֹּאמֶר מֹשֶׁה אֶל־אַהֲרֹן
קְרַב אֶל־הַמִּזְבֵּחַ וַעֲשֵׂה אֶת־חַטָּאתְךָ וְאֶת־עֹלָתֶךָ וְכַפֵּר בַּעַדְךָ וּבְעַד הָעָם וַעֲשֵׂה
אֶת־קָרְבַּן הָעָם וְכַפֵּר בַּעֲדָם כַּאֲשֶׁר צִוָּה יְהֹוָאהדֹנָהִי: וַיִּקְרַב אַהֲרֹן אֶל־הַמִּזְבֵּחַ
וַיִּשְׁחַט אֶת־עֵגֶל הַחַטָּאת אֲשֶׁר־לוֹ: וַיַּקְרִבוּ בְּנֵי אַהֲרֹן אֶת־הַדָּם אֵלָיו וַיִּטְבֹּל אֶצְבָּעוֹ
בַּדָּם וַיִּתֵּן עַל־קַרְנוֹת הַמִּזְבֵּחַ וְאֶת־הַדָּם יָצַק אֶל־יְסוֹד הַמִּזְבֵּחַ: וְאֶת־הַחֵלֶב
וְאֶת־הַכְּלָיֹת וְאֶת־הַיֹּתֶרֶת מִן־הַכָּבֵד מִן־הַחַטָּאת הִקְטִיר הַמִּזְבֵּחָה כַּאֲשֶׁר צִוָּה
יְהֹוָאהדֹנָהִי אֶת־מֹשֶׁה: _Yisrael_ וְאֶת־הַבָּשָׂר וְאֶת־הָעוֹר שָׂרַף בָּאֵשׁ מִחוּץ לַמַּחֲנֶה:
וַיִּשְׁחַט אֶת־הָעֹלָה וַיַּמְצִאוּ בְּנֵי אַהֲרֹן אֵלָיו אֶת־הַדָּם וַיִּזְרְקֵהוּ עַל־הַמִּזְבֵּחַ סָבִיב:
וְאֶת־הָעֹלָה הִמְצִיאוּ אֵלָיו לִנְתָחֶיהָ וְאֶת־הָרֹאשׁ וַיַּקְטֵר עַל־הַמִּזְבֵּחַ: וַיִּרְחַץ אֶת־הַקֶּרֶב
וְאֶת־הַכְּרָעָיִם וַיַּקְטֵר עַל־הָעֹלָה הַמִּזְבֵּחָה: וַיַּקְרֵב אֵת קָרְבַּן הָעָם וַיִּקַּח אֶת־שְׂעִיר
הַחַטָּאת אֲשֶׁר לָעָם וַיִּשְׁחָטֵהוּ וַיְחַטְּאֵהוּ כָּרִאשׁוֹן: וַיַּקְרֵב אֶת־הָעֹלָה וַיַּעֲשֶׂהָ כַּמִּשְׁפָּט:

TAZRIA

וַיְדַבֵּר יְהֹוָאהדֹנָהִי אֶל־מֹשֶׁה לֵּאמֹר: דַּבֵּר אֶל־בְּנֵי יִשְׂרָאֵל לֵאמֹר אִשָּׁה כִּי תַזְרִיעַ
וְיָלְדָה זָכָר וְטָמְאָה שִׁבְעַת יָמִים כִּימֵי נִדַּת דְּוֹתָהּ תִּטְמָא: וּבַיּוֹם הַשְּׁמִינִי יִמּוֹל בְּשַׂר
עָרְלָתוֹ: וּשְׁלֹשִׁים יוֹם וּשְׁלֹשֶׁת יָמִים תֵּשֵׁב בִּדְמֵי טָהֳרָה בְּכָל־קֹדֶשׁ לֹא־תִגָּע
וְאֶל־הַמִּקְדָּשׁ לֹא תָבֹא עַד־מְלֹאת יְמֵי טָהֳרָהּ: _Levi_ וְאִם־נְקֵבָה תֵלֵד וְטָמְאָה שְׁבֻעַיִם
כְּנִדָּתָהּ וְשִׁשִּׁים יוֹם וְשֵׁשֶׁת יָמִים תֵּשֵׁב עַל־דְּמֵי טָהֳרָה: וּבִמְלֹאת | יְמֵי טָהֳרָהּ לְבֵן אוֹ
לְבַת תָּבִיא כֶּבֶשׂ בֶּן־שְׁנָתוֹ לְעֹלָה וּבֶן־יוֹנָה אוֹ־תֹר לְחַטָּאת אֶל־פֶּתַח אֹהֶל־מוֹעֵד
אֶל־הַכֹּהֵן: וְהִקְרִיבוֹ לִפְנֵי יְהֹוָאהדֹנָהִי וְכִפֶּר עָלֶיהָ וְטָהֲרָה מִמְּקֹר דָּמֶיהָ זֹאת תּוֹרַת
הַיֹּלֶדֶת לַזָּכָר אוֹ לַנְּקֵבָה: וְאִם־לֹא תִמְצָא יָדָהּ דֵּי שֶׂה וְלָקְחָה שְׁתֵּי־תֹרִים אוֹ
שְׁנֵי בְּנֵי יוֹנָה אֶחָד לְעֹלָה וְאֶחָד לְחַטָּאת וְכִפֶּר עָלֶיהָ הַכֹּהֵן וְטָהֵרָה: _Yisrael_
וַיְדַבֵּר יְהֹוָאהדֹנָהִי אֶל־מֹשֶׁה וְאֶל־אַהֲרֹן לֵאמֹר: אָדָם כִּי־יִהְיֶה בְעוֹר־בְּשָׂרוֹ
שְׂאֵת אוֹ־סַפַּחַת אוֹ בַהֶרֶת וְהָיָה בְעוֹר־בְּשָׂרוֹ לְנֶגַע צָרָעַת וְהוּבָא אֶל־אַהֲרֹן הַכֹּהֵן
אוֹ אֶל־אַחַד מִבָּנָיו הַכֹּהֲנִים: וְרָאָה הַכֹּהֵן אֶת־הַנֶּגַע בְּעוֹר־הַבָּשָׂר וְשֵׂעָר בַּנֶּגַע
הָפַךְ | לָבָן וּמַרְאֵה הַנֶּגַע עָמֹק מֵעוֹר בְּשָׂרוֹ נֶגַע צָרַעַת הוּא וְרָאָהוּ הַכֹּהֵן וְטִמֵּא אֹתוֹ:
וְאִם־בַּהֶרֶת לְבָנָה הִוא בְּעוֹר בְּשָׂרוֹ וְעָמֹק אֵין־מַרְאֶהָ מִן־הָעוֹר וּשְׂעָרָה לֹא־הָפַךְ לָבָן
וְהִסְגִּיר הַכֹּהֵן אֶת־הַנֶּגַע שִׁבְעַת יָמִים: וְרָאָהוּ הַכֹּהֵן בַּיּוֹם הַשְּׁבִיעִי וְהִנֵּה
הַנֶּגַע עָמַד בְּעֵינָיו לֹא־פָשָׂה הַנֶּגַע בָּעוֹר וְהִסְגִּירוֹ הַכֹּהֵן שִׁבְעַת יָמִים שֵׁנִית:

METZORA

וַיְדַבֵּ֥ר יְהֹוָה֙ אֶל־מֹשֶׁ֣ה לֵּאמֹֽר: זֹ֤את תִּֽהְיֶה֙ תּוֹרַ֣ת הַמְּצֹרָ֔ע בְּי֖וֹם טׇהֳרָת֑וֹ וְהוּבָ֖א
אֶל־הַכֹּהֵֽן: וְיָצָא֙ הַכֹּהֵ֔ן אֶל־מִח֖וּץ לַֽמַּחֲנֶ֑ה וְרָאָה֙ הַכֹּהֵ֔ן וְהִנֵּ֛ה נִרְפָּ֥א נֶֽגַע־הַצָּרַ֖עַת
מִן־הַצָּרֽוּעַ: וְצִוָּה֙ הַכֹּהֵ֔ן וְלָקַ֣ח לַמִּטַּהֵ֗ר שְׁתֵּֽי־צִפֳּרִ֛ים חַיּ֖וֹת טְהֹר֑וֹת וְעֵ֣ץ אֶ֔רֶז וּשְׁנִ֥י תוֹלַ֖עַת
וְאֵזֹֽב: וְצִוָּה֙ הַכֹּהֵ֔ן וְשָׁחַ֖ט אֶת־הַצִּפּ֣וֹר הָֽאֶחָ֑ת אֶל־כְּלִי־חֶ֖רֶשׂ עַל־מַ֥יִם חַיִּֽים: **Levi**
אֶת־הַצִּפֹּ֤ר הַֽחַיָּה֙ יִקַּ֣ח אֹתָ֔הּ וְאֶת־עֵ֥ץ הָאֶ֖רֶז וְאֶת־שְׁנִ֣י הַתּוֹלַ֑עַת וְאֶת־הָֽאֵזֹ֔ב וְטָבַ֣ל אוֹתָ֗ם
וְאֵ֣ת | הַצִּפֹּ֣ר הַֽחַיָּ֗ה בְּדַם֙ הַצִּפֹּ֣ר הַשְּׁחֻטָ֔ה עַ֖ל הַמַּ֥יִם הַֽחַיִּֽים: וְהִזָּ֗ה עַ֤ל הַמִּטַּהֵר֙ מִן־הַצָּרַ֔עַת
שֶׁ֖בַע פְּעָמִ֑ים וְטִ֣הֲר֔וֹ וְשִׁלַּ֛ח אֶת־הַצִּפֹּ֥ר הַֽחַיָּ֖ה עַל־פְּנֵ֥י הַשָּׂדֶֽה: וְכִבֶּס֩ הַמִּטַּהֵ֨ר אֶת־בְּגָדָ֜יו
וְגִלַּ֣ח אֶת־כׇּל־שְׂעָר֗וֹ וְרָחַ֤ץ בַּמַּ֙יִם֙ וְטָהֵ֔ר וְאַחַ֖ר יָב֣וֹא אֶל־הַֽמַּחֲנֶ֑ה וְיָשַׁ֛ב מִח֥וּץ לְאׇהֳל֖וֹ
שִׁבְעַ֥ת יָמִֽים: וְהָיָה֩ בַיּ֨וֹם הַשְּׁבִיעִ֜י יְגַלַּ֣ח אֶת־כׇּל־שְׂעָר֗וֹ אֶת־רֹאשׁ֤וֹ וְאֶת־זְקָנוֹ֙ וְאֵת֙ גַּבֹּ֣ת
עֵינָ֔יו וְאֶת־כׇּל־שְׂעָר֖וֹ יְגַלֵּ֑חַ וְכִבֶּ֣ס אֶת־בְּגָדָ֗יו וְרָחַ֧ץ אֶת־בְּשָׂר֛וֹ בַּמַּ֖יִם וְטָהֵֽר: **Yisrael**
וּבַיּ֣וֹם הַשְּׁמִינִ֗י יִקַּ֤ח שְׁנֵֽי־כְבָשִׂים֙ תְּמִימִ֔ם וְכַבְשָׂ֥ה אַחַ֛ת בַּת־שְׁנָתָ֖הּ תְּמִימָ֑ה וּשְׁלֹשָׁ֣ה
עֶשְׂרֹנִ֗ים סֹ֤לֶת מִנְחָה֙ בְּלוּלָ֣ה בַשֶּׁ֔מֶן וְלֹ֥ג אֶחָ֖ד שָֽׁמֶן: וְהֶֽעֱמִ֞יד הַכֹּהֵ֣ן הַֽמְטַהֵ֗ר אֵ֣ת הָאִ֣ישׁ
הַמִּטַּהֵ֔ר וְאֹתָ֑ם לִפְנֵ֣י יְהֹוָ֔ה פֶּ֖תַח אֹ֥הֶל מוֹעֵֽד: וְלָקַ֨ח הַכֹּהֵ֜ן אֶת־הַכֶּ֤בֶשׂ הָֽאֶחָד֙
וְהִקְרִ֥יב אֹת֛וֹ לְאָשָׁ֖ם וְאֶת־לֹ֣ג הַשָּׁ֑מֶן וְהֵנִ֥יף אֹתָ֛ם תְּנוּפָ֖ה לִפְנֵ֥י יְהֹוָֽה:

ACHAREI MOT

וַיְדַבֵּ֣ר יְהֹוָה֮ אֶל־מֹשֶׁה֒ אַֽחֲרֵ֣י מ֔וֹת שְׁנֵ֖י בְּנֵ֣י אַֽהֲרֹ֑ן בְּקׇרְבָתָ֥ם
לִפְנֵֽי־יְהֹוָ֖ה וַיָּמֻֽתוּ: וַיֹּ֨אמֶר יְהֹוָ֜ה אֶל־מֹשֶׁ֗ה דַּבֵּר֙ אֶל־אַֽהֲרֹ֣ן אָחִ֔יךָ
וְאַל־יָבֹ֤א בְכׇל־עֵת֙ אֶל־הַקֹּ֔דֶשׁ מִבֵּ֖ית לַפָּרֹ֑כֶת אֶל־פְּנֵ֨י הַכַּפֹּ֜רֶת אֲשֶׁ֤ר עַל־הָֽאָרֹן֙ וְלֹ֣א
יָמ֔וּת כִּ֚י בֶּֽעָנָ֔ן אֵֽרָאֶ֖ה עַל־הַכַּפֹּֽרֶת: בְּזֹ֛את יָבֹ֥א אַֽהֲרֹ֖ן אֶל־הַקֹּ֑דֶשׁ בְּפַ֧ר בֶּן־בָּקָ֛ר
לְחַטָּ֖את וְאַ֥יִל לְעֹלָֽה: כְּתֹֽנֶת־בַּ֣ד קֹ֠דֶשׁ יִלְבָּ֡שׁ וּמִֽכְנְסֵי־בַד֩ יִֽהְי֨וּ עַל־בְּשָׂר֜וֹ וּבְאַבְנֵ֥ט בַּ֣ד
יַחְגֹּ֗ר וּבְמִצְנֶ֤פֶת בַּד֙ יִצְנֹ֔ף בִּגְדֵי־קֹ֣דֶשׁ הֵ֔ם וְרָחַ֥ץ בַּמַּ֛יִם אֶת־בְּשָׂר֖וֹ וּלְבֵשָֽׁם: וּמֵאֵ֗ת עֲדַ֛ת
בְּנֵ֥י יִשְׂרָאֵ֖ל יִקַּ֑ח שְׁנֵֽי־שְׂעִירֵ֥י עִזִּ֛ים לְחַטָּ֖את וְאַ֥יִל אֶחָ֥ד לְעֹלָֽה: וְהִקְרִ֧יב אַֽהֲרֹ֛ן אֶת־פַּ֥ר
הַֽחַטָּ֖את אֲשֶׁר־ל֑וֹ וְכִפֶּ֥ר בַּֽעֲד֖וֹ וּבְעַ֥ד בֵּיתֽוֹ: **Levi** וְלָקַ֖ח אֶת־שְׁנֵ֣י הַשְּׂעִירִ֑ם וְהֶֽעֱמִ֤יד אֹתָם֙
לִפְנֵ֣י יְהֹוָ֔ה פֶּ֖תַח אֹ֥הֶל מוֹעֵֽד: וְנָתַ֧ן אַֽהֲרֹ֛ן עַל־שְׁנֵ֥י הַשְּׂעִירִ֖ם גֹּֽרָל֑וֹת גּוֹרָ֤ל אֶחָד֙
לַֽיהֹוָ֔ה וְגוֹרָ֥ל אֶחָ֖ד לַֽעֲזָאזֵֽל: וְהִקְרִ֤יב אַֽהֲרֹן֙ אֶת־הַשָּׂעִ֔יר אֲשֶׁ֨ר עָלָ֥ה עָלָ֛יו
הַגּוֹרָ֖ל לַֽיהֹוָ֑ה וְעָשָׂ֖הוּ חַטָּֽאת: וְהַשָּׂעִ֗יר אֲשֶׁר֩ עָלָ֨ה עָלָ֤יו הַגּוֹרָל֙ לַֽעֲזָאזֵ֔ל יׇֽעֳמַד־
חַ֛י לִפְנֵ֥י יְהֹוָ֖ה לְכַפֵּ֣ר עָלָ֑יו לְשַׁלַּ֥ח אֹת֛וֹ לַֽעֲזָאזֵ֖ל הַמִּדְבָּֽרָה: וְהִקְרִ֨יב אַֽהֲרֹ֜ן
אֶת־פַּ֤ר הַֽחַטָּאת֙ אֲשֶׁר־ל֔וֹ וְכִפֶּ֥ר בַּֽעֲד֖וֹ וּבְעַ֣ד בֵּית֑וֹ וְשָׁחַ֛ט אֶת־פַּ֥ר הַֽחַטָּ֖את אֲשֶׁר־לֽוֹ:
Yisrael וְלָקַ֣ח מְלֹֽא־הַ֠מַּחְתָּ֠ה גַּֽחֲלֵי־אֵ֞שׁ מֵעַ֤ל הַמִּזְבֵּ֙חַ֙ מִלִּפְנֵ֣י יְהֹוָ֔ה וּמְלֹ֣א חׇפְנָ֔יו
קְטֹ֥רֶת סַמִּ֖ים דַּקָּ֑ה וְהֵבִ֖יא מִבֵּ֥ית לַפָּרֹֽכֶת: וְנָתַ֧ן אֶת־הַקְּטֹ֛רֶת עַל־הָאֵ֖שׁ לִפְנֵ֣י
יְהֹוָ֑ה וְכִסָּ֣ה | עֲנַ֣ן הַקְּטֹ֗רֶת אֶת־הַכַּפֹּ֛רֶת אֲשֶׁ֥ר עַל־הָֽעֵד֖וּת וְלֹ֥א יָמֽוּת: וְלָקַח֙
מִדַּ֣ם הַפָּ֔ר וְהִזָּ֧ה בְאֶצְבָּע֛וֹ עַל־פְּנֵ֥י הַכַּפֹּ֖רֶת קֵ֑דְמָה וְלִפְנֵ֣י הַכַּפֹּ֗רֶת יַזֶּ֧ה שֶֽׁבַע־פְּעָמִ֛ים
מִן־הַדָּ֖ם בְּאֶצְבָּעֽוֹ: וְשָׁחַ֞ט אֶת־שְׂעִ֣יר הַֽחַטָּ֗את אֲשֶׁר֙ לָעָ֔ם וְהֵבִיא֙ אֶת־דָּמ֔וֹ אֶל־מִבֵּ֖ית
לַפָּרֹ֑כֶת וְעָשָׂ֣ה אֶת־דָּמ֗וֹ כַּֽאֲשֶׁ֤ר עָשָׂה֙ לְדַ֣ם הַפָּ֔ר וְהִזָּ֥ה אֹת֛וֹ עַל־הַכַּפֹּ֖רֶת וְלִפְנֵ֥י הַכַּפֹּֽרֶת:

וְכִפֶּר עַל־הַקֹּדֶשׁ מִטֻּמְאֹת בְּנֵי יִשְׂרָאֵל וּמִפִּשְׁעֵיהֶם לְכָל־חַטֹּאתָם וְכֵן יַעֲשֶׂה
לְאֹהֶל מוֹעֵד הַשֹּׁכֵן אִתָּם בְּתוֹךְ טֻמְאֹתָם: וְכָל־אָדָם לֹא־יִהְיֶה | בְּאֹהֶל מוֹעֵד בְּבֹאוֹ
לְכַפֵּר בַּקֹּדֶשׁ עַד־צֵאתוֹ וְכִפֶּר בַּעֲדוֹ וּבְעַד בֵּיתוֹ וּבְעַד כָּל־קְהַל יִשְׂרָאֵל:

KEDOSHIM

וַיְדַבֵּר יְהֹוָה אֶל־מֹשֶׁה לֵּאמֹר: דַּבֵּר אֶל־כָּל־עֲדַת בְּנֵי־יִשְׂרָאֵל
וְאָמַרְתָּ אֲלֵהֶם קְדֹשִׁים תִּהְיוּ כִּי קָדוֹשׁ אֲנִי יְהֹוָה אֱלֹהֵיכֶם: אִישׁ אִמּוֹ
וְאָבִיו תִּירָאוּ וְאֶת־שַׁבְּתֹתַי תִּשְׁמֹרוּ אֲנִי יְהֹוָה אֱלֹהֵיכֶם: אַל־תִּפְנוּ
אֶל־הָאֱלִילִם וֵאלֹהֵי מַסֵּכָה לֹא תַעֲשׂוּ לָכֶם אֲנִי יְהֹוָה אֱלֹהֵיכֶם: *Levi*
וְכִי תִזְבְּחוּ זֶבַח שְׁלָמִים לַיהֹוָה לִרְצֹנְכֶם תִּזְבָּחֻהוּ: בְּיוֹם זִבְחֲכֶם יֵאָכֵל
וּמִמָּחֳרָת וְהַנּוֹתָר עַד־יוֹם הַשְּׁלִישִׁי בָּאֵשׁ יִשָּׂרֵף: וְאִם הֵאָכֹל יֵאָכֵל בַּיּוֹם הַשְּׁלִישִׁי
פִּגּוּל הוּא לֹא יֵרָצֶה: וְאֹכְלָיו עֲוֹנוֹ יִשָּׂא כִּי־אֶת־קֹדֶשׁ יְהֹוָה חִלֵּל וְנִכְרְתָה
הַנֶּפֶשׁ הַהִוא מֵעַמֶּיהָ: וּבְקֻצְרְכֶם אֶת־קְצִיר אַרְצְכֶם לֹא תְכַלֶּה פְּאַת שָׂדְךָ לִקְצֹר
וְלֶקֶט קְצִירְךָ לֹא תְלַקֵּט: וְכַרְמְךָ לֹא תְעוֹלֵל וּפֶרֶט כַּרְמְךָ לֹא תְלַקֵּט לֶעָנִי וְלַגֵּר
תַּעֲזֹב אֹתָם אֲנִי יְהֹוָה אֱלֹהֵיכֶם: *Yisrael* לֹא תִּגְנֹבוּ וְלֹא־תְכַחֲשׁוּ וְלֹא־תְשַׁקְּרוּ
אִישׁ בַּעֲמִיתוֹ: וְלֹא־תִשָּׁבְעוּ בִשְׁמִי לַשָּׁקֶר וְחִלַּלְתָּ אֶת־שֵׁם אֱלֹהֶיךָ אֲנִי יְהֹוָה:
לֹא־תַעֲשֹׁק אֶת־רֵעֲךָ וְלֹא תִגְזֹל לֹא־תָלִין פְּעֻלַּת שָׂכִיר אִתְּךָ עַד־בֹּקֶר:
לֹא־תְקַלֵּל חֵרֵשׁ וְלִפְנֵי עִוֵּר לֹא תִתֵּן מִכְשֹׁל וְיָרֵאתָ מֵּאֱלֹהֶיךָ אֲנִי יְהֹוָה:

EMOR

וַיֹּאמֶר יְהֹוָה אֶל־מֹשֶׁה אֱמֹר אֶל־הַכֹּהֲנִים בְּנֵי אַהֲרֹן וְאָמַרְתָּ אֲלֵהֶם לְנֶפֶשׁ
לֹא־יִטַּמָּא בְּעַמָּיו: כִּי אִם־לִשְׁאֵרוֹ הַקָּרֹב אֵלָיו לְאִמּוֹ וּלְאָבִיו וְלִבְנוֹ וּלְבִתּוֹ וּלְאָחִיו:
וְלַאֲחֹתוֹ הַבְּתוּלָה הַקְּרוֹבָה אֵלָיו אֲשֶׁר לֹא־הָיְתָה לְאִישׁ לָהּ יִטַּמָּא: לֹא יִטַּמָּא
בַּעַל בְּעַמָּיו לְהֵחַלּוֹ: לֹא־יִקְרְחוּ (כתיב יקרחה) קָרְחָה בְּרֹאשָׁם וּפְאַת זְקָנָם לֹא יְגַלֵּחוּ
וּבִבְשָׂרָם לֹא יִשְׂרְטוּ שָׂרָטֶת: קְדֹשִׁים יִהְיוּ לֵאלֹהֵיהֶם וְלֹא יְחַלְּלוּ שֵׁם אֱלֹהֵיהֶם
כִּי אֶת־אִשֵּׁי יְהֹוָה לֶחֶם אֱלֹהֵיהֶם הֵם מַקְרִיבִם וְהָיוּ קֹדֶשׁ: *Levi*
אִשָּׁה זֹנָה וַחֲלָלָה לֹא יִקָּחוּ וְאִשָּׁה גְּרוּשָׁה מֵאִישָׁהּ לֹא יִקָּחוּ כִּי־קָדֹשׁ הוּא לֵאלֹהָיו:
וְקִדַּשְׁתּוֹ כִּי־אֶת־לֶחֶם אֱלֹהֶיךָ הוּא מַקְרִיב קָדֹשׁ יִהְיֶה־לָּךְ כִּי קָדוֹשׁ אֲנִי יְהֹוָה
מְקַדִּשְׁכֶם: וּבַת אִישׁ כֹּהֵן כִּי תֵחֵל לִזְנוֹת אֶת־אָבִיהָ הִיא מְחַלֶּלֶת בָּאֵשׁ תִּשָּׂרֵף:
וְהַכֹּהֵן הַגָּדוֹל מֵאֶחָיו אֲשֶׁר־יוּצַק עַל־רֹאשׁוֹ | שֶׁמֶן הַמִּשְׁחָה וּמִלֵּא אֶת־יָדוֹ
לִלְבֹּשׁ אֶת־הַבְּגָדִים אֶת־רֹאשׁוֹ לֹא יִפְרָע וּבְגָדָיו לֹא יִפְרֹם: וְעַל כָּל־נַפְשֹׁת מֵת
לֹא יָבֹא לְאָבִיו וּלְאִמּוֹ לֹא יִטַּמָּא: וּמִן־הַמִּקְדָּשׁ לֹא יֵצֵא וְלֹא יְחַלֵּל אֵת
מִקְדַּשׁ אֱלֹהָיו כִּי נֵזֶר שֶׁמֶן מִשְׁחַת אֱלֹהָיו עָלָיו אֲנִי יְהֹוָה: *Yisrael*
וְהוּא אִשָּׁה בִבְתוּלֶיהָ יִקָּח: אַלְמָנָה וּגְרוּשָׁה וַחֲלָלָה זֹנָה אֶת־אֵלֶּה לֹא יִקָּח כִּי
אִם־בְּתוּלָה מֵעַמָּיו יִקָּח אִשָּׁה: וְלֹא־יְחַלֵּל זַרְעוֹ בְּעַמָּיו כִּי אֲנִי יְהֹוָה מְקַדְּשׁוֹ:

BEHAR

וַיְדַבֵּ֧ר יְהֹוָ֛הاהدוני אֶל־מֹשֶׁ֖ה בְּהַ֣ר סִינַ֣י לֵאמֹֽר: דַּבֵּ֞ר אֶל־בְּנֵ֤י יִשְׂרָאֵל֙ וְאָמַרְתָּ֣ אֲלֵהֶ֔ם כִּ֤י תָבֹ֙אוּ֙ אֶל־הָאָ֔רֶץ אֲשֶׁ֥ר אֲנִ֖י נֹתֵ֣ן לָכֶ֑ם וְשָׁבְתָ֣ה הָאָ֔רֶץ שַׁבָּ֖ת לַֽיהֹוָֽהاהدوני: Levi שֵׁ֤שׁ שָׁנִים֙ תִּזְרַ֣ע שָׂדֶ֔ךָ וְשֵׁ֥שׁ שָׁנִ֖ים תִּזְמֹ֣ר כַּרְמֶ֑ךָ וְאָסַפְתָּ֖ אֶת־תְּבוּאָתָֽהּ: וּבַשָּׁנָ֣ה הַשְּׁבִיעִ֗ת שַׁבַּ֤ת שַׁבָּתוֹן֙ יִהְיֶ֣ה לָאָ֔רֶץ שַׁבָּ֖ת לַיהֹוָ֑הاהدوني שָֽׂדְךָ֙ לֹ֣א תִזְרָ֔ע וְכַרְמְךָ֖ לֹ֥א תִזְמֹֽר: אֵ֣ת סְפִ֤יחַ קְצִֽירְךָ֙ לֹ֣א תִקְצ֔וֹר וְאֶת־עִנְּבֵ֥י נְזִירֶ֖ךָ לֹ֣א תִבְצֹ֑ר שְׁנַ֥ת שַׁבָּת֖וֹן יִהְיֶ֥ה לָאָֽרֶץ: וְֽ֠הָיְתָ֠ה שַׁבַּ֨ת הָאָ֤רֶץ לָכֶם֙ לְאָכְלָ֔ה לְךָ֖ וּלְעַבְדְּךָ֣ וְלַאֲמָתֶ֑ךָ וְלִשְׂכִֽירְךָ֙ וּלְתוֹשָׁ֣בְךָ֔ הַגָּרִ֖ים עִמָּֽךְ: וְלִ֨בְהֶמְתְּךָ֔ וְלַֽחַיָּ֖ה אֲשֶׁ֣ר בְּאַרְצֶ֑ךָ תִּהְיֶ֥ה כָל־תְּבוּאָתָ֖הּ לֶאֱכֹֽל: Yisrael וְסָפַרְתָּ֣ לְךָ֗ שֶׁ֚בַע שַׁבְּתֹ֣ת שָׁנִ֔ים שֶׁ֥בַע שָׁנִ֖ים שֶׁ֣בַע פְּעָמִ֑ים וְהָי֣וּ לְךָ֗ יְמֵי֙ שֶׁ֚בַע שַׁבְּתֹ֣ת הַשָּׁנִ֔ים תֵּ֥שַׁע וְאַרְבָּעִ֖ים שָׁנָֽה: וְהַֽעֲבַרְתָּ֞ שׁוֹפַ֤ר תְּרוּעָה֙ בַּחֹ֣דֶשׁ הַשְּׁבִעִ֔י בֶּעָשׂ֖וֹר לַחֹ֑דֶשׁ בְּיוֹם֙ הַכִּפֻּרִ֔ים תַּעֲבִ֥ירוּ שׁוֹפָ֖ר בְּכָל־אַרְצְכֶֽם: וְקִדַּשְׁתֶּ֗ם אֵ֣ת שְׁנַ֤ת הַחֲמִשִּׁים֙ שָׁנָ֔ה וּקְרָאתֶ֥ם דְּר֛וֹר בָּאָ֖רֶץ לְכָל־יֹשְׁבֶ֑יהָ יוֹבֵ֥ל הִוא֙ תִּהְיֶ֣ה לָכֶ֔ם וְשַׁבְתֶּ֗ם אִ֚ישׁ אֶל־אֲחֻזָּת֔וֹ וְאִ֥ישׁ אֶל־מִשְׁפַּחְתּ֖וֹ תָּשֻֽׁבוּ: יוֹבֵ֣ל הִ֗וא שְׁנַ֛ת הַחֲמִשִּׁ֥ים שָׁנָ֖ה תִּהְיֶ֣ה לָכֶ֑ם לֹ֣א תִזְרָ֗עוּ וְלֹ֤א תִקְצְרוּ֙ אֶת־סְפִיחֶ֔יהָ וְלֹ֥א תִבְצְר֖וּ אֶת־נְזִרֶֽיהָ: כִּ֚י יוֹבֵ֣ל הִ֔וא קֹ֖דֶשׁ תִּהְיֶ֣ה לָכֶ֑ם מִ֨ן־הַשָּׂדֶ֔ה תֹּאכְל֖וּ אֶת־תְּבוּאָתָֽהּ: בִּשְׁנַ֥ת הַיּוֹבֵ֖ל הַזֹּ֑את תָּשֻׁ֕בוּ אִ֖ישׁ אֶל־אֲחֻזָּתֽוֹ:

BECHUKOTAI

אִם־בְּחֻקֹּתַ֖י תֵּלֵ֑כוּ וְאֶת־מִצְוֺתַ֣י תִּשְׁמְר֔וּ וַעֲשִׂיתֶ֖ם אֹתָֽם: וְנָתַתִּ֥י גִשְׁמֵיכֶ֖ם בְּעִתָּ֑ם וְנָתְנָ֤ה הָאָ֙רֶץ֙ יְבוּלָ֔הּ וְעֵ֥ץ הַשָּׂדֶ֖ה יִתֵּ֥ן פִּרְיֽוֹ: וְהִשִּׂ֨יג לָכֶ֥ם דַּ֙יִשׁ֙ אֶת־בָּצִ֔יר וּבָצִ֖יר יַשִּׂ֣יג אֶת־זָ֑רַע וַאֲכַלְתֶּ֤ם לַחְמְכֶם֙ לָשֹׂ֔בַע וִֽישַׁבְתֶּ֥ם לָבֶ֖טַח בְּאַרְצְכֶֽם: Levi וְנָתַתִּ֤י שָׁלוֹם֙ בָּאָ֔רֶץ וּשְׁכַבְתֶּ֖ם וְאֵ֣ין מַחֲרִ֑יד וְהִשְׁבַּתִּ֞י חַיָּ֤ה רָעָה֙ מִן־הָאָ֔רֶץ וְחֶ֖רֶב לֹא־תַעֲבֹ֥ר בְּאַרְצְכֶֽם: וּרְדַפְתֶּ֖ם אֶת־אֹיְבֵיכֶ֑ם וְנָפְל֥וּ לִפְנֵיכֶ֖ם לֶחָֽרֶב: וְרָדְפ֨וּ מִכֶּ֤ם חֲמִשָּׁה֙ מֵאָ֔ה וּמֵאָ֥ה מִכֶּ֖ם רְבָבָ֣ה יִרְדֹּ֑פוּ וְנָפְל֧וּ אֹיְבֵיכֶ֛ם לִפְנֵיכֶ֖ם לֶחָֽרֶב: וּפָנִ֣יתִי אֲלֵיכֶ֗ם וְהִפְרֵיתִ֤י אֶתְכֶם֙ וְהִרְבֵּיתִ֣י אֶתְכֶ֔ם וַהֲקִימֹתִ֥י אֶת־בְּרִיתִ֖י אִתְּכֶֽם: Yisrael וַאֲכַלְתֶּ֥ם יָשָׁ֖ן נוֹשָׁ֑ן וְיָשָׁ֕ן מִפְּנֵ֥י חָדָ֖שׁ תּוֹצִֽיאוּ: וְנָתַתִּ֥י מִשְׁכָּנִ֖י בְּתוֹכְכֶ֑ם וְלֹֽא־תִגְעַ֥ל נַפְשִׁ֖י אֶתְכֶֽם: וְהִתְהַלַּכְתִּי֙ בְּתֽוֹכְכֶ֔ם וְהָיִ֥יתִי לָכֶ֖ם לֵֽאלֹהִ֑ים וְאַתֶּ֖ם תִּהְיוּ־לִ֥י לְעָֽם: אֲנִ֞י יְהֹוָ֣הاהדוני אֱלֹֽהֵיכֶ֗ם אֲשֶׁ֨ר הוֹצֵ֤אתִי אֶתְכֶם֙ מֵאֶ֣רֶץ מִצְרַ֔יִם מִֽהְיֹ֥ת לָהֶ֖ם עֲבָדִ֑ים וָאֶשְׁבֹּר֙ מֹטֹ֣ת עֻלְּכֶ֔ם וָאוֹלֵ֥ךְ אֶתְכֶ֖ם קֽוֹמְמִיּֽוּת:

BEMIDBAR

וַיְדַבֵּ֨ר יְהֹוָ֧הاهدוני אֶל־מֹשֶׁ֛ה בְּמִדְבַּ֥ר סִינַ֖י בְּאֹ֣הֶל מוֹעֵ֑ד בְּאֶחָד֩ לַחֹ֨דֶשׁ הַשֵּׁנִ֜י בַּשָּׁנָ֣ה הַשֵּׁנִ֗ית לְצֵאתָ֛ם מֵאֶ֥רֶץ מִצְרַ֖יִם לֵאמֹֽר: שְׂא֗וּ אֶת־רֹאשׁ֙ כָּל־עֲדַ֣ת בְּנֵֽי־יִשְׂרָאֵ֔ל לְמִשְׁפְּחֹתָ֖ם לְבֵ֣ית אֲבֹתָ֑ם בְּמִסְפַּ֣ר שֵׁמ֔וֹת כָּל־זָכָ֖ר לְגֻלְגְּלֹתָֽם: מִבֶּ֨ן עֶשְׂרִ֤ים שָׁנָה֙ וָמַ֔עְלָה כָּל־יֹצֵ֥א צָבָ֖א בְּיִשְׂרָאֵ֑ל תִּפְקְד֥וּ אֹתָ֛ם לְצִבְאֹתָ֖ם אַתָּ֥ה וְאַהֲרֹֽן: וְאִתְּכֶ֣ם יִהְי֗וּ אִ֣ישׁ אִ֣ישׁ לַמַּטֶּ֔ה אִ֛ישׁ רֹ֥אשׁ לְבֵית־אֲבֹתָ֖יו הֽוּא: Levi

וְאֵלֶּה שְׁמוֹת הָאֲנָשִׁים אֲשֶׁר יַעַמְדוּ אִתְּכֶם לִרְאוּבֵן אֱלִיצוּר בֶּן־שְׁדֵיאוּר:
לְשִׁמְעוֹן שְׁלֻמִיאֵל בֶּן־צוּרִישַׁדָּי: לִיהוּדָה נַחְשׁוֹן בֶּן־עַמִּינָדָב: לְיִשָּׂשכָר נְתַנְאֵל
בֶּן־צוּעָר: לִזְבוּלֻן אֱלִיאָב בֶּן־חֵלֹן: לִבְנֵי יוֹסֵף לְאֶפְרַיִם אֱלִישָׁמָע בֶּן־עַמִּיהוּד
לִמְנַשֶּׁה גַּמְלִיאֵל בֶּן־פְּדָהצוּר: לְבִנְיָמִן אֲבִידָן בֶּן־גִּדְעֹנִי: לְדָן אֲחִיעֶזֶר בֶּן־עַמִּישַׁדָּי:
לְאָשֵׁר פַּגְעִיאֵל בֶּן־עָכְרָן: לְגָד אֶלְיָסָף בֶּן־דְּעוּאֵל: לְנַפְתָּלִי אֲחִירַע בֶּן־עֵינָן:
אֵלֶּה קְרוּאֵי (כתיב קריאי) הָעֵדָה נְשִׂיאֵי מַטּוֹת אֲבוֹתָם רָאשֵׁי אַלְפֵי יִשְׂרָאֵל הֵם: *Yisrael*
וַיִּקַּח מֹשֶׁה וְאַהֲרֹן אֵת הָאֲנָשִׁים הָאֵלֶּה אֲשֶׁר נִקְּבוּ בְּשֵׁמוֹת: וְאֵת כָּל־הָעֵדָה הִקְהִילוּ
בְּאֶחָד לַחֹדֶשׁ הַשֵּׁנִי וַיִּתְיַלְדוּ עַל־מִשְׁפְּחֹתָם לְבֵית אֲבֹתָם בְּמִסְפַּר שֵׁמוֹת מִבֶּן עֶשְׂרִים
שָׁנָה וָמַעְלָה לְגֻלְגְּלֹתָם: כַּאֲשֶׁר צִוָּה יְהֹוָאדֹנָי אֶת־מֹשֶׁה וַיִּפְקְדֵם בְּמִדְבַּר סִינָי:

NASO

וַיְדַבֵּר יְהֹוָאדֹנָי אֶל־מֹשֶׁה לֵּאמֹר: נָשֹׂא אֶת־רֹאשׁ בְּנֵי גֵרְשׁוֹן גַּם־הֵם
לְבֵית אֲבֹתָם לְמִשְׁפְּחֹתָם: מִבֶּן שְׁלֹשִׁים שָׁנָה וָמַעְלָה עַד בֶּן־חֲמִשִּׁים שָׁנָה תִּפְקֹד
אוֹתָם כָּל־הַבָּא לִצְבֹא צָבָא לַעֲבֹד עֲבֹדָה בְּאֹהֶל מוֹעֵד: זֹאת עֲבֹדַת מִשְׁפְּחֹת הַגֵּרְשֻׁנִּי
לַעֲבֹד וּלְמַשָּׂא: וְנָשְׂאוּ אֶת־יְרִיעֹת הַמִּשְׁכָּן וְאֶת־אֹהֶל מוֹעֵד מִכְסֵהוּ וּמִכְסֵה *Levi*
הַתַּחַשׁ אֲשֶׁר־עָלָיו מִלְמָעְלָה וְאֶת־מָסַךְ פֶּתַח אֹהֶל מוֹעֵד: וְאֵת קַלְעֵי הֶחָצֵר וְאֶת־מָסַךְ |
פֶּתַח | שַׁעַר הֶחָצֵר אֲשֶׁר עַל־הַמִּשְׁכָּן וְעַל־הַמִּזְבֵּחַ סָבִיב וְאֵת מֵיתְרֵיהֶם וְאֶת־כָּל־כְּלֵי
עֲבֹדָתָם וְאֵת כָּל־אֲשֶׁר יֵעָשֶׂה לָהֶם וְעָבָדוּ: עַל־פִּי אַהֲרֹן וּבָנָיו
תִּהְיֶה כָּל־עֲבֹדַת בְּנֵי הַגֵּרְשֻׁנִּי לְכָל־מַשָּׂאָם וּלְכֹל עֲבֹדָתָם וּפְקַדְתֶּם עֲלֵהֶם בְּמִשְׁמֶרֶת
אֵת כָּל־מַשָּׂאָם: זֹאת עֲבֹדַת מִשְׁפְּחֹת בְּנֵי הַגֵּרְשֻׁנִּי בְּאֹהֶל מוֹעֵד וּמִשְׁמַרְתָּם
בְּיַד אִיתָמָר בֶּן־אַהֲרֹן הַכֹּהֵן: *Yisrael* בְּנֵי מְרָרִי לְמִשְׁפְּחֹתָם לְבֵית־אֲבֹתָם תִּפְקֹד אֹתָם:
מִבֶּן שְׁלֹשִׁים שָׁנָה וָמַעְלָה וְעַד בֶּן־חֲמִשִּׁים שָׁנָה תִּפְקְדֵם כָּל־הַבָּא לַצָּבָא לַעֲבֹד
אֶת־עֲבֹדַת אֹהֶל מוֹעֵד: וְזֹאת מִשְׁמֶרֶת מַשָּׂאָם לְכָל־עֲבֹדָתָם בְּאֹהֶל מוֹעֵד קַרְשֵׁי
הַמִּשְׁכָּן וּבְרִיחָיו וְעַמּוּדָיו וַאֲדָנָיו: וְעַמּוּדֵי הֶחָצֵר סָבִיב וְאַדְנֵיהֶם וִיתֵדֹתָם וּמֵיתְרֵיהֶם
לְכָל־כְּלֵיהֶם וּלְכֹל עֲבֹדָתָם וּבְשֵׁמֹת תִּפְקְדוּ אֶת־כְּלֵי מִשְׁמֶרֶת מַשָּׂאָם: זֹאת עֲבֹדַת
מִשְׁפְּחֹת בְּנֵי מְרָרִי לְכָל־עֲבֹדָתָם בְּאֹהֶל מוֹעֵד בְּיַד אִיתָמָר בֶּן־אַהֲרֹן הַכֹּהֵן: וַיִּפְקֹד
מֹשֶׁה וְאַהֲרֹן וּנְשִׂיאֵי הָעֵדָה אֶת־בְּנֵי הַקְּהָתִי לְמִשְׁפְּחֹתָם וּלְבֵית אֲבֹתָם: מִבֶּן שְׁלֹשִׁים
שָׁנָה וָמַעְלָה וְעַד בֶּן־חֲמִשִּׁים שָׁנָה כָּל־הַבָּא לַצָּבָא לַעֲבֹדָה בְּאֹהֶל מוֹעֵד: וַיִּהְיוּ
פְקֻדֵיהֶם לְמִשְׁפְּחֹתָם אַלְפַּיִם שְׁבַע מֵאוֹת וַחֲמִשִּׁים: אֵלֶּה פְקוּדֵי מִשְׁפְּחֹת הַקְּהָתִי
כָּל־הָעֹבֵד בְּאֹהֶל מוֹעֵד אֲשֶׁר פָּקַד מֹשֶׁה וְאַהֲרֹן עַל־פִּי יְהֹוָאדֹנָי בְּיַד־מֹשֶׁה:

BEHA'ALOTCHA

וַיְדַבֵּר יְהֹוָאדֹנָי אֶל־מֹשֶׁה לֵּאמֹר: דַּבֵּר אֶל־אַהֲרֹן וְאָמַרְתָּ אֵלָיו
בְּהַעֲלֹתְךָ אֶת־הַנֵּרֹת אֶל־מוּל פְּנֵי הַמְּנוֹרָה יָאִירוּ שִׁבְעַת הַנֵּרוֹת: וַיַּעַשׂ כֵּן אַהֲרֹן
אֶל־מוּל פְּנֵי הַמְּנוֹרָה הֶעֱלָה נֵרֹתֶיהָ כַּאֲשֶׁר צִוָּה יְהֹוָאדֹנָי אֶת־מֹשֶׁה:
וְזֶה מַעֲשֵׂה הַמְּנֹרָה מִקְשָׁה זָהָב עַד־יְרֵכָהּ עַד־פִּרְחָהּ מִקְשָׁה הִוא כַּמַּרְאֶה
אֲשֶׁר הֶרְאָה יְהֹוָאדֹנָי אֶת־מֹשֶׁה כֵּן עָשָׂה אֶת־הַמְּנֹרָה: *Levi*

וַיְדַבֵּר יְהֹוָהָּאֲדֹנָי אֶל־מֹשֶׁה לֵּאמֹר: קַח אֶת־הַלְוִיִּם מִתּוֹךְ בְּנֵי יִשְׂרָאֵל
וְטִהַרְתָּ אֹתָם: וְכֹה־תַעֲשֶׂה לָהֶם לְטַהֲרָם הַזֵּה עֲלֵיהֶם מֵי חַטָּאת וְהֶעֱבִירוּ תַעַר
עַל־כָּל־בְּשָׂרָם וְכִבְּסוּ בִגְדֵיהֶם וְהִטֶּהָרוּ: וְלָקְחוּ פַּר בֶּן־בָּקָר וּמִנְחָתוֹ סֹלֶת בְּלוּלָה
בַשָּׁמֶן וּפַר־שֵׁנִי בֶן־בָּקָר תִּקַּח לְחַטָּאת: וְהִקְרַבְתָּ אֶת־הַלְוִיִּם לִפְנֵי אֹהֶל מוֹעֵד וְהִקְהַלְתָּ
אֶת־כָּל־עֲדַת בְּנֵי יִשְׂרָאֵל: Yisrael וְהִקְרַבְתָּ אֶת־הַלְוִיִּם לִפְנֵי יְהֹוָהָּאֲדֹנָי וְסָמְכוּ
בְנֵי־יִשְׂרָאֵל אֶת־יְדֵיהֶם עַל־הַלְוִיִּם: וְהֵנִיף אַהֲרֹן אֶת־הַלְוִיִּם תְּנוּפָה לִפְנֵי יְהֹוָהָּאֲדֹנָי
מֵאֵת בְּנֵי יִשְׂרָאֵל וְהָיוּ לַעֲבֹד אֶת־עֲבֹדַת יְהֹוָהָּאֲדֹנָי: וְהַלְוִיִּם יִסְמְכוּ אֶת־יְדֵיהֶם
עַל רֹאשׁ הַפָּרִים וַעֲשֵׂה אֶת־הָאֶחָד חַטָּאת וְאֶת־הָאֶחָד עֹלָה לַיהֹוָהָּאֲדֹנָי
לְכַפֵּר עַל־הַלְוִיִּם: וְהַעֲמַדְתָּ אֶת־הַלְוִיִּם לִפְנֵי אַהֲרֹן וְלִפְנֵי בָנָיו וְהֵנַפְתָּ אֹתָם
תְּנוּפָה לַיהֹוָהָּאֲדֹנָי: וְהִבְדַּלְתָּ אֶת־הַלְוִיִּם מִתּוֹךְ בְּנֵי יִשְׂרָאֵל וְהָיוּ לִי הַלְוִיִּם:

SHELACH LECHA

וַיְדַבֵּר יְהֹוָהָּאֲדֹנָי אֶל־מֹשֶׁה לֵּאמֹר: שְׁלַח־לְךָ אֲנָשִׁים וְיָתֻרוּ אֶת־אֶרֶץ כְּנַעַן אֲשֶׁר־
אֲנִי נֹתֵן לִבְנֵי יִשְׂרָאֵל אִישׁ אֶחָד אִישׁ אֶחָד לְמַטֵּה אֲבֹתָיו תִּשְׁלָחוּ כֹּל נָשִׂיא בָהֶם:
וַיִּשְׁלַח אֹתָם מֹשֶׁה מִמִּדְבַּר פָּארָן עַל־פִּי יְהֹוָהָּאֲדֹנָי כֻּלָּם אֲנָשִׁים רָאשֵׁי בְנֵי־
יִשְׂרָאֵל הֵמָּה: Levi וְאֵלֶּה שְׁמוֹתָם לְמַטֵּה רְאוּבֵן שַׁמּוּעַ בֶּן־זַכּוּר: לְמַטֵּה שִׁמְעוֹן שָׁפָט
בֶּן־חוֹרִי: לְמַטֵּה יְהוּדָה כָּלֵב בֶּן־יְפֻנֶּה: לְמַטֵּה יִשָּׂשׂכָר יִגְאָל בֶּן־יוֹסֵף: לְמַטֵּה אֶפְרַיִם
הוֹשֵׁעַ בִּן־נוּן: לְמַטֵּה בִנְיָמִן פַּלְטִי בֶּן־רָפוּא: לְמַטֵּה זְבוּלֻן גַּדִּיאֵל בֶּן־סוֹדִי: לְמַטֵּה יוֹסֵף
לְמַטֵּה מְנַשֶּׁה גַּדִּי בֶּן־סוּסִי: לְמַטֵּה דָן עַמִּיאֵל בֶּן־גְּמַלִּי: לְמַטֵּה אָשֵׁר סְתוּר בֶּן־מִיכָאֵל:
לְמַטֵּה נַפְתָּלִי נַחְבִּי בֶּן־וָפְסִי: לְמַטֵּה גָד גְּאוּאֵל בֶּן־מָכִי: אֵלֶּה שְׁמוֹת הָאֲנָשִׁים
אֲשֶׁר־שָׁלַח מֹשֶׁה לָתוּר אֶת־הָאָרֶץ וַיִּקְרָא מֹשֶׁה לְהוֹשֵׁעַ בִּן־נוּן יְהוֹשֻׁעַ: Yisrael וַיִּשְׁלַח
אֹתָם מֹשֶׁה לָתוּר אֶת־אֶרֶץ כְּנָעַן וַיֹּאמֶר אֲלֵהֶם עֲלוּ זֶה בַּנֶּגֶב וַעֲלִיתֶם אֶת־הָהָר:
וּרְאִיתֶם אֶת־הָאָרֶץ מַה־הִוא וְאֶת־הָעָם הַיֹּשֵׁב עָלֶיהָ הֶחָזָק הוּא הֲרָפֶה הַמְעַט הוּא
אִם־רָב: וּמָה הָאָרֶץ אֲשֶׁר־הוּא יֹשֵׁב בָּהּ הֲטוֹבָה הִוא אִם־רָעָה וּמָה הֶעָרִים
אֲשֶׁר־הוּא יוֹשֵׁב בָּהֵנָּה הַבְּמַחֲנִים אִם בְּמִבְצָרִים: וּמָה הָאָרֶץ הַשְּׁמֵנָה הִוא אִם־רָזָה
הֲיֵשׁ־בָּהּ עֵץ אִם־אַיִן וְהִתְחַזַּקְתֶּם וּלְקַחְתֶּם מִפְּרִי הָאָרֶץ וְהַיָּמִים יְמֵי בִּכּוּרֵי עֲנָבִים:

KORACH

וַיִּקַּח קֹרַח בֶּן־יִצְהָר בֶּן־קְהָת בֶּן־לֵוִי וְדָתָן וַאֲבִירָם בְּנֵי אֱלִיאָב וְאוֹן בֶּן־פֶּלֶת בְּנֵי
רְאוּבֵן: וַיָּקֻמוּ לִפְנֵי מֹשֶׁה וַאֲנָשִׁים מִבְּנֵי־יִשְׂרָאֵל חֲמִשִּׁים וּמָאתָיִם נְשִׂיאֵי עֵדָה קְרִאֵי
מוֹעֵד אַנְשֵׁי־שֵׁם: וַיִּקָּהֲלוּ עַל־מֹשֶׁה וְעַל־אַהֲרֹן וַיֹּאמְרוּ אֲלֵהֶם רַב־לָכֶם כִּי כָל־הָעֵדָה
כֻּלָּם קְדֹשִׁים וּבְתוֹכָם יְהֹוָהָּאֲדֹנָי וּמַדּוּעַ תִּתְנַשְּׂאוּ עַל־קְהַל יְהֹוָהָּאֲדֹנָי: Levi
וַיִּשְׁמַע מֹשֶׁה וַיִּפֹּל עַל־פָּנָיו: וַיְדַבֵּר אֶל־קֹרַח וְאֶל־כָּל־עֲדָתוֹ לֵאמֹר בֹּקֶר
וְיֹדַע יְהֹוָהָּאֲדֹנָי אֶת־אֲשֶׁר־לוֹ וְאֶת־הַקָּדוֹשׁ וְהִקְרִיב אֵלָיו וְאֵת אֲשֶׁר
יִבְחַר־בּוֹ יַקְרִיב אֵלָיו: זֹאת עֲשׂוּ קְחוּ־לָכֶם מַחְתּוֹת קֹרַח וְכָל־עֲדָתוֹ: וּתְנוּ בָהֵן |
אֵשׁ וְשִׂימוּ עֲלֵיהֶן | קְטֹרֶת לִפְנֵי יְהֹוָהָּאֲדֹנָי מָחָר וְהָיָה הָאִישׁ
אֲשֶׁר־יִבְחַר יְהֹוָהָּאֲדֹנָי הוּא הַקָּדוֹשׁ רַב־לָכֶם בְּנֵי לֵוִי: Yisrael

וַיֹּאמֶר מֹשֶׁה אֶל־קֹרַח שִׁמְעוּ־נָא בְּנֵי לֵוִי: הַמְעַט מִכֶּם כִּי־הִבְדִּיל אֱלֹהֵי יִשְׂרָאֵל אֶתְכֶם
מֵעֲדַת יִשְׂרָאֵל לְהַקְרִיב אֶתְכֶם אֵלָיו לַעֲבֹד אֶת־עֲבֹדַת מִשְׁכַּן יְהֹוָהֲדֹנָי וְלַעֲמֹד
לִפְנֵי הָעֵדָה לְשָׁרְתָם: וַיַּקְרֵב אֹתְךָ וְאֶת־כָּל־אַחֶיךָ בְנֵי־לֵוִי אִתָּךְ וּבִקַּשְׁתֶּם גַּם־כְּהֻנָּה:
לָכֵן אַתָּה וְכָל־עֲדָתְךָ הַנֹּעָדִים עַל־יְהֹוָהֲדֹנָי וְאַהֲרֹן מַה־הוּא כִּי תַלִּינוּ (כתיב: תלונו)
עָלָיו: וַיִּשְׁלַח מֹשֶׁה לִקְרֹא לְדָתָן וְלַאֲבִירָם בְּנֵי אֱלִיאָב וַיֹּאמְרוּ לֹא נַעֲלֶה: הַמְעַט כִּי
הֶעֱלִיתָנוּ מֵאֶרֶץ זָבַת חָלָב וּדְבַשׁ לַהֲמִיתֵנוּ בַּמִּדְבָּר כִּי־תִשְׂתָּרֵר עָלֵינוּ גַּם־הִשְׂתָּרֵר:

CHUKAT

וַיְדַבֵּר יְהֹוָהֲדֹנָי אֶל־מֹשֶׁה וְאֶל־אַהֲרֹן לֵאמֹר: זֹאת חֻקַּת הַתּוֹרָה אֲשֶׁר־צִוָּה
יְהֹוָהֲדֹנָי לֵאמֹר | דַּבֵּר אֶל־בְּנֵי יִשְׂרָאֵל וְיִקְחוּ אֵלֶיךָ פָרָה אֲדֻמָּה תְּמִימָה אֲשֶׁר
אֵין־בָּהּ מוּם אֲשֶׁר לֹא־עָלָה עָלֶיהָ עֹל: וּנְתַתֶּם אֹתָהּ אֶל־אֶלְעָזָר הַכֹּהֵן וְהוֹצִיא אֹתָהּ
אֶל־מִחוּץ לַמַּחֲנֶה וְשָׁחַט אֹתָהּ לְפָנָיו: וְלָקַח אֶלְעָזָר הַכֹּהֵן מִדָּמָהּ בְּאֶצְבָּעוֹ וְהִזָּה
אֶל־נֹכַח פְּנֵי אֹהֶל־מוֹעֵד מִדָּמָהּ שֶׁבַע פְּעָמִים: וְשָׂרַף אֶת־הַפָּרָה לְעֵינָיו אֶת־עֹרָהּ
וְאֶת־בְּשָׂרָהּ וְאֶת־דָּמָהּ עַל־פִּרְשָׁהּ יִשְׂרֹף: וְלָקַח הַכֹּהֵן עֵץ אֶרֶז וְאֵזוֹב וּשְׁנִי תוֹלָעַת
וְהִשְׁלִיךְ אֶל־תּוֹךְ שְׂרֵפַת הַפָּרָה: Levi וְכִבֶּס בְּגָדָיו הַכֹּהֵן וְרָחַץ בְּשָׂרוֹ בַּמַּיִם וְאַחַר יָבֹא
אֶל־הַמַּחֲנֶה וְטָמֵא הַכֹּהֵן עַד־הָעָרֶב: וְהַשֹּׂרֵף אֹתָהּ יְכַבֵּס בְּגָדָיו בַּמַּיִם וְרָחַץ בְּשָׂרוֹ
בַּמַּיִם וְטָמֵא עַד־הָעָרֶב: וְאָסַף | אִישׁ טָהוֹר אֵת אֵפֶר הַפָּרָה וְהִנִּיחַ מִחוּץ לַמַּחֲנֶה
בְּמָקוֹם טָהוֹר וְהָיְתָה לַעֲדַת בְּנֵי־יִשְׂרָאֵל לְמִשְׁמֶרֶת לְמֵי נִדָּה חַטָּאת הִוא: Yisrael
וְכִבֶּס הָאֹסֵף אֶת־אֵפֶר הַפָּרָה אֶת־בְּגָדָיו וְטָמֵא עַד־הָעָרֶב וְהָיְתָה לִבְנֵי יִשְׂרָאֵל וְלַגֵּר
הַגָּר בְּתוֹכָם לְחֻקַּת עוֹלָם: הַנֹּגֵעַ בְּמֵת לְכָל־נֶפֶשׁ אָדָם וְטָמֵא שִׁבְעַת יָמִים: הוּא
יִתְחַטָּא־בוֹ בַּיּוֹם הַשְּׁלִישִׁי וּבַיּוֹם הַשְּׁבִיעִי יִטְהָר וְאִם־לֹא יִתְחַטָּא בַּיּוֹם הַשְּׁלִישִׁי וּבַיּוֹם
הַשְּׁבִיעִי לֹא יִטְהָר: כָּל־הַנֹּגֵעַ בְּמֵת בְּנֶפֶשׁ הָאָדָם אֲשֶׁר־יָמוּת וְלֹא יִתְחַטָּא אֶת־מִשְׁכַּן
יְהֹוָהֲדֹנָי טִמֵּא וְנִכְרְתָה הַנֶּפֶשׁ הַהִוא מִיִּשְׂרָאֵל כִּי מֵי נִדָּה לֹא־זֹרַק עָלָיו טָמֵא
יִהְיֶה עוֹד טֻמְאָתוֹ בוֹ: זֹאת הַתּוֹרָה אָדָם כִּי־יָמוּת בְּאֹהֶל כָּל־הַבָּא אֶל־הָאֹהֶל וְכָל־
אֲשֶׁר בָּאֹהֶל יִטְמָא שִׁבְעַת יָמִים: וְכֹל כְּלִי פָתוּחַ אֲשֶׁר אֵין־צָמִיד פָּתִיל עָלָיו טָמֵא הוּא:
וְכֹל אֲשֶׁר־יִגַּע עַל־פְּנֵי הַשָּׂדֶה בַּחֲלַל־חֶרֶב אוֹ בְמֵת אוֹ־בְעֶצֶם אָדָם אוֹ בְקָבֶר יִטְמָא
שִׁבְעַת יָמִים: וְלָקְחוּ לַטָּמֵא מֵעֲפַר שְׂרֵפַת הַחַטָּאת וְנָתַן עָלָיו מַיִם חַיִּים אֶל־כֶּלִי:

BALAK

וַיַּרְא בָּלָק בֶּן־צִפּוֹר אֵת כָּל־אֲשֶׁר־עָשָׂה יִשְׂרָאֵל לָאֱמֹרִי: וַיָּגָר מוֹאָב מִפְּנֵי הָעָם מְאֹד
כִּי רַב־הוּא וַיָּקָץ מוֹאָב מִפְּנֵי בְּנֵי יִשְׂרָאֵל: וַיֹּאמֶר מוֹאָב אֶל־זִקְנֵי מִדְיָן עַתָּה יְלַחֲכוּ
הַקָּהָל אֶת־כָּל־סְבִיבֹתֵינוּ כִּלְחֹךְ הַשּׁוֹר אֵת יֶרֶק הַשָּׂדֶה וּבָלָק בֶּן־צִפּוֹר מֶלֶךְ לְמוֹאָב
בָּעֵת הַהִוא: Levi וַיִּשְׁלַח מַלְאָכִים אֶל־בִּלְעָם בֶּן־בְּעֹר פְּתוֹרָה אֲשֶׁר עַל־הַנָּהָר אֶרֶץ
בְּנֵי־עַמּוֹ לִקְרֹא־לוֹ לֵאמֹר הִנֵּה עַם יָצָא מִמִּצְרַיִם הִנֵּה כִסָּה אֶת־עֵין הָאָרֶץ וְהוּא יֹשֵׁב
מִמֻּלִי: וְעַתָּה לְכָה־נָּא אָרָה־לִּי אֶת־הָעָם הַזֶּה כִּי־עָצוּם הוּא מִמֶּנִּי אוּלַי אוּכַל נַכֶּה־בּוֹ
וַאֲגָרְשֶׁנּוּ מִן־הָאָרֶץ כִּי יָדַעְתִּי אֵת אֲשֶׁר־תְּבָרֵךְ מְבֹרָךְ וַאֲשֶׁר תָּאֹר יוּאָר: וַיֵּלְכוּ זִקְנֵי
מוֹאָב וְזִקְנֵי מִדְיָן וּקְסָמִים בְּיָדָם וַיָּבֹאוּ אֶל־בִּלְעָם וַיְדַבְּרוּ אֵלָיו דִּבְרֵי בָלָק: Yisrael

וַיֹּ֣אמֶר אֲלֵיהֶ֗ם לִ֤ינוּ פֹה֙ הַלַּ֔יְלָה וַהֲשִׁבֹתִ֤י אֶתְכֶם֙ דָּבָ֔ר כַּאֲשֶׁ֛ר יְדַבֵּ֥ר
יְהֹוָ֖ה אֵלָ֑י וַיֵּשְׁב֥וּ שָׂרֵֽי־מוֹאָ֖ב עִם־בִּלְעָֽם: וַיָּבֹ֤א אֱלֹהִים֙ אֶל־בִּלְעָ֔ם
וַיֹּ֕אמֶר מִ֛י הָאֲנָשִׁ֥ים הָאֵ֖לֶּה עִמָּֽךְ: וַיֹּ֥אמֶר בִּלְעָ֖ם אֶל־הָאֱלֹהִ֑ים בָּלָ֧ק בֶּן־צִפֹּ֛ר
מֶ֥לֶךְ מוֹאָ֖ב שָׁלַ֥ח אֵלָֽי: הִנֵּ֤ה הָעָם֙ הַיֹּצֵ֣א מִמִּצְרַ֔יִם וַיְכַ֖ס אֶת־עֵ֣ין הָאָ֑רֶץ
עַתָּ֗ה לְכָ֤ה קָֽבָה־לִּי֙ אֹת֔וֹ אוּלַ֥י אוּכַ֛ל לְהִלָּ֥חֶם בּ֖וֹ וְגֵרַשְׁתִּֽיו: וַיֹּ֤אמֶר אֱלֹהִים֙
אֶל־בִּלְעָ֔ם לֹ֥א תֵלֵ֖ךְ עִמָּהֶ֑ם לֹ֤א תָאֹר֙ אֶת־הָעָ֔ם כִּ֥י בָר֖וּךְ הֽוּא:

PINCHAS

וַיְדַבֵּ֥ר יְהֹוָ֖ה אֶל־מֹשֶׁ֥ה לֵּאמֹֽר: פִּֽינְחָ֨ס בֶּן־אֶלְעָזָ֜ר בֶּן־אַהֲרֹ֣ן הַכֹּהֵ֗ן הֵשִׁ֤יב
אֶת־חֲמָתִי֙ מֵעַ֣ל בְּנֵֽי־יִשְׂרָאֵ֔ל בְּקַנְא֥וֹ אֶת־קִנְאָתִ֖י בְּתוֹכָ֑ם וְלֹא־כִלִּ֥יתִי אֶת־בְּנֵֽי־יִשְׂרָאֵ֖ל
בְּקִנְאָתִֽי: לָכֵ֖ן אֱמֹ֑ר הִנְנִ֨י נֹתֵ֥ן ל֛וֹ אֶת־בְּרִיתִ֖י שָׁלֽוֹם: _Levi_ וְהָ֤יְתָה לּוֹ֙ וּלְזַרְע֣וֹ אַחֲרָ֔יו
בְּרִ֖ית כְּהֻנַּ֣ת עוֹלָ֑ם תַּ֗חַת אֲשֶׁ֤ר קִנֵּא֙ לֵֽאלֹהָ֔יו וַיְכַפֵּ֖ר עַל־בְּנֵ֥י יִשְׂרָאֵֽל: וְשֵׁם֩ אִ֨ישׁ יִשְׂרָאֵ֜ל
הַמֻּכֶּ֗ה אֲשֶׁ֤ר הֻכָּה֙ אֶת־הַמִּדְיָנִ֔ית זִמְרִ֖י בֶּן־סָל֑וּא נְשִׂ֥יא בֵֽית־אָ֖ב לַשִּׁמְעֹנִֽי: וְשֵׁ֨ם הָֽאִשָּׁ֜ה
הַמֻּכָּ֤ה הַמִּדְיָנִית֙ כָּזְבִּ֣י בַת־צ֔וּר רֹ֛אשׁ אֻמּ֥וֹת בֵּֽית־אָ֖ב בְּמִדְיָ֥ן הֽוּא: _Yisrael_
וַיְדַבֵּ֥ר יְהֹוָ֖ה אֶל־מֹשֶׁ֥ה לֵּאמֹֽר: צָר֖וֹר אֶת־הַמִּדְיָנִ֑ים וְהִכִּיתֶ֖ם אוֹתָֽם: כִּ֣י צֹרְרִ֥ים
הֵ֤ם לָכֶם֙ בְּנִכְלֵיהֶ֔ם אֲשֶׁר־נִכְּל֥וּ לָכֶ֖ם עַל־דְּבַר־פְּע֑וֹר וְעַל־דְּבַ֞ר כָּזְבִּ֣י בַת־נְשִׂ֣יא
מִדְיָ֗ן אֲחֹתָ֛ם הַמֻּכָּ֥ה בְיוֹם־הַמַּגֵּפָ֖ה עַל־דְּבַר־פְּעֽוֹר: וַיְהִ֖י אַחֲרֵ֣י הַמַּגֵּפָ֑ה וַיֹּ֤אמֶר
יְהֹוָה֙ אֶל־מֹשֶׁ֔ה וְאֶ֧ל אֶלְעָזָ֛ר בֶּן־אַהֲרֹ֥ן הַכֹּהֵ֖ן לֵאמֹֽר: שְׂא֗וּ אֶת־רֹ֨אשׁ | כָּל־עֲדַ֤ת
בְּנֵֽי־יִשְׂרָאֵל֙ מִבֶּ֨ן עֶשְׂרִ֤ים שָׁנָה֙ וָמַ֔עְלָה לְבֵ֖ית אֲבֹתָ֑ם כָּל־יֹצֵ֥א צָבָ֖א בְּיִשְׂרָאֵֽל: וַיְדַבֵּ֣ר
מֹשֶׁ֗ה וְאֶלְעָזָ֤ר הַכֹּהֵן֙ אֹתָ֔ם בְּעַֽרְבֹ֥ת מוֹאָ֖ב עַל־יַרְדֵּ֥ן יְרֵח֖וֹ לֵאמֹֽר: מִבֶּ֛ן עֶשְׂרִ֥ים שָׁנָ֖ה
וָמַ֑עְלָה כַּאֲשֶׁ֨ר צִוָּ֤ה יְהֹוָה֙ אֶת־מֹשֶׁ֔ה וּבְנֵ֣י יִשְׂרָאֵ֔ל הַיֹּצְאִ֖ים מֵאֶ֥רֶץ מִצְרָֽיִם:

MATOT

וַיְדַבֵּ֤ר מֹשֶׁה֙ אֶל־רָאשֵׁ֣י הַמַּטּ֔וֹת לִבְנֵ֥י יִשְׂרָאֵ֖ל לֵאמֹ֑ר זֶ֣ה הַדָּבָ֔ר אֲשֶׁ֖ר צִוָּ֥ה
יְהֹוָֽה: אִישׁ֩ כִּֽי־יִדֹּ֨ר נֶ֜דֶר לַֽיהֹוָ֗ה אֽוֹ־הִשָּׁ֤בַע שְׁבֻעָה֙ לֶאְסֹ֤ר אִסָּר֙
עַל־נַפְשׁ֔וֹ לֹ֥א יַחֵ֖ל דְּבָר֑וֹ כְּכָל־הַיֹּצֵ֥א מִפִּ֖יו יַעֲשֶֽׂה: וְאִשָּׁ֕ה כִּֽי־תִדֹּ֥ר נֶ֖דֶר לַֽיהֹוָ֑ה
וְאָסְרָ֥ה אִסָּ֛ר בְּבֵ֥ית אָבִ֖יהָ בִּנְעֻרֶֽיהָ: וְשָׁמַ֨ע אָבִ֜יהָ אֶת־נִדְרָ֗הּ וֶֽאֱסָרָהּ֙ אֲשֶׁ֣ר אָֽסְרָ֣ה
עַל־נַפְשָׁ֔הּ וְהֶחֱרִ֥ישׁ לָ֖הּ אָבִ֑יהָ וְקָ֨מוּ֙ כָּל־נְדָרֶ֔יהָ וְכָל־אִסָּ֛ר אֲשֶׁר־אָסְרָ֥ה עַל־נַפְשָׁ֖הּ יָקֽוּם:
וְאִם־הֵנִ֨יא אָבִ֤יהָ אֹתָהּ֙ בְּי֣וֹם שָׁמְע֔וֹ כָּל־נְדָרֶ֨יהָ֙ וֶֽאֱסָרֶ֔יהָ אֲשֶׁר־אָסְרָ֥ה עַל־נַפְשָׁ֖הּ
לֹ֣א יָק֑וּם וַֽיהֹוָה֙ יִֽסְלַח־לָ֔הּ כִּי־הֵנִ֥יא אָבִ֖יהָ אֹתָֽהּ: וְאִם־הָי֤וֹ תִֽהְיֶה֙ לְאִ֔ישׁ
וּנְדָרֶ֖יהָ עָלֶ֑יהָ א֚וֹ מִבְטָ֣א שְׂפָתֶ֔יהָ אֲשֶׁ֥ר אָסְרָ֖ה עַל־נַפְשָֽׁהּ: וְשָׁמַ֥ע אִישָׁ֛הּ
בְּי֥וֹם שָׁמְע֖וֹ וְהֶחֱרִ֣ישׁ לָ֑הּ וְקָ֣מוּ נְדָרֶ֗יהָ וֶֽאֱסָרֶ֛הָ אֲשֶׁר־אָסְרָ֥ה עַל־נַפְשָׁ֖הּ יָקֻֽמוּ:
וְ֠אִם בְּי֨וֹם שְׁמֹ֣עַ אִישָׁהּ֮ יָנִ֣יא אוֹתָהּ֒ וְהֵפֵ֗ר אֶת־נִדְרָהּ֙ אֲשֶׁ֣ר עָלֶ֔יהָ וְאֵת֙
Levi מִבְטָ֣א שְׂפָתֶ֔יהָ אֲשֶׁ֥ר אָסְרָ֖ה עַל־נַפְשָׁ֑הּ וַֽיהֹוָ֖ה יִֽסְלַח־לָֽהּ:

וְנֶ֣דֶר אַלְמָנָ֔ה וּגְרוּשָׁ֑ה כֹּ֛ל אֲשֶׁר־אָסְרָ֥ה עַל־נַפְשָׁ֖הּ יָק֥וּם עָלֶֽיהָ: וְאִם־בֵּ֣ית אִישָׁ֣הּ נָדָ֑רָה

אֽוֹ־אָסְרָ֥ה אִסָּ֛ר עַל־נַפְשָׁ֖הּ בִּשְׁבֻעָֽה: וְשָׁמַ֤ע אִישָׁהּ֙ וְהֶחֱרִ֣שׁ לָ֔הּ לֹ֥א הֵנִ֖יא אֹתָ֑הּ

וְקָ֙מוּ֙ כָּל־נְדָרֶ֔יהָ וְכָל־אִסָּ֛ר אֲשֶׁר־אָסְרָ֥ה עַל־נַפְשָׁ֖הּ יָק֑וּם: וְאִם־הָפֵ֣ר יָפֵר֩ אֹתָ֨ם |

אִישָׁ֜הּ בְּי֣וֹם שָׁמְע֗וֹ כָּל־מוֹצָ֣א שְׂפָתֶ֛יהָ לִנְדָרֶ֥יהָ וּלְאִסַּ֥ר נַפְשָׁ֖הּ לֹ֣א יָק֑וּם

אִישָׁ֣הּ הֲפֵרָ֔ם וַיהֹוָ֥ה יִֽסְלַח־לָֽהּ: *Yisrael* כָּל־נֵ֥דֶר וְכָל־שְׁבֻעַ֖ת אִסָּ֑ר לְעַנֹּ֣ת נָ֑פֶשׁ

אִישָׁ֖הּ יְקִימֶ֑נּוּ וְאִישָׁ֖הּ יְפֵרֶֽנּוּ: וְאִם־הַחֲרֵשׁ֩ יַחֲרִ֨ישׁ לָ֥הּ אִישָׁהּ֘ מִיּ֣וֹם אֶל־י֒וֹם

וְהֵקִים֙ אֶת־כָּל־נְדָרֶ֔יהָ א֥וֹ אֶת־כָּל־אֱסָרֶ֖יהָ אֲשֶׁ֣ר עָלֶ֑יהָ הֵקִ֣ים אֹתָ֔ם כִּֽי־הֶחֱרִ֥שׁ לָ֖הּ בְּי֥וֹם

שָׁמְעֽוֹ: וְאִם־הָפֵ֥ר יָפֵ֛ר אֹתָ֖ם אַחֲרֵ֣י שָׁמְע֑וֹ וְנָשָׂ֖א אֶת־עֲוֹנָֽהּ: אֵ֣לֶּה הַֽחֻקִּ֗ים אֲשֶׁ֨ר

צִוָּ֤ה יְהֹוָה֙ אֶת־מֹשֶׁ֔ה בֵּ֥ין אִ֖ישׁ לְאִשְׁתּ֑וֹ בֵּֽין־אָ֣ב לְבִתּ֔וֹ בִּנְעֻרֶ֖יהָ בֵּ֥ית אָבִֽיהָ:

MASEI

אֵ֣לֶּה מַסְעֵ֣י בְנֵֽי־יִשְׂרָאֵ֗ל אֲשֶׁ֥ר יָצְא֛וּ מֵאֶ֥רֶץ מִצְרַ֖יִם לְצִבְאֹתָ֑ם בְּיַד־מֹשֶׁ֖ה וְאַהֲרֹֽן:

וַיִּכְתֹּ֨ב מֹשֶׁ֜ה אֶת־מוֹצָאֵיהֶ֛ם לְמַסְעֵיהֶ֖ם עַל־פִּ֣י יְהֹוָ֑ה וְאֵ֥לֶּה מַסְעֵיהֶ֖ם

לְמוֹצָאֵיהֶֽם: וַיִּסְע֤וּ מֵֽרַעְמְסֵס֙ בַּחֹ֣דֶשׁ הָֽרִאשׁ֔וֹן בַּחֲמִשָּׁ֥ה עָשָׂ֛ר י֖וֹם לַחֹ֣דֶשׁ הָֽרִאשׁ֑וֹן

מִֽמָּחֳרַ֣ת הַפֶּ֗סַח יָצְא֤וּ בְנֵֽי־יִשְׂרָאֵל֙ בְּיָ֣ד רָמָ֔ה לְעֵינֵ֖י כָּל־מִצְרָֽיִם: *Levi* וּמִצְרַ֣יִם מְקַבְּרִ֗ים

אֵת֩ אֲשֶׁ֨ר הִכָּ֤ה יְהֹוָה֙ בָּהֶ֔ם כָּל־בְּכ֑וֹר וּבֵאלֹ֣הֵיהֶ֔ם עָשָׂ֥ה יְהֹוָ֖ה

שְׁפָטִֽים: וַיִּסְע֥וּ בְנֵֽי־יִשְׂרָאֵ֖ל מֵרַעְמְסֵ֑ס וַיַּחֲנ֖וּ בְּסֻכֹּֽת: וַיִּסְע֖וּ מִסֻּכֹּ֑ת וַיַּחֲנ֣וּ בְאֵתָ֔ם

אֲשֶׁ֖ר בִּקְצֵ֥ה הַמִּדְבָּֽר: *Yisrael* וַיִּסְעוּ֙ מֵֽאֵתָ֔ם וַיָּ֙שָׁב֙ עַל־פִּ֣י הַֽחִירֹ֔ת אֲשֶׁ֥ר עַל־פְּנֵ֖י

בַּ֣עַל צְפ֑וֹן וַֽיַּחֲנ֖וּ לִפְנֵ֥י מִגְדֹּֽל: וַיִּסְעוּ֙ מִפְּנֵ֣י הַֽחִירֹ֔ת וַיַּֽעַבְר֥וּ בְתוֹךְ־הַיָּ֖ם הַמִּדְבָּ֑רָה וַיֵּ֨לְכ֜וּ

דֶּ֣רֶךְ שְׁלֹ֤שֶׁת יָמִים֙ בְּמִדְבַּ֣ר אֵתָ֔ם וַֽיַּחֲנ֖וּ בְּמָרָֽה: וַיִּסְעוּ֙ מִמָּרָ֔ה וַיָּבֹ֖אוּ אֵילִ֑מָה וּבְאֵילִ֗ם

שְׁתֵּ֣ים עֶשְׂרֵ֞ה עֵינֹ֥ת מַ֙יִם֙ וְשִׁבְעִ֣ים תְּמָרִ֔ים וַיַּחֲנוּ־שָֽׁם: וַיִּסְע֖וּ מֵאֵילִ֑ם וַֽיַּחֲנ֖וּ עַל־יַם־סֽוּף:

DEVARIM

אֵ֣לֶּה הַדְּבָרִ֗ים אֲשֶׁ֨ר דִּבֶּ֤ר מֹשֶׁה֙ אֶל־כָּל־יִשְׂרָאֵ֔ל בְּעֵ֖בֶר הַיַּרְדֵּ֑ן בַּמִּדְבָּ֣ר בָּֽעֲרָבָ֡ה

מ֣וֹל סוּף֩ בֵּֽין־פָּארָ֨ן וּבֵֽין־תֹּ֜פֶל וְלָבָ֤ן וַחֲצֵרֹת֙ וְדִ֣י זָהָ֔ב: אַחַ֨ד עָשָׂ֥ר יוֹם֙ מֵֽחֹרֵ֔ב דֶּ֛רֶךְ

הַר־שֵׂעִ֖יר עַ֣ד קָדֵ֣שׁ בַּרְנֵ֑עַ: וַיְהִ֞י בְּאַרְבָּעִ֣ים שָׁנָ֗ה בְּעַשְׁתֵּֽי־עָשָׂ֥ר חֹ֛דֶשׁ בְּאֶחָ֥ד לַחֹ֖דֶשׁ

דִּבֶּ֤ר מֹשֶׁה֙ אֶל־בְּנֵ֣י יִשְׂרָאֵ֔ל כְּכֹ֛ל אֲשֶׁ֥ר צִוָּ֧ה יְהֹוָ֛ה אֹת֖וֹ אֲלֵהֶֽם: *Levi*

אַחֲרֵ֣י הַכֹּת֗וֹ אֵ֚ת סִיחֹן֙ מֶ֣לֶךְ הָֽאֱמֹרִ֔י אֲשֶׁ֥ר יוֹשֵׁ֖ב בְּחֶשְׁבּ֑וֹן וְאֵ֗ת ע֚וֹג מֶ֣לֶךְ הַבָּשָׁ֔ן

אֲשֶׁר־יוֹשֵׁ֥ב בְּעַשְׁתָּרֹ֖ת בְּאֶדְרֶֽעִי: בְּעֵ֥בֶר הַיַּרְדֵּ֖ן בְּאֶ֣רֶץ מוֹאָ֑ב הוֹאִ֣יל מֹשֶׁ֔ה בֵּאֵ֛ר

אֶת־הַתּוֹרָ֥ה הַזֹּ֖את לֵאמֹֽר: יְהֹוָ֧ה אֱלֹהֵ֛ינוּ דִּבֶּ֥ר אֵלֵ֖ינוּ בְּחֹרֵ֣ב לֵאמֹ֑ר רַב־לָכֶ֥ם

שֶׁ֖בֶת בָּהָ֥ר הַזֶּֽה: פְּנ֣וּ | וּסְע֣וּ לָכֶ֗ם וּבֹ֨אוּ הַ֥ר הָֽאֱמֹרִי֮ וְאֶל־כָּל־שְׁכֵנָיו֒ בָּֽעֲרָבָ֥ה בָהָ֣ר

וּבַשְּׁפֵלָ֣ה וּבַנֶּ֔גֶב וּבְח֖וֹף הַיָּ֑ם אֶ֤רֶץ הַֽכְּנַעֲנִי֙ וְהַלְּבָנ֔וֹן עַד־הַנָּהָ֥ר הַגָּדֹ֖ל נְהַר־פְּרָֽת: *Yisrael*

רְאֵ֛ה נָתַ֥תִּי לִפְנֵיכֶ֖ם אֶת־הָאָ֑רֶץ בֹּ֚אוּ וּרְשׁ֣וּ אֶת־הָאָ֔רֶץ אֲשֶׁ֣ר נִשְׁבַּ֣ע יְהֹוָ֗ה

לַאֲבֹֽתֵיכֶ֞ם לְאַבְרָהָ֛ם לְיִצְחָ֥ק וּֽלְיַעֲקֹ֖ב לָתֵ֣ת לָהֶ֑ם וּלְזַרְעָ֖ם אַחֲרֵיהֶֽם: וָאֹמַ֣ר אֲלֵכֶ֔ם

בָּעֵ֥ת הַהִ֖וא לֵאמֹ֑ר לֹא־אוּכַ֥ל לְבַדִּ֖י שְׂאֵ֥ת אֶתְכֶֽם: יְהֹוָ֧ה אֱלֹהֵיכֶ֛ם

הִרְבָּ֥ה אֶתְכֶ֑ם וְהִנְּכֶ֣ם הַיּ֔וֹם כְּכֽוֹכְבֵ֥י הַשָּׁמַ֖יִם לָרֹֽב: יְהֹוָ֞ה אֱלֹהֵ֣י

אֲבֽוֹתֵכֶ֗ם יֹסֵ֧ף עֲלֵיכֶ֛ם כָּכֶ֖ם אֶ֣לֶף פְּעָמִ֑ים וִיבָרֵ֣ךְ אֶתְכֶ֔ם כַּאֲשֶׁ֖ר דִּבֶּ֥ר לָכֶֽם:

VA'ETCHANAN

וָאֶתְחַנַּ֖ן אֶל־יְהֹוָ֑הֱאלֹהִֽיאהדונהי בָּעֵ֥ת הַהִ֖וא לֵאמֹֽר: אֲדֹנָ֣י יֱהֹוִהֱאלֹהֽיאהדונהי אַתָּ֣ה הַחִלּ֗וֹתָ
לְהַרְא֣וֹת אֶֽת־עַבְדְּךָ֔ אֶ֨ת־גָּדְלְךָ֔ וְאֶת־יָדְךָ֖ הַחֲזָקָ֑ה אֲשֶׁ֤ר מִי־אֵל֙ בַּשָּׁמַ֣יִם וּבָאָ֔רֶץ
אֲשֶׁר־יַעֲשֶׂ֥ה כְמַעֲשֶׂ֖יךָ וְכִגְבוּרֹתֶֽךָ: אֶעְבְּרָה־נָּ֗א וְאֶרְאֶה֙ אֶת־הָאָ֣רֶץ הַטּוֹבָ֔ה אֲשֶׁ֖ר
בְּעֵ֣בֶר הַיַּרְדֵּ֑ן הָהָ֥ר הַטּ֛וֹב הַזֶּ֖ה וְהַלְּבָנֹֽן: _Levi_ וַיִּתְעַבֵּ֨ר יְהֹוָ֥הֱאלֹהֽיאהדונהי בִּי֙ לְמַ֣עַנְכֶ֔ם וְלֹ֥א
שָׁמַ֖ע אֵלָ֑י וַיֹּ֨אמֶר יְהֹוָ֤הֱאלֹהֽיאהדונהי אֵלַי֙ רַב־לָ֔ךְ אַל־תּ֗וֹסֶף דַּבֵּ֥ר אֵלַ֛י ע֖וֹד בַּדָּבָ֥ר הַזֶּֽה:
עֲלֵ֣ה ׀ רֹ֣אשׁ הַפִּסְגָּ֗ה וְשָׂ֥א עֵינֶ֛יךָ יָ֧מָּה וְצָפֹ֛נָה וְתֵימָ֥נָה וּמִזְרָ֖חָה וּרְאֵ֣ה בְעֵינֶ֑יךָ כִּי־לֹ֥א
תַעֲבֹ֖ר אֶת־הַיַּרְדֵּ֥ן הַזֶּֽה: וְצַ֣ו אֶת־יְהוֹשֻׁ֗עַ וְחַזְּקֵ֣הוּ וְאַמְּצֵ֑הוּ כִּי־ה֣וּא יַעֲבֹ֗ר לִפְנֵי֙ הָעָ֣ם הַזֶּ֔ה
וְהוּא֙ יַנְחִ֣יל אוֹתָ֔ם אֶת־הָאָ֖רֶץ אֲשֶׁ֥ר תִּרְאֶֽה: וַנֵּ֣שֶׁב בַּגָּ֔יְא מ֖וּל בֵּ֥ית פְּעֽוֹר: וְעַתָּ֣ה יִשְׂרָאֵ֗ל
שְׁמַ֤ע אֶל־הַֽחֻקִּים֙ וְאֶל־הַמִּשְׁפָּטִ֔ים אֲשֶׁ֧ר אָנֹכִ֛י מְלַמֵּ֥ד אֶתְכֶ֖ם לַעֲשׂ֑וֹת לְמַ֣עַן תִּֽחְי֗וּ
וּבָאתֶם֙ וִֽירִשְׁתֶּ֣ם אֶת־הָאָ֔רֶץ אֲשֶׁ֧ר יְהֹוָ֛הֱאלֹהֽיאהדונהי אֱלֹהֵ֥י אֲבֹתֵיכֶ֖ם נֹתֵ֥ן לָכֶֽם: לֹ֣א תֹסִ֗פוּ
עַל־הַדָּבָר֙ אֲשֶׁ֤ר אָנֹכִי֙ מְצַוֶּ֣ה אֶתְכֶ֔ם וְלֹ֥א תִגְרְע֖וּ מִמֶּ֑נּוּ לִשְׁמֹ֗ר אֶת־מִצְוֺת֙ יְהֹוָ֤הֱאלֹהֽיאהדונהי
אֱלֹֽהֵיכֶ֔ם אֲשֶׁ֥ר אָנֹכִ֖י מְצַוֶּ֥ה אֶתְכֶֽם: עֵֽינֵיכֶם֙ הָֽרֹא֔וֹת אֵ֛ת אֲשֶׁר־עָשָׂ֥ה יְהֹוָ֖הֱאלֹהֽיאהדונהי
בְּבַ֣עַל פְּע֑וֹר כִּ֣י כָל־הָאִ֗ישׁ אֲשֶׁ֤ר הָלַךְ֙ אַחֲרֵ֣י בַֽעַל־פְּע֔וֹר הִשְׁמִיד֛וֹ יְהֹוָ֥הֱאלֹהֽיאהדונהי
אֱלֹהֶ֖יךָ מִקִּרְבֶּֽךָ: וְאַתֶּם֙ הַדְּבֵקִ֔ים בַּֽיהֹוָ֖הֱאלֹהֽיאהדונהי אֱלֹהֵיכֶ֑ם חַיִּ֥ים כֻּלְּכֶ֖ם הַיּֽוֹם: _Yisrael_
רְאֵ֣ה ׀ לִמַּ֣דְתִּי אֶתְכֶ֗ם חֻקִּים֙ וּמִשְׁפָּטִ֔ים כַּאֲשֶׁ֥ר צִוַּ֖נִי יְהֹוָ֣הֱאלֹהֽיאהדונהי אֱלֹהָ֑י
לַעֲשׂ֣וֹת כֵּ֔ן בְּקֶ֣רֶב הָאָ֔רֶץ אֲשֶׁ֥ר אַתֶּ֛ם בָּאִ֥ים שָׁ֖מָּה לְרִשְׁתָּֽהּ: וּשְׁמַרְתֶּם֮ וַעֲשִׂיתֶם֒
כִּ֣י הִ֤וא חָכְמַתְכֶם֙ וּבִ֣ינַתְכֶ֔ם לְעֵינֵ֖י הָעַמִּ֑ים אֲשֶׁ֣ר יִשְׁמְע֗וּן אֵ֚ת כָּל־הַחֻקִּ֣ים הָאֵ֔לֶּה
וְאָמְר֗וּ רַ֚ק עַם־חָכָ֣ם וְנָב֔וֹן הַגּ֥וֹי הַגָּד֖וֹל הַזֶּֽה: כִּ֚י מִי־ג֣וֹי גָּד֔וֹל אֲשֶׁר־ל֥וֹ אֱלֹהִ֖ים
קְרֹבִ֣ים אֵלָ֑יו כַּֽיהֹוָ֣הֱאלֹהֽיאהדונהי אֱלֹהֵ֔ינוּ בְּכָל־קָרְאֵ֖נוּ אֵלָֽיו: וּמִי֙ גּ֣וֹי גָּד֔וֹל אֲשֶׁר־ל֛וֹ
חֻקִּ֥ים וּמִשְׁפָּטִ֖ים צַדִּיקִ֑ם כְּכֹל֙ הַתּוֹרָ֣ה הַזֹּ֔את אֲשֶׁ֧ר אָנֹכִ֛י נֹתֵ֥ן לִפְנֵיכֶ֖ם הַיּֽוֹם:

EKEV

וְהָיָ֣ה ׀ עֵ֣קֶב תִּשְׁמְע֗וּן אֵ֤ת הַמִּשְׁפָּטִים֙ הָאֵ֔לֶּה וּשְׁמַרְתֶּ֥ם וַעֲשִׂיתֶ֖ם אֹתָ֑ם
וְשָׁמַר֩ יְהֹוָ֨הֱאלֹהֽיאהדונהי אֱלֹהֶ֜יךָ לְךָ֗ אֶֽת־הַבְּרִית֙ וְאֶת־הַחֶ֔סֶד אֲשֶׁ֥ר נִשְׁבַּ֖ע לַאֲבֹתֶֽיךָ:
וַאֲהֵ֣בְךָ֔ וּבֵרַכְךָ֖ וְהִרְבֶּ֑ךָ וּבֵרַ֣ךְ פְּרִי־בִטְנְךָ֣ וּפְרִֽי־אַדְמָתֶ֗ךָ דְּגָ֨נְךָ֜ וְתִֽירֹשְׁךָ֣ וְיִצְהָרֶ֗ךָ
שְׁגַר־אֲלָפֶ֨יךָ֙ וְעַשְׁתְּרֹ֣ת צֹאנֶ֔ךָ עַ֚ל הָֽאֲדָמָ֔ה אֲשֶׁר־נִשְׁבַּ֥ע לַאֲבֹתֶ֖יךָ לָ֥תֶת לָֽךְ: בָּר֥וּךְ תִּֽהְיֶ֖ה
מִכָּל־הָעַמִּ֑ים לֹא־יִֽהְיֶ֥ה בְךָ֛ עָקָ֥ר וַֽעֲקָרָ֖ה וּבִבְהֶמְתֶּֽךָ: וְהֵסִ֧יר יְהֹוָ֛הֱאלֹהֽיאהדונהי מִמְּךָ֖
כָּל־חֹ֑לִי וְכָל־מַדְוֵי֩ מִצְרַ֨יִם הָרָעִ֜ים אֲשֶׁ֣ר יָדַ֗עְתָּ לֹ֤א יְשִׂימָם֙ בָּ֔ךְ וּנְתָנָ֖ם בְּכָל־שֹׂנְאֶֽיךָ:
וְאָכַלְתָּ֣ אֶת־כָּל־הָֽעַמִּ֗ים אֲשֶׁ֨ר יְהֹוָ֤הֱאלֹהֽיאהדונהי אֱלֹהֶ֨יךָ֙ נֹתֵ֣ן לָ֔ךְ לֹא־תָח֥וֹס עֵֽינְךָ֖ עֲלֵיהֶ֑ם
וְלֹ֤א תַעֲבֹד֙ אֶת־אֱלֹ֣הֵיהֶ֔ם כִּֽי־מוֹקֵ֥שׁ ה֖וּא לָֽךְ: כִּ֤י תֹאמַר֙ בִּלְבָ֣בְךָ֔ רַבִּ֛ים הַגּוֹיִ֥ם הָאֵ֖לֶּה
מִמֶּ֑נִּי אֵיכָ֥ה אוּכַ֖ל לְהֽוֹרִישָֽׁם: לֹ֥א תִירָ֖א מֵהֶ֑ם זָכֹ֣ר תִּזְכֹּ֗ר אֵ֤ת אֲשֶׁר־עָשָׂה֙
יְהֹוָ֤הֱאלֹהֽיאהדונהי אֱלֹהֶ֨יךָ֙ לְפַרְעֹ֖ה וּלְכָל־מִצְרָֽיִם: הַמַּסֹּ֨ת הַגְּדֹלֹ֜ת אֲשֶׁר־רָא֣וּ עֵינֶ֗יךָ
וְהָאֹתֹ֤ת וְהַמֹּֽפְתִים֙ וְהַיָּ֤ד הַחֲזָקָה֙ וְהַזְּרֹ֣עַ הַנְּטוּיָ֔ה אֲשֶׁ֥ר הוֹצִֽאֲךָ֖ יְהֹוָ֣הֱאלֹהֽיאהדונהי אֱלֹהֶ֑יךָ
כֵּֽן־יַעֲשֶׂ֞ה יְהֹוָ֤הֱאלֹהֽיאהדונהי אֱלֹהֶ֨יךָ֙ לְכָל־הָ֣עַמִּ֔ים אֲשֶׁר־אַתָּ֥ה יָרֵ֖א מִפְּנֵיהֶֽם:
וְגַם֙ אֶת־הַצִּרְעָ֔ה יְשַׁלַּ֛ח יְהֹוָ֥הֱאלֹהֽיאהדונהי אֱלֹהֶ֖יךָ בָּ֑ם עַד־אֲבֹ֗ד הַנִּשְׁאָרִ֛ים וְהַנִּסְתָּרִ֖ים
מִפָּנֶֽיךָ: _Levi_ לֹ֥א תַעֲרֹ֖ץ מִפְּנֵיהֶ֑ם כִּֽי־יְהֹוָ֤הֱאלֹהֽיאהדונהי אֱלֹהֶ֨יךָ֙ בְּקִרְבֶּ֔ךָ אֵ֥ל גָּד֖וֹל וְנוֹרָֽא:

וְנָשַׁל יְהֹוָ֣הִדֹנָיאהדונהי אֱלֹהֶ֜יךָ אֶת־הַגּוֹיִ֣ם הָאֵ֗ל מִפָּנֶ֛יךָ מְעַ֣ט מְעָ֑ט לֹ֣א תוּכַ֤ל כַּלֹּתָם֙ מַהֵ֔ר
פֶּן־תִּרְבֶּ֥ה עָלֶ֖יךָ חַיַּ֥ת הַשָּׂדֶֽה: וּנְתָנָ֞ם יְהֹוָ֣הִדֹנָיאהדונהי אֱלֹהֶ֖יךָ לְפָנֶ֑יךָ וְהָמָם֙ מְהוּמָ֣ה גְדֹלָ֔ה
עַ֖ד הִשָּֽׁמְדָֽם: וְנָתַ֤ן מַלְכֵיהֶם֙ בְּיָדֶ֔ךָ וְהַֽאֲבַדְתָּ֣ אֶת־שְׁמָ֔ם מִתַּ֖חַת הַשָּׁמָ֑יִם לֹא־יִתְיַצֵּ֥ב אִישׁ֙
בְּפָנֶ֔יךָ עַ֥ד הִשְׁמִֽדְךָ֖ אֹתָֽם: פְּסִילֵ֤י אֱלֹֽהֵיהֶם֙ תִּשְׂרְפ֣וּן בָּאֵ֔שׁ לֹֽא־תַחְמֹ֨ד כֶּ֤סֶף וְזָהָב֙
עֲלֵיהֶ֔ם וְלָקַחְתָּ֖ לָ֑ךְ פֶּ֚ן תִּוָּקֵ֣שׁ בּ֔וֹ כִּ֧י תֽוֹעֲבַ֛ת יְהֹוָ֥הִדֹנָיאהדונהי אֱלֹהֶ֖יךָ הֽוּא: וְלֹֽא־תָבִ֤יא
תֽוֹעֵבָה֙ אֶל־בֵּיתֶ֔ךָ וְהָיִ֥יתָ חֵ֖רֶם כָּמֹ֑הוּ שַׁקֵּ֧ץ | תְּשַׁקְּצֶ֣נּוּ וְתַעֵ֣ב | תְּֽתַעֲבֶ֗נּוּ כִּי־חֵ֥רֶם הֽוּא:
כָּל־הַמִּצְוָ֗ה אֲשֶׁ֨ר אָֽנֹכִ֧י מְצַוְּךָ֛ הַיּ֖וֹם תִּשְׁמְר֣וּן לַֽעֲשׂ֑וֹת לְמַ֨עַן תִּֽחְי֜וּן וּרְבִיתֶ֗ם וּבָאתֶם֙
וִֽירִשְׁתֶּ֣ם אֶת־הָאָ֔רֶץ אֲשֶׁר־נִשְׁבַּ֥ע יְהֹוָ֖הִדֹנָיאהדונהי לַֽאֲבֹֽתֵיכֶֽם: וְזָֽכַרְתָּ֣ אֶת־כָּל־הַדֶּ֗רֶךְ
אֲשֶׁ֨ר הֹֽלִֽיכְךָ֜ יְהֹוָ֧הִדֹנָיאהדונהי אֱלֹהֶ֛יךָ זֶ֛ה אַרְבָּעִ֥ים שָׁנָ֖ה בַּמִּדְבָּ֑ר לְמַ֨עַן עַנֹּֽתְךָ֜ לְנַסֹּֽתְךָ֗
לָדַ֜עַת אֶת־אֲשֶׁ֧ר בִּֽלְבָֽבְךָ֛ הֲתִשְׁמֹ֥ר מִצְוֹתָ֖ו אִם־לֹֽא: וַיְעַנְּךָ֮ וַיַּרְעִבֶךָ֒ וַיַּֽאֲכִֽלְךָ֤
אֶת־הַמָּן֙ אֲשֶׁ֣ר לֹֽא־יָדַ֔עְתָּ וְלֹ֥א יָֽדְע֖וּן אֲבֹתֶ֑יךָ לְמַ֣עַן הֽוֹדִֽעֲךָ֗ כִּ֠י לֹ֣א עַל־הַלֶּ֤חֶם
לְבַדּוֹ֙ יִֽחְיֶ֣ה הָֽאָדָ֔ם כִּ֛י עַל־כָּל־מוֹצָ֥א פִֽי־יְהֹוָ֖הִדֹנָיאהדונהי יִֽחְיֶ֥ה הָֽאָדָֽם: *Yisrael*
שִׂמְלָֽתְךָ֞ לֹ֤א בָֽלְתָה֙ מֵֽעָלֶ֔יךָ וְרַגְלְךָ֖ לֹ֣א בָצֵ֑קָה זֶ֖ה אַרְבָּעִ֥ים שָׁנָֽה: וְיָֽדַעְתָּ֖ עִם־לְבָבֶ֑ךָ
כִּ֗י כַּֽאֲשֶׁ֨ר יְיַסֵּ֥ר אִישׁ֙ אֶת־בְּנ֔וֹ יְהֹוָ֥הִדֹנָיאהדונהי אֱלֹהֶ֖יךָ מְיַסְּרֶֽךָ: וְשָׁ֣מַרְתָּ֔ אֶת־מִצְוֺ֖ת
יְהֹוָ֣הִדֹנָיאהדונהי אֱלֹהֶ֑יךָ לָלֶ֥כֶת בִּדְרָכָ֖יו וּלְיִרְאָ֥ה אֹתֽוֹ: כִּ֚י יְהֹוָ֣הִדֹנָיאהדונהי אֱלֹהֶ֔יךָ מְבִֽיאֲךָ֖
אֶל־אֶ֣רֶץ טוֹבָ֑ה אֶ֚רֶץ נַ֣חֲלֵי מָ֔יִם עֲיָנֹת֙ וּתְהֹמֹ֔ת יֹֽצְאִ֥ים בַּבִּקְעָ֖ה וּבָהָֽר: אֶ֤רֶץ חִטָּה֙
וּשְׂעֹרָ֔ה וְגֶ֥פֶן וּתְאֵנָ֖ה וְרִמּ֑וֹן אֶֽרֶץ־זֵ֥ית שֶׁ֖מֶן וּדְבָֽשׁ: אֶ֗רֶץ אֲשֶׁ֨ר לֹ֤א בְמִסְכֵּנֻת֙ תֹּֽאכַל־בָּ֣הּ
לֶ֔חֶם לֹֽא־תֶחְסַ֥ר כֹּ֖ל בָּ֑הּ אֶ֚רֶץ אֲשֶׁ֣ר אֲבָנֶ֣יהָ בַרְזֶ֔ל וּמֵֽהֲרָרֶ֖יהָ תַּחְצֹ֥ב נְחֹֽשֶׁת:
וְאָֽכַלְתָּ֖ וְשָׂבָ֑עְתָּ וּבֵֽרַכְתָּ֙ אֶת־יְהֹוָ֣הִדֹנָיאהדונהי אֱלֹהֶ֔יךָ עַל־הָאָ֥רֶץ הַטֹּבָ֖ה אֲשֶׁ֥ר נָֽתַן־לָֽךְ:

RE'EH

רְאֵ֗ה אָֽנֹכִ֛י נֹתֵ֥ן לִפְנֵיכֶ֖ם הַיּ֑וֹם בְּרָכָ֖ה וּקְלָלָֽה: אֶֽת־הַבְּרָכָ֔ה אֲשֶׁ֣ר תִּשְׁמְע֔וּ אֶל־מִצְוֺ֗ת
יְהֹוָ֣הִדֹנָיאהדונהי אֱלֹֽהֵיכֶ֔ם אֲשֶׁ֧ר אָֽנֹכִ֛י מְצַוֶּ֥ה אֶתְכֶ֖ם הַיּֽוֹם: וְהַקְּלָלָ֗ה אִם־לֹ֤א תִשְׁמְעוּ֙
אֶל־מִצְוֺת֙ יְהֹוָ֣הִדֹנָיאהדונהי אֱלֹֽהֵיכֶ֔ם וְסַרְתֶּ֣ם מִן־הַדֶּ֔רֶךְ אֲשֶׁ֧ר אָֽנֹכִ֛י מְצַוֶּ֥ה אֶתְכֶ֖ם הַיּ֑וֹם
לָלֶ֗כֶת אַֽחֲרֵ֛י אֱלֹהִ֥ים אֲחֵרִ֖ים אֲשֶׁ֥ר לֹֽא־יְדַעְתֶּֽם: וְהָיָ֗ה כִּ֤י יְבִֽיאֲךָ֙ יְהֹוָ֣הִדֹנָיאהדונהי אֱלֹהֶ֔יךָ
אֶל־הָאָ֕רֶץ אֲשֶׁר־אַתָּ֥ה בָא־שָׁ֖מָּה לְרִשְׁתָּ֑הּ וְנָֽתַתָּ֤ה אֶת־הַבְּרָכָה֙ עַל־הַ֣ר גְּרִזִ֔ים
וְאֶת־הַקְּלָלָ֖ה עַל־הַ֣ר עֵיבָֽל: הֲלֹא־הֵ֜מָּה בְּעֵ֣בֶר הַיַּרְדֵּ֗ן אַֽחֲרֵי֙ דֶּ֚רֶךְ מְב֣וֹא הַשֶּׁ֔מֶשׁ בְּאֶ֨רֶץ֙
הַֽכְּנַֽעֲנִ֔י הַיֹּשֵׁ֖ב בָּֽעֲרָבָ֑ה מ֚וּל הַגִּלְגָּ֔ל אֵ֖צֶל אֵֽלוֹנֵ֥י מֹרֶֽה: כִּ֥י אַתֶּ֛ם עֹֽבְרִ֥ים אֶת־הַיַּרְדֵּ֖ן לָבֹא֙
לָרֶ֣שֶׁת אֶת־הָאָ֔רֶץ אֲשֶׁר־יְהֹוָ֥הִדֹנָיאהדונהי אֱלֹֽהֵיכֶ֖ם נֹתֵ֣ן לָכֶ֑ם וִֽירִשְׁתֶּ֥ם אֹתָ֖הּ וְאַתָּ֤ה *Levi*
וִֽישַׁבְתֶּם־בָּֽהּ: וּשְׁמַרְתֶּ֣ם לַֽעֲשׂ֔וֹת אֵ֥ת כָּל־הַֽחֻקִּ֖ים וְאֶת־הַמִּשְׁפָּטִ֑ים אֲשֶׁ֧ר אָֽנֹכִ֛י נֹתֵ֥ן
לִפְנֵיכֶ֖ם הַיּֽוֹם: אֵ֣לֶּה הַֽחֻקִּ֣ים וְהַמִּשְׁפָּטִים֮ אֲשֶׁ֣ר תִּשְׁמְר֣וּן לַֽעֲשׂוֹת֒ בָּאָ֕רֶץ אֲשֶׁ֨ר נָתַ֜ן
יְהֹוָ֣הִדֹנָיאהדונהי אֱלֹהֵ֧י אֲבֹתֶ֛יךָ לְךָ֖ לְרִשְׁתָּ֑הּ כָּ֨ל־הַיָּמִ֔ים אֲשֶׁר־אַתֶּ֥ם חַיִּ֖ים עַל־הָֽאֲדָמָֽה:
אַבֵּ֣ד תְּֽאַבְּד֞וּן אֶֽת־כָּל־הַמְּקֹמ֗וֹת אֲשֶׁ֣ר עָֽבְדוּ־שָׁ֣ם הַגּוֹיִ֗ם אֲשֶׁ֥ר אַתֶּ֛ם יֹֽרְשִׁ֥ים
אֹתָ֖ם אֶת־אֱלֹֽהֵיהֶ֑ם עַל־הֶֽהָרִ֤ים הָֽרָמִים֙ וְעַל־הַגְּבָע֔וֹת וְתַ֖חַת כָּל־עֵ֥ץ רַֽעֲנָֽן:

וְנִתַּצְתֶּם אֶת־מִזְבְּחֹתָם וְשִׁבַּרְתֶּם אֶת־מַצֵּבֹתָם וַאֲשֵׁרֵיהֶם תִּשְׂרְפוּן בָּאֵשׁ וּפְסִילֵי
אֱלֹהֵיהֶם תְּגַדֵּעוּן וְאִבַּדְתֶּם אֶת־שְׁמָם מִן־הַמָּקוֹם הַהוּא: לֹא־תַעֲשׂוּן כֵּן לַיהֹוָאֲדֹנָי
אֱלֹהֵיכֶם: כִּי אִם־אֶל־הַמָּקוֹם אֲשֶׁר־יִבְחַר יְהֹוָאֲדֹנָי אֱלֹהֵיכֶם מִכָּל־שִׁבְטֵיכֶם
לָשׂוּם אֶת־שְׁמוֹ שָׁם לְשִׁכְנוֹ תִדְרְשׁוּ וּבָאתָ שָׁמָּה: *Yisrael* וַהֲבֵאתֶם שָׁמָּה עֹלֹתֵיכֶם
וְזִבְחֵיכֶם וְאֵת מַעְשְׂרֹתֵיכֶם וְאֵת תְּרוּמַת יֶדְכֶם וְנִדְרֵיכֶם וְנִדְבֹתֵיכֶם וּבְכֹרֹת בְּקַרְכֶם
וְצֹאנְכֶם: וַאֲכַלְתֶּם־שָׁם לִפְנֵי יְהֹוָאֲדֹנָי אֱלֹהֵיכֶם וּשְׂמַחְתֶּם בְּכֹל מִשְׁלַח יֶדְכֶם אַתֶּם
וּבָתֵּיכֶם אֲשֶׁר בֵּרַכְךָ יְהֹוָאֲדֹנָי אֱלֹהֶיךָ: לֹא תַעֲשׂוּן כְּכֹל אֲשֶׁר אֲנַחְנוּ עֹשִׂים פֹּה
הַיּוֹם אִישׁ כָּל־הַיָּשָׁר בְּעֵינָיו: כִּי לֹא־בָאתֶם עַד־עָתָּה אֶל־הַמְּנוּחָה וְאֶל־הַנַּחֲלָה אֲשֶׁר־
יְהֹוָאֲדֹנָי אֱלֹהֶיךָ נֹתֵן לָךְ: וַעֲבַרְתֶּם אֶת־הַיַּרְדֵּן וִישַׁבְתֶּם בָּאָרֶץ אֲשֶׁר־יְהֹוָאֲדֹנָי
אֱלֹהֵיכֶם מַנְחִיל אֶתְכֶם וְהֵנִיחַ לָכֶם מִכָּל־אֹיְבֵיכֶם מִסָּבִיב וִישַׁבְתֶּם־בֶּטַח:

SHOFTIM

שֹׁפְטִים וְשֹׁטְרִים תִּתֶּן־לְךָ בְּכָל־שְׁעָרֶיךָ אֲשֶׁר יְהֹוָאֲדֹנָי אֱלֹהֶיךָ נֹתֵן לְךָ לִשְׁבָטֶיךָ
וְשָׁפְטוּ אֶת־הָעָם מִשְׁפַּט־צֶדֶק: לֹא־תַטֶּה מִשְׁפָּט לֹא תַכִּיר פָּנִים וְלֹא־תִקַּח שֹׁחַד כִּי
הַשֹּׁחַד יְעַוֵּר עֵינֵי חֲכָמִים וִיסַלֵּף דִּבְרֵי צַדִּיקִם: צֶדֶק צֶדֶק תִּרְדֹּף לְמַעַן תִּחְיֶה וְיָרַשְׁתָּ
אֶת־הָאָרֶץ אֲשֶׁר־יְהֹוָאֲדֹנָי אֱלֹהֶיךָ נֹתֵן לָךְ: *Levi* לֹא־תִטַּע לְךָ אֲשֵׁרָה כָּל־עֵץ
אֵצֶל מִזְבַּח יְהֹוָאֲדֹנָי אֱלֹהֶיךָ אֲשֶׁר תַּעֲשֶׂה־לָּךְ: וְלֹא־תָקִים לְךָ מַצֵּבָה אֲשֶׁר שָׂנֵא
יְהֹוָאֲדֹנָי אֱלֹהֶיךָ: לֹא־תִזְבַּח לַיהֹוָאֲדֹנָי אֱלֹהֶיךָ שׁוֹר וָשֶׂה אֲשֶׁר יִהְיֶה בוֹ מוּם
כֹּל דָּבָר רָע כִּי תוֹעֲבַת יְהֹוָאֲדֹנָי אֱלֹהֶיךָ הוּא: כִּי־יִמָּצֵא בְקִרְבְּךָ בְּאַחַד שְׁעָרֶיךָ
אֲשֶׁר־יְהֹוָאֲדֹנָי אֱלֹהֶיךָ נֹתֵן לָךְ אִישׁ אוֹ־אִשָּׁה אֲשֶׁר יַעֲשֶׂה אֶת־הָרַע
בְּעֵינֵי יְהֹוָאֲדֹנָי ־אֱלֹהֶיךָ לַעֲבֹר בְּרִיתוֹ: וַיֵּלֶךְ וַיַּעֲבֹד אֱלֹהִים אֲחֵרִים וַיִּשְׁתַּחוּ לָהֶם
וְלַשֶּׁמֶשׁ | אוֹ לַיָּרֵחַ אוֹ לְכָל־צְבָא הַשָּׁמַיִם אֲשֶׁר לֹא־צִוִּיתִי: וְהֻגַּד־לְךָ וְשָׁמָעְתָּ וְדָרַשְׁתָּ
הֵיטֵב וְהִנֵּה אֱמֶת נָכוֹן הַדָּבָר נֶעֶשְׂתָה הַתּוֹעֵבָה הַזֹּאת בְּיִשְׂרָאֵל: וְהוֹצֵאתָ אֶת־הָאִישׁ
הַהוּא אוֹ אֶת־הָאִשָּׁה הַהִוא אֲשֶׁר עָשׂוּ אֶת־הַדָּבָר הָרָע הַזֶּה אֶל־שְׁעָרֶיךָ אֶת־הָאִישׁ
אוֹ אֶת־הָאִשָּׁה וּסְקַלְתָּם בָּאֲבָנִים וָמֵתוּ: עַל־פִּי | שְׁנַיִם עֵדִים אוֹ שְׁלֹשָׁה עֵדִים יוּמַת
הַמֵּת לֹא יוּמַת עַל־פִּי עֵד אֶחָד: יַד הָעֵדִים תִּהְיֶה־בּוֹ בָרִאשֹׁנָה לַהֲמִיתוֹ וְיַד כָּל־הָעָם
בָּאַחֲרֹנָה וּבִעַרְתָּ הָרָע מִקִּרְבֶּךָ: כִּי יִפָּלֵא מִמְּךָ דָבָר לַמִּשְׁפָּט בֵּין־דָּם | לְדָם בֵּין־דִּין
לְדִין וּבֵין נֶגַע לָנֶגַע דִּבְרֵי רִיבֹת בִּשְׁעָרֶיךָ וְקַמְתָּ וְעָלִיתָ אֶל־הַמָּקוֹם אֲשֶׁר יִבְחַר
יְהֹוָאֲדֹנָי אֱלֹהֶיךָ בּוֹ: וּבָאתָ אֶל־הַכֹּהֲנִים הַלְוִיִּם וְאֶל־הַשֹּׁפֵט אֲשֶׁר יִהְיֶה בַּיָּמִים
הָהֵם וְדָרַשְׁתָּ וְהִגִּידוּ לְךָ אֵת דְּבַר הַמִּשְׁפָּט: וְעָשִׂיתָ עַל־פִּי הַדָּבָר אֲשֶׁר יַגִּידוּ לְךָ
מִן־הַמָּקוֹם הַהוּא אֲשֶׁר יִבְחַר יְהֹוָאֲדֹנָי וְשָׁמַרְתָּ לַעֲשׂוֹת כְּכֹל אֲשֶׁר יוֹרוּךָ:
Yisrael עַל־פִּי הַתּוֹרָה אֲשֶׁר יוֹרוּךָ וְעַל־הַמִּשְׁפָּט אֲשֶׁר־יֹאמְרוּ לְךָ תַּעֲשֶׂה לֹא תָסוּר
מִן־הַדָּבָר אֲשֶׁר־יַגִּידוּ לְךָ יָמִין וּשְׂמֹאל: וְהָאִישׁ אֲשֶׁר־יַעֲשֶׂה בְזָדוֹן לְבִלְתִּי
שְׁמֹעַ אֶל־הַכֹּהֵן הָעֹמֵד לְשָׁרֶת שָׁם אֶת־יְהֹוָאֲדֹנָי אֱלֹהֶיךָ אוֹ אֶל־הַשֹּׁפֵט
וּמֵת הָאִישׁ הַהוּא וּבִעַרְתָּ הָרָע מִיִּשְׂרָאֵל: וְכָל־הָעָם יִשְׁמְעוּ וְיִרָאוּ וְלֹא יְזִידוּן עוֹד:

KI TETZE

כִּי־תֵצֵא לַמִּלְחָמָה עַל־אֹיְבֶיךָ וּנְתָנוֹ יהוה^{אלהים}אלהינו אֱלֹהֶיךָ בְּיָדֶךָ וְשָׁבִיתָ שִׁבְיוֹ:
וְרָאִיתָ בַּשִּׁבְיָה אֵשֶׁת יְפַת־תֹּאַר וְחָשַׁקְתָּ בָהּ וְלָקַחְתָּ לְךָ לְאִשָּׁה: וַהֲבֵאתָהּ אֶל־תּוֹךְ
בֵּיתֶךָ וְגִלְּחָה אֶת־רֹאשָׁהּ וְעָשְׂתָה אֶת־צִפָּרְנֶיהָ: וְהֵסִירָה אֶת־שִׂמְלַת שִׁבְיָהּ מֵעָלֶיהָ
וְיָשְׁבָה בְּבֵיתֶךָ וּבָכְתָה אֶת־אָבִיהָ וְאֶת־אִמָּהּ יֶרַח יָמִים וְאַחַר כֵּן תָּבוֹא אֵלֶיהָ וּבְעַלְתָּהּ
וְהָיְתָה לְךָ לְאִשָּׁה: וְהָיָה אִם־לֹא חָפַצְתָּ בָּהּ וְשִׁלַּחְתָּהּ לְנַפְשָׁהּ וּמָכֹר לֹא־תִמְכְּרֶנָּה
בַּכָּסֶף לֹא־תִתְעַמֵּר בָּהּ תַּחַת אֲשֶׁר עִנִּיתָהּ: *Levi* כִּי־תִהְיֶיןָ לְאִישׁ שְׁתֵּי נָשִׁים הָאַחַת
אֲהוּבָה וְהָאַחַת שְׂנוּאָה וְיָלְדוּ־לוֹ בָנִים הָאֲהוּבָה וְהַשְּׂנוּאָה וְהָיָה הַבֵּן הַבְּכוֹר לַשְּׂנִיאָה:
וְהָיָה בְּיוֹם הַנְחִילוֹ אֶת־בָּנָיו אֵת אֲשֶׁר־יִהְיֶה לוֹ לֹא יוּכַל לְבַכֵּר אֶת־בֶּן־הָאֲהוּבָה
עַל־פְּנֵי בֶן־הַשְּׂנוּאָה הַבְּכֹר: כִּי אֶת־הַבְּכֹר בֶּן־הַשְּׂנוּאָה יַכִּיר לָתֶת לוֹ פִּי שְׁנַיִם
בְּכֹל אֲשֶׁר־יִמָּצֵא לוֹ כִּי־הוּא רֵאשִׁית אֹנוֹ לוֹ מִשְׁפַּט הַבְּכֹרָה: *Yisrael* כִּי־יִהְיֶה לְאִישׁ
בֵּן סוֹרֵר וּמוֹרֶה אֵינֶנּוּ שֹׁמֵעַ בְּקוֹל אָבִיו וּבְקוֹל אִמּוֹ וְיִסְּרוּ אֹתוֹ וְלֹא יִשְׁמַע אֲלֵיהֶם:
וְתָפְשׂוּ בוֹ אָבִיו וְאִמּוֹ וְהוֹצִיאוּ אֹתוֹ אֶל־זִקְנֵי עִירוֹ וְאֶל־שַׁעַר מְקֹמוֹ: וְאָמְרוּ
אֶל־זִקְנֵי עִירוֹ בְּנֵנוּ זֶה סוֹרֵר וּמֹרֶה אֵינֶנּוּ שֹׁמֵעַ בְּקֹלֵנוּ זוֹלֵל וְסֹבֵא: וּרְגָמֻהוּ
כָּל־אַנְשֵׁי עִירוֹ בָאֲבָנִים וָמֵת וּבִעַרְתָּ הָרָע מִקִּרְבֶּךָ וְכָל־יִשְׂרָאֵל יִשְׁמְעוּ וְיִרָאוּ:

KI TAVO

וְהָיָה כִּי־תָבוֹא אֶל־הָאָרֶץ אֲשֶׁר יהוה^{אלהים}אלהינו אֱלֹהֶיךָ נֹתֵן לְךָ נַחֲלָה וִירִשְׁתָּהּ
וְיָשַׁבְתָּ בָּהּ: וְלָקַחְתָּ מֵרֵאשִׁית | כָּל־פְּרִי הָאֲדָמָה אֲשֶׁר תָּבִיא מֵאַרְצְךָ
אֲשֶׁר יהוה^{אלהים}אלהינו אֱלֹהֶיךָ נֹתֵן לָךְ וְשַׂמְתָּ בַטֶּנֶא וְהָלַכְתָּ אֶל־הַמָּקוֹם אֲשֶׁר יִבְחַר
יהוה^{אלהים}אלהינו אֱלֹהֶיךָ לְשַׁכֵּן שְׁמוֹ שָׁם: וּבָאתָ אֶל־הַכֹּהֵן אֲשֶׁר יִהְיֶה בַּיָּמִים הָהֵם
וְאָמַרְתָּ אֵלָיו הִגַּדְתִּי הַיּוֹם לַיהוה^{אלהים}אלהינו אֱלֹהֶיךָ כִּי־בָאתִי אֶל־הָאָרֶץ אֲשֶׁר נִשְׁבַּע
יהוה^{אלהים}אלהינו לַאֲבֹתֵינוּ לָתֶת לָנוּ: *Levi* וְלָקַח הַכֹּהֵן הַטֶּנֶא מִיָּדֶךָ וְהִנִּיחוֹ לִפְנֵי
מִזְבַּח יהוה^{אלהים}אלהינו אֱלֹהֶיךָ: וְעָנִיתָ וְאָמַרְתָּ לִפְנֵי | יהוה^{אלהים}אלהינו אֱלֹהֶיךָ
אֲרַמִּי אֹבֵד אָבִי וַיֵּרֶד מִצְרַיְמָה וַיָּגָר שָׁם בִּמְתֵי מְעָט וַיְהִי־שָׁם לְגוֹי גָּדוֹל עָצוּם וָרָב:
וַיָּרֵעוּ אֹתָנוּ הַמִּצְרִים וַיְעַנּוּנוּ וַיִּתְּנוּ עָלֵינוּ עֲבֹדָה קָשָׁה: וַנִּצְעַק אֶל־יהוה^{אלהים}אלהינו אֱלֹהֵי
אֲבֹתֵינוּ וַיִּשְׁמַע יהוה^{אלהים}אלהינו אֶת־קֹלֵנוּ וַיַּרְא אֶת־עָנְיֵנוּ וְאֶת־עֲמָלֵנוּ וְאֶת־לַחֲצֵנוּ:
וַיּוֹצִאֵנוּ יהוה^{אלהים}אלהינו מִמִּצְרַיִם בְּיָד חֲזָקָה וּבִזְרֹעַ נְטוּיָה וּבְמֹרָא גָּדֹל וּבְאֹתוֹת
וּבְמֹפְתִים: וַיְבִאֵנוּ אֶל־הַמָּקוֹם הַזֶּה וַיִּתֶּן־לָנוּ אֶת־הָאָרֶץ הַזֹּאת אֶרֶץ זָבַת חָלָב וּדְבָשׁ:
וְעַתָּה הִנֵּה הֵבֵאתִי אֶת־רֵאשִׁית פְּרִי הָאֲדָמָה אֲשֶׁר־נָתַתָּה לִּי יהוה^{אלהים}אלהינו
וְהִנַּחְתּוֹ לִפְנֵי יהוה^{אלהים}אלהינו אֱלֹהֶיךָ וְהִשְׁתַּחֲוִיתָ לִפְנֵי יהוה^{אלהים}אלהינו אֱלֹהֶיךָ:
וְשָׂמַחְתָּ בְכָל־הַטּוֹב אֲשֶׁר נָתַן־לְךָ יהוה^{אלהים}אלהינו אֱלֹהֶיךָ וּלְבֵיתֶךָ אַתָּה וְהַלֵּוִי
וְהַגֵּר אֲשֶׁר בְּקִרְבֶּךָ: *Yisrael* כִּי תְכַלֶּה לַעְשֵׂר אֶת־כָּל־מַעְשַׂר תְּבוּאָתְךָ בַּשָּׁנָה
הַשְּׁלִישִׁת שְׁנַת הַמַּעֲשֵׂר וְנָתַתָּה לַלֵּוִי לַגֵּר לַיָּתוֹם וְלָאַלְמָנָה וְאָכְלוּ בִשְׁעָרֶיךָ וְשָׂבֵעוּ:
וְאָמַרְתָּ לִפְנֵי יהוה^{אלהים}אלהינו אֱלֹהֶיךָ בִּעַרְתִּי הַקֹּדֶשׁ מִן־הַבַּיִת וְגַם נְתַתִּיו לַלֵּוִי וְלַגֵּר
לַיָּתוֹם וְלָאַלְמָנָה כְּכָל־מִצְוָתְךָ אֲשֶׁר צִוִּיתָנִי לֹא־עָבַרְתִּי מִמִּצְוֹתֶיךָ וְלֹא שָׁכָחְתִּי:

לֹא־אָכַלְתִּי בְאֹנִי מִמֶּנּוּ וְלֹא־בִעַרְתִּי מִמֶּנּוּ בְּטָמֵא וְלֹא־נָתַתִּי מִמֶּנּוּ לְמֵת שָׁמַעְתִּי בְּקוֹל יְהֹוָהֱלֹהִיאהדונהי אֱלֹהָי עָשִׂיתִי כְּכֹל אֲשֶׁר צִוִּיתָנִי: הַשְׁקִיפָה מִמְּעוֹן קָדְשְׁךָ מִן־הַשָּׁמַיִם וּבָרֵךְ אֶת־עַמְּךָ אֶת־יִשְׂרָאֵל וְאֵת הָאֲדָמָה אֲשֶׁר נָתַתָּה לָנוּ כַּאֲשֶׁר נִשְׁבַּעְתָּ לַאֲבֹתֵינוּ אֶרֶץ זָבַת חָלָב וּדְבָשׁ:

NITZAVIM

אַתֶּם נִצָּבִים הַיּוֹם כֻּלְּכֶם לִפְנֵי יְהֹוָהֱלֹהִיאהדונהי אֱלֹהֵיכֶם רָאשֵׁיכֶם שִׁבְטֵיכֶם זִקְנֵיכֶם וְשֹׁטְרֵיכֶם כֹּל אִישׁ יִשְׂרָאֵל: טַפְּכֶם נְשֵׁיכֶם וְגֵרְךָ אֲשֶׁר בְּקֶרֶב מַחֲנֶיךָ מֵחֹטֵב עֵצֶיךָ עַד שֹׁאֵב מֵימֶיךָ: לְעָבְרְךָ בִּבְרִית יְהֹוָהֱלֹהִיאהדונהי אֱלֹהֶיךָ וּבְאָלָתוֹ אֲשֶׁר יְהֹוָהֱלֹהִיאהדונהי אֱלֹהֶיךָ כֹּרֵת עִמְּךָ הַיּוֹם: Levi לְמַעַן הָקִים־אֹתְךָ הַיּוֹם | לוֹ לְעָם וְהוּא יִהְיֶה־לְּךָ לֵאלֹהִים כַּאֲשֶׁר דִּבֶּר־לָךְ וְכַאֲשֶׁר נִשְׁבַּע לַאֲבֹתֶיךָ לְאַבְרָהָם לְיִצְחָק וּלְיַעֲקֹב: וְלֹא אִתְּכֶם לְבַדְּכֶם אָנֹכִי כֹּרֵת אֶת־הַבְּרִית הַזֹּאת וְאֶת־הָאָלָה הַזֹּאת: כִּי אֶת־אֲשֶׁר יֶשְׁנוֹ פֹּה עִמָּנוּ עֹמֵד הַיּוֹם לִפְנֵי יְהֹוָהֱלֹהִיאהדונהי אֱלֹהֵינוּ וְאֵת אֲשֶׁר אֵינֶנּוּ פֹּה עִמָּנוּ הַיּוֹם: Yisrael כִּי־אַתֶּם יְדַעְתֶּם אֵת אֲשֶׁר־יָשַׁבְנוּ בְּאֶרֶץ מִצְרָיִם וְאֵת אֲשֶׁר־עָבַרְנוּ בְּקֶרֶב הַגּוֹיִם אֲשֶׁר עֲבַרְתֶּם: וַתִּרְאוּ אֶת־שִׁקּוּצֵיהֶם וְאֵת גִּלֻּלֵיהֶם עֵץ וָאֶבֶן כֶּסֶף וְזָהָב אֲשֶׁר עִמָּהֶם: פֶּן־יֵשׁ בָּכֶם אִישׁ אוֹ־אִשָּׁה אוֹ מִשְׁפָּחָה אוֹ־שֵׁבֶט אֲשֶׁר לְבָבוֹ פֹנֶה הַיּוֹם מֵעִם יְהֹוָהֱלֹהִיאהדונהי אֱלֹהֵינוּ לָלֶכֶת לַעֲבֹד אֶת־אֱלֹהֵי הַגּוֹיִם הָהֵם פֶּן־יֵשׁ בָּכֶם שֹׁרֶשׁ פֹּרֶה רֹאשׁ וְלַעֲנָה: וְהָיָה בְּשָׁמְעוֹ אֶת־דִּבְרֵי הָאָלָה הַזֹּאת וְהִתְבָּרֵךְ בִּלְבָבוֹ לֵאמֹר שָׁלוֹם יִהְיֶה־לִּי כִּי בִּשְׁרִרוּת לִבִּי אֵלֵךְ לְמַעַן סְפוֹת הָרָוָה אֶת־הַצְּמֵאָה: לֹא־יֹאבֶה יְהֹוָהֱלֹהִיאהדונהי סְלֹחַ לוֹ כִּי אָז יֶעְשַׁן אַף־יְהֹוָהֱלֹהִיאהדונהי וְקִנְאָתוֹ בָּאִישׁ הַהוּא וְרָבְצָה בּוֹ כָּל־הָאָלָה הַכְּתוּבָה בַּסֵּפֶר הַזֶּה וּמָחָה יְהֹוָהֱלֹהִיאהדונהי אֶת־שְׁמוֹ מִתַּחַת הַשָּׁמָיִם: וְהִבְדִּילוֹ יְהֹוָהֱלֹהִיאהדונהי לְרָעָה מִכֹּל שִׁבְטֵי יִשְׂרָאֵל כְּכֹל אָלוֹת הַבְּרִית הַכְּתוּבָה בְּסֵפֶר הַתּוֹרָה הַזֶּה: וְאָמַר הַדּוֹר הָאַחֲרוֹן בְּנֵיכֶם אֲשֶׁר יָקוּמוּ מֵאַחֲרֵיכֶם וְהַנָּכְרִי אֲשֶׁר יָבֹא מֵאֶרֶץ רְחוֹקָה וְרָאוּ אֶת־מַכּוֹת הָאָרֶץ הַהִוא וְאֶת־תַּחֲלֻאֶיהָ אֲשֶׁר־חִלָּה יְהֹוָהֱלֹהִיאהדונהי בָּהּ: גָּפְרִית וָמֶלַח שְׂרֵפָה כָל־אַרְצָהּ לֹא תִזָּרַע וְלֹא תַצְמִחַ וְלֹא־יַעֲלֶה בָהּ כָּל־עֵשֶׂב כְּמַהְפֵּכַת סְדֹם וַעֲמֹרָה אַדְמָה וּצְבֹיִים אֲשֶׁר הָפַךְ יְהֹוָהֱלֹהִיאהדונהי בְּאַפּוֹ וּבַחֲמָתוֹ: וְאָמְרוּ כָּל־הַגּוֹיִם עַל־מֶה עָשָׂה יְהֹוָהֱלֹהִיאהדונהי כָּכָה לָאָרֶץ הַזֹּאת מֶה חֳרִי הָאַף הַגָּדוֹל הַזֶּה: וְאָמְרוּ עַל אֲשֶׁר עָזְבוּ אֶת־בְּרִית יְהֹוָהֱלֹהִיאהדונהי אֱלֹהֵי אֲבֹתָם אֲשֶׁר כָּרַת עִמָּם בְּהוֹצִיאוֹ אֹתָם מֵאֶרֶץ מִצְרָיִם: וַיֵּלְכוּ וַיַּעַבְדוּ אֱלֹהִים אֲחֵרִים וַיִּשְׁתַּחֲווּ לָהֶם אֱלֹהִים אֲשֶׁר לֹא־יְדָעוּם וְלֹא חָלַק לָהֶם: וַיִּחַר־אַף יְהֹוָהֱלֹהִיאהדונהי בָּאָרֶץ הַהִוא לְהָבִיא עָלֶיהָ אֶת־כָּל־הַקְּלָלָה הַכְּתוּבָה בַּסֵּפֶר הַזֶּה: וַיִּתְּשֵׁם יְהֹוָהֱלֹהִיאהדונהי מֵעַל אַדְמָתָם בְּאַף וּבְחֵמָה וּבְקֶצֶף גָּדוֹל וַיַּשְׁלִכֵם אֶל־אֶרֶץ אַחֶרֶת כַּיּוֹם הַזֶּה: הַנִּסְתָּרֹת לַיהֹוָהֱלֹהִיאהדונהי אֱלֹהֵינוּ וְהַנִּגְלֹת לָנוּ וּלְבָנֵינוּ עַד־עוֹלָם לַעֲשׂוֹת אֶת־כָּל־דִּבְרֵי הַתּוֹרָה הַזֹּאת:

TORAH READING

VAYELECH

וַיֵּ֖לֶךְ מֹשֶׁ֑ה וַיְדַבֵּ֛ר אֶת־הַדְּבָרִ֥ים הָאֵ֖לֶּה אֶל־כׇּל־יִשְׂרָאֵֽל׃ וַיֹּ֣אמֶר אֲלֵהֶ֗ם בֶּן־מֵאָה֩
וְעֶשְׂרִ֨ים שָׁנָ֤ה אָנֹכִי֙ הַיּ֔וֹם לֹא־אוּכַ֥ל ע֖וֹד לָצֵ֣את וְלָב֑וֹא וַיהוָֽה־אֲדֹנָי אָמַ֣ר אֵלַ֔י לֹ֥א
תַעֲבֹ֖ר אֶת־הַיַּרְדֵּ֥ן הַזֶּֽה׃ יְהוָֽה־אֲדֹנָי אֱלֹהֶ֜יךָ ה֣וּא ׀ עֹבֵ֣ר לְפָנֶ֗יךָ הֽוּא־יַשְׁמִ֞יד
אֶת־הַגּוֹיִ֥ם הָאֵ֛לֶּה מִלְּפָנֶ֖יךָ וִֽירִשְׁתָּ֑ם יְהוֹשֻׁ֗עַ ה֚וּא עֹבֵ֣ר לְפָנֶ֔יךָ כַּאֲשֶׁ֖ר דִּבֶּ֥ר
יְהוָֽה־אֲדֹנָי׃ *Levi* וְעָשָׂ֤ה יְהוָֽה־אֲדֹנָי לָהֶ֔ם כַּאֲשֶׁ֣ר עָשָׂ֗ה לְסִיח֤וֹן וּלְע֙וֹג֙ מַלְכֵ֣י
הָאֱמֹרִ֔י וּלְאַרְצָ֖ם אֲשֶׁ֣ר הִשְׁמִ֣יד אֹתָֽם׃ וּנְתָנָ֥ם יְהוָֽה־אֲדֹנָי לִפְנֵיכֶ֑ם וַעֲשִׂיתֶ֣ם לָהֶ֔ם
כְּכׇ֨ל־הַמִּצְוָ֔ה אֲשֶׁ֥ר צִוִּ֖יתִי אֶתְכֶֽם׃ חִזְק֣וּ וְאִמְצ֔וּ אַל־תִּֽירְא֥וּ וְאַל־תַּֽעַרְצ֖וּ מִפְּנֵיהֶ֑ם כִּ֣י ׀
יְהוָֽה־אֲדֹנָי אֱלֹהֶ֗יךָ ה֚וּא הַהֹלֵ֣ךְ עִמָּ֔ךְ לֹ֥א יַרְפְּךָ֖ וְלֹ֥א יַֽעַזְבֶֽךָּ׃ *Yisrael* וַיִּקְרָ֨א מֹשֶׁ֜ה
לִיהוֹשֻׁ֗עַ וַיֹּ֨אמֶר אֵלָ֜יו לְעֵינֵ֣י כׇל־יִשְׂרָאֵל֮ חֲזַ֣ק וֶֽאֱמָץ֒ כִּ֣י אַתָּ֗ה תָּבוֹא֙ אֶת־הָעָ֣ם הַזֶּ֔ה
אֶל־הָאָ֕רֶץ אֲשֶׁ֨ר נִשְׁבַּ֧ע יְהוָֽה־אֲדֹנָי לַאֲבֹתָ֖ם לָתֵ֣ת לָהֶ֑ם וְאַתָּ֖ה תַּנְחִילֶ֥נָּה אוֹתָֽם׃
וַֽיהוָֽה־אֲדֹנָי ה֣וּא ׀ הַהֹלֵ֣ךְ לְפָנֶ֗יךָ ה֚וּא יִהְיֶ֣ה עִמָּ֔ךְ לֹ֥א יַרְפְּךָ֖ וְלֹ֣א יַֽעַזְבֶ֑ךָּ לֹ֥א תִירָ֖א
וְלֹ֥א תֵחָֽת׃ וַיִּכְתֹּ֣ב מֹשֶׁה֮ אֶת־הַתּוֹרָ֣ה הַזֹּאת֒ וַֽיִּתְּנָ֗הּ אֶל־הַכֹּהֲנִים֙ בְּנֵ֣י לֵוִ֔י הַנֹּ֣שְׂאִ֔ים
אֶת־אֲר֖וֹן בְּרִ֣ית יְהוָֽה־אֲדֹנָי וְאֶל־כׇּל־זִקְנֵ֥י יִשְׂרָאֵֽל׃ וַיְצַ֥ו מֹשֶׁ֖ה אוֹתָ֣ם לֵאמֹ֑ר מִקֵּ֣ץ ׀
שֶׁ֣בַע שָׁנִ֗ים בְּמֹעֵ֛ד שְׁנַ֥ת הַשְּׁמִטָּ֖ה בְּחַ֥ג הַסֻּכּֽוֹת׃ בְּב֣וֹא כׇל־יִשְׂרָאֵ֗ל לֵרָאוֹת֙ אֶת־פְּנֵי֙
יְהוָֽה־אֲדֹנָי אֱלֹהֶ֔יךָ בַּמָּק֖וֹם אֲשֶׁ֣ר יִבְחָ֑ר תִּקְרָ֞א אֶת־הַתּוֹרָ֥ה הַזֹּ֛את נֶ֥גֶד כׇּל־יִשְׂרָאֵ֖ל
בְּאׇזְנֵיהֶֽם׃ הַקְהֵ֣ל אֶת־הָעָ֗ם הָאֲנָשִׁ֤ים וְהַנָּשִׁים֙ וְהַטַּ֔ף וְגֵרְךָ֖ אֲשֶׁ֣ר בִּשְׁעָרֶ֑יךָ לְמַ֨עַן יִשְׁמְע֜וּ
וּלְמַ֣עַן יִלְמְד֗וּ וְיָֽרְאוּ֙ אֶת־יְהוָֽה־אֲדֹנָי אֱלֹֽהֵיכֶ֔ם וְשָֽׁמְר֣וּ לַעֲשׂ֔וֹת אֶת־כׇּל־דִּבְרֵ֖י הַתּוֹרָ֥ה
הַזֹּֽאת׃ וּבְנֵיהֶ֞ם אֲשֶׁ֣ר לֹֽא־יָדְע֗וּ יִשְׁמְעוּ֙ וְלָ֣מְד֔וּ לְיִרְאָ֖ה אֶת־יְהוָֽה־אֲדֹנָי אֱלֹהֵיכֶ֑ם כׇּל־
הַיָּמִ֗ים אֲשֶׁ֨ר אַתֶּ֤ם חַיִּים֙ עַל־הָ֣אֲדָמָ֔ה אֲשֶׁ֨ר אַתֶּ֜ם עֹבְרִ֧ים אֶת־הַיַּרְדֵּ֛ן שָׁ֖מָּה לְרִשְׁתָּֽהּ׃

HA'AZINU

אִמְרֵי־פִֽי׃	הָאָ֑רֶץ	וְתִשְׁמַ֥ע	וַאֲדַבֵּ֑רָה	הַשָּׁמַ֖יִם	הַאֲזִ֥ינוּ
אִמְרָתִ֔י	כַּטַּל֙	תִּזַּ֤ל	לִקְחִ֔י	כַּמָּטָר֙	יַעֲרֹ֤ף
עֲלֵי־עֵֽשֶׂב׃	וְכִרְבִיבִ֖ים		עֲלֵי־דֶ֔שֶׁא	כִּשְׂעִירִם֙	
Levi	לֵאלֹהֵֽינוּ׃	גֹּ֖דֶל	הָב֥וּ	אֶקְרָ֑א	יְהוָֽה־אֲדֹנָי שֵׁ֣ם	כִּ֥י
מִשְׁפָּ֔ט	כׇּל־דְּרָכָ֣יו	כִּ֤י	פׇּעֳל֔וֹ	תָּמִ֣ים	הַצּוּר֙
הֽוּא׃	וְיָשָׁ֖ר	צַדִּ֥יק	עָ֔וֶל	וְאֵ֣ין	אֱמוּנָה֙	אֵ֤ל
וּפְתַלְתֹּֽל׃	עִקֵּ֥שׁ	דּ֖וֹר	מוּמָ֑ם	בָּנָ֖יו	לֹ֥א	שִׁחֵ֥ת
וְכֶ֔ם	וְלֹ֣א	נָבָ֖ל	עַ֥ם	תִּגְמְלוּ־זֹ֔את	הֲלַֽיהוָֽה־אֲדֹנָי	
Yisrael	וַֽיְכֹנְנֶֽךָ׃	עָֽשְׂךָ֖	ה֥וּא	קָּנֶ֔ךָ	אָבִ֣יךָ	הֲלוֹא־ה֤וּא
דֹר־וָדֹ֑ר	שְׁנ֣וֹת	בִּ֖ינוּ	עוֹלָ֔ם	יְמ֣וֹת	זְכֹר֙
לָֽךְ׃	וְיֹ֣אמְרוּ	זְקֵנֶ֖יךָ	וְיַגֵּ֔דְךָ	אָבִ֙יךָ֙	שְׁאַ֤ל
אָדָ֑ם	בְּנֵ֣י	בְּהַפְרִיד֖וֹ	גּוֹיִ֔ם	עֶלְיוֹן֙	בְּהַנְחֵ֤ל
יִשְׂרָאֵֽל׃	בְּנֵ֥י	לְמִסְפַּ֖ר	עַמִּ֔ים	גְּבֻלֹ֣ת	יַצֵּב֙
נַחֲלָתֽוֹ׃	חֶ֖בֶל	יַעֲקֹ֔ב	עַמּ֑וֹ	יְהוָֽה־אֲדֹנָי	כִּ֛י	וְזֶ֗לֶק

יִשְׂמַן	יֶלֶל	וּבְתֹהוּ	מִדְבָּר	בְּאֶרֶץ		יִמְצָאֵהוּ
עֵינוֹ		כְּאִישׁוֹן	יִצְּרֶנְהוּ	יְבוֹנְנֵהוּ		יְסֹבְבֶנְהוּ
יְרַחֵף		עַל־גּוֹזָלָיו	קִנּוֹ	יָעִיר	כְּנֶשֶׁר	
עַל־אֶבְרָתוֹ:			יִשָּׂאֵהוּ	יִקָּחֵהוּ	כְּנָפָיו	יִפְרֹשׂ
נֵכָר:	אֵל	עִמּוֹ	וְאֵין	יַנְחֶנּוּ	בָּדָד	יְהֹוָה

VEZOT HABERACHA

וְזֹאת הַבְּרָכָה אֲשֶׁר בֵּרַךְ מֹשֶׁה אִישׁ הָאֱלֹהִים אֶת־בְּנֵי יִשְׂרָאֵל לִפְנֵי מוֹתוֹ: וַיֹּאמַר
יְהֹוָה מִסִּינַי בָּא וְזָרַח מִשֵּׂעִיר לָמוֹ הוֹפִיעַ מֵהַר פָּארָן וְאָתָה מֵרִבְבֹת קֹדֶשׁ
מִימִינוֹ אֵשׁ דָּת (כתיב: אשדת) לָמוֹ: אַף חֹבֵב עַמִּים כָּל־קְדֹשָׁיו בְּיָדֶךָ וְהֵם תֻּכּוּ לְרַגְלֶךָ
יִשָּׂא מִדַּבְּרֹתֶיךָ: תּוֹרָה צִוָּה־לָנוּ מֹשֶׁה מוֹרָשָׁה קְהִלַּת יַעֲקֹב: וַיְהִי בִישֻׁרוּן מֶלֶךְ
בְּהִתְאַסֵּף רָאשֵׁי עָם יַחַד שִׁבְטֵי יִשְׂרָאֵל: יְחִי רְאוּבֵן וְאַל־יָמֹת וִיהִי מְתָיו מִסְפָּר:
וְזֹאת לִיהוּדָה וַיֹּאמַר שְׁמַע יְהֹוָה קוֹל יְהוּדָה וְאֶל־עַמּוֹ תְּבִיאֶנּוּ יָדָיו רָב לוֹ
וְעֵזֶר מִצָּרָיו תִּהְיֶה: Levi וּלְלֵוִי אָמַר תֻּמֶּיךָ וְאוּרֶיךָ לְאִישׁ חֲסִידֶךָ אֲשֶׁר נִסִּיתוֹ בְּמַסָּה
תְּרִיבֵהוּ עַל־מֵי מְרִיבָה: הָאֹמֵר לְאָבִיו וּלְאִמּוֹ לֹא רְאִיתִיו וְאֶת־אֶחָיו לֹא הִכִּיר
וְאֶת־בָּנָו לֹא יָדָע כִּי שָׁמְרוּ אִמְרָתֶךָ וּבְרִיתְךָ יִנְצֹרוּ: יוֹרוּ מִשְׁפָּטֶיךָ לְיַעֲקֹב וְתוֹרָתְךָ
לְיִשְׂרָאֵל יָשִׂימוּ קְטוֹרָה בְּאַפֶּךָ וְכָלִיל עַל־מִזְבְּחֶךָ: בָּרֵךְ יְהֹוָה חֵילוֹ וּפֹעַל יָדָיו
תִּרְצֶה מְחַץ מָתְנַיִם קָמָיו וּמְשַׂנְאָיו מִן־יְקוּמוּן: לְבִנְיָמִן אָמַר יְדִיד יְהֹוָה יִשְׁכֹּן
לָבֶטַח עָלָיו חֹפֵף עָלָיו כָּל־הַיּוֹם וּבֵין כְּתֵפָיו שָׁכֵן: Yisrael וּלְיוֹסֵף אָמַר מְבֹרֶכֶת
יְהֹוָה אַרְצוֹ מִמֶּגֶד שָׁמַיִם מִטָּל וּמִתְּהוֹם רֹבֶצֶת תָּחַת: וּמִמֶּגֶד תְּבוּאֹת שָׁמֶשׁ
וּמִמֶּגֶד גֶּרֶשׁ יְרָחִים: וּמֵרֹאשׁ הַרְרֵי־קֶדֶם וּמִמֶּגֶד גִּבְעוֹת עוֹלָם: וּמִמֶּגֶד אֶרֶץ וּמְלֹאָהּ
וּרְצוֹן שֹׁכְנִי סְנֶה תָּבוֹאתָה לְרֹאשׁ יוֹסֵף וּלְקָדְקֹד נְזִיר אֶחָיו: בְּכוֹר שׁוֹרוֹ הָדָר לוֹ וְקַרְנֵי
רְאֵם קַרְנָיו בָּהֶם עַמִּים יְנַגַּח יַחְדָּו אַפְסֵי־אָרֶץ וְהֵם רִבְבוֹת אֶפְרַיִם וְהֵם אַלְפֵי מְנַשֶּׁה:

READING FOR ROSH CHODESH (NUMBERS 28:1-15)

וַיְדַבֵּר יְהֹוָה אֶל־מֹשֶׁה לֵּאמֹר: צַו אֶת־בְּנֵי יִשְׂרָאֵל וְאָמַרְתָּ אֲלֵהֶם
אֶת־קָרְבָּנִי לַחְמִי לְאִשַּׁי רֵיחַ נִיחֹחִי תִּשְׁמְרוּ לְהַקְרִיב לִי בְּמוֹעֲדוֹ: Levi starts
וְאָמַרְתָּ לָהֶם זֶה הָאִשֶּׁה אֲשֶׁר תַּקְרִיבוּ לַיהֹוָה כְּבָשִׂים בְּנֵי־שָׁנָה תְמִימִם
שְׁנַיִם לַיּוֹם עֹלָה תָמִיד: Kohen ends (for second aliya start from the former verse "ve'amarta lahem")
אֶת־הַכֶּבֶשׂ אֶחָד תַּעֲשֶׂה בַבֹּקֶר וְאֵת הַכֶּבֶשׂ הַשֵּׁנִי תַּעֲשֶׂה בֵּין הָעַרְבָּיִם:
וַעֲשִׂירִית הָאֵיפָה סֹלֶת לְמִנְחָה בְּלוּלָה בְּשֶׁמֶן כָּתִית רְבִיעִת הַהִין: Yisrael
עֹלַת תָּמִיד הָעֲשֻׂיָה בְּהַר סִינַי לְרֵיחַ נִיחֹחַ אִשֶּׁה לַיהֹוָה: וְנִסְכּוֹ רְבִיעִת הַהִין
לַכֶּבֶשׂ הָאֶחָד בַּקֹּדֶשׁ הַסֵּךְ נֶסֶךְ שֵׁכָר לַיהֹוָה: וְאֵת הַכֶּבֶשׂ הַשֵּׁנִי תַּעֲשֶׂה
בֵּין הָעַרְבָּיִם כְּמִנְחַת הַבֹּקֶר וּכְנִסְכּוֹ תַּעֲשֶׂה אִשֵּׁה רֵיחַ נִיחֹחַ לַיהֹוָה:
וּבְיוֹם הַשַּׁבָּת שְׁנֵי־כְבָשִׂים בְּנֵי־שָׁנָה תְּמִימִם וּשְׁנֵי עֶשְׂרֹנִים סֹלֶת מִנְחָה בְּלוּלָה
בַשֶּׁמֶן וְנִסְכּוֹ: Forth Aliya עֹלַת שַׁבַּת בְּשַׁבַּתּוֹ עַל־עֹלַת הַתָּמִיד וְנִסְכָּהּ:

וּבְרָאשֵׁי חָדְשֵׁיכֶם תַּקְרִיבוּ עֹלָה לַיהוָֹהֱאלֹהִים פָּרִים בְּנֵי־בָקָר שְׁנַיִם
וְאַיִל אֶחָד כְּבָשִׂים בְּנֵי־שָׁנָה שִׁבְעָה תְּמִימִם: וּשְׁלֹשָׁה עֶשְׂרֹנִים סֹלֶת מִנְחָה
בְּלוּלָה בַשֶּׁמֶן לַפָּר הָאֶחָד וּשְׁנֵי עֶשְׂרֹנִים סֹלֶת מִנְחָה בְּלוּלָה בַשֶּׁמֶן
לָאַיִל הָאֶחָד: וְעִשָּׂרֹן עִשָּׂרוֹן סֹלֶת מִנְחָה בְּלוּלָה בַשֶּׁמֶן לַכֶּבֶשׂ הָאֶחָד עֹלָה
רֵיחַ נִיחֹחַ אִשֶּׁה לַיהוָֹהֱאלֹהִים: וְנִסְכֵּיהֶם חֲצִי הַהִין יִהְיֶה לַפָּר וּשְׁלִישִׁת
הַהִין לָאַיִל וּרְבִיעִת הַהִין לַכֶּבֶשׂ יָיִן זֹאת עֹלַת חֹדֶשׁ בְּחָדְשׁוֹ לְחָדְשֵׁי הַשָּׁנָה:
וּשְׂעִיר עִזִּים אֶחָד לְחַטָּאת לַיהוָֹהֱאלֹהִים עַל־עֹלַת הַתָּמִיד יֵעָשֶׂה וְנִסְכּוֹ:

READING FOR CHANUKAH (NUMBERS 6:22-8:4)
FIRST DAY

וַיְדַבֵּר יְהוָֹהֱאלֹהִים אֶל־מֹשֶׁה לֵּאמֹר: דַּבֵּר אֶל־אַהֲרֹן וְאֶל־בָּנָיו לֵאמֹר כֹּה תְבָרֲכוּ
אֶת־בְּנֵי יִשְׂרָאֵל אָמוֹר לָהֶם: יְבָרֶכְךָ יְהוָֹהֱאלֹהִים וְיִשְׁמְרֶךָ: יָאֵר יְהוָֹהֱאלֹהִים | פָּנָיו
אֵלֶיךָ וִיחֻנֶּךָּ: יִשָּׂא יְהוָֹהֱאלֹהִים | פָּנָיו אֵלֶיךָ וְיָשֵׂם לְךָ שָׁלוֹם: וְשָׂמוּ אֶת־שְׁמִי עַל־בְּנֵי
יִשְׂרָאֵל וַאֲנִי אֲבָרֲכֵם: וַיְהִי בְּיוֹם כַּלּוֹת מֹשֶׁה לְהָקִים אֶת־הַמִּשְׁכָּן וַיִּמְשַׁח אֹתוֹ וַיְקַדֵּשׁ
אֹתוֹ וְאֶת־כָּל־כֵּלָיו וְאֶת־הַמִּזְבֵּחַ וְאֶת־כָּל־כֵּלָיו וַיִּמְשָׁחֵם וַיְקַדֵּשׁ אֹתָם: וַיַּקְרִיבוּ נְשִׂיאֵי
יִשְׂרָאֵל רָאשֵׁי בֵּית אֲבֹתָם הֵם נְשִׂיאֵי הַמַּטֹּת הֵם הָעֹמְדִים עַל־הַפְּקֻדִים: וַיָּבִיאוּ
אֶת־קָרְבָּנָם לִפְנֵי יְהוָֹהֱאלֹהִים שֵׁשׁ־עֶגְלֹת צָב וּשְׁנֵי עָשָׂר בָּקָר עֲגָלָה עַל־שְׁנֵי
הַנְּשִׂאִים וְשׁוֹר לְאֶחָד וַיַּקְרִיבוּ אוֹתָם לִפְנֵי הַמִּשְׁכָּן: וַיֹּאמֶר יְהוָֹהֱאלֹהִים אֶל־מֹשֶׁה
לֵּאמֹר: קַח מֵאִתָּם וְהָיוּ לַעֲבֹד אֶת־עֲבֹדַת אֹהֶל מוֹעֵד וְנָתַתָּה אוֹתָם אֶל־הַלְוִיִּם אִישׁ
כְּפִי עֲבֹדָתוֹ: וַיִּקַּח מֹשֶׁה אֶת־הָעֲגָלֹת וְאֶת־הַבָּקָר וַיִּתֵּן אוֹתָם אֶל־הַלְוִיִּם: אֵת | שְׁתֵּי
הָעֲגָלוֹת וְאֵת אַרְבַּעַת הַבָּקָר נָתַן לִבְנֵי גֵרְשׁוֹן כְּפִי עֲבֹדָתָם: וְאֵת | אַרְבַּע הָעֲגָלֹת וְאֵת
שְׁמֹנַת הַבָּקָר נָתַן לִבְנֵי מְרָרִי כְּפִי עֲבֹדָתָם בְּיַד אִיתָמָר בֶּן־אַהֲרֹן הַכֹּהֵן: וְלִבְנֵי קְהָת
לֹא נָתָן כִּי־עֲבֹדַת הַקֹּדֶשׁ עֲלֵהֶם בַּכָּתֵף יִשָּׂאוּ: וַיַּקְרִיבוּ הַנְּשִׂאִים אֵת חֲנֻכַּת הַמִּזְבֵּחַ
בְּיוֹם הִמָּשַׁח אֹתוֹ וַיַּקְרִיבוּ הַנְּשִׂיאִם אֶת־קָרְבָּנָם לִפְנֵי הַמִּזְבֵּחַ: וַיֹּאמֶר יְהוָֹהֱאלֹהִים
אֶל־מֹשֶׁה נָשִׂיא אֶחָד לַיּוֹם נָשִׂיא אֶחָד לַיּוֹם יַקְרִיבוּ אֶת־קָרְבָּנָם לַחֲנֻכַּת הַמִּזְבֵּחַ: *Levi*
וַיְהִי הַמַּקְרִיב בַּיּוֹם הָרִאשׁוֹן אֶת־קָרְבָּנוֹ נַחְשׁוֹן בֶּן־עַמִּינָדָב לְמַטֵּה יְהוּדָה:
וְקָרְבָּנוֹ קַעֲרַת־כֶּסֶף אַחַת שְׁלֹשִׁים וּמֵאָה מִשְׁקָלָהּ מִזְרָק אֶחָד כֶּסֶף
שִׁבְעִים שֶׁקֶל בְּשֶׁקֶל הַקֹּדֶשׁ שְׁנֵיהֶם | מְלֵאִים סֹלֶת בְּלוּלָה בַשֶּׁמֶן לְמִנְחָה:
כַּף אַחַת עֲשָׂרָה זָהָב מְלֵאָה קְטֹרֶת: *Yisrael* פַּר אֶחָד בֶּן־בָּקָר אַיִל אֶחָד
כֶּבֶשׂ־אֶחָד בֶּן־שְׁנָתוֹ לְעֹלָה: שְׂעִיר־עִזִּים אֶחָד לְחַטָּאת: וּלְזֶבַח הַשְּׁלָמִים בָּקָר שְׁנַיִם
אֵילִם חֲמִשָּׁה עַתּוּדִים חֲמִשָּׁה כְּבָשִׂים בְּנֵי־שָׁנָה חֲמִשָּׁה זֶה קָרְבַּן נַחְשׁוֹן בֶּן־עַמִּינָדָב:

SECOND DAY (for Yisrael read from the beginning)

בַּיּוֹם הַשֵּׁנִי הִקְרִיב נְתַנְאֵל בֶּן־צוּעָר נְשִׂיא יִשָּׂשכָר: הִקְרִב אֶת־קָרְבָּנוֹ
קַעֲרַת־כֶּסֶף אַחַת שְׁלֹשִׁים וּמֵאָה מִשְׁקָלָהּ מִזְרָק אֶחָד כֶּסֶף שִׁבְעִים שֶׁקֶל
בְּשֶׁקֶל הַקֹּדֶשׁ שְׁנֵיהֶם | מְלֵאִים סֹלֶת בְּלוּלָה בַשֶּׁמֶן לְמִנְחָה: כַּף אַחַת
עֲשָׂרָה זָהָב מְלֵאָה קְטֹרֶת: *Levi* פַּר אֶחָד בֶּן־בָּקָר אַיִל אֶחָד כֶּבֶשׂ־אֶחָד
בֶּן־שְׁנָתוֹ לְעֹלָה: שְׂעִיר־עִזִּים אֶחָד לְחַטָּאת: וּלְזֶבַח הַשְּׁלָמִים בָּקָר שְׁנַיִם
אֵילִם חֲמִשָּׁה עַתֻּדִים חֲמִשָּׁה כְּבָשִׂים בְּנֵי־שָׁנָה חֲמִשָּׁה זֶה קָרְבַּן נְתַנְאֵל בֶּן־צוּעָר:

THIRD DAY (for Yisrael read from the beginning)

בַּיּוֹם הַשְּׁלִישִׁי נָשִׂיא לִבְנֵי זְבוּלֻן אֱלִיאָב בֶּן־חֵלֹן: קׇרְבָּנוֹ קַעֲרַת־כֶּסֶף אַחַת שְׁלֹשִׁים
וּמֵאָה מִשְׁקָלָהּ מִזְרָק אֶחָד כֶּסֶף שִׁבְעִים שֶׁקֶל בְּשֶׁקֶל הַקֹּדֶשׁ שְׁנֵיהֶם | מְלֵאִים סֹלֶת
בְּלוּלָה בַשֶּׁמֶן לְמִנְחָה: Levi כַּף אַחַת עֲשָׂרָה זָהָב מְלֵאָה קְטֹרֶת: פַּר אֶחָד בֶּן־בָּקָר אַיִל
אֶחָד כֶּבֶשׂ־אֶחָד בֶּן־שְׁנָתוֹ לְעֹלָה: שְׂעִיר־עִזִּים אֶחָד לְחַטָּאת: וּלְזֶבַח הַשְּׁלָמִים בָּקָר
שְׁנַיִם אֵילִם חֲמִשָּׁה עַתֻּדִים חֲמִשָּׁה כְּבָשִׂים בְּנֵי־שָׁנָה חֲמִשָּׁה זֶה קׇרְבַּן זֶה אֱלִיאָב בֶּן־חֵלֹן:

FIURTH DAY (for Yisrael read from the beginning)

בַּיּוֹם הָרְבִיעִי נָשִׂיא לִבְנֵי רְאוּבֵן אֱלִיצוּר בֶּן־שְׁדֵיאוּר: קׇרְבָּנוֹ
קַעֲרַת־כֶּסֶף אַחַת שְׁלֹשִׁים וּמֵאָה מִשְׁקָלָהּ מִזְרָק אֶחָד כֶּסֶף שִׁבְעִים שֶׁקֶל
בְּשֶׁקֶל הַקֹּדֶשׁ שְׁנֵיהֶם | מְלֵאִים סֹלֶת בְּלוּלָה בַשֶּׁמֶן לְמִנְחָה: כַּף אַחַת
עֲשָׂרָה זָהָב מְלֵאָה קְטֹרֶת: פַּר אֶחָד בֶּן־בָּקָר אַיִל אֶחָד כֶּבֶשׂ־אֶחָד Levi
בֶּן־שְׁנָתוֹ לְעֹלָה: שְׂעִיר־עִזִּים אֶחָד לְחַטָּאת: וּלְזֶבַח הַשְּׁלָמִים בָּקָר שְׁנַיִם אֵילִם
חֲמִשָּׁה עַתֻּדִים חֲמִשָּׁה כְּבָשִׂים בְּנֵי־שָׁנָה חֲמִשָּׁה זֶה קׇרְבַּן אֱלִיצוּר בֶּן־שְׁדֵיאוּר:

FIFTH DAY (for Yisrael read from the beginning)

בַּיּוֹם הַחֲמִישִׁי נָשִׂיא לִבְנֵי שִׁמְעוֹן שְׁלֻמִיאֵל בֶּן־צוּרִישַׁדָּי: קׇרְבָּנוֹ
קַעֲרַת־כֶּסֶף אַחַת שְׁלֹשִׁים וּמֵאָה מִשְׁקָלָהּ מִזְרָק אֶחָד כֶּסֶף שִׁבְעִים שֶׁקֶל
בְּשֶׁקֶל הַקֹּדֶשׁ שְׁנֵיהֶם | מְלֵאִים סֹלֶת בְּלוּלָה בַשֶּׁמֶן לְמִנְחָה: כַּף אַחַת
עֲשָׂרָה זָהָב מְלֵאָה קְטֹרֶת: פַּר אֶחָד בֶּן־בָּקָר אַיִל אֶחָד כֶּבֶשׂ־אֶחָד Levi
בֶּן־שְׁנָתוֹ לְעֹלָה: שְׂעִיר־עִזִּים אֶחָד לְחַטָּאת: וּלְזֶבַח הַשְּׁלָמִים בָּקָר שְׁנַיִם אֵילִם
חֲמִשָּׁה עַתֻּדִים חֲמִשָּׁה כְּבָשִׂים בְּנֵי־שָׁנָה חֲמִשָּׁה זֶה קׇרְבַּן שְׁלֻמִיאֵל בֶּן־צוּרִישַׁדָּי:

SIXTH DAY

(On *Rosh Chodesh*, the reading begins on page 516 – the first *aliya* until "*olah tmid*", the second *aliah* until "*veniska*", the third *aliyah* until "*venisko*" (the end of the reading for *Rosh Chodesh*)and the fourth *aliyah* will read here for *Chanukah*).

בַּיּוֹם הַשִּׁשִּׁי נָשִׂיא לִבְנֵי גָד אֶלְיָסָף בֶּן־דְּעוּאֵל: קׇרְבָּנוֹ קַעֲרַת־כֶּסֶף אַחַת שְׁלֹשִׁים וּמֵאָה
מִשְׁקָלָהּ מִזְרָק אֶחָד כֶּסֶף שִׁבְעִים שֶׁקֶל בְּשֶׁקֶל הַקֹּדֶשׁ שְׁנֵיהֶם | מְלֵאִים סֹלֶת בְּלוּלָה
בַשֶּׁמֶן לְמִנְחָה: כַּף אַחַת עֲשָׂרָה זָהָב מְלֵאָה קְטֹרֶת: פַּר אֶחָד בֶּן־בָּקָר אַיִל אֶחָד Levi
כֶּבֶשׂ־אֶחָד בֶּן־שְׁנָתוֹ לְעֹלָה: שְׂעִיר־עִזִּים אֶחָד לְחַטָּאת: וּלְזֶבַח הַשְּׁלָמִים בָּקָר שְׁנַיִם
אֵילִם חֲמִשָּׁה עַתֻּדִים חֲמִשָּׁה כְּבָשִׂים בְּנֵי־שָׁנָה חֲמִשָּׁה זֶה קׇרְבַּן אֶלְיָסָף בֶּן־דְּעוּאֵל:

SEVENTH DAY (for Yisrael read from the beginning)

(On *Rosh Chodesh*, the reading begins on page 516 – the first *aliya* until "*olah tmid*", the second *aliah* until "*veniska*", the third *aliyah* until "*venisko*" (the end of the reading for *Rosh Chodesh*)and the fourth *aliyah* will read here for *Chanukah*).

בַּיּוֹם הַשְּׁבִיעִי נָשִׂיא לִבְנֵי אֶפְרָיִם אֱלִישָׁמָע בֶּן־עַמִּיהוּד: קָרְבָּנוֹ

קַעֲרַת־כֶּסֶף אַחַת שְׁלֹשִׁים וּמֵאָה מִשְׁקָלָהּ מִזְרָק אֶחָד כֶּסֶף שִׁבְעִים

שֶׁקֶל בְּשֶׁקֶל הַקֹּדֶשׁ שְׁנֵיהֶם | מְלֵאִים סֹלֶת בְּלוּלָה בַשֶּׁמֶן לְמִנְחָה: כַּף אַחַת

עֲשָׂרָה זָהָב מְלֵאָה קְטֹרֶת: Levi פַּר אֶחָד בֶּן־בָּקָר אַיִל אֶחָד כֶּבֶשׂ־אֶחָד

בֶּן־שְׁנָתוֹ לְעֹלָה: שְׂעִיר־עִזִּים אֶחָד לְחַטָּאת: וּלְזֶבַח הַשְּׁלָמִים בָּקָר שְׁנַיִם אֵילִם

חֲמִשָּׁה עַתּוּדִים חֲמִשָּׁה כְּבָשִׂים בְּנֵי־שָׁנָה חֲמִשָּׁה זֶה קָרְבַּן אֱלִישָׁמָע בֶּן־עַמִּיהוּד:

EIGHTH DAY

בַּיּוֹם הַשְּׁמִינִי נָשִׂיא לִבְנֵי מְנַשֶּׁה גַּמְלִיאֵל בֶּן־פְּדָהצוּר: קָרְבָּנוֹ

קַעֲרַת־כֶּסֶף אַחַת שְׁלֹשִׁים וּמֵאָה מִשְׁקָלָהּ מִזְרָק אֶחָד כֶּסֶף שִׁבְעִים שֶׁקֶל

בְּשֶׁקֶל הַקֹּדֶשׁ שְׁנֵיהֶם | מְלֵאִים סֹלֶת בְּלוּלָה בַשֶּׁמֶן לְמִנְחָה: כַּף אַחַת

עֲשָׂרָה זָהָב מְלֵאָה קְטֹרֶת: Levi פַּר אֶחָד בֶּן־בָּקָר אַיִל אֶחָד כֶּבֶשׂ־אֶחָד

בֶּן־שְׁנָתוֹ לְעֹלָה: שְׂעִיר־עִזִּים אֶחָד לְחַטָּאת: וּלְזֶבַח הַשְּׁלָמִים בָּקָר שְׁנַיִם אֵילִם

חֲמִשָּׁה עַתּוּדִים חֲמִשָּׁה כְּבָשִׂים בְּנֵי־שָׁנָה חֲמִשָּׁה זֶה קָרְבַּן גַּמְלִיאֵל בֶּן־פְּדָהצוּר:

Yisrael בַּיּוֹם הַתְּשִׁיעִי נָשִׂיא לִבְנֵי בִנְיָמִן אֲבִידָן בֶּן־גִּדְעֹנִי: קָרְבָּנוֹ

קַעֲרַת־כֶּסֶף אַחַת שְׁלֹשִׁים וּמֵאָה מִשְׁקָלָהּ מִזְרָק אֶחָד כֶּסֶף שִׁבְעִים שֶׁקֶל

בְּשֶׁקֶל הַקֹּדֶשׁ שְׁנֵיהֶם | מְלֵאִים סֹלֶת בְּלוּלָה בַשֶּׁמֶן לְמִנְחָה: כַּף אַחַת

עֲשָׂרָה זָהָב מְלֵאָה קְטֹרֶת: פַּר אֶחָד בֶּן־בָּקָר אַיִל אֶחָד כֶּבֶשׂ־אֶחָד בֶּן־שְׁנָתוֹ לְעֹלָה:

שְׂעִיר־עִזִּים אֶחָד לְחַטָּאת: וּלְזֶבַח הַשְּׁלָמִים בָּקָר שְׁנַיִם אֵילִם וְחֲמִשָּׁה

עַתּוּדִים חֲמִשָּׁה כְּבָשִׂים בְּנֵי־שָׁנָה חֲמִשָּׁה זֶה קָרְבַּן אֲבִידָן בֶּן־גִּדְעֹנִי:

בַּיּוֹם הָעֲשִׂירִי נָשִׂיא לִבְנֵי דָן אֲחִיעֶזֶר בֶּן־עַמִּישַׁדָּי: קָרְבָּנוֹ

קַעֲרַת־כֶּסֶף אַחַת שְׁלֹשִׁים וּמֵאָה מִשְׁקָלָהּ מִזְרָק אֶחָד כֶּסֶף שִׁבְעִים שֶׁקֶל

בְּשֶׁקֶל הַקֹּדֶשׁ שְׁנֵיהֶם | מְלֵאִים סֹלֶת בְּלוּלָה בַשֶּׁמֶן לְמִנְחָה: כַּף אַחַת

עֲשָׂרָה זָהָב מְלֵאָה קְטֹרֶת: פַּר אֶחָד בֶּן־בָּקָר אַיִל אֶחָד כֶּבֶשׂ־אֶחָד

בֶּן־שְׁנָתוֹ לְעֹלָה: שְׂעִיר־עִזִּים אֶחָד לְחַטָּאת: וּלְזֶבַח הַשְּׁלָמִים בָּקָר שְׁנַיִם אֵילִם

חֲמִשָּׁה עַתּוּדִים חֲמִשָּׁה כְּבָשִׂים בְּנֵי־שָׁנָה חֲמִשָּׁה זֶה קָרְבַּן אֲחִיעֶזֶר בֶּן־עַמִּישַׁדָּי:

בַּיּוֹם עַשְׁתֵּי עָשָׂר יוֹם נָשִׂיא לִבְנֵי אָשֵׁר פַּגְעִיאֵל בֶּן־עָכְרָן: קָרְבָּנוֹ

קַעֲרַת־כֶּסֶף אַחַת שְׁלֹשִׁים וּמֵאָה מִשְׁקָלָהּ מִזְרָק אֶחָד כֶּסֶף שִׁבְעִים שֶׁקֶל

בְּשֶׁקֶל הַקֹּדֶשׁ שְׁנֵיהֶם | מְלֵאִים סֹלֶת בְּלוּלָה בַשֶּׁמֶן לְמִנְחָה: כַּף אַחַת

עֲשָׂרָה זָהָב מְלֵאָה קְטֹרֶת: פַּר אֶחָד בֶּן־בָּקָר אַיִל אֶחָד כֶּבֶשׂ־אֶחָד

בֶּן־שְׁנָתוֹ לְעֹלָה: שְׂעִיר־עִזִּים אֶחָד לְחַטָּאת: וּלְזֶבַח הַשְּׁלָמִים בָּקָר שְׁנַיִם אֵילִם

חֲמִשָּׁה עַתּוּדִים חֲמִשָּׁה כְּבָשִׂים בְּנֵי־שָׁנָה חֲמִשָּׁה זֶה קָרְבַּן פַּגְעִיאֵל בֶּן־עָכְרָן:

בְּיוֹם שְׁנֵים עָשָׂר יוֹם נָשִׂיא לִבְנֵי נַפְתָּלִי אֲחִירַע בֶּן־עֵינָן: קָרְבָּנוֹ
קַעֲרַת־כֶּסֶף אַחַת שְׁלֹשִׁים וּמֵאָה מִשְׁקָלָהּ מִזְרָק אֶחָד כֶּסֶף שִׁבְעִים שֶׁקֶל
בְּשֶׁקֶל הַקֹּדֶשׁ שְׁנֵיהֶם | מְלֵאִים סֹלֶת בְּלוּלָה בַשֶּׁמֶן לְמִנְחָה: כַּף אַחַת
עֲשָׂרָה זָהָב מְלֵאָה קְטֹרֶת: פַּר אֶחָד בֶּן־בָּקָר אַיִל אֶחָד כֶּבֶשׂ־אֶחָד
בֶּן־שְׁנָתוֹ לְעֹלָה: שְׂעִיר־עִזִּים אֶחָד לְחַטָּאת: וּלְזֶבַח הַשְּׁלָמִים בָּקָר שְׁנַיִם אֵילִם
חֲמִשָּׁה עַתֻּדִים חֲמִשָּׁה כְּבָשִׂים בְּנֵי־שָׁנָה חֲמִשָּׁה זֶה קָרְבַּן אֲחִירַע בֶּן־עֵינָן:
זֹאת | חֲנֻכַּת הַמִּזְבֵּחַ בְּיוֹם הִמָּשַׁח אֹתוֹ מֵאֵת נְשִׂיאֵי יִשְׂרָאֵל קַעֲרֹת כֶּסֶף שְׁתֵּים עֶשְׂרֵה
מִזְרְקֵי־כֶסֶף שְׁנֵים עָשָׂר כַּפּוֹת זָהָב שְׁתֵּים עֶשְׂרֵה: שְׁלֹשִׁים וּמֵאָה הַקְּעָרָה הָאַחַת כֶּסֶף
וְשִׁבְעִים הַמִּזְרָק הָאֶחָד כֹּל כֶּסֶף הַכֵּלִים אַלְפַּיִם וְאַרְבַּע־מֵאוֹת בְּשֶׁקֶל הַקֹּדֶשׁ:
כַּפּוֹת זָהָב שְׁתֵּים־עֶשְׂרֵה מְלֵאֹת קְטֹרֶת עֲשָׂרָה עֲשָׂרָה הַכַּף בְּשֶׁקֶל הַקֹּדֶשׁ
כָּל־זְהַב הַכַּפּוֹת עֶשְׂרִים וּמֵאָה: כָּל־הַבָּקָר לָעֹלָה שְׁנֵים עָשָׂר פָּרִים אֵילִם
שְׁנֵים־עָשָׂר כְּבָשִׂים בְּנֵי־שָׁנָה שְׁנֵים עָשָׂר וּמִנְחָתָם וּשְׂעִירֵי עִזִּים שְׁנֵים עָשָׂר לְחַטָּאת:
וְכֹל בְּקַר | זֶבַח הַשְּׁלָמִים עֶשְׂרִים וְאַרְבָּעָה פָּרִים אֵילִם שִׁשִּׁים עַתֻּדִים שִׁשִּׁים
כְּבָשִׂים בְּנֵי־שָׁנָה שִׁשִּׁים זֹאת חֲנֻכַּת הַמִּזְבֵּחַ אַחֲרֵי הִמָּשַׁח אֹתוֹ: וּבְבֹא מֹשֶׁה
אֶל־אֹהֶל מוֹעֵד לְדַבֵּר אִתּוֹ וַיִּשְׁמַע אֶת־הַקּוֹל מִדַּבֵּר אֵלָיו מֵעַל הַכַּפֹּרֶת אֲשֶׁר
עַל־אֲרֹן הָעֵדֻת מִבֵּין שְׁנֵי הַכְּרֻבִים וַיְדַבֵּר אֵלָיו: וַיְדַבֵּר יְהֹוָה אֶל־מֹשֶׁה
לֵּאמֹר: דַּבֵּר אֶל־אַהֲרֹן וְאָמַרְתָּ אֵלָיו בְּהַעֲלֹתְךָ אֶת־הַנֵּרֹת אֶל־מוּל פְּנֵי הַמְּנוֹרָה
יָאִירוּ שִׁבְעַת הַנֵּרוֹת: וַיַּעַשׂ כֵּן אַהֲרֹן אֶל־מוּל פְּנֵי הַמְּנוֹרָה הֶעֱלָה נֵרֹתֶיהָ כַּאֲשֶׁר
צִוָּה יְהֹוָה אֶת־מֹשֶׁה: וְזֶה מַעֲשֵׂה הַמְּנֹרָה מִקְשָׁה זָהָב עַד־יְרֵכָהּ עַד־פִּרְחָהּ
מִקְשָׁה הִוא כַּמַּרְאֶה אֲשֶׁר הֶרְאָה יְהֹוָה אֶת־מֹשֶׁה כֵּן עָשָׂה אֶת־הַמְּנֹרָה:

READING FOR PURIM (EXODUS 17:8-16)

וַיָּבֹא עֲמָלֵק וַיִּלָּחֶם עִם־יִשְׂרָאֵל בִּרְפִידִם: וַיֹּאמֶר מֹשֶׁה אֶל־יְהוֹשֻׁעַ בְּחַר־לָנוּ אֲנָשִׁים
וְצֵא הִלָּחֵם בַּעֲמָלֵק מָחָר אָנֹכִי נִצָּב עַל־רֹאשׁ הַגִּבְעָה וּמַטֵּה הָאֱלֹהִים בְּיָדִי:
וַיַּעַשׂ יְהוֹשֻׁעַ כַּאֲשֶׁר אָמַר־לוֹ מֹשֶׁה לְהִלָּחֵם בַּעֲמָלֵק וּמֹשֶׁה אַהֲרֹן וְחוּר
עָלוּ רֹאשׁ הַגִּבְעָה: Levi וְהָיָה כַּאֲשֶׁר יָרִים מֹשֶׁה יָדוֹ וְגָבַר יִשְׂרָאֵל וְכַאֲשֶׁר
יָנִיחַ יָדוֹ וְגָבַר עֲמָלֵק: וִידֵי מֹשֶׁה כְּבֵדִים וַיִּקְחוּ־אֶבֶן וַיָּשִׂימוּ תַחְתָּיו וַיֵּשֶׁב עָלֶיהָ
וְאַהֲרֹן וְחוּר תָּמְכוּ בְיָדָיו מִזֶּה אֶחָד וּמִזֶּה אֶחָד וַיְהִי יָדָיו אֱמוּנָה עַד־בֹּא הַשָּׁמֶשׁ:
וַיַּחֲלֹשׁ יְהוֹשֻׁעַ אֶת־עֲמָלֵק וְאֶת־עַמּוֹ לְפִי־חָרֶב: Yisrael וַיֹּאמֶר יְהֹוָה
אֶל־מֹשֶׁה כְּתֹב זֹאת זִכָּרוֹן בַּסֵּפֶר וְשִׂים בְּאָזְנֵי יְהוֹשֻׁעַ כִּי־מָחֹה
אֶמְחֶה אֶת־זֵכֶר עֲמָלֵק מִתַּחַת הַשָּׁמָיִם: וַיִּבֶן מֹשֶׁה מִזְבֵּחַ וַיִּקְרָא שְׁמוֹ יְהֹוָה |
נִסִּי: וַיֹּאמֶר כִּי־יָד עַל־כֵּס יָהּ מִלְחָמָה לַיהֹוָה בַּעֲמָלֵק מִדֹּר דֹּר:

The last verse ("Vayomer") is recited twice

The Torah Reading for Communal Fast Days
(Exodus 32:11-14, 34:1-10)

וַיְחַל מֹשֶׁה אֶת־פְּנֵי יְהֹוָה אֱלֹהָיו וַיֹּאמֶר לָמָה יְהֹוָה יֶחֱרֶה אַפְּךָ בְּעַמֶּךָ אֲשֶׁר הוֹצֵאתָ מֵאֶרֶץ מִצְרַיִם בְּכֹחַ גָּדוֹל וּבְיָד חֲזָקָה׃ לָמָּה יֹאמְרוּ מִצְרַיִם לֵאמֹר בְּרָעָה הוֹצִיאָם לַהֲרֹג אֹתָם בֶּהָרִים וּלְכַלֹּתָם מֵעַל פְּנֵי הָאֲדָמָה (all together) שׁוּב מֵחֲרוֹן אַפֶּךָ וְהִנָּחֵם עַל־הָרָעָה לְעַמֶּךָ׃ זְכֹר לְאַבְרָהָם לְיִצְחָק וּלְיִשְׂרָאֵל עֲבָדֶיךָ אֲשֶׁר נִשְׁבַּעְתָּ לָהֶם בָּךְ וַתְּדַבֵּר אֲלֵהֶם אַרְבֶּה אֶת־זַרְעֲכֶם כְּכוֹכְבֵי הַשָּׁמָיִם וְכָל־הָאָרֶץ הַזֹּאת אֲשֶׁר אָמַרְתִּי אֶתֵּן לְזַרְעֲכֶם וְנָחֲלוּ לְעֹלָם׃ וַיִּנָּחֶם יְהֹוָה עַל־הָרָעָה אֲשֶׁר דִּבֶּר לַעֲשׂוֹת לְעַמּוֹ׃ *Levi* וַיֹּאמֶר יְהֹוָה אֶל־מֹשֶׁה פְּסָל־לְךָ שְׁנֵי־לֻחֹת אֲבָנִים כָּרִאשֹׁנִים וְכָתַבְתִּי עַל־הַלֻּחֹת אֶת־הַדְּבָרִים אֲשֶׁר הָיוּ עַל־הַלֻּחֹת הָרִאשֹׁנִים אֲשֶׁר שִׁבַּרְתָּ׃ וֶהְיֵה נָכוֹן לַבֹּקֶר וְעָלִיתָ בַבֹּקֶר אֶל־הַר סִינַי וְנִצַּבְתָּ לִי שָׁם עַל־רֹאשׁ הָהָר׃ וְאִישׁ לֹא־יַעֲלֶה עִמָּךְ וְגַם־אִישׁ אַל־יֵרָא בְּכָל־הָהָר גַּם־הַצֹּאן וְהַבָּקָר אַל־יִרְעוּ אֶל־מוּל הָהָר הַהוּא׃ *Yisrael* וַיִּפְסֹל שְׁנֵי־לֻחֹת אֲבָנִים כָּרִאשֹׁנִים וַיַּשְׁכֵּם מֹשֶׁה בַבֹּקֶר וַיַּעַל אֶל־הַר סִינַי כַּאֲשֶׁר צִוָּה יְהֹוָה אֹתוֹ וַיִּקַּח בְּיָדוֹ שְׁנֵי לֻחֹת אֲבָנִים׃ וַיֵּרֶד יְהֹוָה בֶּעָנָן וַיִּתְיַצֵּב עִמּוֹ שָׁם וַיִּקְרָא בְשֵׁם יְהֹוָה׃ וַיַּעֲבֹר יְהֹוָה ׀ עַל־פָּנָיו וַיִּקְרָא יְהֹוָה ׀ יְהֹוָה אֵל רַחוּם וְחַנּוּן אֶרֶךְ אַפַּיִם וְרַב־חֶסֶד וֶאֱמֶת׃ נֹצֵר חֶסֶד לָאֲלָפִים נֹשֵׂא עָוֺן וָפֶשַׁע וְחַטָּאָה וְנַקֵּה לֹא יְנַקֶּה פֹּקֵד ׀ עֲוֺן אָבוֹת עַל־בָּנִים וְעַל־בְּנֵי בָנִים עַל־שִׁלֵּשִׁים וְעַל־רִבֵּעִים׃ וַיְמַהֵר מֹשֶׁה וַיִּקֹּד אַרְצָה וַיִּשְׁתָּחוּ׃ וַיֹּאמֶר אִם־נָא מָצָאתִי חֵן בְּעֵינֶיךָ אֲדֹנָי יֵלֶךְ־נָא אֲדֹנָי בְּקִרְבֵּנוּ כִּי עַם־קְשֵׁה־עֹרֶף הוּא (all together) וְסָלַחְתָּ לַעֲוֺנֵנוּ וּלְחַטָּאתֵנוּ וּנְחַלְתָּנוּ׃ וַיֹּאמֶר הִנֵּה אָנֹכִי כֹּרֵת בְּרִית נֶגֶד כָּל־עַמְּךָ אֶעֱשֶׂה נִפְלָאֹת אֲשֶׁר לֹא־נִבְרְאוּ בְכָל־הָאָרֶץ וּבְכָל־הַגּוֹיִם וְרָאָה כָל־הָעָם אֲשֶׁר־אַתָּה בְקִרְבּוֹ אֶת־מַעֲשֵׂה יְהֹוָה כִּי־נוֹרָא הוּא אֲשֶׁר אֲנִי עֹשֶׂה עִמָּךְ׃

The Haftara for Communal Fast Days
(Isaiah 55-56)

(The one who reads the *Haftarah* should say the first blessing of the *Haftarah* before the reading).

דִּרְשׁוּ יְהֹוָה בְּהִמָּצְאוֹ קְרָאֻהוּ בִּהְיוֹתוֹ קָרוֹב׃ יַעֲזֹב רָשָׁע דַּרְכּוֹ וְאִישׁ אָוֶן מַחְשְׁבֹתָיו וְיָשֹׁב אֶל־יְהֹוָה וִירַחֲמֵהוּ וְאֶל־אֱלֹהֵינוּ כִּי־יַרְבֶּה לִסְלוֹחַ׃ כִּי לֹא מַחְשְׁבוֹתַי מַחְשְׁבוֹתֵיכֶם וְלֹא דַרְכֵיכֶם דְּרָכָי נְאֻם יְהֹוָה׃ כִּי־גָבְהוּ שָׁמַיִם מֵאָרֶץ כֵּן גָּבְהוּ דְרָכַי מִדַּרְכֵיכֶם וּמַחְשְׁבֹתַי מִמַּחְשְׁבֹתֵיכֶם׃ כִּי כַּאֲשֶׁר יֵרֵד הַגֶּשֶׁם וְהַשֶּׁלֶג מִן־הַשָּׁמַיִם וְשָׁמָּה לֹא יָשׁוּב כִּי אִם־הִרְוָה אֶת־הָאָרֶץ וְהוֹלִידָהּ וְהִצְמִיחָהּ וְנָתַן זֶרַע לַזֹּרֵעַ וְלֶחֶם לָאֹכֵל׃ כֵּן יִהְיֶה דְבָרִי אֲשֶׁר יֵצֵא מִפִּי לֹא־יָשׁוּב אֵלַי רֵיקָם כִּי אִם־עָשָׂה אֶת־אֲשֶׁר חָפַצְתִּי וְהִצְלִיחַ אֲשֶׁר שְׁלַחְתִּיו׃ כִּי־בְשִׂמְחָה תֵצֵאוּ וּבְשָׁלוֹם תּוּבָלוּן הֶהָרִים וְהַגְּבָעוֹת יִפְצְחוּ לִפְנֵיכֶם רִנָּה וְכָל־עֲצֵי הַשָּׂדֶה יִמְחֲאוּ־כָף׃ תַּחַת הַנַּעֲצוּץ יַעֲלֶה בְרוֹשׁ וְתַחַת (כתיב תחת) הַסִּרְפַּד יַעֲלֶה הֲדַס וְהָיָה לַיהֹוָה לְשֵׁם לְאוֹת עוֹלָם לֹא יִכָּרֵת׃ כֹּה אָמַר יְהֹוָה שִׁמְרוּ מִשְׁפָּט וַעֲשׂוּ צְדָקָה כִּי־קְרוֹבָה יְשׁוּעָתִי לָבוֹא וְצִדְקָתִי לְהִגָּלוֹת׃ אַשְׁרֵי אֱנוֹשׁ יַעֲשֶׂה־זֹּאת וּבֶן־אָדָם יַחֲזִיק בָּהּ שֹׁמֵר שַׁבָּת מֵחַלְּלוֹ וְשֹׁמֵר יָדוֹ מֵעֲשׂוֹת כָּל־רָע׃ וְאַל־יֹאמַר בֶּן־הַנֵּכָר הַנִּלְוָה אֶל־יְהֹוָה לֵאמֹר הַבְדֵּל יַבְדִּילַנִי יְהֹוָה מֵעַל עַמּוֹ וְאַל־יֹאמַר הַסָּרִיס הֵן אֲנִי עֵץ יָבֵשׁ׃

כִּי־כֹה ׀ אָמַר יְהֹוָה לַסָּרִיסִים אֲשֶׁר יִשְׁמְרוּ אֶת־שַׁבְּתוֹתַי וּבָחֲרוּ בַּאֲשֶׁר חָפָצְתִּי וּמַחֲזִיקִים בִּבְרִיתִי: וְנָתַתִּי לָהֶם בְּבֵיתִי וּבְחוֹמֹתַי יָד וָשֵׁם טוֹב מִבָּנִים וּמִבָּנוֹת שֵׁם עוֹלָם אֶתֶּן־לוֹ אֲשֶׁר לֹא יִכָּרֵת: וּבְנֵי הַנֵּכָר הַנִּלְוִים עַל־יְהֹוָה לְשָׁרְתוֹ וּלְאַהֲבָה אֶת־שֵׁם יְהֹוָה לִהְיוֹת לוֹ לַעֲבָדִים כָּל־שֹׁמֵר שַׁבָּת מֵחַלְּלוֹ וּמַחֲזִיקִים בִּבְרִיתִי: וַהֲבִיאוֹתִים אֶל־הַר קָדְשִׁי וְשִׂמַּחְתִּים בְּבֵית תְּפִלָּתִי עוֹלֹתֵיהֶם וְזִבְחֵיהֶם לְרָצוֹן עַל־מִזְבְּחִי כִּי בֵיתִי בֵּית־תְּפִלָּה יִקָּרֵא לְכָל־הָעַמִּים: נְאֻם אֲדֹנָי יֱהֹוִה מְקַבֵּץ נִדְחֵי יִשְׂרָאֵל עוֹד אֲקַבֵּץ עָלָיו לְנִקְבָּצָיו:

(At the end the one who reads the *Haftarah* should say the three last blessings of the *Haftarah* – until *Magen David*)

THE TORAH READING FOR TISHA B'AV
(DEUTERONOMY 4:25-40)

כִּי־תוֹלִיד בָּנִים וּבְנֵי בָנִים וְנוֹשַׁנְתֶּם בָּאָרֶץ וְהִשְׁחַתֶּם וַעֲשִׂיתֶם פֶּסֶל תְּמוּנַת כֹּל וַעֲשִׂיתֶם הָרַע בְּעֵינֵי יְהֹוָה־אֱלֹהֶיךָ לְהַכְעִיסוֹ: הַעִידֹתִי בָכֶם הַיּוֹם אֶת־הַשָּׁמַיִם וְאֶת־הָאָרֶץ כִּי־אָבֹד תֹּאבֵדוּן מַהֵר מֵעַל הָאָרֶץ אֲשֶׁר אַתֶּם עֹבְרִים אֶת־הַיַּרְדֵּן שָׁמָּה לְרִשְׁתָּהּ לֹא־תַאֲרִיכֻן יָמִים עָלֶיהָ כִּי הִשָּׁמֵד תִּשָּׁמֵדוּן: וְהֵפִיץ יְהֹוָה אֶתְכֶם בָּעַמִּים וְנִשְׁאַרְתֶּם מְתֵי מִסְפָּר בַּגּוֹיִם אֲשֶׁר יְנַהֵג יְהֹוָה אֶתְכֶם שָׁמָּה: וַעֲבַדְתֶּם־שָׁם אֱלֹהִים מַעֲשֵׂה יְדֵי אָדָם עֵץ וָאֶבֶן אֲשֶׁר לֹא־יִרְאוּן וְלֹא יִשְׁמְעוּן וְלֹא יֹאכְלוּן וְלֹא יְרִיחֻן: וּבִקַּשְׁתֶּם מִשָּׁם אֶת־יְהֹוָה אֱלֹהֶיךָ וּמָצָאתָ כִּי תִדְרְשֶׁנּוּ בְּכָל־לְבָבְךָ וּבְכָל־נַפְשֶׁךָ: *Levi* בַּצַּר לְךָ וּמְצָאוּךָ כֹּל הַדְּבָרִים הָאֵלֶּה בְּאַחֲרִית הַיָּמִים וְשַׁבְתָּ עַד־יְהֹוָה אֱלֹהֶיךָ וְשָׁמַעְתָּ בְּקֹלוֹ: כִּי אֵל רַחוּם יְהֹוָה אֱלֹהֶיךָ לֹא יַרְפְּךָ וְלֹא יַשְׁחִיתֶךָ וְלֹא יִשְׁכַּח אֶת־בְּרִית אֲבֹתֶיךָ אֲשֶׁר נִשְׁבַּע לָהֶם: כִּי שְׁאַל־נָא לְיָמִים רִאשֹׁנִים אֲשֶׁר־הָיוּ לְפָנֶיךָ לְמִן־הַיּוֹם אֲשֶׁר בָּרָא אֱלֹהִים ׀ אָדָם עַל־הָאָרֶץ וּלְמִקְצֵה הַשָּׁמַיִם וְעַד־קְצֵה הַשָּׁמָיִם הֲנִהְיָה כַּדָּבָר הַגָּדוֹל הַזֶּה אוֹ הֲנִשְׁמַע כָּמֹהוּ: הֲשָׁמַע עָם קוֹל אֱלֹהִים מְדַבֵּר מִתּוֹךְ־הָאֵשׁ כַּאֲשֶׁר־שָׁמַעְתָּ אַתָּה וַיֶּחִי: אוֹ ׀ הֲנִסָּה אֱלֹהִים לָבוֹא לָקַחַת לוֹ גוֹי מִקֶּרֶב גּוֹי בְּמַסֹּת בְּאֹתֹת וּבְמוֹפְתִים וּבְמִלְחָמָה וּבְיָד חֲזָקָה וּבִזְרוֹעַ נְטוּיָה וּבְמוֹרָאִים גְּדֹלִים כְּכֹל אֲשֶׁר־עָשָׂה לָכֶם יְהֹוָה אֱלֹהֵיכֶם בְּמִצְרַיִם לְעֵינֶיךָ: אַתָּה הָרְאֵתָ לָדַעַת כִּי יְהֹוָה הוּא הָאֱלֹהִים אֵין עוֹד מִלְּבַדּוֹ: מִן־הַשָּׁמַיִם הִשְׁמִיעֲךָ אֶת־קֹלוֹ לְיַסְּרֶךָּ וְעַל־הָאָרֶץ הֶרְאֲךָ אֶת־אִשּׁוֹ הַגְּדוֹלָה *Yisrael* וּדְבָרָיו שָׁמַעְתָּ מִתּוֹךְ הָאֵשׁ: וְתַחַת כִּי אָהַב אֶת־אֲבֹתֶיךָ וַיִּבְחַר בְּזַרְעוֹ אַחֲרָיו וַיּוֹצִאֲךָ בְּפָנָיו בְּכֹחוֹ הַגָּדֹל מִמִּצְרָיִם: לְהוֹרִישׁ גּוֹיִם גְּדֹלִים וַעֲצֻמִים מִמְּךָ מִפָּנֶיךָ לַהֲבִיאֲךָ לָתֶת־לְךָ אֶת־אַרְצָם נַחֲלָה כַּיּוֹם הַזֶּה: וְיָדַעְתָּ הַיּוֹם וַהֲשֵׁבֹתָ אֶל־לְבָבֶךָ כִּי יְהֹוָה הוּא הָאֱלֹהִים בַּשָּׁמַיִם מִמַּעַל וְעַל־הָאָרֶץ מִתָּחַת אֵין עוֹד: וְשָׁמַרְתָּ אֶת־חֻקָּיו וְאֶת־מִצְוֹתָיו אֲשֶׁר אָנֹכִי מְצַוְּךָ הַיּוֹם אֲשֶׁר יִיטַב לְךָ וּלְבָנֶיךָ אַחֲרֶיךָ וּלְמַעַן תַּאֲרִיךְ יָמִים עַל־הָאֲדָמָה אֲשֶׁר יְהֹוָה אֱלֹהֶיךָ נֹתֵן לְךָ כָּל־הַיָּמִים:

THE HAFTARA FOR TISHA B'AV
(JEREMIAH 8-9)

(The one who reads the *Haftarah* should say the first blessing of the *Haftarah* before the reading)

אָסֹף אֲסִיפֵם נְאֻם־יְהֹוָה אֵין עֲנָבִים בַּגֶּפֶן וְאֵין תְּאֵנִים בַּתְּאֵנָה וְהֶעָלֶה נָבֵל וָאֶתֵּן לָהֶם יַעַבְרוּם: עַל־מָה אֲנַחְנוּ יֹשְׁבִים הֵאָסְפוּ וְנָבוֹא אֶל־עָרֵי הַמִּבְצָר וְנִדְּמָה־שָּׁם כִּי יְהֹוָה אֱלֹהֵינוּ הֲדִמָּנוּ וַיַּשְׁקֵנוּ מֵי־רֹאשׁ כִּי חָטָאנוּ לַיהֹוָה:

קַוֵּה לְעָלוֹם וְאֵין טוֹב לְעֵת מַרְפֵּא וְהִנֵּה בְעָתָה: מִדָּן נִשְׁמַע נַחֲרַת סוּסָיו מִקּוֹל
מִצְהֲלוֹת אַבִּירָיו רָעֲשָׁה כָּל־הָאָרֶץ וַיָּבוֹאוּ וַיֹּאכְלוּ אֶרֶץ וּמְלוֹאָהּ עִיר וְיֹשְׁבֵי בָהּ: כִּי
הִנְנִי מְשַׁלֵּחַ בָּכֶם נְחָשִׁים צִפְעֹנִים אֲשֶׁר אֵין־לָהֶם לָחַשׁ וְנִשְּׁכוּ אֶתְכֶם
נְאֻם־יְהוָֹה אהדהיאהדונהי: מַבְלִיגִיתִי עֲלֵי יָגוֹן עָלַי לִבִּי דַוָּי: הִנֵּה־קוֹל שַׁוְעַת בַּת־עַמִּי מֵאֶרֶץ
מַרְחַקִּים הַיהוָֹה אהדהיאהדונהי אֵין בְּצִיּוֹן אִם־מַלְכָּהּ אֵין בָּהּ מַדּוּעַ הִכְעִסוּנִי בִּפְסִלֵיהֶם
בְּהַבְלֵי נֵכָר: עָבַר קָצִיר כָּלָה קָיִץ וַאֲנַחְנוּ לוֹא נוֹשָׁעְנוּ: עַל־שֶׁבֶר בַּת־עַמִּי הָשְׁבַּרְתִּי
קָדַרְתִּי שַׁמָּה הֶחֱזִקָתְנִי: הַצֳּרִי אֵין בְּגִלְעָד אִם־רֹפֵא אֵין שָׁם כִּי מַדּוּעַ לֹא עָלְתָה
אֲרֻכַת בַּת־עַמִּי:

(At the end the one who reads the *Haftarah* should say the three last blessings of the *Haftarah* – until *Magen David*)

Amelioration of the Dream

During our waking hours, a constant struggle is waged between our body, which seeks the material satisfaction of the 1 percent physical world, and our soul, which aspires to the higher 99 percent true reality. When we sleep, our soul—the true self—rises out of the limited realm of time and space, out of our physical body, and enters the true reality to get recharged and nourished.

According to Kabbalah, dreams are messages from the 99 percent true reality that we receive when we are least attached to the 1 percent world — when our souls are elevated while we sleep. And because of this, every dream deserves our attention.

Our dreams and nightmares are purification experiences related to negative actions we've taken in our *present* life so that the pain associated with those spiritual corrections is not fully experienced in this physical world. Making a spiritual correction (*tikkun*) in a dream is simply a more merciful way to achieve the objective. The more we seek to transform ourselves in the physical realm, the more opportunities we have to discharge our baggage and pay off our spiritual debts in a dream state.

Hatavat Chalom - Amelioration of the Dream

However, if a person experienced an extremely negative dream that caused him or her anxiety, a process to better or cancel the dream known as *Hatavat Chalom* is required and is performed within three days of the dream. A negative dream indicates a separation between the Upper Worlds and the Lower World—our world. This separation between the Upper and Lower Worlds creates a void and sense of lack both in the dreamer's life as well as in the world.

Hatavat Chalom involves the dreamer coming before three men who, together with the dreamer, go through a set interactive discourse in Hebrew/Aramaic emphasizing that the dream is a good dream. (It is not necessary to tell these three men the dream).

The three men represent the Upper Worlds—the true reality—that nourish our physical world. The technology of *Hatavat Chalom* brings the Upper Worlds closer to our world, bridging the space between the two worlds and filling the void with Light causing the negativity from the dream to disappear.

Themes and Symbols in a dream that require *Hatavat Chalom*

Being naked and performing a negative action or being naked in a negative environment.

People who have passed away are taking something away from you. This is especially so if it's a shoe.

Black or purple Grapes is a negative sign of judgment. It is a warning of something going wrong.

Light blue color is a negative indication of evil eye, or judgment.

Eyes and/or Fish are both warnings of evil eye.

Death: This might mean spiritual death in the person's life or physical death.

Symbols with Double Meanings: According to the *Talmud,* the appearance of the following symbols is either very positive or very negative: **River; Bird; Pot; Mountain; Dog; Lion; Ox; Haircut.** So in these cases it is highly recommended to discuss it with a Kabbalah teacher.

General note: For an accurate interpretation of a dream, you need the overall frame as well as the details.

If you had a disturbing dream that causes you anxiety you should gather three men (the beneficents) and together make the following connection.

The three beneficents represent the three letters *Yud, Hei* and *Vav* יה״ו and when they are connected to the last letter *Hei* ה, which is represented by the dreamer, they (the letters *Yud, Hei* and *Vav*) infuse abundance and fulfilling the last letter *Hei*.

FIRST TIME - CHESED

The dreamer (*Hei - Malchut*):

Meditate to draw abundance from *Chochmah, Binah, Da'at* of *Chochmah, Binah, Da'at* of *Chesed* to the Seven Lower *Sefirot* of *Chesed* of *Malchut* in order to sweeten the Judgments.

Chochmah of Chochmah of Chesed – וזכמה דוזכמה דוזסד

וְזֶלְבְּמָא chelma היה והוה ויהיה ע״ה

Binah of Chochmah of Chesed – בינה דוזכמה דוזסד

טָבָא tava אהיה אהֹהי איהה היהא היאה ההיא יהאה יההא יאהה האהי האיה ההאי

Da'at of Chochmah of Chesed – דעת דוזכמה דוזסד

וְזָזָאִי chazai יהוה.

Chochmah of Binah of Chesed – וזכמה דבינה דוזסד

וְזֶלְבְּמָא chelma היה והוה ויהיה ע״ה

Binah of Binah of Chesed – בינה דבינה דוזסד

טָבָא tava אהיה אהֹהי איהה היהא היאה ההיא יהאה יההא יאהה האהי האיה ההאי

Da'at of Binah of Chesed – דעת דבינה דוזסד

וְזָזָאִי chazai יהוה.

Chochmah of Da'at of Chesed – וזכמה דדעת דוזסד

וְזֶלְבְּמָא chelma היה והוה ויהיה ע״ה

Binah of Da'at of Chesed – בינה דדעת דוזסד

טָבָא tava אהיה אהֹהי איהה היהא היאה ההיא יהאה יההא יאהה האהי האיה ההאי

Da'at of Da'at of Chesed – דעת דדעת דוזסד

וְזָזָאִי chazai יהוה.

HATAVAT CHALOM – AMELIORATION OF THE DREAM
FIRST TIME - CHESED
I have seen a good dream (x3)

The three beneficents (*Yud-Chochmah, Hei-Binah, Vav-Da'at*):

Meditate to draw abundance from *Chochmah, Binah, Da'at* of *Chochmah, Binah, Da'at* of *Chesed* of *Zeir Anpin* to *Chochmah, Binah, Da'at* of *Chochmah, Binah, Da'at* of *Chesed* of *Nukva* (the dreamer).

Chochmah of Chochmah of Chesed – וֹזְכמה דְוֹזְכמה דְחֹסד

וְזֶלְמָא chelma היה והוה ויהיה ע"ה

Binah of Chochmah of Chesed – בינה דְוֹזְכמה דְחֹסד

טָבָא tava אהיה אהֹהי איֹהא היֹהא היֹא הֹהא יֹהאה יֹהאה יֹההא יֹאהה האֹיה האֹי הֹהאי

Da'at of Chochmah of Chesed – דְעת דְוֹזְכמה דְחֹסד

וְזְוְיתָא chazeta.

Chochmah of Binah of Chesed – וֹזְכמה דְבינה דְחֹסד

וְזֶלְמָא chelma היה והוה ויהיה ע"ה

Binah of Binah of Chesed – בינה דְבינה דְחֹסד

טָבָא tava אהֹיה אהֹהי איֹהה היֹהא היֹא הֹהא יֹהאה יֹהאה יֹההא יֹאהה האֹיה האֹי הֹהאי

Da'at of Binah of Chesed – דְעת דְבינה דְחֹסד

וְזְוְיתָא chazeta.

Chochmah of Da'at of Chesed – וֹזְכמה דְדְעת דְחֹסד

וְזֶלְמָא chelma היה והוה ויהיה ע"ה

Binah of Da'at of Chesed – בינה דְדְעת דְחֹסד

טָבָא tava אהֹיה אהֹהי איֹהה היֹהא היֹא הֹהא יֹהאה יֹהאה יֹההא יֹאהה האֹיה האֹי הֹהאי

Da'at of Da'at of Chesed – דְעת דְדְעת דְחֹסד

וְזְוְיתָא chazeta.

vetava וְטָבָא, hu הוא tava טָבָא didach דִידָךְ chelma וְזֶלְמָא

letav לְטַב leshav'ye לְשַׁוְיֵיהּ rachamana רַוֹזְמָנָא lehevei לֶהֱוֵי

alei עֲלֵיהּ פהל yigzerun יִגְזְרוּן zimnin זִימְנִין sheva שְׁבַע

tava טָבָא diyehevei דִיהֱוֵי shemaya שְׁמַיָא min מִן

lehevei לֶהֱוֵי vetava וְטָבָא, hu הוא tava טָבָא

The dreamer says silently (or scans):

ase עֲשֵׂה bemitzvot בְּמִצְוֹת pasha'ti פָּשַׁעְתִּי aviti עָוִיתִי chatati חָטָאתִי וְזֶטָאתִי

hateluyim הַתְּלוּיִים ta'aseh תַעֲשֶׂה lo לֹא uvemitzvot וּבְמִצְוֹת

alai עֲלַי dini דִינִי matz'dik מַצְדִיק vehareni וְהֲרֵינִי, beChesed בְּוֹזְסד

You have seen a good dream (x3), Your dream is good and may it be good. The Merciful One turns it to good. Seven times it will be decreed from the Heaven so it will be good. It is good and may it be good. (The dreamer says silently: I have transgressed, committed iniquity, and sinned in positive or negative commandments that are relying on Chesed and I accept the judgments upon me.)

SECOND TIME - GEVURAH

The dreamer (*Hei - Malchut*):

Meditate to draw abundance from *Chochmah, Binah, Da'at* of *Chochmah, Binah, Da'at* of *Gevurah* to the Seven Lower *Sefirot* of *Gevurah* of *Malchut* in order to sweeten the Judgments.

Chochmah of Chochmah of Gevurah — חכמה דחכמה דגבורה

וְחֶלְמָא chelma הוה והוה ויהיה ע"ה

Binah of Chochmah of Gevurah — בינה דחכמה דגבורה

טָבָא tava אהיה אהֹי איהֹה היֹהֹא היֹאה הֹהֹיא יֹהֹאה יֹאהֹה האהֹי האיה הֹהֹאי

Da'at of Chochmah of Gevurah — דעת דחכמה דגבורה

וְחֲזָאי chazai יֹהוֹה.

Chochmah of Binah of Gevurah — חכמה דבינה דגבורה

וְחֶלְמָא chelma הוה והוה ויהיה ע"ה

Binah of Binah of Gevurah — בינה דבינה דגבורה

טָבָא tava אהיה אהֹי איהֹה היֹהֹא היֹאה הֹהֹיא יֹהֹאה יֹאהֹה האהֹי האיה הֹהֹאי

Da'at of Binah of Gevurah — דעת דבינה דגבורה

וְחֲזָאי chazai יֹהוֹה.

Chochmah of Da'at of Gevurah — חכמה דדעת דגבורה

וְחֶלְמָא chelma הוה והוה ויהיה ע"ה

Binah of Da'at of Gevurah — בינה דדעת דגבורה

טָבָא tava אהיה אהֹי איהֹה היֹהֹא היֹאה הֹהֹיא יֹהֹאה יֹאהֹה האהֹי האיה הֹהֹאי

Da'at of Da'at of Gevurah — דעת דדעת דגבורה

וְחֲזָאי chazai יֹהוֹה.

SECOND TIME - GEVURAH
I have seen a good dream (x3)

The three beneficents (*Yud-Chochmah, Hei-Binah, Vav-Da'at*):

Meditate to draw abundance from *Chochmah, Binah, Da'at* of *Chochmah, Binah, Da'at* of *Gevurah* of *Zeir Anpin* to *Chochmah, Binah, Da'at* of *Chochmah, Binah, Da'at* of *Gevurah* of *Nukva* (the dreamer).

Chochmah of Chochmah of Gevurah – חכמה דוחכמה דגבורה

וְלֶלְמָא chelma היה והוה ויהיה ע"ה

Binah of Chochmah of Gevurah – בינה דוחכמה דגבורה

טָבָא tava אהיה אהֹהי איהה היהא היאה ההיא יהאה יההא יאהה האהי האיה ההאי

Da'at of Chochmah of Gevurah – דעת דוחכמה דגבורה

וְחֲזֵיתָא chazeta.

Chochmah of Binah of Gevurah – וחכמה דבינה דגבורה

וְלֶלְמָא chelma היה והוה ויהיה ע"ה

Binah of Binah of Gevurah – בינה דבינה דגבורה

טָבָא tava אהיה אהֹהי איהה היהא היאה ההיא יהאה יההא יאהה האהי האיה ההאי

Da'at of Binah of Gevurah – דעת דבינה דגבורה

וְחֲזֵיתָא chazeta.

Chochmah of Da'at of Gevurah – וחכמה דדעת דגבורה

וְלֶלְמָא chelma היה והוה ויהיה ע"ה

Binah of Da'at of Gevurah – בינה דדעת דגבורה

טָבָא tava אהיה אהֹהי איהה היהא היאה ההיא יהאה יההא יאהה האהי האיה ההאי

Da'at of Da'at of Gevurah – דעת דדעת דגבורה

וְחֲזֵיתָא chazeta.

vetava וְטָבָא, hu הוּא tava טָבָא didach דִּידָךְ chelma וְלֶלְמָא

◆letav לְטַב leshav'ye לְשַׁוְּיֵיהּ rachamana רַחֲמָנָא ◆lehevei לֶהֱוֵי

alei פהל עֲלֵיהּ yigzerun יִגְזְרוּן zimnin זִימְנִין sheva שְׁבַע

◆tava טָבָא diyehevei דִּיהֱוֵי shemaya שְׁמַיָּא min מִן

‡lehevei לֶהֱוֵי vetava וְטָבָא, hu הוּא tava טָבָא

The dreamer says silently (or scans):

ase עֲשֵׂה bemitzvot בְּמִצְוֹת pasha'ti פָּשַׁעְתִּי aviti עָוִיתִי chatati חָטָאתִי וְטָאתִי

hateluyim הַתְּלוּיִים ta'aseh תַעֲשֶׂה lo לֹא uvemitzvot וּבְמִצְוֹת

◆alai עָלַי dini דִּינִי matz'dik מַצְדִּיק vehareni וְהֲרֵינִי, beGevurah בִּגְבוּרָה

You have seen a good dream (x3), Your dream is good and may it be good. The Merciful One turns it to good. Seven times it will be decreed from the Heaven so it will be good. It is good and may it be good. (The dreamer says silently: I have transgressed, committed iniquity, and sinned in positive or negative commandments that are relying on Gevurah and I accept the judgments upon me.)

THIRD TIME - TIFERET

The dreamer (*Hei - Malchut*):

Meditate to draw abundance from *Chochmah, Binah, Da'at* of *Chochmah, Binah, Da'at* of *Tiferet* to the Seven Lower *Sefirot* of *Tiferet* of *Malchut* in order to sweeten the Judgments.

Chochmah of Chochmah of Tiferet — וזכמה דוזכמה דתפארת

היה והוה ויהיה ע"ה chelma וְזִלְמָא

Binah of Chochmah of Tiferet — בינה דוזכמה דתפארת

אהיה אתהי איהה היהא היאה ההיא יאהה יההא יאהה האהי האיה ההאי tava טָבָא

Da'at of Chochmah of Tiferet — דעת דוזכמה דתפארת

יהוה. chazai וְזָזָאי

Chochmah of Binah of Tiferet — וזכמה דבינה דתפארת

היה והוה ויהיה ע"ה chelma וְזִלְמָא

Binah of Binah of Tiferet — בינה דבינה דתפארת

אהיה אתהי איהה היהא היאה ההיא יאהה יההא יאהה האהי האיה ההאי tava טָבָא

Da'at of Binah of Tiferet — דעת דבינה דתפארת

יהוה. chazai וְזָזָאי

Chochmah of Da'at of Tiferet — וזכמה דדעת דתפארת

היה והוה ויהיה ע"ה chelma וְזִלְמָא

Binah of Da'at of Tiferet — בינה דדעת דתפארת

אהיה אתהי איהה היהא היאה ההיא יאהה יההא יאהה האהי האיה ההאי tava טָבָא

Da'at of Da'at of Tiferet — דעת דדעת דתפארת

יהוה. chazai וְזָזָאי

THIRD TIME - TIFERET
I have seen a good dream (x3)

The three beneficents (*Yud-Chochmah, Hei-Binah, Vav-Da'at*):

Meditate to draw abundance from *Chochmah, Binah, Da'at* of *Chochmah, Binah, Da'at* of *Tiferet* of *Zeir Anpin* to *Chochmah, Binah, Da'at* of *Chochmah, Binah, Da'at* of *Tiferet* of *Nukva* (the dreamer).

Chochmah of Chochmah of Tiferet – וזכמה דוזכמה דתפארת

וְזֵלְמָא chelma היה והוה ויהיה ע״ה

Binah of Chochmah of Tiferet – בינה דוזכמה דתפארת

טָבָא tava אהיה אההי איהה היהא היאה ההיא יהאה יההא יאהה האהי האיה ההאי

Da'at of Chochmah of Tiferet – דעת דוזכמה דתפארת

וְזֵזִיתָא. chazeta

Chochmah of Binah of Tiferet – וזכמה דבינה דתפארת

וְזֵלְמָא chelma היה והוה ויהיה ע״ה

Binah of Binah of Tiferet – בינה דבינה דתפארת

טָבָא tava אהיה אההי איהה היהא היאה ההיא יהאה יההא יאהה האהי האיה ההאי

Da'at of Binah of Tiferet – דעת דבינה דתפארת

וְזֵזִיתָא. chazeta

Chochmah of Da'at of Tiferet – וזכמה דדעת דתפארת

וְזֵלְמָא chelma היה והוה ויהיה ע״ה

Binah of Da'at of Tiferet – בינה דדעת דתפארת

טָבָא tava אהיה אההי איהה היהא היאה ההיא יהאה יההא יאהה האהי האיה ההאי

Da'at of Da'at of Tiferet – דעת דדעת דתפארת

וְזֵזִיתָא. chazeta

vetava וְטָבָא ,hu הוּא tava טָבָא didach דִּידָךְ chelma וְזֵלְמָא

◆letav לְטַב leshav'ye לְשַׁוְּיֵיהּ rachamana רַוְזֲמָנָא ◆lehevei לֶהֱוֵי

פהל alei עֲלֵיהּ yigzerun יִגְזְרוּן zimnin זִמְנִין sheva שְׁבַע

◆tava טָבָא diyehevei דְּיֶהֱוֵי shemaya שְׁמַיָּא min מִן

‡lehevei לֶהֱוֵי vetava וְטָבָא ,hu הוּא tava טָבָא

The dreamer says silently (or scans):

ase עֲשֵׂה bemitzvot בְּמִצְוֹת pasha'ti פָּשַׁעְתִּי aviti עָוִיתִי chatati וְזֵטָאתִי

hateluyim הַתְּלוּיִים ta'aseh תַעֲשֶׂה lo לֹא uvemitzvot וּבְמִצְוֹת

◆alai עֲלַי dini דִּינִי matz'dik מַצְדִּיק vehareni וְהֲרֵינִי ,beTiferet בְּתִפְאֶרֶת

You have seen a good dream (x3), Your dream is good and may it be good. The Merciful One turns it to good. Seven times it will be decreed from the Heaven so it will be good. It is good and may it be good. (The dreamer says silently: I have transgressed, committed iniquity, and sinned in positive or negative commandments that are relying on Tiferet and I accept the judgments upon me.)

FOURTH TIME - NETZACH

The dreamer (Hei - Malchut):

Meditate to draw abundance from *Chochmah, Binah, Da'at* of *Chochmah, Binah, Da'at* of *Netzach* to the Seven Lower *Sefirot* of *Netzach* of *Malchut* in order to sweeten the Judments.

Chochmah of *Chochmah* of *Netzach* – חוכמה דוזכמה דנצוז

וְזַלְמָא chelma היה והוה ויהיה ע"ה

Binah of *Chochmah* of *Netzach* – בינה דוזכמה דנצוז

טָבָא tava אהיה אההי איהה היהה היהא היאה ההיא ההיא יהאה יההא יאהה האהי האיה ההאי

Da'at of *Chochmah* of *Netzach* – דעת דוזכמה דנצוז

וְזֵזָאִי chazai יהוה.

Chochmah of *Binah* of *Netzach* – חוכמה דבינה דנצוז

וְזַלְמָא chelma היה והוה ויהיה ע"ה

Binah of *Binah* of *Netzach* – בינה דבינה דנצוז

טָבָא tava אהיה אההי איהה היהה היהא היאה ההיא ההיא יהאה יההא יאהה האהי האיה ההאי

Da'at of *Binah* of *Netzach* – דעת דבינה דנצוז

וְזֵזָאִי chazai יהוה.

Chochmah of *Da'at* of *Netzach* – חוכמה דדעת דנצוז

וְזַלְמָא chelma היה והוה ויהיה ע"ה

Binah of *Da'at* of *Netzach* – בינה דדעת דנצוז

טָבָא tava אהיה אההי איהה היהה היהא היאה ההיא ההיא יהאה יההא יאהה האהי האיה ההאי

Da'at of *Da'at* of *Netzach* – דעת דדעת דנצוז

וְזֵזָאִי chazai יהוה.

FOURTH TIME - NETZACH
I have seen a good dream (x3)

The three beneficents (*Yud-Chochmah, Hei-Binah, Vav-Da'at*):

Meditate to draw abundance from *Chochmah, Binah, Da'at* of *Chochmah, Binah, Da'at* of *Netzach* of *Zeir Anpin* to *Chochmah, Binah, Da'at* of *Chochmah, Binah, Da'at* of *Netzach* of *Nukva* (the dreamer).

Chochmah of Chochmah of Netzach – וחכמה דוחכמה דנצוז

וְחֶלְמָא chelma היה והוה ויהיה ע"ה

Binah of Chochmah of Netzach – בינה דוחכמה דנצוז

טָבָא tava אהיה אההי איהי איהה היאה היאה ההיא יהאה יההא יאהה האהה האיה ההאי

Da'at of Chochmah of Netzach – דעת דוחכמה דנצוז

וַחֲזִיתָא chazeta.

Chochmah of Binah of Netzach – וחכמה דבינה דנצוז

וְחֶלְמָא chelma היה והוה ויהיה ע"ה

Binah of Binah of Netzach – בינה דבינה דנצוז

טָבָא tava אהיה אההי איהי איהא היאה היאה ההיא יהאה יההא יאהה האהה האיה ההאי

Da'at of Binah of Netzach – דעת דבינה דנצוז

וַחֲזִיתָא chazeta.

Chochmah of Da'at of Netzach – וחכמה דדעת דנצוז

וְחֶלְמָא chelma היה והוה ויהיה ע"ה

Binah of Da'at of Netzach – בינה דדעת דנצוז

טָבָא tava אהיה אההי איהי היאה היאה ההיא יהאה יההא יאהה האהה האיה ההאי

Da'at of Da'at of Netzach – דעת דדעת דנצוז

וַחֲזִיתָא chazeta.

וְחֶלְמָא chelma דִּידָךְ didach טָבָא tava הוּא ,hu וְטָבָא vetava

לֶהֱוֵי lehevei◆ רַחֲמָנָא rachamana לְשַׁוְּיֵיהּ leshav'ye לְטַב letav◆

שְׁבַע sheva זִמְנִין zimnin יִגְזְרוּן yigzerun עֲלֵיהּ alei פהל

מִן min שְׁמַיָּא shemaya דִּיהֱוֵי diyehevei טָבָא tava◆

טָבָא tava הוּא ,hu וְטָבָא vetava לֶהֱוֵי lehevei:

The dreamer says silently (or scans):

וְחָטָאתִי chatati עָוִיתִי aviti פָּשַׁעְתִּי pasha'ti בְּמִצְוֹת bemitzvot עֲשֵׂה ase

וּבְמִצְוֹת uvemitzvot לֹא lo תַעֲשֶׂה ta'aseh הַתְּלוּיִּים hateluyim

בְּנֶצַח beNetzach, וְהָרֵינִי vehareni מַצְדִּיק matz'dik דִּינִי dini עָלַי alai◆

You have seen a good dream (x3), Your dream is good and may it be good. The Merciful One turns it to good. Seven times it will be decreed from the Heaven so it will be good. It is good and may it be good. (The dreamer says silently: I have transgressed, committed iniquity, and sinned in positive or negative commandments that are relying on Netzach and I accept the judgments upon me.)

FIFTH TIME - HOD

The dreamer (Hei - Malchut):

Meditate to draw abundance from *Chochmah, Binah, Da'at* of *Chochmah, Binah, Da'at* of *Hod* to the Seven Lower *Sefirot* of *Hod* of *Malchut* in order to sweeten the Judgments.

Chochmah of Chochmah of Hod – וחכמה דוחכמה דהוד

וְזֶלְמָא chelma היה והוה ויהיה ע"ה

Binah of Chochmah of Hod – בינה דוחכמה דהוד

טָבָא tava אהיה אההי איהה היהה היהא היהי ההיא יהאה יההא יאהה האהי האיה ההאי

Da'at of Chochmah of Hod – דעת דוחכמה דהוד

וְזֶזָאִי chazai יהוה.

Chochmah of Binah of Hod – וחכמה דבינה דהוד

וְזֶלְמָא chelma היה והוה ויהיה ע"ה

Binah of Binah of Hod – בינה דבינה דהוד

טָבָא tava אהיה אההי איהה היהה היהא היהי ההיא יהאה יההא יאהה האהי האיה ההאי

Da'at of Binah of Hod – דעת דבינה דהוד

וְזֶזָאִי chazai יהוה.

Chochmah of Da'at of Hod – וחכמה דדעת דהוד

וְזֶלְמָא chelma היה והוה ויהיה ע"ה

Binah of Da'at of Hod – בינה דדעת דהוד

טָבָא tava אהיה אההי איהה היהה היהא היהי ההיא יהאה יההא יאהה האהי האיה ההאי

Da'at of Da'at of Hod – דעת דדעת דהוד

וְזֶזָאִי chazai יהוה.

FIFTH TIME - HOD
I have seen a good dream (x3)

The three beneficents (*Yud-Chochmah, Hei-Binah, Vav-Da'at*):

Meditate to draw abundance from *Chochmah, Binah, Da'at* of *Chochmah, Binah, Da'at* of *Hod* of *Zeir Anpin* to *Chochmah, Binah, Da'at* of *Chochmah, Binah, Da'at* of *Hod* of *Nukva* (the dreamer).

Chochmah of Chochmah of Hod — חוכמה דוחכמה דהוד

וְחֶלְמָא chelma היה והוה ויהיה ע"ה

Binah of Chochmah of Hod — בינה דוחכמה דהוד

טָבָא tava אהיה אההי איהי היהא היאה ההיא יהאה יההא יאהה האהי האיה ההאי

Da'at of Chochmah of Hod — דעת דוחכמה דהוד

וַחֲזֵיתָא. chazeta

Chochmah of Binah of Hod — וחכמה דבינה דהוד

וְחֶלְמָא chelma היה והוה ויהיה ע"ה

Binah of Binah of Hod — בינה דבינה דהוד

טָבָא tava אהיה אההי איהי היהא היאה ההיא יהאה יההא יאהה האהי האיה ההאי

Da'at of Binah of Hod — דעת דבינה דהוד

וַחֲזֵיתָא. chazeta

Chochmah of Da'at of Hod — וחכמה דדעת דהוד

וְחֶלְמָא chelma היה והוה ויהיה ע"ה

Binah of Da'at of Hod — בינה דדעת דהוד

טָבָא tava אהיה אההי איהי היהא היאה ההיא יהאה יההא יאהה האהי האיה ההאי

Da'at of Da'at of Hod — דעת דדעת דהוד

וַחֲזֵיתָא. chazeta

vetava וְטָבָא	,hu הוּא	tava טָבָא	didach דִּידָךְ	chelma וְחֶלְמָא	
letav♦ לְטַב	leshav'ye לְשַׁוְיֵיהּ	rachamana רַחֲמָנָא	lehevei♦ לֶהֱוֵי		
alei עֲלֵיהּ פהל	yigzerun יִגְזְרוּן	zimnin זִמְנִין	sheva שְׁבַע		
tava♦ טָבָא	diyehevei דִּיהֱוֵי	shemaya שְׁמַיָּא	min מִן		
lehevei‡ לֶהֱוֵי	vetava וְטָבָא	,hu הוּא	tava טָבָא		

The dreamer says silently (or scans):

ase עָשֶׂה	bemitzvot בְּמִצְוֹת	pasha'ti פָּשַׁעְתִּי	aviti עָוִיתִי	chatati חָטָאתִי	וְטָאתִי
hateluyim הַתְּלוּיִים	ta'aseh תַעֲשֶׂה	lo לֹא	uvemitzvot וּבְמִצְוֹת		
alai♦ עָלַי	dini דִּינִי	matz'dik מַצְדִּיק	vehareni וְהֲרֵינִי	beHod, בְּהוֹד	

You have seen a good dream (x3), Your dream is good and may it be good. The Merciful One turns it to good. Seven times it will be decreed from the Heaven so it will be good. It is good and may it be good. (The dreamer says silently: I have transgressed, committed iniquity, and sinned in positive or negative commandments that are relying on Hod and I accept the judgments upon me.)

SIXTH TIME - YESOD

The dreamer (*Hei - Malchut*):

Meditate to draw abundance from *Chochmah, Binah, Da'at* of *Chochmah, Binah, Da'at* of *Yesod* to the Seven Lower *Sefirot* of *Yesod* of *Malchut* in order to sweeten the Judgments.

Chochmah of *Chochmah* of *Yesod* — חכמה דחכמה דיסוד

וֶֽלְֽכְמָֽא chelma היה והוה ויהיה ע״ה

Binah of *Chochmah* of *Yesod* — בינה דחכמה דיסוד

טָֽבָֽא tava אהיה אההי איהה היהא היאה ההיא יהאה יההא יאהה האהה האיה ההאי

Da'at of *Chochmah* of *Yesod* — דעת דחכמה דיסוד

וֶֽחֲֽזָֽאִי chazai יהוה.

Chochmah of *Binah* of *Yesod* — חכמה דבינה דיסוד

וֶֽלְֽכְמָֽא chelma היה והוה ויהיה ע״ה

Binah of *Binah* of *Yesod* — בינה דבינה דיסוד

טָֽבָֽא tava אהיה אההי איהה היהא היאה ההיא יהאה יההא יאהה האהה האיה ההאי

Da'at of *Binah* of *Yesod* — דעת דבינה דיסוד

וֶֽחֲֽזָֽאִי chazai יהוה.

Chochmah of *Da'at* of *Yesod* — חכמה דדעת דיסוד

וֶֽלְֽכְמָֽא chelma היה והוה ויהיה ע״ה

Binah of *Da'at* of *Yesod* — בינה דדעת דיסוד

טָֽבָֽא tava אהיה אההי איהה היהא היאה ההיא יהאה יההא יאהה האהה האיה ההאי

Da'at of *Da'at* of *Yesod* — דעת דדעת דיסוד

וֶֽחֲֽזָֽאִי chazai יהוה.

SIXTH TIME - YESOD

I have seen a good dream (x3)

The three beneficents (*Yud-Chochmah, Hei-Binah, Vav-Da'at*):

Meditate to draw abundance from *Chochmah, Binah, Da'at* of *Chochmah, Binah, Da'at* of *Yesod* of *Zeir Anpin* to *Chochmah, Binah, Da'at* of *Chochmah, Binah, Da'at* of *Yesod* of *Nukva* (the dreamer).

Chochmah of Chochmah of Yesod – וחכמה דוחכמה דיסוד

הָיָה והוה ויהיה ע"ה chelma וְחֶלְמָא

Binah of Chochmah of Yesod – בינה דוחכמה דיסוד

אהיה אהֹהי איהה היהא היהא הֹיהא ֹיהא יהֹהא יההא יאהה הֹאהה הֹאיה הֹאהי ההאי tava טָבָא

Da'at of Chochmah of Yesod – דעת דוחכמה דיסוד

chazeta וְחֲזֵיתָא.

Chochmah of Binah of Yesod – וחכמה דבינה דיסוד

הָיָה והוה ויהיה ע"ה chelma וְחֶלְמָא

Binah of Binah of Yesod – בינה דבינה דיסוד

אהיה אהֹהי איהה היהא היאה היהא הֹיהא יהֹהא יאהה הֹאהה הֹאיה הֹאהי ההאי tava טָבָא

Da'at of Binah of Yesod – דעת דבינה דיסוד

chazeta וְחֲזֵיתָא.

Chochmah of Da'at of Yesod – וחכמה דדעת דיסוד

הָיָה והוה ויהיה ע"ה chelma וְחֶלְמָא

Binah of Da'at of Yesod – בינה דדעת דיסוד

אהיה אהֹהי איהה היהא היהא היאה ֹיהא הֹיהא יאהה הֹאהה הֹאיה הֹאהי ההאי tava טָבָא

Da'at of Da'at of Yesod – דעת דדעת דיסוד

chazeta וְחֲזֵיתָא.

vetava וְטָבָא	,hu הוא	tava טָבָא	didach דִּידָךְ	chelma וְחֶלְמָא		
◆letav לְטַב	leshav'ye לְשַׁוְיֵיהּ	rachamana רַחֲמָנָא	◆lehevei לֶהֱוֵי			
פהל alei עֲלֵיהּ	yigzerun יִגְזְרוּן	zimnin זִמְנִין	sheva שְׁבַע			
◆tava טָבָא	diyehevei דִּיהֱוֵי	shemaya שְׁמַיָּא	min מִן			
‡lehevei לֶהֱוֵי	vetava וְטָבָא	,hu הוא	tava טָבָא			

The dreamer says silently (or scans):

ase עֲשֵׂה	bemitzvot בְּמִצְוֹת	pasha'ti פָּשַׁעְתִּי	aviti עָוִיתִי	chatati וְחָטָאתִי
hateluyim הַתְלוּיִים	ta'aseh תַעֲשֶׂה	lo לֹא	uvemitzvot וּבְמִצְוֹת	
◆alai עָלַי	dini דִּינִי	matz'dik מַצְדִּיק	vehareni וַהֲרֵינִי	,beYesod בִּיסוֹד

You have seen a good dream (x3), Your dream is good and may it be good. The Merciful One turns it to good. Seven times it will be decreed from the Heaven so it will be good. It is good and may it be good. (The dreamer says silently: I have transgressed, committed iniquity, and sinned in positive or negative commandments that are relying on Yesod and I accept the judgments upon me.)

SEVENTH TIME – MALCHUT OF ZEIR ANPIN

The dreamer (*Hei - Malchut*):

Meditate to draw abundance from *Chochmah, Binah, Da'at* of *Chochmah, Binah, Da'at* of *Malchut* of *Zeir Anpin* to the Seven Lower *Sefirot* of *Malchut* of *Zeir Anpin* in order to sweeten the Judments.

Chochmah of *Chochmah* of *Malchut* of *Zeir Anpin* – וזומה דוזוכמה דמלכות דז"א

וְזַלְמָא chelma היה והוה ויהיה ע"ה

Binah of *Chochmah* of *Malchut* of *Zeir Anpin* – בינה דוזוכמה דמלכות דז"א

טָבָא tava אהיה אההי איהי איהה היהא היא היהא יהאה יההא יאהה האהי האיה ההאי

Da'at of *Chochmah* of *Malchut* of *Zeir Anpin* – דעת דוזוכמה דמלכות דז"א

וְזָזָאִי chazai יהוה.

Chochmah of *Binah* of *Malchut* of *Zeir Anpin* – וזומה דבינה דמלכות דז"א

וְזַלְמָא chelma היה והוה ויהיה ע"ה

Binah of *Binah* of *Malchut* of *Zeir Anpin* – בינה דבינה דמלכות דז"א

טָבָא tava אהיה אההי איהי איהה היהא היא היהא יהאה יההא יאהה האהי האיה ההאי

Da'at of *Binah* of *Malchut* of *Zeir Anpin* – דעת דבינה דמלכות דז"א

וְזָזָאִי chazai יהוה.

Chochmah of *Da'at* of *Malchut* of *Zeir Anpin* – וזומה דדעת דמלכות דז"א

וְזַלְמָא chelma היה והוה ויהיה ע"ה

Binah of *Da'at* of *Malchut* of *Zeir Anpin* – בינה דדעת דמלכות דז"א

טָבָא tava אהיה אההי איהי איהה היהא היא היהא יהאה יההא יאהה האהי האיה ההאי

Da'at of *Da'at* of *Malchut* of *Zeir Anpin* – דעת דדעת דמלכות דז"א

וְזָזָאִי chazai יהוה.

SEVENTH TIME – MALCHUT OF ZEIR ANPIN
I have seen a good dream (x3)

The three beneficents (*Yud-Chochmah, Hei-Binah, Vav-Da'at*):

Meditate to draw abundance from *Chochmah, Binah, Da'at* of *Chochmah, Binah, Da'at* of *Malchut* of *Zeir Anpin* to *Chochmah, Binah, Da'at* of *Chochmah, Binah, Da'at* of *Malchut* of *Nukva* (the dreamer).

Chochmah of Chochmah of Malchut of Zeir Anpin – וחכמה דוחכמה דמלכות דז"א

וְזֶלְמָא chelma היה והוה ויהיה ע"ה

Binah of Chochmah of Malchut of Zeir Anpin – בינה דוחכמה דמלכות דז"א

טָבָא tava אהיה אההי איהי איהה היהא היאה היאי יהאה יאהה האהי האיה ההאי

Da'at of Chochmah of Malchut of Zeir Anpin – דעת דוחכמה דמלכות דז"א

וְזֶזִיתָא chazeta.

Chochmah of Binah of Malchut of Zeir Anpin – וחכמה דבינה דמלכות דז"א

וְזֶלְמָא chelma היה והוה ויהיה ע"ה

Binah of Binah of Malchut of Zeir Anpin – בינה דבינה דמלכות דז"א

טָבָא tava אהיה אההי איהי איהה היהא היאה היאי יהאה יהאה יאהה האהי האיה ההאי

Da'at of Binah of Malchut of Zeir Anpin – דעת דבינה דמלכות דז"א

וְזֶזִיתָא chazeta.

Chochmah of Da'at of Malchut of Zeir Anpin – וחכמה דדעת דמלכות דז"א

וְזֶלְמָא chelma היה והוה ויהיה ע"ה

Binah of Da'at of Malchut of Zeir Anpin – בינה דדעת דמלכות דז"א

טָבָא tava אהיה אההי איהי איהה היהא היאה היאי יהאה יהאה יאהה האהי האיה ההאי

Da'at of Da'at of Malchut of Zeir Anpin – דעת דדעת דמלכות דז"א

וְזֶזִיתָא chazeta.

vetava וְטָבָא ,hu הוּא tava טָבָא didach דִּידָך chelma וְזֶלְמָא

◆letav לְטָב leshav'ye לְשַׁוְּיֵיה rachamana רַוֲזְמָנָא ◆lehevei לֶהֱוֵי

פהל alei עֲלֵיה yigzerun יִגְזְרוּן zimnin זִימְנִין sheva שֶׁבַע

◆tava טָבָא diyehevei דִּיהֱוֵי shemaya שְׁמַיָּא min מִן

‡lehevei לֶהֱוֵי vetava וְטָבָא ,hu הוּא tava טָבָא

The dreamer says silently (or scans):

ase עֲשֵׂה bemitzvot בְּמִצְוֹת pasha'ti פָּשַׁעְתִּי aviti עָוִיתִי chatati וְזֶטָאתִי

beMalchut בְּמַלְכוּת hateluyim הַתְּלוּיִים ta'aseh תַעֲשֶׂה lo לֹא uvemitzvot וּבְמִצְוֹת

◆alai עֲלַי dini דִּינִי matz'dik מַצְדִּיק vehareni וַהֲרֵינִי ,Anpin diZeir ז"א

You have seen a good dream (x3), Your dream is good and may it be good. The Merciful One turns it to good. Seven times it will be decreed from the Heaven so it will be good. It is good and may it be good. (The dreamer say silently: I have transgressed, committed iniquity, and sinned in positive or negative commandments that are relying on Malchut of Zeir Anpin and I exept the judgments upon me.)

The word *tava* טבא (good) appears in the above connection 63 times (21 times as the beneficents recite the verse "*chelma tava chazeta*" and another 42 times in the final section of each round "*chelma didach tave hu...*"). Therefore, the three beneficents should meditate here on the Name: יה"ו אהיה as it has the same numerical value of 42 and on the Name: יוד הי ואו הי as it has the numerical value of 63. Then, by adding three (the basic number of the word *tava* in each round), meditate on the Name: אדנ"י ע"ה which is the name of the *Malchut* - the dreamer. Then, by adding six (the basic number of the word *tava* in the verse "*chelma didach tave hu...*"), meditate on the Name: יוד הי ויו הי which has the same numerical value of Mercy (72 – וַֹסד).

In the following verses the word *hafachta* (turned over, or derivatives of it) appears three times. The three beneficents and the dreamer should meditate here to draw abundance from the Three Upper *Sefirot* of *Binah* to the Seven Lower *Sefirot* (as each is included of ten — and together equal 70), and thereby turn over and cancel a life time (70 years) of Judgment.

The dreamer (*Hei - Malchut*):

	li כלי	lemachol לְמָחוֹל	mispedi מִסְפְּדִי	hafachta הָפַכְתָּ
		vate'azreni וַתְּאַזְּרֵנִי	saki שַׂקִי	pitachta פִּתַּחְתָּ
		simcha שִׂמְחָה:		

The three beneficents (*Yud-Chochmah, Hei-Binah, Vav-Da'at*):

bemachol בְּמָחוֹל	betula בְּתוּלָה	tismach תִּשְׂמַח	az אָז
yachdav יַחְדָּו	uzkenim וּזְקֵנִים	uvachurim וּבַחוּרִים	
lesason לְשָׂשׂוֹן	evlam אֶבְלָם	vehafach'ti וְהָפַכְתִּי	
migonam מִיגוֹנָם:	vesimach'tim וְשִׂמַּחְתִּים	venichamtim וְנִחַמְתִּים	
lishmo'a לִשְׁמֹעַ	Elohecha אֱלֹהֶיךָ	Adonai יְהֹוָאדֹנָיאהרונהי	ava אָבָה	velo וְלֹא-
Adonai יְהֹוָאדֹנָיאהרונהי	vayahafoch וַיַּהֲפֹךְ	Bil'am בִּלְעָם	el אֶל-
livracha לִבְרָכָה	hakelala הַקְּלָלָה	et אֶת-	lecha לְךָ	Elohecha אֱלֹהֶיךָ
Elohecha אֱלֹהֶיךָ:	Adonai יְהֹוָאדֹנָיאהרונהי	ahevcha אֲהֵבְךָ	ki כִּי

"You have turned my mourning into a celebration for me. You have undone my sackcloth and have girded me with joy." *(Psalms 30:12)* "The young women will dance for joy, and the men—old and young—will join in the celebration. I will turn their mourning into joy." *(Jeremiah 31:12)* "But the Lord your God refused to listen to Balaam. He turned the intended curse into a blessing because the Lord your God loves you." *(Deuteronomy 23:6)*

In the following verses the word *pada* (redeem, or derivatives of it) appears three times. The three beneficents and the dreamer should meditate here to draw abundance from the Three Upper *Sefirot* of *Chochmah* to the Seven Lower *Sefirot* (as each is included of ten — and together equal 70), and thereby redeem and cancel a life time (70 years) of Judgment.

The dreamer (*Hei - Malchut*):

li כִּי   mikerav מִקְרָב־   nafshi נַפְשִׁי   veshalom בְשָׁלוֹם   pada פָּדָה

imadi עִמָּדִי   hayu הָיוּ   verabim בְרַבִּים   ki כִּי־

The three beneficents (*Yud-Chochmah, Hei-Binah, Vav-Da'at*):

Shaul שָׁאוּל   el אֶל־   ha'am הָעָם   vayomer וַיֹּאמֶר

asa עָשָׂה   asher אֲשֶׁר   yamut יָמוּת   haYonatan הֲיוֹנָתָן

beYisrael בִּיִשְׂרָאֵל   hazot הַזֹּאת   hagedola הַגְּדוֹלָה   hayeshu'a הַיְשׁוּעָה

Adonai יְהֹוָה   chai חַי־   chalila חָלִילָה

artza אָרְצָה   rosho רֹאשׁוֹ   misa'arat מִשַּׂעֲרַת   yipol יִפֹּל   im אִם־

haze הַזֶּה   hayom הַיּוֹם   asa עָשָׂה   Elohim אֱלֹהִים   im עִם־   ki כִּי־

met מֵת   velo וְלֹא־   Yonatan יוֹנָתָן   et אֶת־   ha'am הָעָם   vayifdu וַיִּפְדּוּ

uva'u וּבָאוּ   yeshuvun יְשֻׁבוּן   Adonai יְהֹוָה   ufduyei וּפְדוּיֵי

vesimchat וְשִׂמְחַת   berina בְרִנָּה   Tziyon צִיּוֹן

sason שָׂשׂוֹן   rosham רֹאשָׁם   al עַל־   olam עוֹלָם

va'anacha וַאֲנָחָה   yagon יָגוֹן   venasu וְנָסוּ   yasigu יַשִּׂיגוּ   vesimcha וְשָׂמְחָה

"He redeems me and keeps me safe from the battle waged against me, though many still oppose me." (Psalms 55:19) *"But the people broke in and said to Saul, "Jonathan has won this great victory for Israel. Should he die? Far from it! As surely as the Lord lives, not one hair on his head will be touched, for God helped him do a great deed today. So the people redeemed Jonathan, and he was not put to death."* (I Samuel 14:45) *"And the redeemed of the Lord shall return, and they shall come to Zion with song and with everlasting happiness upon their heads. Gladness and joy they shall attain, and sorrow and sigh shall withdraw."* (Isaiah 35:10)

In the following verses the word *shalom* (peace/completion, or derivatives of it) appears nine times. The three beneficents and the dreamer should meditate here to draw abundance from the Three Upper *Sefirot* of *Keter* (each included of three) to the Seven Lower *Sefirot* (as each is included of ten – and together equal 70), and thereby turnover and cancel a life time (70 years) of Judgment.

The dreamer (Hei - Malchut):

bore בּוֹרֵא   niv נִיב   (כתיב: נוב)   sefatayim שְׂפָתָיִם

shalom שָׁלוֹם   shalom שָׁלוֹם   larachok לָרָחוֹק עדי   velakarov וְלַקָּרוֹב

amar אָמַר   Adonai יְהֹוָאדְנִיאהדונהי   urfativ וּרְפָאתִיו:

The three beneficents (Yud-Chochmah, Hei-Binah, Vav-Da'at):

veru'ach וְרוּחַ   lavsha לָבְשָׁה   et אֶת־   Amasai עֲמָשַׂי

rosh רֹאשׁ ריבוע אלהים אלהים דיודין ע"ה   hashalishim הַשָּׁלִישִׁים (כתיב: השלושים)

lecha לְךָ   David דָּוִיד   ve'imcha וְעִמְּךָ   ven בֶן   Yishai יִשַׁי

shalom שָׁלוֹם   shalom שָׁלוֹם   lecha לְךָ   veshalom וְשָׁלוֹם   le'ozrecha לְעֹזְרֶךָ

ki כִּי   azarcha עֲזָרֶךָ   Elohecha אֱלֹהֶיךָ ילה   vaykablem וַיְקַבְּלֵם

David דָּוִיד   vayitnem וַיִּתְּנֵם   berashei בְּרָאשֵׁי   hagedud הַגְּדוּד:

The dreamer (Hei - Malchut):

va'amartem וַאֲמַרְתֶּם   ko כֹה   lechai לֶחָי

The three beneficents (Yud-Chochmah, Hei-Binah, Vav-Da'at):

ve'ata וְאַתָּה   shalom שָׁלוֹם   uvetcha וּבֵיתְךָ ב"פ ראה   shalom שָׁלוֹם   vechol וְכֹל

asher אֲשֶׁר   lecha לְךָ   shalom שָׁלוֹם: Adonai יְהֹוָאדְנִיאהדונהי   oz עֹז

le'amo לְעַמּוֹ   yiten יִתֵּן   Adonai יְהֹוָאדְנִיאהדונהי   yevarech יְבָרֵךְ עסמ"ב, הברכה

et אֶת־ (למתק את ז' המלכים שמתו)   amo עַמּוֹ   vashalom בַשָּׁלוֹם ר"ת ע"ב, ריבוע יהוה:

"I create fruit of the lips. Peace, peace for the far and the near, says the Lord, and I shall heal him." (Isaiah 57:19) "A spirit clothed Amasai, the head of the officers, for your sake, David, and to be with you, the son of Ishai. Peace, peace to you, and peace to the one who helps you, for your God had helped you. David accepted them and appointed them heads of the group." (I Chronicles 12:19) "And you shall say: So may it be as long as you live. Peace for you, peace for your household and peace for all that is with you." (I Samuel 25:6) "The Lord endows His nation with strength, the Lord blesses His nation with peace." (Psalms 29:11)

The three beneficents and the dreamer meditate here to draw abundance from *Keter* to *Chochmah*.

The dreamer (*Hei - Malchut*):

Adonai יְהֹוָאדְנִיאהדונהי   shama'ti שָׁמַעְתִּי   shim'acha שִׁמְעֲךָ   yareti יָרֵאתִי

The three beneficents (*Yud-Chochmah, Hei-Binah, Vav-Da'at*):

Adonai יְהֹוָאדְנִיאהדונהי   pa'ol'cha פָּעָלְךָ   bekerev בְּקֶרֶב

shanim שָׁנִים   chayehu וְחַיֵּיהוּ   bekerev בְּקֶרֶב   shanim שָׁנִים

todi'a תּוֹדִיעַ   berogez בְּרֹגֶז   rachem רַחֵם   tizkor תִּזְכּוֹר׃

The three beneficents and the dreamer meditate here to draw abundance from *Chochmah* to *Binah*.

The dreamer (*Hei - Malchut*):

Adonai יְהֹוָאדְנִיאהדונהי   shama'ti שָׁמַעְתִּי   shim'acha שִׁמְעֲךָ   yareti יָרֵאתִי

The three beneficents (*Yud-Chochmah, Hei-Binah, Vav-Da'at*):

Adonai יְהֹוָאדְנִיאהדונהי   pa'ol'cha פָּעָלְךָ   bekerev בְּקֶרֶב

shanim שָׁנִים   chayehu וְחַיֵּיהוּ   bekerev בְּקֶרֶב   shanim שָׁנִים

todi'a תּוֹדִיעַ   berogez בְּרֹגֶז   rachem רַחֵם   tizkor תִּזְכּוֹר׃

The three beneficents and the dreamer meditate here to draw abundance from *Binah* to *Da'at*.

The dreamer (*Hei - Malchut*):

Adonai יְהֹוָאדְנִיאהדונהי   shama'ti שָׁמַעְתִּי   shim'acha שִׁמְעֲךָ   yareti יָרֵאתִי

The three beneficents (*Yud-Chochmah, Hei-Binah, Vav-Da'at*):

Adonai יְהֹוָאדְנִיאהדונהי   pa'ol'cha פָּעָלְךָ   bekerev בְּקֶרֶב

shanim שָׁנִים   chayehu וְחַיֵּיהוּ   bekerev בְּקֶרֶב   shanim שָׁנִים

todi'a תּוֹדִיעַ   berogez בְּרֹגֶז   rachem רַחֵם   tizkor תִּזְכּוֹר׃

(x3) *"I have heard all about You, Lord.*
I am filled with awe by Your amazing works. In this time of our deep need,
help us again as you did in years gone by. And in Your anger, remember Your mercy." (Habakuk 3:2)

The three beneficents and the dreamer meditate here to draw abundance from *Da'at* to *Chesed*.

The dreamer (*Hei - Malchut*):

שִׁיר shir לַמַּעֲלוֹת lama'alot אֶשָּׂא esa עֵינַי enai רִיבוּע מ"ה

אֶל el הֶהָרִים heharim מֵאַיִן me'ayin יָבֹא yavo עֶזְרִי ezri

עֶזְרִי ezri מֵעִם me'im יְהֹוָה Adonai

עֹשֵׂה ose שָׁמַיִם shamayim וי"פ טל, י"פ כוזו וָאָרֶץ va'aretz

The three beneficents (*Yud-Chochmah, Hei-Binah, Vav-Da'at*) sy:

אַל al יִתֵּן yiten לַמּוֹט lamot רַגְלֶךָ raglecha

אַל al יָנוּם yanum שֹׁמְרֶךָ shomrecha

The dreamer (*Hei - Malchut*):

הִנֵּה hine לֹא lo יָנוּם yanum וְלֹא velo יִישָׁן yishan ע"ע נהורין דא"א

שׁוֹמֵר shomer כ"א ההויות שבתפילין יִשְׂרָאֵל Yisrael

The three beneficents (*Yud-Chochmah, Hei-Binah, Vav-Da'at*):

יְהֹוָה Adonai שֹׁמְרֶךָ shomrecha יְהֹוָה Adonai צִלְּךָ tzilecha

עַל al יַד yad יְמִינֶךָ yeminecha הי"י יוֹמָם yomam הַשֶּׁמֶשׁ hashemesh

לֹא lo יַכֶּכָּה yakeka ר"ת ילה וְיָרֵחַ veyare'ach בַּלַּיְלָה balayla

יְהֹוָה Adonai יִשְׁמָרְךָ yishmorcha מִכָּל mikol רָע ra

יִשְׁמֹר yishmor אֶת et נַפְשֶׁךָ nafshecha

יְהֹוָה Adonai יִשְׁמֹר yishmor צֵאתְךָ tzetcha

וּבוֹאֶךָ uvo'echa מֵעַתָּה me'ata וְעַד ve'ad עוֹלָם olam

"A Song of Ascents: I lift up my eyes to the mountains; from where will my help come? My help is from the Lord, Creator of the Heavens and the Earth. He will not allow your legs to falter. Your Guardian shall not sleep. Behold: the Guardian of Israel shall neither slumber nor sleep. The Lord is your Guardian. The Lord is your protective shade at your right hand. During the day, the sun shall not harm you, nor shall the moon, at night. The Lord shall protect you from all evil, He will guard your soul. He shall guard you when you leave and when you come, from now and for eternity." (Psalms 121)

The three beneficents and the dreamer meditate here to draw abundance from Chesed *to* Gevurah.

The dreamer (Hei - Malchut):

שִׁיר shir לַמַּעֲלוֹת lama'alot אֶשָּׂא esa עֵינַי enai מ"ה רִיבּוּע

אֶל־ el הֶהָרִים heharim מֵאַיִן me'ayin יָבֹא yavo עֶזְרִי ezri:

עֶזְרִי ezri מֵעִם me'im יְהֹוָﬡﬞﬢﬠﬣﬤ Adonai

עֹשֶׂה ose שָׁמַיִם shamayim י"פ טל, י"פ י"פ כוזו וָאָרֶץ va'aretz:

The three beneficents (Yud-Chochmah, Hei-Binah, Vav-Da'at):

אַל־ al יִתֵּן yiten לַמּוֹט lamot רַגְלֶךָ raglecha

אַל־ al יָנוּם yanum שֹׁמְרֶךָ shomrecha:

The dreamer (Hei - Malchut):

הִנֵּה hine לֹא־ lo יָנוּם yanum וְלֹא velo יִישָׁן yishan ש"ע נהורין דא"א

שׁוֹמֵר shomer כ"א ההויות שבתפילין ישראל Yisrael:

The three beneficents (Yud-Chochmah, Hei-Binah, Vav-Da'at):

יְהֹוָﬡﬞﬢﬠﬣﬤ Adonai שֹׁמְרֶךָ shomrecha יְהֹוָﬡﬞﬢﬠﬣﬤ Adonai צִלְּךָ tzilecha

עַל־ al יַד yad יְמִינֶךָ yeminecha היי יוֹמָם yomam הַשֶּׁמֶשׁ hashemesh

לֹא־ lo יַכֶּכָּה yakeka ר"ת ילה וְיָרֵחַ veyare'ach בַּלַּיְלָה balayla מלה:

יְהֹוָﬡﬞﬢﬠﬣﬤ Adonai יִשְׁמָרְךָ yishmorcha מִכָּל־ mikol ילי רָע ra

יִשְׁמֹר yishmor אֶת־ et נַפְשֶׁךָ nafshecha מיכ:

יְהֹוָﬡﬞﬢﬠﬣﬤ Adonai יִשְׁמֹר yishmor צֵאתְךָ tzetcha

וּבוֹאֶךָ uvo'echa מֵעַתָּה me'ata וְעַד־ ve'ad עוֹלָם olam וולי:

"A Song of Ascents: I lift up my eyes to the mountains; from where will my help come? My help is from the Lord, Creator of the Heavens and the Earth. He will not allow your legs to falter. Your Guardian shall not sleep. Behold: the Guardian of Israel shall neither slumber nor sleep. The Lord is your Guardian. The Lord is your protective shade at your right hand. During the day, the sun shall not harm you, nor shall the moon, at night. The Lord shall protect you from all evil, He will guard your soul. He shall guard you when you leave and when you come, from now and for eternity." (Psalms 121)

The three beneficents and the dreamer meditate here to draw abundance from *Gevurah* to *Tiferet*.

The dreamer (*Hei - Malchut*):

שִׁיר shir לַמַּעֲלוֹת lama'alot אֶשָּׂא esa עֵינַי enai רִיבוּעַ מ״ה

אֶל־ el הֶהָרִים heharim מֵאַיִן me'ayin יָבֹא yavo עֶזְרִי ‡ezri

עֶזְרִי ezri מֵעִם me'im יְהֹוָ֘אֲדֹנִיאהדונהי Adonai

עֹשֵׂה ose שָׁמַיִם shamayim י״פ טַל, טל, י״פ כחו וָאָרֶץ va'aretz‡

The three beneficents (*Yud-Chochmah, Hei-Binah, Vav-Da'at*):

אַל־ al יִתֵּן yiten לַמּוֹט lamot רַגְלֶךָ raglecha

אַל־ al יָנוּם yanum שֹׁמְרֶךָ shomrecha‡

The dreamer (*Hei - Malchut*):

הִנֵּה hine לֹא־ lo יָנוּם yanum וְלֹא velo יִישָׁן yishan ש״ע נהורין דא״א

שׁוֹמֵר shomer כ״א ההויות שובתפילין יִשְׂרָאֵל Yisrael‡

The three beneficents (*Yud-Chochmah, Hei-Binah, Vav-Da'at*):

יְהֹוָ֘אֲדֹנִיאהדונהי Adonai שֹׁמְרֶךָ shomrecha יְהֹוָ֘אֲדֹנִיאהדונהי Adonai צִלְּךָ tzilecha

עַל־ al יַד yad יְמִינֶךָ yeminecha הי״ם יוֹמָם yomam הַשֶּׁמֶשׁ hashemesh

לֹא־ lo יַכֶּכָּה yakeka ר״ת ילה וְיָרֵחַ veyare'ach בַּלַּיְלָה balayla מלה:

יְהֹוָ֘אֲדֹנִיאהדונהי Adonai יִשְׁמָרְךָ yishmorcha מִכָּל־ mikol ילי רָע ra

יִשְׁמֹר yishmor אֶת־ et נַפְשֶׁךָ nafshecha מ״כ:

יְהֹוָ֘אֲדֹנִיאהדונהי Adonai יִשְׁמֹר yishmor צֵאתְךָ tzetcha

וּבוֹאֶךָ uvo'echa מֵעַתָּה me'ata וְעַד־ ve'ad עוֹלָם olam וול:

"A Song of Ascents: I lift up my eyes to the mountains; from where will my help come? My help is from the Lord, Creator of the Heavens and the Earth. He will not allow your legs to falter. Your Guardian shall not sleep. Behold: the Guardian of Israel shall neither slumber nor sleep. The Lord is your Guardian. The Lord is your protective shade at your right hand. During the day, the sun shall not harm you, nor shall the moon, at night. The Lord shall protect you from all evil, He will guard your soul. He shall guard you when you leave and when you come, from now and for eternity." (Psalms 121)

The three beneficents and the dreamer meditate here to draw abundance from *Tiferet* to *Netzach*.

The dreamer (*Hei - Malchut*):

chayim וֺֿחַיִּים orach אֹרַח todi'eni תּוֹדִיעֵנִי

The three beneficents (*Yud-Chochmah, Hei-Binah, Vav-Da'at*):

panecha פָּנֶיךָ et אֶת semachot שְׂמָחוֹת sova שֹׂבַע

:netzach נֶצַח bimin'cha בִּימִינְךָ ne'imot נְעִמוֹת

The three beneficents and the dreamer meditate here to draw abundance from *Netzach* to *Hod*.

The dreamer (*Hei - Malchut*):

chayim וֺֿחַיִּים orach אֹרַח todi'eni תּוֹדִיעֵנִי

The three beneficents (*Yud-Chochmah, Hei-Binah, Vav-Da'at*):

panecha פָּנֶיךָ et אֶת semachot שְׂמָחוֹת sova שֹׂבַע

:netzach נֶצַח bimin'cha בִּימִינְךָ ne'imot נְעִמוֹת

The three beneficents and the dreamer meditate here to draw abundance from *Hod* to *Yesod*.

The dreamer (*Hei - Malchut*):

chayim וֺֿחַיִּים orach אֹרַח todi'eni תּוֹדִיעֵנִי

The three beneficents (*Yud-Chochmah, Hei-Binah, Vav-Da'at*):

panecha פָּנֶיךָ et אֶת semachot שְׂמָחוֹת sova שֹׂבַע

:netzach נֶצַח bimin'cha בִּימִינְךָ ne'imot נְעִמוֹת

(x3) *"You will show me the way of life,
granting me the joy of your presence and the pleasures of living with you forever."* (Psalms 16:11)

The dreamer (Hei - Malchut):

וַיְדַבֵּר vaydaber   ראה   יְהֹוָה/אדני־יאהדונהי Adonai   אֶל־ el   מֹשֶׁה Moshe

מהׁע, ע״ב בריבוע קס״א, אל עדי, ד״פ אלהים ע״ה lemor: לֵאמֹר   דַּבֵּר daber ראה

אֶל־ el   אַהֲרֹן Aharon   וְאֶל־ ve'el   בָּנָיו banav   לֵאמֹר lemor

כֹּה ko   היי   תְבָרֲכוּ tevarchu   יהוה ריבוע יהוה ריבוע מ״ה

אֶת־ et   בְּנֵי benei   יִשְׂרָאֵל Yisrael   אָמוֹר amor   לָהֶם lahem:

The initials of the three verses give us the Holy Name: יי״.
In this section, there are 15 words, which are equal to the numerical value of the Holy Name: יהה.

The three beneficents (Yud-Chochmah, Hei-Binah, Vav-Da'at):

(Right – Chesed) The three beneficents meditate here to draw abundance to:
Chochmah, Chesed, Netzach (Right Column) of Chochmah of Malchut.

יְבָרֶכְךָ yevarechecha   יְהֹוָה/אדני־יאהדונהי Adonai   וְיִשְׁמְרֶךָ veyishmerecha

ר״ת = יהוה ; וס״ת = מ״ה:

(Left - Gevurah) The three beneficents meditate here to draw abundance to:
Binah, Gevurah, Hod (Left Column) of Binah of Malchut.

יָאֵר ya'er   כף   ויו   זין   ויו   יהֹוָה/אדני־יאהדונהי Adonai | פָּנָיו panav

אֵלֶיךָ elecha   וִיחֻנֶּךָּ vichuneka   מגד ;   יהה   אותיות   בפסוק:

(Central – Tiferet) The three beneficents meditate here to draw abundance to:
Da'at, Tiferet, Yesod (Central Column) of Tiferet of Malchut.

יִשָּׂא yisa   יְהֹוָה/אדני־יאהדונהי Adonai | פָּנָיו panav   אֵלֶיךָ elecha

וְיָשֵׂם veyasem   לְךָ lecha   שָׁלוֹם shalom   האא   תיבות   בפסוק:

"And the Lord spoke to Moses and said: Speak to Aaron and his sons saying:
So shall you bless the Children of Israel, say to them:
May the Lord bless you and protect you.
May the Lord enlighten His countenance for you and give you grace.
May the Lord lift His countenance towards you and give you peace." (Numbers 6:22-26)

The dreamer (Hei - Malchut):

Moshe מֹשֶׁה el אֶל־ Adonai יְהֹוָאֱדִנִיאהדונהי ראה vaydaber וַיְדַבֵּר

מהיע, ע"ב בריבוע קס"א, אל שדי, ד"פ אלהים ע"ה daber דַּבֵּר lemor לֵאמֹר: ראה

lemor לֵאמֹר banav בָּנָיו ve'el וְאֶל־ Aharon אַהֲרֹן el אֶל־

כה ko היי tevarchu תְבָרְכוּ יהוה ריבוע יהוה ריבוע יהוה מ"ה

lahem לָהֶם: amor אָמוֹר Yisrael יִשְׂרָאֵל benei בְּנֵי et אֶת־

> The initials of the three verses give us the Holy Name: יהוה.
> In this section, there are 15 words, which are equal to the numerical value of the Holy Name: יהה.

The three beneficents (Yud-Chochmah, Hei-Binah, Vav-Da'at):

(Right – Chesed) The three beneficents meditate here to draw abundance to:
Chochmah, Chesed, Netzach (Right Column) of Chochmah of Malchut.

veyishmerecha וְיִשְׁמְרֶךָ Adonai יְהֹוָאֱדִנִיאהדונהי yevarechecha יְבָרֶכְךָ

ר"ת = יהוה ; וס"ת = מ"ה:

(Left - Gevurah) The three beneficents meditate here to draw abundance to:
Binah, Gevurah, Hod (Left Column) of Binah of Malchut.

panav פָּנָיו | Adonai יְהֹוָאֱדִנִיאהדונהי ויו זין ויו כף ya'er יָאֵר

elecha אֵלֶיךָ vichuneka וִיחֻנֶּךָ מגד ; יהוה אותיות בפסוק:

(Central – Tiferet) The three beneficents meditate here to draw abundance to:
Da'at, Tiferet, Yesod (Central Column) of Tiferet of Malchut.

elecha אֵלֶיךָ panav פָּנָיו | Adonai יְהֹוָאֱדִנִיאהדונהי yisa יִשָּׂא

veyasem וְיָשֵׂם lecha לְךָ shalom שָׁלוֹם האא תיבות בפסוק:

"And the Lord spoke to Moses and said: Speak to Aaron and his sons saying:
So shall you bless the Children of Israel, say to them:
May the Lord bless you and protect you.
May the Lord enlighten His countenance for you and give you grace.
May the Lord lift His countenance towards you and give you peace." (Numbers 6:22-26)

The dreamer (*Hei - Malchut*):

Moshe מֹשֶׁה   el אֶל־   Adonai יְהֹוָה   ראה   vaydaber וַיְדַבֵּר

מהע, ע"ב בר-בוע קס"א, ד"ף אלהים ע"ה :lemor לֵאמֹר   daber דַּבֵּר   ראה

lemor לֵאמֹר   banav בָּנָיו   ve'el וְאֶל־   Aharon אַהֲרֹן   el אֶל־

מ"ה   ריבוע יהוה   ריבוע יהוה   tevarchu תְּבָרְכוּ   הײ   ko כֹּה

:lahem לָהֶם   amor אָמוֹר   Yisrael יִשְׂרָאֵל   benei בְּנֵי   et אֶת־

The initials of the three verses give us the Holy Name: יי.
In this section, there are 15 words, which are equal to the numerical value of the Holy Name: יהה.

The three beneficents (*Yud-Chochmah, Hei-Binah, Vav-Da'at*):

(Right – *Chesed*) The three beneficents meditate here to draw abundance to:
Chochmah, Chesed, Netzach (Right Column) of *Chochmah* of *Malchut*.

veyishmerecha וְיִשְׁמְרֶךָ   Adonai יְהֹוָה   yevarechecha יְבָרֶכְךָ

ר"ת = יהוה ; וס"ת = מ"ה:

(Left - *Gevurah*) The three beneficents meditate here to draw abundance to:
Binah, Gevurah, Hod (Left Column) of *Binah* of *Malchut*.

panav פָּנָיו | Adonai יְהֹוָה   ויו   זין   ויו   כף   ya'er יָאֵר

elecha אֵלֶיךָ   vichuneka וִיחֻנֶּךָּ   מגד ;   יהה   אותיות   בפסוק:

(Central – *Tiferet*) The three beneficents meditate here to draw abundance to:
Da'at, Tiferet, Yesod (Central Column) of *Tiferet* of *Malchut*.

elecha אֵלֶיךָ   panav פָּנָיו | Adonai יְהֹוָה   yisa יִשָּׂא

veyasem וְיָשֵׂם   lecha לְךָ   shalom שָׁלוֹם   האא   תיבות   בפסוק:

lach'mecha לַחְמֶךָ   besimcha בְּשִׂמְחָה   echol אֱכֹל   lech לֵךְ

ki כִּי   yenecha יֵינֶךָ   tov טוֹב   velev בְלֶב־   ush'te וּשֲׁתֵה

:ma'asecha מַעֲשֶׂיךָ   et אֶת   haElohim הָאֱלֹהִים   ratza רָצָה   kevar כְּבָר

The dreamer should give three coins for *Tzedakah* (chrity).

"And the Lord spoke to Moses and said: Speak to Aaron and his sons saying: So shall you bless the Children of Israel, say to them: May the Lord bless you and protect you. May the Lord enlighten His countenance for you and give you grace. May the Lord lift His countenance towards you and give you peace." (Numbers 6:22-26) "So go ahead. Eat your food with joy, and drink your wine with a happy heart, for God approves of this!" (Ecclesiastes 9:7)

Guide to Using the Kabbalistic Transliterated Siddur

There is no uniformly applied system for Hebrew-Aramaic transliteration. So in the kabbalistic transliterated Siddur we have adhered to what is called: "Sephardic pronunciation" as it follows the kabbalistic method of pronunciation and also it is the easiest of use (and not to be scientifically accurate).

The Hebrew and Aramaic letters are consonants. The vowels are symbolized by the markings under or over or next to the letters. The vowels in this transliteration are as spoken in the simplest way.

The consonants below are just to give the vowels a consonant to which to relate:

a – (or **ah** in the end of some words) – sounds as in "jump" (represents *kamatz* and *patach*).

ai – sounds as in "chai" (<u>only</u> in the end of a word with the letter *Yud*).

e – (or **eh** in the end of some words) - sounds as in"rest" (represents *segol* and *tzere* and *sheva na*).

ee – sounds as "free" (only in some words like "Beresheet").

ei – sounds as "day" (only in the end of a word with the letter *Yud*).

i – sounds as in "ink" (represents *chirik*).

o – (or **oh** in the end of some words) - sounds as in "off" (represents *cholam* and *kamatz gadol*)

oi – sounds as in "decoy" (<u>only</u> in the end of a word with the letter *Yud*).

u – sounds as in "room" (represents *shuruk* and *kubutz*)

We use a coma to separate syllables (For example: "*veyit'hadar*") and to separate the sounds of two vowels (For example: "*ha'ola*"). This clarifies pronunciation, and simplifies the words.

Consonants which have a different form as the final letter in a word but sound the same:

Hebrew letter	Letter's Name	Sounds like:	comments
ך (כ)	Kaf	k	K as in "Kenya"
ך (כ)	without dagesh	ch	As in "loch" (Scottish) - a very soft "ch" sound made from the throat.
ם (מ)	Mem	m	M as in "Mars"
ן (נ)	Nun	n	N as in "Norway"
ף (פ)	Pei	p	P as in "Panama"
ף (פ)	without dagesh	f	F as in "France"
ץ (צ)	Tzadik	tz	Tz as in "its"

Hebrew letter	Letter's Name	Sounds like:	comments
א	Alef	a, e, i, o, u	Depend of the vowel – could be sound as "apple." Could be as vowel stop letter.
בּ	Bet	b	B as in "Brazil"
ב	without dagesh	v	V as in "Venus"
ג	Gimel	g	G as in "goal" or "grand"
ד	Dalet	d	D as in "David"
ה	Hei	h	H as in "Hawaii" or could be silent when come in the end of the word
ו	Vav	v, u, o	V as in "Venus" or U as in "Saudi" or could be vowel as O (without any sound).
ז	Zayin	z	Z as in "zebra"
ח	Chet	ch	As in "loch" (Scottish) - a very soft "ch" sound made from the throat.
ט	Tet	t	T as in "Turkey"
י	Yud	i,y	I (in the end of a word) as in "Australia" Y (in the middle of a word) as in "Yugoslavia."
כ	Kaf	k	K as in "Kenya"
כ	without dagesh	ch	As in "loch" (Scottish) - a very soft "ch" sound made from the throat.
ל	Lamed	l	L as in "Libya"
מ	Mem	m	M as in "Mars"
נ	Nun	n	N as in "Norway"
ס	Samech	s	S as in "Scotland"
ע	Ayin	a, e, i, o, u	deep throat sound (Oriental) -intermediate in standard Hebrew.
פ	Pei	p	P as in "Panama"
פ	without dagesh	f	F as in "France"
צ	Tzadik	tz	Tz as in "its"
ק	Kuf	k	K as in "Kenya"
ר	Resh	r	R as in "Russia"
שׁ	Shin	sh	Dot over the right side – sh as in "show."
שׂ		s	Dot over the left side - s as in "Scotland."
ת	Tav	T	T as in "Turkey."

APPENDIX

KADDISH EXPLANATIONS

TWICE LIGHT

Kabbalist Rav Isaac Luria (the Ari), reveals that the *Kaddish* קדיש has the power of *Twice Light*. One Light is the Light within all of us, the spark that is our soul and life force. The second Light is the Light we draw from our surroundings. The *Kaddish* marries these two Lights in the same way it links two worlds.

The numerical value of the Aramaic word *Kaddish* is 414, the same numerical value as the Aramaic word for Light, *Or*—207 x 2 = 414.

TWICE THE POWER OF 28

The Aramaic word for power is *ko'ach*. Its numerical value is 28. Within the *Kaddish*, there are two important verses, one that contains 28 letters: "*yehe shemei... almaya*" and the other that contains 28 words: "*yehe shemei... be'alma*". As we utter both verses, the vibration of the letters helps to generate spiritual power within us.

TWICE THE POWER OF 42

The *Ana Beko'ach* is perhaps the most powerful prayer in the universe and is known as the 42-letter Name of God. When we make a connection to the 42-letter Name, we are tapping the primordial force of Creation.

In the *Kaddish*, we tap this powerful force of Creation twice. The verse: "*veyish'tabach... veyit'halal*" contains seven words starting with the Aramaic letter *Vav* (ו). The numerical value of *Vav* is six, and 7 (words) x 6 (*Vav*) = 42, providing us with a link to the 42-letter Name.

The second connection to 42 is found within the seven words themselves. Each word contains six letters. If you add the two 42s, you get 84, which is the value of the Aramaic word *yeda* ידע, meaning knowledge! The Bible states that "Adam knew (*yada*) Eve and Eve bore Cain." The *Zohar* asks why the Bible uses the Aramaic word *knew* to imply sexual relations, and reveals that the Bible is a code and that the word *knew* reveals to us that *knowledge* is the connection to the Light of the Creator. Information alone is not power—knowledge is power, which is why we should always ask the question *why*. Blind ritual by uninformed people will never activate the power of prayer. We must know the *whys* behind any spiritual act, prayer, or ritual.

TEN TIMES THE 72 NAMES OF GOD

The 72 Names of God refers to a formula of 72 Aramaic words that Moses used to part the Red Sea. The 72 Names of God have the power to overcome the laws of nature and the laws of human nature. The word *yishtabach* ישתבח has a numerical value of 720, which imbues us with ten times the power of the 72 Names of God. We arouse this power by saying the word with great passion.

THE POWER OF IMMORTALITY

The 16th century Kabbalist Rav Abraham Azulai teaches us that the Aramaic word *veyitnase* ויתנשא channels the power of immortality. In 1995, The Kabbalah Centre made public Rav Azulai's secret teachings concerning the idea of immortality and its connection to the Aramaic word *veyitnase*. According to Kabbalah, when knowledge is made public, the energy-intelligence of it begins to permeate the consciousness of all humanity and the cosmos. It is interesting to note that within six months, a remarkable book by physicist Frank J. Tipler appeared in the marketplace. The book, *The Physics of Immortality: Modern Cosmology, God, and the Resurrection of the Dead*, dealt with a topic once considered taboo by science. The barrier was now broken. In January of 1998, The Los Angeles Times stated the following on its front pages: "Breaking a biological barrier once thought out of reach, scientists for the first time have apparently endowed healthy human cells growing in a dish with a quality that alchemists, explorers, and mystics have vainly sought for ages: immortality."

Interestingly, the energy of immortality is found within the *Kaddish*, a prayer we recite when a direct family member passes on. *Veyitnase* also connects to the fourth verse of the *Ana Beko'ach*. After reciting the word *veyitnase,* we can further intensify the force of immortality by reciting the fourth verse of the *Ana Beko'ach* with great enthusiasm: *Barchem taharem rachamei tzedkatecha tamid gomlem*. The powers that will bring about the Resurrection of the Dead and the eventual end of death are concealed inside this connection.

THE *AMEN*

When we recite the word *Amen* we meditate on the combination of the two Holy Names: יהוה and אדני. The Tetragrammaton, which is the most powerful Name of God, draws Light that is so immense that we cannot handle its power, so we do not speak it out aloud. Instead, the kabbalists gave us another Name, אדני *Adonai*, which we utter in its place, while meditating upon the letters of the Tetragrammaton יהוה. This action connects the Upper World with our physical reality, creating a pipeline through which the Light flows into our physical world.

The first combination (יאהדונהי) is meditated upon while uttering the *Amens* we say after blessings. When we intertwine the letters from the *Adonai* sequence—our physical world—with the Tetragrammaton, we marry the Upper and Lower Worlds together.

In the *Kaddish*, we meditate on a slightly different combination (אידהנויה) when uttering *Amen*. Here, the *Alef* (א) of the Name אדני begins the sequence as opposed to the *Yud* (י). The reason being that in most other prayers the Creator initiates the connection and the Light usually emanates into our world through the letter *Yud* (י) of the Tetragrammaton. In the *Kaddish*, we initiate the connection upward; therefore, the *Alef* (א) from *Adonai* starts the sequence because the action originates from this world.

THE *AMIDAH*

We bow forward in four places during the *Amidah* connection: twice in the First Blessing and twice at the end during the Eighteenth (on *Shabbat* – the Fifth) Blessing. The action of bowing brings the Upper Worlds and the Name יהוה to our level. When we straighten up, we elevate our world, our consciousness and the Name אדני to create a connection between the two Worlds. All our spiritual work is designed to join these two Worlds, because this is how the Light is revealed in our life.

First Bow: (beginning of the First Blessing): Bend your knees at *'baruch,'* bow at *'Ata'* and straighten up at *'Adonai,'* and meditate to connect the *Yud* of יהוה with the *Alef* of אדני—(אי).

Second Bow: (end of the First Blessing): Bend your knees at *'baruch,'* bow at *'Ata'* and straighten up at *'Adonai,'* and meditate to connect the *Hei* of יהוה with the *Dalet* of אדני—(הד).

Third Bow: (beginning of the Eighteenth Blessing): Bow your entire body at *'modim'* and straighten up at *'Adonai,'* and meditate to connect the *Vav* of יהוה with the *Nun* of אדני—(ון).

Fourth Bow: (end of the Eighteenth Blessing): Bend your knees at *'baruch,'* bow at *'Ata'* and straighten up at *'Adonai,'* and meditate to connect the *Hei* of יהוה with the *Yud* of אדני—(הי).

BOTH FEET TOGETHER AS ONE

In the *Amidah*, we stand with both our feet together. Our left and right legs denote the Left and Right Columns. Joining them creates a third or Central Column for complete circuitry.

GLOSSARY

Abba (Father) - The second *Partzuf* that encloses the Light of *Chayah*.

Angel – Manifested Supernal energy-intelligent beings of Light dedicated to a specific purpose not subjected to free will.

Arich Anpin (Long Face) – The Lower *Partzuf* of *Keter* of *Atzilut*, which encloses the Seven Lower *Sefirot* of *Atik* (the Upper *Partzuf* of *Keter* of *Atzilut*).

Atik (Ancient) – *Malchut* of *Malchut* of the Upper *Partzuf* becomes the Upper *Partzuf* of *Keter* of *Atzilut* of the Lower *Partzuf*.

Atika Kadisha (Holy Ancient) – represents the head of *Atik* and the three heads of *Arich Anpin*.

Binah (Understanding) – The word *Binah* means: understanding the process of cause and effect. The third of the *Ten Sefirot*. *Binah* contains all the energy that motivates the human endeavor and tugs at the Earthly tides that keep galaxies spinning and stars burning.

Chayah - The fourth level of the soul. The Light that is enclosed in *Chochmah*.

Chesed (Mercy) – The fourth of the *Ten Sefirot*. Right column energy. Chariot Abraham. *Chesed* represents the pure positive energy of sharing and holds the still undifferentiated seed of all that has taken place between *Chochmah* and *Binah*.

Chochmah (Wisdom) – The word *Chochmah* means: having the wisdom to know the final destination of the process. The second of the *Ten Sefirot*. *Chochmah* represents the beginning of the Zodiac. It contains the totality of the Light and stands as the universal "father figure."

Da'at (Knowledge) – not considered a *Sefirah* but a funnel for the energy that is created by the Unification of *Abba* and *Ima*.

Gadlut (Adulthood) – Illumination of the Light of *Chochmah* in a *Partzuf*.

Gevurah (Judgment) – the fifth of the *Ten Sefirot*. Left column energy. Chariot Isaac.

Gimel Rishonot (Three Upper *Sefirot*) – The Three Upper *Sefirot* (*Keter*, *Chochmah* and *Binah*) of the *Ten Sefirot* in a *Partzuf*. It represents the head and the brains of each *Partzuf*.

Hechal (Chamber) – The spiritual space in which we receive all the good that exist for eternity.

Hitlabshut (Enclosing) – Since the *Tzimtzum*, the Upper Light can be revealed in the lower Vessel only by Returning Light. Therefore, the Returning Light is considered as enclosing the Upper Light.

Hitpashtut (Expansion) – The result of the *Hitlabshut*. When the Light is enclosed by the Returning Light it expands in the Vessel.

Hod (Glory) – The eighth of the *Ten Sefirot*. Chariot Aaron.

Ima (Mother) – The third *Partzuf* that encloses the Light of *Neshamah*.

Kavanah (Intention, meditation) – Centering one's inner consciousness with the attention appropriate to the situation or connection.

Keli (Vessel) – the Desire to Receive in the emanated.

Ken (Nest) – Infrequent illumination. Usually will be used to describe a temporary situation when *Malchut* of *Atzilut* is in *Beriah* before She ascends back (like in *Rosh Chodesh*).

Keter (Crown) – The head and the first of the *Ten Sefirot*, the Link between the Endless and the *Sefirot* structure, and the seed of all physical manifestation and activity. *Keter* contains all the incarnations of all the souls in existence. *Keter* is the source of everything, an undifferentiated potential state.

Klipa (Shell, plural-*klipot*) – A spiritual entity existing outside the clothing of *Atzilut* (*Beriah*, *Yetzirah* and *Asiyah*) causing people to be superficial and lazy in their spiritual work. Their essence is total Desire to Receive for the Self Alone.

Leah – Name of the *Partzuf* of the Upper part of *Nukva*, known as the "hidden world."

Levush (Clothing) – When a *Partzuf* receives assistant from a Lower *Partzuf* it is considered as if the Lower *Partzuf* becomes clothing to this *Partzuf* (see also *Hitlabshut*).

Malchut (Kingdom) – The tenth and final *Sefirah*. The *Sefirah* in which the greatest Desire to Receive is manifest and in which all correction takes place. *Malchut* contains the world of physicality.

Masach (Curtain) – A spiritual curtain that delays the Vessel from receiving the Light and also delays the Light from entering the Vessel.

Mayin Duchrin – (Male Water) – Awakening from Above, in order to give energy for the Unification.

Mayin Nukvin (Female Water) – Awakening from Below, in order to give energy to the Female for the Unification. There are two kinds of *Mayin Nukvin*: The first is the effort that the Female makes in order to be unified with Her Male. The second is when the Lower *Partzuf* will make an extra effort in order to give this energy to the Upper *Partzuf* and thereby the Upper *Partzuf* will be able to be unified and give back higher illuminations to this Lower *Partzuf*.

Milui (Spelled out) – When a Name or a word is writen or named by the the letters that comprise the conventionally accepted form of it, it is called *Milui*. Like the word "Light" will be spelled out as: El-Ai-Gi-Eich-Ti. When a name is spelled out this diminishes some of its power and represents a spiritual thickness.

Mochin (Brains) – When a *Partzuf* is missing the aspect of *Chayah* there cannot be a *Zivug*. Therefore, this *Partzuf* needs to draw the Light of *Neshamah* into His Three Upper *Sefirot*. This Light is called *Mochin*.

Nefesh – The first and lowest level of the soul that allows the *klipot* to connect. The Light that is enclosed in *Malchut*.

Neshamah – The third level of the soul. The Light that is enclosed in *Binah*.

Neshikin (Kisses) – The Upper Unification (in order to correct the Three Upper *Sefirot* of a *Partzuf*). Illuminations from the Upper to the Lower resulting from the connection the Returning Light creates before It goes down.

Netzach (Victory) – The seventh of the *Ten Sefirot*. Chariot Moses.

Nitzotz (Spark) – Comes from the word *hetziz* (glance). There are two systems of Sparks. The first is called *Shach* (320) and represents the male aspect of Judgment. The second is called *Par* (280) and represents the female aspect of Judgment.

Nukva (Female) – The lowest *Partzuf* or the female aspect of each *Partzuf*. Comes from the word *nekev* (aperture) meaning that the Light needs to puncture a spiritual hole in order to be revealed and therefore the Light becomes weaker.

Olam (World) – Spiritual structure of five *Partzufim*, when *Netzach*, *Hod* and *Yesod* of the Upper *Partzuf* are inside the Lower *Partzuf*. The end of *Olam* is when *Netzach*, *Hod* and *Yesod* of the Upper *Partzuf* are above the Lower *Partzuf*. Before Adam and Eve fell, the Worlds of *Beriah*, *Yetzirah* and *Asiyah* were included in the World of *Atzilut* where there is protection from the *klipot*.

Olam Adam Kadmon (World of Primordial Man) - The first of the Worlds. It receives directly from the Endless. The root and the archetype for Adam (man) of our World.

Olam Asiyah (World of Action) – The lowest of the Worlds. It was created from *Nukva* and is considered the closest World to the *klipa* domain. Our Physical World is in the bottom of *Olam Asiyah*.

Olam Atzilut (World of Emanation) – The second World; considered as the World of Correction and is totally protected from the *klipot*.

Olam Beriah (World of Creation) – The third World. It was created from *Ima* and is considered as almost completely protected from the *klipot*.

Olam Yetzirah (World of Formation) – The fourth World. It was created from *Zeir Anpin* and is considered to be 50/50 controlled by the *klipot*.

Or (Light) – The total energy of what is received in the Worlds including everything except the Vessel material – Desire to Receive.

Or Chozer (Returning Light) – The Supernal Light as it is relative to Its revelation because it is the Light that is not received by the Fourth Phase.

Or DeChasadim (Light of Mercy) – The Light that encloses the Light of *Chochmah* and reveals it.

Or DeChochmah (Light of Wisdom) – The Light that is drawn to the Vessel in its entirety.

Or Makif (Surrounding Light) – The future and potential Light of a Vessel.

Or Penimi (Inner Light) – The Light that currently exists within a Vessel.

Or Yashar (Direct Light) – The Supernal Light as it is relative to itself because it is the Light that emanates from the Endless.

Partzuf (Face) – A complete structure of the *Ten Sefirot* creates a spiritual form called *Partzuf*. The perfect relationship between the Light and the Vessel so It can emanate to the Lower Worlds.

Rachel – Name of the *Partzuf* of the Lower part of *Nukva*, known as the "revealed world".

Ruach - The second, lowest level of the soul (prior to the sin of Adam, Ruach was the lowest aspect of the soul and, therefore, beyond time space and motion). The Light that is enclosed in *Zeir Anpin*.

Ten Sefirot - A series of ten curtains or veils that were used to conceal the blazing raw Light of the Endless and protect us from it.

Tetragrammaton – The Holy Name of God, composed from the four letters: *Yud, Hei, Vav* and *Hei*.

Tevunah - (Intelligence) – The Name of the *Partzuf* created as a result of the Second *Tzimzum* and enclosed in the Seven Lower *Sefirot* of the *Partzuf* of *Ima*.

Tiferet (Splendor) – The sixth of the *Ten Sefirot*. *Tiferet* is the balancing point between the Right and Left Columns. Chariot Jacob.

Tikkun (Correction) – The process of spiritual correction made by the soul. It is also the process of correction that the Upper Worlds go through in order to be able to receive the Light.

Tipa (Drop) – Although the illumination that is drawn from the *Mochin* in the time of the Unification is momentary, it is enough for the Female to collect it. This illumination is called "drop" (in the *Shema* connection).

Tzelem (Image, shadow) – The clothing of the *Mochin* as They go to the Lower *Partzuf*. This clothing is created by the Returning Light of the Lower *Partzuf*. The *Tzelem* is divided into three main aspects. The first and highest is called *Mem* (מ) of the *Tzelem*. The second is called *Lamed* (ל) of the *Tzelem*. And the third and the lowest is called *Tzadik* (צ) of the *Tzelem*.

Tzimtzum – The ability to restrain the Desire to Receive. The original restriction. In the process of the spiritual Creation we have two *Tzimtzumim*. The First *Tzimtzum* was in the Endless World in order to give the Vessel the opportunity to remove Bread of Shame. The Second *Tzimtzum* came to complete and to correct the shattered Vessel.

Vav Ketzavot (Six Edges) – Any spiritual structure that does not include the *Mochin*.

Yaakov - The outer *Partzuf* of *Zeir Anpin* and corresponds to the Six Edges of *Zeir Anpin*.

Yechidah - The fifth and highest level of the soul. This Light is enclosed in *Keter*.

Yesod (Foundation) – The ninth of the *Ten Sefirot*. *Yesod* sits like a great reservoir or funnel feeding spiritual Light in a manageable way into our physical world. Chariot Joseph the Righteous.

Yisrael – The inner *Partzuf* of *Zeir Anpin* corresponding to the *Mochin* of *Zeir Anpin* (also known as "*Moshe*").

Yisrael Saba (Surrounded *Yisrael* or *Yisrael* Grandfather) – The name of the *Partzuf* that was created as a result of the Second *Tzimzum* enclosed in the Seven Lower *Sefirot* of the *Partzuf* of *Abba*.

Zayin Tachtonot (the Seven Lower *Sefirot*) – The Seven Lower *Sefirot* of the *Ten Sefirot* of a *Partzuf*. We consider *Zayin Tachtonot* as a separate entity when we speak of the revelation of Ten *Sefirot* below the *Masach* (Curtain).

Zeir Anpin (Small Face) – The fourth *Partzuf* that encloses the Light of *Ruach*. The six *Sefirot* - Chesed, Gevurah, Tiferet, Netzach, Hod and Yesod - tightly folded within each other, compacted in a dimension known cumulatively as *Zeir Anpin*.

Zivug (Unification) – The Nature of the Supernal Light is to emanate illumination to the Lower Worlds for all eternity. Because of the *Masach*, the Vessel cannot connect. Therefore, when the Vessel is ready (by Returning Light or by elevating *Mayin Nukvin*) to connect with the Light it is called *Zivug*.

Zivug Panim Befanim (Face-to-Face Unification) – When the Female receives the Supernal Light directly to the Vessels of Her Face from the Face (front) of the Male.

GLOSSARY

3 *Binah* Left Brain יְהֹוָה	1 *Keter* Skull יְהוָה	2 *Chochmah* Right Brain יַהַוַה
5 Left Eye יהוה יהוה יהוה יהוה יהוה	9 8 Nose יְ יְ הַ הַ אֶ אֶ הַ הַ	4 Right Eye יהוה יהוה יהוה יהוה יהוה
7 Left Ear יוד הי ואו הה		6 Right Ear יוד הי ואו הה

10
Mouth

יוד הי ואו הי (אהיה)

אוזה״ע ג׳יכ״ק דטלנ״ת זסער״ץ בומ״ף

12 *Gevurah* Left Arm יְהֹוָה	13 *Tiferet* Body יְהוָה	11 *Chesed* Right Arm יְהֹוָה
15 *Hod* Left Leg יְהוָה	16 *Yesod* Reproductive Organs יו הו וו הו	14 *Netzach* Right Leg יְהוָה
	17 *Malchut* עטרה יְהוָאדני	

יום אֱ - Sunday

יְהֹוָה

יוּד הֵי וָיו הֵי יְוּד הֵי וָאו הֵי

אל עָדִי יאולדפההייואודההיי

אָנָא בכחֹ גְדוּלֹת יְמִינְךָ תַּתִּיר צְרוּרָה

אבְגֵיתַץ יהוה יֱהֶוֶה

סְמְטְורִיֶה גְּזְרִיאֵל וְעְנָאֵל לְמֵוָאֵל

ר"ת סֶגּוֹל

יום בֱ - Monday

יוּד הֵי וָאו הֵי וֵאו הֵי יוד הֵי וְאו הֵי יוד הֵי וָאו הֵא

אל יהוה יאולדפההאאויאוודההאא

קַבֵּל רְנַת עַמְּךָ שַׂגְּבֵנוּ טַהֲרֵנוּ נוֹרָא

קְרַעְשְׂטַן יהוה יֱהֶוֶה

שְׂמַעֵיאֵל בְּרְכִיאֵל אהניאל

ר"ת שׂוֹא

יום גֱ - Tuesday

יוֹד הֵא וָאו הֵא הֵא יוד הֵה וָו הֵה

אל אדני יאולדפההההויוודההההה

נָא גְבוֹר דּוֹרְשֵׂי יְחוּדְךָ כְּבָבַת שָׂמְרֵם

נַגְדִּיכֵשׂ יֱהֶוֶה יהוה

וְנִיאֵל לְהַדִיאֵל מווזניאל

ר"ת ווֹלֹם

Wednesday - יום דְּ

יוֹד הֵא וָאו הֵא יוֹד הֵהּ וָו הֵהּ

אֵל אֲדֹנָי יאולדדפההההויוווודההההה

בּרכֵם טהרם רוֹזמִי צדִקתך תמִיד גְמלֵם

בַּטְרְצָתַג יְהֶוֶה יְהוָה

וֶחֶזְקִיאֵל רָהטִיאֵל קָדְשִׁיאֵל

ר״ת ווֹרק

Thursday - יום הֵ

יֵוַד הֵי וָאו הֵי יוֹד הֵי וָאו הֵי יוֹד הֵא וָאו הֵא

אֵל יהוה יאולדדפההאאוִיאוודההאא

וֶזסִין קָדוֹשׁ בְּרוֹב טוֹבֶר נֹהֵל עֹדֶתך

וְחֶקבְטֹנֶע יַהֶוֶה יְהוָה

שִׁמוְעָאֵל רָעֶבְמִיאֵל קֹנִיאֵל

ר״ת שֹׁרק

(הקבוּץ מלאכיו בר״ת שוֹרק)

Friday - יום וּו

יֵוַד הֵי וָיו הַי יֵוֵד הֵי וָאו הֵי

אֵל שֹׁדִי יאולדדפההיִיאוודהההֹיִי

יוֹזִיד גָאה לְעַמך פָּנֹה זוֹכרִי קְדוֹשׁתך

יַגְלְפֹזֶק יְהֶוֶה יִהּוָוֹדֹוּ

עוֹבמוֹעִיואוֹלוּ רוֹפוּאוֹלוּ קֹדוֹשִׁיוּאוֹלוּ

ר״ת שֹׁרק